The Economics of Money, Banking, and Financial Markets

First Canadian Edition

Frederic S. Mishkin
Columbia University

Apostolos Serletis
University of Calgary

Toronto

To Aglaia

Canadian Cataloguing in Publication Data

Mishkin, Frederic S.
    The economics of money, banking and financial markets

1st Canadian ed.
ISBN 0-201-47766-1

1. Finance. 2. Money. 3. Banks and banking. I. Serletis, Apostolos, 1954-   . II. Title.

HG173.M57 2002   332   C2001-903132-7

ISBN 0-201-47766-1

Vice President, Editorial Director: Michael Young
Executive Editor: Dave Ward
Marketing Manager: Deborah Meredith
Senior Developmental Editor: Suzanne Schaan
Production Editor: Mary Ann McCutcheon
Copy Editor: Jennifer Therriault
Production Coordinator: Deborah Starks
Content Coordinator: Bhavin Desai
Page Layout: Joan M. Wilson
Permissions Research: Beth McAuley
Art Director: Mary Opper
Interior and Cover Design: Julia Hall
Cover Image: Stone

2 3 4 5   06 05 04 03 02

Printed and bound in the United States.

Statistics Canada information is used with permission of the Minister of Industry, as Minister responsible for Statistics Canada. Information on the availability of the wide range of data from Statistics Canada can be obtained from Statistics Canada's Regional Offices, its World Wide Web site at **http://www.statcan.ca** and its toll-free access number, 1-800-263-1136.

CONTENTS IN BRIEF

CONTENTS

PART II   *Financial Markets* *57*

CHAPTER 15

MULTIPLE DEPOSIT CREATION AND THE MONEY SUPPLY PROCESS 342

CHAPTER 16

DETERMINANTS OF THE MONEY SUPPLY 363

PREFACE

In preparing the First Canadian Edition of *The Economics of Money, Banking, and Financial Markets*, I retained the basic hallmarks that have made this text the best-selling textbook on money and banking in the past six U.S. editions:

- A unifying, analytic framework that uses a few basic economic principles to organize students' thinking about the structure of financial markets, the foreign exchange markets, financial institution management, and the role of monetary policy in the economy
- A careful, step-by-step development of models, an approach found in the best principles of economics textbooks, that makes it easier for students to learn
- A complete integration of an international perspective throughout the text
- A thoroughly up-to-date treatment of the latest developments in monetary theory
- Special features called "Following the Financial News" and "Reading the Financial Pages" to encourage reading of a financial newspaper
- An applications-oriented perspective with numerous applications and special-topic boxes that increase students' interest by showing them how to apply theory to real-world examples

THE CANADIAN PERSPECTIVE

The First Canadian Edition of *The Economics of Money, Banking, and Financial Markets* is based on the sixth U.S. edition and has an unabashedly international perspective, because we in Canada have a lot to learn from the monetary experience in other countries. Here is a sample of what is covered:

Monetary Policy Strategy: The International Experience

This edition includes:

- A full discussion of monetary targeting and inflation targeting, two prominent monetary policy strategies used by central banks throughout the world (Chapter 20), and an extensive treatment of current Canadian monetary policy (Chapters 14 and 18)
- A discussion of exchange-rate strategies, including currency boards and dollarization, both of which have received a lot of attention lately

Increased International Perspective

The growing importance of the global economy has encouraged us to add material with an international perspective. The book provides:

- Extensive treatment of the crisis in East Asia, with applications on the sequence of events in the financial crisis (Chapter 8), the specifics of the banking crisis in the affected countries (Chapter 11), and the currency crisis (Chapter 19)

- A discussion of capital controls and the role of the International Monetary Fund in preventing financial crises (Chapter 19)
- Detailed analysis of the introduction of the euro, including discussion of whether it will benefit Europe (Chapter 3), how it has fared in the currency markets so far (Chapter 7), and whether it will challenge the U.S. dollar as a reserve currency (Chapter 19)
- Examination of the structure and independence of the newly created European Central Bank, the U.S. Federal Reserve, the Bank of England, and the Bank of Japan (Chapter 14)
- A full discussion of recent events in the Japanese economy and why they have occurred, including the appearance of negative interest rates (Chapters 4 and 5), the banking crisis (Chapter 11), the recent reforms affecting the Bank of Japan and the Ministry of Finance (Chapter 14), and recent monetary policy (Chapter 20)

Material on Financial Markets and Institutions

Continuing changes in financial markets and institutions have prompted us to include the following material:

- Analysis of recent developments in financial consolidation and the possible return of the financial supermarket (Chapters 10 and 12)
- A section on hedge funds, outlining the factors that caused the near failure of Long-Term Capital Management (Chapter 12)
- Discussion of the most recent developments regarding deposit insurance and risk management, including the modernization of the CDIC's *Standards of Sound Business and Financial Practices* (Chapter 12)
- A full discussion of the key elements of the proposed new legislation based on the MacKay Report on the Future of the Canadian Financial Services Sector (Chapter 10). This legislation is regarded as one of the most significant revisions to the Bank Act in Canadian history, scheduled for no later than 2002

Monetary Theory and Policy

The text discusses recent developments in Canada regarding monetary theory and policy:

- Extensive treatment of the Large Value Transfer System (LVTS) framework within which the Bank of Canada conducts monetary policy (Chapter 17)
- A full discussion of the operating band for the overnight interest rate and the Bank of Canada's standing facilities (Chapter 17)
- A section on the market for settlement balances and the determination of the overnight interest rate (Chapter 17)
- A section on the role of NAIRU, the Phillips curve, and the Taylor rule in the conduct of monetary policy (Chapter 18)
- Examination of the effects of the favourable supply shocks on the economy during 1995–2000 (Chapter 20)

FLEXIBILITY

There are as many ways to teach money, banking, and financial markets as there are instructors. To satisfy the diverse needs of instructors, the text achieves flexibility as follows:

- Core chapters provide the basic analysis used throughout the book, and other chapters or sections of chapters can be used or omitted according to instructor preferences. For example, Chapter 2 introduces the financial system and basic concepts such as transaction costs, adverse selection, and moral hazard. After covering Chapter 2, the instructor may decide to give more detailed coverage of financial structure by assigning Chapter 8, or may choose to skip Chapter 8 and take any of a number of different paths through the book.

- The text also allows instructors to cover the most important issues in monetary theory and policy without having to use the *ISLM* model in Chapters 22 and 23, while more complete treatments of monetary theory make use of the *ISLM* chapters.

- The internationalization of the text through marked international sections within chapters as well as through complete separate chapters on the foreign exchange market and the international monetary system is comprehensive yet flexible. Although many instructors will teach all the international material, others will not. Instructors who want less emphasis on international topics can easily skip Chapter 7, on the foreign exchange market, and Chapter 19, on the international financial system and monetary policy. The international sections within chapters are self-contained and can be omitted with little loss of continuity. Instructors who would like to teach material on the foreign exchange market later in the course can teach Chapter 7 just before Chapter 19.

To illustrate how this book can be used for courses with varying emphases, several course outlines are suggested for a semester teaching schedule. More detailed information about how the text can be used flexibly in your course is available in the Instructor's Manual.

- *General Money and Banking Course*: Chapters 1–5, 9–11, 14, 17, 18, 24, 26, with a choice of 6 of the remaining 14 chapters.
- *General Money and Banking Course with an International Emphasis*: Chapters 1–5, 7, 9–11, 14, 17–19, 24, with a choice of 4 of the remaining 12 chapters.
- *Financial Markets and Institutions Course*: Chapters 1–6, 8–13, 27, with a choice of 6 of the remaining 14 chapters.
- *Monetary Theory and Policy Course*: Chapters 1–5, 14–18, 20, 21, 24–26, with a choice of 4 of the remaining 13 chapters.

PEDAGOGICAL AIDS

In teaching theory or its applications, a textbook must be a solid motivational tool. To this end, I have incorporated a wide variety of pedagogical features to make the material easy to learn.

1. **Previews** at the beginning of each chapter tell students where the chapter is heading, why specific topics are important, and how they relate to other topics in the book.

2. **Applications**, numbering over 50, demonstrate how the analysis in the book can be used to explain many important real-world situations. A special set of applications, called "Reading the Financial Pages," shows students how to read daily columns in leading financial newspapers.

3. **"Following the Financial News" boxes** introduce students to relevant news articles and data that are reported daily in the press, and explain how to read them.

4. **Special-interest boxes** highlight dramatic historical episodes, interesting ideas, and intriguing facts related to the subject matter.

5. **Study Guides** are highlighted statements scattered throughout the text that provide hints to the student on how to think about or approach a topic.

6. **Summary tables** provide a useful study aid in reviewing material.

7. **Key statements** are important points set in boldface italic type so that students can easily find them for later reference.

8. **Graphs** with captions, numbering over 150, help students clearly understand the interrelationship of the variables plotted and the principles of analysis.

9. **Weblinks** direct students to Web sites for further research on economics and finance.

10. **Summary** at the end of each chapter lists the main points covered.

11. **Key terms** are important words or phrases, boldfaced when they are defined for the first time and listed by page number at the end of the chapter.

12. **End-of-chapter questions and problems**, numbering over 400, help students learn the subject matter by applying economic concepts, including a special class of problems that students find particularly relevant, under the heading "Using Economic Analysis to Predict the Future."

13. **Glossary** at the back of the book provides definitions of all the key terms.

14. **Answers section** at the back of the book provides solutions to half of the questions and problems (marked by *).

SUPPLEMENTS PROGRAM TO ACCOMPANY THE FIRST CANADIAN EDITION

The Economics of Money, Banking, and Financial Markets includes a comprehensive program of supplements. The following items are available to qualified adopters:

- **Instructor's Resource Manual**, a print supplement prepared by us and offering sample course outlines, chapter outlines, and answers to questions and problems in the text.

- **Test Item File**, a printed test bank comprising more than 3500 multiple-choice questions.

- **Test Manager**, testing software allowing the instructor to produce quizzes and exams efficiently. This product contains all the multiple-choice items from the printed Test Item File and offers the capability to select and edit existing questions as well as create new questions.

- **Electronic Transparencies**, more than 300 PowerPoint® slides, including figures and tables from the text plus lecture notes.

- **Web Site**, an online source for materials such as minicases and appendices on supplementary topics. Visit the site at www.pearsoned.ca/text/mishkin.

ACKNOWLEDGMENTS

This book is the result of efforts by many people. First of all, I would like to thank Rick Mishkin for his excellent comments on my contributions. I am extremely grateful to Dave Ward, Publisher, Suzanne Schaan, Senior Developmental Editor, Jennifer Therriault, copy editor, Mary Ann McCutcheon, Supervising Editor, and many others at Pearson Education Canada who have contributed to the completion of this first Canadian edition.

I am also grateful to all of the many people who commented on various chapters of the book, made valuable suggestions, and kindly provided me with data. I would particularly like to thank Jim Armstrong, Kevin Clinton, Stan Eakins, Doug Fisher, Chris Graham, Periklis Gogas, Zisimos Koustas, Terry Molik, Ricardo Rangel-Ruiz, Jack Selody, and Mark Zelmer.

I would like to join Pearson in thanking reviewers who provided comparative market reviews and feedback on the U.S. edition of *The Economics of Money, Banking, and Financial Markets*:

Frank Atkins, University of Calgary

Wilson B. Brown, University of Winnipeg

Patrick Crowley, Texas A&M University–Corpus Christi

Harvey King, University of Regina

Kam Hon Chu, Memorial University of Newfoundland

Victor Olshevski, University of Winnipeg

I would also like to thank the following reviewers whose comments on the manuscript contributed to the development of the Canadian edition:

Joe Amoako-Tuffour, St. Francis Xavier University

Niels Anthonisen, Mount Allison University

Wilson B. Brown, University of Winnipeg

Douglas Curtis, Trent University

Jagdish Handa, McGill University

Muhammed Kabir, University of New Brunswick

Ralph Kolinski, University of Windsor

Charles Nunn, University of Alberta

John P. Palmer, University of Western Ontario

Wimal Rankaduwa, University of Prince Edward Island

T.K. Rymes, Carleton University

Special thanks are also due to Donna Howard and Joseph Atta-Mensah of the Department of Monetary and Financial Analysis at the Bank of Canada for their help in clarifying Bank of Canada operations.

And finally, I would like to dedicate this book to my (wife and) best friend, Aglaia. I owe more than I can say to her love and support.

Although I have done my best to make the first Canadian edition as complete and error-free as possible, as most of you know, perfection is impossible. I would greatly appreciate any suggestions for improvement. Please send your comments to me at serletis@ucalgary.ca.

Apostolos Serletis

2002

ABOUT THE AUTHORS

Frederic S. Mishkin is the Alfred Lerner Professor of Banking and Financial Institutions at the Graduate School of Business, Columbia University. He is also a Research Associate at the National Bureau of Economic Research. Since receiving his Ph.D. from the Massachusetts Institute of Technology in 1976, he has taught at the University of Chicago, Northwestern University, Princeton University, and Columbia. He has also received an honorary professorship from the Peoples (Renmin) University of China. From 1994 to 1997 he was Executive Vice President and Director of Research at the Federal Reserve Bank of New York and an associate economist of the Federal Open Market Committee of the Federal Reserve System.

Professor Mishkin's research focuses on monetary policy and its impact on financial markets and the aggregate economy. He is the author of more than ten books, including *Financial Markets and Institutions*, 3rd edition (Addison Wesley Longman, 2000), *Inflation Targeting: Lessons from the International Experience* (Princeton University Press, 1999), *Money, Interest Rates, and Inflation* (Edward Elgar, 1993), and *A Rational Expectations Approach to Macroeconometrics: Testing Policy Ineffectiveness and Efficient Markets Models* (University of Chicago Press, 1983). In addition, he has published more than 100 articles in such journals as the *American Economic Review*, the *Journal of Political Economy*, *Econometrica*, the *Quarterly Journal of Economics*, the *Journal of Finance*, and the *Journal of Monetary Economics*.

Professor Mishkin has served on the editorial board of the *American Economic Review* and has been an associate editor at the *Journal of Business and Economic Statistics*; he also served as the editor of the Federal Reserve Bank of New York's *Economic Policy Review*. He is currently an associate editor (member of the editorial board) at eight academic journals, including the *Journal of Money, Credit and Banking, Macroeconomics and Monetary Economics Abstracts, Journal of International Money and Finance, International Finance, Finance India*, the *Journal of Applied Econometrics, Economic Policy Review*, and the *Journal of Economic Perspectives*. He has been a consultant to the Board of Governors of the Federal Reserve System, the World Bank, and the International Monetary Fund, as well as to many central banks throughout the world. He is currently an academic consultant to and serves on the Economic Advisory Panel of the Federal Reserve Bank of New York.

Apostolos Serletis is Professor of Economics at the University of Calgary. Since receiving his Ph.D. from McMaster University in 1984, he has held visiting appointments at the University of Texas at Austin, the Athens University of Economics and Business, and the Research Department of the Federal Reserve Bank of St. Louis.

Professor Serletis's research focuses on monetary and financial economics, macroeconometrics, and nonlinear and complex dynamics. He is the author of three books, including *The Theory of Monetary Aggregation*, co-edited with William A. Barnett (North-Holland, 2000), and *The Demand for Money: Theoretical and Empirical Approaches* (Kluwer Academic Publishers, 2001).

In addition, he has published more than 100 articles in such journals as the *Journal of Economic Literature*, the *Journal of Monetary Economics*, the *Journal of Money, Credit and Banking*, the *Journal of Econometrics*, the *Canadian Journal of Economics*, the *Journal of Economic Dynamics and Control*, the *Journal of Business and Economic Statistics*, and the *Journal of Applied Econometrics*.

Chapter 1

Why Study Money, Banking, and Financial Markets?

PREVIEW   On the evening news you hear that the Bank of Canada is raising the bank rate by one-half of a percentage point. What effect might this have on the interest rate of an automobile loan when you finance your purchase of a sleek new sports car? Does it mean that a house will be more or less affordable in the future? Will it make it easier or harder for you to get a job next year?

This book provides answers to these and other questions by examining how financial markets (such as those for bonds, stocks, and foreign exchange) and financial institutions (chartered banks, trust and mortgage loan companies, credit unions and *caisses populaires*, insurance companies, mutual fund companies, and other institutions) work and by exploring the role of money in the economy. Financial markets and institutions not only affect your everyday life but also involve huge flows of funds (billions of dollars) through our economy, in turn affecting business profits, the production of goods and services, and even the economic well-being of countries other than Canada. What happens to financial markets, financial institutions, and money is of great concern to our politicians and can have a major impact on our elections. The study of money, banking, and financial markets will reward you with an understanding of many exciting issues. In this chapter we provide a road map of the book by outlining these issues and exploring why they are worth studying.

WHY STUDY FINANCIAL MARKETS?

Part II of this book focuses on **financial markets**, markets in which funds are transferred from people who have an excess of available funds to people who have a shortage. Financial markets such as the bond and stock markets are important in channelling funds from people who do not have a productive use for them to those who do, a process that results in greater economic efficiency. Activities in financial markets also have direct effects on personal wealth, the behaviour of businesses and consumers, and the overall performance of the economy.

1

The Bond Market and Interest Rates

A **security** (also called a *financial instrument*) is a claim on the issuer's future income or **assets** (any financial claim or piece of property that is subject to ownership). A **bond** is a debt security that promises to make payments periodically for a specified period of time.[1] The bond market is especially important to economic activity because it enables corporations or governments to borrow to finance their activities and because it is where interest rates are determined. An **interest rate** is the cost of borrowing or the price paid for the rental of funds (usually expressed as a percentage of the rental of $100 per year). There are many interest rates in the economy—mortgage interest rates, car loan rates, and interest rates on many different types of bonds.

Interest rates are important on a number of levels. On a personal level, high interest rates could deter you from buying a house or a car because the cost of financing it would be high. Conversely, high interest rates could encourage you to save because you can earn more interest income by putting aside some of your earnings as savings. On a more general level, interest rates have an impact on the overall health of the economy because they affect not only consumers' willingness to spend or save but also businesses' investment decisions. High interest rates, for example, may cause a corporation to postpone building a new plant that would ensure more jobs.

Because changes in interest rates have important effects on individuals, financial institutions, businesses, and the overall economy, it is important to explain fluctuations in interest rates that have been substantial over the past twenty years. For example, at the end of the 1970s, the interest rate on three-month Treasury bills was around 13% and reached a peak of over 20% in August 1981. This interest rate then fell to a low of less than 3% in 1997, rose to near 5% in 1998, and has fluctuated around that level since then.

Because different interest rates have a tendency to move in unison, economists frequently lump interest rates together and refer to "the" interest rate. As Figure 1-1 shows, however, interest rates on several types of bonds can differ substantially. The interest rate on three-month Treasury bills, for example, fluctuates more than the other interest rates and is lower on average. The interest rate on long-term corporate bonds is higher on average than the other interest rates and the spread between it and the other rates fluctuates over time.

In Chapter 2 we study the role of bond markets in the economy, and in Chapters 4 through 6 we examine what an interest rate is, how the common movements in interest rates come about, and why the interest rates on different bonds vary.

The Stock Market

A **stock** represents a share of ownership in a corporation. It is a security that is a claim on the earnings and assets of the corporation. Issuing stock and selling it to the public is a way for corporations to raise funds to finance their activities. The stock market, in which claims on the earnings of corporations (shares of stock) are traded, is the most widely followed financial market in Canada (it is often called simply "the market"). A big swing in the prices of shares in the stock market is always a big story on the evening news. People often express their opinion about where the market is heading and will frequently tell you about their latest "big killing" (although you seldom hear about their latest "big loss"!). The attention the

---

[1]The definition of *bond* used throughout this book is the broad one in common use by academics, which covers short- as well as long-term debt instruments. However, some practitioners in financial markets use the word *bond* only to describe specific long-term debt instruments such as corporate bonds or Canada bonds.

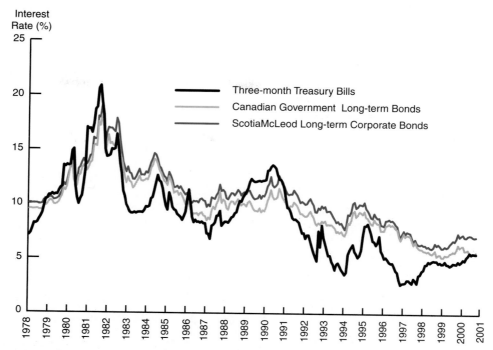

FIGURE 1-1   Interest Rates on Selected Bonds, 1978–2001

Source: Statistics Canada CANSIM Series B14060, B14072, and B14048.

market receives can probably be best explained by one simple fact: it is a place where people can get rich quickly.

As Figure 1-2 indicates, stock prices have been extremely volatile. They climbed steadily in the 1950s, reached a peak in 1966, and then fluctuated up and down until 1974, when they fell sharply. Stock prices had recovered substantially by the early 1980s when a major stock market boom began, sending the Toronto Stock Exchange 300 (TSE 300) index to a peak in August 1987. After a 12.5% decline over the next month and a half, the stock market experienced the worst one-day drop in its entire history on "Black Monday," October 19, 1987, when the TSE 300 fell by more than 400 points, an 11% decline. The stock market then recovered, climbing to above the 11 000 level in 2000, but falling again to the 7500 level in early 2001. These considerable fluctuations in stock prices affect the size of people's wealth and, as a result, may affect their willingness to spend.

The stock market is also an important factor in business investment decisions because the price of shares affects the amount of funds that can be raised by selling newly issued stock to finance investment spending. A higher price for a firm's shares allows the firm to raise a larger amount of funds that can be used to buy production facilities and equipment.

In Chapter 2 we examine the role that the stock market plays in the financial system, and we return to the issue of how stock prices behave and respond to information in the marketplace in Chapter 27.

The Foreign Exchange Market

For funds to be transferred from one country to another, they have to be converted from the currency in the country of origin (say, dollars) into the currency of the country to which they are going (say, francs). The **foreign exchange market** is where this conversion takes place and it is instrumental in moving funds between countries. It is also important because it is where the **foreign exchange rate**, the price of one country's currency in terms of another's, is determined.

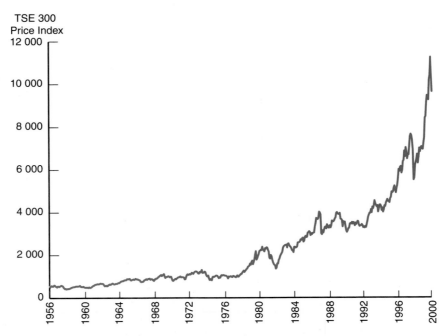

FIGURE 1-2   Stock Prices as Measured by the TSE 300 Price Index, 1956–2000
Source: Statistics Canada CANSIM Series B4237.

Because the foreign exchange rate is the relative price of two national currencies, there are two ways of quoting an exchange rate: either as the amount of domestic currency that can be purchased with a unit of foreign currency or as the amount of foreign currency that can be purchased with a unit of domestic currency. Throughout this book, we always use the latter quoting convention—that is, we express the exchange rate as units of foreign currency per Canadian dollar. In these terms, when the exchange rate increases so that a Canadian dollar buys more units of foreign currency, we say that the Canadian dollar has had an **appreciation**. A decline in the exchange rate is associated with a **depreciation** of the Canadian dollar.

Figure 1-3 shows exchange rates for the Canadian dollar from 1971 to 1999 in terms of the U.S. dollar and ten major foreign currencies. The Canada–U.S. exchange rate is defined as the U.S. dollar price of one Canadian dollar. The G-10 Index line shows the Canadian dollar in terms of a basket of ten currencies of major industrialized countries. It is expressed as an index, with the 1981 value set equal to 100.

The United States is Canada's major trading partner so the two exchange rates move closely together. In the early 1970s, the exchange rate was fixed, but since then the fluctuations in the exchange rate have been substantial: the Canadian dollar weakened considerably in the late 1970s and early 1980s and reached a low point in 1986. From 1987 to the end of 1991, the dollar appreciated dramatically in value, but since then it has fallen substantially.

What have these fluctuations in the exchange rate meant to the Canadian public and businesses? A change in the exchange rate has a direct effect on Canadian consumers because it affects the cost of foreign goods. In 1984, when the British currency, the pound sterling, cost approximately $1.30, £100 of British goods (say, Shetland sweaters) would cost $130. When a weaker dollar raised the cost of a pound to $2.20 in 2000, the same £100 of Shetland sweaters cost $220. Thus a weaker dollar leads to more expensive foreign goods, makes vacationing abroad

FIGURE 1-3 Exchange Rates for the Canadian Dollar, 1971–1999

Source: Statistics Canada CANSIM Series B3418 and B3400.

more expensive, and raises the cost of indulging your desire for imported delicacies. When the value of the dollar drops, Canadians will decrease their purchases of foreign goods and increase their consumption of domestic goods (such as travel in Canada or Canadian-made sweaters).

Conversely, a strong dollar means that Canadian goods exported abroad will cost more in foreign countries and foreigners will buy fewer of them. Exports of steel, for example, declined sharply when the dollar strengthened in the late 1980s. A strong dollar benefited Canadian consumers by making foreign goods cheaper but hurt Canadian businesses and eliminated some jobs by cutting both domestic and foreign sales of their products. The decline in the value of the dollar since 1992 has had the opposite effect: it has made foreign goods more expensive but has made Canadian businesses more competitive. Fluctuations in the foreign exchange markets have major consequences in the Canadian economy.

In Chapter 7 we study how exchange rates are determined in the foreign exchange market in which dollars are bought and sold for foreign currencies.

WHY STUDY BANKING AND FINANCIAL INSTITUTIONS?

Part III of this book focuses on financial institutions and the business of banking. Banks and other financial institutions are what make financial markets work. Without them, financial markets would not be able to move funds from people who save to people who have productive investment opportunities. Therefore, they have important effects on the performance of the economy as a whole.

Structure of the Financial System

The financial system is complex, comprising many different types of private sector financial institutions, including banks, insurance companies, mutual funds, finance companies, and investment banks, all of which are heavily regulated by the government. If an individual wanted to make a loan to Bombardier or Nortel, for example, they would not go directly to the president of the company and offer a loan. Instead, they would lend to such companies indirectly through **financial intermediaries**, institutions that borrow funds from people who have saved and in turn make loans to others.

Why are financial intermediaries so crucial to well-functioning financial markets? Why do they extend credit to one party but not to another? Why do they usually write complicated legal documents when they extend loans? Why are they the most heavily regulated businesses in the economy?

We answer these questions in Chapter 8 by developing a coherent framework for analyzing financial structure in Canada and in the rest of the world.

Banks and Other Financial Institutions

Banks are financial institutions that accept deposits and make loans. Included under the term *banks* are firms such as chartered banks, trust and mortgage loan companies, and credit unions and *caisses populaires*. Banks are the financial intermediaries that the average person interacts with most frequently. A person who needs a loan to buy a house or a car usually obtains it from a local bank. Most Canadians keep a large proportion of their financial wealth in banks in the form of chequing accounts, savings accounts, or other types of bank deposits. Because banks are the largest financial intermediaries in our economy, they deserve the most careful study. However, banks are not the only important financial institutions. Indeed, in recent years, other financial institutions such as insurance companies, finance companies, pension funds, mutual funds, and investment banks have been growing at the expense of banks, and so we need to study them as well.

In Chapter 9 we examine how banks and other financial institutions manage their assets and liabilities to make profits. In Chapter 10 we extend the economic analysis from Chapter 8 to understand why bank regulation takes the form it does and what can go wrong in the regulatory process. In Chapters 11 and 12 we look at the banking industry and at nonbank financial institutions; we examine how the competitive environment has changed in these industries and learn why some financial institutions have been growing at the expense of others. Because the economic environment for banks and other financial institutions has become increasingly risky, these institutions must find ways to manage risk. How they manage risk with financial derivatives is the topic of Chapter 13.

Financial Innovation

In the good old days, when you took cash out of the bank or wanted to check your account balance, you got to say hello to the friendly teller. Nowadays you are more likely to interact with an automated teller machine when withdrawing cash and you can get your account balance from your home computer. To see why these options have developed, in Chapters 9, 10, and 13 we study why and how financial innovation takes place. We also study financial innovation because it shows us how creative thinking on the part of financial institutions can lead to higher profits. By seeing how and why financial institutions have been creative in the past, we obtain a better grasp of how they may be creative in the future. This knowledge provides us with useful clues about how the financial system may change over time and will help keep our knowledge about banks and other financial institutions from becoming obsolete.

WHY STUDY MONEY AND MONETARY POLICY?

Money is defined as anything that is generally accepted in payment for goods or services or in the repayment of debts. Money is linked to changes in economic variables that affect all of us and are important to the health of the economy. The final two parts of the book examine the role of money in the economy.

Money and Business Cycles

In 1981–1982, total production of goods and services (called **aggregate output**) in the economy fell, the number of people out of work rose to close to 12% of the labour force. After 1982, the economy began to expand rapidly, and by 1989, the **unemployment rate** (the percentage of the available labour force unemployed) had declined to 7.5%. In 1990, the eight-year expansion came to an end, and the economy began to decline again, with unemployment rising above 11%. The economy bottomed out in 1991, and the subsequent recovery has been the longest in Canadian history, with unemployment rates falling to around 6% in 2000.

Why did the economy contract in 1981–1982, boom thereafter, and begin to contract again in 1990? Evidence suggests that money plays an important role in generating **business cycles**, the upward and downward movement of aggregate output produced in the economy. Business cycles affect all of us in immediate and important ways. When output is rising, for example, it is easier to find a good job; when output is falling, finding a good job might be difficult. Figure 1-4 shows the movements of the rate of money growth from 1915 to 2000, with the shaded areas representing **recessions**, periods when aggregate output is declining. What we see is that every recession in the twentieth century has been preceded by a decline in the rate of money growth, indicating that changes in money might also be a driving force behind business cycle fluctuations. However, not every decline in the rate of money growth is followed by a recession.

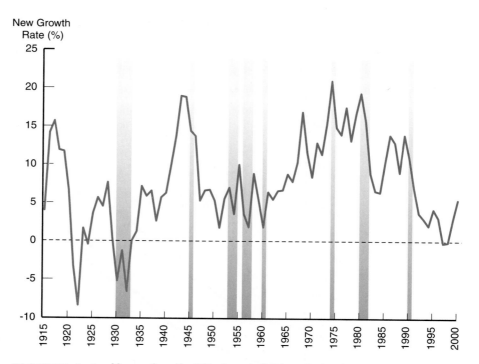

FIGURE 1-4 Money Growth (M2 Annual Rate) and the Business Cycle in Canada, 1915–2000

Note: Shaded areas represent recessions.

Source: From 1914 to 1967 the M2 series is from Cherie Metcalf, Angela Redish, and Ronald Shearer, "New Estimates of the Canadian Money Stock: 1871–1967," *Canadian Journal of Economics* 31, no. 1 (February 1998): 104–24. Reprinted with permission of Blackwell Publishers. From 1968 to 2000 it is Statistics Canada CANSIM Series B3418 and B3400.

We explore how money might affect aggregate output in Chapters 21 through 28, where we study **monetary theory**, the theory that relates changes in the quantity of money to changes in aggregate economic activity and the price level.

Money and Inflation

Thirty years ago, the movie you may have paid $11 to see last week would have set you back only a dollar or two. In fact, for $11 you could probably have had dinner, seen the movie, and bought yourself a big bucket of hot buttered popcorn. As shown in Figure 1-5, which illustrates the movement of average prices in the Canadian economy from 1968 to 2000, the prices of most items are quite a bit higher now than they were then. The average price of goods and services in an economy is called the **aggregate price level** or, more simply, the *price level* (a more precise definition is found in the appendix to this chapter). From 1968 to 2000, the price level has increased by about fivefold. **Inflation**, a continual increase in the price level, affects individuals, businesses, and the government. Inflation is generally regarded as an important problem to be solved and has often been a primary concern of politicians and policymakers. To solve the inflation problem, we need to know something about its causes.

What explains inflation? One clue to answering this question is found in Figure 1-5. As we can see, the price level and the money supply generally move closely together. These data seem to indicate that a continuing increase in the money supply might be an important factor in causing the continuing increase in the price level that we call inflation.

Further evidence that inflation may be tied to continuing increases in the money supply is found in Figure 1-6. For a number of countries, it plots the average **inflation rate** (the rate of change of the price level, usually measured as a

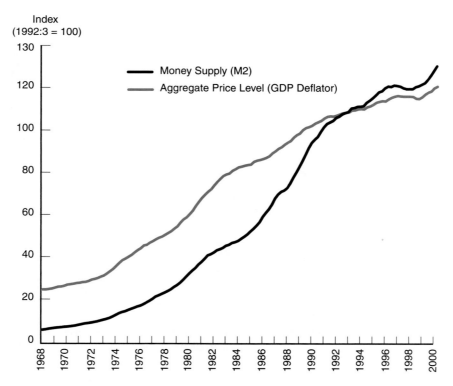

FIGURE 1-5 Aggregate Price Level and the Money Supply in Canada, 1968–2000
Source: Statistics Canada CANSIM Series B1630 and D15612.

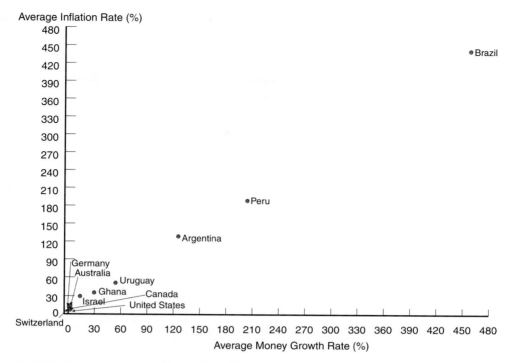

FIGURE 1-6 Average Inflation Rate Versus Average Rate of Money Growth for Selected Countries, 1989–1999

Source: International Financial Statistics.

percentage change per year) over the ten-year period 1989–1999 against the average rate of money growth over the same period.[2] As you can see, there is a positive association between inflation and the growth rate of the money supply: the countries with the highest inflation rates are also the ones with the highest money growth rates. Brazil, Peru, and Argentina, for example, experienced very high inflation during this period, and their rates of money growth were high. By contrast, Switzerland and Germany had very low inflation rates over the same period, and their rates of money growth have been low. Such evidence led Milton Friedman, a Nobel laureate in economics, to make the famous statement "Inflation is always and everywhere a monetary phenomenon."[3] We look at money's role in creating inflation by studying in detail the relationship between changes in the quantity of money and changes in the price level in Chapter 26.

Money and Interest Rates

In addition to other factors, money plays an important role in the interest-rate fluctuations that are of such great concern to businesses and consumers. Figure 1-7 shows the changes in the interest rate on long-term Canada bonds and the rate of money growth. As the money growth rate rose in the late 1970s, the long-term bond

---

[2]If the aggregate price level at time t is denoted by P_t, the inflation rate from time $t - 1$ to t, denoted as π_t, is defined as

$$\pi_t = \frac{P_t - P_{t-1}}{P_{t-1}}$$

[3]Milton Friedman, *Dollars and Deficits* (Upper Saddle River, N.J.: Prentice Hall, 1968), p. 39.

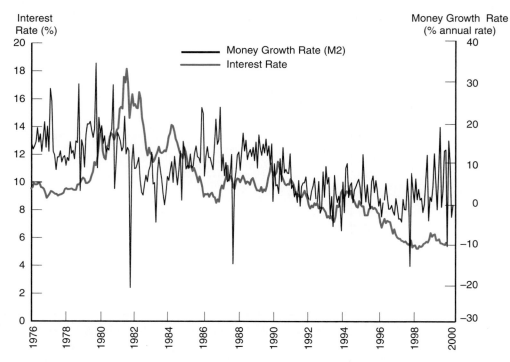

FIGURE 1-7   Money Growth (M2 Annual Rate) and Interest Rates (Long-Term Government of Canada Bonds), 1976–2000

Source: Statistics Canada CANSIM Series B1630 and B14072.

rate rose with it. However, the relationship between money growth and interest rates was less clear-cut in the late 1990s. We analyze the relationship between money and interest rates when we examine the behaviour of interest rates in Chapter 5.

Conduct of Monetary Policy

Bank of Canada
www.bankofcanada.ca

Because money can affect many economic variables that are important to the well-being of our economy, politicians and policymakers throughout the world care about the conduct of **monetary policy**, the management of money and interest rates. The organization responsible for the conduct of a nation's monetary policy is the **central bank**. Canada's central bank is the **Bank of Canada** (also called simply **the Bank**). In Chapters 14 through 20 we study how central banks like the Bank of Canada can affect interest rates and the quantity of money in the economy. We then look at how monetary policy is actually conducted in Canada and elsewhere.

Budget Deficits and Monetary Policy

The **budget deficit** is the excess of government expenditures over tax revenues for a particular time period, typically a year. The government must finance any deficit by borrowing. As Figure 1-8 shows, the budget deficit, relative to the size of our economy, peaked in 1993 at 12% of national output (as calculated by the *gross domestic product*, or *GDP*, a measure of aggregate output described in the appendix to this chapter). Since then, the budget deficit declined and the budget actually went into surplus in 1999. Budget deficits have been the subject of bitter battles between Canadian politicians. Some argue that deficits increase the national debt and make us vulnerable to increases in world interest rates. They propose to cut government spending to pay down the debt and to reduce taxes. Others argue that the ability to issue public debt allows the government to smooth taxes and inflation over time.

Percent of GDP

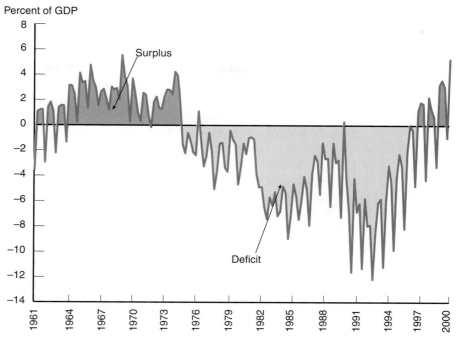

FIGURE 1·8 Government Budget Surplus or Deficit as a Percentage of Gross Domestic Product, 1961–2000

Source: Statistics Canada CANSIM Series D15875, D15885, and D15689.

You may have seen or heard statements in newspapers or on TV that budget deficits are undesirable. We explore the accuracy of such statements in Chapter 26 by examining why deficits might lead to a higher rate of money growth, a higher rate of inflation, and higher interest rates.

HOW WE WILL STUDY MONEY, BANKING, AND FINANCIAL MARKETS

This textbook stresses the economic way of thinking by developing a unifying framework to study money, banking, and financial markets. This analytic framework uses a few basic economic concepts to organize your thinking about the determination of asset prices, the structure of financial markets, bank management, and the role of money in the economy. It encompasses the following basic concepts:

- A simplified approach to the demand for assets
- The concept of equilibrium
- Basic supply and demand to explain behaviour in financial markets
- The search for profits
- An approach to financial structure based on transaction costs and asymmetric information
- Aggregate supply and demand analysis.

The unifying framework used in this book will keep your knowledge from becoming obsolete and make the material more interesting. It will enable you to learn what *really* matters without having to memorize a mass of dull facts that you will forget soon after the final exam. This framework will also provide you with the tools to understand trends in the financial marketplace and in variables such as interest rates, exchange rates, inflation, and aggregate output.

To help you understand and apply the unifying analytic framework, simple models are constructed in which the variables held constant are carefully delineated, each step in the derivation of the model is clearly and carefully laid out, and the models are then used to explain various phenomena by focusing on changes in one variable at a time, holding all other variables constant.

To reinforce the models' usefulness, this text uses case studies, applications, and special-interest boxes to present evidence that supports or casts doubts on the theories being discussed. This exposure to real-life events and data should dissuade you from thinking that all economists make abstract assumptions and develop theories that have little to do with actual behaviour.

To function better in the real world outside the classroom, you must have the tools to follow the financial news that appears in leading financial publications such as the *Globe and Mail: Report on Business*, and the *National Post: Financial Post*. These tools are presented in two formats. The first is a set of special boxed inserts titled "Following the Financial News," which contain actual columns and data from the media that appear daily or periodically. These boxes give you the detailed information and definitions you need to evaluate the data being presented. The second is a set of special applications titled "Reading the Financial Pages" that expand on the "Following the Financial News" boxes. These applications show you how the analytic framework in the book can be used directly to make sense of the daily columns in Canada's leading financial newspapers.

Globe and Mail
www.globeandmail.com

National Post
www.nationalpost.com

CONCLUDING REMARKS

The topic of money, banking, and financial markets is an exciting field that directly affects your life—interest rates influence earnings on your savings and the payments on loans you may seek on a car or a house, and monetary policy may affect your job prospects and the prices of goods in the future. Your study of money, banking, and financial markets will introduce you to many of the controversies about the conduct of economic policy that are currently the subject of hot debate in the political arena and will help you gain a clearer understanding of economic phenomena you frequently hear about in the news media. The knowledge you gain will stay with you long after the course is done.

SUMMARY

1. Activities in financial markets have direct effects on individuals' wealth, the behaviour of businesses, and the efficiency of our economy. Three financial markets deserve particular attention: the bond market (where interest rates are determined), the stock market (which has a major effect on people's wealth and on firms' investment decisions), and the foreign exchange market (because fluctuations in the foreign exchange rate have major consequences for the Canadian economy).

2. Banks and other financial institutions channel funds from people who might not put them to productive use to people who can do so and thus play a crucial role in improving the efficiency of the economy.

3. Money appears to be a major influence on inflation, business cycles, and interest rates. Because these economic variables are so important to the health of the economy, we need to understand how monetary policy is and should be conducted. We also need to study government budget deficits because they can be an influential factor in the conduct of monetary policy.

4. This textbook stresses the economic way of thinking by developing a unifying analytic framework for the study of money, banking, and financial markets using a few basic economic principles. This textbook also emphasizes the interaction of theoretical analysis and empirical data.

KEY TERMS

aggregate income
  (appendix), p. 14

aggregate output, p. 7

aggregate price level, p. 8

appreciation, p. 4

asset, p. 2

Bank of Canada (the Bank), p. 10

banks, p. 6

bond, p. 2

budget deficit, p. 10

business cycles, p. 7

central bank, p. 10

depreciation, p. 4

financial intermediaries, p. 6

financial markets, p. 1

foreign exchange market, p. 3

foreign exchange rate, p. 3

gross domestic product
  (appendix), p. 14

inflation, p. 8

inflation rate, p. 8

interest rate, p. 2

monetary policy, p. 10

monetary theory, p. 8

money, p. 6

recession, p. 7

security, p. 2

stock, p. 2

unemployment rate, p. 7

QUESTIONS AND PROBLEMS

Questions marked with an asterisk are answered at the end of the book in an appendix, "Answers to Selected Questions and Problems."

1. Has the inflation rate in Canada increased or decreased in the past few years? What about interest rates?

*2. What is the typical relationship between the rate of money growth and
  a. real output
  b. the inflation rate, and
  c. interest rates?

3. When was the most recent recession?

*4. When interest rates fall, how might you change your economic behaviour?

5. Can you think of any financial innovation in the past ten years that has affected you personally? Has it made you better off or worse off? Why?

*6. Is everybody worse off when interest rates rise?

7. What is the basic activity of banks?

*8. Why are financial markets important to the health of the economy?

9. What is the typical relationship among interest rates on three-month Treasury bills, long-term Canada bonds, and long-term corporate bonds?

*10. What effect might a fall in stock prices have on business investment?

11. What effect might a rise in stock prices have on consumers' decisions to spend?

*12. How does a fall in the value of the pound sterling affect British consumers?

13. How does an increase in the value of the pound sterling affect Canadian businesses?

*14. Looking at Figure 1-3, in what years would you have chosen to visit the Canadian Rockies rather than the Tower of London?

15. When the dollar is worth more in relation to currencies of other countries, are you more likely to buy Canadian-made or foreign-made jeans? Are Canadian companies that make jeans happier when the dollar is strong or when it is weak? What about a Canadian company that is in the business of importing jeans into Canada?

Appendix to Chapter 1

Defining Aggregate Output, Income, and the Price Level

The terms *aggregate output, income*, and *price level* are used so frequently throughout the text that we need to have a clear understanding of their definitions.

AGGREGATE OUTPUT AND INCOME

The most commonly reported measure of aggregate output, the **gross domestic product** (GDP), is the value of all final goods and services produced in a country during the course of the year.[1] This measure excludes two sets of items that at first glance you might think would be included. Purchases of goods that have been produced in the past, whether a Rembrandt painting or a house built 20 years ago, are not counted as part of GDP, nor are purchases of stocks or bonds. None of these enter into GDP because they are not goods and services produced during the course of the year. Intermediate goods, which are used up in producing final goods and services, such as the sugar in a candy bar or the energy used to produce steel, are also not counted separately as part of GDP. They are not counted separately because to do so would be to count them twice, as the value of the final goods already includes the value of the intermediate goods.

Aggregate income, the total income of *factors of production* (land, labour, and capital) from producing goods and services in the economy during the course of the year, is best thought of as being equal to aggregate output. Because the payments for final goods and services must eventually flow back to the owners of the factors of production as income, income payments must equal payments for final goods and services. For example, if the economy has an aggregate output of $10 billion, total income payments in the economy (aggregate income) are also $10 billion.

---

[1]Another measure of aggregate output is *gross national product (GNP)*, the value of all final goods and services produced by domestically owned factors of production during a year. It differs from GDP in that a part of Canadian GNP is earned abroad by Canadian individuals and corporations. Also, earnings by foreign companies in Canada are excluded from Canadian GNP but included in GDP.

REAL VERSUS NOMINAL MAGNITUDES

When the total value of final goods and services is calculated using current prices, the resulting GDP measure is referred to as *nominal GDP*. The word *nominal* indicates that values are measured using current prices. If all prices doubled but actual production of goods and services remained the same, nominal GDP would double even though people would not enjoy the benefits of twice as many goods and services. As a result, nominal variables can be misleading measures of economic well-being.

A more reliable measure of economic well-being expresses values in terms of prices for an arbitrary base year, currently 1996. GDP measured with constant prices is referred to as *real GDP*, the word *real* indicating that values are measured in terms of fixed prices. Real variables thus measure the quantities of goods and services and do not change because prices have changed but rather only if actual quantities have changed.

A brief example will make the distinction clearer. Suppose that you have a nominal income of $30 000 in 2001 and that your nominal income was $15 000 in 1996. If all prices doubled between 1996 and 2001, are you better off? The answer is no: although your income has doubled, your $30 000 buys you the same amount of goods because prices have also doubled. A real income measure indicates that your income in terms of the goods it can buy is the same. Measured in 1996 prices, the $30 000 of nominal income in 2001 turns out to be only $15 000 of real income. Because your real income is actually the same in the two years, you are no better or worse off in 2001 than you were in 1996.

Because real variables measure quantities in terms of real goods and services, they are typically of more interest than nominal variables. In this text, discussion of aggregate output or aggregate income always refers to real measures (such as real GDP).

AGGREGATE PRICE LEVEL

In Chapter 1 we defined the aggregate price level as a measure of average prices in the economy. Two measures of the aggregate price level are commonly encountered in economic data. The first is the *GDP deflator*, which is defined as

$$\text{GDP deflator} = 100 \times \frac{\text{Nominal GDP}}{\text{Real GDP}}$$

Typically, we multiply by 100 to obtain a measure of the price level in the form of a price index, which expresses the price level for the base year as 100. Thus if 2001 nominal GDP is $9 billion but 2001 real GDP in 1996 prices is $6 billion,

$$\text{GDP deflator} = 100 \times \frac{\$9 \text{ billion}}{\$6 \text{ billion}} = 150.$$

The GDP deflator indicates that, on average, prices have risen 50% since 1996.

Another popular measure of the aggregate price level (and the one that is most frequently reported in the press) is the *consumer price index (CPI)*. The CPI is measured by pricing a "basket" list of goods and services bought by a typical urban household over a given period, say, one month. If over the course of the year the cost of this basket of goods and services rises from $500 to $600, the CPI has risen by 20%. The CPI is also expressed as a price index with the base year equal to 100.

Both the CPI and the GDP deflator measures of the price level can be used to convert or deflate a nominal magnitude into a real magnitude. This is accomplished by dividing the nominal magnitude by the price index:

$$\text{Real GDP} = 100 \times \frac{\text{Nominal GDP}}{\text{GDP deflator}}$$

In our example, in which the GDP deflator for 2001 is 150, real GDP for 2001 equals

$$\text{Real GDP} = 100 \times \frac{\$9 \text{ billion}}{150} = \$6 \text{ billion in 1996 prices}$$

which corresponds to the real GDP figure for 2001 mentioned earlier.

Chapter 2

An Overview of the Financial System

PREVIEW   Inez the Inventor has designed a low-cost robot that cleans house (even does windows), washes the car, and mows the lawn, but she has no funds to put her wonderful invention into production. Walter the Widower has plenty of savings, which he and his wife accumulated over the years. If we could get Inez and Walter together so that Walter could provide funds to Inez, Inez's robot would see the light of day, and the economy would be better off: we would have cleaner houses, shinier cars, and more beautiful lawns.

Financial markets (bond and stock markets) and financial intermediaries (banks, insurance companies, pension funds) have the basic function of getting people like Inez and Walter together by moving funds from those who have a surplus of funds (Walter) to those who have a shortage of funds (Inez). More realistically, when IBM invents a better computer, it may need funds to bring it to market. Similarly, when a local government needs to build a road or a school, it may need more funds than local property taxes provide. Well-functioning financial markets and financial intermediaries are needed to improve economic well-being and efficiency and are crucial to economic health. Indeed, when the financial system breaks down, as it has in Russia and in East Asia recently, severe economic hardship results.

To study the effects of financial markets and financial intermediaries on the economy, we must first acquire an understanding of their general structure and operation. In this chapter we learn about the major financial intermediaries and the instruments that are traded in financial markets as well as how these markets are regulated.

This chapter presents an overview of the fascinating study of financial markets and institutions. We return to a more detailed treatment of the regulation, structure, and evolution of financial markets in Chapters 8 through 13.

FUNCTION OF FINANCIAL MARKETS

Financial markets perform the essential economic function of channelling funds from people who have saved surplus funds by spending less than their income to people who have a shortage of funds because they wish to spend more than their income. This function is shown schematically in Figure 2-1. Those who have saved and are lending funds, the lender-savers, are at the left, and those who must borrow funds to finance their spending, the borrower-spenders, are at the right. The principal lender-savers are households, but business enterprises and the government (particularly state and local government), as well as foreigners and their governments, sometimes also find themselves with excess funds and so lend them out. The most important borrower-spenders are businesses and the government (particularly the federal government), but households and foreigners also borrow to finance their purchases of cars, furniture, and houses. The arrows show that funds flow from lender-savers to borrower-spenders via two routes.

In *direct finance* (the route at the bottom of Figure 2-1), borrowers borrow funds directly from lenders in financial markets by selling them *securities* (also called *financial instruments*), which are claims on the borrower's future income or assets. Securities are assets for the person who buys them but **liabilities** (IOUs or debts) for the individual or firm that sells (issues) them. For example, if Nortel needs to borrow funds to pay for a new factory to manufacture telecommunications equipment, it might borrow the funds from savers by selling them *bonds*, debt securities that promise to make payments periodically for a specified period of time.

Nortel Networks
www.nortelnetworks.com

Why is this channelling of funds from savers to spenders so important to the economy? The answer is that the people who save are frequently not the same people who have profitable investment opportunities available to them, the entrepreneurs. Let's first think about this on a personal level. Suppose that you have saved $1000 this year, but no borrowing or lending is possible because there are no financial markets. If you do not have an investment opportunity that will permit you to earn income with your savings, you will just hold on to the $1000 and

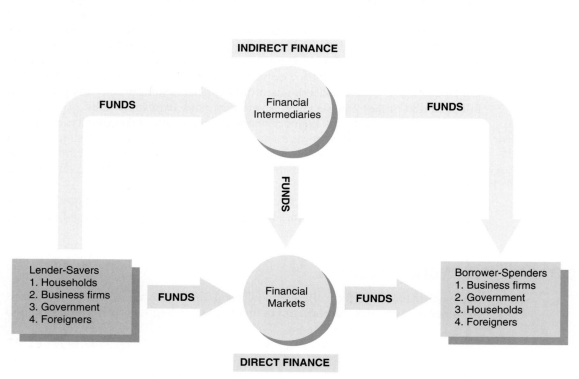

FIGURE 2-1 Flows of Funds Through the Financial System

will earn no interest. However, Carl the Carpenter has a productive use for your $1000: he can use it to purchase a new tool that will shorten the time it takes him to build a house, thereby earning an extra $200 per year. If you could get in touch with Carl, you could lend him the $1000 at a rental fee (interest) of $100 per year, and both of you would be better off. You would earn $100 per year on your $1000, instead of the zero amount that you would earn otherwise, while Carl would earn $100 more income per year (the $200 extra earnings per year minus the $100 rental fee for the use of the funds).

In the absence of financial markets, you and Carl the Carpenter might never get together. Without financial markets, it is hard to transfer funds from a person who has no investment opportunities to one who has them; you would both be stuck with the status quo, and both of you would be worse off. Financial markets are thus essential to promoting economic efficiency.

The existence of financial markets is also beneficial even if someone borrows for a purpose other than increasing production in a business. Say that you are recently married, have a good job, and want to buy a house. You earn a good salary, but because you have just started to work, you have not yet saved much. Over time you would have no problem saving enough to buy the house of your dreams, but by then you would be too old to get full enjoyment from it. Without financial markets, you are stuck; you cannot buy the house and must continue to live in your tiny apartment.

If a financial market were set up so that people who had built up savings could lend you the money to buy the house, you would be more than happy to pay them some interest in order to own a home while you are still young enough to enjoy it. Then, when you had saved up enough funds, you would pay back your loan. The overall outcome would be such that you would be better off, as would the persons who made you the loan. They would now earn some interest, whereas they would not if the financial market did not exist.

Now we can see why financial markets have such an important function in the economy. They allow funds to move from people who lack productive investment opportunities to people who have such opportunities. By so doing, financial markets contribute to higher production and efficiency in the overall economy. They also directly improve the well-being of consumers by allowing them to time their purchases better. They provide funds to young people to buy what they need and can eventually afford without forcing them to wait until they have saved up the entire purchase price. Financial markets that are operating efficiently improve the economic welfare of everyone in the society.

STRUCTURE OF FINANCIAL MARKETS

Now that we understand the basic function of financial markets, let's look at their structure. The following descriptions of several categorizations of financial markets illustrate essential features of these markets.

Debt and Equity Markets

A firm or an individual can obtain funds in a financial market in two ways. The most common method is to issue a debt instrument, such as a bond or a mortgage, which is a contractual agreement by the borrower to pay the holder of the instrument fixed dollar amounts at regular intervals (interest and principal payments) until a specified date (the maturity date), when a final payment is made. The **maturity** of a debt instrument is the time (term) to that instrument's expiration date. A debt instrument is **short-term** if its maturity is less than a year and **long-term** if its maturity is ten years or longer. Debt instruments with a maturity between one and ten years are said to be **medium-term**.

The second method of raising funds is by issuing **equities**, such as common stock, which are claims to share in the net income (income after expenses and taxes) and the assets of a business. If you own one share of common stock in a company that has issued one million shares, you are entitled to one-millionth of the firm's net income and one-millionth of the firm's assets. Equities usually make periodic payments (**dividends**) to their holders and are considered long-term securities because they have no maturity date. In addition, owning stock means that you own a portion of the firm and thus have the right to vote on issues important to the firm and to elect its directors.

The main disadvantage of owning a corporation's equities rather than its debt is that an equity holder is a *residual claimant*; that is, the corporation must pay all its debt holders before it pays its equity holders. The advantage of holding equities is that equity holders benefit directly from any increases in the corporation's profitability or asset value because equities confer ownership rights on the equity holders. Debt holders do not share in this benefit because their dollar payments are fixed. We examine the pros and cons of debt versus equity instruments in more detail in Chapter 8, which provides an economic analysis of financial structure.

The total value of equities in Canada has typically fluctuated between $20 billion and $300 billion since the early 1970s, depending on the prices of shares. Although the average person is more aware of the stock market than any other financial market, the size of the debt market is almost on par with that of the equities market: the value of debt instruments was $183 billion at the end of 2000 while the value of equities was $242 billion at the end of 2000.

Primary and Secondary Markets

A **primary market** is a financial market in which new issues of a security, such as a bond or a stock, are sold to initial buyers by the corporation or government agency borrowing the funds. A **secondary market** is a financial market in which securities that have been previously issued (and are thus second-hand) can be resold.

The primary markets for securities are not well known to the public because the selling of securities to initial buyers often takes place behind closed doors. An important financial institution that assists in the initial sale of securities in the primary market is the **investment bank**. It does this by **underwriting** securities: it guarantees a price for a corporation's securities and then sells them to the public.

Toronto Stock Exchange
www.tse.com

Montreal Stock Exchange
www.me.org

Canadian Venture Capital Exchange
www.cdnx.com

The Toronto and Montreal stock exchanges and the Canadian Venture Capital Exchange (CDNX), in which previously issued stocks are traded, are the best-known examples of secondary markets, although the bond markets, in which previously issued bonds of major corporations and the Canadian government are bought and sold, actually have a larger trading volume. Other examples of secondary markets are foreign exchange markets, futures markets, and options markets. Securities brokers and dealers are crucial to a well-functioning secondary market. **Brokers** are agents of investors who match buyers with sellers of securities; **dealers** link buyers and sellers by buying and selling securities at stated prices.

When an individual buys a security in the secondary market, the person who has sold the security receives money in exchange for the security, but the corporation that issued the security acquires no new funds. A corporation acquires new funds only when its securities are first sold in the primary market. Nonetheless, secondary markets serve two important functions. First, they make it easier to sell these financial instruments to raise cash; that is, they make the financial instruments more **liquid**. The increased liquidity of these instruments then makes them more desirable and thus easier for the issuing firm to sell in the primary market. Second, they determine the price of the security that the issuing firm sells in the primary market. The investors that buy securities in the primary market will pay the issuing corporation no more than the price they think the secondary market will set for this security. The higher the security's price in the secondary market, the higher will be the price that the issuing firm will receive for a new security in the primary market and hence the greater the amount of financial capital it can raise. Conditions in the secondary market are therefore the most relevant to corporations issuing securities. It is for this reason that books like this one, which deal with financial markets, focus on the behaviour of secondary markets rather than that of primary markets.

Exchanges and Over-the-Counter Markets

Winnipeg Commodity
Exchange
www.wce.mb.ca

Secondary markets can be organized in two ways. One is to organize **exchanges**, where buyers and sellers of securities (or their agents or brokers) meet in one central location to conduct trades. The Toronto and Montreal stock exchanges for stocks and the Winnipeg Commodity Exchange for commodities (wheat, oats, barley, and other agricultural commodities) are examples of organized exchanges.

The other method of organizing a secondary market is to have an **over-the-counter (OTC) market**, in which dealers at different locations who have an inventory of securities stand ready to buy and sell securities "over the counter" to anyone who comes to them and is willing to accept their prices. Because over-the-counter dealers are in computer contact and know the prices set by one another, the OTC market is very competitive and not very different from a market with an organized exchange.

Many common stocks are traded over-the-counter, although the largest corporations usually have their shares traded at organized stock exchanges such as the Toronto Stock Exchange. The Canadian government bond market is set up as an over-the-counter market. Dealers establish a "market" in these securities by standing ready to buy and sell Canadian government bonds. Other over-the-counter markets include those that trade other types of financial instruments such as negotiable certificates of deposit, overnight funds, banker's acceptances, and foreign exchange.

Money and Capital Markets

Another way of distinguishing between markets is on the basis of the maturity of the securities traded in each market. The **money market** is a financial market in which only short-term debt instruments (generally those with original maturity of less than one year) are traded; the **capital market** is the market in which longer-term debt (generally those with original maturity of one year or greater) and equity instruments are traded. Money market securities are usually more widely traded than longer-term securities and so tend to be more liquid. In addition, as we will see in Chapter 4, short-term securities have smaller fluctuations in prices than long-term securities, making them safer investments. As a result, corporations and banks actively use the money market to earn interest on surplus funds that they expect to have only temporarily. Capital market securities, such as stocks and long-term bonds, are often held by financial intermediaries such as insurance companies and pension funds, which have more certainty about the amount of funds they will have available in the future.

FINANCIAL MARKET INSTRUMENTS

To complete our understanding of how financial markets perform the important role of channelling funds from lender-savers to borrower-spenders, we need to examine the securities (instruments) traded in financial markets. We first focus on the instruments traded in the money market and then turn to those traded in the capital market.

Money Market Instruments

Because of their short terms to maturity, the debt instruments traded in the money market undergo the fewest price fluctuations and so are the least risky investments. The money market has undergone great changes in the past three decades, with the amount of some financial instruments growing at a far more rapid rate than others.

The principal money market instruments are listed in Table 2-1 along with the amount outstanding at the end of 1970, 1980, 1990, and 2000.

Department of
Finance Canada
www.fin.gc.ca

Government of Canada Treasury Bills   These short-term debt instruments of the Canadian government are issued in 1-, 3-, 6-, and 12-month maturities to finance the federal government. They pay a set amount at maturity and have no interest payments, but they effectively pay interest by initially selling at a discount, that is, at a price lower than the set amount paid at maturity. For instance, you might buy in May 2001 for $9000 a one-year Treasury bill that can be redeemed in May 2002 for $10 000.

Treasury bills are the most liquid of all the money market instruments because they are the most actively traded. They are also the safest of all money market instruments because there is almost no possibility of **default**, a situation in which the party issuing the debt instrument (the federal government in this case) is unable to make interest payments or pay off the amount owed when the instrument matures. The federal government is always able to meet its debt obligations because it can raise taxes to pay off its debts. Treasury bills are held mainly by banks, although households, corporations, and other financial intermediaries hold small amounts.

Certificates of Deposit   A *certificate of deposit* (CD) is a debt instrument sold by a bank to depositors that pays annual interest of a given amount and at maturity pays back the original purchase price. CDs are often negotiable, meaning that they can be traded, and in bearer form (called **bearer deposit notes**), meaning that the buyer's name is neither recorded in the issuer's books nor on the security itself. These negotiable CDs are issued in multiples of $100 000 and with maturities of 30 to 365 days, and can be resold in a secondary market, thus offering the purchaser both yield and liquidity.

TABLE 2-1   Principal Money Market Instruments

Type of Instrument	Amount Outstanding (in millions of dollars)			
	1970	1980	1990	2000
Treasury bills				
Government of Canada	2762	13 709	113 654	77 309
Provincial governments	428	905	12 602	17 399
Municipal governments	25	113	514	160
Short-term paper				
Banker's acceptances	291	4 874	46 738	53 461
Finance paper	–	3 828	9 939	17 574
Commercial paper	588	2 555	12 971	24 782

Source: Statistics Canada CANSIM Series B2477, B15021, B15022, B2313, B4117, and B2329.

Chartered banks also issue non-negotiable CDs. That is, they cannot be sold to someone else and cannot be redeemed from the bank before maturity without paying a substantial penalty. Non-negotiable CDs are issued in denominations ranging from $5000 to $100 000 and with maturities of 1 day to 5 years. They are also known as **term deposit receipts** or **term notes**.

CDs are also an extremely important source of funds for trust and mortgage loan companies (to be discussed later in this chapter). These institutions issue CDs under a variety of names such as, for example, DRs (Deposit Receipts), GTCs (Guaranteed Trust Certificates), GICs (Guaranteed Investment Certificates), and GIRs (Guaranteed Investment Receipts).

General Motors
www.gmcanada.com

DaimlerChrysler
www.daimlerchrysler.ca

Finance Paper and Commercial Paper *Finance paper* is an unsecured short-term debt instrument issued in either Canadian dollars or other currencies by sales finance and consumer loan companies. *Commercial paper* is similar to finance paper and is issued by large banks and well-known corporations such as General Motors and DaimlerChrysler. The interest rate on commercial paper is slightly higher than that on finance paper, but both rates are low relative to those on other corporate fixed-income securities and slightly higher than rates on government of Canada Treasury bills. Finance and commercial paper are issued in minimum denominations of $50 000 and in maturities of 30 to 365 days for finance paper and 1 to 365 days for commercial paper. They are usually held to maturity and as a result the secondary market for both types of paper is limited.

Before the 1960s, corporations usually borrowed their short-term funds from banks, but since then they have come to rely more heavily on selling commercial paper to other financial intermediaries and corporations for their immediate borrowing needs; in other words, they engage in direct finance. Growth of the commercial paper market has been substantial: the amount of commercial paper outstanding increased by over 4000% (from $588 million to $24 billion) in the period 1970–2000. We will discuss why the commercial paper market has had such tremendous growth in Chapter 10.

Banker's Acceptances These money market instruments are created in the course of carrying out international trade and have been in use for hundreds of years. A *banker's acceptance* is a bank draft (a promise of payment similar to a cheque) issued by a firm, payable at some future date, and guaranteed for a fee by the bank that stamps it "accepted." The firm issuing the instrument is required to deposit the required funds into its account to cover the draft. If the firm fails to do so, the bank's guarantee means that it is obligated to make good on the draft. The advantage to the firm is that the draft is more likely to be accepted when purchasing goods abroad because the foreign exporter knows that even if the company purchasing the goods goes bankrupt, the bank draft will still be paid off. These "accepted" drafts are often resold in a secondary market at a discount and so are similar in function to Treasury bills. Typically, they are held by many of the same parties that hold Treasury bills, and the amount outstanding has experienced phenomenal growth, rising by over 18 000% ($291 million to $53 billion) from 1970 to 2000.

The phenomenal growth in banker's acceptances in Canada is due to the growth of the Canadian money market and the fact that Canadian chartered banks enjoy stronger credit ratings than all but the largest corporations. Moreover, revisions in the Bank Act have removed certain restrictions regarding the issuance of banker's acceptances and the banks have reduced the stamping fees that they charge for banker's acceptances—these fees vary from 0.20% to 0.75%.

large corporations [handwritten]

Repurchase Agreements   *Repurchase agreements (repos)* are effectively short-term loans (usually with a maturity of less than two weeks) in which Treasury bills serve as *collateral,* an asset that the lender receives if the borrower does not pay back the loan. Repos are made as follows: a large corporation, such as General Motors, may have some idle funds in its bank account, say $1 million, which it would like to lend for a week. GM uses this excess $1 million to buy Treasury bills from a bank, which agrees to repurchase them the next week at a price slightly above GM's purchase price. The effect of this agreement is that GM makes a loan of $1 million to the bank and holds $1 million of the bank's Treasury bills until the bank repurchases the bills to pay off the loan. Repurchase agreements are a fairly recent innovation in financial markets, having been introduced in 1969. They are now an important source of bank funds. The most important lenders in this market are large corporations.

Overnight Funds   These are typically overnight loans made by banks to other banks. The *overnight funds* designation is somewhat confusing because these loans are not made the federal government or by the Bank of Canada but rather by banks to other banks. One reason why a bank might borrow in the overnight funds market is that it might find it does not have enough settlement balances at the Bank of Canada. It can then borrow these balances from another bank with excess settlement balances.

↑ *interest rate = banks low on $* [handwritten]

The overnight market is very sensitive to the credit needs of the deposit-taking institutions, so the interest rate on overnight loans, called the **overnight interest rate**, is a closely watched barometer of the tightness of credit market conditions in the banking system and the stance of monetary policy. When it is high, it indicates that the banks are strapped for funds, whereas when it is low, banks' credit needs are low. As you will learn in Chapter 17, the overnight interest rate is the operating target of the Bank of Canada's monetary policy.

Capital Market Instruments

Capital market instruments are debt and equity measurements with maturities greater than one year. They have far wider price fluctuations than money market instruments and are considered to be fairly risky investments. The principal capital market instruments are listed in Table 2-2, which shows the amount outstanding at the end of 1970, 1980, 1990, and 2000.

Stocks   *Stocks* are equity claims on the net income and assets of a corporation. Their value was $242 billion at the end of 2000. The amount of new stock issues in any given year is typically quite small, less than 1% of the total value of shares outstanding. Individuals hold around half of the value of stocks; pension funds, mutual funds, and insurance companies hold the rest.

Mortgages   *Mortgages* are loans to households or firms to purchase housing, land, or other real structures, where the structure or land serves as collateral for the loans. The mortgage market is the largest debt market in Canada, with the amount of residential mortgages (used to purchase residential housing) outstanding more than tenfold the amount of commercial and farm mortgages. Trust and mortgage loan companies and credit unions and *caisses populaires* were the primary lenders in the residential mortgage market until 1967. The revision of the Bank Act in 1967, however, extended the authority of chartered banks to

Money Market Rates

The *Globe and Mail: Report on Business* and the *National Post: Financial Post* publish daily a listing of interest rates on many different financial instruments. In the *Globe and Mail: Report on Business*, this listing can be found in the "Money Rates" column.

The interest rates in the "Money Rates" column that are discussed most frequently in the media are:

Bank rate: The interest rate charged by the Bank of Canada on loans made to members of the Canadian Payments Association.

Prime rate: The base interest rate on corporate bank loans, an indicator of the cost of business borrowing from banks.

Treasury bill rates: The interest rates on Government of Canada Treasury bills, an indicator of general interest-rate movements.

Selected U.S. interest rates: Selected U.S. interest rates such as the federal funds rate, prime rate, and commercial paper rate. These are indicators of general interest-rate movements in the United States.

MONEY RATES

ADMINISTERED RATES

Bank of Canada	6.00%
Central bank call range	5.50-6.00%
Canadian prime	7.5%

MONEY MARKET RATES
(for transactions of $1-million or more)

3-month treasury bills	5.67%
6-month treasury bills	5.81%
1-year treasury bills	5.91%
10-year Canada bonds	5.64%
30-year Canada bonds	5.54%
1-month banker's accept	5.82%
2-month banker's accept	5.85%
3-month banker's accept	5.88%

Commercial Paper (R-1 Low)

1-month	5.84%
2-month	5.86%
3-month	5.88%
Call money	5.75%

UNITED STATES

New York (AP)—Money rates for Friday as reported by Bridge Telerate as of 4 p.m.:
Prime Rate: 9.50
Discount Rate: 6.00
Broker call loan rate: 8.25
Federal funds market rate: High 6.5625; low 6.5625; last 6.5625
Dealers commercial paper:
30-180 days: 6.49-6.43
Commercial paper by finance company: 30-270 days: 6.49-6.28
Bankers acceptances dealer indications: 30 days, 6.51; 60 days, 6.63; 90 days, 6.55; 120 days, 6.52; 150 days, 6.48; 180 days, 6.45
Certificates of Deposit Primary: 30 days, 4.82, 90 days, 5.61; 180 days, 5.86

Certificates of Deposit by dealer: 30 days, 6.55; 60 days, 6.67; 90 days, 6.64; 120 days, 6.63; 150 days, 6.62; 180 days, 6.63; 150 days, 6.62; 180 days, 6.61
Eurodollar rates: Overnight, 6.50-6.56; 1 month, 6.53-6.58; 3 months 6.64-6.70; 6 months, 6.70; 1 year, 6.67
Treasury Bill auction results: average discount rate: 3-month as of Nov. 20: 6.175; 6-month as of Nov. 20: 6.050; 52-week as of Aug 29: 5.88
Treasury Bill annualized rate on weekly average basis, yield adjusted for constant maturity, 1-year, as of Nov. 20: 6.09
Treasury Note market rate, 10-year, 5.64

make conventional residential mortgage loans and chartered banks have entered this market very aggressively in the last two decades. In fact, their market share of residential mortgages has increased from about 50% in 1989 to about 65% in 2000.

TABLE 2-2   Principal Capital Market Instruments

Type of Instrument	Amount Outstanding (in millions of dollars)			
	1970	**1980**	**1990**	**2000**
Corporate stocks (market value)	24 761	42 568	110 097	242 532
Residential mortgages	17 139	90 544	243 737	424 129
Corporate bonds	11 307	29 997	72 631	183 521
Government of Canada securities (marketable)	9 772	27 862	124 577	302 019
Bank commercial loans	11 299	58 751	102 574	131 972
Consumer loans	11 439	42 741	97 453	182 038
Commercial and farm mortgages	3 189	15 129	56 143	49 232

Source: Statistics Canada CANSIM Series B142, B942, B2318, B2478, B2300, B2303, B2304, B230, B2306, B2334, and B2319.

Canada Mortgage and
Housing Corporation
www.cmhc.ca

Banks and life insurance companies make the majority of commercial and farm mortgages. The federal government also plays an active role in the mortgage market via the Canada Mortgage and Housing Corporation (CMHC), which provides funds to the mortgage market by selling bonds and using the proceeds to buy mortgages. An important development in the residential mortgage market in recent years is the mortgage-backed security (see Box 2-1).

Corporate Bonds   These are long-term bonds issued by corporations with very strong credit ratings. The typical *corporate bond* pays the holder an interest payment twice a year and pays off the face value when the bond matures. Some corporate bonds, called *convertible bonds,* have the additional feature of allowing the holder to convert them into a specified number of shares of stock at any time up to the maturity date. This feature makes these convertible bonds more desirable to prospective purchasers than bonds without it and allows the corporation to reduce its interest payments because these bonds can increase in value if the price of the stock appreciates sufficiently. Because the outstanding amount of both convertible and nonconvertible bonds for any given corporation is small, they are not nearly as liquid as other securities such as Government of Canada bonds.

Although the size of the corporate bond market is substantially smaller than that of the stock market, the volume of new corporate bonds issued each year is substantially greater than the volume of new stock issues. Thus the behaviour of the corporate bond market is probably far more important to a firm's financing decisions than the behaviour of the stock market. The principal buyers of corporate bonds are life insurance companies; pension funds and households are other large holders.

Government of Canada Medium- and Long-Term Bonds   Medium-term bonds (those with initial maturities from 3 to 10 years) and long-term bonds (those with initial maturities greater than 10 years) are issued by the federal government to finance its deficit. Because they are the most widely traded bonds in Canada, they are the most liquid security traded in the capital market. They are held by the Bank of Canada, banks, households, and foreign investors.

BOX 2 · 1

Mortgage-Backed Securities

A major change in the residential mortgage market in recent years has been the creation of an active secondary market for mortgages. Because mortgages have different terms and interest rates, they are not sufficiently liquid to trade as securities on secondary markets. To stimulate mortgage lending, in late 1986 the government of Canada introduced the concept of a pass-through *mortgage-backed security*, patterned after the U.S. Government National Mortgage Association (GNMA, called "Ginnie Mae"). Mortgage-backed securities are not government of Canada securities but they are guaranteed by the Canada Mortgage and Housing Corporation (CMHC)—a federal government agency.

Under this program, private financial institutions such as chartered banks, trust and mortgage loan companies, and credit unions and *caisses populaires* gather a group of residential first mortgages with similar interest rates and terms to maturity (usually five years) into a bundle (of, say, $1 million). These mortgages must be individually guaranteed under the National Housing Act. This bundle is then sold as a security to a third party, usually a large institutional investor such as a pension fund. When individuals make their mortgage payments to the financial institution, the financial institution passes the payments through to the owner of the security by sending a cheque for the total of all payments. Because CMHC guarantees the payments, these pass-through securities have a very low default risk and are very popular.

Mortgage-backed securities have been so successful that they have completely transformed the residential mortgage market. Throughout the 1970s, over 80% of residential mortgages were owned outright by trust and mortgage loan companies, credit unions and *caisses populaires*, and chartered banks. Now only a fraction is owned outright by these institutions, with the rest held as mortgage-backed securities.

These debt instruments are issued in either bearer or registered form and in denominations of $1000, $5000, $25 000, $100 000, and $1 million. In the case of **registered bonds**, the name of the owner appears on the bond certificate and is also recorded at the Bank of Canada. Some issues have the additional **call** or **redemption** feature of allowing them to be "called" on specified notice (usually 30 to 60 days).

Canada Savings Bonds These are non-marketable bonds issued by the government of Canada once a year, generally for about two weeks ending on November 1. *Canada Savings Bonds* (*CSBs*) are floating-rate bonds, available in denominations from $100 to $10 000, and offered exclusively to individuals, estates, and specified trusts. They are issued as registered bonds and can be purchased from financial institutions or through payroll savings plans.

CSBs are different from all other bonds issued by the government of Canada in that they do not rise or fall in value, like other bonds do. They have the valuable option of being redeemable at face value plus accrued interest, at any time prior to maturity, by being presented at any financial institution. In October 1998 the government of Canada introduced another type of bonds that are similar to CSBs—the Canada Premium Bonds (CPBs). CPBs offer a slightly higher coupon rate than the CSBs, but can be redeemed only once a year, on the anniversary of the issue date and during the month after that date.

Provincial and Municipal Government Bonds Provincial and municipal governments also issue bonds to finance expenditures on schools, roads, and other large programs. The securities issued by provincial governments are referred to as

provincial bonds or **provincials** and those issued by municipal governments as **municipal bonds** or **municipals**—the securities issued by the federal government are referred to as **Canadas**. Provincials and municipals are denominated in either domestic currency or foreign currencies, mostly U.S. dollars, Swiss francs, and Japanese yen. They are mainly held by trusteed pension plans, social security funds (predominantly the Canada Pension Plan), and foreigners.

Government Agency Securities These are long-term bonds issued by various government agencies such as the Ontario Municipal Improvement Corporation and the Alberta Municipal Financing Corporation to assist municipalities to finance such items as mortgages, farm loans, or power-generating equipment. The provincial governments guarantee many of these securities. They function much like Canadas, provincials, and municipals and are held by similar parties.

Consumer and Bank Commercial Loans These are loans to consumers and businesses made principally by banks but, in the case of consumer loans, also by finance companies. There are often no secondary markets in these loans, which makes them the least liquid of the capital market instruments listed in Table 2-2. However, secondary markets are developing.

INTERNATIONALIZATION OF FINANCIAL MARKETS

The growing internationalization of financial markets has become an important trend. The extraordinary growth of foreign financial markets has been the result of both large increases in the pool of savings in foreign countries such as Japan and the deregulation of foreign financial markets, which has enabled them to expand their activities. Canadian corporations and banks are now more likely to tap international capital markets to raise needed funds, and Canadian investors often seek investment opportunities abroad. Similarly, foreign corporations and banks raise funds from Canadians, and foreigners have become important investors in Canada. A look at international bond markets and world stock markets will give us a picture of how this globalization of financial markets is taking place.

International Bond Market, Eurobonds, and Eurocurrencies

The traditional instruments in the international bond market are known as **foreign bonds**. Foreign bonds are sold in a foreign country and are denominated in that country's currency. For example, if the Swedish automaker Volvo sells a bond in Canada denominated in Canadian dollars, it is classified as a foreign bond. Foreign bonds have been an important instrument in the international capital market for centuries. In fact, a large percentage of U.S. railroads built in the nineteenth century were financed by sales of foreign bonds in Britain.

A more recent innovation in the international bond market is the **Eurobond**, a bond denominated in a currency other than that of the country in which it is sold—for example, a bond issued by a Canadian corporation that is denominated in Japanese yen and sold in Germany. Currently, over 80% of the new issues in the international bond market are Eurobonds, and the market for these securities has grown very rapidly.

A variant of the Eurobond is **Eurocurrencies**, which are foreign currencies deposited in banks outside the home country. The most important of the Eurocurrencies are **Eurodollars**, which are U.S. dollars deposited in foreign banks outside the United States or in foreign branches of U.S. banks. Because these short-term deposits earn interest, they are similar to short-term Eurobonds. Canadian banks borrow Eurodollar deposits from other banks or from their own foreign branches, and Eurodollars are now an important source of funds for Canadian banks.

World Stock Markets

New York Stock Exchange
www.nyse.com

London Stock Exchange
www.londonstock
exchange.com

Tokyo Stock Exchange
www.tse.or.jp/english

Until recently, the U.S. stock market was by far the largest in the world, but stock markets in other countries have been growing in importance (Table 2-3). Now the United States is not always number one: since the mid-1980s, the value of stocks traded in Japan has at times exceeded the value of stocks traded in the United States. The increased interest in foreign stocks has prompted the development in Canada of mutual funds specializing in trading in foreign stock markets. Canadian investors now pay attention not only to the Canadian stock markets (the Toronto and Montreal stock exchanges and the Canadian Venture Capital Exchange) but also to stock price indexes for foreign stock markets such as the Dow Jones Industrial Average (New York), the Nikkei 225 Average (Tokyo) and the Financial Times–Stock Exchange 100-Share Index (London).

The internationalization of financial markets is having profound effects on Canada. Foreigners are not only providing funds to corporations in Canada but are also helping finance the federal government. Without these foreign funds, the Canadian economy would have grown far less rapidly in the 1980s and 1990s. The internationalization of financial markets is also leading the way to a more integrated world economy in which flows of goods and technology between countries are more commonplace. In later chapters we will encounter many examples of the important roles that international factors play in our economy.

FUNCTION OF FINANCIAL INTERMEDIARIES

Canadian Pacific
www.canadianpacific.com

As shown in Figure 2-1, funds can move from lenders to borrowers by a second route, called *indirect finance* because it involves a financial intermediary that stands between the lender-savers and the borrower-spenders and helps transfer funds from one to the other. A financial intermediary does this by borrowing funds from the lender-savers and then using these funds to make loans to borrower-spenders. For example, a bank might acquire funds by issuing a liability to the public in the form of savings deposits. It might then use the funds to acquire an asset by making a loan to Canadian Pacific or by buying a Canadian Pacific bond in the financial market. The ultimate result is that funds have been transferred from

TABLE 2-3 Top 10 Stock Exchanges in the World		
Exchange	**Market value (in millions of U.S. dollars)**	**Rank in 1996**
NYSE	6 841 987.6	1
Tokyo	3 011 161.4	2
London	1 642 582.4	3
Nasdaq	1 511 824.4	4
Germany	664 913.2	5
Paris	586 873.0	6
Canada (TSE)	486 977.9	7
Hong Kong	449 218.8	8
Switzerland	400 285.4	9
Amsterdam	375 357.2	10

Source: Annual Report: International Federation of Stock Exchanges 1999, p. 60. Reproduced with permission.

FOLLOWING THE FINANCIAL NEWS

Foreign Stock Market Indexes

Foreign stock market indexes are published daily in the *Globe and Mail: Report on Business* and the *National Post: Financial Post*. In the *National Post: Financial Post* they can be found in the "International Indexes" column, which reports developments in foreign stock markets.

The third column identifies the market index of the country under consideration. The first column, "high," gives the highest value of the index in the past 52 weeks, which was 20 833.21 for the Nikkei 225

Average on December 21. The second column, "low," gives the lowest value of the index in the past 52 weeks, which was 13 914.43 for the Nikkei 225 Average. The fourth column, "Close," gives the closing value of the index, which was 13 914.43 for the Nikkei 225 Average on December 21. The "Net chg" column indicates the change in the index from the previous trading day, -217.94, and the "% chg" column indicates the percentage change in the index, -1.54.

INTERNATIONAL INDEXES

52 week high	52 week low		Close	Net chg	%chg
Japan					
20833.21	13914.43	Nikkel	13914.43	-217.94	-1.54
1754.78	1289.31	Topix	1289.31	-25.32	-1.93
Britain					
4156.80	3321.70	FT Ords	378.10	-27.40	-0.76
6930.20	5994.60	FTSE 100	6176.70	-118.30	-1.88
3421.63	2913.30	FT 500	2913.30	-46.87	-1.58
3261.57	2852.60	FT All Shr	298.46	-50.57	-1.68
3934.25	3404.15	FT EurTop	3494.45	-121.46	-3.36
Germany					
2502.47	1944.53	FAZ	1945.29	-28.43	-1.44
8064.97	6248.76	DAX	6248.76	-230.52	-3.56
Australia					
3330.40	2920.00	All Ords	3190.90	-12.90	-0.40
5823.00	5137.70	All Inds	5533.80	-28.80	-0.52
785.20	592.10	All Mng	65100	-1.10	-0.17
Hong Kong					
18301.69	13722.70	HangSeng	14930.72	-257.32	-1.69
Taiwan					
10202.20	4845.21	Weighted	4947.89	-92.36	-1.83
China					
654.37	396.33	Shenzhen	637.06	6.16	0.98
2119.44	1348.82	Shanghai	2071.27	22.24	1.09
Indonesia					
703.48	404.12	JSX	414.87	-3.91	-0.93
Philippines					
2153.18	1251.23	Comp	1447.65	33.66	2.38
Singapore					
2582.94	1795.13	Straits	1929.32	-31.54	-1.61
Thailand					
498.46	250.60	SET	269.91	-1.18	-0.44
France					
6856.76	5450.11	CAC 40	5766.30	-192.56	-3.23
Italy					
2182.34	166.36	BancaCml	1880.65	-17.69	-0.93

52 week high	52 week low		Close	Net chg	%chg
51093	38736	MIB 30	43253	-973.00	-2.20
Switzerland					
8377.00	6781.40	SwissMrk	7993.70	-74.60	-0.92
Netherlands					
991.80	850.30	CBS Gen	877.20	-21.90	-2.44
Belgium					
19075.97	15270.60	Genreal	18049.70	5.79	0.03
Sweden					
6960.60	4730.67	Affrsvldn	4730.67	-223.83	-4.52
Spain					
1146.21	857.93	Madrid	857.93	-31.28	-3.52
South Africa					
8513.90	5980.70	All Share	783.50	-68.30	-0.87
Mexico					
8319.67	5231.85	Gen IPC	5231.85	-274.70	-4.99
Argentina					
645.29	396.55	BUSE	404.68	-7.45	-1.80
Brazil					
18951	13287	BRSP	14622.41	-713.70	-4.65
Venezuela					
7457.65	5012.63	IBC	644.75	-91.54	-1.36
Chile					
143.05	89.82	IPSA	95.30	-1.57	-1.62
India					
5933.56	3593.63	Sensex	4086.41	-66.53	-1.60
Turkey					
19577.27	7329.61	ISE Nati	9485.45	-161.07	-1.72
Malaysia					
1013.27	700.44	KLSE Cmp	705.51	-5.35	-0.75
Israel					
578.27	455.19	TA-100	490.97	-11.75	-2.34
Greece					
5794.85	3213.42	General	3454.28	-8.20	-0.24

Source: Excerpted with permission from *The Financial Post*, Thursday, December 21, 2000, p. D5.

the public (the lender-savers) to Canadian Pacific (the borrower-spender) with the help of the financial intermediary (the bank).

The process of indirect finance using financial intermediaries, called **financial intermediation**, is the primary route for moving funds from lenders to borrowers. Indeed, although the media focus much of their attention on securities markets, particularly the stock market, financial intermediaries are a far more important source of financing for corporations than securities markets are. This is true not only for Canada but for other industrialized countries as well (see Box 2-2). Why are financial intermediaries and indirect finance so important in financial markets? To answer this question, we need to understand the role of transaction costs and information costs in financial markets.

Transaction Costs

Transaction costs, the time and money spent in carrying out financial transactions, are a major problem for people who have excess funds to lend. As we have seen, Carl the Carpenter needs $1000 for his new tool, and you know that it is an excellent investment opportunity. You have the cash and would like to lend him the money, but to protect your investment, you have to hire a lawyer to write up the loan contract that specifies how much interest Carl will pay you, when he will make these interest payments, and when he will repay you the $1000. Obtaining the contract will cost you $500. When you include this transaction cost for making the loan, you realize that you can't earn enough from the deal (you spend $500 to make perhaps $100) and reluctantly tell Carl that he will have to look elsewhere.

This example illustrates that small savers like you or potential borrowers like Carl might be frozen out of financial markets and thus be unable to benefit from them. Can anyone come to the rescue? Financial intermediaries can.

Financial intermediaries can substantially reduce transaction costs because they have developed expertise in lowering costs and because their large size allows them to take advantage of **economies of scale**, the reduction in transaction costs per dollar of transactions as the size (scale) of transactions increases. For example, a bank knows how to find a good lawyer to produce an airtight loan contract, and this contract can be used over and over again in its loan transactions, thus lowering the legal cost per transaction. Instead of a loan contract (which may not be all that well written) costing $500, a bank can hire a topflight lawyer for $5000 to draw up an airtight loan contract that can be used for 2000 loans at a cost of $2.50 per loan. At a cost of $2.50 per loan, it now becomes profitable for the financial intermediary to lend Carl the $1000.

Because financial intermediaries are able to reduce transaction costs substantially, they make it possible for you to provide funds indirectly to people like Carl with productive investment opportunities. In addition, a financial intermediary's low transaction costs mean that it can provide its customers with liquidity services, services that make it easier for customers to conduct transactions. For example, banks provide depositors with chequing accounts that enable them to pay their bills easily. In addition, depositors can earn interest on chequing and savings accounts and yet still convert them into goods and services whenever necessary.

Asymmetric Information: Adverse Selection and Moral Hazard

The presence of transaction costs in financial markets explains, in part, why financial intermediaries and indirect finance play such an important role in financial markets. An additional reason is that in financial markets, one party often does not know enough about the other party to make accurate decisions. This inequality is called **asymmetric information**. For example, a borrower who takes out a loan

BOX 2·2

The Importance of Financial Intermediaries to Securities Markets: An International Comparison

Patterns of financing corporations differ across countries, but one key fact emerges. Studies of the major developed countries, including Canada, the United States, Great Britain, Japan, Italy, Germany, and France, show that when businesses go looking for funds to finance their activities, they usually obtain them indirectly through financial intermediaries and not directly from securities markets.* Even in Canada and the United States, which have the most developed securities markets in the world, loans from financial intermediaries are far more important for corporate finance than securities markets are. The countries that have made the least use of securities markets are Germany and Japan; in these two countries, financing from financial intermediaries has been almost ten times greater than that from securities markets. However, with the deregulation of Japanese securities markets in recent years, the share of corporate financing by financial intermediaries has been declining relative to the use of securities markets.

Although the dominance of financial intermediaries over securities markets is clear in all countries, the relative importance of bond versus stock markets differs widely across countries. In the United States, the bond market is far more important as a source of corporate finance. On average, the amount of new financing raised using bonds is ten times the amount using stocks. By contrast, countries such as France and Italy make more use of equities markets than of the bond market to raise capital.

*See, for example, Colin Mayer, "Financial Systems, Corporate Finance, and Economic Development," in *Asymmetric Information, Corporate Finance, and Investment*, ed. R. Glenn Hubbard (Chicago: University of Chicago Press, 1990), pp. 307–332.

usually has better information about the potential returns and risk associated with the investment projects for which the funds are earmarked than the lender does. Lack of information creates problems in the financial system on two fronts: before the transaction is entered into and after.[1]

Adverse selection is the problem created by asymmetric information *before* the transaction occurs. Adverse selection in financial markets occurs when the potential borrowers who are the most likely to produce an undesirable *(adverse)* outcome—the bad credit risks—are the ones who most actively seek out a loan and are thus most likely to be selected. Because adverse selection makes it more likely that loans might be made to bad credit risks, lenders may decide not to make any loans even though there are good credit risks in the marketplace.

To understand why adverse selection occurs, suppose that you have two aunts to whom you might make a loan—Aunt Sheila and Aunt Louise. Aunt Louise is a conservative type who borrows only when she has an investment she is quite sure will pay off. Aunt Sheila, by contrast, is an inveterate gambler who has just come across a get-rich-quick scheme that will make her a millionaire if she can just borrow $1000 to invest in it. Unfortunately, as with most get-rich-quick schemes, there is a high probability that the investment won't pay off and that Aunt Sheila will lose the $1000.

Which of your aunts is more likely to call you to ask for a loan? Aunt Sheila, of course, because she has so much to gain if the investment pays off. You, how-

---

[1]Asymmetric information and the adverse selection and moral hazard concepts are also crucial problems for the insurance industry (see Chapter 12).

ever, would not want to make a loan to her because there is a high probability that her investment will turn sour and she will be unable to pay you back.

If you knew both your aunts very well—that is, if your information were not asymmetric—you wouldn't have a problem because you would know that Aunt Sheila is a bad risk and so you would not lend to her. Suppose, though, that you don't know your aunts well. You are more likely to lend to Aunt Sheila than to Aunt Louise because Aunt Sheila would be hounding you for the loan. Because of the possibility of adverse selection, you might decide not to lend to either of your aunts, even though there are times when Aunt Louise, who is an excellent credit risk, might need a loan for a worthwhile investment.

Moral hazard is the problem created by asymmetric information *after* the transaction occurs. Moral hazard in financial markets is the risk (*hazard*) that the borrower might engage in activities that are undesirable (*immoral*) from the lender's point of view because they make it less likely that the loan will be paid back. Because moral hazard lowers the probability that the loan will be repaid, lenders may decide that they would rather not make a loan.

As an example of moral hazard, suppose that you made a $1000 loan to another relative, Uncle Melvin, who needs the money to purchase a word processor so he can set up a business typing students' term papers. Once you have made the loan, however, Uncle Melvin is more likely to slip off to the track and play the horses. If he bets on a 20-to-1 long shot and wins with your money, he is able to pay you back your $1000 and live high off the hog with the remaining $19 000. But if he loses, as is likely, you don't get paid back, and all he has lost is his reputation as a reliable, upstanding uncle. Uncle Melvin therefore has an incentive to go to the track because his gains ($19 000) if he bets correctly may be much greater than the cost to him (his reputation) if he bets incorrectly. If you knew what Uncle Melvin was up to, you would prevent him from going to the track, and he would not be able to increase the moral hazard. However, because it is hard for you to keep informed about his whereabouts—that is, because information is asymmetric—there is a good chance that Uncle Melvin will go to the track and you will not get paid back. The risk of moral hazard might therefore discourage you from making the $1000 loan to Uncle Melvin, even if you were sure that you would be paid back if he used it to set up his business.

Study Guide

Because the concepts of adverse selection and moral hazard are extremely useful in understanding the behaviour we examine in this and many of the later chapters (and in life in general), you must understand them fully. One way to distinguish between them is to remember that adverse selection is a problem of asymmetric information before entering into a transaction, whereas moral hazard is a problem of asymmetric information after the transaction has occurred. A helpful way to nail down these concepts is to think of other examples, for financial or other types of transactions, in which adverse selection or moral hazard plays a role. Several problems at the end of the chapter provide additional examples of situations involving adverse selection and moral hazard.

The problems created by adverse selection and moral hazard are an important impediment to well-functioning financial markets. Again, financial intermediaries can alleviate these problems.

With financial intermediaries in the economy, small savers can provide their funds to the financial markets by lending these funds to a trustworthy intermediary, say, the Honest John Bank, which in turn lends the funds out either by making loans or by buying securities such as stocks or bonds. Successful financial intermediaries have higher earnings on their investments than small savers because they are better equipped than individuals to screen out good from bad credit risks, thereby reducing losses due to adverse selection. In addition, financial intermediaries have high earnings because they develop expertise in monitoring the parties they lend to, thus reducing losses due to moral hazard. The result is that financial intermediaries can afford to pay lender-savers interest or provide substantial services and still earn a profit.

The success of financial intermediaries is evidenced by the fact that most Canadians invest their savings with them and also obtain their loans from them. Financial intermediaries play a key role in improving economic efficiency because they help financial markets channel funds from lender-savers to people with productive investment opportunities. Without a well-functioning set of financial intermediaries, it is very hard for an economy to reach its full potential. We will explore further the role of financial intermediaries in the economy in Part III.

FINANCIAL INTERMEDIARIES

We have seen why financial intermediaries play such an important role in the economy. Now we look at the principal financial intermediaries and how they perform the intermediation function. They fall into three categories: depository institutions (banks and near banks), contractual savings institutions, and investment intermediaries. Table 2-4 provides a guide to the discussion of the financial intermediaries that fit into these three categories by describing their primary liabilities (sources of funds) and assets (uses of funds). The relative size of these intermediaries in Canada is indicated in Table 2-5.

Depository Institutions

Depository institutions (which for simplicity we refer to as *banks* throughout this text) are financial intermediaries that accept deposits from individuals and institutions and make loans. The study of money and banking focuses special attention on this group of financial institutions because they are involved in the creation of deposits, an important component of the money supply. These institutions include chartered banks and the so-called near banks: trust and mortgage loan companies and credit unions and *caisses populaires*. Their behaviour plays an important role in determining the money supply.

Chartered Banks   These financial intermediaries raise funds primarily by issuing chequable deposits (deposits on which cheques can be written), savings deposits (deposits that are payable on demand but do not allow their owner to write cheques), and time deposits (deposits with fixed terms to maturity). They then use these funds to make commercial, consumer, and mortgage loans and to buy Canadian government securities and provincial and municipal bonds. There are 53 chartered banks in Canada, and as a group they are the largest financial intermediary and have the most diversified portfolios (collections) of assets.

Trust and Mortgage Loan Companies   Trust and Mortgage Loan Companies (TMLs) obtain funds primarily through chequable and non-chequable savings deposits, term deposits, guaranteed investment certificates, and debentures. The acquired funds have traditionally been used to make loans. TMLs are the second group of depository institutions, numbering around 65. In the 1950s and 1960s, TMLs grew much more rapidly than chartered banks, but when interest rates climbed sharply from the late 1960s to the early 1980s, TMLs encountered difficulties that slowed their rapid growth. Because most mortgages are long-term loans, with maturities in excess of 25 years, many were made years earlier when interest rates were substantially lower. When interest rates rose, TMLs frequently found that the income

TABLE 2-4   Primary Assets and Liabilities of Financial Intermediaries

Type of Intermediary	Primary Liabilities (Sources of Funds)	Primary Assets (Uses of Funds)
Depository institutions (banks)		
Chartered banks	Deposits	Loans, mortgages, government bonds
Trust and mortgage loan companies	Deposits	Mortgages
Credit unions and *caisses populaires*	Deposits	Mortgages
Contractual savings institutions		
Life insurance companies	Premiums from policies	Corporate bonds and mortgages
P and C insurance companies	Premiums from policies	Corporate bonds and stocks
Pension funds	Retirement contributions	Corporate bonds and stocks
Investment Intermediaries		
Finance companies	Finance paper, stock, bonds	Consumer and business loans
Mutual funds	Shares	Stocks and bonds
Money market mutual funds	Shares	Money market instruments

TABLE 2-5   (Estimated) Relative Shares of Total Financial Intermediary Assets

Type of Intermediary	Total assets (in millions of dollars)	Percent (%)
Depository institutions		
Chartered banks*	1 508 941	45.27
Trust and mortgage loan companies*	202 678	6.08
Credit unions and *caisses populaires***	106 988	3.21
Contractual savings institutions		
Life insurance companies*	277 507	8.33
P and C insurance companies*	54 356	1.63
Pension funds***	846 313	25.39
Investment intermediaries		
Finance companies*	56 463	1.69
Mutual funds**	280 100	8.40
Total	3 333 346	100.00

Source: *OSFI Annual Report 1999–2000. **The MacKay Report, p. 43. ***Canadian Life and Health Insurance Facts 2000, p. 12.

from their mortgages was well below the cost of acquiring funds. In the early 1980s, 30 TMLs suffered large losses and 15 went out of business.

Until 1954, Canadian chartered banks were restricted to making commercial loans and could not make mortgage loans. Following the 1954 revisions in the *Bank Act* and the *National Housing Act* (NHA), chartered banks were allowed for the first time to make residential mortgage loans, but under NHA terms. The *Bank Act* in 1967, however, extended the authority of chartered banks to issue mortgage loans, by allowing them to make conventional mortgage loans and thereby directly compete with TMLs. Also, until 1991, TMLs were restricted to making mortgage loans and could not make commercial loans. The *Bank Act* of 1991 opened new business opportunities for TMLs by permitting them to make commercial loans. The net result of these legislative changes is that the distinction between TMLs and chartered banks has blurred, and these intermediaries have become more alike and much more competitive with each other.

Credit Unions and *Caisses Populaires* Credit unions and *caisses populaires* (CUCPs), numbering about 2200, are very small cooperative lending institutions organized around a particular group: union members, employees of a particular firm, and so forth. Almost 10 million Canadians are members of CUCPs and more than 61 000 are employed in the credit union and *caisse populaire* system. CUCPs acquire funds from deposits and primarily make mortgage and consumer loans.

Contractual Savings Institutions

Contractual savings institutions, such as insurance companies and pension funds, are financial intermediaries that acquire funds at periodic intervals on a contractual basis. Because they can predict with reasonable accuracy how much they will have to pay out in benefits in the coming years, they do not have to worry as much as depository institutions about losing funds. As a result, the liquidity of assets is not as important a consideration for them as it is for depository institutions, and they tend to invest their funds primarily in long-term securities such as corporate bonds, stocks, and mortgages.

Life Insurance Companies Life insurance companies insure people against financial hazards following a death and sell annuities (annual income payments upon retirement). They acquire funds from the premiums that people pay to keep their policies in force and use them mainly to buy corporate bonds and mortgages. They also purchase stocks but are restricted in the amount that they can hold. Currently, with $277 billion of assets, they are among the largest of the contractual savings institutions.

Property and Casualty (P & C) Insurance Companies These companies insure their policyholders against loss from theft, fire, and accidents. They are very much like life insurance companies, receiving funds through premiums for their policies, but they have a greater possibility of loss of funds if major disasters occur. For this reason, they use their funds to buy more liquid assets than life insurance companies do. Their largest holding of assets is government bonds and debentures; they also hold corporate bonds and stocks.

Pension Funds and Government Retirement Funds Private pension funds and provincial and municipal retirement funds provide retirement income in the form of annuities to employees who are covered by a pension plan. Funds are acquired by contributions from employers and/or from employees, who either have a contribution automatically deducted from their paycheques or contribute voluntarily. The largest asset holdings of pension funds are corporate bonds and stocks. The establishment of pension funds has been actively encouraged by the federal government both through legislation requiring pension plans and through tax incentives to encourage contributions.

Investment Intermediaries

This category of financial intermediaries includes finance companies, mutual funds, and money market mutual funds.

Finance Companies   Finance companies raise funds by selling commercial paper (a short-term debt instrument) and by issuing stocks and bonds. They lend these funds to consumers, who make purchases of such items as furniture, automobiles, and home improvements, and to small businesses. Some finance companies are organized by a parent corporation to help sell its product. For example, Ford Credit makes loans to consumers who purchase Ford automobiles.

Mutual Funds   These financial intermediaries acquire funds by selling shares to many individuals and use the proceeds to purchase diversified portfolios of stocks and bonds. Mutual funds allow shareholders to pool their resources so that they can take advantage of lower transaction costs when buying large blocks of stocks or bonds. In addition, mutual funds allow shareholders to hold more diversified portfolios than they otherwise would. Shareholders can sell (redeem) shares at any time, but the value of these shares will be determined by the value of the mutual fund's holdings of securities. Because these fluctuate greatly, the value of mutual fund shares will too; therefore, investments in mutual funds can be risky. Mutual funds have experienced extraordinary growth in recent years. By 2000, their assets had climbed to $280 billion.

REGULATION OF THE FINANCIAL SYSTEM

The financial system is among the most heavily regulated sectors of the Canadian economy. The government regulates financial markets for three main reasons: to increase the information available to investors, to ensure the soundness of the financial system, and to improve control of monetary policy. We will examine how these three reasons have led to the present regulatory environment. As a study aid, the principal regulatory agencies of the Canadian financial system are listed in Table 2-6.

Increasing Information Available to Investors

Asymmetric information in financial markets means that investors may be subject to adverse selection and moral hazard problems that may hinder the efficient operation of financial markets. Risky firms or outright crooks may be the most eager to sell securities to unwary investors, and the resulting adverse selection problem may keep investors out of financial markets. Furthermore, once an investor has bought a security, thereby lending money to a firm, the borrower may have incentives to engage in risky activities or to commit outright fraud. The presence of this moral hazard problem may also keep investors away from financial markets. Government regulation can reduce adverse selection and moral hazard problems in financial markets and increase their efficiency by increasing the amount of information available to investors.

Provincial securities commissions, the most significant being the Ontario Securities Commission (OSC), administer provincial acts requiring corporations issuing securities to disclose certain information about their sales, assets, and earnings to the public and restrict trading by the largest stockholders in the corporation. By requiring disclosure of this information and by discouraging insider trading, which could be used to manipulate security prices, regulators hope that investors will be better informed and be protected from abuses in financial markets. Indeed, in recent years, the OSC has been particularly active in prosecuting people involved in insider trading in Canada's largest stock exchange, the Toronto Stock Exchange (TSE).

Ontario Securities
Commission
www.osc.gov.on.ca

TABLE 2-6	Principal Regulatory Agencies of the Canadian Financial System	
Regulatory Agency	**Subject of Regulation**	**Nature of Regulations**
Provincial securities and exchange commissions	Organized exchanges and financial markets	Require disclosure of information and restrict insider trading
Bank of Canada	Chartered banks, TMLs, and CUCPs	Examines the books of the deposit-taking institutions and coordinates with the federal agencies that are responsible for financial institution regulation: OSFI and CDIC
Office of the Superintendent of Financial Institutions (OSFI)	All federally regulated chartered banks, TMLs, CUCPs, life insurance companies, P & C insurance companies, and pension plans	Sets capital adequacy, accounting, and board-of-directors responsibility standards. Conducts bank audits and coordinates with provincial securities commissions
Canada Deposit Insurance Corporation (CDIC)	Chartered banks, TMLs, CUCPs	Provides insurance of up to $60 000 for each depositor at a bank, examines the books of insured banks, and imposes restrictions on assets they can hold
Québec Deposit Insurance Board	TMLs and credit cooperatives in Québec	Similar role as the CDIC
Canadian Life and Health Insurance Compensation Corporation (CompCorp)	Life insurance companies	Compensates policyholders if the issuing life insurance company goes bankrupt
P & C Insurance Compensation Corporation (PACIC)	Property and casualty insurance companies	Compensates policyholders if the issuing P & C insurance company goes bankrupt

Ensuring the Soundness of Financial Intermediaries

Asymmetric information can also lead to widespread collapse of financial intermediaries, referred to as a **financial panic**. Because providers of funds to financial intermediaries may not be able to assess whether the institutions holding their funds are sound or not, if they have doubts about the overall health of financial intermediaries they may want to pull their funds out of both sound and unsound institutions. The possible outcome is a financial panic that produces large losses for the public and causes serious damage to the economy. To protect the public and the economy from financial panics, the government has implemented six types of regulations.

Office of the
Superintendent of
Financial Institutions
www.osfi-bsif.gc.ca

Restrictions on Entry   Provincial banking and insurance commissions, the Bank of Canada, and the Office of the Superintendent of Financial Institutions (OSFI), an agency of the federal government, have created very tight regulations governing who is allowed to set up a financial intermediary. Individuals or groups that want to establish a financial intermediary, such as a bank or an insurance company, must obtain a charter from the provincial or federal government. Only if they are upstanding citizens with impeccable credentials and a large amount of initial funds will they be given a charter.

Disclosure   There are stringent reporting requirements for financial intermediaries. Their bookkeeping must follow certain strict principles, their books are subject to periodic inspection, and they must make certain information available to the public.

Restrictions on Assets and Activities   There are restrictions on what financial intermediaries are allowed to do and what assets they can hold. Before you put your funds into a chartered bank or some other such institution, you would want to know that your funds are safe and that the bank or other financial intermediary will be able to meet its obligations to you. One way of doing this is to restrict the financial intermediary from engaging in certain risky activities. Another way is to restrict financial intermediaries from holding certain risky assets, or at least from holding a greater quantity of these risky assets than is prudent. For example, chartered banks and other depository institutions are not allowed to hold common stock because stock prices experience substantial fluctuations. Insurance companies are allowed to hold common stock, but their holdings cannot exceed a certain fraction of their total assets.

Canada Deposit Insurance
Corporation
www.cdic.ca

Deposit Insurance   The most important government agency that provides this type of insurance is the Canada Deposit Insurance Corporation (CDIC), created by an act of Parliament in 1967. It insures each depositor at a member deposit-taking financial institution up to a loss of $60 000 per account. Except for certain wholesale branches of foreign banks, credit unions, and some provincial institutions, all deposit-taking financial institutions in Canada are members of the CDIC. All CDIC members make contributions into the CDIC fund, which are used to pay off depositors in the case of a bank's failure. The Québec Deposit Insurance Board, an organization similar to CDIC and set up at the same time as CDIC, provides insurance for TMLs and credit cooperatives in Québec.

Limits on Competition   Politicians have often declared that unbridled competition among financial intermediaries promotes failures that will harm the public. Although the evidence that competition does this is extremely weak, it has not stopped the provincial and federal governments from imposing many restrictive regulations. For example, from 1967 to 1980 the entry of foreign banks into Canadian banking was prohibited. Since 1980, the incorporation of foreign bank subsidiaries has been regulated, but according to the *World Competitiveness Survey*, Canada ranks 41st out of 53 countries surveyed with respect to the degree of competition from foreign banks.[2]

---

[2]Institute for International Management Development, *The World Competitiveness Yearbook 1997*, June 1997.

Improving Control of Monetary Policy

Because banks play a very important role in determining the supply of money (which in turn affects many aspects of the economy), much regulation of these financial intermediaries is intended to improve control over the money supply. One such regulation is **settlement balances**, which make it obligatory for depository institutions to keep in accounts with the Bank of Canada (the Bank), the central bank in Canada. Settlement balances are held to facilitate the clearing of cheques and other transfers and help the Bank of Canada exercise more precise control over the money supply. Deposit insurance regulation can also be rationalized along these lines: the CDIC gives depositors confidence in the banking system and eliminates bank failures, which could cause large, uncontrollable fluctuations in the quantity of money. We will discuss these issues in detail in Chapter 11.

In later chapters we will look more closely at government regulation of financial markets and will see whether it has improved the functioning of financial markets.

Financial Regulation Abroad

Not surprisingly, given the similarity of the economic system here and in the United States, Japan, and the nations of Western Europe, financial regulation in these countries is similar to financial regulation in Canada. The provision of information is improved by requiring corporations issuing securities to report details about assets and liabilities, earnings, and sales of stock, and by prohibiting insider trading. The soundness of intermediaries is ensured by licensing, periodic inspection of financial intermediaries' books, and the provision of deposit insurance.

The major differences between financial regulation in Canada and abroad relate to bank regulation. In the past, for example, the United States was the only industrialized country to subject banks to restrictions on branching, which limited banks' size and restricted them to certain geographic regions. These restrictions were abolished by legislation in 1994. U.S. and Canadian banks are also the most restricted in the range of assets they may hold. Banks in other countries frequently hold shares in commercial firms; in Japan and Germany, those stakes can be sizable.

The Basel Accord

Financial institutions are also required by regulatory authorities to hold capital to protect depositors, policyholders, and liability guarantors. This capital is known as **regulatory capital**. In recent years, regulators in different countries, under the sponsorship of the Bank of International Settlements, have developed a set of capital adequacy standards with the objective of levelling the playing field among international financial institutions and promoting global standards for financial institutions regulation. These capital adequacy standards are known as the Basel Accord and we will discuss it in detail in Chapter 11.

SUMMARY

1. The basic function of financial markets is to channel funds from savers who have an excess of funds to spenders who have a shortage of funds. Financial markets can do this either through direct finance, in which borrowers borrow funds directly from lenders by selling them securities, or through indirect finance, which involves a financial intermediary who stands between the lender-savers and the borrower-spenders and helps transfer funds from one to the other. This channelling of funds improves the economic welfare of everyone in the society because it allows funds to move from people who have no productive investment opportunities to those who have such opportunities, thereby contributing to increased efficiency in the economy. In addition, channelling of funds directly benefits consumers by allowing them to make purchases when they need them most.

2. Financial markets can be classified as debt and equity markets, primary and secondary markets, exchanges and over-the-counter markets, and money and capital markets.

3. The principal money market instruments (debt instruments with maturities of less than one year) are Canada Treasury bills, negotiable bank certificates of deposit, commercial paper, banker's acceptances, repurchase agreements, overnight funds, and Eurodollars. The principal capital market instruments (debt and equity instruments with maturities greater than one year) are stocks, mortgages, corporate bonds, Canadian government securities, Canadian government agency securities, provincial and municipal government bonds, and consumer and bank commercial loans.

4. An important trend in recent years is the growing internationalization of financial markets. Eurobonds, which are denominated in a currency other than that of the country in which they are sold, are now the dominant security in the international bond market. Eurodollars, which are dollars deposited in foreign banks, are an important source of funds for Canadian banks.

5. Financial intermediaries are financial institutions that acquire funds by issuing liabilities and in turn use those funds to acquire assets by purchasing securities or making loans. Financial intermediaries play such an important role in the financial system because they reduce transaction costs and solve problems created by adverse selection and moral hazard. As a result, financial intermediaries allow small savers and borrowers to benefit from the existence of financial markets, thereby increasing the efficiency of the economy.

6. The principal financial intermediaries fall into three categories: (a) banks—chartered banks, trust and mortgage loan companies, and credit unions and *caisses populaires*; (b) contractual savings institutions—life insurance companies, property and casualty insurance companies, and pension funds; and (c) investment intermediaries—finance companies, mutual funds, and money market mutual funds.

7. The government regulates financial markets and financial intermediaries for three main reasons: to increase the information available to investors, to ensure the soundness of the financial system, and to improve control of monetary policy. Regulations include requiring disclosure of information to the public, restrictions on who can set up a financial intermediary, restrictions on what assets financial intermediaries can hold, the provision of deposit insurance, reserve requirements, and the setting of maximum interest rates that can be paid on chequing accounts and savings deposits.

KEY TERMS

adverse selection, p. 32

asymmetric information, p. 31

bearer deposit notes, p. 22

brokers, p. 20

call (redemption), p. 27

Canadas, p. 28

capital market, p. 21

dealers, p. 20

default, p. 22

dividends, p. 20

economies of scale, p. 31

equities, p. 20

Eurobond, p. 28

Eurocurrencies, p. 28

Eurodollars, p. 28

exchanges, p. 21

financial intermediation, p. 31

financial panic, p. 38

foreign bonds, p. 28

investment bank, p. 20

liabilities, p. 18

liquid, p. 20

long-term, p. 19

maturity, p. 19

money market, p. 21

moral hazard, p. 33

municipal bonds (municipals), p. 28

over-the-counter (OTC) market, p. 21

overnight interest rate, p. 24

primary market, p. 20

provincial bonds (provincials), p. 28

registered bonds, p. 27

regulatory capital, p. 40

secondary market, p. 20

settlement balances, p. 40

short-term, p. 19

term deposit receipts (term notes), p. 23

transaction costs, p. 31

underwriting, p. 20

QUESTIONS AND PROBLEMS

Questions marked with an asterisk are answered at the end of the book in an appendix, "Answers to Selected Questions and Problems."

*1. Why is a share of IBM common stock an asset for its owner and a liability for IBM?

2. If I can buy a car today for $5000 and it is worth $10 000 in extra income next year to me because it enables me to get a job as a travelling anvil seller, should I take out a loan from Larry the Loan Shark at a 90% interest rate if no one else will give me a

loan? Will I be better or worse off as a result of taking out this loan? Can you make a case for legalizing loan-sharking?

*3. Some economists suspect that one of the reasons that economies in developing countries grow so slowly is that they do not have well-developed financial markets. Does this argument make sense?

4. Describe how authority over deposit-based financial intermediaries is split between the Bank of Canada, the OSFI, and the CDIC.

*5. "Because corporations do not actually raise any funds in secondary markets, they are less important to the economy than primary markets." Comment.

6. If you suspect that a company will go bankrupt next year, which would you rather hold, bonds issued by the company or equities issued by the company? Why?

*7. How can the adverse selection problem explain why you are more likely to make a loan to a family member than to a stranger?

8. Think of one example in which you have had to deal with the adverse selection problem.

*9. Why do loan sharks worry less about moral hazard in connection with their borrowers than some other lenders do?

10. If you are an employer, what kinds of moral hazard problems might you worry about with your employees?

*11. If there were no asymmetry in the information that a borrower and a lender had, could there still be a moral hazard problem?

12. "In a world without information and transaction costs, financial intermediaries would not exist." Is this statement true, false, or uncertain? Explain your answer.

*13. Why might you be willing to make a loan to your neighbour by putting funds in a savings account earning a 5% interest rate at the bank and having the bank lend her the funds at a 10% interest rate rather than lend her the funds yourself?

14. In two lists, rank the following money market instruments in terms of their liquidity and their safety:
    a. Canada Treasury bills
    b. Negotiable CDs
    c. Repurchase agreements
    d. Commercial paper

*15. Discuss some of the manifestations of the globalization of world capital markets.

Chapter 3

What Is Money?

PREVIEW   If you lived in Canada before the creation of the central bank, the Bank of Canada, in 1935, your money might have consisted primarily of gold and silver coins and paper notes, called *banknotes*, issued by private banks. Today you use not only coins and dollar bills as means of payment but also cheques written on accounts held at banks, credit cards, debit cards, stored-value cards, and electronic cash and cheques. Money has been a different thing at different times; however, it has always been important to people and to the economy.

To understand the effects of money on the economy, we must understand exactly what money is. In this chapter we develop precise definitions by exploring the functions of money, looking at why and how it promotes economic efficiency, tracing how its forms have evolved over time, and examining how money is currently measured.

MEANING OF MONEY

As the word *money* is used in everyday conversation, it can mean many things, but to economists it has a very specific meaning. To avoid confusion, we must clarify how economists' use of the word *money* differs from conventional usage.

Economists define *money* as anything that is generally accepted in payment for goods or services or in the repayment of debts. Currency, consisting of dollar bills and coins, clearly fits this definition and is one type of money. When most people talk about money, they're talking about currency. If, for example, someone comes up to you and says, "Your money or your life," you should quickly hand over all your currency rather than ask, "What exactly do you mean by 'money'?"

To define money merely as currency is much too narrow for economists. Because cheques are also accepted as payment for purchases, chequing account deposits are considered money as well. An even broader definition of money is often needed because other items such as savings deposits can in effect function as money if they can be quickly and easily converted into currency or chequing account deposits. As you can see, there is no single, precise definition of money or the money supply, even for economists.

43

To complicate matters further, the word money is frequently used synonymously with wealth. When people say, "Joe is rich—he has an awful lot of money," they probably mean that Joe not only has a lot of currency and a high balance in his chequing account but also has stocks, bonds, four cars, three houses, and a yacht. Thus while "currency" is too narrow a definition of money, this other popular usage is much too broad. Economists make a distinction between money in the form of currency, demand deposits, and other items that are used to make purchases and **wealth**, the total collection of pieces of property that serve to store value. Wealth includes not only money but also other assets such as bonds, common stock, art, land, furniture, cars, and houses.

People also use the word *money* to describe what economists call *income*, as in the sentence "Sheila would be a wonderful catch; she has a good job and earns a lot of money." **Income** is a *flow* of earnings per unit of time. Money, by contrast, is a stock: it is a certain amount at a given point in time. If someone tells you that he has an income of $1000, you cannot tell whether he earned a lot or a little without knowing whether this $1000 is earned per year, per month, or even per day. But if someone tells you that she has $1000 in her pocket, you know exactly how much this is.

Keep in mind that the money discussed in this book refers to anything that is generally accepted in payment for goods and services or in the repayment of debts and is distinct from income and wealth.

FUNCTIONS OF MONEY

Whether money is shells or rocks or gold or paper, it has three primary functions in any economy: as a medium of exchange, as a unit of account, and as a store of value. Of the three functions, its function as a medium of exchange is what distinguishes money from other assets such as stocks, bonds, and houses.

Medium of Exchange

In almost all market transactions in our economy, money in the form of currency or cheques is a **medium of exchange**; it is used to pay for goods and services. The use of money as a medium of exchange promotes economic efficiency by eliminating much of the time spent in exchanging goods and services. To see why, let's look at a barter economy, one without money, in which goods and services are exchanged directly for other goods and services.

Take the case of Ellen the Economics Professor, who can do just one thing well: give brilliant economics lectures. In a barter economy, if Ellen wants to eat, she must find a farmer who not only produces the food she likes but also wants to learn economics. As you might expect, this search will be difficult and time-consuming, and Ellen may spend more time looking for such an economics-hungry farmer than she will teaching. It is even possible that she will have to quit lecturing and go into farming herself. Even so, she may still starve to death.

The time spent trying to exchange goods or services is called a *transaction cost*. In a barter economy, transaction costs are high because people have to satisfy a "double coincidence of wants"—they have to find someone who has a good or service they want and who also wants the good or service they have to offer.

Let's see what happens if we introduce money into Ellen the Economics Professor's world. Ellen can teach anyone who is willing to pay money to hear her lecture. She can then go to any farmer (or his representative at the supermarket) and buy the food she needs with the money she has been paid. The problem of the double coincidence of wants is avoided and Ellen saves a lot of time, which she may spend doing what she does best: teaching.

As this example shows, money promotes economic efficiency by eliminating much of the time spent exchanging goods and services. It also promotes efficiency by allowing people to specialize in what they do best. Money is therefore essential in an economy: it is a lubricant that allows the economy to run more smoothly by lowering transaction costs, thereby encouraging specialization and the division of labour.

The need for money is so strong that almost every society beyond the most primitive invents it. For a commodity to function effectively as money, it has to meet several criteria: (1) It must be easily standardized, making it simple to ascertain its value; (2) it must be widely accepted; (3) it must be divisible so that it is easy to "make change"; (4) it must be easy to carry; and (5) it must not deteriorate quickly. Forms of money that have satisfied these criteria have taken many unusual forms throughout human history, ranging from wampum (strings of beads), used by Native Americans, to tobacco and whiskey, used by the early American colonists, to cigarettes, used in prisoner-of-war camps during World War II. The diversity of forms of money that have been developed over the years is as much a testament to the inventiveness of the human race as the development of tools and language.[1]

Unit of Account   The second role of money is to provide a **unit of account**; that is, it is used to measure value in the economy. We measure the value of goods and services in terms of money, just as we measure weight in terms of kilograms or distance in terms of kilometres. To see why this function is important, let's look again at a barter economy where money does not perform this function. If the economy has only three goods, say, peaches, economics lectures, and movies, then we need to know only three prices to tell us how to exchange one for another: the price of peaches in terms of economics lectures (that is, how many economics lectures you have to pay for a peach), the price of peaches in terms of movies, and the price of economics lectures in terms of movies. If there were ten goods, we would need to know 45 prices in order to exchange one good for another; with 100 goods, we would need 4950 prices; and with 1000 goods, 499 500 prices.[2]

Imagine how hard it would be in a barter economy to shop at a supermarket with 1000 different items on its shelves, having to decide whether chicken or fish is a better buy if the price of a kilogram of chicken were quoted as 4 kilograms of butter and the price of a kilogram of fish as 8 kilograms of tomatoes. To make it possible to compare prices, the tag on each item would have to list up to 999 different prices, and the time spent reading them would result in very high transaction costs.

The solution to the problem is to introduce money into the economy and have all prices quoted in terms of units of that money, enabling us to quote the price of economics lectures, peaches, and movies in terms of, say, dollars. If there were

---

[1]An extremely entertaining article on the development of money in a prisoner-of-war camp during World War II is R. A. Radford's "The Economic Organization of a P.O.W. Camp," *Economica* 12 (November 1945): 189–201.

[2]The formula for telling us the number of prices we need when we have N goods is the same formula that tells us the number of pairs when there are N items. It is

$$\frac{N(N-1)}{2}$$

In the case of ten goods, for example, we would need

$$\frac{10(10-1)}{2} = \frac{90}{2} = 45$$

only three goods in the economy, this would not be a great advantage over the barter system because we would still need three prices to conduct transactions. But for ten goods we now need only ten prices; for 100 goods, 100 prices; and so on. At the 1000-good supermarket, there are now only 1000 prices to look at, not 499 500!

We can see that using money as a unit of account reduces transaction costs in an economy by reducing the number of prices that need to be considered. The benefits of this function of money grow as the economy becomes more complex.

Store of Value

Money also functions as a **store of value**; it is a repository of purchasing power over time. A store of value is used to save purchasing power from the time income is received until the time it is spent. This function of money is useful because most of us do not want to spend our income immediately upon receiving it but rather prefer to wait until we have the time or the desire to shop.

Money is not unique as a store of value; any asset, whether money, stocks, bonds, land, houses, art, or jewellery, can be used to store wealth. Many such assets have advantages over money as a store of value: they often pay the owner a higher interest rate than money, experience price appreciation, and deliver services such as providing a roof over one's head. If these assets are a more desirable store of value than money, why do people hold money at all?

The answer to this question relates to the important economic concept of **liquidity**, the relative ease and speed with which an asset can be converted into a medium of exchange. Liquidity is highly desirable. Money is the most liquid asset of all because it is the medium of exchange; it does not have to be converted into anything else in order to make purchases. Other assets involve transaction costs when they are converted into money. When you sell your house, for example, you have to pay a brokerage commission (usually 5% to 7% of the sales price), and if you need cash immediately to pay some pressing bills, you might have to settle for a lower price in order to sell the house quickly. The fact that money is the most liquid asset, then, explains why people are willing to hold it even if it is not the most attractive store of value.

How good a store of value money is depends on the price level, because its value is fixed in terms of the price level. A doubling of all prices, for example, means that the value of money has dropped by half; conversely, a halving of all prices means that the value of money has doubled. During an inflation, when the price level is increasing rapidly, money loses value rapidly, and people will be more reluctant to hold their wealth in this form. This is especially true during periods of extreme inflation, known as **hyperinflation**, in which the inflation rate exceeds 50% per month.

Hyperinflation occurred in Germany after World War I, with inflation rates sometimes exceeding 1000% per month. By the end of the hyperinflation in 1923, the price level had risen to more than 30 billion times what it had been just two years before. The quantity of money needed to purchase even the most basic items became excessive. There are stories, for example, that near the end of the hyperinflation, a wheelbarrow of cash would be required to pay for a loaf of bread. Money was losing its value so rapidly that workers were paid and given time off several times during the day to spend their wages before the money became worthless. No one wanted to hold on to money, and so the use of money to carry out transactions declined and barter became more and more dominant. Transaction costs skyrocketed, and as we would expect, output in the economy fell sharply.

EVOLUTION OF THE PAYMENTS SYSTEM

We can obtain a better picture of the functions of money and the forms it has taken over time by looking at the evolution of the **payments system**, the method of conducting transactions in the economy. The payments system has been evolving over centuries, and with it the form of money. At one point, precious metals such as gold were used as the principal means of payment and were the main form of money. Later, paper assets such as cheques and currency began to be used in the payments system and viewed as money. Where the payments system is heading has an important bearing on how money will be defined in the future.

To obtain perspective on where the payments system is heading, it is worth exploring how it has evolved. For any object to function as money, it must be universally acceptable; everyone must be willing to take it in payment for goods and services. An object that clearly has value to everyone is a likely candidate to serve as money, and a natural choice is a precious metal such as gold or silver. Money made up of precious metals or another valuable commodity is called **commodity money**, and from ancient times until several hundred years ago commodity money functioned as the medium of exchange in all but the most primitive societies. The problem with a payments system based exclusively on precious metals is that such a form of money is very heavy and is hard to transport from one place to another. Imagine the holes you'd wear in your pockets if you had to buy things only with coins! Indeed, for large purchases such as a house, you'd have to rent a truck to transport the money payment.

The next development in the payments system was paper currency (pieces of paper that function as a medium of exchange). Initially, paper currency embodied a promise that it was convertible into coins or into a quantity of precious metal. However, currency has evolved into **fiat money**, paper currency decreed by governments as legal tender (meaning that legally it must be accepted as payment for debts) but not convertible into coins or precious metal. Paper currency has the advantage of being much lighter than coins or precious metal, but it can be accepted as a medium of exchange only if there is some trust in the authorities who issue it and printing has reached a sufficiently advanced stage that counterfeiting is extremely difficult. Because paper currency has evolved into a legal arrangement, countries can change the currency that they use at will. Indeed, this is currently a hot topic of debate in Europe, which is adopting a unified currency (see Box 3-1).

Major drawbacks of paper currency and coins are that they are easily stolen and can be expensive to transport because of their bulk if there are large amounts. To combat this problem, another step in the evolution of the payments system occurred with the development of modern banking: the invention of cheques.

Cheques are a type of IOU payable on demand that allows transactions to take place without the need to carry around large amounts of currency. The introduction of cheques was a major innovation that improved the efficiency of the payments system. Frequently, payments made back and forth cancel each other; without cheques, this would involve the movement of a lot of currency. With cheques, payments that cancel each other can be settled by cancelling the cheques, and no currency need be moved. The use of cheques thus reduces the transportation costs associated with the payments system and improves economic efficiency. Another advantage of cheques is that they can be written for any amount up to the balance in the account, making transactions for large amounts much easier. Cheques are advantageous in that loss from theft is greatly reduced, and they provide convenient receipts for purchases.

BOX 3-1

Birth of the Euro: Will It Benefit Europe?

As part of the December 1991 Maastricht Treaty of European Union, the European Economic Commission outlined a plan to achieve the creation of a single European currency starting in 1999. Despite concerns that the plan might blow up, the new common currency, the euro, came into existence right on schedule in January 1999, with 11 countries of the 15 European Union countries participating in the monetary union: Austria, Belgium, Finland, France, Germany, Ireland, Italy, Luxembourg, the Netherlands, Portugal, and Spain. Denmark, Sweden, and the United Kingdom chose not to participate initially, and Greece failed to meet the economic criteria specified by the Maastricht Treaty (such as having a budget deficit less than 3% of GDP and total government debt less than 60% of GDP).

Starting January 1, 1999, the exchange rates of countries entering the monetary union were fixed permanently to the euro (which became a unit of account), the European Central Bank took over monetary policy from the individual national central banks, and the governments of the member countries began to issue debt in euros. By early 2002, euro notes and coins will begin to circulate and by June 2002, the old national currencies will be phased out com-

pletely and only euros will be used in the member countries.

Advocates of monetary union point out the advantages that the single currency has in eliminating the transaction costs incurred in exchanging one currency for another. In addition, the use of a single currency may promote further integration of the European economies and enhance competition. Skeptics who think that monetary union may be bad for Europe suggest that, because labour will not be very mobile across national boundaries and because fiscal transfers (i.e., tax income from one region being spent on another) from better-performing regions to worse-performing regions will not take place as occurs in the United States, a single currency may lead to some regions of Europe being depressed for substantial periods of time while other regions are booming.

Whether the euro will be good for the economies of Europe and increase their GDP is an open question. However, the motive behind monetary union may be more political than economic. European monetary union may encourage political union, producing a unified Europe that can play a stronger economic and political role on the world stage.

There are, however, two problems with a payments system based on cheques. First, it takes time to get cheques from one place to another, a particularly serious problem if you are paying someone in a different location who needs to be paid quickly. In addition, if you have a chequing account, you know that it takes several business days before a bank will allow you to make use of the funds from a cheque you have deposited. If your need for cash is urgent, this feature of paying by cheque can be frustrating. Second, all the paper shuffling required to process cheques is costly.

With the development of the computer and advanced telecommunications technology, there would seem to be a better way to organize our payments system. All paperwork could be eliminated by converting completely to what is known as an electronic means of payment in which all payments are made using electronic telecommunications.

Although not widely recognized, electronic means of payment have been around for many years. Prior to 1999, Canadian financial institutions used the Interbank International Payments System (IIPS) to make large-value electronic payments. Starting on February 4, 1999, however, the core of the Canadian payments system has been the Large Value Transfer System (LVTS), introduced by the Canadian Payments Association (CPA). The CPA, formed in 1980 by an act of Parliament, operates Canada's clearing and settlement system and plans for the evolution of that system. Wire transfers using the LVTS (to be discussed in detail in Chapter 17) are typically for amounts greater than $50 000, so even though fewer than 1% of the number of transactions use the LVTS, over 95% of the dollar value of transactions is conducted electronically. Indeed, when we say that a corporation is paying something by a cheque, it is frequently paying with an electronic wire transfer.

For international large-value wholesale transactions, Canadian financial institutions use Fedwire, CHIPS (Clearing House Interbank Payment System), or SWIFT (Society for Worldwide Intertelecommunications Financial Transfers). Fedwire is a telecommunications system owned by the Federal Reserve System (the U.S. central bank) and allows all financial institutions that maintain accounts with the Federal Reserve to wire funds to each other without having to send cheques. CHIPS is a privately owned network that is used by almost all banks in the world to clear payments denominated in U.S. dollars. SWIFT is a secure network for international payments and documentary advice. Banks, near banks, money market mutual funds, securities dealers, and corporations make extensive use of these systems to wire (transfer) funds.

Smaller wire transfers are carried out with automatic clearing houses (ACHs). It is becoming increasingly common for companies to pay their employees electronically by direct deposit of employees' pay into their bank accounts using an ACH system. Households are also now able to make bill payments by telephone using ACHs or to preauthorize regularly recurring bill payments such as mortgage payments, insurance premiums, and utility bills.

Electronic Money: A Coming Global Phenomenon

The development of cheap computer technology has meant that we are beginning to enter a new stage of a worldwide evolution of the payments system with the advent of electronic money. **Electronic money** (also known as **e-money**) is money that is stored electronically, and it takes several forms.

Debit Cards Debit cards, which look like credit cards, enable consumers to purchase goods by electronically transferring funds directly from their bank accounts to a merchant's account. Debit cards are used in many of the same places that accept credit cards and are now often becoming faster to use than cash. At many supermarkets, for example, when you buy groceries you can swipe your debit card through the card reader at the checkout station and press a few buttons, and the amount of your purchases is deducted from your bank account. Most banks issue debit cards, and your ATM card typically can function as a debit card.

Stored-Value Cards Stored-value cards also look like debit and credit cards but differ in that they contain a fixed amount of digital cash. The simplest form of stored-value cards is purchased for a preset dollar amount that the consumer spends down. The more sophisticated stored-value card is known as a smart card. It contains its own computer chip so that it can be loaded with digital cash from its owner's bank account whenever needed. Smart cards can be loaded from ATM machines, personal computers, or specially equipped telephones.

Stored-value cards are also making inroads in Canada, with major programs implemented or planned in Australia, Chile, Colombia, Denmark, France, Italy, Portugal, Singapore, Spain, Taiwan, the United Kingdom and the United States. One of the most ambitious programs was developed by London-based Mondex Corporation, which started running a test in Swindon, England, in July 1995. Not only can the Mondex smart card be used to transfer funds between consumers and retailers or between the consumer and the bank, but it also allows electronic money transfers between individuals. Funds can be transferred from one person's card to another's by using a handheld wireless device that has been dubbed an electronic wallet because it can carry out all the functions of a standard wallet, including storing phone numbers and other bits and pieces of information as well as holding money.

Electronic Cash *Electronic cash*, or *e-cash*, is a form of electronic money that can be used on the Internet to purchase goods or services. A consumer gets e-cash by setting up an account with a bank that has links to the Internet and then has the e-cash transferred to her PC. A consumer who wants to buy something with e-cash surfs to an Internet store and selects the buy option for a particular item, whereupon the e-cash is automatically transferred from her computer to the merchant's computer. The merchant can then have the funds transferred from the consumer's bank account to his before the goods are shipped. E-cash was pioneered by a Dutch company called DigiCash.

Electronic Cheques Electronic cheques allow users of the Internet to pay their bills directly over the Internet without having to send a paper cheque. The user has his PC write the equivalent of a cheque and then sends the electronic cheque to the other party, who in turn sends it to her bank. Once the recipient's bank verifies that the electronic cheque is valid, it transfers money from the originator's bank account to the recipient's. Because this whole process is done electronically, it is far cheaper and more convenient than using paper cheques. Experts estimate that the cost of using an electronic cheque is less than one-third the cost of conducting a transaction with a paper cheque. These cost advantages have led some organizations to begin paying bills with electronic cheques.

Are We Moving to a Cashless Society?

Given the advantages of electronic money, you might think that we would move quickly to the cashless society in which all payments are made electronically. However, a true cashless society is probably not around the corner. Indeed, predictions of such a society have been around for two decades but have not yet come to fruition. Why has the movement to a cashless society been so slow in coming?

Although electronic means of payment may be more efficient than a payments system based on paper, several factors work against the disappearance of the paper system. First, it is very expensive to set up the computer, card reader, and telecommunications networks necessary to make electronic money the dominant form of payment. Second, paper cheques have the advantage that they provide receipts, something that many consumers are unwilling to give up. Third, the use of paper cheques gives consumers several days of "float"—it takes several days before a cheque is cashed and funds are withdrawn from the issuer's account, which means that the writer of the cheque can earn interest on the funds in the meantime. Because electronic payments are immediate, they eliminate the float for the consumer.

Fourth, electronic means of payment may raise security and privacy concerns. We often hear media reports that a hacker has been able to access a computer database and to alter information stored there. The fact that this is not an uncommon occurrence means that unscrupulous persons might be able to access bank accounts in electronic payments systems and steal funds by moving them from someone else's accounts into their own. Indeed, this happened in 1995, when a Russian computer programmer got access to Citibank's computers and moved funds electronically into his and his conspirators' accounts. The prevention of this type of fraud is no easy task, and a whole new field of computer science is developing to cope with security issues. A further concern is that the use of electronic means of payment leaves an electronic trail that contains a large amount of personal data on buying habits. There are concerns that government, employers, and marketers might be able to access these data, thereby encroaching on our privacy.

The conclusion from this discussion seems to be that we are moving to a payments system in which the use of paper will diminish, although it is likely to be a gradual process.

MEASURING MONEY

The definition of money as anything that is generally accepted in payment for goods and services tells us that money is defined by people's behaviour. What makes an asset money is that people believe it will be accepted by others when making payment. As we have seen, many different assets have performed this role over the centuries, ranging from gold to paper currency to chequing accounts. For that reason, this behavioural definition does not tell us exactly what assets in our economy should be considered money. To measure money, we need a precise definition that tells us exactly what assets should be included.

The Bank of Canada's Monetary Aggregates

The Bank of Canada (the Bank), the central banking authority responsible for monetary policy in Canada, has conducted many studies on how to measure money. The problem of measuring money has become especially crucial because extensive financial innovation has produced new types of assets that might properly belong in a measure of money. Since 1980, the Bank of Canada has modified its measures of money several times and has settled on the following measures of the money supply, which are also referred to as **monetary aggregates** (Table 3-1).

The narrowest measure of money that the Bank of Canada reports is **M1**, which includes currency, personal chequing accounts, and current accounts. Personal chequing accounts consist of personal chequing demand accounts at chartered banks and personal demand deposits held at investment dealer subsidiaries. Current accounts are mostly held by businesses and make up the largest component of M1. Personal chequing accounts and current accounts together are referred to as demand deposits, meaning that they can be withdrawn on demand. These assets pay little or no interest, but are clearly money because they can be used directly as a medium of exchange.

The **M2** monetary aggregate adds to M1 personal savings and non-personal notice deposits at chartered banks. The **M3** aggregate adds to M2 chartered bank non-personal term deposits and foreign currency deposits of Canadian residents. The non-personal term deposits are held by provincial and municipal governments, corporations, and institutions, and also include deposits held by one bank with another, known as *interbank deposits*. The foreign currency deposits are mostly denominated in U.S. dollars. Notice that the M1, M2, and M3 monetary aggregates do not include deposits with near banks, such as trust and mortgage loan companies (TMLs) and credit unions and *caisses populaires* (CUCPs).

With the financial innovation that has occurred (discussed more extensively in Chapter 9), TMLs and CUCPs can also offer deposits that function as media of exchange. The Bank of Canada has responded to this by introducing new measures of money. The **M1+** monetary aggregate adds to M1 other assets that have cheque-writing features—all chequable (personal or non-personal) notice deposits at chartered banks, TMLs, and CUCPs. These assets are also extremely liquid because they can be turned into cash quickly at very little cost. The **M1++** aggregate adds to M1+ all non-chequable (personal or non-personal) notice deposits at

TABLE 3-1   Measures of the Monetary Aggregates

M1

Currency outside banks

Personal chequing accounts

Current accounts

M2 = M1 plus the following:

Personal savings deposits at chartered banks

Non-personal notice deposits at chartered banks

M3 = M2 plus the following:

Non-personal term deposits at chartered banks

Foreign currency deposits at chartered banks

M1+ = M1 plus the following:

Personal chequable savings deposits at chartered banks, TMLs, and CUCPs

Non-personal chequable notice deposits at chartered banks, TMLs, and CUCPs

M1++ = M1+ plus the following:

Personal non-chequable savings deposits at chartered banks, TMLs, and CUCPs

Non-personal non-chequable notice deposits at chartered banks, TMLs, and CUCPs

M2+ = M2 plus the following:

Deposits at trust and mortgage loan companies

Deposits at credit unions and *caisses populaires*

Life insurance company individual annuities

Personal deposits at government-owned savings institutions

Money market mutual funds

M2++ = M2+ plus the following:

Canada Savings Bonds

Non-money market mutual funds

Source: Apostolos Serletis and Terence E. Molik, "Monetary Aggregates and Monetary Policy." In *Money, Monetary Policy, and Transmission Mechanisms*, Bank of Canada (2000): 103-135.

chartered banks, TMLs, and CUCPs. Both the M1+ and M1++ monetary aggregates internalize the substitution between demand and notice deposits and are good at capturing information about changes in savings behaviour, as well as transactions intentions.

The **M2+** monetary aggregate includes M2 plus deposits at near banks, life insurance company annuities, and money market mutual funds. Finally, **M2++**

adds to M2+ Canada Savings Bonds and non-money market mutual funds (i.e., bond and equity mutual funds). This broader monetary aggregate is good at capturing information about the long-run spending plans and expectations of the household sector of the economy.[3]

Because we cannot be sure which of the monetary aggregates is the true measure of money, it is logical to wonder if their movements closely parallel one another. If they do, then using one monetary aggregate to predict future economic performance and to conduct policy will be the same as using another, and the fact that we are not sure of the appropriate definition of money for a given policy decision is not too costly. However, if the monetary aggregates do not move together, then what one monetary aggregate tells us is happening to the money supply might be quite different from what another monetary aggregate would tell us. The conflicting stories might present a confusing picture that would make it hard for policymakers to decide on the right course of action.

Figure 3-1 plots the growth rates of M1, M1+ and M2++ from 1968 to 2000. The growth rates of these three aggregates do tend to move together; the timing of their rise and fall is roughly similar until the 1990s, and they all show a higher growth rate on average in the 1970s.

Yet some glaring discrepancies exist in the movements of these aggregates. The average growth rate of money in the 1970s was 10% according to M1, 11.7% according to M1++, and 14.5% according to M2++. Similarly, the average monetary growth rate in the 1990s was 2.3% according to M1++, 6.9% according to M2++, and 7.9% according to M1. Thus, the different measures of money tell a very different story about the course of monetary policy.

From the data in Figure 3-1, you can see that obtaining a single precise, correct measure of money does seem to matter and that it does make a difference which monetary aggregate policymakers and economists choose as the true measure of money.

Money as a Weighted Aggregate

The measures of the money supply listed in Table 3-1 make black-and-white decisions about whether a given asset is money by including it or excluding it. In addition, these measures are simple-sum indices in which all monetary components are assigned a constant and equal (unitary) weight. This index is M in

$$M = x_1 + x_2 + \ldots + x_n$$

where x_j is one of the n monetary components of the monetary aggregate M. This summation index implies that all monetary components contribute equally to the money total and it views all components as dollar-for-dollar perfect substitutes. Such an index, there is no question, represents an index of the stock of nominal monetary wealth, but cannot, in general, represent a valid structural economic variable for the services of the quantity of money.

Over the years, there has been a steady stream of attempts at properly weighting monetary components within a simple-sum aggregate. With no theory, however, any weighting scheme is questionable. Recently, attention has been focused on the gains that can be achieved by a rigorous use of microeconomic theory, aggregation theory, and index number theory. This new approach to monetary

---

[3]Joseph Atta-Mensah and Loretta Nott, "Recent Developments in the Monetary Aggregates and their Implications," *Bank of Canada Review* (Spring 1999): 5–19, provide an excellent discussion of the recent behaviour of Canada's monetary aggregates.

Annual Growth Rate (%)

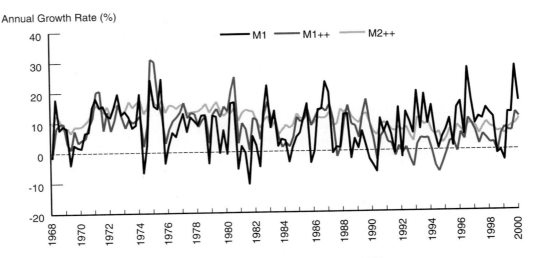

FIGURE 3-1 Growth Rates of M1, M1++, and M2++, 1968–2000
Source: Statistics Canada CANSIM Series B1627, B1652, and B1650.

aggregation led to the construction of *weighted monetary aggregates*.[4] These aggregates represent a viable and theoretically appropriate alternative to the simple-sum aggregates. Moreover, recent research indicates that these new measures of money seem to predict inflation and the business cycle somewhat better than more conventional measures.[5]

HOW RELIABLE ARE THE MONEY DATA?

The difficulties of measuring money arise not only because it is hard to decide what is the best definition of money but also because the Bank of Canada frequently revises earlier estimates of the monetary aggregates by large amounts later on. There are two reasons why the Bank revises its figures. First, because small depository institutions need to report the amounts of their deposits only infrequently, the Bank has to estimate these amounts until these institutions provide the actual figures at some future date. Second, the adjustment of the data for seasonal variation is revised substantially as more data become available. To see why this happens, let's look at an example of the seasonal variation of the money data around Christmastime. The monetary aggregates always rise around Christmas because of increased spending during the holiday season; the rise is greater in some years than in others. This means that the factor that adjusts the data for the seasonal variation due to Christmas must be estimated from several years of data, and the estimates of this seasonal factor become more precise only as more data become available. When the data on the monetary aggregates are revised, the seasonal adjustments often change dramatically from the initial calculation.

The conclusion we can draw is that the initial data on the monetary aggregates reported by the Bank of Canada are not a reliable guide to what is happening to short-run movements in the money supply, such as the one-month growth rates.

[4]William Barnett, Douglas Fisher, and Apostolos Serletis, "Consumer Theory and the Demand for Money," *Journal of Economic Literature* 30 (1992): 2086-2119, provide a state-of-the-art-survey of this literature. See also William Barnett and Apostolos Serletis, *The Theory of Monetary Aggregation* (Amsterdam: North-Holland, 2000) and Apostolos Serletis, *The Demand for Money: Theoretical and Empirical Approaches* (Kluwer Academic Publishers, Norwell, MA, USA, 2001).

[5]See, for example, Apostolos Serletis and Terence E. Molik, "Monetary Aggregates and Monetary Policy." In *Money, Monetary Policy, and Transmission Mechanisms*, Bank of Canada (2000): 103-135.

However, the initial money data are reasonably reliable for longer periods, such as a year. The moral is that ***we probably should not pay much attention to short-run movements in the money supply numbers but should be concerned only with longer-run movements***.

SUMMARY

1. To economists, the word *money* has a different meaning from income or wealth. Money is anything that is generally accepted as payment for goods or services or in the repayment of debts.

2. Money serves three primary functions: as a medium of exchange, as a unit of account, and as a store of value. Money as a medium of exchange avoids the problem of double coincidence of wants that arises in a barter economy by lowering transaction costs and encouraging specialization and the division of labour. Money as a unit of account reduces the number of prices needed in the economy, which also reduces transaction costs. Money also functions as a store of value but performs this role poorly if it is rapidly losing value due to inflation.

3. The payments system has evolved over time. Until several hundred years ago, the payments system in all but the most primitive societies was based primarily on precious metals. The introduction of paper currency lowered the cost of transporting money. The next major advance was the introduction of cheques, which lowered transaction costs still further. We are currently moving toward an electronic payments system in which paper is eliminated and all transactions are handled by computers. Despite the potential efficiency of such a system, obstacles are slowing the movement to the chequeless society and the development of new forms of electronic money.

4. The Bank of Canada has defined seven different measures of the money supply—M1, M1+, M1++, M2, M2+, M2++, and M3. These measures are not equivalent and do not always move together, so they cannot be used interchangeably by policymakers. Obtaining the precise, correct measure of money does seem to matter and has implications for the conduct of monetary policy.

5. Another problem in the measurement of money is that the data are not always as accurate as we would like. Substantial revisions in the data do occur; they indicate that initially released money data are not a reliable guide to short-run (say, month-to-month) movements in the money supply, although they are more reliable over longer periods of time, such as a year.

KEY TERMS

commodity money, p. 47

electronic money (e-money), p. 49

fiat money, p. 47

hyperinflation, p. 46

income, p. 44

liquidity, p. 46

M1, p. 51

M1+, p. 51

M1++, p. 51

M2, p. 51

M2+, p. 52

M2++, p. 52

M3, p. 51

medium of exchange, p. 44

monetary aggregates, p. 51

payments system, p. 47

store of value, p. 46

unit of account, p. 45

wealth, p. 44

QUESTIONS AND PROBLEMS

Questions marked with an asterisk are answered at the end of the book in an appendix, "Answers to Selected Questions and Problems."

1. Which of the following three expressions uses the economists' definition of money?
   a. "How much money did you earn last week?"
   b. "When I go to the store, I always make sure that I have enough money."
   c. "The love of money is the root of all evil."

*2. There are three goods produced in an economy by three individuals:

Good	Producer
Apples	Orchard owner
Bananas	Banana grower
Chocolate	Chocolatier

If the orchard owner likes only bananas, the banana grower likes only chocolate, and the chocolatier likes only apples, will any trade among these three persons take place in a barter economy? How will introducing money into the economy benefit these three producers?

3. Why did cavemen not need money?

*4. Why were people in Canada in the nineteenth century sometimes willing to be paid by cheque rather than with gold, even though they knew that there was a possibility that the cheque might bounce?

5. In ancient Greece, why was gold a more likely candidate for use as money than wine was?

*6. Was money a better store of value in Canada in the 1950s than it was in the 1970s? Why or why not? In which period would you have been more willing to hold money?

7. Would you be willing to give up your chequebook and instead use an electronic means of payment if it were made available? Why or why not?

8. Rank the following assets from most liquid to least liquid:
    a. Chequing account deposits
    b. Houses
    c. Currency
    d. Washing machines
    e. Savings deposits
    f. Common stock

*9. Why have some economists described money during a hyperinflation as a "hot potato" that is quickly passed from one person to another?

10. In Brazil, a country that was undergoing a rapid inflation before 1994, many transactions were conducted in dollars rather than in reals, the domestic currency. Why?

*11. Suppose that a researcher discovers that a measure of the total amount of debt in the Canadian economy over the past 20 years was a better predictor of inflation and the business cycle than M1, M1+, M1++, M2, M2+, M2++, or M3. Does this discovery mean that we should define money as equal to the total amount of debt in the economy?

12. Look up the M1, M1+, M1++, M2, M2+, M2++, and M3 numbers in the *Bank of Canada Review* for the most recent one-year period. Have their growth rates been similar? What implications do their growth rates have for the conduct of monetary policy?

*13. Which of the Bank of Canada's measures of the monetary aggregates, M1, M1+, M1++, M2, M2+, M2++, or M3, is composed of the most liquid assets? Which is the largest measure?

14. In a weighted monetary aggregate, which of the following assets would probably receive the highest weights? Which would receive the lowest weights?
    a. Currency
    b. Savings account deposits
    c. Foreign currency deposits
    d. Canada Savings Bonds
    e. Houses
    f. Furniture

*15. Why are revisions of monetary aggregates less of a problem for measuring long-run movements of the money supply than they are for measuring short-run movements?

Chapter 4

Understanding Interest Rates

PREVIEW   Interest rates are among the most closely watched variables in the economy. Their movements are reported almost daily by the news media because they directly affect our everyday lives and have important consequences for the health of the economy. They affect personal decisions such as whether to consume or save, whether to buy a house, and whether to purchase bonds or put funds into a savings account. Interest rates also affect the economic decisions of businesses and households, such as whether to use their funds to invest in new equipment for factories or to save their money in a bank.

Before we can go on with the study of money, banking, and financial markets, we must understand exactly what the phrase *interest rates* means. In this chapter we see that a concept known as the *yield to maturity* is the most accurate measure of interest rates; the yield to maturity is what economists mean when they use the term *interest rate*. We discuss how the yield to maturity is measured on many of the credit market instruments mentioned in Chapter 2 and examine alternative (but less accurate) ways in which interest rates are quoted. We also see that a bond's interest rate does not necessarily indicate how good an investment the bond is because what it earns (its rate of return) can differ from its interest rate. Finally, we explore the distinction between real interest rates, which are adjusted for changes in the price level, and nominal interest rates, which are not.

Although learning definitions is not always the most exciting of pursuits, it is important to read carefully and understand the concepts presented in this chapter. Not only are they continually used throughout the remainder of this text, but a firm grasp of these terms will give you a clearer understanding of the role that interest rates play in your life as well as in the general economy.

MEASURING INTEREST RATES

In Chapter 2 you were introduced to a number of credit market instruments, which fall into four types:

1. A **simple loan** provides the borrower with an amount of funds (principal) that must be repaid to the lender at the maturity date along with an additional amount known as an interest payment. For example, if a bank made you a simple loan of $100 for one year, you would have to repay the principal of $100 in one year's time along with an additional interest payment of, say, $10. Commercial loans to businesses are often of this type.

2. A **fixed-payment loan** provides a borrower with an amount of funds that is to be repaid by making the same payment every month, consisting of part of the principal and interest for a set number of years. For example, if you borrowed $1000, a fixed-payment loan might require you to pay $126 every year for 25 years. Instalment loans (such as auto loans) and mortgages are frequently of the fixed-payment type.

3. A **coupon bond** pays the owner of the bond a fixed interest payment (coupon payment) every year until the maturity date, when a specified final amount (**face value** or **par value**) is repaid. The coupon payment is so named because the bondholder used to obtain payment by clipping a coupon off the bond and sending it to the bond issuer, who then sent the payment to the holder. Nowadays, for most coupon bonds it is no longer necessary to send in coupons to receive these payments. A coupon bond with $1000 face value, for example, might pay you a coupon payment of $100 per year for ten years and at the maturity date repay you the face value amount of $1000. (The face value of a bond is usually in $1000 increments.)

    A coupon bond is identified by three pieces of information. First is the corporation or government agency that issues the bond. Second is the maturity date of the bond. Third is the bond's **coupon rate**, the dollar amount of the yearly coupon payment expressed as a percentage of the face value of the bond. In our example, the coupon bond has a yearly coupon payment of $100 and a face value of $1000. The coupon rate is then $100/$1000 = 0.10, or 10%. Canada bonds and corporate bonds are examples of coupon bonds.

4. A **discount bond** (also called a **zero-coupon bond**) is bought at a price below its face value (at a discount), and the face value is repaid at the maturity date. Unlike a coupon bond, a discount bond does not make any interest payments; it just pays off the face value. For example, a discount bond with a face value of $1000 might be bought for $900 and in a year's time the owner would be repaid the face value of $1000. Canadian government Treasury bills and long-term zero-coupon bonds are examples of discount bonds.

These four types of instruments require payments at different times: simple loans and discount bonds make payment only at their maturity dates, whereas fixed-payment loans and coupon bonds have payments periodically until maturity. How would you decide which of these instruments provides you with more income? They all seem so different because they make payments at different times. To solve this problem, we use the concept of *present value* to provide us with a procedure for measuring interest rates on these different types of instruments.

Present Value

The concept of **present value** is based on the commonsense notion that a dollar paid to you one year from now is less valuable to you than a dollar paid to you today; this notion is true because you can deposit the dollar in a savings account that earns interest and have more than a dollar in one year. We will now define this concept more formally.

In the case of a simple loan, the interest payment divided by the amount of the loan is a natural and sensible way to measure the cost of borrowing funds: the measure of the cost is the *simple interest rate*. In the example we used to describe the simple loan, a loan of $100 today requires the borrower to repay the $100 a year from now and to make an additional interest payment of $10. Hence, using the definition just given, the simple interest rate i is

$$i = \frac{\$10}{\$100} = 0.10 = 10\%$$.

If you make this $100 loan, at the end of the year you would receive $110, which can be rewritten as

$$\$100 \times (1 + 0.10) = \$110$$

If you then lent out the $110, at the end of the second year you would receive

$$\$110 \times (1 + 0.10) = \$121$$

or, equivalently,

$$\$100 \times (1 + 0.10) \times (1 + 0.10) = \$100 \times (1 + 0.10)^2 = \$121$$

Continuing with the loan again, you would receive at the end of the third year

$$\$121 \times (1 + 0.10) = \$100 \times (1 + 0.10)^3 = \$133$$

The amounts you would have at the end of each year by making a $100 loan today can be seen in the following time line:

Today 0	Year 1	Year 2	Year 3
$100	$110	$121	$133

These calculations of the proceeds from a sequence of simple loans can be generalized as follows: if the simple interest rate i is expressed as a decimal fraction (such as 0.10 for the 10% interest rate in our example), then after making these loans for n years, you will receive a total payment of

$$\$100 \times (1 + i)^n$$

We can also work these calculations backward. Because $100 today will turn into $110 next year when the simple interest rate is 10%, we could say that $110 next year is worth only $100 today. Or we could say that no one would pay more than $100 today to get $110 next year. Similarly, we could say that $121 two years from now or $133 three years from now is worth $100 today. This process of calculating what dollars received in the future are worth today is called *discounting the future*. We have been implicitly solving our forward-looking equations for today's value of a future dollar amount. For example, in the case of the $133 received three years from now, when $i = 0.10$,

Today	Future
$100	$100 \times (1 + i)^3 = \$133$

so that

$$\$100 = \frac{\$133}{(1 + i)^3}$$

More generally, we can solve this equation to tell us the present value *(PV)*, or **present discounted value**, of the future $1, that is, today's value of a $1 payment received *n* years from now when the simple interest rate is *i*:

$$PV \text{ of future } \$1 = \frac{\$1}{(1 + i)^n} \qquad (1)$$

Intuitively, what Equation 1 tells us is that if you were promised $1 for certain ten years from now, this dollar would not be as valuable to you as $1 is today because if you had the $1 today, you could invest it and end up with more than $1 in ten years.

The concept of present value is extremely useful because it allows us to figure out today's value of a credit market instrument at a given simple interest rate *i* by just adding up the individual present values of all the future payments received. This information allows us to compare the value of two instruments with very different timing of their payments, such as a discount bond and a coupon bond. As we will see, this concept also allows us to obtain an equivalent measure of the interest rate on all four types of credit market instruments discussed here.

Yield to Maturity   Of the several common ways of calculating interest rates, the most important is the **yield to maturity,** the interest rate that equates the present value of payments received from a debt instrument with its value today.[1] Because the concept behind the calculation of the yield to maturity makes good economic sense, economists consider it the most accurate measure of interest rates.

To understand the yield to maturity better, we now look at how it is calculated for the four types of credit market instruments.

Simple Loan   Using the concept of present value, the yield to maturity on a simple loan is easy to calculate. For the one-year loan we discussed, today's value is $100, and the payments in one year's time would be $110 (the repayment of $100 plus the interest payment of $10). We can use this information to solve for the yield to maturity *i* by recognizing that the present value of the future payments must equal today's value of a loan. Making today's value of the loan ($100) equal to the present value of the $110 payment in a year (using Equation 1) gives us

$$\$100 = \frac{\$110}{1 + i}$$

Solving for *i*,

$$i = \frac{\$110 - \$100}{\$100} = \frac{\$10}{\$100} = 0.10 = 10\%$$

This calculation of the yield to maturity should look familiar because it equals the interest payment of $10 divided by the loan amount of $100; that is, it equals the simple interest rate on the loan. An important point to recognize is that *for simple loans, the simple interest rate equals the yield to maturity.* Hence the same term *i* is used to denote both the yield to maturity and the simple interest rate.

---

[1] In other contexts, it is also called the *internal rate of return*.

The key to understanding the calculation of the yield to maturity is equating today's value of the debt instrument with the present value of all of its future payments. The best way to learn this principle is to apply it to other specific examples of the four types of credit market instruments in addition to those we discuss here. See if you can develop the equations that would allow you to solve for the yield to maturity in each case.

Fixed-Payment Loan   Recall that this type of loan has the same payment every period throughout the life of the loan. On a fixed-rate mortgage, for example, the borrower makes the same payment to the bank every month until the maturity date, when the loan will be completely paid off. To calculate the yield to maturity for a fixed-payment loan, we follow the same strategy we used for the simple loan—we equate today's value of the loan with its present value. Because the fixed-payment loan involves more than one payment, the present value of the fixed-payment loan is calculated as the sum of the present values of all payments (using Equation 1).

In the case of our earlier example, the loan is $1000 and the yearly payment is $126 for the next 25 years. The present value is calculated as follows: at the end of one year, there is a $126 payment with a PV of $\$126/(1 + i)$; at the end of two years, there is another $126 payment with a PV of $\$126/(1 + i)^2$; and so on until at the end of the twenty-fifth year, the last payment of $126 with a PV of $\$126/(1 + i)^{25}$ is made. Making today's value of the loan ($1000) equal to the sum of the present values of all the yearly payments gives us

$$\$1000 = \frac{\$126}{1 + i} + \frac{\$126}{(1 + i)^2} + \frac{\$126}{(1 + i)^3} + \cdots + \frac{\$126}{(1 + i)^{25}}$$

More generally, for any fixed-payment loan,

$$LV = \frac{FP}{1 + i} + \frac{FP}{(1 + i)^2} + \frac{FP}{(1 + i)^3} + \cdots + \frac{FP}{(1 + i)^n} \qquad (2)$$

where
$$LV = \text{loan value}$$
$$FP = \text{fixed yearly payment}$$
$$n = \text{number of years until maturity}$$

For a fixed-payment loan amount, the fixed yearly payment and the number of years until maturity are known quantities, and only the yield to maturity is not. So we can solve this equation for the yield to maturity i. Because this calculation is not easy, tables have been created that allow you to find i given the loan's numbers for LV, FP, and n. For example, in the case of the 25-year loan with yearly payments of $126, the yield to maturity taken from the table that solves Equation 2 is 12%. Real estate brokers always have such a table handy (or a pocket calculator that can solve such equations) so that they can immediately tell the prospective house buyer exactly what the yearly (or monthly) payments will be if the house purchase is financed by taking out a mortgage.[2]

Coupon Bond To calculate the yield to maturity for a coupon bond, follow the same strategy used for the fixed-payment loan: equate today's value of the bond with its present value. Because coupon bonds also have more than one payment, the present value of the bond is calculated as the sum of the present values of all the coupon payments plus the present value of the final payment of the face value of the bond.

The present value of a $1000-face-value bond with ten years to maturity and yearly coupon payments of $100 (a 10% coupon rate) can be calculated as follows: at the end of one year, there is a $100 coupon payment with a *PV* of $100/(1 + i); at the end of the second year, there is another $100 coupon payment with a *PV* of $100/(1 + i)^2$; and so on until, at maturity, there is a $100 coupon payment with a *PV* of $100/(1 + i)^{10}$ plus the repayment of the $1000 face value with a *PV* of $1000/(1 + i)^{10}$. Setting today's value of the bond (its current price, denoted by *P*) equal to the sum of the present values of all the payments for this bond gives

$$P = \frac{\$100}{1 + i} + \frac{\$100}{(1 + i)^2} + \frac{\$100}{(1 + i)^3} + \cdots + \frac{\$100}{(1 + i)^{10}} + \frac{\$1000}{(1 + i)^{10}}$$

More generally, for any coupon bond,[3]

$$P = \frac{C}{1 + i} + \frac{C}{(1 + i)^2} + \frac{C}{(1 + i)^3} + \cdots + \frac{C}{(1 + i)^n} + \frac{F}{(1 + i)^n} \tag{3}$$

where

P = price of coupon bond
C = yearly coupon payment
F = face value of the bond
n = years to maturity date

In Equation 3, the coupon payment, the face value, the years to maturity, and the price of the bond are known quantities, and only the yield to maturity is not. Hence we can solve this equation for the yield to maturity i. Just as in the case of the fixed-payment loan, this calculation is not easy, so business-oriented pocket calculators have built-in programs that solve this equation for you.[4]

Let's look at some examples of the solution for the yield to maturity on our 10%-coupon-rate bond that matures in ten years. If the purchase price of the bond is $1000, then, either using a pocket calculator with the built-in program or looking at a bond table, we will find that the yield to maturity is 10%. If the price is $900, we find that the yield to maturity is 11.75%. Table 4-1 shows the yields to maturity calculated for several bond prices.

---

[2]The calculation with a pocket calculator programmed for this purpose requires simply that you enter the value of the loan *LV*, the number of years to maturity *n*, and the interest rate *i* and then run the program.

[3]Most coupon bonds actually make coupon payments on a semi-annual basis rather than once a year as assumed here. The effect on the calculations is only very slight and will be ignored here.

[4]The calculation of a bond's yield to maturity with the programmed pocket calculator requires simply that you enter the amount of the yearly coupon payment *C*, the face value *F*, the number of years to maturity *n*, and the price of the bond *P* and then run the program.

TABLE 4-1	Yields to Maturity on a 10% Coupon Rate Bond Maturing in Ten Years (Face Value = $1000)
Price of Bond ($)	**Yield to Maturity (%)**
1200	7.13
1100	8.48
1000	10.00
900	11.75
800	13.81

Table 4-1 illustrates three interesting facts:

1. When the coupon bond is priced at its face value, the yield to maturity equals the coupon rate.
2. The price of a coupon bond and the yield to maturity are negatively related; that is, as the yield to maturity rises, the price of the bond falls. As the yield to maturity falls, the price of the bond rises.
3. The yield to maturity is greater than the coupon rate when the bond price is below its face value.

These three facts are true for any coupon bond and are really not surprising if you think about the reasoning behind the calculation of the yield to maturity. When you put $1000 in a bank account with an interest rate of 10%, you can take out $100 every year and you will be left with the $1000 at the end of ten years. This is similar to buying the $1000 bond with a 10% coupon rate analyzed in Table 4-1, which pays a $100 coupon payment every year and then repays $1000 at the end of ten years. If the bond is purchased at the par value of $1000, its yield to maturity must equal 10%, which is also equal to the coupon rate of 10%. The same reasoning applied to any coupon bond demonstrates that if the coupon bond is purchased at its par value, the yield to maturity and the coupon rate must be equal.

It is straightforward to show that the bond price and the yield to maturity are negatively related. As *i,* the yield to maturity, rises, all denominators in the bond price formula must necessarily rise. Hence a rise in the interest rate as measured by the yield to maturity means that the price of the bond must fall. Another way to explain why the bond price falls when the interest rises is that a higher interest rate implies that the future coupon payments and final payment are worth less when discounted back to the present; hence the price of the bond must be lower.

There is one special case of a coupon bond that is worth discussing because its yield to maturity is particularly easy to calculate. This bond is called a **consol** or a **perpetuity**; it is a perpetual bond with no maturity date and no repayment of principal that makes fixed coupon payments of $C forever. Consols were first sold by the British Treasury during the Napoleonic Wars and are still traded today;

they are quite rare, however, in Canadian capital markets. The formula in Equation 3 for the price of the consol *P* simplifies to the following:[5]

$$P = \frac{C}{i} \qquad (4)$$

where
$$P = \text{price of the consol}$$
$$C = \text{yearly payment}$$

One nice feature of consols is that you can immediately see that as *i* goes up, the price of the bond falls. For example, if a consol pays $100 per year forever and the interest rate is 10%, its price will be $1000 = $100/0.10. If the interest rate rises to 20%, its price will fall to $500 = $100/0.20. We can also rewrite this formula as

$$i = \frac{C}{P} \qquad (5)$$

We see then that it is also easy to calculate the yield to maturity for the consol (despite the fact that it never matures). For example, with a consol that pays $100 yearly and has a price of $2000, the yield to maturity is easily calculated to be 5% (= $100/$2000).

Discount Bond   The yield-to-maturity calculation for a discount bond is similar to that for the simple loan. Let us consider a discount bond such as a one-year Canadian Treasury bill, which pays off a face value of $1000 in one year's time. If the current purchase price of this bill is $900, then equating this price to the present value of the $1000 received in one year, using Equation 1, gives

$$\$900 = \frac{\$1000}{1 + i}$$

and solving for *i*,

$$(1 + i) \times \$900 = \$1000$$
$$\$900 + \$900i = \$1000$$

$$\$900i = \$1000 - \$900$$

$$i = \frac{\$1000 - \$900}{\$900} = 0.111 = 11.1\%$$

More generally, for any one-year discount bond, the yield to maturity can be written as

$$i = \frac{F - P}{P} \qquad (6)$$

---

[5]The bond price formula for a consol is

$$P = \frac{C}{1 + i} + \frac{C}{(1 + i)^2} + \frac{C}{(1 + i)^3} + \cdots$$

which can be written as

$$P = C (x + x^2 + x^3 + \cdots)$$

in which $x = 1/(1 + i)$. The formula for an infinite sum is:

$$1 + x + x^2 + x^3 + \cdots = \frac{1}{1 - x} \quad \text{for} \quad x < 1$$

and so

$$P = C \left(\frac{1}{1 - x} - 1 \right) = C \left(\frac{1}{1 - 1/(1 + i)} - 1 \right)$$

which by suitable algebraic manipulation becomes

$$P = C \left(\frac{1 + i}{i} - \frac{i}{i} \right) = \frac{C}{i}$$

Negative T-Bill Rates? Japan Shows the Way

We normally assume that interest rates must always be positive. Negative interest rates would imply that you are willing to pay more for a bond today than you will receive for it in the future (as our formula for yield to maturity on a discount bond demonstrates). Negative interest rates therefore seem like an impossibility because you would do better by holding cash that has the same value in the future as it does today.

The Japanese have demonstrated that this reasoning is not quite correct. In November 1998, interest rates on Japanese six-month Treasury bills became negative, yielding an interest rate of −0.004%, with investors paying more for the bills than their face value. This is an extremely unusual event because no other country in the world has seen negative interest

rates during the last fifty years. How could this happen?

As we will see in Chapter 5, the weakness of the Japanese economy and a negative inflation rate drove Japanese interest rates to low levels, but these two factors can't explain the negative rates. The answer is that large investors found it more convenient to hold these six-month bills as a store of value rather than holding cash because the bills are denominated in larger amounts and can be stored electronically. For that reason, some investors were willing to hold them, despite their negative rates, even though in monetary terms the investors would be better off holding cash. Clearly, the convenience of T-bills only goes so far, and thus their interest rates can go only a little bit below zero.

where

F = face value of the discount bond
P = current price of the discount bond

In other words, the yield to maturity equals the increase in price over the year, $F - P$, divided by the initial price P. In normal circumstances, investors earn positive returns from holding these securities and so they sell at a discount, meaning that the current price of the bond is below the face value. Therefore, $F - P$ should be positive, and the yield to maturity should be positive as well. However, this is not always the case, as recent extraordinary events in Japan indicate (see Box 4-1).

An important feature of this equation is that it indicates that for a discount bond, the yield to maturity is negatively related to the current bond price. This is the same conclusion that we reached for a coupon bond. For example, Equation 6 shows that a rise in the bond price from $900 to $950 means that the bond will have a smaller increase in its price at maturity, and the yield to maturity falls from 11.1 to 5.3%. Similarly, a fall in the yield to maturity means that the price of the discount bond has risen.

Summary   The concept of present value tells you that a dollar in the future is not as valuable to you as a dollar today because you can earn interest on this dollar. Specifically, a dollar received n years from now is worth only $\$1/(1 + i)^n$ today. The present value of a set of future payments on a debt instrument equals the sum of the present values of each of the future payments. The yield to maturity for an instrument is the interest rate that equates the present value of the future payments on that instrument to its value today. Because the procedure for calculating the yield to maturity is based on sound economic principles, this is the measure that economists think most accurately describes the interest rate.

Our calculations of the yield to maturity for a variety of bonds reveal the important fact that *current bond prices and interest rates are negatively related:* *when the interest rate rises, the price of the bond falls, and vice versa*.

OTHER MEASURES OF INTEREST RATES

The yield to maturity is the most accurate measure of interest rates and is what economists mean when they use the term *interest rate*. Unless otherwise specified, the terms *interest rate* and *yield to maturity* are used synonymously in this book. However, because the yield to maturity is sometimes difficult to calculate, other, less accurate measures of interest rates have come into common use in bond markets. You will frequently encounter two of these measures, the *current yield* and the *yield on a discount basis,* when reading the newspaper, and it is important for you to understand what they mean and how they differ from the more accurate measure of interest rates, the yield to maturity.

Current Yield

The **current yield** is an approximation of the yield to maturity on coupon bonds that is often reported because, in contrast to the yield to maturity, it is easily calculated. It is defined as the yearly coupon payment divided by the price of the security,

$$i_c = \frac{C}{P} \tag{7}$$

where

i_c = current yield
P = price of the coupon bond
C = yearly coupon payment

This formula is identical to the formula in Equation 5, which describes the calculation of the yield to maturity for a consol. Hence, for a consol, the current yield is an exact measure of the yield to maturity. When a coupon bond has a long term to maturity (say, 20 years or more), it is very much like a consol, which pays coupon payments forever. Thus you would expect the current yield to be a rather close approximation of the yield to maturity for a long-term coupon bond, and you can safely use the current-yield calculation instead of looking up the yield to maturity in a bond table. However, as the time to maturity of the coupon bond shortens (say, it becomes less than five years), it behaves less and less like a consol and so the approximation afforded by the current yield becomes worse and worse.

We have also seen that when the bond price equals the par value of the bond, the yield to maturity is equal to the coupon rate (the coupon payment divided by the par value of the bond). Because the current yield equals the coupon payment divided by the bond price, the current yield is also equal to the coupon rate when the bond price is at par. This logic leads us to the conclusion that when the bond price is at par, the current yield equals the yield to maturity. This means that the closer the bond price is to the bond's par value, the better the current yield will approximate the yield to maturity.

The current yield is negatively related to the price of the bond. In the case of our 10%-coupon-rate bond, when the price rises from $1000 to $1100, the current yield falls from 10% (= $100/$1000) to 9.09% (= $100/$1100). As Table 4-1 indicates, the yield to maturity is also negatively related to the price of the bond; when the price rises from $1000 to $1100, the yield to maturity falls from 10 to 8.48%. In this we see an important fact: *the current yield and the yield to maturity always move together; a rise in the current yield always signals that the yield to maturity has also risen..*

The general characteristics of the current yield (the yearly coupon payment divided by the bond price) can be summarized as follows: the current yield better approximates the yield to maturity when the bond's price is nearer to the bond's par value and the maturity of the bond is longer. It becomes a worse approximation when the bond's price is further from the bond's par value and the bond's maturity is shorter. Regardless of whether the current yield is a good approximation of the yield to maturity, a change in the current yield *always* signals a change in the same direction of the yield to maturity.

Yield on a Discount Basis

In calculating the yield to maturity on discount bonds we assumed a maturity of one year. The typical Treasury bill, however, has a maturity less than a year, perhaps 30 or 91 days. The interest rate on such bills with less than one year to maturity is quoted as a **yield on a discount basis** (or **discount yield**). Formally, the discount yield is defined, on an **annualized rate basis**, by the following formula:

$$i_{db} = \frac{F - P}{P} \times \frac{365}{\text{days to maturity}} \qquad (8)$$

where

i_{db} = yield on a discount basis
F = face value of the discount bond
P = purchase price of the discount bond

The discount yield understates the interest rate on bills as measured by the yield to maturity. For example, a 91-day Treasury bill which is selling for $988 and has a face value of $1000 has a discount yield of

$$i_{db} = \frac{\$1000 - \$988}{\$988} \times \frac{365}{91} = 0.0487 \ \ or \ \ (4.87\%)$$

Over 91 days, however, the investor receives a rate of return of

$$\frac{\$1000 - \$988}{\$988} = 0.01215 \ \ or \ \ (1.215\%)$$

and if the proceeds were reinvested at the same rate four times over, the actual rate of return (i.e., the **annual percentage rate**) would have been $1.01215^4 - 1 = 0.0495$ (or 4.95%).

Even though the discount yield is a somewhat misleading measure of the interest rate, however, a change in the discount yield always indicates a change in the same direction for the yield to maturity.[6]

---

[6]The method used to calculate the yield on a discount basis in the United States is different from that used in Canada in two respects. First, the percentage gain on the face value of the bill (F-P)/F, rather than the percentage gain on the purchase price of the bill (F-P)/P, is used in calculating the discount yield. Moreover, it puts the yield on an annual basis by taking the year to be 360 days long rather than 365 days. Formally, the U.S. i_{db} is defined as

$$i_{db} = \frac{F - P}{F} \times \frac{360}{\text{days to maturity}}$$

Because of these peculiarities, the U.S. discount yield further understates the interest rate on bills as measured by the yield to maturity.

APPLICATION   *Reading the Bond Page*

Now that we understand the different interest-rate definitions, let's apply our knowledge and take a look at what kind of information appears on the bond page of a typical newspaper, in this case the *Globe and Mail: Report on Business*. The "Following the Financial News" box on page 70 contains listings for government of Canada bonds, provincial bonds, municipal bonds, and corporate bonds on Monday, November 20, 2000. Panel (a) contains the information on Canada bonds.

The information found in the "Coupon" and "Maturity" columns identifies the bonds by coupon rate and maturity date. For example, Bond 1 has a coupon rate of 5.25%, indicating that it pays out $52.50 per year on a $1000-face-value, and is a short-term bond maturing on December 1, 2001. In bond market parlance, it is referred to as the Canada 5.25% of 2001. The next column tells us about the bond's price. By convention, all prices in the bond market are quoted per $100 of face value. In the case of Bond 1, the price of 99.31 represents an actual price of $993.10 for a $1000-face-value bond. Furthermore, this quoted price is the bid price. The bid price tells you what price you will receive if you sell the bond, and the asked price tells you what you must pay for the bond. (You might want to think of the bid price as the "wholesale" price and the asked price as the "retail" price.)

For all the bonds, the asked price is more than the bid price, with the bid-ask difference being generally $0.10 to $0.15 per $1000 of face value. Can you guess why this is so? The difference between the two (the *spread*) provides the bond dealer who trades these securities with a profit. This profit is what enables the dealer to make a living and provide the service of allowing you to buy and sell bonds at will.

The "Yield" column provides the yield to maturity, which is 5.95% for Bond 1. It is calculated with the method described earlier in this chapter using the asked price as the price of the bond. The asked price is used in the calculation because the yield to maturity is most relevant to a person who is going to buy and hold the security and thus earn the yield. The person selling the security is not going to be holding it and hence is less concerned with the yield.

The figure for the current yield is not usually included in the newspaper's quotations, but it has been added in panel (a) to give you some real-world examples of how well the current yield approximates the yield to maturity. Our previous discussion provided us with some rules for deciding when the current yield is likely to be a good approximation and when it is not.

Bonds 3 and 4 mature in more than 20 years, meaning that their characteristics are like those of a consol. The current yields should then be a good approximation of the yield to maturity, and they are: the current yields are within 50 basis points of the value for the yield to maturity. This approximation is reasonable even for Bond 4, which has a price over 30% above its face value. Notice that when financial analysts talk about differences in yields (or changes in the yield), they frequently describe it in terms of **basis points**, which are hundredths of a percentage point. For example, a financial analyst would describe the 0.38 difference between the current yield and the yield to maturity for the 8%, 2027 Canada bond, by saying that it is 38 basis points.

Now let's take a look at Bonds 1 and 2, which have a much shorter time to maturity. The current yield is a good approximation when the price is very near the par value of 100, as it is for Bond 1. However, the price of Bond 2 differs by less than 4% from the par value, and look how poor an approximation the current yield is for the yield to maturity; it overstates the yield to maturity by more than 2 percentage points. This bears out what we learned earlier about the current yield: it can be a very misleading guide to the value of the yield to maturity for a short-term bond if the bond price is not very close to par.

Hydro-Québec
www.hydroquebec.com

Ontario Power Generation
www.opg.com

Two other categories of government bonds are reported much like the Canada bonds in the newspaper. Provincial bonds, in the first part of panel (b), include securities issued by the provinces and by provincial authorities, such as Hydro-Québec and Ontario Power Generation. Municipal bonds, in the second part of panel (b), include securities issued by large cities.

Panel (c) has quotations for corporate bonds, traded mostly in the over-the-counter market where about 100 dealers and a few banks and trust companies are active. These corporate bonds are reported in like manner: the first column identifies the bond by indicating the corporation that issued it. The bonds we are looking at have all been issued by BC Telephone. The next two columns tell the coupon rate and the maturity date (9.15% and April 8, 2002 for Bond 1). The "Price" column reports the last traded price that day per $100 of face value. The price of 102.67 represents $1026.70 for a $1000-face-value bond. The "Yield" column reports the yield to maturity, calculated with the method described earlier in this chapter.

The current yield is also given for two bonds. This information is not provided in the newspaper, but it is included here because it shows how misleading the current yield can be for a bond with a short maturity such as the 9.15%, of April 8, 2002. The current yield of 8.9% is a misleading measure of the interest rate because the yield to maturity is actually 7.07%. By contrast, for the 9.65%, of April 8, 2022, with over 20 years to maturity, the current yield is just over two-tenths of a percentage point of the value for the yield to maturity.

THE DISTINCTION BETWEEN INTEREST RATES AND RETURNS

Many people think that the interest rate on a bond tells them all they need to know about how well off they are as a result of owning it. If Irving the Investor thinks he is better off when he owns a long-term bond yielding a 10% interest rate and the interest rate rises to 20%, he will have a rude awakening: as we will see shortly, if he has to sell the bond, Irving has lost his shirt! How well a person does by holding a bond or any other security over a particular time period is accurately measured by the **return** or, in more precise terminology, the **rate of return**. For any security, the rate of return is defined as the payments to the owner plus the change in its value, expressed as a fraction of its purchase price. To make this definition clearer, let us see what the return would look like for a $1000-face-value coupon bond with a coupon rate of 10% that is bought for $1000, held for one year, and then sold for $1200. The payments to the owner are the yearly coupon payments of $100, and the change in its value is $1200 − $1000 = $200. Adding these together and expressing them as a fraction of the purchase price of $1000 gives us the one-year holding-period return for this bond:

$$\frac{\$100 + \$200}{\$1000} = \frac{\$300}{\$1000} = 0.30 = 30\%$$

You may have noticed something quite surprising about the return that we have just calculated: it equals 30%, yet as Table 4-1 indicates, initially the yield to maturity was only 10%. This demonstrates that ***the return on a bond will not necessarily equal the interest rate on that bond***. We now see that the distinction between interest rate and return can be important, although for many securities the two may be closely related.

FOLLOWING THE FINANCIAL NEWS

Selected Bond Prices and Interest Rates

Bond prices and interest rate are published weekly. In the *Globe and Mail: Report on Business* they can be found in the "Canadian Bonds" section of the paper. The format for quoting bond prices and yields is illustrated here.

(a)   Government of Canada bonds

GOVERNMENT OF CANADA

	Issuer	Coupon	Maturity	Price	Yield	
Bond 1—	Canada	5.250	Dec 01/01	99.31	5.95	—Current yield = 5.29%
Bond 2—	Canada	8.500	Apr 01/02	103.31	5.92	—Current yield = 8.23%
	Canada	13.500	Jun 01/04	123.90	5.89	
	Canada	12.500	Mar 01/06	129.60	5.89	
	Canada	7.250	Jun 01/07	107.69	5.82	
	Canada	9.500	Jun 01/10	127.02	5.77	
Bond 3—	Canada	8.000	Jun 01/23	127.68	5.79	—Current yield = 6.27%
Bond 4—	Canada	8.000	Jun 01/27	130.83	5.73	—Current yield = 6.11%

(b)   Provincial and municipal bonds

PROVINCIAL					MUNICIPAL				
Issuer	Coupon	Maturity	Price	Yield	Issuer	Coupon	Maturity	Price	Yield
Alberta	7.750	May 05/03	104.01	5.97	BC Mun Fin	9.625	May 13/02	104.86	6.13
Alberta	5.100	Dec 01/03	97.59	5.98	BC Mun Fin	8.300	Jan 12/03	104.28	6.13
BC	9.000	Jan 09/02	103.18	6.04	Edmonton	12.875	Dec 13/04	123.70	6.18
BC	7.750	Jun 16/03	104.00	6.04	Edmonton	11.250	Dec 17/05	121.42	6.25
BC Hydro	14.500	Apr 14/06	103.20	6.07	OntSclBdFin	7.200	Jun 09/25	103.28	6.92
Manitoba	9.750	Sep 03/02	106.01	6.12	Ottawa	6.200	Sep 10/19	97.64	6.42
New Brunswick	9.125	Apr 01/02	103.95	6.04	Toronto-Met	7.750	Dec 01/05	106.97	6.12
Newfoundland	12.875	Apr 06/03	102.41	6.12	Toronto-Met	7.850	Jun 28/06	107.96	6.15
Nova Scotia	5.250	Jun 02/03	98.04	6.10	Vancouver	6.000	Oct 07/09	98.25	6.26
Ontario	10.500	Dec 12/01	104.49	6.04	Winnipeg	8.875	Feb19/02	103.14	6.20

(c)   Corporate bonds

CORPORATE

	Issuer	Coupon	Maturity	Price	Yield	
Bond 1—	BC Telephone	9.150	Apr 08/02	102.67	7.07	—Current yield = 8.91%
	BC Telephone	12.000	May 31/10	129.41	7.60	
	BC Telephone	11.900	Nov 22/15	131.99	8.16	
	BC Telephone	10.650	Jun19/21	123.15	8.29	
Bond 2—	BC Telephone	9.650	Apr 08/22	113.54	8.29	—Current yield = 8.50%

Source: The Globe and Mail: Report on Business, Monday, November 20, 2000, p. B12. Reprinted with permission.

Study Guide

The concept of return discussed here is extremely important because it is used continually throughout the book. Make sure that you understand how a return is calculated and why it can differ from the interest rate. This understanding will make the material presented later in the book easier to follow.

More generally, the return on a bond held from time t to time $t + 1$ can be written as

$$RET = \frac{C + P_{t+1} - P_t}{P_t} \qquad (9)$$

where

RET = return from holding the bond from time t to time $t + 1$
P_t = price of the bond at time t
P_{t+1} = price of the bond at time $t + 1$
C = coupon payment

A convenient way to rewrite the return formula in Equation 9 is to recognize that it can be split into two separate terms:

$$RET = \frac{C}{P_t} + \frac{P_{t+1} - P_t}{P_t}$$

The first term is the current yield i_c (the coupon payment over the purchase price):

$$\frac{C}{P_t} = i_c$$

The second term is the **rate of capital gain**, or the change in the bond's price relative to the initial purchase price:

$$\frac{P_{t+1} - P_t}{P_t} = g$$

where g = rate of capital gain. Equation 9 can then be rewritten as

$$RET = i_c + g \qquad (10)$$

which shows that the return on a bond is the current yield i_c plus the rate of capital gain g. This rewritten formula illustrates the point we just discovered. Even for a bond for which the current yield i_c is an accurate measure of the yield to maturity, the return can differ substantially from the interest rate. Returns will differ from the interest rate especially if there are sizable fluctuations in the price of the bond that produce substantial capital gains or losses.

To explore this point even further, let's look at what happens to the returns on bonds of different maturities when interest rates rise. Table 4-2 calculates the one-year return on several 10%-coupon-rate bonds all purchased at par when interest rates on all these bonds rise from 10 to 20%. Several key findings in this table are generally true of all bonds:

- The only bond whose return equals the initial yield to maturity is one whose time to maturity is the same as the holding period (see the last bond in Table 4-2).

- A rise in interest rates is associated with a fall in bond prices, resulting in capital losses on bonds whose terms to maturity are longer than the holding period.

- The more distant a bond's maturity, the greater the size of the percentage price change associated with an interest-rate change.

- The more distant a bond's maturity, the lower the rate of return that occurs as a result of the increase in the interest rate.

- Even though a bond has a substantial initial interest rate, its return can turn out to be negative if interest rates rise.

	TABLE 4-2	One-Year Returns on Different-Maturity 10% Coupon Rate Bonds When Interest Rates Rise from 10% to 20%				

(1) Years to Maturity When Bond is Purchased	(2) Initial Current Yield (%)	(3) Initial Price ($)	(4) Price Next Year* ($)	(5) Rate of Capital Gain (%)	(6) Rate of Return (2 + 5) (%)
30	10	1000	503	−49.7	−39.7
20	10	1000	516	−48.4	−38.4
10	10	1000	597	−40.3	−30.3
5	10	1000	741	−25.9	−15.9
2	10	1000	917	−8.3	+1.7
1	10	1000	1000	0.0	+10.0

*Calculated using Equation 3.

At first it frequently puzzles students (as it puzzles poor Irving the Investor) that a rise in interest rates can mean that a bond has been a poor investment. The trick to understanding this is to recognize that a rise in the interest rate means that the price of a bond has fallen. A rise in interest rates therefore means that a capital loss has occurred, and if this loss is large enough, the bond can be a poor investment indeed. For example, we see in Table 4-2 that the bond that has 30 years to maturity when purchased has a capital loss of 49.7% when the interest rate rises from 10% to 20%. This loss is so large that it exceeds the current yield of 10%, resulting in a negative return (loss) of −39.7%. If Irving does not sell the bond, his capital loss is often referred to as a "paper loss." This is a loss nonetheless because if he had not bought this bond and had instead put his money in the bank, he would now be able to buy more bonds at their lower price than he presently owns.

Maturity and the Volatility of Bond Returns: Interest-Rate Risk

The finding that the prices of longer-maturity bonds respond more dramatically to changes in interest rates helps explain an important fact about the behaviour of bond markets: *prices and returns for long-term bonds are more volatile than those for shorter-term bonds*. Price changes of +20% and −20% within a year, with corresponding variations in returns, are common for bonds more than 20 years away from maturity.

We now see that changes in interest rates make investments in long-term bonds quite risky. Indeed, the riskiness of an asset's return that results from interest-rate changes is so important that it has been given a special name, **interest-rate risk**. Dealing with interest-rate risk is a major concern of managers of financial institutions and investors, as we will see in later chapters (see also Box 4-2).

Although long-term debt instruments have substantial interest-rate risk, short-term debt instruments do not. Indeed, bonds with a maturity that is as short as the holding period have no interest-rate risk.[7] We see this for the coupon bond at the

---

[7]The statement that there is no interest-rate risk for any bond whose time to maturity matches the holding period is literally true only for discount bonds and zero-coupon bonds that make no intermediate

BOX 4·2

Helping Investors to Select Desired Interest-Rate Risk

Because many investors want to know how much interest-rate risk they are exposed to, some mutual fund companies try to educate investors about the perils of interest-rate risk, as well as to offer investment alternatives that match their investors' preferences.

For example, one U.S. company, Vanguard Group, offers eight separate high-grade bond mutual funds. In its prospectus, Vanguard separates the funds by the average maturity of the bonds they hold and demonstrates the effect of interest-rate changes by computing the percentage change in bond value resulting from a 1% increase and decrease in interest rates.

Three of the bond funds invest in bonds with average maturities of one to three years, which Vanguard rates as having the lowest interest-rate risk. Three other funds hold bonds with average maturities of five to ten years, which Vanguard rates as having medium interest-rate risk. Two funds hold long-term bonds with maturities of 15 to 30 years, which Vanguard rates as having high interest-rate risk.

By providing this information, Vanguard hopes to increase its market share in the sale of bond funds. Not surprisingly, Vanguard is one of the most successful mutual fund companies in the business.

Vanguard Group
www.vanguard.com

bottom of Table 4-2, which has no uncertainty about the rate of return because it equals the yield to maturity, which is known at the time the bond is purchased. The key to understanding why there is no interest-rate risk for any bond whose time to maturity matches the holding period is to recognize that (in this case) the price at the end of the holding period is already fixed at the face value. The change in interest rates can then have no effect on the price at the end of the holding period for these bonds, and the return will therefore be equal to the yield to maturity known at the time the bond is purchased.[8]

---

cash payments before the holding period is over. A coupon bond that makes an intermediate cash payment before the holding period is over requires that this payment be reinvested. Because the interest rate at which this payment can be reinvested is uncertain, there is some uncertainty about the return on this coupon bond even when the time to maturity equals the holding period. However, the riskiness of the return on a coupon bond from reinvesting the coupon payments is typically quite small, and so the basic point that a coupon bond with a time to maturity equalling the holding period has very little risk still holds true.

[8]In the text, we are assuming that all holding periods are short and equal to the maturity on short-term bonds and are thus not subject to interest-rate risk. However, if an investor's holding period is longer than the term to maturity of the bond, the investor is exposed to a type of interest-rate risk called *reinvestment risk*. Reinvestment risk occurs because the proceeds from the short-term bond need to be reinvested at a future interest rate that is uncertain.

To understand reinvestment risk, suppose that Irving the Investor has a holding period of two years and decides to purchase a $1000 one-year bond at face value and will then purchase another one at the end of the first year. If the initial interest rate is 10%, Irving will have $1100 at the end of the year. If the interest rate rises to 20%, as in Table 4-2, Irving will find that buying $1100 worth of another one-year bond will leave him at the end of the second year with $1100 × (1 + 0.20) = $1320. Thus Irving's two-year return will be ($1320 − $1000)/1000 = 0.32 = 32%, which equals 14.9% at an annual rate. In this case, Irving has earned more by buying the one-year bonds than if he had initially purchased the two-year bond with an interest rate of 10%. Thus when Irving has a holding period that is longer than the term to maturity of the bonds he purchases, he benefits from a rise in interest rates. Conversely, if interest rates fall to 5%, Irving will have only $1155 at the end of two years: $1100 × (1 + 0.05). Thus his two-year return will be ($1155 − $1000)/1000 = 0.155 = 15.5%, which is 7.2% at an annual rate. With a holding period greater than the term to maturity of the bond, Irving now loses from a fall in interest rates.

We have thus seen that when the holding period is longer than the term to maturity of a bond, the return is uncertain because the future interest rate when reinvestment occurs is also uncertain—in short, there is reinvestment risk. We also see that if the holding period is longer than the term to maturity of the bond, the investor benefits from a rise in interest rates and is hurt by a fall in interest rates.

Summary   The return on a bond, which tells you how good an investment it has been over the holding period, is equal to the yield to maturity in only one special case: when the holding period and the maturity of the bond are identical. Bonds whose term to maturity is longer than the holding period are subject to interest-rate risk: changes in interest rates lead to capital gains and losses that produce substantial differences between the return and the yield to maturity known at the time the bond is purchased. Interest-rate risk is especially important for long-term bonds, where the capital gains and losses can be substantial. This is why long-term bonds are not considered to be safe assets with a sure return over short holding periods.

THE DISTINCTION BETWEEN REAL AND NOMINAL INTEREST RATES

So far in our discussion of interest rates, we have ignored the effects of inflation on the cost of borrowing. What we have up to now been calling the interest rate makes no allowance for inflation, and it is more precisely referred to as the **nominal interest rate**, which is to distinguish it from the **real interest rate**, the interest rate that is adjusted for expected changes in the price level so that it more accurately reflects the true cost of borrowing.[9] The real interest rate is more accurately defined by the *Fisher equation,* named for Irving Fisher, one of the great monetary economists of the twentieth century. The Fisher equation states that the nominal interest rate i equals the real interest rate i_r plus the expected rate of inflation π^e:[10]

$$i = i_r + \pi^e \tag{11}$$

Rearranging terms, we find that the real interest rate equals the nominal interest rate minus the expected inflation rate:

$$i_r = i - \pi^e \tag{12}$$

To see why this definition makes sense, let us first consider a situation in which you have made a one-year simple loan with a 5% interest rate ($i = 5\%$) and you expect the price level to rise by 3% over the course of the year ($\pi^e = 3\%$). As a result of making the loan, at the end of the year you will have 2% more in **real terms**, that is, in terms of real goods and services you can buy. In this case, the interest rate you have earned in terms of real goods and services is 2%; that is,

$$i_r = 5\% - 3\% = 2\%$$

as indicated by the Fisher definition.

Now what if the interest rate rises to 8%, but you expect the inflation rate to be 10% over the course of the year? Although you will have 8% more dollars at

---

[9]The real interest rate defined in the text is more precisely referred to as the *ex ante real interest rate* because it is adjusted for *expected* changes in the price level. This is the real interest rate that is most important to economic decisions, and typically it is what economists mean when they make reference to the "real" interest rate. The interest rate that is adjusted for *actual* changes in the price level is called the *ex post real interest rate.* It describes how well a lender has done in real terms after the fact.

[10]A more precise formulation of the Fisher equation is

$$i = i_r + \pi^e + (i_r \times \pi^e)$$

because

$$1 + i = (1 + i_r)(1 + \pi^e) = 1 + i_r + \pi^e + (i_r \times \pi^e)$$

and subtracting 1 from both sides gives us the first equation. For small values of i_r and π^e, the term $i_r \times \pi^e$ is so small that we ignore it, as in the text.

the end of the year, you will be paying 10% more for goods; the result is that you will be able to buy 2% fewer goods at the end of the year and you are 2% worse off *in real terms*. This is also exactly what the Fisher definition tells us because

$$i_r = 8\% - 10\% = -2\%$$

As a lender, you are clearly less eager to make a loan in this case because in terms of real goods and services you have actually earned a negative interest rate of 2%. By contrast, as the borrower, you fare quite well because at the end of the year, the amounts you will have to pay back will be worth 2% less in terms of goods and services—you as the borrower will be ahead by 2% in real terms. **When the real interest rate is low, there are greater incentives to borrow and fewer incentives to lend.**

A similar distinction can be made between nominal returns and real returns. Nominal returns, which do not allow for inflation, are what we have been referring to as simply "returns." When inflation is subtracted from a nominal return, we have the real return, which indicates the amount of extra goods and services that can be purchased as a result of holding the security.

The distinction between real and nominal interest rates is important because the real interest rate, which reflects the real cost of borrowing, is likely to be a better indicator of the incentives to borrow and lend. It appears to be a better guide to how people will be affected by what is happening in credit markets. Figure 4-1, which presents estimates from 1974 to 2000 of the real and nominal interest rates on three-month Canadian Treasury bills, shows us that nominal and real rates often do not move together. (This is also true for nominal and real interest rates in the rest of the world.) In particular, when nominal rates in Canada were high in the 1970s, real rates were actually extremely low, sometimes negative. By the standard of nominal interest rates, you would have thought that credit market conditions were tight in this period because it was expensive to borrow.

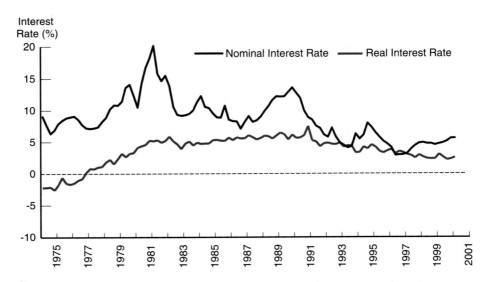

FIGURE 4-1   Real and Nominal Interest Rates (Three-Month Treasury Bill), 1974–2000

Source: Statistics Canada CANSIM Series B3400 and B14060. The real interest rate is constructed using the procedure outlined in Frederic S. Mishkin, "The Real Interest Rate: An Empirical Investigation," *Carnegie-Rochester Conference Series on Public Policy* 15 (1981):151-200. This involves estimating the expected inflation rate as a function of past interest rates, inflation, and time trends and then subtracting the expected inflation rate measure from the nominal interest rate.

With Real Return Bonds, Real Interest Rates Have Become Observable in Canada

On December 10, 1991, the Canadian government issued coupon bonds whose coupon payment and face value are indexed to the Consumer Price Index (CPI). These securities are known as *Real Return Bonds* and are designed to provide investors with a known real return if held to maturity. Other countries such as the United Kingdom, Australia, and Sweden also issue similar indexed securities and the U.S. Treasury joined the group in September 1998 by issuing TIPS (Treasury Inflation Protection Securities).

These indexed securities have successfully acquired a niche in the bond market, enabling governments to raise more funds. In addition, because their interest and principal payments are adjusted for changes in the price level, the interest rate on these bonds provides a direct measure of a real interest rate. These indexed bonds are very useful to policymakers, especially monetary policymakers, because by subtracting their interest rate from a nominal interest rate on a nonindexed bond, they generate more insight into expected inflation, a valuable piece of information.

For example, on December 10, 1991, the interest rate on long-term Canada bonds was 9.12%, while that on the long-term Real Return Bond was 4.25%. Thus, the implied expected inflation rate, derived from the difference between these two rates, was 4.87%. The private sector finds the information provided by Real Return Bonds very useful: many financial institutions routinely publish the expected Canadian inflation rate derived from these bonds.

However, the estimates of the real rates indicate that you would have been mistaken. In real terms, the cost of borrowing was actually quite low.[11]

Until recently, real interest rates in Canada were not observable; only nominal rates were reported. This all changed when, on December 10, 1991, the government of Canada began to issue **indexed bonds**, whose interest and principal payments are adjusted for changes in the price level (see Box 4-3).

---

[11]Because most interest income in Canada is subject to income taxes, the true earnings in real terms from holding a debt instrument are not reflected by the real interest rate defined by the Fisher equation but rather by the *after-tax real interest rate,* which equals the nominal interest rate *after income tax payments have been subtracted,* minus the expected inflation rate. For a person facing a 30% tax rate, the after-tax interest rate earned on a bond yielding 10% is only 7% because 30% of the interest income must be paid to the CCRA. Thus the after-tax real interest rate on this bond when expected inflation is 5% equals 2% (= 7% − 5%). More generally, the after-tax real interest rate can be expressed as

$$i(1 - \tau) - \pi^e$$

where τ = the income tax rate.

This formula for the after-tax real interest rate also provides a better measure of the effective cost of borrowing for many corporations in Canada because in calculating income taxes, they can deduct interest payments on loans from their income. Thus if you face a 30% tax rate and take out a business loan with a 10% interest rate, you are able to deduct the 10% interest payment and thus lower your business taxes by 30% of this amount. Your after-tax nominal cost of borrowing is then 7% (10% minus 30% of the 10% interest payment), and when the expected inflation rate is 5%, the effective cost of borrowing in real terms is again 2% (= 7% − 5%).

As the example (and the formula) indicates, after-tax real interest rates are always below the real interest rate defined by the Fisher equation. For a further discussion of measures of after-tax real interest rates, see Frederic S. Mishkin, "The Real Interest Rate: An Empirical Investigation," *Carnegie-Rochester Conference Series on Public Policy* 15 (1981): 151 -200.

SUMMARY

1. The yield to maturity, which is the measure that most accurately reflects the interest rate, is the interest rate that equates the present value of future payments of a debt instrument with its value today. Application of this principle reveals that bond prices and interest rates are negatively related: when the interest rate rises, the price of the bond must fall, and vice versa.

2. Two less accurate measures of interest rates are commonly used to quote interest rates on coupon and discount bonds. The current yield, which equals the coupon payment divided by the price of a coupon bond, is a less accurate measure of the yield to maturity the shorter the maturity of the bond and the greater the gap between the price and the par value. The yield on a discount basis (also called the discount yield) also understates the yield to maturity on a discount bond. Even though these measures are misleading guides to

the size of the interest rate, a change in them always signals a change in the same direction for the yield to maturity.

3. The return on a security, which tells you how well you have done by holding this security over a stated period of time, can differ substantially from the interest rate as measured by the yield to maturity. Long-term bond prices have substantial fluctuations when interest rates change and thus bear interest-rate risk. The resulting capital gains and losses can be large, which is why long-term bonds are not considered to be safe assets with a sure return.

4. The real interest rate is defined as the nominal interest rate minus the expected rate of inflation. It is a better measure of the incentives to borrow and lend than the nominal interest rate, and it is a more accurate indicator of the tightness of credit market conditions than the nominal interest rate.

KEY TERMS

annual percentage rate, p. 67

annualized rate basis, p. 67

basis point, p. 68

consol (perpetuity), p. 63

coupon bond, p. 58

coupon rate, p. 58

current yield, p. 66

discount bond (zero-coupon bond), p. 58

face value (par value), p. 58

fixed-payment loan, p. 58

indexed bond, p. 76

interest-rate risk, p. 72

nominal interest rate, p. 74

present discounted value, p. 60

present value, p. 58

rate of capital gain, p. 71

real interest rate, p. 74

real terms, p. 74

return (rate of return), p. 69

simple loan, p. 58

yield on a discount basis (discount yield), p. 67

yield to maturity, p. 60

QUESTIONS AND PROBLEMS

Questions marked with an asterisk are answered at the end of the book in an appendix, "Answers to Selected Questions and Problems."

*1. Would a dollar tomorrow be worth more or less to you today when the interest rate is 20% or when it is 10%?

2. You have just won $20 million in a provincial lottery, which promises to pay you $1 million (tax free) every year for the next 20 years. Have you really won $20 million?

*3. If the interest rate is 10%, what is the present value of a security that pays you $1100 next year, $1210 the year after, and $1331 the year after that?

4. If the security in Problem 3 sold for $4000, is the yield to maturity greater or less than 10%? Why?

*5. Write down the formula that is used to calculate the yield to maturity on a 20-year 10% coupon bond with $1000 face value that sells for $2000.

6. What is the yield to maturity on a $1000-face-value discount bond maturing in one year that sells for $800?

*7. What is the yield to maturity on a simple loan for $1 million that requires a repayment of $2 million in five years' time?

8. To pay for university, you have just taken out a $1000 government loan that makes you pay $126 per year for 25 years. However, you don't have to

start making these payments until you graduate from college two years from now. Why is the yield to maturity necessarily less than 12%, the yield to maturity on a normal $1000 fixed-payment loan in which you pay $126 per year for 25 years?

*9. Which $1000 bond has the higher yield to maturity, a 20-year bond selling for $800 with a current yield of 15% or a one-year bond selling for $800 with a current yield of 5%?

10. Pick five Canada bonds from the bond page of the newspaper, and calculate the current yield. Note when the current yield is a good approximation of the yield to maturity.

*11. You are offered two bonds, a one-year Canada bond with a yield to maturity of 9% and a one-year Treasury bill with a yield on a discount basis of 8.9%. Which would you rather own?

12. If there is a decline in interest rates, which would you rather be holding, long-term bonds or short-term bonds? Why? Which type of bond has the greater interest-rate risk?

*13. Francine the Financial Adviser has just given you the following advice: "Long-term bonds are a great investment because their interest rate is over 20%." Is Francine necessarily right?

14. If mortgage rates rise from 5% to 10% but the expected rate of increase in housing prices rises from 2% to 9%, are people more or less likely to buy houses?

*15. Interest rates were lower in the mid-1980s than they were in the late 1970s, yet many economists have commented that real interest rates were actually much higher in the mid-1980s than in the late 1970s. Does this make sense? Do you think that these economists are right?

Chapter 5

The Behaviour of Interest Rates

P R E V I E W In the early 1950s, nominal interest rates on three-month Treasury bills were about 1% at an annual rate; by 1981, they had reached over 20%, then fell to 3% in 1997, rose to about 5% in 1998, and have been around that level since. What explains these substantial fluctuations in interest rates? One reason why we study money, banking, and financial markets is to provide some answers to this question.

In this chapter we examine how the overall level of *nominal* interest rates (which we refer to as simply "interest rates") is determined and what factors influence their behaviour. We learned in Chapter 4 that interest rates are negatively related to the price of bonds, so if we can explain why bond prices change, we can also explain why interest rates fluctuate. To do this, we make use of supply and demand analysis for markets for bonds and money to examine how interest rates change.

In order to derive a demand curve for assets like money or bonds, the first step in our analysis, we must first understand what determines the demand for these assets. We do this by developing an economic theory known as the *theory of asset demand,* which outlines criteria that are important when deciding how much of an asset to buy. Armed with this theory, we can then go on to derive the demand curve for bonds or money. After deriving supply curves for these assets, we develop the concept of market equilibrium, the point at which the quantity supplied equals the quantity demanded. Then we use this model to explain changes in equilibrium interest rates.

Because interest rates on different securities tend to move together, in this chapter we will act as if there is only one type of security and a single interest rate in the entire economy. In the following chapter, we expand our analysis to look at why interest rates on different types of securities differ.

DETERMINANTS OF ASSET DEMAND

Before going on to our supply and demand analysis of the bond market and the market for money, we must first understand what determines the quantity demanded of an asset. Recall that an asset is a piece of property that is a store of value. Items such as money, bonds, stocks, art, land, houses, farm equipment, and manufacturing machinery are all assets. Facing the question of whether to buy and hold an asset or whether to buy one asset rather than another, an individual must consider the following factors:

1. **Wealth**, the total resources owned by the individual, including all assets
2. **Expected return** (the return expected over the next period) on one asset relative to alternative assets
3. **Risk** (the degree of uncertainty associated with the return) on one asset relative to alternative assets
4. **Liquidity** (the ease and speed with which an asset can be turned into cash) relative to alternative assets.

Study Guide As we discuss each factor that influences asset demand, remember that we are always holding all the other factors constant. Also, think of additional examples of how changes in each factor would influence your decision to purchase a particular asset, say, a house or a share of common stock. This intuitive approach will help you understand how the theory works in practice.

Wealth

When we find that our wealth has increased, we have more resources available with which to purchase assets, and so, not surprisingly, the quantity of assets we demand increases. Therefore, the effect of changes in wealth on the quantity demanded of an asset can be summarized as follows: ***holding everything else constant, an increase in wealth raises the quantity demanded of an asset***.

Expected Returns

In Chapter 4 we saw that the return on an asset (such as a bond) measures how much we gain from holding that asset. When we make a decision to buy an asset, we are influenced by what we expect the return on that asset to be. If a Nortel Networks Corp. bond, for example, has a return of 15% half the time and 5% the other half of the time, its expected return (which you can think of as the average return) is 10%.[1] If the expected return on the Nortel Networks bond rises relative to expected returns on alternative assets, holding everything else constant, then it becomes more desirable to purchase it, and the quantity demanded increases. This can occur in either of two ways: (1) when the expected return on the Nortel

---

[1]More generally, the expected return equals a weighted sum of each possible realized return multiplied by the probability of its occurring:

$$RET^e = \Sigma\, p_i \times RET_i$$

where RET^e = expected return

p_i = probability of getting the realization RET_i

RET_i = realization of the return

For a Nortel bond,

$$RET^e = \left(\frac{1}{2} \times 15\%\right) + \left(\frac{1}{2} \times 5\%\right) = 10\%$$

TD Canada Trust
www.tdcanadatrust.
com

Networks bond rises while the return on an alternative asset—say, stock in TD Canada Trust—remains unchanged or (2) when the return on the alternative asset, the TD Canada Trust stock, falls while the return on the Nortel bond remains unchanged. To summarize, ***an increase in an asset's expected return relative to that of an alternative asset, holding everything else unchanged, raises the quantity demanded of the asset***.

Risk

The degree of risk or uncertainty of an asset's returns also affects the demand for the asset. Consider two assets, stock in Fly-by-Night Airlines and stock in Feet-on-the-Ground Bus Company. Suppose that Fly-by-Night stock has a return of 15% half the time and 5% the other half of the time, making its expected return 10%, while stock in Feet-on-the-Ground has a fixed return of 10%. Fly-by-Night stock has uncertainty associated with its returns and so has greater risk than stock in Feet-on-the-Ground, whose return is a sure thing.[2]

A *risk-averse* person prefers stock in Feet-on-the-Ground (the sure thing) to Fly-by-Night stock (the riskier asset), even though the stocks have the same expected return, 10%. By contrast, a person who prefers risk is a *risk preferrer* or *risk lover*. Most people are risk-averse: everything else being equal, they prefer to hold the less risky asset. Hence, ***holding everything else constant, if an asset's risk rises relative to that of alternative assets, its quantity demanded will fall***.

Liquidity

Another factor that affects the demand for an asset is how quickly it can be converted into cash without incurring large costs—its liquidity. An asset is liquid if the market in which it is traded has depth and breadth, that is, if the market has many buyers and sellers. A house is not a very liquid asset because it may be hard to find a buyer quickly; if a house must be sold to pay off bills, it might have to be sold for a much lower price. And the transaction costs in selling a house (broker's commissions, lawyer's fees, and so on) are substantial. A Canadian government Treasury bill, by contrast, is a highly liquid asset. It can be sold in a well-organized market where there are many buyers, so it can be sold quickly at low cost. ***The more liquid an asset is relative to alternative assets, holding everything else unchanged, the more desirable it is, and the greater will be the quantity demanded***.

Theory of Asset Demand

All the determining factors we have just discussed can be assembled into the **theory of asset demand**, which states that, holding all of the other factors constant:

1. The quantity demanded of an asset is positively related to wealth.
2. The quantity demanded of an asset is positively related to its expected return relative to alternative assets.

---

[2]One frequently used formal measure of risk is the standard deviation, σ:

$$\sigma = \sqrt{\Sigma p_i \times (RET_i - RET^e)^2}$$

where all the variables are as defined in footnote 1. For Fly-by-Night Airlines stock it equals $\sqrt{0.5 \times (15\% - 10\%)^2 + 0.5 \times (5\% - 10\%)^2} = 5\%$; for stock in Feet-on-the-Ground Bus Company it is $\sqrt{1 \times (10\% - 10\%)^2} = 0\%$. As you would expect, Fly-by-Night stock, the riskier asset, has a higher standard deviation of its returns. If there is another asset, such as High Flyer, Inc., stock with a return of 0% half the time and 20% the other half of the time, its expected return is also 10%. This asset is riskier than either of the other two assets, as the standard deviation of its returns shows. For High Flyer stock, the standard deviation is $\sqrt{0.5 \times (0\% - 10\%)^2 + 0.5 \times (20\% - 10\%)^2} = 10\%$, which is higher than the standard deviations for stock in Fly-by-Night or Feet-on-the-Ground.

TABLE 5-1 Response of the Quantity of an Asset Demanded to Changes in Income or Wealth, Expected Returns, Risk, and Liquidity

Variable	Change in Variable	Change in Quantity Demanded
Income or wealth	↑	↑
Expected return relative to other assets	↑	↑
Risk relative to other assets	↑	↓
Liquidity relative to other assets	↑	↑

Note: Only increases (↑) in the variables are shown. The effect of decreases in the variables on the change in demand would be the opposite of those indicated in the rightmost column.

3. The quantity demanded of an asset is negatively related to the risk of its returns relative to alternative assets.

4. The quantity demanded of an asset is positively related to its liquidity relative to alternative assets.

These results are summarized in Table 5-1.

LOANABLE FUNDS FRAMEWORK: SUPPLY AND DEMAND IN THE BOND MARKET

Our first approach to the analysis of interest-rate determination looks at supply and demand in the bond market. The first step in the analysis is to obtain a bond **demand curve**, which shows the relationship between the quantity demanded and the price when all other economic variables are held constant (that is, values of other variables are taken as given). You may recall from previous economics courses that the assumption that all other economic variables are held constant is called *ceteris paribus*, which means "other things being equal" in Latin.

Demand Curve

To clarify our analysis, let us consider the demand for one-year discount bonds, which make no coupon payments but pay the owner the $1000 face value in a year. If the holding period is one year, then, as we saw in Chapter 4, the return on the bonds is known absolutely and is equal to the interest rate as measured by the yield to maturity. This means that the expected return on this bond is equal to the interest rate i, which, using Equation 6 in Chapter 4, is

$$i = RET^e = \frac{F - P}{P}$$

where

i = interest rate = yield to maturity

RET^e = expected return

F = face value of the discount bond

P = initial purchase price of the discount bond.

This formula shows that a particular value of the interest rate corresponds to each bond price. If the bond sells for $950, the interest rate and expected return is

$$\frac{\$1000 - \$950}{\$950} = 0.053 = 5.3\%$$

At this 5.3% interest rate and expected return corresponding to a bond price of $950, let us assume that the quantity of bonds demanded is $100 billion, which is plotted as point A in Figure 5-1. To display both the bond price and the corresponding interest rate, Figure 5-1 has two vertical axes. The left vertical axis shows the bond price, with the price of bonds increasing from $750 near the bottom of the axis toward $1000 at the top. The right vertical axis shows the interest rate, which increases in the *opposite* direction from 0% at the top of the axis to 33% near the bottom. The right and left vertical axes run in opposite directions because, as we learned in Chapter 4, bond price and interest rate are always negatively related: as the price of the bond rises, the interest rate on the bond necessarily falls.

At a price of $900, the interest rate and expected return equals

$$\frac{\$1000 - \$900}{\$900} = 0.111 = 11.1\%$$

Because the expected return on these bonds is higher, with all other economic variables (such as income, expected returns on other assets, risk, and liquidity) held constant, the quantity demanded of bonds will be higher as predicted by the theory of asset demand. Point B in Figure 5-1 shows that the quantity of bonds

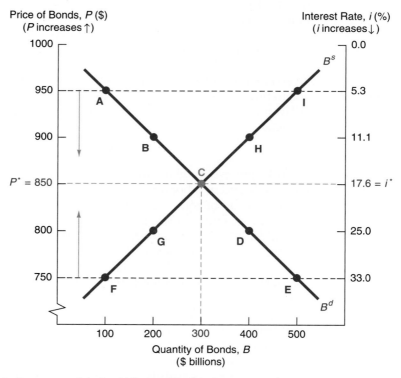

FIGURE 5·1   Supply and Demand for Bonds

Equilibrium in the bond market occurs at point C, the intersection of the demand curve B^d and the bond supply curve B^s. The equilibrium price is $P^* = \$850$, and the equilibrium interest rate is $i^* = 17.6\%$. (*Note*: P and i increase in opposite directions. P on the left vertical axis increases as we go up the axis from $750 near the bottom to $1000 at the top, while i on the right vertical axis increases as we go down the axis from 0% at the top to 33% near the bottom.)

demanded at the price of $900 has risen to $200 billion. Continuing with this reasoning, if the bond price is $850 (interest rate and expected return = 17.6%), the quantity of bonds demanded (point C) will be greater than at point B. Similarly, at the lower prices of $800 (interest rate = 25%) and $750 (interest rate = 33.3%), the quantity of bonds demanded will be even higher (points D and E). The curve B^d, which connects these points, is the demand curve for bonds. It has the usual downward slope, indicating that at lower prices of the bond (everything else being equal), the quantity demanded is higher.[3]

Supply Curve

An important assumption behind the demand curve for bonds in Figure 5-1 is that all other economic variables besides the bond's price and interest rate are held constant. We use the same assumption in deriving a **supply curve**, which shows the relationship between the quantity supplied and the price when all other economic variables are held constant.

When the price of the bonds is $750 (interest rate = 33.3%), point F shows that the quantity of bonds supplied is $100 billion for the example we are considering. If the price is $800, the interest rate is the lower rate of 25%. Because at this interest rate it is now less costly to borrow by issuing bonds, firms will be willing to borrow more through bond issues, and the quantity of bonds supplied is at the higher level of $200 billion (point G). An even higher price of $850, corresponding to a lower interest rate of 17.6%, results in a larger quantity of bonds supplied of $300 billion (point C). Higher prices of $900 and $950 result in even greater quantities of bonds supplied (points H and I). The B^s curve, which connects these points, is the supply curve for bonds. It has the usual upward slope found in supply curves, indicating that as the price increases (everything else being equal), the quantity supplied increases.

Market Equilibrium

In economics, **market equilibrium** occurs when the amount that people are willing to buy (*demand*) equals the amount that people are willing to sell (*supply*) at a given price. In the bond market, this is achieved when the quantity of bonds demanded equals the quantity of bonds supplied:

$$B^d = B^s \tag{1}$$

In Figure 5-1, equilibrium occurs at point C, where the demand and supply curves intersect at a bond price of $850 (interest rate of 17.6%) and a quantity of bonds of $300 billion. The price of $P^* = $850, where the quantity demanded equals the quantity supplied, is called the *equilibrium* or *market-clearing* price. Similarly, the interest rate of $i^* = 17.6\%$ that corresponds to this price is called the equilibrium or market-clearing interest rate.

The concepts of market equilibrium and equilibrium price or interest rate are useful because there is a tendency for the market to head toward them. We can see that it does in Figure 5-1 by first looking at what happens when we have a bond price that is above the equilibrium price. When the price of bonds is set too high, at, say, $950, the quantity of bonds supplied at point I is greater than the quantity of bonds demanded at point A. A situation like this, in which the quantity of bonds supplied exceeds the quantity of bonds demanded, is called a condition of **excess supply**. Because people want to sell more bonds than others want to buy, the price of the bonds will fall, and this is why the downward arrow is drawn in the figure at the bond price of $950. As long as the bond price

---

[3]Note that although our analysis indicates that the demand curve is downward-sloping, it does not imply that the curve is a straight line. For ease of exposition, however, we will draw demand curves and supply curves as straight lines.

remains above the equilibrium price, there will continue to be an excess supply of bonds, and the price will continue to fall. This will stop only when the price has reached the equilibrium price of $850, where the excess supply of bonds has been eliminated.

Now let's look at what happens when the price of bonds is below the equilibrium price. If the price of the bonds is set too low, at, say, $750, the quantity demanded at point E is greater than the quantity supplied at point F. This is called a condition of **excess demand**. People now want to buy more bonds than others are willing to sell, and so the price of bonds will be driven up. This is illustrated by the upward arrow drawn in the figure at the bond price of $750. Only when the excess demand for bonds is eliminated by the price rising to the equilibrium level of $850 is there no further tendency for the price to rise.

We can see that the concept of equilibrium price is a useful one because it indicates where the market will settle. Because each price on the left vertical axis of Figure 5-1 corresponds to a value of the interest rate on the right vertical axis, the same diagram also shows that the interest rate will head toward the equilibrium interest rate of 17.6%. When the interest rate is below the equilibrium interest rate, as it is when it is at 5.3%, the price of the bond is above the equilibrium price, and there will be an excess supply of bonds. The price of the bond then falls, leading to a rise in the interest rate toward the equilibrium level. Similarly, when the interest rate is above the equilibrium level, as it is when it is at 33.3%, there is excess demand for bonds, and the bond price will rise, driving the interest rate back down to the equilibrium level of 17.6%.

Supply and Demand Analysis

Our Figure 5-1 is a conventional supply and demand diagram with price on the left vertical axis and quantity on the horizontal axis. Because the interest rate that corresponds to each bond price is also marked on the right vertical axis, this diagram allows us to read the equilibrium interest rate, giving us a model that describes the determination of interest rates. It is important to recognize that a supply and demand diagram like Figure 5-1 can be drawn for *any* type of bond because the interest rate and price of a bond are *always* negatively related for any type of bond, whether a discount bond or a coupon bond.

One disadvantage of the diagram in Figure 5-1 is that interest rates run in an unusual direction on the right vertical axis: as we go up the right axis, interest rates fall. Because economists are typically more concerned with the value of interest rates than with the price of bonds, we could plot the supply of and demand for bonds on a diagram that has only a left vertical axis that provides the values of the interest rates running in the usual direction, rising as we go up the axis. Figure 5-2 is such a diagram, in which points A through I match the corresponding points in Figure 5-1.

However, making interest rates run in the "usual" direction on the vertical axis presents us with a problem. Our demand curve for bonds, points A through E, now looks peculiar because it has an upward slope. This upward slope is, however, completely consistent with our usual demand analysis, which produces a negative relationship between price and quantity. The inverse relationship between bond prices and interest rates means that in moving from point A to point B to point C, bond prices are falling and, consistent with usual demand analysis, the quantity demanded is rising. Similarly, our supply curve for bonds, points F through I, has an unusual-looking downward slope but is completely consistent with the usual view that price and the quantity supplied are positively related.

One way to give the demand curve the usual downward slope and the supply curve the usual upward slope is to rename the horizontal axis and the demand and supply curves. Because a firm supplying bonds is in fact taking out a loan from a person buying a bond, "supplying a bond" is equivalent to "demanding a loan."

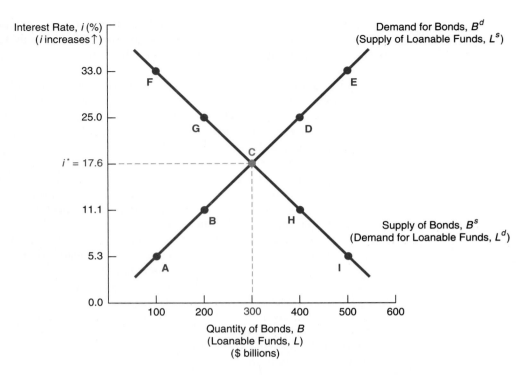

Interest Rate, i (%)
(i increases ↑)

Demand for Bonds, B^d
(Supply of Loanable Funds, L^s)

Supply of Bonds, B^s
(Demand for Loanable Funds, L^d)

Quantity of Bonds, B
(Loanable Funds, L)
($ billions)

FIGURE 5-2   A Comparison of Terminology: Loanable Funds and Supply and Demand for Bonds

The demand for bonds is equivalent to the supply of loanable funds, and the supply of bonds is equivalent to the demand for loanable funds. (*Note:* i increases as we go up the vertical axis, in contrast to Figure 5-1, in which the opposite occurs.)

Thus the supply curve for bonds can be reinterpreted as indicating the *quantity of loans demanded* for each value of the interest rate. If we rename the horizontal axis **loanable funds**, defined as the quantity of loans, the supply of bonds can be reinterpreted as the *demand for loanable funds*. Similarly, the demand curve for bonds can be re-identified as the *supply of loanable funds* because buying (demanding) a bond is equivalent to supplying a loan. Figure 5-2 relabels the curves and the horizontal axis using the loanable funds terminology in parentheses, and now the renamed loanable funds demand curve has the usual downward slope and the renamed loanable funds supply curve the usual upward slope.

Because supply and demand diagrams that explain how interest rates are determined in the bond market most commonly use the loanable funds terminology, this analysis is frequently referred to as the **loanable funds framework**. However, because in later chapters describing the conduct of monetary policy we focus on how the demand for and supply of bonds is affected, we will continue to conduct supply and demand analysis in terms of bonds, as in Figure 5-1, rather than loanable funds. Whether the analysis is done in terms of loanable funds or in terms of the demand for and supply of bonds, the results are the same; the two ways of analyzing the determination of interest rates are equivalent.

An important feature of the analysis here is that supply and demand are always in terms of *stocks* (amounts at a given point in time) of assets, not in terms of *flows*. This approach is somewhat different from certain loanable funds analyses, which are conducted in terms of flows (loans per year). The **asset market approach** for understanding behaviour in financial markets—which emphasizes stocks of assets rather than flows in determining asset prices—is now the dominant methodology used by economists because correctly conducting analyses in terms of flows is very tricky, especially when we encounter inflation.

CHANGES IN EQUILIBRIUM INTEREST RATES

We will now use the supply and demand framework for bonds to analyze why interest rates change. To avoid confusion, it is important to make the distinction between *movements along* a demand (or supply) curve and *shifts in* a demand (or supply) curve. When quantity demanded (or supplied) changes as a result of a change in the price of the bond (or, equivalently, a change in the interest rate), we have a *movement along* the demand (or supply) curve. The change in the quantity demanded when we move from point A to B to C in Figure 5-1 or Figure 5-2, for example, is a movement along a demand curve. A *shift in* the demand (or supply) curve, by contrast, occurs when the quantity demanded (or supplied) changes *at each given price (or interest rate)* of the bond in response to a change in some other factor besides the bond's price or interest rate. When one of these factors changes, causing a shift in the demand or supply curve, there will be a new equilibrium value for the interest rate.

In the following pages we will look at how the supply and demand curves shift in response to changes in variables, such as expected inflation and wealth, and what effects these changes have on the equilibrium value of interest rates.

Shifts in the Demand for Bonds

The theory of asset demand developed at the beginning of the chapter provides a framework for deciding what factors cause the demand curve for bonds to shift. These factors include changes in four parameters:

1. Wealth
2. Expected returns on bonds relative to alternative assets
3. Risk of bonds relative to alternative assets
4. Liquidity of bonds relative to alternative assets.

To see how a change in each of these factors (holding all other factors constant) can shift the demand curve, let us look at some examples. (As a study aid, Table 5-2 summarizes the effects of changes in these factors on the bond demand curve.)

Wealth When the economy is growing rapidly in a business cycle expansion and wealth is increasing, the quantity of bonds demanded at each bond price (or interest rate) increases as shown in Figure 5-3. To see how this works, consider point B on the initial demand curve for bonds B_1^d. It tells us that at a bond price of $900 and an interest rate of 11.1%, the quantity of bonds demanded is $200 billion. With higher wealth, the quantity of bonds demanded at the same interest rate must rise, say, to $400 billion (point B'). Similarly, the higher wealth causes the quantity demanded at a bond price of $800 and an interest rate of 25% to rise from $400 billion to $600 billion (point D to D'). Continuing with this reasoning for every point on the initial demand curve B_1^d, we can see that the demand curve shifts to the right from B_1^d to B_2^d as is indicated by the arrows.

The conclusion we have reached is that *in a business cycle expansion with growing wealth, the demand for bonds rises and the demand curve for bonds shifts to the right*. Using the same reasoning, *in a recession, when income and wealth are falling, the demand for bonds falls, and the demand curve shifts to the left*.

TABLE 5-2 Factors That Shift the Demand Curve for Bonds

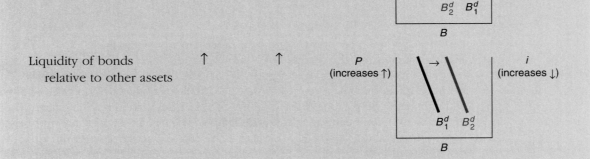

Variable	Change in Variable	Change in Quantity Demanded	Shift in Demand Curve
Wealth	↑	↑	
Expected interest rate	↑	↓	
Expected inflation	↑	↓	
Riskiness of bonds relative to other assets	↑	↓	
Liquidity of bonds relative to other assets	↑	↑	

Note: P and *i* increase in opposite directions: *P* on the left vertical axis increases as we go up the axis, while *i* on the right vertical axis increases as we go down the axis. Only increases (↑) in the variables are shown. The effect of decreases in the variables on the change in demand would be the opposite of those indicated in the remaining columns.

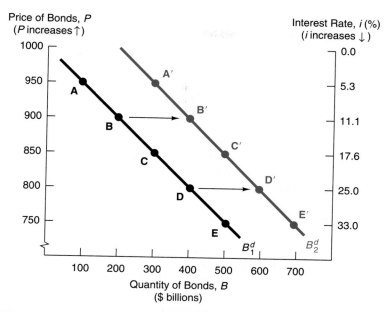

FIGURE 5-3   Shift in the Demand Curve for Bonds

When the demand for bonds increases, the demand curve shifts to the right as shown. (*Note:* P and i increase in opposite directions. P on the left vertical axis increases as we go up the axis, while i on the right vertical axis increases as we go down the axis.)

Another factor that affects wealth is the public's propensity to save. If households save more, wealth increases and, as we have seen, the demand for bonds rises and the demand curve for bonds shifts to the right. Conversely, if people save less, wealth and the demand for bonds will fall and the demand curve shifts to the left.

Expected Returns   For a one-year discount bond and a one-year holding period, the expected return and the interest rate are identical, so nothing besides today's interest rate affects the expected return.

For bonds with maturities of greater than one year, the expected return may differ from the interest rate. For example, we saw in Chapter 4, Table 4-2, that a rise in the interest rate on a long-term bond from 10 to 20% would lead to a sharp decline in price and a very negative return. Hence if people begin to think that interest rates will be higher next year than they had originally anticipated, the expected return today on long-term bonds will fall, and the quantity demanded will fall at each interest rate. ***Higher expected interest rates in the future lower the expected return for long-term bonds, decrease the demand, and shift the demand curve to the left.***

By contrast, a revision downward of expectations of future interest rates would mean that long-term bond prices would be expected to rise more than originally anticipated, and the resulting higher expected return today would raise the quantity demanded at each bond price and interest rate. ***Lower expected interest rates in the future increase the demand for long-term bonds and shift the demand curve to the right*** (as in Figure 5-3).

Changes in expected returns on other assets can also shift the demand curve for bonds. If people suddenly became more optimistic about the stock market and began to expect higher stock prices in the future, both expected capital gains and expected returns on stocks would rise. With the expected return on bonds held constant, the expected return on bonds today relative to stocks would fall, lowering the demand for bonds and shifting the demand curve to the left.

A change in expected inflation is likely to alter expected returns on physical assets (also called *real assets*) such as automobiles and houses, which affect the demand for bonds. An increase in expected inflation, say, from 5% to 10%, will lead to higher prices on cars and houses in the future and hence higher nominal capital gains. The resulting rise in the expected returns today on these real assets will lead to a fall in the expected return on bonds relative to the expected return on real assets today and thus cause the demand for bonds to fall. Alternatively, we can think of the rise in expected inflation as lowering the real interest rate on bonds, and the resulting decline in the relative expected return on bonds causes the demand for bonds to fall. ***An increase in the expected rate of inflation lowers the expected return for bonds, causing their demand to decline and the demand curve to shift to the left.***

Risk   If prices in the bond market become more volatile, the risk associated with bonds increases, and bonds become a less attractive asset. ***An increase in the riskiness of bonds causes the demand for bonds to fall and the demand curve to shift to the left.***
Conversely, an increase in the volatility of prices in another asset market, such as the stock market, would make bonds more attractive. ***An increase in the riskiness of alternative assets causes the demand for bonds to rise and the demand curve to shift to the right*** (as in Figure 5-3).

Liquidity   If more people started trading in the bond market and as a result it became easier to sell bonds quickly, the increase in their liquidity would cause the quantity of bonds demanded at each interest rate to rise. ***Increased liquidity of bonds results in an increased demand for bonds, and the demand curve shifts to the right*** (see Figure 5-3). ***Similarly, increased liquidity of alternative assets lowers the demand for bonds and shifts the demand curve to the left.*** The reduction of brokerage commissions for trading common stocks that occurred when the fixed-rate commission structure was abolished in 1975, for example, increased the liquidity of stocks relative to bonds, and the resulting lower demand for bonds shifted the demand curve to the left.

Shifts in the Supply of Bonds

Certain factors can cause the supply curve for bonds to shift, among them:

1. Expected profitability of investment opportunities
2. Expected inflation
3. Government activities.

We will look at how the supply curve shifts when each of these factors changes (all others remaining constant). (As a study aid, Table 5-3 summarizes the effects of changes in these factors on the bond supply curve.)

Expected Profitability of Investment Opportunities   The more profitable plant and equipment investments that a firm expects it can make, the more willing it will be to borrow and increase the amount of its outstanding debt in order to finance these investments. When the economy is growing rapidly, as in a business cycle expansion, investment opportunities that are expected to be profitable abound, and the quantity of bonds supplied at any given bond price and interest rate will increase (see Figure 5-4). ***Therefore, in a business cycle expansion, the supply of bonds increases, and the supply curve shifts to the right. Likewise, in a recession, when there are far fewer expected profitable investment opportunities, the supply of bonds falls, and the supply curve shifts to the left.***

SUMMARY

TABLE 5-3 Factors That Shift the Supply Curve of Bonds

Variable	Change in Variable	Change in Quantity Supplied	Shift in Supply Curve		
Profitability of investments	↑	↑	P (increases ↑)		i (increases ↓)
Expected inflation	↑	↑	P (increases ↑)		i (increases ↓)
Government deficit	↑	↑	P (increases ↑)		i (increases ↓)

Note: P and *i* increase in opposite directions: *P* on the left vertical axis increases as we go up the axis, while *i* on the right vertical axis increases as we go down the axis. Only increases (↑) in the variables are shown. The effect of decreases in the variables on the change in supply would be the opposite of those indicated in the remaining columns.

Expected Inflation As we saw in Chapter 4, the real cost of borrowing is more accurately measured by the real interest rate, which equals the (nominal) interest rate minus the expected inflation rate. For a given interest rate, when expected inflation increases, the real cost of borrowing falls; hence the quantity of bonds supplied increases at any given bond price and interest rate. ***An increase in expected inflation causes the supply of bonds to increase and the supply curve to shift to the right*** (see Figure 5-4).

Government Activities The activities of the government can influence the supply of bonds in several ways. The Canadian government issues bonds to finance government deficits, the gap between the government's expenditures and its revenues. When these deficits are large, the government sells more bonds, and the quantity of bonds supplied at each bond price and interest rate increases. ***Higher government deficits increase the supply of bonds and shift the supply***

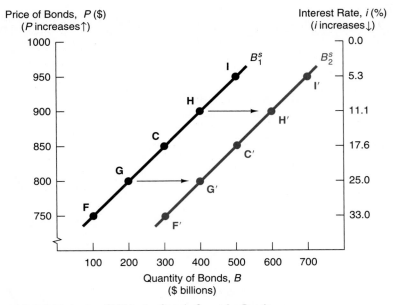

FIGURE 5-4 Shift in the Supply Curve for Bonds

When the supply of bonds increases, the supply curve shifts to the right. *Note: P* and *i* increase in opposite directions. *P* on the left vertical axis increases as we go up the axis, while *i* on the right vertical axis increases as we go down the axis.)

curve to the right (see Figure 5-4). **On the other hand, government surpluses, as have occurred in recent years, decrease the supply of bonds and shift the supply curve to the left.**

Provincial and municipal governments and other government agencies also issue bonds to finance their expenditures, and this can also affect the supply of bonds. We will see in later chapters that the conduct of monetary policy involves the purchase and sale of bonds, which in turn influences the supply of bonds.

APPLICATION | *Changes in the Equilibrium Interest Rate Due to Expected Inflation or Business Cycle Expansions*

We now can use our knowledge of how supply and demand curves shift to analyze how the equilibrium interest rate can change. The best way to do this is to pursue several applications that are particularly relevant to our understanding of how monetary policy affects interest rates.

Study Guide

Supply and demand analysis for the bond market is best learned by practicing applications. When there is an application in the text and we look at how the interest rate changes because some economic variable increases, see if you can draw the appropriate shifts in the supply and demand curves when this same economic variable decreases. While you are practicing applications, keep two things in mind:

1. When you examine the effect of a variable change, remember that we are assuming that all other variables are unchanged; that is, we are making use of the *ceteris paribus* assumption.

2. Remember that the interest rate is negatively related to the bond price, so when the equilibrium bond price rises, the equilibrium interest rate falls. Conversely, if the equilibrium bond price moves downward, the equilibrium interest rate rises.

Changes in Expected Inflation: The Fisher Effect

We have already done most of the work to evaluate how a change in expected inflation affects the nominal interest rate in that we have already analyzed how a change in expected inflation shifts the supply and demand curves. Figure 5-5 shows the effect on the equilibrium interest rate of an increase in expected inflation.

Suppose that expected inflation is initially 5% and the initial supply and demand curves B_1^s and B_1^d intersect at point 1, where the equilibrium bond price is P_1 and the equilibrium interest rate is i_1. If expected inflation rises to 10%, the expected return on bonds relative to real assets falls for any given bond price and interest rate. As a result, the demand for bonds falls, and the demand curve shifts to the left from B_1^d to B_2^d. The rise in expected inflation also shifts the supply curve. At any given bond price and interest rate, the real cost of borrowing has declined, causing the quantity of bonds supplied to increase, and the supply curve shifts to the right, from B_1^s to B_2^s.

When the demand and supply curves shift in response to the change in expected inflation, the equilibrium moves from point 1 to point 2, the intersection of B_2^d and B_2^s. The equilibrium bond price has fallen from P_1 to P_2, and because the bond price is negatively related to the interest rate (as is indicated by the interest rate rising as we go down the right vertical axis), this means that the interest rate has risen from i_1 to i_2. Note that Figure 5-5 has been drawn so that the equilibrium quantity of bonds remains the same for both point 1 and point 2. However, depending on the size of the shifts in the supply and demand curves, the equilibrium quantity of bonds could either rise or fall when expected inflation rises.

Our supply and demand analysis has led us to an important observation: ***when expected inflation rises, interest rates will rise***. This result has been named

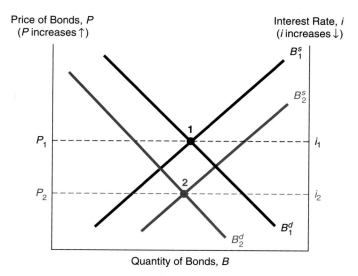

Price of Bonds, *P*
(*P* increases ↑)

Interest Rate, *i*
(*i* increases ↓)

Quantity of Bonds, *B*

FIGURE 5-5   Response to a Change in Expected Inflation

When expected inflation rises, the supply curve shifts from B_1^s to B_2^s, and the demand curve shifts from B_1^d to B_2^d. The equilibrium moves from point 1 to point 2, with the result that the equilibrium bond price (left axis) falls from P_1 to P_2 and the equilibrium interest rate (right axis) rises from i_1 to i_2. (*Note: P* and *i* increase in opposite directions. *P* on the left vertical axis increases as we go up the axis, while *i* on the right vertical axis increases as we go down the axis.)

the **Fisher effect**, after Irving Fisher, the economist who first pointed out the relationship of expected inflation to interest rates. The accuracy of this prediction is shown in Figure 5-6. The interest rate on three-month Treasury bills has usually moved along with the expected inflation rate. Consequently, it is understandable that many economists recommend that inflation must be kept low if we want to keep interest rates low.

Business Cycle Expansion

Figure 5-7 analyzes the effects of a business cycle expansion on interest rates. In a business cycle expansion, the amount of goods and services being produced in the economy rises, so national income increases. When this occurs, businesses will be more willing to borrow because they are likely to have many profitable investment opportunities for which they need financing. Hence at a given bond price and interest rate, the quantity of bonds that firms want to sell (that is, the supply of bonds) will increase. This means that in a business cycle expansion, the supply curve for bonds shifts to the right (see Figure 5-7) from B_1^s to B_2^s.

Expansion in the economy will also affect the demand for bonds. The theory of asset demand tells us that as the business cycle expands and wealth increases, the demand for bonds will rise as well. We see this in Figure 5-7, where the demand curve has shifted to the right, from B_1^d to B_2^d.

Given that both the supply and demand curves have shifted to the right, we know that the new equilibrium reached at the intersection of B_2^d and B_2^s must also move to the right. However, depending on whether the supply curve shifts more than the demand curve or vice versa, the new equilibrium interest rate can either rise or fall.

The supply and demand analysis used here gives us an ambiguous answer to the question of what will happen to interest rates in a business cycle expansion. The figure has been drawn so that the shift in the supply curve is greater than the shift in the demand curve, causing the equilibrium bond price to fall to P_2, leading to a rise in the equilibrium interest rate to i_2. The reason the figure has been drawn so that a business cycle expansion and a rise in income lead to a higher interest rate is that this is the outcome we actually see in the data. Figure 5-8 plots the movement of the interest rate on three-month Treasury bills from 1953 to 2000

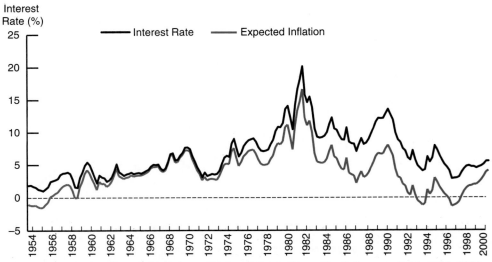

FIGURE 5-6   Expected Inflation and Interest Rates (Three-Month Treasury Bills), 1953–2000

Source: Statistics Canada CANSIM Series B14060. The expected inflation rate is constructed using the procedure outlined in Frederic S. Mishkin, "The Real Interest Rate: An Empirical Investigation," *Carnegie-Rochester Conference Series on Public Policy* 15 (1981): 151-200. This involves estimating the expected inflation rate as a function of past interest rates, inflation, and time trends and then subtracting the expected inflation rate measure from the nominal interest rate.

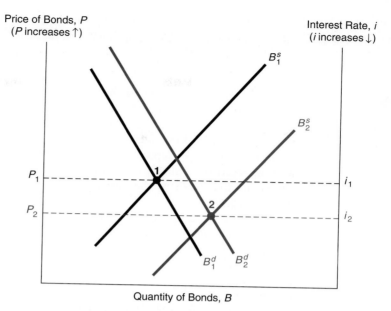

FIGURE 5-7   Response to a Business Cycle Expansion

In a business cycle expansion, when income and wealth are rising, the demand curve shifts rightward from B_1^d to B_2^d, and the supply curve shifts rightward from B_1^s to B_2^s. If the supply curve shifts to the right more than the demand curve, as in this figure, the equilibrium bond price (left axis) moves down from P_1 to P_2, and the equilibrium interest rate (right axis) rises from i_1 to i_2. (*Note:* P and i increase in opposite directions. P on the left vertical axis increases as we go up the axis, while i on the right vertical axis increases as we go down the axis.)

and indicates when the business cycle is undergoing recessions (shaded areas). As you can see, the interest rate rises during business cycle expansions and falls during recessions, which is what the supply and demand diagram indicates.

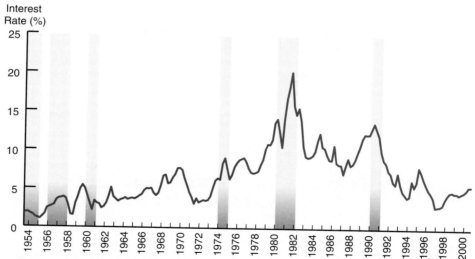

FIGURE 5-8   Business Cycle and Interest Rates (Three-Month Treasury Bills), 1953–2000

Shaded areas indicate periods of recession. The figure shows that interest rates rise during business cycle expansions and fall during contractions, which is what Figure 5-7 suggests would happen.

Source: Statistics Canada CANSIM Series B14060.

APPLICATION | *Explaining Low Japanese Interest Rates*

In the 1990s, Japanese interest rates became the lowest in the world. Indeed, in November 1998, an extraordinary event occurred: interest rates on Japanese six-month Treasury bills turned slightly negative (see Chapter 4). Why did Japanese rates drop to such low levels?

In the late 1990s, Japan experienced a prolonged recession, which has been accompanied by deflation, a negative inflation rate. Using these facts, analysis similar to that used in the preceding application explains the low Japanese interest rates.

Negative inflation caused the demand for bonds to rise because the expected return on real assets fell, thereby raising the relative expected return on bonds and in turn causing the demand curve to shift to the right. The negative inflation also raised the real interest rate and therefore the real cost of borrowing for any given nominal rate, thereby causing the supply of bonds to contract and the supply curve to shift to the left. The outcome was then exactly the opposite of that graphed in Figure 5-5: the rightward shift of the demand curve and leftward shift of the supply curve led to a rise in the bond price and a fall in interest rates.

The business cycle contraction and the resulting lack of investment opportunities in Japan also led to lower interest rates by decreasing the supply of bonds and shifting the supply curve to the left. Although the demand curve also would shift to the left because wealth decreased during the business cycle contraction, we have seen in the preceding application that the demand curve would shift less than the supply curve. Thus, the bond price rose and interest rates fell (the opposite outcome to that in Figure 5-7).

Usually, we think that low interest rates are a good thing because they make it cheap to borrow. But the Japanese example shows that just as there is a fallacy in the adage "You can never be too rich or too thin" (maybe you can't be too rich, but you can certainly be too thin and do damage to your health) there is a fallacy in always thinking that lower interest rates are better. In Japan, the low and even negative interest rates were a sign that the Japanese economy was in real trouble, with falling prices and a contracting economy. Only when the Japanese economy returns to health will interest rates rise back to more normal levels.

APPLICATION | *Reading the* **Wall Street Journal's** *"Credit Markets" Column*

Wall Street Journal
www.wsj.com

Now that we have an understanding of how supply and demand determine prices and interest rates in the bond market, we can use our analysis to understand discussions about bond prices and interest rates appearing in the financial press. Every day, the *Wall Street Journal* reports on developments in the bond market on the previous business day in its "Credit Markets" column, an example of which is found in the "Following the Financial News" box. Let's see how statements in the "Credit Markets" column can be explained using our supply and demand framework.

The column begins by indicating that the U.S. Treasury announced a larger buy-back of debt than the market expected and that this sparked a rally in Treasurys. This is exactly what our supply and demand analysis predicts would happen.

The larger than expected Treasury buyback will reduce the supply of bonds in the future and thus will shift the supply curve to the left, thereby raising the price of these bonds in the future by more than expected. The resulting increase in the expected return on these bonds because of their higher future price will lead to an immediate rightward shift in the demand for these bonds today. The outcome is thus a rise in their equilibrium price and a decline in their interest rate.

Our analysis thus demonstrates why, even though the Treasury has not increased its buying of bonds today, the price of these bonds rises immediately nonetheless.

FOLLOWING THE FINANCIAL NEWS

The "Credit Markets" Column

The "Credit Markets" column appears daily in the *Wall Street Journal*; an example is presented here. It is found in the third section, "Money and Investing."

CREDIT MARKETS

Treasury Announces Its Plan to Buy Back Debt Of As Much As $30 Billion, Above Expectations

By Youchi J. Dreazen
And Gregory Zuckerman
Staff Reporters of The Wall Street Journal

The Treasury Department, enjoying a surging federal budget surplus, said it would buy back as much as $30 billion in debt outstanding held by the public by the end of the year.

While bond traders were counting down to such an announcement, the size of the prospective bond buyback is greater than expected, helping to spark a rally in Treasurys.

Yesterday's announcement comes nearly five months after the department first raised the idea of offering cash for securities that haven't yet matured as a way of easing federal borrowing costs and keeping interest rates low.

The Treasury estimates that every hundredth of a percentage point reduction in federal interest costs saves the government about $300 million annually, savings that would ultimately be passed on to taxpayers.

"We will very literally be taking the burden of debt off the backs of American taxpayers by buying back federal debt,"

Treasury Secretary Lawrence Summers said.

Wall Street traders, who expected a buyback sized at just $20 billion to $25 billion, cheered the announcement, which helped the bond market shake off the effects of strong economic data. In late trading, the benchmark 30-year Treasury bond was up 22/32, or $6.875 per $1,000 bond, to yield 6.652%, down from 6.708% on Wednesday, as yields move inversely to prices.

"The size was a bit larger than expected, and it looks like they'll be buying the debt back sooner than we thought," said Tom Juterbock, Morgan Stanley Dean Witter & Co.'s head of U.S. government-bond trading.

The Treasury will purchase off-the-run securities, or those that haven't been issued lately and usually trade at a yield significantly higher than recently issued securities like the 30-year bond. Some of these securities have been trading at yields approaching 7% in recent days as investors flocked to more liquid issues such as the long bond, but yesterday's announcement sent prices on off-the-run securities higher compared with other bonds.

"Any time you reduce supply it helps prices," said Lou Crandall of Wrightson Associates.

Although the buyback is unusual, the Treasury has been paying down the debt steadily for the past few years by issuing fewer new bonds as old ones mature. Indeed, Mr. Summers estimated that by the time President Clinton leaves office next January, his administration will have paid down roughly $250 billion of the debt, which now stands at $5.76 trillion.

Of that amount about $3.6 trillion is held by the public in the form of Treasury securities. This is the portion that would be bought back. The rest of the debt, more than $2 trillion, is held by the government's large trust funds, most significantly the Social Security trust fund.

Since first raising the issue in August, officials have steadily emphasized what they consider the positive influence debt buybacks would have on interest costs, cash management and overall liquidity in the Treasury market. Curtailing the government's need to borrow would reduce interest rates for businesses and consumers, and ultimately the government itself, they argue.

Source: Wall Street Journal, Friday, January 14, 2000, p. C19.

APPLICATION | *Have Low Savings Rates in Canada Led to Higher Interest Rates?*

Since 1980, Canada has experienced a sharp drop in personal savings rates, with record lows in recent years. Many commentators, including high officials of the Bank of Canada, have blamed the profligate spending habits of the Canadian public for high interest rates. Are they right?

Our supply and demand analysis of the bond market indicates that they could be right. The decline in savings means that the wealth of Canadian households is lower than would otherwise be the case. This smaller amount of wealth decreases the demand for bonds and shifts the demand curve to the left from B_1^d to B_2^d, as shown in Figure 5-9. The result is that the equilibrium bond price drops from P_1 to P_2 and the interest rate rises from i_1 to i_2. Low savings can thus raise interest rates, and the higher rates may retard investment in capital goods. The low savings rate of Canadians may therefore lead to a less productive economy and is of serious concern to both economists and policymakers. Suggested remedies for the problem range from changing the tax code to encourage saving to forcing Canadians to save more by mandating increased contributions into retirement plans.

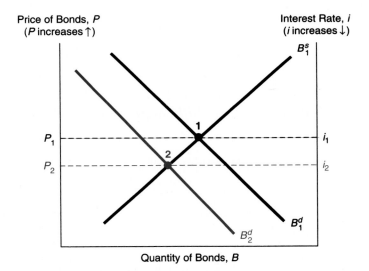

FIGURE 5-9 Response to a Lower Savings Rate

With a lower savings rate, all other things equal, wealth decreases, and the demand curve shifts from B_1^d to B_2^d. The equilibrium moves from point 1 to point 2, with the result that the equilibrium bond price (left axis) drops from P_1 to P_2 and the equilibrium interest rate (right axis) rises from i_1 to i_2. (Note: P and i increase in opposite directions. P on the left vertical axis increases as we go up the axis, while i on the right vertical axis increases as we go down the axis.)

LIQUIDITY PREFERENCE FRAMEWORK:
SUPPLY AND DEMAND IN THE MARKET FOR MONEY

Whereas the loanable funds framework determines the equilibrium interest rate using the supply of and demand for bonds, an alternative model developed by John Maynard Keynes, known as the **liquidity preference framework,** determines the equilibrium interest rate in terms of the supply of and demand for money. Although the two frameworks look different, the liquidity preference analysis of the market for money is closely related to the loanable funds framework of the bond market.[4]

The starting point of Keynes's analysis is his assumption that there are two main categories of assets that people use to store their wealth: money and bonds. Therefore, total wealth in the economy must equal the total quantity of bonds plus money in the economy, which equals the quantity of bonds supplied B^s plus the quantity of money supplied M^s. The quantity of bonds B^d and money M^d that people want to hold and thus demand must also equal the total amount of wealth, because people cannot purchase more assets than their available resources allow. The conclusion is that the quantity of bonds and money supplied must equal the quantity of bonds and money demanded:

$$B^s + M^s = B^d + M^d \tag{2}$$

Collecting the bond terms on one side of the equation and the money terms on the other, this equation can be rewritten as

$$B^s - B^d = M^d - M^s \tag{3}$$

The rewritten equation tells us that if the market for money is in equilibrium ($M^s = M^d$), the right-hand side of Equation 3 equals zero, implying that $B^s = B^d$, meaning that the bond market is also in equilibrium.

Thus it is the same to think about determining the equilibrium interest rate by equating the supply and demand for bonds or by equating the supply and demand for money. In this sense, the liquidity preference framework, which analyzes the market for money, is equivalent to the loanable funds framework, which analyzes the bond market. In practice, the approaches differ because by assuming that there are only two kinds of assets, money and bonds, the liquidity preference approach implicitly ignores any effects on interest rates that arise from changes in the expected returns on real assets such as automobiles and houses. In most instances, however, both frameworks yield the same predictions.

The reason that we approach the determination of interest rates with both frameworks is that the loanable funds framework is easier to use when analyzing the effects from changes in expected inflation, whereas the liquidity preference framework provides a simpler analysis of the effects from changes in income, the price level, and the supply of money.

Because the definition of money that Keynes used includes currency (which earns no interest) and chequing account deposits (which in his time typically earned little or no interest), he assumed that money has a zero rate of return.

[4]Note that the term *market for money* refers to the market for the medium of exchange, money. This market differs from the *money market* referred to by finance practitioners, which is the financial market in which short-term debt instruments are traded.

Bonds, the only alternative asset to money in Keynes's framework, have an expected return equal to the interest rate *i*.[5] As this interest rate rises (holding everything else unchanged), the expected return on money falls relative to the expected return on bonds, and as the theory of asset demand tells us, this causes the demand for money to fall.

We can also see that the demand for money and the interest rate should be negatively related by using the concept of **opportunity cost**, the amount of interest (expected return) sacrificed by not holding the alternative asset—in this case, a bond. As the interest rate on bonds *i* rises, the opportunity cost of holding money rises, and so money is less desirable and the quantity of money demanded must fall.

Figure 5-10 shows the quantity of money demanded at a number of interest rates, with all other economic variables, such as income and the price level, held constant. At an interest rate of 25%, point A shows that the quantity of money demanded is $100 billion. If the interest rate is at the lower rate of 20%, the opportunity cost of money is lower, and the quantity of money demanded rises to $200 billion, as indicated by the move from point A to point B. If the interest rate is even lower, the quantity of money demanded is even higher, as is indicated by points C, D, and E. The curve M^d connecting these points is the demand curve for money, and it slopes downward.

At this point in our analysis, we will assume that a central bank controls the amount of money supplied at a fixed quantity of $300 billion, so the supply curve for money M^s in the figure is a vertical line at $300 billion. The equilibrium where the quantity of money demanded equals the quantity of money supplied occurs at the intersection of the supply and demand curves at point C, where

$$M^d = M^s \qquad (4)$$

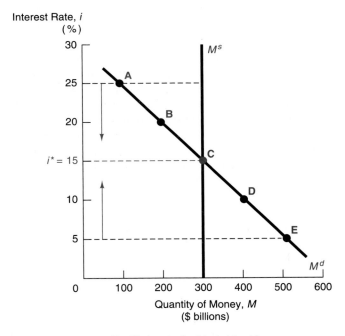

FIGURE 5-10   Equilibrium in the Market for Money

---

[5]Keynes did not actually assume that the expected returns on bonds equalled the interest rate but rather argued that they were closely related (see Chapter 23). This distinction makes no appreciable difference in our analysis.

The resulting equilibrium interest rate is at $i^* = 15\%$.

We can again see that there is a tendency to approach this equilibrium by first looking at the relationship of money demand and supply when the interest rate is above the equilibrium interest rate. When the interest rate is 25%, the quantity of money demanded at point A is $100 billion, yet the quantity of money supplied is $300 billion. The excess supply of money means that people are holding more money than they desire, so they will try to get rid of their excess money balances by trying to buy bonds. Accordingly, they will bid up the price of bonds, and as the bond price rises, the interest rate will fall toward the equilibrium interest rate of 15%. This tendency is shown by the downward arrow drawn at the interest rate of 25%.

Likewise, if the interest rate is 5%, the quantity of money demanded at point E is $500 billion, but the quantity of money supplied is only $300 billion. There is now an excess demand for money because people want to hold more money than they currently have. To try to obtain more money, they will sell their only other asset—bonds—and the price will fall. As the price of bonds falls, the interest rate will rise toward the equilibrium rate of 15%. Only when the interest rate is at its equilibrium value will there be no tendency for it to move further, and the interest rate will settle to its equilibrium value.

CHANGES IN EQUILIBRIUM INTEREST RATES

Analyzing how the equilibrium interest rate changes using the liquidity preference framework requires that we understand what causes the demand and supply curves for money to shift.

Study Guide

Learning the liquidity preference framework also requires practicing applications. When there is an application in the text to examine how the interest rate changes because some economic variable increases, see if you can draw the appropriate shifts in the supply and demand curves when this same economic variable decreases. And remember to use the *ceteris paribus* assumption: when examining the effect of a change in one variable, hold all other variables constant.

Shifts in the Demand for Money

In Keynes's liquidity preference analysis, two factors cause the demand curve for money to shift: income and the price level.

Income Effect   In Keynes's view, there were two reasons why income would affect the demand for money. First, as an economy expands and income rises, wealth increases and people will want to hold more money as a store of value. Second, as the economy expands and income rises, people will want to carry out more transactions using money, with the result that they will also want to hold more money. The conclusion is that *a higher level of income causes the demand for money to increase and the demand curve to shift to the right*.

Price-Level Effect   Keynes took the view that people care about the amount of money they hold in real terms, that is, in terms of the goods and services that it can buy. When the price level rises, the same nominal quantity of money is no longer as valuable; it cannot be used to purchase as many real goods or services.

To restore their holdings of money in real terms to their former level, people will want to hold a greater nominal quantity of money, so *a rise in the price level causes the demand for money to increase and the demand curve to shift to the right*.

Shifts in the Supply of Money

We will assume that the supply of money is completely controlled by the central bank, which in Canada is the Bank of Canada. (Actually, the process that determines the money supply is substantially more complicated, involving banks, depositors, and borrowers from banks. We will study it in more detail later in the book.) For now, all we need to know is that *an increase in the money supply engineered by the Bank of Canada will shift the supply curve for money to the right*.

APPLICATION   *Changes in the Equilibrium Interest Rate Due to Changes in Income, the Price Level, or the Money Supply*

To see how the liquidity preference framework can be used to analyze the movement of interest rates, we will again look at several applications that will be useful in evaluating the effect of monetary policy on interest rates. (As a study aid, Table 5-4 summarizes the shifts in the demand and supply curves for money.)

Changes in Income

When income is rising during a business cycle expansion, we have seen that the demand for money will rise. It is shown in Figure 5-11 by the shift rightward in the demand curve from M_1^d to M_2^d. The new equilibrium is reached at point 2 at the intersection of the M_2^d curve with the money supply curve M^s. As you can see, the equilibrium interest rate rises from i_1 to i_2. The liquidity preference framework thus generates the conclusion that *when income is rising during a business cycle expansion (holding other economic variables constant), interest rates will rise*. This conclusion is unambiguous when contrasted to the conclusion reached about the effects of a change in income on interest rates using the loanable funds framework.

Changes in the Price Level

When the price level rises, the value of money in terms of what it can purchase is lower. To restore their purchasing power in real terms to its former level, people will want to hold a greater nominal quantity of money. A higher price level shifts the demand curve for money to the right from M_1^d to M_2^d (see Figure 5-11). The equilibrium moves from point 1 to point 2, where the equilibrium interest rate has risen from i_1 to i_2, illustrating that *when the price level increases, with the supply of money and other economic variables held constant, interest rates will rise*.

Changes in the Money Supply

An increase in the money supply due to an expansionary monetary policy by the Bank of Canada implies that the supply curve for money shifts to the right. As is shown in Figure 5-12 by the movement of the supply curve from M_1^s to M_2^s, the equilibrium moves from point 1 down to point 2, where the M_2^s supply curve intersects with the demand curve M^d and the equilibrium interest rate has fallen

SUMMARY

TABLE 5-4 Factors That Shift the Demand for and Supply of Money

Variable	Change in Variable	Change in Money Demand (M^d) or Supply (M^s)	Change in Interest Rate	
Income	↑	M^d ↑	↑	
Price level	↑	M^d ↑	↑	
Money supply	↑	M^s ↑	↓	

Note: Only increases (↑) in the variables are shown. The effect of decreases in the variables on the change in demand would be the opposite of those indicated in the remaining columns.

from i_1 to i_2. **When the money supply increases (everything else remaining equal), interest rates will decline.**[6]

---

[6]This same result can be generated using the loanable funds framework. As we will see in Chapters 15 and 16, the primary way that a central bank produces an increase in the money supply is by buying bonds and thereby decreasing the supply of bonds to the public. The resulting shift to the left of the supply curve for bonds will lead to a decline in the equilibrium interest rate.

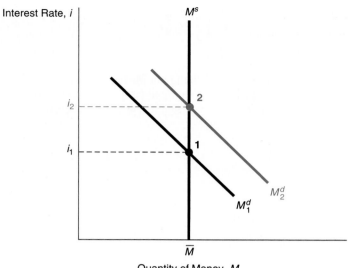

FIGURE 5-11   Response to a Change in Income or the Price Level

In a business cycle expansion, when income is rising, or when the price level rises, the demand curve shifts from M_1^d to M_2^d. The supply curve is fixed at $M^s = \overline{M}$. The equilibrium interest rate rises from i_1 to i_2.

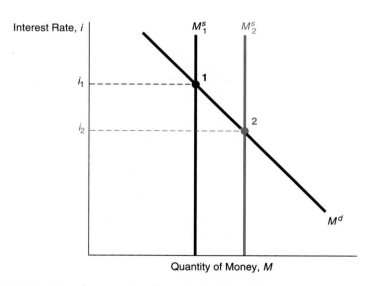

FIGURE 5-12   Response to a Change in the Money Supply

When the money supply increases, the supply curve shifts from M_1^s to M_2^s, and the equilibrium interest rate falls from i_1 to i_2.

| APPLICATION | *Money and Interest Rates* |

The liquidity preference analysis in Figure 5-12 seems to lead to the conclusion that an increase in the money supply will lower interest rates. This conclusion has important policy implications because it has frequently caused politicians to call for a more rapid growth of the money supply in order to drive down interest rates.

But is this conclusion that money and interest rates should be negatively related correct? Might there be other important factors left out of the liquidity preference analysis in Figure 5-12 that would reverse this conclusion? We will provide answers to these questions by applying the supply and demand analysis we have used in this chapter to obtain a deeper understanding of the relationship between money and interest rates.

Milton Friedman, a Nobel laureate in economics, has raised an important criticism of the conclusion that a rise in the money supply lowers interest rates. He acknowledges that the liquidity preference analysis is correct and calls the result—that an increase in the money supply (*everything else remaining equal*) lowers interest rates—the *liquidity effect*. However, he views the liquidity effect as merely part of the story: an increase in the money supply might not leave "everything else equal" and will have other effects on the economy that may make interest rates rise. If these effects are substantial, it is entirely possible that when the money supply rises, interest rates too may rise.

We have already laid the groundwork to discuss these other effects because we have shown how changes in income, the price level, and expected inflation affect the equilibrium interest rate.

Study Guide

To get further practice with the loanable funds and liquidity preference frameworks, show how the effects discussed here work by drawing the supply and demand diagrams that explain each effect. This exercise will also improve your understanding of the effect of money on interest rates.

1. *Income Effect.* Because an increasing money supply is an expansionary influence on the economy, it should raise national income and wealth. Both the liquidity preference and loanable funds frameworks indicate that interest rates will then rise (see Figures 5-7 and 5-11). Thus **the income effect of an increase in the money supply is a rise in interest rates in response to the higher level of income**.

2. *Price-Level Effect.* An increase in the money supply can also cause the overall price level in the economy to rise. The liquidity preference framework predicts that this will lead to a rise in interest rates. So **the price-level effect from an increase in the money supply is a rise in interest rates in response to the rise in the price level**.

3. *Expected-Inflation Effect.* The rising price level (the higher inflation rate) that results from an increase in the money supply also affects interest rates by affecting the expected inflation rate. Specifically, an increase in the money supply may lead people to expect a higher price level in the future—hence the expected inflation rate will be higher. The loanable funds framework has shown us that this increase in expected inflation will lead to a higher level of interest rates. Therefore, ***the expected-inflation effect of an increase in the money supply is a rise in interest rates in response to the rise in the expected inflation rate***.

At first glance it might appear that the price-level effect and the expected-inflation effect are the same thing. They both indicate that increases in the price level induced by an increase in the money supply will raise interest rates. However, there is a subtle difference between the two, and this is why they are discussed as two separate effects.

Suppose that there is a onetime increase in the money supply today that leads to a rise in prices to a permanently higher level by next year. As the price level rises over the course of this year, the interest rate will rise via the price-level effect. Only at the end of the year, when the price level has risen to its peak, will the price-level effect be at a maximum.

The rising price level will also raise interest rates via the expected-inflation effect because people will expect that inflation will be higher over the course of the year. However, when the price level stops rising next year, inflation and the expected inflation rate will fall back down to zero. Any rise in interest rates as a result of the earlier rise in expected inflation will then be reversed. We thus see that in contrast to the price-level effect, which reaches its greatest impact next year, the expected-inflation effect will have its smallest impact (zero impact) next year. The basic difference between the two effects, then, is that the price-level effect remains even after prices have stopped rising, whereas the expected-inflation effect disappears.

An important point is that the expected-inflation effect will persist only as long as the price level continues to rise. As we will see in our discussion of monetary theory in subsequent chapters, a onetime increase in the money supply will not produce a continually rising price level; only a higher rate of money supply growth will. Thus a higher rate of money supply growth is needed if the expected-inflation effect is to persist.

Does a Higher Rate of Growth of the Money Supply Lower Interest Rates?

We can now put together all the effects we have discussed to help us decide whether our analysis supports the politicians who advocate a greater rate of growth of the money supply when they feel that interest rates are too high. Of all the effects, only the liquidity effect indicates that a higher rate of money growth will cause a decline in interest rates. In contrast, the income, price-level, and expected-inflation effects indicate that interest rates will rise when money growth is higher. Which of these effects are largest, and how quickly do they take effect? The answers are critical in determining whether interest rates will rise or fall when money supply growth is increased.

Generally, the liquidity effect from the greater money growth takes effect immediately because the rising money supply leads to an immediate decline in the equilibrium interest rate. The income and price-level effects take time to work because it takes time for the increasing money supply to raise the price level and income, which in turn raise interest rates. The expected-inflation effect, which also raises interest rates, can be slow or fast, depending on whether people adjust their expectations of inflation slowly or quickly when the money growth rate is increased.

Three possibilities are outlined in Figure 5-13; each shows how interest rates respond over time to an increased rate of money supply growth starting at time *T*. Panel (a) shows a case in which the liquidity effect dominates the other effects so that the interest rate falls from i_1 at time *T* to a final level of i_2. The liquidity effect operates quickly to lower the interest rate, but as time goes by the other effects start to reverse some of the decline. Because the liquidity effect is larger than the others, however, the interest rate never rises back to its initial level.

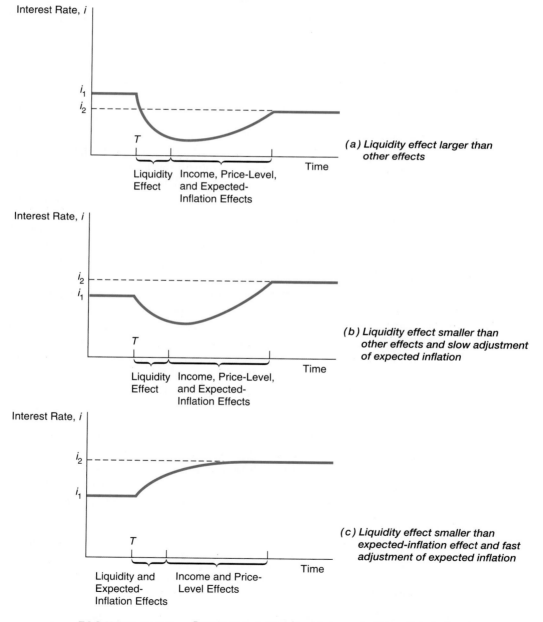

FIGURE 5-13   Response over Time to an Increase in Money Supply Growth

Panel (b) has a smaller liquidity effect than the other effects, with the expected-inflation effect operating slowly because expectations of inflation are slow to adjust upward. Initially, the liquidity effect drives down the interest rate. Then the income, price-level, and expected-inflation effects begin to raise it. Because these effects are dominant, the interest rate eventually rises above its initial level to i_2. In the short run, lower interest rates result from increased money growth, but eventually they end up climbing above the initial level.

Panel (c) has the expected-inflation effect dominating as well as operating rapidly because people quickly raise their expectations of inflation when the rate of money growth increases. The expected-inflation effect begins immediately to overpower the liquidity effect, and the interest rate immediately starts to climb. Over time, as the income and price-level effects start to take hold, the interest rate rises even higher, and the eventual outcome is an interest rate that is substantially above the initial interest rate. The result shows clearly that increasing money supply growth is not the answer to reducing interest rates; rather, money growth should be reduced in order to lower interest rates!

An important issue for economic policymakers is which of these three scenarios is closest to reality. If a decline in interest rates is desired, then an increase in money supply growth is called for when the liquidity effect dominates the other effects, as in panel (a). A decrease in money growth is appropriate if the other effects dominate the liquidity effect and expectations of inflation adjust rapidly, as in panel (c). If the other effects dominate the liquidity effect but expectations of inflation adjust only slowly, as in panel (b), then whether you want to increase or decrease money growth depends on whether you care more about what happens in the short run or the long run.

Which scenario does the evidence support? The relationship of interest rates and money growth from 1950 to 1999 is plotted in Figure 5-14. When the rate of money supply growth began to climb in the mid-1960s, interest rates rose, indicating that the price-level, income, and expected-inflation effects dominated the liquidity effect. By the 1970s, interest rates reached levels unprecedented in the post-World War II period, as did the rate of money supply growth.

The scenario depicted in panel (a) of Figure 5-13 seems doubtful, and the case for lowering interest rates by raising the rate of money growth is much weakened. Looking back at Figure 5-6, which shows the relationship between interest rates and expected inflation, you should not find this too surprising. The rise in the rate of money supply growth in the 1960s and 1970s is matched by a large rise in expected inflation, which would lead us to predict that the expected-inflation effect would be dominant. It is the most plausible explanation for why interest rates rose in the face of higher money growth. However, Figure 5-14 does not really tell us which one of the two scenarios, panel (b) or panel (c) of Figure 5-13, is more accurate. It depends critically on how fast people's expectations about inflation adjust. However, recent research using more sophisticated methods than just looking at a graph like Figure 5-14 do indicate that increased money growth temporarily lowers short-term interest rates.[7]

---

[7]See Lawrence J. Christiano and Martin Eichenbaum, "Identification and the Liquidity Effect of a Monetary Policy Shock," in *Business Cycles, Growth, and Political Economy,* ed. Alex Cukierman, Zvi Hercowitz, and Leonardo Leiderman (Cambridge, Mass.: MIT Press, 1992), pp. 335–370; Eric M. Leeper and David B. Gordon, "In Search of the Liquidity Effect," *Journal of Monetary Economics* 29 (1992): 341–370; Steven Strongin, "The Identification of Monetary Policy Disturbances: Explaining the Liquidity Puzzle," *Journal of Monetary Economics* 35 (1995): 463–497; and Adrian Pagan and John C. Robertson, "Resolving the Liquidity Effect," *Federal Reserve Bank of St. Louis Review* 77 (May-June 1995): 33–54.

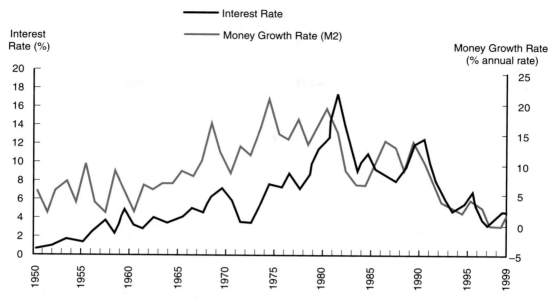

FIGURE 5-14   Money Growth (M2, Annual Rate) and Interest Rates (Three-Month Treasury Bills), 1950–1999

Source: Statistics Canada CANSIM Series B14060. From 1950 to 1967 the M2 series is from Cherie Metcalf, Angela Redish, and Ronald Shearer, "New Estimates of the Canadian Money Stock: 1871-1967," The University of British Columbia, Discussion Paper No.: 96-17. From 1968 to 1999 it is Statistics Canada CANSIM Series B1630.

FOLLOWING THE FINANCIAL NEWS

Forecasting Interest Rates

Forecasting interest rates is a time-honoured profession. Economists are hired (sometimes at very high salaries) to forecast interest rates because businesses need to know what the rates will be in order to plan their future spending, and banks and investors require interest-rate forecasts in order to decide which assets to buy.

The media frequently reports interest rate forecasts by leading prognosticators. These forecasts are produced using a wide range of statistical models and a number of different sources of information. One of the most popular methods is based on the loanable funds framework described earlier in the chapter. Using this framework, analysts predict what will happen to the factors that affect the supply of and demand for bonds and then use the supply and demand analysis outlined in the chapter to come up with their interest-rate forecasts.

An alternative method of forecasting interest rates makes use of **econometric models**, models whose equations are estimated with statistical procedures using past data. Many of these econometric models are quite large, involving hundreds and sometimes over a thousand interlocking equations. They produce simultaneous forecasts for many variables, including interest rates, under the assumption that the estimated relationships between variables do not change over time.

Good forecasts of future interest rates are extremely valuable to households and businesses, which, not surprisingly, would be willing to pay a lot for accurate forecasts. Unfortunately, forecasting interest rates is a perilous business. To their embarrassment, even the top experts are frequently far off in their forecasts.

SUMMARY

1. The theory of asset demand tells us that the quantity demanded of an asset is (a) positively related to wealth, (b) positively related to the expected return on the asset relative to alternative assets, (c) negatively related to the riskiness of the asset relative to alternative assets, and (d) positively related to the liquidity of the asset relative to alternative assets.

2. The supply and demand analysis for bonds, known as the loanable funds framework, provides one theory of how interest rates are determined. It predicts that interest rates will change when there is a change in demand because of changes in income (or wealth), expected returns, risk, or liquidity or when there is a change in supply because of changes in the attractiveness of investment opportunities, the real cost of borrowing, or government activities.

3. An alternative theory of how interest rates are determined is provided by the liquidity preference framework, which analyzes the supply of and demand for money. It shows that interest rates will change when there is a change in the demand for money because of changes in income or the price level or when there is a change in the supply of money.

4. There are four possible effects of an increase in the money supply on interest rates: the liquidity effect, the income effect, the price-level effect, and the expected-inflation effect. The liquidity effect indicates that a rise in money supply growth will lead to a decline in interest rates; the other effects work in the opposite direction. The evidence seems to indicate that the income, price-level, and expected-inflation effects dominate the liquidity effect such that an increase in money supply growth leads to higher rather than lower interest rates.

KEY TERMS

asset market approach, p. 86

demand curve, p. 82

excess demand, p. 85

excess supply, p. 84

expected return, p. 80

Fisher effect, p. 94

liquidity, p. 80

liquidity preference framework, p. 99

loanable funds, p. 86

loanable funds framework, p. 86

market equilibrium, p. 84

opportunity cost, p. 100

risk, p. 80

supply curve, p. 84

theory of asset demand, p. 81

wealth, p. 80

QUESTIONS AND PROBLEMS

Questions marked with an asterisk are answered at the end of the book in an appendix, "Answers to Selected Questions and Problems."

1. Explain why you would be more or less willing to buy a share of Air Canada stock in the following situations:
   a. Your wealth falls.
   b. You expect the stock to appreciate in value.
   c. The bond market becomes more liquid.
   d. You expect gold to appreciate in value.
   e. Prices in the bond market become more volatile.

*2. Explain why you would be more or less willing to buy a house under the following circumstances:
   a. You just inherited $100 000.
   b. Real estate commissions fall from 6% of the sales price to 5% of the sales price.
   c. You expect Air Canada stock to double in value next year.

   d. Prices in the stock market become more volatile.
   e. You expect housing prices to fall.

3. Explain why you would be more or less willing to buy gold under the following circumstances:
   a. Gold again becomes acceptable as a medium of exchange.
   b. Prices in the gold market become more volatile.
   c. You expect inflation to rise, and gold prices tend to move with the aggregate price level.
   d. You expect interest rates to rise.

*4. Explain why you would be more or less willing to buy long-term Nortel bonds under the following circumstances:
   a. Trading in these bonds increases, making them easier to sell.
   b. You expect a bear market in stocks (stock prices are expected to decline).
   c. Brokerage commissions on stocks fall.

d. You expect interest rates to rise.

e. Brokerage commissions on bonds fall.

5. What would happen to the demand for Rembrandts if the stock market undergoes a boom? Why?

Answer each question by drawing the appropriate supply and demand diagrams.

*6. An important way in which the Bank of Canada decreases the money supply is by selling bonds to the public. Using the loanable funds framework, show what effect this action has on interest rates. Is your answer consistent with what you would expect to find with the liquidity preference framework?

7. Using both the liquidity preference and loanable funds frameworks, show why interest rates are procyclical (rising when the economy is expanding and falling during recessions).

*8. Why should a rise in the price level (but not in expected inflation) cause interest rates to rise when the nominal money supply is fixed?

9. What effect will a sharp increase in personal savings rates have on Canadian interest rates?

10. What effect will a sudden increase in the volatility of gold prices have on interest rates?

*11. How might a sudden increase in people's expectations of future real estate prices affect interest rates?

12. Explain what effect a large federal deficit might have on interest rates.

*13. Using both the loanable funds and liquidity preference frameworks, show what the effect is on

interest rates when the riskiness of bonds rises. Are the results the same in the two frameworks?

14. If the price level falls next year, remaining fixed thereafter, and the money supply is fixed, what is likely to happen to interest rates over the next two years? (Hint: Take account of both the price-level effect and the expected-inflation effect.)

*15. Will there be an effect on interest rates if brokerage commissions on stocks fall? Explain your answer.

Using Economic Analysis to Predict the Future

16. The governor of the Bank of Canada announces in a press conference that he will fight the higher inflation rate with a new anti-inflation program. Predict what will happen to interest rates if the public believes him.

*17. The governor of the Bank of Canada announces that interest rates will rise sharply next year, and the market believes him. What will happen to today's interest rate on long-term corporate bonds?

18. Predict what will happen to interest rates if the public suddenly expects a large increase in stock prices.

*19. Predict what will happen to interest rates if prices in the bond market become more volatile.

20. If the next governor of the Bank of Canada has a reputation for advocating an even slower rate of money growth than the current governor, what will happen to interest rates? Discuss the possible resulting situations.

Chapter 6

The Risk and Term Structure of Interest Rates

PREVIEW   In our supply and demand analysis of interest-rate behaviour in Chapter 5, we examined the determination of just one interest rate. Yet we saw earlier that there are enormous numbers of bonds on which the interest rates can and do differ. In this chapter we complete the interest-rate picture by examining the relationship of the various interest rates to one another. Understanding why they differ from bond to bond can help businesses, banks, insurance companies, and private investors decide which bonds to purchase as investments and which ones to sell.

We first look at why bonds with the same term to maturity have different interest rates. The relationship among these interest rates is called the **risk structure of interest rates**, although risk and liquidity both play a role in determining the risk structure. A bond's term to maturity also affects its interest rate, and the relationship among interest rates on bonds with different terms to maturity is called the **term structure of interest rates**. In this chapter we examine the sources and causes of fluctuations in interest rates relative to one another and look at a number of theories that explain these fluctuations.

RISK STRUCTURE OF INTEREST RATES

Figure 6-1 shows the yields to maturity for several categories of long-term bonds from 1980 to 2000. It shows us two important features of interest-rate behaviour for bonds of the same maturity: interest rates on different categories of bonds differ from one another in any given year, and the spread (or difference) between the interest rates varies over time. The interest rates on corporate bonds, for example, are above those on Canada bonds and provincial bonds. In addition, the spread between the interest rates on corporate bonds and Canada bonds is very large during the 1980–1982 and 1990–1991 recessions, is smaller during the mid-1990s, and then widens again in the late 1990s (see also Figure 6-3).

FIGURE 6-1   Long-Term Bond Yields, 1980–2000

Source: Statistics Canada CANSIM Series B14072, B14047, and B14048.

Default Risk

One attribute of a bond that influences its interest rate is its **default risk**, the chance that the issuer of the bond will default, that is, be unable to make interest payments or pay off the face value when the bond matures. A corporation suffering big losses, such as Canadian Airlines did in the 1990s, might be more likely to suspend interest payments on its bonds.[1] The default risk on its bonds would therefore be quite high. By contrast, Canadian government bonds have usually been considered to have no default risk because the federal government can always increase taxes or even print money to pay off its obligations. Bonds like these with no default risk are called **default-free bonds**. The spread between the interest rates on bonds with default risk and default-free bonds, called the **risk premium**, indicates how much additional interest people must earn in order to be willing to hold a risky bond. Our supply and demand analysis of the bond market in Chapter 5 can be used to explain why a bond with default risk always has a positive risk premium and why the higher the default risk is, the larger the risk premium will be.

Study Guide

Two exercises will help you gain a better understanding of the risk structure:

1. Put yourself in the shoes of an investor—see how your purchase decision would be affected by changes in risk and liquidity.

2. Practice drawing the appropriate shifts in the supply and demand curves when risk and liquidity change. For example, see if you can draw the appropriate shifts in the supply and demand curves when, in contrast to the examples in the text, a corporate bond has a decline in default risk or an improvement in its liquidity.

---

[1]Canadian Airlines did not default on its loans in this period, but it would have were it not for a government bailout plan intended to preserve jobs that in effect provided Canadian Airlines with funds that were used to pay off creditors.

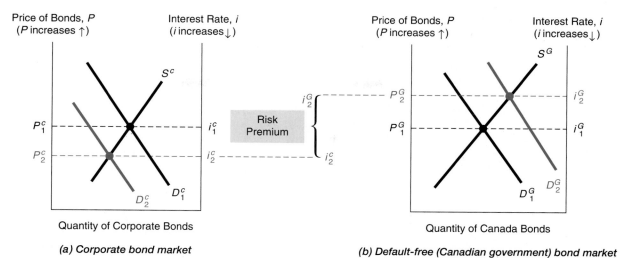

FIGURE 6-2 Response to an Increase in Default Risk on Corporate Bonds

An increase in default risk on corporate bonds shifts the demand curve from D_1^c to D_2^c. Simultaneously, it shifts the demand curve for Canada bonds from D_1^G to D_2^G. The equilibrium price for corporate bonds (left axis) falls from P_1^c to P_2^c, and the equilibrium interest rate on corporate bonds (right axis) rises from i_1^c to i_2^c. In the Canada bond market, the equilibrium bond price rises from P_1^G to P_2^G, and the equilibrium interest rate falls from i_1^G to i_2^G. The brace indicates the difference between i_2^c and i_2^G, the risk premium on corporate bonds. (*Note*: P and i increase in opposite directions. P on the left vertical axis increases as we go up the axis, while i on the right vertical axis increases as we go down the axis.)

To examine the effect of default risk on interest rates, let us look at the supply and demand diagrams for the default-free (Canadian government) and corporate long-term bond markets in Figure 6-2. To make the diagrams somewhat easier to read, let's assume that initially corporate bonds have the same default risk as Canada bonds. In this case, these two bonds have the same attributes (identical risk and maturity); their equilibrium prices and interest rates will initially be equal ($P_1^c = P_1^G$ and $i_1^c = i_1^G$), and the risk premium on corporate bonds ($i_1^c - i_1^G$) will be zero.

If the possibility of a default increases because a corporation begins to suffer large losses, the default risk on corporate bonds will increase, and the expected return on these bonds will decrease. In addition, the corporate bond's return will be more uncertain as well. The theory of asset demand predicts that because the expected return on the corporate bond falls relative to the expected return on the default-free Canada bond while its relative riskiness rises, the corporate bond is less desirable (holding everything else equal), and demand for it will fall. The demand curve for corporate bonds in panel (a) of Figure 6-2 then shifts to the left, from D_1^c to D_2^c.

At the same time, the expected return on default-free Canada bonds increases relative to the expected return on corporate bonds while their relative riskiness declines. The Canada bonds thus become more desirable, and demand rises, as shown in panel (b) by the rightward shift in the demand curve for these bonds from D_1^G to D_2^G.

As we can see in Figure 6-2, the equilibrium price for corporate bonds (left axis) falls from P_1^c to P_2^c, and since the bond price is negatively related to the interest rate, the equilibrium interest rate on corporate bonds (right axis) rises from i_1^c to i_2^c. At the same time, however, the equilibrium price for the Canada bonds rises from P_1^G to P_2^G, and the equilibrium interest rate falls from i_1^G to i_2^G. The spread between the interest rates on corporate and default-free bonds—that is, the risk premium on corporate bonds—has risen from zero to $i_2^c - i_2^G$. We can now conclude that ***a bond with default risk will always have a positive risk premium, and an increase in its default risk will raise the risk premium***.

Because default risk is so important to the size of the risk premium, purchasers of bonds need to know whether a corporation is likely to default on its bonds. Two main investment advisory firms, the Canadian Bond Rating Service (CBRS) and the Dominion Bond Rating Service (DBRS), provide default risk information by rating the quality of the majority of corporate bonds in terms of their probability of default—in the United States, Moody's Investor Service and Standard & Poor's Corporation provide similar information. Since October 31, 2000 Standard & Poor's and the Canadian Bond Rating Service have combined operations in Canada. The ratings and their description are contained in Table 6-1. Bonds with relatively low risk of default are called *investment-grade* securities and have a rating of B++ (or BBB) and above. Bonds with ratings below B++ (or BBB) have higher default risk and have been aptly dubbed speculative-grade or **junk bonds**. Because these bonds always have higher interest rates than investment-grade securities, they are also referred to as high-yield bonds. Investment-grade securities whose rating has fallen to junk levels are referred to as **fallen angels**.

Next let's look back at Figure 6-1 and see if we can explain the relationship between interest rates on corporate and Canada bonds. Corporate bonds always have higher interest rates than Canada bonds because they always have some risk of default, whereas Canada bonds do not. Because corporate bonds have a greater default risk than the Canada bonds, their risk premium is greater, and the corporate bond rate therefore always exceeds the Canada bond rate. We can use the same analysis to explain the huge jump in the risk premium on corporate bond rates during the 1980–1982 and 1990–1991 recessions (Figure 6-3). The recession periods saw a very high rate of business failures and defaults. As we would expect, these factors led to a substantial increase in default risk for bonds issued by vulnerable corporations, and the risk premium for corporate bonds reached unprecedented high levels.

Dominion Bond Rating Service
www.dbrs.com

Moody's Investor Service
www.moodys.com

Standard & Poor's Corporation
www.standardandpoors.com/canada

TABLE 6-1   Bond Ratings by Standard & Poor's and DBRS

Standard & Poor's	DBRS	Descriptions	Examples of Corporations with Bonds Outstanding in 2000
A++	AAA	Highest quality	Government of Canada, Mobil Oil
A+	AA	Superior quality	Imperial Oil, Shell Canada, DuPont
A	A	Good quality	Dofasco, Nortel, MacMillan Bloedel
B++	BBB	Medium quality	Noranda, Nova Chemicals
B+	BB	Lower medium quality	Air Canada, Saskatchewan Wheat Pool
B	B	Moderately speculative	Algoma Steel, Scott Paper Ltd.
C	CCC	Highly speculative	Telesystems International Wireless Inc.
D	CC	Default	Canadian Airlines, Laidlaw Inc.
—	C	In default	

APPLICATION | ***The Stock Market Crash of 1987 and the Junk Bond–Canada Spread***

The stock market crash on "Black Monday," October 19, 1987, when the TSE 300 fell more than 400 points, an 11% decline, had a major impact not only on prices of stocks but on the bond market as well. Let's see how our supply and demand analysis explains the behaviour of the spread between interest rates on junk bonds and government of Canada securities in the aftermath of the crash using Figure 6-2.

As a consequence of the Black Monday crash, many investors began to worry about the possibility of a financial crisis and so to doubt the financial health of corporations with lower credit ratings that had issued junk bonds. The increase in default risk for junk bonds made them less desirable at any given interest rate, decreased the quantity demanded, and shifted the demand curve for junk bonds to the left. As shown in panel (a) of Figure 6-2, the interest rate on junk bonds should have risen, which is indeed what happened: interest rates on junk bonds shot up by about one percentage point. But the increase in the perceived default risk for junk bonds after the crash made default-free Canada bonds relatively more attractive and shifted the demand curve for these securities to the right—an outcome described by some analysts as a "flight to quality." Just as our analysis predicts in Figure 6-2, interest rates on government of Canada securities fell by about one percentage point. The overall outcome was that the spread between interest rates on junk bonds and government bonds rose by two percentage points, from 4% before the crash to 6% immediately after.

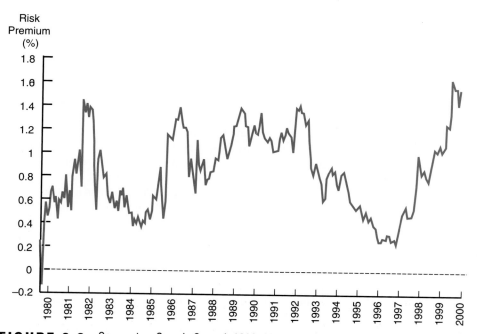

FIGURE 6-3   Corporates–Canada Spread, 1980–2000
Source: Statistics Canada CANSIM Series B14072 and B14048.

APPLICATION | *What If Canada Bonds Were No Longer Default-Risk Free?*

Throughout our history, the Canadian government has never defaulted on its securities. In the early 1990s, however, because of government overspending and a lower average growth rate for real GDP, the federal government's debt/GDP ratio climbed up to 75%. Because of this and of an international concern about political instability in Canada (for example, Québec separation), U.S. bond rating agencies such as S&P's and Moody's (which have also been in the practice of rating Canadian government bonds) threatened to lower their rating of the federal government's debt. What would have been the impact of a lower rating?

Our analysis in Figure 6-2 provides the answer. A lower rating on Canada bonds would mean that they would no longer be considered default-risk free and would now have the attributes of corporate bonds in panel (a) of Figure 6-2. The increase in default risk would decrease the quantity of Canada bonds demanded at any given interest rate and would thus cause their demand curve to shift to the left. As we see in panel (a), this would result in a fall in their bond price and a rise in their interest rate.

Liquidity

Another attribute of a bond that influences its interest rate is its liquidity. As we learned in Chapter 4, a liquid asset is one that can be quickly and cheaply converted into cash if the need arises. The more liquid an asset is, the more desirable it is (holding everything else constant). Canada bonds are the most liquid of all long-term bonds because they are so widely traded that they are the easiest to sell quickly and the cost of selling them is low. Corporate bonds are not as liquid because fewer bonds for any one corporation are traded; thus it can be costly to sell these bonds in an emergency because it may be hard to find buyers quickly.

How does the reduced liquidity of the corporate bonds affect their interest rates relative to the interest rate on Canadian government bonds? We can use supply and demand analysis with the same figure that was used to analyze the effect of default risk, Figure 6-2, to show that the lower liquidity of corporate bonds relative to Canada bonds increases the spread between the interest rates on these two bonds. Let us start the analysis by assuming that initially corporate and Canada bonds are equally liquid and all their other attributes are the same. As shown in Figure 6-2, their equilibrium prices and interest rates will initially be equal: $P_1^c = P_1^T$ and $i_1^c = i_1^T$. If the corporate bond becomes less liquid than the Canada bond because it is less widely traded, then as the theory of asset demand indicates, its demand will fall, shifting its demand curve from D_1^c to D_2^c as in panel (a). The Canada bond now becomes relatively more liquid in comparison with the corporate bond, so its demand curve shifts rightward from D_1^T to D_2^T as in panel (b). The shifts in the curves in Figure 6-2 show that the price of the less liquid corporate bond falls and its interest rate rises, while the price of the more liquid Canada bond rises and its interest rate falls.

The result is that the spread between the interest rates on the two bond types has risen. Therefore, the differences between interest rates on corporate bonds and Canada bonds (that is, the risk premiums) reflect not only the corporate bond's default risk but its liquidity too. This is why a risk premium is sometimes called a *liquidity premium*. Most accurately, it should be called a "risk and liquidity premium," but convention dictates that it be called a *risk premium*.

Income Tax Considerations

In Canada, coupon payments on fixed-income securities are taxed as ordinary income in the year they are received. In some other countries, however, certain government bonds are not taxable. In the United States, for example, interest payments on municipal bonds are exempt from federal income taxes, and these bonds have had lower interest rates than U.S. Treasury bonds for at least 40 years. How does taxation affect the interest rate on bonds?

Let us imagine that you have a high enough income to put you in the 40% income tax bracket, where for every extra dollar of income you have to pay 40 cents to the government. If you own a $1000-face-value taxable bond that sells for $1000 and has a coupon payment of $100, you get to keep only $60 of the payment after taxes. Although the bond has a 10% interest rate, you actually earn only 6% after taxes.

Suppose, however, that you put your savings into a $1000-face-value tax-exempt bond that sells for $1000 and pays only $80 in coupon payments. Its interest rate is only 8%, but because it is a tax-exempt security, you pay no taxes on the $80 coupon payment, so you earn 8% after taxes. Clearly, you earn more on the tax-exempt bond, so you are willing to hold the bond even though it has a lower interest rate than the taxable bond. Notice that the tax-exempt status of a bond becomes a significant advantage when income-tax rates are very high.

Summary

In general, the risk structure of interest rates (the relationship among interest rates on bonds with the same maturity) is explained by three factors: default risk, liquidity, and the income tax treatment of the bond's interest payments. As a bond's default risk increases, the risk premium on that bond (the spread between its interest rate and the interest rate on a default-free Canadian government bond) rises. The greater liquidity of Canada bonds also explains why their interest rates are lower than interest rates on less liquid bonds. If a bond has a favourable tax treatment, as do municipal bonds in the United States whose interest payments are exempt from federal income taxes, its interest rate will be lower.

TERM STRUCTURE OF INTEREST RATES

We have seen how risk, liquidity, and tax considerations (collectively embedded in the risk structure) can influence interest rates. Another factor that influences the interest rate on a bond is its term to maturity: bonds with identical risk, liquidity, and tax characteristics may have different interest rates because the time remaining to maturity is different. A plot of the yields on bonds with differing terms to maturity but the same risk, liquidity, and tax considerations is called a **yield curve**, and it describes the term structure of interest rates for particular types of bonds, such as government bonds. The "Following the Financial News" box shows several yield curves for Canadian government securities that were published in the *Globe and Mail: Report on Business*. Yield curves can be classified as upward-sloping, flat, and downward-sloping (the last sort is often referred to as an **inverted yield curve**). When yield curves slope upward, the long-term interest rates are above the short-term interest rates; when yield curves are flat, short- and long-term interest rates are the same; and when yield curves are inverted, as in the "Following the Financial News" box, long-term interest rates are below short-term interest rates. Yield curves can also have more complicated shapes in which they first slope up and then down, or vice versa. Why do we usually see upward slopes of the yield curve?

FOLLOWING THE FINANCIAL NEWS

Yield Curves

The *Globe and Mail: Report on Business* publishes a weekly plot of the yield curves for government of Canada securities, an example of which is presented here. It is typically found in the "Canadian Bonds" column.

The numbers on the vertical axis indicate the interest rate for the government of Canada security, with the maturity given by the numbers on the horizontal axis. For example, the yield curve marked "Last Friday" indicates that the interest rate on the three-month Treasury bill last Friday was 5.45%, while the one-year bill had an interest rate of 5.95% and the ten-year bond had an interest rate of 5.65%. As you can see, the yield curves in the plot first slope up and then down.

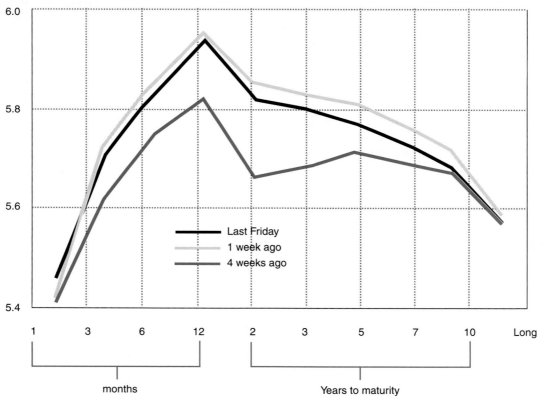

Source: Royal Bank of Canada, as it appeared in *The Globe and Mail: Report on Business*, Monday, November 27, 2000, p. B11. Reproduced with permission of Royal Bank of Canada

Besides explaining why yield curves take on different shapes at different times, a good theory of the term structure of interest rates must explain the following three important empirical facts.

1. As we see in Figure 6-4, interest rates on bonds of different maturities move together over time.

2. When short-term interest rates are low, yield curves are more likely to have an upward slope; when short-term interest rates are high, yield curves are more likely to slope downward and be inverted.

3. Yield curves almost always slope upward, unlike the yield curves in the "Following the Financial News" box.

Three theories have been put forward to explain the term structure of interest rates, that is, the relationship among interest rates on bonds of different maturities reflected in yield curve patterns: (1) the expectations theory, (2) the segmented markets theory, and (3) the liquidity premium theory. The expectations theory does a good job of explaining the first two facts on our list but not the third. The segmented markets theory can explain fact 3 but not the other two facts, which are well explained by the expectations theory. Because each theory explains facts that the others cannot, a natural way to seek a better understanding of the term structure is to combine features of all three theories, which leads us to the liquidity premium theory, which can explain all three facts.

If the liquidity premium theory does a better job of explaining the facts and is hence the most widely accepted theory, why do we spend time discussing the other two theories? There are two reasons. First, the ideas in these two theories provide the groundwork for the liquidity premium theory. Second, it is important to see how economists modify theories to improve them when they find that the predicted results are inconsistent with the empirical evidence.

Expectations Theory

The **expectations theory** of the term structure states the following commonsense proposition: the interest rate on a long-term bond will equal an average of short-term

FIGURE 6-4   Movements over Time of Interest Rates on Government of Canada Bonds with Different Maturities, 1962–2000

Source: Statistics Canada CANSIM Series B14060, B14010, and B14013.

interest rates that people expect to occur over the life of the long-term bond. For example, if people expect that short-term interest rates will be 10% on average over the coming five years, the expectations theory predicts that the interest rate on bonds with five years to maturity will be 10% too. If short-term interest rates were expected to rise even higher after this five-year period so that the average short-term interest rate over the coming 20 years is 11%, then the interest rate on 20-year bonds would equal 11% and would be higher than the interest rate on five-year bonds. We can see that the explanation provided by the expectations theory for why interest rates on bonds of different maturities differ is that short-term interest rates are expected to have different values at future dates.

The key assumption behind this theory is that buyers of bonds do not prefer bonds of one maturity over another, so they will not hold any quantity of a bond if its expected return is less than that of another bond with a different maturity. Bonds that have this characteristic are said to be *perfect substitutes*. What this means in practice is that if bonds with different maturities are perfect substitutes, the expected return on these bonds must be equal.

To see how the assumption that bonds with different maturities are perfect substitutes leads to the expectations theory, let us consider the following two investment strategies:

1. Purchase a one-year bond, and when it matures in one year, purchase another one-year bond.
2. Purchase a two-year bond and hold it until maturity.

Because both strategies must have the same expected return if people are holding both one- and two-year bonds, the interest rate on the two-year bond must equal the average of the two one-year interest rates. For example, let's say that the current interest rate on the one-year bond is 9% and you expect the interest rate on the one-year bond next year to be 11%. If you pursue the first strategy of buying the two one-year bonds, the expected return over the two years will average out to be (9% + 11%)/2 = 10% per year. You will be willing to hold both the one- and two-year bonds only if the expected return per year of the two-year bond equals this. Therefore, the interest rate on the two-year bond must equal 10%, the average interest rate on the two one-year bonds.

We can make this argument more general. For an investment of $1, consider the choice of holding, for two periods, a two-period bond or two one-period bonds. Using the definitions

i_t = today's (time t) interest rate on a one-period bond

i_{t+1}^e = interest rate on a one-period bond expected for next period (time $t + 1$)

i_{2t} = today's (time t) interest rate on the two-period bond

the expected return over the two periods from investing $1 in the two-period bond and holding it for the two periods can be calculated as

$$(1 + i_{2t})(1 + i_{2t}) - 1 = 1 + 2i_{2t} + (i_{2t})^2 - 1 = 2i_{2t} + (i_{2t})^2$$

After the second period, the $1 investment is worth $(1 + i_{2t})(1 + i_{2t})$. Subtracting the $1 initial investment from this amount and dividing by the initial $1 investment gives the rate of return calculated in the above equation. Because $(i_{2t})^2$ is extremely small—if i_{2t} = 10% = 0.10, then $(i_{2t})^2$ = 0.01—we can simplify the expected return for holding the two-period bond for the two periods to

$$2i_{2t}$$

With the other strategy, in which one-period bonds are bought, the expected return on the $1 investment over the two periods is

$$(1 + i_t)(1 + i^e_{t+1}) - 1$$

After the first period, the \$1 investment becomes $1 + i_t$, and this is reinvested in the one-period bond for the next period, yielding an amount $(1 + i_t)(1 + i^e_{t+1})$. Subtracting the \$1 initial investment from this amount and dividing by the initial investment of \$1 gives the expected return for the strategy of holding one-period bonds for the two periods. Because $i_t(i^e_{t+1})$ is also extremely small—if $i_t = i^e_{t+1} = 0.10$, then $i_t(i^e_{t+1}) = 0.01$—we can simplify this to

$$i_t + i^e_{t+1}$$

Both bonds will be held only if these expected returns are equal, that is, when

$$2i_{2t} = i_t + i^e_{t+1}$$

Solving for i_{2t} in terms of the one-period rates, we have

$$i_{2t} = \frac{i_t + i^e_{t+1}}{2} \qquad (1)$$

which tells us that the two-period rate must equal the average of the two one-period rates. Graphically, this can be shown as:

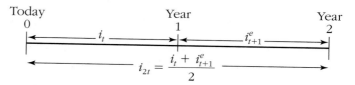

We can conduct the same steps for bonds with a longer maturity so that we can examine the whole term structure of interest rates. Doing so, we will find that the interest rate of i_{nt} on an n-period bond must equal

$$i_{nt} = \frac{i_t + i^e_{t+1} + i^e_{t+2} + \ldots + i^e_{t+(n-1)}}{n} \qquad (2)$$

Equation 2 states that the n-period interest rate equals the average of the one-period interest rates expected to occur over the n-period life of the bond. This is a restatement of the expectations theory in more precise terms.[2]

A simple numerical example might clarify what the expectations theory in Equation 2 is saying. If the one-year interest rate over the next five years is expected to be 5, 6, 7, 8, and 9%, Equation 2 indicates that the interest rate on the two-year bond would be

$$\frac{5\% + 6\%}{2} = 5.5\%$$

while for the five-year bond it would be

$$\frac{5\% + 6\% + 7\% + 8\% + 9\%}{5} = 7\%$$

Doing a similar calculation for the one-, three-, and four-year interest rates, you should be able to verify that the one- to five-year interest rates are 5.0, 5.5, 6.0,

[2]The analysis here has been conducted for discount bonds. Formulas for interest rates on coupon bonds would differ slightly from those used here but would convey the same principle.

6.5, and 7.0%, respectively. Thus we see that the rising trend in expected short-term interest rates produces an upward-sloping yield curve along which interest rates rise as maturity lengthens.

The expectations theory is an elegant theory that provides an explanation of why the term structure of interest rates (as represented by yield curves) changes at different times. When the yield curve is upward-sloping, the expectations theory suggests that short-term interest rates are expected to rise in the future, as we have seen in our numerical example. In this situation, in which the long-term rate is currently above the short-term rate, the average of future short-term rates is expected to be higher than the current short-term rate, which can occur only if short-term interest rates are expected to rise. This is what we see in our numerical example. When the yield curve is inverted (slopes downward), the average of future short-term interest rates is expected to be below the current short-term rate, implying that short-term interest rates are expected to fall, on average, in the future. Only when the yield curve is flat does the expectations theory suggest that short-term interest rates are not expected to change, on average, in the future.

The expectations theory also explains fact 1, that interest rates on bonds with different maturities move together over time. Historically, short-term interest rates have had the characteristic that if they increase today, they will tend to be higher in the future. Hence a rise in short-term rates will raise people's expectations of future short-term rates. Because long-term rates are the average of expected future short-term rates, a rise in short-term rates will also raise long-term rates, causing short- and long-term rates to move together.

The expectations theory also explains fact 2, that yield curves tend to have an upward slope when short-term interest rates are low and are inverted when short-term rates are high. When short-term rates are low, people generally expect them to rise to some normal level in the future, and the average of future expected short-term rates is high relative to the current short-term rate. Therefore, long-term interest rates will be substantially above current short-term rates, and the yield curve would then have an upward slope. Conversely, if short-term rates are high, people usually expect them to come back down. Long-term rates would then drop below short-term rates because the average of expected future short-term rates would be below current short-term rates and the yield curve would slope downward and become inverted.[3]

The expectations theory is an attractive theory because it provides a simple explanation of the behaviour of the term structure, but unfortunately it has a major shortcoming: it cannot explain fact 3, that yield curves usually slope upward. The typical upward slope of yield curves implies that short-term interest rates are usually expected to rise in the future. In practice, short-term interest rates are just as likely to fall as they are to rise, and so the expectations theory suggests that the typical yield curve should be flat rather than upward-sloping.

Segmented Markets Theory

As the name suggests, the **segmented markets theory** of the term structure sees markets for different-maturity bonds as completely separate and segmented. The interest rate for each bond with a different maturity is then determined by the

---

[3]The expectations theory explains another important fact about the relationship between short-term and long-term interest rates. As you can see looking back at Figure 6-4, short-term interest rates are more volatile than long-term rates. If interest rates are mean-reverting—that is, if they tend to head back down after they are at unusually high levels or go back up when they are at unusually low levels—then an average of these short-term rates must necessarily have lower volatility than the short-term rates themselves. Because the expectations theory suggests that the long-term rate will be an average of future short-term rates, it implies that the long-term rate will have lower volatility than short-term rates.

supply of and demand for that bond with no effects from expected returns on other bonds with other maturities.

The key assumption in the segmented markets theory is that bonds of different maturities are not substitutes at all, so the expected return from holding a bond of one maturity has no effect on the demand for a bond of another maturity. This theory of the term structure is at the opposite extreme to the expectations theory, which assumes that bonds of different maturities are perfect substitutes.

The argument for why bonds of different maturities are not substitutes is that investors have strong preferences for bonds of one maturity but not for another, so they will be concerned with the expected returns only for bonds of the maturity they prefer. This might occur because they have a particular holding period in mind, and if they match the maturity of the bond to the desired holding period, they can obtain a certain return with no risk at all.[4] (We have seen in Chapter 4 that if the term to maturity equals the holding period, the return is known for certain because it equals the yield exactly, and there is no interest-rate risk.) For example, people who have a short holding period would prefer to hold short-term bonds. Conversely, if you were putting funds away for your young child to go to college, your desired holding period might be much longer, and you would want to hold longer-term bonds.

In the segmented markets theory, differing yield curve patterns are accounted for by supply and demand differences associated with bonds of different maturities. If, as seems sensible, investors have short desired holding periods and generally prefer bonds with shorter maturities that have less interest-rate risk, the segmented markets theory can explain fact 3, that yield curves typically slope upward. Because in the typical situation the demand for long-term bonds is relatively lower than that for short-term bonds, long-term bonds will have lower prices and higher interest rates, and hence the yield curve will typically slope upward.

Although the segmented markets theory can explain why yield curves usually tend to slope upward, it has a major flaw in that it cannot explain facts 1 and 2. Because it views the market for bonds of different maturities as completely segmented, there is no reason for a rise in interest rates on a bond of one maturity to affect the interest rate on a bond of another maturity. Therefore, it cannot explain why interest rates on bonds of different maturities tend to move together (fact 1). Second, because it is not clear how demand and supply for short- versus long-term bonds change with the level of short-term interest rates, the theory cannot explain why yield curves tend to slope upward when short-term interest rates are low and to be inverted when short-term interest rates are high (fact 2).

Because each of our two theories explains empirical facts that the other cannot, a logical step is to combine the theories, which leads us to the liquidity premium theory.

Liquidity Premium Theory

The **liquidity premium theory** of the term structure states that the interest rate on a long-term bond will equal an average of short-term interest rates expected to occur over the life of the long-term bond plus a liquidity premium (also referred to as a term premium) that responds to supply and demand conditions for that bond.

---

[4]The statement that there is no uncertainty about the return if the term to maturity equals the holding period is literally true only for a discount bond. For a coupon bond with a long holding period, there is some risk because coupon payments must be reinvested before the bond matures. Our analysis here is thus being conducted for discount bonds. However, the gist of the analysis remains the same for coupon bonds because the amount of this risk from reinvestment is small when coupon bonds have the same term to maturity as the holding period.

The liquidity premium theory's key assumption is that bonds of different maturities are substitutes, which means that the expected return on one bond *does* influence the expected return on a bond of a different maturity, but it allows investors to prefer one bond maturity over another. In other words, bonds of different maturities are assumed to be substitutes but not perfect substitutes. Investors tend to prefer shorter-term bonds because these bonds bear less interest-rate risk. For these reasons, investors must be offered a positive liquidity premium to induce them to hold longer-term bonds. Such an outcome would modify the expectations theory by adding a positive liquidity premium to the equation that describes the relationship between long- and short-term interest rates. The liquidity premium theory is thus written as:

$$i_{nt} = \frac{i_t + i_{t+1}^e + i_{t+2}^e + \cdots + i_{t+(n-1)}^e}{n} + l_{nt} \qquad (3)$$

where l_{nt} = the liquidity (term) premium for the n-period bond at time t, which is always positive and rises with the term to maturity of the bond, n.

The relationship between the expectations theory and the liquidity premium theory is shown in Figure 6-5. There we see that because the liquidity premium is always positive and grows as the term to maturity increases, the yield curve implied by the liquidity premium theory is always above the yield curve implied by the expectations theory and has a steeper slope.[5]

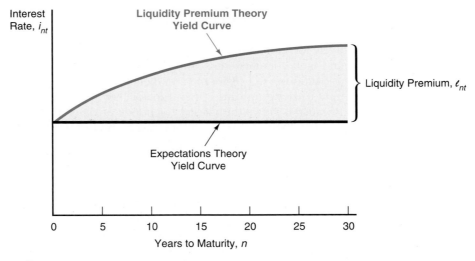

FIGURE 6-5 The Relationship Between the Liquidity Premium and Expectations Theory

Because the liquidity premium is always positive and grows as the term to maturity increases, the yield curve implied by the liquidity premium theory is always above the yield curve implied by the expectations theory and has a steeper slope. Note that the yield curve implied by the expectations theory is drawn under the scenario of unchanging future one-year interest rates.

[5]The liquidity premium theory is closely related to the preferred habitat theory, which takes a somewhat less direct approach to modifying the expectations hypothesis but comes up with a similar conclusion. It assumes that investors have a preference for bonds of one maturity over another, a particular bond maturity (preferred habitat) in which they prefer to invest. Because they prefer bonds of one maturity over another they will be willing to buy bonds that do not have the preferred maturity only if they earn a somewhat higher expected return. Because investors are likely to prefer the habitat of short-term bonds to that of longer-term bonds, they are willing to hold long-term bonds only if they have higher expected return. This reasoning leads to the same Equation 3 implied by the liquidity premium theory with a term premium that rises with maturity.

A simple numerical example similar to the one we used for the expectations hypothesis further clarifies what the liquidity premium theory in Equation 3 is saying. Again suppose that the one-year interest rate over the next five years is expected to be 5%, 6%, 7%, 8%, and 9%, while investors' preferences for holding short-term bonds means that the liquidity premiums for one- to five-year bonds are 0%, 0.25%, 0.5%, 0.75%, and 1.0%, respectively. Equation 3 then indicates that the interest rate on the two-year bond would be

$$\frac{5\% + 6\%}{2} + 0.25\% = 5.75\%$$

while for the five-year bond it would be

$$\frac{5\% + 6\% + 7\% + 8\% + 9\%}{5} + 1\% = 8\%$$

Doing a similar calculation for the one-, three-, and four-year interest rates, you should be able to verify that the one- to five-year interest rates are 5.0%, 5.75%, 6.5%, 7.25%, and 8.0%, respectively. Comparing these findings with those for the expectations theory, we see that the liquidity premium theory produces yield curves that slope more steeply upward because of investors' preferences for short-term bonds.

Let's see if the liquidity premium theory is consistent with all three empirical facts we have discussed. It explains fact 1, that interest rates on different-maturity bonds move together over time: a rise in short-term interest rates indicates that short-term interest rates will, on average, be higher in the future, and the first term in Equation 3 then implies that long-term interest rates will rise along with them.

It also explains why yield curves tend to have an especially steep upward slope when short-term interest rates are low and to be inverted when short-term rates are high (fact 2). Because investors generally expect short-term interest rates to rise to some normal level when they are low, the average of future expected short-term rates will be high relative to the current short-term rate. With the additional boost of a positive liquidity premium, long-term interest rates will be substantially above current short-term rates, and the yield curve would then have a steep upward slope. Conversely, if short-term rates are high, people usually expect them to come back down. Long-term rates would then drop below short-term rates because the average of expected future short-term rates would be so far below current short-term rates that despite positive liquidity premiums, the yield curve would slope downward.

The liquidity premium theory explains fact 3, that yield curves typically slope upward, by recognizing that the liquidity premium rises with a bond's maturity because of investors' preferences for short-term bonds. Even if short-term interest rates are expected to stay the same on average in the future, long-term interest rates will be above short-term interest rates, and yield curves will typically slope upward.

How can the liquidity premium theory explain the occasional appearance of inverted yield curves if the liquidity premium is positive? It must be that at times short-term interest rates are expected to fall so much in the future that the average of the expected short-term rates is well below the current short-term rate. Even when the positive liquidity premium is added to this average, the resulting long-term rate will still be below the current short-term interest rate.

As our discussion indicates, a particularly attractive feature of the liquidity premium theory is that it tells you what the market is predicting about future short-term interest rates just from the slope of the yield curve. A steeply rising yield curve, as in panel (a) of Figure 6-6, indicates that short-term interest rates are expected to

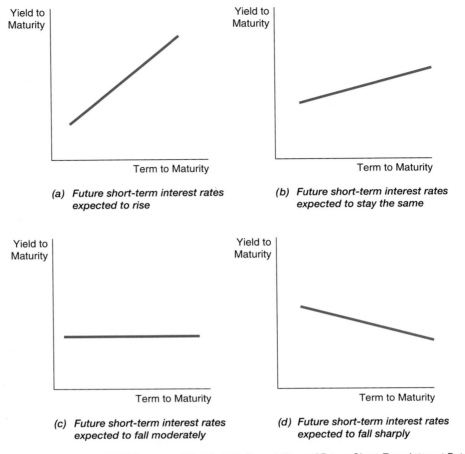

(a) *Future short-term interest rates expected to rise*

(b) *Future short-term interest rates expected to stay the same*

(c) *Future short-term interest rates expected to fall moderately*

(d) *Future short-term interest rates expected to fall sharply*

FIGURE 6-6   Yield Curves and the Market's Expectations of Future Short-Term Interest Rates According to the Liquidity Premium Theory

rise in the future. A moderately steep yield curve, as in panel (b), indicates that short-term interest rates are not expected to rise or fall much in the future. A flat yield curve, as in panel (c), indicates that short-term rates are expected to fall moderately in the future. Finally, an inverted yield curve, as in panel (d), indicates that short-term interest rates are expected to fall sharply in the future.

The Predictive Power of the Yield Curve

People often think that the slope of the yield curve can be used to forecast future short-term interest rates. The yield curve has this practical use only if it is determined by the expectations theory of the term structure that views long-term interest rates as equalling the average of future short-term interest rates. If, however, there are liquidity (term) premiums in the term structure, then it will be difficult to extract a reliable forecast of future short-term interest rates without good measures of these premiums.

In the 1980s, researchers examining the term structure of interest rates questioned whether the slope of the yield curve provides information about movements of future short-term interest rates.[6] They found that the spread between

[6]Robert J. Shiller, John Y. Campbell, and Kermit L. Schoenholtz, "Forward Rates and Future Policy: Interpreting the Term Structure of Interest Rates," *Brookings Papers on Economic Activity* 1 (1983): 173–217; N. Gregory Mankiw and Lawrence H. Summers, "Do Long-Term Interest Rates Overreact to Short-Term Interest Rates?" *Brookings Papers on Economic Activity* 1 (1984): 223–242.

long- and short-term interest rates does not always help predict future short-term interest rates, a finding that may stem from substantial fluctuations in the liquidity premium for long-term bonds. More recent research using more discriminating tests now favours a different view. It shows that the term structure contains quite a bit of information for the very short run, over the next several months, and the long run, over several years, but is unreliable at predicting movements in interest rates over the intermediate term, the time in between.[7]

Summary

The liquidity premium theory is the most widely accepted theory of the term structure of interest rates because it explains the major empirical facts about the term structure so well. It combines the features of both the expectations theory and the segmented markets theory by asserting that a long-term interest rate will be the sum of a liquidity (term) premium and the average of the short-term interest rates that are expected to occur over the life of the bond.

The liquidity premium theory explains the following facts: (1) Interest rates on bonds of different maturities tend to move together over time, (2) yield curves usually slope upward, and (3) when short-term interest rates are low, yield curves are more likely to have a steep upward slope, whereas when short-term interest rates are high, yield curves are more likely to be inverted.

The theory also helps us predict the movement of short-term interest rates in the future. A steep upward slope of the yield curve means that short-term rates are expected to rise, a mild upward slope means that short-term rates are expected to remain the same, a flat slope means that short-term rates are expected to fall moderately, and an inverted yield curve means that short-term rates are expected to fall sharply.

APPLICATION | *Interpreting Yield Curves, 1990–2000*

Figure 6-7 illustrates several yield curves that have appeared for Canadian government bonds in recent years. What do these yield curves tell us about the public's expectations of future movements of short-term interest rates?

Study Guide

Try to answer the preceding question before reading further in the text. If you have trouble answering it with the liquidity premium theory, first try answering it with the expectations theory (which is simpler because you don't have to worry about the liquidity premium). When you understand what the expectations of future interest rates are in this case, modify your analysis by taking the liquidity premium into account.

[7]Eugene Fama, "The Information in the Term Structure," *Journal of Financial Economics* 13 (1984): 509–528; Eugene Fama and Robert Bliss, "The Information in Long-Maturity Forward Rates," *American Economic Review* 77 (1987): 680–692; John Y. Campbell and Robert J. Shiller, "Cointegration and Tests of the Present Value Models," *Journal of Political Economy* 95 (1987): 1062–1088; John Y. Campbell and Robert J. Shiller, "Yield Spreads and Interest Rate Movements: A Bird's Eye View," *Review of Economic Studies* 58 (1991): 495–514.

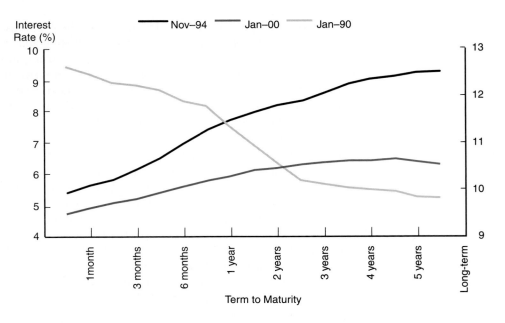

FIGURE 6-7   Yield Curves for Government of Canada Bonds, 1990–2000

Source: Statistics Canada CANSIM Series B14059, B14060, B14061, B14062, B14067, B14068, B14069, B14071, B14072, and the author's calculations.

The steep inverted yield curve that occurred in January 1990 indicated that short-term interest rates were expected to decline sharply in the future. In order for longer-term interest rates with their positive liquidity premium to be well below the short-term interest rate, short-term interest rates must be expected to decline so sharply that their average is far below the current short-term rate. Indeed, the public's expectations of sharply lower short-term interest rates evident in the yield curve were realized soon after January 1990; by June 1991, one-month Treasury bill rates had declined from over 12% to less than 9%.

The steep upward-sloping yield curve in November 1994, indicates that short-term interest rates would climb in the future. The long-term interest rate is above the short-term interest rate when short-term interest rates are expected to rise because their average plus the liquidity premium will be above the current short-term rate. The moderately upward-sloping yield curve in January 2000 indicates that short-term interest rates were expected neither to rise nor to fall in the near future. In this case, their average remains the same as the current short-term rate, and the positive liquidity premium for longer-term bonds explains the moderate upward slope of the yield curve.

SUMMARY

1. Bonds with the same maturity will have different interest rates because of three factors: default risk, liquidity, and tax considerations. The greater a bond's default risk, the higher its interest rate rela- tive to other bonds; the greater a bond's liquidity, the lower its interest rate; and bonds with tax- exempt status will have lower interest rates than they otherwise would. The relationship among

interest rates on bonds with the same maturity that arises because of these three factors is known as the risk structure of interest rates.

2. Three theories of the term structure provide explanations of how interest rates on bonds with different terms to maturity are related. The expectations theory views long-term interest rates as equalling the average of future short-term interest rates expected to occur over the life of the bond; by contrast, the segmented markets theory treats the determination of interest rates for each bond's maturity as the outcome of supply and demand in that market only. Neither of these theories by itself can explain the fact that interest rates on bonds of different maturities move together over time and that yield curves usually slope upward.

3. The liquidity premium theory combines the features of the other two theories and by so doing is able to explain the facts just mentioned. It views long-term interest rates as equalling the average of future short-term interest rates expected to occur over the life of the bond plus a liquidity premium. This theory allows us to infer the market's expectations about the movement of future short-term interest rates from the yield curve. A steeply upward-sloping curve indicates that future short-term rates are expected to rise, a mildly upward-sloping curve indicates that short-term rates are expected to stay the same, a flat curve indicates that short-term rates are expected to decline slightly, and an inverted yield curve indicates that a substantial decline in short-term rates is expected in the future.

KEY TERMS

default-free bonds, p. 114

default risk, p. 114

expectations theory, p. 121

fallen angels, p. 116

inverted yield curve, p. 119

junk bonds, p. 116

liquidity premium theory, p. 125

risk premium, p. 114

risk structure of interest rates, p. 113

segmented markets theory, p. 124

term structure of interest rates, p. 113

yield curve, p. 119

QUESTIONS AND PROBLEMS

Questions marked with an asterisk are answered at the end of the book in an appendix, "Answers to Selected Questions and Problems."

1. Which should have the higher risk premium on its interest rates, a corporate bond with a S & P B++ rating or a corporate bond with a C rating? Why?

*2. Why do Canadian Treasury bills have lower interest rates than large-denomination negotiable bank CDs?

3. Risk premiums on corporate bonds are usually anticyclical; that is, they decrease during business cycle expansions and increase during recessions. Why is this so?

*4. "If bonds of different maturities are close substitutes, their interest rates are more likely to move together." Is this statement true, false, or uncertain? Explain your answer.

5. If yield curves, on average, were flat, what would this say about the liquidity (term) premiums in the term structure? Would you be more or less willing to accept the expectations theory?

*6. Assuming that the expectations theory is the correct theory of the term structure, calculate the interest rates in the term structure for maturities of one to five years, and plot the resulting yield curves for the following series of one-year interest rates over the next five years:
   (a) 5%, 7%, 7%, 7%, 7%
   (b) 5%, 4%, 4%, 4%, 4%
   How would your yield curves change if people preferred shorter-term bonds to longer-term bonds?

7. Assuming that the expectations theory is the correct theory of the term structure, calculate the interest rates in the term structure for maturities of one to five years, and plot the resulting yield curves for the following path of one-year interest rates over the next five years:
   (a) 5%, 6%, 7%, 6%, 5%
   (b) 5%, 4%, 3%, 4%, 5%
   How would your yield curves change if people preferred shorter-term bonds to longer-term bonds?

*8. If a yield curve looks like the one shown in (a), what is the market predicting about the movement of future short-term interest rates? What might the yield curve indicate about the market's predictions about the inflation rate in the future?

9. If a yield curve looks like the one shown in (b), what is the market predicting about the movement of future short-term interest rates? What might the yield curve indicate about the market's predictions about the inflation rate in the future?

*10. What are the financial implications of a firm with a high default risk?

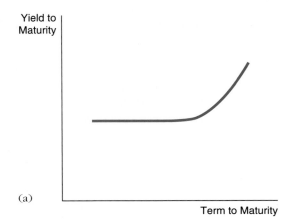

(a)

Yield to Maturity

Term to Maturity

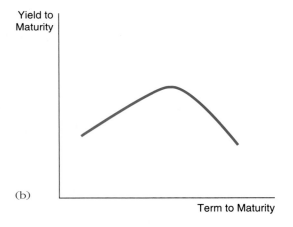

(b)

Yield to Maturity

Term to Maturity

Using Economic Analysis to Predict the Future

11. Predict what will happen to interest rates on a corporation's bonds if the federal government guarantees today that it will pay creditors if the corporation goes bankrupt in the future. What will happen to the interest rates on Canada bonds?

*12. Predict what would happen to the risk premiums on corporate bonds if brokerage commissions were lowered in the corporate bond market.

13. Predict what would happen to yield spreads in response to the following macroeconomic events: recession, high inflation, and stock market increase.

*14. If the yield curve suddenly becomes steeper, how would you revise your predictions of interest rates in the future?

15. If expectations of future short-term interest rates suddenly fall, what would happen to the slope of the yield curve?

Chapter 7

The Foreign Exchange Market

PREVIEW   More foreigners are travelling to Canada now than in the early 1980s. The increase in foreigners travelling to Canada did not occur because foreigners suddenly increased their taste for adventure. The increase occurred because Canadian dollars had become cheaper in terms of foreign currencies—a change that made it less expensive for foreigners to travel here.

The price of one currency in terms of another (say euros per dollar) is called the **exchange rate**. It affects the economy and our daily lives because when the Canadian dollar becomes less valuable relative to foreign currencies, foreign goods and overseas travel become more expensive. When the Canadian dollar rises in value, foreign goods and travel become cheaper. We begin our study of international finance by examining the **foreign exchange market**, the financial market where exchange rates are determined.

In the 1980s, exchange rates were highly volatile. As shown in Figure 7-1, from the beginning of 1980 to early 1985 the dollar strengthened, and its value relative to many other currencies (such as the German mark, the British pound, and the French franc) climbed sharply—54% against the pound sterling, 38% against the German mark, and 24% against the Swiss franc. From early 1992 to the end of 1999, the dollar weakened and fell in value relative to other currencies—over 27% against the Japanese yen, 13% against the Swiss franc, and 19% against the U.S. dollar. What factors explain the former strength and later weakness of the dollar that has caused foreign goods to be more expensive since 1985 and has made overseas travel less of a bargain? Why are exchange rates so volatile from day to day?

To answer these questions, we develop a modern view of exchange rate determination that explains recent behaviour in the foreign exchange market.

FOREIGN EXCHANGE MARKET

Most countries of the world have their own currencies: Canada has its dollar; the European Monetary Union, the euro; Brazil, its real; and India, its rupee. Trade between countries involves the mutual exchange of different currencies (or,

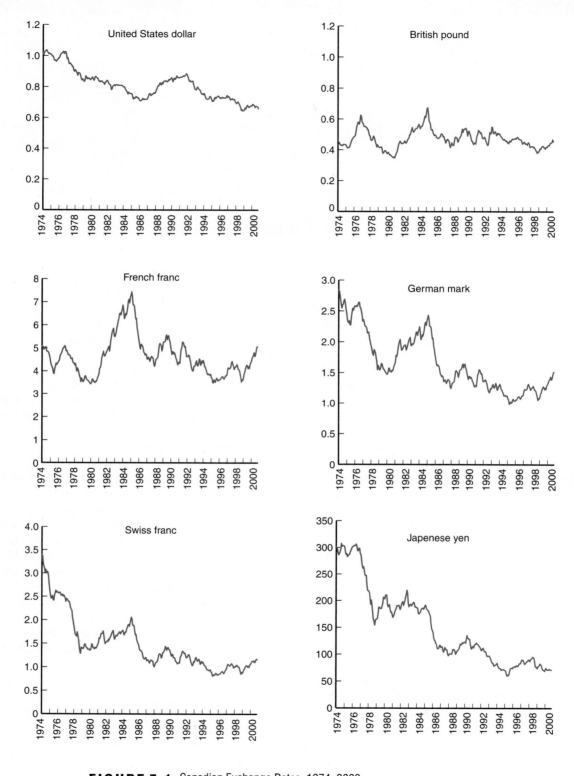

FIGURE 7-1 Canadian Exchange Rates, 1974–2000

Dollar prices of selected foreign currencies (monthly averages). Note that a decline in these plots means a strengthening of the dollar, and an increase indicates a weakening of the dollar.

Source: Statistics Canada CANSIM Series B3400, B3412, B3404, B3405, B43411, and B3407.

more usually, bank deposits denominated in different currencies). When a Canadian firm buys foreign goods, services, or financial assets, for example, Canadian dollars (typically, bank deposits denominated in Canadian dollars) must be exchanged for foreign currency (bank deposits denominated in the foreign currency).

The trading of currency and bank deposits denominated in particular currencies takes place in the foreign exchange market. Transactions conducted in the foreign exchange market determine the rates at which currencies are exchanged, which in turn determine the cost of purchasing foreign goods and financial assets.

What Are Foreign Exchange Rates?

There are two kinds of exchange rate transactions. The predominant ones, called **spot transactions**, involve the immediate (two-day) exchange of bank deposits. **Forward transactions** involve the exchange of bank deposits at some specified future date. The **spot exchange rate** is the exchange rate for the spot transaction, and the **forward exchange rate** is the exchange rate for the forward transaction.

When a currency increases in value, it experiences **appreciation**; when it falls in value and is worth fewer Canadian dollars, it undergoes **depreciation**. At the beginning of 1999, for example, the euro was valued at 1.76 dollars, and as indicated in the "Following the Financial News" box, on November 17, 2000, it was valued at 1.32 dollars. The euro *depreciated* by 25%: $(1.32 - 1.76)/1.76 = -0.25 = -25\%$. Equivalently, we could say that the Canadian dollar, which went from a value of 0.56 euros per dollar at the beginning of 1999 to a value of 0.75 euros per dollar on November 17, 2000, *appreciated* by 33%: $(0.75 - 0.56)/0.56 = 0.33 = 33\%$.

Why Are Exchange Rates Important?

Exchange rates are important because they affect the relative price of domestic and foreign goods. The dollar price of French goods to a Canadian is determined by the interaction of two factors: the price of French goods in francs and the franc/dollar exchange rate.

Suppose that Wanda the Winetaster, a Canadian, decides to buy a bottle of 1961 (a very good year) Château Lafite Rothschild to complete her wine cellar. If the price of the wine in France is 1000 euros and the exchange rate is $1.32 to the euro, the wine will cost Wanda $1320 (1000 euros × $1.32/euro). Now suppose that Wanda delays her purchase by two months, at which time the euro has appreciated to $1.50 per euro. If the domestic price of the bottle of Lafite Rothschild remains 1000 euros, its dollar cost will have risen from $1320 to $1500.

The same currency appreciation, however, makes the price of foreign goods in that country less expensive. At an exchange rate of $1.32 per euro, a Compaq computer priced at $2000 costs Pierre the Programmer 1515 euros; if the exchange rate increases to $1.50 per euro, the computer will cost only 1333 euros.

A depreciation of the euro lowers the cost of French goods in Canada but raises the cost of Canadian goods in France. If the euro drops in value to $1.20, Wanda's bottle of Lafite Rothschild will cost her only $1200 instead of $1320, and the Compaq computer will cost Pierre 1667 euros rather than 1515.

Such reasoning leads to the following conclusion: ***when a country's currency appreciates (rises in value relative to other currencies), the country's goods abroad become more expensive and foreign goods in that country become cheaper (holding domestic prices constant in the two countries). Conversely, when a country's currency depreciates, its goods abroad become cheaper and foreign goods in that country become more expensive.***

Appreciation of a currency can make it harder for domestic manufacturers to sell their goods abroad and can increase competition at home from foreign goods because they cost less. From early 1986 to early 1992, the appreciating Canadian dollar against the U.S. dollar hurt Canadian industries. For example, the Canadian

FOLLOWING THE FINANCIAL NEWS

Foreign Exchange Rates

Foreign exchange rates are published daily and appear in the "Foreign Exchange" column of the *Globe and Mail: Report on Business*. The entries from one such column, shown here, are explained in the text.

Panel (a) gives the cross rates for several currencies in Toronto on March 22, 2001. For example, we find that $/Can $ = 0.6359 by looking across the U.S. dollar row for the Canadian dollar column. To find the U.S dollar price of euros, we look across the U.S. dollar row for the euro column and see that $/euro = 0.8972. By dividing $/euro by $/Can $, we find the

implied cross rate for Can $/euro = 1.4109, which is the same as the rate that we find by looking across the Canadian dollar column for the euro column.

In panel (b), the first entry for the euro lists the exchange rate for the spot transaction (the spot exchange rate) on March 22, 2001, and is quoted in two ways: Cdn.$ 1.4109 per euro and U.S.$ 0.8972 per euro. The entries immediately after the spot exchange rate for some currencies give the rates for forward transactions (the forward exchange rates) that will take place 1 month, 2 months, and so on, in the future.

FOREIGN EXCHANGE

CROSS RATES

	Canadian dollar	U.S. dollar	German mark	British pound	Japanese yen	Swiss franc	French franc	Euro	Italian lira
Canadian dollar	—	1.5726	2.2499	0.7214	0.012720	0.9203	0.2151	1.4109	0.000729
U.S. dollar	0.6359	—	1.4307	0.457	0.008089	0.5852	0.1368	0.8972	0.000464
British pound	0.4445	0.6990	—	-0.3206	0.005654	0.4090	0.0956	0.6271	0.000324
German mark	1.3862	2.1799	3.1188	—	0.017632	1.2757	0.2982	1.9558	0.001011
Japanese yen	78.62	123.63	176.88	56.71	—	72.35	16.91	110.92	0.057311
Swiss franc	1.0866	1.7088	2.4447	0.7839	0.013822	—	0.2337	1.5331	0.000792
French franc	4.6490	7.3110	10.4598	3.3538	0.059135	4.2785	—	6.5593	0.003389
Euro	0.7088	1.1146	1.5947	0.5113	0.009016	0.6523	0.1525	—	0.000517
Italian lira	1371.74	2157.20	3086.28	989.57	17.448560	1262.41	295.06	1935.39	—

Mid-market rates in Toronto at noon, Mar. 21, 2001. Prepared by BMP Nesbitt Burns, Capital Markets.

		$1 U.S. in Cdn.$ =	$1 Cdn. in U.S.$ =
U.S./Canada spot		1.5726	0.6359
1 month forward		1.5724	0.6360
2 months forward		1.5720	0.6361
3 months forward		1.5717	0.6363
6 months forward		1.5710	0.6365
12 months forward		1.5699	0.6370
3 years forward		1.5641	0.6393
5 years forward		1.5554	0.6429
7 years forward		1.5531	0.6439
10 years forward		1.5591	0.6414
Canadian dollar in 2001:	High	1.4901	0.6711
	Low	1.5772	0.6340
	Average	1.5230	0.6466

Country	Currency	Cdn. $ per unit	U.S. per unit
Britain	Pound	2.2499	1.4307
1 month forward		2.287	1.4301
2 months forward		2.2472	1.4295
3 months forward		2.2455	1.4287
6 months forward		2.2409	1.4264
12 months forward		2.2335	1.4227
Europe	Euro	1.4109	0.8972
1 month forward		1.4110	0.8974
3 months forward		1.4107	0.8976
6 months forward		1.4103	0.8977
12 months forward		1.4113	0.8990
Japan	Yen	0.012720	0.008089
1 month forward		0.012772	0.008123
3 months forward		0.012869	0.008188
6 months forward		0.013005	0.008278
12 months forward		0.013278	0.008458
Algeria	Dinar	0.02126	0.0135
Antigua, Grenada and St. Lucia	E.C. Dollar	0.5890	0.3745
Argentina	Peso	1.57291	1.00020
Australia	Dollar	0.7772	0.4942
Austria	Schill	0.10253	0.06520
Bahamas	Dollar	1.5726	1.0000
Barbados	Dollar	0.7903	0.5025
Belgium	Franc	0.03498	0.02224
Bermuda	Dollar	1.5726	1.0000
Brazil	Real	0.7471	0.4751
Bulgaria	Lev	0.72134	0.4598
Chile	Peso	0.002678	0.001703
China	Renminbi	0.1900	0.1208
Cyprus	Pound	2.4314	1.5461
Czech Rep	Krouna	0.0408	0.0259
Denmark	Krone	0.1890	0.1202
Egypt	Pound	0.4053	0.2577
Fiji	Dollar	0.6868	0.4367

Country	Currency	Cdn. $ per unit	U.S. per unit
Finland	Markka	0.2373	0.1509
France	Franc	0.2151	0.1368
Germany	Mark	0.7214	0.4587
Greece	Drachma	0.004141	0.002633
Hong Kong	Dollar	0.2016	0.1282
Hungary	Forint	0.00529	0.00336
Iceland	Krona	0.01785	0.01135
India	Rupee	0.03370	0.02143
Indonesia	Rupiah	0.000151	0.000096
Ireland	Punt	1.7915	1.1392
Israel	N Shekel	0.3744	0.2381
Italy	Lira	0.000729	0.000464
Jamaica	Dollar	0.03456	0.02198
Jordan	Dinar	2.2212	1.4124
Lebanon	Pound	0.001039	0.000661
Luxenbourg	Franc	0.03498	0.02224
Malaysia	Ringgit	0.4139	0.2632
Mexico	N Peso	0.1650	0.1049
Netherlands	Guildr	0.6402	0.4071
New Zealand	Dollar	0.6523	0.4148
Norway	Krone	0.1736	0.1104
Pakistan	Rupee	0.02625	0.01669
Panama	Balboa	1.5726	1.0000
Philippines	Peso	0.03253	0.02068
Poland	Zloty	0.3822	0.2430
Portugal	Escudo	0.00704	0.00448
Romania	Leu	0.000057	0.000036
Russia	Ruble	0.054737	0.034807
Saudi Arabia	Riyal	0.4193	0.2666
Singapore	Dollar	0.8812	0.5603
Slovakia	Krouna	0.0323	0.0206
South Africa	Rand	0.1967	0.1251
South Korea	Won	0.001214	0.000772
Spain	Peseta	0.00848	0.00539
Sudan	Dinar	0.00611	0.0039
Sweden	Krona	0.1535	0.0976
Switzerland	Franc	0.9203	0.5852
Taiwan	Dollar	0.04806	0.0306
Thailand	Baht	0.2520	0.1603
Trinidad, Tobago	Dollar	0.2520	0.1603
Turkey	Lira	0.0000016	0.0000010
Venezuela	Bolivar	0.002231	0.00142
Zambia	Kwacha	0.000467	0.000297
Spec Draw Right S.D.R.		1.9969	1.2698

The U.S. dollar closed at $1.5759 in terms of Canadian funds, up $0.0102 from Tuesday. The pound sterling closed at $2.2550, up $0.0071.
In New York, the Canadian dollar closed down $0.0041 at $0.6346 in terms of U.S. funds. The pound sterling was down $0.0048 to $1.4309.

Source: The Globe and Mail: Report on Business, Thursday, March 22, 2001, p. B21. Reprinted with permission.

steel industry was hurt because sales in the United States of the more expensive Canadian steel declined but also because sales of relatively cheap steel from other countries increased. Although appreciation of the Canadian dollar hurt some domestic businesses, consumers benefited because U.S. goods were less expensive. Canadian consumers also benefited in the 1980-1985 period when the cost of vacationing in Europe and the United States fell in price as a result of the strong Canadian dollar against the major European currencies and the U.S. dollar.

How Is Foreign Exchange Traded?

You cannot go to a centralized location to watch exchange rates being determined; currencies are not traded on exchanges such as the Toronto Stock Exchange. Instead, the foreign exchange market is organized as an over-the-counter market in which several hundred dealers (mostly banks) stand ready to buy and sell deposits denominated in foreign currencies. Because these dealers are in constant telephone and computer contact, the market is very competitive; in effect, it functions no differently from a centralized market.

An important point to note is that while banks, companies, and governments talk about buying and selling currencies in foreign exchange markets, they do not take a fistful of dollar bills and sell them for British pound notes. Rather, most trades involve the buying and selling of bank deposits denominated in different currencies. So when we say that a bank is buying dollars in the foreign exchange market, what we actually mean is that the bank is buying *deposits denominated in dollars*. The volume in this market is colossal, exceeding $1 trillion per day.

Trades in the foreign exchange market consist of transactions in excess of $1 million. The market that determines the exchange rates in the "Following the Financial News" box is not where one would buy foreign currency for a trip abroad. Instead, we buy foreign currency in the retail market from dealers such as Thomas Cook or from banks. Because retail prices are higher than wholesale, when we buy foreign exchange, we obtain fewer units of foreign currency per dollar than exchange rates in the box indicate.

EXCHANGE RATES IN THE LONG RUN

Like the price of any good or asset in a free market, exchange rates are determined by the interaction of supply and demand. To simplify our analysis of exchange rates in a free market, we divide it into two parts. First, we examine how exchange rates are determined in the long run; then we use our knowledge of the long-run determinants of the exchange rate to help us understand how they are determined in the short run.

Law of One Price

The starting point for understanding how exchange rates are determined is a simple idea called the **law of one price**: if two countries produce an identical good, and transportation costs and trade barriers are very low, the price of the good should be the same throughout the world no matter which country produces it.

Suppose that Canadian steel costs $100 per ton and identical Japanese steel costs 10 000 yen per ton. The law of one price suggests that the exchange rate between the yen and the dollar must be 100 yen per dollar ($0.01 per yen) in order for one ton of Canadian steel to sell for 10 000 yen in Japan (the price of Japanese steel) and one ton of Japanese steel to sell for $100 in Canada (the price of Canadian steel). If the exchange rate were 200 yen to the dollar, Japanese steel would sell for $50 per ton in Canada or half the price of Canadian steel, and Canadian steel would sell for 20 000 yen per ton in Japan, twice the price of Japanese steel. Because Canadian steel would be more expensive than Japanese steel in both countries and is identical to Japanese steel, the demand for Canadian steel would go to zero. Given a fixed dollar price for Canadian steel, the resulting excess supply of Canadian steel will be eliminated only if the exchange rate falls to 100 yen per dollar, making the price of Canadian steel and Japanese steel the same in both countries.

Theory of Purchasing Power Parity

One of the most prominent theories of how exchange rates are determined is the **theory of purchasing power parity** (**PPP**). It states that exchange rates between any two currencies will adjust to reflect changes in the price levels of the two countries. The theory of PPP is simply an application of the law of one price to national price levels rather than to individual prices. Suppose that the yen price of Japanese steel rises 10% (to 11 000 yen) relative to the dollar price of Canadian steel (unchanged at $100). For the law of one price to hold, the exchange rate must rise to 110 yen to the dollar, a 10% appreciation of the dollar. Applying the law of one price to the price levels in the two countries produces the theory of purchasing power parity, which maintains that if the Japanese price level rises 10% relative to the Canadian price level, the dollar will appreciate by 10%.

As our Canadian/Japanese example demonstrates, the theory of PPP suggests that if one country's price level rises relative to another's, its currency should depreciate (the other country's currency should appreciate). As you can see in Figure 7-2, this prediction is borne out in the long run. From 1973 to 2000, the U.S. price level fell 5% relative to the Canadian price level, and as the theory of PPP predicts, the Canadian dollar depreciated against the U.S. dollar, though by 31%, an amount larger than the 5% decrease predicted by PPP.

Yet, as the same figure indicates, PPP theory often has little predictive power in the short run. From early 1985 to the end of 1992, for example, the U.S. price level fell relative to that of Canada. Instead of depreciating, as PPP theory predicts, the Canadian dollar actually appreciated by 7.2% against the U.S. dollar. So even though PPP theory provides some guidance to the long-run movement of exchange rates, it is not perfect and in the short run is a particularly poor predictor (see Box 7-1). What explains PPP theory's failure to predict well?

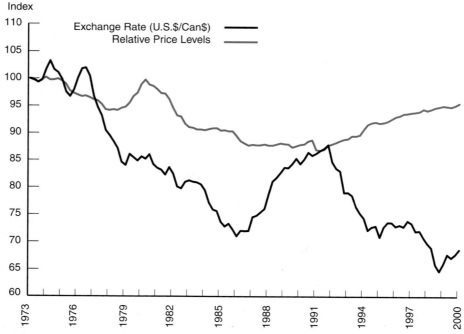

FIGURE 7-2 Purchasing Power Parity, Canada/United States, 1973–2000

Source: International Monetary Fund, *International Financial Statistics.* Reprinted with permission.

```
BOX 7-1
```

The Purchasing Power Parity Puzzle

The theory of purchasing power parity has attracted a great deal of attention and has been explored extensively in the recent literature using recent advances in the field of applied econometrics. Based on the law of one price, the theory asserts that relative goods prices are not affected by exchange rates—or, equivalently, that exchange rate changes will be proportional to relative inflation. The relationship is important not only because it has been a cornerstone of exchange rate models in international economics, but also because of its policy implications—it provides a benchmark exchange rate and therefore has some practical appeal for policymakers and exchange rate arbitragers.

Empirical studies generally fail to find support for long-run purchasing power parity, especially during the recent floating exchange rate period. In fact, the empirical consensus is that purchasing power parity does not hold over this period. But there are also studies covering different groups of countries as well as studies covering periods of long duration or country pairs experiencing large differentials in price movements that report evidence consistent with the theory of purchasing power parity. For an excellent discussion of the purchasing power parity puzzle, see Kenneth Rogoff, "The Purchasing Power Parity Puzzle," *Journal of Economic Literature* 34 (1996): 647-668.

Why the Theory of Purchasing Power Parity Cannot Fully Explain Exchange Rates

The PPP conclusion that exchange rates are determined solely by changes in relative price levels rests on the assumption that all goods are identical in both countries and that transportation costs and trade barriers are very low. When this assumption is true, the law of one price states that the relative prices of all these goods (that is, the relative price level between the two countries) will determine the exchange rate. The assumption that goods are identical may not be too unreasonable for Canadian and Japanese steel, but is it a reasonable assumption for Canadian and Japanese cars? Is a Toyota the equivalent of a Chevrolet?

Because Toyotas and Chevys are obviously not identical, their prices do not have to be equal. Toyotas can be more expensive relative to Chevys and both Canadians and Japanese will still purchase Toyotas. Because the law of one price does not hold for all goods, a rise in the price of Toyotas relative to Chevys will not necessarily mean that the yen must depreciate by the amount of the relative price increase of Toyotas over Chevys.

PPP theory furthermore does not take into account that many goods and services (whose prices are included in a measure of a country's price level) are not traded across borders. Housing, land, and services such as restaurant meals, haircuts, and golf lessons are not traded goods. So even though the prices of these items might rise and lead to a higher price level relative to another country's, there would be little direct effect on the exchange rate.

Factors That Affect Exchange Rates in the Long Run

Our analysis indicates that in the long run, four major factors affect the exchange rate: relative price levels, tariffs and quotas, preferences for domestic versus foreign goods, and productivity. We examine how each of these factors affects the exchange rate while holding the others constant.

The basic reasoning proceeds along the following lines: anything that increases the demand for domestic goods relative to foreign goods tends to appreciate the domestic currency because domestic goods will continue to sell well even when the value of the domestic currency is higher. Similarly, anything that increases the demand for foreign goods relative to domestic goods tends to depreciate the domestic currency because domestic goods will continue to sell well only if the value of the domestic currency is lower.

Relative Price Levels   In line with PPP theory, when prices of Canadian goods rise (holding prices of foreign goods constant), the demand for Canadian goods falls and the dollar tends to depreciate so that Canadian goods can still sell well. By contrast, if prices of Japanese goods rise so that the relative prices of Canadian goods fall, the demand for Canadian goods increases, and the dollar tends to appreciate because Canadian goods will continue to sell well even with a higher value of the domestic currency. *In the long run, a rise in a country's price level (relative to the foreign price level) causes its currency to depreciate, and a fall in the country's relative price level causes its currency to appreciate.*

Tariffs and Quotas   Barriers to free trade such as **tariffs** (taxes on imported goods) and **quotas** (restrictions on the quantity of foreign goods that can be imported) can affect the exchange rate. Suppose that Canada imposes a tariff or a quota on Japanese cars. These trade barriers increase the demand for Canadian cars, and the dollar tends to appreciate because Canadian cars will still sell well even with a higher value of the dollar. *Tariffs and quotas cause a country's currency to appreciate in the long run.*

Preferences for Domestic Versus Foreign Goods   If the Japanese develop an appetite for Canadian goods—say, for Bombardier's high-speed trains and Canadian beef and pork—the increased demand for Canadian goods (exports) tends to appreciate the dollar because the Canadian goods will continue to sell well even at a higher value for the dollar. Likewise, if Canadians decide that they prefer Japanese cars to Canadian cars, the increased demand for Japanese goods (imports) tends to depreciate the dollar. *Increased demand for a country's exports causes its currency to appreciate in the long run; conversely, increased demand for imports causes the domestic currency to depreciate.*

Productivity   If one country becomes more productive than other countries, businesses in that country can lower the prices of domestic goods relative to foreign goods and still earn a profit. As a result, the demand for domestic goods rises, and the domestic currency tends to appreciate because domestic goods will continue to sell well at a higher value for the currency. If, however, its productivity lags behind that of other countries, its goods become relatively more expensive, and the currency tends to depreciate. *In the long run, as a country becomes more productive relative to other countries, its currency appreciates.*[1]

Study Guide

The trick to figuring out what long-run effect a factor has on the exchange rate is to remember the following: **if a factor increases the demand for domestic goods relative to foreign goods, the domestic currency will appreciate, and if a factor decreases the relative demand for domestic goods, the domestic currency will depreciate**. See how this works by explaining what happens to the exchange rate when any of the factors in Table 7-1 declines rather than increases.

---

[1] A country might be so small that a change in productivity or the preferences for domestic or foreign goods would have no effect on prices of these goods relative to foreign goods. In this case, changes in productivity or changes in preferences for domestic or foreign goods affect the country's income but will not necessarily affect the value of the currency. In our analysis, we are assuming that these factors can affect relative prices and consequently the exchange rate.

TABLE 7-1 Factors That Affect Exchange Rates in the Long Run

Factor	Change in Factor	Response of the Exchange Rate, E^*
Domestic price level†	↑	↓
Tariffs and quotas†	↑	↑
Import demand	↑	↓
Export demand	↑	↑
Productivity†	↑	↑

*Units of foreign currency per dollar: ↑ indicates domestic currency appreciation; ↓, depreciation.

†Relative to other countries.

Note: Only increases (↑) in the factors are shown; the effects of decreases in the variables on the exchange rate are the opposite of those indicated in the "Response" column.

Our long-run theory of exchange rate behaviour is summarized in Table 7-1. We use the convention that the exchange rate E is quoted so that an appreciation of the currency corresponds to a rise in the exchange rate. In the case of Canada, this means that we are quoting the exchange rate as units of foreign currency per dollar (say, yen per dollar).[2]

EXCHANGE RATES IN THE SHORT RUN

We have developed a theory of the long-run behaviour of exchange rates. However, if we are to understand why exchange rates exhibit such large changes (sometimes several percent) from day to day, we must develop a theory of how current exchange rates (spot exchange rates) are determined in the short run.

The key to understanding the short-run behaviour of exchange rates is to recognize that an exchange rate is the price of domestic bank deposits (those denominated in the domestic currency) in terms of foreign bank deposits (those denominated in the foreign currency). Because the exchange rate is the price of one asset in terms of another, the natural way to investigate the short-run determination of exchange rates is through an asset market approach that relies heavily on the theory of asset demand developed in Chapter 5. As you will see, however, the long-run determinants of the exchange rate we have just outlined also play an important role in the short-run asset market approach.[3]

Earlier approaches to exchange rate determination emphasized the role of import and export demand. The more modern asset market approach used here does not emphasize the flows of purchases of exports and imports over short periods because these transactions are quite small relative to the amount of domestic and foreign bank deposits at any given time. For example, foreign exchange transactions in Canada each year are well over 25 times greater than

---

[2]Exchange rates can be quoted either as units of foreign currency per domestic currency or alternatively as units of domestic currency per foreign currency. In professional writing, many economists quote exchange rates as units of domestic currency per foreign currency so that an appreciation of the domestic currency is portrayed as a fall in the exchange rate. The opposite convention is used in the text here because it is more intuitive to think of an appreciation of the domestic currency as a rise in the exchange rate.

[3]For a further description of the modern asset market approach to exchange rate determination that we use here, see Paul Krugman and Maurice Obstfeld, *International Economics*, 5th ed. (Reading, Mass.: Addison Wesley Longman, 2000).

the amount of Canadian exports and imports. Thus over short periods such as a year, decisions to hold domestic or foreign assets play a much greater role in exchange rate determination than the demand for exports and imports does.

Comparing Expected Returns on Domestic and Foreign Deposits

In this analysis, we treat Canada as the home country, so as an example domestic bank deposits are denominated in Canadian dollars. For simplicity, we use euros to stand for any foreign country's currency; so foreign bank deposits are denominated in euros. The theory of asset demand suggests that the most important factor affecting the demand for domestic (dollar) deposits and foreign (euro) deposits is the expected return on these assets relative to each other. When Canadians or foreigners expect the return on dollar deposits to be high relative to the return on foreign deposits, there is a higher demand for dollar deposits and a correspondingly lower demand for euro deposits. To understand how the demands for dollar and foreign deposits change, we need to compare the expected returns on dollar deposits and foreign deposits.

To illustrate further, suppose that dollar deposits have an interest rate (expected return payable in dollars) of i^D, and foreign bank deposits have an interest rate (expected return payable in the foreign currency, euros) of i^F. To compare the expected returns on dollar deposits and foreign deposits, investors must convert the returns into the currency unit they use.

First let us examine how François the Foreigner compares the returns on dollar deposits and foreign deposits denominated in his currency, the euro. When he considers the expected return on dollar deposits in terms of euros, he recognizes that it does not equal i^D; instead, the expected return must be adjusted for any expected appreciation or depreciation of the dollar. If the dollar were expected to appreciate by 7%, for example, the expected return on dollar deposits in terms of euros would be 7% higher because the dollar has become worth 7% more in terms of euros. Thus if the interest rate on dollar deposits is 10%, with an expected appreciation of the dollar of 7%, the expected return on dollar deposits in terms of euros is 17%: the 10% interest rate plus the 7% expected appreciation of the dollar. Conversely, if the dollar were expected to depreciate by 7% over the year, the expected return on dollar deposits in terms of euros would be only 3%: the 10% interest rate minus the 7% expected depreciation of the dollar.

Writing the currency exchange rate (the spot exchange rate) as E_t and the expected exchange rate for the next period as E^e_{t+1}, we can write the expected rate of appreciation of the dollar as $(E^e_{t+1} - E_t)/E_t$. Our reasoning indicates that the expected return on dollar deposits RET^D in terms of foreign currency can be written as the sum of the interest rate on dollar deposits plus the expected appreciation of the dollar:[4]

---

[4]This expression is actually an approximation of the expected return in terms of euros, which can be more precisely calculated by thinking how a foreigner invests in the dollar deposit. Suppose that François decides to put one euro into dollar deposits. First he buys $1/E_t$ of Canadian dollar deposits (recall that E_t, the exchange rate between dollar and euro deposits, is quoted in euros per dollar), and at the end of the period he is paid $(1 + i^D)(1/E_t)$ in dollars. To convert this amount into the number of euros he expects to receive at the end of the period, he multiplies this quantity by E^e_{t+1}. François's expected return on his initial investment of one euro can thus be written as $(1 + i^D)(E^e_{t+1}/E_t)$ minus his initial investment of one euro:

$$(1 + i^D)\left(\frac{E^e_{t+1}}{E_t}\right) - 1$$

which can be rewritten as

$$i^D\left(\frac{E^e_{t+1}}{E_t}\right) + \frac{E^e_{t+1} - E_t}{E_t}$$

which is approximately equal to the expression in the text because E^e_{t+1}/E_t is typically close to 1.

$$RET^D \text{ in terms of euros} = i^D + \frac{E^e_{t+1} - E_t}{E_t}$$

However, François's expected return on foreign deposits RET^F in terms of euros is just i^F. Thus in terms of euros, the relative expected return on dollar deposits (that is, the difference between the expected return on dollar deposits and euro deposits) is calculated by subtracting i^F from the expression just given to yield

$$\text{Relative } RET^D = i^D - i^F + \frac{E^e_{t+1} - E_t}{E_t} \qquad (1)$$

As the relative expected return on dollar deposits increases, foreigners will want to hold more dollar deposits and fewer foreign deposits.

Next let us look at the decision to hold dollar deposits versus euro deposits from Al the Canadian's point of view. Following the same reasoning we used to evaluate the decision for François, we know that the expected return on foreign deposits RET^F in terms of dollars is the interest rate on foreign deposits i^F plus the expected appreciation of the foreign currency, equal to minus the expected appreciation of the dollar, $-(E^e_{t+1} - E_t)/E_t$, that is,

$$RET^F \text{ in terms of dollars} = i^F - \frac{E^e_{t+1} - E_t}{E_t}$$

If the interest rate on euro deposits is 5%, for example, and the dollar is expected to appreciate by 4%, then the expected return on euro deposits in terms of dollars is 1%. Al earns the 5% interest rate, but he expects to lose 4% because he expects the euro to be worth 4% less in terms of dollars as a result of the dollar's appreciation.

Al's expected return on the dollar deposits RET^D in terms of dollars is just i^D. Hence in terms of dollars, the relative expected return on dollar deposits is calculated by subtracting the expression just given from i^D to obtain

$$\text{Relative } RET^D = i^D - \left(i^F - \frac{E^e_{t+1} - E_t}{E_t}\right) = i^D - i^F + \frac{E^e_{t+1} - E_t}{E_t}$$

This equation is the same as the one describing François's relative expected return on dollar deposits (calculated in terms of euros). The key point here is that the relative expected return on dollar deposits is the same whether it is calculated by François in terms of euros or by Al in terms of dollars. Thus as the relative expected return on dollar deposits increases, both foreigners and domestic residents respond in exactly the same way—both will want to hold more dollar deposits and fewer foreign deposits.

Interest Parity Condition

We currently live in a world in which there is **capital mobility**: foreigners can easily purchase Canadian assets such as dollar deposits, and Canadians can easily purchase foreign assets such as euro deposits. Because foreign bank deposits and Canadian bank deposits have similar risk and liquidity and because there are few impediments to capital mobility, it is reasonable to assume that the deposits are perfect substitutes (that is, equally desirable). When capital is mobile and when bank deposits are perfect substitutes, if the expected return on dollar deposits is above that on foreign deposits, both foreigners and Canadians will want to hold only dollar deposits and will be unwilling to hold foreign deposits. Conversely, if the expected return on foreign deposits is higher than on dollar deposits, both foreigners and Canadians will not want to hold any dollar deposits and will want to hold only foreign deposits. For existing supplies of both dollar deposits and foreign deposits to be held, it must therefore be true that there is no difference in their expected returns; that is, the relative expected return in Equation 1 must equal zero. This condition can be rewritten as

$$i^D = i^F - \frac{E^e_{t+1} - E_t}{E_t} \qquad (2)$$

This equation is called the **interest parity condition**, and it states that the domestic interest rate equals the foreign interest rate minus the expected appreciation of the domestic currency. Equivalently, this condition can be stated in a more intuitive way: the domestic interest rate equals the foreign interest rate plus the expected appreciation of the foreign currency. If the domestic interest rate is above the foreign interest rate, this means that there is a positive expected appreciation of the foreign currency, which compensates for the lower foreign interest rate. A domestic interest rate of 15% versus a foreign interest rate of 10% means that the expected appreciation of the foreign currency must be 5% (or, equivalently, that the expected depreciation of the dollar must be 5%).

There are several ways to look at the interest parity condition. First, we should recognize that interest parity means simply that the expected returns are the same on both dollar deposits and foreign deposits. To see this, note that the left side of the interest parity condition (Equation 2) is the expected return on dollar deposits, while the right side is the expected return on foreign deposits, both calculated in terms of a single currency, the Canadian dollar. Given our assumption that domestic and foreign bank deposits are perfect substitutes (equally desirable), the interest parity condition is an equilibrium condition for the foreign exchange market. Only when the exchange rate is such that expected returns on domestic and foreign deposits are equal—that is, when interest parity holds—will the outstanding domestic and foreign deposits be willingly held.

Equilibrium in the Foreign Exchange Market

To see how the interest parity equilibrium condition works in determining the exchange rate, our first step is to examine how the expected returns on euro and dollar deposits change as the current exchange rate changes.

Expected Return on Euro Deposits   As we demonstrated earlier, the expected return in terms of dollars on foreign deposits RET^F is the foreign interest rate minus the expected appreciation of the domestic currency: $i^F - (E^e_{t+1} - E_t)/E_t$. Suppose that the foreign interest rate i^F is 10% and that the expected exchange rate next period E^e_{t+1} is 0.80 euros per dollar. When the current exchange rate E_t is 0.75 euros per dollar, the expected appreciation of the dollar is $(0.80 - 0.75)/0.75 = 0.066 = 6.6\%$, so the expected return on euro deposits RET^F in terms of dollars is 3.4% (equal to the 10% foreign interest rate minus the 6.6% dollar appreciation). This expected return when $E_t = 0.75$ euros per dollar is plotted as point A in Figure 7-3. At a higher current exchange rate of $E_t = 0.80$ euros per dollar, the expected appreciation of the dollar is zero because E^e_{t+1} also equals 0.80 euros per dollar. Hence RET^F, the expected dollar return on euro deposits, is now just $i^F = 10\%$. This expected return on euro deposits when $E_t = 0.80$ euros per dollar is plotted as point B. At an even higher exchange rate of $E_t = 0.85$ euros per dollar, the expected change in the value of the dollar is now -5.8% [$=(0.80 - 0.85)/0.85 = -0.058$], so the expected dollar return on foreign deposits RET^F has now risen to 15.8% [$= 10\% - (-5.8\%)$]. This combination of exchange rate and expected return on euro deposits is plotted as point C.

The curve connecting these points is the schedule for the expected return on euro deposits in Figure 7-3, labelled RET^F, and as you can see, it slopes upward;

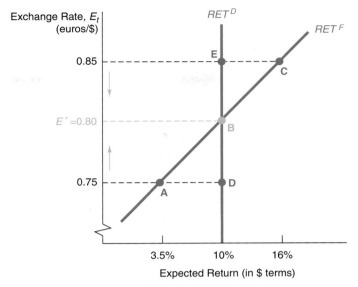

FIGURE 7-3   Equilibrium in the Foreign Exchange Market
Equilibrium in the foreign exchange market occurs at the intersection of the schedules for the expected return on euro deposits RET^F and the expected return on dollar deposits RET^D at point B. The equilibrium exchange rate is $E^* = 0.80$ euros per dollar.

that is, as the exchange rate E_t rises, the expected return on euro deposits rises. The intuition for this upward slope is that because the expected next-period exchange rate is held constant as the current exchange rate rises, there is less expected appreciation of the dollar. Hence a higher current exchange rate means a greater expected appreciation of the foreign currency in the future, which increases the expected return on foreign deposits in terms of dollars.

Expected Return on Dollar Deposits   The expected return on dollar deposits in terms of dollars RET^D is always the interest rate on dollar deposits i^D no matter what the exchange rate is. Suppose that the interest rate on dollar deposits is 10%. The expected return on dollar deposits, whether at an exchange rate of 0.75, 0.80, or 0.85 euros per dollar, is always 10% (points D, B, and E) since no foreign-exchange transaction is needed to convert the interest payments into dollars. The line connecting these points is the schedule for the expected return on dollar deposits, labelled RET^D in Figure 7-3.

Equilibrium   The intersection of the schedules for the expected return on dollar deposits RET^D and the expected return on euro deposits RET^F is where equilibrium occurs in the foreign exchange market; in other words,

$$RET^D = RET^F$$

At the equilibrium point B where the exchange rate E^* is 0.80 euros per dollar, the interest parity condition is satisfied because the expected returns on dollar deposits and on euro deposits are equal.

To see that the exchange rate actually heads toward the equilibrium exchange rate E^*, let's see what happens if the exchange rate is 0.85 euros per dollar, a value above the equilibrium exchange rate. As we can see in Figure 7-3, the expected return on euro deposits at point C is greater than the expected return on dollar deposits at point E. Since dollar and euro deposits are perfect substitutes, people will not want to hold any dollar deposits, and holders of dollar deposits will try to sell them for euro deposits in the foreign exchange market (which is referred to as "selling dollars" and "buying euros"). However, because the expected return on these dollar deposits is below that on euro deposits, no one holding euros will be willing to exchange them for dollar deposits. The resulting excess supply of dollar deposits means that the price of the dollar deposits relative to euro deposits must fall; that is, the exchange rate (amount of euros per dollar) falls as is illustrated by the downward arrow drawn in the figure at the exchange rate of 0.85 euros per dollar. The decline in the exchange rate will continue until point B is reached at the equilibrium exchange rate of 0.80 euros per dollar, where the expected return on dollar and euro deposits is now equalized.

Now let us look at what happens when the exchange rate is 0.75 euros per dollar, a value below the equilibrium level. Here the expected return on dollar deposits is greater than that on euro deposits. No one will want to hold euro deposits, and everyone will try to sell them to buy dollar deposits ("sell euros" and "buy dollars"), thus driving up the exchange rate as illustrated by the upward arrow. As the exchange rate rises, there is a higher expected depreciation of the dollar and so a higher expected appreciation of the euro, thereby increasing the expected return on euro deposits. Finally, when the exchange rate has risen to $E^* = 0.80$ euros per dollar, the expected return on euro deposits has risen enough so that it again equals the expected return on dollar deposits.

EXPLAINING CHANGES IN EXCHANGE RATES

To explain how an exchange rate changes over time, we have to understand the factors that shift the expected-return schedules for domestic (dollar) deposits and foreign (euro) deposits.

Shifts in the Expected-Return Schedule for Foreign Deposits

As we have seen, the expected return on foreign (euro) deposits depends on the foreign interest rate i^F minus the expected appreciation of the dollar $(E^e_{t+1} - E_t)/E_t$. Because a change in the current exchange rate E_t results in a movement along the expected-return schedule for euro deposits, factors that shift this schedule must work through the foreign interest rate i^F and the expected future exchange rate E^e_{t+1}. We examine the effect of changes in these factors on the expected-return schedule for euro deposits RET^F, holding everything else constant.

Study Guide

To grasp how the expected-return schedule for euro deposits shifts, just think of yourself as an investor who is considering putting funds into foreign deposits. When a variable changes (i^F for example), decide whether at a given level of the current exchange rate, holding all other variables constant, you would earn a higher or lower expected return on euro deposits.

Changes in the Foreign Interest Rate If the interest rate on foreign deposits i^F increases, holding everything else constant, the expected return on these deposits must also increase. Hence at a given exchange rate, the increase in i^F leads to a rightward shift in the expected-return schedule for euro deposits from RET^F_1 to RET^F_2 in Figure 7-4. As you can see in the figure, the outcome is a depreciation of the dollar from E_1 to E_2. An alternative way to see this is to recognize that the increase in the expected return on euro deposits at the original equilibrium exchange rate resulting from the rise in i^F means that people will want to buy euros and sell dollars, so the value of the dollar must fall. Our analysis thus generates the following conclusion: *an increase in the foreign interest rate i^F*

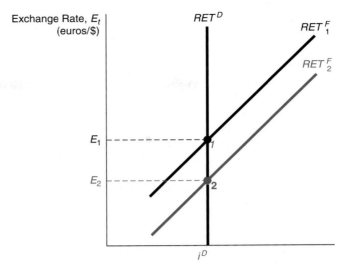

FIGURE 7-4 Shifts in the Schedule for the Expected Return on Foreign Deposits RET^F

An increase in the expected return on foreign deposits, which occurs when either the foreign interest rate rises or the expected future exchange rate falls, shifts the schedule for the expected return on foreign deposits from RET_1^F to RET_2^F, and the exchange rate falls from E_1 to E_2.

shifts the RET^F schedule to the right and causes the domestic currency to depreciate ($E\downarrow$).

Conversely, if i^F falls, the expected return on euro deposits falls, the RET^F schedule shifts to the left, and the exchange rate rises. This yields the following conclusion: ***a decrease in i^F shifts the RET^F schedule to the left and causes the domestic currency to appreciate ($E\uparrow$).***

Changes in the Expected Future Exchange Rate Any factor that causes the expected future exchange rate E_{t+1}^e to fall decreases the expected appreciation of the dollar and hence raises the expected appreciation of the euro. The result is a higher expected return on euro deposits, which shifts the schedule for the expected return on euro deposits to the right and leads to a decline in the exchange rate as in Figure 7-4. Conversely, a rise in E_{t+1}^e raises the expected appreciation of the dollar, lowers the expected return on foreign deposits, shifts the RET^F schedule to the left, and raises the exchange rate. To summarize, ***a rise in the expected future exchange rate shifts the RET^F schedule to the left and causes an appreciation of the domestic currency; a fall in the expected future exchange rate shifts the RET^F schedule to the right and causes a depreciation of the domestic currency***.

Summary Our analysis of the long-run determinants of the exchange rate indicates the factors that influence the expected future exchange rate: the relative price level, relative tariffs and quotas, import demand, export demand, and relative productivity (refer to Table 7-1). The theory of purchasing power parity suggests that if a higher Canadian price level relative to the foreign price level is expected to persist, the dollar will depreciate in the long run. A higher expected relative Canadian price level should thus have a tendency to raise the expected return on euro deposits, shift the RET^F schedule to the right, and lower the current exchange rate.

Similarly, the other long-run determinants of the exchange rate we discussed earlier can also influence the expected return on euro deposits and the current exchange rate. Briefly, the following changes will increase the expected return on euro deposits, shift the RET^F schedule to the right, and cause a depreciation of the domestic currency, the dollar: (1) expectations of a rise in the Canadian price level relative to the foreign price level, (2) expectations of lower Canadian tariffs and quotas relative to foreign tariffs and quotas, (3) expectations of higher Canadian import demand, (4) expectations of lower foreign demand for Canadian exports, and (5) expectations of lower Canadian productivity relative to foreign productivity.

Shifts in the Expected-Return Schedule for Domestic Deposits

Since the expected return on domestic (dollar) deposits is just the interest rate on these deposits i^D, this interest rate is the only factor that shifts the schedule for the expected return on dollar deposits.

Changes in the Domestic Interest Rate   A rise in i^D raises the expected return on dollar deposits, shifts the RET^D schedule to the right, and leads to a rise in the exchange rate, as is shown in Figure 7-5. Another way of seeing this is to recognize that a rise in i^D, which raises the expected return on dollar deposits, creates an excess demand for dollar deposits at the original equilibrium exchange rate, and the resulting purchases of dollar deposits cause an appreciation of the dollar. *A rise in the domestic interest rate i^D shifts the RET^D schedule to the right and causes an appreciation of the domestic currency; a fall in i^D shifts the RET^D schedule to the left and causes a depreciation of the domestic currency.*

Study Guide

As a study aid, the factors that shift the RET^F and RET^D schedules and lead to changes in the current exchange rate E_t are listed in Table 7-2. The table shows what happens to the exchange rate when there is an increase in each of these variables, holding everything else constant. To give yourself practice, see if you can work out what happens to the RET^F and RET^D schedules and to the exchange rate if each of these factors falls rather than rises. Check your answers by seeing if you get the opposite change in the exchange rate to those indicated in Table 7-2.

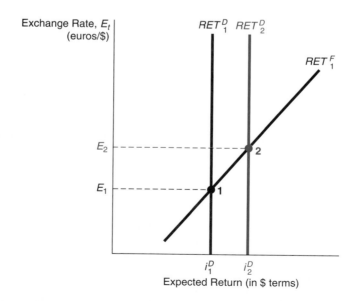

FIGURE 7-5   Shifts in the Schedule for the Expected Return on Domestic Deposits RET^D

An increase in the expected return on dollar deposits i^D shifts the expected return on domestic (dollar) deposits from RET^D_1 to RET^D_2 and the exchange rate from E_1 to E_2.

SUMMARY

TABLE 7-2   Factors that Shift the RET^F and RET^D Schedules and Affect the Exchange Rate

Factor	Change in Factor	Response of Exchange Rate, E_t	
Domestic interest rate, i^D	↑	↑	
Foreign interest rate, i^F	↑	↓	
Expected domestic price level*	↑	↓	
Expected tariffs and quotas*	↑	↑	
Expected import demand	↑	↓	
Expected export demand	↑	↑	
Expected productivity*	↑	↑	

*Relative to other countries.

Note: Only increases (↑) in the factors are shown; the effects of decreases in the variables on the exchange rate are the opposite of those indicated in the "Response" column.

| APPLICATION | *Changes in the Equilibrium Exchange Rate: Two Examples* |

Our analysis has revealed the factors that affect the value of the equilibrium exchange rate. Now we use this analysis to take a close look at the response of the exchange rate to changes in interest rates and money growth.

Changes in Interest Rates

Changes in domestic interest rates i^D are often cited as a major factor affecting exchange rates. For example, we see headlines in the financial press like this one: "Dollar Recovers As Interest Rates Edge Upward." But is the view presented in this headline always correct?

Not necessarily, because to analyze the effects of interest rate changes, we must carefully distinguish the sources of the changes. The Fisher equation (Chapter 4) states that a (nominal) interest rate equals the *real* interest rate plus expected inflation: $i = i_r + \pi^e$. The Fisher equation indicates that an interest rate i can change for two reasons: either the real interest rate i_r changes or the expected inflation rate π^e changes. The effect on the exchange rate is quite different, depending on which of these two factors is the source of the change in the nominal interest rate.

Suppose that the domestic real interest rate increases so that the nominal interest rate i^D rises while expected inflation remains unchanged. In this case, it is reasonable to assume that the expected appreciation of the dollar will be unchanged because expected inflation is unchanged, and so the expected return on foreign deposits will remain unchanged for any given exchange rate. The result is that the RET^F schedule stays put and the RET^D schedule shifts to the right, and we end up with the situation depicted in Figure 7-5, which analyzes an increase in i^D, holding everything else constant. Our model of the foreign exchange market produces the following result: ***when domestic real interest rates rise, the domestic currency appreciates***.

When the nominal interest rate rises because of an increase in expected inflation, we get a different result from the one shown in Figure 7-5. The rise in expected domestic inflation leads to an expected depreciation of the dollar (a higher appreciation of the euro), which is typically thought to be larger than the increase in the domestic interest rate i^D.[5] As a result, at any given exchange rate, the expected return on foreign deposits rises more than the expected return on dollar deposits. Thus, as we see in Figure 7-6, the RET^F schedule shifts to the right more than the RET^D schedule, and the exchange rate falls. Our analysis leads to this conclusion: ***when domestic interest rates rise due to an expected increase in inflation, the domestic currency depreciates***.

Because this conclusion is completely different from the one reached when the rise in the domestic interest rate is associated with a higher real interest rate, we

---

[5]This conclusion is standard in asset market models of exchange rate determination; see Rudiger Dornbusch, "Expectations and Exchange Rate Dynamics," *Journal of Political Economy* 84 (1976): 1061–1076. It is also consistent with empirical evidence that suggests that nominal interest rates do not rise one-for-one with increases in expected inflation. See Frederic S. Mishkin, "The Real Interest Rate: An Empirical Investigation," *Carnegie-Rochester Conference Series on Public Policy* 15 (1981): 151–200; and Lawrence Summers, "The Nonadjustment of Nominal Interest Rates: A Study of the Fisher Effect," in *Macroeconomics, Prices and Quantities*, ed. James Tobin (Washington, D.C.: Brookings Institution, 1983), pp. 201–240.

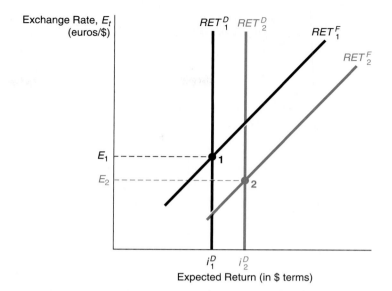

FIGURE 7-6   Effect of a Rise in the Domestic Nominal Interest Rate as a Result of an Increase in Expected Inflation

Because a rise in domestic expected inflation leads to an expected dollar depreciation that is larger than the resulting increase in the domestic interest rate, the expected return on foreign deposits rises by more than the expected return on domestic (dollar) deposits. RET^F shifts to the right more than RET^D, and the equilibrium exchange rate falls from E_1 to E_2.

must always distinguish between *real* and *nominal* measures when analyzing the effects of interest rates on exchange rates.

Changes in the Money Supply

Suppose that the Bank of Canada decides to increase the level of the money supply in order to reduce unemployment, which it believes to be excessive. The higher money supply will lead to a higher Canadian price level in the long run (as we will see in Chapter 24) and hence to a lower expected future exchange rate. The resulting expected depreciation of the dollar increases the expected return on foreign deposits at any given current exchange rate and so shifts the RET^F schedule rightward from RET^F_1 to RET^F_2 in Figure 7-7. In addition, the higher money supply will lead to a higher real money supply M/P because the price level does not immediately increase in the short run. As suggested in Chapter 5, the resulting rise in the real money supply causes the domestic interest rate to fall from i^D_1 to i^D_2, which lowers the expected return on domestic (dollar) deposits, shifting the RET^D schedule leftward from RET^D_1 to RET^D_2. As we can see in Figure 7-7, the result is a decline in the exchange rate from E_1 to E_2. The conclusion is this: ***a higher domestic money supply causes the domestic currency to depreciate***.

Exchange Rate Overshooting

Our analysis of the effect of an increase in the money supply on the exchange rate is not yet over—we still need to look at what happens to the exchange rate in the long run. A basic proposition in monetary theory, called **monetary neutrality**, states that in the long run, a onetime percentage rise in the money supply is matched by the same onetime percentage rise in the price level, leaving

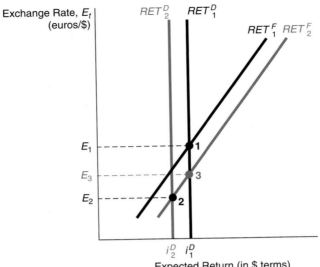

FIGURE 7-7   Effect of a Rise in the Money Supply

A rise in the money supply leads to a higher domestic price level in the long run, which in turn leads to a lower expected future exchange rate. The resulting decline in the expected appreciation of the dollar raises the expected return on foreign deposits, shifting the RET^F schedule rightward from RET_1^F to RET_2^F. In the short run, the domestic interest rate i^D falls, shifting RET^D from RET_1^D to RET_2^D. The short-run outcome is that the exchange rate falls from E_1 to E_2. In the long run, however, the interest rate returns to i_1^D and RET^D returns to RET_1^D. The exchange rate thus rises from E_2 to E_3 in the long run.

unchanged the real money supply and all other economic variables such as interest rates. An intuitive way to understand this proposition is to think of what would happen if our government announced overnight that an old dollar would now be worth 100 new dollars. The money supply in new dollars would be 100 times its old value and the price level would also be 100 times higher, but nothing in the economy would really have changed; real and nominal interest rates and the real money supply would remain the same. Monetary neutrality tells us that in the long run, the rise in the money supply would not lead to a change in the domestic interest rate and so it would return to i_1^D in the long run, and the schedule for the expected return on domestic deposits would return to RET_1^D. As we can see in Figure 7-7, this means that the exchange rate would rise from E_2 to E_3 in the long run.

The phenomenon we have described here in which the exchange rate falls by more in the short run than it does in the long run when the money supply increases is called **exchange rate overshooting**. It is important because, as we will see in the following application, it can help explain why exchange rates exhibit so much volatility.

Another way of thinking about why exchange rate overshooting occurs is to recognize that when the domestic interest rate falls in the short run, equilibrium in the foreign exchange market means that the expected return on foreign deposits must be lower. With the foreign interest rate given, this lower expected return on foreign deposits means that there must be an expected appreciation of the dollar (depreciation of the euro) in order for the expected return on foreign deposits to decline when the domestic interest rate falls. This can occur only if the current exchange rate falls below its long-run value.

APPLICATION	*Why Are Exchange Rates So Volatile?*

The high volatility of foreign exchange rates surprises many people. Thirty or so years ago, economists generally believed that allowing exchange rates to be determined in the free market would not lead to large fluctuations in their values. Recent experience has proved them wrong. If we return to Figure 7-1, we see that exchange rates over the 1980–1999 period have been very volatile.

The asset market approach to exchange rate determination that we have outlined in this chapter gives a straightforward explanation of volatile exchange rates. Because expected appreciation of the domestic currency affects the expected return on foreign deposits, expectations about the price level, inflation, tariffs and quotas, productivity, import demand, export demand, and the money supply play important roles in determining the exchange rate. When expectations about any of these variables change, our model indicates that there will be an immediate effect on the expected return on foreign deposits and therefore on the exchange rate. Since expectations on all these variables change with just about every bit of news that appears, it is not surprising that the exchange rate is volatile. In addition, we have seen that our exchange rate analysis produces exchange rate overshooting when the money supply increases. Exchange rate overshooting is an additional reason for the high volatility of exchange rates.

Because earlier models of exchange rate behaviour focused on goods markets rather than asset markets, they did not emphasize changing expectations as a source of exchange rate movements, and so these earlier models could not predict substantial fluctuations in exchange rates. The failure of earlier models to explain volatility is one reason why they are no longer so popular. The more modern approach developed here emphasizes that the foreign exchange market is like any other asset market in which expectations of the future matter. The foreign exchange market, like other asset markets such as the stock market, displays substantial price volatility, and foreign exchange rates are notoriously hard to forecast.

APPLICATION	*The Euro's First Year*

With much fanfare the euro debuted on January 1, 1999, at an exchange rate of 1.18 U.S. dollars per euro. Despite initial hopes that the euro would be a strong currency, it actually proved to be weak, declining 15% to 1.00 U.S. dollars per euro by the beginning of 2000. Why was the euro so weak in its first year?

The previous application has shown that changes in real interest rates are an important factor determining the exchange rate. When the domestic real interest rate falls relative to the foreign real interest rate, the domestic currency declines in value. This is exactly what has happened to the euro. While the euro was coming into existence, European economies were experiencing only slow recoveries from recession, thus causing both real and nominal interest rates to fall. In contrast, in 1999, the United States was experiencing a boom that kept real and nominal interest rates high and substantially above their European counterparts. As in the analysis of the previous application, the low real interest rates in Europe relative to those in the United States led to a decline in the value of the euro.

APPLICATION | *Reading the* Wall Street Journal's *"Foreign Exchange" Column*

Now that we have an understanding of how exchange rates are determined, we can use our analysis to understand discussions about developments in the foreign exchange market reported in the financial press.

Every day, the *Wall Street Journal* reports on developments in the foreign exchange market on the previous business day in its "Foreign Exchange" column, an example of which is presented in the "Following the Financial News" box.

The column indicates that the higher interest rate outlook in the euro area has led to a rise in the euro relative to the dollar, while talk of intervention to weaken the yen has led to a decline in the yen. Our analysis of the foreign exchange market explains why these developments have led to a stronger euro and a weaker yen.

The column indicates that the euro initially fell after announcement of large wage increases in Germany, which might have caused inflation concerns for the euro area. Higher inflation in Europe would imply a lower value of the euro in the future, lowering the expected return on foreign (euro) deposits. As a result, the RET^F curve would shift to the left, causing the dollar to rise and the euro to fall. However, the fall in the price in U.S. Treasurys on inflation fears suggests a lower value of the dollar in the future, therefore a larger expected appreciation of the euro and a shift of the RET^F curve to the right, which would cause the dollar to fall and the euro to rise. In addition, the outlook for strong euro-zone growth indicates that euro rates are likely to be high in the future, raising the value of the euro. The resulting future increase in the euro means a higher expected return on euro deposits, which would shift the RET^F curve to the right and cause the dollar to fall and the euro to rise. By the end of the day, these latter two effects that caused the euro to rise outweighed the initial weakness in the euro.

The talk of G-7 intervention to weaken the yen raises the possibility that the yen would decline in the future, which would decrease the expected return on foreign (yen) deposits, thus shifting the RET^F curve to the left. The result is that the dollar would rise relative to the yen.

FOLLOWING THE FINANCIAL NEWS

The "Foreign Exchange" Column

The "Foreign Exchange" column appears daily in the *Wall Street Journal*; an example is presented here. It is found in the third section, "Money and Investing."

FOREIGN EXCHANGE

Rate Outlook Aids Euro Against Dollar; Yen Is Hurt by Talk of G-7 Intervention

BY UMBERTO TORRESAN
Dow Jones Newswires

NEW YORK–The dollar lost ground against the euro but ended higher against the yen as renewed prospects for higher interest rates in the euro zone supported the common currency against its major counterparts.

A higher-than-expected demand for wage increases by a major German union sparked fears the European Central Bank will have to face increasing wage pressures from the dominant economy in the European Union.

Germany's biggest union, IG Metall, demanded a 5.5 % increase for the 3.4 million workers in Germany's metals and electronics industry this year. This is about four times the current rate of Germany's inflation, which has ranged between 1.2% and 1.5% in recent months. The aggressive wage demands ensure a tough collective-bargaining process.

After an initial drop in tandem with the European bond market, the euro gradually gained ground on the dollar. The dollar weakened further as U.S. bonds resumed Monday's sell-off. The bellwether 30-year U.S. Treasurys dropped by more than a point in price on inflation fears, with the yield hitting its highest level since September 1997.

The modest performance of the U.S. stock market, pressured by profit-taking after Monday's rally, didn't help the U.S. currency either.

Late yesterday in New York, the dollar was trading at 106.06 yen, up from 105.19 yen late Monday. The euro was trading at $1.0333, up from $1.0258 late Monday. Sterling was trading at $1.6478, up from $1.6373.

On a day with no major U.S. economic indicators on the calendar, the dollar continued to hover around the 106-yen level on speculation whether central-bank and finance ministers will launch a coordinated intervention to weaken the yen after the next Group of Seven meeting Jan. 22.

Meanwhile, the euro also benefited from remarks by Bundesbank President Ernst Welteke, who said the November ECB rate increase has improved the basis for sustained euro-zone growth and a strong euro has substantial potential to rise.

Source: Wall Street Journal, Wednesday, January 12, 2000, p. C23.

SUMMARY

1. Foreign exchange rates (the price of one country's currency in terms of another's) are important because they affect the price of domestically produced goods sold abroad and the cost of foreign goods bought domestically.

2. The theory of purchasing power parity suggests that long-run changes in the exchange rate between two countries are determined by changes in the relative price levels in the two countries. Other factors that affect exchange rates in the long run are tariffs and quotas, import demand, export demand, and productivity.

3. Exchange rates are determined in the short run by the interest parity condition, which states that the expected return on domestic deposits is equal to the expected return on foreign deposits.

4. Any factor that changes the expected returns on domestic or foreign deposits will lead to changes in the exchange rate. Such factors include changes in the interest rates on domestic and foreign deposits as well as changes in any of the factors that affect the long-run exchange rate and hence the expected future exchange rate. Changes in the money supply lead to exchange rate overshooting, causing the exchange rate to change by more in the short run than in the long run.

5. The asset market approach to exchange rate determination can explain both the volatility of exchange rates and the rise of the dollar in the 1980–1985 period and its subsequent fall.

KEY TERMS

appreciation, p. 135

capital mobility, p. 143

depreciation, p. 135

exchange rate, p. 133

exchange rate overshooting, p. 152

foreign exchange market, p. 133

forward exchange rate, p. 135

forward transaction, p. 135

interest parity condition, p. 144

law of one price, p. 137

monetary neutrality, p. 151

quotas, p. 140

spot exchange rate, p. 135

spot transaction, p. 135

tariffs, p. 140

theory of purchasing power parity (PPP), p. 138

QUESTIONS AND PROBLEMS

Questions marked with an asterisk are answered at the end of the book in an appendix, "Answers to Selected Questions and Problems."

1. When the euro appreciates, are you more likely to drink Canadian or French wine?

*2. "A country is always worse off when its currency is weak (falls in value)." Is this statement true, false, or uncertain? Explain your answer.

3. In a newspaper, check the exchange rates for the foreign currencies listed in the "Following the Financial News" box on page 136. Which of these currencies have appreciated and which have depreciated since November 17, 2000?

*4. If the Japanese price level rises by 5% relative to the price level in Canada, what does the theory of purchasing power parity predict will happen to the value of the Japanese yen in terms of dollars?

5. If the demand for a country's exports falls at the same time that tariffs on imports are raised, will the country's currency tend to appreciate or depreciate in the long run?

*6. In the mid- to late 1970s, the yen appreciated relative to the U.S. dollar even though Japan's inflation rate was higher than America's. How can this be explained by an improvement in the productivity of Japanese industry relative to American industry?

Using Economic Analysis to Predict the Future

Answer the remaining questions by drawing the appropriate exchange market diagrams.

7. The governor of the Bank of Canada announces that he will reduce inflation with a new anti-inflation program. If the public believes him, predict what will happen to the Canadian exchange rate.

*8. If the British central bank prints money to reduce unemployment, what will happen to the value of the pound in the short run and the long run?

9. If the Canadian government unexpectedly announces that it will be imposing higher tariffs and quotas on foreign goods one year from now, what will happen to the value of the Canadian dollar today?

*10. If nominal interest rates in Canada rise but real interest rates fall, predict what will happen to the Canadian exchange rate.

11. If Canadian auto companies make a breakthrough in automobile technology and are able to produce a car that gets 100 kilometres to the litre, what will happen to the Canadian exchange rate?

*12. If Canadians go on a spending spree and buy twice as much French perfume, Japanese TVs, English sweaters, Swiss watches, and Italian wine, what will happen to the value of the Canadian dollar?

13. If expected inflation drops in Europe so that interest rates fall there, predict what will happen to the Canadian exchange rate.

*14. If the European central bank decides to contract the money supply in order to fight inflation, what will happen to the value of the Canadian dollar?

15. If there is a strike in France, making it harder to buy French goods, what will happen to the value of the euro?

Chapter 8

An Economic Analysis of Financial Structure

P R E V I E W
A healthy and vibrant economy requires a financial system that moves funds from people who save to people who have productive investment opportunities. But how does the financial system make sure that your hard-earned savings get channelled to Paula the Productive Investor rather than to Benny the Bum?

This chapter answers that question by providing an economic analysis of how our financial structure is designed to promote economic efficiency. The analysis focuses on a few simple but powerful economic concepts that enable us to explain features of our financial system such as why financial contracts are written as they are and why financial intermediaries are more important than securities markets for getting funds to borrowers. The analysis also demonstrates the important link between the financial system and the performance of the aggregate economy, which is the subject of Part V of the book. The economic analysis of financial structure explains how the performance of the financial sector affects economic growth and why financial crises occur and have such severe consequences for aggregate economic activity.

BASIC PUZZLES ABOUT FINANCIAL STRUCTURE THROUGHOUT THE WORLD

The financial system is complex in structure and function throughout the world. It includes many different types of institutions: banks, insurance companies, mutual funds, stock and bond markets, and so on—all of which are regulated by government. The financial system channels billions of dollars per year from savers to people with productive investment opportunities. If we take a close look at financial structure all over the world, we find eight basic puzzles that we need to solve in order to understand how the financial system works.

The pie charts in Figure 8-1 indicate how Canadian and American businesses financed their activities using external funds (those obtained from outside the business itself) in the period 1970–1985. The *loans* category is made up primarily of bank loans, but it also includes loans made by other financial intermediaries; the

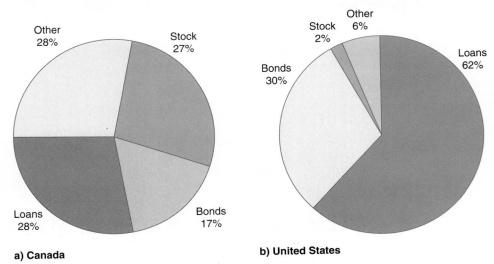

a) Canada   b) United States

FIGURE 8-1   Sources of External Funds for Nonfinancial Businesses in Canada and the
United States

Source: Colin Mayer, "Financial Systems, Corporate Finance, and Economic Development," in
Asymmetric Information, Corporate Finance, and Investment, ed. R. Glenn Hubbard (Chicago:
University of Chicago Press, 1990), p. 312.

bonds category includes marketable debt securities such as corporate bonds and
commercial paper; *stock* consists of stock market shares; and *other* includes other
loans such as government loans, loans by foreigners, and trade debt (loans made
by businesses to other businesses when they purchase goods). Figure 8-2 uses the
same classifications as Figure 8-1 and compares the Canadian and U.S. data to
those of four other industrialized countries: France, Germany, Japan, and the
United Kingdom.

Now let us explore the eight financial puzzles.

1. ***Stocks are not the most important source of external financing for
   businesses.*** Because so much attention in the media is focused on the
   stock market, many people have the impression that stocks are the most
   important source of financing for corporations. However, as we can see
   from the pie charts in Figure 8-1 and from Figure 8-2, the stock markets
   accounted for only a small fraction of the external financing of business in
   the 1970-1985 period (2.1% in the United States, 14.2% in the United
   Kingdom, 17.9% in France, 5.5% in Germany, 5.3% in Japan, and 26.5% in
   Canada). Only in Canada, France, and the United Kingdom do stock markets raise a significant proportion of external finance for businesses.[1] (In
   fact, in the mid- to late 1980s, American corporations generally stopped issu-

---

[1]The figures for the percentage of external financing provided by stocks are based on the flows of
external funds to corporations. However, this flow figure is somewhat misleading because when a
share of stock is issued, it raises funds permanently, whereas when a bond is issued, it raises funds
only temporarily until they are paid back at maturity. To see this, suppose that a firm raises $1000 by
selling a share of stock and another $1000 by selling a $1000 one-year bond. In the case of the stock
issue, the firm can hold on to the $1000 it raised this way, but to hold on to the $1000 it raised through
debt, it has to issue a new $1000 bond every year. If we look at the flow of funds to corporations over
a 15-year period, as in Figures 8-1 and 8-2, the firm will have raised $1000 with a stock issue only once
in the 15-year period, while it will have raised $1000 with debt 15 times, once in each of the 15 years.
Thus it will look as though debt is 15 times more important than stocks in raising funds, even though
our example indicates that they are actually equally important for the firm.

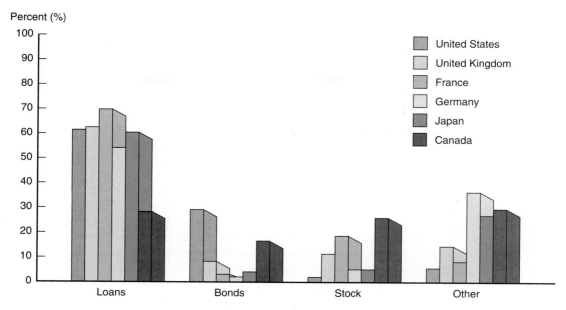

FIGURE 8-2   Sources of External Funds for Nonfinancial Businesses: A Comparison of Canada, the United States, and Four Other Industrialized Countries

The categories of external funds are the same as in Figure 8-1.

Source: Colin Mayer, "Financial Systems, Corporate Finance, and Economic Development," in *Asymmetric Information, Corporate Finance, and Investment,* ed. R. Glenn Hubbard (Chicago: University of Chicago Press, 1990), p. 312.

ing shares to finance their activities; instead they purchased large numbers of shares, meaning that the stock market was actually a *negative* source of corporate finance in those years.) Why is the stock market less important than other sources of financing?

2. ***Issuing marketable debt and equity securities is not the primary way in which businesses finance their operations.*** The pie chart for the United States in Figure 8-1 shows that bonds are a far more important source of financing than stocks in that country (29.8% versus 2.1%). However, as you can see in Figure 8-2, bonds are less important than stocks in each of the other countries (9% versus 14.2% in the United Kingdom, 3.9% versus 17.9% in France, 1.8% versus 5.5% in Germany, 4.7% versus 5.3% in Japan, and 16.7% versus 26.5% in Canada). But stocks and bonds combined, which make up the total share of marketable securities, are still not the dominant source of external finance in all countries (31.9% in the United States, 23.2% in the United Kingdom, 21.8% in France, 7.3% in Germany, 10% in Japan, and 43.2% in Canada). Why don't businesses use marketable securities to finance their activities?

3. ***Indirect finance, which involves the activities of financial intermediaries, is many times more important than direct finance, in which businesses raise funds directly from lenders in financial markets.*** Direct finance involves the sale to households of marketable securities such as stocks and bonds. The shares of stocks and bonds that we mentioned as a source of external financing for businesses actually greatly overstate the importance of direct finance in the financial system throughout the world. In general, only a small fraction of newly issued corporate bonds and commercial paper and

around 50% of stocks are sold directly to households. The rest of these securities are bought primarily by financial intermediaries such as insurance companies, pension funds, and mutual funds. This strengthens the argument that direct finance is a far less important source of finance than indirect finance. Why are financial intermediaries and indirect finance so important in financial markets throughout the world?

4. ***Banks are the most important source of external funds used to finance businesses.*** As we can see in Figures 8-1 and 8-2, the primary sources of external funds for businesses throughout the world are loans (61.9% in the United States, 62.2% in the United Kingdom, 70.2% in France, 55% in Germany, 61.3% in Japan, and 28.5% in Canada). Most of these loans are bank loans, so the data suggest that banks have the most important role in financing business activities throughout the world. Banks are more important in countries such as France, the United Kingdom, the United States, and Japan, but less important in countries such as Germany and Canada. Moreover, banks play an even more important role in the financial system of developing countries than they do in the industrialized countries. What makes banks so important to the working of the financial system?

5. ***The financial system is among the most heavily regulated sectors of the economy.*** You learned in Chapter 2 that the financial system is heavily regulated, not only in Canada but in all other developed countries as well. Governments regulate financial markets primarily to promote the provision of information and to ensure the soundness of the financial system. Why are financial markets so extensively regulated throughout the world?

6. ***Only large, well-established corporations have access to securities markets to finance their activities.*** Individuals and smaller businesses that are not well established almost never raise funds by issuing marketable securities. Instead, they obtain their financing from banks. Why do only large, well-known corporations have the ability to raise funds in securities markets?

7. ***Collateral is a prevalent feature of debt contracts for both households and businesses.*** **Collateral** is property that is pledged to the lender to guarantee payment in the event that the borrower is unable to make debt payments. Collateralized debt (also known as **secured debt** to contrast it with **unsecured debt**, such as credit card debt, which is not collateralized) is the predominant form of household debt and is widely used in business borrowing as well. The majority of household debt in Canada consists of collateralized loans: your automobile is collateral for your auto loan, and your house is collateral for your mortgage. Commercial and farm mortgages, for which property is pledged as collateral, make up one-quarter of borrowing by nonfinancial businesses; corporate bonds and other bank loans also often involve pledges of collateral. Why is collateral such an important feature of debt contracts?

8. ***Debt contracts typically are extremely complicated legal documents that place substantial restrictions on the behaviour of the borrower.*** Many students think of a debt contract as a simple IOU that can be written on a single piece of paper. The reality of debt contracts is far different, however. In all countries, bond or loan contracts typically are long legal documents with provisions (called **restrictive covenants**) that restrict and specify certain activities that the borrower can engage in. Restrictive covenants are

not just a feature of debt contracts for businesses; for example, personal automobile loan and home mortgage contracts have covenants that require the borrower to maintain sufficient insurance on the automobile or house purchased with the loan. Why are debt contracts so complex and restrictive?

As you may recall from Chapter 2, an important feature of financial markets is that they have substantial transaction and information costs. An economic analysis of how these costs affect financial markets provides us with solutions to the eight puzzles, which in turn provide us with a much deeper understanding of how our financial system works. In the next section we examine the impact of transaction costs on the structure of our financial system. Then we turn to how information costs affect financial structure.

TRANSACTION COSTS

Transaction costs are a major problem in financial markets. An example will make this clear.

How Transaction Costs Influence Financial Structure

Say you have $5000 you would like to invest, and you think about investing in the stock market. Because you have only $5000, you can buy only a small number of shares. The stockbroker tells you that your purchase is so small that the brokerage commission for buying the stock you picked will be a large percentage of the purchase price of the shares. If instead you decide to buy a bond, the problem is even worse because the smallest denomination for some bonds you might want to buy is as much as $10 000 and you do not have that much to invest. Indeed, the broker may not be interested in your business at all because the small size of your account doesn't make spending time on it worthwhile. You are disappointed and realize that you will not be able to use financial markets to earn a return on your hard-earned savings. You can take some consolation, however, in the fact that you are not alone in being stymied by high transaction costs. This is a fact of life for many of us.

You also face another problem because of transaction costs. Because you have only a small amount of funds available, you can make only a restricted number of investments. That is, you have to put all your eggs in one basket, and your inability to diversify will subject you to a lot of risk.

How Financial Intermediaries Reduce Transaction Costs

This example of the problems posed by transaction costs and the example outlined in Chapter 2 when legal costs kept you from making a loan to Carl the Carpenter illustrate that small savers like you are frozen out of financial markets and are unable to benefit from them. Fortunately, financial intermediaries, an important part of the financial structure, have evolved to reduce transaction costs and allow small savers and borrowers to benefit from the existence of financial markets.

Economies of Scale   One solution to the problem of high transaction costs is to bundle the funds of many investors together so that they can take advantage of *economies of scale,* the reduction in transaction costs per dollar of investment as the size (scale) of transactions increases. By bundling investors' funds together, transaction costs for each individual investor are far smaller. Economies of scale exist because the total cost of carrying out a transaction in financial markets increases only a little as the size of the transaction grows. For example, the cost of arranging a purchase of 10 000 shares of stock is not much greater than the cost of arranging a purchase of 50 shares of stock.

The presence of economies of scale in financial markets helps explain why financial intermediaries developed and have become such an important part of our financial structure. The clearest example of a financial intermediary that arose because of economies of scale is a mutual fund. A *mutual fund* is a financial intermediary that sells shares to individuals and then invests the proceeds in bonds or stocks. Because it buys large blocks of stocks or bonds, a mutual fund can take advantage of lower transaction costs. These cost savings are then passed on to individual investors after the mutual fund has taken its cut in the form of management fees for administering their accounts. An additional benefit for individual investors is that a mutual fund is large enough to purchase a widely diversified portfolio of securities. The increased diversification for individual investors reduces their risk, thus making them better off.

Economies of scale are also important in lowering the costs of things such as computer technology that financial institutions need to accomplish their tasks. Once a large mutual fund has invested a lot of money in setting up a telecommunications system, for example, the system can be used for a huge number of transactions at a low cost per transaction.

Expertise   Financial intermediaries also arise because they are better able to develop expertise to lower transaction costs. Their expertise in computer technology enables them to offer customers convenient services like being able to call a toll-free number for information on how well their investments are doing and to write cheques on their accounts.

An important outcome of a financial intermediary's low transaction costs is the ability to provide its customers with *liquidity services,* services that make it easier for customers to conduct transactions. Some money market mutual funds, for example, not only pay shareholders high interest rates, but also allow them to write cheques for convenient bill-paying.

ASYMMETRIC INFORMATION: ADVERSE SELECTION AND MORAL HAZARD

The presence of transaction costs in financial markets explains in part why financial intermediaries and indirect finance play such an important role in financial markets (puzzle 3). To understand financial structure more fully, however, we turn to the role of information in financial markets.[2]

Asymmetric information—one party's having insufficient knowledge about the other party involved in a transaction to make accurate decisions—is an important aspect of financial markets. For example, managers of a corporation know whether they are honest or have better information about how well their business is doing than the stockholders do. The presence of asymmetric information leads to adverse selection and moral hazard problems, which were introduced in Chapter 2.

Adverse selection is an asymmetric information problem that occurs *before* the transaction occurs: potential bad credit risks are the ones who most actively seek out loans. Thus the parties who are the most likely to produce an undesirable outcome are the ones most likely to want to engage in the transaction. For example, big risk takers or outright crooks might be the most eager to take out a loan

---

[2]An excellent survey of the literature on information and financial structure that expands on the topics discussed in the rest of this chapter is contained in Mark Gertler, "Financial Structure and Aggregate Economic Activity: An Overview," *Journal of Money, Credit and Banking* 20 (1988): 559–588.

because they know that they are unlikely to pay it back. Because adverse selection increases the chances that a loan might be made to a bad credit risk, lenders may decide not to make any loans even though there are good credit risks in the marketplace.

Moral hazard arises *after* the transaction occurs: the lender runs the risk that the borrower will engage in activities that are undesirable from the lender's point of view because they make it less likely that the loan will be paid back. For example, once borrowers have obtained a loan, they may take on big risks (which have possible high returns but also run a greater risk of default) because they are playing with someone else's money. Because moral hazard lowers the probability that the loan will be repaid, lenders may decide that they would rather not make a loan.

THE LEMONS PROBLEM: HOW ADVERSE SELECTION INFLUENCES FINANCIAL STRUCTURE

A particular characterization of the adverse selection problem and how it interferes with the efficient functioning of a market was outlined in a famous article by George Akerlof. It is referred to as the "lemons problem" because it resembles the problem created by lemons in the used-car market.[3] Potential buyers of used cars are frequently unable to assess the quality of the car; that is, they can't tell whether a particular used car is a good car that will run well or a lemon that will continually give them grief. The price that a buyer pays must therefore reflect the *average* quality of the cars in the market, somewhere between the low value of a lemon and the high value of a good car.

The owner of a used car, by contrast, is more likely to know whether the car is a peach or a lemon. If the car is a lemon, the owner is more than happy to sell it at the price the buyer is willing to pay, which, being somewhere between the value of a lemon and a good car, is greater than the lemon's value. However, if the car is a peach, the owner knows that the car is undervalued by the price the buyer is willing to pay, and so the owner may not want to sell it. As a result of this adverse selection, very few good used cars will come to the market. Because the average quality of a used car available in the market will be low and because very few people want to buy a lemon, there will be few sales. The used-car market will then function poorly, if at all.

Lemons in the Stock and Bond Markets

A similar lemons problem arises in securities markets, that is, the debt (bond) and equity (stock) markets. Suppose that our friend Irving the Investor, a potential buyer of securities such as common stock, can't distinguish between good firms with high expected profits and low risk and bad firms with low expected profits and high risk. In this situation, Irving will be willing to pay only a price that reflects the *average* quality of firms issuing securities—a price that lies between the value of securities from bad firms and the value of those from good firms. If the owners or managers of a good firm have better information than Irving and *know* that they are a good firm, they know that their securities are undervalued and will not want to sell them to Irving at the price he is willing to pay. The only firms willing to sell

[3]George Akerlof, "The Market for 'Lemons': Quality, Uncertainty and the Market Mechanism," *Quarterly Journal of Economics* 84 (1970): 488–500. Two important papers that have applied the lemons problem analysis to financial markets are Stewart Myers and N. S. Majluf, "Corporate Financing and Investment Decisions When Firms Have Information That Investors Do Not Have," *Journal of Financial Economics* 13 (1984): 187–221, and Bruce Greenwald, Joseph E. Stiglitz, and Andrew Weiss, "Information Imperfections in the Capital Market and Macroeconomic Fluctuations," *American Economic Review* 74 (1984): 194–199.

Irving securities will be bad firms (because the price is higher than the securities are worth). Our friend Irving is not stupid; he does not want to hold securities in bad firms, and hence he will decide not to purchase securities in the market. In an outcome similar to that in the used-car market, this securities market will not work very well because few firms will sell securities in it to raise capital.

The analysis is similar if Irving considers purchasing a corporate debt instrument in the bond market rather than an equity share. Irving will buy a bond only if its interest rate is high enough to compensate him for the average default risk of the good and bad firms trying to sell the debt. The knowledgeable owners of a good firm realize that they will be paying a higher interest rate than they should, and so they are unlikely to want to borrow in this market. Only the bad firms will be willing to borrow, and because investors like Irving are not eager to buy bonds issued by bad firms, they will probably not buy any bonds at all. Few bonds are likely to sell in this market, and so it will not be a good source of financing.

The analysis we have just conducted explains puzzle 2—why marketable securities are not the primary source of financing for businesses in any country in the world. It also partly explains puzzle 1—why stocks are not the most important source of financing for Canadian businesses. The presence of the lemons problem keeps securities markets such as the stock and bond markets from being effective in channelling funds from savers to borrowers.

Tools to Help Solve Adverse Selection Problems

In the absence of asymmetric information, the lemons problem goes away. If buyers know as much about the quality of used cars as sellers so that all involved can tell a good car from a bad one, buyers will be willing to pay full value for good used cars. Because the owners of good used cars can now get a fair price, they will be willing to sell them in the market. The market will have many transactions and will do its intended job of channelling good cars to people who want them.

Similarly, if purchasers of securities can distinguish good firms from bad, they will pay the full value of securities issued by good firms, and good firms will sell their securities in the market. The securities market will then be able to move funds to the good firms that have the most productive investment opportunities.

Private Production and Sale of Information   The solution to the adverse selection problem in financial markets is to eliminate asymmetric information by furnishing people supplying funds with full details about the individuals or firms seeking to finance their investment activities. One way to get this material to saver-lenders is to have private companies collect and produce information that distinguishes good from bad firms and then sell it to purchasers of securities. In Canada, companies such as Standard & Poor's and the Dominion Bond Rating Service gather information on firms' balance sheet positions and investment activities, publish these data, and sell them to subscribers (individuals, libraries, and financial intermediaries involved in purchasing securities).

The system of private production and sale of information does not completely solve the adverse selection problem in securities markets, however, because of the so-called **free-rider problem**. The free-rider problem occurs when people who do not pay for information take advantage of the information that other people have paid for. The free-rider problem suggests that the private sale of information will be only a partial solution to the lemons problem. To see why, suppose that you have just purchased information that tells you which firms are good and which are bad. You believe that this purchase is worthwhile because you can make up the cost of acquiring this information, and then some, by purchasing the securities of good firms that are undervalued. However, when our savvy (free-riding) investor Irving sees you buying certain securities, he buys right along with you, even though he has not paid for any information. If many other investors act as Irving does, the increased demand for the undervalued good securities will cause their low price to be bid up immediately to reflect the securities' true value. Because of all these free riders, you can no longer buy the securities for less than their true value. Now because you will not gain any extra profits from purchasing the information, you realize that you never should have paid for this information in the first place. If other investors come to the same realization, private firms and individuals may not be able to sell enough of this information to make it worth their while to gather and produce it. The weakened ability of private firms to profit from selling information will mean that less information is produced in the marketplace, and so adverse selection (the lemons problem) will still interfere with the efficient functioning of securities markets.

Government Regulation   The free-rider problem prevents the private market from producing enough information to eliminate all the asymmetric information that leads to adverse selection. Could financial markets benefit from government intervention? The government could, for instance, produce information to help investors distinguish good from bad firms and provide it to the public free of charge. This solution, however, would involve the government in releasing negative information about firms, a practice that might be politically difficult. A second possibility (and one followed by Canada and most governments throughout the world) is for the government to regulate securities markets in a way that encourages firms to reveal honest information about themselves so that investors can determine how good or bad the firms are. In Canada, government regulation exists that requires firms selling their securities in public markets to adhere to standard accounting principles and to disclose information about their sales, assets, and earnings. Similar regulations are found in other countries.

The asymmetric information problem of adverse selection in financial markets helps explain why financial markets are among the most heavily regulated sectors in the economy (puzzle 5). Government regulation to increase information for investors is needed to reduce the adverse selection problem, which interferes with the efficient functioning of securities (stock and bond) markets.

Although government regulation lessens the adverse selection problem, it does not eliminate it. Even when firms provide information to the public about their sales, assets, or earnings, they still have more information than investors: there is a lot more to knowing the quality of a firm than statistics can provide. Furthermore, bad firms have an incentive to make themselves look like good firms because this would enable them to fetch a higher price for their securities. Bad firms will slant the information they are required to transmit to the public, thus making it harder for investors to sort out the good firms from the bad.

Financial Intermediation   So far we have seen that private production of information and government regulation to encourage provision of information lessen but do not eliminate the adverse selection problem in financial markets. How, then, can the financial structure help promote the flow of funds to people with productive investment opportunities when there is asymmetric information? A clue is provided by the structure of the used-car market.

An important feature of the used-car market is that most used cars are not sold directly by one individual to another. An individual considering buying a used car might pay for privately produced information by subscribing to a magazine like *Consumer Reports* to find out if a particular make of car has a good repair record. Nevertheless, reading *Consumer Reports* does not solve the adverse selection problem because even if a particular make of car has a good

Consumer Reports
www.consumerreports.org

reputation, the specific car someone is trying to sell could be a lemon. The prospective buyer might also bring the used car to a mechanic for a once-over. But what if the prospective buyer doesn't know a mechanic who can be trusted or if the mechanic would charge a high fee to evaluate the car?

Because these roadblocks make it hard for individuals to acquire enough information about used cars, most used cars are not sold directly by one individual to another. Instead, they are sold by an intermediary, a used-car dealer who purchases used cars from individuals and resells them to other individuals. Used-car dealers produce information in the market by becoming experts in determining whether a car is a peach or a lemon. Once they know that a car is good, they can sell it with some form of a guarantee: either a guarantee that is explicit, such as a warranty, or an implicit guarantee in which they stand by their reputation for honesty. People are more likely to purchase a used car because of a dealer's guarantee, and the dealer is able to make a profit on the production of information about automobile quality by being able to sell the used car at a higher price than the dealer paid for it. If dealers purchase and then resell cars on which they have produced information, they avoid the problem of other people free-riding on the information they produced.

Just as used-car dealers help solve adverse selection problems in the automobile market, financial intermediaries play a similar role in financial markets. A financial intermediary such as a bank becomes an expert in the production of information about firms so that it can sort out good credit risks from bad ones. Then it can acquire funds from depositors and lend them to the good firms. Because the bank is able to lend mostly to good firms, it is able to earn a higher return on its loans than the interest it has to pay to its depositors. The resulting profit that the bank earns allows it to engage in this information production activity.

An important element in the ability of the bank to profit from the information it produces is that it avoids the free-rider problem by primarily making private loans rather than by purchasing securities that are traded in the open market. Because a private loan is not traded, other investors cannot watch what the bank is doing and bid up the loan's price to the point that the bank receives no compensation for the information it has produced. The bank's role as an intermediary that holds mostly nontraded loans is the key to its success in reducing asymmetric information in financial markets.

Our analysis of adverse selection indicates that financial intermediaries in general, and banks in particular because they hold a large fraction of nontraded loans, should play a greater role in moving funds to corporations than securities markets do. Our analysis thus explains puzzles 3 and 4: why indirect finance is so much more important than direct finance and why banks are the most important source of external funds for financing businesses.

Another important fact that is explained by the analysis here is the greater importance of banks in the financial systems of developing countries. As we have seen, when the quality of information about firms is better, asymmetric information problems will be less severe, and it will be easier for firms to issue securities. Information about private firms is harder to collect in developing countries than in industrialized countries; therefore, the smaller role played by securities markets leaves a greater role for financial intermediaries such as banks. A corollary of this analysis is that as information about firms becomes easier to acquire, the role of banks should decline. A major development in the past 20 years has been huge improvements in information technology. Thus the analysis here suggests that the lending role of financial institutions such as banks should have declined, and this is exactly what has occurred (see Chapter 10).

Our analysis of adverse selection also explains which firms are more likely to obtain funds from banks and financial intermediaries, an indirect route, rather than directly from the securities markets. The better known a corporation is, the more information about its activities is available in the marketplace. Thus it is easier for investors to evaluate the quality of the corporation and determine whether it is a good firm or a bad one. Because investors have fewer worries about adverse selection with well-known corporations, they will be willing to invest directly in their securities. Hence we have an explanation for puzzle 6: the larger and more mature a corporation is, the more information investors have about it, and the more likely it is that the corporation can raise funds in securities markets.

Collateral and Net Worth Adverse selection interferes with the functioning of financial markets only if a lender suffers a loss when a borrower is unable to make loan payments and thereby defaults. Collateral, property promised to the lender if the borrower defaults, reduces the consequences of adverse selection because it reduces the lender's losses in the event of a default. If a borrower defaults on a loan, the lender can sell the collateral and use the proceeds to make up for the losses on the loan. For example, if you fail to make your mortgage payments, the lender can take title to your house, auction it off, and use the receipts to pay off the loan. Lenders are thus more willing to make loans secured by collateral, and borrowers are willing to supply collateral because the reduced risk for the lender makes it more likely they will get the loan in the first place and perhaps at a better loan rate. The presence of adverse selection in credit markets thus provides an explanation for why collateral is an important feature of debt contracts (puzzle 7).

Net worth (also called **equity capital**), the difference between a firm's assets (what it owns or is owed) and its liabilities (what it owes), can perform a similar role to collateral. If a firm has a high net worth, then even if it engages in investments that cause it to have negative profits and so defaults on its debt payments, the lender can take title to the firm's net worth, sell it off, and use the proceeds to recoup some of the losses from the loan. In addition, the more net worth a firm has in the first place, the less likely it is to default because the firm has a cushion of assets that it can use to pay off its loans. Hence when firms seeking credit have high net worth, the consequences of adverse selection are less important and lenders are more willing to make loans. This analysis lies behind the often-heard lament, "Only the people who don't need money can borrow it!"

Summary So far we have used the concept of adverse selection to explain seven of the eight puzzles about financial structure introduced earlier: the first four emphasize the importance of financial intermediaries and the relative unimportance of securities markets for the financing of corporations; the fifth, that financial markets are among the most heavily regulated sectors of the economy; the sixth, that only large, well-established corporations have access to securities markets; and the seventh, that collateral is an important feature of debt contracts. In the next section we will see that the other asymmetric information concept of moral hazard provides additional reasons for the importance of financial intermediaries and the relative unimportance of securities markets for the financing of corporations, the prevalence of government regulation, and the importance of collateral in debt contracts. In addition, the concept of moral hazard can be used to explain our final puzzle (puzzle 8) of why debt contracts are complicated legal documents that place substantial restrictions on the behaviour of the borrower.

HOW MORAL HAZARD AFFECTS THE CHOICE BETWEEN DEBT AND EQUITY CONTRACTS

Moral hazard is the asymmetric information problem that occurs after the financial transaction takes place, when the seller of a security may have incentives to hide information and engage in activities that are undesirable for the purchaser of the security. Moral hazard has important consequences for whether a firm finds it easier to raise funds with debt than with equity contracts.

Moral Hazard in Equity Contracts: The Principal–Agent Problem

Equity contracts, such as common stock, are claims to a share in the profits and assets of a business. Equity contracts are subject to a particular type of moral hazard called the **principal–agent problem**. When managers own only a small fraction of the firm they work for, the stockholders who own most of the firm's equity (called the *principals*) are not the same people as the managers of the firm, who are the *agents* of the owners. This separation of ownership and control involves moral hazard in that the managers in control (the agents) may act in their own interest rather than in the interest of the stockholder-owners (the principals) because the managers have less incentive to maximize profits than the stockholder-owners do.

To understand the principal–agent problem more fully, suppose that your friend Steve asks you to become a silent partner in his ice-cream store. The store requires an investment of $10 000 to set up and Steve has only $1000. So you purchase an equity stake (stock shares) for $9000, which entitles you to 90% of the ownership of the firm, while Steve owns only 10%. If Steve works hard to make tasty ice cream, keeps the store clean, smiles at all the customers, and hustles to wait on tables quickly, after all expenses (including Steve's salary), the store will have $50 000 in profits per year, of which Steve receives 10% ($5000) and you receive 90% ($45 000).

But if Steve doesn't provide quick and friendly service to his customers, uses the $50 000 in income to buy artwork for his office, and even sneaks off to the beach while he should be at the store, the store will not earn any profit. Steve can earn the additional $5000 (his 10% share of the profits) over his salary only if he works hard and forgoes unproductive investments (such as art for his office). Steve might decide that the extra $5000 just isn't enough to make him want to expend the effort to be a good manager; he might decide that it would be worth his while only if he earned an extra $10 000. If Steve feels this way, he does not have enough incentive to be a good manager and will end up with a beautiful office, a good tan, and a store that doesn't show any profits. Because the store won't show any profits, Steve's decision not to act in your interest will cost you $45 000 (your 90% of the profits if he had chosen to be a good manager instead).

The moral hazard arising from the principal–agent problem might be even worse if Steve were not totally honest. Because his ice-cream store is a cash business, Steve has the incentive to pocket $50 000 in cash and tell you that the profits were zero. He now gets a return of $50 000, but you get nothing.

Further indications that the principal–agent problem created by equity contracts can be severe are provided by examples of managers who build luxurious offices for themselves or drive high-priced corporate automobiles. Besides pursuing personal benefits, managers might also pursue corporate strategies (such as the acquisition of other firms) that enhance their personal power but do not increase the corporation's profitability.

The principal–agent problem would not arise if the owners of a firm had complete information about what the managers were up to and could prevent wasteful expenditures or fraud. The principal–agent problem, which is an example of moral hazard, arises only because a manager, like Steve, has more information about his activities than the stockholder does—that is, there is asymmetric information. The principal–agent problem would also not arise if Steve alone owned the store and there were no separation of ownership and control. If this were the case, Steve's hard work and avoidance of unproductive investments would yield him a profit (and extra income) of $50 000, an amount that would make it worth his while to be a good manager.

Tools to Help Solve the Principal–Agent Problem

Production of Information: Monitoring   You have seen that the principal–agent problem arises because managers have more information about their activities and actual profits than stockholders do. One way for stockholders to reduce this moral hazard problem is for them to engage in a particular type of information production, the monitoring of the firm's activities: auditing the firm frequently and checking on what the management is doing. The problem is that the monitoring process can be expensive in terms of time and money, as reflected in the name economists give it, **costly state verification**. Costly state verification makes the equity contract less desirable, and it explains, in part, why equity is not a more important element in our financial structure.

As with adverse selection, the free-rider problem decreases the amount of information production that would reduce the moral hazard (principal–agent) problem. In this example, the free-rider problem decreases monitoring. If you know that other stockholders are paying to monitor the activities of the company you hold shares in, you can take a free ride on their activities. Then you can use the money you save by not engaging in monitoring to vacation on a Caribbean island. If you can do this, though, so can other stockholders. Perhaps all the stockholders will go to the islands, and no one will spend any resources on monitoring the firm. The moral hazard problem for shares of common stock will then be severe, making it hard for firms to issue them to raise capital.

Government Regulation to Increase Information   As with adverse selection, the government has an incentive to try to reduce the moral hazard problem created by asymmetric information. Governments everywhere have laws to force firms to adhere to standard accounting principles that make profit verification easier. They also pass laws to impose stiff criminal penalties on people who commit the fraud of hiding and stealing profits. However, these measures can only be partly effective. Catching this kind of fraud is not easy; fraudulent managers have the incentive to make it very hard for government agencies to find or prove fraud.

Financial Intermediation   Financial intermediaries have the ability to avoid the free-rider problem in the face of moral hazard. One financial intermediary that helps reduce the moral hazard arising from the principal–agent problem is the **venture capital firm**. Venture capital firms pool the resources of their partners and use the funds to help budding entrepreneurs start new businesses. In exchange for the use of the venture capital, the firm receives an equity share in the new business. Because verification of earnings and profits is so important in eliminating moral hazard, venture capital firms usually insist on having several of their own people participate as members of the managing body of the firm, the board of directors, so that they can keep a close watch on the firm's activities. When a venture capital firm supplies start-up funds, the equity in the firm is not marketable to anyone *but* the venture capital firm. Thus other investors are unable to take a free ride on the venture capital firm's verification activities. As a result of this arrangement, the venture capital firm is able to garner the full benefits of its verification activities and is given the appropriate incentives to reduce the moral hazard problem.

Debt Contracts   Moral hazard arises with an equity contract, which is a claim on profits in all situations, whether the firm is making or losing money. If a contract could be structured so that moral hazard would exist only in certain situations, there would be a reduced need to monitor managers, and the contract would be more attractive than the equity contract. The debt contract has exactly these attributes because it is a contractual agreement by the borrower to pay the lender *fixed* dollar amounts at periodic intervals. When the firm has high profits, the lender receives the contractual payments and does not need to know the exact profits of the firm. If the managers are hiding profits or are pursuing activities that are personally beneficial but don't increase profitability, the lender doesn't care as long as these activities do not interfere with the ability of the firm to make its debt payments on time. Only when the firm cannot meet its debt payments, thereby being in a state of default, is there a need for the lender to verify the state of the firm's profits. Only in this situation do lenders involved in debt contracts need to act more like equity holders; now they need to know how much income the firm has in order to get their fair share.

The advantage of a less frequent need to monitor the firm, and thus a lower cost of state verification, helps explain why debt contracts are used more frequently than equity contracts to raise capital. The concept of moral hazard thus helps explain puzzle 1, why stocks are not the most important source of financing for businesses.[4]

HOW MORAL HAZARD INFLUENCES FINANCIAL STRUCTURE IN DEBT MARKETS

Even with the advantages just described, debt contracts are still subject to moral hazard. Because a debt contract requires the borrowers to pay out a fixed amount and lets them keep any profits above this amount, the borrowers have an incentive to take on investment projects that are riskier than the lenders would like.

For example, suppose that because you are concerned about the problem of verifying the profits of Steve's ice-cream store, you decide not to become an equity partner. Instead, you lend Steve the $9000 he needs to set up his business and have a debt contract that pays you an interest rate of 10%. As far as you are concerned, this is a surefire investment because there is a strong and steady demand for ice cream in your neighbourhood. However, once you give Steve the funds, he might use them for purposes other than you intended. Instead of opening up the ice-cream store, Steve might use your $9000 loan to invest in chemical research equipment because he thinks he has a 1-in-10 chance of inventing a diet ice cream that tastes every bit as good as the premium brands but has no fat or calories.

Obviously, this is a very risky investment, but if Steve is successful, he will become a multimillionaire. He has a strong incentive to undertake the riskier investment with your money because the gains to him would be so large if he succeeded. You would clearly be very unhappy if Steve used your loan for the riskier investment because if he were unsuccessful, which is highly likely, you would lose most, if not all, of the money you gave him. And if he were successful, you wouldn't share in his success—you would still get only a 10% return on the loan because the principal and interest payments are fixed. Because of the potential moral hazard (that Steve might use your money to finance a very risky venture), you would probably not make the loan to Steve, even though an ice-cream store in the neighbourhood is a good investment that would provide benefits for everyone.

---

[4]Another factor that encourages the use of debt contracts rather than equity contracts is our tax code. Debt interest payments are a deductible expense for Canadian firms, whereas dividend payments to equity shareholders are not.

Tools to Help Solve Moral Hazard in Debt Contracts

Net Worth   When borrowers have more at stake because their *net worth* (the difference between their assets and their liabilities) is high, the risk of moral hazard—the temptation to act in a manner that lenders find objectionable—will be greatly reduced because the borrowers themselves have a lot to lose. Let's return to Steve and his ice-cream business. Suppose that the cost of setting up either the ice-cream store or the research equipment is $100 000 instead of $10 000. So Steve needs to put $91 000 of his own money into the business (instead of $1000) in addition to the $9000 supplied by your loan. Now if Steve is unsuccessful in inventing the no-calorie nonfat ice cream, he has a lot to lose, the $91 000 of net worth ($100 000 in assets minus the $9000 loan from you). He will think twice about undertaking the riskier investment and is more likely to invest in the ice-cream store, which is more of a sure thing. Hence when Steve has more of his own money (net worth) in the business, you are more likely to make him the loan.

One way of describing the solution that high net worth provides to the moral hazard problem is to say that it makes the debt contract **incentive-compatible**; that is, it aligns the incentives of the borrower with those of the lender. The greater the borrower's net worth, the greater the borrower's incentive to behave in the way that the lender expects and desires, the smaller the moral hazard problem in the debt contract is, and the easier it is for the firm to borrow. Conversely, when the borrower's net worth is lower, the moral hazard problem is greater, and it is harder for the firm to borrow.

Monitoring and Enforcement of Restrictive Covenants   As the example of Steve and his ice-cream store shows, if you could make sure that Steve doesn't invest in anything riskier than the ice-cream store, it would be worth your while to make him the loan. You can ensure that Steve uses your money for the purpose *you* want it to be used for by writing provisions (restrictive covenants) into the debt contract that restrict his firm's activities. By monitoring Steve's activities to see whether he is complying with the restrictive covenants and enforcing the covenants if he is not, you can make sure that he will not take on risks at your expense. Restrictive covenants are directed at reducing moral hazard either by ruling out undesirable behaviour or by encouraging desirable behaviour. There are four types of restrictive covenants that achieve this objective:

1. Covenants can be designed to lower moral hazard by keeping the borrower from engaging in the undesirable behaviour of undertaking risky investment projects. Some such covenants mandate that a loan can be used only to finance specific activities, such as the purchase of particular equipment or inventories. Others restrict the borrowing firm from engaging in certain risky business activities, such as purchasing other businesses.

2. Restrictive covenants can encourage the borrower to engage in desirable activities that make it more likely that the loan will be paid off. One restrictive covenant of this type requires the breadwinner in a household to carry life insurance that pays off the mortgage upon that person's death. Restrictive covenants of this type for businesses focus on encouraging the borrowing firm to keep its net worth high because higher borrower net worth reduces moral hazard and makes it less likely that the lender will suffer losses. These restrictive covenants typically specify that the firm must maintain minimum holdings of certain assets relative to the firm's size.

3. Because collateral is an important protection for the lender, restrictive covenants can encourage the borrower to keep the collateral in good condition and make sure that it stays in the possession of the borrower. This is the type of covenant ordinary people encounter most often. Automobile loan contracts, for example, require the car owner to maintain a minimum amount

of collision and theft insurance and prevent the sale of the car unless the loan is paid off. Similarly, the recipient of a home mortgage must have adequate insurance on the home and must pay off the mortgage when the property is sold.

4. Restrictive covenants also require a borrowing firm to provide information about its activities periodically in the form of quarterly financial statements, thereby making it easier for the lender to monitor the firm and reduce moral hazard. This type of covenant may also stipulate that the lender has the right to audit and inspect the firm's books at any time.

We now see why debt contracts are often complicated legal documents with numerous restrictions on the borrower's behaviour (puzzle 8): debt contracts require complicated restrictive covenants to lower moral hazard.

Financial Intermediation   Although restrictive covenants help reduce the moral hazard problem, they do not eliminate it completely. It is almost impossible to write covenants that rule out *every* risky activity. Furthermore, borrowers may be clever enough to find loopholes in restrictive covenants that make them ineffective.

Another problem with restrictive covenants is that they must be monitored and enforced. A restrictive covenant is meaningless if the borrower can violate it knowing that the lender won't check up or is unwilling to pay for legal recourse. Because monitoring and enforcement of restrictive covenants are costly, the free-rider problem arises in the debt securities (bond) market just as it does in the stock market. If you know that other bondholders are monitoring and enforcing the restrictive covenants, you can free-ride on their monitoring and enforcement. But other bondholders can do the same thing, so the likely outcome is that not enough resources are devoted to monitoring and enforcing the restrictive covenants. Moral hazard therefore continues to be a severe problem for marketable debt.

As we have seen before, financial intermediaries, particularly banks, have the ability to avoid the free-rider problem as long as they primarily make private loans. Private loans are not traded, so no one else can free-ride on the intermediary's monitoring and enforcement of the restrictive covenants. The intermediary making private loans thus receives the benefits of monitoring and enforcement and will work to shrink the moral hazard problem inherent in debt contracts. The concept of moral hazard has provided us with additional reasons why financial intermediaries play a more important role in channelling funds from savers to borrowers than marketable securities do, as described in puzzles 1 through 4.

Summary

The presence of asymmetric information in financial markets leads to adverse selection and moral hazard problems that interfere with the efficient functioning of those markets. Tools to help solve these problems involve the private production and sale of information, government regulation to increase information in financial markets, the importance of collateral and net worth to debt contracts, and the use of monitoring and restrictive covenants. A key finding from our analysis is that the existence of the free-rider problem for traded securities such as stocks and bonds indicates that financial intermediaries, particularly banks, should play a greater role than securities markets in financing the activities of businesses. Economic analysis of the consequences of adverse selection and moral hazard has helped explain the basic features of our financial system and has provided solutions to the eight puzzles about our financial structure outlined at the beginning of this chapter.

APPLICATION	*Financial Development and Economic Growth*

Recent research has found that an important reason why many developing countries or ex-communist countries like Russia (which are referred to as transition countries) experience very low rates of growth is that their financial systems are underdeveloped (a situation referred to as *financial repression*).[5] The economic analysis of financial structure helps explain how an underdeveloped financial system leads to a low state of economic development and economic growth.

The financial systems in developing and transition countries face several difficulties that keep them from operating efficiently. As we have seen, two important tools used to help solve adverse selection and moral hazard problems in credit markets are collateral and restrictive covenants. In many developing countries, the legal system functions poorly, making it hard to make effective use of these two tools. In these countries, bankruptcy procedures are often extremely slow and cumbersome. For example, in many countries, **creditors** (holders of debt) must first sue the defaulting debtor for payment, which can take several years, and then once a favourable judgment has been obtained, the creditor has to sue again to obtain title to the collateral. The process can take in excess of five years, and by the time the lender acquires the collateral, it may have been neglected and thus have little value. In addition, governments often block lenders from foreclosing on borrowers in politically powerful sectors such as agriculture. Where the market is unable to use collateral effectively, the adverse selection problem will be worse because the lender will need even more information about the quality of the borrower in order to screen out a good loan from a bad one. The result is that it will be harder for lenders to channel funds to borrowers with the most productive investment opportunities, thereby leading to less productive investment and hence a slower-growing economy. Similarly, a poorly developed legal system may make it extremely difficult for borrowers to enforce restrictive covenants. Thus they may have a much more limited ability to reduce moral hazard on the part of borrowers and so will be less willing to lend. Again the outcome will be less productive investment and a lower growth rate for the economy.

Governments in developing and transition countries have also often decided to use their financial systems to direct credit to themselves or to favoured sectors of the economy by setting interest rates at artificially low levels for certain types of loans, by creating so-called development finance institutions to make specific types of loans, or by directing existing institutions to lend to certain entities. As we have seen, private institutions have an incentive to solve adverse selection and moral hazard problems and lend to borrowers with the most productive investment opportunities. Governments have less incentive to do so because they are not driven by the profit motive and so their directed credit programs may not channel funds to sectors that will produce high growth for the economy. The outcome is again likely to result in less efficient investment and slower growth.

In addition, banks in many developing and transition countries have been nationalized by their governments. Again because of the absence of the profit

---

[5]See Nouriel Roubini and Xavier Sala-i-Martin, "A Growth Model of Inflation, Tax Evasion and Financial Repression," *Journal of Monetary Economics* 35 (1995): 275–301, for a survey of this literature and a list of further references.

motive, these nationalized banks have little incentive to allocate their capital to the most productive uses. Indeed, the primary loan customer of these nationalized banks is often the government, which does not always use the funds wisely.

We have seen that government regulation can increase the amount of information in financial markets to make them work more efficiently. Many developing and transition countries have an underdeveloped regulatory apparatus that retards the provision of adequate information to the marketplace. For example, these countries often have weak accounting standards, making it very hard to ascertain the quality of a borrower's balance sheet. As a result, asymmetric information problems are more severe, and the financial system is severely hampered in channelling funds to the most productive uses.

The institutional environment of a poor legal system, weak accounting standards, inadequate government regulation, and government intervention through directed credit programs and nationalization of banks all help explain why many countries stay poor while others grow richer.

FINANCIAL CRISES AND AGGREGATE ECONOMIC ACTIVITY

Our economic analysis of the effects of adverse selection and moral hazard can help us understand **financial crises**, major disruptions in financial markets that are characterized by sharp declines in asset prices and the failures of many financial and nonfinancial firms. Financial crises have been common in most countries throughout modern history. Canada experienced major financial crises in 1866, 1879, 1923, 1930–1933, and 1985 but has had none since then.[6] Studying financial crises is worthwhile because they have led to severe economic downturns in the past and have the potential for doing so in the future.

Financial crises occur when there is a disruption in the financial system that causes such a sharp increase in adverse selection and moral hazard problems in financial markets that the markets are unable to channel funds efficiently from savers to people with productive investment opportunities. As a result of this inability of financial markets to function efficiently, economic activity contracts sharply.

Factors Causing Financial Crises

To understand why banking and financial crises occur and more specifically how they lead to contractions in economic activity, we need to examine the factors that cause them. Four categories of factors can trigger financial crises: increases in interest rates, increases in uncertainty, asset market effects on balance sheets, and problems in the banking sector.

Increases in Interest Rates As we saw earlier, individuals and firms with the riskiest investment projects are exactly those who are willing to pay the highest interest rates. If market interest rates are driven up sufficiently because of increased demand for credit or because of a decline in the money supply, good credit risks

---

[6]Although we in Canada have not experienced any financial crises since the Great Depression, we have had several close calls—the October 1987 stock market crash, for example. An important reason why we have escaped financial crises is the timely action of the Bank of Canada to prevent them during episodes like that of October 1987. We look at the issue of the Bank's role in preventing financial crises in Chapter 17.

are less likely to want to borrow while bad credit risks are still willing to borrow. Because of the resulting increase in adverse selection, lenders will no longer want to make loans. The substantial decline in lending will lead to a substantial decline in investment and aggregate economic activity.

Increases in Uncertainty   A dramatic increase in uncertainty in financial markets, due perhaps to the failure of a prominent financial or nonfinancial institution, a recession, or a stock market crash, makes it harder for lenders to screen good from bad credit risks. The resulting inability of lenders to solve the adverse selection problem makes them less willing to lend, which leads to a decline in lending, investment, and aggregate activity.

Asset Market Effects on Balance Sheets   The state of firms' balance sheets has important implications for the severity of asymmetric information problems in the financial system. A sharp decline in the stock market is one factor that can cause a serious deterioration in firms' balance sheets that can increase adverse selection and moral hazard problems in financial markets and provoke a financial crisis. A decline in the stock market means that the net worth of corporations has fallen because share prices are the valuation of a corporation's net worth. The decline in net worth as a result of a stock market decline makes lenders less willing to lend because, as we have seen, the net worth of a firm plays a role similar to that of collateral. When the value of collateral declines, it provides less protection to lenders, meaning that losses on loans are likely to be more severe. Because lenders are now less protected against the consequences of adverse selection, they decrease their lending, which in turn causes investment and aggregate output to decline. In addition, the decline in corporate net worth as a result of a stock market decline increases moral hazard by providing incentives for borrowing firms to make risky investments, as they now have less to lose if their investments go sour. The resulting increase in moral hazard makes lending less attractive—another reason why a stock market decline and hence a decline in net worth leads to decreased lending and economic activity.

In economies in which inflation has been moderate, which characterizes most industrialized countries, many debt contracts are typically of fairly long maturity with fixed interest rates. In this institutional environment, unanticipated declines in the aggregate price level also decrease the net worth of firms. Because debt payments are contractually fixed in nominal terms, an unanticipated decline in the price level raises the value of firms' liabilities in *real* terms (increases the burden of the debt) but does not raise the real value of firms' assets. The result is that net worth in *real* terms (the difference between assets and liabilities in *real* terms) declines. A sharp drop in the price level therefore causes a substantial decline in real net worth and an increase in adverse selection and moral hazard problems facing lenders. An unanticipated decline in the aggregate price level thus leads to a drop in lending and economic activity.

Because of uncertainty about the future value of the domestic currency in developing countries (and in some industrialized countries), many nonfinancial firms, banks, and governments in these countries find it easier to issue debt denominated in foreign currencies. This can lead to a financial crisis in a similar fashion to an unanticipated decline in the price level. With debt contracts denominated in foreign currency, when there is an unanticipated depreciation or devaluation of the domestic currency, the debt burden of domestic firms increases. Since assets are typically denominated in domestic currency, there is a resulting deterioration in firms' balance sheets and a decline in net worth, which then increases adverse selection and moral hazard problems along the lines just described. The increase in asymmetric information problems leads to a decline in investment and economic activity.

Although we have seen that increases in interest rates have a direct effect on increasing adverse selection problems, increases in interest rates also play a role in promoting a financial crisis through their effect on both firms' and households' balance sheets. A rise in interest rates and therefore in households' and firms' interest payments decreases firms' **cash flow**, the difference between cash receipts and cash expenditures. The decline in cash flow causes a deterioration in the balance sheet because it decreases the liquidity of the household or firm and thus makes it harder for lenders to know whether the firm or household will be able to pay its bills. As a result, adverse selection and moral hazard problems become more severe for potential lenders to these firms and households, leading to a decline in lending and economic activity. There is thus an additional reason why sharp increases in interest rates can be an important factor leading to financial crises.

Problems in the Banking Sector   Banks play a major role in financial markets because they are well positioned to engage in information-producing activities that facilitate productive investment for the economy. The state of banks' balance sheets has an important effect on bank lending. If banks suffer a deterioration in their balance sheets and so have a substantial contraction in their capital, they will have fewer resources to lend, and bank lending will decline. The contraction in lending then leads to a decline in investment spending, which slows economic activity.

If the deterioration in bank balance sheets is severe enough, banks will start to fail and fear can spread from one bank to another, causing even healthy banks to go under. The multiple bank failures that result are known as a **bank panic**. The source of the contagion is again asymmetric information. In a panic, depositors, fearing for the safety of their deposits (in the absence of deposit insurance) and not knowing the quality of banks' loan portfolios, withdraw their deposits to the point that the banks fail. The failure of a large number of banks in a short period of time means that there is a loss of information production in financial markets and hence a direct loss of financial intermediation by the banking sector. The decrease in bank lending during a financial crisis also decreases the supply of funds to borrowers, which leads to higher interest rates. The outcome of a bank panic is an increase in adverse selection and moral hazard problems in credit markets: these problems produce an even sharper decline in lending to facilitate productive investments that lead to an even more severe contraction in economic activity.

APPLICATION | *Financial Crises in Canada*

As mentioned, Canada had a number of banking and financial crises in the nineteenth and twentieth centuries—in 1866, 1879, 1923, 1930–1933, and 1985. Our analysis of the factors that lead to a financial crisis can explain why these crises took place and why they were so damaging to the Canadian economy.

Study Guide   To understand fully what took place in a Canadian financial crisis, make sure that you can state the reasons why each of the factors—increases in interest rates, increases in uncertainty, asset market effects on balance sheets, and problems in the banking sector—increases adverse selection and moral hazard problems, which in turn lead to a decline in economic activity. To help you understand these crises, you might want to refer to Figure 8-3, a diagram that traces the sequence of events in a Canadian financial crisis.

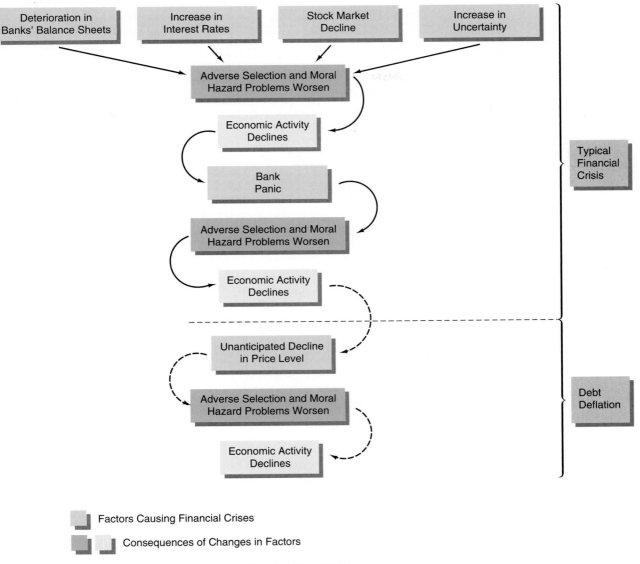

Factors Causing Financial Crises

Consequences of Changes in Factors

FIGURE 8-3 Sequence of Events in Canadian Financial Crises

The solid arrows trace the sequence of events in a typical financial crisis; the dotted arrows show the additional set of events that occur if the crisis develops into a debt deflation.

As shown in Figure 8-3, most financial crises in Canada have begun with a deterioration in banks' balance sheets, a sharp rise in interest rates (frequently stemming from increases in interest rates in the United States), a steep stock market decline, and an increase in uncertainty resulting from a failure of major financial or nonfinancial firms (the Bank of Upper Canada in 1866 and the Home Bank in 1923) or from a bank panic (the panic of 1879). During these crises, deterioration in banks' balance sheets, the increase in uncertainty, the rise in interest rates, and the stock market decline increased the severity of adverse selection problems in credit markets; the stock market decline, the deterioration in banks' balance sheets, and the rise in interest rates, which decreased firms' cash flow, also increased moral hazard problems. The rise in adverse selection and moral hazard problems then made it less attractive for lenders to lend and led to a decline in investment and aggregate economic activity.

BOX 8·1

Case Study of a Financial Crisis

The Great Depression. Federal Reserve officials viewed the stock market boom of 1928 and 1929, during which stock prices doubled, as excessive speculation. To curb it, they pursued a tight monetary policy to raise interest rates. The Fed got more than it bargained for when the stock market crashed in October 1929.

Although the 1929 crash had a great impact on the minds of a whole generation, most people forget that by the middle of 1930, more than half of the stock market decline had been reversed. What might have been a normal recession turned into something far different, however, with adverse shocks to the agricultural sector, a continuing decline in the stock market after the middle of 1930, and a sequence of bank collapses from October 1930 until March 1933 in which over one-third of the banks in the United States went out of business. It is worth noting, however, that no Canadian banks failed during this period—we will describe these events in more detail in Chapter 18.

The continuing decline in stock prices after mid-1930 (by mid-1932 stocks had declined to 10% of their value at the 1929 peak) and the increase in uncertainty from the unsettled business conditions created by the economic contraction made adverse selection and moral hazard problems worse in the credit markets. The loss of one-third of the banks reduced the amount of financial intermediation. This intensified adverse selection and moral hazard problems, thereby decreasing the ability of financial markets to channel funds to firms with productive investment opportunities. As our analysis predicts, the amount of outstanding commercial loans fell by half from 1929 to 1933, and investment spending collapsed, declining by 90% from its 1929 level.

The short-circuiting of the process that kept the economy from recovering quickly, which it does in most recessions, occurred because of a fall in the price level by 25% in the 1930–1933 period. This huge decline in prices triggered a debt deflation in which net worth fell because of the increased burden of indebtedness borne by firms. The decline in net worth and the resulting increase in adverse selection and moral hazard problems in the credit markets led to a prolonged economic contraction in which unemployment rose to 25% of the labour force. The financial crisis in the Great Depression was the worst ever experienced in the United States, and it explains why this economic contraction was also the most severe one ever experienced by the nation.*

*See Ben Bernanke, "Nonmonetary Effects of the Financial Crisis in the Propagation of the Great Depression," *American Economic Review* 73 (1983): 257–276, for a discussion of the role of asymmetric information problems in the Great Depression period.

Because of the worsening business conditions and uncertainty about their bank's health (perhaps banks would go broke), depositors began to withdraw their funds from banks, which led to bank panic. The resulting decline in the number of banks raised interest rates even further and decreased the amount of financial intermediation by banks. Worsening of the problems created by adverse selection and moral hazard led to further economic contraction.

Finally, there was a sorting out of firms that were **insolvent** (had a negative net worth and hence were bankrupt) from healthy firms by bankruptcy proceedings. The same process occurred for banks, often with the help of public and private authorities. Once this sorting out was complete, uncertainty in financial markets declined, the stock market underwent a recovery, and interest rates fell. The overall result was that adverse selection and moral hazard problems diminished and the financial crisis subsided. With the financial markets able to operate well again, the stage was set for the recovery of the economy.

If, however, the economic downturn led to a sharp decline in prices, the recovery process was short-circuited. In this situation, shown in Figure 8-3, a process called **debt deflation** occurred, in which a substantial decline in the price level set in, leading to a further deterioration in firms' net worth because of the increased burden of indebtedness. When debt deflation set in, the adverse selection and moral hazard problems continued to increase so that lending, investment spending, and aggregate economic activity remained depressed for a long time. The most significant financial crisis that included debt deflation was the Great Depression, the worst economic contraction in history (see Box 8-1).

APPLICATION	*Financial Crises in Emerging-Market Countries: Mexico, 1994–1995, and East Asia, 1997–1998*

In recent years, many emerging-market countries have experienced financial crises, the most dramatic of which were the Mexican crisis, which started in December 1994, and the East Asian crisis, which started in July 1997. An important puzzle is how a developing country can shift dramatically from a path of high growth before a financial crisis—as was true for Mexico and particularly the East Asian countries of Thailand, Malaysia, Indonesia, the Philippines, and South Korea—to a sharp decline in economic activity. We can apply our asymmetric information analysis of financial crises to explain this puzzle and to understand the Mexican and East Asian financial situations.[7]

Because of the different institutional features of emerging-market countries' debt markets, the sequence of events in the Mexican and East Asian crises is different from that occurring in Canada in the nineteenth and twentieth centuries. Figure 8-4 diagrams the sequence of events that occurred in Mexico and East Asia.

An important factor leading up to both financial crises was the deterioration in banks' balance sheets because of increasing loan losses. When financial markets in these countries were deregulated in the early 1990s, a lending boom ensued in which bank credit to the private nonfinancial business sector accelerated sharply. Because of weak supervision by bank regulators and a lack of expertise in screening and monitoring borrowers at banking institutions, losses on the loans began to mount, causing an erosion of banks' net worth (capital). As a result of this erosion, banks had fewer resources to lend, and this lack of lending eventually led to a contraction in economic activity.

Banco de Mexico
www.banxico.org.mx

Another precipitating factor to the Mexican (but not East Asian) financial crisis was a rise in interest rates abroad. Beginning in February 1994, the Federal Reserve in the United States began to raise the federal funds rate to head off inflationary pressures. Although the policy was quite successful in keeping inflation in check in the United States, it put upward pressure on Mexican interest rates. In addition, the Mexican central bank, the Banco de Mexico, raised interest rates to protect the value of the peso in the foreign exchange market. The rise in interest rates directly added to increased adverse selection in Mexican financial markets because, as discussed earlier, it made it more likely that the parties willing to take on the most risk would seek loans.

---

[7]This chapter does not examine two other recent crises, those in Brazil and Russia. Russia's financial crisis in August 1998 can also be explained with the asymmetric information story here, but it is more appropriate to view it as a symptom of a wider breakdown in the economy—and this is why we do not focus on it here. The Brazilian crisis in January 1999 has features of a more traditional balance-of-payments crisis (see Chapter 19), rather than a financial crisis.

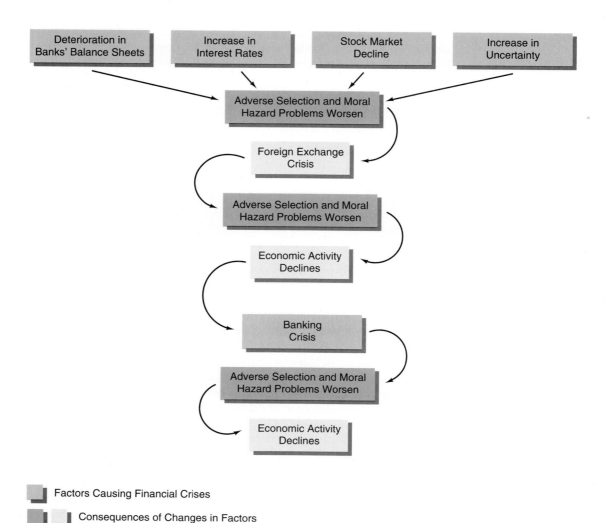

FIGURE 8-4 Sequence of Events in the Mexican and East Asian Financial Crises

The arrows trace the sequence of events during the financial crisis.

Also, stock market declines and increases in uncertainty occurred prior to and contributed to full-blown crises in Mexico, Thailand, and South Korea. (The stock market declines in Malaysia, Indonesia, and the Philippines, on the other hand, occurred simultaneously with the onset of the crisis.) The Mexican economy was hit by political shocks in 1994 that created uncertainty, specifically the assassination of Luis Donaldo Colosio, the ruling party's presidential candidate, and an uprising in the southern state of Chiapas. By the middle of December 1994, stock prices on the Bolsa (stock exchange) had fallen nearly 20% from their September 1994 peak. In January 1997, a major Korean chaebol (conglomerate), Hanbo Steel, collapsed; it was the first bankruptcy of a chaebol in a decade. Shortly thereafter, Sammi Steel and Kia Motors also declared bankruptcy. In Thailand, Samprosong Land, a major real estate developer, defaulted on its foreign debt in early February 1997, and Thai financial institutions that had lent heavily in the real estate market began to encounter serious difficulties, requiring over $8 billion of loans from the Thai central bank to prop them up. Finally, in June, the failure of a major Thai finance company, Finance One, imposed substantial losses on both domestic and

Mexican Stock Exchange
www.bmv.com.mx

Bank of Thailand
www.bot.or.th

foreign creditors. These events increased general uncertainty in the financial markets of Thailand and South Korea, and both experienced substantial declines in their securities markets. From peak values in early 1996, Korean stock prices fell by 25% and Thai stock prices by 50%.

As we have seen, an increase in uncertainty and a decrease in net worth as a result of a stock market decline increase asymmetric information problems. It becomes harder to screen out good from bad borrowers, and the decline in net worth decreases the value of firms' collateral and increases their incentives to make risky investments because there is less equity to lose if the investments are unsuccessful. The increase in uncertainty and stock market declines that occurred before the crisis, along with the deterioration in banks' balance sheets, worsened adverse selection and moral hazard problems (shown at the top of the diagram in Figure 8-4) and made the economies ripe for a serious financial crisis.

At this point, full-blown speculative attacks developed in the foreign exchange market plunging these countries into a full-scale crisis. With the Colosio assassination, the Chiapas uprising, and the growing weakness in the banking sector, the Mexican peso came under attack. Even though the Mexican central bank intervened in the foreign exchange market and raised interest rates sharply, it was unable to stem the attack and was forced to devalue the peso on December 20, 1994. In the case of Thailand, concerns about the large current account deficit and weakness in the Thai financial system, culminating with the failure of Finance One, led to a successful speculative attack that forced the Thai central bank to allow the baht to float downward. Soon thereafter, speculative attacks developed against the other countries in the region, leading to the collapse of the Philippine peso, the Indonesian rupiah, the Malaysian ringgit, and the South Korean won.

The institutional structure of debt markets in Mexico and East Asia now interacted with the currency devaluations to propel the economies into full-fledged financial crises. Because so many firms in these countries had debt denominated in foreign currencies like the dollar and the yen, depreciation of their currencies resulted in increases in their indebtedness in domestic currency terms, even though the value of their assets remained unchanged. When the peso lost half its value by March 1995 and the Thai, Philippine, Malaysian, and South Korean currencies lost between a third and half of their value by the beginning of 1998, firms' balance sheets took a big negative hit, causing a dramatic increase in adverse selection and moral hazard problems. This negative shock was most severe for Indonesia, which saw the value of its currency fall by an astronomical 80%, resulting in insolvency for any firm with substantial amounts of debt denominated in foreign currencies.

The collapse of currencies also led to a rise in actual and expected inflation in these countries, and market interest rates rose sky-high (to over 100% in Mexico). The resulting increase in interest payments caused reductions in households' and firms' cash flow, which led to further deterioration in their balance sheets. A feature of debt markets in emerging-market countries, like those in Mexico and East Asia, is that debt contracts have very short durations, typically less than one month. Thus the rise in short-term interest rates in these countries meant that the effect on cash flow and hence on balance sheets was substantial. As our asymmetric information analysis suggests, this deterioration in households' and firms' balance sheets increased adverse selection and moral hazard problems in the credit markets, making lenders even less willing to lend.

In addition, in the aftermath of the currency crises, stock markets crashed. The Mexican market declined 50% from its peak value, and the Thai, Philippine, Malaysian, Indonesian, and South Korean markets declined 50% to 80%. The collapse of stock market values further worsened adverse selection and moral hazard problems.

These asymmetric information problems were severe not only for domestic lenders but for foreign lenders as well because they had difficulty obtaining information regarding these economies. Foreign lenders were thus eager to pull their funds out of Mexico and the East Asian crisis countries, and that is what they did. Foreign portfolio investment inflows to Mexico, which had been on the order of $20 billion a year in 1993, reversed course, and the outflows exceeded $10 billion a year by the fourth quarter of 1994. Similarly in East Asia, capital flows for Thailand, Malaysia, the Philippines, Indonesia, and South Korea reversed from an inflow of close to $100 billion in 1996 to an outflow of more than $10 billion in 1997. Consistent with the theory of financial crises outlined in this chapter, the sharp decline in lending helped lead to a collapse of economic activity, with real GDP growth falling sharply.

As shown in Figure 8-4, further deterioration in the economy occurred because the collapse in economic activity and the deterioration in the cash flow and balance sheets of both firms and households led to a worsening banking crisis. The problems of firms and households meant that many of them were no longer able to pay off their debts, resulting in substantial losses for the banks. Even more problematic for the banks was that they had many short-term liabilities denominated in foreign currencies, and the sharp increase in the value of these liabilities after the devaluation led to a further deterioration in the banks' balance sheets. Under these circumstances, the banking system would have collapsed in the absence of a government safety net, but with the assistance of the International Monetary Fund, these countries were in some cases able to protect depositors and avoid a bank panic. However, given the loss of bank capital and the need for the government to intervene to prop up the banks, the banks' ability to lend was nevertheless sharply curtailed. As we have seen, a banking crisis of this type hinders the ability of the banks to lend and also makes adverse selection and moral hazard problems worse in financial markets because banks are less capable of playing their traditional financial intermediation role. The banking crisis, along with other factors that increased adverse selection and moral hazard problems in the credit markets of Mexico and East Asia, explains the collapse of lending and hence economic activity in the aftermath of the crisis.

In the aftermath of their crises, Mexico began to recover in 1996, while the crisis countries in East Asia saw a glimmer of recovery in 1999. In all these countries, the economic hardship caused by the financial crises was tremendous. Unemployment rose sharply, poverty increased substantially, and even the social fabric of society was stretched thin. For example, Mexico City has become one of the most crime-ridden cities in the world, while Indonesia has experienced waves of ethnic violence.

International Monetary Fund
www.imf.org

SUMMARY

1. There are eight basic puzzles about financial structure throughout the world. The first four emphasize the importance of financial intermediaries and the relative unimportance of securities markets for the financing of corporations; the fifth recognizes that financial markets are among the most heavily regulated sectors of the economy; the sixth states that only large, well-established corporations have access to securities markets; the seventh indicates that collateral is an important feature of debt contracts; and the eighth presents debt contracts as complicated legal documents that place substantial restrictions on the behaviour of the borrower.

2. Transaction costs freeze many small savers and borrowers out of direct involvement with financial markets. Financial intermediaries can take advantage of economies of scale and are better able to develop expertise to lower transaction costs, thus enabling savers and borrowers to benefit from the existence of financial markets.

3. Asymmetric information results in two problems: adverse selection, which occurs before the transaction, and moral hazard, which occurs after the transaction. Adverse selection refers to the fact that bad credit risks are the ones most likely to seek loans, and moral hazard refers to the risk of the borrower's engaging in activities that are undesirable from the lender's point of view.

4. Adverse selection interferes with the efficient functioning of financial markets. Tools to help reduce the adverse selection problem include private production and sale of information, government regulation to increase information, financial intermediation, and collateral and net worth. The free-rider problem occurs when people who do not pay for information take advantage of information that other people have paid for. This problem explains why financial intermediaries, particularly banks, play a more important role in financing the activities of businesses than securities markets do.

5. Moral hazard in equity contracts is known as the principal–agent problem because managers (the agents) have less incentive to maximize profits than stockholders (the principals). The principal–agent problem explains why debt contracts are so much more prevalent in financial markets than equity contracts. Tools to help reduce the principal–agent problem include monitoring, government regulation to increase information, and financial intermediation.

6. Tools to reduce the moral hazard problem in debt contracts include net worth, monitoring and enforcement of restrictive covenants, and financial intermediaries.

7. Financial crises are major disruptions in financial markets. They are caused by increases in adverse selection and moral hazard problems that prevent financial markets from channelling funds to people with productive investment opportunities, leading to a sharp contraction in economic activity. The four types of factors that lead to financial crises are increases in interest rates, increases in uncertainty, asset market effects on balance sheets, and problems in the banking sector.

KEY TERMS

bank panic, p. 176

cash flow, p. 176

collateral, p. 160

costly state verification, p. 169

creditor, p. 173

debt deflation, p. 179

financial crisis, p. 174

free-rider problem, p. 164

incentive-compatible, p. 171

insolvent, p. 178

net worth (equity capital), p. 167

principal–agent problem, p. 168

restrictive covenants, p. 160

secured debt, p. 160

unsecured debt, p. 160

venture capital firm, p. 169

QUESTIONS AND PROBLEMS

Questions marked with an asterisk are answered at the end of the book in an appendix, "Answers to Selected Questions and Problems."

1. How can economies of scale help explain the existence of financial intermediaries?

*2. Describe two ways in which financial intermediaries help lower transaction costs in the economy.

3. Would moral hazard and adverse selection still arise in financial markets if information were not asymmetric? Explain.

*4. How do standard accounting principles required by the government help financial markets work more efficiently?

5. Do you think the lemons problem would be more severe for stocks traded on the Toronto Stock Exchange or those traded over-the-counter? Explain.

*6. Which firms are most likely to use bank financing rather than to issue bonds or stocks to finance their activities? Why?

7. How can the existence of asymmetric information provide a rationale for government regulation of financial markets?

*8. Would you be more willing to lend to a friend if she put all of her life savings into her business than you would if she had not done so? Why?

9. Rich people often worry that others will seek to marry them only for their money. Is this a problem of adverse selection?

*10. The more collateral there is backing a loan, the less the lender has to worry about adverse selection. Is this statement true, false, or uncertain? Explain your answer.

11. How does the free-rider problem aggravate adverse selection and moral hazard problems in financial markets?

*12. Explain how the separation of ownership and control in Canadian corporations might lead to poor management.

13. Is a financial crisis more likely to occur when the economy is experiencing deflation or inflation? Explain.

*14. How can a stock market crash provoke a financial crisis?

15. How can a sharp rise in interest rates provoke a financial crisis?

Chapter 9

The Banking Firm and the Management of Financial Institutions

PREVIEW   Because banks (depository institutions) play such a major role in channelling funds to borrowers with productive investment opportunities, they are important in ensuring that the financial system and the economy run smoothly and efficiently. In Canada, banks provide loans to businesses, help us finance our college and university educations or the purchase of a new car or home, and provide us with services such as chequing and savings accounts.

In this chapter we examine how banks, the most important of all the financial intermediaries, operate to earn the highest profits possible: how and why they make loans, how they acquire funds and manage their assets and liabilities (debts), and how they earn income. Although we focus on chartered banks because they are the most important financial intermediaries, many of the same principles are equally applicable to other types of banking institutions, such as trust and mortgage loan companies and credit unions and *caisses populaires,* and to other nonbank financial institutions as well.

THE BANK BALANCE SHEET

To understand how a bank operates, first we need to examine its **balance sheet**, a list of the bank's assets and liabilities. As the name implies, this list balances; that is, it has the characteristic that

$$\text{Total assets} = \text{total liabilities} + \text{capital}$$

Furthermore, a bank's balance sheet lists *sources* of bank funds (liabilities) and *uses* to which they are put (assets). Banks obtain funds by borrowing and by issuing other liabilities such as deposits. They then use these funds to acquire assets such as securities and loans. Banks make profits by earning an interest rate on their holdings of securities and loans that is higher than the expenses on their liabilities. The balance sheet of all chartered banks, as of September 30, 2000, appears in Table 9-1.

TABLE 9-1 Balance Sheet of All Banks in Canada, in millions (as of September 30, 2000)

Assets (Uses of Funds)	Amount ($)	Percent (%)
Coins and bank notes	5 648	0.37
Deposits with the Bank of Canada	507	0.03
Deposits with other financial institutions	86 507	5.73
Cheques and other items in transit	3 533	0.23
Total cash reserves	96 195	6.38
Securities		
Issued by the government of Canada	90 351	5.99
Issued by provinces and municipalities	17 857	1.18
Issued by other entities	235 230	15.59
Total securities	343 438	22.76
Loans		
To investment dealers and brokers	11 219	0.74
To regulated financial institutions	15 801	1.05
Other loans	551 167	36.53
Mortgage loans	292 717	19.40
Total loans	870 904	57.72
Fixed and other assets		
Customer liabilities under acceptances	53 970	3.58
Other assets	144 434	9.57
Total fixed and other assets	198 404	13.15
Total assets	1 508 941	100.00

Liabilities (Sources of Funds)	Amount ($)	Percent (%)
Demand deposits	127 529	8.45
Notice deposits	178 704	11.84
Fixed-term deposits	733 754	48.63
Total deposits	1 039 987	68.92
Nondeposit liabilities		
Cheques and other items in transit	294	0.02
Advances from the Bank of Canada	309	0.02
Banker's acceptances	53 970	3.58
Nondeposit liabilities of subsidiaries	8 755	0.58
Insurance related liabilities	2 343	0.16
Accrued interest payable	14 360	0.95
Obligations related to borrowed securities	67 851	4.50
Obligations related to assets sold under repo	90 941	6.03
Derivative contract obligations	80 355	5.33
Other liabilities	42 935	2.85
Noncontrolling interest in subsidiaries	4 521	0.30
Total nondeposit liabilities	366 634	24.30
Subordinated debt	29 036	1.92
Bank capital	73 284	4.86
Total liabilities and bank capital	1 508 941	100.00

Source: Office of the Superintendent of Financial Institutions Canada. Website: http://www.osfi-bsif.gc.ca. Reproduced with permission.

Liabilities

A bank acquires funds by issuing (selling) liabilities, which are consequently also referred to as *sources of funds*. The funds obtained from issuing liabilities are used to purchase income-earning assets. Chartered banks have three main sources of funds: deposits, borrowings, and equity. Table 9-1 shows that deposits make up 69% of bank liabilities, borrowings 26%, and equity 5%.

Demand and Notice Deposits   Demand deposits are payable on demand; that is, if a depositor shows up at the bank and requests payment by making a withdrawal, the bank must pay the depositor immediately. Similarly, if a person, who receives a cheque written on an account from a bank, presents that cheque at the bank, the bank must pay the funds out immediately (or credit them to that person's account).

Notice deposits are more important as a source of funds for the banks than are demand deposits (11.84% versus 8.45% in Table 9-1). Although notice deposits have a notice requirement in the contractual agreement with the client, the banks never enforce this clause, and so in fact most notice deposits are really just like demand deposits in this sense.

Demand deposits and notice deposits are bank accounts that allow the owner to write cheques to third parties. Table 9-1 shows that this category of chequable deposits is an important low-cost source of bank funds, making up 20% of bank liabilities. Once, chequable deposits were the most important source of bank funds, but with the appearance of new, more attractive financial instruments, the share of chequable deposits in total bank liabilities has shrunk over time.

A chequable deposit is an asset for the depositor because it is part of his or her wealth. Conversely, because the depositor can withdraw from an account funds that the bank is obligated to pay, chequable deposits are a liability for the bank. They are usually the lowest-cost source of bank funds because depositors are willing to forgo some interest in order to have access to a liquid asset that can be used to make purchases. The bank's costs of maintaining chequable deposits include interest payments and the costs incurred in servicing these accounts—processing and storing cancelled cheques, preparing and sending out monthly statements, providing efficient tellers (human or otherwise), maintaining an impressive building and conveniently located branches, and advertising and marketing to entice customers to deposit their funds with a given bank. In recent years, interest paid on deposits (chequable and time) has accounted for around 56% of total bank operating expenses, while the costs involved in servicing accounts (employee salaries, building rent, and so on) have been approximately 35% of operating expenses.

Fixed-Term Deposits   Fixed-term deposits are the primary source of bank funds (almost 49% of bank liabilities in Table 9-1). Owners (retail customers, small- and medium-sized businesses, large corporations, governments, and other financial institutions) cannot write cheques on fixed-term deposits, but the interest rates are usually higher than those on chequable deposits. There are two main types of fixed-term deposits: savings accounts and time deposits (also called certificates of deposit, or CDs).

Savings accounts were once the most common type of fixed-term deposit. In these accounts, to which funds can be added or from which funds can be withdrawn at any time, transactions and interest payments are recorded in a monthly statement or in a small book (the passbook) held by the owner of the account.

Time deposits have a fixed maturity length, ranging from several months to over five years, and have substantial penalties for early withdrawal (the forfeiture of several months' interest). Small-denomination time deposits (deposits of less than $100 000) are less liquid for the depositor than passbook savings, earn higher interest rates, and are a more costly source of funds for the banks.

Large-denomination time deposits (CDs) are available in denominations of $100 000 or over and are typically bought by corporations or other banks. Large-denomination CDs are negotiable; like bonds, they can be resold in a secondary market before they mature. For this reason, negotiable CDs are held by corporations, money market mutual funds, and other financial institutions as alternative assets to Treasury bills and other short-term bonds. Since 1964, when they first appeared in Canada, negotiable CDs have become an important source of bank funds.

Borrowings   Banks obtain funds by borrowing from the Bank of Canada, other banks, and corporations. Borrowings from the Bank of Canada are called **overdrafts loans** (also known as **advances**). Banks also borrow reserves overnight in the overnight market from other Canadian banks and financial institutions. Banks borrow funds overnight in order to have enough **settlement balances** at the Bank of Canada to facilitate the clearing of cheques and other transfers (these clearing and settlement processes will be investigated in detail in Chapter 17).

Banks also have liabilities under banker's acceptances (BAs). These liabilities are very similar to negotiable CDs in that both are short-term bank promises to pay a specified amount on a specified date. In particular, upon the maturity of a banker's acceptance, the bank makes payment of its face amount, but at the same time the client reimburses the bank in the amount of the banker's acceptance. It is for this reason that banker's acceptances are also treated like corporate short-term assets of the bank and they appear on both sides of the balance sheet (in Table 9-1), in the same amount.

Other major sources of borrowed funds are loan arrangements with corporations, such as short sales and repurchase agreements (the latter is discussed in Chapter 2); they exceed 15% of bank liabilities, reflecting banks' increasing investment banking activities. A **short sale** involves borrowing a security from an investor or another financial institution for a fixed time period and selling it in the market with the intention of repurchasing it when it is due to be returned to the lender. When an investment bank short sells a security, it generates cash for itself and shows the obligation to repay the loan as "Obligations related to borrowed securities" on the liabilities side of the balance sheet, as in Table 9-1.

Borrowings have become a more important source of bank funds over time: in 1960, they made up only a small fraction of bank liabilities; currently, they are about 25% of bank liabilities.

Bank Capital   The final category on the liabilities side of the balance sheet is bank capital, the bank's net worth, which equals the difference between total assets and liabilities (close to 5% of total bank assets in Table 9-1). The funds are raised by selling new equity (stock) or from retained earnings. Bank capital is a cushion against a drop in the value of its assets, which could force the bank into insolvency (having liabilities in excess of assets, meaning that the bank is bankrupt). One important component of bank capital is *loan loss reserves*, which are described in Box 9-1.

Assets

A bank uses the funds that it has acquired by issuing liabilities to purchase income-earning assets. Bank assets are thus naturally referred to as *uses of funds,* and the interest payments earned on them are what enable banks to make profits.

Cash Reserves   All banks hold some of the funds they acquire as deposits in an account at the Bank of Canada, in the form of settlement balances. **Cash reserves** are these settlement balances plus currency that is physically held by banks (called **vault cash** because it is stored in bank vaults overnight). Although Canadian

> ### BOX 9-1
>
> ## *Understanding Loan Loss Reserves*
>
> Perhaps you have seen headlines in the press about a bank's large increase in loan loss (bad debt) reserves. Often there is confusion about loan loss reserves, perhaps because they have a name that sounds similar to the "reserves" item on a bank's balance sheet. Actually, loan loss reserves have nothing to do with the reserves shown on the assets side of the balance sheet; rather, they are a component of the liabilities item known as bank capital.
>
> To see how loan loss reserves work, suppose that a bank suspects that some of its loans, say $1 million worth, might prove to be bad debts that will have to be written off (valued at zero) in the future. The bank can set aside $1 million of its earnings and put it into its loan loss reserves account. Because the $1 million is now retained earnings, it adds to the difference between the bank's assets and liabilities and so increases bank capital. The fact that adding to loan loss reserves increases bank capital explains why loan loss reserves are counted as a component of capital. As a result of adding to loan loss reserves, the bank reduces its reported earnings by $1 million, even though it has not yet actually lost the $1 million—in
>
> effect, taking its lumps even before the bad debt is written off.
>
> If the bank eventually determines that the $1 million loan will never be paid back and formally writes it off, it reduces the value of its assets by $1 million. The resulting $1 million decline in bank capital is reflected as a decrease in the loan loss reserves account by $1 million. At this time, however, reported earnings are unaffected by the loan write-off because they were reduced earlier when the bank set aside $1 million of earnings as loan loss reserves.
>
> Banks add to loan loss reserves before some loans have to be written off because it is better for them to allow for potential losses when they have plenty of earnings rather than to wait and find that they must take the loss when they have little in earnings to write the loan off against. In addition, adding to loan loss reserves, which reduces reported earnings, can reduce the amount of taxes a bank has to pay and is also a way of informing the bank's stockholders, depositors, and regulators of potential future losses on loans. Bank regulators also sometimes force banks to add to loan loss reserves if they believe the bank will suffer future loan losses.

banks are not required to hold reserves in some proportion to their deposits (Canada removed all such legal requirements in June 1994), banks hold cash reserves in order to facilitate the clearing of cheques and to keep the automated banking machines with adequate amounts. Currently, cash reserves do not pay any interest and account for only 0.4% of bank assets.

Deposits at Other Banks These deposits are known as **interbank deposits** and account for close to 6% of bank assets. About 85% of these interbank deposits are in foreign currencies and are connected to the large banks' extensive eurocurrency operations and corresponding banking relationships. The main advantage of interbank deposits has been the flexibility they have provided banks to manage their own short-term liquidity requirements and respond to the liquidity needs of their clients.

Cash Items in Process of Collection Suppose that a cheque written on an account at another bank is deposited in your bank and the funds for this cheque have not yet been received (collected) from the other bank. The cheque is classified as a cash item in process of collection, and it is an asset for your bank because it is a claim on another bank for funds that will be paid within a few days. Items in process of collection are also called **items in transit** or bank **float**.

Collectively, cash reserves, cash items in process of collection, and deposits at other banks are often referred to as **total cash reserves** or simply **reserves**. In Table 9-1 they constitute only 6% of total assets, and their importance has been shrinking over time: in 1960, for example, they accounted for over 20% of total assets. Although Canadian banks are not required to hold reserves and there is a requirement of zero settlement balances with the Bank of Canada at the end of each banking day, banks hold some reserves, which we call **desired excess reserves** or simply **desired reserves**.

Banks hold reserves because of their desire to manage their own short-term liquidity requirements and respond to predictable clearing drains and predictable across-the-counter and automated banking machine drains. Moreover, banks hold reserves in order to meet unpredictable and potentially large withdrawals by their liability holders. The risk that net cash withdrawals might be negative is known as **banker's risk**, and from the perspective of this risk, banks hold reserves to meet unpredictable cash and clearing drains. We will refer to the fraction of deposits banks hold in the form of reserves (5%, for example) as the **desired reserve ratio**.

Securities A bank's holdings of securities are an important income-earning asset: securities (made up entirely of debt instruments for commercial banks because banks are not allowed to hold stock) account for close to 23% of bank assets in Table 9-1, and they provide commercial banks with about 15% of their revenue. These securities can be classified into three categories: government of Canada, provincial and municipal securities, and other securities. The government of Canada securities are the most liquid because they can be easily traded and converted into cash with low transaction costs. Because of their high liquidity, short-term Canadian government securities (such as Treasury bills) are called **secondary reserves**.

Provincial and municipal government securities are desirable for banks to hold primarily because provincial and municipal governments are more likely to do business with banks that hold their securities. Provincial and municipal government and other securities are less marketable (hence less liquid) and are also riskier than government of Canada securities, primarily because of default risk: there is some possibility that the issuer of the securities may not be able to make its interest payments or pay back the face value of the securities when they mature.

Loans Banks make their profits primarily by issuing loans. In Table 9-1, some 58% of bank assets are in the form of loans, and in recent years they have generally produced more than half of bank revenues. A loan is a liability for the individual or corporation receiving it but an asset for a bank because it provides income to the bank. Loans are typically less liquid than other assets because they cannot be turned into cash until the loan matures. If the bank makes a one-year loan, for example, it cannot get its funds back until the loan comes due in one year. Loans also have a higher probability of default than other assets. Because of the lack of liquidity and higher default risk, the bank earns its highest return on loans.

As you can see in Table 9-1, the largest categories of loans for chartered banks are commercial and industrial loans made to businesses and real estate loans. Chartered banks also make consumer loans and lend to each other. The bulk of these interbank loans are overnight loans lent in the overnight market. As the balance sheet in Table 9-1 considers both foreign and domestic assets of both Canadian and Canadian foreign-owned banks, it shows that corporate loans exceed mortgage loans (36.53% versus 19.4% of bank assets). This is so because a larger portion of the foreign activities of Canadian banks is in corporate loans rather than mortgages. In fact, the major difference in the balance sheets of the various depository institutions is primarily the type of loan they specialize in. Trust and mortgage loan companies and credit unions and *caisses populaires*, for example, specialize in residential mortgages.

Fixed and Other Assets   The physical capital (bank buildings, computers, and other equipment) owned by the banks is included in this category.

BASIC OPERATION OF A BANK

Before proceeding to a more detailed study of how a bank manages its assets and liabilities in order to make the highest profit, you should understand the basic operation of a bank.

In general terms, banks make profits by selling liabilities with one set of characteristics (a particular combination of liquidity, risk, and return) and using the proceeds to buy assets with a different set of characteristics. This process is often referred to as *asset transformation*. For example, a savings deposit held by one person can provide the funds that enable the bank to make a mortgage loan to another person. The bank has, in effect, transformed the savings deposit (an asset held by the depositor) into a mortgage loan (an asset held by the bank). Another way this process of asset transformation is described is to say that the bank "borrows short and lends long" because it makes long-term loans and funds them by issuing short-dated deposits.

The process of transforming assets and providing a set of services (cheque clearing, record keeping, credit analysis, and so forth) is like any other production process in a firm. If the bank produces desirable services at low cost and earns substantial income on its assets, it earns profits; if not, the bank suffers losses.

To make our analysis of the operation of a bank more concrete, we use a tool called a **T-account**. A T-account is a simplified balance sheet, with lines in the form of a T, which lists only the changes that occur in balance sheet items starting from some initial balance sheet position.

The key characteristic of banks is their ability to buy assets by issuing their own deposit liabilities. Suppose that the First Bank has found some profitable loans that it wants to add to its portfolio. It makes a loan in the amount of $100 to a business and credits the business's chequable deposit in that amount. The business accepts the First Bank's deposit liabilities because they have the characteristic of being the medium of exchange and are accepted as money by others. The T-accounts for the First Bank and the business look like these:

FIRST BANK				BUSINESS			
Assets		Liabilities		Assets		Liabilities	
Loans	+100	Chequable deposits	+100	Chequable deposits	+100	Bank loans	+100

Note that the transaction is simply an exchange of assets and liabilities, with no change in the net worth of both the First Bank and the business. The bank's act of making a new loan to the business increases chequable deposits, and thus the money supply, by the amount of the loan. Note, however, that the bank's objective is not to create deposits and increase the money supply; ***the bank is in the business of making a profit for its shareholders and the creation of deposits occurs as a byproduct of the bank's financing decisions***.

Acquiring income-producing assets is not the only way in which the First Bank can create new chequable deposits. Let's say that Jane Brown has heard that the First Bank provides excellent service, so she opens a chequing account with a $100 bill. She now has a $100 chequable deposit at the bank, which shows up as a $100 liability on the bank's balance sheet. The bank now puts her $100 bill into its vault so that the bank's assets rise by the $100 increase in vault cash. The T-account for the bank looks like this:

FIRST BANK		
Assets	Liabilities	
Vault cash +$100	Chequable deposits +$100	

Since vault cash is also part of the bank's reserves, we can rewrite the T-account as follows:

Assets	Liabilities	
Reserves +$100	Chequable deposits +$100	

Note that Jane Brown's opening of a chequing account leads to ***an increase in the bank's reserves equal to the increase in chequable deposits***.

If Jane had opened her account with a $100 cheque written on an account at another bank, say, the Second Bank, we would get the same result. The initial effect on the T-account of the First Bank is as follows:

Assets	Liabilities	
Cash items in process of collection +$100	Chequable deposits +$100	

Chequable deposits increase by $100 as before, but now the First Bank is owed $100 by the Second Bank. This asset for the First Bank is entered in the T-account as $100 of cash items in process of collection because the First Bank will now try to collect the funds that it is owed. It could go directly to the Second Bank and ask for payment of the funds, but if the two banks are in separate provinces, that would be a time-consuming and costly process. Instead, the First Bank deposits the cheque in its account at the Bank of Canada, and the Bank of Canada collects the funds from the Second Bank. The result is that the Bank of Canada transfers $100 of reserves from the Second Bank to the First Bank, and the final balance sheet positions of the two banks are as follows:

FIRST BANK		**SECOND BANK**	
Assets	Liabilities	Assets	Liabilities
Reserves +$100	Chequable deposits +$100	Reserves −$100	Chequable deposits −$100

The process initiated by Jane Brown can be summarized as follows: when a cheque written on an account at one bank is deposited in another, the bank receiving the deposit gains reserves equal to the amount of the cheque, while the bank on which the cheque is written sees its reserves fall by the same amount. Therefore, **when a bank receives additional deposits, it gains an equal amount of reserves; when it loses deposits, it loses an equal amount of reserves**.

Study Guide

T-accounts are used to study various topics throughout this text. Whenever you see a T-account, try to analyze what would happen if the opposite action were taken; for example, what would happen if Jane Brown decided to close her $100 account at the First Bank by writing a $100 cheque and depositing it in a new chequing account at the Second Bank?

Now that you understand how banks gain and lose reserves, we can examine how a bank rearranges its balance sheet to make a profit when it experiences a change in its deposits. Let's return to the situation when the First Bank has just received the extra $100 of chequable deposits. As you know, the bank wants to keep a certain fraction of its chequable deposits as reserves. If the fraction (the desired reserve ratio) is 10%, the First Bank's desired reserves have increased by $10, and we can rewrite its T-account as follows:

FIRST BANK

Assets		Liabilities	
Desired reserves	+$10	Chequable deposits	+$100
Excess reserves	+$90		

Let's see how well the bank is doing as a result of the additional chequable deposits. Because reserves pay no interest, it has no income from the additional $100 of assets. But servicing the extra $100 of chequable deposits is costly because the bank must keep records, pay tellers, return cancelled cheques, pay for cheque clearing, and so forth. The bank is making a loss! The situation is even worse if the bank makes interest payments on the deposits. If it is to make a profit, the bank must put to productive use all or part of the $90 of excess reserves it has available.

Let us assume that the bank chooses not to hold any excess reserves but to make loans instead. Assuming that the bank gives up its cash directly, the T-account then looks like this:

Assets		Liabilities	
Desired reserves	+$10	Chequable deposits	+$100
Loans	+$90		

The bank is now making a profit because it holds short-term liabilities such as chequable deposits and uses the proceeds to buy longer-term assets such as loans with higher interest rates. As mentioned earlier, this process of asset transformation is frequently described by saying that banks are in the business of "borrowing short and lending long." For example, if the loans have an interest rate of 10% per year, the bank earns $9 in income from its loans over the year. If the $100 of chequable deposits is in an account with a 5% interest rate and it costs another $3 per year to service the account, the cost per year of these deposits is $8. The bank's profit on the new deposits is then $1 per year (a 1% return on assets).

GENERAL PRINCIPLES OF BANK MANAGEMENT

Now that you have some idea of how a bank operates, let's look at how a bank manages its assets and liabilities in order to earn the highest possible profit. The bank manager has four primary concerns. The first is to make sure that the bank has enough ready cash to pay its depositors when there are **deposit outflows**, that is, when deposits are lost because depositors make withdrawals and demand payment. To keep enough cash on hand, the bank must engage in **liquidity management**, the acquisition of sufficiently liquid assets to meet the bank's obligations to depositors. Second, the bank manager must pursue an acceptably low level of risk by acquiring assets that have a low rate of default and by diversifying asset holdings (**asset management**). The third concern is to acquire funds at low cost (**liability management**). Finally, the manager must decide the amount of capital the bank should maintain and then acquire the needed capital (**capital adequacy management**).

To understand bank and other financial institution management fully, we must go beyond the general principles of bank asset and liability management described next and look in more detail at how a financial institution manages its assets. The two sections following this one provide an in-depth discussion of how a financial institution manages **credit risk**, the risk arising because borrowers may default, and how it manages **interest-rate risk**, the riskiness of earnings and returns on bank assets that results from interest-rate changes.

Liquidity Management and the Role of Reserves

Let us see how a typical bank, the First Bank, can deal with deposit outflows that occur when its depositors withdraw cash from chequing or savings accounts or write cheques that are deposited in other banks. In the example that follows, we assume that the bank has ample excess reserves and that all deposits have the same desired reserve ratio of 10% (the bank wants to keep 10% of its time and chequable deposits as reserves). Suppose that the First Bank's initial balance sheet is as follows:

Assets		Liabilities	
Reserves	$20 million	Deposits	$100 million
Loans	$80 million	Bank capital	$ 10 million
Securities	$10 million		

The bank's desired reserves are 10% of $100 million, or $10 million. Since it holds $20 million of reserves, the First Bank has excess reserves of $10 million. If a deposit outflow of $10 million occurs, the bank's balance sheet becomes

Assets		Liabilities	
Reserves	$10 million	Deposits	$90 million
Loans	$80 million	Bank capital	$10 million
Securities	$10 million		

The bank loses $10 million of deposits *and* $10 million of reserves, but since its desired reserves are now 10% of only $90 million ($9 million), its reserves still exceed this amount by $1 million. In short, ***if a bank has ample reserves, a deposit out-flow does not necessitate changes in other parts of its balance sheet***.

The situation is quite different when a bank holds insufficient excess reserves. Let's assume that instead of initially holding $10 million in excess reserves, the First Bank makes loans of $10 million, so that it holds no excess reserves. Its initial balance sheet would be

Assets		Liabilities	
Reserves	$10 million	Deposits	$100 million
Loans	$90 million	Bank capital	$ 10 million
Securities	$10 million		

When it suffers the $10 million deposit outflow, its balance sheet becomes

Assets		Liabilities	
Reserves	$ 0	Deposits	$90 million
Loans	$90 million	Bank capital	$10 million
Securities	$10 million		

After $10 million has been withdrawn from deposits and hence reserves, the bank has a problem: its desired reserves are 10% of $90 million, or $9 million, but it has no reserves! To eliminate this shortfall, the bank has four basic options. One is to acquire reserves to meet a deposit outflow by borrowing them from other banks in the overnight market or by borrowing from corporations.[1] If the First Bank acquires the $9 million shortfall in reserves by borrowing it from other banks or corporations, its balance sheet becomes

Assets		Liabilities	
Reserves	$ 9 million	Deposits	$90 million
Loans	$90 million	Borrowings from other banks or corporations	$ 9 million
Securities	$10 million	Bank capital	$10 million

The cost of this activity is the interest rate on these loans, such as the overnight interest rate.

A second alternative is for the bank to sell some of its securities to help cover the deposit outflow. For example, it might sell $9 million of its securities and deposit the proceeds with the Bank of Canada, resulting in the following balance sheet:

---

[1]One way that the First Bank can borrow from other banks and corporations is by selling negotiable certificates of deposit. This method for obtaining funds is discussed in the section on liability management.

Assets		Liabilities	
Reserves	$ 9 million	Deposits	$90 million
Loans	$90 million	Bank capital	$10 million
Securities	$ 1 million		

The bank incurs some brokerage and other transaction costs when it sells these securities. The government of Canada securities that the bank holds are very liquid, so the transaction costs of selling them are quite modest. However, the other securities the bank holds are less liquid, and the transaction costs can be appreciably higher.

A third way that the bank can meet a deposit outflow is to acquire reserves by borrowing from the Bank of Canada. In our example, the First Bank could leave its security and loan holdings the same and borrow $9 million in loans from the Bank of Canada. Its balance sheet would be

Assets		Liabilities	
Reserves	$ 9 million	Deposits	$90 million
Loans	$90 million	Advances from the Bank of Canada	$ 9 million
Securities	$10 million	Bank capital	$10 million

There are two costs associated with advances from the Bank of Canada. First is the interest rate that must be paid to the Bank of Canada (called the **bank rate**). The second is a nonexplicit cost resulting from the Bank's discouragement of too much borrowing from it and increased scrutiny of the bank by the Bank of Canada.

Finally, a bank can acquire the $9 million of reserves to meet the deposit outflow by reducing its loans by this amount and depositing the $9 million it then receives with the Bank of Canada, thereby increasing its reserves by $9 million. This transaction changes the balance sheet as follows:

Assets		Liabilities	
Reserves	$ 9 million	Deposits	$90 million
Loans	$81 million	Bank capital	$10 million
Securities	$10 million		

The First Bank is once again in good shape because its $9 million of reserves satisfies the reserve requirement.

However, this process of reducing its loans is the bank's costliest way of acquiring reserves when there is a deposit outflow. If the First Bank has numerous short-term loans renewed at fairly short intervals, it can reduce its total amount of loans outstanding fairly quickly by *calling in* loans—that is, by not renewing some loans when they come due. Unfortunately for the bank, this is likely to antagonize the customers whose loans are not being renewed because they have not done anything to deserve such treatment. Indeed, they are likely to take their business elsewhere in the future, a very costly consequence for the bank.

A second method for reducing its loans is for the bank to sell them off to other banks. Again, this is very costly because other banks do not personally know the customers who have taken out the loans and so may not be willing to buy the loans at their full value.

The foregoing discussion explains why banks hold excess reserves even though loans or securities earn a higher return. When a deposit outflow occurs, holding excess reserves allows the bank to escape the costs of (1) borrowing from other banks or corporations, (2) selling securities, (3) borrowing from the Bank of Canada, or (4) calling in or selling off loans. ***Excess reserves are insurance against the costs associated with deposit outflows. The higher the costs associated with deposit outflows, the more excess reserves banks will want to hold.***

Just as you and I would be willing to pay an insurance company to insure us against a casualty loss such as the theft of a car, a bank is willing to pay the cost of holding excess reserves (the opportunity cost, which is the earnings forgone by not holding income-earning assets such as loans or securities) in order to insure against losses due to deposit outflows. Because excess reserves, like insurance, have a cost, banks also take other steps to protect themselves; for example, they might shift their holdings of assets to more liquid securities.

Study *Guide*	Bank management is easier to grasp if you put yourself in the banker's shoes and imagine what you would do in the situations described. To understand a bank's possible responses to deposit outflows, imagine how you as a banker might respond to two successive deposit outflows of $10 million.

Asset Management

Now that you understand why a bank has a need for liquidity, we can examine the basic strategy a bank pursues in managing its assets. To maximize its profits, a bank must simultaneously seek the highest returns possible on loans and securities, reduce risk, and make adequate provisions for liquidity by holding liquid assets. Banks try to accomplish these three goals in four basic ways.

First, banks try to find borrowers who will pay high interest rates and are unlikely to default on their loans. They seek out loan business by advertising their borrowing rates and by approaching corporations directly to solicit loans. It is up to the bank's loan officer to decide if potential borrowers are good credit risks who will make interest and principal payments on time. Typically, banks are conservative in their loan policies; the default rate is usually less than 1%. It is important, however, that banks not be so conservative that they miss out on attractive lending opportunities that earn high interest rates.

Second, banks try to purchase securities with high returns and low risk. Third, in managing their assets, banks must attempt to lower risk by diversifying. They accomplish this by purchasing many different types of assets (short- and long-term, government of Canada, and municipal bonds) and approving many types of loans to a number of customers. Banks that have not sufficiently sought the benefits of diversification often come to regret it later. For example, banks that had overspecialized in making loans to energy companies, real estate developers, or farmers suffered huge losses in the 1980s with the slump in energy, property, and farm prices. Indeed, some of these banks (e.g., the Canadian Commercial Bank and the Northland Bank) went broke because they had "put too many eggs in one basket."

Finally, the bank must manage the liquidity of its assets so that it can pay depositors when there are deposit outflows without bearing huge costs. This means that it will hold liquid securities even if they earn a somewhat lower return than other assets. In addition, it will want to hold government securities so that even if a deposit outflow forces some costs on the bank, these will not be terribly high. Again, it is not wise for a bank to be too conservative. If it avoids all costs associated with deposit outflows by holding only excess reserves, losses are suffered because reserves earn no interest, while the bank's liabilities are costly to maintain. The bank must balance its desire for liquidity against the increased earnings that can be obtained from less liquid assets such as loans.

Liability Management

Before the 1960s, liability management was a staid affair: for the most part, banks took their liabilities as fixed and spent their time trying to achieve an optimal mix of assets. There were two main reasons for the emphasis on asset management. First, a large part of the sources of bank funds was obtained through demand deposits that did not pay any interest. Thus banks could not actively compete with one another for these deposits, and so their amount was effectively a given for an individual bank. Second, because the markets for making overnight loans between banks were not well developed, banks rarely borrowed from other banks to meet their reserve needs.

Starting in the 1960s, however, large banks (called **money centre banks**) began to explore ways in which the liabilities on their balance sheets could provide them with reserves and liquidity. This led to an expansion of overnight loan markets, such as the federal funds market in the United States and the overnight funds market in Canada, and the development of new financial instruments such as negotiable CDs (first developed in 1961), which enabled money centre banks to acquire funds quickly.[2]

This new flexibility in liability management meant that banks could take a different approach to bank management. They no longer needed to depend on chequable deposits as the primary source of bank funds and as a result no longer treated their sources of funds (liabilities) as given. Instead, they aggressively set target goals for their asset growth and tried to acquire funds (by issuing liabilities) as they were needed.

For example, today, when a money centre bank finds an attractive loan opportunity, it can acquire funds by selling a negotiable CD. Or if it has a reserve shortfall, funds can be borrowed from another bank in the overnight market without incurring high transaction costs. The overnight market can also be used to finance loans. Because of the increased importance of liability management most banks now manage both sides of the balance sheet together in a so-called asset–liability management (ALM) committee.

The emphasis on liability management explains some of the important changes over the past three decades in the composition of banks' balance sheets. While negotiable CDs and bank borrowings have greatly increased in importance as a source of bank funds in recent years, chequable deposits have decreased in importance. Newfound flexibility in liability management and the search for higher profits have also stimulated banks to increase the proportion of their assets held in loans, which earn higher income.

---

[2]Because small banks are not as well known as money centre banks and so might be a higher credit risk, they find it harder to raise funds in the negotiable CD market. Hence they do not engage nearly as actively in liability management.

Capital Adequacy Management

Banks have to make decisions about the amount of capital they need to hold for three reasons. First, bank capital helps prevent *bank failure,* a situation in which the bank cannot satisfy its obligations to pay its depositors and other creditors and so goes out of business. Second, the amount of capital affects returns for the owners (equity holders) of the bank. Third, regulatory authorities require a minimum amount of bank capital (bank capital requirements).

How Bank Capital Helps Prevent Bank Failure   Let's consider two banks with identical balance sheets, except that the High Capital Bank has a ratio of capital to assets of 10% while the Low Capital Bank has a ratio of 4%.

HIGH CAPITAL BANK					LOW CAPITAL BANK			
Assets		**Liabilities**			**Assets**		**Liabilities**	
Reserves	$10 million	Deposits	$90 million		Reserves	$10 million	Deposits	$96 million
Loans	$90 million	Bank			Loans	$90 million	Bank	
		capital	$10 million				capital	$ 4 million

Suppose that both banks got caught up in the euphoria of the real estate market in the 1980s, only to find that $5 million of their real estate loans became worthless in the 1990s. When these bad loans are written off (valued at zero), the total value of assets declines by $5 million, and so bank capital, which equals total assets minus liabilities, also declines by $5 million. The balance sheets of the two banks now look like this:

HIGH CAPITAL BANK					LOW CAPITAL BANK			
Assets		**Liabilities**			**Assets**		**Liabilities**	
Reserves	$10 million	Deposits	$90 million		Reserves	$10 million	Deposits	$96 million
Loans	$85 million	Bank			Loans	$85 million	Bank	
		capital	$ 5 million				capital	−$ 1 million

The High Capital Bank takes the $5 million loss in stride because its initial cushion of $10 million in capital means that it still has a positive net worth (bank capital) of $5 million after the loss. The Low Capital Bank, however, is in big trouble. The value of its assets has fallen below its liabilities and its net worth is now −$1 million. Because the bank has a negative net worth, it is insolvent (bankrupt): it does not have sufficient assets to pay off all holders of its liabilities (creditors). When a bank becomes insolvent, government regulators close the bank, its assets are sold off, and its managers are fired. Since the owners of the Low Capital Bank will find their investment wiped out, they would clearly have preferred the bank to have had a large enough cushion of bank capital to absorb the losses, as was the case for the High Capital Bank. We therefore see an important rationale for a bank to maintain a high level of capital: ***a bank maintains bank capital to lessen the chance that it will become insolvent***.

How the Amount of Bank Capital Affects Returns to Equity Holders   Because owners of a bank must know whether their bank is being managed well, they need good measures of bank profitability. A basic measure of bank profitability is the **return on assets** (*ROA*), the net profit after taxes per dollar of assets:

$$ROA = \frac{\text{net profit after taxes}}{\text{assets}}$$

The return on assets provides information on how efficiently a bank is being run because it indicates how much profits are generated on average by each dollar of assets.

However, what the bank's owners (equity holders) care about most is how much the bank is earning on their equity investment. This information is provided by the other basic measure of bank profitability, the **return on equity** (*ROE*), the net profit after taxes per dollar of equity capital:

$$ROE = \frac{\text{net profit after taxes}}{\text{equity capital}}$$

There is a direct relationship between the return on assets (which measures how efficiently the bank is run) and the return on equity (which measures how well the owners are doing on their investment). This relationship is determined by the so-called **equity multiplier** (*EM*), which is the amount of assets per dollar of equity capital:

$$EM = \frac{\text{assets}}{\text{equity capital}}$$

To see this, we note that

$$\frac{\text{Net profit after taxes}}{\text{Equity capital}} = \frac{\text{net profit after taxes}}{\text{assets}} \times \frac{\text{assets}}{\text{equity capital}}$$

which, using our definitions, yields

$$ROE = ROA \times EM \tag{1}$$

The formula in Equation 1 tells us what happens to the return on equity when a bank holds a smaller amount of capital (equity) for a given amount of assets. As we have seen, the High Capital Bank initially has $100 million of assets and $10 million of equity, which gives it an equity multiplier of 10 (= $100 million/$10 million). The Low Capital Bank, by contrast, has only $4 million of equity, so its equity multiplier is higher, equalling 25 (= $100 million/$4 million). Suppose that these banks have been equally well run so that they both have the same return on assets, 1%. The return on equity for the High Capital Bank equals 1% × 10 = 10%, while the return on equity for the Low Capital Bank equals 1% × 25 = 25%. The equity holders in the Low Capital Bank are clearly a lot happier than the equity holders in the High Capital Bank because they are earning more than twice as high a return. We now see why owners of a bank may not want it to hold a lot of capital. ***Given the return on assets, the lower the bank capital, the higher the return for the owners of the bank.***

Trade-Off Between Safety and Returns to Equity Holders   We now see that bank capital has benefits and costs. Bank capital benefits the owners of a bank in that it makes their investment safer by reducing the likelihood of bankruptcy. But bank capital is costly because the higher it is, the lower will be the return on equity for a given return on assets. In determining the amount of bank capital, managers must decide how much of the increased safety that comes with higher capital (the benefit) they are willing to trade off against the lower return on equity that comes with higher capital (the cost).

In more uncertain times, when the possibility of large losses on loans increases, bank managers might want to hold more capital to protect the equity holders. Conversely, if they have confidence that loan losses won't occur, they might want to reduce the amount of bank capital, have a high equity multiplier, and thereby increase the return on equity.

Bank Capital Requirements   Banks also hold capital because they are required to do so by regulatory authorities. Because of the high costs of holding capital for the reasons just described, bank managers often want to hold less bank capital than is required by the regulatory authorities. In this case, the amount of bank capital is determined by the bank capital requirements. We discuss the details of bank capital requirements and why they are such an important part of bank regulation in Chapter 11.

APPLICATION	*Strategies for Managing Bank Capital*

Suppose that as the manager of the First Bank, you have to make decisions about the appropriate amount of bank capital. Looking at the balance sheet of the bank, which like the High Capital Bank has a ratio of bank capital to assets of 10% ($10 million of capital and $100 million of assets), you are concerned that the large amount of bank capital is causing the return on equity to be too low. You conclude that the bank has a capital surplus and should increase the equity multiplier to increase the return on equity. What should you do?

To lower the amount of capital relative to assets and raise the equity multiplier, you can do any of three things: (1) you can reduce the amount of bank capital by buying back some of the bank's stock; (2) you can reduce the bank's capital by paying out higher dividends to its stockholders, thereby reducing the bank's retained earnings; (3) you can keep bank capital constant but increase the bank's assets by acquiring new funds, say, by issuing CDs, and then seeking out loan business or purchasing more securities with these new funds. Because you think that it would enhance your position with the stockholders, you decide to pursue the second alternative and raise the dividend on the First Bank stock.

Now suppose that the First Bank is in a similar situation to the Low Capital Bank and has a ratio of bank capital to assets of 4%. You now worry that the bank is short on capital relative to assets because it does not have a sufficient cushion to prevent bank failure. To raise the amount of capital relative to assets, you now have the following three choices: (1) you can raise capital for the bank by having it issue equity (common stock); (2) you can raise capital by reducing the bank's dividends to shareholders, thereby increasing retained earnings that it can put into its capital account; (3) you can keep capital at the same level but reduce the bank's assets by making fewer loans or by selling off securities and then using the proceeds to reduce its liabilities. Suppose that raising bank capital is not easy to do at the current time because capital markets are tight or because shareholders will protest if their dividends are cut. Then you might have to choose the third alternative and decide to shrink the size of the bank.

In past years, many banks experienced capital shortfalls and have had to restrict asset growth, as you might have had to do if the First Bank were short of capital. The important consequences of this for the credit markets are discussed in the application that follows.

APPLICATION	*Did the Capital Crunch Cause a Credit Crunch in the Early 1990s?*

During the 1990–1991 recession and the year following, there occurred a slow-down in the growth of credit that was unprecedented in the post–World War II era. Many economists and politicians have claimed that there was a "credit crunch" during this period in which credit was hard to get, and as a result the performance of the economy in 1990–1992 was very weak. Was the slowdown in credit growth a manifestation of a credit crunch, and if so, what caused it?

Our analysis of how a bank manages bank capital suggests that a credit crunch was likely to have occurred in 1990–1992 and that it was caused at least in part by the so-called capital crunch in which shortfalls of bank capital led to slower credit growth.

The period of the late 1980s saw a boom and then a major bust in the real estate market that led to huge losses for banks on their real estate loans. As our example of how bank capital helps prevent bank failures demonstrates, the loan losses caused a substantial fall in the amount of bank capital. At the same time, regulators were raising capital requirements (a subject discussed in Chapter 11). The resulting capital shortfalls meant that banks had to either raise new capital or restrict their asset growth by cutting back on lending. Because of the weak economy at the time, raising new capital was extremely difficult for banks, so they chose the latter course. Banks did restrict their lending, and borrowers found it harder to obtain loans, leading to complaints from banks' customers. Only with the stronger recovery of the economy in 1993, helped by a low-interest-rate policy at the Bank of Canada, did these complaints subside.

MANAGING CREDIT RISK

As seen in the earlier discussion of general principles of asset management, banks and other financial institutions must make successful loans that are paid back in full (and so subject the institution to little credit risk) in order to earn high profits. The economic concepts of adverse selection and moral hazard (introduced in Chapter 2) provide a framework for understanding the principles that financial institutions have to follow to reduce credit risk and make successful loans.[3]

Adverse selection in loan markets occurs because bad credit risks (those most likely to default on their loans) are the ones who usually line up for loans; in other words, those who are most likely to produce an *adverse* outcome are the most likely to be *selected*. Borrowers with very risky investment projects have much to gain if their projects are successful, and so they are the most eager to obtain loans. Clearly, however, they are the least desirable borrowers because of the greater possibility that they will be unable to pay back their loans.

Moral hazard exists in loan markets because borrowers may have incentives to engage in activities that are undesirable from the lender's point of view. In such situations, it is more likely that the lender will be subjected to the *hazard* of default. Once borrowers have obtained a loan, they are more likely to invest in

---

[3]Other financial intermediaries, such as trust and mortgage loan companies, credit unions and *caisses populaires*, insurance companies, pension funds, and finance companies, also make private loans, and the credit risk management principles we outline here apply to them as well.

high-risk investment projects—projects that pay high returns to the borrowers if successful. The high risk, however, makes it less likely that they will be able to pay the loan back.

To be profitable, financial institutions must overcome the adverse selection and moral hazard problems that make loan defaults more likely. The attempts of financial institutions to solve these problems help explain a number of principles for managing credit risk: screening and monitoring, establishment of long-term customer relationships, loan commitments, collateral and compensating balance requirements, and credit rationing.

Screening and Monitoring

Asymmetric information is present in loan markets because lenders have less information about the investment opportunities and activities of borrowers than borrowers do. This situation leads to two information-producing activities by banks and other financial institutions—screening and monitoring. Indeed, Walter Wriston, a former head of Citicorp, the largest bank corporation in the United States, was often quoted as stating that the business of banking is the production of information.

Screening   Adverse selection in loan markets requires that lenders screen out the bad credit risks from the good ones so that loans are profitable to them. To accomplish effective screening, lenders must collect reliable information from prospective borrowers. Effective screening and information collection together form an important principle of credit risk management.

When you apply for a consumer loan (such as a car loan or a mortgage to purchase a house), the first thing you are asked to do is fill out forms that elicit a great deal of information about your personal finances. You are asked about your salary, your bank accounts and other assets (such as cars, insurance policies, and furnishings), and your outstanding loans; your record of loan, credit card, and charge account repayments; the number of years you've worked and who your employers have been. You also are asked personal questions such as your age, marital status, and number of children. The lender uses this information to evaluate how good a credit risk you are by calculating your "credit score," a statistical measure derived from your answers that predicts whether you are likely to have trouble making your loan payments. Deciding on how good a risk you are cannot be entirely scientific, so the lender must also use judgment. The loan officer, whose job is to decide whether you should be given the loan, might call your employer or talk to some of the personal references you supplied. The officer might even make a judgment based on your demeanour or your appearance. (This is why most people dress neatly and conservatively when they go to a bank to apply for a loan.)

The process of screening and collecting information is similar when a financial institution makes a business loan. It collects information about the company's profits and losses (income) and about its assets and liabilities. The lender also has to evaluate the likely future success of the business. So in addition to obtaining information on such items as sales figures, a loan officer might ask questions about the company's future plans, how the loan will be used, and the competition in the industry. The officer may even visit the company to obtain a firsthand look at its operations. The bottom line is that, whether for personal or business loans, bankers and other financial institutions need to be nosy.

Specialization in Lending   One puzzling feature of bank lending is that a bank often specializes in lending to local firms or to firms in particular industries, such as energy. In one sense, this behaviour seems surprising because it means that the bank is not diversifying its portfolio of loans and thus is exposing itself to more risk. But from another perspective such specialization makes perfect sense. The adverse selection problem requires that the bank screen out bad credit risks. It is easier for the bank to collect information about local firms and determine their creditworthiness than to collect comparable information on firms that are far away. Similarly, by concentrating its lending on firms in specific industries, the bank becomes more knowledgeable about these industries and is therefore better able to predict which firms will be able to make timely payments on their debt.

Monitoring and Enforcement of Restrictive Covenants   Once a loan has been made, the borrower has an incentive to engage in risky activities that make it less likely that the loan will be paid off. To reduce this moral hazard, financial institutions must adhere to the principle for managing credit risk that a lender should write provisions (restrictive covenants) into loan contracts that restrict borrowers from engaging in risky activities. By monitoring borrowers' activities to see whether they are complying with the restrictive covenants and by enforcing the covenants if they are not, lenders can make sure that borrowers are not taking on risks at their expense. The need for banks and other financial institutions to engage in screening and monitoring explains why they spend so much money on auditing and information-collecting activities.

Long-Term Customer Relationships

An additional way for banks and other financial institutions to obtain information about their borrowers is through long-term customer relationships, another important principle of credit risk management.

If a prospective borrower has had a chequing or savings account or other loans with a bank over a long period of time, a loan officer can look at past activity on the accounts and learn quite a bit about the borrower. The balances in the chequing and savings accounts tell the banker how liquid the potential borrower is and at what time of year the borrower has a strong need for cash. A review of the cheques the borrower has written reveals the borrower's suppliers. If the borrower has borrowed previously from the bank, the bank has a record of the loan payments. Thus long-term customer relationships reduce the costs of information collection and make it easier to screen out bad credit risks.

The need for monitoring by lenders adds to the importance of long-term customer relationships. If the borrower has borrowed from the bank before, the bank has already established procedures for monitoring that customer. Therefore, the costs of monitoring long-term customers are lower than those for new customers.

Long-term relationships benefit the customers as well as the bank. A firm with a previous relationship will find it easier to obtain a loan at a low interest rate because the bank has an easier time determining if the prospective borrower is a good credit risk and incurs fewer costs in monitoring the borrower.

A long-term customer relationship has another advantage for the bank. No bank can think of every contingency when it writes a restrictive covenant into a loan contract; there will always be risky borrower activities that are not ruled out. However, what if a borrower wants to preserve a long-term relationship with a bank because it will be easier to get future loans at low interest rates? The borrower then has the incentive to avoid risky activities that would upset the bank, even if restrictions on these risky activities were not specified in the loan contract. Indeed, if a bank doesn't like what a borrower is doing even when the borrower isn't violating any restrictive covenants, it has some power to discourage the borrower from such activity: the bank can threaten not to let the borrower have new loans in the future. Long-term customer relationships therefore enable banks to deal with even unanticipated moral hazard contingencies.

Loan Commitments

Banks also create long-term relationships and gather information by issuing **loan commitments** to commercial customers. A loan commitment is a bank's commitment (for a specified future period of time) to provide a firm with loans up to a given amount at an interest rate that is tied to some market interest rate. The majority of commercial and industrial loans are made under the loan commitment arrangement. The advantage for the firm is that it has a source of credit when it needs it. The advantage for the bank is that the loan commitment promotes a long-term relationship, which in turn facilitates information collection. In addition, provisions in the loan commitment agreement require that the firm continually supply the bank with information about the firm's income, asset and liability position, business activities, and so on. A loan commitment arrangement is a powerful method for reducing the bank's costs for screening and information collection.

Collateral and Compensating Balances

Collateral requirements for loans are important credit risk management tools. Collateral, which is property promised to the lender as compensation if the borrower defaults, lessens the consequences of adverse selection because it reduces the lender's losses in the case of a loan default. If a borrower defaults on a loan, the lender can sell the collateral and use the proceeds to make up for its losses on the loan. One particular form of collateral required when a bank makes commercial loans is called **compensating balances**: a firm receiving a loan must keep a required minimum amount of funds in a chequing account at the bank. For example, a business getting a $10 million loan may be required to keep compensating balances of at least $1 million in its chequing account at the bank. This $1 million in compensating balances can then be taken by the bank to make up some of the losses on the loan if the borrower defaults.

Besides serving as collateral, compensating balances help increase the likelihood that a loan will be paid off. They do this by helping the bank monitor the borrower and consequently reduce moral hazard. Specifically, by requiring the borrower to use a chequing account at the bank, the bank can observe the firm's cheque payment practices, which may yield a great deal of information about the borrower's financial condition. For example, a sustained drop in the borrower's chequing account balance may signal that the borrower is having financial trouble, or account activity may suggest that the borrower is engaging in risky activities; perhaps a change in suppliers means that the borrower is pursuing new lines of business. Any significant change in the borrower's payment procedures is a signal to the bank that it should make inquiries. Compensating balances therefore make it easier for banks to monitor borrowers more effectively and are another important credit risk management tool.

Credit Rationing

Another way in which financial institutions deal with adverse selection and moral hazard is through **credit rationing**: refusing to make loans even though borrowers are willing to pay the stated interest rate or even a higher rate. Credit rationing takes two forms. The first occurs when a lender refuses to make a loan *of any amount* to a borrower, even if the borrower is willing to pay a higher interest rate. The second occurs when a lender is willing to make a loan but restricts the size of the loan to less than the borrower would like.

At first you might be puzzled by the first type of credit rationing. After all, even if the potential borrower is a credit risk, why doesn't the lender just extend the loan but at a higher interest rate? The answer is that adverse selection prevents this solution. Individuals and firms with the riskiest investment projects are exactly those that are willing to pay the highest interest rates. If a borrower took on a high-risk investment and succeeded, the borrower would become extremely rich. But a lender wouldn't want to make such a loan precisely because the investment risk is high; the likely outcome is that the borrower will *not* succeed and the lender will not be paid back. Charging a higher interest rate just makes adverse selection worse for the lender; that is, it increases the likelihood that the lender is lending to a bad credit risk. The lender would therefore rather not make any loans at a higher interest rate; instead, it would engage in the first type of credit rationing and would turn down loans.

Financial institutions engage in the second type of credit rationing to guard against moral hazard: they grant loans to borrowers, but not loans as large as the borrowers want. Such credit rationing is necessary because the larger the loan, the greater the benefits from moral hazard. If a bank gives you a $1000 loan, for example, you are likely to take actions that enable you to pay it back because you don't want to hurt your credit rating for the future. However, if the bank lends you $10 million, you are more likely to fly down to Rio to celebrate. The larger your loan, the greater your incentives to engage in activities that make it less likely that you will repay the loan. Since more borrowers repay their loans if the loan amounts are small, financial institutions ration credit by providing borrowers with smaller loans than they seek.

MANAGING INTEREST-RATE RISK

With the increased volatility of interest rates that occurred in the 1980s, banks and other financial institutions became more concerned about their exposure to interest-rate risk, the riskiness of earnings and returns that is associated with changes in interest rates. To see what interest-rate risk is all about, let's again take a look at the First Bank, which has the following balance sheet:

FIRST BANK

Assets		Liabilities	
Rate-sensitive assets	$20 million	Rate-sensitive liabilities	$50 million
Variable-rate loans		Variable-rate CDs	
Short-term securities		Variable-rate chequable	
Overnight funds		deposits	
Fixed-rate assets	$80 million	Fixed-rate liabilities	$50 million
Reserves		Chequable deposits	
Long-term loans		Savings deposits	
Long-term securities		Long-term CDs	
		Equity capital	

A total of $20 million of its assets are rate-sensitive, with interest rates that change frequently (at least once a year), and $80 million of its assets are fixed-rate, with interest rates that remain unchanged for a long period (over a year). On the liabilities side, the First Bank has $50 million of rate-sensitive liabilities and $50 million of fixed-rate liabilities. Suppose that interest rates rise by 5 percentage points on average, from 10% to 15%. The income on the assets rises by $1 million (= 5% × $20 million of rate-sensitive assets), while the payments on the liabilities rise by $2.5 million (= 5% × $50 million of rate-sensitive liabilities). The First Bank's profits now decline by $1.5 million (= $1 million − $2.5 million). Conversely, if interest rates fall by 5 percentage points, similar reasoning tells us that the First Bank's profits rise by $1.5 million. This example illustrates the following point: *if a bank has more rate-sensitive liabilities than assets, a rise in interest rates will reduce bank profits and a decline in interest rates will raise bank profits*.

Gap and Duration Analysis

The sensitivity of bank profits to changes in interest rates can be measured more directly using **gap analysis**, in which the amount of rate-sensitive liabilities is subtracted from the amount of rate-sensitive assets. In our example, this calculation (called the "gap") is −$30 million (= $20 million − $50 million). By multiplying the gap times the change in the interest rate, we can immediately obtain the effect on bank profits. For example, when interest rates rise by 5 percentage points, the change in profits is 5% × −$30 million, which equals −$1.5 million, as we saw.

The analysis we just conducted is known as *basic gap analysis,* and it can be refined in two ways. Clearly, not all assets and liabilities in the fixed-rate category have the same maturity. One refinement, the *maturity bucket approach,* is to measure the gap for several maturity subintervals, called *maturity buckets,* so that effects of interest-rate changes over a multiyear period can be calculated. The second refinement, called *standardized gap analysis,* accounts for the differing degrees of rate sensitivity for different rate-sensitive assets and liabilities.

An alternative method for measuring interest-rate risk, called **duration analysis**, examines the sensitivity of the market value of the bank's total assets and liabilities to changes in interest rates. Duration analysis is based on what is known as Macaulay's concept of *duration,* which measures the average lifetime of a security's stream of payments.[4] Duration is a useful concept because it provides a good approximation of the sensitivity of a security's market value to a change in its interest rate:

$$\text{Percent change in market value of security} \approx$$
$$- \text{percentage-point change in interest rate} \times \text{duration in years}$$

where ≈ denotes "approximately equals."

Duration analysis involves using the average (weighted) duration of a financial institution's assets and of its liabilities to see how its net worth responds to a change in interest rates. Going back to our example of the First Bank, suppose that the average duration of its assets is three years (that is, the average lifetime of the stream of payments is three years), while the average duration of its liabilities is two years. In addition, the First Bank has $100 million of assets and $90 million of liabilities, so its bank capital is 10% of assets. With a 5-percentage-point increase in interest rates, the market value of the bank's assets falls by 15% (= −5% × 3 years), a decline of $15 million on the $100 million of assets. However, the market value of the liabilities falls by 10% (= −5% × 2 years), a decline of $9 million on the $90 million of liabilities. The net result is that the net worth (the market value of the assets minus the liabilities) has declined by $6 million, or 6% of the total original asset value. Similarly, a 5-percentage-point decline in interest rates increases the net worth of the First Bank by 6% of the total asset value.

As our example makes clear, both duration analysis and gap analysis indicate that the First Bank will suffer if interest rates rise but will gain if they fall. Duration analysis and gap analysis are thus useful tools for telling a manager of a financial institution its degree of exposure to interest-rate risk.

---

[4]Algebraically, Macaulay's duration, D, is defined as

$$D = \sum_{\tau=1}^{N} \tau \, \frac{CP_\tau}{(1+i)^\tau} \Big/ \sum_{\tau=1}^{N} \frac{CP_\tau}{(1+i)^\tau}$$

where $\quad$ τ $\quad$ = time until cash payment is made
$\qquad\qquad$ CP_τ = cash payment (interest plus principal) at time τ
$\qquad\qquad$ i $\quad$ = interest rate
$\qquad\qquad$ N $\quad$ = time to maturity of the security

APPLICATION	*Strategies for Managing Interest-Rate Risk*

Suppose that as the manager of the First Bank, you have done a duration and gap analysis for the bank as discussed in the text. Now you need to decide what alternative strategies you should pursue to manage the interest-rate risk.

If you firmly believe that interest rates will fall in the future, you may be willing to take no action because you know that the bank has more rate-sensitive liabilities than rate-sensitive assets and so will benefit from the expected interest-rate decline. However, you also realize that the First Bank is subject to substantial interest-rate risk because there is always a possibility that interest rates will rise rather than fall. What should you do to eliminate this interest-rate risk? One thing you could do is to shorten the duration of the bank's assets to increase their rate sensitivity. Alternatively, you could lengthen the duration of the liabilities. By this adjustment of the bank's assets and liabilities, the bank will be less affected by interest-rate swings.

One problem with eliminating the First Bank's interest-rate risk by altering the balance sheet is that doing so might be very costly in the short run. The bank may be locked in to assets and liabilities of particular durations because of where its expertise lies. Fortunately, recently developed financial instruments known as financial derivatives—financial forwards and futures, options, and swaps—can help the bank reduce its interest-rate risk exposure but do not require that the bank rearrange its balance sheet. We discuss these instruments and how banks and other financial institutions can use them to manage interest-rate risk in Chapter 13.

OFF-BALANCE-SHEET ACTIVITIES

Although asset and liability management has traditionally been the major concern of banks, in the more competitive environment of recent years banks have been aggressively seeking out profits by engaging in off-balance-sheet activities. **Off-balance-sheet activities** involve trading financial instruments and generating income from fees and loan sales, activities that affect bank profits but do not appear on bank balance sheets. Indeed, off-balance-sheet activities have been growing in importance for banks: the income from these activities as a percentage of assets has nearly doubled since 1979.

Loan Sales

One type of off-balance-sheet activity that has grown in importance in recent years involves income generated by loan sales. A **loan sale**, also called a *secondary loan participation*, involves a contract that sells all or part of the cash stream from a specific loan and thereby removes the loan from the bank's balance sheet. Banks earn profits by selling loans for an amount slightly greater than the amount of the original loan. Because the high interest rate on these loans makes them attractive, institutions are willing to buy them even though the higher price means that they earn a slightly lower interest rate than the original interest rate on the loan, usually on the order of 0.15 percentage points.

Generation of Fee Income

Another type of off-balance-sheet activity involves the generation of income from fees that banks receive for providing specialized services to their customers, such as making foreign exchange trades on a customer's behalf, servicing a mortgage-backed security by collecting interest and principal payments and then paying them out, guaranteeing debt securities such as banker's acceptances (by which the bank promises to make interest and principal payments if the party issuing the security cannot), and providing backup lines of credit. There are several types of backup lines of credit. We have already mentioned the most important, the loan commitment, under which for a fee the bank agrees to provide a loan at the customer's request, up to a given dollar amount, over a specified period of time. Credit lines are also now available to bank depositors with "overdraft privileges"— these bank customers can write cheques in excess of their deposit balances and, in effect, write themselves a loan.

Off-balance-sheet activities involving guarantees of securities and backup credit lines increase the risk a bank faces. Even though a guaranteed security does not appear on a bank balance sheet, it still exposes the bank to default risk: if the issuer of the security defaults, the bank is left holding the bag and must pay off the security's owner. Backup credit lines also expose the bank to risk because the bank may be forced to provide loans when it does not have sufficient liquidity or when the borrower is a very poor credit risk.

Trading Activities and Risk Management Techniques

We have already mentioned that banks' attempts to manage interest-rate risk led them to trading in financial futures, options for debt instruments, and interest-rate swaps. Banks engaged in international banking also conduct transactions in the foreign exchange market. All transactions in these markets are off-balance-sheet activities because they do not have a direct effect on the bank's balance sheet. Although bank trading in these markets is often directed toward reducing risk or facilitating other bank business, banks also try to outguess the markets and engage in speculation. This speculation can be a very risky business and indeed has led to bank insolvencies, the most dramatic being the failure of Barings, a British bank, in 1995.

Trading activities, although often highly profitable, are dangerous because they make it easy for financial institutions and their employees to make huge bets quickly. A particular problem for management of trading activities is that the principal–agent problem, discussed in Chapter 8, is especially severe. Given the ability to place large bets, a trader (the agent), whether she trades in bond markets, in foreign exchange markets, or in financial derivatives, has an incentive to take on excessive risks: if her trading strategy leads to large profits, she is likely to receive a high salary and bonuses, but if she takes large losses, the financial institution (the principal) will have to cover them. As the Barings Bank failure in 1995 so forcefully demonstrated, a trader subject to the principal–agent problem can take an institution that is quite healthy and drive it into insolvency very fast (Box 9-2).

To reduce the principal–agent problem, managers of financial institutions must set up internal controls to prevent debacles like the one at Barings. Such controls include the complete separation of the people in charge of trading activities from those in charge of the bookkeeping for trades. In addition, managers must set limits on the total amount of traders' transactions and on the institution's risk exposure. Managers must also scrutinize risk assessment procedures using the latest computer technology. One such method involves the so-called value-at-risk approach. In this approach, the institution develops a statistical model with which it can calculate the maximum loss that its portfolio is likely to sustain over a given time interval, dubbed the value at risk, or VAR. For example, a bank might estimate that the maximum loss it would be likely to sustain over one day with a probability of 1 in 100 is $1 million; the $1 million figure is the bank's calculated value at risk. Another approach is called "stress testing." In this approach, a manager asks models what would happen if a doomsday scenario occurs; that is, she looks at the losses the institution would sustain if an unusual combination of bad events occurred. With the value-at-risk approach and stress testing, a financial institution can assess its risk exposure and take steps to reduce it.

BOX 9-2

Barings, Daiwa, and Sumitomo

Rogue Traders and the Principal–Agent Problem. The demise of Barings, a venerable British bank over a century old, is a sad morality tale of how the principal–agent problem operating through a rogue trader can take a financial institution that has a healthy balance sheet one month and turn it into an insolvent tragedy the next.

In July 1992, Nick Leeson, Barings's new head clerk at its Singapore branch, began to speculate on the Nikkei, the Japanese version of the Dow Jones index. By late 1992, Leeson had suffered losses of $3 million, which he hid from his superiors by stashing the losses in a secret account. He even fooled his superiors into thinking he was generating large profits, thanks to a failure of internal controls at his firm, which allowed him to execute trades on the Singapore exchange *and* oversee the book-keeping of those trades. (As anyone who runs a cash business, such as a bar, knows, there is always a lower likelihood of fraud if more than one person handles the cash. Similarly for trading operations, you never mix management of the back room with management of the front room; this principle was grossly violated by Barings management.)

Things didn't get better for Leeson, who by late 1994 had losses exceeding $250 million. In January and February 1995, he bet the bank. On January 17, 1995, the day of the Kobe earthquake, he lost $75 million, and by the end of the week had lost more than $150 million. When the stock market declined on February 23, leaving him with a further loss of $250 million, he called it quits and fled Singapore. Three days later, he turned himself in at the Frankfurt airport. By the end of his wild ride, Leeson's losses, $1.3 billion in all, ate up Barings's capital and caused the bank to fail. Leeson was subsequently convicted and sent to jail in Singapore for his activities. He was released in 1999 and apologized for his actions.

Our asymmetric information analysis of the principal–agent problem explains Leeson's behaviour and the danger of Barings's management lapse. By letting Leeson control both his own trades and the back room, it increased asymmetric information because it reduced the principal's (Barings's) knowledge about Leeson's trading activities. This lapse increased the moral hazard incentive for him to take risks at the bank's expense, as he was now less likely to be caught. Furthermore, once he had experienced large losses, he had even greater incentives to take on even higher risk because if his bets worked out, he could reverse his losses and keep in good standing with the company, whereas if his bets soured, he had little to lose since he was out of a job anyway. Indeed, the bigger his losses, the more he had to gain by bigger bets, which explains the escalation of the amount of his trades as his losses mounted. If Barings's managers had understood the principal–agent problem, they would have been more vigilant at finding out what Leeson was up to, and the bank might still be here today.

Unfortunately, Nick Leeson is no longer a rarity in the rogue traders' billionaire club, those who have lost more than $1 billion. Over 11 years, Toshihide Iguchi, an officer in the New York branch of Daiwa Bank, also had control of both the bond trading operation and the back room, and he racked up $1.1 billion in losses over the period. In July 1995, Iguchi disclosed his losses to his superiors, but the management of the bank did not disclose them to its regulators. The result was that Daiwa was slapped with a $340 million fine and the bank was thrown out of the country by U.S. bank regulators. Yasuo Hamanaka is the latest member of the billionaire club. In July 1996, he topped Leeson's and Iguchi's record, losing $2.6 billion for his employer, the Sumitomo Corporation, one of Japan's top trading companies. The moral of these stories is that management of firms engaged in trading activities must reduce the principal–agent problem by closely monitoring their traders' activities.

Because of the increased risk that banks are facing from their off-balance-sheet activities, Canadian bank regulators have become concerned about increased risk from banks' off-balance-sheet activities and, as we will see in Chapter 11, are encouraging banks to pay increased attention to risk management. In addition, the Bank for International Settlements is developing additional bank capital requirements based on value-at-risk calculations for a bank's trading activities.

FINANCIAL INNOVATION

Like other industries, the financial industry is in business to earn profits by selling its products. If a soap company perceives that there is a need in the marketplace for a laundry detergent with fabric softener, it develops a product to fit the need. Similarly, to maximize their profits, financial institutions develop new products to satisfy their own needs as well as those of their customers; in other words, innovation—which can be extremely beneficial to the economy—is driven by the desire to get (or stay) rich. This view of the innovation process leads to the following simple analysis: *a change in the financial environment will stimulate a search by financial institutions for innovations that are likely to be profitable*.

Starting in the 1960s, individuals and financial institutions operating in financial markets were confronted with drastic changes in the economic environment: inflation and interest rates climbed sharply and became harder to predict, a situation that changed demand conditions in financial markets. The rapid advance in computer technology changed supply conditions. In addition, financial regulations became more burdensome. Financial institutions found that many of the old ways of doing business were no longer profitable; the financial services and products they had been offering to the public were not selling. Many financial intermediaries found that they were no longer able to acquire funds with their traditional financial instruments, and without these funds they would soon be out of business. To survive in the new economic environment, financial institutions had to research and develop new products and services that would meet customer needs and prove profitable, a process referred to as **financial engineering**. In their case, necessity was the mother of innovation.

Our discussion of why financial innovation occurs suggests that there are three basic types of financial innovation: responses to changes in demand conditions, responses to changes in supply conditions, and avoidance of regulations. Now that we have a framework for understanding why financial institutions such as banks produce innovations, let's look at examples of how financial institutions in their search for profits have produced financial innovations of the three basic types.

Responses to Changes in Demand Conditions

The most significant change in the economic environment that altered the demand for financial products in recent years has been the dramatic increase in the volatility of interest rates. In the 1950s, the interest rate on three-month Treasury bills fluctuated between 1.0% and 5.5%; in the 1970s, it fluctuated between 3% and 14%. This volatility became even more pronounced in the 1980s, during which the three-month T-bill rate ranged from 7% to over 20%. We saw in Table 4-2 that a rise in the interest rate from 10% to 20% would result in a capital loss of nearly 50% on a 30-year bond and a negative return of almost 40%. Large fluctuations in interest rates lead to substantial capital gains or losses and greater uncertainty about returns on investments. Recall that the risk that is related to the uncertainty about interest-rate movements and returns is called *interest-rate risk,* and high volatility of interest rates, such as we saw in the 1970s and 1980s, leads to a higher level of interest-rate risk.

We would expect the increase in interest-rate risk to increase the demand for financial products and services that could reduce that risk. This change in the economic environment would thus stimulate a search for profitable innovations by financial institutions that meet this new demand and would spur the creation of new financial instruments that help lower interest-rate risk. One financial innovation in the banking industry that appeared in the 1970s confirms this prediction: the development of adjustable-rate mortgages.

Adjustable-Rate Mortgages   Like other investors, financial institutions find that lending is more attractive if interest-rate risk is lower. They would not want to make a mortgage loan at a 10% interest rate and two months later find that they could obtain 12% in interest on the same mortgage. To reduce interest-rate risk, financial institutions recently began to issue adjustable-rate mortgages, that is, mortgage loans on which the interest rate changes when a market interest rate (usually the Treasury bill rate) changes. Initially, an adjustable-rate mortgage might have a 5% interest rate. In six months, this interest rate might increase or decrease by the amount of the increase or decrease in, say, the six-month Treasury bill rate, and the mortgage payment would change. Because adjustable-rate mortgages allow mortgage-issuing institutions to earn higher interest rates on mortgages when rates rise, profits are kept higher during these periods. This was the case in the early 1980s when the three-month T-bill rate exceeded 20%.

This attractive feature of adjustable-rate mortgages has encouraged mortgage-issuing institutions to issue adjustable-rate mortgages with lower initial interest rates than on conventional fixed-rate mortgages, making them popular with many households. However, because the mortgage payment on an adjustable-rate mortgage can increase, many households continue to prefer fixed-rate mortgages. Hence both types of mortgages are widespread.

Responses to Changes in Supply Conditions

The most important source of the changes in supply conditions that stimulate financial innovation has been the improvement in computer and telecommunications technology. These changes have made it profitable for financial institutions to create new financial products and services to the public. When computer technology that substantially lowered the cost of processing financial transactions became available, financial institutions conceived new financial products and instruments dependent on this technology that might appeal to the public, including the bank credit card and electronic banking facilities.

Bank Credit and Debit Cards

American Express
www.americanexpress.
com

Diners Club
www.dinersclub.com

Credit cards have been around since well before World War II. Many individual stores (Sears, Eaton's, the Bay) institutionalized charge accounts by providing customers with credit cards that allowed them to make purchases at these stores without cash. Nationwide credit cards were not established until after World War II, when Diners Club developed one to be used in restaurants. Similar credit card programs were started by American Express and Carte Blanche, but because of the high cost of operating these programs, cards were issued only to selected persons and businesses that could afford expensive purchases.

A firm issuing credit cards earns income from loans it makes to credit card holders and from payments made by stores on credit card purchases (a percentage of the purchase price, say 5%). A credit card program's costs arise from loan defaults, stolen cards, and the expense involved in processing credit card transactions.

Seeing the success of Diners Club, American Express, and Carte Blanche, bankers wanted to share in the profitable credit card business. Several chartered banks attempted to expand the credit card business to a wider market in the 1950s, but the cost per transaction of running these programs was so high that their early attempts failed.

In the late 1960s, improved computer technology, which lowered the transaction costs for providing credit card services, made it more likely that bank credit card programs would be profitable. The banks tried to enter this business again, and this time their efforts led to the creation of two successful bank credit card programs: Visa and MasterCard. These programs have become phenomenally successful; more than 1.1 million merchants in Canada accepted Visa and MasterCard in 1999. Indeed, bank credit cards have been so profitable that nonfinancial institutions such as Sears, General Motors, and Wal-Mart have also entered the credit card business. Consumers have benefited because credit cards are more widely accepted than cheques to pay for purchases (particularly abroad), and they allow consumers to take out loans more easily.

Wal-Mart
www.walmart.com

The success of bank credit cards has led these institutions to come up with a new financial innovation, *debit cards*. Debit cards often look just like credit cards and can be used to make purchases in an identical fashion. However, in contrast to credit cards, which extend the purchaser a loan that does not have to be paid off immediately, a debit card purchase is immediately deducted from the cardholder's bank account. Debit cards depend even more on low costs of processing transactions, since their profits are generated entirely from the fees paid by merchants on debit card purchases at their stores. Debit cards have grown increasingly popular in recent years. In fact, today over 57% of payment transactions in Canada are made by debit or credit card.

Electronic Banking Facilities   The wonders of modern computer technology have also enabled banks to lower the cost of bank transactions by having the customer interact with an electronic banking facility rather than with a human being. One important form of electronic banking facility is the automated banking machine (ABM), which has the advantage that it does not have to be paid overtime and never sleeps, thus being available for use 24 hours a day. Not only does this result in cheaper transactions for the bank, but it also provides more convenience for the customer. Furthermore, because of their low cost, ABMs can be put at locations other than a bank or its branches, further increasing customer convenience. The low cost of ABMs has meant that they have sprung up everywhere, now numbering over 17 000 in Canada alone (and over 100 000 in the United States). Furthermore, it is now as easy to get foreign currency from an ABM when you are travelling in Europe as it is to get cash from your local bank. In addition, transactions with ABMs are so much cheaper for the bank than ones conducted with human tellers that some banks charge customers less if they use the ABM than if they use a human teller.

With the drop in the cost of telecommunications, banks have developed another financial innovation, home banking. It is now cost-effective for banks to set up an electronic banking facility in which the bank's customer is linked up with the bank's computer to carry out transactions either by phone or by personal computer. Now a bank's customers can conduct many of their bank transactions without ever leaving home. The advantage for the customer is the convenience of home banking, while banks find that the cost of transactions is substantially less than having the customer come to the bank. Also, as we saw in Chapter 3, we are entering a new world in which computer banking is evolving to electronic payment methods that eliminate paper transactions and their associated costs.

With the decline in the price of personal computers and their increasing presence in the home, we have seen a further innovation in the home banking area, the appearance of a new type of banking institution, the **virtual bank**, a bank that has no physical location but rather exists only in cyberspace. ING, Citizens Bank, and Wells Fargo (one of the largest U.S. banks) became the first virtual banks, planning to offer an array of banking services on the Internet—accepting chequing account and savings deposits, selling certificates of deposit, issuing ABM cards, providing bill-paying facilities, and so on. Subsequently, many other banks, including the largest, have entered the virtual banking market, providing home banking services via the Internet. The virtual bank thus takes home banking one step further, enabling a customer to have a full set of banking services at home, 24 hours a day.

Canadian Bankers
Association
www.cba.ca

The acceptance of these new technologies in Canada has been phenomenal. A March 2000 survey conducted by the Strategic Counsel Inc. for the Canadian Bankers Association shows that 63% of Canadians currently use ABMs, the telephone, or computer banking as the main way of conducting financial transactions. In fact, when it comes to ABM use, Canadians are number one in the world, followed by the United States and Sweden. We also lead the way in the use of debit cards, followed by the Netherlands and France.

Avoidance of Existing Regulations

The process of financial innovation we have discussed so far is much like innovation in other areas of the economy: it occurs in response to changes in demand and supply conditions. However, because the financial industry is more heavily regulated than other industries, government regulation is a much greater spur to innovation in this industry. Government regulation leads to financial innovation by creating incentives for firms to skirt regulations that restrict their ability to earn profits. Edward Kane, an economist at Boston College, describes this process of avoiding regulations as "loophole mining."[5] The economic analysis of innovation suggests that when the economic environment changes such that regulatory constraints are so burdensome that large profits can be made by avoiding them, loophole mining and innovation are more likely to occur.

Because banking is one of the most heavily regulated industries, loophole mining is especially likely to occur. The rise in inflation and interest rates from the late 1960s to 1980 made the regulatory constraints imposed on this industry even more burdensome. Under these circumstances, we would expect the pace of financial innovation in banking to be rapid, and, indeed, it has been.

Two sets of regulations have seriously restricted the ability of U.S. banks to make profits: reserve requirements that force banks to keep a certain fraction of their deposits as reserves (deposits in the Federal Reserve System) and restrictions on the interest rates that can be paid on deposits. For the following reasons, these regulations have been among the major forces behind financial innovation in recent years.

Reserve Requirements The key to understanding why reserve requirements affect financial innovation is to recognize that they act, in effect, as a tax on deposits. Because the central bank does not pay interest on reserves, the opportunity cost of holding them is the interest that a bank could otherwise earn by lending the reserves out. For each dollar of deposits, reserve requirements therefore impose a cost on the bank equal to the interest rate that could be earned if the reserves could be lent out, i, times the fraction of deposits required as reserves, r_D. The cost of $i \times r_D$ imposed on the bank is just like a tax on bank deposits of $i \times r_D$.

As you will learn in Chapter 17, the current Canadian situation is that banks earn interest on positive settlement balances with the Bank of Canada. The interest rate is the bank rate less 50 basis points. There is still an opportunity cost for Canadian banks, but not of the order of magnitude when the central bank does not pay any interest on bank reserves.

---

[5]"Banking Takes a Beating," *Time,* December 3, 1984, p. 49.

It is a great tradition to avoid taxes if possible, and banks also play this game. Just as taxpayers look for loopholes to lower their tax bills, banks seek to increase their profits by mining loopholes and by producing financial innovations that allow them to escape the tax on deposits imposed by reserve requirements.

Restrictions on Interest Paid on Deposits   Although Canadian banks have never been subject to deposit rate ceilings, for decades after 1933, U.S. banks were prohibited from paying interest on chequing accounts. In addition, until 1986, the U.S. Federal Reserve System had the power under **Regulation Q** to set maximum interest rates that banks could pay on time deposits. The desire to avoid these **deposit rate ceilings** also led to financial innovations.

If market interest rates rose above the maximum rates that banks paid on time deposits under Regulation Q, depositors withdrew funds from banks to put them into higher-yielding securities. This loss of deposits from the banking system restricted the amount of funds that banks could lend (called **disintermediation**) and thus limited bank profits. Banks had an incentive to get around deposit rate ceilings because by so doing, they could acquire more funds to make loans and earn higher profits.

We can now look at how the desire to avoid restrictions on interest payments and the tax effect of reserve requirements led to several important financial innovations.

Eurodollars and Bank Commercial Paper   In the late 1960s, inflation was accelerating, and (as we would expect from our analysis of the Fisher effect in Chapter 5) interest rates began to rise. The tax on deposits from reserve requirements $i \times r_D$ also began to rise, and the incentives to avoid this tax increased. In addition, higher interest rates meant that market interest rates exceeded the maximum rate payable on time deposits under Regulation Q, and as market interest rates climbed to then record highs in 1969, investors reduced their time deposits to invest in higher-yielding securities. By the late 1960s, commercial banks had a strong incentive to search for new funds that would not be subject to reserve requirements and so escape the tax of $i \times r_D$ and not be subject to the interest rate ceiling set by Regulation Q.

As the economic analysis of innovation predicts, the banks began to mine loopholes and discovered two sources of funds that avoided both reserve requirements and deposit rate ceilings: Eurodollars and bank commercial paper. Because Eurodollars (deposits abroad denominated in dollars) were borrowed from banks outside the United States, they were not subject to reserve requirements or to Regulation Q. Similarly, commercial paper issued by a bank's parent holding company was not treated as deposits and so was also exempt from these regulations. Not surprisingly, the markets for Eurodollars and bank commercial paper have experienced phenomenal growth since then, even though the motivating U.S. regulations have been changed.

Sweep Accounts, and Overnight Repos   Another innovation that enables banks to pay interest on corporate chequing accounts is the **sweep account**. In this type of arrangement, any balances above a certain amount in a corporation's chequing account at the end of a business day are "swept out" of the account and invested in overnight repos that pay the corporation interest. (As you may recall from Chapter 2, the repo is an agreement whereby a corporation purchases Treasury bills that the bank agrees to repurchase the next day at a slightly higher price.) Again, although the chequing account does not legally pay interest, in effect the corporation is receiving interest on balances that are available for writing cheques.

The financial innovations of sweep accounts and overnight repo arrangements were stimulated not only by deposit rate ceilings but also by new technology. Without low-cost computers to process inexpensively the additional transactions required by these accounts, neither of these innovations would be profitable and therefore would have been developed. Technological factors often combine with other incentives, such as the desire to get around restrictions on deposit rates, to produce financial innovation.

Conclusion Our discussion of financial innovation and the challenges that are facing managers of banks indicate that banking is no longer the staid profession it once was. As one banker put it, "Despite all the dark suits worn by its leaders, banking is a very dynamic industry."[6]

SUMMARY

1. The balance sheet of commercial banks can be thought of as a list of the sources and uses of bank funds. The bank's liabilities are its sources of funds, which include chequable deposits, time deposits, advances from the Bank of Canada, borrowings from other banks and corporations, and bank capital. The bank's assets are its uses of funds, which include cash reserves, cash items in process of collection, deposits at other banks, securities, loans, and other assets (mostly physical capital).

2. Banks make profits through the process of asset transformation: they borrow short (accept deposits) and lend long (make loans). When a bank takes in additional deposits, it gains an equal amount of reserves; when it pays out deposits, it loses an equal amount of reserves.

3. Although more-liquid assets tend to earn lower returns, banks still desire to hold them. Specifically, banks hold reserves because they provide insurance against the costs of a deposit outflow. Banks manage their assets to maximize profits by seeking the highest returns possible on loans and securities while at the same time trying to lower risk and making adequate provisions for liquidity. Although liability management was once a staid affair, large (money centre) banks now actively seek out sources of funds by issuing liabilities such as negotiable CDs or by actively borrowing from other banks and corporations. Banks manage the amount of capital they hold to prevent bank failure and to meet bank capital requirements set by the regulatory authorities. However, they do not want to hold too much capital because by so doing they will lower the returns to equity holders.

4. The concepts of adverse selection and moral hazard explain many credit risk management principles involving loan activities: screening and monitoring, establishment of long-term customer relationships and loan commitments, collateral and compensating balances, and credit rationing.

5. With the increased volatility of interest rates that occurred in the 1980s, financial institutions became more concerned about their exposure to interest-rate risk. Gap and duration analyses tell a financial institution if it has more rate-sensitive liabilities than assets (in which case a rise in interest rates will reduce profits and a fall in interest rates will raise profits). Financial institutions manage their interest-rate risk by modifying their balance sheets but can also use strategies (outlined in Chapter 13) involving financial derivatives.

6. Off-balance-sheet activities consist of trading financial instruments and generating income from fees and loan sales, all of which affect bank profits but are not visible on bank balance sheets. Because these off-balance-sheet activities expose banks to increased risk, bank management must pay particular attention to risk assessment procedures and internal controls to restrict employees from taking on too much risk.

7. A change in the economic environment will stimulate financial institutions to search for financial innovations that are likely to be profitable. Changes in demand conditions, especially the rise in interest-rate risk, have stimulated a search for profits that has resulted in financial innovations such as adjustable-rate mortgages, while changes in supply conditions because of advances in computer technology have led to financial innovations such as bank credit cards and electronic banking facilities. Regulation leads to financial innovation by encouraging loophole mining. Starting in the late 1960s, for example, higher interest rates (resulting from higher inflation) encouraged financial innovations, including Eurodollars, bank commercial paper, and overnight repos.

---

[6]Ibid.

KEY TERMS

asset management, p. 194

balance sheet, p. 185

bank rate, p. 196

banker's risk, p. 190

capital adequacy management, p. 194

compensating balance, p. 205

credit rationing, p. 205

credit risk, p. 194

deposit outflows, p. 194

deposit rate ceiling, p. 215

desired excess reserves (desired reserves), p. 190

desired reserve ratio, p. 190

disintermediation, p. 215

duration analysis, p. 207

equity multiplier (*EM*), p. 200

financial engineering, p. 211

gap analysis, p. 207

interbank deposits, p. 189

interest-rate risk, p. 194

items in transit (float), p. 189

liability management, p. 194

liquidity management, p. 194

loan commitment, p. 204

loan sale, p. 208

money centre banks, p. 198

off-balance-sheet activities, p. 208

overdraft loans (advances), p. 190

Regulation Q, p. 215

return on assets (*ROA*), p. 200

return on equity (*ROE*), p. 200

secondary reserves, p. 190

settlement balances, p. 188

short sale, p. 188

sweep account, p. 215

T-account, p. 191

total cash reserves (reserves), p. 190

vault cash, p. 188

virtual bank, p. 213

QUESTIONS AND PROBLEMS

Questions marked with an asterisk are answered at the end of the book in an appendix, "Answers to Selected Questions and Problems."

1. Why might a bank be willing to borrow funds from other banks at a higher rate than it can borrow from the Bank of Canada?

*2. Rank the following bank assets from most to least liquid:
   a. Commercial loans
   b. Securities
   c. Reserves
   d. Physical capital

3. Using the T-accounts of the First Bank and the Second Bank, describe what happens when Jane Brown writes a $50 cheque on her account at the First Bank to pay her friend Joe Green, who in turn deposits the cheque in his account at the Second Bank.

*4. What happens to reserves at the First Bank if one person withdraws $1000 of cash and another person deposits $500 of cash? Use T-accounts to explain your answer.

5. The bank you own has the following balance sheet:

Assets		Liabilities	
Reserves	$ 75 million	Deposits	$500 million
Loans	$525 million	Bank	
		capital	$100 million

If the bank suffers a deposit outflow of $50 million and has a desired reserve ratio on deposits of 10%, what actions must you take to keep your bank from failing?

*6. If a deposit outflow of $50 million occurs, which balance sheet would a bank rather have initially, the balance sheet in Problem 5 or the following balance sheet? Why?

Assets		Liabilities	
Reserves	$100 million	Deposits	$500 million
Loans	$500 million	Bank	
		capital	$100 million

7. Why has the development of overnight loan markets made it more likely that banks will hold fewer reserves?

*8. If the bank you own has no excess reserves and a sound customer comes in asking for a loan, should you automatically turn the customer down, explaining that you don't have any excess reserves to lend out? Why or why not? What options are available for you to provide the funds your customer needs?

9. If a bank finds that its *ROE* is too low because it has too much bank capital, what can it do to raise its *ROE*?

*10. If a bank is falling short of meeting its capital requirements by $1 million, what three things can it do to rectify the situation?

11. Why is being nosy a desirable trait for a banker?

*12. A bank almost always insists that the firms it lends to keep compensating balances at the bank. Why?

13. "Because diversification is a desirable strategy for avoiding risk, it never makes sense for a bank to

specialize in making specific types of loans." Is this statement true, false, or uncertain? Explain your answer.

*14. Suppose that you are the manager of a bank whose $100 billion of assets have an average duration of four years and whose $90 billion of liabilities have an average duration of six years. Conduct a duration analysis for the bank, and show what will happen to the net worth of the bank if interest rates rise by 2 percentage points.

What actions could you take to reduce the bank's interest-rate risk?

15. Suppose that you are the manager of a bank that has $15 million of fixed-rate assets, $30 million of rate-sensitive assets, $25 million of fixed-rate liabilities, and $20 million of rate-sensitive liabilities. Conduct a gap analysis for the bank, and show what will happen to bank profits if interest rates rise by 5 percentage points. What actions could you take to reduce the bank's interest-rate risk?

Chapter 10

Banking Industry: Structure and Competition

P R E V I E W   The operations of individual banks (how they acquire, use, and manage funds to make a profit) are roughly similar throughout the world. In all countries, banks are financial intermediaries in the business of earning profits. When you consider the structure and operation of the banking industry as a whole, however, Canada is in a class by itself, with a comparatively concentrated banking industry and small financial institutions. Unlike the United States where there are over 8500 commercial banks, 1200 savings and loan associations, 400 mutual savings banks, and 12 000 credit unions, Canada has six large commercial banks, commonly called chartered banks, that typically dominate the banking industry.[1]

Is fewer better? Does it mean that the Canadian banking system is more stable and competitive and therefore more economically efficient and sound than banking systems in other countries? What in the Canadian economic and political system explains this small number of banking institutions? In this chapter we try to answer these questions by examining the historical trends in the banking industry and its overall structure.

We start by examining the chartered banking industry in detail and then go on to look at the near banking industry, which includes trust and mortgage loan companies, credit unions and *caisses populaires*. We spend more time on chartered banks because they are by far the largest depository institutions, accounting for over two-thirds of the deposits in the banking system. In addition to looking at our domestic banking system, we also examine forces behind the growth in international banking to see how it has affected us in Canada. Finally, we examine how financial innovation has increased the competitive environment for the banking industry and is causing fundamental changes in it.

---

[1]Commercial banks in Canada are called chartered banks, because they can be established only by charter granted either in a special Act of the federal Parliament or by the minister of finance.

HISTORICAL DEVELOPMENT OF THE CANADIAN BANKING SYSTEM

The modern Canadian banking industry began with the creation of the Bank of Montreal in 1817, by nine merchants in Montreal. Initially, the Bank of Montreal was without statutory authority, but a charter was approved by the legislature of Lower Canada and confirmed by royal assent in 1822. Meanwhile, other banks opened for business, and the Canadian banking industry was off and running; the Bank of New Brunswick received royal assent in 1820 and the Chartered Bank of Upper Canada in York (Toronto) in 1821. (As a study aid, Figure 10-1 provides a time line of the most important dates in the history of Canadian commercial banking before World War II.)

All these banks were authorized to issue notes (redeemable in specie, essentially British or American gold or silver coins, on demand), receive deposits, and lend for commercial purposes only; no bank was allowed to lend funds on mortgages, land, or real property. There were, however, some differences between the charters of these banks. For example, the terms of the charter of the Bank of New Brunswick followed the banking tradition of New England. The charter of the Bank of Montreal almost duplicated the terms governing the Bank of the United States (Box 10-1), which had elements of both a private and a **central bank**, a government institution that has responsibility for the amount of money and credit supplied in the economy as a whole. Also, the Bank of New Brunswick had to submit regular annual statements to the government and was not allowed to open **branches** (additional offices for the conduct of banking operations), whereas the Bank of Montreal had to provide statements only on request and was allowed to open branches in any part of Upper or Lower Canada.

Bank of Montreal
www.bankofmontreal.com

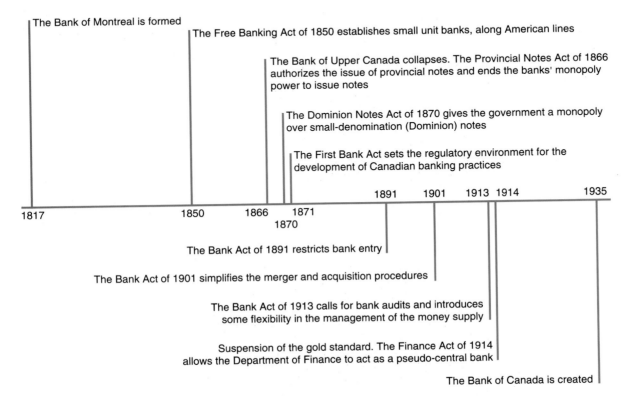

FIGURE 10-1   Time Line of the Early History of Commercial Banking in Canada

BOX 10·1

The Dual Banking System in the United States

The banking industry in the United States began when the Bank of North America was chartered in Philadelphia in 1782. A major controversy involving the U.S. banking industry in its early years was whether the federal government or the states should charter banks. The Federalists, particularly Alexander Hamilton, advocated greater centralized control of banking and federal chartering of banks. Their efforts led to the creation in 1791 of the Bank of the United States.

Until 1863, all commercial banks in the United States were chartered by the banking commission of the state in which they operated. No national currency existed, and banks obtained funds primarily by issuing banknotes. Because banking regulations were extremely lax in many states, banks regularly failed due to

fraud or lack of sufficient bank capital; their banknotes became worthless.

To eliminate the abuses of the state-chartered banks (called **state banks**), the National Bank Act of 1863 (and subsequent amendments to it) created a new banking system of federally chartered banks (called **national banks**). This legislation was originally intended to dry up sources of funds to state banks by imposing a prohibitive tax on their banknotes while leaving the banknotes of the federally chartered banks untaxed. The state banks cleverly escaped extinction by acquiring funds through deposits. As a result, today the United States has a **dual banking system** in which banks supervised by the federal government and banks supervised by the states operate side by side.

The Free Banking Experiment

Until 1850, no national currency existed in Canada, and banks obtained funds primarily by issuing *banknotes* (currency circulated by the banks that could be redeemed for gold). Although no banks failed, because banking regulations were extremely lax banks regularly experienced substantial declines in bank capital due to business failures; their banknotes tended to become scarce. The government tried various schemes to guarantee the provision of stable money, including the issuing of its own notes, but it was significantly influenced by the concept of **free banking**, implemented in New York in 1837. This system, as the name suggests, permitted the organization of a bank by any group that met certain established criteria concerning the amount of equity capital and maintenance of reserves.

The Free Banking Act was passed in Canada in 1850, with the purpose of facilitating the entry of small unit banks along American lines. It allowed the establishment of a bank, without a legislative charter, by any group that met the lax requirements set out in the free banking legislation. Under this legislation, the minimum amount of net worth to organize a bank was $100 000, branching was not allowed, and although the banknotes of the free banks were untaxed, the amount of note issue was limited to the amount of government debt held by the banks. The move to free banking was a step in the right direction, but Canada's experience with free banking was a failure. It did not lead to the establishment of a large number of new banks; only five new banks were established, two of which soon failed, and the other three converted to legislative charters.

The restriction on branching and the issue of banknotes based on government debt, rather than on commercial loans, were blamed for the failure of Canada's free banking experiment. The most important factor, however, was the fact that the option of a legislative charter was still available, unlike the situation in the United States where the provision of a legislative charter was simultaneously abolished in those states where free banking was established. In Canada, free banking with its restrictive provisions, particularly the restriction on branches and the less liberal provision for note issue, proved to be less profitable than banking under legislative charters.

In 1850, there were 15 chartered banks in Canada; 8 in Central Canada and 7 in what was to become Atlantic Canada. From 1850 until Confederation in 1867, and except for a short period after 1857, the Canadian provinces experienced an economic expansion and 30 new banks were established. However, 11 of these failed or closed their doors for other reasons, leaving 34 chartered banks with a total of 127 branches at the end of 1867.

The Provincial Notes Act, 1866

In the years before confederation, governments were anxious about the chartered banks' control of the note issue. They believed that the best way to protect the public from some of the consequences of bank failures would be to separate the currency of the country from the banking interests. In 1860, Alexander Galt, finance minister of the Province of Canada, proposed the substitution of a government-issued paper currency for banknotes. His proposal, however, was defeated by his critics, especially the chartered banks, for obvious reasons; the substitution of interest-free government debt for interest-free bank debt would have directly reduced their profits.

In the midst of a minor financial crisis in 1866, with the collapse of the Bank of Upper Canada (Canada's first chartered bank failure), the proponents of government-issued paper money finally achieved their objective with the enactment of the Provincial Notes Act. The Act authorized the issue of provincial notes, which because of their legal reserve status could be substituted for specie. With the co-operation of the Bank of Montreal, which had become the government's fiscal agent in 1864 by replacing the Bank of Upper Canada, the banks began to hold the new currency, thereby surrendering their power to issue notes.

The Dominion Notes Act, 1870

Canada was created by the British North America Act in 1867. The Act granted the new federal government of Canada exclusive jurisdiction over all matters pertaining to currency and banking, and the first problem to be tackled was the issue of paper money. With the failure in 1867 of the Chartered Bank of Canada (the second chartered bank failure in Canadian history), the Dominion Notes Act was passed in 1870. The Act confirmed the rights of banks to issue banknotes on their own credit, but restricted to large-denomination (over $5) notes, thereby giving the government a monopoly over small-denomination ($1 and $2) notes, the Dominion notes.

Although the Dominion Notes Act of 1870 did not set any reserve requirements, it required banks to hold at least half of their reserves in Dominion notes, thereby giving the government a share of the profits from the issuance of money, which is called **seignorage**. The Dominion notes themselves were fractionally backed by gold, and in this sense the Dominion Notes Act of 1870 confirmed that Canada would operate under the **gold standard**, meaning that its currency was convertible directly into gold.

Canada operated under the gold standard, keeping its currency backed by and convertible into gold, until World War I. During the years 1870–1935, Dominion notes increased in importance, but they never accounted for a major fraction of currency in circulation. They were superseded, together with the banknotes, by Bank of Canada notes, soon after the creation of the Bank of Canada (Canada's central bank) in 1935.

The First Bank Act, 1871

The first Bank Act came into effect in 1871. It was to be revised every 10 years, in light of experience and changing conditions; this "sunset" clause has effectively ensured that governments over the years paid periodic attention to banking reform. The Bank Act set the regulatory environment for Canadian chartered banks and for the future development of Canadian banking practices.

The Act continued the legislative chartering of banks, with each charter running for a 10-year period, then to be reviewed and renewed. New banks had to meet minimum capital requirements: $100 000 paid up before they opened for business against a total of $500 000. The banks' note issue continued to be restricted to large-denomination (over $5) notes and limited to the amount of their paid-up capital plus reserves. There were no reserve requirements, but one-third of a bank's cash reserves were required to be in the form of Dominion notes.

The Act continued the prohibition against mortgage lending and real estate loans, but it reinforced the commercial nature of banking, by allowing banks to make loans on the security of most kinds of merchandise. Also, for the greater security of the public, bank shareholders were liable for double the amount of their subscription. Finally, each bank was required to submit a detailed statement to the government on a monthly basis, but there was no provision for government inspection or audit.

The Bank Act, 1881–1913

A depression followed Confederation and lasted from 1873–1879. During the depression years, the banks were hard hit and 13 bank failures (4 in 1878, 5 in 1887, and another 4 in 1890) wiped out the savings of many noteholders. To prevent future losses from such failures, the early decennial revisions of the Bank Act, in 1881, 1891, 1901, and 1913 (postponed since 1911), were intended to provide better protection for the holders of banknotes, but the Act was not substantially changed.

In particular, in the Bank Act revision of 1891, the capital requirement was increased to $250 000 paid up, thereby restricting entry into the industry. The proportion of Dominion notes in bank cash reserves was increased to 40%, and the notes of a failed bank were made a first charge against its assets in the event of liquidation. Moreover, in the Bank Act revision of 1891, a Bank Circulation Redemption Fund was created, each bank contributing an amount equal to 5% of its average note circulation, to insure noteholders against loss.

In the years between mid-1890 and the outbreak of World War I, the Canadian economy experienced a phenomenal economic expansion. While bank entry was restrained (due to the increase in capital requirements in the Bank Act of 1891), the Bank Act revision of 1901 simplified the merger and acquisition procedures, by requiring only approval of Cabinet; previously a special Act of Parliament was required for all mergers. As a result of these legislative changes, 13 mergers took place before the end of 1914, relative to only 6 in the previous 33-year period, and the number of banks declined from 41 in 1890 to 22 in 1914. Over the same period, however, the number of bank branches increased from 426 to over 3000.

Another important legislative change occurred in the 1913 revision of the Bank Act. The Act called for a *bank audit*; annual, independent verification of the financial statements of the banks, with the results distributed to the shareholders and the minister of finance. The objective was to limit adverse selection and moral hazard problems that had increased over the years and been found to be the cause of a number of bank failures, particularly the failure of the Farmers Bank in 1910.

An additional noteworthy change was the excess circulation provision that introduced some flexibility in the management of the money supply. The economic expansion in the period after mid-1890 caused banknote issues to reach the ceiling that the Bank Act of 1871 had fixed at the amount of paid-up capital plus reserves. The banks did not increase their capital (and thus their note-issuing capacity), producing a shortage of currency. In order to achieve expansion in the money supply with the growth of economic activity, the Bank Act of 1913 allowed for the issuing of banknotes in excess of a bank's paid-up capital plus reserves.

The Finance Act, 1914

At the end of July 1914, less than a year after the revision of the Bank Act in 1913, World War I looked more and more inescapable. Canada's established banking legislation appeared to be inadequate and the immediate problem was to preserve the stability and liquidity of the financial system. Panic had taken hold, with depositors converting their money into gold for hoarding, and the banks and the government being concerned about their ability to convert money into gold on demand, since their gold reserves were a small fraction of their combined monetary liabilities. In light of these developments, on August 3, 1914, the government suspended the convertibility of Dominion notes and banknotes into gold, thereby ending the gold standard that had emerged over 40 years earlier in 1870. The gold standard was re-established in 1926 and suspended again in 1929, when the Great Depression hit the world.

A major legislative change, following the suspension of the gold standard, was the Finance Act of 1914. Patterned on the episode of 1907, during which banks could obtain cash reserves from the Department of Finance to prevent bank runs (which were triggered by bank failures in the United States), the Finance Act allowed the Department of Finance to act as a **lender of last resort**, that is, to provide Dominion notes to banks (on the pledge of approved securities) when no one else would, thereby preventing bank and financial panics. The Finance Act foreshadowed the increased flexibility in the management of the money supply that was provided by the Bank of Canada in 1935. We will examine in detail the economic forces that led to the creation of the Bank of Canada in Chapter 14.

Department of Finance
Canada
www.fin.gc.ca

STRUCTURE OF THE CANADIAN CHARTERED BANKING INDUSTRY

TD Canada Trust
www.tdcanadatrust.com

Canadian Imperial Bank
of Commerce
www.cibc.com

Royal Bank of Canada
www.royalbank.com

National Bank of Canada
www.bnc.ca

Scotiabank
www.scotiabank.com

As of June 2000, there were 49 chartered banks in Canada with over 8000 branches and over 222 000 employees (Figure 10-2). As Table 10-1 indicates, however, the six largest chartered banks, the Royal Bank of Canada, Canadian Imperial Bank of Commerce (CIBC), Bank of Montreal, Scotiabank, TD Canada Trust, and the National Bank of Canada, together hold over 92% of the assets in the industry. These banks are often called the **Big Six**.

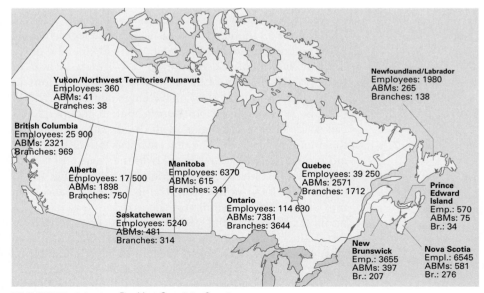

FIGURE 10-2   Banking Coast-to-Coast

Source: Canadian Bankers Association website: http://www.cba.ca. Information is updated annually. Reprinted with permission.

TABLE 10-1 Canadian Banks as of July 31, 2000			
Bank	**Date of establishment**	**Assets (in millions)**	**Percent (%) of bank assets**
The Big Six			
Royal Bank of Canada	1869	277 559.2	18.71
Canadian Imperial Bank of Commerce	1961	265 780.0	17.91
Bank of Montreal	1822	235 645.5	15.88
Scotiabank	1832	243 123.8	16.39
TD Canada Trust	1955	272 742.1	18.38
National Bank of Canada	1980	73 611.8	4.96
Big Six Subtotal		1 368 462.4	92.23
Laurentian Bank of Canada	1987	15 208.5	1.03
Canadian Western Bank	1988	2 944.6	0.20
8 Domestic Banks Subtotal		1 386 615.5	93.46
Other Banks			
Domestic Banks		1 719.7	0.12
Foreign Banks		95 301.8	6.42
Total		1 483 637.0	100.00

Source: Canadian Bankers Association website: http://www.cba.ca. Information is updated annually. Reprinted with permission.

Schedule I, Schedule II, and Schedule III Banks

Vancity Savings
www.vancity.com

Manulife Bank
www.manulifebank.com

The Big Six, together with the Laurentian Bank of Canada and the Canadian Western Bank, are Canada's **Schedule I** banks. Of the remaining 41 banks, 39 are **Schedule II** banks; they include three domestic Schedule II banks, Citizen Bank (owned by Vancity Savings), First Nations Bank (owned by TD Canada Trust), and Manulife Bank (owned by Manulife Insurance), and 36 subsidiaries (i.e., separate Canadian legal entities) of foreign banks.

Until 1981, foreign banks were not allowed to operate in Canada and there was no distinction between Schedule I and Schedule II banks. The 1981 revisions to the Bank Act focused on introducing more competition into the Canadian financial services industry. Domestic Canadian banks became Schedule I banks and subsidiaries of foreign banks became Schedule II banks.

Schedule I and Schedule II banks have identical powers; the only difference between them is the ownership structure permitted. In particular, according to current ownership policy, all Schedule I banks must be widely held: no individual can own more than 10% of any class of shares. Schedule II banks, however, are exceptions to this rule if small. In fact, there are three categories of exception. The first exception is that widely held foreign banks can own 100% of a Canadian bank subsidiary. The second exception is that a Schedule II bank may have a significant shareholder (more than 10%) for up to 10 years after chartering, as a transition measure to becoming a Schedule I bank. The third exception, introduced in the 1992 revision of the Bank Act, is that any widely held and regulated Canadian financial institution, other than a bank, may own 100% of a bank. In the case of big Schedule II banks (those with over $5 billion in equity capital), the same widely held ownership rule that applies to Schedule I banks applies.

With the passage of Bill C-67 in June 1999, a foreign bank may enter the Canadian banking industry as either a Schedule II or a **Schedule III** bank. The difference between Schedule II and Schedule III banks is that a Schedule II bank is a Canadian subsidiary of a foreign bank whereas a Schedule III bank is a foreign bank allowed to branch directly into Canada, under certain restrictions (to be discussed later in the chapter). As of June 2000, there were only 2 Schedule III banks in Canada, but recently the OSFI has approved branching for a large number of foreign banks.

Competition and Technology

ING Bank of Canada
www.ingdirect.ca

MBNA America Bank
www.mbna.com

Wells Fargo
www.wellsfargo.com

Capital One Financial Corporation
www.capitalone.com

Although Canada has a small number of banks relative to other countries, Canadians enjoy one of the most dynamic and competitive financial services industries. Besides chartered banks, there are over 3000 financial institutions providing financial services. These include trust and mortgage loan companies, credit unions and *caisses populaires*, government savings institutions, insurance companies, pension funds, mutual funds, and investment dealers.

New technology and the Internet have also helped in the development of a more competitive and innovative banking system in Canada. They have enabled new entrants to enter the Canadian financial services market and provide increased competition to the Big Six. For example, ING Bank of Canada, a new Canadian banking subsidiary of a major Netherlands banking and insurance conglomerate, and Citizen Bank, a subsidiary of Vancity Savings, are virtual banks offering an array of banking services on the Internet. Moreover, U.S. credit card banks, such as MBNA and Capital One Financial Corporation, are now offering specialized credit card products in Canada, and Wells Fargo, one of the largest banks in the United States, provides loans to Canadian small businesses from the United States.

COMPARISON WITH THE UNITED STATES

Microsoft Corporation
www.microsoft.com

Ford Motor Company
www.ford.com

Toyota Motor Corporation
www.toyota.com

The structure of the commercial banking industry in Canada, although similar to that in many other industrialized countries, is radically different from that in the United States. There are around 8500 commercial banks in the United States, whereas every other industrialized country in the world has well under 1000 commercial banks. Japan, for example, has fewer than 100 commercial banks—a mere fraction of the number of banks in the United States, even though its economy and population are half the size of the United States—and, as already noted, Canada has 49 chartered banks. Moreover, banks in the United States tend to be much smaller than banks in other countries; 14% of the commercial banks in the United States have less than $25 million in assets, and the 10 largest U.S. banks together hold just 36% of the assets in the industry.

The presence of so many commercial banks in the United States reflects past regulations that restricted the ability of these financial institutions to open branches. The result was that many small banks stayed in existence because a large bank capable of driving them out of business was often restricted from opening a branch nearby. Indeed, it was often easier for a U.S. bank to open a branch in a foreign country than to open one in another state in the United States! In fact, most industries in the United States have far fewer firms than the commercial banking industry. For example, Microsoft dominates the computer software industry and General Motors, Ford, DaimlerChrysler, Toyota, and Honda dominate the automobile industry.

Does the large number of banks in the commercial banking industry in the United States and the absence of a few dominant firms suggest that commercial banking is more competitive than other industries? Advocates of restrictive state branching regulations in the United States argued that regulations foster competition by keeping so many banks in business. But the existence of large numbers of banks in the United States should be seen as an indication of a *lack* of competition, *not* the presence of vigorous competition. Inefficient banks were able to remain in business because their customers could not find a conveniently located branch of another bank.

Response to Branching Restrictions in the United States

An important feature of the U.S. banking industry is that competition can be repressed by regulation but not completely quashed. As we saw in Chapter 9, the existence of restrictive regulation will stimulate banking institutions to go "loophole mining," coming up with financial innovations that get around these regulations in the banks' search for profits. Regulations restricting branching have stimulated similar economic forces and have promoted the development of three financial innovations: bank holding companies, nonbank banks, and automated banking machines.

Bank Holding Companies   A **bank holding company** is a corporation that owns several different companies. This form of corporate ownership has important advantages for banks. First, it has allowed them to circumvent restrictive branching regulations, because the holding company can own a controlling interest in several banks even if branching is not permitted. Second, a bank holding company can engage in other activities related to banking, such as the provision of investment advice, data processing and transmission services, leasing, credit card services, and servicing of loans in other states. Finally, the holding company can issue commercial paper, allowing the bank to tap into nondeposit sources of funds.

Bank holding companies also have the advantage that many states would allow bank holding companies headquartered in other states to purchase banks in their state. In addition, starting in 1982, banks were permitted to purchase out-of-state banks that were failing. For example, bank holding companies headquartered in New York, Ohio, North Carolina, Michigan, and California gained entry into the Texas market by purchasing failing institutions in that state.

The growth of the bank holding companies in the United States has been dramatic over the past three decades. Today bank holding companies own almost all large banks, and over 90% of all commercial bank deposits are held in banks owned by holding companies.

Nonbank Banks   Another way banks could avoid branching restrictions was through a loophole in the Bank Holding Act of 1956, which defined a bank as a financial institution that accepts deposits *and* makes loans. Once bank holding companies recognized this loophole, they realized that if they opened limited-service banks that either took deposits but did not make commercial loans or did not take deposits but made commercial loans, these so-called **nonbank banks** would not be subject to branching regulations. Thus the bank holding companies discovered a way of branching across state lines. However, the Competitive Equality Act passed in 1987 placed a moratorium on new nonbank banks, thus closing this loophole.

Automated Banking Machines   Another financial innovation that avoided the restrictions on branching is the electronic banking facility known as the automated banking machine (ABM). Banks realized that if they did not own or rent the ABM, but instead let it be owned by someone else and paid for each transaction with a fee, the ABM would probably not be considered a branch of the bank and thus would not be subject to branching regulations. This is exactly what the regulatory agencies and courts in most states in the United States concluded. Because they enable banks to widen their markets, a number of these shared facilities (such as Cirrus and NYCE) have been established nationwide. Furthermore, even when an ABM is owned by a bank, states typically have special provisions that allow wider establishment of ABMs than is permissible for traditional "brick and mortar" branches.

As we saw in Chapter 9, avoiding regulation was not the only reason for the development of the ABM. The advent of cheaper computer and telecommunications technology enabled banks to provide ABMs at low cost, making them a profitable innovation. This further illustrates that technological factors often combine with incentives such as the desire to avoid restrictive regulations like branching restrictions to produce financial innovations.

COMPETITION ACROSS ALL FOUR PILLARS

Another important feature of the structure of the banking industry in Canada until recently was the separation of the banking and other financial services industries—such as securities, insurance, and real estate. Regulations enforced the separation of institutions according to their core financial service, and only four distinct types of financial services were identified: banking, brokerage, trusts, and insurance. This approach to regulation by institution (versus regulation by function) has been known as the **four-pillar approach**. The separation of the four pillars prohibited chartered banks from engaging in insurance and real estate activities. In turn, it prevented investment banks and insurance companies from engaging in commercial banking activities and thus protected banks from competition.

Convergence   In recent years, however, financial markets have opened up and Canada's traditional four-pillar system has changed. Despite the prohibitions in the legislation, the pursuit of profits and financial innovation stimulated both banks and other financial institutions to bypass the intent of the legislation and encroach on each other's traditional territory. For example, credit unions long offered insurance to their members and brokerage firms engaged in the traditional banking business of issuing deposit instruments with the development of money market mutual funds and cash management accounts.

Not surprisingly, the regulatory barriers between banking and other financial services markets have been coming down, in response to these forces. Before the 1950s, for example, legislation allowed chartered banks to make loans for commercial purposes only and prohibited them from making residential mortgage loans. It was only after the 1967 revision of the Bank Act that banks were allowed to make conventional residential mortgage loans, thereby directly competing with trust and mortgage loan companies and credit unions and *caisses populaires*.

In the 1980s, the Bank Act was amended to allow Canadian and foreign financial institutions to own up to 100% of securities firms. Moreover, the 1990s revisions to the Bank Act allowed cross-ownership via subsidiaries between financial institutions. Chartered banks, for example, can either buy independent investment dealers or expand on their own into capital raising, brokerage, and other securities activities. As a result, as is shown in Table 10-2, the Big Six now dominate the investment banking industry through their investment brokerage subsidiaries; they hold a 70% share in the business.

TABLE 10-2   The Canadian Investment Banking Industry

Investment bank	Owner	Total financing volume, 1997 (Cdn $ billions)	Market share
RBC Dominion Securities	Royal Bank	7.9	16.0
Nesbitt Burns Inc.	Bank of Montreal	7.3	14.8
CIBC World Markets	CIBC	7.1	14.5
Scotia McLeod	Bank of Nova Scotia	5.7	14.5
TD Securities	Toronto Dominion	3.3	6.7
Midland Walwyn	Independent	3.3	6.7
Lévesque Beaubien	National Bank	1.6	3.2
Goldman Sachs	Independent	1.5	3.1
First Marathon	Independent	1.4	2.9
Merrill Lynch	Independent	1.1	2.3

Source: Mckinsey, *The Changing Landscape for Canadian Financial Services: New forces, new competitors, new choices*. Final Report for the Task Force on the Future of the Canadian Financial Services Sector (Ottawa, September 1998), Exhibit 2–16. Reproduced with the permission of the Minister of Public Works and Government Services Canada, 2001.

As a result of these recent legislative changes, Canada's traditional four pillars of financial services—banking, brokerage, trusts, and insurance—have now converged into a single financial services marketplace. Similar trends are also appearing in the United States as old rules and laws are overturned. With the Citicorp-Travelers merger in 1998 (Box 10-2), the Gramm-Leach-Bliley Financial Services Modernization Act of 1999 overturned the Glass-Steagall separation of the banking and securities industries and allowed securities firms and insurance companies to purchase banks and banks to underwrite insurance and securities and engage in real estate activities.

Implications for Financial Consolidation

As we have seen, recent legislation has stimulated consolidation of the banking industry. The financial consolidation process will be even further speeded up in the future, because the way is now open to consolidation in terms not only of the number of banking institutions, but also across financial service activities. Mergers of banks with other financial service firms like that of Citicorp and Travelers in the United States should become increasingly common, and more mega-mergers are likely to be on the way. Banking institutions will become not only larger, but also increasingly complex organizations, engaging in the full gamut of financial service activities.

Separation of Banking and Other Financial Services Industries Throughout the World

Not many other countries in the aftermath of the Great Depression followed the lead of Canada and the United States in separating the banking and other financial services industries. In fact, in the past this separation was the most prominent difference between banking regulation in Canada and the United States and in other countries. Around the world there are three basic frameworks for the banking and securities industries.

The first framework is *universal banking*, which exists in Germany, the Netherlands, and Switzerland. It provides no separation at all between the banking

---

BOX 10-2

The Citicorp-Travelers Merger

On April 6, 1998, the financial world was rocked by the announcement of what was expected to be the largest corporate merger ever, between Citicorp, the second-largest bank in the United States, and Travelers Group, which was in the insurance business and also owned the third-largest securities firm in the country, Salomon Smith Barney. (Because of a decline in the value of Citicorp by the time the merger actually took place, it turned out only to be the second-largest corporate merger in history; the Bank of America and NationsBank merger around the same time edged it out slightly.) The merged bank holding company, called Citigroup, would be one of the largest financial services firms in the world, with 100 million customers in 100 countries, over 150 000 employees, and $700 billion in assets.

The merger was remarkable not only for its size but also because under the Glass-Steagall Act of 1933 and the Bank Holding Company Act of 1956, the combination of these two corporations would be illegal. However, the marriage was approved by the Federal Reserve in September 1998 and was consummated in early October. As part of the approval process, the Federal Reserve produced a waiver giving Citigroup two to five years to sell off prohibited businesses like insurance underwriting. However, Citicorp and Travelers were betting that by the time the five-year period was up, Congress would pass legislation eliminating the restrictions imposed by Glass-Steagall and the Bank Holding Company Acts, thereby enabling Citigroup to engage in all financial service activities. The Citicorp and Travelers bet was a good one—Congress finally did pass the Gramm-Leach-Bliley Act overturning Glass-Steagall in 1999.

Citibank
www.citibank.com

Bank of America
www.bankofamerica.com

Salomon Smith Barney
www.salomonsmithbarney.com

and securities industries. In a universal banking system, commercial banks provide a full range of banking, securities, real estate, and insurance services, all within a single legal entity. Banks are allowed to own sizable equity shares in commercial firms, and often they do.

The British-style universal banking system, the second framework, is found in the United Kingdom and countries with close ties to it, such as Australia, Canada, and now the United States. The British-style universal bank engages in securities underwriting, but it differs from the German-style universal bank in three ways: separate legal subsidiaries are more common, bank equity holdings of commercial firms are less common, and combinations of banking and insurance firms are less common.

The third framework features some legal separation of the banking and other financial services industries, as in Japan. A major difference between British-style and Japanese banking systems is that Japanese banks are allowed to hold substantial equity stakes in commercial firms, whereas British-style universal banks cannot. Although the banking and securities industries are legally separated in Japan under Section 65 of the Japanese Securities Act, commercial banks are increasingly being allowed to engage in securities activities and are thus becoming more like British-style universal banks.

THE NEAR BANKS: REGULATION AND STRUCTURE

Not surprisingly, the regulation and structure of the near banks (trust and mortgage loan companies and credit unions and *caisses populaires*) closely parallels the regulation and structure of the chartered banking industry.

Trust and Mortgage Loan Companies

Over the years, the Bank Acts have denied to chartered banks the power to function as corporate **trustees** (or fiduciaries). Unlike the situation in the United States, legislators in Canada reasoned that deposit-taking financial institutions might face a conflict of interest if they were to act as both financial fiduciaries and banks. So beginning in 1843, trust companies were established, under a variety of provincial and federal laws, and specialized in the provision of fiduciary services. As financial fiduciaries, trust companies administer estates, trusts, and agencies (i.e., assets that belong to someone else), for a fee, and under conditions prescribed in a contract.

Over the years, the structure of the trust industry has changed significantly and the trust companies became closely associated with the chartered banks. In the early 1900s, the trust companies were also allowed to act as financial intermediaries. In this role, trust companies borrow funds by issuing deposit liabilities and then use these funds to make loans and purchase assets. Moreover, over the years the Bank Acts have allowed regulated federal financial institutions (domestic chartered banks and life insurance companies) to own trust companies. As a result, and with the acquisition of Canada Trust (Canada's largest trust company) by the Toronto Dominion Bank in early 2000, trust companies now constitute a relatively small market segment.

The development of trust companies was paralleled by the growth of mortgage loan companies. The concept of mortgage loan companies came from the building societies in the United Kingdom (during the early part of the 19th century), whose purpose was to enable members to acquire land, build homes, or develop farms. Today's mortgage loan companies take deposits and primarily make residential mortgage loans. They do not act as trustees, unless they are licensed specifically for that purpose. Over the years, the mortgage loan companies together with the trust companies formed the second pillar of the traditional financial services industry in Canada. However, as you will see later in the chapter, financial innovation, competition, and regulatory evolution significantly changed the competitive position of financial institutions in recent years.

Trust and mortgage loan companies (TMLs) operate under a charter issued by either the federal government or one of the provincial governments. Federally incorporated TMLs come under the federal Trust and Loan Companies Act and are regulated and supervised by the Office of the Superintendent of Financial Institutions (OSFI). They must also register in all of the provinces in which they operate and must conform to the regulations of those provinces. In the case of trust companies, the fiduciary component of their business is only subject to provincial legislation, even if the company is federally incorporated. Deposit insurance for TMLs outside Québec is provided by the CDIC (up to $60 000 per account). The Québec Deposit Insurance Board (QDIB) insures deposits for Québec TMLs, on terms similar to the CDIC's.

Table 10-3 shows the aggregate balance sheet of trust and mortgage loan companies, excluding those that are subsidiaries of chartered banks. They are funded almost entirely by chequable and non-chequable savings deposits, term deposits, guaranteed investment certificates, and debentures; together, they account for 87.6% of the balance sheet. Their risk asset portfolio is made up mostly by residential mortgages and personal loans; together they account for 62.5% of assets. The low-risk assets are largely in short-term paper (10%) and Canadian bonds (over 11%).

Cooperative Banks: Credit Unions and *Caisses Populaires*

Cooperative banks are small lending institutions organized around a particular group of individuals with a common bond (union members or employees of a particular firm). Alphonse Desjardins formed Canada's first cooperative bank in 1900 in Québec, and it was based on the cooperative movements in Europe, which, among other things, stressed the provision of credit to the "little man." Today, there are two cooperative financial systems in Canada: the *caisses populaires* system in Québec and the credit union system in other parts of the country.

TABLE 10-3	Balance Sheet of All Trust and Mortgage Loan Companies (in millions, as of December 1999)

Assets	Amount ($)	Percent (%)	Liabilities	Amount ($)	Percent (%)
Cash, items in transit, and gross demand and notice deposits	1 003	1.72	Savings deposits		
			Chequable	8 134	13.94
Term deposits	441	0.76	Non-chequable	4 001	6.86
Short-term paper	5 846	10.02	Term deposits, GICs, and debentures	38 987	66.83
Canadian bonds			Other liabilities	4 937	8.46
Government of Canada	3 512	6.02	Shareholders' equity	2 279	3.91
Provincial and municipal	229	0.39	Total liabilities	58 338	100.00
Corporate	2 846	4.88			
Loans and leases					
Residential mortgages	19 223	32.95			
Personal loans	17 237	29.55			
Non-residential mortgages	1 394	2.39			
Other loans and assets	6 607	11.32			
Total assets	58 338	100.00			

Source: *Bank of Canada Banking and Financial Statistics*, March 2000. Reprinted with permission.

The business importance of the cooperative banks in Canada varies significantly from province to province. In Québec, the *Mouvement Desjardins*, named after its founder, accounts for over 36% of the assets of all deposit-taking institutions, with strong presence in many financial product lines. For example, it accounts for 44% of deposits, 39% of residential mortgages, and almost 45% of agricultural credit in the province. In Saskatchewan and Manitoba the credit union movement accounts for about 35% and 25%, respectively, of the assets of deposit-taking institutions. In other provinces, the cooperative banks have a much less significant presence.

There are more than 2200 credit unions and *caisses populaires* in Canada, with almost 10 million members and more than 61 000 employees, carrying on retail financial services businesses. Because their members share a common goal, credit unions and *caisses populaires* are typically quite small; most are about the size of a single bank branch and hold less than $10 million of assets, with the largest being Vancity Savings with assets close to $6 billion. The credit unions and *caisses populaires* are established under provincial legislation and are non-profit-seeking financial institutions. Unlike chartered banks that accept deposits from and lend funds to the general public, the cooperative banks accept deposits from and lend funds only to their members. Members have voting rights and elect a board of directors, which determines the union's lending and investment policies.

As member-owned, independent financial firms, credit unions and *caisses populaires* constitute an alternative financial system, different from the profit-seeking banking system. They have also developed their own set of institutions, including central banking and deposit insurance arrangements. In particular, each province has a central credit union, owned by the member credit unions, that provides financial services to individual credit unions. All central credit unions outside Québec are members of the Credit Union Central of Canada (CUCC), also known as Canadian Central. The Canadian Central serves as the third tier for the credit union movement; it coordinates various functions and provides cheque-clearing services for all provincial central credit unions.

Credit Union Central of Canada
www.cucentral.ca

In Québec, *caisses populaires* are organized into eleven regional federations that in turn belong to *the Confédération des caisses populaires et d'économie Desjardins du Québec*, which has a similar structure as the provincial central credit unions in the rest of Canada but with considerably broader regulatory responsibilities. The confederation dominates retail and corporate financial intermediation in Québec. It owns a P&C insurance company, *Assurances Générales*; a life insurance company, Desjardins Laurentian Life; an American banking subsidiary, Desjardins Federal Savings Bank; an investment dealer and discount brokerage, Desjardins Securities Inc. and Disnat; and an industrial investment subsidiary, *Investissement Desjardins*. It also owns *Caisse centrale Desjardins*, which functions as a central bank, as the CUCC does for the rest of Canada.

Desjardins
www.desjardins.com

Credit unions and *caisses populaires* are not directly covered by the CDIC. However, each provincial government has an agency, commonly called a stabilization fund, which has a line of credit with the provincial treasury and provides deposit guarantees for credit unions on terms similar to those of the CDIC. In Québec, the Québec Deposit Insurance Board, the same provincial government agency that insures deposits in other deposit-taking financial institutions in Québec, also provides deposit guarantees for *caisses populaires*, on terms similar to the CDIC's.

The aggregate balance sheet of credit unions and *caisses populaires* is shown in Table 10-4. Their main source of funds is deposits—they account for almost 86% of liabilities—followed by members' equity (7.14% of liabilities). Their asset portfolio is made up largely by residential and non-residential mortgages (54.43% of the balance sheet) and cash loans to members (13.11%). Low-risk assets, such as cash and deposits (primarily with central credit unions) also represent a significant proportion of the balance sheet (close to 15%). The rest of the balance sheet consists of fixed assets, and shares in central credit unions.

Government Savings Institutions

In addition to the near banks (trust and mortgage loans companies and credit unions and *caisses populaires*), there are some government-operated deposit-taking institutions such as the Province of Ontario Savings Office and the Alberta Treasury Branches.

The Province of Ontario Savings Office was established in 1921 with the objective to gather funds from the public and lend them to farmers. Today, however, the Savings Office only lends funds to the Treasurer of Ontario for provincial government purposes. In fact, its deposit liabilities are a debt of the province of Ontario and are guaranteed by the province.

The province of Alberta established Treasury branches back in 1938 in response to Albertans' needs in remote areas. Today, there are 278 branches in 109 communities across the province operating in three target markets: individual financial services, agricultural operations, and independent business. Alberta Treasury Branches are funded almost entirely by demand, notice, and fixed-term deposits, and their risk asset portfolio is made up largely of residential mortgages, and personal, commercial, and agricultural loans.

Alberta Treasury Branches
www.atb.com

TABLE 10-4	Balance Sheet of All Credit Unions and *Caisses Populaires* (in millions, as of December 1999)					
Assets	**Amount ($)**	**Percent (%)**	**Liabilities**	**Amount ($)**	**Percent (%)**	
Cash and demand and			Deposits			
notice deposits	8 479	7.09	Chequable	23 903	19.99	
Term deposits	9 070	7.59	Non-chequable	9 719	8.13	
Short-term paper	472	0.39	Term	69 042	57.74	
Canadian bonds			Loans	6 021	5.04	
Government of Canada	480	0.40	Other liabilities	2 345	1.96	
Provincial and municipal	275	0.23	Members' equity	8 542	7.14	
Other	460	0.38	Total liabilities	119 572	100.00	
Shares central credit unions	605	0.51				
Loans and other assets						
Personal loans	15 674	13.11				
Residential mortgages	56 861	47.55				
Non-residential mortgages	8 230	6.88				
Other loans and assets	18 966	15.86				
Total assets	119 572	100.00				

Source: Bank of Canada Banking and Financial Statistics, March 2000. Reprinted with permission.

INTERNATIONAL BANKING

Canadian banks have a well-developed presence in the global financial services marketplace, which varies among the individual institutions. From its inception, for example, the Bank of Montreal found some of its best opportunities in international operations and was soon joined by the Canadian Imperial Bank of Commerce and the Bank of Nova Scotia. Currently, around 37% of the assets of the Big Six are employed in international operations, generating 35% of their net income, which varies from 58% for the Bank of Montreal, to 49% for Scotiabank, to 28% for the Royal Bank of Canada. The spectacular growth in international banking can be explained by three factors.

First is the rapid growth in international trade and multinational (worldwide) corporations that has occurred in recent years. When Canadian firms operate abroad, they need banking services in foreign countries to help finance international trade. For example, they might need a loan in a foreign currency to operate a factory abroad. And when they sell goods abroad, they need to have a bank exchange the foreign currency they have received for their goods into Canadian dollars. Although these firms could use foreign banks to provide them with these international banking services, many of them prefer to do business with the Canadian banks with which they have established long-term relationships and which understand Canadian business customs and practices. As international trade has grown, international banking has grown with it.

Second, Canadian banks have been able to earn substantial profits by being very active in global investment banking, in which they underwrite foreign securities. They also sell insurance abroad, and they derive substantial profits from these investment banking and insurance activities.

Third, Canadian banks have wanted to tap into the large pool of Eurocurrencies—currencies deposited in banks outside the home country. To understand the structure of Canadian banking overseas, let us first look at the Eurocurrencies market, an important source for international banking.

Eurocurrencies Market

The most important of the Eurocurrencies are Eurodollars, originated after World War II with U.S. dollar deposits in European banks. They were created when deposits in accounts in the United States were transferred to a bank outside the United States and were kept in the form of U.S. dollars. For example, if Rolls Royce PLC deposits a $1 million cheque, written on an account at an American bank, in its bank in London—specifying that the deposit be payable in U.S. dollars—$1 million in Eurodollars is created.[2] Over 90% of Eurodollar deposits are time deposits, more than half of them certificates of deposit with maturities of 30 days or more. The total amount of Eurodollars outstanding is on the order of U.S. $5 trillion, making the Eurodollar market (which was born in an ironic way—see Box 10-3) one of the most important financial markets in the world economy.

The main centre of the Eurocurrencies market is London, a major international financial centre for hundreds of years. Eurocurrencies are also held outside Europe in locations that provide offshore status to these deposits—for example, Singapore, the Bahamas, and the Cayman Islands.

The minimum transaction in the Eurocurrencies market is typically $1 million, and banks hold approximately 75% of Eurocurrencies deposits. Plainly, you and I are unlikely to come into direct contact with Eurocurrencies. The Eurocurrencies market is, however, an important source of funds to Canadian banks. Rather than using an intermediary and borrowing all the deposits from foreign banks, Canadian banks decided that they could earn higher profits by opening their own branches abroad to attract these deposits. Consequently, the Eurocurrencies market has been an important stimulus to Canadian banking overseas.

Canadian Banking Overseas

Canadian banks have been present in international financial markets for over 100 years, providing services to Canadians and multinational businesses. As Table 10-5 shows, the international presence of the Big Six varies among the individual institutions. In particular, the Bank of Montreal, the Canadian Imperial Bank of Commerce, and TD Canada Trust have significant presence in the United States, whereas Scotiabank has established a presence in South America, and the Royal Bank in Europe and Asia.

During the 1970s and early 1980s a large proportion of the banks' foreign lending was in **sovereign loans**; loans to foreign governments and their agencies in the less developed countries (LDCs), particularly Mexico, Brazil, Venezuela, Argentina, and Chile. Most of this activity in international lending was unregulated, with near disastrous consequences. One example is the international debt crisis, which had its origin in the oil price shocks of the 1970s. In particular, the 1973–1974 increase in the price of oil was a bonanza for some oil exporting countries like Mexico, but a disaster for oil importing countries like Brazil, which had to either cut their living standards or borrow massively abroad in order to pay their higher oil bills. At the time, real interest rates were very low (in fact negative) and the oil importers couldn't resist the temptation to borrow abroad.

---

[2]Note that the bank in London keeps the $1 million on deposits at the American bank, so the creation of Eurodollars has not caused a reduction in the amount of bank deposits in the United States.

BOX 10·3

Ironic Birth of the Eurodollar Market

One of capitalism's great ironies is that the Eurodollar market, one of the most important financial markets used by capitalists, was fathered by the Soviet Union. In the early 1950s, during the height of the Cold War, the Soviets had accumulated a substantial amount of dollar balances held by banks in the United States. Because the Russians feared that the U.S. government might freeze these assets in the United States, they wanted to move the deposits to Europe, where they would be safe from expropriation. (This fear was not unjustified—consider the U.S. freeze on Iranian assets in 1979 and Iraqi assets in 1990.) However, they also wanted to keep the deposits in dollars so that they could be used in their international transactions. The solution to the problem was to transfer the deposits to European banks but to keep the deposits denominated in dollars. When the Soviets did this, the Eurodollar was born.

Although most offshore deposits are denominated in U.S. dollars, some are also denominated in other currencies. Collectively, these offshore deposits are referred to as Eurocurrencies. A Canadian dollar-denominated deposit held in London, for example, is called a Euro Canadian dollar, and a French franc-denominated deposit held in London is called a Eurofranc. Why would companies like Rolls Royce want to hold Eurocurrencies? First, some currencies are widely used in international trade, so Rolls Royce might want to hold deposits in these currencies to conduct its international transactions. Second, Eurocurrencies are "offshore" deposits—they are held in countries that will not subject them to regulations such as reserve requirements or restrictions (called *capital controls*) on taking the deposits outside the country.

TABLE 10-5 International Activity of the Big Six

Bank	Primary Focus	International Assets (Cdn $ billions)	Percent of International Assets in Total Assets (%)
Bank of Montreal	United States, Mexico	87.3	44
CIBC	United States	99.4	42
Scotiabank	South America, Mexico	62.8	37
TD Canada Trust	United States	51.9	32
Royal Bank	Europe, Asia	60.1	28
National Bank	No significant international presence	8.6	16

Source: Mckinsey, *The Changing Landscape for Canadian Financial Services: New forces, new competitors, new choices.* Final Report for the Task Force on the Future of the Canadian Financial Services Sector (Ottawa, September 1998), Exhibit 5–24. Reproduced with the permission of the Minister of Public Works and Government Services Canada, 2001.

At the same time the oil exporters were depositing huge sums in banks and as a result the banks were lending not only to the oil importing countries but also to the oil exporting countries, because the latter had large oil reserves and seemed like good credit risks. The banks underestimated the **indebtedness** of these countries—the total amount these countries had borrowed from banks—and, as a result, were severely punished in the early 1980s when the recession hit and real interest rates increased significantly. With Argentina, Brazil, Mexico, and Peru threatening to default on their loans, the banks had two choices: to reschedule their loans and make more loans to these countries (to enable them to pay the interest on the debt), or to declare these countries in default and acknowledge large losses on their balance sheets. The banks chose to make more loans, because in many cases the losses would have been large enough to destroy them.

Today, the LDC debt is no longer a significant threat to the international banking system, because of other arrangements as well. In recent years, for example, a variety of debt conversion schemes have been proposed to alleviate the debt service obligations of the major indebted LDCs. There are three main forms of debt conversion: **debt-debt swaps** (where banks holding the debt of one LDC exchange it for the debt of another LDC), **debt-currency swaps** (where the debt denominated in foreign currency is converted into domestic currency), and **debt-equity swaps** (where the debt is converted into the equity of public and private domestic enterprises). The main impetus of all these debt conversion schemes has been the recognition that the true value of the sovereign debt is well below its face value.

As a result of their lending experience in Latin America, the Big Six have withdrawn from certain countries and focused more of their international activities in the United States (Figure 10-3). Moreover, the international activities of Canadian banking organizations are now regulated, primarily by the Office of the Superintendent of Financial Institutions (OSFI), created in 1987 to succeed two separate regulatory bodies: the Inspector General of Banks and the Department of Insurance. In particular, in 1991, the OSFI asked the chartered banks to set up special reserves in the amount of 35%–45% of their exposure to a number of LDCs.

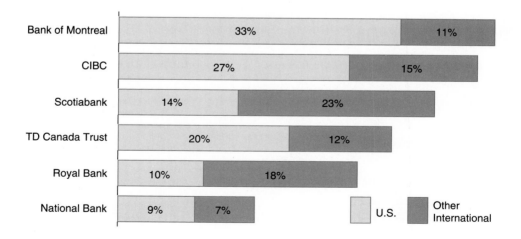

FIGURE 10-3 International Focus of the Big Six

Source: Mckinsey, *The Changing Landscape for Canadian Financial Services: New forces, new competitors, new choices.* Final Report for the Task Force on the Future of the Canadian Financial Services Sector (Ottawa, September 1998), Exhibit 5–24. Reproduced with the permission of the Minister of Public Works and Government Services Canada, 2001. Reproduced with the permission of the Minister of Public Works and Government Services Canada, 2001.

Foreign Banks in Canada

HSBC Bank of Canada
www.hsbc.ca

The growth in international trade has not only encouraged Canadian banks to open offices overseas but has also encouraged foreign banks to establish offices in Canada. Foreign banks have been extremely successful in Canada. Over the past 20 years, since the 1981 revision to the Bank Act, globally prominent foreign banks have set up and expanded banking subsidiaries in Canada. Foreign banks are a highly fragmented group and as shown in Table 10-6 they currently hold about 12% of total Canadian bank assets, with HSBC Bank of Canada (the former Hong Kong and Shanghai Banking Corp.) enjoying a national market share of 3.1%. It should be noted, however, that these institutions target specific groups, achieving a higher representation within their target groups than their national share would suggest. For example, HSBC, the largest of the Schedule II banks, enjoys a strong presence and success in the Chinese communities of British Columbia and Ontario.

Foreign banks may enter the Canadian financial services industry as either Schedule II or Schedule III banks. As already noted, Schedule II banks don't have to be widely held if small. If, however, their equity capital exceeds $1 billion then at least 35% of it must be widely held. In the case that their equity capital exceeds $5 billion then the same widely held ownership rule applies as for Schedule I banks. The major difference between Schedule II and Schedule III banks is that Schedule III banks can branch directly into Canada, following authorization by the Minister of Finance, whereas Schedule II banks can add branches to their initial branch only with ministerial approval. However, Schedule III banks cannot take retail deposits (i.e., deposits less than $150 000) and, as a result, have the advantage of not being subject to regulations that apply to full-service banks (such as requirements for CDIC

TABLE 10-6   Schedule II Banks in Canada

Institution	Domestic assets (Cdn $ billions)	Share (%)
HSBC Bank of Canada	23.9	3.1
Deutsche Bank	8.7	1.1
Citibank	7.2	0.9
Bank of America	5.0	0.6
Société Générale	4.5	0.6
ABN Amro Bank	3.9	0.5
BT Bank of Canada	3.8	0.5
Bank of Tokyo-Mitsubishi	3.1	0.4
Crédit Lyonnais	2.7	0.3
Banque Nationale de Paris	2.6	0.3
Union Bank of Switzerland	2.6	0.3
Crédit Suisse First Boston	2.6	0.3
Banca Commerciale Italiana	2.0	0.2
Other	20.8	2.7
Total	**93.4**	**11.8**

Source: Mckinsey, *The Changing Landscape for Canadian Financial Services: New forces, new competitors, new choices.* Final Report for the Task Force on the Future of the Canadian Financial Services Sector (Ottawa, September 1998), Exhibit 2–12. Reproduced with the permission of the Minister of Public Works and Government Services Canada, 2001.

insurance). Given that most Schedule II banks do little retail deposit gathering, it is likely that in the future many Schedule II banks will become Schedule III banks.

The internationalization of banking, both by Canadian banks going abroad and by foreign banks entering Canada, has meant that financial markets throughout the world have become more integrated. As a result, there is a growing trend toward international coordination of bank regulation, one example of which is the 1988 Basel agreement to standardize minimum capital requirements in industrialized countries, discussed in Chapter 11. Financial market integration has also encouraged bank consolidation abroad, culminating in the creation of the first trillion-dollar bank with the proposed merger of the Industrial Bank of Japan, Dai-Ichi Kangyo Bank, and Fuji Bank, announced in August 1999, but to take place in 2002. Another development has been the importance of foreign banks in international banking. As is shown in Table 10-7, in 1998, 54 of the largest banks in the world were foreign. The implications of this financial market integration for the operation of our economy is examined further in Chapter 19 when we discuss the international financial system in more detail.

Industrial Bank of Japan
www.ibjbank.co.jp

Fuji Bank
www.fujibank.co.jp

Dai-Ichi Kangyo Bank
www.dkb.co.jp

FINANCIAL INNOVATION AND THE DECLINE OF TRADITIONAL BANKING

The traditional financial intermediation role of banking has been to make long-term loans and fund them by issuing short-dated deposits, a process of asset transformation commonly referred to as "borrowing short and lending long." Earlier in

TABLE 10-7 Largest Banks in the World at Fiscal 1998

Bank	Asset ranking	Asset size (in billions of Cdn $)
Deutsche Bank	1	1123.0
UBS	2	1051.5
Citigroup	3	1025.0
Bank of America Corp.	4	946.9
Bank of Tokyo-Mitsubishi	5	917.8
ABN Amro Bank	6	772.8
HSBC Holdings	7	743.0
Crédit Suisse Group	8	726.6
Crédit Agricole Groupe	9	700.6
Société Générale	10	686.1
CIBC	55	281.4
Royal Bank of Canada	57	274.4
Scotiabank	62	233.6
Bank of Montreal	64	222.6
TD Canada Trust	79	181.8
National Bank of Canada	154	70.7

Source: Canadian Bankers Association website, http://www.cba.ca. Information updated annually. Reprinted with permission.

the chapter, we saw that changes in regulations have been increasing the competitive environment in the banking industry in Canada. Another source of increasing competition for this industry is coming from financial innovations. Here we examine how the same economic forces we examined in Chapter 9 have generated financial innovations that present the banking industry with competitive challenges that are causing traditional banking business to decline. The decline in traditional banking has important implications for the future of the banking industry and creates new challenges for regulators.

Behind the Decline: Four Financial Innovations

Four financial innovations have played an important role in the decline of traditional banking: mutual funds, junk bonds, the rise of the commercial paper market, and securitization.

Mutual Funds As we saw in Chapter 9, the financial behaviours of Canadians have been evolving. People are relying less and less on bank branches for basic transactions, switching to automated banking machines, telephone banking, and Internet banking. Moreover, consumers are widening their investment choices, putting more of their wealth into the stock market and new financial innovations such as mutual funds. In fact, mutual funds have experienced extraordinary growth and already exceed personal deposits at chartered banks. As Figure 10-4 shows, industry experts expect that in the near future, mutual funds will exceed personal deposits at chartered banks, trust and mortgage loan companies, credit unions and *caisses populaires*, and government saving institutions.

More important has been the development of money market mutual funds. These relatively new financial instruments have the characteristics of a mutual fund but also function to some extent as a depository institution because they offer deposit-type accounts. In particular, money market mutual funds issue shares that are redeemable at a fixed price (usually $1). For example, if you buy 5000 shares for $5000, the money market fund uses these funds to invest in short-term money market securities (Treasury bills, certificates of deposit, commercial paper) that provide you with inter-

Investment Funds
Institute of Canada
www.ific.ca

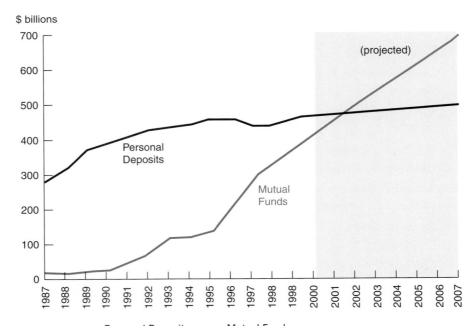

FIGURE 10-4 Personal Deposits versus Mutual Funds

Source: Canadian Bankers Association website: http://www.cba.ca. Reproduced with the permission of the Minister of Public Works and Government Services Canada, 2001.

est payments. Although money market fund shares effectively function as deposits that earn interest, they are not legally deposits and so are not insured by the CDIC.

In the United States, money market mutual funds also offer chequing privileges, effectively functioning as chequing account deposits. For this reason, money market mutual funds in that country have experienced extraordinary growth since 1971, when they first appeared. By 1999, their assets had climbed to nearly $1500 billion. As consumers shift to mutual funds, deposit-taking financial institutions (throughout the world) risk losing a low-cost source of funds.

Junk Bonds   Before the advent of computers and advanced telecommunications, it was difficult to acquire information about the financial situation of firms that might want to sell securities. Because of the difficulty in screening out bad from good credit risks, the only firms that were able to sell bonds were very well established corporations that had high credit ratings.[3] Before the 1980s, then, only corporations that could issue bonds with ratings of B++ or above could raise funds by selling newly issued bonds. Some firms that had fallen on bad times, so-called *fallen angels,* had previously issued long-term corporate bonds that now had ratings that had fallen below B++, bonds that were pejoratively dubbed "junk bonds."

With the improvement in information technology in the 1970s, it became easier for investors to screen out bad from good credit risks, thus making it more likely that they would buy long-term debt securities from less well-known corporations with lower credit ratings. With this change in supply conditions, we would expect that some smart individual would pioneer the concept of selling new public issues of junk bonds, not for fallen angels but for companies that had not yet achieved investment-grade status. This is exactly what Michael Milken of Drexel Burnham, an investment-banking firm, started to do in 1977. Junk bonds became an important factor in the corporate bond market. Although there was a sharp slowdown in activity in the junk bond market after Milken was indicted for securities law violations in 1989, it has heated up again in the 1990s.

Commercial Paper Market   Recall that *commercial paper* is a short-term debt security issued by large banks and corporations. As we saw in Chapter 2, the commercial paper market has undergone tremendous growth since 1970, when there was $588 million outstanding, to over $24 billion outstanding at the end of 2000. Indeed, commercial paper has been one of the fastest-growing money market instruments.

Improvements in information technology also help provide an explanation for the rapid rise of the commercial paper market. We have seen that the improvement in information technology made it easier for investors to screen out bad from good credit risks, thus making it easier for corporations to issue debt securities. Not only did this make it easier for corporations to issue long-term debt securities as in the junk bond market, but it also meant that they could raise funds by issuing short-term debt securities like commercial paper more easily. Many corporations that used to do their short-term borrowing from banks now frequently raise short-term funds in the commercial paper market instead.

The development of money market mutual funds has been another factor in the rapid growth in the commercial paper market. Because money market mutual funds need to hold liquid, high-quality, short-term assets such as commercial paper, the growth of assets in these funds has created a ready market in commercial paper. The growth of pension and other large funds that invest in commercial paper has also stimulated the growth of this market.

---

[3]The discussion of adverse selection problems in Chapter 8 provides a more detailed analysis of why only well-established firms with high credit ratings were able to sell securities.

Securitization   An important example of a financial innovation arising from improvements in both transaction and information technology is securitization, one of the most important financial innovations in the past two decades. **Securitization** is the process of transforming otherwise illiquid financial assets (such as residential mortgages), which have typically been the bread and butter of banking institutions, into marketable capital market securities. As we have seen, improvements in the ability to acquire information have made it easier to sell marketable capital market securities. In addition, with low transaction costs because of improvements in computer technology, financial institutions find that they can cheaply bundle together a portfolio of loans (such as mortgages) with varying small denominations (often less than $100 000), collect the interest and principal payments on the mortgages in the bundle, and then "pass them through" (pay them out) to third parties. By dividing the portfolio of loans into standardized amounts, the financial institution can then sell the claims to these interest and principal payments to third parties as securities. The standardized amounts of these securitized loans make them liquid securities, and the fact that they are made up of a bundle of loans helps diversify risk, making them desirable. The financial institution selling the securitized loans makes a profit by servicing the loans (collecting the interest and principal payments and paying them out) and charging a fee to the third party for this service.

Securitization first started in the United States in 1970 when the GNMA (now known as Ginnie Mae) began a program in which it guaranteed interest and principal payments on bundles of standardized mortgages, thereby encouraging the creation of a new financial instrument, the mortgage-backed security. The guarantee of the interest and principal payments makes it easy for private financial institutions to sell a bundle of guaranteed mortgages as a security and to pass through these payments to the owner of the security. Securitization, however, has not stopped with mortgages: numerous types of assets are now routinely securitized, including residential mortgages, automobile loans, credit card receivables, and commercial and computer leases.

Computer technology has also enabled financial institutions to tailor securitization to produce securities that have payment streams considered especially desirable by the market. Collateralized mortgage obligations (CMOs), which are bonds that pass through the payments from a portfolio of mortgages, are a good example of such tailoring; they first appeared in 1983. Computerization enables a CMO to be split into several classes known as *tranches*. The first tranches receive interest payments according to the coupon rate on the CMO, with class 1 first receiving all principal payments and prepayments from the collateralized pool of mortgages. After the class 1 bonds have been paid off, the principal payments and prepayments are used to retire the remaining classes sequentially. The last class, called *accrual* or *Z bonds*, receives interest and principal payments only after the other classes have been paid off. The basic CMO described here has the advantage of containing bonds of both short maturity (class 1) and long maturity (the later classes or the accrual bond), thus increasing its potential market. Indeed, the financial innovation process has led to even more complicated CMOs that fit additional niches in the marketplace.

In Canada, securitization has not yet developed to the same degree as in the United States. Recently, however, the popularity of securitization has been growing, primarily because of the benefits it provides to all stakeholders. For example, it benefits investors by increasing the variety of available instruments and offering a greater degree of liquidity than other investments. It benefits borrowers by offering greater flexibility in product choice and perhaps lower borrowing costs. It also allows financial institutions to move assets off their balance sheet, thereby reducing the need to hold regulatory capital. In Canada, by the end of June 1998, the total amount of asset-backed securities outstanding was $40.9 billion, a 326% increase from the $9.6 billion in 1995.

Decline of Traditional Banking

Clearly, the traditional financial intermediation role of banking, whereby banks make loans that are funded with deposits, is no longer as important in our financial system. However, the decline in the market share of banks in total lending and total financial intermediary assets does not indicate that the banking industry is in decline. If we look at bank profitability relative to GDP, there is no evidence of a declining trend. As we can see in Figure 10-5, after a dismal performance in the late 1980s and early 1990s, bank profits have rebounded sharply, with strong profits since 1992. In fact, in recent years the profit margins of Canadian banks have climbed close to those in the United States and the United Kingdom.

However, overall bank profitability is not a good indicator of the profitability of traditional banking because it includes an increasing amount of income from nontraditional off-balance-sheet activities discussed in Chapter 9. As you can see in Figure 10-6, noninterest income derived from off-balance-sheet activities, as a share of total bank income, increased from around 30% in 1988 to 60% of total bank income by 2000. Given that the overall profitability of banks has not risen, the increase in income from off-balance-sheet activities implies that the profitability of traditional banking business has declined. This decline in profitability then explains why banks have been reducing their traditional business.

Reasons for the Decline

To understand why traditional banking business has declined in both size and profitability, we need to look at how the financial innovations described earlier have caused banks to suffer declines in their cost advantages in acquiring funds, that is, on the liabilities side of their balance sheet, while at the same time they have lost income advantages on the assets side of their balance sheet. The simultaneous decline of cost and income advantages has resulted in the reduced profitability of traditional banking and an effort by banks to leave this business and engage in new and more profitable activities.

Decline in Cost Advantages in Acquiring Funds (Liabilities)   Before the 1980s, banks were paying low interest rates on chequable deposits. This worked to the banks' advantage because their major source of funds was chequable deposits. Unfortunately,

FIGURE 10-5   Commercial Bank Profitability, 1986–2000

Source: Bank of Canada and CANSIM Series D15689. Reproduced with the permission of the Minister of Public Works and Government Services Canada, 2001.

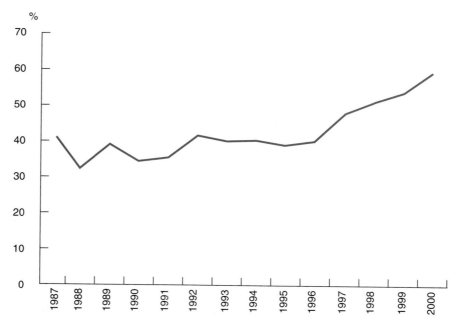

FIGURE 10-6   Share of Noninterest Income in Total Bank Income, 1987–2000
Source: Bank of Canada. Reprinted with permission.

this cost advantage for banks did not last. The rise in inflation from the late 1960s on led to higher interest rates, which made investors more sensitive to yield differentials on different assets. The result was the so-called disintermediation process, in which people began to take their money out of banks, with their low interest rates on both chequable and time deposits, and began to seek out higher-yielding investments. Also, as we have seen, at the same time, financial innovation led to money market mutual funds, which put the banks at an even further disadvantage because depositors could now obtain deposit-like services while earning high interest on their money market mutual fund accounts. One manifestation of these changes in the financial system was that the low-cost source of funds declined dramatically in importance for banks.

Decline in Income Advantages on Uses of Funds (Assets)   The loss of cost advantages on the liabilities side of the balance sheet for Canadian banks is one reason that they have become less competitive, but they have also been hit by a decline in income advantages on the assets side from the financial innovations we discussed earlier—junk bonds, securitization, and the rise of the commercial paper market.

We have seen that improvements in information technology have made it easier for firms to issue securities directly to the public. This has meant that instead of going to banks to finance short-term credit needs, many of the banks' best business customers now find it cheaper to go instead to the commercial paper market for funds. The loss of this competitive advantage for banks is evident in the fact that before 1970, nonfinancial commercial paper equalled 5% of commercial bank loans, whereas the figure has risen to close to 19% today.

The rise of the junk bond market has also eaten into banks' loan business. Improvements in information technology have made it easier for corporations to sell their bonds to the public directly, thereby bypassing banks. Although well-established companies started taking this route in the 1970s, now lower-quality corporate borrowers are using banks less often because they have access to the junk bond market.

We have also seen that improvements in computer technology have led to securitization, whereby illiquid financial assets such as bank loans and mortgages are transformed into marketable securities. Computers enable other financial institutions to originate loans because they can now accurately evaluate credit risk with statistical methods, while computers have lowered transaction costs, making it possible to bundle these loans and sell them as securities. When default risk can be easily evaluated with computers, banks no longer have an advantage in making loans. Without their former advantages, banks have lost loan business to other financial institutions even though the banks themselves are involved in the process of securitization.

Banks' Responses

Canadian banks have sought to maintain former profit levels by pursuing new off-balance-sheet activities that are more profitable. As we saw in Figure 10-6, chartered banks did this during the 1990s, significantly increasing the share of their income from off-balance-sheet, noninterest-income activities.[4] This strategy, however, has generated concerns about what are proper activities for banks and about whether nontraditional activities might be riskier and result in banks taking excessive risks.

The decline of banks' traditional business has thus meant that the banking industry has been driven to seek out new lines of business. This could be beneficial because by so doing, banks can keep vibrant and healthy. Indeed, bank profitability has been high in recent years, and nontraditional, off-balance-sheet activities have been playing an important role in the resurgence of bank profits. However, there is a danger that the new directions in banking could lead to increased risk taking, and thus the decline in traditional banking requires regulators to be more vigilant. It also poses new challenges for bank regulators, who, as we will see in Chapter 11, must now be far more concerned about banks' off-balance-sheet activities.

Decline of Traditional Banking in Other Industrialized Countries

Forces similar to those in Canada have been leading to the decline of traditional banking in other industrialized countries. The loss of banks' monopoly power over depositors has occurred outside Canada as well. Financial innovation and deregulation are occurring worldwide and have created attractive alternatives for both depositors and borrowers. In the United States, for example, the importance of commercial banks as a source of funds to nonfinancial borrowers has shrunk dramatically. In 1974, commercial banks provided close to 40% of these funds; by 1999, their market share was down to below 30%. The decline in market share for thrift institutions has been even more precipitous: from over 20% in the late 1970s to below 10% today. In Japan, deregulation has opened a wide array of new financial instruments to the public, causing a disintermediation process similar to that in Canada and the United States. In European countries, innovations have steadily eroded the barriers that have traditionally protected banks from competition.

In other countries, banks have also faced increased competition from the expansion of securities markets. Both financial deregulation and fundamental economic forces in other countries have improved the availability of information in securities markets, making it easier and less costly for firms to finance their activities by issuing securities rather than going to banks. Further, even in countries where securities markets have not grown, banks have still lost loan business because their best corporate customers have had increasing access to foreign and

---

[4]Note that some off-balance-sheet activities, such as loan commitments and letters of credit, which produce fee income, can be classified as being in the category of traditional banking business. The data in Figure 10-5 overstate somewhat the importance of nontraditional banking business.

offshore capital markets, such as the Eurobond market. In smaller economies, like Australia, which still do not have well-developed corporate bond or commercial paper markets, banks have lost loan business to international securities markets.

The increase in the competitive environment for foreign banks has meant that some of them have found themselves in financial difficulties. Return on assets and return on equity have fallen in Japan and many European countries, and banks in these countries have sometimes been finding themselves in financial difficulties. France's largest bank, Crédit Lyonnais, required a $10 billion bailout in 1995, with additional infusions of over $1 billion in 1996 and 1997, and in 1996, the Italian government injected over $1 billion to help keep the Banco di Napoli afloat. Even in countries like Switzerland and Germany, banks have been running into trouble. For example, in January 1993, BfG Bank, a German bank, needed a capital infusion from its parent company, Crédit Lyonnais, because it suffered huge losses in 1992. In the following chapter, we will discuss the extensive problems in the Japanese banking industry. Canada is not unique in seeing its banks face a more difficult competitive environment.

FINANCIAL SERVICES REFORM FOR THE 21ˢᵀ CENTURY

We have seen that fundamental structural changes make possible new financial products and services, increasing the competitive environment in the financial services industry and changing the financial intermediation role of banking at Internet speed. It is against this backdrop of phenomenal change that the federal government has recently introduced legislation reforming the policy framework of the Canadian financial services sector. This legislation is mostly based on the Report of the Task Force on the Future of the Canadian Financial Services Sector, also known as the MacKay Report, and it has been called one of the most significant revisions to the Bank Act in Canadian history, scheduled for no later than 2002.

In what follows we provide an overview of the key elements of this important proposed legislation that has the potential to dramatically change the face of competition in Canada's financial services marketplace. As you will see, the new legislation establishes the regulatory framework to accelerate changes already taking place throughout the Canadian and world economies and introduces new opportunities for strategic alliances and partnerships, with the objective of fostering more competition and providing more innovative products and services to Canadians.

Bank Holding Companies

The current organizational structure of Canada's bank financial groups is based on the "bank-as-parent" model, where all banking functions and all subsidiaries of the bank are subject to the same regulation. Under the new legislation, bank financial groups will have the option of organizing themselves under a holding company. A holding company is a corporation that owns several different companies. Most developed countries permit bank holding company structures and the growth of bank holding companies has been dramatic over the past three decades. Today, in the United States, for example, bank holding companies own almost all large banks, and over 90% of all commercial bank deposits are held in banks owned by holding companies. In fact, the Gramm-Leach-Bliley Act of 1999 modernized the holding company rules in the United States (which have been in place since 1956) to allow a new and more flexible holding company model–the financial holding company.

The holding company form of corporate ownership has important advantages for bank financial groups in that (1) it allows them to engage in other activities related to banking, such as the provision of investment advice, data processing and transmission services, leasing, and credit card services; (2) a holding company structure allows for lighter regulation throughout the bank financial group because certain activities (those not involving retail deposit-taking and insurance) can be undertaken by less-regulated, non-bank-affiliated companies held by the holding company parent rather than the regulated operating bank; and (3) the holding company model provides bank financial groups increased flexibility to achieve economies of scale and scope through strategic partnerships, alliances, and joint ventures.[5]

The big advantage of the proposed new regime for establishing holding companies is that bank financial groups will be able to move parts of their heavily regulated business into less regulated affiliates under a common holding company. The holding company, however, would be a viable option for bank financial groups, if the transition to a holding company would be tax-neutral and without increased costs or regulatory burdens. If, for example, additional taxes or heavier regulation were to arise as a result of a restructuring into a holding company, then the holding company option wouldn't be feasible. For this reason, the proposed legislation provides a set of transitional rules to address unintended cost consequences that would be triggered by the transition to a holding company.

The Permitted Investment Regime

A second item of the proposed legislation pertains to the type of investments Canadian bank financial groups are allowed to make. At present, there is a restrictive list of activities beyond banking that banks can get involved in. The new legislation, however, provides greater flexibility for bank involvement in the information technology area (and in particular the Internet and wireless technology). It permits bank financial groups to establish and operate information services entities utilizing recent advances in Internet and wireless banking and voice recognition technologies.

New information technologies are critical in the ability of Canadian bank financial groups to provide new financial products and services and adapt to the changing marketplace. Although bank involvement in the information technology area is subject to regulation, the new permitted investment regime will enhance the ability of banks to pursue strategic alliances and joint ventures and will further accelerate the technological advances that are already taking place and revolutionize the financial services sector.

New Ownership Rules

A third policy measure that can change significantly the face of competition in Canada's financial services marketplace is the new ownership regime that enables investors to take a greater equity interest in widely held bank financial groups. In particular, the proposed legislation increases the limit a single shareholder can own of a widely held financial institution (either a bank holding company or a bank subsidiary under the holding company) from 10% of any class of shares to 20% of voting shares and 30% of non-voting shares. The new legislation, however, does not permit a single shareholder to own more than 10% of both a bank holding company and a bank subsidiary under the holding company at the same time. Moreover, acquisitions of more than 10% are subject to approval by the Minister of Finance based on a "fit and proper person" test.

The new legislation also includes a three-tiered ownership regime. Small banks (those with equity capital under $1 billion) don't have to be widely held and can be wholly owned (have one particular investor own 100% of their shares). Medium

---

[5]Recently, for example, the British-based banking group HSBC entered into a joint venture with the U.S.-based securities dealer Merrill Lynch, to create a global on-line banking and investment company, called Merrill Lynch HSBC.

sized banks (and bank holding companies) with shareholders' equity between $1 billion and $5 billion can be closely held provided that there is a 35% public float (that is, they could have a single shareholder own up to 65% of their shares). Large banks (and bank holding companies), those with shareholders' equity in excess of $5 billion, are required to be widely held.

The proposed ownership regime, together with other provisions in the legislation, such as the lowering of the capital needed to create a bank from $10 million to $5 million and the allowance of domestic and foreign commercial enterprises (such as department stores and grocery chains) to establish small and medium-sized banks, will fundamentally change Canada's financial sector.

Access to the Payments and Clearance System

Another regulatory change that will significantly affect Canada's financial services marketplace is the decision to allow non-deposit-taking financial institutions, such as life insurance companies, securities dealers, and money market mutual funds, access to the payments and clearance system. This will allow these organizations to provide bank-like services, such as chequing accounts and debit cards, without being banks, thereby directly competing with banks, trust and mortgage loan companies, and credit unions and *caisses populaires*.

Expanding access to the payments and clearance system, by allowing non-deposit-taking financial institutions to participate, will further accelerate the process of the blurring of distinction among deposit-taking and non-deposit-taking financial institutions. As already noted, this process started in 1987, when securities dealers were allowed to own banks, and was reinforced by the 1992 federal financial reforms that permitted cross ownership of financial institutions.

Merger Review Policy

The government has also issued a statement establishing a process for reviewing mergers involving large banks—banks like the Bank of Montreal and CIBC with shareholder equity in excess of $5 billion. By doing so, the government acknowledges that mergers are a legitimate business option that should be available to Canadian bank financial groups. The bank merger review process, however, unlike those in other countries such as the United States and the United Kingdom, is political having the Parliament directly involved in it.

The government has also indicated that it will not allow mergers between large banks and large demutualized life insurance companies such as Manulife and Clarica Life. We would note, however, that in other countries such as Australia, Germany, the Netherlands, Switzerland, the United Kingdom, and the United States, mergers of banks, insurance companies, and other financial services providers are not prohibited.

Implications for the Canadian Banking Industry

A bank holding company structure (as an alternative to the current "bank-as-parent" structure), new ownership rules, expanded permitted investments, expanded access to the payments and clearance system, and a transparent merger review policy, offer new opportunities for strategic alliances and joint ventures that have the potential to reshape the Canadian financial services marketplace. These developments, together with new information technologies, make possible new financial products and services and a more vibrant and dynamic market for financial services.

As we have seen, the 1992 federal financial reforms have stimulated consolidation of the Canadian banking industry. The financial consolidation process will be even further speeded up by the proposed legislation, because the way is now open to both mergers and acquisitions, and strategic alliances, partnerships, and joint ventures. As already noted, bank financial groups will become not only larger, but increasingly complex organizations, engaging in a full gamut of financial activities.

SUMMARY

1. The history of banking in Canada has left us with a small number of banks chartered by the federal government. Multiple agencies regulate chartered banks: the Office of the Superintendent of Financial Institutions (OSFI), the Bank of Canada, and the Canada Deposit Insurance Corporation (CDIC).

2. The Big Six (the Royal Bank of Canada, Canadian Imperial Bank of Commerce, Bank of Montreal, Scotiabank, TD Canada Trust, and the National Bank of Canada) together with the *Mouvement Desjardins* dominate the deposit-taking industry in Canada.

3. In the United States there is a dual banking system, with commercial banks chartered by the states and the federal government. Restrictive state branching regulations which prohibited branching across state lines, led to a large number of small commercial banks in the United States. The large number of commercial banks in the United States reflects the past *lack* of competition, not the presence of vigorous competition.

4. The regulation and structure of the near banks (trust and mortgage loan companies and credit unions and *caisses populaires*) parallel closely the regulation and structure of the chartered banks. Federally incorporated near banks are regulated and super-

vised by the OSFI. They must also register in all the provinces in which they do business and must conform to the regulations of those provinces.

5. With the rapid growth of world trade since 1960, international banking has grown dramatically. Canadian banks engage in international banking activities by opening branches abroad and owning controlling interests in foreign banks. Foreign banks operate in Canada by owning a subsidiary Canadian bank or by operating branches or agency offices in Canada.

6. Until 1981, foreign banks were not allowed to operate in Canada. Today, we have 43 foreign bank subsidiaries, operating as Schedule II banks. They have the same powers as the domestic banks but differ in the ownership structure permitted. That is, all Schedule I banks must be widely held whereas Schedule II banks can be closely held if small.

7. Financial innovation has caused banks to suffer declines in cost advantages in acquiring funds and in income advantages on their assets. The resulting squeeze has hurt profitability in banks' traditional lines of business and has led to a decline in traditional banking.

KEY TERMS

bank holding companies, p. 227

Big Six, p. 224

branches, p. 220

central bank, p. 220

debt-currency swaps, p. 237

debt-debt swaps, p. 237

debt-equity swaps, p. 237

dual banking system, p. 221

four-pillar approach, p. 228

free banking, p. 221

gold standard, p. 222

indebtedness, p. 237

lender of last resort, p. 224

national banks, p. 221

nonbank banks, p. 227

Schedule I banks, p. 225

Schedule II banks, p. 225

Schedule III banks, p. 225

securitization, p. 242

seigniorage, p. 222

sovereign loans, p. 235

state banks, p. 221

trustees, p. 231

QUESTIONS AND PROBLEMS

Questions marked with an asterisk are answered at the end of the book in an appendix, "Answers to Selected Questions and Problems."

1. Describe how early revisions to the Bank Act attempted to introduce more flexibility in the management of the money supply.

*2. Which regulatory agency has the primary responsibility for supervising the following categories of financial institutions?

a. chartered banks
b. trust and mortgage loans companies
c. credit unions and *caisses populaires*

3. "The commercial banking industry in Canada is less competitive than the commercial banking industry in the United States because in Canada only a few large banks dominate the industry, while in the United States there are around 8500 commercial banks." Is this statement true, false, or uncertain? Explain your answer.

*4. How did new technology cause banks' traditional lending activities to decline in balance-sheet importance?

5. Contrast the activities of a Schedule I bank, a Schedule II bank, a trust company, and a credit union.

*6. Explain how sovereign loans in the 1970s and early 1980s caused problems for the Big Six.

7. Explain how the early development of chartered banks in Canada differed from the development of commercial banks in the United States.

*8. What incentives do Canadian regulatory agencies have to encourage the establishment of foreign banks in Canada?

9. Explain how securitization can be used to change illiquid assets into liquid assets.

*10. If the bank at which you keep your chequing account is owned by Saudi Arabians, should you worry that your deposits are less safe than if Canadians owned the bank?

11. What are the essential differences between chartered banks, trust and mortgage loan companies, and credit unions and *caisses populaires?*

*12. Why have banks been losing cost advantages in acquiring funds in recent years?

13. "If inflation had not risen in the 1960s and 1970s, the banking industry might be healthier today." Is this statement true, false, or uncertain? Explain your answer.

*14. Why have banks been losing income advantages on their assets in recent years?

15. "The invention of the computer is the major factor behind the decline of the banking industry." Is this statement true, false, or uncertain? Explain your answer.

Chapter 11

Economic Analysis of Banking Regulation

P R E V I E W   As we have seen in the previous chapters, the financial system is among the most heavily regulated sectors of the economy, and banks are among the most heavily regulated of financial institutions. In this chapter we develop an economic analysis of why regulation of banking takes the form it does.

Unfortunately, the regulatory process may not always work very well, as evidenced by recent crises in the banking systems, not only in Canada but also in many countries throughout the world. Here we also use our economic analysis of banking regulation to explain the worldwide crises in banking and how the regulatory system can be reformed to prevent future disasters.

ASYMMETRIC INFORMATION AND BANK REGULATION

In earlier chapters we have seen how asymmetric information, the fact that different parties in a financial contract do not have the same information, leads to adverse selection and moral hazard problems that have an important impact on our financial system. The concepts of asymmetric information, adverse selection, and moral hazard are especially useful in understanding why government has chosen the form of banking regulation we see in Canada and in other countries. There are seven basic categories of banking regulation: the government safety net, restrictions on bank asset holdings, capital requirements, chartering and bank examination, disclosure requirements, consumer protection, and restrictions on competition.

Government Safety Net: Deposit Insurance and the CDIC

As we saw in Chapter 8, banks are particularly well suited to solving adverse selection and moral hazard problems because they make private loans that help avoid the free-rider problem. However, this solution to the free-rider problem creates another asymmetric information problem because depositors lack information about the quality of these private loans. This asymmetric information problem leads to two reasons why the banking system might not function well.

First, before the CDIC started operations in 1967, a **bank failure** (in which a bank is unable to meet its obligations to pay its depositors and other creditors and so must go out of business) meant that depositors would have to wait to get their deposit funds until the bank was liquidated (until its assets had been turned into cash); at that time, they would be paid only a fraction of the value of their deposits. Unable to learn if bank managers were taking on too much risk or were outright crooks, depositors would be reluctant to put money in the bank, thus making banking institutions less viable. Second is that depositors' lack of information about the quality of bank assets can lead to bank panics, which, as we saw in Chapter 8, can have serious harmful consequences for the economy. To see this, consider the following situation. There is no deposit insurance, and an adverse shock hits the economy. As a result of the shock, 5% of the banks have such large losses on loans that they become insolvent (have a negative net worth and so are bankrupt). Because of asymmetric information, depositors are unable to tell whether their bank is a good bank or one of the 5% that are insolvent. Depositors at bad *and* good banks recognize that they may not get back 100 cents on the dollar for their deposits and will want to withdraw them. Indeed, because banks operate on a "sequential service constraint" (a first-come, first-served basis), depositors have a very strong incentive to show up at the bank first because if they are last in line, the bank may run out of funds and they will get nothing. Uncertainty about the health of the banking system in general can lead to runs on banks both good and bad, and the failure of one bank can hasten the failure of others (referred to as the *contagion effect*). If nothing is done to restore the public's confidence, a bank panic can ensue.

A government safety net for depositors can short-circuit runs on banks and bank panics, and by providing protection for the depositor, it can overcome reluctance to put funds in the banking system. One form of the safety net is deposit insurance, a guarantee such as that provided by the Canada Deposit Insurance Corporation (CDIC) in Canada in which depositors are paid off in full on the first $60 000 they have deposited in the bank no matter what happens to the bank. With fully insured deposits, depositors don't need to run to the bank to make withdrawals—even if they are worried about the bank's health—because their deposits will be worth 100 cents on the dollar no matter what.

Canada Deposit Insurance
Corporation
www.cdic.ca

The CDIC uses two primary methods to handle a failed bank. In the first, called the *payoff method,* the CDIC allows the bank to fail and pays off deposits up to the $60 000 insurance limit (with funds acquired from the insurance premiums paid by the banks who have bought CDIC insurance). After the bank has been liquidated, the CDIC lines up with other creditors of the bank and is paid its share of the proceeds from the liquidated assets. Typically, when the payoff method is used, account holders with deposits in excess of the $60 000 limit get back more than 90 cents on the dollar, although the process can take several years to complete.

In the second method, called the *purchase and assumption method,* the CDIC reorganizes the bank, typically by finding a willing merger partner who assumes (takes over) all of the failed bank's deposits so that no depositor loses a penny. The CDIC may help the merger partner by providing it with subsidized loans or by buying some of the failed bank's weaker loans. The net effect of the purchase and assumption method is that the CDIC has guaranteed *all* deposits, not just those under the $60 000 limit.

Deposit insurance is not the only way in which governments provide a safety net for depositors. Governments have often stood ready to provide support to domestic banks when they face runs even in the absence of explicit deposit insurance. This support is sometimes provided by lending from the central bank to troubled institutions and is often referred to as the "lender of last resort" role of the central bank. In other cases, funds are provided directly by the government to troubled institutions, or these institutions are taken over by the government and the government then guarantees that depositors will receive their money in full.

Moral Hazard and the Government Safety Net   Although a government safety net has been successful at protecting depositors and preventing bank panics, it is a mixed blessing. The most serious drawback of the government safety net stems from moral hazard, the incentives of one party to a transaction to engage in activities detrimental to the other party. Moral hazard is an important concern in insurance arrangements in general because the existence of insurance provides increased incentives for taking risks that might result in an insurance payoff. For example, some drivers with automobile collision insurance that has a low deductible might be more likely to drive recklessly because if they get into an accident, the insurance company pays most of the costs for damage and repairs.

Moral hazard is a prominent concern in government arrangements to provide a safety net. Because with a safety net depositors know that they will not suffer losses if a bank fails, they do not impose the discipline of the marketplace on banks by withdrawing deposits when they suspect that the bank is taking on too much risk. Consequently, banks with a government safety net have an incentive to take on greater risks than they otherwise would.

Adverse Selection and the Government Safety Net   A further problem with a government safety net like deposit insurance arises because of adverse selection, the fact that the people who are most likely to produce the adverse outcome insured against (bank failure) are those who most want to take advantage of the insurance. For example, bad drivers are more likely than good drivers to take out automobile collision insurance with a low deductible. Because depositors protected by a government safety net have little reason to impose discipline on the bank, risk-loving entrepreneurs might find the banking industry a particularly attractive one to enter—they know that they will be able to engage in highly risky activities. Even worse, because protected depositors have so little reason to monitor the bank's activities, without government intervention outright crooks might also find banking an attractive industry for their activities because it is easy for them to get away with fraud and embezzlement.

"Too Big to Fail"   The moral hazard created by a government safety net and the desire to prevent bank failures have presented bank regulators with a particular quandary. Because the failure of a very large bank makes it more likely that a major financial disruption will occur, bank regulators are naturally reluctant to allow a big bank to fail and cause losses to its depositors.

One problem with the too-big-to-fail policy is that it increases the moral hazard incentives for big banks. If the CDIC were willing to close a bank using the alternative payoff method, paying depositors only up to the $60 000 limit, large depositors with more than $60 000 would suffer losses if the bank failed. Thus they would have an incentive to monitor the bank by examining the bank's activities closely and pulling their money out if the bank was taking on too much risk. To prevent such a loss of deposits, the bank would be more likely to engage in less risky activities. However, once large depositors know that a bank is too big to fail, they have no incentive to monitor the bank and pull out their deposits when it takes on too much risk: no matter what the bank does, large depositors will not suffer any losses. The result of the too-big-to-fail policy is that big banks might take on even greater risks, thereby making bank failures more likely.

Financial Consolidation and the Government Safety Net   As we saw in Chapter 10, financial consolidation has been proceeding at a rapid pace, leading to both larger and more complex banking organizations. Financial consolidation poses two challenges to banking regulation because of the existence of the government safety net. First, the increased size of banks as a result of financial consolidation increases the too-big-to-fail problem because there will now be more large institutions whose failure exposes the financial system to systemic (system-wide) risk. Thus more banking institutions are likely to be treated as too big to fail, and the increased moral hazard incentives for these large institutions to take on greater risk can then increase the fragility of the financial system. Second, financial consolidation of banks with other financial services firms means that the government safety net may be extended to new activities such as securities underwriting, insurance, or real estate activities, thereby increasing incentives for greater risk taking in these activities that can also weaken the fabric of the financial system. Limiting the moral hazard incentives for the larger, more complex financial organizations that are resulting from recent changes in legislation will be one of the key issues facing banking regulators in the future.

Restrictions on Asset Holdings and Bank Capital Requirements

As we have seen, the moral hazard associated with a government safety net encourages too much risk taking on the part of banks. Bank regulations that restrict asset holdings and bank capital requirements are directed at minimizing this moral hazard, which can cost the taxpayers dearly.

Even in the absence of a government safety net, banks still have the incentive to take on too much risk. Risky assets may provide the bank with higher earnings when they pay off; but if they do not pay off and the bank fails, depositors are left holding the bag. If depositors were able to monitor the bank easily by acquiring information on its risk-taking activities, they would immediately withdraw their deposits if the bank were taking on too much risk. To prevent such a loss of deposits, the bank would be more likely to reduce its risk-taking activities. Unfortunately, acquiring information on a bank's activities to learn how much risk the bank is taking can be a difficult task. Hence most depositors are incapable of imposing discipline that might prevent banks from engaging in risky activities. A strong rationale for government regulation to reduce risk taking on the part of banks therefore existed even before the establishment of deposit insurance.

Bank regulations that restrict banks from holding risky assets such as common stock are a direct means of making banks avoid too much risk. Bank regulations also promote diversification, which reduces risk by limiting the amount of loans in particular categories or to individual borrowers. Requirements that banks have sufficient bank capital are another way to change the bank's incentives to take on less risk. When a bank is forced to hold a large amount of equity capital, the bank has more to lose if it fails and is thus more likely to pursue less risky activities.

Bank capital requirements take three forms. The first type is based on the so-called **leverage ratio**, the amount of capital divided by the bank's total assets. To be classified as well capitalized, a bank's leverage ratio must exceed 5%; a lower leverage ratio, especially one below 3%, triggers increased regulatory restrictions on the bank.

In the past decade, regulators in Canada and the rest of the world have become increasingly worried about banks' holdings of risky assets and about the increase in banks' **off-balance-sheet activities**, activities that involve trading financial instruments and generating income from fees, which do not appear on bank balance sheets but nevertheless expose banks to risk. Under an agreement among banking officials from industrialized nations (who met under the auspices of the Basel Committee on Bank Supervision at the Bank for International Settlements in Basel, Switzerland), the Bank of Canada, the CDIC, and the OSFI have implemented a second type of bank-based capital requirement, which was fully phased in by December 1992 and has been modified since then (see Box 11-1). Under this risk-based capital requirement, which the banks must meet along with the leverage ratio capital requirement, minimum capital standards are linked to off-balance-sheet activities such as interest-rate swaps and trading positions in futures and options.

Bank for International
Settlements
www.bis.org

Bank Supervision: Chartering and Examination

Overseeing who operates banks and how they are operated, referred to as **bank supervision** or more generally as **prudential supervision**, is an important method for reducing adverse selection and moral hazard in the banking business. Because banks can be used by crooks or overambitious entrepreneurs to engage in highly speculative activities, such undesirable people would be eager to run a bank. Chartering banks is one method for preventing this adverse selection problem; through chartering, proposals for new banks are screened to prevent undesirable people from controlling them.

Regular on-site bank examinations, which allow regulators to monitor whether the bank is complying with capital requirements and restrictions on asset holdings, also function to limit moral hazard. Bank examiners give banks a so-called *CAMELS rating* (the acronym is based on the six areas assessed: capital adequacy, asset quality, management, earnings, liquidity, and sensitivity to market risk). With this information about a bank's activities, regulators can enforce regulations by taking such formal actions as *cease and desist orders* to alter the bank's behaviour or even close a bank if its CAMELS rating is sufficiently low. Actions taken to reduce moral hazard by restricting banks from taking on too much risk help reduce the adverse selection problem further because with less opportunity for risk taking, risk-loving entrepreneurs will be less likely to be attracted to the banking industry. Note that the methods regulators use to cope with adverse selection and moral hazard have their counterparts in private financial markets (see Chapter 8). Chartering is similar to the screening of potential borrowers, regulations restricting risky asset holdings are similar to restrictive covenants that prevent borrowing firms from engaging in risky investment activities, bank capital requirements act like restrictive covenants that require minimum amounts of net worth for borrowing firms, and regular bank examinations are similar to the monitoring of borrowers by lending institutions.

A chartered bank obtains a charter either by Act of Parliament or through application to the minister of finance, who has the authority to issue a charter. To obtain a charter, the people planning to organize the bank must submit an application that shows how they plan to operate the bank. In evaluating the application, the regulatory authority looks at whether the bank is likely to be sound by examining the quality of the bank's intended management, the likely earnings of the bank, and the amount of the bank's initial capital. Moreover, the chartering agency typically explores the issue of whether the community needs a new bank. Often a new bank charter would not be granted if existing banks in a community would be hurt by its presence. Today this anticompetitive stance (justified by the desire to prevent bank failures of existing banks) is no longer as strong.

Once a bank has been chartered, it is required to file periodic (usually quarterly) *call reports* that reveal the bank's assets and liabilities, income and dividends, ownership, foreign exchange operations, and other details. The bank is also subject to examination by the bank regulatory agencies to ascertain its financial condition at least once a year. To avoid duplication of effort, the three federal agencies work together and usually accept each other's examinations. This means that, typically, chartered banks are examined by the Bank of Canada, the CDIC, and the OSFI.

Bank examinations are conducted by bank examiners, who study a bank's books to see whether it is complying with the rules and regulations that apply to its holdings of assets. If a bank is holding securities or loans that are too risky, the bank examiner can force the bank to get rid of them. If a bank examiner decides that a loan is unlikely to be repaid, the examiner can force the bank to declare the loan worthless (to write off the loan). If, after examining the bank, the examiner feels that it does not have sufficient capital or has engaged in dishonest practices, the bank can be declared a "problem bank" and will be subject to more frequent examinations.

The Basel Accord on Risk-Based Capital Requirements: Where Is It Heading?

The increased integration of financial markets across countries and the need to make the playing field level for banks from different countries led to the June 1988 Basel Accord to standardize bank capital requirements internationally. The stated purposes of the agreement were (1) to promote world financial stability by coordinating supervisory definitions of capital, risk assessments, and standards for capital adequacy across countries and (2) to link a bank's capital requirements systematically to the riskiness of its activities, including various off-balance-sheet forms of risk exposure.

The Basel Accord required that banks hold as capital at least 8% of their risk-weighted assets. Assets and off-balance-sheet activities were allocated into four categories, each with a different weight to reflect the degree of credit risk. The first category carried a zero weight and included items that have little default risk, such as reserves and government securities in the OECD (industrialized) countries. The second category had a 20% weight and included claims on banks in OECD countries. The third category had a weight of 50% and included municipal bonds and residential mortgages. The fourth category had the maximum weight of 100% and included loans to consumers and corporations. Off-balance-sheet activities are treated in a similar manner by assigning a credit-equivalent percentage that converts them to on-balance-sheet items to which the

appropriate risk weight applies. The 1996 Market Risk Amendment to the accord set minimum capital requirements for risks in banks' trading accounts.

Over time, limitations of the accord have become apparent because the regulatory measure of bank risk as stipulated by the risk weights can differ substantially from the actual risk the bank faces. To address these limitations, the Basel Committee on Bank Supervision released a proposal in June 1999 to expand on the 1988 accord in four main areas. First, minimum capital requirements are to be changed by expanding the number of risk categories and by using credit ratings provided by commercial credit rating agencies or by banks themselves to assign assets into these categories. Second, banks will be able to use their own credit risk models for setting capital requirements. Third, the internal management procedures banks use to decide on how much capital to hold should be subject to supervisory review, after which banks could be required to hold capital beyond the regulatory minimum in some circumstances. Fourth, there should be increased disclosure of banks' capital requirements and risk exposure.

The Basel Committee's work on bank capital requirements is never-ending. As the banking industry changes, the regulation of bank capital must change with it to ensure the safety and soundness of the banking institutions.

OECD
www.oecd.org

A New Trend in Bank Supervision: Assessment of Risk Management

Traditionally, on-site bank examinations have focused primarily on assessment of the quality of the bank's balance sheet at a point in time and whether it complies with capital requirements and restrictions on asset holdings. Although the traditional focus is important for reducing excessive risk taking by banks, it is no longer felt to be adequate in today's world, in which financial innovation has produced new markets and instruments that make it easy for banks and their employees to make huge bets easily and quickly. In this new financial environment, a bank that is quite healthy at a particular point in time can be driven into insolvency extremely rapidly from trading losses, as forcefully demonstrated by the failure of Barings in 1995 (discussed in Chapter 9). Thus an examination that focuses only on a bank's position at a point in time may not be effective in indicating whether a bank will in fact be taking on excessive risk in the near future.

This change in the financial environment for banking institutions has resulted in a major shift in thinking about the bank supervisory process throughout the world. Bank examiners are now placing far greater emphasis on evaluating the soundness of a bank's management processes with regard to controlling risk. This shift in thinking is now reflected in a new focus on risk management in the guidelines to examiners on trading and derivatives activities. Now bank examiners focus on four elements of sound risk management: (1) the quality of oversight provided by the board of directors and senior management, (2) the adequacy of policies and limits for all activities that present significant risks, (3) the quality of the risk measurement and monitoring systems, and (4) the adequacy of internal controls to prevent fraud or unauthorized activities on the part of employees.

This shift toward focusing on management processes is also reflected in recent guidelines adopted by the Canadian bank regulatory authorities to deal with interest-rate risk. At one point, Canadian regulators were contemplating requiring banks to use a standard model to calculate the amount of capital a bank would need to have to allow for the interest-rate risk it bears. Because coming up with a one-size-fits-all model that would work for all banks has proved difficult, the regulatory agencies have instead decided to adopt guidelines for the management of interest-rate risk, although bank examiners will continue to consider interest-rate risk in deciding on the bank's capital requirements. These guidelines require the bank's board of directors to establish interest-rate risk limits, appoint officials of the bank to manage this risk, and monitor the bank's risk exposure. The guidelines also require that senior management of a bank develop formal risk management policies and procedures to ensure that the board of director's risk limits are not violated and to implement internal controls to monitor interest-rate risk and compliance with the board's directives.

Disclosure Requirements

The free-rider problem described in Chapter 8 indicates that individual depositors and other bank creditors will not have enough incentive to produce private information about the quality of a bank's assets. To ensure that there is better information for depositors and the marketplace, regulators can require that banks adhere to certain standard accounting principles and disclose a wide range of information that helps the market assess the quality of a bank's portfolio and the amount of the bank's exposure to risk. More public information about the risks incurred by banks and the quality of their portfolio can better enable stockholders, creditors, and depositors to evaluate and monitor banks and so act as a deterrent to excessive risk taking. This view is consistent with a recent position paper issued by the Eurocurrency Standing Committee of the G-10 Central Banks, which recommends that estimates of financial risk generated by firms' own internal risk management systems be adapted for public disclosure purposes.[1] Such information would supplement disclosures based on traditional accounting conventions by providing information about risk exposure and risk management that is not normally included in conventional balance sheet and income statement reports.

Consumer Protection

The existence of asymmetric information also suggests that consumers may not have enough information to protect themselves fully. Consumer protection regulation has taken several forms. First is "truth in lending," which requires all lenders, not just banks, to provide information to consumers about the cost of borrowing

---

[1]See Eurocurrency Standing Committee of Central Banks of Group of Ten Countries (Fisher Group), "Discussion Paper on Public Disclosure of Markets and Credit Risks by Financial Intermediaries," September 1994, and a companion piece to this report, Federal Reserve Bank of New York, "A Discussion Paper on Public Disclosure of Risks Related to Market Activity," September 1994.

including a standardized interest rate (called the annual percentage rate, or APR) and the total finance charges on the loan. Legislation also requires creditors, especially credit card issuers, to provide information on the method of assessing finance charges and requires that billing complaints be handled quickly.

Restrictions on Competition

Increased competition can also increase moral hazard incentives for banks to take on more risk. Declining profitability as a result of increased competition could tip the incentives of bankers toward assuming greater risk in an effort to maintain former profit levels. Thus governments in many countries have instituted regulations to protect banks from competition. These regulations have taken different forms in the past, one being preventing nonbank institutions from competing with banks by engaging in banking business.

Before 1987, Canada's chartered banks were not allowed to engage in investment banking activities. Because investment banking is inherently risky, it was thought that allowing banks to pursue these activities might have increased their moral hazard opportunities for risk taking. Legislation also prohibited investment banks from engaging in commercial banking activities and thus protected banks from competition. Additional regulations prohibited banks from selling insurance and engaging in other nonbank activities that were considered risky.

The past ten years, however, have seen the erosion of these restrictions as a result of the pursuit of profits, financial innovation, as well as concerns that these restrictions put Canadian banks at a competitive disadvantage relative to foreign banks that were not subject to similar restrictions. The Financial Institutions and Deposit Insurance System Amendment Act of 1987 allowed chartered banks to own investment banking subsidiaries, thereby rendering the separation of banking, insurance, and securities industries in Canada a thing of the past.

Although restricting competition propped up the health of banks, restrictions on competition also had serious disadvantages: they led to higher charges to consumers and decreased the efficiency of banking institutions, which did not have to compete as hard. Thus, although the existence of asymmetric information provided a rationale for anticompetitive regulations, it did not mean that they would be beneficial. Indeed, in recent years, the impulse of governments in industrialized countries to restrict competition has been waning.

Study Guide

Because so many laws regulating banking have been passed in Canada, it is hard to keep track of them all. As a study aid, Table 11-1 lists the major banking legislation in the twentieth century and its key provisions.

INTERNATIONAL BANKING REGULATION

Because asymmetric information problems in the banking industry are a fact of life throughout the world, bank regulation in other countries is similar to that in Canada. Banks are chartered and supervised by government regulators, just as they are in Canada. Deposit insurance is also a feature of the regulatory systems in most other developed countries, although its coverage is often different than in Canada. We have also seen that bank capital requirements are in the process of being standardized across countries with agreements like the Basel Accord.

The BCCI Scandal

The Bank of Credit and Commerce International (BCCI) was chartered in Luxembourg in 1972 by a Pakistani businessman, Agha Hasan Abedi. The bank grew rapidly to $20 billion in assets and by 1991 was operating in more than 70 countries. Unfortunately, the bank was siphoning off funds to secret accounts in the Cayman Islands, where much of this money was stolen. Indeed, estimates suggest that nearly half of the bank's assets may have "disappeared." Fraud was not the only shady activity BCCI engaged in. BCCI supposedly helped dictators such as Saddam Hussein of Iraq, Manuel Noriega of Panama, and Ferdinand Marcos of the Philippines steal huge sums from their countries, helped the CIA channel funds to the *contra* rebels in Nicaragua, and acted as a banker for the notorious Abu Nidal terrorist group. Not surprisingly, BCCI has been dubbed the "Bank of Crooks and Criminals, Inc."

How did BCCI get away with these fraudulent activities for so long? The answer illustrates the difficulties of regulating banks with operations in many countries. Although BCCI's headquarters were in London, regulatory oversight fell to the chartering country, Luxembourg, whose tiny bank regulator, the Institut Monétaire Luxembourgeois (IML), was not up to the task. As a result, BCCI effectively operated free of government regulatory oversight for 15 years. In 1987, the IML reached an agreement with seven other countries' regulators to oversee BCCI jointly, but even this larger group was unable to keep track of the bank's activities. Only in spring 1990 did these regulators uncover some evidence of fraud, and not until July 1991 did the Price Waterhouse accounting firm document the pervasiveness of the fraud to the Bank of England, which then closed BCCI down.

The losses to depositors and stockholders from the BCCI collapse were immense, and national regulators, particularly the Bank of England, have been severely criticized for their slowness in uncovering the scandal. A year after the BCCI collapse, in July 1992, the Basel Committee announced an agreement to further standardize the regulation of international banks. Now a bank's worldwide operations will be under the scrutiny of a single home-country regulator with enhanced powers to acquire information on the bank's activities. Furthermore, regulators in other countries will have the right to restrict operations of a foreign bank if they feel that it lacks effective oversight. Despite this improvement in the regulation of international banks, fears remain that another BCCI-like scandal could happen again.

Problems in Regulating International Banking

Particular problems in bank regulation occur when banks are engaged in international banking and thus can readily shift their business from one country to another. Bank regulators closely examine the domestic operations of banks in their country, but they often do not have the knowledge or ability to keep a close watch on bank operations in other countries, either by domestic banks' foreign affiliates or by foreign banks with domestic branches. In addition, when a bank operates in many countries, it is not always clear which national regulatory authority should have primary responsibility for keeping the bank from engaging in overly risky activities. The difficulties inherent in regulating international banking are highlighted by the BCCI scandal discussed in Box 11-2. Cooperation among regulators in different countries and standardization of regulatory requirements provide potential solutions to the problems of regulating international banking. The world has been moving in this direction through agreements like the Basel Accord on

TABLE 11-1 Major Banking Legislation in Canada in the Twentieth Century

Bank of Canada Act (1934)

Created the Bank of Canada following the recommendations of the Macmillan Commission

Bank Act of 1936

Prohibited banks from issuing banknotes
Imposed reserve requirements on depository institutions to be held with the Bank of Canada

Bank Act of 1954

Increased reserve requirements on depository institutions
Allowed chartered banks to offer mortgages issued under the National Housing Act

Canada Deposit Insurance Corporation Act (1967)

Created the CDIC to insure deposits with all federally chartered banks and near banks

Bank Act of 1967

Removed the 6% loan interest rate ceiling
Restricted foreign competition
Imposed secondary reserve requirements on depository institutions
Put chartered banks and near banks on equal footing regarding mortgage lending

Bank Act of 1981

Created the Canadian Payments Association to operate the national payments system and plan its development
Lowered reserve requirements on Canadian dollar deposits
Increased competition by introducing a less complicated procedure for obtaining a licence to operate as a bank
Allowed foreign banks to establish subsidiaries in Canada, subject to reciprocal treatment of Canadian banks
Extended banks' business powers to include financial leasing, factoring, and data processing
Redesigned corporate clauses to ensure consistency between the Bank Act and the Canada Business Corporations Act
Provided a simpler incorporation method for new banks (letters patent) while retaining incorporation through a special Act of Parliament

Office of the Superintendent of Financial Institutions Act (1987)

Created the OSFI to succeed two separate federal regulatory bodies (the Department of Insurance and the Inspector General of Banks) in the supervision of financial institutions

capital requirements in 1988 and the new regulatory oversight procedures announced by the Basel Committee in July 1992 (see Box 11-1). However, whether agreements of this type will solve the problem of regulating international banking in the future is an open question.

TABLE 11-1   Major Banking Legislation in Canada in the Twentieth Century (*continued*)

Financial Institutions and Deposit Insurance System Amendment Act (1987)

Allowed chartered banks to own investment banking subsidiaries, thereby initiating the merging of the four pillars

Savings and Credit Union Act of the Province of Québec (1988)

Set rules for credit unions, federations, and confederations, with specific reference to the *Mouvement Desjardins*

Bank Act of 1992

Comprehensive banking law
Allowed chartered banks to own trust companies
Allowed trust companies to make commercial loans
Made provisions for the phasing out of reserve requirements
Set rules regarding the supervisory role of the Bank of Canada and the OSFI with respect to chartered banks
Reset the "sunset" clause from 10 years to 5 years to address the changing Canadian financial services marketplace

Cooperative Credit Associations Act (1992)

Replaced the Cooperative Credit Association Act of 1952–1953 and set rules for federally chartered credit unions
Followed the same format as the Bank Act

Insurance Companies Act (1992)

Replaced the Canadian and British Insurance Companies Act and the Foreign Insurance Companies Act, both passed in 1932
Set rules for life insurance companies and property and casualty (P&C) insurance companies
Allowed insurance companies to own Schedule II chartered banks
Followed the same format as the Bank Act

Trust and Loan Companies Act (1992)

Replaced the Trust Companies Act and the Loan Companies Act, both passed in 1914
Set rules for federally incorporated TMLs and provincially incorporated TMLs reporting to the OSFI
Required large, formerly closely held TMLs to become 35% widely held
Followed the same format as the Bank Act

Bank Act of 1997

Yielded minor changes because the government was waiting for the recommendations of the Mackay Task Force

Summary

Asymmetric information analysis explains what types of banking regulations are needed to reduce moral hazard and adverse selection problems in the banking system. However, understanding the theory behind regulation does not mean that regulation and supervision of the banking system are easy in practice. Getting bank regulators and supervisors to do their job properly is difficult for several reasons. First, as we learned in the discussion of financial innovation in Chapter 9, in their search for profits, financial institutions have strong incentives to avoid existing regulations by loophole mining. Thus regulation applies to a moving target: regulators are continually playing cat and mouse with financial institutions—financial institutions think up clever ways to avoid regulations, which then causes regulators to modify their regulation activities. Regulators continually face new challenges in a dynamically changing financial system, and unless they can respond rapidly to change, they may not be able to keep financial institutions from taking on excessive risk. This problem can be exacerbated if regulators and supervisors do not have the resources or expertise to keep up with clever people in financial institutions who think up ways to hide what they are doing or to get around the existing regulations.

Bank regulation and supervision are difficult for two other reasons. In the regulation and supervision game, the devil is in the details. Subtle differences in the details may have unintended consequences; unless regulators get the regulation and supervision just right, they may be unable to prevent excessive risk taking. In addition, regulators and supervisors may be subject to political pressure not to do their jobs properly. For all these reasons, there is no guarantee that bank regulators and supervisors will be successful in promoting a healthy financial system. Indeed, as we will see, bank regulation and supervision have not always worked well, leading to banking crises in Canada and throughout the world.

THE 1980s CANADIAN BANKING CRISIS: WHY?

The period from 1923 (when the Home Bank failed) to 1985 was one in which the failure of Canadian chartered banks was thought to be impossible. During the same period, failures of deposit-taking financial institutions in the United States were averaging about 20 a year. In the mid-1980s, however, the situation in Canada changed dramatically with the failure of two chartered banks and the financial difficulties of a large number of other financial institutions. Why did this happen? How did a stable banking system that seemed to be working well find itself in trouble?

Early Stages of the Crisis

The story starts with the oil boom in western Canada in the 1970s. It led to the creation of several western banks, including two Alberta-based Schedule I banks, the Canadian Commercial Bank and the Northland Bank, both formed in 1975. Unfortunately, the managers of these banks did not have the expertise that would have enabled them to manage risk appropriately; they excessively concentrated in a few borrowers in western Canada and placed a large percentage of their total loans in real estate.

The existence of deposit insurance increased moral hazard for the Canadian Commercial and Northland banks, because insured depositors had little incentive to keep the banks from taking on too much risk. Regardless of how much risk the banks were taking, deposit insurance guaranteed that depositors would not suffer any losses.

Canadian Commercial and Northland pursued rapid growth and took on risky projects, attracting the necessary funds by issuing large denomination certificates of deposit with high interest rates. Without deposit insurance, high interest rates would not have induced depositors to provide the high-rolling banks with funds because of the realistic expectation that they might not get the funds back. But with deposit insurance, the government was guaranteeing that the deposits were safe, so depositors were more than happy to make deposits in the Canadian Commercial and Northland banks with the higher interest rates.

As already noted, the managers of Canadian Commercial and Northland did not have the required expertise to manage risk in the permissive atmosphere of western Canada. Even if the required expertise was available initially, rapid credit growth may outstrip the available information resources of the banking institution, resulting in excessive risk taking. Also, the lending boom meant that the activities of Canadian Commercial and Northland were expanding in scope and were becoming more complicated, requiring an expansion of regulatory resources to monitor these activities appropriately. Unfortunately, regulators of chartered banks at the Inspector General of Banks (the predecessor of the Office of the Superintendent of Financial Institutions) had neither the expertise nor the resources that would have enabled them to sufficiently monitor the activities of Canadian Commercial and Northland. Given the lack of expertise in both the banks and the Inspector General of Banks, the weakening of the regulatory apparatus, and the moral hazard incentives provided by deposit insurance, it is no surprise that Canadian Commercial and Northland took on excessive risks, which led to huge losses on bad loans.

In addition, the incentives of moral hazard were increased dramatically by a historical accident: the combination of sharp increases in interest rates from late 1979 until 1981 and a severe recession in 1981–1982, both of which were engineered by the Federal Reserve in the United States to bring down inflation. The sharp rise in interest rates produced rapidly rising costs of funds for the banks that were not matched by higher earnings on their principal asset, long-term residential mortgages (whose rates had been fixed at a time when interest rates were far lower). The 1981–1982 recession and a collapse in the prices of energy and farm products hit the economy of Alberta very hard. As a result, there were defaults on many loans. Losses for Canadian Commercial and Northland mounted and the banks had a negative net worth and were thus insolvent by the beginning of 1985.

Later Stages of the Crisis: Regulatory Forbearance

At this point, a logical step might have been for the regulators—the Bank of Canada and the Inspector General of Banks—to close the insolvent banks. Instead, the regulators adopted a stance of **regulatory forbearance**: they refrained from exercising their regulatory right to put the insolvent Canadian Commercial Bank and Northland Bank out of business.

There were two main reasons why the Bank of Canada and the Inspector General of Banks opted for regulatory forbearance. First, the CDIC did not have sufficient funds in its insurance fund to close the insolvent banks and pay off their deposits. Second, because bureaucrats do not like to admit that their own agency is in trouble, the regulators preferred to sweep their problems under the rug in the hope that they would go away.

When Canadian Commercial and Northland were declared insolvent in September of 1985, rumours of financial trouble caused many large depositors to withdraw large deposits from the Bank of British Columbia, Mercantile Bank, and Continental Bank. By the time Mercantile was acquired by the National Bank of Canada, Bank of British Columbia by the Hong Kong Bank of Canada, and Continental by Lloyds Bank of Canada (a subsidiary of a U.K.-based banking powerhouse), the Bank of Canada lent over $5 billion.

The loss of public confidence in the Canadian banking system led to the financial reforms of 1987–1992 (see Table 11-1) and the consolidating of financial institution supervision under the Office of the Superintendent of Financial Institutions.

POLITICAL ECONOMY OF THE BANKING CRISIS

Although we now have a grasp of the regulatory and economic forces that created the 1980s Canadian banking crisis, we still need to understand the political forces that produced the regulatory structure and activities that led to it. The key to understanding the political economy of the crisis is to recognize that the relationship between voter-taxpayers and the regulators and politicians creates a particular type of moral hazard problem, discussed in Chapter 8: the *principal–agent problem,* which occurs when representatives (agents) such as managers have incentives that differ from those of their employer (the principal) and so act in their own interest rather than in the interest of the employer.

Principal–Agent Problem for Regulators and Politicians

Regulators and politicians are ultimately agents for voter-taxpayers (principals) because in the final analysis, taxpayers bear the cost of any losses by the deposit insurance agency. The principal–agent problem occurs because the agent (a politician or regulator) does not have the same incentives to minimize costs to the economy as the principal (the taxpayer).

To act in the taxpayers' interest and lower costs to the deposit insurance agency, regulators have several tasks, as we have seen. They must set tight restrictions on holding assets that are too risky, must impose high capital requirements, and must not adopt a stance of regulatory forbearance, which allows insolvent institutions to continue to operate. However, because of the principal–agent problem, regulators have incentives to do the opposite. Indeed, as our sad saga of the Canadian Commercial and Northland debacle indicates, they have at times loosened capital requirements and restrictions on risky asset holdings and pursued regulatory forbearance. One important incentive for regulators that explains this phenomenon is their desire to escape blame for poor performance by their agency. By loosening capital requirements and pursuing regulatory forbearance, regulators can hide the problem of an insolvent bank and hope that the situation will improve. Edward Kane characterizes such behaviour on the part of regulators as "bureaucratic gambling."

CDIC DEVELOPMENTS

The Canada Deposit Insurance Corporation (CDIC) insures each depositor at member institutions up to a loss of $60 000 per account. All federally incorporated financial institutions and all provincially incorporated trust and mortgage loan companies are members of the CDIC. Insurance companies, credit unions, *caisses populaires*, and investment dealers are not eligible for CDIC membership; the Québec Deposit Insurance Board (QDIB) insures provincially incorporated financial institutions in Québec and the other provinces have deposit insurance corporations that insure the deposits of credit unions in their jurisdiction, on terms similar to the CDIC's.

The CDIC is allowed to insure only deposits in Canadian currency and payable in Canada; foreign currency deposits, such as accounts in U.S. dollars, are not insured. Moreover, not all deposits and investments offered by CDIC member institutions are insurable. Insurable deposits include savings and chequing accounts, term deposits with a maturity date of less than five years, money orders and drafts, certified drafts and cheques, and traveller's cheques. The CDIC does not insure term deposits with an initial maturity date of more than five years, Treasury bills, bonds and debentures issued by governments and corporations (including the chartered banks), and investments in stocks, mutual funds, and mortgages.

The primary rationale for deposit insurance is protecting depositors from bank insolvency and thus ensuring financial stability. Deposit insurance could also promote competition among financial institutions by removing barriers to entry for new deposit-taking institutions. In the absence of deposit insurance it is difficult for new banks to attract deposits. Most depositors, for example, are not capable of making appropriate risk calculations to assess the risk of a new bank. Those depositors would tend to place their deposits in banks that are considered as too big to fail, thereby producing significant barriers to entry and unfair disadvantages for small new entrants. By insuring deposits at all deposit-taking financial institutions, the CDIC effectively removes barriers to entry for new deposit takers.

Differential Premiums

Until recently, CDIC premium revenue was not tied to the risk profile of the financial institutions; the premium rate was the same for all deposit-taking institutions, irrespective of their risk profile. For example, in the 1998/1999 fiscal year, the flat-rate insurance premium was 1/6 of 1%, or 0.1667%, meaning that each deposit-taking financial institution paid an insurance premium of close to 17 cents per $100. This was one of the reasons that the Big Six, represented by the Canadian Bankers Association, vigorously opposed the establishment of the CDIC in 1967; it was argued that deposit insurance would be a subsidy to small banks paid by the big banks.

Over the years, the Canadian Bankers Association strongly promoted the reform of the Canadian deposit insurance system. As a result, the CDIC developed the Differential Premiums By-law, which came into force on March 31, 1999. The important feature of this legislation is its implicit, prompt corrective action provisions, which require the CDIC to intervene earlier and more vigorously when a bank gets into trouble. CDIC member institutions are now classified into four premium groups based on their risk profile. An institution's risk profile is determined using a variety of quantitative and qualitative criteria, including capital adequacy, profitability, asset concentration, income volatility, regulatory ratings, and adherence to CDIC's Standards of Sound Business and Financial Practices, with capital adequacy dominating the criteria, accounting for 25% of the score.

Under the new system the premium rates for CDIC member institutions are those shown in Table 11-2; they vary from 4 cents to 33 cents per $100. Group 1, classified as "best," is well-capitalized banks that significantly exceed minimum requirements. On the other hand, banks in group 4, classified as "worst," are significantly (and perhaps critically) undercapitalized and the insurance premium that they pay is 33 basis points, the maximum allowed under the CDIC Act. In addition, for group 4 banks, the CDIC is required to take prompt corrective actions such as requiring them to submit a capital restoration plan, restrict their asset growth, and seek regulatory approval to open new branches or develop new lines of business. Today, over 90% of CDIC member institutions are classified in categories 1 and 2, but as in other countries, the premium category and related supervisory information applicable to individual CDIC members are confidential.

Canadian Bankers
Association
www.cba.ca

TABLE 11-2   Premium Structure and Rates for CDIC Member Institutions

Premium category	Premium rate (as a % of insured deposits)
1	1/24 of 1%, or 0.0417%
2	1/12 of 1%, or 0.0833%
3	1/6 of 1%, or 0.1667%
4	1/3 of 1%, or 0.3333%

Source: CDIC website: http://www.cdic.ca. Reprinted with permission of the Canadian Deposit Insurance Corporation.

Opting-Out

Another interesting recent development is the Opting-Out By-law that came into effect on October 15, 1999. This legislation permits Schedule III banks that accept primarily wholesale deposits (defined as $150 000 or more) to opt out of CDIC membership and therefore to operate without deposit insurance. The new legislation, however, includes provisions to protect depositors who hold deposits eligible for CDIC protection. In particular, it requires an opted-out bank to inform all depositors, by posting notices in its branches, that their deposits will not be protected by the CDIC, and not to charge any early withdrawal penalties for depositors who choose to withdraw.

Probably the most important feature of the opting-out legislation is its minimization of CDIC exposure to uninsured deposits. This represents a significant departure from past practices, when the CDIC showed generosity to uninsured depositors. For example, in the Canadian Commercial and Northland failures of the mid-1980s, the CDIC paid 100 cents on the dollar to all depositors, both insured and uninsured. By compensating only the insured depositors rather than all depositors, the opting-out legislation increases the incentives of uninsured depositors to monitor the risk-taking activities of banks, thereby reducing moral hazard risk.

APPLICATION | *Evaluating CDIC and Other Proposed Reforms of the Banking Regulatory System*

The new system of risk-based premiums and opting-out rules is a major step in reformulating the banking regulatory system. How well will it work to solve the adverse selection and moral hazard problems of the bank regulatory system? Let's use the analysis in the chapter to evaluate the new legislation to answer this question.

Study Guide

Before looking at the evaluation for each set of provisions and proposals in this application, try to reason out how well they will solve the current problems with banking regulation. This exercise will help you develop a deeper understanding of the material in this chapter.

Limits on the Scope of Deposit Insurance

CDIC's reductions of the scope of deposit insurance by limiting insurance to insured deposits might have increased the incentives for uninsured depositors to monitor banks and to withdraw funds if the bank is taking on too much risk. Because banks might now fear the loss of deposits when they engage in risky activities, they might have less incentive to take on too much risk.

Although the cited new elements of deposit insurance strengthen the incentive of depositors to monitor banks, some critics would take these limitations on the scope of deposit insurance even further. Some suggest that deposit insurance should be eliminated entirely or should be reduced in amount from the current $60 000 limit to, say, $20 000 or $10 000. Another proposed reform would institute a system of **coinsurance** in which only a percentage of a deposit, say 90%, would be covered by insurance. In this system, the insured depositor would suffer a percentage of the losses along with the deposit insurance agency. Because depositors facing a lower limit on deposit insurance or coinsurance would suffer losses if the bank goes broke, they would have an incentive to monitor the bank's activities.

However, other experts do not believe that depositors are capable of monitoring banks and imposing discipline on them. The basic problem with reducing the scope of deposit insurance even further as proposed is that banks would be subject to runs, sudden withdrawals by nervous investors. Such runs could by themselves lead to bank failures. In addition to protecting individual depositors, the purpose of deposit insurance is to prevent a large number of bank failures, which would lead to an unstable banking system and an unstable economy. From this perspective, deposit insurance has been a resounding success. Bank panics, in which there are simultaneous failures of many banks and consequent disruption of the financial system, have not occurred since deposit insurance was established.

Eliminating the too-big-to-fail policy altogether would also cause some of the same problems that would occur if deposit insurance were eliminated or reduced: the probability of bank panics would increase. If a bank were allowed to fail, the repercussions in the financial system might be immense. Other banks with a correspondent relationship with the failed bank (those that have deposits at the bank in exchange for services) would suffer large losses and might fail in turn, leading to full-scale panic. In addition, the problem of liquidating the big bank's loan portfolio might create a major disruption in the financial system.

Prompt Corrective Action

The prompt corrective action provisions of CDIC should also substantially reduce incentives for bank risk taking and reduce taxpayer losses. CDIC uses a carrot-and-stick approach to get banks to hold more capital. If they are well capitalized, they receive better ratings and are placed in a better premium rate category; if their capital ratio falls, they are subject to more and more onerous regulation. Increased bank capital reduces moral hazard for the bank because the bank now has more to lose if it fails and so is less likely to take on too much risk. In addition, encouraging banks to hold more capital reduces potential losses for the CDIC because increased bank capital is a cushion that makes bank failure less likely.

Prompt corrective action, which requires regulators to intervene early when bank capital begins to fall, is a serious attempt to reduce the principal–agent problem for politicians and regulators. With prompt corrective action provisions, regulators no longer have the option of regulatory forbearance, which, as we have seen, can greatly increase moral hazard incentives for banks.

Risk-Based Insurance Premiums

Under the Differential Premiums By-law, banks deemed to be taking on greater risk, in the form of lower capital or riskier assets, are subjected to higher insurance premiums. Risk-based insurance premiums consequently reduce the moral hazard incentives for banks to take on higher risk. In addition, the fact that risk-based premiums drop as the bank's capital increases encourages the banks to hold more capital, which has the benefits already mentioned.

One problem with risk-based premiums is that the scheme for determining the amount of risk the bank is taking may not be very accurate. For example, it might be hard for regulators to determine when a bank's loans are risky. Some critics have also pointed out that the classification of banks by such measures as the Basel risk-based capital standard solely reflects credit risk and does not take sufficient account of interest-rate risk. The regulatory authorities, however, are encouraged to modify existing risk-based standards to include interest-rate risk.

Other CDIC Provisions

CDIC's requirements that regulators perform frequent bank examinations and member institutions file a Standards report at least once a year are necessary for monitoring banks' compliance with bank capital requirements and asset restrictions. As the Canadian Commercial and Northland debacles illustrate, frequent supervisory examinations of banks are necessary to keep them from taking on too much risk or committing fraud. Similarly, beefing up the ability of the regulators to monitor foreign banks might help dissuade international banks from engaging in these undesirable activities.

The stricter and more burdensome reporting requirements for banks have the advantage of providing more information to regulators to help them monitor bank activities. However, these reporting requirements have been criticized by banks, which claim that the requirements make it harder to lend to small businesses. As a result, the CDIC recently developed the Modernized Standards By-law, adopted in early 2001, that enables the CDIC to determine the frequency of a member institution's reporting based on its categorization under the Differential Premiums By-law.

The new legislation allows CDIC discretion in examining the performance of problem member institutions. Under the new regime, well capitalized, category 1 banks will be required to file a Standards report every five years. However, banks in categories 3 and 4 may be subjected to special examination at any time, the cost of which will be chargeable to the institution. The Modernized Standards By-law, in addition to increasing the regulatory supervision of problem banks, also increases the accountability of the CDIC. Moreover, it decreases the incentives of banks to take on excessive risk and increases their incentives to hold capital.

Other Proposed Changes in Banking Regulations

Regulatory Consolidation The current bank regulatory system in Canada has banking institutions supervised by three federal agencies: the Bank of Canada, the Office of the Superintendent of Financial Institutions, and the CDIC. Critics of this system of multiple regulatory agencies with overlapping jurisdictions believe it creates a system that is too complex and too costly because it is rife with duplication. For example, although the CDIC has no direct supervisory role, its Standards of Sound Business and Financial Practices overlap with those of the OSFI.

The MacKay Task Force, named after its chairman Harold MacKay and set up by the government in 1996 to review the financial services sector and propose a framework for its future, considered whether the CDIC and the OSFI should be amalgamated. Although the task force recommended that the regulator (OSFI) and the insurer (CDIC) should not be combined in a single institution, it proposed that the CDIC's mandate be amended to remove the overlap with the OSFI's mandate.

Market-Value Accounting for Capital Requirements We have seen that the requirement that a bank have substantial equity capital makes the bank less likely to fail. The requirement is also advantageous because a bank with high equity capital has more to lose if it takes on risky investments and so will have less incentive to hold risky assets. Unfortunately, capital requirements, including new risk-based measures, are calculated on a historical-cost (book value) basis in which the value of an asset is set at its initial purchase price. The problem with historical-cost accounting is that changes in the value of assets and liabilities because of changes in interest rates or default risk are not reflected in the calculation of the firm's equity capital. Yet changes in the market value of assets and liabilities and hence changes in the market value of equity capital are what indicate if a firm is truly insolvent. Furthermore, it is the market value of capital that determines the incentives for a bank to hold risky assets.

Market-value accounting when calculating capital requirements is another reform that receives substantial support. All assets and liabilities could be updated to market value periodically, say every three months, to determine if a bank's capital is sufficient to meet the minimum requirements. This market-value accounting information would let the deposit insurance agency know quickly when a bank was falling below its capital requirement. The bank could then be closed down before its net worth fell below zero, thus preventing a loss to the deposit insurance agency. The market-value-based capital requirement would also ensure that banks would not be operating with negative capital, thereby preventing the bet-the-bank strategy of taking on excessive risk.

Objections to market-value-based capital requirements centre on the difficulty of making accurate and straightforward market-value estimates of capital. Historical-cost accounting has an important advantage in that accounting rules are easier to define and standardize when the value of an asset is simply set at its purchase price. Market-value accounting, by contrast, requires estimates and approximations that are harder to standardize. For example, it might be hard to assess the market value of your friend Joe's car loan, whereas it would be quite easy to value a government bond. In addition, conducting market-value accounting would prove costly to banks because estimation of market values requires the collection of more information about the characteristics of assets and liabilities. Nevertheless, proponents of market-value accounting for capital requirements point out that although market-value accounting involves some estimates and approximations, it would still provide regulators with a more accurate assessment of bank equity capital than historical-cost accounting does.

Overall Evaluation

The recent CDIC developments appear to be an important step in the right direction because they increase the incentives for banks to hold capital and decrease their incentives to take on excessive risk. However, more could be done to improve the incentives for banks to limit their risk taking. Yet eliminating deposit insurance and the too-big-to-fail policy altogether may be going too far because these proposals might make the banking system too prone to a banking panic.

BANKING CRISES THROUGHOUT THE WORLD

Because misery loves company, it may make you feel better to know that Canada has by no means been alone in suffering a banking crisis. Indeed, as Table 11-3 and Figure 11-1 illustrate, banking crises have struck a large number of countries throughout the world, and many of them have been substantially worse than ours. We will examine what took place in several of these other countries and see that the same forces that produced a banking crisis in Canada have been at work elsewhere too.

United States

Federal Deposit Insurance Corporation
www.fdic.gov

Before the establishment of the Federal Deposit Insurance Corporation (FDIC) in 1934, bank failures were a fact of American life, with major ones occurring every 20 years or so in 1819, 1837, 1857, 1873, 1884, 1893, 1907, and 1930–1933. Bank failures were a serious problem even during the boom years of the 1920s, when the number of bank failures averaged around 600 per year. In contrast to the pre-1934 period, the period from 1934 to 1980 was one in which bank failures were a rarity, averaging 15 a year for commercial banks and fewer than 5 a year for savings and loans. After 1981, however, this rosy picture changed dramatically. Failures in both commercial banks and savings and loans (S&Ls) climbed to levels more than ten times greater than in earlier years. Why did this happen? How did a deposit insurance system that seemed to be working well for half a century find itself in so much trouble?

FIGURE 11-1 Banking Crises Throughout the World Since 1970

Source: Gerard Caprio and Daniela Klingbiel, "Episodes of Systemic and Borderline Financial Crises" mimeo., World Bank, October 1999.

The story starts with the burst of financial innovation in the 1960s, 1970s, and early 1980s: NOW accounts, money market mutual funds, junk bonds, securitization and the rise of the commercial paper market. Financial innovation decreased the profitability of certain traditional business for commercial banks. Banks now faced increased competition for their sources of funds from new financial institutions such as money market mutual funds while they were losing commercial lending business to the commercial paper market and securitization. With the decreasing profitability of their traditional business, by the mid-1980s commercial banks were forced to seek out new and potentially risky business to keep their profits up, by placing a greater percentage of their total loans in real estate and in credit extended to assist corporate takeovers and leveraged buyouts (called *highly leveraged transaction loans*).

Adding fuel to the fire, financial innovation produced new financial instruments that widened the scope for risk taking. New markets in financial futures, swaps, and other instruments made it easier for banks to take on extra risk—making the moral hazard problem more severe. New legislation that deregulated the banking industry in the early 1980s, the Depository Institutions Deregulation and Monetary Control Act (DIDMCA) of 1980 and the Depository Institutions (Garn–St. Germain) Act of 1982, gave expanded powers to the S&Ls and mutual savings banks to engage in new risky activities. In addition, DIDMCA increased the mandated amount of federal deposit insurance from $40 000 per account to $100 000, increasing moral hazard for banks because insured depositors had little incentive to keep the banks from taking on too much risk.

TABLE 11-3	The Cost of Rescuing Banks in Several Countries	
Date	**Country**	**Cost as a % of GDP**
1980–1982	Argentina	55
1997–ongoing	Indonesia	50–55
1981–1983	Chile	41
1997–ongoing	Thailand	33
1997–ongoing	South Korea	27
1997–ongoing	Malaysia	21
1994–ongoing	Venezuela	20+
1995	Mexico	20
1990s	Japan	12+
1989–ongoing	Czech Republic	12+
1991–1994	Finland	11
1991–1995	Hungary	10
1994–1995	Brazil	5–10
1987–1993	Norway	8
1998	Russia	5–7
1991–1994	Sweden	4
1984–1991	United States	3

Source: Gerard Caprio and Daniela Klingbiel, "Episodes of Systemic and Borderline Financial Crises" mimeo., World Bank, October 1999.

Another financial innovation that made it even easier for high-rolling banks to raise funds is known as **brokered deposits**, which enable depositors to circumvent the $100 000 limit on deposit insurance. Brokered deposits work as follows: a large depositor with $10 million goes to a broker, who breaks the $10 million into 100 packages of $100 000 each and then buys $100 000 CDs at 100 different banks. Because the amount of each CD is within the $100 000 limit for deposits at each bank, the large depositor has in effect obtained deposit insurance on all $10 million.

Financial innovation and deregulation in the permissive atmosphere of the Reagan years led to expanded powers for the S&Ls industry that led to several problems. First, many S&Ls managers did not have the required expertise to manage risk appropriately in these new lines of business. Second, the new expanded powers meant that there was a rapid growth in new lending, particularly to the real estate sector. Third, regulators of the S&Ls at the Federal Savings and Loan Insurance Corporation (FSLIC) had neither the expertise nor the resources that would have enabled them to monitor these new activities sufficiently. It is no surprise then that the S&Ls took on excessive risks. As a result, when the 1981–1982 recession hit hard the economies of certain parts of the country such as Texas, there were defaults on many S&Ls' loans. Losses mounted to $10 billion in 1981–1982, and by some estimates over half of the S&Ls in the United States had a negative net worth and were thus insolvent by the end of 1982.

At that point, a logical step might have been for the S&L regulators to close the insolvent S&Ls. Instead, the regulators opted for regulatory forbearance, mainly because the FSLIC did not have sufficient funds in its insurance fund to close the insolvent S&Ls and pay off their depositors. Regulatory forbearance, however, increases moral hazard dramatically because an operating but insolvent S&L (nicknamed a "zombie S&L" by economist Edward Kane because it is the "living dead") has almost nothing to lose by taking on great risk and "betting the bank": if it gets lucky and its risky investments pay off, it gets out of insolvency. Unfortunately, if, as is likely, the risky investments don't pay off, the zombie S&L's losses will mount, and the deposit insurance agency will be left holding the bag.

Given the sequence of events we have discussed here, it should be no surprise that savings and loans began to take huge risks: they built shopping centres in the desert, bought manufacturing plants to convert manure to methane, and purchased billions of dollars of high-risk, high yield junk bonds. Consistent with our analysis, the situation deteriorated rapidly. Losses in the savings and loan industry surpassed $10 billion in 1988 and approached $20 billion in 1989. The crisis was reaching epidemic proportions. The collapse of the real estate market in the late 1980s led to additional huge loan losses that greatly exacerbated the problem.

The S&Ls problem was dealt with by the Bush administration immediately after taking office in 1989. The new legislation, the Financial Institutions Reform, Recovery, and Enforcement Act (FIRREA), was the most significant legislation to affect the thrift industry since the 1930s. The cost of the bailout ended up on the order of $150 billion. FIRREA eliminated the Federal Home Loan Bank Board and gave its regulatory role to the Office of Thrift Supervision. It also eliminated the FSLIC and turned its insurance role over to the FDIC. Moreover, FIRREA imposed new restrictions on thrift activities that in essence reregulated the S&L industry to the asset choices it had before 1982. S&Ls can no longer purchase junk bonds and had to sell their holdings by 1994. Commercial real estate loans are restricted to four times capital rather than the previous limit of 40% of assets, and so this new restriction is a reduction for all institutions whose capital is less than 10% of assets. S&Ls must also hold at least 70%—up from 60%—of their assets in investments that are primarily housing-related. Troubled S&Ls are not allowed to accept brokered deposits. FIRREA also enhanced the enforcement powers of thrift regulators by making it easier for them to remove managers, issue cease and desist orders, and impose civil money penalties.

FIRREA did not focus on the underlying adverse selection and moral hazard problems created by deposit insurance. FIRREA did, however, mandate that the U.S. Treasury produce a comprehensive study and plan for reform of the federal deposit insurance system. After this study appeared in 1991, Congress passed the Federal Deposit Insurance Corporation Improvement Act (FDICIA), which engendered major reforms in the U.S. bank regulatory system.

Scandinavia

As in the United States, an important factor in the banking crises in Norway, Sweden, and Finland was the financial liberalization that occurred in the 1980s. Before the 1980s, banks in these Scandinavian countries were highly regulated and subject to restrictions on the interest rates they could pay to depositors and on the interest rates they could earn on loans. In this noncompetitive environment, and with artificially low rates on both deposits and loans, these banks lent only to the best credit risks, and both banks and their regulators had little need to develop expertise in screening and monitoring borrowers. With the deregulated environment, a lending boom ensued, particularly in the real estate sector. Given the lack of expertise in both the banking industry and its regulatory authorities in keeping risk taking in check, banks engaged in risky lending. When real estate prices collapsed in the late 1980s, massive loan losses resulted. The outcome of this process forced the government to bail out almost the entire banking industry in these countries in the late 1980s and early 1990s on a scale that was even larger relative to GDP than in the United States (see Table 11-3).

Latin America

The Latin American banking crises show a pattern similar to those in Canada, the United States, and in Scandinavia. Before the 1980s, banks in many Latin American countries were owned by the government and were subject to interest-rate restrictions as in Scandinavia. Their lending was restricted to the government and other low-risk borrowers. With the deregulation trend that was occurring world-wide, many of these countries liberalized their credit markets and privatized their banks. We then see the same pattern we saw in the United States and Scandinavia, a lending boom in the face of inadequate expertise on the part of both bankers and regulators. The result was again massive loan losses and the inevitable government bailout. What is particularly striking about the Latin American experience is the high cost of the bailout relative to GDP. For example, in the recent banking crises in Mexico and Venezuela, the cost to the taxpayer of the government bailouts were on the order of 20% of GDP.

Russia and Eastern Europe

Before the end of the Cold War, in the communist countries of Eastern Europe and the Soviet Union, banks were owned by the state. When the downfall of communism occurred, banks in these countries had little expertise in screening and monitoring loans. Furthermore, bank regulatory and supervisory apparatus that could rein in the banks and keep them from taking on excessive risk barely existed. Given the lack of expertise on the part of regulators and banks, not surprisingly, substantial loan losses ensued, resulting in the failure or government bailout of many banks. For example, in the second half of 1993, eight banks in Hungary with 25% of the financial system's assets were insolvent, and in Bulgaria, an estimated 75% of all loans in the banking system were estimated to be substandard in 1995.

On August 24, 1995, a bank panic requiring government intervention occurred in Russia when the interbank loan market seized up and stopped functioning because of concern about the solvency of many new banks. This was not the end of troubles in the Russian banking system. On August 17, 1998, the Russian government announced that Russia would impose a moratorium on the repayment of foreign debt because of insolvencies in the banking system. In November the Russian central bank announced that nearly half of the country's 1500 commercial banks were likely to go under and the cost of the bailout is expected to be on the order of $15 billion.

Japan

Japan was a latecomer to the banking crisis game. Before 1990, the vaunted Japanese economy looked unstoppable. Unfortunately, it has recently experienced many of the same pathologies that we have seen in other countries. Before the 1980s, Japan's financial markets were among the most heavily regulated in the world, with very strict restrictions on the issuing of securities and interest rates. Financial deregulation and innovation produced a more competitive environment that set off a lending boom, with banks lending aggressively in the real estate sector. As in the other countries we have examined here, financial disclosure and monitoring by regulators did not keep pace with the new financial environment. The result was that banks could and did take on excessive risks. When property values collapsed in the early 1990s, the banks were left holding massive amounts of bad loans. For example, Japanese banks decided to get into the mortgage lending market by setting up the so-called *jusen,* home mortgage lending companies that raised funds by borrowing from banks and then lending these funds out to households. Seven of these *jusen* became insolvent, leaving banks with $60 billion or so of bad loans.

As a result the Japanese have experienced their first bank failures since World War II. In July 1995, Tokyo-based Cosmo Credit Corporation, Japan's fifth-largest credit union, failed and on August 30, the Osaka authorities announced the imminent closing of Kizu Credit Cooperative, Japan's second-largest credit union. (Kizu's story is remarkably similar to that of many U.S. savings and loans. Kizu, like many American S&Ls, began offering high rates on large time deposits and grew at a blistering pace, with deposits rising from $2.2 billion in 1988 to $12 billion by 1995 and real estate loans growing by a similar amount. When the property market collapsed, so did Kizu.) On the same day, the Ministry of Finance announced that it was liquidating Hyogo Bank, a midsize Kobe bank that was the first commercial bank to fail. Larger banks now began to follow the same path. In late 1996, the Hanwa Bank, a large regional bank, was liquidated, followed in 1997 by a government-assisted restructuring of the Nippon Credit Bank, Japan's seventeenth-largest bank. In November 1997, Hokkaido Takushoku Bank was forced to go out of business, making it the first city bank (a large commercial bank) to be closed during the crisis.

The Japanese have been going through a cycle of forbearance similar to the one that occurred in the United States in the 1980s. The Japanese regulators in the Ministry of Finance enabled banks to meet capital standards and to keep operating by allowing them to artificially inflate the value of their assets. For example, they were allowed to value their large holdings of equities at historical value, rather than market value, which was much lower. Inadequate amounts were allocated for recapitalization of the banking system, and the extent of the problem was grossly underestimated by government officials. Furthermore, until the closing of the Hokkaido Takushoku Bank, the bank regulators in the Ministry of Finance were unwilling to close down city banks and impose any losses on stockholders or any uninsured creditors.

By the middle of 1998, the Japanese government began to take some steps to attack these problems. In June, supervisory authority over financial institutions was taken away from the Ministry of Finance and transferred to the Financial Supervisory Agency (FSA), which reports directly to the prime minister. This was the first instance in half a century in which the all-powerful Ministry of Finance was stripped of some of its authority. In October, the parliament passed a bailout package of $500 billion (60 trillion yen). However, disbursement of the funds depends on the voluntary cooperation of the banks. The law does not require insolvent banks to close or to accept funds if they are insolvent. Indeed, acceptance of the funds requires the bailed-out bank to open up its books and restructure its operations, say by reducing its workforce and shutting down unprofitable branches. Thus it is not at all clear whether this new rescue plan will work, although in March 1999, 15 of the large banks applied for 7 trillion yen of funds from this plan. Furthermore, immediately after the law was passed in October 1998, one of the ailing city banks, Long-Term Credit Bank of Japan, was taken over by the government and declared insolvent. It was later sold to a consortium of U.S. investors. Then in December 1998, the Nippon Credit Bank was finally put out of its misery and closed down by the government. These closings are further signs that the Japanese may be getting more serious about cleaning up their banking mess.

East Asia

We discussed the banking and financial crisis in the East Asian countries (Thailand, Malaysia, Indonesia, the Philippines, and South Korea) in Chapter 8. Due to inadequate supervision of the banking system, the lending booms that arose in the aftermath of financial liberalization led to substantial loan losses, which became huge after the currency collapses that occurred in the summer of 1997. An estimated 15% to 35% of all bank loans have turned sour in Thailand, Indonesia, Malaysia, and South Korea, and the cost of the bailout for the banking system is estimated at more than 20% of GDP in these countries and over 50% of GDP in Indonesia. The Philippines is expected to fare somewhat better, with the cost below 10% of GDP.

"Déjà Vu All Over Again"	What we see in banking crises in these different countries is that history has kept on repeating itself. The parallels between the banking crisis episodes in all these countries are remarkably similar, leaving us with a feeling of déjà vu. Although financial liberalization is generally a good thing because it promotes competition and can make a financial system more efficient, as we have seen in the countries examined here, it can lead to an increase in moral hazard, with more risk taking on the part of banks if there is lax regulation and supervision; the result can then be banking crises. However, these episodes do differ in that deposit insurance has not played an important role in many of the countries experiencing banking crises. For example, the size of the Japanese equivalent of the CDIC, the Deposit Insurance Corporation, was so tiny relative to the CDIC that it did not play a prominent role in the banking system and exhausted its resources almost immediately with the first bank failures. This means that deposit insurance is not to blame for some of these banking crises. However, what is common to all the countries discussed here is the existence of a government safety net, in which the government stands ready to bail out banks whether deposit insurance is an important feature of the regulatory environment or not. It is the existence of a government safety net, and not deposit insurance per se, that increases moral hazard incentives for excessive risk taking on the part of banks.

SUMMARY

1. The concepts of asymmetric information, adverse selection, and moral hazard help explain the seven types of banking regulation that we see in Canada and other countries: the government safety net, restrictions on bank asset holdings, capital requirements, bank supervision, disclosure requirements, consumer protection, and restrictions on competition.

2. Because asymmetric information problems in the banking industry are a fact of life throughout the world, bank regulation in other countries is similar to that in Canada. It is particularly problematic to regulate banks engaged in international banking because they can readily shift their business from one country to another.

3. Because of financial innovation, deregulation, and a set of historical accidents, adverse selection and moral hazard problems increased in the 1980s and resulted in huge losses for the Canadian banking industry and for taxpayers.

4. Regulators and politicians are subject to the principal–agent problem, meaning that they may not have sufficient incentives to minimize the costs of deposit insurance to taxpayers. As a result, regulators and politicians relaxed capital standards, removed restrictions on holdings of risky assets, and relied on regulatory forbearance, thereby increasing the costs of the 1980s banking crisis.

5. The Financial Institutions Reform, Recovery, and Enforcement Act (FIRREA) of 1989 was the most significant legislation to affect the thrift industry in the United States since the Great Depression. It imposed restrictions on S&Ls' activities similar to those in effect before 1982; increased the capital requirements to those adhered to by commercial banks; and increased the enforcement powers of thrift regulators.

6. Recent CDIC legislation includes reforms for the deposit insurance and regulatory system so that taxpayer losses would be minimized. This legislation mandated prompt corrective action to deal with troubled deposit-taking financial institutions and instituted risk-based deposit insurance premiums. These provisions have helped reduce the incentives of banks to take on excessive risk and so should help reduce taxpayer exposure in the future.

7. Proposals for reforming the banking regulatory system include elimination of deposit insurance, lower limits on the amount of deposit insurance, outright elimination of the too-big-to-fail policy, coinsurance, risk-based insurance premiums, regulatory consolidation, and market-value accounting for capital requirements.

8. The parallels between the banking crisis episodes that have occurred in countries throughout the world are striking, indicating that similar forces are at work.

KEY TERMS

bank failure, p. 251

bank supervision (prudential
    supervision), p. 255

brokered deposits, p. 271

coinsurance, p. 266

leverage ratio, p. 254

off-balance-sheet activities, p. 254

regulatory forbearance, p. 263

QUESTIONS AND PROBLEMS

Questions marked with an asterisk are answered at the end of the book in an appendix, "Answers to Selected Questions and Problems."

1. Give one example each of moral hazard and adverse selection in private insurance arrangements.

*2. If property and casualty insurance companies provided fire insurance without any restrictions, what kind of adverse selection and moral hazard problems might result?

3. What bank regulation is designed to reduce adverse selection problems for deposit insurance? Will it always work?

*4. What bank regulations are designed to reduce moral hazard problems created by deposit insurance? Will they completely eliminate the moral hazard problem?

5. What are the costs and benefits of a too-big-to-fail policy?

*6. Why did the S&L crisis not occur until the 1980s?

7. Why is regulatory forbearance a dangerous strategy for a deposit insurance agency?

*8. The FIRREA legislation of 1989 is the most comprehensive banking legislation since the 1930s. Describe its major features.

9. What steps were taken in recent CDIC legislation to improve the functioning of deposit insurance?

*10. What are the advantages and disadvantages of the CDIC's risk-based insurance premiums?

11. How can the 1980s Canadian banking crisis be blamed on the principal–agent problem?

*12. Do you think that eliminating or limiting the amount of deposit insurance would be a good idea? Explain your answer.

13. Should the overlap between the OSFI and CDIC be eliminated? Why or why not?

*14. How could higher deposit insurance premiums for banks with riskier assets benefit the economy?

15. How could market-value accounting for bank capital requirements benefit the economy? How difficult would it be to implement?

Chapter 12

Nonbank Financial Institutions

PREVIEW   Although banks (depository institutions) may be the financial institutions we deal with most often, they are not the only financial institutions we come in contact with. Suppose that you purchase insurance from an insurance company, take out an instalment loan on your new car from a finance company, or buy a share of common stock with the help of a broker. In each of these transactions, you are dealing with a nonbank financial institution. In our economy, nonbank financial institutions also play an important role in channelling funds from lender-savers to borrower-spenders.

    Furthermore, the process of financial innovation has increased the importance of nonbank financial institutions. Through innovation, nonbank financial institutions now compete more directly with banks by providing banklike services to their customers. This chapter examines in more detail how the major nonbank financial institutions operate, how they are regulated, and recent trends in the nonbank financial industry. Table 12-1 shows the estimated relative shares of financial intermediary assets for each of the financial intermediaries discussed in this chapter.

INSURANCE COMPANIES

Every day we face the possibility of the occurrence of certain catastrophic events that could lead to large financial losses. A spouse's earnings might disappear due to death or illness; a car accident might result in costly repair bills or payments to an injured party. Because financial losses from crises could be large relative to our financial resources, we protect ourselves against them by purchasing insurance coverage that will pay a sum of money if catastrophic events occur. Life insurance companies sell policies that provide income if a person dies, is incapacitated by illness, or retires. Property and casualty companies specialize in policies that pay for losses incurred as a result of accidents, fire, or theft.

TABLE 12-1	(Estimated) Relative Shares of Total Financial Intermediary Assets		
Non-bank Financial Institution	**Number of Companies**	**Total Assets (in millions)**	**Percent (%)**
Insurance Companies			
Life Insurance*	121	277 507	8.33
Property and Casualty*	208	54 356	1.63
Pension Plans***			
Private	15 213	586 640	17.60
Personal		259 673	7.79
Finance Companies		56 463	1.69
Mutual Funds**	78	280 100	8.40
Depository Institutions			
Chartered Banks*	53	1 508 941	45.27
Trust and Loan Companies*	65	202 678	6.08
Credit Unions and *Caisses Populaires***	2 289	106 988	3.21
Total		3 333 346	100.00

Source: *OSFI Annual Report 1999-2000. **The MacKay Report, p. 43. ***Canadian Life and Health Insurance Facts 2000, p. 12.

Life Insurance Companies

Canada Life
www.canadalife.com

Clarica
www.clarica.com

Manulife Financial
www.manulife.com

Sun Life
www.sunlife.com

Industrial Alliance
www.inalco.com

CompCorp
www.compcorp.ca

As you can see in Table 12-1, there are currently 121 life insurance companies in Canada, which are organized as either stock companies or mutuals. Shareholders own stock companies; mutuals are technically similar to credit unions, owned by the policyholders. Prior to 1999, half of the life insurance companies in Canada were organized as mutuals. In 1999, however, five large mutual life insurance companies, Canada Life, Clarica, Manulife Financial, Sun Life, and Industrial-Alliance, started a process called **demutualization**, and have now converted to stock companies.

Life insurance company regulation is the responsibility of the OSFI and the Canadian Life and Health Insurance Compensation Corporation (CompCorp).[1] OSFI regulation is directed at sales practices, the provision of adequate liquid assets to cover losses, and restrictions on the amount of risky assets (such as common stock) the companies can hold. In other words, OSFI performs the same oversight functions as it does for banks and near banks. CompCorp has no regulatory role in overseeing individual life insurance companies. It is a federally incorporated private, not-for-profit corporation established and funded by the Canadian life insurance industry to provide liability insurance to policyholders: it compensates policyholders if the issuing company goes bankrupt.[2]

---

[1]Of the 127 life insurance companies, 100 are registered under federal laws and 27 under provincial.

[2]Since the establishment of CompCorp, a large insurance company, Confederation Life, went bankrupt in 1994 and two smaller ones, Sovereign Life and Les Coopérants, in 1992—no life insurance company had failed in Canada prior to CompCorp's establishment.

TABLE 12-2 Consolidated Balance Sheet of Canadian Life Insurance Companies, in millions (as of December 1999)

Assets	Amount ($)	Percent (%)	Liabilities	Amount ($)	Percent (%)
Cash and short-term investments	14 893	5.24	Net actuarial liabilities under insurance policies and annuity contracts	199 314	70.18
Accrued investment income	3 090	1.09	Other insurance policy and contract liabilities	16 122	5.68
Bonds	148 758	52.38	Trust and banking deposits	4 428	1.56
Policy loans	12 969	4.57			
Mortgage loans	54 235	19.10	Accounts payable	6 424	2.26
Shares	15 910	5.60	Net deferred gains (losses) on disposal of portfolio investments	11 206	3.94
Real estate	9 952	3.50			
Other loans and investments	3 254	1.14	Deferred income taxes	526	0.19
Accounts receivable	5 445	1.92	Other liabilities	15 626	5.50
Other assets	15 502	5.46			
Total assets excluding segregated funds	284 008	100.00	Total liabilities	253 646	89.31
			Policyholders' equity	8 884	3.13
Segregated funds	186 843		Shareholders' equity		
			Capital stock	5 730	2.02
			Other	15 748	5.54
			Total liabilities and equity	284 008	100.00

Source: OSFI website: http://www.osfi-bsif.gc.ca. Reprinted with permission.

Because death rates for the population as a whole are predictable with a high degree of certainty, life insurance companies can accurately predict what their payouts to policyholders will be in the future. Consequently, as shown in Table 12-2, they hold long-term assets that are not particularly liquid—corporate bonds (52% of assets) and commercial mortgages (19% of assets) as well as some corporate stock. Actuarial liabilities make up 70% of the liabilities of the Canadian life insurance industry. These are the present values of expected claims of policyholders.

There are two basic classes of life insurance, distinguished by the way they are sold: individual life insurance and group life insurance. **Individual life insurance**, as its name implies, is sold one policy at a time, whereas **group life insurance** is sold to a group of people under a single policy. At the end of 1999, the life insurance industry in Canada administered almost 13 million individual life insurance policies and over 121 400 group life insurance policies. At the same time, Canadians owned about $2 trillion of life insurance, about twice the country's GDP.

There are two principal forms of individual life insurance policies: **permanent life insurance** (such as the traditional whole life insurance) and **temporary insurance** (such as term insurance). Permanent life insurance policies have a constant premium throughout the life of the policy. In the early years of the policy, the size of this premium exceeds the amount needed to insure against death because the probability of death is low. Thus the policy builds up a cash value in its early years, but in later years the cash value declines because the constant premium falls below the amount needed to insure against death, the probability of which is now higher. The policyholder can borrow against the cash value of the permanent life policy or can claim it by cancelling the policy. For this reason, permanent insurance is also called **endowment insurance**.

Term insurance, by contrast, has a premium that is matched every year to the amount needed to insure against death during the period of the term (such as one year or five years). As a result, term policies have premiums that rise over time as the probability of death rises (or level premiums with a decline in the amount of death benefits). Term policies have no cash value and thus, in contrast to permanent life policies, provide insurance only, with no savings aspect.

Beginning in the mid-1970s, life insurance companies began to restructure their business to become managers of assets for pension funds. Now more than half of the assets managed by life insurance companies are for pension funds and not for life insurance. Insurance companies have also begun to sell investment vehicles for retirement such as **annuities**, arrangements whereby the customer pays an annual premium in exchange for a future stream of annual payments beginning at a set age, say 65, and continuing until death. In 1999, Canadians paid about $20 billion in premiums or contributions for individual and group annuities. This figure was almost 15% higher than the 1998 figure of $17.4 billion.

Property and Casualty Insurance Companies

Royal & Sun Alliance Insurance Company of Canada
www.royalsunalliance. com

CGU Insurance Company of Canada
www.cgu.ca

Property and Casualty Insurance Compensation Corporation
www.pacic.com

There are 208 property and casualty (P&C) insurance companies in Canada (see Table 12-1), the two largest of which are Royal & Sun Alliance Insurance Company of Canada and General Accident Assurance Company of Canada, now a part of CGU Insurance Company of Canada. More than 64% of the industry, measured by assets held, is foreign-controlled. Most property and casualty insurance companies in Canada are federally registered and subject to regulation by OSFI and the Property and Casualty Insurance Compensation Corporation (PACIC). PACIC was set up in 1988 and performs the same role for property and casualty companies as CompCorp does for life insurance companies. Some lines of P&C insurance, such as, for example, auto insurance, are also subject to provincial laws and regulations.

Property insurance covers losses of real property and casualty insurance protects against legal liability exposures. Although property and casualty insurance companies have seen a slight increase in their share of total financial intermediary assets since 1960, in recent years they have not fared well, and insurance rates have skyrocketed. With the high interest rates in the 1970s, insurance companies had high investment income that enabled them to keep insurance rates low. Since then, however, investment income has fallen with the decline in interest rates, while the growth in lawsuits involving property and casualty insurance and the explosion in amounts awarded in such cases have produced substantial losses for companies.

To return to profitability, insurance companies have raised their rates dramatically—sometimes doubling or even tripling premiums—and have refused to provide coverage for some people. They have also campaigned actively for limits on insurance payouts, particularly for medical malpractice. In the search for profits, insurance companies are also branching out into uncharted territory by insuring the payment of interest on corporate bonds and mortgage-backed securities. One worry is that the insurance companies may be taking on excessive risk in order to boost their profits. One result of the concern about the health of the property and casualty insurance industry is that insurance regulators have proposed new rules that would impose capital requirements on these companies based on the riskiness of their assets and operations.

The investment policies of these companies are affected by the fact that property losses are very uncertain. In fact, because property losses are more uncertain than the death rate in a population, these insurers are less able to predict how much they will have to pay policyholders than life insurance companies are. Natural disasters such as the ice storm of 1998 and the Calgary hailstorm of 1991 exposed the property and casualty insurance companies to billions of dollars of losses.[3] Therefore, property and casualty insurance companies hold more liquid assets than life insurance companies. Table 12-3 shows the aggregate balance sheet of all federally regulated P&C companies: cash, due and accrued investment income, money market instruments, and receivables amount to over a third of their assets, and most of the remainder is held in bonds, debentures, and stocks. Their largest liability relates to unpaid claims and adjustment expenses, followed by unearned premiums (premiums representing the unexpired part of policies).

TABLE 12-3 Consolidated Balance Sheet of Federally Registered Property and Casualty Insurance Companies, in millions (as of December 1999)

Assets	Amount ($)	Percent (%)	Liabilities	Amount ($)	Percent (%)
Cash	310	0.84	Accounts payable	1 620	4.40
Investment income due and accrued	243	0.66	Unpaid claims and adjustment expenses	16 981	46.14
Term deposits	1 500	4.08	Unearned premiums	7 509	20.40
Bonds and debentures	14 476	39.33	Other liabilities	693	1.88
Mortgage loans	802	2.18	Total liabilities	26 803	72.82
Preferred shares	2 652	7.20			
Common shares	3 256	8.85	Subordinated debentures	24	0.06
Real estate	332	0.90	Deferred income taxes	93	0.25
Other investments	329	0.89	Reserves required (by OSFI)	1 383	3.76
Receivable from agents and policyholders	2 942	7.99	Capital stock and contributed surplus	4 037	10.97
Receivable from subsidiaries and affiliates	310	0.84	Earned surplus	4 456	12.11
Other accounts receivable	1 077	2.93	General and contingency reserves	11	0.03
Recoverables	5 757	15.64			
Investments in subsidiaries	505	1.37	Total liabilities and equities	36 807	100.00
Deferred policy acquisition expenses	1 335	3.63			
Other assets	981	2.67			
Total assets	36 807	100.00			

Source: OSFI website: http://www.osfi-bsif.gc.ca. Reprinted with permission.

[3]For example, the freezing rains of January 1998 triggered about 840 000 insurance claims. As a result, Canadian P&C insurance companies paid out over $1.44 billion.

The Woes of Lloyd's of London

In June 1993, Lloyd's of London announced the biggest loss in its history, $4.33 billion for the year 1990 (Lloyd's waits three years to allow all claims to be processed before reporting profits or losses). The chairman of Lloyd's stated that the 1990 deficit "represents in every way the low point of Lloyd's history in the last 305 years."* Things continued to get worse for Lloyd's, with losses continuing until 1992, for a cumulative amount of more than $12 billion over the five-year period 1988–1992.

Lloyd's began in 1688 in a London coffee-house owned by Edward Lloyd, which was a meeting place for merchants, shipowners, and sea captains. Lloyd's became a marketplace in which members, known as "names," trade pieces of insurance policies in order to spread the risk, a process called *reinsurance.* An unusual feature of Lloyd's is that names are directly exposed to losses because they accept unlimited personal liability for any claims they have to pay. Many of those participating in Lloyd's have come to regret it in recent years,

having lost their entire personal fortunes. Indeed, the average loss per name was over $150 000 in 1990. The losses at Lloyd's have also resulted in a slew of lawsuits, with members suing each other right and left over who should be responsible for paying claims.

To survive, the basic structure of Lloyd's has had to change. Lloyd's has opened itself up to corporate capital with only limited liability, has taken measures to lower central spending by the organization, and has altered the way it is governed. In 1996, Lloyd's was able to announce record profits for the year 1993, and profits have been high in subsequent years. However, to settle its lawsuits, Lloyd's offered a $4.8 billion rescue package to its 34 000 names, including the creation of a new corporation called Equitas that took over Lloyd's liabilities incurred before 1993. A result of these changes is that the number of names has shrunk by over 80% to 4000. A victim of the worldwide woes of the property and casualty insurance industry, Lloyd's of London, after three centuries, will never be the same.

*"Lloyd's of London Posts Big Loss, Raising Fears on Market's Viability," *Wall Street Journal,* June 23, 1993, p. A10.

Lloyd's of London
**www.lloydsoflondon.
com**

Property and casualty insurance companies will insure against losses from almost any type of event, including fire, theft, negligence, malpractice, earthquakes, and automobile accidents. If a possible loss being insured is too large for any one firm, several firms may join together to write a policy in order to share the risk. Insurance companies may also reduce their risk exposure by obtaining **reinsurance**. Reinsurance allocates a portion of the risk to another company in exchange for a portion of the premium and is particularly important for small insurance companies. You can think of reinsurance as insurance for the insurance company. The most famous risk-sharing operation is Lloyd's of London, an association in which different insurance companies can underwrite a fraction of an insurance policy. Lloyd's of London has claimed that it will insure against any contingency—for a price. Unfortunately, even the venerable Lloyd's of London has recently found itself in trouble (Box 12-1).

The Competitive Threat from the Banking Industry

Until recently, banks have been restricted in their ability to sell life insurance products. This has been changing rapidly, however. Banks are now allowed to sell life insurance in one form or another. In fact, one of the recommendations of *The MacKay Report* is to allow large banks to offer insurance to consumers through their branches, as some provincially regulated deposit-taking institutions do.

Are Independent Insurance Agents Going the Way of the Milkman?

Twenty years ago, most insurance was sold by independent insurance agents, small independent businessmen who acted as agents for insurance companies but were not employees of the insurance companies. Today, independent insurance agents are facing two competitive challenges that threaten their livelihood. First, new competitors such as banks have been entering the insurance field, taking away some of the independent agents' business. Second, new technology and ways of selling insurance are enabling insurance companies to bypass the independent agents. Insurance companies and banks have used mass-marketing techniques such as toll-free phone numbers and targeted mailings to sell insurance policies. Selling insurance has even begun to enter cyberspace, with customers able to purchase insurance over the Internet. Just as technology and new merchandising techniques have all but eliminated the door-to-door milkman, independent insurance agents may be on their way out.

American International Group (AIG), a publicly traded company that is the largest seller of commercial insurance, recently jettisoned most of its agents. The result of these competitive forces is that independent insurance agents now sell less than one-third of personal insurance policies.

American International Group
www.aig.com

Getting into insurance would help diversify banks' business, thereby improving their economic health and making bank failures less likely.

Insurance companies and their agents reacted to this competitive threat with lobbying actions to block banks from entering the insurance business. They argue that allowing banks to sell insurance directly through their branches will lead to the disappearance of an independent insurance industry. Clearly, competition from banks and other financial institutions will rapidly change the way insurance is sold and will perhaps threaten the livelihood of independent insurance agents (Box 12-2).

APPLICATION | *Insurance Management*

Insurance companies, like banks, are in the financial intermediation business of transforming one type of asset into another for the public. Insurance companies use the premiums paid on policies to invest in assets such as bonds, stocks, mortgages, and other loans; the earnings from these assets are then used to pay out claims on the policies. In effect, insurance companies transform assets such as bonds, stocks, and loans into insurance policies that provide a set of services (for example, claim adjustments, savings plans, friendly insurance agents). If the insurance company's production process of asset transformation efficiently provides its customers with adequate insurance services at low cost and if it can earn high returns on its investments, it will make profits; if not, it will suffer losses.

In Chapter 9 the economic concepts of adverse selection and moral hazard allowed us to understand principles of bank management related to managing credit risk; many of these same principles also apply to the lending activities of insurance companies. Here again we apply the adverse selection and moral hazard concepts to explain many management practices specific to the insurance industry.

In the case of an insurance policy, moral hazard arises when the existence of insurance encourages the insured party to take risks that increase the likelihood of an insurance payoff. For example, a person covered by burglary insurance might not take as many precautions to prevent a burglary because the insurance company will reimburse most of the losses if a theft occurs. Adverse selection holds that the people most likely to receive large insurance payoffs are the ones who will want to purchase insurance the most. For example, a person suffering from a terminal disease would want to take out the biggest life and medical insurance policies possible, thereby exposing the insurance company to potentially large losses. Both adverse selection and moral hazard can result in large losses to insurance companies because they lead to higher payouts on insurance claims. Lowering adverse selection and moral hazard to reduce these payouts is therefore an extremely important goal for insurance companies, and this goal explains the insurance practices we will discuss here.

Screening

To reduce adverse selection, insurance companies try to screen out good insurance risks from poor ones. Effective information collection procedures are therefore an important principle of insurance management.

When you apply for auto insurance, the first thing your insurance agent does is ask you questions about your driving record (number of speeding tickets and accidents), the type of car you are insuring, and certain personal matters (age, marital status). If you are applying for life insurance, you go through a similar grilling, but you are asked even more personal questions about such things as your health, smoking habits, and drug and alcohol use. The life insurance company even orders a medical evaluation (usually done by an independent company) that involves taking blood and urine samples. Just as a bank calculates a credit score to evaluate a potential borrower, the insurance company uses the information you provide to allocate you to a risk class—a statistical estimate of how likely you are to have an insurance claim. Based on this information, the insurance company can decide whether to accept you for the insurance or to turn you down because you pose too high a risk and thus would be an unprofitable customer for the insurance company.

Risk-Based Premiums

Charging insurance premiums on the basis of how much risk a policyholder poses for the insurance company is a time-honoured principle of insurance management. Adverse selection explains why this principle is so important to insurance company profitability.

To understand why an insurance company finds it necessary to have risk-based premiums, let's examine an example of risk-based insurance premiums that at first glance seems unfair. Harry and Sally, both college students with no accidents or speeding tickets, apply for auto insurance. Normally, Harry will be charged a much higher premium than Sally. Insurance companies do this because young males have a much higher accident rate than young females. Suppose, though, that one insurance company did not base its premiums on a risk classification but rather just charged a premium based on the average combined risk for males and females. Then Sally would be charged too much and Harry too little. Sally could go to another insurance company and get a lower rate, while Harry would sign up for the insurance. Because Harry's premium isn't high enough to cover the accidents he is likely to have, on average the company would lose money on Harry. Only with a premium based on a risk classification, so that Harry is charged more, can the insurance company make a profit.[4]

---

[4]Note that the example here is in fact the lemons problem described in Chapter 8.

Restrictive Provisions

Restrictive provisions in policies are an insurance management tool for reducing moral hazard. Such provisions discourage policyholders from engaging in risky activities that make an insurance claim more likely. For example, life insurance companies have provisions in their policies that eliminate death benefits if the insured person commits suicide within the first two years that the policy is in effect. Restrictive provisions may also require certain behaviour on the part of the insured. A company renting motor scooters may be required to provide helmets for renters in order to be covered for any liability associated with the rental. The role of restrictive provisions is not unlike that of restrictive covenants on debt contracts described in Chapter 8. Both serve to reduce moral hazard by ruling out undesirable behaviour.

Prevention of Fraud

Insurance companies also face moral hazard because an insured person has an incentive to lie to the company and seek a claim even if the claim is not valid. For example, a person who has not complied with the restrictive provisions of an insurance contract may still submit a claim. Even worse, a person may file claims for events that did not actually occur. Thus an important management principle for insurance companies is conducting investigations to prevent fraud so that only policyholders with valid claims receive compensation.

Cancellation of Insurance

Being prepared to cancel policies is another insurance management tool. Insurance companies can discourage moral hazard by threatening to cancel a policy when the insured person engages in activities that make a claim more likely. If your auto insurance company makes it clear that coverage will be cancelled if a driver gets too many speeding tickets, you will be less likely to speed.

Deductibles

The **deductible** is the fixed amount by which the insured's loss is reduced when a claim is paid off. A $250 deductible on an auto policy, for example, means that if you suffer a loss of $1000 because of an accident, the insurance company will pay you only $750. Deductibles are an additional management tool that helps insurance companies reduce moral hazard. With a deductible, you experience a loss along with the insurance company when you make a claim. Because you also stand to lose when you have an accident, you have an incentive to drive more carefully. A deductible thus makes a policyholder act more in line with what is profitable for the insurance company; moral hazard has been reduced. And because moral hazard has been reduced, the insurance company can lower the premium by more than enough to compensate the policyholder for the existence of the deductible. Another function of the deductible is to eliminate the administrative costs of handling small claims by forcing the insured to bear these losses.

Coinsurance

When a policyholder shares a percentage of the losses along with the insurance company, their arrangement is called *coinsurance*. For example, some medical insurance plans provide coverage for 80% of medical bills, and the insured person pays 20% after a certain deductible has been met. Coinsurance works to reduce moral hazard in exactly the same way that a deductible does. A policyholder who suffers a loss along with the insurance company has less incentive to take actions, such as going to a specialist unnecessarily, that involve higher claims. Coinsurance is thus another useful management tool for insurance companies.

Limits on the Amount of Insurance

Another important principle of insurance management is that there should be limits on the amount of insurance provided, even though a customer is willing to pay for more coverage. The higher the insurance coverage, the more the insured person can gain from risky activities that make an insurance payoff more likely and hence the greater the moral hazard. For example, if Zelda's car were insured for more than its true value, she might not take proper precautions to prevent its theft, such as making sure that the key is always removed or putting in an alarm system. If it were stolen, she comes out ahead because the excessive insurance payment would allow her to buy an even better car. By contrast, when the insurance payments are lower than the value of her car, she will suffer a loss if it is stolen and will thus take precautions to prevent this from happening. Insurance companies must always make sure that their coverage is not so high that moral hazard leads to large losses.

Summary

Effective insurance management requires several practices: information collection and screening of potential policyholders, risk-based premiums, restrictive provisions, prevention of fraud, cancellation of insurance, deductibles, coinsurance, and limits on the amount of insurance. All of these practices reduce moral hazard and adverse selection by making it harder for policyholders to benefit from engaging in activities that increase the amount and likelihood of claims. With smaller benefits available, the poor insurance risks (those who are more likely to engage in the activities in the first place) see less benefit from the insurance and are thus less likely to seek it out.

PENSION FUNDS

In performing the financial intermediation function of asset transformation, pension funds provide the public with another kind of protection: income payments on retirement. Employers, unions, or private individuals can set up pension plans, which acquire funds through contributions paid in by the plan's participants or their employees. Table 12-1 shows that pension plans have grown in importance, with their share of total financial intermediary assets rising from about 10% at the end of 1977 to over 25% at the end of 2000. Federal tax policy has been a major factor behind the rapid growth of pension funds because employer contributions to employee pension plans are tax-deductible. Furthermore, tax policy has also encouraged employee contributions to pension funds by making them tax-deductible as well and enabling self-employed individuals to open up their own tax-sheltered pension plans.

Because the benefits paid out of the pension fund each year are highly predictable, pension funds invest in long-term securities, with the bulk of their asset holdings in bonds, stocks, and long-term mortgages. The key management issues for pension funds revolve around asset management. Pension fund managers try to hold assets with high expected returns and to lower risk through diversification. They also use techniques we discussed in Chapter 9 to manage credit and interest-rate risk. The investment strategies of pension plans have changed radically over time. In the aftermath of World War II, most pension fund assets were held in government bonds. However, the strong performance of stocks in the 1950s and 1960s afforded pension plans higher returns, causing them to shift their portfolios into stocks, currently on the order of over one-third of their assets. As a result, pension plans now have a much stronger presence in the stock market.

Although the purpose of all pension plans is the same, they can differ in a number of attributes. First is the method by which payments are made: if the benefits are determined by the contributions into the plan and their earnings, the pension is a **defined-contribution plan**; if future income payments (benefits) are set in advance, the pension is a **defined-benefit plan**. In the case of a defined-benefit plan, a further attribute is related to how the plan is funded. A defined-benefit plan is **fully funded** if the contributions into the plan and their earnings over the years are sufficient to pay out the defined benefits when they come due. If the contributions and earnings are not sufficient, the plan is **underfunded**. For example, if Jane Brown contributes $100 per year into her pension plan and the interest rate is 10%, after ten years the contributions and their earnings would be worth $1753.[5] If the defined benefit on her pension plan pays her $1753 or less after ten years, the plan is fully funded because her contributions and earnings will fully pay for this payment. But if the defined benefit is $2000, the plan is underfunded because her contributions and earnings do not cover this amount.

A second characteristic of pension plans is their *vesting,* the length of time that a person must be enrolled in the pension plan (by being a member of a union or an employee of a company) before being entitled to receive benefits. Typically, firms require that an employee work two years for the company before being vested and qualifying to receive pension benefits; if the employee leaves the firm before the two years are up, either by quitting or being fired, all rights to benefits are lost.

Private Pension Plans

Ontario Teachers' Pension Plan Board
www.otpp.com

Ontario Municipal Employees' Retirement System
www.omers.com

Caisse de dépôt et placement du Québec
www.lacaisse.com

Private pension plans are voluntary, employer-sponsored plans, with the contributions usually shared between employer and employee. At the beginning of 1998, there were over 15 000 private pension plans in Canada, covering over 5 million members, with total accumulated assets of $587 billion. Trusteed pension plans account for the majority of private pension plans in Canada. Typically, a pension plan sponsor (such as a government or private-sector employer) will hire a bank, a life insurance company, or a pension fund manager to manage the fund, for the benefit of the plan members. The largest trusteed pension funds in Canada are the Ontario Teachers' Pension Plan Board and the Ontario Municipal Employees' Retirement System (OMERS). Among the largest pension fund managers are the *Caisse de dépôt et Placement du Québec* and Royal Trust, a subsidiary of the Royal Bank.

Many private pension plans are underfunded because they plan to meet their pension obligations out of current earnings when the benefits come due. As long as companies have sufficient earnings, underfunding creates no problems, but if not, they may not be able to meet their pension obligations. Because of potential problems caused by corporate underfunding, mismanagement, fraudulent practices, and other abuses of private pension funds, these funds are heavily regulated. As with insurance companies, the regulatory system governing pension funds is split between OSFI and provincial superintendents of pensions. Pension funds administered for people working in businesses that are federal in scope (for example, railways, air transport, telecommunications, and banking) are the responsibility of OSFI. However, most trusteed pension funds are registered under provincial acts. These acts and regulations tend to be similar across provinces. They establish minimum standards for the reporting and disclosure of information, set rules for vesting and the degree of underfunding, and place restrictions on investment practices.

---

[5]The $100 contributed in year 1 would be worth $100 \times (1 + 0.10)^{10} = \$259.37$ at the end of ten years; the $100 contributed in year 2 would be worth $100 \times (1 + 0.10)^9 = \$235.79$; and so on until the $100 contributed in year 10 would be worth $100 \times (1 + 0.10) = \$110$. Adding these together, we get the total value of these contributions and their earnings at the end of ten years:

$$\$259.37 + \$235.79 + \$214.36 + \$194.87 + \$177.16$$
$$+ \$161.05 + \$146.41 + \$133.10 + \$121.00 + \$110.00 = \$1753.11$$

Social Security and Public Pension Plans

The most important government pension plan is Social Security—Old Age Security (OAS) and Guaranteed Income Supplement (GIS)—which covers all Canadians, subject to claw-back provisions. It makes monthly flat payments (out of federal government revenues) to retired or disabled workers or their surviving spouses. The public pension plans are the Canada Pension Plan (CPP) and, in Québec, the Québec Pension Plan (QPP), both supported by contributions from employees and their employers. The accumulated funds of the CPP are managed by an investment board, called the CPP Investment Board, and those of the QPP are managed by the *Caisse de dépôt et placement du Québec.*

When the government pension plans were established, the federal government intended to operate them like private pension plans. However, unlike private pension plans, benefits are typically paid out from current contributions, not from the contributions previously made by the participant. This "pay as you go" system led to a massive underfunding. The problems of the public pension plans could become worse in the future because of the growth in the number of retired people relative to the working population. The government has been grappling with the problems of the public pension plans for years, but the prospect of a huge bulge of new retirees has resulted in calls for radical surgery (Box 12-3). In 1999, for example, the CPP was given authority to sharply increase contribution levels from $969 to a maximum of $1635 by the year 2003. It was also given the authority to invest its accumulated assets (estimated to rise to $100 billion by 2006 and to $300 billion by 2015) in the market in order to earn a higher return so that future increases in contribution levels will not be needed.

Canada Pension Plan
www.cpp-rpc.gc.ca

Provincial and local governments and the federal government, like private employers, have also set up pension plans for their employees. These plans are almost identical in operation to private pension plans and hold similar assets. Underfunding of the plans is also prevalent, and some investors in municipal bonds worry that it may lead to future difficulties in the ability of state and local governments to meet their debt obligations.

Personal Pension Plans

These are the Registered Retirement Savings Plans (RRSPs) that Canadians set up with financial institutions. They provide tax-sheltered, self-financed retirement funds. At the end of 1999, RRSP accumulated assets totalled about $260 billion. This is an increase of 273% over the $95 billion of total RRSP accumulated assets a decade ago.

Upon retirement, an RRSP must be converted into an annuity or a Registered Retirement Income Fund (RRIF), which provides taxable annuity payments. Since RRIFs are less popular than annuities, which may only be offered by insurance companies, the insurance industry has benefited from the introduction of the RRSP.

FINANCE COMPANIES

Finance companies are nondeposit-taking financial institutions that acquire funds by issuing commercial paper or stocks and bonds or borrowing from banks, and that use the proceeds to make loans (often for small amounts) that are particularly well suited to consumer and business needs. The financial intermediation process of finance companies can be described by saying that they borrow in large amounts but often lend in small amounts—a process quite different from that of banking institutions, which collect deposits in small amounts and then often make large loans.

A key feature of finance companies is that although they lend to many of the same customers that borrow from banks, they are virtually unregulated compared to chartered banks and near banks. Provinces regulate the maximum amount they can loan to individual consumers and the terms of the debt contract, but there are no restrictions on branching, the assets they hold, or how they raise their funds.

BOX 12-3

Should Public Pension Plans Be Privatized?

In recent years, public confidence in the public pension plans has reached a new low. Some surveys suggest that young people have more confidence in the existence of flying saucers than they do in the government's promise to pay them their public pension plan benefits. Without some overhaul of the system, public pension plans will not be able to meet their future obligations. The government has set up advisory commissions and has been holding hearings to address this problem.

Currently, the assets of the public pension plans, which reside in trust funds, are all invested in government securities. Because stocks and corporate bonds have higher returns than government securities, many proposals to save the public pension plans suggest investing part of the trust fund in corporate securities and thus partially privatizing the systems.

Suggestions for privatization take three basic forms:

1. *Government investment of trust fund assets in corporate securities.* This plan has the advantage of possibly improving the trust funds' overall return, while minimizing transactions costs because it exploits the economies of scale of the trust funds. Critics warn that government ownership of private assets could lead to increased government intervention in the private sector.

2. *Shift of trust fund assets to individual accounts that can be invested in private assets.* This option has the advantage of possibly increasing the return on investments and does not involve the government in the ownership of private assets. However, critics warn that it might expose individuals to greater risk and to transaction costs on individual accounts that might be very high because of the small size of many of these accounts.

3. *Individual accounts in addition to those in the trust funds.* This option has advantages and disadvantages similar to those of option 2 and may provide more funds to individuals at retirement. However, some increase in contributions would be required to fund these accounts.

Whether some privatization of the public pension plans occurs is an open question. In the short term public pension plan reform is likely to involve an increase in contributions, a reduction in benefits, or both. For example, under the 1997 changes to the CPP Act, the percentage of liabilities of CPP that are funded is expected to increase from the current 8% to 20% by 2018.

The lack of restrictions enables finance companies to tailor their loans to customer needs better than banking institutions can.

There are three types of finance companies: sales, consumer, and business.

1. *Sales finance companies* are owned by a particular retailing or manufacturing company and make loans to consumers to purchase items from that company. Sears Roebuck Acceptance Corporation, for example, finances consumer purchases of all goods and services at Sears stores, and General Motors Acceptance Corporation finances purchases of GM cars. Sales finance companies compete directly with banks for consumer loans and are used by consumers because loans can frequently be obtained faster and more conveniently at the location where an item is purchased.

2. *Consumer finance companies* make loans to consumers to buy particular items such as furniture or home appliances, to make home improvements, or to help refinance small debts. Consumer finance companies are separate corporations or are owned by banks. Typically, these companies make loans to consumers who cannot obtain credit from other sources and charge higher interest rates.

3. *Business finance companies* provide specialized forms of credit to businesses by making loans and purchasing accounts receivable (bills owed to the firm) at a discount; this provision of credit is called *factoring*. For example, a dress-

making firm might have outstanding bills (accounts receivable) of $100 000 owed by the retail stores that have bought its dresses. If this firm needs cash to buy 100 new sewing machines, it can sell its accounts receivable for, say, $90 000 to a finance company, which is now entitled to collect the $100 000 owed to the firm. Besides factoring, business finance companies also specialize in leasing equipment (such as railroad cars, jet planes, and computers), which they purchase and then lease to businesses for a set number of years.

Table 12-4 presents the consolidated finance company balance sheet. It shows that leasing dominates the business credit side (24.7% of assets), while personal loans dominate the household credit side (21.94% of assets). Together, leasing and personal loans account for almost half the balance sheet. On the liabilities side, you can see that finance companies source their funds from the capital and money markets. It is for this reason that they must maintain good credit ratings, so that institutional investors will purchase their paper.

TABLE 12-4   Consolidated Balance Sheet of Finance Companies, in millions (as of December 1999)

Assets	Amount ($)	Percent (%)	Liabilities	Amount ($)	Percent (%)
Cash and deposits	1 399	2.48	Short-term paper	17 855	31.62
Business credit			Long-term debt	23 819	42.19
Retail sales financing	7 934	14.05	Owed to parent and		
Wholesale financing	6 264	11.09	affiliated companies	7 854	13.91
Business financing	942	1.67	Bank loans	510	0.90
Leasing and retail contracts	13 945	24.70	Total major liabilities	50 038	88.62
Non-residential mortgages	54	0.10	Other liabilities	2 962	5.25
			Shareholders' equity	3 463	6.13
Total business credit	30 538	54.09	Total liabilities and equity	56 463	100.00
Household credit					
Residential mortgages	1 815	3.21			
Personal loans	12 390	21.94			
Total household credit	14 205	25.15			
Other receivables	1 279	2.27			
Allowance for doubtful accounts	(524)	(0.93)			
Investments and advances	79	0.14			
Investments in subsidiaries	10 000	17.71			
Other assets	886	1.57			
Total assets	56 463	100.00			

Source: Bank of Canada Review, March 2000. Reprinted with permission.

MUTUAL FUNDS

Fidelity Investments
www.fidelity.com

Investors Group
www.investorsgroup. com

Mutual funds are financial intermediaries that pool the resources of many small investors by selling them shares and using the proceeds to buy securities. Through the asset transformation process of issuing shares in small denominations and buying large blocks of securities, mutual funds can take advantage of volume discounts on brokerage commissions and purchase diversified holdings (portfolios) of securities. Mutual funds allow the small investor to obtain the benefits of lower transaction costs in purchasing securities and to take advantage of the reduction of risk by diversifying the portfolio of securities held. Many mutual funds are run by brokerage firms, but others are run by banks or independent investment advisers such as Fidelity or Investors Group.

Mutual funds have seen a large increase in their market share since 1980, due primarily to the booming stock market. Another source of growth has been mutual funds that specialize in debt instruments, which first appeared in the 1970s. Before 1970, mutual funds invested almost solely in common stocks. Funds that purchase common stocks may specialize even further and invest solely in foreign securities or in specialized industries, such as energy or high technology. Funds that purchase debt instruments may specialize further in corporate, government, or municipal bonds or in long-term or short-term securities.

Mutual funds are primarily held by households (around 80%) with the rest held by other financial institutions and nonfinancial businesses. Mutual funds have become increasingly important in household savings. For example, between 1995 and 1997, total personal deposits of Canadians declined from $449 billion to $429 billion. Between 1991 and 1997, however, mutual fund assets grew sixfold, from $50 billion to over $280 billion. In fact, today over 35% of Canadian households hold mutual fund shares. The age group with the greatest participation in mutual fund ownership includes individuals between 50 and 70, which makes sense because they are the most interested in saving for retirement. Interestingly, Generation X (ages 18 to 30) is the second most active age group in mutual fund ownership, suggesting that they have a greater tolerance for investment risk than those who are somewhat older.

The growing importance of mutual funds and pension funds, so-called **institutional investors**, has resulted in their controlling a large share of total financial sector assets. For example, in the 10-year period from 1987 to 1997, mutual fund companies increased their share of total financial sector assets from 2.9% to over 8%. Over the same period, trusteed pension funds increased their share from 14.6% to 17%. Thus, institutional investors are important players in Canadian financial markets (see Table 12-1). They are also the predominant players in the stock markets, with over 70% of the total daily volume in the stock market due to their trading. Increased ownership of stocks has also meant that institutional investors have more clout with corporate boards, often forcing changes in leadership or in corporate policies.

Mutual funds are structured in two ways. The more common structure is an **open-end fund**, from which shares can be redeemed at any time at a price that is tied to the asset value of the fund. Mutual funds also can be structured as a **closed-end fund**, in which a fixed number of nonredeemable shares are sold at an initial offering and are then traded like a common stock. The market price of these shares fluctuates with the value of the assets held by the fund. In contrast to the open-end fund, however, the price of the shares may be above or below the value of the assets held by the fund, depending on factors such as the liquidity of the shares or the quality of the management. The greater popularity of the open-end funds is explained by the greater liquidity of their redeemable shares relative to that of the nonredeemable shares of closed-end funds.

Originally, shares of most open-end mutual funds were sold by salespeople (usually brokers) who were paid a commission. Since this commission is paid at the time of purchase and is immediately subtracted from the redemption value of the shares, these funds are called **load funds**. Most mutual funds are currently **no-load funds**; they are sold directly to the public with no sales commissions. In both types of funds, the managers earn their living from management fees paid by the shareholders. These fees amount to approximately 0.5% of the asset value of the fund per year.

Mutual funds are regulated by a variety of agencies. As securities distributed by investment dealers and financial advisers, they fall within provincial jurisdiction. As services provided by financial institutions, they fall under the Bank Act, Trust and Loan Companies Act, Insurance Companies Act, etc., and are the responsibility of OSFI. Regulations require periodic disclosure of information on these funds to the public and restrictions on the methods of soliciting business.

The industry has also a national association, the Investment Funds Institute of Canada (IFIC). The IFIC, however, has no regulatory role; its main function is to reflect the industry's concerns and to disburse information regarding the industry. The Mutual Funds Dealers' Association, established in 2000, is the self-regulatory organization for the distribution end of the mutual funds industry.

Investment Funds
Institute of Canada
www.ific.ca

Money Market Mutual Funds

An important addition to the family of mutual funds resulting from the financial innovation process described in earlier chapters is the money market mutual fund. Recall that this type of mutual fund invests in short-term debt (money market) instruments of very high quality, such as Treasury bills, commercial paper, and bank certificates of deposit. There is some fluctuation in the market value of these securities, but because their maturity is typically less than six months, the change in the market value is small enough that these funds allow their shares to be redeemed at a fixed value. Changes in the market value of the securities are figured into the interest paid out by the fund.

In the United States, many money market mutual funds allow their shareholders to redeem shares by writing cheques above some minimum amount (usually $500) on the fund's account at a commercial bank. In this way, shares in money market mutual funds effectively function as chequable deposits that earn market interest rates on short-term debt securities. For this reason, in the United States the share of money market mutual funds in total financial intermediary assets has increased to over 5% and currently money market mutual funds account for around one-quarter of the asset value of all mutual funds.

There is a debate about how much of the recent phenomenal growth of money market mutual funds is due to low interest rates and buoyant stock markets and whether, when interest rates rise and markets correct, investors will get out of money market mutual funds and back into deposits. Most observers believe that the trend away from deposits and into money market mutual funds is irreversible.

Hedge Funds

Hedge funds are a United States phenomenon that received considerable attention recently due to the shock to the financial system resulting from the near collapse of Long-Term Capital Management, once one of the most important hedge funds (Box 12-4). Well-known hedge funds in the United States include Moore Capital Management and the Quantum group of funds associated with George Soros. Like mutual funds, hedge funds accumulate money from many people and invest on their behalf, but several features distinguish them from traditional mutual funds. Hedge funds have a minimum investment requirement between $100 000 and $20 million, with the typical minimum investment being $1 million. Long-Term Capital Management required a $10 million minimum investment.

BOX 12·4

The Long-Term Capital Management Debacle

Long-Term Capital Management was a hedge fund with a star cast of managers, including 25 Ph.D.s, two Nobel Prize winners in economics (Myron Scholes and Robert Merton), a former vice-chairman of the Federal Reserve System (David Mullins), and one of Wall Street's most successful bond traders (John Meriwether). It made headlines in September 1998 because its near collapse roiled markets and required a private rescue plan organized by the Federal Reserve Bank of New York.

The experience of Long-Term Capital demonstrates that hedge funds are far from risk-free, despite their use of market-neutral strategies. Long-Term Capital got into difficulties when it thought that the high spread between prices on long-term Treasury bonds and long-term corporate bonds was too high, and bet that this "anomaly" would disappear and the spread would narrow. In the wake of the collapse of the Russian financial system in August 1998, investors increased their assessment of the riskiness of corporate securities and the spread between corporates and Treasuries rose rather than narrowed as Long-Term Capital had predicted. The result was that Long-Term Capital took big losses on its positions, eating up much of its equity position.

By mid-September, Long-Term Capital was unable to raise sufficient funds to meet the demands of its creditors. With Long-Term Capital facing the potential need to liquidate its

portfolio of $80 billion in securities and more than $1 trillion of notional value in derivatives (discussed in Chapter 13), the Federal Reserve Bank of New York stepped in on September 23 and organized a rescue plan with its creditors. The Fed's rationale for stepping in was that a sudden liquidation of Long-Term Capital's portfolio would create unacceptable systemic risk. Tens of billions of dollars of illiquid securities would be dumped on an already jittery market, causing potentially huge losses to numerous lenders and other institutions. The rescue plan required creditors, banks and investment banks to supply an additional $3.6 billion of funds to Long-Term Capital in exchange for much tighter management control of funds and a 90% reduction in the managers' equity stake. In the middle of 1999, John Meriwether began to wind down the funds operations.

Even though no public funds were expended, the Fed's involvement in organizing the rescue of Long-Term Capital was highly controversial. Some critics argue that the Fed intervention increased moral hazard by weakening discipline imposed by the market on fund managers because future Fed interventions of this type would be expected. Others think that the Fed's action was necessary to prevent a major shock to the financial system that could have provoked a financial crisis. The debate on whether the Fed should have intervened is likely to go on for some time.

Federal law limits hedge funds to have no more than 99 investors (limited partners) who must have steady annual incomes of $200 000 or more or a net worth of $1 million, excluding their homes. These restrictions are aimed at allowing hedge funds to be largely unregulated, on the theory that the rich can look out for themselves. Many of the 4000 U.S. hedge funds are located offshore to escape regulatory restrictions.

Hedge funds also differ from traditional mutual funds in that they usually require that investors commit their money for long periods of time, often several years. The purpose of this requirement is to give managers breathing room to pursue long-run strategies. Hedge funds also typically charge large fees to investors. The typical fund charges a 1% annual fee on the assets it manages plus 20% of profits, and some charge significantly more. Long-Term Capital, for example, charged investors a 2% asset management fee and took 25% of the profits.

The term *hedge fund* is highly misleading because the word hedge typically is used to indicate strategies to avoid risk. As the near failure of Long-Term Capital illustrates, despite their name, these funds can and do take big risks. Many hedge funds engage in what are called "market neutral" strategies where they buy a security, such as a bond, that seems cheap and sell an equivalent amount of a similar security that appears to be overvalued. If interest rates as a whole go up or down, the fund is hedged because the decline in value of one security is matched by the rise in value of the other. However, the fund is speculating on whether the spread between the prices on the two securities moves in the direction predicted by the fund managers. If the fund bets wrong, it can lose a lot of money, particularly if it has leveraged up its positions, that is, has borrowed heavily against these positions so that its equity stake is small relative to the size of its portfolio. When Long-Term Capital was rescued it had a leverage ratio of 50 to 1, that is, its assets were fifty times larger than its equity, and even before it got into trouble it was leveraged 20 to 1.

In the wake of the near collapse of Long-Term Capital, many U.S. politicians have called for regulation of these funds. However, because these funds operate offshore in places like the Cayman Islands and are outside U.S. jurisdiction, they would be extremely hard to regulate. What U.S. regulators can do is ensure that U.S. banks and investment banks have clear guidelines on the amount of lending they can provide to hedge funds and require that these institutions get the appropriate amount of disclosure from hedge funds as to the riskiness of their positions.

GOVERNMENT FINANCIAL INTERMEDIATION

The government has become involved in financial intermediation in two basic ways: first, by setting up government finance companies that directly engage in financial intermediation, and second, by supplying government guarantees for private loans.

Crown Finance Companies

To promote housing and community development, the government has created the Canada Mortgage and Housing Corporation (CMHC) to provide funds to the mortgage market by borrowing from the federal government and also from the private sector by issuing mortgage-backed securities. The CMHC is not a bank; it doesn't take deposits and is not governed by the Bank Act, but as a financial intermediary makes direct loans and investments primarily for social housing.

Agriculture is another area in which government financial intermediation plays an important role. Farm Credit Canada (FCC), headquartered in Regina, was set up as a Crown corporation in 1959 and is the successor of the Canadian Farm Loan Board, which was established in 1927 to help Canadian farmers. It makes direct loans to new and established farmers for any agricultural or farm-related operation, including the purchase of land, equipment, and livestock. It sources its funds from the federal government and from selling its notes to domestic and foreign capital markets.

To stimulate the export of Canadian goods and services, the Export Development Corporation (EDC) was established in 1969 as the successor to the Export Credits Insurance Corporation, which dated from 1944. The EDC, with its head office in Ottawa, provides loans to Canadian exporters to finance the working capital buildup associated with international trade. It also provides medium-term, low-interest-rate loans to foreign concerns for the purchase of Canadian goods, equipment, and services.

To promote and assist in the establishment and development of business enterprises in Canada, in 1995 the government created the Business Development Bank of Canada (BDC), headquartered in Montreal. It is the successor to the Federal Business Development Bank (FBDB), which had been set up in 1975 to succeed

Canada Mortgage and
Housing Corporation
www.cmhc.ca

Farm Credit Canada
www.fcc-sca.ca

Export Development
Corporation
www.edc.ca

Business Development
Bank of Canada
www.bdc.ca

the Industrial Development Bank (IDB), which dated from 1944. The BDC issues notes in domestic and foreign financial markets and then uses the proceeds to make loans to small and medium-sized businesses.

In recent years, government financial intermediaries have been experiencing financial difficulties. The farm credit assistance program is one example. The rising tide of farm bankruptcies meant losses in the billions of dollars for Farm Credit Canada. One potential solution to problems like this is to set up new rules that require government finance companies to increase their capital to provide a greater cushion to offset any potential losses.

Government Loan Guarantees

Another important government role in promoting financial intermediation has been the provision of government loan guarantees. A government loan guarantee acts just like insurance: it insures the lender, say a bank, from any loss if the borrower defaults. In the housing market, government loan guarantees are provided by the CMHC, which insures private mortgages issued by financial institutions to individuals with insufficient down payment, thereby protecting these institutions against the risk of default.

Government loan guarantees have been growing at a rapid rate and they have been particularly attractive because they subsidize activities that our politicians believe in, like going to university and owning a home, and yet do not involve any direct expenditure on the part of the government. An important economic principle that you hear all the time is "You don't get something for nothing," and this is just as true for the government. The problem with government loan guarantees is the same as that with government deposit insurance. Both are insurance schemes that create moral hazard problems that result in losses to the government. Because banks and other institutions making the loans don't suffer any losses if the loans default, they have little incentive to be careful to whom they make their loans.

The resulting lax lending practices can cause substantial losses for the government agencies that provide the loan guarantees. Notorious is the nearly one-in-three default rate on government-guaranteed loans for students in trade schools. An additional problem is that the government bureaucracy to screen and monitor these loans has been shrinking, potentially making the adverse selection and moral hazard problems worse for these loans. Unless the government does a good job of coping with the adverse selection and moral hazard problems inherent in their loan guarantees, taxpayers may be hit with costly bailouts in the future.

SECURITIES MARKET INSTITUTIONS

The smooth functioning of securities markets, in which bonds and stocks are traded, involves several financial institutions, including securities brokers and dealers, investment banks, and organized exchanges. None of these institutions were included in our list of financial intermediaries because they do not perform the intermediation function of acquiring funds by issuing liabilities and then using the funds to acquire financial assets. Nonetheless, they are important in the process of channelling funds from savers to spenders.

First, however, we must recall the distinction between primary and secondary securities markets discussed in Chapter 2. In a primary market, new issues of a security are sold to buyers by the corporation or government agency borrowing the funds. A secondary market then trades the securities that have been sold in the primary market (and so are secondhand). *Investment banks* (also called *investment dealers*) assist in the initial sale of securities in the primary market;

securities brokers and *dealers* assist in the trading of securities in the secondary markets, some of which are organized into exchanges.

Investment Banks

ScotiaMcLeod
www.scotiamcleod.com

RBC Dominion Securities
www.rbcds.com

BMO Nesbitt Burns
www.nesbittburns.com

When a corporation wishes to borrow (raise) funds, it normally hires the services of an investment bank to help sell its securities. Despite its name, an investment bank is not a bank in the ordinary sense; that is, it is not a financial intermediary that takes in deposits and then lends them out. Some of the well-known Canadian investment banking firms are ScotiaMcLeod, RBC Dominion Securities, and BMO Nesbitt Burns.

Investment bankers assist in the sale of securities as follows. First, they advise the corporation on whether it should issue bonds or stock. If they suggest that the corporation issue bonds, investment bankers give advice on what the maturity and interest payments on the bonds should be. If they suggest that the corporation should sell stock, they give advice on what the price should be. This is fairly easy to do if the firm has prior issues currently selling in the market, called **seasoned issues**. However, when a firm issues stock for the first time in what is called an **initial public offering** (IPO), it is more difficult to determine what the correct price should be. All the skills and expertise of the investment-banking firm then need to be brought to bear to determine the most appropriate price. IPOs have become very important in the Canadian economy because they are a major source of financing for Internet companies, which became all the rage on Bay Street in the late 1990s. Not only have IPOs helped these companies to acquire capital to substantially expand their operations, but they have also made the original owners of these firms very rich. Many a nerdy 20- to 30-year-old became an instant millionaire when his stake in his Internet company was given a high valuation after the initial public offering of shares in the company.

When the corporation decides which kind of financial instrument it will issue, it offers them to **underwriters**—investment banks that guarantee the corporation a price on the securities and then sell them to the public. If the issue is small, only one investment bank underwrites it (usually the original investment banking firm hired to provide advice on the issue). If the issue is large, several investment-banking firms form a syndicate to underwrite the issue jointly, thus limiting the risk that any one investment bank must take. The underwriters sell the securities to the general public by contacting potential buyers, such as banks and insurance companies, directly and by placing advertisements in newspapers like the *National Post* and the *Globe and Mail*.

The activities of investment banks and the operation of primary markets are heavily regulated by the provinces and the federal government. The Ontario Securities Commission (OSC), for example, is responsible for administering the Ontario Securities Act, Canada's first provincial securities act passed in 1945. Other provinces and territories have generally tended to follow Ontario's lead and passed Securities Acts regulating investment banking and the trading of securities. Canada doesn't have a Securities Act, but portions of the Criminal Code of Canada specifically apply to securities trading.

Ontario Securities
Commission
www.osc.gov.on.ca

Securities Brokers and Dealers

Securities brokers and dealers conduct trading in secondary markets. Brokers are pure intermediaries who act as agents for investors in the purchase or sale of securities. Their function is to match buyers with sellers, a function for which they are paid brokerage commissions. In contrast to brokers, dealers link buyers and sellers by standing ready to buy and sell securities at given prices. Therefore, dealers hold inventories of securities and make their living by selling these securities for a slightly higher price than they paid for them—that is, on the "spread" between the asked price and the bid price. This can be a high-risk business because dealers hold securities that can rise or fall in price; in recent years, several firms specializing in bonds have collapsed. Brokers, by contrast, are not as exposed to risk because they do not own the securities involved in their business dealings.

Brokerage firms engage in all three securities market activities, acting as brokers, dealers, and investment bankers. That is, the same investment banks that handle the sale of securities in the primary markets also are involved in the retail business of trading for clients on the stock exchanges. However, the provinces and the federal government regulate the investment banking operation of the firms and also restrict brokers and dealers from misrepresenting securities and from trading on *insider information*, nonpublic information known only to the management of a corporation.

Organized Exchanges

As discussed in Chapter 2, secondary markets can be organized either as over-the-counter markets, in which trades are conducted using dealers, or as organized exchanges, in which trades are conducted in one central location. The Canadian stock exchanges reorganized in 2000. The former Alberta and Vancouver stock exchanges combined and formed the Canadian Venture Capital Exchange (CDNX), located in Vancouver; the CDNX is now a subsidiary of the TSE. The Toronto Stock Exchange consolidated its position as the country's senior equity exchange, trading thousands of securities. The Montreal Exchange expanded its coverage of derivatives by assuming the derivatives business formerly at the TSE.

Organized stock exchanges actually function as a hybrid of an auction market (in which buyers and sellers trade with each other in a central location) and a dealer market (in which dealers make the market by buying and selling securities at given prices). Securities are traded on the floor of the exchange with the help of a special kind of dealer-broker called a **specialist**. A specialist matches buy and sell orders submitted at the same price and so performs a brokerage function. However, if buy and sell orders do not match up, the specialist buys stocks or sells from a personal inventory of securities, in this manner performing a dealer function. By assuming both functions, the specialist maintains orderly trading of the securities for which he or she is responsible.

Organized exchanges are also heavily regulated. In particular, government regulatory bodies, such as the Ontario Securities Commission, impose regulations that govern the behaviour of brokers and dealers involved with exchanges. Furthermore, recent advances in computers and telecommunications, which reduce the costs of linking these markets, have encouraged the expansion of a national market system. We thus see that legislation and modern computing technology are leading the way to a more competitive securities industry. Another development is the growing importance of the Internet in securities markets (Box 12-5).

The growing internationalization of capital markets has encouraged another trend in securities trading. Increasingly, Canadian companies are being listed on U.S. stock exchanges, and the markets are moving toward trading stocks internationally, 24 hours a day.

The Internet Comes to Bay and Wall Streets

An important development in recent years is the growing importance of the Internet in securities markets. Initial public offerings of stock are now being sold on the Internet, and many brokerage firms allow clients to conduct securities trades online or to transmit buy and sell orders via e-mail. In June of 1999, Wall Street was rocked by the announcement that its largest full-service brokerage firm, Merrill Lynch, would begin offering online trading for as little as $29.95 a trade to its five million customers. The major Canadian banks have also added wireless banking and brokerage services along with secure e-commerce solutions to help their clients manage their financial operations. Moreover, the Canadian Payments Association continues to pursue new opportunities to enhance Canadians' confidence in Internet payments. The banking and brokerage business will never be the same.

Merrill Lynch
www.merrilllynch.com

SUMMARY

1. Insurance companies, which are regulated by the OSFI and the provinces, acquire funds by selling policies that pay out benefits if catastrophic events occur. Property and casualty insurance companies hold more liquid assets than life insurance companies because of greater uncertainty regarding the benefits they will have to pay out. All insurance companies face moral hazard and adverse selection problems that explain the use of insurance management tools, such as information collection and screening of potential policyholders, risk-based premiums, restrictive provisions, prevention of fraud, cancellation of insurance, deductibles, coinsurance, and limits on the amount of insurance.

2. Pension plans provide income payments to people when they retire after contributing to the plans for many years. Pension funds have experienced very rapid growth as a result of encouragement by federal tax policy and now play an important role in the stock market. Many pension plans are underfunded, which means that in future years they will have to pay out higher benefits than the value of their contributions and earnings. The problem of underfunding is especially acute for public pension plans such as Social Security.

3. Finance companies raise funds by issuing commercial paper and stocks and bonds and use the proceeds to make loans that are particularly suited to consumer and business needs. Virtually unregulated in comparison to chartered banks and near banks, finance companies have been able to tailor their loans to customer needs very quickly and have grown rapidly.

4. Mutual funds sell shares and use the proceeds to buy securities. Open-end funds issue shares that can be redeemed at any time at a price tied to the asset value of the firm. Closed-end funds issue nonredeemable shares, which are traded like common stock. They are less popular than open-end funds because their shares are not as liquid. Money market mutual funds hold only short-term, high-quality securities, allowing shares to be redeemed at a fixed value.

5. Investment banks are firms that assist in the initial sale of securities in primary markets, whereas securities brokers and dealers assist in the trading of securities in the secondary markets, some of which are organized into exchanges. The provinces and the federal government regulate the financial institutions in the securities markets and ensure that adequate information reaches prospective investors.

KEY TERMS

annuities, p. 280

brokerage firms, p. 297

closed-end fund, p. 291

deductible, p. 285

defined-benefit plan, p. 286

defined-contribution plan, p. 286

demutualization, p. 278

endowment insurance, p. 280

fully funded, p. 287

group life insurance, p. 279

hedge fund, p. 292

individual life insurance, p. 279

initial public offering (IPO), p. 296

institutional investors, p. 291

load funds, p. 292

no-load funds, p. 292

open-end fund, p. 291

permanent life insurance, p. 279

reinsurance, p. 282

seasoned issue, p. 296

specialist, p. 297

temporary insurance, p. 279

underfunded, p. 287

underwriters, p. 296

QUESTIONS AND PROBLEMS

Questions marked with an asterisk are answered at the end of the book in an appendix, "Answers to Selected Questions and Problems."

*1. If death rates were to become less predictable than they are, how would life insurance companies change the types of assets they hold?

2. Why do property and casualty insurance companies have large holdings of liquid assets but life insurance companies do not?

*3. Why are all defined contribution pension plans fully funded?

4. How can favourable tax treatment of pension plans encourage saving?

*5. "In contrast to private pension plans, government pension plans are rarely underfunded." Is this statement true, false, or uncertain? Explain your answer.

6. What explains the widespread use of deductibles in insurance policies?

*7. Why might insurance companies restrict the amount of insurance a policyholder can buy?

8. Why are restrictive provisions a necessary part of insurance policies?

*9. If you needed to take out a loan, why might you first go to your local bank rather than to a finance company?

10. Explain why shares in closed-end mutual funds typically sell for less than the market value of the stocks they hold.

*11. Why might you buy a no-load mutual fund instead of a load fund?

12. Why can a money market mutual fund allow its shareholders to redeem shares at a fixed price but other mutual funds cannot?

*13. Why might government loan guarantees be a high-cost way for the government to subsidize certain activities?

14. If you like to take risks, would you rather be a dealer, a broker, or a specialist? Why?

*15. Is investment banking a good career for someone who is afraid of taking risks? Why or why not?

Chapter 13

Financial Derivatives

PREVIEW Starting in the 1970s and increasingly in the 1980s and 1990s, the world became a riskier place for the financial institutions described in this part of the book. Swings in interest rates widened, and the bond and stock markets went through some episodes of increased volatility. As a result of these developments, managers of financial institutions have become more concerned with reducing the risk their institutions face. Given the greater demand for risk reduction, the process of financial innovation described in Chapter 9 came to the rescue by producing new financial instruments that help financial institution managers manage risk better. These instruments, called **financial derivatives**, have payoffs that are linked to previously issued securities and are extremely useful risk reduction tools.

In this chapter we look at the most important financial derivatives that managers of financial institutions use to reduce risk: forward contracts, financial futures, options, and swaps. We examine not only how markets for each of these financial derivatives work but also how they can be used by financial institutions to manage risk. We also study financial derivatives because they have become an important source of profits for financial institutions, particularly larger banks, which, as we saw in Chapter 10, have found their traditional business declining.

FORWARD MARKETS

Forward contracts are agreements by two parties to engage in a financial transaction at a future (forward) point in time. Here we focus on forward contracts that are linked to debt instruments, called **interest-rate forward contracts**; later in the chapter we discuss forward contracts for foreign currencies.

Interest-Rate Forward Contracts

Interest-rate forward contracts involve the future sale of a debt instrument and have several dimensions: (1) specification of the actual debt instrument that will be delivered at a future date, (2) amount of the debt instrument to be delivered, (3) price (interest rate) on the debt instrument when it is delivered, and (4) date on which delivery will take place. An example of an interest-rate forward contract might be an agreement for the First Bank to sell to the Rock Solid Insurance Company, one year from today, $5 million face value of 8% coupon Canada bonds that mature in 2015 at a price that yields the same interest rate on these bonds as today's, say 8%. Because Rock Solid will buy the securities at a future date, it is said to have taken a **long position**, while the First Bank, which will sell the securities, is said to have taken a **short position**.

| APPLICATION | *Hedging with Interest-Rate Forward Contracts* |

Why would the First Bank want to enter into this forward contract with Rock Solid Insurance Company in the first place?

The reason is that the First Bank is able to **hedge** (protect itself) against interest-rate risk in case it wants to sell the bonds before they mature. For its part, the First Bank, which is currently holding the $5 million of the 8% coupon bonds maturing in 2015, may worry that if interest rates rise in the future, the price of these bonds will fall and expose it to a capital loss if they are sold. When it enters into the forward contract, it locks in the future price and eliminates the price risk it faces from interest-rate changes. We thus see that interest-rate forward contracts can allow financial institution managers to reduce (hedge against) interest-rate risk.

Why would the Rock Solid Insurance Company want to enter into the forward contract with the First Bank? Rock Solid expects to receive premiums of $5 million in one year's time that it will want to invest in the 8% coupon bonds maturing in 2015, but worries that interest rates on these bonds will decline between now and next year. By using the forward contract, it is able to lock in the 8% interest rate on the Canada bonds (which will be sold to it by the First Bank).

Pros and Cons of Forward Contracts

The advantage of forward contracts is that they can be as flexible as the parties involved want them to be. This means that an institution like the First Bank may be able to hedge completely the interest-rate risk for the exact security it is holding in its portfolio, just as it has in our example.

However, forward contracts suffer from two problems that severely limit their usefulness. The first is that it may be very hard for an institution like the First Bank to find another party (called a *counterparty*) to make the contract with. There are brokers to facilitate the matching up of parties like the First Bank and Rock Solid Insurance Company, but there may be few institutions that want to engage in a forward contract specifically for the 8% coupon bond maturing in 2015. This means that it may prove impossible to find a counterparty when a financial institution like the First Bank wants to make a specific type of forward contract. Furthermore, even if the First Bank finds a counterparty, it may not get as high a price as it wants because there may not be anyone else to make the deal with. A serious problem for the market in interest-rate forward contracts, then, is that it may be difficult to make the financial transaction or that it will have to be made at a disadvantageous price; in the parlance of financial economists, this market suffers from a *lack of liquidity*. (Note that this use of the term *liquidity* when it is applied to a market is somewhat broader than its use when it is applied to an asset. For an asset, liquidity refers to the ease with which the asset can be turned into cash, whereas for a market, liquidity refers to the ease of carrying out financial transactions.)

The second problem with forward contracts is that they are subject to default risk. Suppose that in one year's time, interest rates rise so that the price of the 8% coupon bonds maturing in 2015 falls. The Rock Solid Insurance Company might then decide that it would like to default on the forward contract with the First Bank because it can now buy the bonds at a price lower than the agreed price in the forward contract. Or perhaps Rock Solid may not have been rock solid after all and will have gone bust during the year and so is no longer available to complete the terms of the forward contract. Because there is no outside organization guaranteeing the contract, the only recourse is for the First Bank to go to the courts to sue Rock Solid, but this process will be costly. Furthermore, if Rock Solid is already bankrupt, the First Bank will suffer a loss; the bank can no longer sell the 8% coupon bonds maturing in 2015 at the price it had agreed on with Rock Solid but instead will have to sell at a price well below that because the price of these bonds has fallen.

The presence of default risk in forward contracts means that parties to these contracts must check each other out to be sure that the counterparty is both financially sound and likely to be honest and live up to its contractual obligations. Because this is a costly process and because all the adverse selection and moral hazard problems discussed in earlier chapters apply, default risk is a major barrier to the use of interest-rate forward contracts. When the default risk problem is combined with a lack of liquidity, we see that these contracts may be of limited usefulness to financial institutions. Although there is a market for interest-rate forward contracts, it is not nearly as large as the financial futures market, to which we turn next.

FINANCIAL FUTURES MARKETS

Chicago Board of Trade
www.cbot.com

Given the default risk and liquidity problems in the interest-rate forward market, another solution to hedging interest-rate, stock market, and foreign exchange risk was needed. This solution was provided by the development of financial futures contracts by the Chicago Board of Trade starting in 1975.

Financial futures are classified as (1) interest-rate futures, (2) stock index futures, and (3) currency futures. In Canada, such contracts are traded in the Montreal Exchange (which maintains active markets in short-term and long-term Canadian government bond futures) and the Toronto Futures Exchange (which maintains active markets in the Toronto 35 and Toronto 100 stock indexes futures). In what follows, we discuss interest-rate and stock index futures. Later in the chapter we also discuss currency futures.

Interest-Rate Futures Contracts

An **interest-rate futures contract** is similar to an interest-rate forward contract in that it specifies that a financial instrument must be delivered by one party to another on a stated future date. However, it differs from an interest-rate forward contract in several ways that overcome some of the liquidity and default problems of forward markets.

To understand what interest-rate futures contracts are all about, let's look at one of the most widely traded futures contracts, that for 10-year Canadian government bonds, which are traded on the Montreal Exchange (ME). (An illustration of how prices on these contracts are quoted can be found in the "Following the Financial News" box.) The contract value is for $100 000 face value of bonds. Prices are quoted in points, with each point equal to $1000, and the smallest change in price is one hundredth of a point ($10). This contract specifies that the bonds to be delivered must have 10 years to maturity at the delivery date. If the Canada bonds delivered to settle the futures contract have a coupon rate different from the 8% specified in the futures contract, the amount of bonds to be delivered is adjusted to reflect the difference in value between the delivered bonds and the 8% coupon bond. In line with the terminology used for forward contracts, parties who have bought a futures contract and thereby agreed to buy (take delivery of) the bonds are said to

---

FOLLOWING THE FINANCIAL NEWS

Interest-Rate Futures

The prices for interest-rate futures contracts are published daily. In the *National Post: Financial Post*, these prices are found in the "Futures Prices" columns under the "Interest Rate" heading. An excerpt is reproduced here.

Lifetime				Daily				
High	Low	Mth	Open	High	Low	Settle	Chg	Prev. op. int

Interest Rate

Canadian Govt. Bonds 5 Years (ME)

$100 000, points of 100%; 0.01=$10 per contract

Vol. 0		Prev. vol. 0		Prev. open int. 0				

Canadian Govt. Bonds 10 years (ME)

$100 000, points of 100%; 0.01=$10 per contract

High	Low	Mth	Open	High	Low	Settle	Chg	Prev. op. int
102.64	100.55	Dec00	101.26	101.51	101.20	101.25	+0.01	62 409

Vol. 4230   Prev. vol. 5214   Prev. open int. 62 410

The following information is included in each column. The Montreal Exchange's contract for delivery of 10-year Canadian government bonds in December 2000 is used as an example.

Lifetime High: Highest price ever; each point corresponds to $1000 of face value—102.64 is $102 640 (for $100 000 face value) for the December 2000 contract.

Lifetime Low: Lowest price ever—100.55 is $100 550 for the December contract.

Mth: Maturity month of the futures contract.

Open: Opening price—101.26 is $101 260 for the December contract.

High: Highest traded price that day—101.51 is $101 510 for the December contract.

Low: Lowest traded price that day—101.20 is $101 200 for the December contract.

Settle: Settlement price, the closing price that day—101.25 is $101 250 for the December contract.

Chg: Change in the settlement price from the previous day—+0.01 is +$10 for the December contract.

Prev. op. int.: Number of contracts outstanding—62 409 for the December contract, with a face value of $6.2 billion (62 409 × $100 000).

Source: Excerpted with permission from *The Financial Post*, October 31, 2000, p. C17.

have taken a *long position,* and parties who have sold a futures contract and thereby agreed to sell (deliver) the bonds have taken a *short position.*

To make our understanding of this contract more concrete, let's consider what happens when you buy or sell one of these 10-year Canadian government bond futures contracts. Let's say that on February 1, you sell one $100 000 June contract at a price of 115 (that is, $115 000). By selling this contract, you agree to deliver $100 000 face value of the long-term Canada bonds to the contract's counterparty at the end of June for $115 000. By buying the contract at a price of 115, the buyer has agreed to pay $115 000 for the $100 000 face value of bonds when you deliver them at the end of June. If interest rates on long-term bonds rise so that when the contract matures at the end of June the price of these bonds has fallen to 110 ($110 000 per $100 000 of face value), the buyer of the contract will have lost $5000 because he or she paid $115 000 for the bonds but can sell them only for the market price of $110 000. But you, the seller of the contract, will have gained $5000 because you can now sell the bonds to the buyer for $115 000 but have to pay only $110 000 for them in the market.

It is even easier to describe what happens to the parties who have purchased futures contracts and those who have sold futures contracts if we recognize the following fact. ***At the expiration date of a futures contract, the price of the contract is the same as the price of the underlying asset to be delivered.*** To see why this is the case, consider what happens on the expiration date of the June contract at the end of June when the price of the underlying $100 000 face value Canada bond is 110 ($110 000). If the futures contract is selling below 110, say at 109, a trader can buy the contract for $109 000, take delivery of the bond, and immediately sell it for $110 000, thereby earning a quick profit of $1000. Because earning this profit involves no risk, it is a great deal that everyone would like to get in on. That means that everyone will try to buy the contract, and as a result, its price will rise. Only when the price rises to 110 will the profit opportunity cease to exist and the buying pressure disappear. Conversely, if the price of the futures contract is above 110, say at 111, everyone will want to sell the contract. Now the sellers get $111 000 from selling the futures contract but have to pay only $110 000 for the Canada bonds that they must deliver to the buyer of the contract, and the $1000 difference is their profit. Because this profit involves no risk, traders will continue to sell the futures contract until its price falls back down to 110, at which price there are no longer any profits to be made. The elimination of riskless profit opportunities in the futures market is referred to as **arbitrage**, and it guarantees that the price of a futures contract at expiration equals the price of the underlying asset to be delivered.[1]

Armed with the fact that a futures contract at expiration equals the price of the underlying asset makes it even easier to see who profits and who loses from such a contract when interest rates change. When interest rates have risen so that the price of the Canada bond is 110 on the expiration day at the end of June, the June Canada bond futures contract will also have a price of 110. Thus if you bought the contract for 115 in February, you have a loss of 5 points, or $5000 (5% of $100 000). But if you sold the futures contract at 115 in February, the decline in price to 110 means that you have a profit of 5 points, or $5000.

---

[1] In actuality, futures contracts sometimes set conditions for delivery of the underlying assets that cause the price of the contract at expiration to differ slightly from the price of the underlying assets. Because the difference in price is extremely small, we ignore it in this chapter.

APPLICATION | *Hedging with Interest-Rate Futures*

First Bank can also use interest-rate futures contracts to hedge the interest-rate risk on its holdings of $5 million of the 8% coupon bonds maturing in 2015. To see how it can do this, suppose that the 8% coupon bonds maturing in 2015 are the long-term bonds that would be delivered in the Canada bond futures contract expiring one year in the future and that the interest rate on these bonds is expected to remain at 8% over the next year so that both the 8% coupon bonds maturing in 2015 and the futures contract are selling at par. It should be easy for you to see that First Bank can hedge its interest-rate risk by selling $5 million of the Canada bond futures contract, that is, 50 contracts ($5 million divided by $100 000 per contract). Then if the interest rate on this bond rises from 8% to, say, 10% next year when the contract expires, both the futures contract and the bond price will fall by exactly the same percentage so that the capital loss on the bonds is exactly matched by the capital gain on First Bank's sale of the futures contracts.[2]

The hedge just described is called a **micro hedge** because the financial institution is hedging the interest-rate risk for a specific asset it is holding. A second type of hedge that financial institutions engage in is called a **macro hedge**, in which the hedge is for the institution's entire portfolio. For example, we have seen in Chapter 9 that if a bank has more rate-sensitive liabilities than assets, a rise in interest rates will cause the value of the bank to decline. By selling interest-rate future contracts that will yield a profit when interest rates rise, the bank can offset the losses on its overall portfolio from an interest-rate rise and thereby hedge its interest-rate risk.

Organization of Trading in Financial Futures Markets

Chicago Mercantile Exchange
www.cme.com

Financial futures contracts are traded on organized exchanges such as the Chicago Board of Trade, the Chicago Mercantile Exchange, the Montreal Exchange, the London International Financial Futures and Options Exchange, and the Marché à Terme International de France. These futures exchanges are highly competitive with one another, and each organization tries to design contracts and set rules that will increase the amount of futures trading on its exchange. The exchanges are also regulated to ensure that prices in the market are not being manipulated. The most widely traded financial futures contracts listed in the *Wall Street Journal* and the exchanges where they are traded (along with the number of contracts outstanding, called **open interest**, on February 16, 2000) are listed in Table 13-1 (interest-rate futures), Table 13-2 (stock-index futures), and Table 13-3 (currency futures).[3]

Given the globalization of other financial markets in recent years, it is not surprising that increased international competition has been occurring in financial futures markets as well.

---

[2]In the real world, designing a hedge is somewhat more complicated than the example here because the bond that is most likely to be delivered might not be an 8% coupon bond maturing in 2015. See Frederic S. Mishkin and Stanley Eakins, *Financial Markets and Institutions.* 3rd ed. (Reading, Mass.: Addison Wesley Longman, 2000), for a discussion of how to construct the hedge in a more realistic case.

[3]For a more detailed treatment of financial futures and option markets, see Franklin R. Edwards and Cindy W. Ma, *Futures and Options* (New York: McGraw-Hill, 1992).

TABLE 13-1 Widely Traded Interest-Rate Futures Contracts

Type of Contract	Contract Size	Exchange*	Open Interest February 15, 2000
A. Short-term debt contracts			
U.S. Treasury bills	$1 million	CME	2 492
30-day Federal funds	$5 million	CBT	22 596
1-month LIBOR	euro 1 million	LIFFE	32 689
Eurodollar	$1 million	CME	1 334 181
Euroyen	100 million	CME	88 112
Sterling	£500 000	LIFFE	777 857
Euro	euro 1 million	LIFFE	1 364 326
Euroswiss franc	SF 1 million	LIFFE	187 837
Canadian banker's acceptance	C$1 million	ME	294 548
B. Long-term debt contracts			
U.S. Treasury bonds	$100 000	CBT	666 993
U.S. Treasury bonds	$50 000	MCE	9 575
U.S. Treasury notes	$100 000	CBT	658 017
5-year U.S. Treasury notes	$100 000	CBT	505 173
2-year U.S. Treasury notes	$200 000	CBT	40 650
Municipal Bond Index	$1000	CBT	24 860
Long Gilt	£50 000	LIFFE	64 976
5-year German govt. bonds	euro 100 000	Eurex	421 919
10-year German govt. bonds	euro 100 000	Eurex	672 716
10-year Canadian govt. bonds	C$100 000	ME	35 066

*Exchange abbreviations:

CME, Chicago Mercantile Exchange;

CBT, Chicago Board of Trade;

LIFFE, London International Financial Futures and Options Exchange;

ME, Montreal Exchange;

MCE, MidAmerica Commodity Exchange.

Source: *Wall Street Journal*, February 16, 2000, p. C20.

The Globalization of Financial Futures Markets

Because futures exchanges in the United States were the first to develop financial futures, they dominated the trading of financial futures in the early 1980s. For example, in 1985, all of the top ten futures contracts were traded on exchanges in the United States. With the rapid growth of financial futures markets and the resulting high profits made by the American exchanges, exchanges in other countries saw a profit opportunity and began to enter this business. By the 1990s, Eurodollar contracts traded on the London International Financial Futures and Options Exchange,

TABLE 13-2   Widely Traded Stock Index Futures Contracts

Type of Contract	Contract Size	Exchange*	Open Interest February 15, 2000
Standard & Poor's 500 Index	$250 × index	CME	365 383
Standard & Poor's MIDCAP 400	$500 × index	CME	12 972
Nasdaq 100	$100 × index	CME	32 495
Nikkei 225 Stock Average	$5 × index	CME	16 526
Financial Times—Stock Exchange 100	£10 per point	LIFFE	244 855

*Exchange abbreviations:

CME, Chicago Merchantile Exchange;

LIFFE, London International Financial Futures Exchange.

Source: *Wall Street Journal*, February 16, 2000, p. C20.

TABLE 13-3   Widely Traded Currency Futures Contracts

Type of Contract	Contract Size	Exchange*	Open Interest February 15, 2000
Japanese yen	12 500 000 yen	CME	122 393
Canadian dollar	100 000 C$	CME	66 877
British pound	62 500 pounds	CME	48 047
Swiss franc	125 000 francs	CME	70 946
Mexican peso	500 000 new pesos	CME	20 802

*Exchange abbreviations: CME, Chicago Mercantile Exchange.

Source: *Wall Street Journal*, February 16, 2000, p. C20.

London International
Financial Futures and
Options Exchange
www.liffe.com

Tokyo Stock Exchange
www.tse.or.jp/english

Marché à Terme
International de France
www.matif.fr

Osaka Securities
Exchange
www.ose.or.jp

Japanese government bond contracts and Euroyen contracts traded on the Tokyo Stock Exchange, French government bond contracts traded on the Marché à Terme International de France, and Nikkei 225 contracts traded on the Osaka Securities Exchange. All became among the most widely traded futures contracts in the world.

International competition has also spurred knockoffs of the most popular financial futures contracts initially developed in the United States. These contracts traded on financial futures exchanges in other countries are virtually identical to those traded in the United States and have the advantage that they can be traded when the American exchanges are closed. The movement to 24-hour-a-day trading in financial futures has been further stimulated by the development of the Globex electronic trading system, which allows traders throughout the world to trade futures even when the exchanges are not officially open. Financial futures trading has thus become completely internationalized, and competition between financial futures exchanges in the U.S. and other countries will be intense in the future.

Explaining the Success of Futures Markets

There are several differences between financial futures and forward contracts and in the organization of their markets that help explain why financial futures markets like those for Canadian government bonds have been so successful.

Several features of futures contracts were designed to overcome the liquidity problem inherent in forward contracts. The first feature is that, in contrast to forward contracts, the quantities delivered and the delivery dates of futures contracts are standardized, making it more likely that different parties can be matched up in the futures market, thereby increasing the liquidity of the market. In the case of the 10-year Canadian government bond futures contract, the quantity delivered is $100 000 face value of bonds, and the delivery dates are set to be the last business day of March, June, September, and December. The second feature is that after the futures contract has been bought or sold, it can be traded (bought or sold) again at any time until the delivery date. In contrast, once a forward contract is agreed on, it typically cannot be traded. The third feature is that in a futures contract, not just one specific type of Canada bond is deliverable on the delivery date, as in a forward contract. In the case, for example, of the 10-year Canadian government bond futures contract, any Canada bond that matures in 8 to $10\frac{1}{2}$ years is eligible for delivery. Allowing continuous trading also increases the liquidity of the futures market, as does the ability to deliver a range of Canada bonds rather than one specific bond.

Another reason futures contracts specify that more than one bond is eligible for delivery is to limit the possibility that someone might corner the market and "squeeze" traders who have sold contracts. To corner the market, someone buys up all the deliverable securities so that investors with a short position cannot obtain from anyone else the securities that they contractually must deliver on the delivery date. As a result, the person who has cornered the market can set exorbitant prices for the securities that investors with a short position must buy to fulfill their obligations under the futures contract. The person who has cornered the market makes a fortune, but investors with a short position take a terrific loss. Clearly, the possibility that corners might occur in the market will discourage people from taking a short position and might therefore decrease the size of the market. By allowing many different securities to be delivered, the futures contract makes it harder for anyone to corner the market because a much larger amount of securities would have to be purchased to establish the corner. Corners are a concern to both regulators and the organized exchanges that design futures contracts.

Trading in the futures market has been organized differently from trading in forward markets to overcome the default risk problems arising in forward contracts. In both types, for every contract, there must be a buyer who is taking a long position and a seller who is taking a short position. However, the buyer and seller of a futures contract make their contract not with each other but with the clearinghouse associated with the futures exchange. This setup means that the buyer of the futures contract does not need to worry about the financial health or trustworthiness of the seller, or vice versa, as in the forward market. As long as the clearinghouse is financially solid, buyers and sellers of futures contracts do not have to worry about default risk.

To make sure that the clearinghouse is financially sound and does not run into financial difficulties that might jeopardize its contracts, buyers or sellers of futures contracts must put an initial deposit, called a **margin requirement**, of perhaps $2000 per Canada bond contract into a margin account kept at their brokerage firm. Futures contracts are then **marked to market** every day. What this means is that at the end of every trading day, the change in the value of the futures contract is added to or subtracted from the margin account. Suppose that after you buy the Canada bond contract at a price of 115 on Wednesday morning, its closing price at the end of the day, the *settlement price,* falls to 114. You now have a loss of 1 point, or $1000, on the contract, and the seller who sold you the contract has a gain of 1 point, or $1000. The $1000 gain is added to the seller's margin account, making a total of $3000 in that account, and the $1000 loss is subtracted from your account, so you now only have $1000 in your account. If the amount in this margin account falls below the maintenance margin requirement (which can be the same as the initial requirement but is usually a little less), the trader is required to add money to the account. For example, if the maintenance margin requirement is also $2000, you would have to add $1000 to your account to bring it up to $2000. Margin requirements and marking to market make it far less likely that a trader will default on a contract, thus protecting the futures exchange from losses.

A final advantage that futures markets have over forward markets is that most futures contracts do not result in delivery of the underlying asset on the expiration date, whereas forward contracts do. A trader who sold a futures contract is allowed to avoid delivery on the expiration date by making an offsetting purchase of a futures contract. Because the simultaneous holding of the long and short positions means that the trader would in effect be delivering the bonds to itself, under the exchange rules the trader is allowed to cancel both contracts. Allowing traders to cancel their contracts in this way lowers the cost of conducting trades in the futures market relative to the forward market in that a futures trader can avoid the costs of physical delivery, which is not so easy with forward contracts.

APPLICATION | *Hedging Foreign Exchange Risk*

As we discussed in Chapter 7, foreign exchange rates have been highly volatile in recent years. The large fluctuations in exchange rates subject financial institutions and other businesses to significant foreign exchange risk because they generate substantial gains and losses. Luckily for financial institution managers, the financial derivatives discussed in this chapter—forward and financial futures contracts—can be used to hedge foreign exchange risk.

To understand how financial institution managers manage foreign exchange risk, let's suppose that in January, the First Bank's customer Frivolous Luxuries, Inc. is due a payment of 20 million deutsche marks (DM) in two months for $10 million worth of goods it has just sold in Germany—we assume that the deutsche mark per dollar exchange rate is DM 2. Frivolous Luxuries is concerned that if the value of the deutsche mark falls substantially from its current value of 50 cents, the company might suffer a large loss because the DM 20 million payment will no longer be worth $10 million. So Sam, the CEO of Frivolous Luxuries, calls up his friend Mona, the manager of the First Bank, and asks her to hedge this foreign exchange risk for his company. Let's see how the bank manager does this using forward and financial futures contracts.

Hedging Foreign Exchange Risk with Forward Contracts

Forward markets in foreign exchange have been highly developed by commercial banks and investment banking operations that engage in extensive foreign exchange trading and so are widely used to hedge foreign exchange risk. Mona knows that she can use this market to hedge the foreign exchange risk for Frivolous Luxuries. Such a hedge is quite straightforward for her to execute. She just enters a forward contract that obligates her to sell DM 20 million two months from now in exchange for dollars at the current forward rate of $0.50 per mark.[4]

In two months, when her customer receives the DM 20 million, the forward contract ensures that it is exchanged for dollars at an exchange rate of $0.50 per mark, thus yielding $10 million. No matter what happens to future exchange rates, Frivolous Luxuries will be guaranteed $10 million for the goods it sold in Germany. Mona calls up her friend Sam to let him know that his company is now protected from any foreign exchange movements, and he thanks her for her help.

Hedging Foreign Exchange Risk with Futures Contracts

As an alternative, Mona could have used the currency futures market to hedge the foreign exchange risk. In this case, she would see that the Chicago Mercantile Exchange has a March deutsche mark contract with a contract amount of DM 125 000 and a price of $0.50 per mark. To do the hedge, Mona must sell DM 20 million of the March futures, and since the contract size is DM 125 000, she sells 20 million ÷ 125 000 = 160 contracts. Given the $0.50-per-mark price, the sale of the contracts yields 160 × DM 125 000 × $0.50 = $10 million. The futures hedge thus again enables her to lock in the exchange rate for Frivolous Luxuries so that it gets its payment of $10 million.

One advantage of using the futures market is that the contract size of DM 125 000, worth $62 500, is quite a bit smaller than the minimum size of a forward contract, which is usually $1 million or more. However, in this case, the bank manager is making a large enough transaction that she can use either the forward or the futures market. Her choice depends on whether the transaction costs are lower in one market than in the other. If the First Bank is active in the forward market, that market would probably have the lowest transaction costs, but if First Bank rarely deals in foreign exchange forward contracts, the bank manager may do better by sticking with the futures market.

Stock Index Futures Contracts

Kansas City Board of Trade
www.kcbt.com

New York Mercantile Exchange
www.nymex.com

As we saw in Chapter 12, institutional investors, including pension and mutual funds, have become a more important force in the stock market. In addition, many small investors recognized that mutual funds have a hard time beating the market, and index funds (mutual funds that focus on producing returns similar to those on broad market indexes) became increasingly popular. The increased importance of institutional investors along with the increased focus on tracking market indexes led to an increased demand for a more liquid market in a basket of stocks that track the market.

Given this need in the marketplace, a natural extension to the already successful markets in interest-rate futures occurred in 1982. The financial innovation was futures trading in stock price indexes at the Chicago Board of Trade (CBT), the Chicago Mercantile Exchange (CME), the Kansas City Board of Trade (KCBT), and the New York Futures Exchange (NYFE), a subsidiary of the New York Stock Exchange. In Canada, futures contracts on stock indexes are traded in the Toronto Futures Exchange (TFE), a subsidiary of the Toronto Stock Exchange. The futures trading in stock price indexes is now quite controversial because critics assert that

---

[4]The forward exchange rate will probably differ slightly from the spot rate of 50 cents per mark because the interest rates in Germany and Canada may not be equal. In that case, as we saw in Equation 2 in Chapter 7, the future expected exchange rate will not equal the spot rate and neither will the forward rate. However, since interest differentials have typically been less than 6% at an annual rate (1% bimonthly), the expected appreciation or depreciation of the mark over a two-month period has always been less than 1%. Thus the forward rate is always close to the spot rate, and so our assumption in the example that the forward rate and the spot rate are the same is a reasonable one.

it has led to substantial increases in market volatility, especially in such episodes as 1987's Black Monday crash.

Stock index futures differ from most other financial futures in that they are settled with a cash delivery rather than with the delivery of a security. Cash settlement gives these contracts the advantage of a high degree of liquidity and also rules out the possibility of anyone's cornering the market. The "Following the Financial News" box provides an illustration of how prices on stock index futures contracts are quoted. Note that the price quotes are in terms of index points, and that a change of 1 point represents a change of $500 in the contract's value. Let's look at the Toronto 35 Index futures contract, the most widely traded stock index futures contract in Canada.[5] On March 1, 1999, the settlement price of the March 1999 futures contract for the Toronto 35 Index was $500 times the index, that is, $175 250 ($500 × 350.50).

To understand what all this means, let's look at what happens when you buy or sell this futures contract. Suppose that on February 1, you sell one June contract at a price of 350 (that is, $175 000). By selling the contract, you agree to a delivery amount due of $500 times the Toronto 35 Index on the expiration date at the end of June. By buying the contract at a price of 350, the buyer has agreed to pay $175 000 for the delivery amount due of $500 times the Toronto 35 Index at the expiration date at the end of June. If the stock market falls so that the Toronto

---

FOLLOWING THE FINANCIAL NEWS

Stock Index Futures

The prices for stock index futures contracts are published daily. In the *National Post: Financial Post*, these prices are found in the "Future Prices" columns under the "Indexes" heading. An excerpt is reproduced here.

Lifetime				Daily				
High	Low	Mth	Open	High	Low	Settle	Chg	Prev. op. int
Indexes								
Toronto 35 (TFE)								
500 × index points; 0.05 pt.=$25 per contract								
381.70	338.90	Mar99	349.80	351.00	347.20	350.50	-0.50	22 591
351.60	351.60	June99	...	...	...	352.97	...	2975
Vol. 8097	Prev. vol. 1584	Open int. 25 566						
Toronto 100 (TFE)								
500 × index points; 0.05 pt.=$25 per contract								
417.00	383.00	Mar99	...	...	...	385.50	...	1228
Vol. 0	Prev. vol. 0	Open int. 1555						

Source: Excerpted with permission from *The Financial Post*, March 2, 1999, p.C18.

Like interest-rate futures contracts, the price quotes of stock index futures are also in points. Each point equals $500 and the smallest change in price is one twentieth of a point ($25.00). In the case, for example, of the Toronto Futures Exchange's March 1999 futures contract on the Toronto 35 Index, the settlement price on March 1, 1999 was 350.50 times the index, that is, $175 250 ($500 × 350.50).

---

[5]The Toronto 35 Index is made up of 35 of Canada's largest publicly listed companies.

35 Index declines to 300 on the expiration date, the buyer of the contract will have lost $25 000 because he or she has agreed to pay $175 000 for the contract but has a delivery amount due of only $150 000 (300 × $500). But you, the seller of the contract, will have a profit of $25 000 because you agreed to receive a $175 000 purchase price for the contract but have a delivery amount due of only $150 000. Because the amounts payable and due are netted out, only $25 000 will change hands; you, the seller of the contract, receive $25 000 from the buyer.

OPTIONS

Another vehicle for hedging interest-rate, foreign exchange, and stock market risk involves the use of options on financial instruments. **Options** are contracts that give the purchaser the option, or *right,* to buy or sell the underlying financial instrument at a specified price, called the **exercise price** or **strike price**, within a specific period of time (the *term to expiration*). The seller (sometimes called the *writer*) of the option is *obligated* to buy or sell the financial instrument to the purchaser if the owner of the option exercises the right to sell or buy. These option contract features are important enough to be emphasized: the *owner* or buyer of an option does not have to exercise the option; he or she can let the option expire without using it. Hence the *owner* of an option is *not obligated* to take any action but rather has the *right* to exercise the contract if he or she so chooses. The *seller* of an option, by contrast, has no choice in the matter; he or she *must* buy or sell the financial instrument if the owner exercises the option.

Because the right to buy or sell a financial instrument at a specified price has value, the buyer of an option is willing to pay an amount for it called a **premium**. There are two types of option contracts. **American options** can be exercised *at any time up to* the expiration date of the contract, and **European options** can be exercised only *on* the expiration date.

Option contracts are written on a number of financial instruments (an example of which is shown in the "Following the Financial News" box). Options on individual stocks are called **stock options**, and such options have existed for a long time. Option contracts on financial futures called **financial futures options** or, more commonly, **futures options**, were developed in 1982 and have become the most widely traded option contracts.

You might wonder why option contracts are more likely to be written on financial futures than on underlying financial instruments such as bonds. As you saw earlier in the chapter, at the expiration date, the price of the futures contract and of the deliverable debt instrument will be the same because of arbitrage. So it would seem that investors should be indifferent about having the option written on the financial instrument or on the futures contract. However, financial futures contracts have been so well designed that their markets are often more liquid than the markets in the underlying financial instruments. So investors would rather have the option contract written on the more liquid instrument, in this case the futures contract. That explains why the most popular futures options are written on many of the same futures contracts listed in Tables 13-1, 13-2, and 13-3.

In Canada, the regulation of option markets is the responsibility of the Canadian Derivatives Clearing Corporation (CDCC), a firm that since March 31, 2000 is owned by the Montreal Exchange (now Bourse de Montreal Inc.) The regulation of U.S. option markets is split between the Securities and Exchange Commission (SEC), which regulates stock options, and the Commodity Futures Trading Commission (CFTC), which regulates futures options. Regulation focuses on ensuring that writers of options have enough capital to make good on their contractual obligations and on overseeing traders and exchanges to prevent fraud and ensure that the market is not being manipulated.

Canadian Derivatives
Clearing Corporation
www.cdcc.ca

FOLLOWING THE FINANCIAL NEWS

Futures Options

The prices for financial futures options are published daily. In the *National Post: Financial Post*, they are found in the section "Futures Options." An excerpt from this listing is reproduced here.

Interest Rate

Canadian Govt. Bonds 9% (ME)
$100 000, points of 100%

Strike	Calls-Settle			Puts-Settle		
	Apr	May	June	Apr	May	June
124	0.32	0.62	0.89	0.90	1.20	1.47
125	0.09	0.31	0.54	1.68	1.89	2.11
126	0.02	0.14	0.31	2.60	2.71	2.87
127	r	0.05	0.16	3.59	3.62	3.71

Prev. open int. 0   Prev. open int. 0

Information for each contract is reported in columns, as follows. (The Montreal Exchange's option on its Canada bonds futures contract is used as an example.)

Strike Price: Strike (exercise) price of each contract, which runs from 124 to 127

Calls-Settle: Premium (price) at settlement for call options on the Canada bond futures expiring in the month listed, with each full point representing $1000; at a strike price of 125, the April call option's premium is 0.09, or $90 per contract

Puts-Settle: Premium (price) at settlement for put options on the Canada bond futures expiring in the month listed, with each full point representing $1000; at a strike price of 125, the April put option's premium is 1.68, or $1680 per contract

Source: Excerpted with permission from *The Financial Post*, March 2, 1999, p. C18.

Option Contracts

A **call option** is a contract that gives the owner the right to *buy* a financial instrument at the exercise price within a specific period of time. A **put option** is a contract that gives the owner the right to *sell* a financial instrument at the exercise price within a specific period of time.

Study Guide

Remembering which is a call option and which is a put option is not always easy. To keep them straight, just remember that having a call option to buy a financial instrument is the same as having the option to call in the instrument for delivery at a specified price. Having a put option to sell a financial instrument is the same as having the option to put up an instrument for the other party to buy.

Profits and Losses on Option and Futures Contracts

To understand option contracts more fully, let's first examine the option on the same June 10-year Canadian government bond futures contract that we looked at earlier in the chapter. Recall that if you buy this futures contract at a price of 115 (that is, $115 000), you have agreed to pay $115 000 for $100 000 face value of long-term Canada bonds when they are delivered to you at the end of June. If you sold this futures contract at a price of 115, you agreed, in exchange for $115 000, to deliver $100 000 face value of the long-term Canada bonds at the end of June. An option contract on the Canada bond futures contract has several key features: (1) It has the same expiration date as the underlying futures contract, (2) it is an American option and so can be exercised at any time before the expiration date, and (3) the premium (price) of the option is quoted in points that are the same as in the futures contract, so each point corresponds to $1000. If, for a premium of $2000, you buy one call option contract on the June Canada bond contract with an exercise price of 115, you have purchased the right to buy (call in) the June Canada bond futures contract for a price of 115 ($115 000 per contract) at any time through the expiration date of this contract at the end of June. Similarly, when for $2000 you buy a put option on the June Canada bond contract with an exercise price of 115, you have the right to sell (put up) the June Canada bond futures contract for a price of 115 ($115 000 per contract) at any time until the end of June.

Futures option contracts are somewhat complicated, so to explore how they work and how they can be used to hedge risk, let's first examine how profits and losses on the call option on the June Canada bond futures contract occur. In February, our old friend Irving the Investor buys, for a $2000 premium, a call option on the $100 000 June Canada bond futures contract with a strike price of 115. (We assume that if Irving exercises the option, it is on the expiration date at the end of June and not before.) On the expiration date at the end of June, suppose that the underlying Canada bond for the futures contract has a price of 110. Recall that on the expiration date, arbitrage forces the price of the futures contract to be the same as the price of the underlying bond, so it too has a price of 110 on the expiration date at the end of June. If Irving exercises the call option and buys the futures contract at an exercise price of 115, he will lose money by buying at 115 and selling at the lower market price of 110. Because Irving is smart, he will not exercise the option, but he will be out the $2000 premium he paid. In such a situation, in which the price of the underlying financial instrument is below the exercise price, a call option is said to be "out of the money." At the price of 110 (less than the exercise price), Irving thus suffers a loss on the option contract of the $2000 premium he paid. This loss is plotted as point A in panel (a) of Figure 13-1.

On the expiration date, if the price of the futures contract is 115, the call option is "at the money," and Irving is indifferent whether he exercises his option to buy the futures contract or not, since exercising the option at 115 when the market price is also at 115 produces no gain or loss. Because he has paid the $2000 premium, at the price of 115 his contract again has a net loss of $2000, plotted as point B.

If the futures contract instead has a price of 120 on the expiration day, the option is "in the money," and Irving benefits from exercising the option. He would buy the futures contract at the exercise price of 115 and then sell it for 120, thereby earning a 5-point gain ($5000 profit) on the $100 000 Canada bond futures contract. Because Irving paid a $2000 premium for the option contract, however, his net profit is $3000 ($5000 − $2000). The $3000 profit at a price of 120 is plotted as point C. Similarly, if the price of the futures contract rose to 125, the option contract would yield a net profit of $8000 ($10 000 from exercising the option minus the $2000 premium), plotted as point D. Plotting these points, we get the kinked profit curve for the call option that we see in panel (a).

Suppose that instead of purchasing the futures *option* contract in February, Irving decides instead to buy the $100 000 June Canada bond *futures* contract at the price of 115. If the price of the bond on the expiration day at the end of June declines to 110, meaning that the price of the futures contract also falls to 110, Irving suffers a loss of 5 points, or $5000. The loss of $5000 on the futures contract at a price of 110 is plotted as point A′ in panel (a). At a price of 115 on the

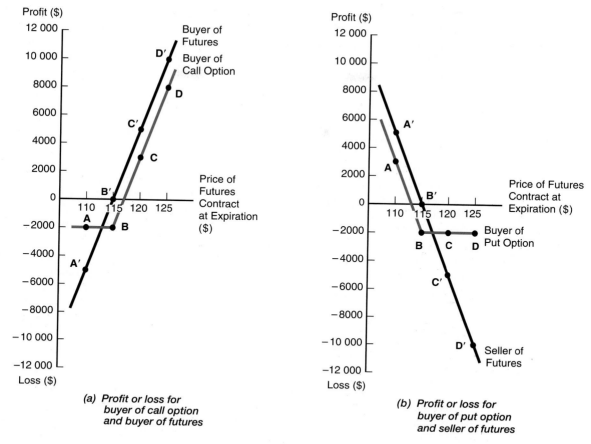

FIGURE 13·1 Profits and Losses on Options Versus Futures Contracts

The futures contract is the $100 000 June Canada bond contract, and the option contracts are written on this futures contract with an exercise price of 115. Panel (a) shows the profits and losses for the buyer of the call option and the buyer of the futures contract, and panel (b) shows the profits and losses for the buyer of the put option and the seller of the futures contract.

expiration date, Irving would have a zero profit on the futures contract, plotted as point B'. At a price of 120, Irving would have a profit on the contract of 5 points, or $5000 (point C'), and at a price of 125, the profit would be 10 percentage points, or $10 000 (point D'). Plotting these points, we get the linear (straight-line) profit curve for the futures contract that appears in panel (a).

Now we can see the major difference between a futures contract and an option contract. As the profit curve for the futures contract in panel (a) indicates, the futures contract has a linear profit function: profits grow by an equal dollar amount for every point increase in the price of the underlying financial instrument. By contrast, the kinked profit curve for the option contract is nonlinear, meaning that profits do not always grow by the same amount for a given change in the price of the underlying financial instrument. The reason for this nonlinearity is that the call option protects Irving from having losses that are greater than the amount of the $2000 premium. In contrast, Irving's loss on the futures contract is $5000 if the price on the expiration day falls to 110, and if the price falls even further, Irving's loss will be even greater. This insurance-like feature of option contracts explains why their purchase price is referred to as a premium. Once the underlying financial instrument's price rises above the exercise price, however, Irving's profits grow linearly. Irving has given up something by buying an option rather than a futures contract. As we see in panel (a), when the price of the underlying financial instrument rises above the exercise price, Irving's profits are always less than that on the futures contract by exactly the $2000 premium he paid.

Panel (b) plots the results of the same profit calculations if Irving buys not a call but a put option (an option to sell) with an exercise price of 115 for a premium of $2000 and if he sells the futures contract rather than buying one. In this case, if on the expiration date the Canada bond futures have a price above the 115-exercise price, the put option is "out of the money." Irving would not want to exercise the put option and then have to sell the futures contract he owns as a result at a price below the market price and lose money. He would not exercise his option, and he would be out only the $2000 premium he paid. Once the price of the futures contract falls below the 115 exercise price, Irving benefits from exercising the put option because he can sell the futures contract at a price of 115 but can buy it at a price below this. In such a situation, in which the price of the underlying instrument is below the exercise price, the put option is "in the money," and profits rise linearly as the price of the futures contract falls. The profit function for the put option illustrated in panel (b) of Figure 13-1 is kinked, indicating that Irving is protected from losses greater than the amount of the premium he paid. The profit curve for the sale of the futures contract is just the negative of the profit for the futures contract in panel (a) and is therefore linear.

Panel (b) of Figure 13-1 confirms the conclusion from panel (a) that profits on option contracts are nonlinear but profits on futures contracts are linear.

Study Guide

To make sure you understand how profits and losses on option and futures contracts are generated, calculate the net profits on the put option and the short position in the futures contract at prices on the expiration day of 110, 115, 120, and 125. Then verify that your calculations correspond to the points plotted in panel (b) of Figure 13-1.

Two other differences between futures and option contracts must be mentioned. The first is that the initial investment on the contracts differs. As we saw earlier in the chapter, when a futures contract is purchased, the investor must put up a fixed amount, the margin requirement, in a margin account. But when an option contract is purchased, the initial investment is the premium that must be paid for the contract. The second important difference between the contracts is that the futures contract requires money to change hands daily when the contract is marked to market, whereas the option contract requires money to change hands only when it is exercised.

APPLICATION | *Hedging with Futures Options*

Earlier in the chapter, we saw how the First Bank could hedge the interest-rate risk on its $5 million holdings of 8% coupon bonds maturing in 2015 by selling $5 million of Canada bond futures. A rise in interest rates and the resulting fall in bond prices and bond futures contracts would lead to profits on the bank's sale of the futures contracts that would exactly offset the losses on the 8% coupon bonds maturing in 2015 the bank is holding.

As panel (b) of Figure 13-1 suggests, an alternative way for the manager to protect against a rise in interest rates and hence a decline in bond prices is to buy $5 million of put options written on the same Canada bond futures. As long as the exercise price is not too far from the current price as in panel (b), the rise in interest rates and decline in bond prices will lead to profits on the futures and the futures put options, profits that will offset any losses on the $5 million of Canada bonds.

The one problem with using options rather than futures is that the First Bank will have to pay premiums on the options contracts, thereby lowering the bank's profits in order to hedge the interest-rate risk. Why might the bank manager be willing to use options rather than futures to conduct the hedge? The answer is that the option contract, unlike the futures contract, allows the First Bank to gain if interest rates decline and bond prices rise. With the hedge using futures contracts, the First Bank does not gain from increases in bond prices because the profits on the bonds it is holding are offset by the losses from the futures contracts it has sold. However, as panel (b) of Figure 13-1 indicates, the situation when the hedge is conducted with put options is quite different. Once bond prices rise above the exercise price, the bank does not suffer additional losses on the option contracts. At the same time, the value of the Canada bonds the bank is holding will increase, thereby leading to a profit for the bank. Thus using options rather than futures to conduct the micro hedge allows the bank to protect itself from rises in interest rates but still allows the bank to benefit from interest-rate declines (although the profit is reduced by the amount of the premium).

Similar reasoning indicates that the bank manager might prefer to use options to conduct the macro hedge to immunize the entire bank portfolio from interest-rate risk. Again, the strategy of using options rather than futures has the disadvantage that the First Bank has to pay the premiums on these contracts up front. By contrast, using options allows the bank to keep the gains from a decline in interest rates (which will raise the value of the bank's assets relative to its liabilities) because these gains will not be offset by large losses on the option contracts.

In the case of a macro hedge, there is another reason why the bank might prefer option contracts to futures contracts. Profits and losses on futures contracts can cause accounting problems for banks because such profits and losses are not allowed to be offset by unrealized changes in the value of the rest of the bank's portfolio. Consider the case when interest rates fall. If First Bank sells futures contracts to conduct the macro hedge, then when interest rates fall and the prices of the Canada bond futures contracts rise, it will have large losses on these contracts. Of course, these losses are offset by unrealized profits in the rest of the bank's portfolio, but the bank is not allowed to offset these losses in its accounting statements. So even though the macro hedge is serving its intended purpose of immunizing the bank's portfolio from interest-rate risk, the bank would experience large accounting losses when interest rates fall. Indeed, bank managers have lost their jobs when perfectly sound hedges with interest-rate futures have led to large accounting losses. Not surprisingly, bank managers might shrink from using financial futures to conduct macro hedges for this reason.

Futures options, however, can come to the rescue of the managers of banks and other financial institutions. Suppose that First Bank conducted the macro hedge by buying put options instead of selling Canada bond futures. Now if interest rates fall and bond prices rise well above the exercise price, the bank will not have large losses on the option contracts because it will just decide not to exercise its options. The bank will not suffer the accounting problems produced by hedging with financial futures. Because of the accounting advantages of using futures options to conduct macro hedges, option contracts have become important to financial institution managers as tools for hedging interest-rate risk.

Factors Affecting the Prices of Option Premiums

If we again look closely at the *National Post: Financial Post* entry for Canada bond futures options in the "Following the Financial News" box, we learn several interesting facts about how the premiums on option contracts are priced. The first thing you may have noticed is that when the strike (exercise) price is higher, the premium for the call option is lower and the premium for the put option is higher. For example, when the strike price rises from 124 to 126, the premium for the May call option falls from 0.62 to 0.14, and the premium for the May put option rises from 1.20 to 2.71.

Our understanding of the profit function for option contracts illustrated in Figure 13-1 helps explain this fact. As we saw in panel (a), a higher price for the underlying financial instrument (in this case a Canada bond futures contract) relative to the option's exercise price results in higher profits on the call (buy) option. Thus the lower the strike price, the higher the profits on the call option contract and the greater the call premium that investors like Irving are willing to pay. Similarly, we saw in panel (b) that a higher price for the underlying financial instrument relative to the exercise price lowers profits on the put (sell) option, so that a higher strike price increases profits and thus causes the put premium to increase.

The second thing you may have noticed in the *National Post: Financial Post* entry is that as the period of time over which the option can be exercised (the term to expiration) gets longer, the premiums for both call and put options rise. For example, at a strike price of 125, the premium on the call option increases from 0.09 in April to 0.31 in May and to 0.54 in June. Similarly, the premium on the put option increases from 1.68 in April to 1.89 in May and to 2.11 in June. The fact that premiums increase with the term to expiration is also explained by the nonlinear profit function for option contracts. As the term to expiration lengthens, there is a greater chance that the price of the underlying financial instrument will be very high or very low by the expiration date. If the price becomes very high and goes well above the exercise price, the call (buy) option will yield a high profit, but if the price becomes very low and goes well below the exercise price, the losses will be small because the owner of the call option will simply decide not to exercise the option. The possibility of greater variability of the underlying financial instrument as the term to expiration lengthens raises profits on average for the call option.

Similar reasoning tells us that the put (sell) option will become more valuable as the term to expiration increases because the possibility of greater price variability of the underlying financial instrument increases as the term to expiration increases. The greater chance of a low price increases the chance that profits on the put option will be very high. But the greater chance of a high price does not produce substantial losses for the put option because the owner will again just decide not to exercise the option.

Another way of thinking about this reasoning is to recognize that option contracts have an element of "heads, I win; tails, I don't lose too badly." The greater variability of where the prices might be by the expiration date increases the value of both kinds of options. Since a longer term to the expiration date leads to greater variability of where the prices might be by the expiration date, a longer term to expiration raises the value of the option contract.

The reasoning that we have just developed also explains another important fact about option premiums. When the volatility of the price of the underlying instrument is great, the premiums for both call and put options will be higher. Higher volatility of prices means that for a given expiration date, there will again be greater variability of where the prices might be by the expiration date. The "heads,

I win; tails, I don't lose too badly" property of options then means that the greater variability of possible prices by the expiration date increases average profits for the option and thus increases the premium that investors are willing to pay.

Summary

Our analysis of how profits on options are affected by price movements for the underlying financial instrument leads to the following conclusions about the factors that determine the premium on an option contract:

1. The higher the strike price, everything else being equal, the lower the premium on call (buy) options and the higher the premium on put (sell) options.

2. The greater the term to expiration, everything else being equal, the higher the premiums for both call and put options.

3. The greater the volatility of prices of the underlying financial instrument, everything else being equal, the higher the premiums for both call and put options.

The results we have derived here appear in more formal models, such as the Black-Scholes model, which analyze how the premiums on options are priced. You might study such models in finance courses.

INTEREST-RATE SWAPS

In addition to forwards, futures, and options, financial institutions use one other important financial derivative to manage risk. **Swaps** are financial contracts that obligate one party to exchange (swap) a set of payments it owns for another set of payments owned by another party. There are two basic kinds of swaps. **Currency swaps** involve the exchange of a set of payments in one currency for a set of payments in another currency. **Interest-rate swaps** involve the exchange of one set of interest payments for another set of interest payments, all denominated in the same currency.

Interest-Rate Swap Contracts

Interest-rate swaps are an important tool for managing interest-rate risk, and they first appeared in the United States in 1982 when there was an increase in the demand for financial instruments that could be used to reduce interest-rate risk. The most common type of interest-rate swap (called the *plain vanilla swap*) specifies (1) the interest rate on the payments that are being exchanged; (2) the type of interest payments (variable or fixed-rate); (3) the amount of **notional principal**, which is the amount on which the interest is being paid; and (4) the time period over which the exchanges continue to be made. There are many other more complicated versions of swaps, including forward swaps and swap options (called *swaptions*), but here we will look only at the plain vanilla swap. Figure 13-2 illustrates an interest-rate swap between First Trust and the Friendly Finance Company. First Trust agrees to pay Friendly Finance a fixed rate of 7% on $1 million of notional principal for the next ten years, and Friendly Finance agrees to pay First Trust the one-year Treasury bill rate plus 1% on $1 million of notional principal for the same period. Thus as shown in Figure 13-2, every year First Trust would be paying the Friendly Finance Company 7% on $1 million, while Friendly Finance would be paying First Trust the one-year T-bill rate plus 1% on $1 million.

| APPLICATION | *Hedging with Interest-Rate Swaps* |

You might wonder why these two parties find it advantageous to enter into this swap agreement. The answer is that it may help both of them hedge interest-rate risk.

Suppose that First Trust, which tends to borrow short-term and then lend long-term in the mortgage market, has $1 million less of rate-sensitive assets than it has of rate-sensitive liabilities. As we learned in Chapter 9, this situation means that as interest rates rise, the rise in the cost of funds (liabilities) is greater than the rise in interest payments it receives on its assets, many of which are fixed-rate. The result of rising interest rates is thus a shrinking of First Trust's net interest margin and a decline in its profitability. As we saw in Chapter 9, to avoid this interest-rate risk, First Trust would like to convert $1 million of its fixed-rate assets into $1 million of rate-sensitive assets, in effect making rate-sensitive assets equal rate-sensitive liabilities, thereby eliminating the gap. This is exactly what happens when it engages in the interest-rate swap. By taking $1 million of its fixed-rate income and exchanging it for $1 million of Treasury bill rate-sensitive income, it has converted income on $1 million of fixed-rate assets into income on $1 million of rate-sensitive assets. Now when interest rates increase, the rise in rate-sensitive income on its assets exactly matches the rise in the rate-sensitive cost of funds on its liabilities, leaving the net interest margin and bank profitability unchanged.

The Friendly Finance Company, which issues long-term bonds to raise funds and uses them to make short-term loans, finds that it is in exactly the opposite situation to First Trust: it has $1 million more of rate-sensitive assets than of rate-sensitive liabilities. It is therefore concerned that a fall in interest rates, which will result in a larger drop in income from its assets than the decline in the cost of funds on its liabilities, will cause a decline in profits. By doing the interest-rate swap, it eliminates this interest-rate risk because it has converted $1 million of rate-sensitive income into $1 million of fixed-rate income. Now the Friendly Finance Company finds that when interest rates fall, the decline in rate-sensitive income is smaller and so is matched by the decline in the rate-sensitive cost of funds on its liabilities, leaving its profitability unchanged.

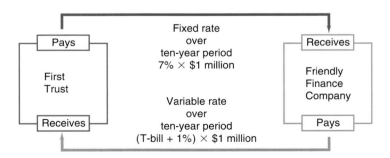

FIGURE 13-2 Interest-Rate Swap Payments
In this swap arrangement with a notional principal of $1 million and a term of ten years, First Trust pays a fixed rate of 7% × $1 million to the Friendly Finance Company, which in turn agrees to pay the one-year Treasury bill rate plus 1% × $1 million to First Trust.

Advantages of Interest-Rate Swaps

To eliminate interest-rate risk, both First Trust and the Friendly Finance Company could have rearranged their balance sheets by converting fixed-rate assets into rate-sensitive assets, and vice versa, instead of engaging in an interest-rate swap. However, this strategy would have been costly for both financial institutions for several reasons. The first is that financial institutions incur substantial transaction costs when they rearrange their balance sheets. Second, different financial institutions have informational advantages in making loans to certain customers who may prefer certain maturities. Thus, adjusting the balance sheet to eliminate interest-rate risk may result in a loss of these informational advantages, which the financial institution is unwilling to give up. Interest-rate swaps solve these problems for financial institutions because in effect they allow the institutions to convert fixed-rate assets into rate-sensitive assets without affecting the balance sheet. Large transaction costs are avoided, and the financial institutions can continue to make loans where they have an informational advantage.

We have seen that financial institutions can also hedge interest-rate risk with other financial derivatives such as futures contracts and futures options. Interest-rate swaps have one big advantage over hedging with these other derivatives: they can be written for very long horizons, sometimes as long as 20 years, whereas financial futures and futures options typically have much shorter horizons, not much more than a year. If a financial institution needs to hedge interest-rate risk for a long horizon, financial futures and option markets may not do it much good. Instead it can turn to the swap market.

Disadvantages of Interest-Rate Swaps

Although interest-rate swaps have important advantages that make them very popular with financial institutions, they also have disadvantages that limit their usefulness. Swap markets, like forward markets, can suffer from a lack of liquidity. Let's return to looking at the swap between First Trust and the Friendly Finance Company. As with a forward contract, it might be difficult for First Trust to link up with the Friendly Finance Company to arrange the swap. In addition, even if First Trust could find a counterparty like the Friendly Finance Company, it might not be able to negotiate a good deal because it couldn't find any other institution with which to negotiate.

Swap contracts also are subject to the same default risk that we encountered for forward contracts. If interest rates rise, the Friendly Finance Company would love to get out of the swap contract because the fixed-rate interest payments it receives are less than it could get in the open market. It might then default on the contract, exposing First Trust to a loss. Alternatively, the Friendly Finance Company could go bust, meaning that the terms of the swap contract would not be fulfilled.

Financial Intermediaries in Interest-Rate Swaps

As we have just seen, financial institutions do have to be aware of the possibility of losses from a default on swaps. As with a forward contract, each party to a swap must have a lot of information about the other party to make sure that the contract is likely to be fulfilled. The need for information about counterparties and the liquidity problems in swap markets could limit the usefulness of these markets. However, as we saw in Chapter 8, when informational and liquidity problems crop up in a market, financial intermediaries come to the rescue. That is exactly what happens in swap markets. Intermediaries such as investment banks and especially large banks have the ability to acquire information cheaply about the creditworthiness and reliability of parties to swap contracts and are also able to match up parties to a swap. Hence large chartered banks and investment banks have set up swap markets in which they act as intermediaries.

APPLICATION | *Are Financial Derivatives a Worldwide Time Bomb?*

Bank of England
**www.bankofengland.
co.uk**

Commodity Futures
Trading Commission
www.cftc.gov

With the bankruptcy of the Barings Bank in 1995 (discussed in Chapter 9), and the near failure of Long-Term Capital Management in 1998 (discussed in Chapter 12)—both of which involved trades in financial derivatives—politicians, the media, and regulators have become very concerned about the dangers of derivatives. This concern is international and has spawned a slew of reports issued by such organizations as the Bank for International Settlements (BIS), the Bank of England, the Group of Thirty, and the U.S. Commodity Futures Trading Commission (CFTC). Particularly scary are the notional amounts of derivatives contracts—tens of trillions of dollars worldwide—and the fact that banks, which are subject to bank panics, are major players in the derivatives markets. As a result of these fears, some politicians have called for restrictions on banks' involvement in the derivatives markets. Are financial derivatives a time bomb that could bring down the world financial system?

There are three major concerns about financial derivatives. First is that financial derivatives allow financial institutions to increase their leverage; that is, they can in effect control a proportion of the underlying asset that is many times greater than the amount of money they have had to put up. Increasing their leverage enables them to take huge bets on currency and interest-rate movements, which if they are wrong can bring down the bank, as was the case for Barings in 1995. This concern is valid. As we saw earlier in the chapter, the amount of money placed in margin accounts is only a small fraction of the price of the futures contract, meaning that small movements in the price of a contract can produce losses that are many times the size of the initial amount put in the margin account. Thus although financial derivatives can be used to hedge risk, they can also be used by financial institutions to take on excessive risk.

The second concern is that financial derivatives are too sophisticated for managers of financial institutions because they are so complicated. Although it is true that some financial derivatives can be so complex that some financial managers are not sophisticated enough to use them, this seems unlikely to apply to the big international financial institutions that are the major players in the derivatives markets. Indeed, in the Barings case, the bank was brought down not by trades in complex derivatives but rather by trades in one of the simplest of derivatives, stock index futures. (Recall from Chapter 9 that Barings's problem was more a lack of internal controls at the bank than a problem with derivatives per se.)

A third concern is that banks have holdings of huge notional amounts of financial derivatives, particularly swaps, that greatly exceed the amount of bank capital, and so these derivatives expose the banks to serious risk of failure. Banks are indeed major players in the financial derivatives markets, particularly the swaps market, where our earlier analysis has shown that they are the natural market-makers because they can act as intermediaries between two counterparties who would not make the swap without their involvement. However, looking at the notional amount of swaps at banks gives a very misleading picture of their risk exposure. Because banks act as intermediaries in the swap markets, they are typically exposed only to credit risk—a default by one of their counterparties. Furthermore, swaps, unlike loans, do not involve payments of the notional amount but rather the much smaller interest payments based on the notional amounts. For example, in the case of a 7% interest rate, the payment is only $70 000 for a $1 million swap. Estimates of the credit exposure from swap contracts indicate that they are on the order of 1% of the notional value of the contracts and that credit exposure at banks from derivatives is generally less than a quarter of their total credit exposure from loans. Banks' credit exposure from their derivatives activities is thus not out of line with other credit exposures they face.

The conclusion is that financial derivatives do present dangers for financial institutions, but some of these dangers have been overplayed. The biggest danger occurs in trading activities of financial institutions, and as we have seen in Chapter 11, regulators have been paying increased attention to this danger and have issued new disclosure requirements and regulatory guidelines for how derivatives trading should be done. The credit risk exposure posed by derivatives, by contrast, seems to be manageable with standard methods of dealing with credit risk, by both managers of financial institutions and their regulators.

SUMMARY

1. Interest-rate forward contracts, which are agreements to sell a debt instrument at a future (forward) point in time, can be used to hedge interest-rate risk. The advantage of forward contracts is that they are flexible, but the disadvantages are that they are subject to default risk and their market is illiquid.

2. A financial futures contract is similar to an interest-rate forward contract in that it specifies that a debt instrument must be delivered by one party to another on a stated future date. However, it has advantages over a forward contract in that it is not subject to default risk and is more liquid. Forward and futures contracts can be used by financial institutions to hedge (protect) against interest-rate risk.

3. An option contract gives the purchaser the right to buy (call option) or sell (put option) a security at the exercise (strike) price within a specific period of time. The profit function for options is nonlinear—profits do not always grow by the same amount for a given change in the price of the underlying financial instrument. The nonlinear profit function for options explains why their value (as reflected by the premium paid for them) is negatively related to the exercise price for call options, positively related to the exercise price for put options, positively related to the term to expiration for both call and put options, and positively related to the volatility of the prices of the underlying financial instrument for both call and put options. Financial institutions use

futures options to hedge interest-rate risk in a similar fashion to the way they use financial futures and forward contracts. Futures options may be preferred for macro hedges because they suffer from fewer accounting problems than financial futures.

4. Interest-rate swaps involve the exchange of one set of interest payments for another set of interest payments and have default risk and liquidity problems similar to those of forward contracts. As a result, interest-rate swaps often involve intermediaries such as large commercial banks and investment banks that make a market in swaps. Financial institutions find that interest-rate swaps are useful ways to hedge interest-rate risk. Interest-rate swaps have one big advantage over financial futures and options: they can be written for very long horizons.

5. There are three concerns about the dangers of derivatives. They allow financial institutions more easily to increase their leverage and take big bets (by effectively enabling them to hold a larger amount of the underlying assets than the amount of money put down), they are too complex for managers of financial institutions to understand, and they expose financial institutions to large credit risks because the huge notional amounts of derivative contracts greatly exceed the capital of these institutions. The second two dangers seem to be overplayed, but the danger from increased leverage using derivatives is real.

KEY TERMS

American option, p. 312

arbitrage, p. 304

call option, p. 313

currency swap, p. 319

European option, p. 312

exercise price (strike price), p. 312

financial derivatives, p. 300

financial futures, p. 302

financial futures option (futures option), p. 312

forward contract, p. 300

hedge, p. 301

interest-rate forward contract, p. 300

interest-rate futures contract, p. 302

QUESTIONS AND PROBLEMS

Questions marked with an asterisk are answered at the end of the book in an appendix, "Answers to Selected Questions and Problems."

1. If the pension fund you manage expects to have an inflow of $120 million six months from now, what forward contract would you seek to enter into to lock in current interest rates?

*2. If the portfolio you manage is holding $25 million Canada bonds with a price of 110, what forward contract would you enter into to hedge the interest-rate risk on these bonds over the coming year?

3. If at the expiration date, the deliverable Canada bond is selling for 101 but the Canada bond futures contract is selling for 102, what will happen to the futures price? Explain your answer.

*4. If you buy a $100 000 June Canada bond contract for 108 and the price of the deliverable Canada bond at the expiration date is 102, what is your profit or loss on the contract?

5. Suppose that the pension you are managing is expecting an inflow of funds of $100 million next year and you want to make sure that you will earn the current interest rate of 8% when you invest the incoming funds in long-term bonds. How would you use the futures market to do this?

*6. How would you use the options market to accomplish the same thing as in Problem 5? What are the advantages and disadvantages of using an options contract rather than a futures contract?

7. If you buy a put option on a $100 000 Canada bond futures contract with an exercise price of 95 and the price of the Canada bond is 120 at expiration, is the contract in the money, out of the money, or at the money? What is your profit or loss on the contract if the premium was $4000?

*8. Suppose that you buy a call option on a $100 000 Canada bond futures contract with an exercise price of 110 for a premium of $1500. If on expiration the futures contract has a price of 111, what is your profit or loss on the contract?

9. Explain why greater volatility or a longer term to maturity leads to a higher premium on both call and put options.

*10. Why does a lower strike price imply that a call option will have a higher premium and a put option a lower premium?

11. If the finance company you manage has a gap of +$5 million (rate-sensitive assets greater than rate-sensitive liabilities by $5 million), describe an interest-rate swap that would eliminate the company's income gap.

*12. If the bank you manage has a gap of −$42 million, describe an interest-rate swap that would eliminate the bank's income risk from changes in interest rates.

13. If your company has a payment of 200 million deutsche marks due one year from now, how would you hedge the foreign exchange risk in this payment with DM 125 000 futures contracts?

*14. If your company has to make a DM 10 million payment to a German company in June, three months from now, how would you hedge the foreign exchange risk in this payment with a DM 125 000 futures contract?

15. Suppose that your company will be receiving 30 million euros six months from now and the euro is currently selling for 1 euro per dollar. If you want to hedge the foreign exchange risk in this payment, what kind of forward contract would you want to enter into?

Chapter 14

Structure of Central Banks and the Bank of Canada

PREVIEW   Among the most important players in financial markets throughout the world are central banks, the government authorities in charge of monetary policy. Central banks' actions affect interest rates, the amount of credit, and the money supply, all of which have direct impacts not only on financial markets but also on aggregate output and inflation. To understand the role that central banks play in financial markets and the overall economy, we need to understand how these organizations work. Who controls central banks and determines their actions? What motivates their behaviour? Who holds the reins of power?

In this chapter we look at the institutional structure of major central banks and particularly focus on the Bank of Canada, Canada's central bank, often just called the Bank. We start by focusing on the formal institutional structure of the Bank and then examine the more relevant informal structure that determines who has the ultimate responsibility for monetary policy in Canada. By understanding who makes the decisions, we will have a better idea of how they are made. We then look at several other major central banks and see how they are organized. With this information, we will be more able to comprehend the actual conduct of monetary policy described in the following chapters.

ORIGINS OF THE BANK OF CANADA

Scattered agricultural settlements over vast geographical areas in Canada were for years individually served by local banks which, influenced by the British tradition, depended on a small number of banks with multiple branches. As long as the needs of the rural economy were satisfied by the evolution of a branch-banking system, the imperative for a central bank was downgraded and early attempts to establish such an institution in Canada were unsuccessful. In time, as the central government's needs for funding of its debt and managing fiat money became more important and as the worth of monetary policy came to be more appreciated, the creation of a central bank proved inevitable.

BOX 14-1

Establishment of Selected Central Banks

Canada did not have a central bank for almost the first 70 years after Confederation. By the time the Bank of Canada began operations in 1935, most other countries already had a central bank. In fact, as you can see in the table, Sweden and the United Kingdom created their central banks back in the seventeenth century. These early central banks, however, were initially privately owned and gradually evolved into modern publicly owned central banks.

Country	Year central bank was established
Sweden	1656
United Kingdom	1694
France	1800
Belgium	1850
Germany	1875
Japan	1882
Italy	1893
Switzerland	1905
United States	1913
Canada	1935

Source: Forrest H. Capie, Terence C. Mills, and Geoffrey E. Wood, "Central Bank Dependence and Inflation Performance: An Exploratory Data Analysis," in *Varieties of Monetary Reform: Lessons and Experiences on the Road to Monetary Union*, ed. Pierre L. Siklos (Dordrecht, The Netherlands: Kluwer Academic Publishers, 1994), pp. 95-132. Reprinted with permission of the publisher.

The devastation of the Great Depression was of fundamental importance in the creation of the Bank of Canada. From 1929 to 1933, Canadian real GDP fell by almost 30% and the unemployment rate increased sevenfold from less than 3% to close to 20%. The Great Depression involved not only the largest decline in the level of economic activity in the history of Canada, but was also followed by an extremely slow recovery. Being such a cataclysmic event, the Great Depression contributed to significant changes in government policy, including fiscal policy, monetary policy, banking policy, and international policy.

In particular, as the depth of the Great Depression was blamed on the operation of the monetary system, in 1933 the federal Conservative government established a royal commission to study the problems of the Great Depression. Based on a recommendation of the royal commission, Parliament passed the Bank of Canada Act in 1934 and the newly founded Bank of Canada started operations on March 11, 1935. By this time, most other countries already had a central bank (Box 14-1). Although the primary motivation for the formation of the Bank of Canada was economic (or monetary), other motives within the government were the need for Canada to reflect its growing political independence from Britain and the need to coordinate its international economic policy.

Initially the Bank of Canada was a private institution but was nationalized in 1938, so it is now a national institution with headquarters in Ottawa. The Bank also has regional offices in Toronto, Vancouver, Calgary, Montreal, and Halifax. Unlike a private bank that operates in pursuit of profit, the Bank of Canada is responsible for the country's monetary policy and for the regulation of Canada's deposit-based financial institutions.

FORMAL STRUCTURE OF THE BANK OF CANADA

The overall responsibility for the operation of the Bank of Canada rests with a **Board of Directors**, which consists of fifteen members—the governor, the senior deputy governor, the deputy minister of finance, and twelve outside directors. The Board appoints the governor and senior deputy governor with the government's

The Political Environment and the Bank of Canada

Since the inception of the Bank of Canada there have been seven governors:

1935–1954, Graham Towers
1955–1961, James Coyne
1961–1973, Louis Rasminsky
1973–1987, Gerald Bouey
1987–1994, John Crow
1994–2000, Gordon Thiessen
2001–, David Dodge

It is interesting to note that during the same period Canadians went to the polls twenty times to elect a federal government. The Bank of Canada is not completely independent from the government. For example, the government can directly influence the Bank by not renewing the governor's appointment when it expires, as the Liberal government did in 1994 when it didn't renew the appointment of John Crow, who was appointed by the Conservative government in 1987.

approval, for a renewable term of seven years. The outside directors are appointed by the minister of finance, with cabinet approval, for a three-year term and they are required to come from all regions of Canada representing a variety of occupations with the exception of banking. The governor of the Bank is the chief executive officer and chairman of the Board of Directors. Currently, the governor of the Bank of Canada is David Dodge (Box 14-2).

In 1994 the Board of Directors made some changes in the internal organization of the Bank. Most prominently the Board established a new senior decision-making authority within the Bank called the **Governing Council**. The Council is chaired by the governor and is composed of the senior deputy governor and the four deputy governors. Since this change, the six members of the Governing Council of the Bank collectively assume responsibility for the Bank's new semi-annual *Monetary Policy Report*, issued in May and November, and its *Update*, issued in January and July. This system of "collective responsibility" ensures that the Bank's governor is not personally identified with the Bank's policy.

THE FUNCTIONS OF THE BANK OF CANADA

In the words of the preamble of the Bank of Canada Act, the functions of the Bank of Canada are

"to regulate credit and currency in the best interests of the economic life of the nation, to control and protect the external value of the national monetary unit and to mitigate by its influence fluctuations in the general level of production, trade, prices and employment, so far as may be possible within the scope of monetary action, and generally to promote the economic and financial welfare of Canada."

Bank of Canada
www.bankofcanada.ca

This is a vague mandate, leaving a lot of room for interpretation. To explore this subject, we discuss four functions of the Bank of Canada as they are mentioned in the Bank's web page:

- bank note issue
- government debt and asset management services
- central banking services, and
- monetary policy management.

Bank Note Issue

Before the creation of the Bank of Canada, the federal government and the early banks issued notes designed to circulate as currency. The day it began operations, the Bank replaced the outstanding issue of federal government notes and provision was also made for the gradual removal of notes issued by banks. By 1945 the Bank had a monopoly over note issue. Although the original Bank Act required the Bank to redeem its notes in gold, this provision was never used. In fact, it was removed with the 1967 revision of the Bank Act, thereby providing the Bank with unlimited powers to issue legal tender.

The Bank also conducts ongoing research, working closely with private sector partnerships and note-issuing authorities in other countries, in order to improve cost-effectiveness, increase the durability of bank notes, and reduce counterfeiting. In its role as provider of paper money, the Bank's overall objective is to preserve the integrity and safety of Canadian currency in the most economical and efficient manner possible.

Government Debt and Asset Management Services

In its role as the federal government's fiscal agent, the Bank of Canada provides debt-management services for the federal government such as advising on borrowings, managing new debt offerings, and servicing outstanding debt. Before 1995 these services were provided for all of the federal government's debt. In 1995, however, a special agency of the Department of Finance was created, known as Canada Investment and Savings, to be responsible for the federal government's debt held by individuals, commonly known as retail debt.

Canada Investment and Savings handles government of Canada securities such as Canada Savings Bonds, Treasury bills, and marketable bonds, and is also responsible for the development of new investment products and marketing initiatives. The Bank of Canada, however, continues to be responsible for all of the government's securities after they are issued, administering millions of bondholder accounts and making payments on behalf of the federal government for interest and debt redemption.

In its role as fiscal agent, the Bank of Canada also manages the government's foreign exchange reserves held by the **Exchange Fund Account** of the Department of Finance. In particular, the Bank assists the Department of Finance in investing these foreign reserves and in borrowing when necessary to maintain an adequate level of reserves. The Bank also engages in international financial transactions, on behalf of the government, in order to influence exchange rates. (We discuss the Bank's foreign exchange interventions more formally in Chapter 19.)

Department of
Finance Canada
www.fin.gc.ca

Central Banking Services

Office of the
Superintendent of
Financial Institutions
www.osfi-bsif.gc.ca

Canada Deposit Insurance
Corporation
www.cdic.ca

The Bank of Canada serves as the lender of last resort if a deposit-taking financial institution faces a liquidity crisis. Because of its unique power to create base money, the Bank can ease the liquidity problems of any financial institution, by extending advances, and therefore deter bank runs and panics. **Base money** (also called **monetary base**) consists of the monetary liabilities of the central bank and, as you will see in the next chapter, is an important part of the money supply, because changes in it lead to multiple changes in the money supply. Of course, lender-of-last-resort lending is closely coordinated with the two federal regulatory agencies that are set up specifically to regulate financial institutions—the Office of the Superintendent of Financial Institutions and the Canada Deposit Insurance Corporation.[1] Moreover, such lending is done judiciously, explicitly considering the effects on other financial institutions, the money supply, and government policy.

---

[1]The Office of the Superintendent of Financial Institutions was created in 1987 to succeed the Department of Insurance and the Inspector General of Banks whereas the Canada Deposit Insurance Corporation was created by act of Parliament in 1967 to insure deposits, up to $60 000 per account, of member deposit-taking institutions.

The Bank also plays a central role in Canada's national payments system (to be discussed in some detail in Chapter 17). This is essentially an electronic system that clears and settles payments and transactions including securities and foreign exchange, currently handling 15 times our gross domestic product per year. Although this system is operated by the Canadian Payments Association, federal legislation that came into force in 1996 gave the Bank explicit responsibility for the regulatory oversight of this system. The Bank's main concern is whether problems that affect one participant in the clearing and settlement system will spread to other participants.

Canadian Payments
Association
www.cdnpay.ca

Finally, the Bank acts as the holder of deposit accounts of the federal government, the directly clearing members of the Canadian Payments Association, international organizations such as the International Monetary Fund, and other central banks. As the federal government's banker, the Bank is also responsible for the government's operating accounts. In this role, as you will see in Chapter 17, the Bank shifts government balances between the government's transactions account with the Bank and the government's non-transactions accounts with the direct clearers.

International
Monetary Fund
www.imf.org

Monetary Policy

The Bank of Canada employs such tools as **open market operations** (the purchase and sale of government securities that affect both interest rates and the amount of reserves in the banking system) and, to a lesser extent, the shifting of government balances between it and the directly clearing members of the Canadian Payments Association to implement changes in the money supply. The Bank's ultimate objective is to keep inflation low. The Bank has a staff of professional economists, which provides economic analysis that the Board of Directors uses in making its decisions. (Box 14-3 discusses the role of the research staff.)

The Bank's goal of low inflation is closely related to the goal of steady economic growth, because businesses are more likely to invest in capital equipment to increase productivity and economic growth when inflation is low. Low inflation is also desirable because it protects the purchasing power of pensioners and those on fixed incomes.

Although the Bank determines monetary policy, in the following section you will learn that the ultimate responsibility for policy rests with the government, since it is the government that must answer to Parliament. This system of "joint responsibility" dates back to 1967 when the Bank of Canada Act was amended to give responsibility for monetary policy to the government.

HOW INDEPENDENT IS THE BANK OF CANADA?

When we look, in the next four chapters, at how the Bank of Canada conducts monetary policy, we will want to know why it decides to take certain policy actions but not others. To understand its actions, we must understand the incentives that motivate the Bank's behaviour. How free is the Bank from the whims of the government? Do economic, bureaucratic, or political considerations guide it? Is the Bank truly independent of outside pressures?

The Bank's degree of independence has evolved over time, in part because of changing circumstances, in part because a clear division of authority was not established in the original Bank of Canada Act. Initially the Bank of Canada was privately owned, with about 12 000 individual shareholders, and so was largely free of political pressures. It was also free of private interference, because of regulations regarding who could hold how much stock in the Bank. The Conservative government in office at the time of the Bank's creation believed that the Bank should possess a large share of the responsibility for the development of monetary policy.

BOX 14-3

Role of the Bank's Research Staff

The Bank of Canada is the largest employer of economists in Canada. What do all these economists do?

The most important task of the Bank's economists is to follow the incoming data from government agencies and private sector organizations on the economy and provide guidance to the policymakers on where the economy may be heading and what the impact of monetary policy actions on the economy might be. Moreover, the Bank's economists maintain large econometric models (models whose equations are estimated with statistical procedures) that help them produce forecasts of the national economy, and brief the governor and the senior management of the Bank on their forecasts for the Canadian economy.

Because of the increased influence of developments in foreign countries on the Canadian economy, the research staff produces reports on the major foreign economies. They also conduct research on developments in the foreign exchange market because of its growing importance in the monetary policy process and to support the activities of the Bank's foreign exchange desk.

Staff economists also engage in basic research on the effects of monetary policy on output and inflation, developments in the labour markets, international trade, international capital markets, banking and other financial institutions, financial markets, and regional economy, among other topics. This research is published widely in academic journals and in Bank of Canada publications. (Bank of Canada publications, such as the *Bank of Canada Review*, the *Bank of Canada Banking and Financial Statistics*, and the *Monetary Policy Report*, are a good source of supplemental material for money and banking students.)

Another important activity of the research staff is in the public education area. Staff economists are called on frequently to make presentations to the public.

Significant changes in the balance of power occurred with the election of a majority Liberal government in the fall of 1935. The Liberals moved the Bank in the direction of public ownership, culminating in its complete nationalization by 1938. This was done to further isolate the Bank from the pressures of the private system. However, the nationalization of the Bank did tilt the balance of authority for monetary policy back towards the federal cabinet and the Parliament. The Liberals believed that the Bank should have discretion in internal management and in implementing monetary policy yet the policies being implemented should be in harmony with the views of the government.

In June 1954, the first governor of the Bank of Canada, Graham Towers, retired after 19 years of service. Graham Towers was replaced by James Coyne (see Box 14-2). Like many Canadians at the time, James Coyne was concerned about the level of foreign ownership and the increase in consumer prices during the Korean War. He was convinced that the solution to these problems was a tighter monetary policy stance. A decline in the supply of bank reserves would increase interest rates, thereby raising national savings and reducing Canada's dependence on foreign capital inflows. The tighter monetary policy led to rising unemployment and weak output growth. As a result, the Bank's policies were criticized by commentary in the popular press and by most of the academic community. In fact, thirty economists signed a letter to the minister of finance calling for Coyne's dismissal.[2]

---

[2]See H. S. Gordon, *The Economists versus the Bank of Canada*, (Toronto: The Ryerson Press, 1961): v-vi.

James Coyne, however, did not change his mind. He was convinced that there was no long-run relationship between inflation and unemployment, despite the publication of a famous paper in 1958 by the British economist A. W. Phillips, showing that higher inflation was typically associated with a lower unemployment rate.[3] Although the Phillips hypothesis attracted widespread support in Canada and was replicated with Canadian data, Coyne was anticipating the pathbreaking work by Milton Friedman and Edmund Phelps on the vertical Phillips curve, to be published 10 years later in 1968.[4] But as a former governor of the Bank of Canada, Gordon Thiessen, put it in a recent speech,

> "[t]here was one critical area, however, where Coyne and many other policy analysts, both within and outside the Bank, appear to have been misguided. Those who had questioned the effectiveness of monetary policy in earlier years had failed to appreciate that it was likely to be much stronger than fiscal policy under a flexible exchange rate system, especially when capital was highly mobile. The large capital movements triggered by any change in interest rates would put significant pressure on the exchange rate, amplifying the effects of monetary policy while undercutting the effects of any opposing fiscal policy. Coyne did not realize that, for similar reasons, it was unlikely that a tighter monetary policy would ever raise national savings or reduce foreign investment inflows."[5]

To avoid accepting blame for this state of affairs, the Liberal government in office reversed its previous stand and disavowed its position that the government was responsible for monetary policy. The government was criticized for this reversal and the new hands-off approach to monetary policy. When the government changed hands on June 10, 1957 and Donald Fleming became the federal minister of finance, the stage was set for a confrontation with the governor of the Bank, James Coyne. After a long and acrimonious debate the so-called "Coyne Affair" was resolved in 1961 with the resignation of Governor Coyne.

On July 24, 1961, Louis Rasminsky accepted the position as the third governor of the Bank of Canada on the condition that the relationship between the government and the Bank be clearly defined. Soon after he assumed office, he issued a public statement containing two main principles reflecting his views on that relationship

> "...(1) in the ordinary course of events, the Bank has the responsibility for monetary policy, and (2) if the government disapproves of the monetary policy being carried out by the Bank, it has the right and the responsibility to direct the Bank as to the policy which the Bank is to carry out."[6]

A royal commission, whose appointment was partly initiated by the Coyne Affair, accepted Governor Rasminsky's views regarding the relationship between the Bank and the government. The commission recommended a system of joint responsibility under which the Bank has considerable autonomy in the conduct of day-to-day monetary policy but the government must accept full responsibility for the policy being followed.

[3]A. W. Phillips, "The Relation between Unemployment and the Rate of Change of Money Wages in the United Kingdom," *Economica* 24 (1958): 283-299.

[4]Milton Friedman, "The Role of Monetary Policy," *American Economic Review* 58 (1968): 1-17; Edmund Phelps, "Money-Wage Dynamics and Labour Market Equilibrium," *Journal of Political Economy* 76 (1968): 678-711.

[5]Gordon Thiessen, "Can a Bank Change? The Evolution of Monetary Policy at the Bank of Canada 1935-2000," Lecture to the Faculty of Social Science, University of Western Ontario.

[6]Bank of Canada, *Annual Report*, 1961, p. 3.

The Bank of Canada Act was amended in 1967 to confirm the joint responsibility system, and this state of affairs regarding monetary policy has generally remained in order to this day. Under this joint responsibility system, the governor of the Bank of Canada and the minister of finance, acting on behalf of the government, consult regularly and, in the event of a serious disagreement over the conduct of monetary policy, the government has the right to override the Bank's decisions. In particular, the minister of finance can issue a directive to the Bank indicating the specific policy changes that the Bank must follow. The directive, however, must be published indicating not only the new policy that the Bank is supposed to undertake but also the period during which it is to apply.

Hence, ultimate responsibility for monetary policy rests with the democratically elected government. However, because of the consequences of issuing a directive, it is unlikely that such a directive would be issued, and none has been issued to date.

THE CHANGING FACE OF THE BANK OF CANADA

The legislation governing the Bank of Canada's responsibility for monetary policy has remained relatively unchanged since the Bank Act of 1967. Over the past decade, however, the Bank has undertaken a broad range of initiatives and made significant institutional changes to the way it operates. The impetus for change came from the interaction of experience and economic theory, the desire to explain and build confidence in the Bank's actions, and (to a smaller extent) from technological change and globalization.

Clarifying objectives is an important starting point for any successful monetary policy framework. The legislation by which the Bank of Canada is governed does not facilitate a clear understanding of objectives. For example, the preamble to legislation governing the Bank refers to multiple, and potentially inconsistent, policy objectives. Over the past few decades, however, the performance of the Canadian economy, together with the evolution of economic theory, led to the view that price stability is the most important goal of monetary policy. As John Crow put it, in his January 1988 Hanson Memorial Lecture at the University of Alberta,

> "[t]heory and experience—much of this experience not overly cheerful but certainly instructive—both point to a very clear answer. Monetary policy should be conducted so as to achieve a pace of monetary expansion that promotes stability in the value of money. This means pursuing a policy aimed at achieving and maintaining stable prices."[7]

The Hanson lecture was designed to explicitly identify price stability as the objective of Bank of Canada policy. This message was reinforced on February 26, 1991, through a joint announcement by the governor of the Bank and the minister of finance regarding the establishment of formal inflation targets (to be discussed in detail in Chapters 18 and 20). Clearly defined targets can be appealed as an institutional way of improving the macroeconomic outcomes of monetary policy.

The effectiveness of such an institutional framework, however, depends on two fundamental requirements: "independence" and "accountability". Although the Bank of Canada has not been given "goal independence"—the goal of price stability has been set jointly by the Bank and the Department of Finance—over the last decade the Bank placed increased emphasis on its responsibility to achieve

---

[7]John Crow, "The Work of Canadian Monetary Policy," The Eric J. Hanson Memorial Lecture, University of Alberta, Edmonton, Alberta. *Bank of Canada Review* (1988): 3-17.

the goal of price stability and its greater freedom to take whatever action is needed to do so. This freedom is referred to as "operational" (or "instrument") independence and, although it hasn't been explicitly legislated, it exists in practice. Increased operational independence has also raised the standards for accountability. As already noted, for example, the governor of the Bank has delegated the authority for monetary policy decisions to a committee—the seven-member internal Governing Council. Moreover, it has become a de facto standard for the governor to appear before a parliamentary committee following the release of the Bank's *Monetary Policy Report*.

The Bank has also improved its communications activities by moving towards greater "transparency" in its operations and objectives. In 1999, for example, the Bank started a twice-yearly *Update* to the *Monetary Policy Report*, both published by the Bank's Governing Council. The *Monetary Policy Report* is published every May and November while the *Update* is published every February and August giving an account of the Bank's management of monetary policy. Moreover, the Bank has noticeably increased the number of press conferences, press releases, and speeches, and also reorganized its regional offices in 1996–1997 with the objective of improving communication, transparency, and its assessment of economic conditions across Canada. For example, the Bank's regional offices, by maintaining contact with provincial governments, industries, and the general public, present quarterly "grassroots" assessments of current and prospective economic developments to the Bank's Governing Council—information that complements economic projections prepared by the Bank's staff. Finally, the Bank maintains a comprehensive website (at http://www.bankofcanada.ca) to disseminate information regarding financial statistics, publications, the transmission of monetary policy, and Bank-related material.

The direction taken in the recent evolution of the monetary policy framework in Canada has been heavily influenced by the role that the institutional monetary structure plays in influencing the monetary conduct.[8] As the Bank's former governor, Gordon Thiessen, put it in his October 17, 2000 speech to the Faculty of Social Science of the University of Western Ontario,

> "[t]he Bank tries to work with the markets, rather than against them, to avoid surprising them with unexpected actions. Greater transparency facilitates the policy-transmission process by conditioning market expectations, and helps avoid unnecessary confusion about the reasons for our actions."[9]

STRUCTURE AND INDEPENDENCE OF FOREIGN CENTRAL BANKS

In contrast to the Bank of Canada, which is a centralized unit owned by the government, central banks in other industrialized countries have a more decentralized structure. Here we examine the structure and degree of independence of four of the most important foreign central banks: the Bank of England, the Bank of Japan, the European Central Bank, and the Federal Reserve System of the United States.

---

[8]For a discussion of similar changes implemented by other central banks around the world, see Graydon Paulin, "The Changing Face of Central Banking in the 1990s," *Bank of Canada Review* (Summer 2000): 3-13.

[9]Gordon Thiessen, "Can a Bank Change? The Evolution of Monetary Policy at the Bank of Canada 1935-2000," Lecture to the Faculty of Social Science, University of Western Ontario.

Bank of England

Bank of England
**www.bankofengland.
co.uk**

Founded in 1694, the Bank of England is one of the oldest central banks. The Bank Act of 1946 gave the government statutory authority over the Bank of England. The governor of the Bank of England is appointed by the government for a five-year term.

Until 1997, the Bank of England was the least independent of the central banks examined in this chapter because the decision to raise or lower interest rates resided not within the Bank of England but with the chancellor of the exchequer (the equivalent of the Canadian minister of finance). All of this changed when the new Labour government came to power in May 1997. At this time, the new chancellor of the exchequer, Gordon Brown, made a surprise announcement that the Bank of England would henceforth have the power to set interest rates. However, the Bank was not granted total independence. The government can overrule the Bank and set rates "in extreme economic circumstances" and "for a limited period." Nonetheless, as in Canada, because overruling the Bank would be so public and is supposed to occur only in highly unusual circumstances and for a limited time, it is likely to be a rare occurrence.

The decision to set interest rates resides in the Monetary Policy Committee, made up of the governor, two deputy governors, two members appointed by the governor after consultation with the chancellor (normally central bank officials), plus four outside economic experts appointed by the chancellor. (Surprisingly, two of the four outside experts initially appointed to this committee were not British citizens—one was Dutch and the other American, although both were residents of the United Kingdom.)

Bank of Japan

Bank of Japan
www.boj.or.jp

The Bank of Japan (Nippon Ginko) was founded in 1882 during the Meiji Restoration. Monetary policy is determined by the Policy Board, which is composed of the governor; two vice governors; and six outside members appointed by the cabinet and approved by the parliament, all of whom serve for five-year terms.

Until recently, the Bank of Japan was not formally independent of the government, with the ultimate power residing with the Ministry of Finance. However, the new Bank of Japan Law, which took effect in April 1998 and was the first major change in the powers of the Bank of Japan in 55 years, has changed this. In addition to stipulating that the objective of monetary policy is to attain price stability, the law granted greater independence to the Bank of Japan. Before this, the government had two voting members on the Policy Board, one from the Ministry of Finance and the other from the Economic Planning Agency. Now the government may send two representatives from these agencies to board meetings, but they no longer have voting rights, although they do have the ability to request delays in monetary policy decisions. In addition, the Ministry of Finance lost its authority to oversee many of the operations of the Bank of Japan, particularly the right to dismiss senior officials. However, the Ministry of Finance continues to have control over the part of the Bank's budget that is unrelated to monetary policy. Some critics of the new law argue that giving the ministry veto power over most of the Bank's budget may substantially limit the independence of the Bank of Japan.

European Central Bank

European Central Bank
www.ecb.int

The Maastricht Treaty established the European Central Bank (ECB) and the European System of Central Banks (ESCB), which began operation in January 1999. The structure of the central bank is patterned after the U.S. Federal Reserve System in that central banks for each country have a role similar to that of the Federal Reserve banks. The executive board of the ECB is made up of the president, a vice president, and four other members, who are appointed for eight-year terms. The monetary policymaking body of the bank includes the six members of the executive board and the central-bank governors from the 11 euro countries, all of whom must have five-year terms at a minimum.

Swiss National Bank
www.snb.ch

The European Central Bank will be the most independent in the world, even more independent than the German central bank, the Bundesbank, which, before the establishment of the ECB, was considered the world's most independent central bank, along with the Swiss National Bank. The ECB is independent of both the European Union and the national governments and has complete control over monetary policy. In addition, the ECB's mandated mission is the pursuit of price stability. The ECB is far more independent than any other central bank in the world because its charter cannot be changed by legislation. It can be changed only by revision of the Maastricht Treaty, a difficult process because all signatories to the treaty would have to agree.

Federal Reserve System

Federal Reserve
www.federalreserve.gov

Of all the central banks in the world, the United States' **Federal Reserve System** (also called simply **the Fed**) probably has the most unusual structure. It includes the following entities: the **Board of Governors**, the 12 **Federal Reserve Banks**, the **Federal Open Market Committee** (FOMC), the Federal Advisory Council, and around 3000 member commercial banks.

At the head of the Federal Reserve System is the seven-member Board of Governors, headquartered in Washington, D.C. Each governor is appointed by the president of the United States and confirmed by the Senate. To limit the president's control over the Fed and insulate the Fed from other political pressures, the governors serve one nonrenewable 14-year term, with one governor's term expiring every other January. The chairman of the Board of Governors is chosen from among the seven governors and serves a 4-year term. It is expected that once a new chairman is chosen, the old chairman resigns from the Board of Governors, even if there are many years left to his or her term as a governor.

Federal Reserve Bank
of New York
www.ny.frb.org

Federal Reserve Bank
of Chicago
www.chicagofed.org

Federal Reserve Bank
of San Francisco
www.frbsf.org

Each of the 12 Federal Reserve banks is a quasi-public (part private, part government) institution owned by the private commercial banks in the district, which are members of the Federal Reserve System.[10] The three largest Federal Reserve banks in terms of assets are those of New York, Chicago, and San Francisco—combined they hold 50% of the assets (discount loans, securities, and other holdings) of the Federal Reserve System. The New York bank, with around one-quarter of the assets, is the most important of the Federal Reserve banks. The 12 Federal Reserve banks and the Board of Governors are actively involved in decisions concerning the conduct of monetary policy. In particular, all seven governors are voting members of the FOMC together with the president of the Federal Reserve Bank of New York and presidents of four other Federal Reserve banks. The FOMC usually meets eight times a year (about every six weeks) and makes decisions regarding the conduct of monetary policy in the United States.

The Federal Reserve appears to be remarkably free of the political pressures that influence other government agencies in the United States. Yet it is still subject to the influence of the president of the United States, since the president appoints members to the Board of Governors. The power of the United States president in appointing members to the Board of Governors is limited, however. Because the term of the chairman of the Board of Governors is not necessarily concurrent with that of the president of the United States, a president may have to deal with a chairman of the Board of Governors appointed by a previous administration. Alan Greenspan, for example, was appointed chairman in 1987 by President Ronald Reagan and was reappointed to another term by another Republican president,

---

[10]Currently, around one-third of the commercial banks in the United States are members of the Federal Reserve System. However, there is no distinction between member and nonmember banks, as they all are on equal footing in terms of reserve requirements and access to the Federal Reserve facilities, such as the discount window and Fed cheque clearing.

George Bush. When Bill Clinton, a Democrat, became president in 1993, Greenspan had several years left to his term. Clinton was put under tremendous pressure to reappoint Greenspan when his term expired and did so in 1996, even though Greenspan is a Republican.[11]

You can see that the Federal Reserve has extraordinary independence for a government agency and is one of the most independent central banks in the world. Moreover, the Fed's independence is reinforced by the fact that it faces less constraint than any other central bank from the behaviour of other central banks; other central banks, including the Bank of Canada, have to pay considerable attention to the behaviour of the U.S. Federal Reserve.

The Trend Toward Greater Independence

Reserve Bank
of New Zealand
www.rbnz.govt.nz

Sveriges Riksbank
www.riksbank.se

As our survey of the structure and independence of the major central banks indicates, in recent years we have been seeing a remarkable trend toward increasing independence. It used to be that the Federal Reserve was substantially more independent than almost all other central banks, with the exception of those in Germany and Switzerland. Now the newly established European Central Bank is far more independent than the Fed, and greater independence has been granted to central banks like the Bank of England and the Bank of Japan, putting them more on a par with the Fed, as well as to central banks in such diverse countries as New Zealand, Sweden, and the euro nations. Both theory and experience suggest that more independent central banks produce better monetary policy, thus providing an impetus for this trend.

EXPLAINING CENTRAL BANK BEHAVIOUR

One view of government bureaucratic behaviour is that bureaucracies serve the public interest (this is the *public interest view*). Yet some economists have developed a theory of bureaucratic behaviour that suggests other factors that influence how bureaucracies operate. The *theory of bureaucratic behaviour* suggests that the objective of a bureaucracy is to maximize its own welfare, just as a consumer's behaviour is motivated by the maximization of personal welfare and a firm's behaviour is motivated by the maximization of profits. The welfare of a bureaucracy is related to its power and prestige. Thus this theory suggests that an important factor affecting a central bank's behaviour is its attempt to increase its power and prestige.

What predictions does this view of a central bank like the Bank of Canada suggest? One is that the Bank will fight vigorously to preserve its autonomy, a prediction verified time and time again as the Bank has continually counterattacked attempts to control its functions. Another prediction is that the Bank of Canada will try to avoid conflict with powerful groups that may threaten to curtail its power and reduce its autonomy. The Bank's behaviour may take several forms. One possible factor explaining why the Bank is sometimes slow to increase interest rates and so smoothes out their fluctuations is that it wishes to avoid a conflict with the government over increases in interest rates. The desire to avoid conflict may also explain why some central banks devised clever stratagems to avoid blame for their mistakes (Box 14-4).

The theory of bureaucratic behaviour seems applicable to the Bank of Canada's actions, but we must recognize that this view of the Bank as being solely concerned

---

[11]Similarly, William McChesney Martin Jr., the chairman from 1951 to 1970, was appointed by President Truman (Dem.) but was reappointed by Presidents Eisenhower (Rep.), Kennedy (Dem.), and Nixon (Rep.). Also Paul Volcker, the chairman from 1979 to 1987, was appointed by President Carter (Dem.) but was reappointed by President Reagan (Rep.).

Games Central Banks Play

As the theory of bureaucratic behaviour predicts, central banks may play games to obscure their actions in order to avoid governmental interference in their activities. For example, in 1975, the U.S. Congress passed a resolution which instructed the Fed to report quarterly its target ranges for the growth in the monetary aggregates over the next 12 months and how successful it had been in achieving its previous targets. One game that the Fed played was to report on several monetary aggregates (such as M1, M2, and M3) rather than on one. When the Fed testified to Congress on its success in achieving its past targets, it would focus on the particular monetary aggregate whose growth rate was closest to the target range.

In addition to this clever tactic, the Fed devised a procedure for setting its target for monetary aggregates (called *base drift*) that made it more likely that it would hit its targets, thereby avoiding conflict with Congress. Every quarter, the Fed would revise the target values for monetary aggregates by applying target growth rates to the amount at which the aggregate had ended up (a new base). When the Fed overshot its targets, as frequently occurred after 1975, it revised future target values upward, making it less likely that the monetary aggregates would exceed target ranges in the future. Similarly, if the Fed undershot its targets, it revised future target values downward, making it less likely that the monetary aggregates would fall below the target ranges in the future. Subsequent legislation now restricts the Fed to changing the base for its target ranges only once a year, reducing the extent of base drift.

with its own self-interest is too extreme. Maximizing one's welfare does not rule out altruism. (You might give generously to a charity because it makes you feel good about yourself, but in the process you are helping a worthy cause.) The Bank is surely concerned that it conducts monetary policy in the public interest. However, much uncertainty and disagreement exist over what monetary policy should be.[12] When it is unclear what is in the public interest, other motives may influence the Bank's behaviour. In these situations, the theory of bureaucratic behaviour may be a useful guide to predicting what motivates the Bank.

SHOULD THE BANK OF CANADA BE INDEPENDENT?

As we have seen, the Bank of Canada is probably the most independent government agency in Canada. Every few years, the question arises whether the independence of the Bank of Canada should be curtailed. Politicians who strongly oppose a Bank policy often want to bring it under their supervision in order to impose a policy more to their liking. Should the Bank of Canada be independent, or would we be better off with a central bank under the control of the government?

The Case for Independence

The strongest argument for an independent Bank of Canada rests on the view that subjecting the Bank to more political pressures would impart an inflationary bias to monetary policy. In the view of many observers, politicians in a democratic society are shortsighted because they are driven by the need to win their next elec-

---

[12]One example of the uncertainty over how best to conduct monetary policy was discussed in Chapter 3: economists are not sure how to measure money. So even if economists agreed that controlling the quantity of money is the appropriate way to conduct monetary policy (a controversial position, as we will see in later chapters), the Bank of Canada cannot be sure which monetary aggregate it should control.

tion. With this as the primary goal, they are unlikely to focus on long-run objectives, such as promoting a stable price level. Instead, they will seek short-run solutions to problems, like high unemployment and high interest rates, even if the short-run solutions have undesirable long-run consequences. For example, we saw in Chapter 5 that high money growth might lead initially to a drop in interest rates but might cause an increase later as inflation heats up. Would a Bank of Canada under the control of the government be more likely to pursue a policy of excessive money growth when interest rates are high, even though it would eventually lead to inflation and even higher interest rates in the future? The advocates of an independent central bank say yes. They believe that a politically insulated central bank is more likely to be concerned with long-run objectives and thus be a defender of a sound dollar and a stable price level.

A variation on the preceding argument is that the political process in Canada leads to the so-called **political business cycle**, in which just before an election, expansionary policies are pursued to lower unemployment and interest rates. After the election, the bad effects of these policies—high inflation and high interest rates—come home to roost, requiring contractionary policies that politicians hope the public will forget before the next election. Although the issue has not been completely settled, recent work by Apostolos Serletis and Panos Afxentiou of the University of Calgary indicates that there is no credible evidence that such a political business cycle exists in Canada (Box 14-5).

Putting the Bank of Canada under the control of the government is also considered dangerous because the Bank can be used to facilitate government financing of large budget deficits by its purchases of government bonds in the open market. Such open-market purchases by the Bank increase the money supply and lead to inflation. Government pressure on the Bank to "help out" might lead to a more inflationary bias in the economy. An independent Bank of Canada is better able to resist this pressure from the government.

Another argument for Bank of Canada independence is that control of monetary policy is too important to leave to politicians, a group that has repeatedly demonstrated a lack of expertise at making hard decisions on issues of great economic importance, such as reducing the budget deficit or reforming the banking system. Another way to state this argument is in terms of the principal–agent problem discussed in Chapters 8 and 11. Both the Bank of Canada and politicians are agents of the public (the principals), and as we have seen, both politicians and the Bank have incentives to act in their own interest rather than in the interest of the public. The argument supporting Bank of Canada independence is that the principal–agent problem is worse for politicians than for the Bank because politicians have fewer incentives to act in the public interest.

Indeed, some politicians may prefer to have an independent Bank of Canada, which can be used as a public "whipping boy" to take some of the heat off their backs. It is possible that a politician who in private opposes an inflationary monetary policy will be forced to support such a policy in public for fear of not being re-elected. An independent Bank of Canada can pursue policies that are politically unpopular yet in the public interest.

The Case Against Independence

Proponents of a Bank of Canada under the control of the government argue that it is undemocratic to have monetary policy (which affects almost everyone in the economy) controlled by an elite group responsible to no one. The current lack of de facto accountability of the Bank of Canada has serious consequences: if the Bank performs badly, there is no provision for replacing members (as there is with politicians). True, the Bank of Canada needs to pursue long-run objectives, but elected government officials vote on long-run issues also (foreign policy, for

BOX 14·5

Electoral and Partisan Cycle Regularities

Recent politico-institutional approaches to the theory of economic policy emphasize the incentives of rational and maximizing policymakers in explaining movements in macroeconomic variables. Central to this perspective is the general assumption that policymakers respond to incentives and constraints just like the rest of the economic agents. As a consequence, the actual policies of government give rise to political cycles, which on the basis of the primary motivational force involved are distinguished into opportunistic and partisan cycles.

In opportunistic (or electoral) business cycle models, politicians maximize their popularity or their probability of re-election by following pre-election expansionary fiscal policies in order to please the fiscally knowledgeable voters. As a consequence, their actual policies give rise to electoral cycles, that is, persistent cyclical patterns of key policy and target variables across electoral terms, regardless of the political orientation of the incumbent government. In particu-

lar, models of opportunistic cycles predict pre-election high growth and low unemployment, increasing inflation around the election time, and a post-election contraction, regardless of the political party in power. In the more accepted partisan cycle models, politicians are ideological, that is, they represent the interests of different pressure groups and, when in office, follow policies which are favourable to their supporting groups. For example, the left-wing parties pursue expansionary policies in order to reduce unemployment, while the right-wing parties tend to induce post-election contractions in economic performance in order to reduce inflation. The outcome, therefore, is partisan cycles, that is, systematic and permanent differences in macroeconomic outcomes that differ by political party.

Recent work by Apostolos Serletis and Panos Afxentiou of the University of Calgary indicates that there is no credible evidence that such a political business cycle exists in Canada.*

* Apostolos Serletis and Panos C. Afxentiou, "Electoral and Partisan Cycle Regularities in Canada," *Canadian Journal of Economics* 31 (1998): 28-46.

example). If we push the argument further that policy is always performed better by elite groups like the Bank of Canada, we end up with such conclusions as Canada Customs and Revenue Agency (formerly Revenue Canada) should set tax policies with no oversight from the government. Would you advocate this degree of independence for Canada Customs and Revenue Agency?

The public holds government responsible for the economic well-being of the country, yet it lacks control over the government agency that may well be the most important factor in determining the health of the economy. In addition, to achieve a cohesive program that will promote economic stability, monetary policy must be coordinated with fiscal policy (management of government spending and taxation). Only by placing monetary policy under the control of the politicians who also control fiscal policy can these two policies be prevented from working at cross-purposes.

Central Bank Independence and Macroeconomic Performance in Seventeen Countries

There is no consensus on whether Bank of Canada independence is a good thing, although public support for independence of the central bank seems to have been growing in both Canada and abroad. As you might expect, people who like the Bank's policies are more likely to support its independence, while those who dislike its policies advocate a less independent Bank of Canada.

We have seen that advocates of **central bank independence** believe that macroeconomic performance will be improved by making the central bank more independent. Recent research seems to support this conjecture: when central banks

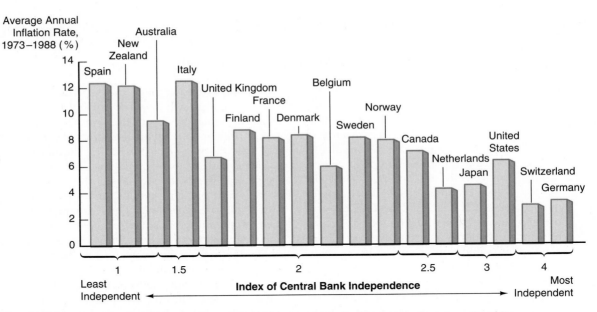

FIGURE 14-1 Central Bank Independence and Macroeconomic Performance in Seventeen Countries
On the horizontal axis, the 17 central banks are rated from 1 (least independent) to 4 (most independent). More independent banks have generally produced lower inflation than less independent central banks.
Source: Alberto Alesina and Lawrence H. Summers, "Central Bank Independence and Macroeconomic Performance: Some Comparative Evidence," *Journal of Money, Credit and Banking* 25 (1993): 151–162.

Banco de España
www.bde.es

are ranked from 1 (least independent) to 4 (most independent), inflation performance is found to be the best for countries with the most independent central banks.[13] As you can see in Figure 14-1, Germany and Switzerland, with the two most independent central banks, were also the countries with the lowest inflation rates in the 1973–1988 period. By contrast, the countries with the highest inflation in those years—Spain, New Zealand, Australia, and Italy—were also the countries with the least independent central banks. (The Spanish and New Zealand central banks have since gained greater independence.) Although a more independent central bank appears to lead to a lower inflation rate, this is not achieved at the expense of poorer real economic performance. Countries with independent central banks are no more likely to have high unemployment or greater output fluctuations than countries with less independent central banks.

SUMMARY

1. The Bank of Canada was created by act of Parliament in 1934 and began operations on March 11, 1935. Initially it was privately owned but became a crown corporation in 1938.

2. The overall responsibility for the operation of the Bank of Canada rests with a Board of Directors, consisting of the governor, the senior deputy governor, the deputy minister of finance, and twelve out-

---

[13]Alberto Alesina and Lawrence H. Summers, "Central Bank Independence and Macroeconomic Performance: Some Comparative Evidence," *Journal of Money, Credit and Banking* 25 (1993): 151–162. However, Adam Posen, "Central Bank Independence and Disinflationary Credibility: A Missing Link," *Oxford Economic Papers* 50 (1998): 335–359, has cast some doubt on whether the causality runs from central bank independence to improved inflation performance.

side directors. The Bank's governor (currently David Dodge) is the chief executive officer and chairman of the Board of Directors.

3. Although on paper the Bank of Canada is an arm of the government, in practice the Bank has more independence than the Bank of Canada Act suggests.

4. The Bank of Canada is more independent than most agencies of the Canadian government, but it is still subject to political pressures. The theory of bureaucratic behaviour indicates that one factor driving the Bank's behaviour is its attempt to increase its power and prestige. This view explains many of the Bank's actions, although the agency may also try to act in the public interest.

5. The case for an independent Bank of Canada rests on the view that curtailing the Bank's independence and subjecting it to more political pressures would impart an inflationary bias to monetary policy. An independent Bank of Canada can afford to take the long view and not respond to short-run problems that will result in expansionary monetary policy and a political business cycle. The case against an independent Bank of Canada holds that it is undemocratic to have monetary policy (so important to the public) controlled by an elite that is not accountable to the public. An independent Bank of Canada also makes the coordination of monetary and fiscal policy difficult.

KEY TERMS

base money (monetary base), p. 328

Board of Directors, p. 326

Board of Governors, p. 335

central bank independence, p. 339

Exchange Fund Account, p. 328

Federal Open Market Committee (FOMC), p. 335

Federal Reserve Banks, p. 335

Federal Reserve System (the Fed), p. 335

Governing Council, p. 327

open market operations, p. 329

political business cycle, p. 338

QUESTIONS AND PROBLEMS

Questions marked with an asterisk are answered at the end of the book in an appendix, "Answers to Selected Questions and Problems."

*1. What political realities might explain the creation of the Bank of Canada in 1934?

2. In what ways can the government influence the conduct of monetary policy?

*3. Who is responsible for monetary policy in Canada?

4. Do you think that the 7-year renewable term for the governor of the Bank of Canada effectively insulates the Bank from political pressure?

*5. How did the "Coyne Affair" motivate the current system of joint responsibility for monetary policy?

6. Over time, which entities have gained power in the conduct of monetary policy in Canada and which have lost power? Why do you think this has happened?

*7. "The strongest argument for an independent Bank of Canada rests on the view that subjecting the Bank to more political pressures would impart an inflationary bias to monetary policy." Is this statement true, false, or uncertain? Explain your answer.

8. The Bank of Canada is the most independent of all Canadian government agencies. What is the main difference between it and other government agencies that explains its greater independence?

*9. How can the government directly influence the Bank of Canada?

10. How is the responsibility for monetary policy shared in the Eurosystem?

*11. "The theory of bureaucratic behaviour indicates that the Bank of Canada never operates in the public interest." Is this statement true, false, or uncertain? Explain your answer.

12. Why might eliminating the Bank's independence lead to a more pronounced political business cycle?

*13. "The independence of the Bank leaves it completely unaccountable for its actions." Is this statement true, false, or uncertain? Explain your answer.

14. "The independence of the Bank has meant that it takes the long view and not the short view." Is this statement true, false, or uncertain? Explain your answer.

*15. Why did Canada show little interest in the establishment of a central bank during the first 60 or so years of Confederation?

Chapter 15

Multiple Deposit Creation and the Money Supply Process

PREVIEW   As we saw in Chapter 5 and will see in later chapters on monetary theory, movements in the money supply affect interest rates and the overall health of the economy and thus affect us all. Because of its far-reaching effects on economic activity, it is important to understand how the money supply is determined. Who controls it? What causes it to change? How might control of it be improved? In this and subsequent chapters we answer these questions by providing a detailed description of the *money supply process*, the mechanism that determines the level of the money supply.

Because deposits at banks are by far the largest component of the money supply, understanding how these deposits are created is the first step in understanding the money supply process. This chapter provides an overview of how the banking system creates deposits. In addition, it outlines the basic building blocks needed in later chapters for you to understand in greater depth how the money supply is determined.

FOUR PLAYERS IN THE MONEY SUPPLY PROCESS

The "cast of characters" in the money supply story is as follows:

1. The central bank—the government agency that oversees the banking system and is responsible for the conduct of monetary policy; in Canada, the Bank of Canada

2. Banks (depository institutions)—the financial intermediaries that accept deposits from individuals and institutions and make loans: chartered banks and near banks

3. Depositors—individuals and institutions that hold deposits in banks

4. Borrowers from banks—individuals and institutions that borrow from the depository institutions and institutions that issue bonds that are purchased by the depository institutions.

Of the four players, the central bank, the Bank of Canada, is the most important. Its conduct of monetary policy involves actions that affect its balance sheet (holdings of assets and liabilities), to which we turn now.

THE BANK OF CANADA'S BALANCE SHEET AND THE MONETARY BASE

Just as any other bank has a balance sheet that lists its assets and liabilities, so does the Bank of Canada. We examine each of its categories of assets and liabilities because changes in them are an important way the Bank affects the reserve position of banks and manipulates interest rates and the money supply.

Assets

1. *Government of Canada securities.* These are the Bank's holdings of government of Canada securities. The total amount of securities is controlled by open market operations (the Bank's purchase and sale of these securities). As shown in Table 15-1, "Government of Canada securities" is by far the Bank's largest category of assets, accounting for over 80% of the balance sheet.

2. *Other investments.* This category mostly includes investments held under short-term foreign currency swap arrangements with the **Exchange Fund**

TABLE 15-1 Balance Sheet of the Bank of Canada ($ millions, end of 2000)

Assets	Amount	Percent	Liabilities	Amount	Percent
Government of Canada securities			Bank of Canada notes outstanding	36 775.3	92.99
Treasury bills	9 134.7	23.10	Deposits		
Securities maturing within three years	8 342.5	21.09	Government of Canada	16.1	0.04
Securities not maturing within three years	15 293.8	38.67	Chartered banks	1 669.2	4.22
Other investments	3 167.0	8.01	Other members of the CPA	101.8	0.26
Advances to members of the CPA	952.3	2.41	Other deposits	267.0	0.67
Foreign currency assets			Securities sold under repurchase agreements	—	—
U.S. dollars	742.0	1.88	Other liabilities	718.7	1.82
Other currencies	4.9	0.01	Total	39 548.1	100.00
Securities purchased under resale agreements	1 357.5	3.43			
Other assets	553.4	1.40			
Total	39 548.1	100.00			

Source: Bank of Canada *Annual Report* 2000. Reprinted with permission.

Banco de Mexico
www.banxico.org.mx

Canadian Payments
Association
www.cdnpay.ca

Account (**EFA**) of the Department of Finance.[1] In particular, as part of its cash-management operations within the Canadian banking system, the Bank of Canada temporarily acquires foreign currency investments from the EFA at the prevailing exchange rate with a commitment to reverse the transaction at the same exchange rate at a future date. Moreover, the Bank of Canada is a participant in two foreign currency swap facilities with foreign central banks—the U.S. Federal Reserve (in the amount of U.S. $2 billion) and the Banco de Mexico (in the amount of Can $1 billion).

3. *Advances.* These are loans the Bank of Canada makes to members of the Canadian Payments Association. There is a big difference between normal advances and extraordinary advances (to be discussed in detail in Chapter 17) lent by the Bank of Canada to troubled banks to prevent bank and financial panics. Normal advances are fully collateralized and generally overnight in duration. The Bank of Canada charges the **bank rate** on advances under the Large Value Transfer System (LVTS) and the bank rate plus a margin, which was 150 basis points at the end of December 1999, on advances under the Automated Clearing Settlement System (ACSS)—we will discuss the Canadian payments system in detail in Chapter 17.

4. *Foreign currency assets.* These include deposits denominated in foreign currencies, which the Bank keeps with domestic and foreign banks and with other central banks. Although these assets are part of Canada's foreign exchange reserves, they must not be confused with the foreign currency assets held by the Exchange Fund Account of the government of Canada.

5. *Securities purchased under resale agreements.* These are **Special Purchase and Resale Agreements (SPRAs)** with primary dealers, a subgroup of government securities distributors, in which the Bank of Canada purchases government of Canada securities with an agreement to sell them back the next business day at a predetermined price. The balance sheet entry "Securities purchased under resale agreements" represents the value receivable by the Bank of Canada upon resale of the securities. As you will see in Chapter 17, the Bank enters into SPRAs at the target rate for the overnight interest rate if overnight funds in the money market are traded above the target rate.

   These first five assets are important because they earn interest. Because the liabilities of the Bank generally pay low interest rates, the Bank makes millions of dollars every year—its assets earn income, and its liabilities cost little. Although it returns most of its earnings to the federal government, the Bank does spend some of it on "worthy causes," such as supporting economic research.

6. *All other assets.* These include securities denominated in foreign currencies as well as physical goods such as computers, office equipment, and buildings owned by the Bank of Canada.

Liabilities

1. *Bank of Canada notes outstanding.* The Bank of Canada issues notes (those blue, purple, green, red, and brown pieces of paper in your wallet that say "Bank of Canada"). The Bank of Canada notes outstanding is the amount of these notes that is in the hands of the public and the depository institutions. Coins issued by the Canadian Mint are not a liability of the Bank of Canada. The coins and Bank of Canada notes that we use in Canada today are collectively known as *currency.*

---

[1]Regarding the government of Canada's official international reserves and the Exchange Fund Account, see Jacobo De León, "The Bank of Canada's Management of Foreign Currency Reserves," *Bank of Canada Review* (Winter 2000-2001): 13-21.

Laurentian
Bank of Canada
www.laurentianbank.ca

Alberta Treasury
Branches
www.atb.com

HSBC Bank Canada
www.hsbc.ca

Credit Union
Central of Canada
www.cucentral.ca

Bank of Canada notes are IOUs from the Bank to the bearer and are also liabilities, but unlike most liabilities, they promise to pay back the bearer solely with Bank of Canada notes; that is, they pay off IOUs with other IOUs. Accordingly, if you bring a $100 bill to the Bank of Canada and demand payment, you will receive two $50s, five $20s, ten $10s, or twenty $5 bills.

People are more willing to accept IOUs from the Bank of Canada than from you or me because Bank of Canada notes are a recognized medium of exchange; that is, they are accepted as a means of payment and so function as *money*. Unfortunately, neither you nor I can convince people that our IOUs are worth anything more than the paper they are written on.[2]

2. *Reserves*. All the direct clearers have accounts at the Bank of Canada in which they hold settlement deposits. As of January 2001, there were twelve direct clearers in addition to the Bank of Canada: the Big Six, Alberta Treasury Branches, La Caisse centrale Desjardins du Québec, Canada Trustco Mortgage Company, Credit Union Central of Canada, HSBC Bank Canada, and the Laurentian Bank of Canada.

Reserves consist of **settlement balances** at the Bank of Canada plus currency that is physically held by banks (called vault cash because it is held in bank vaults, cash tills, and automated banking machines). Under the LVTS (to be discussed in detail in Chapter 17), positive settlement balances held by direct clearers earn the bank rate less 50 basis points. **Reserves** are assets for the banks but liabilities for the Bank of Canada because the banks can demand payment on them at any time and the Bank of Canada is required to satisfy its obligation by paying Bank of Canada notes. As you will see, an increase in reserves leads to an increase in the level of deposits and hence in the money supply.

As already noted in Chapter 9, Canadian banks are no longer required to hold reserves (Box 15-1). Banks, however, hold some reserves in order to manage their own short-term liquidity requirements and respond to predictable clearing drains and across-the-counter and automated banking machine drains. We call these reserves desired excess reserves or simply **desired reserves**. For example, banks might desire that for every dollar of deposits, a certain fraction (say, 10 cents) is held as reserves. This fraction (10%) is called the **desired reserve ratio**. Reserves in excess of the desired amounts are called unwanted or **excess reserves**.

3. *Government of Canada deposits*. The government keeps deposits at the Bank of Canada, against which it writes all its cheques. The government also maintains deposit accounts with the direct clearers. The maintenance of these government accounts with the Bank of Canada and the direct clearers gives the Bank of Canada an additional instrument of monetary control, called **government deposit transfers** (that we shall discuss in detail in Chapter 17).

---

[2]The "Bank of Canada notes outstanding" item on the Bank's balance sheet refers only to currency in circulation, the amount in the hands of the public. Currency that has been printed is not automatically a liability of the Bank. For example, consider the importance of having $1 million of your own IOUs printed up. You give out $100 worth to other people and keep the other $999 900 in your pocket. The $999 900 of IOUs does not make you richer or poorer and does not affect your indebtedness. You care only about the $100 of liabilities from the $100 of circulated IOUs. The same reasoning applies for the Bank in regard to its notes.

For similar reasons, the currency component of the money supply, no matter how it is defined, includes only currency in circulation. It does not include any additional currency that is not yet in the hands of the public. The fact that currency has been printed but is not circulating means that it is not anyone's asset or liability and thus cannot affect anyone's behaviour. Therefore, it makes sense not to include it in the money supply.

The Worldwide Decline in Reserve Requirements

In order to meet the demand for withdrawals by depositors or to pay the cheques drawn on depositors' accounts, depository institutions need to keep sufficient reserves on hand. In most countries, banks hold a certain amount of noninterest-bearing reserves because of legally imposed reserve requirements. These reserves are called **required reserves**. The rationale for reserve requirements is that reserves are necessary for monetary control purposes and, to a lesser extent, for the protection of depositors and the stability of the banking system.

In recent years, however, central banks in many countries in the world have been reducing or eliminating their reserve requirements. In the United States, for example, the Federal Reserve eliminated requirements on time deposits in December 1990 and lowered reserve requirements on chequable deposits from 12% to 10% in April 1992. Canada has gone a step further: financial market legislation taking effect in June 1992 eliminated all reserve requirements over a two-year period. The central banks of Switzerland, New Zealand, and Australia have

also eliminated reserve requirements entirely. What explains the downward trend in reserve requirements in most countries?

You may recall from Chapter 10 that reserve requirements act as a tax on banks. Because central banks typically do not pay interest on reserves, the bank earns nothing on them and loses the interest that could have been earned if the bank held loans instead. The cost imposed on banks from reserve requirements means that banks, in effect, have a higher cost of funds than other deposit-based financial institutions not subject to reserve requirements, making them less competitive. Central banks have thus been reducing reserve requirements to make banks more competitive and stronger.

Although central banks have been reducing or eliminating their reserve requirements, banks still want to hold reserves to protect themselves against predictable and unpredictable cash and clearing drains. Hence, "desired reserves" is the appropriate term to describe the reserves of deposit-taking financial institutions in a system without reserve requirements.

4. *Securities sold under repurchase agreements.* These are **Sale and Repurchase Agreements (SRAs)** with primary dealers, in which the Bank of Canada sells government of Canada securities (Treasury bills and bonds) with an agreement to buy them back the next business day at a predetermined price. The balance sheet entry "Securities sold under repurchase agreements" represents the value payable by the Bank of Canada upon repurchase of the securities. As you will see in Chapter 17, the Bank of Canada enters into SRAs at the target rate for the overnight interest rate if overnight funds in the money market are traded below the target rate.

5. *All other liabilities.* This item includes the deposits with the Bank of Canada owned by foreign governments, foreign central banks, and international agencies (such as the World Bank and the United Nations). It also includes all the remaining Bank of Canada liabilities not included elsewhere on the balance sheet.

World Bank
www.worldbank.org

Monetary Base

The first and third liabilities on the balance sheet, Bank of Canada notes outstanding and bank settlement balances, are often referred to as the *monetary liabilities* of the Bank of Canada. When we add to these liabilities the amount of coins in the hands of the public and depository institutions, we get a construct called the **monetary base**. The monetary base is an important part of the money supply because increases in it will lead to a multiple increase in the money supply (everything else being constant). This is why the monetary base is also called **high-powered money**. The monetary base MB is expressed as

$$MB = \left(\begin{array}{c} \text{Bank of Canada} \\ \text{notes outstanding} \end{array} \right) + \left(\begin{array}{c} \text{Settlement} \\ \text{balances} \end{array} \right) + \left(\begin{array}{c} \text{Coins} \\ \text{outstanding} \end{array} \right)$$

$$= C + R$$

where C denotes currency in circulation (coins and Bank of Canada notes held by the public) and R denotes bank reserves (vault cash plus settlement balances).

The items on the right-hand side of this equation indicate how the base is used and are called the **uses of the base**. Unfortunately, this equation does not tell us the factors that determine the base (the **sources of the base**), but the Bank of Canada balance sheet in Table 15-1 comes to the rescue because it has the property that the total assets on the left-hand side must equal the total liabilities on the right-hand side. Because the "Bank of Canada notes outstanding" and "Settlement balances" items in the uses of the base are Bank of Canada liabilities, the "assets equals liabilities" property of the Bank of Canada balance sheet enables us to solve for those items in terms of the Bank of Canada balance sheet items that are included in the sources of the base. Specifically, Bank of Canada notes outstanding and bank settlement balances equal the sum of all the Bank of Canada assets minus all the other Bank of Canada liabilities:

$$\left(\begin{array}{c} \text{Bank of Canada} \\ \text{notes outstanding} \end{array} \right) + \left(\begin{array}{c} \text{Settlement} \\ \text{balances} \end{array} \right) = \left(\begin{array}{c} \text{Securities} \\ \text{and investments} \end{array} \right) + \text{Advances}$$

$$+ \text{ Foreign assets} + \text{SPRAs} - \text{Government deposits} - \text{SRAs} + \text{Other assets (net)}$$

The two balance sheet items related to other assets and other liabilities have been collected into one term called Other assets (net), defined as "All other assets" minus "All other liabilities." This is a technical item, affecting the monetary base, but is not an instrument of monetary control. Substituting all the right-hand-side items in the equation for "Bank of Canada notes outstanding + Settlement balances" in the uses of the base equation, we obtain the following expression describing the sources of the monetary base:

$$MB = \text{Securities and investments} + \text{Advances} + \text{Foreign assets} + \text{SPRAs} \\ + \text{Other assets (net)} + \text{Coins outstanding} - \text{Government deposits} - \text{SRAs} \quad (1)$$

Accounting logic has led us to a useful equation that clearly identifies the eight factors affecting the monetary base listed in Table 15-2. As Equation 1 and Table 15-2 depict, increases in the first six factors increase the monetary base, and increases in the last two factors reduce the monetary base.

CONTROL OF THE MONETARY BASE

The Bank of Canada exercises control over the monetary base via factors 1, 2, 3, 4, 7, and 8 listed in Table 15-2: through its purchases or sales of government securities in the open market, called **open market operations**, through its extension of advances to banks, through its purchases or sales of foreign exchange in the foreign exchange market, through SPRAs and SRAs in the overnight market, and through its shifting of government balances between the Bank of Canada and the direct clearers.

In what follows we discuss how the Bank exercises control over the monetary base via the first two factors, leaving the Bank's management of settlement

TABLE 15-2 Factors Affecting the Monetary Base

Factor	Change in Factor	Change in Monetary Base
Factors That Increase the Monetary Base		
1. Securities and investments	↑	↑
2. Advances to members of the CPA	↑	↑
3. Foreign currency assets	↑	↑
4. Securities purchased under resale agreements	↑	↑
5. Other assets (net)	↑	↑
6. Currency outstanding	↑	↑
Factors That Decrease the Monetary Base		
7. Government deposits with the Bank of Canada	↑	↓
8. Securities sold under repurchase agreements	↑	↓

balances through SPRAs, SRAs, and government deposit shifting for Chapter 17 and the Bank's open market operations in the foreign exchange market for Chapter 19.

Bank of Canada Open Market Operations

As Table 15-2 suggests, the Bank of Canada can cause changes in the monetary base through its open market operations. A purchase of bonds by the Bank is called an **open market purchase**, and a sale of bonds by the Bank is called an **open market sale**.

Open Market Purchase from a Bank Suppose that the Bank of Canada purchases $100 of bonds from a bank and pays for them with a $100 cheque. The bank will either deposit the cheque in its account with the Bank of Canada (thereby increasing its settlement balances) or cash it in for currency, which will be counted as vault cash. To understand what occurs as a result of this transaction, we look at *T-accounts*, which list only the changes that occur in balance sheet items starting from the initial balance sheet position. Either action means that the bank will find itself with $100 more reserves and a reduction in its holdings of securities of $100. The T-account for the banking system, then, is

BANKING SYSTEM

Assets		Liabilities
Securities	−$100	
Reserves	+$100	

The Bank of Canada meanwhile finds that its liabilities have increased by the additional $100 of settlement balances, while its assets have increased by the $100 of additional securities that it now holds. Its T-account is

BANK OF CANADA

Assets		Liabilities	
Securities	+$100	Settlement balances	+$100

The net result of this open market purchase is that reserves have increased by $100, the amount of the open market purchase. Because bank reserves have increased and there has been no change of currency in circulation, the monetary base has also risen by $100.

Open Market Purchase from the Nonbank Public   To understand what happens when there is an open market purchase from the nonbank public, we must look at two cases. First, let's assume that the person or corporation that sells the $100 of bonds to the Bank of Canada deposits the Bank's cheque in the local bank. The nonbank public's T-account after this transaction is

NONBANK PUBLIC

Assets		Liabilities
Securities	−$100	
Chequable deposits	+$100	

When the bank receives the cheque, it credits the depositor's account with the $100 and then deposits the cheque in its account with the Bank of Canada, thereby increasing its settlement balances and adding to its reserves. The banking system's T-account becomes

BANKING SYSTEM

Assets		Liabilities	
Reserves	+$100	Chequable deposits	+$100

The effect on the Bank of Canada's balance sheet is that it has gained $100 of securities in its assets column, while it has an increase of $100 of settlement balances in its liabilities column:

BANK OF CANADA

Assets		Liabilities	
Securities	+$100	Settlement balances	+$100

As you can see in the previous T-account, when the Bank of Canada's cheque is deposited in a bank, the net result of the Bank of Canada's open market purchase from the nonbank public is identical to the effect of its open market purchase from a bank. Reserves increase by the amount of the open market purchase, and the monetary base increases by the same amount.

If, however, the person or corporation selling the bonds to the Bank of Canada cashes the Bank's cheque at a local bank, the effect on reserves is different.[3] This seller will receive currency of $100 while reducing holdings of securities by $100. The bond seller's T-account will be

NONBANK PUBLIC

Assets		Liabilities
Securities	−$100	
Currency	+$100	

The Bank of Canada now finds that it has exchanged $100 of currency for $100 of securities, so its T-account is

BANK OF CANADA

Assets		Liabilities	
Securities	+$100	Currency in circulation	+$100

The net effect of the open market purchase in this case is that reserves are unchanged, while currency in circulation increases by the $100 of the open market purchase. Thus the monetary base increases by the $100 amount of the open market purchase, while reserves do not. This contrasts with the case in which the seller of the bonds deposits the Bank of Canada's cheque in a bank; in that case, reserves increase by $100, and so does the monetary base.

The analysis reveals that *the effect of an open market purchase on reserves depends on whether the seller of the bonds keeps the proceeds from the sale in currency or in deposits*. If the proceeds are kept in currency, the open market purchase has no effect on reserves; if the proceeds are kept as deposits, reserves increase by the amount of the open market purchase.

The effect of an open market purchase on the monetary base, however, is always the same (the monetary base increases by the amount of the purchase) whether the seller of the bonds keeps the proceeds in deposits or in currency. The impact of an open market purchase on reserves is much more uncertain than its impact on the monetary base.

Open Market Sale If the Bank of Canada sells $100 of bonds to a bank or the nonbank public, the monetary base will decline by $100. For example, if the Bank of

---

[3]If the bond seller cashes the cheque at the local bank, its balance sheet will be unaffected because the $100 of vault cash that it pays out will be exactly matched by the deposit of the $100 cheque at the Bank of Canada. Thus its reserves will remain the same, and there will be no effect on its T-account. That is why a T-account for the banking system does not appear here.

Canada sells the bonds to an individual who pays for them with currency, the buyer exchanges $100 of currency for $100 of bonds, and the resulting T-account is

NONBANK PUBLIC

Assets		Liabilities
Securities	+$100	
Currency	−$100	

The Bank of Canada, for its part, has reduced its holdings of securities by $100 and has also lowered its monetary liability by accepting the currency as payment for its bonds, thereby reducing the amount of currency in circulation by $100:

BANK OF CANADA

Assets		Liabilities	
Securities	−$100	Currency in circulation	−$100

The effect of the open market sale of $100 of bonds is to reduce the monetary base by an equal amount, although reserves remain unchanged. Manipulations of T-accounts in cases in which the buyer of the bonds is a bank or the buyer pays for the bonds with a cheque written on a chequable deposit account at a local bank lead to the same $100 reduction in the monetary base, although the reduction occurs because the level of reserves has fallen by $100.

Study Guide

The best way to learn how open market operations affect the monetary base is to use T-accounts. Using T-accounts, try to verify that an open market sale of $100 of bonds to a bank or to a person who pays with a cheque written on a bank account leads to a $100 reduction in the monetary base.

The following conclusion can now be drawn from our analysis of open market purchases and sales. ***The effect of open market operations on the monetary base is much more certain than the effect on reserves.*** Therefore, the Bank of Canada can control the monetary base with open market operations more effectively than it can control reserves.

Open market operations can also be done in other assets besides government bonds and have the same effects on the monetary base we have described here. One example of this is a foreign exchange intervention by the Bank of Canada (Box 15-2).

Although open market operations are the most important monetary policy tool for most central banks around the world, in 1994 the Bank of Canada stopped conducting open market operations in government of Canada bills and bonds. Since then, the Bank's most common open market operations involve repurchase transactions, either SPRAs or SRAs. As we will discuss in detail in Chapter 17, the Bank of Canada is currently conducting repurchase transactions to reinforce its operating

BOX 15·2

Foreign Exchange Rate Intervention and the Monetary Base

It is common to read in the newspaper about a Bank of Canada intervention in the foreign exchange market to buy or sell dollars. Can this also be a factor that affects the monetary base? The answer is yes because a Bank of Canada intervention in the foreign exchange market involves a purchase or sale of assets denominated in a foreign currency, which affects the "Foreign currency assets" category in the Bank's balance sheet.

Suppose that the Bank purchases $100 of deposits denominated in euros in exchange for $100 of deposits at the Bank (a sale of dollars for euros). A Bank of Canada purchase of any asset, whether it is a government bond or a deposit denominated in a foreign currency, is still just an open market purchase and so leads to an equal rise in the monetary base. One way to see this is to look at Table 15-2 and recog-

nize that $100 of deposits denominated in euros belongs in the "Foreign currency assets" category. Thus a $100 purchase of euro deposits leads to a $100 increase in the "Foreign currency assets" item in Table 15-2 and hence a $100 increase in the monetary base. Similarly, a sale of foreign currency deposits leads to a decline in "Foreign currency assets" and a decline in the monetary base. Another way to see this is to realize that the T-accounts from a $100 purchase or sale of deposits of foreign currency are identical to those in the text for a $100 open market purchase or sale except the word *securities* would be replaced by *foreign-currency-denominated deposits*. Bank of Canada interventions in the foreign exchange market are thus an important influence on the monetary base, a topic that we discuss further in Chapter 19.

target—the midpoint of the operating band for the overnight interest rate. The Bank, however, neutralizes the effect on settlement balances of SPRAs and SRAs, so that at the end of the day there is no change in the level of settlement balances in the banking system.

Shifts from Deposits into Currency

Even if the Bank of Canada does not conduct open market operations, including repurchase transactions, a shift from deposits to currency will affect the reserves in the banking system. However, such a shift will have no effect on the monetary base, another reason why the Bank has more control over the monetary base than over reserves.

Let's suppose that Jane Brown (who opened a $100 chequing account at the First Bank in Chapter 9) decides that tellers are so abusive in all banks that she closes her account by withdrawing the $100 balance in cash and vows never to deposit it in a bank again. The effect on the T-account of the nonbank public is

NONBANK PUBLIC		
Assets		**Liabilities**
Chequable deposits	−$100	
Currency	+$100	

The banking system loses $100 of deposits and hence $100 of reserves:

BANKING SYSTEM

Assets		Liabilities	
Reserves	−$100	Chequable deposits	−$100

For the Bank of Canada, Jane Brown's action means that there is $100 of additional currency circulating in the hands of the public, while reserves in the banking system have fallen by $100. The Bank's T-account is

BANK OF CANADA

Assets		Liabilities	
		Currency in circulation	+$100
		Reserves	−$100

The net effect on the monetary liabilities of the Bank of Canada is a wash; the monetary base is unaffected by Jane Brown's disgust at the banking system. But reserves are affected. Random fluctuations of reserves can occur as a result of random shifts into currency and out of deposits, and vice versa. The same is not true for the monetary base, making it a more stable variable.

Bank of Canada Advances

In this chapter so far we have seen changes in the monetary base solely as a result of open market operations. However, the monetary base is also affected when the Bank of Canada makes a loan to a bank. When the Bank makes a $100 loan to the First Bank, the bank is credited with $100 of reserves (settlement balances) from the proceeds of the loan. The effects on the balance sheet of the banking system and the Bank of Canada are illustrated by the following T-accounts:

BANKING SYSTEM				BANK OF CANADA			
Assets		Liabilities		Assets		Liabilities	
Reserves	+$100	Advances	+$100	Advances	+$100	Reserves	+$100

The monetary liabilities of the Bank have now increased by $100, and the monetary base, too, has increased by this amount. However, if a bank pays off a loan from the Bank of Canada, thereby reducing its borrowings from the Bank by $100, the T-accounts of the banking system and the Bank are as follows:

BANKING SYSTEM				BANK OF CANADA			
Assets		Liabilities		Assets		Liabilities	
Reserves	−$100	Advances	−$100	Advances	−$100	Reserves	−$100

The net effect on the monetary liabilities of the Bank of Canada, and hence on the monetary base, is then a reduction of $100. We see that the monetary base changes one-for-one with the change in the borrowings from the Bank of Canada.

Although the monetary base is affected when the Bank of Canada makes advances to direct clearers, such lending is not under the direct control of the Bank. The Bank can change its lending policy, which primarily involves changes in the bank rate, but the initiative for making and repaying advances rests with the direct clearers. In this sense, advances can be influenced by the Bank of Canada but cannot be considered a positive instrument of controlling the monetary base.

Overview of the Bank's Ability to Control the Monetary Base

The factor that most affects the monetary base is the Bank's holdings of securities, which is completely controlled by the Bank through its open market operations. Factors not directly controlled by the Bank of Canada (for example, the "coins outstanding," "other assets (net)," and "advances" items) undergo substantial short-run variations and can be important sources of fluctuations in the monetary base over time periods as short as a week. However, these fluctuations are quite predictable and so can be offset through open market operations. *Although technical and external factors complicate control of the monetary base, they do not prevent the Bank of Canada from accurately controlling it*.

MULTIPLE DEPOSIT CREATION: A SIMPLE MODEL

With our understanding of how the Bank of Canada controls the monetary base and how banks operate (Chapter 9), we now have the tools necessary to explain how deposits are created. When the Bank supplies the banking system with $1 of additional reserves, deposits increase by a multiple of this amount—a process called **multiple deposit creation**.

Deposit Creation: The Single Bank

Suppose that the $100 open market purchase described earlier was conducted with the First Bank. After the Bank of Canada has bought the $100 bond from the First Bank, the bank finds that it has an increase in reserves of $100. To analyze what the bank will do with these additional reserves, assume that the bank does not want to hold more reserves because it earns no interest on them. We begin the analysis with the following T-account:

FIRST BANK

Assets		Liabilities
Securities	−$100	
Reserves	+$100	

Because the bank has no increase in its chequable deposits, desired reserves remain the same, and the bank finds that its additional $100 of reserves means that its excess reserves (reserves in excess of desired reserves) have increased by $100. Let's say that the bank decides to make a loan equal in amount to the $100 increase in excess reserves. When the bank makes the loan, it sets up a chequing account for the borrower and puts the proceeds of the loan into this account. In this way the bank alters its balance sheet by increasing its liabilities with $100 of chequable deposits and at the same time increasing its assets with the $100 loan. The resulting T-account looks like this:

FIRST BANK

Assets		Liabilities	
Securities	−$100	Chequable deposits	+$100
Reserves	+$100		
Loans	+$100		

The bank has created chequable deposits by its act of lending. Because chequable deposits are part of the money supply, the bank's act of lending has in fact created money.

In its current balance sheet position, the First Bank still has excess reserves and so might want to make additional loans. However, these reserves will not stay at the bank for very long. The borrower took out a loan not to leave $100 idle at the First Bank but to purchase goods and services from other individuals and corporations. When the borrower makes these purchases by writing cheques, they will be deposited at other banks, and the $100 of reserves will leave the First Bank. *A bank cannot safely make loans for an amount greater than the excess reserves it has before it makes the loan.*

The final T-account of the First Bank is

FIRST BANK

Assets		Liabilities
Securities	−$100	
Loans	+$100	

The increase in reserves of $100 has been converted into additional loans of $100 at the First Bank, plus an additional $100 of deposits that have made their way to other banks. (All the cheques written on accounts at the First Bank are deposited in banks rather than converted into cash because we are assuming that the public does not want to hold any additional currency.) Now let's see what happens to these deposits at the other banks.

Deposit Creation: The Banking System

To simplify the analysis, let us assume that the $100 of deposits created by First Bank's loan is deposited at Bank A and that this bank and all other banks hold no excess reserves. Bank A's T-account becomes

BANK A

Assets		Liabilities	
Reserves	+$100	Chequable deposits	+$100

If the desired reserve ratio is 10%, this bank will now find itself with a $10 increase in desired reserves, leaving it $90 of excess reserves. Because Bank A (like the First Bank) does not want to hold on to excess reserves, it will make loans for the entire amount. Its loans and chequable deposits will then increase by $90, but when the borrower spends the $90 of chequable deposits, they and the reserves at Bank A will fall back down by this same amount. The net result is that Bank A's T-account will look like this:

BANK A

Assets		Liabilities	
Reserves	+$10	Chequable deposits	+$100
Loans	+$90		

If the money spent by the borrower to whom Bank A lent the $90 is deposited in another bank, such as Bank B, the T-account for Bank B will be

BANK B

Assets		Liabilities	
Reserves	+$90	Chequable deposits	+$90

The chequable deposits in the banking system have increased by another $90, for a total increase of $190 ($100 at Bank A plus $90 at Bank B). In fact, the distinction between Bank A and Bank B is not necessary to obtain the same result on the overall expansion of deposits. If the borrower from Bank A writes cheques to someone who deposits them at Bank A, the same change in deposits would occur. The T-accounts for Bank B would just apply to Bank A, and its chequable deposits would increase by the total amount of $190.

Bank B will want to modify its balance sheet further. It must keep 10% of $90 ($9) as desired reserves and has 90% of $90 ($81) in excess reserves and so can make loans of this amount. Bank B will make an $81 loan to a borrower, who spends the proceeds from the loan. Bank B's T-account will be

BANK B

Assets		Liabilities	
Reserves	+$ 9	Chequable deposits	+$90
Loans	+$81		

The $81 spent by the borrower from Bank B will be deposited in another bank (Bank C). Consequently, from the initial $100 increase of reserves in the banking system, the total increase of chequable deposits in the system so far is $271 (= $100 + $90 + $81).

Following the same reasoning, if all banks make loans for the full amount of their excess reserves, further increments in chequable deposits will continue (at Banks C, D, E, and so on), as depicted in Table 15-3. Therefore, the total increase in deposits from the initial $100 increase in reserves will be $1000. The increase is tenfold, the reciprocal of the 0.10 desired reserve ratio.

TABLE 15-3	Creation of Deposits (assuming a 10% desired reserve ratio and a $100 increase in reserves)		
Bank	**Increase in Deposits ($)**	**Increase in Loans ($)**	**Increase in Reserves ($)**
First Bank	0.00	100.00	0.00
A	100.00	90.00	10.00
B	90.00	81.00	9.00
C	81.00	72.90	8.10
D	72.90	65.61	7.29
E	65.61	59.05	6.56
F	59.05	53.14	5.91
.	.	.	.
.	.	.	.
.	.	.	.
Total for all banks	1000.00	1000.00	100.00

If the banks choose to invest their excess reserves in securities, the result is the same. If Bank A had taken its excess reserves and purchased securities instead of making loans, its T-account would have looked like this:

BANK A

Assets		Liabilities	
Reserves	+$10	Chequable deposits	+$100
Securities	+$90		

When the bank buys $90 of securities, it writes a $90 cheque to the seller of the securities, who in turn deposits the $90 at a bank such as Bank B. Bank B's chequable deposits rise by $90, and the deposit expansion process is the same as before. **Whether a bank chooses to use its excess reserves to make loans or to purchase securities, the effect on deposit expansion is the same.**

You can now see the difference in deposit creation for the single bank versus the banking system as a whole. Because a single bank can safely create deposits equal only to the amount of its excess reserves, it cannot by itself generate multiple deposit expansion. A single bank cannot make loans greater in amount than its excess reserves because the bank will lose these reserves as the deposits created by the loan find their way to other banks. However, the banking system as a whole can generate a multiple expansion of deposits because when a bank loses its excess reserves, these reserves do not leave the banking system even though they are lost to the individual bank. So as each bank makes a loan and creates deposits, the reserves find their way to another bank, which uses them to make additional loans and create additional deposits. As you have seen, this process continues until the initial increase in reserves results in a multiple increase in deposits.

The multiple increase in deposits generated from an increase in the banking system's reserves is called the **simple deposit multiplier**.[4] In our example, with a 10% desired reserve ratio, the simple deposit multiplier is 10. More generally, the simple deposit multiplier equals the reciprocal of the desired reserve ratio, expressed as a fraction (10 = 1/0.10), so the formula for the multiple expansion of deposits can be written as

$$\Delta D = \frac{1}{r_D} \times \Delta R \tag{2}$$

where ΔD = change in total chequable deposits in the banking system
r_D = desired reserve ratio (0.10 in the example)
ΔR = change in reserves for the banking system ($100 in the example)[5]

Multiple Deposit Contraction

The multiple deposit creation process should also work in reverse; that is, when the Bank of Canada withdraws reserves from the banking system, there should be a multiple contraction of deposits. To prove this, let us trace the effect of a reduction of reserves in the banking system when again we assume that banks do not hold any excess reserves.

Study Guide

Test your understanding of multiple deposit creation by writing out the appropriate T-account for each step in the process of multiple deposit contraction before you look at the T-accounts in the text.

Let's start our analysis with a $100 reduction in the reserves of the First Bank (by the Bank of Canada's sale of a $100 bond to the bank). The First Bank finds that it has lost $100 of reserves, and because it has not been holding any excess reserves, its holdings of reserves are $100 short of the desired amount. It can obtain the reserves needed by selling $100 of securities or by demanding repayment of $100 of loans. When it sells the securities, it will receive $100 of cheques written on an account with another bank that will be deposited at the Bank of Canada, thus raising its reserves by the same amount. Similarly, the repayment of the loan will also be made with cheques written on an account with another bank. In both cases, the reserves at the First Bank will be increased by $100, but the bank on which the cheques are drawn (such as Bank A) will lose $100 of chequable deposits and $100 of reserves. Bank A's T-account will be

---

[4]This multiplier should not be confused with the Keynesian multiplier, which is derived through a similar step-by-step analysis. That multiplier relates an increase in income to an increase in investment, whereas the simple deposit multiplier relates an increase in deposits to an increase in reserves.

[5]A formal derivation of this formula follows. Using the reasoning in the text, the change in chequable deposits is $100 (= $\Delta R \times 1$) plus $90 [= $\Delta R \times (1 - r_D)$] plus $81 [= $\Delta R \times (1 - r_D)^2$] and so on, which can be rewritten as

$$\Delta D = \Delta R \times [1 + (1 - r_D) + (1 - r_D)^2 + (1 - r_D)^3 + \cdots]$$

Using the formula for the sum of an infinite series found in footnote 5 in Chapter 4, this can be rewritten as

$$\Delta D = \Delta R \times \frac{1}{1 - (1 - r_D)} = \frac{1}{r_D} \times \Delta R$$

BANK A

Assets		Liabilities	
Reserves	−$100	Chequable deposits	−$100

Bank A will now find that its holdings of reserves are short of the desired amount—it will be $90 short. Its reserves have fallen by $100, but its desired reserves have also fallen by $10 (10% of the $100 decline in chequable deposits). To meet this reserve shortfall, Bank A will reduce its holdings of loans or securities by $90, transforming its T-account to

BANK A

Assets		Liabilities	
Reserves	−$10	Chequable deposits	−$100
Loans and securities	−$90		

If the cheques that Bank A receives as a result of reducing its loans or securities were written on accounts at Bank B, Bank B would then find itself with the following T-account:

BANK B

Assets		Liabilities	
Reserves	−$90	Chequable deposits	−$90

Bank B now has a reserve shortfall of $81 ($90 minus 10% of $90), and so it reduces its loans and securities by this amount, lowering another bank's chequable deposits by $81. This process keeps on going, with the level of chequable deposits in the banking system changing by

$$-\$100 - \$90 - \$81 - \$72.90 - \$65.61 - \$59.05 - \ldots = -\$1000$$

You can see that the process of multiple deposit contraction is symmetrical to the process of multiple deposit creation.

Deriving the Formula for Multiple Deposit Creation

The formula for the multiple creation of deposits can also be derived directly using algebra. We obtain the same answer for the relationship between a change in deposits and a change in reserves, but more quickly.

Our assumption that banks do not hold on to any excess reserves means that the total amount of desired reserves for the banking system DR will equal the total reserves in the banking system R:

$$DR = R$$

The total amount of desired reserves equals the desired reserve ratio r_D times the total amount of chequable deposits D:

$$DR = r_D \times D$$

Substituting $r_D \times D$ for DR in the first equation,

$$r_D \times D = R$$

and dividing both sides of the preceding equation by r_D gives us

$$D = \frac{1}{r_D} \times R$$

Taking the change in both sides of this equation and using delta to indicate a change,

$$\Delta D = \frac{1}{r_D} \times \Delta R$$

which is the same formula for deposit creation found in Equation 2.

This derivation provides us with another way of looking at the multiple creation of deposits because it forces us to look directly at the banking system as a whole rather than one bank at a time. For the banking system as a whole, deposit creation (or contraction) will stop only when all excess reserves in the banking system are gone; that is, the banking system will be in equilibrium when the total amount of desired reserves equals the total amount of reserves, as seen in the equation $DR = R$. When $r_D \times D$ is substituted for DR, the resulting equation $R = r_D \times D$ tells us how high chequable deposits will have to be in order for desired reserves to equal total reserves. Accordingly, a given level of reserves in the banking system determines the level of chequable deposits when the banking system is in equilibrium (when excess reserves, ER, equal 0); put another way, the given level of reserves supports a given level of chequable deposits.

In our example, the desired reserve ratio is 10%. If reserves increase by $100, chequable deposits must rise to $1000 in order for total desired reserves also to increase by $100. If the increase in chequable deposits is less than this, say $900, then the increase in desired reserves of $90 remains below the $100 increase in reserves, so there are still excess reserves somewhere in the banking system. The banks with the excess reserves will now make additional loans, creating new deposits, and this process will continue until all reserves in the system are used up. This occurs when chequable deposits have risen to $1000.

We can also see this by looking at the T-account of the banking system as a whole (including the First Bank) that results from this process:

BANKING SYSTEM

Assets		Liabilities	
Securities	−$ 100	Chequable deposits	+$1000
Reserves	+$ 100		
Loans	+$1000		

The procedure of eliminating excess reserves by loaning them out means that the banking system (First Bank and Banks A, B, C, D, and so on) continues to make loans up to the $1000 amount until deposits have reached the $1000 level. In this way, $100 of reserves supports $1000 (ten times the quantity) of deposits.

Critique of the Simple Model

Our model of multiple deposit creation seems to indicate that the Bank of Canada is able to exercise complete control over the level of chequable deposits by setting the level of reserves. The actual creation of deposits is much less mechanical than the simple model indicates. If proceeds from Bank A's $90 loan are not deposited but are kept in cash, nothing is deposited in Bank B, and the deposit creation process stops dead in its tracks. The total increase in chequable deposits is only $100—considerably less than the $1000 we calculated. So if some proceeds from loans are used to raise the holdings of currency, chequable deposits will not increase by as much as our streamlined model of multiple deposit creation tells us.

Another situation ignored in our model is one in which the desired reserve ratio can change over time. If Bank A decides to hold on to all $90 of its excess reserves (reflecting an increase in desired reserves), no deposits would be made in Bank B, and this would also stop the deposit creation process. The total increase in deposits would again be only $100 and not the $1000 increase in our example. Hence if the desired reserve ratio increases, the full expansion of deposits predicted by the simple model of multiple deposit creation does not occur.

Our examples rightly indicate that the Bank of Canada is not the only player whose behaviour influences the level of deposits and therefore the money supply. Banks' decisions regarding the amount of reserves they wish to hold, depositors' decisions regarding how much currency to hold, and borrowers' decisions on how much to borrow from banks can cause the money supply to change. In the next chapter we stress the behaviour and interactions of the four players in constructing a more realistic model of the money supply process.

SUMMARY

1. There are four players in the money supply process: the central bank, banks (depository institutions), depositors, and borrowers from banks.

2. The monetary base consists of currency in circulation and reserves. Eight factors affect the monetary base: (1) the Bank of Canada's holdings of securities and investments, (2) advances, (3) foreign currency assets, (4) securities purchased under resale agreements, (5) currency outstanding, (6) other Bank of Canada assets (net), (7) government deposits with the Bank of Canada, and (8) securities sold under repurchase agreements. Increases in the first six factors add to the monetary base; increases in the last two factors reduce the monetary base.

3. The Bank of Canada controls the monetary base through open market operations and extension of advances to banks and has better control over the monetary base than over reserves.

4. A single bank can make loans up to the amount of its excess reserves, thereby creating an equal amount of deposits. The banking system can create a multiple expansion of deposits because as each bank makes a loan and creates deposits, the reserves find their way to another bank, which uses them to make loans and create additional deposits. In the simple model of multiple deposit creation in which banks do not hold on to excess reserves and the public holds no currency, the multiple increase in chequable deposits (simple deposit multiplier) equals the reciprocal of the desired reserve ratio.

5. The simple model of multiple deposit creation has serious deficiencies. Decisions by depositors to increase their holdings of currency or of banks to hold excess reserves will result in a smaller expansion of deposits than the simple model predicts. All four players—the Bank of Canada, banks, depositors, and borrowers from banks—are important in the determination of the money supply.

KEY TERMS

bank rate, p. 344

desired reserve ratio, p. 345

desired reserves, p. 345

excess reserves, p. 345

Exchange Fund Account, p. 343

government deposit transfers, p. 345

high-powered money, p. 347

monetary base, p. 346

multiple deposit creation, p. 354

open market operations, p. 347

open market purchase, p. 348

open market sale, p. 348

required reserves, p. 346

reserves, p. 345

Sale and Repurchase Agreements (SRAs), p. 346

settlement balances, p. 345

simple deposit multiplier, p. 358

Special Purchase and Resale Agreements (SPRAs), p. 344

sources of the base, p. 347

uses of the base, p. 347

QUESTIONS AND PROBLEMS

Questions marked with an asterisk are answered at the end of the book in an appendix, "Answers to Selected Questions and Problems."

1. If the Bank of Canada sells $2 million of bonds to the First Bank, what happens to reserves and the monetary base? Use T-accounts to explain your answer.

*2. If the Bank of Canada sells $2 million of bonds to Irving the Investor, who pays for the bonds with a briefcase filled with currency, what happens to reserves and the monetary base? Use T-accounts to explain your answer.

*3. If the Bank of Canada lends five banks an additional total of $100 million but depositors withdraw $50 million and hold it as currency, what happens to reserves and the monetary base? Use T-accounts to explain your answer.

4. The First Bank receives an extra $100 of reserves but decides not to lend any of these reserves out. How much deposit creation takes place for the entire banking system?

   Unless otherwise noted, the following assumptions are made in all the remaining problems: the desired reserve ratio on chequable deposits is 10%, banks do not hold on to excess reserves, and the public's holdings of currency do not change.

*5. Using T-accounts, show what happens to chequable deposits in the banking system when the Bank of Canada lends an additional $1 million to the First Bank.

6. Using T-accounts, show what happens to chequable deposits in the banking system when the Bank of Canada sells $2 million of bonds to the First Bank.

*7. Suppose that the Bank of Canada buys $1 million of bonds from the First Bank. If the First Bank and all other banks use the resulting increase in reserves to purchase securities only and not to make loans, what will happen to chequable deposits?

8. If the Bank of Canada buys $1 million of bonds from the First Bank, but an additional 10% of any deposit is held as excess reserves, what is the total increase in chequable deposits? (*Hint*: Use T-accounts to show what happens at each step of the multiple expansion process.)

*9. If a bank depositor withdraws $1000 of currency from an account, what happens to reserves and chequable deposits?

10. If reserves in the banking system increase by $1 billion as a result of advances of $1 billion and chequable deposits increase by $9 billion, why isn't the banking system in equilibrium? What will continue to happen in the banking system until equilibrium is reached? Show the T-account for the banking system in equilibrium.

*11. If the Bank of Canada reduces reserves by selling $5 million worth of bonds to the banks, what will the T-account of the banking system look like when the banking system is in equilibrium? What will have happened to the level of chequable deposits?

12. If the desired reserve ratio on chequable deposits increases to 20%, how much multiple deposit creation will take place when reserves are increased by $100?

*13. If a bank decides that it wants to hold $1 million of excess reserves, what effect will this have on chequable deposits in the banking system?

14. If a bank sells $10 million of bonds back to the Bank of Canada in order to pay back $10 million on the advances it owes, what will be the effect on the level of chequable deposits?

*15. If you decide to hold $100 less cash than usual and therefore deposit $100 in cash in the bank, what effect will this have on chequable deposits in the banking system if the rest of the public keeps its holdings of currency constant?

Chapter 16

Determinants of the Money Supply

PREVIEW   In Chapter 15 we developed a simple model of multiple deposit creation that showed how the Bank of Canada can control the level of chequable deposits by setting the level of reserves. Unfortunately for the Bank, life isn't that simple; control of the money supply is far more complicated. Our critique of this model indicated that decisions by depositors about their holdings of currency and by banks about their holdings of reserves also affect the money supply. To deal with this critique, in this chapter we develop a money supply model in which depositors and banks assume their important roles. The resulting framework provides an in-depth description of the money supply process to help you understand the complexity of the Bank's role.

To simplify the analysis, we separate the development of our model into several steps. First, because the Bank of Canada can exert more precise control over the monetary base (currency in circulation plus total reserves in the banking system) than it can over total reserves alone, our model links changes in the money supply to changes in the monetary base. This link is achieved by deriving a **money multiplier** (a ratio that relates the change in the money supply to a given change in the monetary base). Finally, we examine the determinants of the money multiplier.

Study Guide

One reason for breaking the money supply model into its component parts is to help you answer questions using intuitive step-by-step logic rather than memorizing how changes in the behaviour of the Bank of Canada, depositors, or banks will affect the money supply.

In deriving a model of the money supply process, we focus here on a simple definition of money (currency plus all chequable deposits at chartered banks, trust and mortgage loan companies, and credit unions and *caisses populaires*), which corresponds to M1+. Although other definitions of money are frequently used in policymaking, we conduct the analysis with an M1+ definition because it is less complicated and yet provides a basic understanding of the money supply process. Furthermore, all analyses and results using the M1+ definition apply equally well to other definitions. A somewhat more complicated money supply model for the M2+ definition is developed in the appendix to this chapter.

THE MONEY SUPPLY MODEL AND THE MONEY MULTIPLIER

Because, as we saw in Chapter 15, the Bank of Canada can control the monetary base better than it can control reserves, it makes sense to link the money supply M to the monetary base MB through a relationship such as the following:

$$M = m \times MB \qquad (1)$$

The variable m is the money multiplier, which tells us how much the money supply changes for a given change in the monetary base MB. This multiplier tells us what multiple of the monetary base is transformed into the money supply. Because the money multiplier is larger than 1, the alternative name for the monetary base, *high-powered money*, is logical. A \$1 change in the monetary base leads to more than a \$1 change in the money supply.

The money multiplier reflects the effect on the money supply of other factors besides the monetary base, and the following model will explain the factors that determine the size of the money multiplier. Depositors' decisions about their holdings of currency and chequable deposits are one set of factors affecting the money multiplier. Another involves the banks' decisions about reserves.

Deriving the Money Multiplier

In our model of multiple deposit creation in Chapter 15, we ignored the effects on deposit creation of changes in the public's holdings of currency and banks' holdings of reserves. Now we incorporate these changes into our model of the money supply process by assuming that the desired level of currency C, like desired reserves DR, grows proportionally with chequable deposits D; in other words, we assume that the ratios of these items to chequable deposits are constants in equilibrium:

$$c = \text{currency ratio, } C/D$$
$$r_D = \text{desired reserve ratio, } DR/D$$

We will now derive a formula that describes how the currency ratio desired by depositors c and the reserves ratio desired by banks r_D affect the money multiplier m. We begin the derivation of the model of the money supply with the equation

$$R = DR$$

which states that the total amount of reserves in the banking system R equals desired reserves DR. (Note that this equation is the same as the equilibrium condition in Chapter 15, where excess reserves were assumed to be zero.)

The total amount of desired reserves equals the desired reserve ratio r_D times the amount of chequable deposits D:

$$DR = r_D \times D$$

Substituting $r_D \times D$ for DR in the first equation yields an equation that links reserves in the banking system to the amount of chequable deposits they can support:

$$R = r_D \times D$$

A key point here is that banks set the desired reserve ratio r_D to be less than 1. Thus $1 of reserves can support more than $1 of deposits, and the multiple expansion of deposits can occur.

Let's see how this works in practice. If the desired reserve ratio is $r_D = 0.05$, and the level of chequable deposits in the banking system is $800 billion, the amount of reserves needed to support these deposits is $40 billion (= $0.05 \times $800 billion). The $40 billion of reserves can support twenty times this amount in chequable deposits, because multiple deposit creation will occur.

Because the monetary base *MB* equals currency *C* plus reserves *R*, we can generate an equation that links the amount of monetary base to the levels of chequable deposits and currency by adding currency to both sides of the equation:

$$MB = C + R = C + (r_D \times D)$$

Another way of thinking about this equation is to recognize that it reveals the amount of the monetary base needed to support the existing amounts of currency and chequable deposits.

An important feature of this equation is that an additional dollar of *MB* that arises from an additional dollar of currency does not support any additional deposits. This occurs because such an increase leads to an identical increase in the right-hand side of the equation with no change occurring in *D*. The currency component of *MB* does not lead to multiple deposit creation as the reserves component does. Put another way, ***an increase in the monetary base that goes into currency is not multiplied, whereas an increase that goes into supporting deposits is multiplied***.

To derive the money multiplier formula in terms of the currency ratio *c* and the desired reserve ratio, we rewrite the last equation, specifying *C* as $c \times D$:

$$MB = (c \times D) + (r_D \times D)$$
$$= (c + r_D) \times D$$

We next divide both sides of the equation by the term inside the parentheses to get an expression linking chequable deposits *D* to the monetary base *MB*:

$$D = \frac{1}{c + r_D} \times MB \tag{2}$$

Using the definition of the money supply as currency plus chequable deposits ($M = C + D$) and again specifying *C* as $c \times D$

$$M = (c \times D) + D$$
$$= (1 + c) \times D$$

Substituting in this equation the expression for *D* from Equation 2, we have

$$M = \frac{1 + c}{c + r_D} \times MB \tag{3}$$

Finally, we have achieved our objective of deriving an expression in the form of our earlier Equation 1. As you can see, the ratio that multiplies *MB* is the money multiplier that tells how much the money supply changes in response to a given change in the monetary base (high-powered money). The money multiplier *m* is thus

$$m = \frac{1 + c}{c + r_D} \tag{4}$$

and it is a function of the currency ratio set by depositors *c* and the desired reserve ratio set by banks r_D.

Although the algebraic derivation we have just completed shows you how the money multiplier is constructed, you need to understand the basic intuition behind it to understand and apply the money multiplier concept without having to memorize it.

Intuition Behind the Money Multiplier

In order to get a feel for what the money multiplier means, let us again construct a numerical example with realistic numbers for the following variables:

$$r_D = \text{desired reserve ratio} = 0.05$$
$$C = \text{currency in circulation} = \$40 \text{ billion}$$
$$D = \text{chequable deposits} = \$160 \text{ billion}$$
$$M = \text{money supply (M1+)} = C + D = \$200 \text{ billion}$$

From these numbers we can calculate the value for the currency ratio c:

$$c = \frac{\$40 \text{ billion}}{\$160 \text{ billion}} = 0.25$$

The resulting value of the money multiplier is

$$m = \frac{1 + 0.25}{0.25 + 0.05} = \frac{1.25}{0.3} = 4.2$$

The money multiplier of 4.2 tells us that given the behaviour of depositors as represented by $c = 0.25$ and banks as represented by $r_D = 0.05$, a \$1 increase in the monetary base leads to a \$4.20 increase in the money supply (M1+).

An important characteristic of the money multiplier is that it is less than the simple deposit multiplier of 20 one would find if $c = 0$. The key to understanding this result and our money supply model is to realize that **although there is multiple expansion of deposits, there is no such expansion for currency.** Thus if some portion of the increase in high-powered money finds its way into currency, this portion does not undergo multiple deposit expansion. In our analysis in Chapter 15, we did not allow for this possibility, and so the increase in reserves led to the maximum amount of multiple deposit creation. However, in our current model of the money multiplier, the level of currency does increase when the monetary base *MB* and chequable deposits *D* increase because c is greater than zero. As previously stated, any increase in *MB* that goes into an increase in currency is not multiplied, so only part of the increase in *MB* is available to support chequable deposits that undergo multiple expansion. The overall level of multiple deposit expansion must be lower, meaning that the increase in *M*, given an increase in *MB*, is smaller than the simple model in Chapter 15 would indicate.

FACTORS THAT DETERMINE THE MONEY MULTIPLIER

To develop our intuition of the money multiplier even further, let us look at how this multiplier changes in response to changes in the variables in our model: c and r_D. The "game" we are playing is a familiar one in economics: we ask what happens when one of these variables changes, leaving all other variables the same (*ceteris paribus*).

Changes in the Currency Ratio c

What happens to the money multiplier when depositor behaviour causes c to increase with all other variables unchanged? An increase in c means that depositors are converting some of their chequable deposits into currency. As shown before, chequable deposits undergo multiple expansion while currency does not.

Hence when chequable deposits are being converted into currency, there is a switch from a component of the money supply that undergoes multiple expansion to one that does not. The overall level of multiple expansion declines, and so must the multiplier.[1]

We can verify that the foregoing analysis is correct by seeing what happens to the value of the money multiplier in our numerical example when c rises from 0.25 to 0.30 (leaving all the other variables unchanged). The money multiplier becomes

$$m = \frac{1 + 0.30}{0.30 + 0.05} = \frac{1.30}{0.35} = 3.7$$

which, as we would expect, is less than 4.2.

The analysis just conducted can also be applied to the case in which the currency ratio falls. In this case, there would be more multiple expansion for chequable deposits, since there is a switch from a component of the money supply that does not undergo multiple expansion to one that does. For example, if c falls from 0.25 to 0.20, plugging this value into our money multiplier formula (leaving all the other variables unchanged) yields a money multiplier of

$$m = \frac{1 + 0.20}{0.20 + 0.05} = \frac{1.20}{0.25} = 4.8$$

which is above the initial value of 4.2.

We can now state the following result: ***the money multiplier and the money supply are negatively related to the currency ratio* c**.

Changes in the Desired Reserve Ratio r_D

When banks increase their holdings of reserves relative to chequable deposits, the banking system in effect has fewer reserves to support chequable deposits. This means that given the same level of *MB*, banks will reduce their loans, causing a decline in the level of chequable deposits and a decline in the money supply, and the money multiplier will fall.[2]

This reasoning is supported in our numerical example when r_D increases from 5% to 10%. The money multiplier declines from 4.2 to

$$m = \frac{1 + 0.25}{0.25 + 0.10} = \frac{1.25}{0.35} = 3.6$$

Note that although the desired reserve ratio has doubled, there has been only a small decline in the money multiplier. This decline is small because in recent years r_D has been extremely small, so changes in it have only a small impact on the money multiplier. Our final result, however, is still an important one: ***the money multiplier and the money supply are negatively related to the desired reserve ratio* r_D.**

To understand the factors that determine the level of r_D in the banking system, we must look at the costs and benefits to banks of holding reserves. When the costs of holding reserves rise, we would expect the level of desired reserves and hence r_D to fall; when the benefits of holding reserves rise, we would expect the level of desired reserves and r_D to rise. Two primary factors affect these costs and benefits and hence affect the desired reserve ratio: market interest rates and expected deposit outflows.

---

[1] As long as r_D is less than 1 (as is the case using the realistic numbers we have used), an increase in c raises the denominator of the money multiplier proportionally by more than it raises the numerator. The increase in c causes the multiplier to fall.

[2] This result can be demonstrated from the Equation 4 formula as follows: when r_D rises, the denominator of the money multiplier rises, and so the money multiplier must fall.

Market Interest Rates As you may recall from our analysis of bank management in Chapter 9, the cost to a bank of holding reserves is its opportunity cost, the interest that could have been earned on loans or securities if they had been held instead of reserves. For the sake of simplicity, we assume that loans and securities earn the same interest rate i, which we call the market interest rate. If i increases, the opportunity cost of holding reserves rises, and the desired ratio of reserves to deposits will fall. A decrease in i, conversely, will reduce the opportunity cost of reserves, and r_D will rise. ***The banking system's desired reserve ratio r_D is negatively related to the market interest rate i.***

Another way of understanding the negative effect of market interest rates on r_D is to return to the theory of asset demand, which states that if the expected returns on alternative assets rise relative to the expected returns on an asset, the demand for that asset will decrease. As the market interest rate increases, the expected return on loans and securities rises relative to the zero return on reserves, and the desired reserve ratio falls.

Expected Deposit Outflows Our analysis of bank management in Chapter 9 also indicated that the primary benefit to a bank of holding reserves is that they provide insurance against losses due to deposit outflows; that is, they enable the bank experiencing deposit outflows to escape the costs of calling in loans, selling securities, borrowing from the Bank of Canada or other corporations, or bank failure. If banks fear that deposit outflows are likely to increase (that is, if expected deposit outflows increase), they will want more insurance against this possibility and will increase the reserve ratio. Another way to put it is this: if expected deposit outflows rise, the expected benefits, and hence the expected returns for holding reserves, increase. As the theory of asset demand predicts, desired reserves will then rise. Conversely, a decline in expected deposit outflows will reduce the insurance benefit of reserves, and their level should fall. We have the following result: ***the desired reserve ratio r_D is positively related to expected deposit outflows***.

ADDITIONAL FACTORS THAT DETERMINE THE MONEY SUPPLY

So far we have been assuming that the Bank of Canada has complete control over the monetary base. However, whereas the amount of open market purchases or sales is completely controlled by the Bank's placing orders with dealers in bond markets, the central bank lacks complete control over the monetary base because it cannot unilaterally determine, and therefore perfectly predict, the amount of borrowing by banks from the Bank. The Bank of Canada sets the bank rate (interest rate on advances), and then banks make decisions about whether to borrow. The amount of advances, though influenced by the Bank's setting of the bank rate, is not completely controlled by the Bank; banks' decisions play a role too.

Therefore, we might want to split the monetary base into two components: one that the Bank of Canada can control completely and another that is less tightly controlled. The less tightly controlled component is the amount of the base that is created by advances from the Bank. The remainder of the base (called the **nonborrowed monetary base**) is under the Bank's control because it results primarily from open market operations.[3] The nonborrowed monetary base is formally defined as the monetary base minus advances from the Bank of Canada:

---

[3]Actually, there are other items on the Bank's balance sheet (discussed in Chapter 15) that affect the magnitude of the nonborrowed monetary base. Since their effects on the nonborrowed base relative to open market operations are both small and predictable, these other items do not present the Bank with difficulties in controlling the nonborrowed base.

$$MB_n = MB - A$$

where MB_n = nonborrowed monetary base
             MB = monetary base
             A = advances from the Bank of Canada

The reason for distinguishing the nonborrowed monetary base MB_n from the monetary base MB is that the nonborrowed monetary base, which is tied to open market operations, is directly under the control of the Bank of Canada, whereas the monetary base, which is also influenced by advances from the Bank, is not.

To complete the money supply model, we use the fact that $MB = MB_n + A$ and rewrite the money supply model as

$$M = m \times (MB_n + A) \tag{5}$$

where the money multiplier m is defined as in Equation 4. Thus in addition to the effects on the money supply of the currency ratio and the desired reserve ratio, the expanded model stipulates that the money supply is also affected by changes in MB_n and A. Because the money multiplier is positive, Equation 5 immediately tells us that the money supply is positively related to both the nonborrowed monetary base and advances. However, it is still worth developing the intuition for these results.

Changes in the Nonborrowed Monetary Base MB_n

As shown in Chapter 15, the Bank of Canada's open market purchases increase the nonborrowed monetary base, and its open market sales decrease it. Holding all other variables constant, an increase in MB_n arising from an open market purchase increases the amount of the monetary base that is available to support currency and deposits, so the money supply will increase. Similarly, an open market sale that decreases MB_n will shrink the amount of the monetary base available to support currency and deposits, thereby causing the money supply to decrease.

We have the following result: ***the money supply is positively related to the nonborrowed monetary base*** **MB_n**.

Changes in Advances from the Bank of Canada

With the nonborrowed monetary base MB_n unchanged, more advances from the Bank of Canada provide additional reserves (and hence higher MB) to the banking system, and these are used to support more currency and deposits. As a result, the increase in A will lead to a rise in the money supply. If banks reduce the level of their borrowing from the Bank of Canada with all other variables held constant, the amount of MB available to support currency and deposits will decline, causing the money supply to decline.

The result is this: ***the money supply is positively related to the level of advances*** **A** ***from the Bank of Canada***.

Market Interest Rates and the Bank Rate

Our analysis of what determines bank borrowing from the Bank of Canada relies on identifying the costs and benefits of borrowing from the Bank. Two primary factors affect these costs and benefits and subsequently the volume of advances: market interest rates and the bank rate.

The principal benefit for a bank when it borrows from the Bank of Canada is straightforward. With additional borrowed reserves, a bank can acquire loans and securities, which earn the market interest rate i. The primary cost of borrowing for the bank, however, is the bank rate i_b, the interest rate the Bank of Canada charges on its loans to banks.[4] The greater the difference between the benefits

---

[4]Changes in the bank rate i_b can also have an effect on the desired reserve ratio r_D. The cost to a bank experiencing a deposit outflow rises when i_b rises because it is more costly to borrow from the Bank of Canada when an outflow occurs. Thus a rise in i_b increases the benefits of holding reserves and r_D rises. This effect of the bank rate on the desired reserve ratio has not been emphasized in the text because it is believed to be small.

(earnings) obtained from the use of borrowed funds i and the cost of borrowing i_b, the more a bank will borrow from the Bank of Canada. Thus advances are positively related to $i - i_b$. This relationship in turn implies that **the amount of advances A is positively related to the market interest rate i and negatively related to the bank rate i_b.**

However, as we will see in Chapter 17, in the current Canadian framework for monetary policy implementation, the Bank of Canada's standing liquidity facilities have been designed in such a way that it is better for banks to deal directly with each other in the overnight money market than to borrow from the Bank of Canada at the bank rate.

OVERVIEW OF THE MONEY SUPPLY PROCESS

We now have a model of the money supply process in which all four of the players—the Bank of Canada, depositors, banks, and borrowers from banks—directly influence the money supply. As a study aid, Table 16-1 charts the money supply (M1+) response to the five variables discussed and gives a brief synopsis of the reasoning behind each result.

*Study
Guide*

To improve your understanding of the money supply process, slowly work through the logic behind the results in Table 16-1 rather than just memorizing the results. Then see if you can construct your own table in which all the variables decrease rather than increase.

SUMMARY

TABLE 16-1 Money Supply (M1+) Response

Player	Variable	Change in Variable	Money Supply Response	Reason
Bank of Canada	MB_n	↑	↑	More MB to support currency and chequable deposits
	i_b	↑	↓	A ↓ so less MB to support D and C
Depositors	c	↑	↓	Less multiple deposit expansion
Depositors and banks	Expected deposit outflow	↑	↓	r_D ↑ so more reserves to support D
Borrowers from banks and other three players	i	↑	↑	r_D ↓ so more reserves to support D; A ↑ so more MB to support D and C

Note. Only increases (↑) in the variables are shown. The effects of decreases on the money supply would be the opposite of those indicated in the "Response" column.

The variables are grouped by the player or players who either influence the variable or are most influenced by it. The Bank of Canada, for example, influences the money supply by controlling the first two variables—MB_n and i_b, also known as the tools of the Bank. (How these tools are used is discussed in subsequent chapters.) Depositors influence the money supply through their decisions about the currency ratio c, while banks influence the money supply by their decisions about r_D, which is affected by their expectations about deposit outflows. Because depositors' behaviour also influences bankers' expectations about deposit outflows, this variable also reflects the role of both depositors and bankers in the money supply process. Market interest rates, as represented by i, affect the money supply through the desired reserve ratio, r_D. As shown in Chapter 5, the demand for loans by borrowers influences market interest rates, as does the supply of money. Therefore, all four players are important in the determination of i.

We developed a multiplicative relationship between the money supply and the monetary base, suggesting that the Bank of Canada could control the money supply by controlling the quantity of base money or official bank reserves. In Canada, however, there are no official bank reserves, and although a money multiplier exists between the money supply and the aggregate liquidity reserves of deposit-based financial institutions, currently the Bank of Canada and most central banks throughout the world implement monetary policy through their influence on short-term interest rates. As you will see in Chapter 17, in Canada the overnight money market is at the centre of the banking system and the overnight interest rate is the Bank of Canada's operating target.

APPLICATION   *The Great Depression Bank Panics, 1930–1933*

We can also use our money supply model to help us understand major movements in the money supply that have occurred in the past. In this application, we use the model to explain the monetary contraction that occurred in the United States during the Great Depression. In Chapter 8 we discussed bank panics and saw that they could harm the economy by making asymmetric information problems more severe in credit markets, as they did during the Great Depression. Here we can see that another consequence of bank panics is that they can cause a substantial reduction in the money supply. As we will see in the chapters on monetary theory later in the book, such reductions can also cause severe damage to the economy.

Figure 16-1 traces the bank crisis during the Great Depression by showing the volume of deposits at failed commercial banks from 1929 to 1933. In their classic book *A Monetary History of the United States, 1867–1960*, Milton Friedman and Anna Schwartz describe the onset of the first banking crisis in late 1930 as follows:

> Before October 1930, deposits of suspended [failed] commercial banks had been somewhat higher than during most of 1929 but not out of line with experience during the preceding decade. In November 1930, they were more than double the highest value recorded since the start of monthly data in 1921. A crop of bank failures, particularly in Missouri, Indiana, Illinois, Iowa, Arkansas, and North Carolina, led to widespread attempts to convert chequable and time deposits into currency, and also, to a much lesser extent, into postal savings deposits. A contagion of fear spread among depositors, starting from the agricultural areas, which had experienced the heaviest impact of bank failures in the twenties. But failure of 256 banks with $180 million of deposits in November 1930 was

FIGURE 16-1 Deposits of Failed Commercial Banks, 1929–1933

Source: Milton Friedman and Anna Jacobson Schwartz, *A Monetary History of the United States, 1867–1960* (Princeton, N.J.: Princeton University Press, 1963), p. 309.

followed by the failure of 532 with over $370 million of deposits in December (all figures seasonally unadjusted), the most dramatic being the failure on December 11 of the Bank of the United States with over $200 million of deposits. That failure was especially important. The Bank of United States was the largest commercial bank, as measured by volume of deposits, ever to have failed up to that time in U.S. history. Moreover, though it was just an ordinary commercial bank, the Bank of the United States's name had led many at home and abroad to regard it somehow as an official bank, hence its failure constituted more of a blow to confidence than would have been administered by the fall of a bank with a less distinctive name.[5]

The first bank panic, from October 1930 to January 1931, is clearly visible in Figure 16-1 at the end of 1930, when there is a rise in the amount of deposits at failed banks. Because there was no deposit insurance at the time (the FDIC wasn't established until 1934), when a bank failed, depositors would receive only partial repayment of their deposits. Therefore, when banks were failing during a bank panic, depositors knew that they would be likely to suffer substantial losses on deposits and thus the expected return on deposits would be negative. The theory of asset demand predicts that with the onset of the first bank crisis, depositors would shift their holdings from chequable deposits to currency by withdrawing currency from their bank accounts, and c would rise. Our earlier analysis of excess reserves suggests that the resulting surge in deposit outflows would cause the banks to protect themselves by substantially increasing their excess reserves ratio

---

[5]Milton Friedman and Anna Jacobson Schwartz, *A Monetary History of the United States, 1867–1960* (Princeton, N.J.: Princeton University Press, 1963), pp. 308–311.

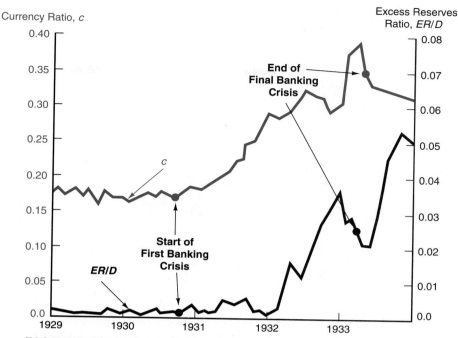

FIGURE 16-2   Excess Reserves Ratio and Currency Ratio, 1929–1933

Source: Federal Reserve *Bulletin*; Milton Friedman and Anna Jacobson Schwartz, *A Monetary History of the United States, 1867–1960* (Princeton, N.J.: Princeton University Press, 1963), p. 333.

ER/D.[6] Both of these predictions are borne out by the data in Figure 16-2. During the first bank panic (October 1930–January 1931) *c* began to climb. Even more striking is the behaviour of *ER/D*, which more than doubled from November 1930 to January 1931.

The money supply model predicts that when *ER/D* and *c* increase, the money supply will fall. The rise in *c* results in a decline in the overall level of multiple deposit expansion, leading to a smaller money multiplier and a decline in the money supply, while the rise in *ER/D* reduces the amount of reserves available to support deposits and also causes the money supply to fall. Thus our model predicts that the rise in *ER/D* and *c* after the onset of the first bank crisis would result in a decline in the money supply—a prediction borne out by the evidence in Figure 16-3. The money supply declined sharply in December 1930 and January 1931 during the first bank panic.

Banking crises continued to occur from 1931 to 1933, and the pattern predicted by our model persisted: *c* continued to rise, and so did *ER/D*. By the end of the crises in March 1933, the money supply (M1) had declined by over 25%— by far the largest decline in all of American history—and it coincided with the nation's worst economic contraction (see Chapter 8). Even more remarkable is that this decline occurred despite a 20% rise in the level of the monetary base— which illustrates how important the changes in *c* and *ER/D* during bank panics can be in the determination of the money supply. It also illustrates that a central bank's job of conducting monetary policy can be complicated by depositor and bank behaviour.

---

[6]In this application we use the term *excess reserves* to mean reserves in excess of required reserves.

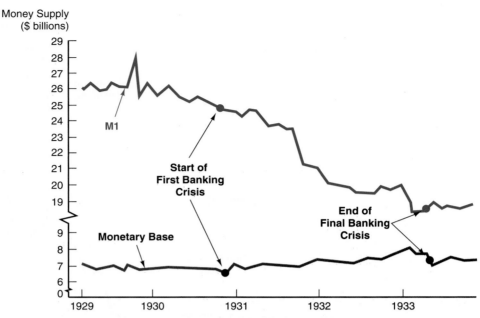

FIGURE 16-3   M1 and the Monetary Base, 1929–1933

Source: Milton Friedman and Anna Jacobson Schwartz, *A Monetary History of the United States, 1867–1960* (Princeton, N.J.: Princeton University Press, 1963), p. 333.

SUMMARY

1. We developed a model to describe how the money supply is determined. First, we linked the monetary base to the money supply using the concept of the money multiplier, which tells us how much the money supply changes when there is a change in the monetary base.

2. The money supply is negatively related to the desired reserve ratio r_D and the currency ratio c. It is positively related to the level of advances A from the Bank of Canada and the nonborrowed base MB_n, which is determined by Bank of Canada open market opera-

tions. The money supply model therefore allows for the behaviour of all four players in the money supply process: the Bank of Canada through its setting of the bank rate and open market operations; depositors through their decisions about the currency ratio; the banks through their decisions about the desired reserve ratio and advances from the Bank of Canada; and borrowers from banks indirectly through their effect on market interest rates, which affect bank decisions regarding the desired reserve ratio and borrowings from the Bank of Canada.

KEY TERMS

money multiplier, p. 363

nonborrowed monetary base, p. 368

QUESTIONS AND PROBLEMS

Questions marked with an asterisk are answered at the end of the book in an appendix, "Answers to Selected Questions and Problems."

*1. "The money multiplier is necessarily greater than 1." Is this statement true, false, or uncertain? Explain your answer.

2. "If the desired reserve ratio on chequable deposits were set at zero, the amount of multiple deposit expansion would go on indefinitely." Is this statement true, false, or uncertain? Explain.

*3. During the Great Depression years 1930–1933, the currency ratio c rose dramatically. What do you think happened to the money supply? Why?

4. During the Great Depression, the excess reserves ratio ER/D rose dramatically. What do you think happened to the money supply? Why?

*5. Suppose that traveller's cheques were included in the M1+ measure of the money supply and had no reserve requirements. When people travel during the summer and convert some of their chequing account deposits into traveller's cheques, what would happen to the money supply? Why?

6. If Jane Brown closes her account at the First Bank and uses the money instead to open a money market mutual fund account, what happens to M1+ and M2++? Why?

*7. What happens to M2+ when chequable deposits are converted into time deposits?

8. Why might the procyclical behaviour of interest rates (rising during business cycle expansions and falling during recessions) lead to procyclical movements in the money supply?

Using Economic Analysis to Predict the Future

*9. The Bank of Canada buys $100 million of bonds from the public and banks lower r_D. What will happen to the money supply?

10. If the Bank of Canada paid interest on bank reserves, what would happen to r_D?

*11. If the Bank of Canada sells $1 million of bonds and banks reduce their borrowing from the Bank of Canada by $1 million, predict what will happen to the money supply.

12. Predict what will happen to the money supply if there is a sharp rise in the currency ratio.

*13. What do you predict would happen to the money supply if expected inflation suddenly increased?

14. If the economy starts to boom and loan demand picks up, what do you predict will happen to the money supply?

*15. Milton Friedman once suggested that central bank lending should be abolished. Predict what would happen to the money supply if Friedman's suggestion were put into practice.

Appendix to Chapter 16

The M2+ Money Multiplier

The derivation of a money multiplier for the M2+ definition of money requires only slight modifications to the analysis in the chapter. The definition of M2+ is

$$M2+ = C + D + T + MMF$$

where C = currency in circulation
D = all chequable deposits
T = all time and savings deposits
MMF = money market mutual funds

We again assume that all desired quantities of these variables rise proportionally with chequable deposits so that the equilibrium ratios

c = currency ratio, C/D
t = time deposit ratio, T/D
f = money market fund ratio, MMF/D

set by depositors and the desired reserve ratio r_D set by banks are treated as constants. Replacing C by $c \times D$, T by $t \times D$, and MMF by $f \times D$ in the definition of M2+ just given, we get

$$M2+ = (c \times D) + D + (t \times D) + (f \times D)$$
$$= (1 + c + t + f) \times D$$

Substituting in the expression for D from equation 2 in the chapter,[1] we have

$$M2+ = \frac{1 + c + t + f}{c + r_D} \times MB$$

---

[1]From the derivation here it is clear that the quantity of chequable deposits D is unaffected by the depositor ratios t and f even though time deposits and money market mutual funds are included in M2+. This is just a consequence of the fact that the desired reserve ratios on time deposits and money market mutual funds are zero (because they are not payable on demand), so T and MMF do not appear in any of the equations in the derivation of D in the chapter.

To see what this formula implies about the M2+ money multiplier, we continue with the same numerical example in the chapter, with the additional information that T = \$320 billion and MMF = \$80 billion so that t = 2 and f = 0.5. The resulting value of the multiplier for M2+ is

$$m = \frac{1 + 0.25 + 2 + 0.5}{0.25 + 0.05} = \frac{3.75}{0.3} = 12.5$$

An important feature of the M2+ multiplier is that it is substantially above the M1+ multiplier of 4.2 that we found in the chapter. The crucial concept in understanding this difference is that a lower desired reserve ratio for time deposits or money market mutual funds means that they undergo more multiple expansion because fewer reserves are needed to support the same amount of them. Time deposits and $MMFs$ have a lower desired reserve ratio than chequable deposits—zero—and they will therefore have more multiple expansion than chequable deposits will. Thus the overall multiple expansion for the sum of these deposits will be greater than for chequable deposits alone, and so the M2+ money multiplier will be greater than the M1+ money multiplier.

FACTORS THAT DETERMINE THE M2+ MONEY MULTIPLIER

Changes in c and r_D

The economic reasoning analyzing the effect of changes in the desired reserve ratio and the currency ratio on the M2+ money multiplier is identical to that used for the M1+ multiplier in the chapter. An increase in the desired reserve ratio r_D will decrease the amount of multiple deposit expansion, thus lowering the M2+ money multiplier. An increase in c means that depositors have shifted out of chequable deposits into currency, and since currency has no multiple deposit expansion, the overall level of multiple deposit expansion for M2+ must also fall, lowering the M2+ multiplier.

We thus have the same results we found for the M1+ multiplier: **the M2+ money multiplier and M2+ money supply are negatively related to the desired reserve ratio r_D and the currency ratio c.**

Response to Changes in t and f

An increase in either t or f leads to an increase in the M2+ multiplier because the desired reserve ratios on time deposits and money market mutual funds are zero and hence are lower than the desired reserve ratio on chequable deposits.

Both time deposits and money market mutual funds undergo more multiple expansion than chequable deposits. Thus a shift out of chequable deposits into time deposits or money market mutual funds, increasing t or f, implies that the overall level of multiple expansion will increase, raising the M2+ money multiplier.

A decline in t or f will result in less overall multiple expansion, and the M2+ money multiplier will decrease, leading to the following conclusion: **the M2+ money multiplier and M2+ money supply are positively related to both the time deposit ratio t and the money market fund ratio f.**

The response of the M2+ money supply to all the depositor and desired reserve ratios is summarized in Table 16A-1.

	TABLE 16A-1	Response of the M2+ Money Supply to Changes in MB_n, A, r_D, c, t, and f	

Variable	Change in Variable	M2+ Money Supply Response	Reason
MB_n	↑	↑	More MB to support C and D
A	↑	↑	More MB to support C and D
r_D	↑	↓	Less multiple deposit expansion
c	↑	↓	Less overall deposit expansion
t	↑	↑	More multiple deposit expansion
f	↑	↑	More multiple deposit expansion

Note: Only increases (↑) in the variables are shown; the effects of decreases in the variables on the money supply would be the opposite of those indicated in the "Response" column.

Chapter 17

The Framework for the Implementation of Monetary Policy and the Tools of Monetary Policy

PREVIEW   In the chapters describing the structure of the Bank of Canada and the money supply process, we mentioned three policy tools that the Bank can use to manipulate interest rates and the money supply: open market operations, Bank of Canada advances, and government deposit shifting. Because the Bank's use of these tools has such an important impact on interest rates and economic activity, it is important to understand how the Bank wields them in practice and how relatively useful each tool is.

In recent years, the Bank of Canada has increased its focus on the overnight rate, the interest rate on overnight loans of reserves from one bank to another, as the primary indicator of the stance of monetary policy. Since December 2000, the Bank of Canada has announced an overnight rate target eight times throughout the year, an announcement that is watched closely by market participants because it affects interest rates throughout the economy. Thus to fully understand how the Bank's tools are used in the conduct of monetary policy, we must understand their direct effects on the overnight interest rate.

This chapter begins with the institutional framework within which the Bank of Canada conducts monetary policy, followed by a supply and demand analysis of the market for settlement balances, where the overnight interest rate is determined. We then go on to look in more detail at the tools of monetary policy—open market operations, Bank of Canada lending, and government deposit shifting—to see how they are used in practice.

THE FRAMEWORK FOR THE IMPLEMENTATION OF MONETARY POLICY

The tools used by the Bank of Canada to implement monetary policy are closely linked to the institutional arrangements regarding the clearing and settlement systems in the Canadian economy. Understanding the tools of monetary policy therefore requires that we know the key features of the framework for the implementation of monetary policy. As you will see, this framework has been designed to encourage deposit-taking financial institutions to deal directly with the market, rather than with the Bank of Canada.[1]

The Large Value Transfer System (LVTS)

Canadian Payments Association
www.cdnpay.ca

Bank for International Settlements
www.bis.org

The core of the Canadian payments system is the **Large Value Transfer System** (**LVTS**), introduced by the Canadian Payments Association on February 4, 1999. The LVTS is an electronic, real-time net settlement network, designed to provide immediate finality and settlement to time-critical transactions. As of January 2001, in addition to the Bank of Canada, there were thirteen **LVTS participants**—members of the Canadian Payments Association who participate in the LVTS and maintain a settlement account at the Bank of Canada. These are the Big Six, Alberta Treasury Branches, Bank of America Canada, Banque Nationale de Paris Canada, La Caisse centrale Desjardins du Québec, Credit Union Central of Canada, HSBC Bank Canada, and the Laurentian Bank of Canada.

The LVTS has been put in place in order to eliminate **systemic risk**—the risk to the entire payments system due to the inability of one financial institution to fulfill its payment obligations in a timely fashion. Of course, it is not just Canada that is concerned about systemic risk. The United States was the first country to initiate a real-time settlement system, the Fedwire system, in 1918. More recently, real-time settlement systems have been implemented by Sweden in 1986, Germany and Switzerland in 1987, Japan in 1988, Italy in 1989, Belgium and the United Kingdom in 1996, and France, Hong Kong, and the Netherlands in 1997. Moreover, the central banks of the G-10 countries, through the Bank for International Settlements, have developed minimum standards for the operation of the global payment network for large-value funds transfers.

In Canada's LVTS, participants know in real time their large-value, wholesale transactions (over $50 000). Although these transactions account for less than 1% of the total number of transactions, they account for about 94% of the value of transactions in Canada. This information eliminates most of the uncertainty from settlement balance prediction—the largest reason for financial institutions not being able to hit their target settlement balances with the Bank of Canada in the pre-LVTS system. Settlement of payment obligations among LVTS participants takes place, at the end of each banking day, through the transfer of funds in their settlement accounts at the Bank of Canada. The LVTS uses **multilateral netting**, in which only the net credit or debit position of each participant vis-à-vis all other participants is calculated for settlement, thereby reducing the need for a large amount of settlement balances.

Small-Value Transactions— ACSS

Although the LVTS eliminates the uncertainty from daily wholesale settlement balances prediction, there is still a residual stochastic element in settlement balances from non-LVTS (paper-based) payment items, such as cheques. Those items are cleared through the Automated Clearing Settlement System (ACSS), an electronic payments system also operated by the Canadian Payments Association. The ACSS aggregates interbank payments and calculates the net amounts to be transferred from and to each participant's settlement account with the Bank of Canada. The Bank retroactively completes the settlement the next day (at midday) through the LVTS.

---

[1]For more details, see Donna Howard, "A Primer on the Implementation of Monetary Policy in the LVTS Environment," *Bank of Canada Review* (Autumn, 1998): 57-66; Kevin Clinton, "Implementation of Monetary Policy in a Regime with Zero Reserve Requirements," Bank of Canada Working Paper 97-8; and "The Framework for the Implementation of Monetary Policy in the Large Value Transfer System Environment," *Bank of Canada Release*, March 31, 1999.

Direct and Indirect Clearers

A subset of LVTS participants also participates directly in the ACSS and these participants are known as **direct clearers**. However, many deposit-taking financial institutions that are members of the Canadian Payments Association do not have a clearing account with the Bank of Canada. These institutions, known as **indirect clearers**, hold deposits in direct clearers in exchange for a variety of services, including cheque clearing, foreign exchange transactions, and help with securities purchases. This is an aspect of a system called correspondent banking.

The Operating Band for the Overnight Interest Rate

The overnight market in Canada is the key market for finance and monetary policy. This market is very liquid, with an estimated $50 billion traded per day by a broad range of participants, the most active of which are deposit-taking institutions and their investment dealer affiliates.[2] The interest rate at which participants borrow and lend overnight funds to each other in the money market is called the **overnight interest rate**. This rate is the shortest-term rate available and forms the base of any term structure of interest rates.

The Bank of Canada implements monetary policy by changing the overnight interest rate. In fact, the Bank's operational objective is to keep the overnight rate within a band of 50 basis points. Since December 2000, the Bank operates under a system of eight "fixed" dates throughout the year for announcing any changes to the **operating band** for the overnight rate, keeping the option of acting between the fixed dates in "extraordinary circumstances." Early in the morning (at 9:00 a.m.), on each of those specified announcement dates, the Bank of Canada announces an operating band of 50 basis points (1/2 of 1%) for the overnight rate (Box 17-1).

As Figure 17-1 shows, the upper limit of the operating band defines the bank rate i_b. The bank rate is the interest rate the Bank charges LVTS participants that require an overdraft loan to cover negative settlement balances on the books of the Bank at the end of the banking day. The lower limit of the operating band is the rate the Bank pays to LVTS participants with positive settlement balances at the end of the day. The midpoint of the operating band is the operating target of the Bank

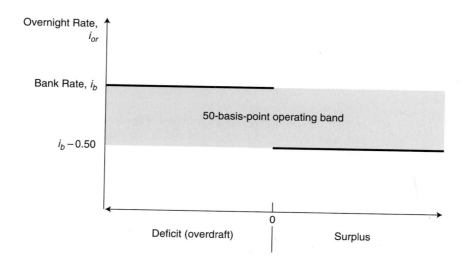

FIGURE 17-1   Operating Band and Target for the Overnight Interest Rate

---

[2]See Eugene Lundrigan and Sari Toll, "The Overnight Market in Canada," *Bank of Canada Review* (Winter 1997-1998): 27-42, for details regarding the evolution of the overnight market.

Monetary Policy Implementation in the LVTS Environment

In the LVTS environment, the Bank of Canada operates under a system of eight fixed dates throughout the year for announcing, via a press release (at 9:00 a.m.), any changes to the operating band for the overnight interest rate. The upper limit of the operating band defines the bank rate and the lower limit is the rate the Bank pays to LVTS participants with positive settlement balances at the end of the day.

The operating band for the overnight interest rate, reinforced by the Bank of Canada's standing facilities, and a target level of settlement balances of roughly $50 million are currently the framework within which the Bank of Canada implements monetary policy. The midpoint of the operating band is the operating target of the Bank's monetary policy.

In targeting the midpoint of the operating band, the Bank uses two rounds of repurchase transactions, either SPRAs or SRAs, although effective April 2, 2001, the Bank discontinued the second round of repurchase transactions, except in extraordinary circumstances.

To maintain the target level of settlement balances, the Bank neutralizes the effects of repurchase transactions and those of certain federal government and Bank of Canada flows that potentially affect settlement balances. The neutralization is effected through the shifting of federal government deposits between the government's account at the Bank of Canada and the government's accounts with LVTS participants. The shifting is made through twice-daily auctions of government term deposits (the first at 9:15 a.m. and the second at 4:15 p.m.).

The LVTS has a pre-settlement trading period of half an hour, at the end of the banking day (6–6:30 p.m.), to permit participating financial institutions to adjust positions with each other at a better return than can be achieved at the Bank of Canada's standing facilities. LVTS participants with settlement imbalances at the end of the banking day use the Bank of Canada's standing facilities to bring their settlement balances to the target level. That is, LVTS participants that

of Canada's monetary policy. When, for example, the operating band is from 3.5% to 4.0%, the bank rate is 4.0%, the rate the Bank pays on deposits to LVTS participants is 3.5%, and the Bank's operating target is an overnight interest rate of 3.75%.

The Bank of Canada's Standing Facilities

LVTS participants can make a payment only if they have, in real time (right now), either positive settlement balances in their accounts with the Bank of Canada, or posted collateral (such as government of Canada Treasury bills and bonds), or explicit lines of credit with other participants. As a result, the large-value clearing and settlement systems will settle at the end of each day even in the face of risk and liquidity problems. Moreover, at the end of each banking day, each participant must bring its settlement balance with the Bank of Canada close to zero. Of course, it can scarcely be expected that LVTS participants will always be successful in ending up with near-zero settlement balances. The Bank of Canada therefore stands ready (we call this **standing facilities**) to lend to or borrow from a participant to bring their settlement balances to zero at the end of the banking day. As already noted, participants also know with certainty the rates applicable to positive and negative settlement balances with the Bank of Canada (see Box 17-1 and Figure 17-1).

To permit participating financial institutions to adjust positions with each other (i.e., reduce the costs of either positive or negative positions), the LVTS has a pre-settlement trading period of half an hour, at the end of the banking day (6-6:30 p.m.)—see Box 17-1. The purpose of the pre-settlement trading period is to provide a window for those participants with excess positions to trade with those in deficit, at a better return than can be achieved at the Bank's facilities, to require an overdraft loan to cover negative settlement balances on the books of the Bank borrow from the Bank at the bank rate. LVTS participants with positive settlement balances at the end of the day earn the bank rate less 50 basis points.

The Market Timetable

9:00 a.m.	Bank of Canada announces changes (if any) to the operating band	4:00 p.m.	Payment exchange for Debt Clearing Service (DCS)
9:15 a.m.	Cutoff time for bids for Receiver General term deposit auction	4:15 p.m.	Cutoff time for bids for Receiver General deposit auction
9:30 a.m.	Release of Receiver General term deposit auction results	4:30 p.m.	Release of Receiver General auction results
11:45 a.m.	Special Purchase and Resale Agreements (SPRAs) or Sale and Repurchase Agreements (SRAs) transacted (if any)	6:00 p.m.	Close of LVTS for client (third-party) transactions
		6:00–6:30 p.m.	Pre-settlement trading
3:00 p.m.	Cutoff time for presentation of government items to Bank of Canada	8:00 p.m. or earlier	Settlement of LVTS balances at the Bank of Canada

Source: Donna Howard, "A Primer on the Implementation of Monetary Policy in the LVTS Environment," *Bank of Canada Review* (Autumn, 1998): 57–66; Kevin Clinton, "Implementation of Monetary Policy in a Regime with Zero Reserve Requirements," Bank of Canada Working Paper 97-8; and "The Framework for the Implementation of Monetary Policy in the Large Value Transfer System Environment," *Bank of Canada Release*, March 31, 1999. Reprinted with permission.

the advantage of both. In fact, the typical bid–ask spread on overnight funds in the interbank market has been less than 1/8%. This is significantly less than the spread of 50 basis points between the rate charged on overdrafts and that paid on deposits by the Bank of Canada at the end of the LVTS day.

In general, pre-settlement trading among participants will achieve a zero settlement balance for each participant on wholesale transactions. However, if at the end of the settlement day a participant has a negative balance on the books of the Bank of Canada, the deficit will be financed by a collateralized advance at the bank rate. Participants with positive settlement balances at the end of the day are paid interest at the bank rate less 50 basis points (i.e., the bottom of the operating band). Hence, as long as the bank rate is set so that the market bid–ask spread is within the operating band, participants will resolve their nonzero settlement balances among themselves rather than through the Bank of Canada's standing facilities. In fact, in a fully competitive market, participants would be expected to trade at the midpoint of the operating band for the overnight interest rate.

Regarding the smaller value or ACSS settlements, the Bank of Canada charges the bank rate plus 150 basis points on ACSS collateralized advances and pays the bank rate less 150 basis points on ACSS positive balances. There is, however, an overnight interbank market in retroactive ACSS balances that allows participating financial institutions to resolve their nonzero retail clearing balances among themselves. In fact, since the rate spread at the Bank of Canada for ACSS balances is 300 basis points (250 basis points wider than that for LVTS balances), participants find that they can resolve their nonzero retail clearing balances at more favourable rates among themselves. This market, however, is thin and the Bank of Canada does not regard the interest rates that are formed in this market as a good indicator of the banking system's supply of overnight funds.

Clearly, the LVTS and the Bank of Canada's standing facilities have been set up in such a way so as to ensure a determinate demand for settlement balances, treating the costs of deficits and surpluses symmetrically. That is, the cost of holding excess settlement balances (an opportunity cost of 25 basis points) equals the cost of holding deficit levels of settlement balances (a premium of 25 basis points for an overdraft borrowing). These cost incentives are very important in the absence of reserve requirements; they encourage banks to target zero settlement balances at the Bank of Canada and in doing so to deal directly with the market rather than to rely on the Bank's automatic standing facilities. Most days banks are within $25 million from zero and, in aggregate, $500 to $700 million away from target.

The Bank's Implementation of the Operating Band

It is through its lending and taking deposits from LVTS participants that the Bank of Canada implements its target band for the overnight interest rate. *If the overnight rate increases towards the upper limit of the operating band, then the Bank will lend at the bank rate to put a ceiling on the overnight rate.* The bank rate is the ceiling on the overnight rate in the money market for LVTS participants, because they are unlikely to borrow overnight funds at a higher interest rate, since they can borrow at the bank rate from the Bank of Canada.

If the overnight rate declines towards the lower limit of the operating band, then the Bank will accept deposits from LVTS participants at the bank rate less 50 basis points, to put a floor on the overnight rate. The bank rate less 50 basis points is the floor on the overnight rate because LVTS participants are unlikely to lend overnight funds at a lower rate, since they can leave funds on deposit at this rate at the Bank of Canada.

THE MARKET FOR SETTLEMENT BALANCES AND THE OVERNIGHT RATE

The overnight market is basically the market in which banks trade their settlement balances at the end of the day. It is helpful to use a supply and demand analysis to analyze what occurs. Our analysis of the market for settlement balances proceeds in a similar fashion to the analysis of the bond market we conducted in Chapter 5. We derive a demand and supply curve for settlement balances. Then the market equilibrium in which the quantity of settlement balances demanded equals the quantity of settlement balances supplied determines the overnight rate, the interest rate charged on the loans of these settlement balances.

Demand Curve

To derive the demand curve for settlement balances, we need to ask what happens to the quantity of settlement balances demanded, holding everything else constant, in a world with zero reserve requirements. In general, in such a context the demand for settlement balances is perfectly inelastic with respect to interest rates.

At a market interest rate at the upper limit of the operating band (the bank rate), the demand curve is horizontal since the demand for negative settlement balances will be indefinitely large. At a market rate at the lower limit of the operating band (the bank rate less 50 basis points), the demand curve is also horizontal, since the demand for positive settlement balances would also be indefinitely large. At rates within the operating band, the demand for settlement balances is zero. Consequently, the demand curve for settlement balances is represented by the horizontal solid lines in Figure 17-2.

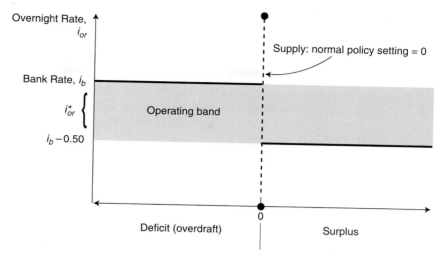

FIGURE 17-2 Equilibrium in the Overnight Market

Supply Curve

As already noted, the Bank of Canada normally targets a daily level of settlement balances of zero, although effective April 2, 2001, the Bank is targeting a level of balances of $50 million (instead of zero), on a trial basis to reduce frictions in the system. Assuming here that the supply of settlement balances is set at zero by the Bank of Canada, the supply curve for settlement balances is a vertical line at the zero quantity, as shown in Figure 17-2.

Equilibrium in the Market for Settlement Balances

Market equilibrium occurs where the quantity of settlement balances demanded equals the quantity supplied. In terms of Figure 17-2, equilibrium occurs at the intersection of the vertical supply curve for settlement balances and the vertical part of the demand curve for settlement balances at the zero quantity. This means that the equilibrium overnight rate is indeterminate and that it could be anywhere within the 50-basis-point operating band. As Kevin Clinton of the Bank of Canada puts it, "[t]he actual rate will be affected by a variety of technical factors, such as the size and distribution of clearing imbalances among banks. This implies that the realized rate will generally differ somewhat from the target indicated at the start of the day by the Bank of Canada."[3]

THE BANK OF CANADA'S APPROACH TO MONETARY POLICY

The goal of the Bank of Canada's current monetary policy is to keep the inflation rate within a target range of 1% to 3%, with the midpoint of the inflation target range, 2%, being the most desirable outcome. In setting its inflation targets, the Bank of Canada uses the rate of change in the consumer price index (CPI), because it is the most commonly used and understood price measure in Canada. Although the Bank's targets are specified in terms of "headline CPI" (all items), the Bank uses "core CPI" which excludes volatile components such as food, energy, and the effect of indirect taxes. Core CPI inflation is useful in assessing whether trend inflation is on track for the medium term. Also, defining the inflation targets

---

[3]Kevin Clinton, "Implementation of Monetary Policy in a Regime with Zero Reserve Requirements," Bank of Canada Working Paper 97-8.

in terms of ranges provides the Bank of Canada sufficient flexibility to deal with supply shocks beyond those already taken care of by the exclusion of volatile components from core inflation.

Figure 17-3 shows what happened to the Canadian inflation rate since February 1991, when the Bank's governor and the minister of finance jointly announced a series of declining inflation targets, with a band of plus and minus one percentage point around them. In what follows, we examine the tools used by the Bank of Canada to implement monetary policy, leaving a detailed analysis of the Bank's monetary policy for Chapters 18 and 20.

How Monetary Policy Affects the Economy

The Bank of Canada affects interest rates and the level of economic activity by changing the operating band for the overnight interest rate. As we saw in Chapter 6, interest rates on different assets tend to move together over time. Hence, changes in the operating band and thus the bank rate influence other rates, such as the prime rate (the interest rate banks charge to their best customers) and the interest rates on bank deposits and mortgages. These changes in interest rates may also lead to changes in the exchange rate. The level of short-term interest rates and the exchange rate of the Canadian dollar determine the **monetary conditions** in which the economy operates.

The concept of monetary conditions, introduced by the Bank in its conduct of monetary policy in the early 1990s, focuses on the effect on the economy of both short-term interest rates and the exchange rate. Changes in monetary conditions affect the economy and the Bank's ultimate objective, the inflation rate, only indirectly and are usually felt over a period of several months to several years. This means that the Bank of Canada must always be forward looking in its conduct of monetary policy, anticipating the level of monetary conditions needed today to achieve its ultimate goal of low and stable inflation in the future.

As an example, suppose that the Bank of Canada expects the economy to slow down and wishes to ease monetary conditions. It lowers the operating band for the overnight interest rate, thereby encouraging banks to borrow reserves either

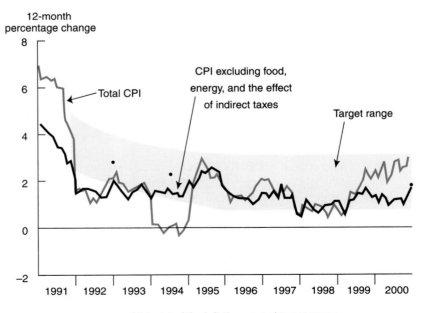

FIGURE 17-3   Inflation Rates and Inflation Targets for Canada, 1991–2000

Source: Bank of Canada *Annual Report*, 2000. Reprinted with permission.

from each other at the overnight rate or from the Bank of Canada at the bank rate.[4] As you can see in Figure 17-4, this reduces interest rates and the value of the dollar and leads to an increase in the supply of money, aggregate demand, and the price level, thereby preventing the inflation rate from falling below the target range of 1% to 3%.

In the opposite case, if the Bank expects the economy to be exceeding its capacity at some point in the future, it raises the operating band in order to prevent inflationary pressures from building. The consequent increase in interest rates and the value of the dollar lead to a decline in the supply of money, aggregate demand, and the price level, thereby preventing the inflation rate from moving above the Bank's target range of 1% to 3%—see Figure 17-5.

Hence, by changing the operating band for the overnight rate, the Bank of Canada sends a signal regarding the direction that it would like interest rates and the money supply to take. A rise in the operating band and thus the bank rate is a signal that the Bank would like to see higher interest rates and less money in the economy. A fall in the operating band is a signal that the Bank would like lower interest rates and more money.

However, the Bank of Canada's direct influence on long-term interest rates diminishes as the time period increases. Long-term interest rates can be either higher or lower than short-term rates depending on expectations about the inflation rate and the level of short-term interest rates in the future, the relative balance between the demand for and supply of loanable funds, the level of interest rates in the Unites States, and the relative stance of monetary policies in the two countries. The Bank of Canada typically changes the operating band for the overnight rate to ratify movements in the general level of interest rates that have already

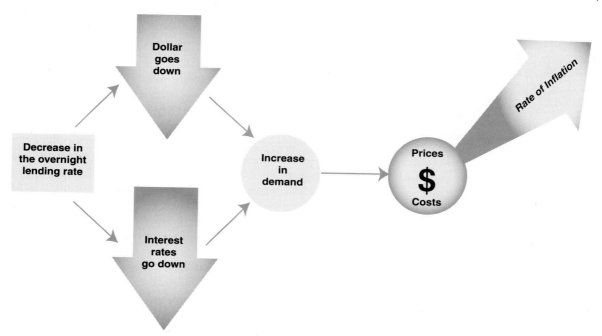

FIGURE 17-4   How the Bank of Canada Keeps the Rate of Inflation from Falling Below the Target Range

Source: Bank of Canada web site: www.bankofcanada.ca. Reprinted with permission.

---

[4]For example, the Bank might lower the operating band by 25 basis points from 3.5% to 4.0% to 3.25% to 3.75%.

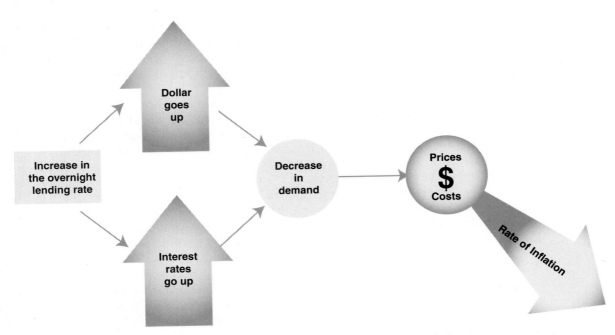

FIGURE 17-5 How the Bank of Canada Keeps the Rate of Inflation from Moving Above the Target Range

Source: Bank of Canada web site: www.bankofcanada.ca. Reprinted with permission.

taken place in the market. The Bank, however, wouldn't ratify interest rate movements in the opposite direction to what it feels is required by the fundamentals.

OPEN MARKET OPERATIONS

Open market operations are an important monetary policy tool for many central banks around the world, because they are the primary determinants of changes in interest rates and the monetary base, the main source of fluctuations in the money supply. Open market purchases expand bank reserves and the monetary base, thereby lowering short-term interest rates and raising the money supply. Open market sales shrink bank reserves and the monetary base, raising short-term interest rates and lowering the money supply.

There are two types of open market operations. **Dynamic open market operations** are intended to change the level of bank reserves and the monetary base. **Defensive open market operations** are intended to offset movements in other factors that affect bank reserves, such as changes in government deposits with the central bank. To avoid conflicts of interest, central banks do not conduct open market operations in privately issued securities.[5] They conduct open market operations in government bills and bonds, because the markets for these securities are the most liquid and have the largest trading volume; these markets have the capacity to absorb the central bank's substantial volume of transactions without experiencing excessive price fluctuations that would disrupt the market.

Over the years, the Bank of Canada introduced additional tools in its conduct of monetary policy. In 1985, the Bank of Canada introduced **repos**, which in Canada are known as Special Purchase and Resale Agreements (SPRAs), as a tool

---

[5]For example, think of the conflict if the Bank of Canada purchased bonds issued by a company owned by the governor's brother-in-law.

to reduce undesired upward pressure on the overnight interest rate. In 1986, the Bank introduced **reverse repos**, known in Canada as Sale and Repurchase Agreements (SRAs), as a tool to reduce undesired downward pressure on the overnight rate. By 1994, the Bank of Canada stopped conducting open market operations in government of Canada Treasury bills and bonds and its most common operations since then have been repurchase transactions, either SPRAs or SRAs, with **primary dealers** (formerly known as jobbers)—the Big Six and the major investment dealers.

SPRAs and SRAs

The operating band for the overnight interest rate, reinforced by the Bank of Canada's standing facilities, and a target level of settlement balances of roughly $50 million are currently the framework within which the Bank of Canada implements monetary policy. As already noted, the Bank's current operation to support the management of settlement balances in targeting the overnight interest rate around the midpoint of the operating band involves repurchase transactions, either SPRAs or SRAs. Between 1994 and the implementation of the LVTS on February 4, 1999, SPRAs were used to reinforce the upper end of the operating band and SRAs the lower end. Since the LVTS, two rounds of SPRAs and SRAs are used to reinforce the target rate in the middle of the operating band, although effective April 2, 2001, the Bank discontinued the second round of repurchase transactions, except in extraordinary circumstances.

Let's see how the Bank of Canada uses SPRAs and SRAs in order to support the management of settlement balances in achieving the desired impact on the overnight rate. Assume that the operating band for the overnight interest rate is 3.5% to 4% and that the Bank of Canada is targeting the overnight rate at the midpoint of the band, at 3.75%. If overnight funds are traded at a rate higher than the target rate of 3.75%, then the Bank of Canada enters into SPRAs, at a price that works out to a 3.75% interest rate, the midpoint of the operating band. That is, the Bank purchases government of Canada T-bills or bonds, with an agreement that the seller will repurchase them one business day later.

Since the securities are placed with the Canadian Depository for Securities (CDS), Canada's central securities depository owned and operated by the financial community, the title of the securities changes hands by electronic instruction. The balance sheets of the Bank of Canada and the direct clearers look like this:

BANK OF CANADA				DIRECT CLEARERS			
Assets		Liabilities		Assets		Liabilities	
SPRAs	+100	Settlement balances	+100	Settlement balances	+100	SPRAs	+100

Hence, *repos, also known as Special Purchase and Resale Agreements (SPRAs), relieve undesired upward pressure on the overnight interest rate.*

If on the other hand overnight funds are traded at a rate below the target rate of 3.75%, then the Bank of Canada enters into SRAs, in which the Bank sells government securities and the buyer agrees to sell them back to the Bank one business day later. The balance sheets of the Bank of Canada and the direct clearers now look like this:

BANK OF CANADA			DIRECT CLEARERS		
Assets	Liabilities		Assets		Liabilities
	Settlement balances	−100	Settlement balances	−100	
	SRAs	+100	SRAs	+100	

Hence, *reverse repos, also known as Sale and Repurchase Agreements (SRAs), alleviate undesired downward pressure on the overnight financing rate.*

Because the effects on settlement balances of SPRAs and SRAs are reversed on the day the agreement matures, SPRAs and SRAs are actually temporary open market operations. Moreover, *because the effects on settlement balances of SPRAs and SRAs are neutralized by the end of the day by the Bank of Canada, there is no change at the end of the day in the level of settlement balances in the system.*

Advantages of SPRAs and SRAs

The Bank of Canada's repurchase transactions, either SPRAs or SRAs, have several advantages over other tools of monetary policy.

1. SPRAs and SRAs occur at the initiative of the Bank of Canada, which has complete control over their volume. This control is not found, for example, in lending operations, in which the Bank can encourage or discourage banks to take out loans by altering the bank rate but cannot directly control the volume of advances.

2. Repurchase transactions are flexible and precise; together with the Bank's standing facilities, they can be used to any extent. No matter how small a change in interest rates is desired, SPRAs or SRAs can achieve it with a small purchase or sale of securities. Conversely, if the desired change in interest rates is very large, the repurchase-transactions tool is strong enough to do the job through a very large purchase or sale of securities.

3. Repurchase transactions are easily reversed. If a mistake is made, the Bank of Canada can immediately reverse it. If, for example, the Bank decides that the overnight rate is too low because it has offered too many SPRAs, it can immediately make a correction by offering SRAs. Reversing, however, repurchase transactions too often will result in a loss of credibility.

4. Repurchase transactions can be implemented quickly; they involve no administrative delays. When the Bank of Canada decides to change interest rates on the fixed action dates, it makes the interest rate announcement at 9:00 a.m. and enters into SPRAs or SRAs.

BANK OF CANADA LENDING

In addition to its use as a standing liquidity facility to reinforce the operating band for the overnight interest rate, Bank of Canada lending is also important in preventing financial panics. In fact, one of the Bank's most important roles is to be the **lender of last resort** in the Canadian economy; it provides reserves to solvent banks in order to prevent bank failures from spinning further out of control, thereby preventing bank and financial panics. In doing so, the Bank always makes a judgment with respect to the trade-off between morally hazardous behaviour and the costs in terms of financial stability. Last-resort lending is a particularly effective way to provide reserves to the banking system during a banking crisis because reserves are immediately channelled to the banks that need them most.

Avoiding financial panics by performing the role of lender of last resort is an extremely important requirement of successful monetary policymaking. As we demonstrated with our money supply analysis in Chapter 16, the bank panics in the United States in the 1930–1933 period were the cause of the sharpest decline in the money supply in U.S. history, which many economists see as the driving force behind the collapse of the world economy during the Great Depression. Financial panics can also severely damage the economy because they interfere with the ability of financial intermediaries and markets to move funds to people with productive investment opportunities (see Chapter 8).

At first glance, it might appear as though the presence of the CDIC, which insures depositors from losses due to a bank's failure up to a limit of $60 000 per account, would make the lender-of-last-resort function of the Bank of Canada superfluous. (The CDIC is described in detail in Chapter 11.) There are two reasons why this is not the case. First, it is important to recognize that the CDIC's insurance fund amounts to a small fraction of the amount of deposits outstanding. If a large number of bank failures occurred, the CDIC would not be able to cover all the depositors' losses. Indeed, the failures of deposit-based financial institutions in the 1980s and early 1990s in Canada, described in Chapter 11, led to large losses and a shrinkage in the CDIC's insurance fund, which reduced the CDIC's ability to cover depositors' losses. This fact has not weakened the confidence of small depositors in the banking system because the Bank of Canada has been ready to stand behind the banks to provide whatever reserves are needed to prevent bank panics. Second, the large-denomination deposits in the banking system are not guaranteed by the CDIC because they exceed the $60 000 limit. A loss of confidence in the banking system could still lead to runs on banks from the large-denomination depositors, and bank panics could still occur despite the existence of the CDIC.

CDIC
www.cdic.ca

The importance of the Bank of Canada's role as lender of last resort is, if anything, more important today because of the bank failures experienced in Canada in the 1980s and early 1990s. Figure 17-6, which shows Bank of Canada advances to members of the Canadian Payments Association, reveals that the Bank of Canada advanced considerable funds in the recent past to financial institutions facing liquidity crises (see also Box 17-2). Unfortunately, the Bank of Canada's lending policy has not always been successful in preventing financial crises. Two examples of the use of the Bank's lending weapon to avoid bank panics are the provisions of huge loans to the Canadian Commercial Bank and the Northland Bank in 1985 (see Box 17-2).

Not only can the central bank be a lender of last resort to banks, but it can also play the same role for the financial system as a whole. The existence of the advances mechanism can help prevent financial panics that are not triggered by bank failures, as was the case in the United States during the Black Monday stock market crash of 1987 (see Box 17-3).

Although the Bank of Canada's role as the lender of last resort has the benefit of preventing bank and financial panics, it does have a cost. If a bank expects that the Bank of Canada will provide it with advances when it gets into trouble, it will be willing to take on more risk knowing that the Bank of Canada will come to the rescue. The Bank of Canada's lender-of-last-resort role has thus created a moral hazard problem similar to the one created by deposit insurance (discussed in Chapter 11). Banks take on more risk, thus exposing the deposit insurance agency, and hence taxpayers, to greater losses. The moral hazard problem is most severe for large banks, which may believe that the Bank of Canada and the CDIC view them as "too big to fail"; that is, they will always receive Bank of Canada advances when they are in trouble because their failure would be likely to precipitate a bank panic.

BOX 17-2

Advances to Troubled Banks

Canadian Commercial and Northland. In 1985, there was public concern over the quality of the assets of two small Alberta-based banks—the Canadian Commercial Bank and the Northland Bank—who had made many bad loans. Larger depositors, whose accounts exceeded the $60 000 limit insured by the CDIC, began to withdraw their deposits, and the failure of the banks was imminent. Because the immediate failure of Canadian Commercial and Northland would have had repercussions on other vulnerable banks, the Bank of Canada, under the advice from the Inspector General of Banks (the predecessor of the Office of the Superintendent of Financial Institutions) made extraordinary advances. Total advances amounted to $1.8 billion so that depositors, including the largest, would not suffer any losses.

In doing this, the Bank of Canada was following the precedent established in 1984 by the Federal Reserve's rescue of Continental Illinois National Bank. Continental Illinois had made bad loans (primarily to businesses in the energy industry and to foreign countries), and rumours of financial trouble in early May 1984 caused large depositors to withdraw over $10 billion of deposits from the bank. The

Federal Deposit Insurance Corporation (FDIC) arranged a rescue effort in July 1984 that culminated in a $4.5 billion commitment of funds to save the bank. Still the Fed had to lend Continental Illinois over $5 billion—making the Bank of Canada's $1.8 billion advances to Canadian Commercial and Northland look like small potatoes! Although Continental Illinois was taken over by the FDIC, the Fed's action prevented further bank failures, and a potential bank panic was averted.

The Bank of Canada, however, was not as successful in preventing a bank crisis. With the failure of Canadian Commercial and Northland, rumours of financial trouble caused many large depositors to withdraw large deposits from the Bank of British Columbia, Mercantile Bank, and Continental Bank. By the time Mercantile was acquired by the National Bank of Canada, Bank of British Columbia by the Hong Kong Bank of Canada, and Continental by Lloyds Bank of Canada, the Bank of Canada had lent over $5 billion (see Figure 17-6). The loss of public confidence in the Canadian banking system led to the financial reforms of 1987–1992 and the consolidating of financial institution supervision under the Office of the Superintendent of Financial Institutions.

Federal Deposit
Insurance
Corporation
www.fdic.gov

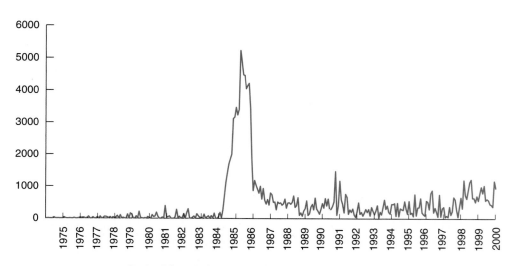

FIGURE 17-6   Bank of Canada Advances to Members of the Canadian Payments Association, 1975–2000 (in millions of dollars)

Source: Statistics Canada CANSIM (monthly) Series B210.

BOX 17-3

Last-Resort Lending to Prevent a Financial Panic

The Black Monday Stock Market Crash of 1987. Although October 19, 1987, dubbed "Black Monday," will go down in the history books as the largest one-day decline in stock prices to date (the Dow Jones Industrial Average declined by more than 500 points), it was on Tuesday, October 20, 1987, that financial markets almost stopped functioning. Felix Rohatyn, one of the most prominent men on Wall Street, stated flatly: "Tuesday was the most dangerous day we had in 50 years."* Much of the credit for prevention of a market meltdown after Black Monday must be given to the Federal Reserve System and the chairman of the Board of Governors, Alan Greenspan.

The stress of keeping markets functioning during the sharp decline in stock prices on Monday, October 19, meant that many brokerage houses and specialists (dealer-brokers who maintain orderly trading on the stock exchanges) were severely in need of additional funds to finance their activities. However, understandably enough, New York banks, as well as foreign and regional U.S. banks, growing very nervous about the financial health of securities firms, began to cut back credit to the securities industry at the very time when it was most needed. Panic was in the air. One chairman of a large specialist firm commented that

on Monday, "from 2 P.M. on, there was total despair. The entire investment community fled the market. We were left alone on the field." It was time for the Fed, like the cavalry, to come to the rescue.

Upon learning of the plight of the securities industry, Alan Greenspan and E. Gerald Corrigan, then president of the Federal Reserve Bank of New York and the Fed official most closely in touch with Wall Street, became fearful of a spreading collapse of securities firms. To prevent this from occurring, Greenspan announced before the market opened on Tuesday, October 20, the Federal Reserve System's "readiness to serve as a source of liquidity to support the economic and financial system." In addition to this extraordinary announcement, the Fed made it clear that it would provide discount loans to any bank that would make loans to the securities industry, although this did not prove to be necessary. As one New York banker said, the Fed's message was, "We're here. Whatever you need, we'll give you."

The outcome of the Fed's timely action was that a financial panic was averted. The markets kept functioning on Tuesday, and a market rally ensued that day, with the Dow Jones Industrial Average climbing over 100 points.

*"Terrible Tuesday: How the Stock Market Almost Disintegrated a Day After the Crash," *Wall Street Journal,* November 20, 1987, p. 1. This article provides a fascinating and more detailed view of the events described here and is the source of all the quotations cited.

Similarly, Bank of Canada actions to prevent financial panic may encourage financial institutions other than banks to take on greater risk. They, too, expect the Bank of Canada to ensure that they could get loans if a financial panic seemed imminent. When the Bank of Canada considers using the lending weapon to prevent panics, it therefore needs to consider the trade-off between the moral hazard cost of its role as lender of last resort and the benefit of preventing financial panics. This trade-off explains why the Bank of Canada must be careful not to perform its role as lender of last resort too frequently.

Advantages and Disadvantages of the Bank's Lending Policy

The most important advantage of the Bank of Canada's lending policy is that the Bank can use it to perform its role of lender of last resort. Experiences in the 1980s and early 1990s, described in Chapter 11, and the Black Monday crash indicate that this role has become more important in the past couple of decades.

However, the use of the Bank's lending policy to control the money supply seems to have little to recommend it. Compared to open market operations, it is less effective for two reasons. Open market operations are completely at the discretion of the Bank of Canada, whereas the volume of normal advances is not—the Bank can change the bank rate, but it can't make banks borrow. In addition, open market operations are more easily reversed than changes in Bank lending policy.

APPLICATION | ***Should Central Bank Lending Be Abolished?***

The disadvantages of central bank lending policy as a tool of monetary control have prompted economists to suggest abolishing central bank lending. Milton Friedman and other economists have proposed that central banks should terminate their lending facilities in order to establish better monetary control.[6] Friedman has contended that the presence of deposit insurance eliminates the possibility of bank panics; therefore, the use of the central bank's lending facilities is no longer as necessary. Abolishing central bank lending would eliminate fluctuations in the monetary base due to changes in the volume of advances and so would reduce unintended fluctuations in the money supply.

Critics of Friedman's proposal, however, emphasize that deposit insurance is effective at preventing bank panics only because the central bank stands behind it and plays the role of lender of last resort. Furthermore, as we have seen in the case of the Black Monday crash, the existence of the central bank's lending facilities and the provision of liquidity to the system as a whole can help avert a financial panic unrelated to bank failures. Because of the increased number of bank failures in recent years, the need for the central bank's use of its lending facility to preserve the health of the financial system has become more apparent. Hence most economists do not support Friedman's proposal.

Should the Bank Rate Be Tied to a Market Rate of Interest?

For most of the last two decades, the Bank of Canada has operated under a **floating bank rate regime**, having the bank rate tied to a specific market interest rate. For example, from March 1980 to February 1996, the bank rate was automatically set each week at 25 basis points above the average interest rate established at the auction of three-month government of Canada Treasury bills. In February 1996, however, in anticipation of the introduction of the LVTS, the Bank switched to a **fixed bank rate regime**, using its discretion to change the bank rate on any business day it deemed appropriate. In fact, since February 1996, the Bank sets the bank rate, which is the upper end of the operating band for the overnight interest rate—see Figure 17-1.

As already noted, in December 2000 the Bank of Canada changed its approach to the conduct of monetary policy by adopting a new system of eight fixed dates throughout the year for announcing changes (if any) to the bank rate. The Bank still has the option to act between the fixed dates in extraordinary circumstances. The new system of pre-set announcement dates for changes in the bank rate is intended to improve the functioning of financial markets and to increase the channels of communication between the Bank of Canada and financial markets, thereby increasing the effectiveness of Canadian monetary policy.

---

[6]Milton Friedman, *A Program for Monetary Stability* (New York: Fordham University Press, 1960); Marvin Goodfriend and Robert G. King, "Financial Deregulation, Monetary Policy, and Central Banking," Federal Reserve Bank of Richmond *Review* 74 (1988): 3-22.

In contrast to the Bank of Canada, the U.S. Federal Reserve does not tie its equivalent of the bank rate (the **discount rate**) to a market rate of interest, although it pursues a policy that is consistent with a floating discount rate regime. It does not let the discount rate move too far away from market rates of interest because it does not want to let the volume of discount loans get out of hand. However, the Fed operates under a system of ten pre-set announcement dates for discount rate changes throughout the year. It is to be noted that the dates on the Bank of Canada's new system of fixed announcement dates for bank rate changes appear to have no correlation with those of the U.S Federal Reserve's system of fixed announcement dates for discount rate changes.

The most important advantage of a fixed bank rate regime is that the Bank of Canada can signal its intentions about future monetary policy. For example, if the Bank decides to slow the expansion of the economy by increasing the overnight rate, it can amplify the announcement that it makes by also raising the bank rate. This signal alone may rein in economic expansion because the public will expect monetary policy to be less expansionary in the future.

The problem with the announcement effect is that it is subject to misinterpretation. When the Bank fixes the bank rate to a pre-determined level, large fluctuations will occur in the spread between market interest rates and the bank rate as market interest rates change. If, for example, the overnight rate is rising relative to the bank rate, the volume of Bank of Canada advances will rise. In such a situation, the Bank may have no intention of amplifying the announcement of an overnight rate increase, but to keep the amount of advances from becoming excessive it may raise the bank rate to keep it more in line with market interest rates. When the bank rate rises, the market may interpret this as a signal that the Bank is moving to a more contractionary policy, even if that is not the case. The announcement effect may be a hindrance rather than a help.

The advantages of a flexible bank rate regime are many. First, by tying the bank rate to a market rate of interest like the overnight rate, the Bank of Canada can continue to perform its role of lender of last resort. Second, most fluctuations in the spread between market interest rates and the bank rate are eliminated, removing a major source of fluctuations in the volume of advances and hence in the money supply (see Figure 17-7). Third, because bank rate changes are automatic, there are no false signals about the Bank of Canada's intentions, and the announcement effect disappears.

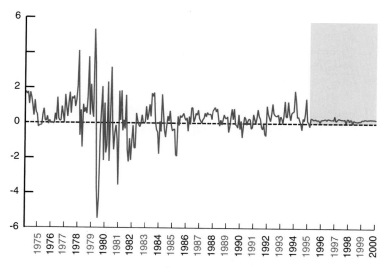

FIGURE 17-7   Spread between Bank Rate and Overnight Interest Rate, 1975–2000
Source: Statistics Canada CANSIM (monthly) Series B14006 and B14044.

Many professional economists support tying the bank rate to a market rate of interest—that is, a flexible bank rate regime. However, other economists oppose this method of setting the bank rate because they think that keeping the bank rate fixed when market interest rates change would reduce fluctuations in market interest rates. Such a policy would cause advances and hence reserves to rise when market interest rates rise, possibly countering some of the rise in market interest rates.

GOVERNMENT DEPOSIT SHIFTING

Prior to the introduction of the LVTS, the management of settlement balances (**cash setting**) was the main mechanism by which the Bank of Canada implemented monetary policy. By shifting federal government deposits between the government's account at the Bank and the government's accounts at the direct clearers, the Bank was essentially implementing its target band for the overnight interest rate.[7] It was also neutralizing certain federal government and Bank of Canada transactions that affect the financial system. With the introduction of the LVTS, however, the Bank introduced a new framework for implementing monetary policy. This involves lending to and taking deposits from LVTS participants, as we discussed earlier.

However, in aiming at a near zero level of settlement balances for the financial system each day, the Bank of Canada continues to use government deposit shifting in order to neutralize certain federal government and Bank of Canada flows that potentially affect settlement balances. These flows (such as, for example, federal government receipts and disbursements) affect settlement balances, because the Bank of Canada acts as the fiscal agent for the federal government. In particular, net government disbursements would increase the direct clearers' settlement balances at the Bank, while net government receipts would reduce them.

In the pre-LVTS system, the transferring of government deposits between the government's accounts at financial institutions and its account at the Bank of Canada was effected by the Bank's daily **drawdowns** (transfers of government deposits from the direct clearers to the Bank of Canada) and **redeposits** (transfers of government deposits from the Bank of Canada to the direct clearers). However, with the instantaneous transfer of funds allowed by the LVTS environment, the drawdown/redeposit mechanism is not a practical tool for government deposit shifting. This is so because the Bank of Canada is not able to debit the government's account with a direct clearer on a day with a net disbursement by the government. *In the LVTS environment, twice-daily auctions of government term deposits (the first at 9:15 a.m. and the second at 4:15 p.m.) are used to effect the transfer (see Box 17-1).*[8]

To illustrate the process for neutralizing federal government flows using government deposit shifting, suppose that there is a net government receipt of $100 (i.e., the government's receipts from the public exceed its payments to the public by $100). Net receipts are drawn on the government's deposits at the direct clearers, creating claims on the direct clearers in favour of the Bank of Canada and ultimately reducing settlement balances by an amount equal to the government's net

---

[7]For detailed descriptions of the process, see the discussion in Kevin Clinton, "Bank of Canada Cash Management: The Main Technique for Implementing Monetary Policy," *Bank of Canada Review*, (1991): 3-25; or Bruce Montador, "The Implementation of Monetary Policy in Canada," *Canadian Public Policy* (1995): 107-120.

[8]For more details, see "The Framework for the Implementation of Monetary Policy in the Large Value Transfer System Environment," *Bank of Canada Release*, March 31, 1999.

receipts. In the absence of any offsetting transactions by the Bank of Canada, through the workings of supply and demand, a decline in settlement balances will normally cause an increase in the overnight interest rate, as many direct clearers would have to borrow more to meet their settlement obligations.

However, in targeting the overnight interest rate, the Bank of Canada will neutralize the net government receipt by morning and afternoon auctions of government term deposits. This procedure results in the following balance sheets for the Bank and the direct clearers:

BANK OF CANADA			DIRECT CLEARERS		
Assets	Liabilities		Assets		Liabilities
	Government deposits	−100	Settlement balances +100	Government deposits	+100
	Settlement balances	+100			

Note that government deposits at the Bank of Canada are reduced by $100 and at the same time the settlement balances of the direct clearers are increased by $100.

If instead of a net receipt by the government, there were a net disbursement of $100 (i.e., the government's payments to the public exceed its receipts from the public by $100), then the financial system's settlement balances would increase by the same amount. This would prompt a fall in the overnight interest rate, as many direct clearers would have to borrow less to meet their settlement obligations. The Bank's neutralization process would prevent a decline in the overnight rate by reducing the banking system's settlement balances. This would involve LVTS transfers of $100 (i.e., the difference between the total amount of government balances maturing and the total amount of government balances auctioned) from the government's accounts at the participating institutions to the government's account at the Bank. This procedure results in the following T-accounts:

BANK OF CANADA			DIRECT CLEARERS		
Assets	Liabilities		Assets		Liabilities
	Government deposits	+100	Settlement balances −100	Government deposits	−100
	Settlement balances	−100			

In this case government deposits at the Bank of Canada are increased by $100 and at the same time the clearing balances of the participants are reduced by $100.

Swaps with the Exchange Fund Account

When the Bank of Canada transfers government balances, it usually brings onto its balance sheet Exchange Fund Account assets to back its liabilities. It does so by arranging a swap with the **Exchange Fund Account**, which holds the country's foreign exchange reserves. This involves a spot purchase and a simultaneous forward sale of foreign exchange. To illustrate the operation, assume that the Bank temporarily buys $100 of foreign currency assets from the Exchange Fund Account. It credits the government's account on its own books and the operation results in the following balance sheets for the Bank and the government:

BANK OF CANADA				GOVERNMENT OF CANADA		
Assets		Liabilities		Assets		Liabilities
Foreign exchange +100		Government deposits +100		Exchange Fund Account −100		
				Deposits at the Bank of Canada +100		

We see that government deposit balances at the Bank of Canada increase and these balances can then be transferred to participants to increase settlement balances, as we saw earlier.

Although the spot transaction adds to the government deposits at the Bank of Canada and enables the Bank to auction government balances, the forward contract between the Bank and the Exchange Fund Account does not affect the settlement balances of participating financial institutions. The Bank simply sells foreign exchange to the Exchange Fund Account in the future at a price agreed upon today. The advantage to the Bank of Canada of using swap transactions with the Exchange Fund Account is that it can bring a temporary change in the level of settlement balances or respond to some event that the Bank thinks will have a significant but not long-lived effect.

As we will learn in Chapter 19, the foreign exchange reserves held in the Exchange Fund Account can also be used by the Bank of Canada in international financial transactions to prevent undesirable movements in the exchange rate. For example, a Bank of Canada sale of domestic currency and corresponding purchase of foreign assets in the foreign exchange market leads to a gain in international reserves, an increase in the monetary base and the money supply, and a depreciation of the domestic currency. A Bank purchase of domestic currency and corresponding sale of foreign exchange leads to a loss of international reserves, a decline in the monetary base and the money supply, and an appreciation of the domestic currency. We shall discuss such foreign exchange interventions in detail in Chapter 19.

AN EXAMPLE OF MONETARY CONTROL

Suppose that the operating band is 4.5% to 5% and the Bank of Canada expects the economy to exceed its capacity in the near future. To prevent inflationary pressures from building, the Bank wishes to tighten monetary policy by raising the operating band by 25 basis points. In one of the eight fixed days for announcing changes to the operating band for the overnight rate, the Bank announces, at 9:00 a.m., that it is adjusting the operating band up from 4.5% to 5% to 4.75% to 5.25%. From this announcement, LVTS participants know that the bank rate shifts from 5% to 5.25%, the rate on positive settlement balances shifts from 4.5% to 4.75%, and that the Bank of Canada's new target overnight rate, the midpoint of the operating band, shifts from 4.75% to 5%.

Later in the day, at 11:45 a.m. (see Box 17-1), if overnight funds are trading below the target overnight rate (the midpoint of the operating band), the Bank of Canada enters into SRAs to enforce the new target for the overnight rate. That is, it sells government securities to primary dealers, who pay for the securities with settlement balances and agree to sell the securities back to the Bank of Canada on the next business day, at a price that works out to an annual interest rate of 5%—the midpoint of the new operating band. Assuming that the Bank of Canada enters into SRAs in the amount of $100, the T-accounts of the Bank of Canada and the direct clearers will be

BANK OF CANADA			**DIRECT CLEARERS**		
Assets	Liabilities		Assets		Liabilities
	Settlement balances	−100	Settlement balances	−100	
	SRAs	+100	SRAs	+100	

The clearing banks find that their settlement balances have declined by $100, and because they had not been holding any excess reserves, their holdings of settlement balances are $100 short of the desired amount. Assuming that no other transactions occur during the day, at 4:15 p.m. (see Box 17-1), the Bank of Canada neutralizes the effect on aggregate settlement balances of its issue of SRAs, by auctioning off government deposits. The Bank's neutralization process involves auctioning off $100 of government deposits and paying those direct clearers taking government deposits with settlement balances, bringing the amount of aggregate settlement balances back to zero. The balance sheets of the Bank of Canada and the direct clearers now look like this:

BANK OF CANADA			**DIRECT CLEARERS**		
Assets	Liabilities		Assets		Liabilities
	Settlement balances	+100	Settlement balances	+100	Government deposits +100
	Government deposits	−100			

The end-of-day effect on the balance sheets of the Bank of Canada and the direct clearers is as follows:

BANK OF CANADA			**DIRECT CLEARERS**		
Assets	Liabilities		Assets		Liabilities
	SRAs	+100	SRAs	+100	Government deposits +100
	Government deposits	−100			

The Bank of Canada's monetary tightening has been effected through the management of settlement balances, during the course of the day, with no change in the aggregate settlement balances of deposit-taking institutions. As already noted, the change in the overnight rate will influence other interest rates and the level of monetary conditions in which the economy operates.

SUMMARY

1. The Bank of Canada views the overnight interest rate as the centrepiece of its monetary policy implementation. At 9:00 a.m. on the fixed action date, the Bank announces an operating band of 50 basis points for the overnight rate. The upper limit of the operating band is the bank rate—the rate the Bank charges LVTS participants that require an overdraft loan to cover negative settlement balances. The lower limit is the rate the Bank pays LVTS participants with positive settlement balances.

2. Prior to the introduction of the LVTS, the Bank reinforced the target band for the overnight rate by offering SPRAs at the upper end of the band and SRAs at the lower end of the band. With the introduction of the LVTS on February 4, 1999, however, the Bank introduced a new framework for implementing monetary policy. This involves the lending and taking deposits from LVTS participants.

3. The Bank of Canada targets the value of the overnight interest rate within its operating band, at the midpoint of the band. In doing so, the Bank inter-

venes in the overnight market using open-market buyback operations at the target rate. If the overnight rate is trading above the target rate, the Bank uses repos in which it purchases government of Canada securities from primary dealers with an agreement to resell them on the next business day. If the overnight rate is too low relative to the target rate, the Bank uses reverse repos in which it sells government of Canada securities to primary dealers with an agreement to buy them back on the next day.

4. The Bank continues to use government deposit shifting to neutralize public sector flows that affect LVTS participants' settlement balances—this in effect is a cash setting, a cash setting that is currently $50 million. Because its holdings of government of Canada securities are often much smaller than its monetary liabilities, the Bank brings onto its balance sheet Exchange Fund Account assets to back its liabilities. These amounts are adjusted daily, depending on factors such as the level of financial institution borrowings and/or deposits.

KEY TERMS

cash setting, p. 396

defensive open market operations, p. 388

direct clearers, p. 381

discount rate, p. 395

drawdowns, p. 396

dynamic open market operations, p. 388

Exchange Fund Account, p. 397

fixed bank rate regime, p. 394

floating bank rate regime, p. 394

indirect clearers, p. 381

Large Value Transfer System (LVTS), p. 380

lender of last resort, p. 390

LVTS participants, p. 380

monetary conditions, p. 386

multilateral netting, p. 380

operating band, p. 381

overnight interest rate, p. 381

primary dealers, p. 389

redeposits, p. 396

repos, p. 388

reverse repos, p. 389

standing facilities, p. 382

systemic risk, p. 380

QUESTIONS AND PROBLEMS

Questions marked with an asterisk are answered at the end of the book in an appendix, "Answers to Selected Questions and Problems."

*1. If government deposits at the Bank of Canada are predicted to increase, what defensive open market operations could be undertaken to neutralize the effect on settlement balances?

2. During the holiday season, when the public's holdings of currency increase, what defensive open market operations typically occur? Why?

*3. If the government has just paid for a supercomputer and as a result its deposits with the Bank of Canada fall, what defensive open market operations could be undertaken?

4. "In the LVTS environment, government deposit shifting is effected by auctions of government balances." Discuss.

*5. Most open market operations are currently repurchase agreements. What does this tell us about the likely volume of defensive open market operations relative to dynamic open market operations?

6. "The only way that the Bank of Canada can affect the level of advances is by adjusting the bank rate." Is this statement true, false, or uncertain? Explain your answer.

*7. If the Bank of Canada did not administer the operating band what do you predict would happen to the money supply if the bank rate were several percentage points below the overnight rate?

8. Discuss how the operating band affects interest rates and the money supply in the economy.

*9. "Last-resort lending is no longer needed because the presence of the CDIC eliminates the possibility of bank panics." Discuss.

10. The benefits of using last-resort lending to prevent bank panics are straightforward. What are the costs?

*11. You often read in the newspaper that the Bank of Canada has just lowered the bank rate. Does this signal that the Bank is moving to a more expansionary monetary policy? Why or why not?

12. How can the procyclical movement of interest rates (rising during business cycle expansions and falling during business cycle contractions) lead to a procyclical movement in the money supply as a result of the Bank of Canada's lending policy? Why might this movement of the money supply be undesirable?

*13. Explain how repos and reverse repos affect the overnight rate.

14. "A fixed bank rate regime would lead to tighter control of the money supply." Discuss.

*15. Compare the use of open market operations and government deposit shifting to control the money supply on the following criteria: flexibility, reversibility, effectiveness, and speed of implementation.

Chapter 18

Conduct of Monetary Policy: Goals and Targets

PREVIEW   Now that we understand the tools central banks like the Bank of Canada use to conduct monetary policy, we can proceed to see how monetary policy is actually conducted. Understanding the conduct of monetary policy is important because it not only affects the money supply and interest rates but also has a major influence on the level of economic activity and hence on our well-being.

To explore this subject, we look at the goals that the Bank of Canada establishes for monetary policy and its strategies for attaining them. After examining the goals and strategies, we can evaluate the Bank's conduct of monetary policy in the past, with the hope that it will give us some clues to where monetary policy may head in the future.

GOALS OF MONETARY POLICY

Six basic goals are continually mentioned by personnel at the Bank of Canada and other central banks when they discuss the objectives of monetary policy: (1) high employment, (2) economic growth, (3) price stability, (4) interest-rate stability, (5) stability of financial markets, and (6) stability in foreign exchange markets. Note that different countries and different regimes may give different weights to these goals. As we shall see, the current Canadian regime and the regimes of most hard currency countries are now strongly attached to the goals of price stability and financial markets stability.

High Employment

High employment is a worthy goal for two main reasons: (1) the alternative situation, high unemployment, causes much human misery, with families suffering financial distress, loss of personal self-respect, and increase in crime (though this last conclusion is highly controversial), and (2) when unemployment is high, the economy has not only idle workers but also idle resources (closed factories and unused equipment), resulting in a loss of output (lower GDP).

Although it is clear that high employment is desirable, how high should it be? At what point can we say that the economy is at full employment? At first, it might seem that full employment is the point at which no worker is out of a job, that is, when unemployment is zero. But this definition ignores the fact that some unemployment, called *frictional unemployment*, which involves searches by workers and firms to find suitable matchups, is beneficial to the economy. For example, a worker who decides to look for a better job might be unemployed for a while during the job search. Workers often decide to leave work temporarily to pursue other activities (raising a family, travel, returning to school), and when they decide to re-enter the job market, it may take some time for them to find the right job. The benefit of having some unemployment is similar to the benefit of having a nonzero vacancy rate in the market for rental apartments. As many of you who have looked for an apartment have discovered, when the vacancy rate in the rental market is too low, you will have a difficult time finding the right apartment.

Another reason that unemployment is not zero when the economy is at full employment is due to what is called *structural unemployment*, a mismatch between job requirements and the skills or availability of local workers. Clearly, this kind of unemployment is undesirable. Nonetheless, it is something that monetary policy can do little about.

The goal for high employment should therefore not seek an unemployment level of zero but rather a level above zero consistent with full employment at which the demand for labour equals the supply of labour. This level is called the **natural rate of unemployment**.

Although this definition sounds neat and authoritative, it leaves a troublesome question unanswered: what unemployment rate is consistent with full employment? On the one hand, in some cases, it is obvious that the unemployment rate is too high. The unemployment rate in excess of 20% during the Great Depression, for example, was clearly far too high. In the early 1960s, on the other hand, policymakers thought that a reasonable goal was 4%, a level that was probably too low because it led to accelerating inflation. Current estimates of the natural rate of unemployment place it between 6% and 7%, but even this estimate is subject to a great deal of uncertainty and disagreement. In addition, it is possible that appropriate government policy, such as the provision of better information about job vacancies or job training programs, might decrease the natural rate of unemployment.

Economic Growth

The goal of steady economic growth is closely related to the high-employment goal because businesses are more likely to invest in capital equipment to increase productivity and economic growth when unemployment is low. Conversely, if unemployment is high and factories are idle, it does not pay for a firm to invest in additional plants and equipment. Although the two goals are closely related, policies can be specifically aimed at promoting economic growth by directly encouraging firms to invest or by encouraging people to save, which provides more funds for firms to invest. In fact, this is the stated purpose of so-called supply-side economics policies, which are intended to spur economic growth by providing tax incentives for businesses to invest in facilities and equipment and for taxpayers to save more. The public, politicians, and the media in Canada have become much more concerned about economic growth in recent years because of substantial changes in the growth rate. In the 1950s and 1960s, real GDP grew in excess of 5% per year on average, whereas from 1973 to 1995, it grew at less than 3%. Only in the late 1990s did the growth rate return to the higher growth rate of the 1950s and 1960s. This has generated an active debate over what can be done to increase our growth rate and whether monetary policy can play a role in boosting growth.

Price Stability

Over the past few decades, policymakers in Canada have become increasingly aware of the social and economic costs of inflation and more concerned with a stable price level as a goal of economic policy. Indeed, price stability is increasingly viewed as the most important goal for monetary policy. (This view is also evident in Europe—see Box 18-1.) Price stability is desirable because a rising price level (inflation) creates uncertainty in the economy, and that may hamper economic growth. For example, when the overall level of prices is changing, the information conveyed by the prices of goods and services is harder to interpret, which complicates decision making for consumers, businesses, and government. Not only do public opinion surveys indicate that the public is very hostile to inflation, but also a growing body of evidence suggests that inflation leads to lower economic growth.[1] The most extreme example of unstable prices is *hyperinflation*, such as Argentina, Brazil, and Russia have experienced in the recent past. Many economists attribute the slower growth that these countries have experienced to their problems with hyperinflation.

Inflation also makes it hard to plan for the future. For example, it is more difficult to decide how much funds should be put aside to provide for a child's college education in an inflationary environment. Further, inflation may strain a country's social fabric. Conflict may result because each group in the society may compete with other groups to make sure that its income keeps up with the rising level of prices.

Interest-Rate Stability

Interest-rate stability is desirable because fluctuations in interest rates can create uncertainty in the economy and make it harder to plan for the future. Fluctuations in interest rates that affect consumers' willingness to buy houses, for example, make it more difficult for consumers to decide when to purchase a house and for construction firms to plan how many houses to build. A central bank may also want to reduce upward movements in interest rates for the reasons we discussed in Chapter 14. Upward movements in interest rates generate hostility toward central banks like the Bank of Canada and lead to demands that their power be curtailed.

Stability of Financial Markets

As our analysis in Chapter 8 showed, financial crises can interfere with the ability of financial markets to channel funds to people with productive investment opportunities, thereby leading to a sharp contraction in economic activity. The promotion of a more stable financial system in which financial crises are avoided is thus an important goal for a central bank. Indeed, as discussed in Chapter 14, the Bank of Canada was created in response to the problems of the Great Depression.

The stability of financial markets is also fostered by interest-rate stability because fluctuations in interest rates create great uncertainty for financial institutions. An increase in interest rates produces large capital losses on long-term bonds and mortgages, losses that can cause the failure of the financial institutions holding them. In recent years, more pronounced interest-rate fluctuations have been a particularly severe problem for financial institutions, many of which got into serious financial trouble in the 1980s (as we have seen in Chapter 11).

Stability in Foreign Exchange Markets

With the increasing importance of international trade to the economy, the value of the dollar relative to other currencies has become a major consideration for the Bank of Canada. As we saw in Chapter 7, a rise in the value of the dollar makes Canadian industries less competitive with those abroad, and declines in the value

---

[1]For example, see Stanley Fischer, "The Role of Macroeconomic Factors in Growth," *Journal of Monetary Economics* 32 (1993): 485–512.

BOX 18-1

The Growing European Commitment to Price Stability

Not surprisingly, given Germany's experience with hyperinflation in the 1920s, Germans have had the strongest commitment to price stability as the primary goal for monetary policy. Other Europeans have been coming around to the view that the primary objective for a central bank should be price stability. The increased importance of this goal was reflected in the December 1991 Treaty of European Union,

known as the Maastricht Treaty. This treaty created the European System of Central Banks, which functions very much like the Federal Reserve System. The statute of the European System of Central Banks sets price stability as the primary objective of this system and indicates that the general economic policies of the European Union are to be supported only if they are not in conflict with price stability.

European System of
Central Banks
www.ecb.int

of the dollar stimulate inflation in Canada. In addition, preventing large changes in the value of the dollar makes it easier for firms and individuals purchasing or selling goods abroad to plan ahead. Stabilizing extreme movements in the value of the dollar in foreign exchange markets is thus viewed as a worthy goal of monetary policy. In other countries, which are even more dependent on foreign trade, stability in foreign exchange markets takes on even greater importance.

Conflict Among Goals

Although many of the goals mentioned are consistent with each other—high employment with economic growth, interest-rate stability with financial market stability—this is not always the case. The goal of price stability often conflicts with the goals of interest-rate stability and high employment in the short run (but probably not in the long run). For example, when the economy is expanding and unemployment is falling, both inflation and interest rates may start to rise. If the central bank tries to prevent a rise in interest rates, this may cause the economy to overheat and stimulate inflation. But if a central bank raises interest rates to prevent inflation, in the short run unemployment may rise. The conflict among goals may thus present central banks like the Bank of Canada with some hard choices.[2] We return to the issue of how central banks should choose conflicting goals in later chapters when we examine how monetary policy affects the economy.

CENTRAL BANK STRATEGY: USE OF TARGETS

The central bank's problem is that it wishes to achieve certain goals, such as price stability with high employment, but it does not directly influence the goals. It has a set of tools to employ (open market operations, changes in the operating band for the overnight rate, etc.) that can affect the goals indirectly after a period of time (typically more than a year). If the central bank waits to see what the price level and employment will be one year later, it will be too late to make any corrections to its policy—mistakes will be irreversible.

---

[2]Strictly speaking, it is not central banks that face hard choices, or at least not once their mandate has been narrowed in the way that it has been in Canada. It is rather the more defined monetary authorities, including the ministry of finance and, for all countries more or less, the International Monetary Fund and the Bank for International Settlements, which face them.

All central banks consequently pursue a different strategy for conducting monetary policy by aiming at variables that lie between its tools and the achievement of its goals. The strategy is as follows: after deciding on its goals for employment and the price level, the central bank chooses a set of variables to aim for, called **intermediate targets**, such as the monetary aggregates (M1+, M2+, or M3) or interest rates (short- or long-term), which have a direct effect on employment and the price level. However, even these intermediate targets are not directly affected by the central bank's policy tools. Therefore, it chooses another set of variables to aim for, called **operating targets**, or alternatively called *instruments*, such as reserve aggregates (reserves or monetary base) or interest rates (overnight rate or Treasury bill rate), which are more responsive to its policy tools.[3]

The central bank pursues this strategy because it is easier to hit a goal by aiming at targets than by aiming at the goal directly. Specifically, by using intermediate and operating targets, it can more quickly judge whether its policies are on the right track, rather than waiting until it sees the final outcome of its policies on employment and the price level.[4] By analogy, a hot air balloon operator employs the strategy of using targets when trying to land the balloon on the ground. He will check to see whether the balloon is positioned correctly as it lands (we can think of this as an "operating target"). If the balloon is off course at this stage, the operator will adjust its thrust (a policy tool) to get it back on target. The operator may check the position of the balloon again when it is halfway to the landing spot (we can think of this as the "intermediate target") and can make further midcourse corrections if necessary.

The central bank's strategy works in a similar way. Suppose that the central bank's employment and price-level goals are consistent with a nominal GDP growth rate of 5%. If the central bank feels that the 5% nominal GDP growth rate will be achieved by a 4% growth rate for M1+ (its intermediate target), which will in turn be achieved by a growth rate of 3% for the monetary base (its operating target), it will carry out open market operations (its tool) to achieve the 3% growth in the monetary base. After implementing this policy, the central bank may find that the monetary base is growing too slowly, say at a 2% rate; then it can correct this too-slow growth by increasing the amount of its open market purchases. Somewhat later, the central bank will begin to see how its policy is affecting the growth rate of the money supply. If M1+ is growing too fast, say at a 7% rate, the central bank may decide to reduce its open market purchases or make open market sales to reduce the M1+ growth rate.

One way of thinking about this strategy (illustrated in Figure 18-1) is that the central bank is using its operating and intermediate targets to direct monetary policy (the hot air balloon) toward the achievement of its goals. After the initial setting of the policy tools, an operating target such as the monetary base, which the central bank can control fairly directly, is used to reset the tools so that monetary policy is channelled toward achieving the intermediate target of a certain rate of money supply growth. Midcourse corrections in the policy tools can be made again when the central bank sees what is happening to its intermediate target, thus directing monetary policy so that it will achieve its goals of high employment and price stability.

---

[3]There is some ambiguity as to whether to call a particular variable an operating target or an intermediate target. The monetary base and the Treasury bill rate are often viewed as possible intermediate targets, even though they may function as operating targets as well. In addition, if the Bank wants to pursue a goal of interest-rate stability, an interest rate can be both a goal and a target.

[4]This reasoning for the use of monetary targets has come under attack because information on employment and the price level can be useful in evaluating policy. See Benjamin M. Friedman, "The Inefficiency of Short-Run Monetary Targets for Monetary Policy," *Brookings Papers on Economic Activity* 2 (1977): 292–346.

Tools of the Central Bank

Open market operations
Government deposit shifting
Operating band for the overnight interest rate

Operating Targets

Reserve aggregates (reserves, monetary base)
Interest rates (short-term such as overnight rate)

Intermediate Targets

Monetary aggregates (M1+, M2+, M3)
Interest rates (short- and long-term)

Goals

High employment, price stability, financial market stability, and so on.

FIGURE 18-1 Central Bank Strategy

CHOOSING THE TARGETS

As we see in Figure 18-1, there are two different types of target variables: interest rates and aggregates (monetary aggregates and reserve aggregates). In our example, the central bank chose a 4% growth rate for M1+ to achieve a 5% rate of growth for nominal GDP. It could have chosen to lower the overnight rate to, say, 3% to achieve the same goal. Can the central bank choose to pursue both of these targets at the same time? The answer is no. The application of the supply and demand analysis of the money market that we covered in Chapter 5 explains why a central bank must choose one or the other.

Let's first see why a monetary aggregate target involves losing control of the interest rate. Figure 18-2 contains a supply and demand diagram for the money market. Although the central bank expects the demand curve for money to be at M^{d*}, it fluctuates between $M^{d'}$ and $M^{d''}$ because of unexpected increases or decreases in output or changes in the price level. The money demand curve might also shift unexpectedly because the public's preferences about holding bonds versus money may change. If the central bank's monetary aggregate target of a 4% growth rate in M1+ results in a money supply of M^*, it expects that the interest rate will be i^*. However, as the figure indicates, the fluctuations in the money demand curve between $M^{d'}$ and $M^{d''}$ will result in an interest rate fluctuating between i' and i''. ***Pursuing a monetary aggregate target implies that interest rates will fluctuate***.

The supply and demand diagram in Figure 18-3 shows the consequences of an interest-rate target set at i^*. Again, the central bank expects the money demand curve to be at M^{d*}, but it fluctuates between $M^{d'}$ and $M^{d''}$ due to unexpected changes in output, the price level, or the public's preferences toward holding money. If the demand curve falls to $M^{d'}$, the interest rate will begin to fall below i^*, and the price of bonds will rise. With an interest-rate target, the central bank will prevent the interest rate from falling by selling bonds to drive their price back down and the interest rate back up to its former level. The central bank will make open market sales until the money supply declines to $M^{s'}$, at which point the equilibrium interest rate is again i^*. Conversely, if the demand curve rises to $M^{d''}$ and

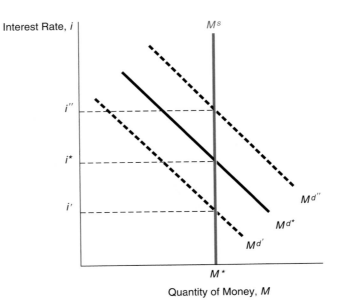

FIGURE 18-2 Result of Targeting on the Money Supply

Targeting on the money supply at M^* will lead to fluctuations in the interest rate between i' and i'' because of fluctuations in the money demand curve between $M^{d'}$ and $M^{d''}$.

drives up the interest rate, the central bank will keep interest rates from rising by buying bonds to keep their prices from falling. The central bank will make open market purchases until the money supply rises to $M^{s''}$ and the equilibrium interest rate is i^*. The central bank's adherence to the interest-rate target thus leads to a fluctuating money supply as well as fluctuations in reserve aggregates such as the monetary base.

The conclusion from the supply and demand analysis is that interest-rate and monetary aggregate targets are incompatible: a central bank can hit one or the other but not both. Because a choice between them has to be made, we need to examine what criteria should be used to decide on the target variable.

Criteria for Choosing Intermediate Targets

The rationale behind a central bank's strategy of using targets suggests three criteria for choosing an intermediate target. It must be measurable, it must be controllable by the central bank, and it must have a predictable effect on the goal.

Measurability Quick and accurate measurement of an intermediate-target variable is necessary because the intermediate target will be useful only if it signals rapidly when policy is off track. What good does it do for the central bank to plan to hit a 4% growth rate for M1+ if it has no way of quickly and accurately measuring M1+? Data on the monetary aggregates are available with about a month's delay, and interest-rate data are available almost immediately. Data on a variable like GDP that serves as a goal, by contrast, are compiled quarterly and are obtained after a two-month delay. In addition, the GDP data are less accurate than data on the monetary aggregates or interest rates. On these grounds alone, focusing on interest rates and monetary aggregates as intermediate targets rather than on a goal like GDP can provide clearer signals about the status of the central bank's policy.

At first glance, interest rates seem to be more measurable than monetary aggregates and hence more useful as intermediate targets. Not only are the data

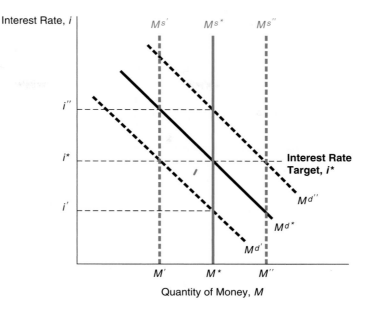

FIGURE 18-3   Result of Targeting on the Interest Rate

Targeting the interest rate at i^* will lead to fluctuations of the money supply between M' and M'' because of fluctuations in the money demand curve between $M^{d'}$ and $M^{d''}$.

on interest rates available more quickly than on monetary aggregates, but they are also measured more precisely and are rarely revised, in contrast to the monetary aggregates, which are subject to a fair amount of revision (as we saw in Chapter 3). However, as we learned in Chapter 4, the interest rate that is quickly and accurately measured, the nominal interest rate, is typically a poor measure of the real cost of borrowing, which indicates with more certainty what will happen to GDP. This real cost of borrowing is more accurately measured by the real interest rate—the interest rate adjusted for expected inflation ($i_r = i - \pi^e$). Until recently, the real interest rate was extremely hard to measure because we didn't have a direct way to measure expected inflation. This all changed, however, when governments in countries like Australia, Canada, Sweden, the United Kingdom, and the United States began to issue indexed bonds (discussed in Box 4-3) that make it possible to observe the real interest rate. Since the interest rate is now more measurable than monetary aggregates, it should be preferred to the monetary aggregates as an intermediate target.

Controllability   A central bank must be able to exercise effective control over a variable if it is to function as a useful target. If the central bank cannot control an intermediate target, knowing that it is off track does little good because the central bank has no way of getting the target back on track. Some economists have suggested that nominal GDP should be used as an intermediate target, but since the central bank has little direct control over nominal GDP, it will not provide much guidance on how the Bank of Canada should set its policy tools. A central bank does, however, have a good deal of control over the monetary aggregates and interest rates.

Our discussion of the money supply process and the central bank's policy tools indicates that a central bank does have the ability to exercise a powerful effect on the money supply, although its control is not perfect. We have also seen that open market operations can be used to set interest rates by directly affecting the price of bonds. Because a central bank can set interest rates directly whereas it cannot completely control the money supply, it might appear that interest rates dominate the monetary aggregates on the controllability criterion. However, a central bank cannot set real interest rates because it does not have control over expectations of inflation. So again, a clear-cut case cannot be made that interest rates are preferable to monetary aggregates as an intermediate target or vice versa.

Predictable Effect on Goals The most important characteristic a variable must have to be useful as an intermediate target is that it must have a predictable impact on a goal. If a central bank can accurately and quickly measure the price of tea in China and can completely control its price, what good will it do? The central bank cannot use the price of tea in China to affect unemployment or the price level in its country. Because the ability to affect goals is so critical to the usefulness of an intermediate-target variable, the linkage of the money supply and interest rates with the goals—output, employment, and the price level—is a matter of much debate. The evidence on whether these goals have a closer (more predictable) link with the money supply than with interest rates is discussed in Chapter 25.

Criteria for Choosing Operating Targets

The choice of an operating target can be based on the same criteria used to evaluate intermediate targets. Both the overnight rate and reserve aggregates are measured accurately and are available daily with almost no delay; both are easily controllable using the policy tools that we discussed in Chapter 17. When we look at the third criterion, however, we can think of the intermediate target as the goal for the operating target. An operating target that has a more predictable impact on the most desirable intermediate target is preferred. If the desired intermediate target is an interest rate, the preferred operating target will be an interest-rate variable like the overnight rate because interest rates are closely tied to each other (as we saw in Chapter 6). However, if the desired intermediate target is a monetary aggregate, our money supply model in Chapters 15 and 16 shows that a reserve aggregate operating target such as the monetary base will be preferred. Because there does not seem to be much reason to choose an interest rate over a reserve aggregate on the basis of measurability or controllability, the choice of which operating target is better rests on the choice of the intermediate target (the goal of the operating target).

BANK OF CANADA POLICY PROCEDURES: HISTORICAL PERSPECTIVE

The well-known adage "The road to hell is paved with good intentions" applies as much to the Bank of Canada as it does to human beings. Understanding a central bank's goals and the strategies it can use to pursue them cannot tell us how monetary policy is actually conducted. To understand the practical results of the theoretical underpinnings, we have to look at how central banks have actually conducted policy in the past. First we will look at the Bank of Canada's past policy procedures: its choice of goals, policy tools, operating targets, and intermediate targets. This historical perspective will not only show us how our central bank carries out its duties but will also help us interpret the Bank's activities and see where Canadian monetary policy may be heading in the future. Once we are done studying the Bank of Canada, we will then examine central banks' experiences in other countries.

The following discussion of the Bank's policy procedures and their effect on the money supply provides a review of the money supply process and how the Bank's policy tools work. If you have trouble understanding how the particular policies described affect the money supply, it might be helpful to review the material in Chapters 15 and 16.

The Early Years

From the end of World War II in 1945 until the early 1970s the world economy operated under a system of fixed exchange rates, known as the Bretton Woods system (to be discussed in detail in Chapter 20). Initially, Canada opted out of this system, but joined in 1962 and participated with the exchange rate fixed at 92.5 U.S. cents. Even before 1962, Canadian monetary policy had been driven by the goal of maintaining a stable exchange rate with the United States and the Bank of Canada therefore kept short-term interest rates more or less in step with U.S. interest rates. This meant that short-term interest rates, or the differential between U.S. and Canadian rates, were the intermediate target of monetary policy. As a result, inflation rates and interest rates followed generally similar patterns in the two countries (see Figures 18-4 and 18-5).

In 1971, Canada switched to a flexible exchange rate regime, but the Bank of Canada continued to adjust short-term interest rates to keep the foreign exchange and domestic bonds markets functioning smoothly, and paid no attention to the growth rate of money. As a result, monetary policy was quite expansionary in the early 1970s and the inflation rate increased to double digits—in fact, the price level increased by 11% in 1974 compared to only 3% in 1971. By the mid-1970s there was little doubt that one consequence of the policy of using interest rates as the intermediate target was that the Bank of Canada did not concern itself with the rate of growth of the money supply, as measured by the monetary aggregates.

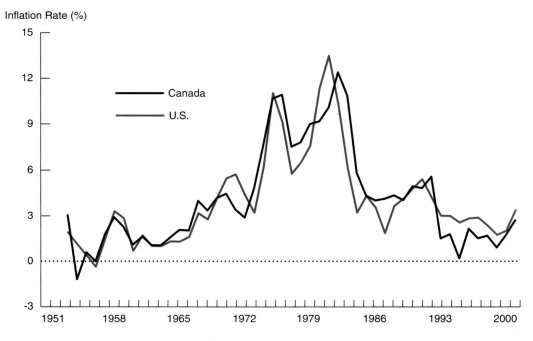

FIGURE 18-4   Inflation Rates, Canada and the United States, 1951-2000

Source: Statistics Canada CANSIM Series P100000 and D139105.

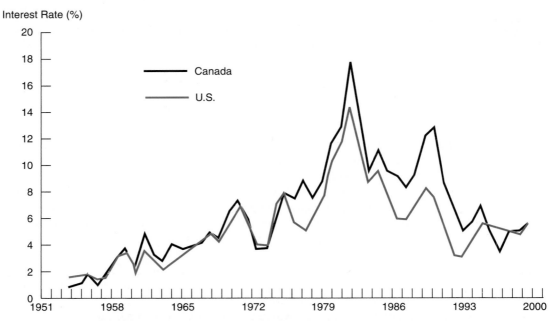

Interest Rate (%)

FIGURE 18-5 Interest Rates (90-Day T-bills), Canada and the United States, 1951–2000
Source: Statistics Canada CANSIM Series B14007 and B54401.

By the end of this period there was also a wide consensus among central banks around the world that fluctuations in money contained useful information about income and prices. This evidence contributed to the rise of **monetarism**, a theory that emphasizes a steady, predictable rate of growth in the monetary aggregates, to be discussed in Chapter 24. It led the Bank of Canada and many other central banks, including the Federal Reserve, the Bank of England, the Bundesbank, the Swiss National Bank, and the Bank of Japan, to adopt key monetary aggregates as the intermediate targets of monetary policy.

Monetary Targeting, 1975–1981

In response to rising inflation in the early 1970s, in 1975 the Bank of Canada introduced a program of "monetary gradualism," under which M1 growth would be controlled within a gradually falling target range (see Table 18-1). The change in monetary strategy did not extend to a change in operating procedures—the Bank continued to use an interest rate as its operating target. The idea was to announce (about one year) in advance the target path for the growth of M1 and then adjust policy during the course of the year to make the actual growth rate lie within the target range. The rationale for announcing the monetary policy targets in advance was to influence people's expectations, with the hope that this would help bring down actual inflation faster than otherwise. Moreover, the Bank decided to target M1 because it was the most prominent measure of money with a very stable demand.

As can be seen from Table 18-1, the Bank of Canada was successful at keeping actual M1 growth within the target range, and the goal of reducing M1 growth was achieved by the end of the decade. However, the inflation rate accelerated, and by the end of the 1970s, it was almost at the same level as when monetary gradualism was introduced in 1975. What went wrong? Why did the inflation rate remain high? The answers to these questions lie in a series of financial innovations that reduced the demand for M1 balances. In particular, the introduction of new kinds of bank deposit accounts, and the development of cash management techniques for corporate accounts, motivated individuals and firms to move out of demand deposits—part of M1—into new chequable savings deposits—part of M2. This increased the growth rate of M2 and reduced the growth rate of M1, at the

TABLE 18-1   Canadian M1 Target Ranges and Actual Growth Rates for 1975–1980

Announcement Date	Base Period	M1 Growth Target (%)	Outcome (%)
November 1975	April–June 1975	10-15	9.3
August 1976	February–April 1976	8-12	7.7
October 1977	June 1977	7-11	9.3
September 1978	June 1978	6-10	5.1
December 1979	April–June 1979	5-9	5.9
February 1981	August–October 1980	4-8	0.4

Notes: Outcomes are annualized growth rates (%) of seasonally adjusted M1 between the base period and the next announcement of new targets. For example, the outcome corresponding to the November 1975 announcement is the annualized growth rate of M1 between April and June 1975 and August 1976.

Source: Ben Bernanke and Frederic Mishkin, "Central Bank Behaviour and the Strategy of Monetary Policy: Observations from Six Industrialised Countries." *NBER Macroeconomics Annual* (1992): 183-228. Reprinted with permission of the authors.

same time that M1 growth was being targeted, thereby rendering what seemed like tight anti-inflationary policy one that was in fact accommodating inflation.

By 1978, only three years after monetary targeting had begun, the Bank of Canada began to distance itself from this strategy out of concern for the nominal exchange rate, which had been depreciating. In particular, when interest rates in the United States increased sharply in late 1979, the Bank of Canada had to choose between allowing Canadian rates to increase to prevent an outflow of financial capital or allowing the exchange rate to depreciate to accommodate the spread in interest rates between the two countries. The Bank responded by an extremely restrictive monetary policy to resist depreciation of the Canadian dollar and the possible inflationary shock from import prices. Not surprisingly, M1 growth was negative in 1981 even though the target range was for growth between 4% and 8% (see Table 18-1), and Canadian interest rates increased to unprecedented levels (see Figure 18-5). The cost was the very deep 1981–1982 recession, the most severe since the 1930s.

Because of the conflict with exchange rate goals, as well as the uncertainty about M1 as a reliable guide to monetary policy, monetary targeting was formally abandoned in November 1982. Gerald Bouey, then governor of the Bank of Canada, described the situation by saying, "We didn't abandon monetary aggregates, they abandoned us."

The Checklist Approach, 1982–1988

The period following 1982 was one of groping. With the abandonment of M1 targets, the Bank of Canada switched its focus to a range of broader monetary aggregates, such as M2 and M2+, but no aggregate was found that would be suitable as a guide for conducting monetary policy. As a result, the Bank adopted what came to be called the "checklist" approach to policy, meaning that it looked at a list of factors in order to design and implement monetary policy. The Bank's checklist included the interest rate, the exchange rate, and with less weight attached to it, the money supply. The goal of monetary policy was inflation containment in the short term and price stability in the long term.

The Bank's anti-inflation policy during the 1982–1988 period can be viewed as one where the interest rate became the operating target and the exchange rate was the intermediate target. Throughout most of the period the Bank targeted interest rates, resisting depreciation of the Canadian dollar (fearing that depreciation would worsen inflation). The Bank's policy, however, had been undertaken against the backdrop of a persistent federal budget deficit that led to higher interest rates, making it difficult for the Bank to control money growth and inflation. In fact inflation had begun to increase again and the Bank responded with a dramatic reversal of its ad hoc monetary strategy. It announced early in 1988 that short-term issues would henceforth less guide policy and that price stability would be the Bank's long-term objective of monetary policy.

Inflation Targeting, 1989–Present

The adoption of inflation targets in Canada followed a three-year campaign by the Bank of Canada to promote price stability as the long-term goal of monetary policy. Beginning with the Hanson Lecture at the University of Alberta in January 1988, the newly appointed Bank of Canada governor, John Crow, announced that the Bank would subsequently pursue an objective of price stability (or zero inflation).[5] Initially, the policy of zero inflation took the form of a return to the high interest rates of the early 1980s. For example, during 1987 through 1989, interest rates increased and the Canadian dollar appreciated by more than would have normally been expected under previous regimes. The idea was that higher interest rates and a stronger dollar would lower aggregate demand and eventually bring inflation down.

In this most recent attempt at lowering inflation, the Bank of Canada, however, followed a different strategy, by announcing explicit targets for its ultimate goal—the inflation rate—rather than for an intermediate variable such as money growth. In particular, in February 1991 the Bank's governor and the minister of finance jointly announced a series of declining inflation targets, with a band of plus and minus one percentage point around them. The targets were 3% by the end of 1992, falling to 2% by the end of 1995, to remain within a range of 1% to 3% thereafter. The 1% to 3% target range for inflation was renewed in December 1995, in early 1998, and again in May 2001, to apply until the end of 2006.[6] The midpoint of the current inflation target range, 2%, is regarded as the most desirable outcome.

In setting its inflation targets, the Bank uses the rate of change in the CPI because of its "headline" quality—it is the most commonly used and understood price measure in Canada. Moreover, the CPI comes out monthly and without revisions, whereas other price indexes, such as the GDP deflator, are frequently revised. However, because headline CPI (all items) includes volatile components such as food, energy, and the effect of indirect taxes, the Bank, in order to avoid responses to short-run fluctuations, prefers to use and report inflation in "core CPI" which excludes volatile components. A core inflation rate is useful in assessing whether trend inflation is on track for the medium term. Also, defining the inflation targets in terms of ranges provides the Bank sufficient flexibility to deal with supply shocks beyond those already taken care of by the exclusion of volatile components from core inflation.

The move to targeting directly a goal of policy rather than an intermediate variable represented a significant shift in Bank of Canada policy procedures. An implication of this change was that the Bank had to broaden its information gathering to include variables containing significant information about future inflation. It has since used the overnight interest rate as the operating target and indicated that a range of monetary aggregates is useful in guiding policy along with an index of monetary conditions based on interest rates and exchange rates. The main purpose

---

[5]Zero inflation should be interpreted as a small positive rate of measured inflation.

[6]The 1995 and 1998 inflation-control agreements between the Bank of Canada and the government had a three-year horizon. The 2001 agreement, however, has a five-year horizon, reflecting the wide acceptance of the targets after almost a decade of operation.

of this index is to capture the two key monetary policy transmission mechanisms in an open economy—the one operating through interest rates and the one operating through exchange rates.

What are the results of Canada's inflation-targeting monetary policy? Figure 18-6 plots the Canadian inflation rate for each year since 1980 and shows the Bank's target range since 1996. Clearly, inflation has fallen dramatically since the adoption of inflation targets, from above the 5% level in 1991 to a 1% rate in 1998, being most of the time in the lower half of the target range. However, this decline was not without cost: unemployment soared to above the 10% level from 1991 until 1994 but has since fallen. What is difficult to say is whether explicit inflation targets are the only way to achieve good macroeconomic outcomes. As the Bank's former governor, Gordon Thiessen, recently put it, "It is too early to draw very strong conclusions about the impact of inflation targets on actual economic performance in Canada. We really do require a longer period of time for targets to demonstrate their ability to deal successfully with the peak of an economic upturn without the trend of inflation moving persistently outside the target range."[7]

International Considerations

The growing integration and interdependence of national economies (a process known as **globalization**) has brought international considerations to the forefront of Bank of Canada policymaking in recent years. With integrated financial markets, the Bank of Canada's monetary policy is also influenced by developments outside Canada. This is not a bad thing, but requires international policy cooperation to reduce potential disruptions to domestic policymaking and promote greater stability in financial markets. International cooperation has been encouraged by the process of **international policy coordination** (agreements among countries to enact policies cooperatively) that led to the Plaza Agreement in 1985 and the Louvre Accord in 1987 (see Box 18-2).

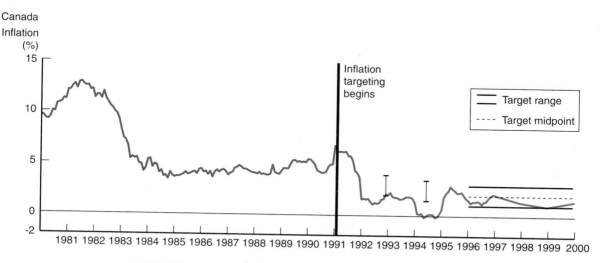

FIGURE 18-6   Inflation Rate and Inflation Targets for Canada, 1980–2000

Source: Ben S. Bernanke, Thomas Laubach, Frederic S. Mishkin, and Adam S. Posen, *Inflation Targeting: Lessons from the International Experience* (Princeton University Press: Princeton, N.J.) and updates from the same sources.

[7]Gordon G. Thiessen, "The Canadian Experience with Targets for Inflation Control," *Canadian Public Policy* 24 (1998), p. 425. For a more detailed discussion of Canada's experience with inflation targets see also Charles Freedman, "Inflation Targeting and the Economy: Lessons from Canada's First Decade," *Contemporary Economic Policy* 19 (2001), pp. 2-19, and Ben Bernanke, Thomas Laubach, Frederic Mishkin, and Adam Posen, *Inflation Targeting: Lessons from the International Experience*, Princeton: Princeton University Press, 1998.

BOX 18-2

International Policy Coordination

The Plaza Agreement and the Louvre Accord. By 1985, the decrease in the competitiveness of American corporations as a result of the strong U.S. dollar was raising strong sentiment in the United States for restricting imports. This protectionist threat to the international trading system stimulated finance ministers and the heads of central banks from the Group of Five (G-5) industrial countries—the United States, the United Kingdom, France, West Germany, and Japan—to reach an agreement at New York's Plaza Hotel in September 1985 to bring down the value of the U.S. dollar. From September 1985 until the beginning of 1987, the value of the U.S. dollar did indeed undergo a substantial decline, falling by 35% on average relative to foreign currencies. At this point, there was growing controversy over the decline in the U.S. dollar, and another meeting of policymakers from the G-5 countries plus Canada took place in February 1987 at the Louvre Museum in Paris. There the policymakers

agreed that exchange rates should be stabilized around the levels currently prevailing. Although the value of the U.S. dollar did continue to fluctuate relative to foreign currencies after the Louvre Accord, its downward trend had been checked as intended.

Because subsequent exchange rate movements were pretty much in line with the Plaza Agreement and the Louvre Accord, these attempts at international policy coordination have been considered successful. However, other aspects of the agreements were not adhered to by all signatories. For example, West German and Japanese policymakers agreed that their countries should pursue more expansionary policies by increasing government spending and cutting taxes, and the United States agreed to try to bring down its budget deficit. At that time, the United States was not particularly successful in lowering its deficit, and the Germans were reluctant to pursue expansionary policies because of their concerns about inflation.

International
Monetary Fund
www.imf.org

Bank for International
Settlements
www.bis.org

International considerations also played a role in the initiatives recently undertaken by the International Monetary Fund and the Bank for International Settlements, following the G-7 Halifax Summit in 1995, to improve the functioning of international financial markets. These initiatives seek to maximize the benefits of financial globalization, reduce the risks of financial instability that unrestrained capital flows may cause, and develop mechanisms for support in times of financial crisis. For example, the issue of international financial stability played a role in the Federal Reserve's decision to lower the federal funds rate by 3/4 of a percentage point in the fall of 1998. Concerns about the potential for worldwide financial crisis in the wake of the collapse of the Russian financial system at that time and weakness in other economies, particularly in Asia, stimulated the Fed to take a dramatic step to calm down markets.

International considerations, although not the primary focus of the Bank of Canada, are likely to also be a major factor in the conduct of Canadian monetary policy in the future.

ADVANTAGES AND DISADVANTAGES OF INFLATION TARGETING

Now that we understand the basic features of the Bank of Canada's inflation-targeting strategy, let's look at its advantages and disadvantages.

Advantages of Inflation Targeting

Inflation targeting has several advantages over other strategies for the conduct of monetary policy. It enables monetary policy to focus on domestic considerations and to respond to shocks to the domestic economy. It also has the key advantage that it is readily understood by the public and is thus highly transparent.

Because an explicit numerical inflation target increases the accountability of the central bank, inflation targeting also has the potential to reduce the likelihood that the Bank of Canada will fall into the time-inconsistency trap (to be discussed in detail in Chapter 20), trying to expand output and employment by pursuing overly expansionary monetary policy. A key advantage of inflation targeting is that it can help focus the political debate on what the Bank of Canada can do in the long run—that is, control inflation, rather than what it cannot do—permanently increase economic growth and the number of jobs through expansionary monetary policy. Thus inflation targeting has the potential to reduce pressures on the Bank of Canada to pursue inflationary monetary policy and thereby to reduce the likelihood of time-inconsistent policymaking.

The Bank of Canada's inflation-targeting regime also puts great stress on making policy transparent and on regular communication with the public. The Bank of Canada has frequent communications with the government, some mandated by law and some in response to informal inquiries, and its officials take every opportunity to make public speeches on the Bank's monetary policy strategy. While these techniques are also commonly used in countries that have not adopted inflation targeting (such as Germany and the United States), the Bank of Canada has taken public outreach a step further: not only does it engage in extended public information campaigns, but it publishes documents like the *Monetary Policy Report* and its *Update*. The publication of these documents is particularly noteworthy because they depart from the usual dull-looking, formal reports of central banks and use fancy graphics, boxes, and other eye-catching design elements to engage the public's interest.

The above channels of communication are used by the Bank of Canada and other inflation-targeting central banks to explain the following concepts to the general public, financial market participants, and the politicians: (1) the goals and limitations of monetary policy, including the rationale for inflation targets; (2) the numerical values of the inflation targets and how they are determined; (3) how the inflation targets are to be achieved, given current economic conditions; and (4) reasons for any deviations from targets. These communications have improved private sector planning by reducing uncertainty about monetary policy, interest rates, and inflation; they have promoted public debate of monetary policy, in part by educating the public about what the Bank of Canada can and cannot achieve; and they have helped clarify the responsibilities of the Bank of Canada and of politicians in the conduct of monetary policy.

Another key feature of Canada's inflation-targeting regime is the tendency toward increased accountability of the Bank of Canada. Indeed, transparency and communication go hand in hand with increased accountability. The transparency of policy associated with inflation targeting has tended to make the Bank of Canada highly accountable to the public and the government. Sustained successes in the conduct of monetary policy as measured against a pre-announced and well-defined inflation target can be instrumental in building public support for the Bank of Canada's independence and for its policies. This building of public support and accountability occurs even in the absence of a rigidly defined and legalistic standard of performance evaluation and punishment.

One remarkable example illustrates the benefits of transparency and accountability in Canada's inflation-targeting framework. It occurred in 1996, when the president of the Canadian Economic Association made a speech criticizing the Bank of Canada for pursuing monetary policy that he claimed was too contractionary. His speech sparked a widespread public debate. In countries not pursuing inflation targeting, such debates often degenerate into calls for the immediate expansion of monetary policy with little reference to the long-run consequences of such a policy change. In this case, however, the very existence of inflation targeting channelled the debate into a discussion over what should be the appropriate target for inflation, with both the Bank and its critics obliged to make explicit their assumptions and estimates of the costs and benefits of different levels of inflation. Indeed, the debate and the Bank's record and responsiveness increased support for the Bank of Canada, with the result that criticism of the Bank and its conduct of monetary policy was not a major issue in the 1997 elections as it had been before the 1993 elections.

Inflation targeting also seems to ameliorate the effects of inflationary shocks. For example, shortly after adopting inflation targets in February 1991, the Bank of Canada was faced with a new goods and services tax (GST), an indirect tax similar to a value-added tax—an adverse supply shock that in earlier periods might have led to a ratcheting up in inflation. Instead the tax increase led to only a one-time increase in the price level; it did not generate second- and third-round increases in wages and prices that would have led to a persistent rise in the inflation rate.

Disadvantages of Inflation Targeting

Critics of inflation targeting cite four disadvantages/criticisms of this monetary policy strategy: delayed signalling, too much rigidity, the potential for increased output fluctuations, and low economic growth. We look at each in turn and examine the validity of these criticisms.

Delayed Signalling   The monetary authorities do not easily control inflation. Furthermore, because of the long lags in the effects of monetary policy, inflation outcomes are revealed only after a substantial lag. Thus, an inflation target is unable to send immediate signals to both the public and markets about the stance of monetary policy. However, as you will learn in Chapter 20, the signals provided by other strategies for the conduct of monetary policy such as monetary targeting and exchange-rate targeting are not very strong either. Hence, a case can be made that other strategies are not superior to inflation targeting on these grounds.

Too Much Rigidity   Some economists have criticized inflation targeting because they believe it imposes a rigid rule on monetary policymakers, limiting their discretion to respond to unforeseen circumstances. For example, policymakers in Canada and other inflation-targeting countries did not foresee the breakdown of the relationship between monetary aggregates and goal variables such as nominal spending or inflation. With rigid adherence to a monetary rule, the breakdown in their relationship could have been disastrous. However, the traditional distinction between rules and discretion can be highly misleading. Useful policy strategies exist that are "rule-like" in that they involve forward-looking behaviour that limits policymakers from systematically engaging in policies with undesirable long-run consequences. Such policies avoid the time-inconsistency problem (to be discussed in detail in Chapter 20) and would best be described as "constrained discretion."

Indeed, inflation targeting can be described exactly in this way. Inflation targeting, as actually practiced by the Bank of Canada, is far from rigid. In particular, inflation targeting does not prescribe simple and mechanical instructions on how the Bank of Canada should conduct monetary policy. Rather, it requires the Bank to use all available information to determine what policy actions are appropriate to achieve the inflation target. Unlike simple policy rules, inflation targeting never requires the Bank of Canada to focus solely on one key variable.

Potential for Increased Output Fluctuations   An important criticism of inflation targeting is that a sole focus on inflation may lead to monetary policy that is too tight when inflation is above target and thus may lead to larger output fluctuations. Inflation targeting does not, however, require a sole focus on inflation. The decision by the Bank of Canada to choose inflation targets above zero reflects the concern that particularly low inflation can have substantial negative effects on real economic activity. Deflation (negative inflation in which the price level actually falls) is especially to be feared because of the possibility that it may promote financial instability and precipitate a severe economic contraction (Chapter 8). The deflation in Japan in recent years has been an important factor in the weakening of the Japanese financial system and economy. Targeting inflation rates of above zero makes periods of deflation less likely. This is one reason why some economists both within and outside Japan have been calling on the Bank of Japan to adopt an inflation target at levels of 2% or above.

Inflation targeting also does not ignore traditional stabilization goals. The Bank of Canada continues to express its concern about fluctuations in output and employment, and the ability to accommodate short-run stabilization goals to some degree is built into its inflation-targeting regime. The Bank of Canada and all inflation-targeting countries have been willing to minimize output declines by gradually lowering medium-term inflation targets toward the long-run goal.

In addition, the Bank of Canada has emphasized that the floor of the target range should be emphasized every bit as much as the ceiling, thus helping to stabilize the real economy when there are negative shocks to demand. Inflation targets can increase the Bank of Canada's flexibility in responding to declines in aggregate spending. Declines in aggregate demand that cause the inflation rate to fall below the floor of the target range will automatically stimulate the Bank of Canada to loosen monetary policy without fearing that its action will trigger a rise in inflation expectations.

Another element of flexibility in inflation-targeting regimes is that deviations from inflation targets are routinely allowed in response to supply shocks, such as restrictions in the supply of energy or raw materials that could have substantial negative effects on output. First, the price index on which the official inflation targets are based, core CPI, excludes the effects of "supply shocks"; for example, core CPI excludes volatile components such as food and energy prices. Second, following (or in anticipation of) a supply shock, such as a rise in a value-added tax (similar to a sales tax), the Bank of Canada would first deviate from its planned policies as needed and then explain to the public the reasons for its action.

Low Economic Growth   Another common concern about inflation targeting is that it will lead to low growth in output and employment. Although inflation reduction has been associated with below-normal output during disinflationary phases, once low inflation levels were achieved, output and employment returned to levels as high as they were before. A conservative conclusion is that once low inflation is achieved, inflation targeting is not harmful to the real economy. Given the strong economic growth after disinflation in Canada and other inflation targeters (such as New Zealand), a case can be made that inflation targeting promotes real economic growth in addition to controlling inflation.

THE TAYLOR RULE, NAIRU, AND THE PHILLIPS CURVE

As we have seen, the Bank of Canada currently conducts monetary policy by setting a target for the overnight rate. But how should this target be chosen?

John Taylor of Stanford University has come up with an answer, his so-called **Taylor rule**. The Taylor rule indicates that the overnight rate should be set equal to the inflation rate plus an "equilibrium" real overnight rate, $\bar{i}_{or}$ (the real overnight rate that is consistent with full employment in the long run), plus a weighted average of two parts: (1) an inflation gap, current inflation, π, minus a target rate, π^*, and (2) an output gap, the percentage deviation of real GDP, y, from an estimate of its potential full employment level, $\bar{y}$.[8] This rule can be written as follows:

$$i_{or} = \pi + \bar{i}_{or} + \frac{1}{2}\left(\pi - \pi^*\right) + \frac{1}{2}\left(y - \bar{y}\right)$$

where $\pi - \pi^*$ is the inflation gap and $y - \bar{y}$ is the output gap.

For an example of the Taylor rule in practice, suppose that the equilibrium real overnight rate is 2%, that an appropriate target for inflation is also 2%, that the inflation rate is at 3%, leading to a positive inflation gap of 1% (= 3% − 2%), and real GDP was 1% above its potential, resulting in a positive output gap of 1%. Then the Taylor rule suggests that the overnight rate should be set at 6%,

$$i_{or} = 3\% + 2\% + \frac{1}{2}\ (1\%\ \text{inflation gap}) + \frac{1}{2}\ (1\%\ \text{output gap}) = 6\%$$

The presence of both an inflation gap and an output gap in the Taylor rule might indicate that the Bank of Canada should care not only about keeping inflation under control, but also about minimizing business cycle fluctuations of output around its potential. Caring about both inflation and output fluctuations is consistent with many statements by Bank of Canada officials that controlling inflation and stabilizing real output are important concerns of the Bank of Canada.

An alternative interpretation of the presence of the output gap in the Taylor rule is that the output gap is an indicator of future inflation as stipulated in **Phillips curve theory**. Phillips curve theory indicates that changes in inflation are influenced by the state of the economy relative to its productive capacity, as well as to other factors. This productive capacity can be measured by potential GDP, which is a function of the natural rate of unemployment, the rate of unemployment consistent with full employment. A related concept is the **NAIRU**, the **nonaccelerating inflation rate of unemployment**, the rate of unemployment at which there is no tendency for inflation to change.[9] Simply put, the theory states that when the unemployment rate is above NAIRU with output below potential, inflation will come down, but if it is below NAIRU with output above potential, inflation will rise. Prior to 1995, the NAIRU was thought to reside around 8%. However, with the decline in unemployment in the late 1990s, with no increase in inflation and even a slight decrease, some critics have questioned the value of Phillips curve theory. Either they claim that it just doesn't work any more or alternatively believe that there is great uncertainty about the value of NAIRU. Phillips curve theory is now highly controversial, and many economists believe that it should not be used as a guide for the conduct of monetary policy.

---

[8]John B. Taylor, "Discretion Versus Policy Rules in Practice," *Carnegie-Rochester Conference Series on Public Policy* 39 (1993): 195-214. A more intuitive discussion with a historical perspective can be found in John B. Taylor, "A Historical Analysis of Monetary Policy Rules," in *Monetary Policy Rules*, ed. John B. Taylor (Chicago: University of Chicago Press, 1999), pp. 319–341.

[9]There are however subtle differences between the two concepts as is discussed in Arturo Estrella and Frederic S. Mishkin, "The Role of NAIRU in Monetary Policy: Implications of Uncertainty and Model Selection," in *Monetary Policy Rules*, ed. John Taylor (Chicago: University of Chicago Press, 1999): 405-430.

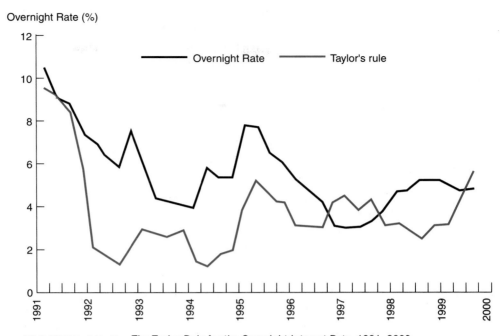

FIGURE 18-7   The Taylor Rule for the Overnight Interest Rate, 1991–2000

Source: Statistics Canada CANSIM Series P119500, B14044, D14872, and authors' calculations.

As Figure 18-7 shows, the Taylor rule does a pretty good job of describing the Bank of Canada's setting of the overnight rate. It also provides a perspective on the Bank's conduct of monetary policy under the inflation-targeting regime. During this period, when the Bank was trying to bring inflation down quickly, the overnight rate was generally higher than that recommended by the Taylor rule. The closer correspondence between the actual overnight rate and the Taylor rule recommendation during the late 1990s may help explain why the Bank's performance has been so successful in recent years.

SUMMARY

1. The six basic goals of monetary policy are high employment, economic growth, price stability, interest-rate stability, stability of financial markets, and stability in foreign exchange markets.

2. By using intermediate and operating targets, a central bank like the Bank of Canada can more quickly judge whether its policies are on the right track and make midcourse corrections, rather than waiting to see the final outcome of its policies on such goals as employment and the price level. The Bank's policy tools directly affect its operating targets, which in turn affect the intermediate targets, which in turn affect the goals.

3. Because interest-rate and monetary aggregate targets are incompatible, a central bank must choose between them on the basis of three criteria: measurability, controllability, and the ability to affect goal variables predictably. Unfortunately, these criteria do not establish an overwhelming case for one set of targets over another.

4. The historical record of the Bank of Canada's conduct of monetary policy reveals that the Bank has switched its targets many times, pursuing inflation targeting in recent years.

5. The Taylor rule indicates that the overnight rate should be set equal to the inflation rate plus an "equilibrium" real overnight rate plus a weighted average of two gaps: (1) an inflation gap, current inflation minus a target rate, and (2) an output gap, the percentage deviation of real GDP from an estimate of its potential full employment level. The output gap in the Taylor rule could represent an indicator of future inflation as stipulated in Phillips curve theory. However, this theory is controversial because high output relative to potential as measured by low unemployment has not seemed to produce higher inflation in recent years.

KEY TERMS

globalization, p. 415

intermediate targets, p. 406

international policy coordination, p. 415

monetarism, p. 412

natural rate of unemployment, p. 403

nonaccelerating inflation rate of unemployment (NAIRU), p. 420

operating target, p. 406

Phillips curve theory, p. 420

Taylor rule, p. 420

QUESTIONS AND PROBLEMS

Questions marked with an asterisk are answered at the end of the book in an appendix, "Answers to Selected Questions and Problems."

*1. "Unemployment is a bad thing, and the government should make every effort to eliminate it." Do you agree or disagree? Explain your answer.

2. Classify each of the following as either an operating target or an intermediate target, and explain why.
   a. The three-month Treasury bill rate
   b. The monetary base
   c. M2+

*3. "If the demand for money did not fluctuate, the Bank of Canada could pursue both a money supply target and an interest-rate target at the same time." Is this statement true, false, or uncertain? Explain your answer.

4. If the Bank has an interest-rate target, why will an increase in money demand lead to a rise in the money supply?

*5. What procedures can the Bank use to control the three-month Treasury bill rate? Why does control of this interest rate imply that the Bank will lose control of the money supply?

6. Compare the monetary base to M2+ on the grounds of controllability and measurability. Which do you prefer as an intermediate target? Why?

*7. "Interest rates can be measured more accurately and more quickly than the money supply. Hence an interest rate is preferred over the money supply as an intermediate target." Do you agree or disagree? Explain your answer.

8. Explain why an inflation-targeting framework is sufficient to hold the Bank of Canada accountable to the public.

*9. How does the Bank of Canada influence interest rates and the money supply by changing the operating band for the overnight interest rate?

10. Has the new inflation-targeting framework for monetary policy improved the credibility of the Bank of Canada?

*11. "When the economy enters a recession, an interest-rate target will lead to a slower rate of growth for the money supply." Explain why this statement is true. What does it say about the use of interest rates as targets?

12. "The failure of the Bank of Canada to control the money supply in the 1970s and 1980s suggests that the Bank is not able to control the money supply." Do you agree or disagree? Explain your answer.

*13. Why might the Bank of Canada say that it wants to control the money supply but in reality not be serious about doing so?

14. How can bank behaviour and the Bank of Canada's behaviour cause money supply growth to be procyclical (rising in booms and falling in recessions)?

Chapter 19

The International Financial System

PREVIEW

Thanks to the growing interdependence between the Canadian economy and the economies of the rest of the world, a country's monetary policy can no longer be conducted without taking international considerations into account. In this chapter we examine how international financial transactions and the structure of the international financial system affect monetary policy. We also examine the evolution of the international financial system during the past half-century and consider where it may be heading in the future.

INTERVENTION IN THE FOREIGN EXCHANGE MARKET

In Chapter 7 we analyzed the foreign exchange market as if it were a completely free market that responds to all market pressures. Like many other markets, however, the foreign exchange market is not free of government intervention; central banks regularly engage in international financial transactions called **foreign exchange interventions** in order to influence exchange rates. In our current international financial arrangement, called a **managed float regime** (or a **dirty float**), exchange rates fluctuate from day to day, but central banks attempt to influence their countries' exchange rates by buying and selling currencies. The exchange rate analysis we developed in Chapter 7 is used here to explain the impact that central bank intervention has on the foreign exchange market.

Foreign Exchange Intervention and the Money Supply

The first step in understanding how central bank intervention in the foreign exchange market affects exchange rates is to see the impact on the monetary base from a central bank sale in the foreign exchange market of some of its holdings of assets denominated in a foreign currency (called **international reserves**). Suppose that the Bank of Canada decides to sell $1 billion of its foreign assets in exchange for $1 billion of Canadian currency. The Bank's purchase of dollars has two effects. First, it reduces the Bank's holding of international reserves by

$1 billion. Second, because its purchase of currency removes it from the hands of the public, currency in circulation falls by $1 billion. We can see this in the following T-account for the Bank of Canada:

Bank of Canada

Assets	Liabilities
Foreign assets (international reserves) −$1 billion	Currency in circulation −$1 billion

Because the monetary base is made up of currency in circulation plus reserves, this decline in currency implies that the monetary base has fallen by $1 billion.

If instead of paying for the foreign assets sold by the Bank of Canada with currency, the persons buying the foreign assets pay for them by cheques written on accounts at domestic banks, then the Bank deducts the $1 billion from the deposit accounts these banks have with the Bank of Canada. The result is that deposits with the Bank of Canada (reserves) decline by $1 billion, as shown in the following T-account:

BANK OF CANADA

Assets	Liabilities
Foreign assets (international reserves) −$1 billion	Deposits with the Bank of Canada (reserves) −$1 billion

In this case, the outcome of the Bank of Canada sale of foreign assets and the purchase of dollar deposits is a $1 billion decline in reserves and a $1 billion decline in the monetary base because reserves are also a component of the monetary base.

We now see that the outcome for the monetary base is exactly the same when a central bank sells foreign assets to purchase domestic bank deposits or domestic currency. This is why when we say that a central bank has purchased its domestic currency, we do not have to distinguish whether it actually purchased currency or bank deposits denominated in the domestic currency. We have thus reached an important conclusion. *A central bank's purchase of domestic currency and corresponding sale of foreign assets in the foreign exchange market leads to an equal decline in its international reserves and the monetary base.*

We could have reached the same conclusion by a more direct route. A central bank sale of a foreign asset is no different from an open market sale of a government bond. We learned in our exploration of the money supply process that an open market sale leads to an equal decline in the monetary base; therefore, a sale of foreign assets also leads to an equal decline in the monetary base. By similar reasoning, a central bank purchase of foreign assets paid for by selling domestic currency, like an open market purchase, leads to an equal rise in the monetary base. Thus we reach the following conclusion. *A central bank's sale of domestic currency to purchase foreign assets in the foreign exchange market results in an equal rise in its international reserves and the monetary base.*

The intervention we have just described, in which a central bank allows the purchase or sale of domestic currency to have an effect on the monetary base, is called an **unsterilized foreign exchange intervention**. But what if the central bank does not want the purchase or sale of domestic currency to affect the monetary base? All it has to do is to counter the effect of the foreign exchange intervention by conducting an offsetting open market operation in the government bond market. For example, in the case of a $1 billion purchase of dollars by the Bank of Canada and a corresponding $1 billion sale of foreign assets, which we have seen would decrease the monetary base by $1 billion, the Bank can conduct an open market purchase of $1 billion of government bonds, which would increase the monetary base by $1 billion. The resulting T-account for the foreign exchange intervention and the offsetting open market operation leaves the monetary base unchanged:

BANK OF CANADA

Assets		Liabilities	
Foreign assets (international reserves)	−$1 billion	Monetary base (reserves)	0
Government bonds	+$1 billion		

A foreign exchange intervention with an offsetting open market operation that leaves the monetary base unchanged is called a **sterilized foreign exchange intervention**.

Now that we understand that there are two types of foreign exchange interventions, unsterilized and sterilized, let's look at how each affects the exchange rate.

Unsterilized Intervention

Your intuition might lead you to suspect that if a central bank wants to lower the value of the domestic currency, it should sell its currency in the foreign exchange market and purchase foreign assets. Indeed, this intuition is correct for the case of an unsterilized intervention.

Recall that in an unsterilized intervention, if the Bank of Canada decides to sell dollars in order to buy foreign assets in the foreign exchange market, this works just like an open market purchase of bonds to increase the monetary base. Hence the sale of dollars leads to an increase in the money supply, and we find ourselves analyzing exactly the situation already described in Figure 7-7, which is reproduced here as Figure 19-1. The higher money supply leads to a higher Canadian price level in the long run and so to a lower expected future exchange rate. The resulting decline in the expected appreciation of the dollar increases the expected return on foreign deposits and shifts the RET^F schedule to the right. In addition, the increase in the money supply will lead to a higher real money supply in the short run, which causes the interest rate on dollar deposits to fall. The resulting lower expected return on dollar deposits translates as a leftward shift in the RET^D schedule. The fall in the expected return on dollar deposits and the increase in the expected return on foreign deposits means that foreign assets have a higher expected return than dollar deposits at the old equilibrium exchange rate. Hence people will try to sell their dollar deposits, and the exchange rate will fall. Indeed, as we saw in Chapter 7, the increase in the money supply will lead to exchange rate overshooting, whereby the exchange rate falls by more in the short run than it does in the long run.

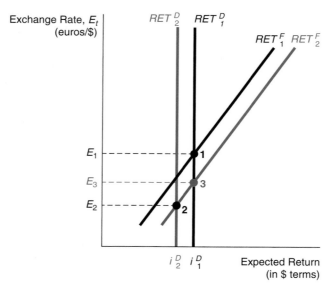

FIGURE 19-1   Effect of a Sale of Canadian Dollars and a Purchase of Foreign Assets

A sale of Canadian dollars and the consequent open market purchase of foreign assets increase the monetary base. The resulting rise in the money supply leads to a higher domestic price level in the long run, which leads to a lower expected future exchange rate. The resulting decline in the expected appreciation of the dollar raises the expected return on foreign deposits, shifting the RET^F schedule rightward from RET^F_1 to RET^F_2. In the short run, the domestic interest rate i^D falls, shifting RET^D from RET^D_1 to RET^D_2. The short-run outcome is that the exchange rate falls from E_1 to E_2. In the long run, however, the interest rate returns to i^D_1, and RET^D returns to RET^D_1. The exchange rate therefore rises from E_2 to E_3 in the long run.

Our analysis leads us to the following conclusion about unsterilized interventions in the foreign exchange market. ***An unsterilized intervention in which domestic currency is sold to purchase foreign assets leads to a gain in international reserves, an increase in the money supply, and a depreciation of the domestic currency.***

The reverse result is found for an unsterilized intervention in which domestic currency is purchased by selling foreign assets. The purchase of domestic currency by selling foreign assets (reducing international reserves) works like an open market sale to reduce the monetary base and the money supply. The decrease in the money supply raises the interest rate on dollar deposits and shifts RET^D rightward while causing RET^F to shift leftward because it leads to a lower Canadian price level in the long run and thus to a higher expected appreciation of the dollar and hence a lower expected return on foreign deposits. The increase in the expected return on dollar deposits relative to foreign deposits will mean that people will want to buy more dollar deposits, and the exchange rate will rise. ***An unsterilized intervention in which domestic currency is purchased by selling foreign assets leads to a drop in international reserves, a decrease in the money supply, and an appreciation of the domestic currency.***

Sterilized Intervention

The key point to remember about a sterilized intervention is that the central bank engages in offsetting open market operations so that there is no impact on the monetary base and the money supply. In the context of the model of exchange rate determination we have developed here, it is straightforward to show that a sterilized intervention has *no effect* on the exchange rate. Remember that in our model, foreign and domestic deposits are perfect substitutes, so equilibrium in the foreign exchange market occurs when the expected returns on foreign and domestic deposits are equal. A sterilized intervention leaves the money supply unchanged and so has no way of directly affecting interest rates or the expected future exchange rate.[1] Because the expected returns on dollar and foreign deposits are unaffected, the expected return schedules remain at RET_1^D and RET_1^F in Figure 19-1, and the exchange rate remains unchanged at E_1.

At first it might seem puzzling that a central bank purchase or sale of domestic currency that is sterilized does not lead to a change in the exchange rate. A central bank purchase of domestic currency cannot raise the exchange rate because, with no effect on the domestic money supply or interest rates, any resulting rise in the exchange rate would mean that the expected return on foreign deposits would be greater than the expected return on domestic deposits. Given our assumption that foreign and domestic deposits are perfect substitutes (equally desirable), this would mean that no one would want to hold domestic deposits.[2] So the exchange rate would have to fall back to its previous level, where the expected returns on domestic and foreign deposits were equal.

BALANCE OF PAYMENTS

Because international financial transactions such as foreign exchange interventions have considerable effects on monetary policy, it is worth knowing how these transactions are measured. The **balance of payments** is a bookkeeping system for recording all payments that have a direct bearing on the movement of funds between a nation (private sector and government) and foreign countries.

The balance-of-payments account in the accompanying "Following the Financial News" box uses a standard double-entry bookkeeping system much like one that you or I might use to keep a record of payments and receipts. All transactions involving payments from foreigners to Canadians are entered in the "Receipts" column with a plus sign (+) to reflect that they are credits; that is, they result in a flow of funds to Canadians. Receipts include foreign purchases of Canadian products such as computers and wheat (exports), purchases by foreign tourists (services), income earned from Canadian investment abroad (investment income), foreign gifts and pensions paid to Canadians (unilateral transfers), and foreign payments for Canadian assets (capital inflows).

All payments to foreigners are entered in the "Payments" column with a minus sign (−) to reflect that they are debits because they result in flows of funds to other countries. Payments include Canadian purchases of foreign products such as French wine and Japanese cars (imports), Canadian travel abroad (services), income earned by foreigners from investments in Canada (investment income), foreign aid and gifts and pensions paid to foreigners (unilateral transfers), and Canadian payments for foreign assets (capital outflows).

---

[1] Note that a sterilized intervention could indicate what central banks want to happen to the future exchange rate and so might provide a signal about the course of future monetary policy. In this way, a sterilized intervention could lead to shifts in the RET^F schedule, but in reality it is the future change in monetary policy, not the sterilized intervention, that is the ultimate source of exchange rate effects. For a discussion of the signalling effect, see Maurice Obstfeld, "The Effectiveness of Foreign Exchange Intervention: Recent Experience, 1985–1988," in *International Policy Coordination and Exchange Rate Fluctuations,* ed. William H. Branson, Jacob A. Frenkel, and Morris Goldstein (Chicago: University of Chicago Press, 1990), pp. 197–237.

[2] If domestic and foreign deposits are not perfect substitutes, a sterilized intervention can affect the exchange rate. However, most studies find little evidence to support the position that sterilized intervention has a significant impact on foreign exchange rates. For a further discussion of the effects of sterilized versus unsterilized intervention, see Paul Krugman and Maurice Obstfeld, *International Economics,* 5th ed. (Reading, Mass.: Addison Wesley Longman, 2000).

FOLLOWING THE FINANCIAL NEWS

The Balance of Payments

The balance of payments summarizes a country's transactions with the rest of the world. The complete set of items in the balance of payments is published on a quarterly basis by Statistics Canada, with the figures released about two months after the end of the quarter to which they apply. An example of the balance-of-payments accounts for Canada appears here.

Statistics Canada
www.statcan.ca

CANADIAN BALANCE OF PAYMENTS, 1999 ($ BILLIONS)

	Receipts (+)	Payments (−)	Balance
Current Account			
(1) Exports	412.4		
(2) Imports		−384.6	
Trade balance			27.8
(3) Net investment income		−32.2	
(4) Net unilateral transfers	1.0		
Current account balance: (1)+(2)+(3)+(4)			−3.4
Capital Account			
(5) Capital outflows		−45.4	
(6) Capital inflows	39.7		
(7) Statistical discrepancy	9.7		
Official reserve transactions balance: (1)+(2)+(3)+(4)+(5)+(6)+(7)			0.6
Method of Financing			
(8) Increase in Canadian official reserve assets		−8.8	
(9) Increase in foreign official assets	8.2		
Total financing of surplus (8)+(9)			−0.6
Balance of Payments			
Sum (1) through (9)			0.0

Source: www.statcan.ca. By convention, an increase in official reserve assets is recorded with a minus sign (debit).

Current Account

The **current account** shows international transactions that involve currently produced goods and services. The difference between exports (line 1) and imports (line 2) is called the **trade balance**. When exports are greater than imports (here by $27.8 billion), we have a trade surplus; if imports are greater than exports, we have a trade deficit.

The next two items in the current account are the net payments or receipts that arise from investment income and unilateral transfers (gifts, pensions, and foreign aid). In 1999, for example, net investment income was minus $32.2 billion (in line 3) for Canada because Canadians received less investment income from abroad than they paid out. Since Canadians made fewer unilateral transfers to foreign countries than foreigners made to Canada, a $1.0 billion receipt is shown in line 4.

The sum of the items in lines 1 through 4 is the current account balance, which in 1999 showed a deficit of $3.4 billion. The current account balance is an important balance-of-payment concept for several reasons. As we can see from the balance-of-payments account, any surplus or deficit in the current account must be balanced either by capital account transactions (lending or borrowing abroad) or by changes in government reserve asset items:

Current account + capital account = change in government reserve assets

The current account balance tells us whether Canada (private sector and government combined) is increasing or decreasing its claims on foreign wealth. A surplus indicates that Canada is increasing its claims on foreign wealth, and a deficit, as in 1999, indicates that the country is reducing its claims on foreign wealth.[3]

Financial analysts follow the current account balance closely because they believe that it can provide information on the future movement of exchange rates. The current account balance provides some indication of what is happening to the demand for imports and exports, which, as we saw in Chapter 7, can affect the exchange rate. In addition, the current account balance provides information about what will be happening to Canadian claims on foreign wealth in the long run. Because a movement of foreign wealth to Canadian residents can affect the demand for dollar assets, changes in Canadian claims on foreign wealth, reflected in the current account balance, can affect the exchange rate over time.[4]

Capital Account

The **capital account** describes the flow of capital between Canada and other countries. Capital outflows are Canadian purchases of foreign assets (a "Payments" item), and capital inflows are foreign purchases of Canadian assets (a "Receipts" item). The capital outflows (line 5) are more than the capital inflows (line 6), resulting in a net outflow of $5.7 billion.

The statistical discrepancy (line 7) represents errors due to unrecorded transactions involving smuggling and other capital flows. The statistical discrepancy, which keeps the balance-of-payments account in balance, is $9.7 billion, which suggests that some of the other items in the balance of payments may not be measured very accurately. Many experts believe that the statistical discrepancy is primarily the result of large hidden capital flows, and so the item has been placed in the capital account part of the balance of payments.

Official Reserve Transactions Balance

The sum of lines 1 through 7, called the **official reserve transactions balance**, equals the current account balance plus the items in the capital account. When we refer to a surplus or a deficit in the balance of payments, we actually mean a surplus or deficit in the official reserve transactions balance. Because the balance-of-payments account must balance, the official reserve transactions balance tells us the net amount of international reserves that must move between central banks to finance international transactions. One reason we are particularly interested in the movements of international reserves is that, as we saw earlier in the chapter, these movements have an important impact on the money supply and exchange rates.

---

[3]The current account balance can also be viewed as showing by how much total saving exceeds private sector and government investment in Canada. We can see this by noting that total Canadian saving equals the increase in total wealth held by the Canadian private sector and government. Total investment equals the increase in the Canadian capital stock (wealth physically in Canada). The difference between them is the increase in Canadian claims on foreign wealth.

[4]If Canadian residents have a greater preference for dollar assets than foreigners do, a movement of foreign wealth to Canadian residents when there is a balance-of-payments surplus will increase the demand for dollar assets over time and will cause the Canadian dollar to appreciate.

Methods of Financing the Balance of Payments

Because most countries' currencies are not held by other countries as international reserves, these countries must finance an excess of payments over receipts (a deficit in the balance of payments) by providing international reserves to foreign governments and central banks. A balance-of-payments deficit is associated with a loss of international reserves; likewise, a balance-of-payments surplus is associated with a gain.

Unlike the Canadian dollar, the U.S. dollar and U.S.-dollar-denominated assets are the major component of international reserves held by other countries. Thus a U.S. balance-of-payments deficit can be financed by a decrease in U.S. international reserves, an increase in foreign central banks' holdings of international reserves (dollar assets), or both. Conversely, a U.S. balance-of-payments surplus can be financed by an increase in U.S. international reserves, a decrease in foreign central banks' international reserves, or both.

For Canada in 1999, the official reserve transactions surplus of $0.6 billion resulted in an $8.8 billion increase in Canadian international reserves (−8.8 in the "Payments" column of line 8) and an $8.2 billion increase of foreign holdings of Canadian dollars (8.2 in the "Receipts" column of line 9).[5] On net, Canada's international reserves increased by $0.6 billion (the $8.8 billion increase in Canadian holdings of international reserves minus the $8.2 billion foreign increase in holdings of Canadian dollars). This $0.6 billion increase in Canadian international reserves just matches the $0.6 billion official reserve transactions surplus, so the sum of lines 1 through 9 is zero, and the account balances.

EVOLUTION OF THE INTERNATIONAL FINANCIAL SYSTEM

Before examining the impact of international financial transactions on monetary policy, we need to understand the past and current structure of the international financial system.

Gold Standard

Before World War I, the world economy operated under the **gold standard**, meaning that the currency of most countries was convertible directly into gold. Canadian dollar bills, for example, could be exchanged for approximately 1/20 ounce of gold. Likewise, the British Treasury would exchange 1/4 ounce of gold for £1 sterling. Because a Canadian could convert $20 into 1 ounce of gold, which could be used to buy £4, the exchange rate between the pound and the Canadian dollar was effectively fixed at approximately $5 to the pound. Tying currencies to gold resulted in an international financial system with fixed exchange rates between currencies. The fixed exchange rates under the gold standard had the important advantage of encouraging world trade by eliminating the uncertainty that occurs when exchange rates fluctuate.

To see how the gold standard operated in practice, let us see what occurs if, under the gold standard, the British pound begins to appreciate above the $5 par value. If a Canadian importer of £100 of English tweed tries to pay for the tweed with dollars, it costs more than the $500 it cost before. Nevertheless, the importer has another option involving the purchase of gold that can reduce the cost of the tweed. Instead of using dollars to pay for the tweed, the Canadian importer can exchange the $500 for gold, ship the gold to Britain, and convert it into £100. The

---

[5]At first it may seem strange that when Canada gains $8.8 billion of international reserves, it is entered in the balance of payments as a payment with a negative sign. Recall, however, that when a central bank gains international reserves, it has bought foreign assets. Thus an increase in international reserves is just like an outflow of capital in the capital account and appears as a payment with a negative sign.

shipment of gold to Britain is cheaper as long as the British pound is above the $5 par value (plus a small amount to pay for the cost of shipping the gold).

The appreciation of the pound leads to a British gain of international reserves (gold) and an equal Canadian loss. Because a change in a country's holdings of international reserves (gold) leads to an equal change in its monetary base, the movement of gold from Canada to Britain causes the British monetary base to rise and the Canadian monetary base to fall. The resulting rise in the British money supply raises the British price level, while the fall in the Canadian money supply lowers the Canadian price level. The resulting increase in the British price level relative to Canada then causes the pound to depreciate. This process will continue until the value of the pound falls back down to its $5 par value.

A depreciation of the pound below the $5 par value, on the contrary, stimulates gold shipments from Britain to Canada. These shipments raise the Canadian money supply and lower the British money supply, causing the pound to appreciate back toward the $5 par value. We thus see that under the gold standard, a rise or fall in the exchange rate sets in motion forces that return it to the par value.

As long as countries abided by the rules under the gold standard and kept their currencies backed by and convertible into gold, exchange rates remained fixed. However, adherence to the gold standard meant that a country had no control over its monetary policy because its money supply was determined by gold flows between countries. Furthermore, monetary policy throughout the world was greatly influenced by the production of gold and gold discoveries. When gold production was low in the 1870s and 1880s, the money supply throughout the world grew slowly and did not keep pace with the growth of the world economy. The result was deflation (falling price levels). Gold discoveries in Alaska and South Africa in the 1890s then greatly expanded gold production, causing money supplies to increase rapidly and price levels to rise (inflation) until World War I.

Bretton Woods System

World War I caused massive trade disruptions. Countries could no longer convert their currencies into gold, and the gold standard collapsed. Despite attempts to revive it in the interwar period, the worldwide depression, beginning in 1929, led to its permanent demise. As the Allied victory in World War II was becoming certain in 1944, the Allies met in Bretton Woods, New Hampshire, to develop a new international monetary system to promote world trade and prosperity after the war. In the agreement worked out among the Allies, central banks bought and sold their own currencies to keep their exchange rates fixed at a certain level (called a **fixed exchange rate regime**). The agreement lasted from 1945 to 1971 and was known as the **Bretton Woods system**.

The Bretton Woods agreement created the **International Monetary Fund (IMF)**, headquartered in Washington, D.C., which had 30 original member countries in 1945 and currently has over 180. The IMF was given the task of promoting the growth of world trade by setting rules for the maintenance of fixed exchange rates and by making loans to countries that were experiencing balance-of-payments difficulties. As part of its role of monitoring the compliance of member countries with its rules, the IMF also took on the job of collecting and standardizing international economic data.

The Bretton Woods agreement also set up the International Bank for Reconstruction and Development, commonly referred to as the **World Bank**, also headquartered in Washington, D.C., which provides long-term loans to help developing countries build dams, roads, and other physical capital that would contribute to their economic development. The funds for these loans are obtained

International Monetary Fund
www.imf.org

World Bank
www.worldbank.org

BOX 19-1

The Euro's Challenge to the U.S. Dollar

With the creation of the European Monetary Union and the euro in 1999, the U.S. dollar may face a challenge to its position as the key reserve currency in international financial transactions. Adoption of the euro may increase integration of Europe's financial markets, which could help them rival those in the United States. The resulting increase in the use of euros in financial markets will make it more likely that international transactions are carried out in the euro. The economic clout of the European Union rivals that of the United States: both have a similar share of world GDP

(around 20%) and world exports (around 15%). If the European Central Bank can make sure that inflation remains low so that the euro becomes a sound currency, this should bode well for the euro.

However, for the euro to eat into the dollar's position as a reserve currency, the European Union must function as a cohesive political entity that is able to exert its influence on the world stage. There are serious doubts on this score, and most analysts think it will be a long time before the euro beats out the dollar in international financial transactions.

primarily by issuing World Bank bonds, which are sold in the capital markets of the developed countries.[6]

Because the United States emerged from World War II as the world's largest economic power, with over half of the world's manufacturing capacity and the greater part of the world's gold, the Bretton Woods system of fixed exchange rates was based on the convertibility of U.S. dollars into gold (for foreign governments and central banks only) at $35 per ounce. The fixed exchange rates were to be maintained by intervention in the foreign exchange market by central banks in countries besides the United States who bought and sold dollar assets, which they held as international reserves. The U.S. dollar, which was used by other countries to denominate the assets that they held as international reserves, was called the **reserve currency**. Thus an important feature of the Bretton Woods system was the establishment of the United States as the reserve currency country. Even after the breakup of the Bretton Woods system, the U.S. dollar has kept its position as the reserve currency in which most international financial transactions are conducted. However, with the creation of the euro in 1999, the supremacy of the U.S. dollar may be subject to a serious challenge (see Box 19-1).

How a Fixed Exchange Rate Regime Works   The most important feature of the Bretton Woods system was that it set up a fixed exchange rate regime. Figure 19-2 shows how a fixed exchange rate regime works in practice using the model of exchange rate determination we learned in Chapter 7. Panel (a) describes a situation in which the domestic currency is initially overvalued. The schedule for the expected return on foreign deposits RET_1^F intersects the schedule for the expected return on domestic deposits RET_1^D at exchange rate E_1, which is lower than the par (fixed) value of the exchange rate E_{par}. To keep the exchange rate at E_{par}, the central bank must intervene in the foreign exchange market to purchase domestic currency by selling foreign assets, and this action, like an open market sale, means that the monetary base and the money supply decline. Because the

---

[6]In 1960, the World Bank established an affiliate, the International Development Association (IDA), which provides particularly attractive loans to third-world countries (with 50-year maturities and zero interest rates, for example). Funds for these loans are obtained by direct contributions of member countries.

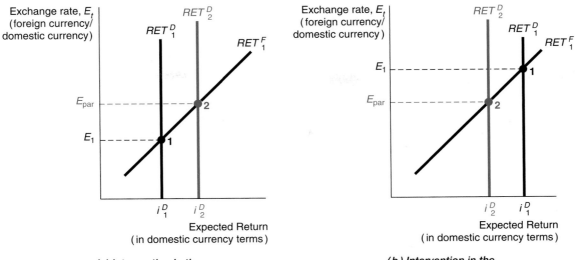

FIGURE 19-2   Intervention in the Foreign Exchange Market Under a Fixed Exchange Rate
Regime

In panel (a), the exchange rate at E_{par} is overvalued. To keep the exchange rate at E_{par} (point 2), the central bank must purchase domestic currency to shift the schedule for the expected return on domestic deposits to RET^D_2. In panel (b), the exchange rate at E_{par} is undervalued, so a central bank sale of domestic currency is needed to shift RET^D to RET^D_2 to keep the exchange rate at E_{par} (point 2).

exchange rate will continue to be fixed at E_{par}, the expected future exchange rate remains unchanged, and so the schedule for the expected return on foreign deposits remains at RET^F_1. However, the purchase of domestic currency, which leads to a fall in the money supply, also causes the interest rate on domestic deposits i^D to rise. This increase in turn shifts the expected return on domestic deposits RET^D to the right. The central bank will continue purchasing domestic currency and selling foreign assets until the RET^D curve reaches RET^D_2 and the equilibrium exchange rate is at E_{par} at point 2 in panel (a).

We have thus come to the conclusion that ***when the domestic currency is overvalued, the central bank must purchase domestic currency to keep the exchange rate fixed, but as a result it loses international reserves.***

Panel (b) in Figure 19-2 shows how a central bank intervention keeps the exchange rate fixed at E_{par} when the exchange rate is initially undervalued, that is, when RET^F_1 and the initial RET^D_1 intersect at exchange rate E_1, which is above E_{par}. Here the central bank must sell domestic currency and purchase foreign assets, and this works like an open market purchase to raise the money supply and lower the interest rate on domestic deposits i^D. The central bank keeps selling domestic currency and lowers i^D until RET^D shifts all the way to RET^D_2, where the equilibrium exchange rate is at E_{par}—point 2 in panel (b). Our analysis thus leads us to the following result: ***when the domestic currency is undervalued, the central bank must sell domestic currency to keep the exchange rate fixed, but as a result it gains international reserves.***

As we have seen, if a country's currency has an overvalued exchange rate, its central bank's attempts to keep the currency from depreciating will result in a loss of international reserves. If the country's central bank eventually runs out of international reserves, it cannot keep its currency from depreciating, and then a **devaluation** must occur, meaning that the par exchange rate is reset at a lower level.

If, by contrast, a country's currency has an undervalued exchange rate, its central bank's intervention to keep the currency from appreciating leads to a gain of international reserves. Because, as we will see shortly, the central bank might not want to acquire these international reserves, it might want to reset the par value of its exchange rate at a higher level (a **revaluation**).

Note that if domestic and foreign deposits are perfect substitutes, as is assumed in the model of exchange rate determination used here, a sterilized exchange rate intervention would not be able to keep the exchange rate at E_{par} because, as we have seen earlier in the chapter, neither RET^F nor RET^D will shift. For example, if the exchange rate is overvalued, a sterilized purchase of domestic currency will still leave the expected return on domestic deposits below the expected return on foreign deposits at the par exchange rate—so pressure for a depreciation of the domestic currency is not removed. If the central bank keeps on purchasing its domestic currency but continues to sterilize, it will just keep on losing international reserves until it finally runs out of them and is forced to let the value of the currency seek a lower level.

One implication of the foregoing analysis is that a country that ties its exchange rate to a larger country's currency loses control of its monetary policy. If the larger country pursues a more contractionary monetary policy and decreases its money supply, this would lead to lower expected inflation in the larger country, thus causing an appreciation of the larger country's currency and a depreciation of the smaller country's currency. The smaller country, having locked in its exchange rate, will now find its currency overvalued and will therefore have to sell the larger country's currency and buy its own to keep its currency from depreciating. The result of this foreign exchange intervention will then be a decline in the smaller country's international reserves, a contraction of the monetary base, and thus a decline in its money supply. Sterilization of this foreign exchange intervention is not an option because this would just lead to a continuing loss of international reserves until the smaller country was forced to devalue. The smaller country no longer controls its monetary policy because movements in its money supply are completely determined by movements in the larger country's money supply.

Another way to see that when a country fixes its exchange rate to a larger country's currency it loses control of its monetary policy is through the interest parity condition discussed in Chapter 7. There we saw that when there is capital mobility, the domestic interest rate equals the foreign interest rate minus the expected appreciation of the domestic currency. With a fixed exchange rate, expected appreciation of the domestic currency is zero, so that the domestic interest rate equals the foreign interest rate. Therefore changes in the monetary policy in the large country that affect its interest rate are directly transmitted to interest rates in the small country. Furthermore, because the monetary authorities in the small country cannot make their interest rate deviate from that of the larger country, they have no way to use monetary policy to affect their economy.

Bretton Woods System of Fixed Exchange Rates   Under the Bretton Woods system, exchange rates were supposed to change only when a country was experiencing a "fundamental disequilibrium," that is, large persistent deficits or surpluses in its balance of payments. To maintain fixed exchange rates when countries had balance-of-payments deficits and were losing international reserves, the IMF would loan deficit countries international reserves contributed by other members. As a result of its power to dictate loan terms to borrowing countries, the IMF could encourage deficit countries to pursue contractionary monetary policies that would strengthen their currency or eliminate their balance-of-payment deficits. If the IMF loans were not sufficient to prevent depreciation of a currency, the country was allowed to devalue its currency by setting a new, lower exchange rate.

A notable weakness of the Bretton Woods system was that although deficit countries losing international reserves could be pressured into devaluing their currency or pursuing contractionary policies, the IMF had no way to force surplus countries to revise their exchange rates upward or pursue more expansionary policies. Particularly troublesome in this regard was the fact that the reserve currency country, the United States, could not devalue its currency under the Bretton Woods system even if the dollar was overvalued. When the United States attempted to reduce its unemployment in the 1960s by pursuing an inflationary monetary policy, a fundamental disequilibrium of an overvalued dollar developed. Because surplus countries were not willing to revise their exchange rates upward, adjustment in the Bretton Woods system did not take place, and the system collapsed in 1971. Attempts to patch up the Bretton Woods system with the Smithsonian Agreement in December 1971 proved unsuccessful, and by 1973, the United States and its trading partners had agreed to allow exchange rates to float.

Managed Float

Although exchange rates are currently allowed to change daily in response to market forces, central banks have not been willing to give up their option of intervening in the foreign exchange market. Preventing large changes in exchange rates makes it easier for firms and individuals purchasing or selling goods abroad to plan into the future. Furthermore, countries with surpluses in their balance of payments frequently do not want to see their currencies appreciate because it makes their goods more expensive abroad and foreign goods cheaper in their country. Because an appreciation might hurt sales for domestic businesses and increase unemployment, surplus countries have often sold their currency in the foreign exchange market and acquired international reserves.

Countries with balance-of-payments deficits do not want to see their currency lose value because it makes foreign goods more expensive for domestic consumers and can stimulate inflation. To keep the value of the domestic currency high, deficit countries have often bought their own currency in the foreign exchange market and given up international reserves.

The current international financial system is a hybrid of a fixed and a flexible exchange rate system. Rates fluctuate in response to market forces but are not determined solely by them. Furthermore, many countries continue to keep the value of their currency fixed against other currencies, as was the case in the European Monetary System (to be described shortly).

Another important feature of the current system is the continuing de-emphasis of gold in international financial transactions. Not only has the United States suspended convertibility of dollars into gold for foreign central banks, but also since 1970 the IMF has been issuing a paper substitute for gold, called **special drawing rights (SDRs)**. Like gold in the Bretton Woods system, SDRs function as international reserves. Unlike gold, whose quantity is determined by gold discoveries and the rate of production, SDRs can be created by the IMF whenever it decides that there is a need for additional international reserves to promote world trade and economic growth.

The use of gold in international transactions was further de-emphasized by the IMF's elimination of the official gold price in 1975 and by the sale of gold by the U.S. Treasury and the IMF to private interests in order to demonetize it. Currently, the price of gold is determined in a free market. Investors who want to speculate in it are able to purchase and sell at will, as are jewellers and dentists who use gold in their businesses.

European Monetary System (EMS)

In March 1979, eight members of the European Economic Community (Germany, France, Italy, the Netherlands, Belgium, Luxembourg, Denmark, and Ireland) set up an exchange rate union, the European Monetary System (EMS), in which they agreed to fix their exchange rates vis-à-vis one another and to float jointly against the U.S. dollar. Spain joined the EMS in June 1989, the United Kingdom in October 1990, and Portugal in April 1992. The EMS created a new monetary unit, the *European currency unit* (ECU), whose value was tied to a basket of specified amounts of European currencies. Each member of the EMS was required to contribute 20% of its holdings of gold and dollars to the European Monetary Cooperation Fund and in return received an equivalent amount of ECUs.

The exchange rate mechanism (ERM) of the European Monetary System worked as follows. The exchange rate between every pair of currencies of the participating countries was not allowed to fluctuate outside narrow limits around a fixed exchange rate. (The limits were typically ±2.25% but were raised to ±15% in August 1993.) When the exchange rate between two countries' currencies moved outside these limits, the central banks of both countries were supposed to intervene in the foreign exchange market. If, for example, the French franc depreciated below its lower limit against the German mark, the Bank of France was required to buy francs and sell marks, thereby giving up international reserves. Similarly, the German central bank was also required to intervene to sell marks and buy francs and consequently increase its international reserves. The EMS thus required that intervention be symmetric when a currency fell outside the limits, with the central bank with the weak currency giving up international reserves and the one with the strong currency gaining them. Central bank intervention was also very common even when the exchange rate was within the limits, but in this case, if one central bank intervened, no others were required to intervene as well.

A serious shortcoming of fixed exchange rate systems such as the Bretton Woods system or the European Monetary System is that they can lead to foreign exchange crises involving a "speculative attack" on a currency—massive sales of a weak currency or purchases of a strong currency to cause a sharp change in the exchange rate. In the following application, we use our model of exchange rate determination to understand how the September 1992 exchange rate crisis that rocked the European Monetary System came about.

APPLICATION | *The Foreign Exchange Crisis of September 1992*

In the aftermath of German reunification in October 1990, the German central bank, the Bundesbank, faced rising inflationary pressures, with inflation having accelerated from below 3% in 1990 to near 5% by 1992. To get monetary growth under control and to dampen inflation, the Bundesbank raised German interest rates to near double-digit levels. Figure 19-3 shows the consequences of these actions by the Bundesbank in the foreign exchange market for sterling. Note that in the diagram, the pound sterling is the domestic currency and RET^D is the expected return on sterling deposits, whereas the foreign currency is the German mark (deutsche mark, DM), so RET^F is the expected return on mark deposits.

The increase in German interest rates i^F shifted the RET^F schedule rightward to RET^F_2 in Figure 19-3, so that the intersection of the RET^D_1 and the RET^F_2 schedules at point 1' was below the lower exchange rate limit (2.778 marks per pound, denoted E_{par}) under the exchange rate mechanism of the European Monetary System. To lower the value of the mark relative to the pound and restore the pound/mark exchange rate to within the ERM limits, either the Bank of England had to pursue a contractionary monetary policy, thereby raising British interest rates to i^D_2 and shifting the RET^D_1 schedule to the right to point 2, or the

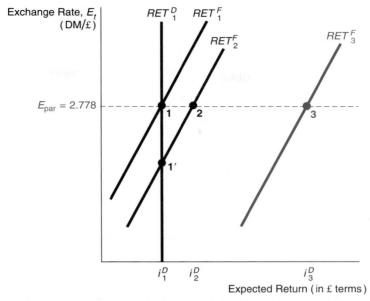

FIGURE 19-3   Foreign Exchange Market for British Pounds in 1992

The realization by speculators that the United Kingdom would soon devalue the pound increased the expected return on foreign (German mark, DM) deposits and shifted RET^F_2 rightward to RET^F_3. The result was the need for a much greater purchase of pounds by the British central bank to raise the interest rate to i^D_3 to keep the exchange rate at 2.778 German marks per pound.

Bundesbank could pursue an expansionary monetary policy, thereby lowering German interest rates, which would shift the RET^F schedule to the left to move back to point 1. (The shift in RET^D to point 2 is not shown in the figure.)

The catch was that the Bundesbank, whose primary goal was fighting inflation, was unwilling to pursue an expansionary monetary policy, and the British, who were facing their worst recession in the postwar period, were unwilling to pursue a contractionary monetary policy to prop up the pound. This impasse became clear when, in response to great pressure from other members of the EMS, the Bundesbank was willing to lower its lending rates by only a token amount on September 14 after a speculative attack was mounted on the currencies of the Scandinavian countries. So at some point in the near future, the value of the pound would have to decline to point 1′. Speculators now knew that the appreciation of the mark was imminent and hence that the value of foreign (mark) deposits would rise in value relative to the pound. As a result, the expected return on mark deposits increased sharply, shifting the RET^F schedule to RET^F_3 in Figure 19-3.

The huge potential losses on pound deposits and potential gains on mark deposits caused a massive sell-off of pounds (and purchases of marks) by speculators. The need for the British central bank to intervene to raise the value of the pound now became much greater and required a huge rise in British interest rates, all the way to i^D_3. After a major intervention effort on the part of the Bank of England, which included a rise in its lending rate from 10% to 15%, which still wasn't enough, the British were finally forced to give up on September 16: they pulled out of the ERM indefinitely, allowing the pound to depreciate by 10% against the mark.

Speculative attacks on other currencies forced devaluation of the Spanish peseta by 5% and the Italian lira by 15%. To defend its currency, the Swedish central bank was forced to raise its daily lending rate to the astronomical level of 500%! By the time the crisis was over, the British, French, Italian, Spanish, and Swedish central banks had intervened to the tune of $100 billion; the Bundesbank alone had laid out $50 billion for foreign exchange intervention. Because foreign exchange crises lead to large changes in central banks' holdings of international reserves and thus affect the official reserve asset items in the balance of payments, these crises are also referred to as **balance-of-payments crises**.

The attempt to prop up the European Monetary System was not cheap for these central banks. It is estimated that they lost $4 to $6 billion as a result of exchange rate intervention during the crisis. What the central banks lost, the speculators gained. A speculative fund run by George Soros ran up $1 billion of profits during the crisis, and Citibank traders are reported to have made $200 million. When an exchange rate crisis comes, life can certainly be sweet for exchange rate speculators.

Citibank
www.citibank.com

APPLICATION | *The Mexican Peso Crisis of December 1994*

As part of a reform plan initiated in 1987 to stabilize the Mexican economy, the Mexican government decided to put limits on the movements of the peso against the U.S. dollar. When the ruling party's presidential candidate was assassinated in March 1994, investors became concerned that the government might devalue the currency despite promises not to do so. The result was a speculative attack on the peso that not only brought down the peso but also threatened to bring down the currencies of other developing countries, particularly those in Latin America (jauntily referred to as the "Tequila effect"). Figure 19-3 can be used to understand the sequence of events during the Mexican peso crisis. We just need to recognize that RET^D is now the expected return on peso deposits and, since the foreign currency is the U.S. dollar, RET^F is the expected return on U.S. dollar deposits, with both denominated in the domestic currency, the peso.

Because of investors' concerns that the peso might be devalued after the March assassination, the expected return on dollar deposits rose, thus moving the RET^F schedule from RET^F_1 to RET^F_2 in Figure 19-3. The result was that the intersection of RET^D_1 and RET^F_2 was below the lower exchange limit E_{par} of around 30 cents per peso. To keep the peso from falling through this limit, the Mexican authorities needed to buy pesos and sell dollars, to raise interest rates to i^D_2 by shifting the RET^D curve to the right. This is exactly what they did, raising interest rates from around 10% to over 20% and losing close to half of their $30 billion in international reserves in the process. For the time being, the peso held, but more bad luck was to hit the Mexicans. An uprising in the southern state of Chiapas, the assassination of another high official in the ruling party, and concerns about the large current account deficit and particularly about the health of the banking system led to further rumours of devaluation. Now the RET^F curve shifted even farther to the right, say to RET^F_3, capital flew out of the country, and the Mexican authorities intervened further, doubling interest rates again and almost completely exhausting the nation's foreign exchange reserves. Once speculators guessed that the Mexicans were running out of reserves, the game was up. With near certainty that the new Mexican government installed on December 1 would be forced to devalue, the expected return on dollar deposits increased sharply, shifting RET^F even farther to the right, making a devaluation inevitable. On December 20, Mexico's government had to devalue the peso; by early 1995 it had less than half its former value.

| APPLICATION | *The East Asian Currency Crisis of 1997* |

The East Asian currency crisis in 1997 started in Thailand. We use Figure 19-3 to demonstrate what happened during this crisis, again assuming that dollars are the foreign currency so that RET^D is the expected return on deposits denominated in the Thai currency, the baht, and RET^F is the expected return on U.S. dollar deposits. (Note that the exchange rate label on the vertical axis would be in terms of dollars/baht and the label on the horizontal axis would be expected return in baht terms.) By May 1997, concerns about the large current account deficit in Thailand and the weakness in the Thai financial system made foreign creditors nervous and caused speculators to suspect that Thailand might be forced to devalue its currency. The result was a rise in the expected return on dollar deposits, which shifted the RET^F schedule from RET_1^F to RET_2^F, so that the intersection of the RET_1^D and RET_2^F curves was below the pegged value E_{par} of around 4 cents per baht. Intervention by the Thai central bank to purchase baht, which raised interest rates to i_2^D, was successful in containing this speculative attack. However, the failure of a major finance company, Finance One, imposed losses on creditors, causing foreign creditors to begin pulling out of the market in earnest. As speculators became even more confident that the Thais could not continue defending the baht, the expected return on dollar deposits shot up further, and RET^F moved much farther to the right, to RET_3^F. Given the weakness in the financial sector and the loss of reserves, the Thai monetary authorities could not continue to intervene. On July 2 they were forced to give up and let the baht depreciate.

Bank of Thailand
www.bot.or.th

Concerns that similar problems might be present in other East Asian countries generated speculative attacks against other currencies as well, leading to a scenario akin to that depicted in Figure 19-3. The result was that one by one, Indonesia, Malaysia, South Korea, and the Philippines were forced to devalue. The outcome was severe depreciations of all these currencies against the U.S. dollar: over 30% for the Thai baht, the Malaysian ringgit, the South Korean won, and the Philippine peso, and over 75% for the Indonesian rupiah. Even Hong Kong, Singapore, and Taiwan were subjected to speculative attacks, but because the financial systems in these countries were healthy, the attacks were successfully averted.

As we saw in Chapter 8, the sharp depreciations in Mexico and East Asia led to full-scale financial crises that severely damaged these countries' economies. The foreign exchange crisis that shocked the European Monetary System in September 1992 cost central banks a lot of money, but the public in European countries was not seriously affected. By contrast, the public in Mexico and the crisis countries of East Asia was not so lucky. The collapse of these currencies triggered by speculative attacks led to the financial crisis described in Chapter 8, producing severe depressions that caused hardship and political unrest.

EUROPEAN MONETARY UNION (EMU)

In January 1999 the members of the European Monetary System formed a currency union—the European Monetary Union (EMU). The new common currency of the European Monetary Union is the euro, managed by the Eurosystem (discussed in Chapter 15 and in Box 19-1). In preparation for monetary unification, countries had to implement policies enabling them to achieve a high degree of economic convergence, including a low inflation rate. Convergence of macro-economic performances was intended to put in place the institutional framework for conducting a single monetary policy.

A **currency union** has two advantages over a fixed exchange rate system such as the Bretton Woods System or an **exchange rate union** such as the European Monetary System. First, transaction costs are lower under a currency union than under fixed exchange rates. Second, foreign exchange crises involving a "specu-lative attack" on a national currency—massive sales of a weak currency or pur-chases of a strong currency to cause a sharp change in the exchange rate—no longer can occur.

CAPITAL CONTROLS

Because capital flows have been an important element in the currency crises in Mexico and East Asia, politicians and some economists have advocated that capi-tal mobility in emerging market countries should be restricted with capital controls in order to avoid financial instability. Are capital controls a good idea?

Controls on Capital Outflows

Capital outflows can promote financial instability in emerging market countries because when domestic residents and foreigners pull their capital out of a country, the resulting capital outflow forces a country to devalue its currency. This is why recently some politicians in emerging market countries have found capital controls particularly attractive. For example, Prime Minister Mahathir of Malaysia instituted capital controls in 1998 to restrict outflows in the aftermath of the East Asian crisis.

Although these controls sound like a good idea, they suffer from several dis-advantages. First, empirical evidence indicates that controls on capital outflows are seldom effective during a crisis because the private sector finds ingenious ways to evade them and has little difficulty moving funds out of the country.[7] Second, the evidence suggests that capital flight may even increase after controls are put into place because confidence in the government is weakened. Third, controls on cap-ital outflows often lead to corruption, as government officials get paid off to look the other way when domestic residents are trying to move funds abroad. Fourth, controls on capital outflows may lull governments into thinking they do not have to take the steps to reform their financial systems to deal with the crisis, with the result that opportunities are lost to improve the functioning of the economy.

Controls on Capital Inflows

Although most economists find the arguments against controls on capital outflows persuasive, controls on capital inflows receive more support. Supporters reason that if speculative capital cannot come in, then it cannot go out suddenly and cre-ate a crisis. Our analysis of the financial crises in East Asia in Chapter 8 provides support for this view by suggesting that capital inflows can lead to a lending boom and excessive risk taking on the part of banks, which then helps trigger a financial crisis.

However, controls on capital inflows have the undesirable feature that they may block from entering a country funds that would be used for productive invest-ment opportunities. Although such controls may limit the fuel supplied to lending booms through capital flows, over time they produce substantial distortions and misallocation of resources as households and businesses try to get around them. Indeed, just as with controls on capital outflows, controls on capital inflows can lead to corruption. There are serious doubts whether capital controls can be

---

[7]See Sebastian Edwards, "How Effective Are Capital Controls?" *Journal of Economic Perspectives*, Winter 2000; vol. 13, no. 4, pp. 65–84.

effective in today's environment, in which trade is open and where there are many financial instruments that make it easier to get around these controls.

On the other hand, there is a strong case for improving bank regulation and supervision so that capital inflows are less likely to produce a lending boom and encourage excessive risk taking by banking institutions. For example, restricting banks in how fast their borrowing could grow might have the impact of substantially limiting capital inflows. Supervisory controls of this type, focusing on the sources of financial fragility rather than the symptoms, can enhance the efficiency of the financial system rather than hamper it.

THE ROLE OF THE IMF

The International Monetary Fund was originally set up under the Bretton Woods system to help countries deal with balance-of-payments problems and stay with the fixed exchange rate by lending to deficit countries. With the collapse of the Bretton Woods system of fixed exchange rates in 1971, the IMF has taken on new roles.

The IMF continues to function as a data collector and provides technical assistance to its member countries. Although the IMF no longer attempts to encourage fixed exchange rates, its role as an international lender has become more important recently. This role first came to the fore in the 1980s during the third-world debt crisis, in which the IMF assisted developing countries in repaying their loans. The financial crises in Mexico in 1994–1995 and in East Asia in 1997–1998 led to huge loans by the IMF to these and other affected countries to help them recover from their financial crises and to prevent the spread of these crises to other countries. This role, in which the IMF acts like an international lender of last resort to cope with financial instability, is indeed highly controversial.

Should the IMF Be an International Lender of Last Resort?

As we saw in Chapter 17, in industrialized countries when a financial crisis occurs and the financial system threatens to seize up, domestic central banks can address matters with a lender-of-last-resort operation to limit the degree of instability in the banking system. In emerging markets, however, where the credibility of the central bank as an inflation-fighter may be in doubt and debt contracts are typically short-term and in foreign currencies, a lender-of-last-resort operation becomes a two-edged sword—as likely to exacerbate the financial crisis as to alleviate it. For example, when the U.S. Federal Reserve engaged in a lender-of-last-resort operation during the 1987 stock market crash, there was almost no sentiment in the markets that there would be substantially higher inflation. However, for a central bank having less inflation-fighting credibility than the Fed, central bank lending to the financial system in the wake of a financial crisis—even under the lender-of-last-resort rhetoric—may well arouse fears of inflation spiralling out of control, causing an even greater currency depreciation and still greater deterioration of balance sheets. The resulting increase in moral hazard and adverse selection problems in financial markets, along the lines discussed in Chapter 8, would only make the financial crisis worse.

Central banks in emerging market countries therefore have only a very limited ability to successfully engage in a lender-of-last-resort operation. However, liquidity provided by an international lender of last resort does not have these undesirable consequences, and in helping to stabilize the value of the domestic currency it strengthens domestic balance sheets. Moreover, an international lender of last resort may be able to prevent contagion, the situation in which a successful speculative attack on one emerging market currency leads to attacks on other emerging market currencies, spreading financial and economic disruption as it goes.

Since a lender of last resort for emerging market countries is needed at times, and since it cannot be provided domestically, there is a strong rationale for an international institution to fill this role. Indeed, since Mexico's financial crisis in 1994, the International Monetary Fund and other international agencies have stepped into the lender-of-last-resort role and provided emergency lending to countries threatened by financial instability.

However, support from an international lender of last resort brings risks of its own, especially the risk that the perception it is standing ready to bail out irresponsible financial institutions may lead to excessive risk taking of the sort that makes financial crises more likely. In the Mexican and East Asian crises, governments in the crisis countries have used IMF support to protect depositors and other creditors of banking institutions from losses. This safety net creates a well-known moral hazard problem because the depositors and other creditors have less incentive to monitor these banking institutions and withdraw their deposits if the institutions are taking on too much risk. Indeed, critics of the IMF contend that its lending in the Mexican crisis, which was used to bail out foreign lenders, set the stage for the East Asian crisis because these lenders expected to be bailed out if things went wrong and thus provided funds which were used to fuel excessive risk taking.

An international lender of last resort must find ways to limit this moral hazard problem, or it can actually make the situation worse. The international lender of last resort can make it clear that it will extend liquidity only to governments that put the proper measures in place to prevent excessive risk taking. In addition, it can reduce the incentives for risk taking by restricting the ability of governments to bail out stockholders and large uninsured creditors of domestic financial institutions. Some critics of the IMF believe that the IMF has not put enough pressure on the governments to which it lends to contain the moral hazard problem.

One problem that arises for international organizations like the IMF engaged in lender-of-last-resort operations is that they know that if they don't come to the rescue, the emerging market country will suffer extreme hardship and possible political instability. Politicians in the crisis country may exploit these concerns and engage in a game of chicken with the international lender of last resort: they resist necessary reforms, hoping that the IMF will cave in. Elements of this game were present in the Mexican crisis of 1995 and were also a particularly important feature of the negotiations between the IMF and Indonesia during the Asian crisis.

The IMF would produce better outcomes if it makes it clear that it will not play this game. Just as giving in to ill-behaved children may be the easy way out in the short run, but supports a pattern of poor behaviour in the long run, some critics worry that the IMF may not be tough enough when confronted by short-run humanitarian concerns. For example, they have been particularly critical of the IMF's lending to the Russian government, which has resisted adopting appropriate reforms to stabilize its financial system.

The IMF has also been criticized for imposing on the East Asian countries so-called austerity programs that focus on tight macroeconomic policies rather than on microeconomic policies to fix the crisis-causing problems in the financial sector. Such programs are likely to increase resistance to IMF recommendations, particularly in emerging market countries. Austerity programs allow these politicians to label institutions such as the IMF as being anti-growth, rhetoric that helps the politicians mobilize the public against the IMF and avoid doing what they really need to do to reform the financial system in their country. IMF programs focused instead on microeconomic policies related to the financial sector would increase the likelihood that the IMF will be seen as a helping hand in the creation of a more efficient financial system.

An important historical feature of successful lender-of-last-resort operations is that the faster the lending is done, the lower is the amount that actually has to be lent. An excellent example occurred in the aftermath of the stock market crash on October 19, 1987. At the end of that day, in order to service their customers' accounts, securities firms needed to borrow several billion dollars to maintain orderly trading. However, given the unprecedented developments, banks were very nervous about extending further loans to these firms. Upon learning this, the U.S. Federal Reserve engaged in an immediate lender-of-last-resort operation, with the Fed making it clear that it would provide liquidity to banks making loans to the securities industry. Indeed, what is striking about this episode is that the extremely quick intervention of the Fed resulted not only in a negligible impact of the stock market crash on the economy, but also meant that the amount of liquidity that the Fed needed to supply to the economy was not very large.

The ability of the Fed to engage in a lender-of-last-resort operation within a day of a substantial shock to the financial system is in sharp contrast to the amount of time it has taken the IMF to supply liquidity during the recent crises in Mexico and Asian countries, which exceeded $50 billion. Because IMF lending facilities were originally designed to provide funds after a country was experiencing a balance-of-payments crisis and because the conditions for the loan had to be negotiated, it took several months before the IMF made funds available. By this time, the crises had gotten much worse—and much larger sums of funds were needed to cope with the crisis, often stretching the resources of the IMF. One reason central banks can lend so much more quickly than the IMF is that they have set up procedures in advance to provide loans, with the terms and conditions for this lending agreed upon beforehand. The need for quick provision of liquidity to keep the loan amount manageable argues for similar credit facilities at the international lender of last resort so that funds can be provided quickly as long as the borrower meets conditions such as properly supervising its banks or keeping budget deficits low. A step in this direction was made in 1999 when the IMF set up a new lending facility, the Contingent Credit Line, so it can provide liquidity faster during a crisis.

The debate on whether the world will be better off with the IMF operating as an international lender of last resort is currently a hot one. Much attention is being focused on making the IMF more effective in performing this role, and redesign of the IMF is at the centre of proposals for a new international financial architecture to help reduce international financial instability.

INTERNATIONAL CONSIDERATIONS AND MONETARY POLICY

Our analysis in this chapter so far has suggested several ways in which monetary policy can be affected by international matters. Awareness of these effects can have significant implications for the way monetary policy is conducted.

Direct Effects of the Foreign Exchange Market on the Money Supply

When central banks intervene in the foreign exchange market, they acquire or sell off international reserves, and their monetary base is affected. When a central bank intervenes in the foreign exchange market, it gives up some control of its money supply. For example, in the early 1970s, the German central bank faced a dilemma. In attempting to keep the German mark from appreciating too much against the U.S. dollar, the Germans acquired huge quantities of international reserves, leading to a rate of money growth that the German central bank considered inflationary.

The Bundesbank could have tried to halt the growth of the money supply by stopping its intervention in the foreign exchange market and reasserting control over its own money supply. Such a strategy has a major drawback when the central bank is under pressure not to allow its currency to appreciate: the lower price of imports and higher price of exports as a result of an appreciation in its currency will hurt domestic producers and increase unemployment.

The ability to conduct monetary policy is typically easier when a country's currency is a reserve currency. For example, because the U.S. dollar has been a reserve currency, the U.S. monetary base and money supply have been less affected by developments in the foreign exchange market. As long as other central banks, rather than the Fed, intervene to keep the value of the dollar from changing, U.S. holdings of international reserves are unaffected. However, the central bank of a reserve currency country must worry about a shift away from the use of its currency for international reserves.

Balance-of-Payments Considerations

Under the Bretton Woods system, balance-of-payments considerations were more important than they are under the current managed float regime. When a nonreserve currency country is running balance-of-payments deficits, it necessarily gives up international reserves. To keep from running out of these reserves, under the Bretton Woods system it had to implement contractionary monetary policy to strengthen its currency. Exactly that occurred in the United Kingdom before its devaluation of the pound in 1967. When policy became expansionary, the balance of payments deteriorated, and the British were forced to "slam on the brakes" by implementing a contractionary policy. Once the balance of payments improved, policy became more expansionary until the deteriorating balance of payments again forced the British to pursue a contractionary policy. Such on-again, off-again actions became known as a "stop-go" policy, and the domestic instability it created was criticized severely.

The situation is different with a major reserve currency country. The United States, for example, can run large balance-of-payments deficits without losing huge amounts of international reserves. This does not mean, however, that the Federal Reserve is never influenced by developments in the U.S. balance of payments. Current account deficits in the United States suggest that American businesses may be losing some of their ability to compete because the value of the dollar is too high. In addition, large U.S. balance-of-payments deficits lead to balance-of-payments surpluses in other countries, which can in turn lead to large increases in their holdings of international reserves (this was especially true under the Bretton Woods system). Because such increases put a strain on the international financial system and may stimulate world inflation, the Fed worries about U.S. balance-of-payments and current account deficits. To help shrink these deficits, the Fed might pursue a more contractionary monetary policy.

Exchange Rate Considerations

Unlike balance-of-payments considerations, which have become less important under the current managed float system, exchange rate considerations now play a greater role in the conduct of monetary policy. If a central bank does not want to see its currency fall in value, it may pursue a more contractionary monetary policy of reducing the money supply to raise the domestic interest rate, thereby strengthening its currency. Similarly, if a country experiences an appreciation in its currency, domestic industry may suffer from increased foreign competition and may pressure the central bank to pursue a higher rate of money growth in order to lower the exchange rate.

SUMMARY

1. An unsterilized central bank intervention in which the domestic currency is sold to purchase foreign assets leads to a gain in international reserves, an increase in the money supply, and a depreciation of the domestic currency. Available evidence suggests, however, that sterilized central bank interventions have little long-term effect on the exchange rate.

2. The balance of payments is a bookkeeping system for recording all payments between a country and foreign countries that have a direct bearing on the movement of funds between them. The official reserve transactions balance is the sum of the current account balance plus the items in the capital account. It indicates the amount of international reserves that must be moved between countries to finance international transactions.

3. Before World War I, the gold standard was predominant. Currencies were convertible into gold, thus fixing exchange rates between countries. After World War II, the Bretton Woods system and the IMF were established to promote a fixed exchange rate system in which the U.S. dollar was convertible into gold. The Bretton Woods system collapsed in 1971. We now have an international financial system that has elements of a managed float and a fixed exchange rate system. Some exchange rates fluctuate from day to day, although central banks intervene in the foreign exchange market, while other exchange rates are fixed, as in the European Monetary System.

4. Controls on capital outflows receive support because they may prevent domestic residents and foreigners from pulling capital out of a country during a crisis and make devaluation less likely. Controls on capital inflows make sense under the theory that if speculative capital cannot flow in, it cannot go out suddenly and create a crisis. However, capital controls suffer from several disadvantages: they are seldom effective, they lead to corruption, and they may allow governments to avoid taking the steps needed to reform their financial systems to deal with the crisis.

5. The IMF has recently taken on the role of an international lender of last resort. Because central banks in emerging market countries are unlikely to be able to perform a lender-of-last-resort operation successfully, an international lender of last resort like the IMF is needed to prevent financial instability. However, the IMF's role as an international lender of last resort creates a serious moral hazard problem that can encourage excessive risk taking and make a financial crisis more likely, but avoiding the problem may be politically hard to do. In addition, the IMF needs to be able to provide liquidity quickly during a crisis in order to keep manageable the amount of funds lent.

6. Three international considerations affect the conduct of monetary policy: direct effects of the foreign exchange market on the money supply, balance-of-payments considerations, and exchange rate considerations. A reserve currency country like the United States is less affected by developments in the foreign exchange market and its balance of payments than are other countries.

KEY TERMS

balance of payments, p. 427
balance-of-payments crisis, p. 438
Bretton Woods system, p. 431
capital account, p. 429
currency union, p. 440
current account, p. 428
devaluation, p. 433
exchange rate union, p. 440
fixed exchange rate regime, p. 431

foreign exchange intervention, p. 423
gold standard, p. 430
International Monetary Fund (IMF), p. 431
international reserves, p. 423
managed float regime (dirty float), p. 423
official reserve transactions balance, p. 429

reserve currency, p. 432
revaluation, p. 434
special drawing rights (SDRs), p. 435
sterilized foreign exchange intervention, p. 425
trade balance, p. 428
unsterilized foreign exchange intervention, p. 425
World Bank, p. 431

QUESTIONS AND PROBLEMS

Questions marked with an asterisk are answered at the end of the book in an appendix, "Answers to Selected Questions and Problems."

1. If the Bank of Canada buys Canadian dollars in the foreign exchange market but conducts an offsetting open market operation to sterilize the intervention,

what will be the impact on international reserves, the money supply, and the exchange rate?

*2. If the Bank of Canada buys Canadian dollars in the foreign exchange market but does not sterilize the intervention, what will be the impact on international reserves, the money supply, and the exchange rate?

3. For each of the following, identify in which part of the balance-of-payments account it appears (current account, capital account, or method of financing) and whether it is a receipt or a payment.
   a. A British subject's purchase of a share of Air Canada stock
   b. A Canadian's purchase of an airline ticket from Air France
   c. The Swiss government's purchase of Canadian Treasury bills
   d. A Japanese's purchase of Canadian salmon
   e. $50 million of foreign aid to Honduras
   f. A loan by a Canadian bank to Mexico
   g. A Canadian bank's borrowing of Eurodollars

*4. Why does a balance-of-payments deficit for Canada have a different effect on its international reserves than a balance-of-payments deficit for the United States?

5. Under the gold standard, if Britain became more productive relative to Canada, what would happen to the money supply in the two countries? Why would the changes in the money supply help preserve a fixed exchange rate between Canada and Britain?

*6. What is the exchange rate between dollars and francs if one dollar is convertible into 1/20 ounce of gold and one franc is convertible into 1/40 ounce of gold?

7. If a country's par exchange rate was undervalued during the Bretton Woods fixed exchange rate regime, what kind of intervention would that country's central bank be forced to undertake, and what effect would it have on its international reserves and the money supply?

*8. How can a large balance-of-payments surplus contribute to the country's inflation rate?

9. "If a country wants to keep its exchange rate from changing, it must give up some control over its money supply." Is this statement true, false, or uncertain? Explain your answer.

*10. Why can balance-of-payments deficits force some countries to implement a contractionary monetary policy?

11. "Balance-of-payments deficits always cause a country to lose international reserves." Is this statement true, false, or uncertain? Explain your answer.

*12. How can persistent U.S. balance-of-payments deficits stimulate world inflation?

13. "Inflation is not possible under the gold standard." Is this statement true, false, or uncertain? Explain your answer.

*14. Why is it that in a pure flexible exchange rate system, the foreign exchange market has no direct effects on the money supply? Does this mean that the foreign exchange market has no effect on monetary policy?

15. "The abandonment of fixed exchange rates after 1973 has meant that countries have pursued more independent monetary policies." Is this statement true, false, or uncertain? Explain your answer.

Chapter 20

Monetary Policy Strategy: The International Experience

PREVIEW   Getting monetary policy right is crucial to the health of the economy. Overly expansionary monetary policy leads to high inflation, which decreases the efficiency of the economy and hampers economic growth. Canada has not been exempt from inflationary episodes, but more extreme cases of inflation, in which the inflation rate climbs to over 100% per year, have been prevalent in some regions of the world such as Latin America, and have been very harmful to the economy. Monetary policy that is too tight can produce serious recessions in which output falls and unemployment rises. It can also lead to deflation, a fall in the price level, as occurred in Canada during the Great Depression and in Japan more recently. As we saw in Chapter 8, deflation can be especially damaging to the economy because it promotes financial instability and can even help trigger financial crises.

In Chapter 18 our discussion of the conduct of monetary policy focused primarily on Canada. However, Canada is not the source of all wisdom about how to do monetary policy well. In thinking about what strategies for the conduct of monetary policy might be best, we need to examine monetary policy experiences in other countries.

A central feature of monetary policy strategies in all countries is the use of a **nominal anchor** (a nominal variable that monetary policymakers use to tie down the price level such as the inflation rate, an exchange rate, or the money supply) as an intermediate target to achieve an ultimate goal such as price stability. We begin the chapter by examining the role a nominal anchor plays in promoting price stability. Then we examine three basic types of monetary policy strategy—exchange-rate targeting, monetary targeting, and inflation targeting—and compare them to the Bank of Canada's current monetary policy regime. We will see that the Bank's inflation targeting has several advantages although there is much to learn from the foreign experience.

THE ROLE OF A NOMINAL ANCHOR

Adherence to a nominal anchor forces a nation's monetary authority to conduct monetary policy so that the nominal anchor variable such as the inflation rate or the money supply stays within a narrow range. A nominal anchor thus keeps the price level from growing or falling too fast and thereby preserves the value of a country's money. Thus, a nominal anchor of some sort is a necessary element in successful monetary policy strategies.

One reason a nominal anchor is necessary for monetary policy is that it can help promote price stability, which most countries now view as the most important goal for monetary policy. A nominal anchor promotes price stability by tying inflation expectations to low levels directly through its constraint on the value of domestic money. A more subtle reason for a nominal anchor's importance is that it can limit the **time-inconsistency problem** in which monetary policy conducted on a discretionary, day-by-day, basis leads to poor long-run outcomes.[1]

The Time-Inconsistency Problem

The time-inconsistency problem of discretionary policy arises because economic behaviour is influenced by what firms and people expect the monetary authorities to do in the future. With firms' and people's expectations assumed to remain unchanged, policymakers think they can boost economic output (or lower unemployment) by pursuing monetary policy that is more expansionary than originally expected, and so they have incentives to pursue this policy. Because decisions about wages and prices reflect expectations about policy, however, workers and firms will raise their expectations not only of inflation but also of wages and prices. On average, output will not be higher under such an expansionary strategy, but inflation will be. (We examine this result more formally in Chapter 28.) Even though a central bank believes it is operating in a sensible manner, it may pursue overly expansionary monetary policy and end up with a poor outcome—high inflation with no gains on the output front. Even if the central bank recognizes the time-inconsistency problem, it may be hard for it to avoid because of the political pressures on the central bank to pursue an overly expansionary monetary policy.

Although this analysis sounds somewhat complicated, the time-inconsistency problem is actually something we encounter in everyday life. For example, a parent may give in to a child to keep the child from acting up. The more the parent gives in, however, the more demanding the child may become. Thus, while giving in may be the right thing to do *if* a child's expectations remain unchanged (that is, if the child does *not* begin to expect that the parent will give in to irresponsible behaviour), it eventually leads to a bad outcome because the child's expectations *are* affected by what the parent does. This is why how-to books on parenting usually suggest that parents should set rules for their children and stick to them.

A nominal anchor is like a behaviour rule: it can help avoid the time-inconsistency problem by providing an expected constraint on discretionary policy. In the following sections, we examine three monetary policy strategies—exchange-rate targeting, monetary targeting, and inflation targeting—that make use of a nominal anchor.

---

[1]The time-inconsistency problem was first outlined in Finn Kydland and Edward Prescott, "Rules Rather Than Discretion: The Inconsistency of Optimal Plans," *Journal of Political Economy* 85 (1977): 473–491; Guillermo Calvo, "On the Time Consistency of Optimal Policy in the Monetary Economy," *Econometrica* 46 (November 1978): 1411–1428; and Robert J. Barro and David Gordon, "A Positive Theory of Monetary Policy in a Natural Rate Model," *Journal of Political Economy* 91 (August 1983).

EXCHANGE-RATE TARGETING

Targeting the exchange rate is a monetary policy strategy with a long history. It can take the form of fixing the value of the domestic currency to a commodity such as gold, the key feature of the gold standard described in Chapter 19. More recently, fixed exchange-rate regimes have involved fixing the value of the domestic currency to that of a large, low-inflation country like the United States or Germany (called the anchor country). Another alternative is to adopt a crawling target or peg, in which a currency is allowed to depreciate at a steady rate so that the inflation rate in the pegging country can be higher than that of the anchor country.

Advantages of Exchange-Rate Targeting

Exchange-rate targeting has several advantages. First, the nominal anchor of an exchange-rate target directly contributes to keeping inflation under control by tying the inflation rate for internationally traded goods to that found in the anchor country. It does this because the foreign price of internationally traded goods is set by the world market, while the domestic price of these goods is fixed by the exchange-rate target. For example, in Argentina the exchange rate for the Argentine peso is exactly one to the dollar, so that a bushel of wheat traded internationally at five dollars has its price set at five pesos. If the exchange-rate target is credible (i.e., expected to be adhered to), the exchange-rate target has the added benefit of anchoring inflation expectations to the inflation rate in the anchor country.

Second, an exchange-rate target provides an automatic rule for the conduct of monetary policy that helps mitigate the time-inconsistency problem. As we saw in Chapter 19, an exchange-rate target forces a tightening of monetary policy when there is a tendency for the domestic currency to depreciate or a loosening of policy when there is a tendency for the domestic currency to appreciate, so that discretionary, time-inconsistent monetary policy is less of an option.

Third, an exchange-rate target has the advantage of simplicity and clarity, which makes it easily understood by the public. A "sound currency" is an easy-to-understand rallying cry for monetary policy. In the past, this aspect was important in France, where an appeal to the "franc fort" (strong franc) was often used to justify tight monetary policy.

Given its advantages, it is not surprising that exchange-rate targeting has been used successfully to control inflation in industrialized countries. Both France and the United Kingdom, for example, successfully used exchange-rate targeting to lower inflation by tying the value of their currencies to the German mark. In 1987, when France first pegged its exchange rate to the mark, its inflation rate was 3%, two percentage points above the German inflation rate. By 1992 its inflation rate had fallen to 2%, a level that can be argued is consistent with price stability, and was even below that in Germany. By 1996, the French and German inflation rates had converged, to a number slightly below 2%. Similarly, after pegging to the German mark in 1990, the United Kingdom was able to lower its inflation rate from 10% to 3% by 1992, when it was forced to abandon the exchange rate mechanism (ERM, discussed in Chapter 19).

Exchange-rate targeting has also been an effective means of reducing inflation quickly in emerging market countries. For example, before the devaluation in Mexico in 1994, its exchange-rate target enabled it to bring inflation down from levels above 100% in 1988 to below 10% in 1994.

Disadvantages of Exchange-Rate Targeting

Despite the inherent advantages of exchange-rate targeting, there are several serious criticisms of this strategy. The problem (as we saw in Chapter 19) is that with capital mobility the targeting country no longer can pursue its own independent monetary policy and so loses its ability to use monetary policy to respond to domestic shocks that are independent of those hitting the anchor country. Furthermore, an exchange-rate target means that shocks to the anchor country are directly transmitted to the targeting country because changes in interest rates in the anchor country lead to a corresponding change in interest rates in the targeting country.

A striking example of these problems occurred when Germany reunified in 1990. In response to concerns about inflationary pressures arising from reunification and the massive fiscal expansion required to rebuild East Germany, long-term German interest rates rose until February 1991 and short-term rates rose until December 1991. This shock to the anchor country in the exchange rate mechanism (ERM) was transmitted directly to the other countries in the ERM whose currencies were pegged to the mark, and their interest rates rose in tandem with those in Germany. Continuing adherence to the exchange-rate target slowed economic growth and increased unemployment in countries such as France that remained in the ERM and adhered to the exchange-rate peg.

A second problem with exchange-rate targets is that they leave countries open to speculative attacks on their currencies. Indeed, one aftermath of German reunification was the foreign exchange crisis of September 1992. As we saw in Chapter 19, the tight monetary policy in Germany following reunification meant that the countries in the ERM were subjected to a negative demand shock that led to a decline in economic growth and a rise in unemployment. It was certainly feasible for the governments of these countries to keep their exchange rates fixed relative to the mark in these circumstances, but speculators began to question whether these countries' commitment to the exchange-rate peg would weaken. Speculators reasoned that these countries would not tolerate the rise in unemployment resulting from keeping interest rates high enough to fend off attacks on their currencies.

At this stage, speculators were, in effect, presented with a one-way bet because the currencies of countries like France, Spain, Sweden, Italy, and the United Kingdom could only go in one direction and depreciate against the mark. Selling these currencies before the likely depreciation occurred gave speculators an attractive profit opportunity with potentially high expected returns. The result was the speculative attack in September 1992 discussed in Chapter 19. Only in France was the commitment to the fixed exchange rate strong enough so that France did not devalue. The governments in the other countries were unwilling to defend their currencies at all costs and eventually allowed their currencies to fall in value.

The different response of France and the United Kingdom after the September 1992 exchange-rate crisis illustrates the potential cost of an exchange-rate target. France, which continued to peg to the mark and was thus unable to use monetary policy to respond to domestic conditions, found that economic growth remained slow after 1992 and unemployment increased. The United Kingdom, on the other hand, which dropped out of the ERM exchange-rate peg and adopted inflation targeting (discussed later in this chapter), had much better economic performance: economic growth was higher, the unemployment rate fell, and yet its inflation was not much worse than France's.

In contrast to industrialized countries, emerging market countries (including the so-called transition countries of Eastern Europe) may not lose much by giving up an independent monetary policy when they target exchange rates. Because many emerging market countries have not developed the political or monetary institutions that allow the successful use of discretionary monetary policy, they may have little to gain from an independent monetary policy, but a lot to lose. Thus, they would be better off by, in effect, adopting the monetary policy of a country like the United States through targeting exchange rates than by pursuing their own independent policy. This is one of the reasons that so many emerging market countries have adopted exchange-rate targeting.

Nonetheless, exchange-rate targeting is highly dangerous for these countries because it leaves them open to speculative attacks that can have far more serious consequences for their economies than for the economies of industrialized countries. Indeed, as we saw in Chapters 8 and 19, the successful speculative attacks in Mexico in 1994 and East Asia in 1997 plunged their economies into full-scale financial crises that devastated their economies.

An additional disadvantage of an exchange-rate target is it can weaken the accountability of policymakers, particularly in emerging market countries. Because exchange-rate targeting fixes the exchange rate, it eliminates an important signal that can help constrain monetary policy from becoming too expansionary. In industrialized countries, the bond market provides an important signal about the stance of monetary policy. Overly expansionary monetary policy or strong political pressure to engage in overly expansionary monetary policy produces an inflation scare in which inflation expectations surge, interest rates rise because of the Fisher effect (described in Chapter 5), and there is a sharp decline in long-term bond prices. Because both central banks and the politicians want to avoid this kind of scenario, overly expansionary, time-inconsistent monetary policy will be less likely.

In many countries, particularly emerging market countries, the long-term bond market is essentially nonexistent. Under a flexible exchange-rate regime, however, if monetary policy is too expansionary, the exchange rate will depreciate. In these countries the daily fluctuations of the exchange rate can, like the bond market in Canada, provide an early warning signal that monetary policy is too expansionary. Just as the fear of a visible inflation scare in the bond market constrains central bankers from pursuing overly expansionary monetary policy and also constrains politicians from putting pressure on the central bank to engage in overly expansionary monetary policy, fear of exchange-rate depreciations can make overly expansionary, time-inconsistent monetary policy less likely.

The need for signals from the foreign exchange market may be even more acute for emerging market countries because the balance sheets and actions of the central banks are not as transparent as they are in industrialized countries. Targeting the exchange rate can make it even harder to ascertain the central bank's policy actions, as was true in Thailand before the July 1997 currency crisis. The public is less able to keep a watch on the central banks and the politicians pressuring it, which makes it easier for monetary policy to become too expansionary.

When Is Exchange-Rate Targeting Desirable for Industrialized Countries?

Given the above disadvantages with exchange-rate targeting, when might it make sense?

In industrialized countries, the biggest cost to exchange-rate targeting is the loss of an independent monetary policy to deal with domestic considerations. If an independent, domestic monetary policy can be conducted responsibly, this can be a serious cost indeed, as the comparison between the post-1992 experience of France and the United Kingdom indicates. However, not all industrialized countries have found that they are capable of conducting their own monetary policy successfully, either because of the lack of independence of the central bank or because political pressures on the central bank lead to an inflation bias in monetary policy. In these cases, giving up independent control of domestic monetary policy may not be a great loss, while the gain of having monetary policy determined by a better-performing central bank in the anchor country can be substantial.

Italy provides an example. It was not a coincidence that the Italian public was the most favourable of all those in Europe to the European Monetary Union. The past record of Italian monetary policy was not good, and the Italian public recognized that having monetary policy controlled by more responsible outsiders had benefits that far outweighed the costs of losing the ability to focus monetary policy on domestic considerations.

A second reason why industrialized countries might find targeting exchange rates useful is that it encourages integration of the domestic economy with its neighbours. Clearly this was the rationale for long-standing pegging of the exchange rate to the deutsche mark by countries such as Austria and the Netherlands, and the more recent exchange-rate pegs that preceded the European Monetary Union.

To sum up, exchange-rate targeting for industrialized countries is probably not the best monetary policy strategy to control the overall economy unless (1) domestic monetary and political institutions are not conducive to good monetary policy-making or (2) there are other important benefits of an exchange-rate target that have nothing to do with monetary policy.

When Is Exchange-Rate Targeting Desirable for Emerging Market Countries?

In countries whose political and monetary institutions are particularly weak and who therefore have been experiencing continued bouts of hyperinflation, a characterization that applies to many emerging market (including transition) countries, exchange-rate targeting may be the only way to break inflationary psychology and stabilize the economy. In this situation, exchange-rate targeting is the stabilization policy of last resort. However, if the exchange-rate targeting regimes in emerging market countries are not always transparent, they are more likely to break down, often resulting in disastrous financial crises.

Are there exchange-rate strategies that make it less likely that the exchange-rate regime will break down in emerging market countries? Two such strategies that have received increasing attention in recent years are currency boards and dollarization.

Currency Boards

One solution to the problem of lack of transparency and commitment to the exchange-rate target is the adoption of a **currency board**, in which the domestic currency is backed 100% by a foreign currency (say, dollars) and in which the note-issuing authority, whether the central bank or the government, establishes a fixed exchange-rate to this foreign currency and stands ready to exchange domestic currency for the foreign currency at this rate whenever the public requests it. A currency board is just a variant of a fixed exchange-rate target in which the commitment to the fixed exchange rate is especially strong because the conduct of monetary policy is in effect put on autopilot, taken completely out of the hands of the central bank and the government. In contrast, the typical fixed or pegged exchange-rate regime does allow the monetary authorities some discretion in their conduct of monetary policy because they can still adjust interest rates or print money.

A currency board arrangement thus has important advantages over a monetary policy strategy that just uses an exchange-rate target. First, the money supply can expand only when dollars are exchanged for domestic currency at the central bank. Thus the increased amount of domestic currency is matched by an equal increase in foreign exchange reserves. The central bank no longer has the ability to print money and thereby cause inflation. Second, the currency board involves a stronger commitment by the central bank to the fixed exchange rate and may therefore be effective in bringing down inflation quickly and in decreasing the likelihood of a successful speculative attack against the currency.

BOX 20·1

Argentina's Currency Board

Argentina has had a long history of monetary instability, with inflation rates fluctuating dramatically and sometimes surging to beyond 1000% a year. To end this cycle of inflationary surges, Argentina decided to adopt a currency board in April 1991. The Argentine currency board works as follows. Under Argentina's convertibility law, the peso/dollar exchange rate is fixed at one to one, and a member of the public can go to the Argentine central bank and exchange a peso for a dollar, or vice versa, at any time.

The early years of Argentina's currency board looked stunningly successful. Inflation, which had been running at an 800% annual rate in 1990, fell to less than 5% by the end of 1994, and economic growth was rapid, averaging an annual rate of almost 8% from 1991 to 1994. In the aftermath of the Mexican peso crisis, however, concern about the health of the Argentine economy resulted in the public's pulling money out of the banks (deposits fell by 18%) and

exchanging pesos for dollars, thus causing a contraction of the Argentine money supply. The result was a sharp drop in Argentine economic activity, with real GDP shrinking by more than 5% in 1995 and the unemployment rate jumping above 15%. Only in 1996 did the economy begin to recover.

Because the central bank of Argentina has no control over monetary policy under the currency board system, it was relatively helpless to counteract the contractionary monetary policy stemming from the public's behaviour. Furthermore, because the currency board does not allow the central bank to create pesos and lend them to the banks, it has very little capability to act as a lender of last resort. With help from international agencies, such as the IMF, the World Bank, and the Interamerican Development Bank, which lent Argentina over $5 billion in 1995 to help shore up its banking system, the currency board survived.

Central Bank of Bosnia and Herzegovina
www.cbbh.gov.ba

Hong Kong Monetary Authority
www.info.gov.hk/hkma

Bank of Estonia
www.ee/epbe

Bank of Lithuania
www.lbank.lt

Bulgarian National Bank
www.bnb.bg

Central Bank of Argentina
www.bcra.gov.ar

Dollarization

Although they solve the transparency and commitment problems inherent in an exchange-rate target regime, currency boards suffer from some of the same shortcomings: the loss of an independent monetary policy and increased exposure of the economy to shocks from the anchor country, and the loss of the central bank's ability to create money and act as a lender of last resort. Other means must therefore be used to cope with potential banking crises. Also, if there is a speculative attack on a currency board, the exchange of the domestic currency for foreign currency leads to a sharp contraction of the money supply, which can be highly damaging to the economy.

Currency boards have been established recently in countries such as Hong Kong (1983), Argentina (1991), Estonia (1992), Lithuania (1994), Bulgaria (1997), and Bosnia (1998). Argentina's currency board, which was established in 1991 and required the central bank to exchange U.S. dollars for new pesos at a fixed exchange rate of 1 to 1, is one of the most interesting. Box 20-1 describes Argentina's experience with its currency board.

Another solution to the problems created by a lack of transparency and commitment to the exchange-rate target is **dollarization**, the adoption of a sound currency, like the U.S. dollar, as a country's money. Indeed, dollarization is just another variant of a fixed exchange-rate target with an even stronger commitment mechanism than a currency board provides. A currency board can be abandoned, allowing a change in the value of the currency, but a change of value is impossible with dollarization: a dollar bill is always worth one dollar whether it is held in the United States or outside of it.

Dollarization has been advocated as a monetary policy strategy for emerging market countries. It has been discussed actively by Argentine officials in the aftermath of the devaluation of the Brazilian real in January 1999 and was adopted by Ecuador in March 2000. Dollarization's key advantage is that it completely avoids the possibility of a speculative attack on the domestic currency (because there is none). (Such an attack is still a danger even under a currency board arrangement.)

Dollarization is subject to the usual disadvantages of an exchange-rate target (the loss of an independent monetary policy, increased exposure of the economy to shocks from the anchor country, and the inability of the central bank to create money and act as a lender of last resort). Dollarization has one additional disadvantage not characteristic of currency boards or other exchange-rate target regimes. Because a country adopting dollarization no longer has its own currency it loses the revenue that a government receives by issuing money, which is called

SUMMARY

TABLE 20-1 Advantages and Disadvantages of Different Monetary Policy Strategies

	Exchange-Rate Targeting	Monetary Targeting	Inflation Targeting	Implicit Nominal Anchor
Advantages				
	Directly ties down inflation of internationally traded goods			
	Automatic rule for conduct of monetary policy			
	Simplicity and clarity of target		Simplicity and clarity of target	
		Independent monetary policy can focus on domestic considerations	Independent monetary policy can focus on domestic considerations	Independent monetary policy can focus on domestic considerations
		Immediate signal on achievement of target		
			Does not rely on stable money–inflation relationship	Does not rely on stable money–inflation relationship
			Increased accountability of central bank	
			Reduced effects of inflationary shocks	
				Demonstrated success in U.S.

seignorage. Because governments (or their central banks) do not have to pay interest on their currency, they earn revenue (seignorage) by using this currency to purchase income-earning assets such as bonds. In the case of the Bank of Canada in recent years, this revenue is on the order of $1 billion per year. If an emerging market country dollarizes and gives up its currency, it needs to make up this loss of revenue somewhere, which is not always easy for a poor country.

Study Guide

As a study aid, the advantages and disadvantages of exchange-rate targeting and the other monetary policy strategies are listed in Table 20-1.

SUMMARY

TABLE 20-1 Advantages and Disadvantages of Different Monetary Policy Strategies *continued*

Exchange-Rate Targeting	Monetary Targeting	Inflation Targeting	Implicit Nominal Anchor
Disadvantages			
Loss of independent monetary policy			
Open to speculative attacks (less for currency board and not a problem for dollarization)			
Loss of exchange-rate signal			
	Relies on stable money–inflation relationship		
		Delayed signal about achievement of target	
		Could impose rigid rule (though not in practice)	
		Larger output fluctuations if sole focus on inflation (though not in practice)	
			Lack of transparency
			Success depends on individuals
			Low accountability

MONETARY TARGETING

In many countries, exchange-rate targeting is not an option because either the country (or bloc of countries) is too large or because there is no country whose currency is an obvious choice to serve as the nominal anchor. Exchange-rate targeting is therefore clearly not an option for the United States, Japan, or the European Monetary Union. These countries must look to other strategies for the conduct of monetary policy, one of which is monetary targeting.

Monetary Targeting in the United States, the United Kingdom, Japan, Germany, and Switzerland

In the 1970s, monetary targeting was adopted by several countries, notably the United States, Germany, Switzerland, the United Kingdom, and Japan, as well as in Canada (already discussed in Chapter 18). This strategy involves using monetary aggregates as an intermediate target of the type described in Chapter 18 to achieve an ultimate goal such as price stability. Monetary targeting as practiced was quite different from Milton Friedman's suggestion that the chosen monetary aggregate be targeted to grow at a constant rate. Indeed, in all these countries the central banks never adhered to strict, ironclad rules for monetary growth and in some of these countries monetary targeting was not pursued very seriously.

The United States   In response to concerns about inflation in the late 1960s, in 1970 the Federal Reserve committed itself to the use of monetary aggregates as intermediate targets. Every six weeks, the Federal Open Market Committee would set target ranges for the growth rate of various monetary aggregates and would determine what federal funds rate (the interest rate on funds loaned overnight between banks) it thought consistent with these aims. The target ranges for the growth in monetary aggregates were fairly broad—a typical range for M1 growth might be 3% to 6%; for M2, 4% to 7%—while the range for the federal funds rate was a narrow band, say, from $7\frac{1}{2}\%$ to $8\frac{1}{4}\%$. The trading desk at the Federal Reserve Bank of New York was then instructed to meet both sets of targets, but as we saw earlier, interest-rate targets and monetary aggregate targets might not be compatible. If the two targets were incompatible, the trading desk was instructed to give precedence to the federal funds target.

The Fed was actually using the federal funds rate as its operating target. During the six-week period between FOMC meetings, an unexpected rise in output (which would cause the federal funds rate to hit the top of its target band) would then induce open market purchases and a too-rapid growth of the money supply. When the FOMC met again, it would try to bring money supply growth back on track by raising the target range on the federal funds rate. However, if income continued to rise unexpectedly, money growth would overshoot again. This is exactly what occurred from June 1972 to June 1973, when the economy boomed unexpectedly. M1 growth greatly exceeded its target, increasing at approximately an 8% rate, while the federal funds rate climbed from $4\frac{1}{2}\%$ to $8\frac{1}{2}\%$. The economy soon became overheated, and inflationary pressures began to mount.

The opposite chain of events occurred at the end of 1974, when the economic contraction was far more severe than anyone had predicted. The federal funds rate fell dramatically, from over 12% to 5%, and persistently bumped against the bottom of its target range. The trading desk conducted open market sales to keep the federal funds rate from falling, and money growth dropped precipitously, actually turning negative by the beginning of 1975. Clearly, this sharp drop in money growth when the United States was experiencing one of the worst economic contractions of the postwar era was a serious mistake.

Using the federal funds rate as an operating target promoted a procyclical monetary policy despite the Fed's lip service to monetary aggregate targets. If the Federal Reserve really intended to pursue monetary aggregate targets, it seems peculiar that it would have chosen an interest rate for an operating target rather than a reserve aggregate. The explanation for the Fed's choice of an interest rate as an operating target is that it was still very concerned with achieving interest-rate stability and was reluctant to relinquish control over interest-rate movements. The incompatibility of the Fed's policy procedure with its stated intent of targeting on the monetary aggregates had become very clear by October 1979, when the Fed's policy procedures underwent drastic revision.

In October 1979, two months after Paul Volcker became chairman of the Board of Governors, the Fed finally de-emphasized the federal funds rate as an operating target by widening its target range more than fivefold. The primary operating target became nonborrowed reserves, which the Fed would set after estimating the volume of discount loans the banks would borrow. Figure 20-1 shows what happened to the federal funds rate and the growth rate of the M1 money supply both before and after October 1979. Not surprisingly, the federal funds rate underwent much greater fluctuations after it was de-emphasized as an operating target. What is surprising, however, is that the de-emphasis of the federal funds target did not

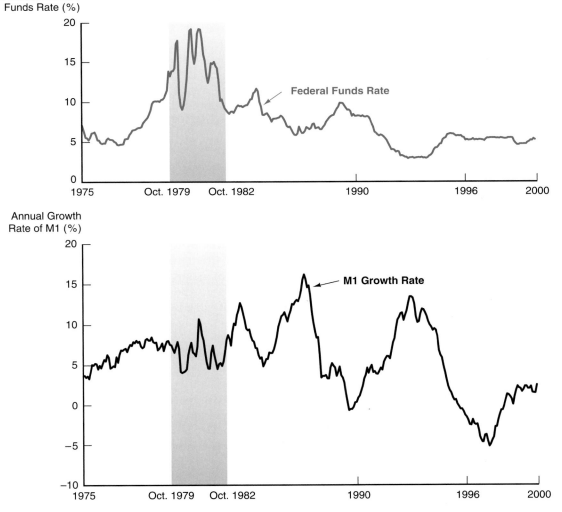

FIGURE 20-1   Federal Funds Rate and Growth Rate of the Money Supply: Before and After October 1979

Source: Federal Reserve: www.bog.frg.fed.us/release/H6.

result in improved monetary control. After October 1979, the fluctuations in the rate of money supply growth *increased* rather than decreased as would have been expected. In addition, the Fed missed its M1 growth target ranges in all three years of the 1979–1982 period. What went wrong?

There are several possible answers to this question, but the most persuasive explanation for poor monetary control is that controlling the money supply was never really the intent of Volcker's policy shift. Despite Volcker's statements about the need to target monetary aggregates, he was not committed to these targets. Rather, he was far more concerned with using interest-rate movements to wring inflation out of the economy. Volcker's primary reason for changing the Fed's operating procedure was to free his hands to manipulate interest rates in order to fight inflation. It was necessary to abandon interest-rate targets if Volcker were to be able to raise interest rates sharply when a slowdown in the economy was required to dampen inflation. This view of Volcker's strategy suggests that the Fed's announced attachment to monetary aggregate targets may have been a smokescreen to keep the Fed from being blamed for the high interest rates that would result from the new policy.

The interest rate movements in Figure 20-1 support this interpretation of Fed strategy. After the October 1979 announcement, short-term interest rates were driven up by nearly 5%, until in March 1980 they exceeded 15%. With the imposition of credit controls in March 1980 and the rapid decline in real GDP in the second quarter of 1980, the Fed eased up on its policy and allowed interest rates to decline sharply. When recovery began in July 1980, inflation remained persistent, still exceeding 10%. Because the inflation fight was not yet won, the Fed tightened the screws again, sending short-term rates above the 15% level for a second time. The 1981–1982 recession and its large decline in output and high unemployment began to bring inflation down. With inflationary psychology apparently broken, interest rates were allowed to fall.

The Fed's anti-inflation strategy during the October 1979–October 1982 period was neither intended nor likely to produce smooth growth in the monetary aggregates. Indeed, the large fluctuations in interest rates and the business cycle, along with financial innovation, helped generate volatile money growth. In October 1982, with inflation in check, the Fed returned, in effect, to a policy of smoothing interest rates. It did this by placing less emphasis on monetary aggregate targets and shifting to borrowed reserves (discount loan borrowings) as an operating target.

The United Kingdom   The British introduced monetary targeting in late 1973, also in response to mounting concerns about inflation. The Bank of England targeted M3, a broader monetary target than the Bank of Canada or the Fed used.

In the United Kingdom, after monetary aggregates overshot their targets and inflation accelerated in the late 1970s, Prime Minister Margaret Thatcher in 1980 introduced the Medium-Term Financial Strategy, which proposed a gradual deceleration of M3 growth. Unfortunately, the M3 targets ran into problems: they were not reliable indicators of the tightness of monetary policy. After 1983, arguing that financial innovation was wreaking havoc with the relationship between M3 and national income, the Bank of England began to de-emphasize M3 in favour of a narrower monetary aggregate, M0 (the monetary base). The target for M3 was temporarily suspended in October 1985 and was completely dropped in 1987.

A feature of monetary targeting in the United Kingdom was that there was substantial game playing. The Bank of England targeted multiple aggregates, allowed base drift (by applying target growth rates to a new base at which the target ended up every period), did not announce targets on a regular schedule, used artificial means to bring down the growth of a targeted aggregate, often overshot its targets without reversing the overshoot later, and often obscured why deviations from the monetary targets occurred. (As discussed in Chapter 18, similar game playing was displayed by the Bank of Canada when it targeted monetary aggregates.)

Japan The increase in oil prices in late 1973 was a major shock for Japan, which experienced a huge jump in the inflation rate, to greater than 20% in 1974—a surge facilitated by money growth in 1973 in excess of 20%. The Bank of Japan, like the other central banks discussed here, began to pay more attention to money growth rates. In 1978, the Bank of Japan began to announce "forecasts" at the beginning of each quarter for M2+ CDs. Although the Bank of Japan was not officially committed to monetary targeting, monetary policy appeared to be more money-focused after 1978. For example, after the second oil price shock in 1979, the Bank of Japan quickly reduced M2+ CDs growth, rather than allowing it to shoot up as occurred after the first oil shock. The Bank of Japan conducted monetary policy with operating procedures that were similar in many ways to those that the Federal Reserve used in the United States. The Bank of Japan used the interest rate in the Japanese interbank market (which has a function similar to that of the overnight money market in Canada and federal funds market in the United States) as its daily operating target.

The Bank of Japan's monetary policy performance during the 1978–1987 period was much better than the Fed's. Money growth in Japan slowed gradually, beginning in the mid-1970s, and was much less variable than in the United States. The outcome was a more rapid braking of inflation and a lower average inflation rate. In addition, these excellent results on inflation were achieved with lower variability in real output in Japan than in the United States.

In parallel with the United States, financial innovation and deregulation in Japan began to reduce the usefulness of the M2 + CDs monetary aggregate as an indicator of monetary policy. Because of concerns about the appreciation of the yen, the Bank of Japan significantly increased the rate of money growth from 1987 to 1989. Many observers blame speculation in Japanese land and stock prices (the so-called bubble economy) on the increase in money growth. To reduce this speculation, in 1989 the Bank of Japan switched to a tighter monetary policy aimed at slower money growth. The aftermath was a substantial decline in land and stock prices and the collapse of the bubble economy.

The 1990s have not been a happy period for the Japanese economy. The collapse of land and stock prices helped provoke a severe banking crisis, discussed in Chapter 11, that has continued to be a severe drag on the economy. The resulting weakness of the economy has even led to bouts of deflation, promoting further financial instability. The outcome has been an economy that has been stagnating for close to a decade. Many critics believe that the Bank of Japan has pursued overly tight monetary policy and needs to substantially increase money growth in order to lift the economy out of its stagnation.

Germany and Switzerland The two countries that have officially engaged in monetary targeting for over 20 years starting at the end of 1974 have been Germany and Switzerland, and this is why we will devote more attention to them. The success of monetary policy in these two countries in controlling inflation is the reason that monetary targeting still has strong advocates and is an element of the official policy regime for the European Central Bank (see Box 20-2).

The monetary aggregate chosen by the Germans was a narrow one known as *central bank money,* the sum of currency in circulation and bank deposits weighted by the 1974 required reserve ratios. In 1988, the Bundesbank switched targets from central bank money to M3. The Swiss began targeting the M1 monetary aggregate, but in 1980 switched to the narrower monetary aggregate, M0, the monetary base.

BOX 20-2

The European Central Bank's Monetary Policy Strategy

The European Central Bank (ECB) has adopted a hybrid monetary policy strategy that has much in common with the monetary targeting strategy previously used by the Bundesbank but also has some elements of inflation targeting. The ECB's strategy has two key "pillars." First is a prominent role for monetary aggregates with a "reference value" for the growth rate of a monetary aggregate (M3). Second is a broadly based assessment of the outlook for future price developments with a goal of price stability defined as a year-on-year increase in the consumer price index below 2%. After critics pointed out that a deflationary situation with negative inflation would satisfy the stated price stability criteria, the ECB provided a clarification that inflation meant positive inflation only, so that the price stability goal should be interpreted as a range for inflation of 0–2%.

The ECB's strategy is somewhat unclear and has been subjected to criticism for this reason. Although the 0–2% range for the goal of price stability sounds like an inflation target, the ECB has not been willing to live with this interpretation—it has repeatedly stated that it does not have an inflation target. On the other hand, the ECB has downgraded the importance of monetary aggregates in its strategy by using the term "reference value" rather than "target" in describing its strategy and has indicated that it will also monitor broadly based developments on the price level. The ECB seems to have decided to try to have its cake and eat it too by not committing too strongly to either a monetary or an inflation-targeting strategy. The resulting difficulty of assessing what the ECB's strategy is likely to be has the potential to reduce the accountability of this new institution.

The key fact about monetary targeting regimes in Germany and Switzerland is that the targeting regimes were very far from a Friedman-type monetary targeting rule in which a monetary aggregate is kept on a constant-growth-rate path and is the primary focus of monetary policy. As Otmar Issing, at the time the chief economist of the Bundesbank, has noted, "One of the secrets of success of the German policy of money-growth targeting was that ... it often did not feel bound by monetarist orthodoxy as far as its more technical details were concerned."[2] The Bundesbank allowed growth outside of its target ranges for periods of two to three years, and overshoots of its targets were subsequently reversed. Monetary targeting in Germany and Switzerland was instead primarily a method of communicating the strategy of monetary policy focused on long-run considerations and the control of inflation.

The calculation of monetary target ranges put great stress on making policy transparent (clear, simple, and understandable) and on regular communication with the public. First and foremost, a numerical inflation goal was prominently featured in the setting of target ranges. Second, monetary targeting, far from being a rigid policy rule, was quite flexible in practice. The target ranges for money growth were missed on the order of 50% of the time in Germany, often because of the Bundesbank's concern about other objectives, including output and exchange rates. Furthermore, the Bundesbank demonstrated its flexibility by allowing its inflation goal to vary over time and to converge gradually to the long-run inflation goal.

When the Bundesbank first set its monetary targets at the end of 1974, it announced a medium-term inflation goal of 4%, well above what it considered to be an appropriate long-run goal. It clarified that this medium-term inflation goal

---

[2]Otmar Issing, "Is Monetary Targeting in Germany Still Adequate?" In *Monetary Policy in an Integrated World Economy: Symposium 1995*, ed. Horst Siebert (Tübingen: Mohr, 1996), p. 120.

differed from the long-run goal by labelling it the "unavoidable rate of price increase." Its gradualist approach to reducing inflation led to a period of nine years before the medium-term inflation goal was considered to be consistent with price stability. When this occurred at the end of 1984, the medium-term inflation goal was renamed the "normative rate of price increase" and was set at 2%. It continued at this level until 1997, when it was changed to 1.5 to 2%. The Bundesbank also responded to negative supply shocks, restrictions in the supply of energy or raw materials that raise the price level, by raising its medium-term inflation goal: specifically, it raised the unavoidable rate of price increase from 3.5% to 4% in the aftermath of the second oil price shock in 1980.

The monetary targeting regimes in Germany and Switzerland demonstrated a strong commitment to clear communication of the strategy to the general public. The money growth targets were continually used as a framework to explain the monetary policy strategy, and both the Bundesbank and the Swiss National Bank expended tremendous effort in their publications and in frequent speeches by central bank officials to communicate to the public what the central bank was trying to achieve. Given that both central banks frequently missed their money growth targets by significant amounts, their monetary targeting frameworks are best viewed as a mechanism for transparently communicating how monetary policy is being directed to achieve inflation goals and as a means for increasing the accountability of the central bank.

The success of Germany's monetary targeting regime in producing low inflation has been envied by many other countries, explaining why it was chosen as the anchor country for the exchange rate mechanism. One clear indication of Germany's success occurred in the aftermath of German reunification in 1990. Despite a temporary surge in inflation stemming from the terms of reunification, high wage demands, and the fiscal expansion, the Bundesbank was able to keep these temporary effects from becoming embedded in the inflation process, and by 1995, inflation fell back down below the Bundesbank's normative inflation goal of 2%.

Monetary targeting in Switzerland has been more problematic than in Germany, suggesting the difficulties of targeting monetary aggregates in a small open economy that also underwent substantial changes in the institutional structure of its money markets. In the face of a 40% trade-weighted appreciation of the Swiss franc from the fall of 1977 to the fall of 1978, the Swiss National Bank decided that the country could not tolerate this high a level of the exchange rate. Thus, in the fall of 1978 the monetary targeting regime was abandoned temporarily, with a shift from a monetary target to an exchange-rate target until the spring of 1979, when monetary targeting was reintroduced (although not announced).

The period from 1989 to 1992 was also not a happy one for Swiss monetary targeting because the Swiss National Bank failed to maintain price stability after it successfully reduced inflation. The substantial overshoot of inflation from 1989 to 1992, reaching levels above 5%, was due to two factors. The first was that the strength of the Swiss franc from 1985 to 1987 caused the Swiss National Bank to allow the monetary base to grow at a rate greater than the 2% target in 1987 and then caused it to raise the money growth target to 3% for 1988. The second arose from the introduction of a new interbank payment system, Swiss Interbank Clearing (SIC), and a wide-ranging revision of the commercial banks' liquidity requirements in 1988. The result of the shocks to the exchange rate and the shift in the demand for monetary base arising from the above institutional changes created a serious problem for its targeted aggregate. As the 1988 year unfolded, it became clear that the Swiss National Bank had guessed wrong in predicting the effects of these shocks so that monetary policy was too easy even though the monetary target was undershot. The result was a subsequent rise in inflation to above the 5% level.

As a result of these problems with monetary targeting Switzerland has substantially loosened its monetary targeting regime. The Swiss National Bank recognized that its money growth targets were of diminished utility as a means of signalling the direction of monetary policy. Thus, its announcement at the end of 1990 of the medium-term growth path did not specify a horizon for the target or the starting point of the growth path. At the end of 1992 the bank specified the starting point for the expansion path and at the end of 1994 it announced a new medium-term path for money base growth for the period 1995 to 1999. By setting this path, the bank revealed retroactively that the horizon of the first path was also five years (1990–1995). Clearly, the Swiss National Bank has moved to a much more flexible framework in which hitting one-year targets for money base growth has been abandoned. Nevertheless, Swiss monetary policy has continued to be successful in controlling inflation, with inflation rates falling back down below the 1% level after the temporary bulge in inflation from 1989 to 1992.

There are two key lessons to be learned from our discussion of German and Swiss monetary targeting. First, a monetary targeting regime can restrain inflation in the longer run, even when the regime permits substantial target misses. Thus adherence to a rigid policy rule has not been found to be necessary to obtain good inflation outcomes. Second, the key reason why monetary targeting has been reasonably successful in these two countries, despite frequent target misses, is that the objectives of monetary policy are clearly stated and both the central banks actively engaged in communicating the strategy of monetary policy to the public, thereby enhancing the transparency of monetary policy and the accountability of the central bank.

As we will see in the next section, these key elements of a successful targeting regime—flexibility, transparency, and accountability—are also important elements in inflation-targeting regimes. German and Swiss monetary policy is actually closer in practice to inflation targeting than it is to Friedman-like monetary targeting, and thus might best be thought of as "hybrid" inflation targeting.

Advantages of Monetary Targeting

A major advantage of monetary targeting over exchange-rate targeting is that it enables a central bank to adjust its monetary policy to cope with domestic considerations. It enables the central bank to choose goals for inflation that may differ from those of other countries and allows some response to output fluctuations. Also, as with an exchange-rate target, information on whether the central bank is achieving its target is known almost immediately—figures for monetary aggregates are typically reported within a couple of weeks. Thus, monetary targets can send almost immediate signals to the public and markets about the stance of monetary policy and the intentions of the policymakers to keep inflation in check. In turn, these signals help fix inflation expectations and produce less inflation. Monetary targets also allow almost immediate accountability for monetary policy to keep inflation low, thus helping to constrain the monetary policymaker from falling into the time-inconsistency trap.

Disadvantages of Monetary Targeting

All of the above advantages of monetary aggregate targeting depend on a big *if*: there must be a strong and reliable relationship between the goal variable (inflation or nominal income) and the targeted aggregate. If the relationship between the monetary aggregate and the goal variable is weak, monetary aggregate targeting will not work, and this seems to have been a serious problem in the United States, the United Kingdom, and Switzerland, as well as in Canada. The weak relationship implies that hitting the target will not produce the desired outcome on the goal variable and thus the monetary aggregate will no longer provide an adequate signal about the stance of monetary policy. As a result, monetary targeting will not help fix inflation expectations and be a good guide for assessing the accountability of the central bank. In addition, an unreliable relationship between monetary aggregates and goal variables makes it difficult for monetary targeting to serve as a communications device that increases the transparency of monetary policy and makes the central bank accountable to the public.

INFLATION TARGETING

Brazil Central Bank
www.bcb.gov.br

Central Bank of Chile
www.bcentral.cl

Bank of Israel
www.bankisrael.gov.il

Bank of Finland
www.bof.fi

Reserve Bank of Australia
www.rba.gov.au

Inflation Targeting in New Zealand and the United Kingdom

Given the breakdown of the relationship between monetary aggregates and goal variables such as inflation, many countries that want to maintain an independent monetary policy have recently adopted inflation targeting as their monetary policy regime. New Zealand was the first country to formally adopt inflation targeting in 1990, with Canada following in 1991, the United Kingdom in 1992, Sweden and Finland in 1993, Australia in 1994, and Spain in 1994. Israel, Chile, and Brazil have also adopted a form of inflation targeting.

Inflation targeting involves several elements: (1) public announcement of medium-term numerical targets for inflation; (2) an institutional commitment to price stability as the primary, long-run goal of monetary policy and a commitment to achieve the inflation goal; (3) an information-inclusive strategy in which many variables and not just monetary aggregates are used in making decisions about monetary policy; (4) increased transparency of the monetary policy strategy through communication with the public and the markets about the plans and objectives of monetary policymakers; and (5) increased accountability of the central bank for attaining its inflation objectives.

We discussed Canada's experience with inflation targeting in Chapter 18. Here, we look at inflation targeting in New Zealand because it was the first country to adopt it. We then go on to look at the experience in the United Kingdom.[3]

New Zealand   As part of a general reform of the government's role in the economy, the New Zealand parliament passed a new Reserve Bank of New Zealand Act in 1989, which became effective on February 1, 1990. Besides increasing the independence of the central bank, moving it from being one of the least independent to one of the most independent among the developed countries, the act also committed the Reserve Bank to a sole objective of price stability. The act stipulated that the minister of finance and the governor of the Reserve Bank should negotiate and make public a Policy Targets Agreement, a statement that sets out the targets by which monetary policy performance will be evaluated, specifying numerical target ranges for inflation and the dates by which they are to be reached. An unusual feature of the New Zealand legislation is that the governor of the Reserve Bank is held highly accountable for the success of monetary policy. If the goals set forth in the Policy Targets Agreement are not satisfied, the governor is subject to dismissal.

The first Policy Targets Agreement, signed by the minister of finance and the governor of the Reserve Bank on March 2, 1990, directed the Reserve Bank to achieve an annual inflation rate within a 3–5% range. Subsequent agreements lowered the range to 0–2% until the end of 1996, when the range was changed to 0–3%. As a result of tight monetary policy, the inflation rate was brought down from above 5% to below 2% by the end of 1992 (see Figure 20-2, panel a), but at

---

[3]For further discussion of experiences with inflation targeting, particularly in other countries, see Leonardo Leiderman and Lars E. O. Svensson, *Inflation Targeting* (London: Centre for Economic Policy Research 1995); Frederic S. Mishkin and Adam Posen, "Inflation Targeting: Lessons from Four Countries," Federal Reserve Bank of New York, *Economic Policy Review* 3 (August 1997) pp. 9–110; and Ben S. Bernanke, Thomas Laubach, Frederic S. Mishkin, and Adam S. Posen, *Inflation Targeting: Lessons from the International Experience* (Princeton University Press: Princeton, N.J., 1999).

(a) New Zealand

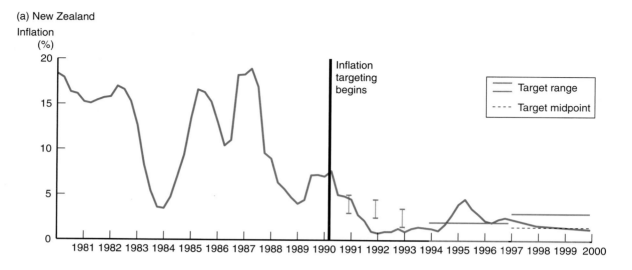

(b) United Kingdom

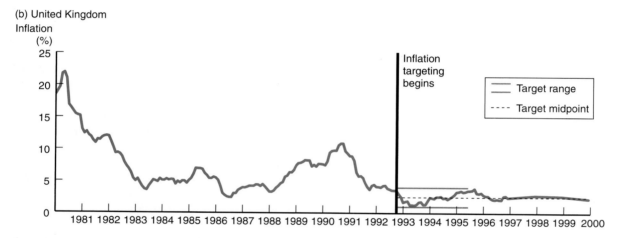

FIGURE 20-2   Inflation Rates and Inflation Targets for New Zealand and the United Kingdom, 1980–2000

Source: Ben S. Bernanke, Thomas Laubach, Frederic S. Mishkin, and Adam S. Posen, *Inflation Targeting: Lessons from the International Experience* (Princeton University Press: Princeton, N.J., 1999) and updates from the same sources.

the cost of a deep recession and a sharp rise in unemployment. Since then, inflation has typically remained within the targeted range with the exception of a brief period in 1995 when it exceeded the range by a few tenths of a percentage point. (Under the Reserve Bank Act, the governor, Donald Brash, could have been dismissed, but after parliamentary debate he was retained in his job.) Since 1992, New Zealand's growth rate has generally been very high, with some years exceeding 5%, and unemployment has come down significantly.

United Kingdom   Once the U.K. left the European Monetary System after the speculative attack on the pound in September 1992 (discussed in Chapter 19), the British decided to turn to inflation targets instead of the exchange rate as their nominal anchor. As you may recall from Chapter 14, the central bank in the U.K., the Bank of England, did not have statutory authority over monetary policy until 1997; it could only make recommendations about monetary policy. Thus it was the chancellor of the Exchequer (the equivalent of the Canadian minister of finance) who announced an inflation target for the U.K. on October 8, 1992. Three weeks later he "invited" the governor of the Bank of England to begin producing *Inflation Report*, a quarterly report on the progress being made in achieving the target—an invitation the governor accepted. The inflation target range was set at 1–4% until the next election, spring 1997 at the latest, with the intent that the inflation rate should settle down to the lower half of the range (below 2.5%). In May 1997, after the new Labour government came into power, it adopted a point target of 2.5% for inflation and gave the Bank of England the power to set interest rates henceforth, granting it a more independent role in monetary policy.

Before the adoption of inflation targets, inflation had already been falling in the U.K. from a peak of 9% at the beginning of 1991 to 4% at the time of adoption (see Figure 20-2, panel b). After a small upward movement in early 1993, inflation continued to fall until, by the third quarter of 1994, it was at 2.2%, within the intended range articulated by the chancellor. Subsequently inflation rose, climbing slightly above the 2.5% level by 1996, but has remained around the 2.5% target since then. Meanwhile, growth of the U.K. economy has been strong, causing a substantial reduction in the unemployment rate.

Advantages of Inflation Targeting

Inflation targeting has several advantages over exchange-rate and monetary targeting as a strategy for the conduct of monetary policy. In contrast to exchange-rate targeting, but like monetary targeting, inflation targeting enables monetary policy to focus on domestic considerations and to respond to shocks to the domestic economy. Inflation targeting also has the advantage that stability in the relationship between money and inflation is not critical to its success because it does not rely on this relationship. An inflation target allows the monetary authorities to use all available information, not just one variable, to determine the best settings for monetary policy.

Inflation targeting, like exchange-rate targeting, also has the key advantage that it is readily understood by the public and is thus highly transparent. Monetary targets, in contrast, are less likely to be easily understood by the public than inflation targets. Moreover, if the relationship between monetary aggregates and the inflation goal variable is subject to unpredictable shifts, as has occurred in many countries, monetary targets lose their transparency because they are no longer able to accurately signal the stance of monetary policy.

As discussed in Chapter 18, inflation-targeting regimes greatly emphasize the transparency and communication of monetary policy. This tends to increase the accountability of the central bank and has the potential to reduce the likelihood that the central bank will fall into the time-inconsistency trap. In fact, transparency and communication go hand in hand with increased accountability. The strongest case of accountability of a central bank in an inflation-targeting regime is in New Zealand, where the government has the right to dismiss the Reserve Bank's governor if the inflation targets are breached, even for one quarter. In other inflation-targeting countries, including Canada, the central bank's accountability is less formalized.

Another example illustrating the benefits of transparency and accountability in the inflation-targeting framework occurred upon the granting of operational independence to the Bank of England on May 6, 1997. Prior to that date, the government, as represented by the chancellor of the Exchequer, controlled the decision to set monetary policy instruments, while the Bank of England was relegated to acting as the government's counterinflationary conscience. On May 6, the new chancellor of the Exchequer, Gordon Brown, announced that the Bank of England would henceforth have the responsibility for setting interest rates and for engaging in short-term exchange-rate interventions. Two factors were cited by Chancellor Brown that justified the government's decision: first was the bank's successful performance over time as measured against an announced clear target; second was the increased accountability that an independent central bank is exposed to under an inflation-targeting framework, making the bank more responsive to political oversight. The granting of operational independence to the Bank of England occurred because it would operate under a monetary policy regime to ensure that monetary policy goals cannot diverge from the interest of society for extended periods of time. Nonetheless monetary policy was to be insulated from short-run political considerations. An inflation-targeting regime makes it more palatable to have an independent central bank that focuses on long-run objectives but is consistent with a democratic society because it is accountable.

The performance of inflation-targeting regimes has been quite good. Inflation-targeting countries seem to have significantly reduced both the rate of inflation and inflation expectations beyond what would likely have occurred in the absence of inflation targets. Furthermore, once down, inflation in these countries has stayed down; following disinflations, the inflation rate in targeting countries has not bounced back up during subsequent cyclical expansions of the economy. But as Charles Freedman of the Bank of Canada recently put it, "[t]his does not mean that inflation targets are necessary for achieving and maintaining low inflation. Indeed, a number of countries have posted good inflation records without them."[4]

We discussed Canada's performance in Chapter 18. Another example is the experience of the United Kingdom and Sweden following their departures from the ERM exchange-rate pegs in 1992. In both cases, devaluation would normally have stimulated inflation because of the direct effects on higher export and import prices from devaluation and the subsequent effects on wage demands and price-setting behaviour. Again it seems reasonable to attribute the lack of inflationary response in these episodes to adoption of inflation targeting, which short-circuited the second- and later-round effects and helped to focus public attention on the temporary nature of the devaluation shocks. Indeed, one reason why inflation targets were adopted in both countries was to achieve exactly this result.

Disadvantages of Inflation Targeting

As discussed in Chapter 18, inflation targeting has several disadvantages. In contrast to exchange rates and monetary aggregates, the monetary authorities do not easily control inflation, so that an inflation target cannot send immediate signals to both the public and markets. However, we have seen that the signals provided by monetary aggregates may not be very strong and that an exchange-rate peg may obscure the ability of the foreign exchange market to signal overly expansionary policies. Hence, it is not at all clear that these other strategies are superior to inflation targeting on these grounds.

It has also been argued that inflation targeting imposes a rigid rule on policymakers. As we have seen, however, inflation targeting as practiced contains a substantial degree of policy discretion. Inflation targets have been modified depending on economic circumstances and central banks under inflation-targeting regimes have left themselves considerable scope to respond to output growth and fluctuations through several devices.

Another concern about inflation targeting is that it may lead to larger output fluctuations when inflation is above target. Experience has shown, however, that inflation targeters do display substantial concern about output fluctuations. In particular, all the inflation targeters have set their inflation targets above zero to avoid the potentially substantial negative effects of low inflation on real economic activity. For example, currently New Zealand has the lowest midpoint for an inflation target, 1.5%, while Canada and Sweden set the midpoint of their inflation target at 2%, and the United Kingdom and Australia currently have their midpoint at 2.5%.

---

[4]Charles Freedman, "Inflation Targeting and the Economy: Lessons from Canada's First Decade," *Contemporary Economic Policy* 19 (2001), 2–19.

Nominal GDP Targeting

The concern that a sole focus on inflation may lead to larger output fluctuations has led some economists to propose a variation on inflation targeting in which central banks would target the growth rate of nominal GDP (real GDP times the price level) rather than inflation. Relative to inflation, nominal GDP growth has the advantage that it does put some weight on output as well as prices in the policy-making process. With a nominal GDP target, a decline in projected real output growth would automatically imply an increase in the central bank's inflation target. This increase would tend to be stabilizing because it would automatically lead to an easier monetary policy.

Nominal GDP targeting is close in spirit to inflation targeting, and although it has the advantages mentioned in the paragraph above, it has disadvantages as well. First, a nominal GDP target forces the central bank or the government to announce a number for potential (long-term) GDP growth. Such an announcement is highly problematic because estimates of potential GDP growth are far from precise and change over time. Announcing a specific number for potential GDP growth may thus indicate a certainty that policymakers do not have and may also cause the public to mistakenly believe that this estimate is actually a fixed target for potential GDP growth. Announcing a potential GDP growth number is likely to be political dynamite because it opens policymakers to the criticism that they are willing to settle for long-term growth rates that the public may consider too low. Indeed, a nominal GDP target may lead to an accusation that the central bank or the targeting regime is anti-growth, when the opposite is true because a low inflation rate is a means to promote a healthy economy with high growth. In addition, if the estimate for potential GDP growth is higher than the true potential for long-term growth and becomes embedded in the public mind as a target, it can lead to a positive inflation bias.

Second, information on prices is timelier and more frequently reported than data on nominal GDP (and could be made even more so)—a practical consideration that offsets some of the theoretical appeal of nominal GDP as a target. Although collecting data on nominal GDP could be improved, measuring nominal GDP requires data on current quantities and current prices, and the need to collect two pieces of information is perhaps intrinsically more difficult to accomplish in a timely manner.

Third, the concept of inflation in consumer prices is much better understood by the public than the concept of nominal GDP, which can easily be confused with real GDP. Consequently, it seems likely that communication with the public and accountability would be better served by using an inflation rather than a nominal GDP growth target. While a significant number of central banks have adopted inflation targeting, none has adopted a nominal GDP target.

Finally, as argued above, inflation targeting, as it is actually practiced, allows considerable flexibility for policy in the short run, and elements of monetary policy tactics based on nominal GDP targeting could easily be built into an inflation-targeting regime. Thus it is doubtful that, in practice, nominal GDP targeting would be more effective than inflation targeting in achieving short-run stabilization.

When all is said and done, inflation targeting has almost all the benefits of nominal GDP targeting, but without the problems that arise from potential confusion about what nominal GDP is or the political complications that arise because nominal GDP requires announcement of a potential GDP growth path.

MONETARY POLICY WITH AN IMPLICIT NOMINAL ANCHOR

In recent years, the United States has achieved excellent macroeconomic performance (including low and stable inflation) without using an explicit nominal anchor such as an exchange rate, a monetary aggregate, or an inflation target. Although the Federal Reserve has not articulated an explicit strategy, a coherent strategy for the conduct of monetary policy exists nonetheless. This strategy involves an implicit but not an explicit nominal anchor in the form of an overriding concern by the Federal Reserve to control inflation in the long run. In addition, it involves forward-looking behaviour in which there is careful monitoring for signs of future inflation using a wide range of information, coupled with periodic "pre-emptive strikes" by monetary policy against the threat of inflation.

As emphasized by Milton Friedman, monetary policy effects have long lags. In industrialized countries with a history of low inflation, the inflation process seems to have tremendous inertia. Estimates from large macroeconometric models of the U.S. economy, for example, suggest that monetary policy takes over a year to affect output and over two years to have a significant impact on inflation. For countries whose economies respond more quickly to exchange-rate changes or that have experienced highly variable inflation, and therefore have more flexible prices, the lags may be shorter.

The presence of long lags means that monetary policy cannot wait to respond until inflation has already reared its ugly head. If the central bank waited until overt signs of inflation appeared, it would already be too late to maintain stable prices, at least not without a severe tightening of policy: inflation expectations would already be embedded in the wage- and price-setting process, creating an inflation momentum that would be hard to halt. Inflation becomes much harder to control once it has been allowed to gather momentum because higher inflation expectations become ingrained in various types of long-term contracts and pricing agreements.

To prevent inflation from getting started, therefore, monetary policy needs to be forward-looking and pre-emptive: that is, depending on the lags from monetary policy to inflation, monetary policy needs to act well before inflationary pressures appear in the economy. For example, suppose it takes roughly two years for monetary policy to have a significant impact on inflation. In this case, even if inflation is currently low but policymakers believe inflation will rise over the next two years with an unchanged stance of monetary policy, they must *now* tighten monetary policy to prevent the inflationary surge.

Under Alan Greenspan, the Federal Reserve has been successful in pursuing a pre-emptive monetary policy. For example, the Fed raised interest rates from 1994 to 1995 before a rise in inflation got a toehold. As a result, inflation not only did not rise, but also fell slightly. This pre-emptive monetary policy strategy is clearly also a feature of inflation-targeting regimes because monetary policy instruments are adjusted to take account of the long lags in their effects in order to hit future inflation targets. However, the Fed's policy regime, which has no nominal anchor and so might best be described as a "just do it" policy, differs from inflation targeting in that it does not officially have a nominal anchor and is much less transparent in its monetary policy strategy.

Advantages of the Fed's Approach

The Fed's "just do it" approach, which has some of the key elements of inflation targeting, has many of the same advantages. It also enables monetary policy to focus on domestic considerations and does not rely on a stable money–inflation relationship. As with inflation targeting, the central bank uses many sources of information to determine the best settings for monetary policy. The Fed's forward-looking behaviour and stress on price stability also help to discourage overly expansionary monetary policy, thereby ameliorating the time-inconsistency problem.

Another key argument for the "just do it" strategy is its demonstrated success. The Federal Reserve has been able to bring down inflation in the United States from double-digit levels in 1980 to around the 3% level by the end of 1991. Since then, inflation has dropped to around the 2% level, which is arguably consistent with the price stability goal. The Fed conducted a successful pre-emptive strike against inflation from February 1994 until early 1995, when in several steps it raised the federal funds rate from 3% to 6% even though inflation was not increasing during this period. The subsequent lengthy business-cycle expansion, the longest in U.S. history, has brought unemployment down to around 4%, a level not seen since the 1960s, while CPI inflation has even fallen to a level near 2%. In addition, the overall U.S. growth rate has continued to remain strong. Indeed, the performance of the U.S. economy became the envy of the industrialized world in the 1990s.

Disadvantages of the Fed's Approach

Given the success of the "just do it" strategy in the United States, why should the United States consider other monetary policy strategies? (If it ain't broke, why fix it?) The answer is that the "just do it" strategy has some disadvantages that may cause it to work less well in the future.

One disadvantage of the strategy is a lack of transparency. The Fed's close-mouthed approach about its intentions gives rise to a constant guessing game about what it is going to do. This high level of uncertainty leads to unnecessary volatility in financial markets and creates doubt among producers and the general public about the future course of inflation and output. Furthermore, the opacity of its policymaking makes it hard to hold the Federal Reserve accountable to Congress and the general public. The Fed can't be held accountable if there are no predetermined criteria for judging its performance. Low accountability may make the central bank more susceptible to the time-inconsistency problem, whereby it may pursue short-term objectives at the expense of long-term ones.

Probably the most serious problem with the "just do it" approach is strong dependence on the preferences, skills, and trustworthiness of the individuals in charge of the central bank. In recent years in the United States, Federal Reserve Chairman Alan Greenspan and other Federal Reserve officials have emphasized forward-looking policies and inflation control, with great success. The Fed's prestige and credibility with the public have risen accordingly. But the Fed's leadership will eventually change, and there is no guarantee that the new team will be committed to the same approach. Nor is there any guarantee that the relatively good working relationship that has existed between the Fed and the executive branch will continue. In a different economic or political environment, the Fed might face strong pressure to engage in over-expansionary policies, raising the possibility that time inconsistency may become a more serious problem. In the past, after a successful period of low inflation, the Federal Reserve has reverted to inflationary monetary policy—the 1970s are one example—and without an explicit nominal anchor, this could certainly happen again.

Another disadvantage of the "just do it" approach is that it has some inconsistencies with democratic principles. As described in Chapter 14, there are good reasons, notably insulation from short-term political pressures, for the central bank to have some degree of independence, as the Federal Reserve currently does, and the evidence does generally support central bank independence. Yet the practical economic arguments for central bank independence coexist uneasily with the presumption that government policies should be made democratically, rather than by an elite group.

In contrast, inflation targeting can make the institutional framework for the conduct of monetary policy more consistent with democratic principles and avoid some of the above problems. The inflation-targeting framework promotes the accountability of the central bank to elected officials, who are given some responsibility for setting the goals for monetary policy and then monitoring the economic outcomes. However, under inflation targeting as it has generally been practiced, the central bank has complete control over operational decisions so that it can be held accountable for achieving its assigned objectives.

Inflation targeting thus can help to promote operational independence of the central bank. The example of the granting of independence to the Bank of England in 1997 indicates how inflation targeting can reduce the tensions between central bank independence and democratic principles and promote central bank independence. When operational independence was granted to the Bank of England in May 1997, the chancellor of the Exchequer made it clear that this action had been made possible by the adoption of an inflation-targeting regime, which had increased the transparency of policy and the accountability of the bank for achieving policy objectives set by the government.

The Fed's monetary policy strategy may also move more toward inflation targeting in the future. Inflation targeting is not too far from the Fed's current policymaking philosophy, which has stressed the importance of price stability as the overriding, long-run goal of monetary policy. Also, a move to inflation targeting is consistent with recent steps by the Fed to increase the transparency of monetary policy, such as shortening the time before the minutes of the FOMC meeting are released, the practice of announcing the FOMC's decision about whether to change the target for the federal funds rates immediately after the conclusion of the FOMC meeting, and the announcement of the "balance of risks" in the future, whether toward higher inflation or toward a weaker economy.

SUMMARY

1. A nominal anchor is a key element in monetary policy strategies. It helps promote price stability by tying down inflation expectations and limiting the time-inconsistency problem, in which monetary policymakers conduct monetary policy in a discretionary way that produces poor long-run outcomes.

2. Exchange-rate targeting has the following advantages: (1) it directly keeps inflation under control by tying the inflation rate for internationally traded goods to that found in the anchor country to whom its currency is pegged; (2) it provides an automatic rule for the conduct of monetary policy that helps mitigate the time-inconsistency problem; and (3) it has the advantage of simplicity and clarity. Exchange-rate targeting also has serious disadvantages: (1) it results in a loss of independent monetary policy and increases the exposure of the economy to shocks from the anchor country; (2) it leaves the currency open to speculative attacks; and (3) it can weaken the accountability of policymakers because the exchange-rate signal is lost. Two strategies that make it less likely that the exchange-rate regime will break down are currency boards, in which the central bank stands ready to automatically exchange domestic for foreign currency at a fixed rate, and dollarization, in which a sound currency like the U.S. dollar is adopted as the country's money.

3. Monetary targeting has two main advantages. It enables a central bank to adjust its monetary policy to cope with domestic considerations, and information on whether the central bank is achieving its target is known almost immediately. On the other hand, monetary targeting suffers from the disadvantage that it works well only if there is a reliable relationship between the monetary aggregate and the goal variable, inflation, a relationship that has often not held in different countries.

4. The Bank of Canada's current strategy is to target the inflation rate and the Bank's current inflation target is 2%. In setting its inflation targets, the Bank uses the rate of change in core CPI, because it excludes volatile components, and also uses the overnight interest rate as the operating target. Recently, inflation targeting has been adopted by several countries, notably, New Zealand, the United Kingdom, Sweden, Finland, and Australia, and more recently by Spain, Israel, Chile, and Brazil.

5. Inflation targeting has several advantages: (1) it enables monetary policy to focus on domestic considerations; (2) stability in the relationship between money and inflation is not critical to its success; (3) it is readily understood by the public and is highly transparent; (4) it increases accountability of the central bank; and (5) it appears to ameliorate the effects of inflationary shocks. It does have some disadvantages, however: (1) inflation is not easily controlled by the monetary authorities, so that an inflation target cannot send immediate signals to both the public and markets; (2) it might impose a rigid rule on policymakers, although this has not been the case in practice; and (3) a sole focus on inflation may lead to larger output fluctuations, although this has also not been the case in practice.

The concern that a sole focus on inflation may lead to larger output fluctuations has led some economists to propose a variant of inflation targeting, nominal GDP targeting, in which central banks target the growth in nominal GDP rather than inflation.

6. The Federal Reserve has a strategy of having an implicit, not an explicit, nominal anchor. This strategy has the following advantages: (1) it enables monetary policy to focus on domestic considerations; (2) it does not rely on a stable money–inflation relationship; and (3) it has had a demonstrated success, producing low inflation with the longest business cycle expansion since World War II. However, it does have some disadvantages: (1) it has a lack of transparency; (2) it is strongly dependent on the preferences, skills, and trustworthiness of individuals in the central bank and the government; and (3) it has some inconsistencies with democratic principles because the central bank is not highly accountable.

KEY TERMS

currency board, p. 452

dollarization, p. 453

nominal anchor, p. 447

seignorage, p. 455

time-inconsistency problem, p. 448

QUESTIONS AND PROBLEMS

Questions marked with an asterisk are answered at the end of the book in an appendix, "Answers to Selected Questions and Problems."

1. What are the benefits of using a nominal anchor for the conduct of monetary policy?

2. Give an example of the time-inconsistency problem that you experience in your everyday life.

3. What incentives arise for a central bank to engage in time-inconsistent behaviour?

*4. What are the key advantages of exchange-rate targeting as a monetary policy strategy?

5. Why did the exchange-rate peg lead to difficulties for the countries in the ERM when German reunification occurred?

*6. How can exchange-rate targets lead to a speculative attack on a currency?

7. Why may the disadvantage of exchange-rate targeting of not having an independent monetary policy be less of an issue for emerging market countries than for industrialized countries?

*8. How can the long-term bond market help reduce the time-inconsistency problem for monetary policy? Can the foreign exchange market also perform this role?

9. When is exchange-rate targeting likely to be a sensible strategy for industrialized countries? When is exchange-rate targeting likely to be a sensible strategy for emerging market countries?

*10. What are the advantages and disadvantages of a currency board over a monetary policy that just uses an exchange-rate target?

11. What are the key advantages and disadvantages of dollarization over other forms of exchange-rate targeting?

*12. What are the advantages of monetary targeting as a strategy for the conduct of monetary policy?

13. What is the big *if* necessary for the success of monetary targeting? Does the experience with monetary targeting suggest that the big *if* is a problem?

*14. What methods have inflation-targeting central banks used to increase communication with the public and increase the transparency of monetary policymaking?

15. Why might inflation targeting increase support for the independence of the central bank to conduct monetary policy?

*16. "Because the public can see whether a central bank hits its monetary targets almost immediately, whereas it takes time before the public can see whether an inflation target is achieved, monetary targeting makes central banks more accountable than inflation targeting does." True, false, or uncertain? Explain.

17. "Because inflation targeting focuses on achieving the inflation target, it will lead to excessive output fluctuations." True, false, or uncertain? Explain.

*18. What are the most important advantages and disadvantages of nominal GDP targeting over inflation targeting?

19. What are the key advantages and disadvantages of the monetary strategy used in the United States under Alan Greenspan in which the nominal anchor is only implicit?

*20. What is the advantage that monetary targeting, inflation targeting, and a monetary strategy with an implicit, but not an explicit, nominal anchor have in common?

Chapter 21

The Demand for Money

PREVIEW   In earlier chapters we spent a lot of time and effort learning what the money supply is, how it is determined, and what role the Bank of Canada plays in it. Now we are ready to explore the role of the money supply in determining the price level and total production of goods and services (aggregate output) in the economy. The study of the effect of money on the economy is called **monetary theory**, and we examine this branch of economics in the chapters of Part V.

When economists mention *supply*, the word *demand* is sure to follow, and the discussion of money is no exception. The supply of money is an essential building block in understanding how monetary policy affects the economy because it suggests the factors that influence the quantity of money in the economy. Not surprisingly, another essential part of monetary theory is the demand for money.

This chapter describes how the theories of the demand for money have evolved. We begin with the classical theories refined at the start of the twentieth century by economists such as Irving Fisher, Alfred Marshall, and A. C. Pigou; then we move on to the Keynesian theories of the demand for money. We end with Milton Friedman's modern quantity theory.

A central question in monetary theory is whether or to what extent the quantity of money demanded is affected by changes in interest rates. Because this issue is crucial to how we view money's effects on aggregate economic activity, we focus on the role of interest rates in the demand for money.[1]

QUANTITY THEORY OF MONEY

Developed by the classical economists in the nineteenth and early twentieth centuries, the quantity theory of money is a theory of how the nominal value of aggregate income is determined. Because it also tells us how much money is held for a given amount of aggregate income, it is also a theory of the demand for money.

---

[1]In Chapter 23 we will see that the responsiveness of the quantity of money demanded to changes in interest rates has important implications for the relative effectiveness of monetary policy and fiscal policy in influencing aggregate economic activity.

The most important feature of this theory is that it suggests that interest rates have no effect on the demand for money.

Velocity of Money and Equation of Exchange

The clearest exposition of the classical quantity theory approach is found in the work of the American economist Irving Fisher, in his influential book *The Purchasing Power of Money*, published in 1911. Fisher wanted to examine the link between the total quantity of money M (the money supply) and the total amount of spending on final goods and services produced in the economy $P \times Y$, where P is the price level and Y is aggregate output (income). (Total spending $P \times Y$ is also thought of as aggregate nominal income for the economy or as nominal GDP.) The concept that provides the link between M and $P \times Y$ is called the **velocity of money** (often reduced simply to *velocity*), the rate of turnover of money, that is, the average number of times per year that a dollar is spent in buying the total amount of goods and services produced in the economy. Velocity V is defined more precisely as total spending $P \times Y$ divided by the quantity of money M:

$$V = \frac{P \times Y}{M} \tag{1}$$

If, for example, nominal GDP ($P \times Y$) in a year is $5 trillion and the quantity of money is $1 trillion, velocity is 5, meaning that the average dollar bill is spent five times in purchasing final goods and services in the economy.

By multiplying both sides of this definition by M, we obtain the **equation of exchange**, which relates nominal income to the quantity of money and velocity:

$$M \times V = P \times Y \tag{2}$$

The equation of exchange thus states that the quantity of money multiplied by the number of times that this money is spent in a given year must be equal to nominal income (the total nominal amount spent on goods and services in that year).[2]

As it stands, Equation 2 is nothing more than an identity—a relationship that is true by definition. It does not tell us, for instance, that when the money supply M changes, nominal income ($P \times Y$) changes in the same direction; a rise in M, for example, could be offset by a fall in V that leaves $M \times V$ (and therefore $P \times Y$) unchanged. To convert the equation of exchange (*an identity*) into a *theory* of how nominal income is determined requires an understanding of the factors that determine velocity.

Irving Fisher reasoned that velocity is determined by the institutions in an economy that affect the way individuals conduct transactions. If people use charge accounts and credit cards to conduct their transactions and consequently use money less often when making purchases, less money is required to conduct the transactions generated by nominal income ($M\downarrow$ relative to $P \times Y$), and velocity ($P \times Y)/M$ will increase. Conversely, if it is more convenient for purchases to be

---

[2]Fisher actually first formulated the equation of exchange in terms of the nominal value of transactions in the economy PT:

$$MV_T = PT$$

where P = average price per transaction
T = number of transactions conducted in a year
$V_T = PT/M$ = transactions velocity of money

Because the nominal value of transactions T is difficult to measure, the quantity theory has been formulated in terms of aggregate output Y, as follows: T is assumed to be proportional to Y so that $T = vY$, where v is a constant of proportionality. Substituting vY for T in Fisher's equation of exchange yields $MV_T = vPY$, which can be written as Equation 2 in the text in which $V = V_T/v$.

paid for with cash or cheques (both of which are money), more money is used to conduct the transactions generated by the same level of nominal income, and velocity will fall. Fisher took the view that the institutional and technological features of the economy would affect velocity only slowly over time, so velocity would normally be reasonably constant in the short run.

Quantity Theory of Money

Fisher's view that velocity is fairly constant in the short run transforms the equation of exchange into the **quantity theory of money**, which states that nominal income is determined solely by movements in the quantity of money. When the quantity of money M doubles, $M \times V$ doubles and so must $P \times Y$, the value of nominal income. To see how this works, let's assume that velocity is 5, nominal income (GDP) is initially \$5 trillion, and the money supply is \$1 trillion. If the money supply doubles to \$2 trillion, the quantity theory of money tells us that nominal income will double to \$10 trillion (= 5 × \$2 trillion).

Because the classical economists (including Fisher) thought that wages and prices were completely flexible, they believed that the level of aggregate output Y produced in the economy during normal times would remain at the full-employment level, so Y in the equation of exchange could also be treated as reasonably constant in the short run. The quantity theory of money then implies that if M doubles, P must also double in the short run because V and Y are constant. In our example, if aggregate output is \$5 trillion, the velocity of 5 and a money supply of \$1 trillion indicate that the price level equals 1 because 1 times \$5 trillion equals the nominal income of \$5 trillion. When the money supply doubles to \$2 trillion, the price level must also double to 2 because 2 times \$5 trillion equals the nominal income of \$10 trillion.

For the classical economists, the quantity theory of money provided an explanation of movements in the price level. ***Movements in the price level result solely from changes in the quantity of money.***

Quantity Theory of Money Demand

Because the quantity theory of money tells us how much money is held for a given amount of aggregate income, it is in fact a theory of the demand for money. We can see this by dividing both sides of the equation of exchange by V, thus rewriting it as

$$M = \frac{1}{V} \times PY$$

where nominal income $P \times Y$ is written as PY. When the money market is in equilibrium, the quantity of money M that people hold equals the quantity of money demanded M^d, so we can replace M in the equation by M^d. Using k to represent the quantity $1/V$ (a constant because V is a constant), we can rewrite the equation as

$$M^d = k \times PY \tag{3}$$

Equation 3 tells us that because k is a constant, the level of transactions generated by a fixed level of nominal income PY determines the quantity of money M^d that people demand. Therefore, Fisher's quantity theory of money suggests that the demand for money is purely a function of income, and interest rates have no effect on the demand for money.

Fisher came to this conclusion because he believed that people hold money only to conduct transactions and have no freedom of action in terms of the amount they want to hold. The demand for money is determined (1) by the level of transactions generated by the level of nominal income PY and (2) by the institutions in the economy that affect the way people conduct transactions that determine velocity and hence k.

CAMBRIDGE APPROACH TO MONEY DEMAND

While Fisher was developing his quantity theory approach to the demand for money, a group of classical economists in Cambridge, England, which included Alfred Marshall and A. C. Pigou, were studying the same topic. Although their analysis led them to an equation identical to Fisher's money demand equation ($M^d = k \times PY$), their approach differed significantly. Instead of studying the demand for money by looking solely at the level of transactions and the institutions that affect the way people conduct transactions as the key determinants, the Cambridge economists asked how much money individuals would want to hold, given a set of circumstances. In the Cambridge model, then, individuals are allowed some flexibility in their decision to hold money and are not completely bound by institutional constraints such as whether they can use credit cards to make purchases. Accordingly, the Cambridge approach did not rule out the effects of interest rates on the demand for money.

The classical Cambridge economists recognized that two properties of money motivate people to want to hold it: its utility as a *medium of exchange* and as a *store of wealth*.

Because it is a medium of exchange, people can use money to carry out transactions. The Cambridge economists agreed with Fisher that the demand for money would be related to (but not determined solely by) the level of transactions and that there would be a transactions component of money demand proportional to nominal income.

That money also functions as a store of wealth led the Cambridge economists to suggest that the level of people's wealth also affects the demand for money. As wealth grows, an individual needs to store it by holding a larger quantity of assets—one of which is money. Because the Cambridge economists believed that wealth in nominal terms is proportional to nominal income, they also believed that the wealth component of money demand is proportional to nominal income.

Concluding that the demand for money would be proportional to nominal income, the Cambridge economists expressed the demand for money function as

$$M^d = k \times PY$$

where k is the constant of proportionality. Because this equation looks just like Fisher's (Equation 3), it would seem that the Cambridge group agreed with Fisher that interest rates play no role in the demand for money in the short run. However, that is not the case.

Although the Cambridge economists often treated k as a constant and agreed with Fisher that nominal income is determined by the quantity of money, their approach allowed individuals to choose how much money they wished to hold. It allowed for the possibility that k could fluctuate in the short run because the decisions about using money to store wealth would depend on the yields and expected returns on other assets that also function as stores of wealth. If these characteristics of other assets changed, k might change too. Although this seems a minor distinction between the Fisher and Cambridge approaches, you will see that when John Maynard Keynes (a later Cambridge economist) extended the Cambridge approach, he arrived at a view very different from that of the quantity theorists on the importance of interest rates to the demand for money.

To summarize, both Irving Fisher and the Cambridge economists developed a classical approach to the demand for money in which the demand for money is proportional to income. However, the two approaches differ in that Fisher's emphasized technological factors and ruled out any possible effect of interest rates on the demand for money in the short run, whereas the Cambridge approach emphasized individual choice and did not rule out the effects of interest rates.

IS VELOCITY A CONSTANT?

The classical economists' conclusion that nominal income is determined by movements in the money supply rested on their belief that velocity PY/M could be treated as reasonably constant.[3] Is it reasonable to assume that velocity is constant? To answer this, let's look at Figure 21-1, which shows the year-to-year changes in velocity from 1915 to 2000 (nominal income is represented by nominal GDP and the money supply by M1 and M2).

What we see in Figure 21-1 is that even in the short run, velocity fluctuates too much to be viewed as a constant. Prior to 1960, velocity exhibited large swings up and down. This may reflect the substantial instability of the economy in this period, which included two world wars and the Great Depression. (Velocity actually falls, or at least its rate of growth declines, in years when recessions are taking place.) After 1960, velocity appears to have more moderate fluctuations, yet there are large differences in the growth rate of velocity from year to year. The percentage change in M1 velocity (GDP/M1) from 1981 to 1982, for example, was 5.4%, whereas from 1980 to 1981 velocity grew at a rate of 10.8%. This difference of 5.4% means that nominal GDP was 5.4% lower than it would have been if velocity had kept growing at the same rate as in 1980–1981.[4] The drop is enough to

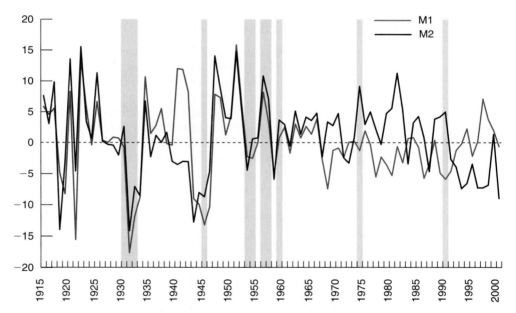

FIGURE 21-1   Change in the Velocity of M1 and M2 from Year to Year, 1915–2000
Shaded areas indicate recessions.

Source: From 1914 to 1967 the M1 and M2 series are from Cherie Metcalf, Angela Redish, and Ronald Shearer, "New Estimates of the Canadian Money Stock: 1871-1967," The University of British Columbia, Discussion Paper No.: 96-17. From 1968 to 2000 they are Statistics Canada CANSIM Series B1627 and B1630. From 1914 to 1967 the GDP series is from M. C. Urquhart, "Canadian Economic Growth, 1870-1985," Institute for Economic Research, Queen's University, Discussion Paper No.: 734. From 1968 to 2000 it is Statistics Canada CANSIM Series D14841.

---

[3]Actually, the classical conclusion still holds if velocity grows at some uniform rate over time that reflects changes in transaction technology. Hence the concept of a constant velocity should more accurately be thought of here as a lack of upward and downward fluctuations in velocity.

[4]However, we do not reach a similar conclusion if we use M2 velocity. The percentage change in M2 velocity (GDP/M2) from 1981 to 1982 was –3.3%, whereas from 1980 to 1981 it was –0.8%. This difference of 2.5% means that nominal GDP was 2.5% lower than it would have been if M2 velocity had kept growing at the same rate as in 1980–1981.

account for the severe recession that took place in 1981–1982. After 1982, velocity (however measured) appears to have become even more volatile, a fact that has puzzled researchers when they examine the empirical evidence on the demand for money (discussed later in this chapter). This led the Bank of Canada to abandon the monetarist prescription and its belief in targeting the money supply, due to a lack of success by this approach in controlling inflation.

Until the Great Depression, economists did not recognize that velocity declines sharply during severe economic contractions. Why did the classical economists not recognize this fact when it is easy to see in the pre-depression period in Figure 21-1? Unfortunately, accurate data on GDP and the money supply did not exist before World War II. (Only after the war did the government start to collect these data.) Economists had no way of knowing that their view of velocity as a constant was demonstrably false. The decline in velocity during the Great Depression years was so great, however, that even the crude data available to economists at that time suggested that velocity was not constant. This explains why, after the Great Depression, economists began to search for other factors influencing the demand for money that might help explain the large fluctuations in velocity.

Let us now examine the theories of money demand that arose from this search for a better explanation of the behaviour of velocity.

KEYNES'S LIQUIDITY PREFERENCE THEORY

In his famous 1936 book *The General Theory of Employment, Interest, and Money,* John Maynard Keynes abandoned the classical view that velocity was a constant and developed a theory of money demand that emphasized the importance of interest rates. Keynes, at Cambridge at the time, naturally enough followed the approach developed by his Cambridge predecessors. His theory of the demand for money, which he called the **liquidity preference theory**, also asked the question, why do individuals hold money? But Keynes was far more precise than his predecessors regarding what influences the individuals' decisions. He postulated that there are three motives behind the demand for money: the transactions motive, the precautionary motive, and the speculative motive.

Transactions Motive

In both the Fisher and the Cambridge classical approaches, individuals are assumed to hold money because it is a medium of exchange that can be used to carry out everyday transactions. Following the classical tradition, Keynes emphasized that this component of the demand for money is determined primarily by the level of people's transactions. Because he believed that these transactions were proportional to income, like the classical economists he took the transactions component of the demand for money to be proportional to income.

Precautionary Motive

Keynes went beyond the classical analysis by recognizing that in addition to holding money to carry out current transactions, people hold money as a cushion against an unexpected need. Suppose that you've been thinking about buying a fancy stereo; you walk by a store that is having a 50%-off sale on the one you want. If you are holding money as a precaution for just such an occurrence, you can purchase the stereo right away; if you are not holding precautionary money balances, you cannot take advantage of the sale. Precautionary money balances also come in handy if you are hit with an unexpected bill, say for car repair or hospitalization.

Keynes believed that the amount of precautionary money balances people want to hold is determined primarily by the level of transactions that they expect to make in the future and that these transactions are proportional to income. Therefore, he postulated, the demand for precautionary money balances is proportional to income.

Speculative Motive

If Keynes had ended his theory with the transactions and precautionary motives, income would be the only important determinant of the demand for money, and he would not have added much to the Cambridge approach. However, Keynes agreed with the classical Cambridge economists that money is a store of wealth and called this reason for holding money the speculative motive. Since he also agreed with the classical Cambridge economists that wealth is tied closely to income, the speculative component of money demand would be related to income. However, Keynes looked more carefully at the factors that influence the decisions regarding how much money to hold as a store of wealth. Unlike the classical Cambridge economists, who were willing to treat the wealth component of money demand as proportional to income, Keynes believed that interest rates, too, have an important role to play.

Keynes divided the assets that can be used to store wealth into two categories: money and bonds. He then asked the following question: why would individuals decide to hold their wealth in the form of money rather than bonds?

Thinking back to the discussion of the theory of asset demand (Chapter 5), you would want to hold money if its expected return was greater than the expected return from holding bonds. Keynes assumed that the expected return on money was zero because in his time, unlike today, most chequable deposits did not earn interest. For bonds, there are two components of the expected return: the interest payment and the *expected* rate of capital gains.

You learned in Chapter 4 that when interest rates rise, the price of a bond falls. If you expect interest rates to rise, you expect the price of the bond to fall and therefore suffer a negative capital gain—that is, a capital loss. If you expect the rise in interest rates to be substantial enough, the capital loss might outweigh the interest payment, and your *expected* return on the bond might be negative. In this case, you would want to store your wealth as money because its expected return is higher; its zero return exceeds the negative return on the bond.

Keynes assumed that individuals believe that interest rates gravitate to some normal value (an assumption less plausible in today's world). If interest rates are below this normal value, individuals expect the interest rate on bonds to rise in the future and so expect to suffer capital losses on them. As a result, individuals will be more likely to hold their wealth as money rather than bonds, and the demand for money will be high.

What would you expect to happen to the demand for money when interest rates are above the normal value? In general, people will expect interest rates to fall, bond prices to rise, and capital gains to be realized. At higher interest rates, they are more likely to expect the return from holding a bond to be positive, thus exceeding the expected return from holding money. They will be more likely to hold bonds than money, and the demand for money will be quite low. From Keynes's reasoning we can conclude that as interest rates rise, the demand for money falls, and therefore ***money demand is negatively related to the level of interest rates.***

Putting the Three Motives Together

In putting the three motives for holding money balances together into a demand for money equation, Keynes was careful to distinguish between nominal quantities and real quantities. Money is valued in terms of what it can buy. If, for example, all prices in the economy double (the price level doubles), the same nominal quantity of money will be able to buy only half as many goods. Keynes thus reasoned that people want to hold a certain amount of **real money balances** (the quantity of money in real terms)—an amount that his three motives indicated would be related to real income Y and to interest rates i. Keynes wrote down the following demand for money equation, known as the *liquidity preference function*, which says that the demand for real money balances M^d/P is a function of (related to) i and Y:[5]

$$\frac{M^d}{P} = f(\underset{-}{i}, \underset{+}{Y})$$

(4)

The minus sign below i in the liquidity preference function means that the demand for real money balances is negatively related to the interest rate i, and the plus sign below Y means that the demand for real money balances and real income Y are positively related. This money demand function is the same one that was used in our analysis of money demand discussed in Chapter 5.

Keynes's conclusion that the demand for money is related not only to income but also to interest rates is a major departure from Fisher's view of money demand, in which interest rates can have no effect on the demand for money, but it is less of a departure from the Cambridge approach, which did not rule out possible effects of interest rates. However, the classical Cambridge economists did not explore the explicit effects of interest rates on the demand for money.

By deriving the liquidity preference function for velocity PY/M, we can see that Keynes's theory of the demand for money implies that velocity is not constant but instead fluctuates with movements in interest rates. The liquidity preference equation can be rewritten as

$$\frac{P}{M^d} = \frac{1}{f(i, Y)}$$

Multiplying both sides of this equation by Y and recognizing that M^d can be replaced by M because they must be equal in money market equilibrium, we solve for velocity:

$$V = \frac{PY}{M} = \frac{Y}{f(i, Y)}$$

(5)

We know that the demand for money is negatively related to interest rates; when i goes up, $f(i, Y)$ declines, and therefore velocity rises. In other words, a rise in interest rates encourages people to hold lower real money balances for a given level of income; therefore, the rate of turnover of money (velocity) must be higher. This reasoning implies that because interest rates have substantial fluctuations, the liquidity preference theory of the demand for money indicates that velocity has substantial fluctuations as well.

An interesting feature of Equation 5 is that it explains some of the velocity movements in Figure 21-1, in which we noted that when recessions occur, velocity falls or its rate of growth declines. What fact regarding the cyclical behaviour of interest rates that we discussed in Chapter 5 might help us explain this phenomenon? You might recall that interest rates are procyclical, rising in expansions and falling in recessions. The liquidity preference theory indicates that a rise in interest rates will cause velocity to rise also. The procyclical movements of interest rates should induce procyclical movements in velocity, and that is exactly what we see in Figure 21-1.

Keynes's model of the speculative demand for money provides another reason why velocity might show substantial fluctuations. What would happen to the demand for money if the view of the normal level of interest rates changes? For

---

[5]The classical economists' money demand equation can also be written in terms of real money balances by dividing both sides of Equation 3 by the price level P to obtain

$$\frac{M^d}{P} = k \times Y$$

example, what if people expect the future normal interest rate to be higher than the current normal interest rate? Because interest rates are then expected to be higher in the future, more people will expect the prices of bonds to fall and will anticipate capital losses. The expected returns from holding bonds will decline, and money will become more attractive relative to bonds. As a result, the demand for money will increase. This means that $f(i, Y)$ will increase and so velocity will fall. Velocity will change as expectations about future normal levels of interest rates change, and unstable expectations about future movements in normal interest rates can lead to instability of velocity. This is one more reason why Keynes rejected the view that velocity could be treated as a constant.

Study Guide | Keynes's explanation of how interest rates affect the demand for money will be easier to understand if you think of yourself as an investor who is trying to decide whether to invest in bonds or to hold money. Ask yourself what you would do if you expected the normal interest rate to be lower in the future than it is currently. Would you rather be holding bonds or money?

To sum up, Keynes's liquidity preference theory is an extension of the classical Cambridge approach but is far more precise about the reasons why people hold money. Specifically, Keynes postulated three motives for holding money: the transactions motive, the precautionary motive, and the speculative motive. Although Keynes took the transactions and precautionary components of the demand for money to be proportional to income, he reasoned that the speculative motive would be negatively related to the level of interest rates.

Keynes's model of the demand for money has the important implication that velocity is not constant but instead is positively related to interest rates, which fluctuate substantially. His theory also rejected the constancy of velocity because changes in people's expectations about the normal level of interest rates would cause shifts in the demand for money that would cause velocity to shift as well. Thus Keynes's liquidity preference theory casts doubt on the classical quantity theory that nominal income is determined primarily by movements in the quantity of money.

FURTHER DEVELOPMENTS IN THE KEYNESIAN APPROACH

After World War II, economists began to take the Keynesian approach to the demand for money even further by developing more precise theories to explain the three Keynesian motives for holding money. Because interest rates were viewed as a crucial element in monetary theory, a key focus of this research was to understand better the role of interest rates in the demand for money.

Transactions Demand

William Baumol and James Tobin independently developed similar demand for money models, which demonstrated that even money balances held for transactions purposes are sensitive to the level of interest rates.[6] In developing their models, they considered a hypothetical individual who receives a payment once a

---

[6]William J. Baumol, "The Transactions Demand for Cash: An Inventory Theoretic Approach," *Quarterly Journal of Economics* 66 (1952): 545–556; James Tobin, "The Interest Elasticity of the Transactions Demand for Cash," *Review of Economics and Statistics* 38 (1956): 241–247.

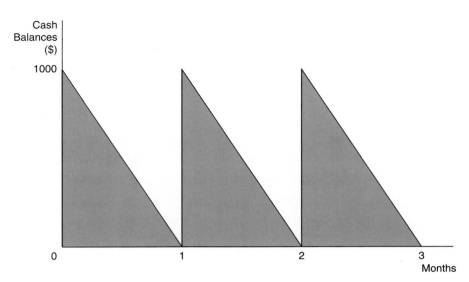

FIGURE 21-2   Cash Balances for an Individual Who Keeps the Entire Monthly Payment in Cash

The $1000 payment at the beginning of each month is held entirely as cash and is spent at a constant rate until it is exhausted by the end of the month. At this point, a new $1000 payment is received, and the whole process begins again.

period and spends it over the course of this period. In their model, money, which earns zero interest, is held only because it can be used to carry out transactions.

To refine this analysis, let's say that Grant Smith receives $1000 at the beginning of the month and spends it on transactions that occur at a constant rate during the course of the month. If Grant keeps the $1000 in cash in order to carry out his transactions, his money balances follow the sawtooth pattern displayed in Figure 21-2. At the beginning of the month he has $1000, and by the end of the month he has no cash left because he has spent it all. Over the course of the month, his holdings of money will on average be $500 (his holdings at the beginning of the month, $1000, plus his holdings at the end of the month, $0, divided by 2).

At the beginning of the next month, Grant receives another $1000 payment, which he holds as cash, and the same decline in money balances begins again. This process repeats monthly, and his average money balance during the course of the year is $500. Since his yearly nominal income is $12 000 and his holdings of money average $500, the velocity of money ($V = PY/M$) is $12 000/$500 = 24.

Suppose that as a result of taking a money and banking course, Grant realizes that he can improve his situation by not always holding cash. In January, then, he decides to hold part of his $1000 in cash and puts part of it into an income-earning security such as bonds. At the beginning of each month, Grant keeps $500 in cash and uses the other $500 to buy a Treasury bond. As you can see in Figure 21-3, he starts out each month with $500 of cash and $500 of bonds, and by the middle of the month, his cash balance has run down to zero. Because bonds cannot be used directly to carry out transactions, Grant must sell them and turn them into cash so that he can carry out the rest of the month's transactions. At the middle of the month, then, Grant's bond holdings drop to zero and his cash balance rises back up to $500. By the end of the month, the cash is gone. When he again receives his next $1000 monthly payment, he again divides it into $500 of cash and $500 of bonds, and the process continues. The net result of this process is that the average cash balance held

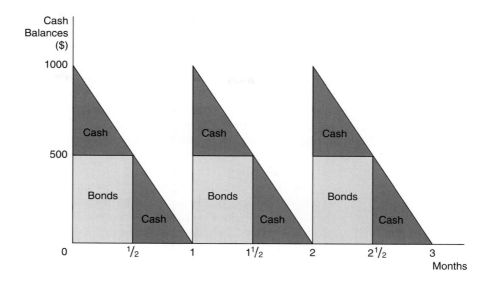

FIGURE 21-3 Cash and Bond Balances for an Individual Who Keeps Only Half the Monthly Payment in Cash

Half of a monthly $1000 payment is put into bonds, and half is held as cash. At the middle of the month, cash balances reach zero, and bonds must be sold to bring balances up to $500. By the end of the month, cash balances dwindle to zero.

during the month is $500/2 = $250—just half of what it was before. Velocity has doubled to $12 000/$250 = 48.

What has Grant Smith gained from his new strategy? He has earned interest on $500 of bonds that he held for half the month. If the interest rate is 1% per month, he has earned an additional $2.50 (= $\frac{1}{2}$ × $500 × 1%) per month.

Sounds like a pretty good deal, doesn't it? In fact, if he had kept $333.33 in cash at the beginning of the month, he would have been able to hold $666.67 in bonds for the first third of the month. Then he could have sold $333.33 of bonds and held on to $333.34 of bonds for the next third of the month. Finally, two-thirds of the way through the month, he would have had to sell the remaining bonds to raise cash. The net result of this is that Grant would have earned $3.33 per month [= ($\frac{1}{3}$ × $666.67 × 1%) + ($\frac{1}{3}$ × $333.34 × 1%)]. This is an even better deal. His average cash holdings in this case would be $333.33/2 = $166.67. Clearly, the lower his average cash balance, the more interest he will earn.

As you might expect, there is a catch to all this. In buying bonds, Grant incurs transaction costs of two types. First, he must pay a straight brokerage fee for the buying and selling of the bonds. These fees increase when average cash balances are lower because Grant will be buying and selling bonds more often. Second, by holding less cash, he will have to make more trips to the bank to get the cash, once he has sold some of his bonds. Because time is money, this must also be counted as part of the transaction costs.

Grant faces a trade-off. If he holds very little cash, he can earn a lot of interest on bonds, but he will incur greater transaction costs. If the interest rate is high, the benefits of holding bonds will be high relative to the transaction costs, and he will hold more bonds and less cash. Conversely, if interest rates are low, the transaction costs involved in holding a lot of bonds may outweigh the interest payments, and Grant would then be better off holding more cash and fewer bonds.

The conclusion of the Baumol-Tobin analysis may be stated as follows: as interest rates increase, the amount of cash held for transactions purposes will decline, which in turn means that velocity will increase as interest rates increase.[7] Put another way, the ***transactions component of the demand for money is negatively related to the level of interest rates***.

The basic idea in the Baumol-Tobin analysis is that there is an opportunity cost of holding money—the interest that can be earned on other assets. There is also a benefit to holding money—the avoidance of transaction costs. When interest rates increase, people will try to economize on their holdings of money for transactions purposes because the opportunity cost of holding money has increased. By using simple models, Baumol and Tobin revealed something that we might not otherwise have seen: that the transactions demand for money, and not just the speculative demand, will be sensitive to interest rates. The Baumol-Tobin analysis presents a nice demonstration of the value of economic modelling.

Study Guide

The idea that as interest rates increase, the opportunity cost of holding money increases so that the demand for money falls can be stated equivalently with the terminology of expected returns used earlier. As interest rates increase, the expected return on the other asset, bonds, increases, causing the relative expected return on money to fall, thereby lowering the demand for money. These two explanations are in fact identical because as we saw in Chapter 5, changes in the opportunity cost of an asset are just a description of what is happening to the relative expected return. Baumol and Tobin used the opportunity cost terminology in their work on the transactions demand for money, and that is why we used this terminology in the text. To make sure you understand the equivalence of the two terminologies, try to translate the reasoning in the precautionary demand discussion from opportunity cost terminology to expected returns terminology.

Precautionary Demand

Models that explore the precautionary motive of the demand for money have been developed along lines similar to the Baumol-Tobin framework, so we will not go into great detail about them here. We have already discussed the benefits of holding precautionary money balances, but weighed against these benefits must be the opportunity cost of the interest forgone by holding money. We therefore have a trade-off similar to the one for transactions balances. As interest rates rise, the opportunity cost of holding precautionary balances rises, and so the holdings of these money balances fall. We then have a result similar to the one found for the Baumol-Tobin analysis.[8] ***The precautionary demand for money is negatively related to interest rates.***

---

[7]Similar reasoning leads to the conclusion that as brokerage fees increase, the demand for transactions money balances increases as well. When these fees rise, the benefits from holding transactions money balances increase because by holding these balances an individual will not have to sell bonds as often, thereby avoiding these higher brokerage costs. The greater benefits to holding money balances relative to the opportunity cost of interest forgone, then, lead to a higher demand for transactions balances.

[8]These models of the precautionary demand for money also reveal that as uncertainty about the level of future transactions grows, the precautionary demand for money increases. This is so because greater uncertainty means that individuals are more likely to incur transaction costs if they are not holding precautionary balances. The benefit of holding such balances then increases relative to the opportunity cost of forgone interest, and so the demand for them rises.

Speculative Demand

Keynes's analysis of the speculative demand for money was open to several serious criticisms. It indicated that an individual holds only money as a store of wealth when the expected return on bonds is less than the expected return on money and holds only bonds when the expected return on bonds is greater than the expected return on money. Solely in the rare instance when people have expected returns on bonds and money that are exactly equal would they hold both. Keynes's analysis therefore implies that practically no one holds a diversified portfolio of bonds and money simultaneously as a store of wealth. Since diversification is apparently a sensible strategy for choosing which assets to hold, the fact that it rarely occurs in Keynes's analysis is a serious shortcoming of his theory of the speculative demand for money.

Tobin developed a model of the speculative demand for money that attempted to avoid this criticism of Keynes's analysis.[9] His basic idea was that not only do people care about the expected return on one asset versus another when they decide what to hold in their portfolio, but they also care about the riskiness of the returns from each asset. Specifically, Tobin assumed that most people are risk-averse—that they would be willing to hold an asset with a lower expected return if it is less risky. An important characteristic of money is that its return is certain; Tobin assumed it to be zero. Bonds, by contrast, can have substantial fluctuations in price, and their returns can be quite risky and sometimes negative. So even if the expected returns on bonds exceed the expected return on money, people might still want to hold money as a store of wealth because it has less risk associated with its return than bonds do.

The Tobin analysis also shows that people can reduce the total amount of risk in a portfolio by diversifying, that is, by holding both bonds and money. The model suggests that individuals will hold bonds and money simultaneously as stores of wealth. Since this is probably a more realistic description of people's behaviour than Keynes's, Tobin's rationale for the speculative demand for money seems to rest on more solid ground.

Tobin's attempt to improve on Keynes's rationale for the speculative demand for money was only partly successful, however. It is still not clear that the speculative demand even exists. What if there are assets that have no risk—like money—but earn a higher return? Will there be any speculative demand for money? No, because an individual will always be better off holding such an asset rather than money. The resulting portfolio will enjoy a higher expected return yet has no higher risk. Do such assets exist in the Canadian economy? The answer is yes. Canadian Treasury bills, money market mutual fund shares, and other assets that have no default risk provide certain returns that are greater than those available on money. Therefore, why would anyone want to hold money balances as a store of wealth (ignoring for the moment transactions and precautionary reasons)?

Although Tobin's analysis did not explain why money is held as a store of wealth, it was an important development in our understanding of how people should choose among assets. Indeed, his analysis was an important step in the development of the academic field of finance, which examines asset pricing and portfolio choice (the decision to buy one asset over another).

To sum up, further developments of the Keynesian approach have attempted to give a more precise explanation for the transactions, precautionary, and speculative demand for money. The attempt to improve Keynes's rationale for the speculative demand for money has been only partly successful; it is still not clear that this demand

---

[9]James Tobin, "Liquidity Preference as Behaviour Towards Risk," *Review of Economic Studies* 25 (1958): 65–86.

even exists. However, the models of the transactions and precautionary demand for money indicate that these components of money demand are negatively related to interest rates. Hence Keynes's proposition that the demand for money is sensitive to interest rates—suggesting that velocity is not constant and that nominal income might be affected by factors other than the quantity of money—is still supported.

FRIEDMAN'S MODERN QUANTITY THEORY OF MONEY

In 1956, Milton Friedman developed a theory of the demand for money in a famous article, "The Quantity Theory of Money: A Restatement."[10] Although Friedman frequently refers to Irving Fisher and the quantity theory, his analysis of the demand for money is actually closer to that of Keynes and the Cambridge economists than it is to Fisher's.

Like his predecessors, Friedman pursued the question of why people choose to hold money. Instead of analyzing the specific motives for holding money, as Keynes did, Friedman simply stated that the demand for money must be influenced by the same factors that influence the demand for any asset. Friedman then applied the theory of asset demand to money.

The theory of asset demand (Chapter 5) indicates that the demand for money should be a function of the resources available to individuals (their wealth) and the expected returns on other assets relative to the expected return on money. Like Keynes, Friedman recognized that people want to hold a certain amount of real money balances (the quantity of money in real terms). From this reasoning, Friedman expressed his formulation of the demand for money as follows:

$$\frac{M^d}{P} = f(\overset{+}{Y_p}, \overset{-}{r_b - r_m}, \overset{-}{r_e - r_m}, \overset{-}{\pi^e - r_m}) \tag{6}$$

where M^d/P = demand for real money balances

Y_p = Friedman's measure of wealth, known as *permanent income* (technically, the present discounted value of all expected future income, but more easily described as expected average long-run income)

r_m = expected return on money

r_b = expected return on bonds

r_e = expected return on equity (common stocks)

π^e = expected inflation rate

and the signs underneath the equation indicate whether the demand for money is positively (+) related or negatively (−) related to the terms that are immediately above them.[11]

Let us look in more detail at the variables in Friedman's money demand function and what they imply for the demand for money.

Because the demand for an asset is positively related to wealth, money demand is positively related to Friedman's wealth concept, permanent income (indicated by the plus sign beneath it). Unlike our usual concept of income, permanent

---

[10]Milton Friedman, "The Quantity Theory of Money: A Restatement," in *Studies in the Quantity Theory of Money*, ed. Milton Friedman (Chicago: University of Chicago Press, 1956), pp. 3–21.

[11]Friedman also added to his formulation a term *h* that represented the ratio of human to nonhuman wealth. He reasoned that if people had more permanent income coming from labour income and thus from their human capital, they would be less liquid than if they were receiving income from financial assets. In this case, they might want to hold more money because it is a more liquid asset than the alternatives. The term *h* plays no essential role in Friedman's theory and has no important implications for monetary theory. That is why we ignore it in the money demand function.

income (which can be thought of as expected average long-run income) has much smaller short-run fluctuations because many movements of income are transitory (short-lived). For example, in a business cycle expansion, income increases rapidly, but because some of this increase is temporary, average long-run income does not change very much. Hence in a boom, permanent income rises much less than income. During a recession, much of the income decline is transitory, and average long-run income (hence permanent income) falls less than income. One implication of Friedman's use of the concept of permanent income as a determinant of the demand for money is that the demand for money will not fluctuate much with business cycle movements.

An individual can hold wealth in several forms besides money; Friedman categorized them into three types of assets: bonds, equity (common stocks), and goods. The incentives for holding these assets rather than money are represented by the expected return on each of these assets relative to the expected return on money, the last three terms in the money demand function. The minus sign beneath each indicates that as each term rises, the demand for money will fall.

The expected return on money r_m, which appears in all three terms, is influenced by two factors:

1. The services provided by banks on deposits included in the money supply, such as provision of receipts in the form of cancelled cheques or the automatic paying of bills. When these services are increased, the expected return from holding money rises.

2. The interest payments on money balances. Deposits that are included in the money supply currently pay interest. As these interest payments rise, the expected return on money rises.

The terms $r_b - r_m$ and $r_e - r_m$ represent the expected return on bonds and equity relative to money; as they rise, the relative expected return on money falls, and the demand for money falls. The final term, $\pi^e - r_m$, represents the expected return on goods relative to money. The expected return from holding goods is the expected rate of capital gains that occurs when their prices rise and hence is equal to the expected inflation rate π^e. If the expected inflation rate is 10%, for example, then goods' prices are expected to rise at a 10% rate, and their expected return is 10%. When $\pi^e - r_m$ rises, the expected return on goods relative to money rises, and the demand for money falls.

DISTINGUISHING BETWEEN THE FRIEDMAN AND KEYNESIAN THEORIES

There are several differences between Friedman's theory of the demand for money and the Keynesian theories. One is that by including many assets as alternatives to money, Friedman recognized that more than one interest rate is important to the operation of the aggregate economy. Keynes, for his part, lumped financial assets other than money into one big category—bonds—because he felt that their returns generally move together. If this is so, the expected return on bonds will be a good indicator of the expected return on other financial assets, and there will be no need to include them separately in the money demand function.

Also in contrast to Keynes, Friedman viewed money and goods as substitutes; that is, people choose between them when deciding how much money to hold. That is why Friedman included the expected return on goods relative to money as a term in his money demand function. The assumption that money and goods are substitutes indicates that changes in the quantity of money may have a direct effect on aggregate spending.

In addition, Friedman stressed two issues in discussing his demand for money function that distinguish it from Keynes's liquidity preference theory. First, Friedman did not take the expected return on money to be a constant, as Keynes did. When interest rates rise in the economy, banks make more profits on their loans, and they want to attract more deposits to increase the volume of their now more profitable loans. If there are no restrictions on interest payments on deposits, banks attract deposits by paying higher interest rates on them. Because the industry is competitive, the expected return on money held as bank deposits then rises with the higher interest rates on bonds and loans. The banks compete to get deposits until there are no excess profits, and in doing so they close the gap between interest earned on loans and interest paid on deposits. The net result of this competition in the banking industry is that $r_b - r_m$ stays relatively constant when the interest rate i rises.[12]

What if there are restrictions on the amount of interest that banks can pay on their deposits? Will the expected return on money be a constant? As interest rates rise, will $r_b - r_m$ rise as well? Friedman thought not. He argued that although banks might be restricted from making pecuniary payments on their deposits, they could still compete on the quality dimension. For example, they can provide more services to depositors by hiring more tellers, paying bills automatically, or making more cash machines available at more accessible locations. The result of these improvements in money services is that the expected return from holding deposits will rise. So despite the restrictions on pecuniary interest payments, we might still find that a rise in market interest rates will raise the expected return on money sufficiently so that $r_b - r_m$ will remain relatively constant. ***Unlike Keynes's theory, which indicates that interest rates are an important determinant of the demand for money, Friedman's theory suggests that changes in interest rates should have little effect on the demand for money.***

Therefore, Friedman's money demand function is essentially one in which permanent income is the primary determinant of money demand, and his money demand equation can be approximated by

$$\frac{M^d}{P} = f(Y_p) \tag{7}$$

In Friedman's view, the demand for money is insensitive to interest rates—not because he viewed the demand for money as insensitive to changes in the incentives for holding other assets relative to money but rather because changes in interest rates should have little effect on these incentive terms in the money demand function. The incentive terms remain relatively constant because any rise in the expected returns on other assets as a result of the rise in interest rates would be matched by a rise in the expected return on money.

The second issue Friedman stressed is the stability of the demand for money function. In contrast to Keynes, Friedman suggested that random fluctuations in the demand for money are small and that the demand for money can be predicted accurately by the money demand function. When combined with his view that the demand for money is insensitive to changes in interest rates, this means that velocity is highly predictable. We can see this by writing down the velocity that is implied by the money demand equation (7):

$$V = \frac{Y}{f(Y_p)} \tag{8}$$

[12]Friedman does suggest that there is some increase in $r_b - r_m$ when i rises because part of the money supply (especially currency) is held in forms that cannot pay interest in a pecuniary or nonpecuniary form. See, for example, Milton Friedman, "Why a Surge of Inflation Is Likely Next Year," *Wall Street Journal*, September 1, 1983, p. 24.

Because the relationship between Y and Y_p is usually quite predictable, a stable money demand function (one that does not undergo pronounced shifts so that it predicts the demand for money accurately) implies that velocity is predictable as well. If we can predict what velocity will be in the next period, a change in the quantity of money will produce a predictable change in aggregate spending. Even though velocity is no longer assumed to be constant, the money supply continues to be the primary determinant of nominal income as in the quantity theory of money. Therefore, Friedman's theory of money demand is indeed a restatement of the quantity theory because it leads to the same conclusion about the importance of money to aggregate spending.

You may recall that we said that the Keynesian liquidity preference function (in which interest rates are an important determinant of the demand for money) can explain the procyclical movements of velocity that we find in the data. Can Friedman's money demand formulation explain this procyclical velocity phenomenon as well?

The key clue to answering this question is the presence of permanent income rather than measured income in the money demand function. What happens to permanent income in a business cycle expansion? Because much of the increase in income will be transitory, permanent income rises much less than income. Friedman's money demand function then indicates that the demand for money rises only a small amount relative to the rise in measured income, and as Equation 8 indicates, velocity rises. Similarly, in a recession, the demand for money falls less than income because the decline in permanent income is small relative to income, and velocity falls. In this way, we have the procyclical movement in velocity.

To summarize, Friedman's theory of the demand for money used a similar approach to that of Keynes and the earlier Cambridge economists but did not go into detail about the motives for holding money. Instead, Friedman made use of the theory of asset demand to indicate that the demand for money will be a function of permanent income and the expected returns on alternative assets relative to the expected return on money. There are two major differences between Friedman's theory and Keynes's. Friedman believed that changes in interest rates have little effect on the expected returns on other assets relative to money. Thus, in contrast to Keynes, he viewed the demand for money as insensitive to interest rates. In addition, he differed from Keynes in stressing that the money demand function does not undergo substantial shifts and so is stable. These two differences also indicate that velocity is predictable, yielding a quantity theory conclusion that money is the primary determinant of aggregate spending.

EMPIRICAL EVIDENCE ON THE DEMAND FOR MONEY

As we have seen, the alternative theories of the demand for money can have very different implications for our view of the role of money in the economy. Which of these theories is an accurate description of the real world is an important question, and it is the reason why evidence on the demand for money has been at the centre of many debates on the effects of monetary policy on aggregate economic activity. Here we examine the empirical evidence in the United States and Canada on the two primary issues that distinguish the different theories of money demand and affect their conclusions about whether the quantity of money is the primary determinant of aggregate spending. Is the demand for money sensitive to changes in interest rates, and is the demand for money function stable over time?

Interest Rates and Money Demand

Earlier in the chapter we saw that if interest rates do not affect the demand for money, velocity is more likely to be a constant—or at least predictable—so that the quantity theory view that aggregate spending is determined by the quantity of money is more likely to be true. However, the more sensitive the demand for money is to interest rates, the more unpredictable velocity will be, and the less clear the link between the money supply and aggregate spending will be. Indeed, there is an extreme case of ultrasensitivity of the demand for money to interest rates, called the *liquidity trap*, in which monetary policy has no effect on aggregate spending because a change in the money supply has no effect on interest rates. (If the demand for money is ultrasensitive to interest rates, a tiny change in interest rates produces a very large change in the quantity of money demanded. Hence in this case, the demand for money is completely flat in the supply and demand diagrams of Chapter 5. Therefore, a change in the money supply that shifts the money supply curve to the right or left results in it intersecting the flat money demand curve at the same unchanged interest rate.)

James Tobin conducted one of the earliest studies on the link between interest rates and money demand using U.S. data.[13] Tobin separated out transactions balances from other money balances, which he called "idle balances," assuming that transactions balances were proportional to income only, and idle balances were related to interest rates only. He then looked at whether his measure of idle balances was inversely related to interest rates in the period 1922–1941 by plotting the average level of idle balances each year against the average interest rate on commercial paper that year. When he found a clear-cut inverse relationship between interest rates and idle balances, Tobin concluded that the demand for money is sensitive to interest rates.[14]

Additional empirical evidence on the demand for money strongly confirms Tobin's finding.[15] Also, studies of the demand for money in Canada, using postwar data, by Kevin Clinton, Norman Cameron, and Stephen Poloz found that the demand for money is sensitive to interest rates.[16] Does this sensitivity ever become so high that we approach the case of the liquidity trap in which monetary policy is ineffective? The answer is almost certainly no. Keynes suggested in *The General Theory* that a liquidity trap might occur when interest rates are extremely low. (However, he did state that he had never yet seen an occurrence of a liquidity trap.)

---

[13]James Tobin, "Liquidity Preference and Monetary Policy," *Review of Economics and Statistics* 29 (1947): 124–131.

[14]A problem with Tobin's procedure is that idle balances are not really distinguishable from transactions balances. As the Baumol-Tobin model of transactions demand for money makes clear, transactions balances will be related to both income and interest rates, just like idle balances.

[15]See David E. W. Laidler, *The Demand for Money: Theories and Evidence*, 4th ed. (New York: HarperCollins, 1993). Only one major study has found that the demand for money is insensitive to interest rates: Milton Friedman, "The Demand for Money: Some Theoretical and Empirical Results," *Journal of Political Economy* 67 (1959): 327–351. He concluded that the demand for money is not sensitive to interest-rate movements, but as later work by David Laidler (using the same data as Friedman) demonstrated, Friedman used a faulty statistical procedure that biased his results: David Laidler, "The Rate of Interest and the Demand for Money: Some Empirical Evidence," *Journal of Political Economy* 74 (1966): 545–555. When Laidler employed the correct statistical procedure, he found the usual result that the demand for money is sensitive to interest rates. In later work, Friedman has also concluded that the demand for money is sensitive to interest rates.

[16]Kevin Clinton, "The Demand for Money in Canada: 1955-1970: Some Single Equation Estimates and Stability Tests," *Canadian Journal of Economics* 6 (1973): 53-61; Norman Cameron, "The Stability of Canadian Demand for Money Functions," *Canadian Journal of Economics* 12 (1979): 258-281; Stephen Poloz, "Simultaneity and the Demand for Money in Canada," *Canadian Journal of Economics* 13 (1980): 407-420.

Typical of the evidence demonstrating that the liquidity trap has never occurred is that of David Laidler, Karl Brunner, and Allan Meltzer, who looked at whether the interest sensitivity of money demand increased in periods when interest rates were very low.[17] Laidler and Meltzer looked at this question by seeing whether the interest sensitivity of money demand differed across periods, especially in periods such as the 1930s when interest rates were particularly low.[18] They found that there was no tendency for interest sensitivity to increase as interest rates fell—in fact, interest sensitivity did not change from period to period. Brunner and Meltzer explored this question by recognizing that higher interest sensitivity in the 1930s as a result of a liquidity trap implies that a money demand function estimated for this period should not predict well in more normal periods. What Brunner and Meltzer found was that a money demand function, estimated mostly with data from the 1930s, accurately predicted the demand for money in the 1950s. This result provided little evidence in favour of the existence of a liquidity trap during the Great Depression period.

The evidence on the interest sensitivity of the demand for money found by different researchers for different countries is remarkably consistent. Neither extreme case is supported by the data. The demand for money is sensitive to interest rates, but there is little evidence that a liquidity trap has ever existed.

Stability of Money Demand

If the money demand function, like Equation 4 or 6, is unstable and undergoes substantial unpredictable shifts, as Keynes thought, then velocity is unpredictable, and the quantity of money may not be tightly linked to aggregate spending, as it is in the modern quantity theory. The stability of the money demand function is also crucial to whether the central bank should target interest rates or the money supply (see Chapter 23). Thus it is important to look at the question of whether or not the money demand function is stable because it has important implications for how monetary policy should be conducted.

As our discussion of the Brunner and Meltzer article indicates, evidence on the stability of the demand for money function is related to the evidence on the existence of a liquidity trap. Brunner and Meltzer's finding that a money demand function estimated using data mostly from the 1930s predicted the demand for money well in the postwar period not only suggests that a liquidity trap did not exist in the 1930s but also indicates that the money demand function has been stable over long periods of time. The evidence that the interest sensitivity of the demand for money did not change from period to period also suggests that the money demand function is stable, since a changing interest sensitivity would mean that the demand for money function estimated in one period would not be used to predict that of another period.

By the early 1970s, the evidence using data from the postwar period strongly supported the stability of the money demand function when M1 was used as the definition of the money supply. For example, a well-known U.S. study by Stephen Goldfeld published in 1973 found not only that the interest sensitivity of M1 money demand did not undergo changes in the postwar period but also that the M1 money demand function predicted extremely well throughout the postwar

[17]David E. W. Laidler, "Some Evidence on the Demand for Money," *Journal of Political Economy* 74 (1966): 55–68; Allan H. Meltzer, "The Demand for Money: The Evidence from the Time Series," *Journal of Political Economy* 71 (1963): 219–246; Karl Brunner and Allan H. Meltzer, "Predicting Velocity: Implications for Theory and Policy," *Journal of Finance* 18 (1963): 319–354.

[18]Interest sensitivity is measured by the interest elasticity of money demand, which is defined as the percentage change in the demand for money divided by the percentage change in the interest rate.

period.[19] Similarly, studies of the demand for money in Canada concluded that narrow money demand functions were quite stable.[20] As a result of this evidence, the M1 money demand function became the conventional money demand function used by economists. In fact, this evidence provided the foundation for the Bank of Canada's experiment with targeting the growth rate of M1 and for its strategy of gradualism from 1975 to 1982.

The Case of the Missing Money   The stability of the demand for money, then, was a well-established fact when, starting in 1974, conventional M1 money demand functions in the United States and Canada began to severely overpredict the demand for money. Stephen Goldfeld labelled this phenomenon of instability in the demand for money function "the case of the missing money."[21] It presented a serious challenge to the usefulness of the money demand function as a tool for understanding how monetary policy affects aggregate economic activity. In addition, it had important implications for how monetary policy should be conducted. As a result, the instability of the M1 money demand function stimulated an intense search for a solution to the mystery of the missing money so that a stable money demand function could be resurrected.

The search for a stable money demand function took three directions. The first direction focused on whether an incorrect definition of money could be the reason why the demand for money function had become so unstable. As Charles Freedman and Ed Fine argue, competition between banks and near-banks, technological innovation, and high interest rates caused the payments mechanism and cash management techniques to undergo rapid changes after the beginning of monetary targeting in 1975.[22] This has led some researchers to suspect that the rapid pace of financial innovation has meant that the conventional definitions of the money supply no longer apply. They searched for a stable money demand function by actually looking directly for the missing money; that is, they looked for financial instruments that have been incorrectly left out of the definition of money used in the money demand function.

Daily interest savings accounts, introduced in 1979, and daily interest chequing accounts, introduced in 1981, are one example. These accounts provided chequing privileges and paid daily interest (computed on the daily closing balance), thereby offering the small saver the opportunity to earn near-market interest rates. As a result, people found these accounts attractive and were encouraged to substitute them for demand deposits (part of M1). These accounts, however, were included in the M2 definition of the money supply and hence the demand for M1 decreased and that for M2 increased. Recent evidence using later data has cast some doubt on whether including daily interest savings and chequing

---

[19]Stephen M. Goldfeld, "The Demand for Money Revisited," *Brookings Papers on Economic Activity* 3 (1973): 577–638.

[20]See, for example, William R. White, "The Demand for Money in Canada and the Control of Monetary Aggregates: Evidence from the Monthly Data," *Bank of Canada Staff Research Study* 12, Ottawa: Bank of Canada, 1976.

[21]Stephen M. Goldfeld, "The Case of the Missing Money," *Brookings Papers on Economic Activity* 3 (1976): 683–730.

[22]Charles Freedman, "Financial Innovation in Canada: Causes and Consequences," *American Economic Review*, Papers and Proceedings, 73 (May 1983): 101-106; Ed Fine, "Institutional Developments Affecting Monetary Aggregates," in *Monetary Seminar 90* (Ottawa: Bank of Canada, 1990): pp. 555-563.

accounts, and other highly liquid assets, in measures of the money supply produces money demand functions that are stable.[23]

The second direction of search for a stable money demand function was to use weighted monetary aggregates (discussed in Chapter 3). However, the results of estimating money demand functions using weighted monetary aggregates do not support the existence of a stable money demand function. For example, David Longworth and Joseph Atta-Mensah of the Bank of Canada compared the empirical performance of weighted monetary aggregates with the corresponding simple-sum aggregates and found that the theoretically superior weighted aggregates do not produce a stable money demand function.[24] This is also consistent with earlier results by John Cockerline and John Murray, also of the Bank of Canada.[25]

The third direction of search for a stable money demand function was to re-evaluate the conventional money demand specifications, by looking for new variables to include in the money demand function that will make it stable. Francesco Caramaza, Doug Hostland, and Kim McPhail, for example, found that the earning-price ratio has a significant negative effect on the demand for broad money.[26] Other researchers, such as Steve Ambler and Alain Paquet, added the real stock of Canada Savings Bonds (CSB) as well as dummy variables (to capture seasonal factors and postal strikes).[27]

These attempts to produce a stable money demand function have been criticized on the grounds that the theoretical justification for including them in the money demand function is weak. Also, later research questions whether these alterations to the money demand function will lead to continuing stability in the future.[28]

Conclusion   The main conclusion from the research on the money demand function seems to be that the most likely cause of its instability is the rapid pace of financial innovation occurring after 1973, which has changed what items can be counted as money. The evidence is still somewhat tentative, however, and a truly stable and satisfactory money demand function has not yet been found. And so the search for a stable money demand function goes on.

The recent instability of the money demand function calls into question whether our theories and empirical analyses are adequate.[29] It also has important implications for the way monetary policy should be conducted because it casts doubt on the usefulness of the money demand function as a tool to provide guid-

---

[23]Francesco Caramaza, "The Demand for M2 and M2+ in Canada," *Bank of Canada Review,* December 1989: 3-19.

[24]David Longworth and Joseph Attah-Mensah, "The Canadian Experience with Weighted Monetary Aggregates," *Bank of Canada Working Paper* 95-10.

[25]John P. Cockerline and John Murray, "A Comparison of Alternative Methods of Monetary Aggregation: Some Preliminary Evidence," *Bank of Canada Technical Report* 28, Ottawa: Bank of Canada, 1981.

[26]Francesco Caramaza, Doug Hostland, and Kim McPhail, "Studies on the Demand for M2 and M2+ in Canada," in *Monetary Seminar 90* (Ottawa: Bank of Canada, 1990): pp. 1-114.

[27]Steve Ambler and Alain Paquet, "Cointegration and the Demand for M2 and M2+ in Canada," in *Monetary Seminar 90* (Ottawa: Bank of Canada, 1990): pp. 125-168.

[28]This research is discussed in John P. Judd and John L. Scadding, "The Search for a Stable Money Demand Function," *Journal of Economic Literature* 20 (1982): 993–1023.

[29]Thomas F. Cooley and Stephen F. Le Roy, "Identification and Estimation of Money Demand," *American Economic Review* 71 (1981): 825–844, is especially critical of the empirical research on the demand for money.

ance to policymakers. In particular, because the money demand function has become unstable, velocity is now harder to predict, and, as discussed in Chapter 20, setting rigid money supply targets in order to control aggregate spending in the economy may not be an effective way to conduct monetary policy.

SUMMARY

1. Irving Fisher developed a transactions-based theory of the demand for money in which the demand for real balances is proportional to real income and is insensitive to interest-rate movements. An implication of his theory is that velocity, the rate of turnover of money, is constant. This generates the quantity theory of money, which implies that aggregate spending is determined solely by movements in the quantity of money.

2. The classical Cambridge approach tried to answer the question of how much money individuals want to hold. This approach also viewed the demand for real balances as proportional to real income, but it differs from Fisher's analysis in that it does not rule out interest-rate effects on the demand for money.

3. The classical view that velocity can be effectively treated as a constant is not supported by the data. The nonconstancy of velocity became especially clear to the economics profession after the sharp drop in velocity during the years of the Great Depression.

4. John Maynard Keynes extended the Cambridge approach by suggesting three motives for holding money: the transactions motive, the precautionary motive, and the speculative motive. His resulting liquidity preference theory views the transactions and precautionary components of money demand as proportional to income. However, the speculative component of money demand is viewed as sensitive to interest rates as well as to expectations

about the future movements of interest rates. This theory, then, implies that velocity is unstable and cannot be treated as a constant.

5. Further developments in the Keynesian approach provided a better rationale for the three Keynesian motives for holding money. Interest rates were found to be important to the transactions and precautionary components of money demand as well as to the speculative component.

6. Milton Friedman's theory of money demand used a similar approach to that of Keynes and the classical Cambridge economists. Treating money like any other asset, Friedman used the theory of asset demand to derive a demand for money that is a function of the expected returns on other assets relative to the expected return on money and permanent income. In contrast to Keynes, Friedman believed that the demand for money is stable and insensitive to interest-rate movements. His belief that velocity is predictable (though not constant) in turn leads to the quantity theory conclusion that money is the primary determinant of aggregate spending.

7. There are two main conclusions from the research on the demand for money. The demand for money is sensitive to interest rates, but there is little evidence that the liquidity trap has ever existed; and since 1973, money demand has been found to be unstable, with the most likely source of the instability being the rapid pace of financial innovation.

KEY TERMS

equation of exchange, p. 474

liquidity preference theory, p. 478

monetary theory, p. 473

quantity theory of money, p. 475

real money balances, p. 479

velocity of money, p. 474

QUESTIONS AND PROBLEMS

Questions marked with an asterisk are answered at the end of the book in an appendix, "Answers to Selected Questions and Problems."

*1. The money supply M has been growing at 10% per year, and nominal GDP PY has been growing at 20% per year. The data are as follows (in billions of dollars):

	2001	2002	2003
M	100	110	121
PY	1000	1200	1440

Calculate the velocity in each year. At what rate is velocity growing?

2. Calculate what happens to nominal GDP if velocity remains constant at 5 and the money supply increases from $200 billion to $300 billion.

*3. What happens to nominal GDP if the money supply grows by 20% but velocity declines by 30%?

4. If credit cards were made illegal by government legislation, what would happen to velocity? Explain your answer.

*5. If velocity and aggregate output are reasonably constant (as the classical economists believed), what happens to the price level when the money supply increases from $1 trillion to $4 trillion?

6. If velocity and aggregate output remain constant at 5 and 1000, respectively, what happens to the price level if the money supply declines from $400 billion to $300 billion?

*7. "Considering that both Fisher and the classical Cambridge economists ended with the same equation for the demand for money, $M^d = k \times PY$, their theories are equivalent." Is this statement true, false, or uncertain? Explain your answer.

8. Using data from the *Bank of Canada Review,* calculate velocity for the M2 definition of the money supply in the past five years. Does velocity appear to be constant?

*9. In Keynes's analysis of the speculative demand for money, what will happen to money demand if people suddenly decide that the normal level of the interest rate has declined? Why?

10. Why is Keynes's analysis of the speculative demand for money important to his view that velocity will undergo substantial fluctuations and thus cannot be treated as constant?

*11. If interest rates on bonds go to zero, what does the Baumol-Tobin analysis suggest Grant Smith's average holdings of money balances should be?

12. If brokerage fees go to zero, what does the Baumol-Tobin analysis suggest Grant Smith's average holdings of money should be?

*13. "In Tobin's analysis of the speculative demand for money, people will hold both money and bonds, even if bonds are expected to earn a positive return." Is this statement true, false, or uncertain? Explain your answer.

14. Both Keynes's and Friedman's theories of the demand for money suggest that as the relative expected return on money falls, demand for it will fall. Why does Friedman think that money demand is unaffected by changes in interest rates, but Keynes thought that it is affected?

*15. Why does Friedman's view of the demand for money suggest that velocity is predictable, whereas Keynes's view suggests the opposite?

Chapter 22

The Keynesian Framework and the *ISLM* Model

PREVIEW In the media, you often see forecasts of GDP and interest rates by economists and government agencies. At times, these forecasts seem to come from a crystal ball, but economists actually make their predictions using a variety of economic models. One model widely used by economic forecasters is the *ISLM* model, which was developed by Sir John Hicks in 1937 and is based on the analysis in John Maynard Keynes's influential book *The General Theory of Employment, Interest, and Money*, published in 1936.[1] The *ISLM* model explains how interest rates and total output produced in the economy (aggregate output or, equivalently, aggregate income) are determined, given a fixed price level.

The *ISLM* model is valuable not only because it can be used in economic forecasting but also because it provides a deeper understanding of how government policy can affect aggregate economic activity. In Chapter 24 we use it to evaluate the effects of monetary and fiscal policy on the economy and to learn some lessons about how monetary policy might best be conducted.

In this chapter we begin by developing the simplest framework for determining aggregate output, in which all economic actors (consumers, firms, and others) except the government play a role. Government fiscal policy (spending and taxes) is then added to the framework to see how it can affect the determination of aggregate output. Finally, we achieve a complete picture of the *ISLM* model by adding monetary policy variables: the money supply and the interest rate.

DETERMINATION OF AGGREGATE OUTPUT

Keynes was especially interested in understanding movements of aggregate output because he wanted to explain why the Great Depression had occurred and how government policy could be used to increase employment in a similar economic situation. Keynes's analysis started with the recognition that the total quantity demanded of an economy's output was the sum of four types of spending: (1) **consumer expenditure** (*C*), the total demand for consumer goods and services

[1]John Hicks, "Mr. Keynes and the Classics: A Suggested Interpretation," *Econometrica* (1937): 147–159.

(hamburgers, stereos, rock concerts, and so on); (2) **planned investment spending** (I), the total planned spending by businesses on new physical capital (machines, computers, factories, raw materials, and the like) plus planned spending on new homes; (3) **government spending** (G), the spending by all levels of government on goods and services (aircraft carriers, government workers, red tape, and so forth); and (4) **net exports** (NX), the net foreign spending on domestic goods and services, equal to exports minus imports.[2] The total quantity demanded of an economy's output, called **aggregate demand** (Y^{ad}), can be written as

$$Y^{ad} = C + I + G + NX \tag{1}$$

Using the commonsense concept from supply and demand analysis, Keynes recognized that equilibrium would occur in the economy when total quantity of output supplied (aggregate output produced), Y, equals quantity of output demanded, Y^{ad}, that is, when

$$Y = Y^{ad} \tag{2}$$

When this equilibrium condition is satisfied, producers are able to sell all of their output and have no reason to change their production. Keynes's analysis explains two things: (1) why aggregate output is at a certain level (which involves understanding what factors affect each component of aggregate demand) and (2) how the sum of these components can add up to an output smaller than the economy is capable of producing, resulting in less than full employment of resources.

Keynes was especially concerned with explaining the low level of output and employment during the Great Depression. Because inflation was not a serious problem during this period, he assumed that output could change without causing a change in prices. ***Keynes's analysis assumes that the price level is fixed;*** that is, dollar amounts for variables such as consumer expenditure, investment, and aggregate output do not have to be adjusted for changes in the price level to tell us how much the real quantities of these variables change. Because the price level is assumed to be fixed, when we talk in this chapter about changes in nominal quantities, we are talking about changes in real quantities as well.

Our discussion of Keynes's analysis begins with a simple framework of aggregate output determination in which the role of government, net exports, and the possible effects of money and interest rates are ignored. Because we are assuming that government spending and net exports are zero ($G = 0$ and $NX = 0$), we need only examine consumer expenditure and investment spending to explain how aggregate output is determined. This simple framework is unrealistic because both government and monetary policy are left out of the picture and because it makes other simplifying assumptions, such as a fixed price level. Still, the model is worth studying because its simplified view helps us understand the key factors that explain how the economy works. It also clearly illustrates the Keynesian idea that the economy can come to rest at a level of aggregate output below the full employment level. Once you understand this simple framework, we can proceed to more complex and more realistic models.

---

[2]Imports are subtracted from exports in arriving at the net exports component of the total quantity demanded of an economy's output because imports are already counted in C, I, and G but do not add to the demand for the economy's output.

Consumer Expenditure and the Consumption Function

Ask yourself what determines how much you spend on consumer goods and services. Your likely response is that your income is the most important factor because if your income rises, you will be willing to spend more. Keynes reasoned similarly that consumer expenditure is related to **disposable income**, the total income available for spending, equal to aggregate income (which is equivalent to aggregate output) minus taxes $(Y - T)$. He called this relationship between disposable income Y_D and consumer expenditure C the **consumption function** and expressed it as

$$C = a + (mpc \times Y_D) \qquad (3)$$

The term mpc, the **marginal propensity to consume**, is the slope of the consumption function line $(\Delta C/\Delta Y_D)$ and reflects the change in consumer expenditure that results from an additional dollar of disposable income. Keynes assumed that mpc was a constant between the values of 0 and 1. If, for example, a $1.00 increase in disposable income leads to an increase in consumer expenditure of $0.50, then $mpc = 0.5$.

The term a stands for **autonomous consumer expenditure**, the amount of consumer expenditure that is independent of disposable income. It tells us how much consumers will spend when disposable income is 0 (they still must have food, clothing, and shelter). If a is $200 billion when disposable income is 0, consumer expenditure will equal $200 billion.[3]

A numerical example of a consumption function using the values of $mpc = 0.5$ and $a = 200$ will clarify the preceding concept. The $200 billion of consumer expenditure at a disposable income of 0 is listed in the first row of Table 22-1 and is plotted as point E in Figure 22-1. (Remember that throughout this chapter, dollar amounts for all variables in the figures correspond to real quantities because Keynes assumed that the price level is fixed.) Because $mpc = 0.5$, when disposable income increases by $400 billion, the change in consumer expenditure ΔC in column 3 of Table 22-1 is $200 billion ($0.5 \times $400 billion). Thus when disposable income is $400 billion, consumer expenditure is $400 billion (initial value of $200 billion when income is 0 plus the $200 billion change in consumer expenditure). This combination of consumer expenditure and disposable income is listed in the second row of Table 22-1 and is plotted as point F in Figure 22-1. Similarly, at point G, where disposable income has increased by another $400 billion to $800 billion, consumer expenditure will rise by another $200 billion to $600 billion. By the same reasoning, at point H, at which disposable income is $1200 billion, consumer expenditure will be $800 billion. The line connecting these points in Figure 22-1 graphs the consumption function.

Study Guide

The consumption function is an intuitive concept that you can readily understand if you think about how your own spending behaviour changes as you receive more disposable income. One way to make yourself more comfortable with this concept is to estimate your marginal propensity to consume (for example, it might be 0.8) and your level of consumer expenditure when your disposable income is 0 (it might be $2000) and then construct a consumption function similar to that in Table 22-1.

[3]Consumer expenditure can exceed income if people have accumulated savings to tide them over bad times. An alternative is to have parents who will give you money for food (or to pay for school) when you have no income. The situation in which consumer expenditure is greater than disposable income is called *dissaving*.

TABLE 22-1   Consumption Function: Schedule of Consumer Expenditure C When $mpc = 0.5$ and $a = 200$ ($ billions)

Point in Figure 22-1	Disposable income Y_D (1)	Change in Disposable Income ΔY_D (2)	Change in Consumer Expenditure ΔC $(0.5 \times \Delta Y_D)$ (3)	Consumer Expenditure C (4)
E	0	—	—	200 (= a)
F	400	400	200	400
G	800	400	200	600
H	1200	400	200	800

Investment Spending

It is important to understand that there are two types of investment. The first type, **fixed investment**, is the spending by firms on equipment (machines, computers, airplanes) and structures (factories, office buildings, shopping centres) and planned spending on residential housing. The second type, **inventory investment**, is spending by firms on additional holdings of raw materials, parts, and finished goods, calculated as the change in holdings of these items in a given time period, say, a year. (Box 22-1 explains how economists' use of the word *investment* differs from everyday use of the term.)

Suppose that Compaq, a company that produces personal computers, has 100 000 computers sitting in its warehouses on December 31, 2000, ready to be shipped to dealers. If each computer has a wholesale price of $1000, Compaq has an inventory worth $100 million. If by December 31, 2001, its inventory of personal computers has risen to $150 million, its inventory investment in 2001 is $50 million, the *change* in the level of its inventory over the course of the year ($150 million minus $100 million). Now suppose that there is a drop in the level of inventories; inventory investment will then be negative.

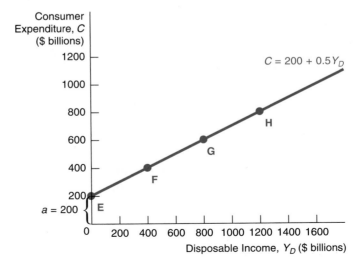

FIGURE 22-1   Consumption Function

The consumption function plotted here is from Table 22-1; $mpc = 0.5$ and $a = 200$.

Compaq may also have additional inventory investment if the level of raw materials and parts that it is holding to produce these computers increases over the course of the year. If on December 31, 2000, it holds $20 million of computer chips used to produce its computers and on December 31, 2001, it holds $30 million, it has an additional $10 million of inventory investment in 2001.

An important feature of inventory investment is that—in contrast to fixed investment, which is always planned—some inventory investment can be unplanned. Suppose that the reason Compaq finds itself with an additional $50 million of computers on December 31, 2001, is that $50 million less of its computers were sold in 2001 than expected. This $50 million of inventory investment in 2001 was unplanned. In this situation, Compaq is producing more computers than it can sell and will cut production.

Planned investment spending, a component of aggregate demand Y^{ad}, is equal to planned fixed investment plus the amount of inventory investment *planned* by firms. Keynes mentioned two factors that influence planned investment spending: interest rates and businesses' expectations about the future. How these factors affect investment spending is discussed later in this chapter. For now, planned investment spending will be treated as a known value. At this stage, we want to see how aggregate output is determined for a given level of planned investment spending; once we understand this, we can examine how interest rates and business expectations influence aggregate output by affecting planned investment spending.

Equilibrium and the Keynesian Cross Diagram

We have now assembled the building blocks (consumer expenditure and planned investment spending) that will enable us to see how aggregate output is determined when we ignore the government. Although unrealistic, this stripped-down analysis clarifies the basic principles of output determination. In the next section, government enters the picture and makes our model more realistic.

The diagram in Figure 22-2, known as the *Keynesian cross diagram*, shows how aggregate output is determined. The vertical axis measures aggregate demand, and the horizontal axis measures the level of aggregate output. The 45° line shows all the points at which aggregate output Y equals aggregate demand Y^{ad}; that is, it shows all the points at which the equilibrium condition $Y = Y^{ad}$ is satisfied. Since government spending and net exports are zero ($G = 0$ and $NX = 0$), aggregate demand is

$$Y^{ad} = C + I$$

Because there is no government sector to collect taxes, there are none in our simplified economy; disposable income Y_D then equals aggregate output Y (remember that aggregate income and aggregate output are equivalent; see the appendix to Chapter 1). Thus the consumption function with $a = 200$ and $mpc = 0.5$ plotted

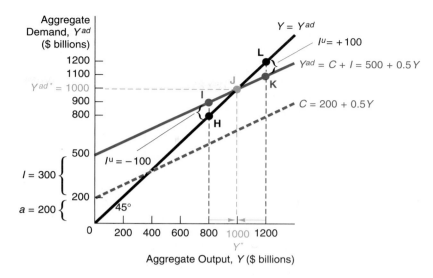

FIGURE 22-2   Keynesian Cross Diagram

When $I = 300$ and $C = 200 + 0.5Y$, equilibrium output occurs at $Y^* = 1000$, where the aggregate demand function $Y^{ad} = C + I$ intersects with the $45°$ line $Y = Y^{ad}$.

in Figure 22-1 can be written as $C = 200 + 0.5Y$ and is plotted in Figure 22-2. Given that planned investment spending is $300 billion, aggregate demand can then be expressed as

$$Y^{ad} = C + I = 200 + 0.5Y + 300 = 500 + 0.5Y$$

This equation, plotted in Figure 22-2, represents the quantity of aggregate demand at any given level of aggregate output and is called the **aggregate demand function**.

The aggregate demand function $Y^{ad} = C + I$ is the vertical sum of the consumption function line ($C = 200 + 0.5Y$) and planned investment spending ($I = 300$). The point at which the aggregate demand function crosses the $45°$ line $Y = Y^{ad}$ indicates the equilibrium level of aggregate demand and aggregate output. In Figure 22-2, equilibrium occurs at point J, with both aggregate output Y^* and aggregate demand Y^{ad*} at $1000 billion.

As you learned in Chapter 5, the concept of equilibrium is useful only if there is a tendency for the economy to settle there. To see whether the economy heads toward the equilibrium output level of $1000 billion, let's first look at what happens if the amount of output produced in the economy is $1200 billion and is therefore above the equilibrium level. At this level of output, aggregate demand is $1100 billion (point K), $100 billion less than the $1200 billion of output (point L on the $45°$ line). Since output exceeds aggregate demand by $100 billion, firms are saddled with $100 billion of unsold inventory. To keep from accumulating unsold goods, firms will cut production. As long as it is above the equilibrium level, output will exceed aggregate demand and firms will cut production, sending aggregate output toward the equilibrium level.

Another way to observe a tendency of the economy to head toward equilibrium at point J is from the viewpoint of inventory investment. When firms do not sell all output produced, they add unsold output to their holdings of inventory, and inventory investment increases. At an output level of $1200 billion, for instance, the $100 billion of unsold goods leads to $100 billion of unplanned inventory investment, which firms do not want. Companies will decrease production to reduce inventory to the desired level, and aggregate output will fall (indicated by the arrow near the horizontal axis). This viewpoint means that unplanned inventory investment for the entire economy I^u equals the excess of output over aggregate demand. In our example, at an output level of $1200 billion, $I^u = \$100$ billion. If I^u is positive, firms will cut production and output will fall. Output will stop falling only when it has returned to its equilibrium level at point J, where $I^u = 0$.

What happens if aggregate output is below the equilibrium level of output? Let's say output is $800 billion. At this level of output, aggregate demand at point I is $900 billion, $100 billion higher than output (point H on the 45° line). At this level, firms are selling $100 billion more goods than they are producing, so inventory falls below the desired level. The negative unplanned inventory investment ($I^u = -\$100$ billion) will induce firms to increase their production in order to raise inventory to desired levels. As a result, output rises toward the equilibrium level, shown by the arrow in Figure 22-2. As long as output is below the equilibrium level, unplanned inventory investment will remain negative, firms will continue to raise production, and output will continue to rise. We again see the tendency for the economy to settle at point J, where aggregate demand Y equals output Y^{ad} and unplanned inventory investment is zero ($I^u = 0$).

Expenditure Multiplier

Now that we understand that equilibrium aggregate output is determined by the position of the aggregate demand function, we can examine how different factors shift the function and consequently change aggregate output. We will find that either a rise in planned investment spending or a rise in autonomous consumer expenditure shifts the aggregate demand function upward and leads to an increase in aggregate output.

Output Response to a Change in Planned Investment Spending Suppose that a new electric motor is invented that makes all factory machines three times more efficient. Because firms are suddenly more optimistic about the profitability of investing in new machines that use this new motor, planned investment spending increases by $100 billion from an initial level of $I_1 = \$300$ billion to $I_2 = \$400$ billion. What effect does this have on output?

The effects of this increase in planned investment spending are analyzed in Figure 22-3 using a Keynesian cross diagram. Initially, when planned investment spending I_1 is $300 billion, the aggregate demand function is Y_1^{ad}, and equilibrium occurs at point 1, where output is $1000 billion. The $100 billion increase in planned investment spending adds directly to aggregate demand and shifts the aggregate demand function upward to Y_2^{ad}. Aggregate demand now equals output at the intersection of Y_2^{ad} with the 45° line $Y = Y^{ad}$ (point 2). As a result of the $100 billion increase in planned investment spending, equilibrium output rises by $200 billion to $1200 billion ($Y_2$). For every dollar increase in planned investment spending, aggregate output has increased twofold.

The ratio of the change in aggregate output to a change in planned investment spending, $\Delta Y/\Delta I$, is called the **expenditure multiplier**. (This multiplier should not be confused with the money supply multiplier developed in Chapter 16, which measures the ratio of the change in the money supply to a change in the monetary base.) In Figure 22-3, the expenditure multiplier is 2.

Why does a change in planned investment spending lead to an even larger change in aggregate output so that the expenditure multiplier is greater than 1? The expenditure multiplier is greater than 1 because an increase in planned investment spending, which raises output, also leads to an additional increase in consumer expenditure ($mpc \times \Delta Y$). The increase in consumer expenditure in turn raises aggregate demand and output further, resulting in a multiple change of output from a given change in planned investment spending. This conclusion can be

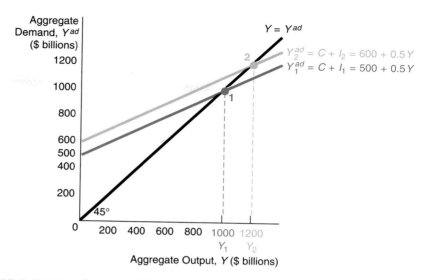

FIGURE 22-3   Response of Aggregate Output to a Change in Planned Investment

A \$100 billion increase in planned investment spending from $I_1 = 300$ to $I_2 = 400$ shifts the aggregate demand function upward from Y^{ad}_1 to Y^{ad}_2. The equilibrium moves from point 1 to point 2, and equilibrium output rises from $Y_1 = 1000$ to $Y_2 = 1200$.

derived algebraically by solving for the unknown value of Y in terms of a, mpc, and I, resulting in the following equation:[4]

$$Y = (a + I) \times \frac{1}{1 - mpc} \tag{4}$$

Because I is multiplied by the term $1/(1 - mpc)$, this equation tells us that a \$1 change in I leads to a $1/(1 - mpc)$ change in aggregate output; thus $1/(1 - mpc)$ is the expenditure multiplier. When $mpc = 0.5$, the change in output for a \$1 change in I is \$2 [$= 1/(1 - 0.5)$]; if $mpc = 0.8$, the change in output for a \$1 change in I is \$5. The larger the marginal propensity to consume, the higher the expenditure multiplier.

Response to Changes in Autonomous Spending   Because a is also multiplied by the term $1/(1 - mpc)$ in Equation 4, a \$1 change in autonomous consumer expenditure a also changes aggregate output by $1/(1 - mpc)$, the amount of the expenditure multiplier. Therefore, we see that the expenditure multiplier applies equally well to changes in autonomous consumer expenditure. In fact, Equation 4 can be rewritten as

$$Y = A \times \frac{1}{1 - mpc} \tag{5}$$

in which A = autonomous spending = $a + I$.

---

[4]Substituting the consumption function $C = a + (mpc \times Y)$ into the aggregate demand function Y^{ad} = $C + I$ yields

$$Y^{ad} = a + (mpc \times Y) + I$$

In equilibrium, where aggregate output equals aggregate demand,

$$Y = Y^{ad} = a + (mpc \times Y) + I$$

Subtracting the term $mpc \times Y$ from both sides of this equation in order to collect the terms involving Y on the left side, we have

$$Y - (mpc \times Y) = Y(1 - mpc) = a + I$$

Dividing both sides by $1 - mpc$ to solve for Y leads to Equation 4 in the text.

This rewritten equation tells us that any change in autonomous spending, whether from a change in a, in I, or in both, will lead to a multiplied change in Y. If both a and I decrease by $100 billion each and $mpc = 0.5$, the expenditure multiplier is 2 [= $1/(1 - 0.5)$], and aggregate output Y will fall by $2 \times 200 billion = $400 billion. Conversely, a rise in I by $100 billion that is offset by a $100 billion decline in a will leave autonomous spending A, and hence Y, unchanged. The expenditure multiplier $1/(1 - mpc)$ can therefore be defined more generally as the ratio of the change in aggregate output to a change in autonomous spending ($\Delta Y / \Delta A$).

Another way to reach this conclusion—that any change in autonomous spending will lead to a multiplied change in aggregate output—is to recognize that the shift in the aggregate demand function in Figure 22-3 did not have to come from an increase in I; it could also have come from an increase in a, which directly raises consumer expenditure and therefore aggregate demand. Alternatively, it could have come from an increase in both a and I. Changes in the attitudes of consumers and firms about the future, which cause changes in their spending, will result in multiple changes in aggregate output.

Keynes believed that changes in autonomous spending are dominated by unstable fluctuations in planned investment spending, which is influenced by emotional waves of optimism and pessimism—factors he labelled "**animal spirits**." His view was coloured by the collapse in investment spending during the Great Depression, which he saw as the primary reason for the economic contraction. We will examine the consequences of this fall in investment spending in the following application.

APPLICATION | *The Collapse of Autonomous Consumer Expenditure and the Great Depression*

From 1929 to 1933, the Canadian economy experienced the largest percentage decline in investment spending ever recorded. One explanation for the investment collapse was the ongoing wave of extreme pessimism during this period. The investment collapse also brought a decrease in autonomous consumer expenditure, a. In 1992 dollars, autonomous consumer expenditure fell by $17.8 billion in the years 1929 through 1933. What does the Keynesian analysis developed so far suggest should have happened to aggregate output in this period?

Figure 22-4 demonstrates how the $17.8 billion drop in autonomous consumer spending would shift the aggregate demand function downward from Y_1^{ad} to Y_2^{ad}, moving the economy from point 1 to point 2. Aggregate output would then fall sharply; real GDP actually fell by $19 billion (a multiple of the $17.8 billion drop in autonomous consumer expenditure), from $65 billion to $46 billion (in 1992 dollars). Because the economy was at full employment in 1929, the fall in output resulted in massive unemployment, with over 20% of the labour force unemployed in 1933.

Government's Role

After witnessing the events in the Great Depression, Keynes took the view that an economy would continually suffer major output fluctuations because of the volatility of autonomous spending, particularly planned investment spending. He was especially worried about sharp declines in autonomous spending, which would inevitably lead to large declines in output and an equilibrium with high unem-

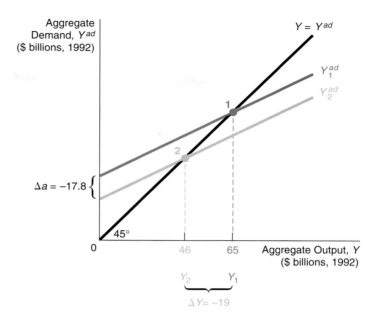

FIGURE 22-4   Response of Aggregate Output to the Collapse of Autonomous Consumer Expenditure, 1929–1933

The decline of $17.8 billion (in 1992 dollars) in autonomous consumer expenditure from 1929 to 1933 shifted the aggregate demand function down from Y_1^{ad} to Y_2^{ad} and caused the economy to move from point 1 to point 2, where output fell by $19 billion.

Source: Statistics Canada, *Historical Statistics of Canada,* Second Edition, F.H. Leacy (ed.), Series F33, F34, and F55.

ployment. If autonomous spending fell sharply, as it did during the Great Depression, how could an economy be restored to higher levels of output and more reasonable levels of unemployment? Not by an increase in autonomous spending, since the business outlook was so grim. Keynes's answer to this question involved looking at the role of government in determining aggregate output.

Keynes realized that government spending and taxation could also affect the position of the aggregate demand function and hence be manipulated to restore the economy to full employment. As shown in the aggregate demand equation $Y^{ad} = C + I + G + NX$, government spending G adds directly to aggregate demand. Taxes, however, do not affect aggregate demand directly, as government spending does. Instead, taxes lower the amount of income that consumers have available for spending and affect aggregate demand by influencing consumer expenditure; that is, when there are taxes, disposable income Y_D does not equal aggregate output; it equals aggregate output Y minus taxes T: $Y_D = Y - T$. The consumption function $C = a + (mpc \times Y_D)$ can be rewritten as follows:

$$C = a + [mpc \times (Y - T)] = a + (mpc \times Y) - (mpc \times T) \qquad (6)$$

This consumption function looks similar to the one used in the absence of taxes, but it has the additional term $-(mpc \times T)$ on the right side. This term indicates that if taxes increase by $100, consumer expenditure declines by mpc times this amount; if $mpc = 0.5$, consumer expenditure declines by $50. This occurs because consumers view $100 of taxes as equivalent to a $100 reduction in income and reduce their expenditure by the marginal propensity to consume times this amount.

To see how the inclusion of government spending and taxes modifies our analysis, first we will observe the effect of a positive level of government spending on

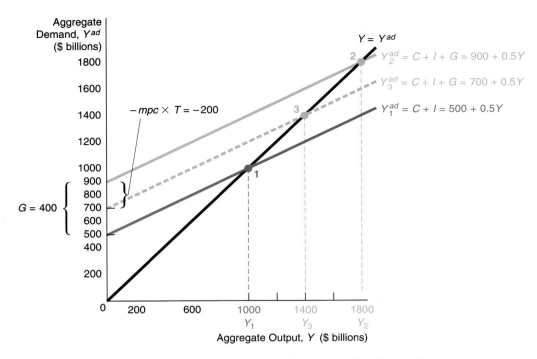

FIGURE 22-5   Response of Aggregate Output to Government Spending and Taxes

With no government spending or taxes, the aggregate demand function is Y_1^{ad}, and equilibrium output is $Y_1 = 1000$. With government spending of $400 billion, the aggregate demand function shifts upward to Y_2^{ad}, and aggregate output rises by $800 billion to $Y_2 = \$1800$ billion. Taxes of $400 billion lower consumer expenditure and the aggregate demand function by $200 billion from Y_2^{ad} to Y_3^{ad}, and aggregate output falls by $400 billion to $Y_3 = \$1400$ billion.

aggregate output in the Keynesian cross diagram of Figure 22-5. Let's say that in the absence of government spending or taxes, the economy is at point 1, where the aggregate demand function $Y_1^{ad} = C + I = 500 + 0.5Y$ crosses the 45° line $Y = Y^{ad}$. Here equilibrium output is at $1000 billion. Suppose, however, that the economy reaches full employment at an aggregate output level of $1800 billion. How can government spending be used to restore the economy to full employment at $1800 billion of aggregate output?

If government spending is set at $400 billion, the aggregate demand function shifts upward to $Y_2^{ad} = C + I + G = 900 + 0.5Y$. The economy moves to point 2, and aggregate output rises by $800 billion to $1800 billion. Figure 22-5 indicates that aggregate output is positively related to government spending and that a change in government spending leads to a multiplied change in aggregate output, equal to the expenditure multiplier, $1/(1 - mpc) = 1/(1 - 0.5) = 2$. Therefore, declines in planned investment spending that produce high unemployment (as occurred during the Great Depression) can be offset by raising government spending.

What happens if the government decides that it must collect taxes of $400 billion to balance the budget? Before taxes are raised, the economy is in equilibrium at the same point 2 found in Figure 22-5. Our discussion of the consumption function (which allows for taxes) indicates that taxes T reduce consumer expenditure by $mpc \times T$ because there is T less income now available for spending. In our example, $mpc = 0.5$, so consumer expenditure and the aggregate demand function shift downward by $200 billion (= 0.5 × 400); at the new equilibrium, point 3, the level of output has declined by twice this amount (the expenditure multiplier) to $1400 billion.

Although you can see that aggregate output is negatively related to the level of taxes, it is important to recognize that the change in aggregate output from the $400 billion increase in taxes ($\Delta Y = -\$400$ billion) is smaller than the change in aggregate output from the $400 billion increase in government spending ($\Delta Y = \$800$ billion). If both taxes and government spending are raised equally, by $400 billion, as occurs in going from point 1 to point 3 in Figure 22-5, aggregate output will rise.

The Keynesian framework indicates that the government can play an important role in determining aggregate output by changing the level of government spending or taxes. If the economy enters a deep recession, in which output drops severely and unemployment climbs, the analysis we have just developed provides a prescription for restoring the economy to health. The government might raise aggregate output by increasing government spending, or it could lower taxes and reverse the process described in Figure 22-5 (that is, a tax cut makes more income available for spending at any level of output, shifting the aggregate demand function upward and causing the equilibrium level of output to rise).

Role of International Trade

International trade also plays a role in determining aggregate output because net exports (exports minus imports) are a component of aggregate demand. To analyze the effect of net exports in the Keynesian cross diagram of Figure 22-6, suppose that initially net exports are equal to zero ($NX_1 = 0$) so that the economy is at point 1, where the aggregate demand function $Y_1^{ad} = C + I + G + NX_1 = 500 + 0.5Y$ crosses the 45° line $Y = Y_1^{ad}$. Equilibrium output is again at $1000 billion. Now foreigners suddenly get an urge to buy more Canadian products so that net exports rise to $100 billion ($NX_2 = 100$). The $100 billion increase in net exports adds directly to aggregate demand and shifts the aggregate demand function upward to $Y_2^{ad} = C + I + G + NX_2 = 600 + 0.5Y$. The economy moves to point 2, and aggregate output rises by $200 billion to $1200 billion ($Y_2$). Figure 22-6 indicates that just as we found for planned investment spending and government spending, a rise in net exports leads to a multiplied rise in aggregate output, equal to the expenditure multiplier, $1/(1 - mpc) = 1/(1 - 0.5) = 2$. Therefore, changes in net exports can be another important factor affecting fluctuations in aggregate output.

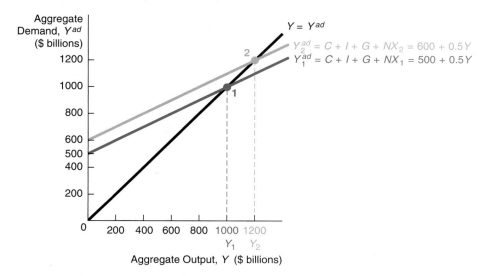

FIGURE 22-6   Response of Aggregate Output to a Change in Net Exports
A $100 billion increase in net exports from $NX_1 = 0$ to $NX_2 = 100$ shifts the aggregate demand function upward from Y_1^{ad} to Y_2^{ad}. The equilibrium moves from point 1 to point 2, and equilibrium output rises from $Y_1 = \$1000$ billion to $Y_2 = \$1200$ billion.

Summary of the Determinants of Aggregate Output

Our analysis of the Keynesian framework so far has identified five autonomous factors (factors independent of income) that shift the aggregate demand function and hence the level of aggregate output:

1. Changes in autonomous consumer expenditure (a)
2. Changes in planned investment spending (I)
3. Changes in government spending (G)
4. Changes in taxes (T)
5. Changes in net exports (NX)

The effects of changes in each of these variables on aggregate output are summarized in Table 22-2 and discussed next in the text.

Changes in Autonomous Consumer Spending (*a*)   A rise in autonomous consumer expenditure a (say, because consumers become more optimistic about the economy when the stock market booms) directly raises consumer expenditure and shifts the aggregate demand function upward, resulting in an increase in aggregate output. A decrease in a causes consumer expenditure to fall, leading ultimately to a decline in aggregate output. Therefore, ***aggregate output is positively related to autonomous consumer expenditure* a**.

Changes in Planned Investment Spending (*I*)   A rise in planned investment spending adds directly to aggregate demand, thus raising the aggregate demand function and aggregate output. A fall in planned investment spending lowers aggregate demand and causes aggregate output to fall. Therefore, ***aggregate output is positively related to planned investment spending* I**.

Changes in Government Spending (*G*)   A rise in government spending also adds directly to aggregate demand and raises the aggregate demand function, increasing aggregate output. A fall directly reduces aggregate demand, lowers the aggregate demand function, and causes aggregate output to fall. Therefore, ***aggregate output is positively related to government spending* G**.

Changes in Taxes (*T*)   A rise in taxes does not affect aggregate demand directly but does lower the amount of income available for spending, reducing consumer expenditure. The decline in consumer expenditure then leads to a fall in the aggregate demand function, resulting in a decline in aggregate output. A lowering of taxes makes more income available for spending, raises consumer expenditure, and leads to higher aggregate output. Therefore, ***aggregate output is negatively related to the level of taxes* T**.

Changes in Net Exports (*NX*)   A rise in net exports adds directly to aggregate demand and raises the aggregate demand function, increasing aggregate output. A fall directly reduces aggregate demand, lowers the aggregate demand function, and causes aggregate output to fall. Therefore, ***aggregate output is positively related to net exports* NX**.

Size of the Effects from the Five Factors   The aggregate demand function in the Keynesian cross diagrams shifts vertically by the full amount of the change in a, I, G, or NX, resulting in a multiple effect on aggregate output through the effects of

SUMMARY

TABLE 22-2 Response of Aggregate Output Y to Autonomous Changes in a, I, G, T, and NX

Variable	Change in Variable	Response of Aggregate Output, Y	
Autonomous consumer expenditure, a	↑	↑	Y^{ad} axis; lines Y^{ad}_2, Y^{ad}_1; 45°; Y_1 Y_2 Y
Investment, I	↑	↑	Y^{ad} axis; lines Y^{ad}_2, Y^{ad}_1; 45°; Y_1 Y_2 Y
Government spending, G	↑	↑	Y^{ad} axis; lines Y^{ad}_2, Y^{ad}_1; 45°; Y_1 Y_2 Y
Taxes, T	↑	↓	Y^{ad} axis; lines Y^{ad}_1, Y^{ad}_2 (↓); 45°; Y_2 Y_1 Y
Net exports, NX	↑	↑	Y^{ad} axis; lines Y^{ad}_2, Y^{ad}_1; 45°; Y_1 Y_2 Y

Note: Only increases (↑) in the variables are shown; the effects of decreases in the variables on aggregate output would be the opposite of those indicated in the "Response" column.

the expenditure multiplier, $1/(1 - mpc)$. A change in taxes has a smaller effect on aggregate output because consumer expenditure changes only by mpc times the change in taxes ($-mpc \times \Delta T$), which in the case of $mpc = 0.5$ means that aggregate demand shifts vertically by only half of the change in taxes.

If there is a change in one of these autonomous factors that is offset by a change in another (say, I rises by \$100 billion, but a, G, or NX falls by \$100 billion or *T* rises by $200 billion when *mpc* = 0.5), the aggregate demand function will remain in the same position, and aggregate output will remain unchanged.[5]

To test your understanding of the Keynesian analysis of how aggregate output changes in response to changes in the factors described, see if you can use Keynesian cross diagrams to illustrate what happens to aggregate output when each variable decreases rather than increases. Also, be sure to do the problems at the end of the chapter that ask you to predict what will happen to aggregate output when certain economic variables change.

THE *ISLM* MODEL

So far our analysis has excluded monetary policy. We now include money and interest rates in the Keynesian framework in order to develop the more intricate *ISLM* model of how aggregate output is determined, in which monetary policy plays an important role. Why another complex model? The *ISLM* model is more versatile and allows us to understand economic phenomena that cannot be analyzed with the simpler Keynesian cross framework used earlier. The *ISLM* model will help you understand how monetary policy affects economic activity and interacts with fiscal policy (changes in government spending and taxes) to produce a certain level of aggregate output; how the level of interest rates is affected by changes in investment spending as well as by changes in monetary and fiscal policy; how best to conduct monetary policy; and how the *ISLM* model generates the aggregate demand curve, an essential building block for the aggregate supply and demand analysis used in Chapter 24 and thereafter.

Like our simplified Keynesian model, the full Keynesian *ISLM* model examines an equilibrium in which aggregate output produced equals aggregate demand,

---

[5]These results can be derived algebraically as follows. Substituting the consumption function allowing for taxes (Equation 6) into the aggregate demand function (Equation 1), we have

$$Y^{ad} = a - (mpc \times T) + (mpc \times Y) + I + G + NX$$

If we assume that taxes *T* are unrelated to income, we can define autonomous spending in the aggregate demand function to be

$$A = a - (mpc \times T) + I + G + NX$$

The expenditure equation can be rewritten as

$$Y^{ad} = A + (mpc \times Y)$$

In equilibrium, aggregate demand equals aggregate output,

$$Y = A + (mpc \times Y)$$

which can be solved for *Y*. The resulting equation,

$$Y = A \times \frac{1}{1 - mpc}$$

is the same equation that links autonomous spending and aggregate output in the text (Equation 5), but it now allows for additional components of autonomous spending in *A*. We see that any increase in autonomous expenditure leads to a multiple increase in output. Thus any component of autonomous spending that enters *A* with a positive sign (*a*, *I*, *G*, and *NX*) will have a positive relationship with output, and any component with a negative sign (*−mpc × T*) will have a negative relationship with output. This algebraic analysis also shows us that any rise in a component of *A* that is offset by a movement in another component of *A*, leaving *A* unchanged, will also leave output unchanged.

and since it assumes a fixed price level, real and nominal quantities are the same. The first step in constructing the *ISLM* model is to examine the effect of interest rates on planned investment spending and hence on aggregate demand. Next we use a Keynesian cross diagram to see how the interest rate affects the equilibrium level of aggregate output. The resulting relationship between equilibrium aggregate output and the interest rate is known as the **IS curve**.

Just as a demand curve alone cannot tell us the quantity of goods sold in a market, the *IS* curve by itself cannot tell us what the level of aggregate output will be because the interest rate is still unknown. We need another relationship, called the **LM curve**, which describes the combinations of interest rates and aggregate output for which the quantity of money demanded equals the quantity of money supplied. When the *IS* and *LM* curves are combined in the same diagram, the intersection of the two determines the equilibrium level of aggregate output as well as the interest rate. Finally, we will have obtained a more complete analysis of the determination of aggregate output in which monetary policy plays an important role.

Equilibrium in the Goods Market: The *IS* Curve

In Keynesian analysis, the primary way that interest rates affect the level of aggregate output is through their effects on planned investment spending and net exports. After explaining why interest rates affect planned investment spending and net exports, we will use Keynesian cross diagrams to learn how interest rates affect equilibrium aggregate output.[6]

Interest Rates and Planned Investment Spending   Businesses make investments in physical capital (machines, factories, and raw materials) as long as they expect to earn more from the physical capital than the interest cost of a loan to finance the investment. When the interest rate is high, few investments in physical capital will earn more than the cost of borrowed funds, so planned investment spending is low. When the interest rate is low, many investments in physical capital will earn more than the interest cost of borrowed funds. Therefore, when interest rates are lower, business firms are more likely to undertake an investment in physical capital, and planned investment spending will be higher.

Even if a company has surplus funds and does not need to borrow to undertake an investment in physical capital, its planned investment spending will be affected by the interest rate. Instead of investing in physical capital, it could purchase a security, such as a bond. If the interest rate on this security is high, the opportunity cost (forgone interest earnings) of an investment is high, and planned investment spending will be low because the firm would probably prefer to purchase the security than to invest in physical capital. As the interest rate and the opportunity cost of investing fall, planned investment spending will increase because investments in physical capital are more likely than the security to earn greater income for the firm.

The relationship between the amount of planned investment spending and any given level of the interest rate is illustrated by the investment schedule in panel (a) of Figure 22-7. The downward slope of the schedule reflects the negative relationship between planned investment spending and the interest rate. At a low interest rate i_1, the level of planned investment spending I_1 is high; for a high interest rate i_3, planned investment spending I_3 is low.

---

[6]More modern Keynesian approaches suggest that consumer expenditure, particularly for consumer durables (cars, furniture, appliances), is influenced by the interest rate. This interest sensitivity of consumer expenditure can be allowed for in the model here by defining planned investment spending more generally to include the interest-sensitive component of consumer expenditure.

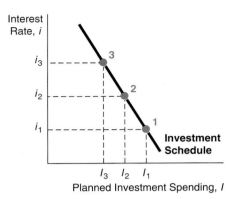

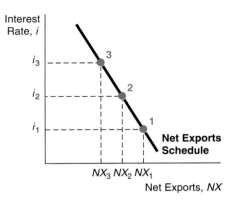

(a) Interest rates and planned
investment spending

(b) Interest rates and net exports

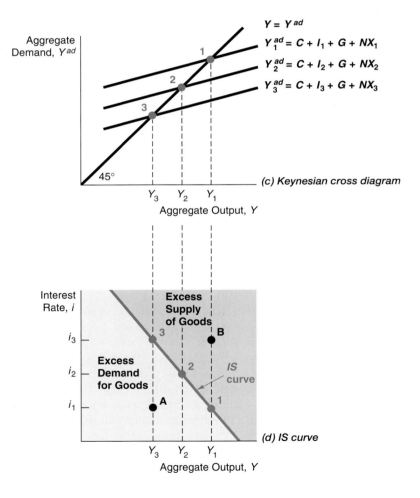

FIGURE 22·7
Deriving the *IS* Curve

The investment schedule in panel (a) shows that as the interest rate rises from i_1 to i_2 to i_3, planned investment spending falls from I_1 to I_2 to I_3, and panel (b) shows that net exports also fall from NX_1 to NX_2 to NX_3 as the interest rate rises. Panel (c) then indicates the levels of equilibrium output Y_1, Y_2, and Y_3 that correspond to those three levels of planned investment and net exports. Finally, panel (d) plots the level of equilibrium output corresponding to each of the three interest rates; the line that connects these points is the *IS* curve.

Interest Rates and Net Exports   As discussed in more detail in Chapter 7, when interest rates rise in Canada (with the price level fixed), Canadian dollar bank deposits become more attractive relative to deposits denominated in foreign currencies, thereby causing a rise in the value of dollar deposits relative to other currency deposits, that is, a rise in the exchange rate. The higher value of the dollar resulting from the rise in interest rates makes domestic goods more expensive than foreign goods, thereby causing a fall in net exports. The resulting negative relationship between interest rates and net exports is shown in panel (b) of Figure 22-7. At a low interest rate i_1, the exchange rate is low and net exports NX_1 are high; at a high interest rate i_3, the exchange rate is high and net exports NX_3 are low.

Deriving the *IS* Curve   We can now use what we have learned about the relationship of interest rates to planned investment spending and net exports in panels (a) and (b) to examine the relationship between interest rates and the equilibrium level of aggregate output (holding government spending and autonomous consumer expenditure constant). The three levels of planned investment spending and net exports in panels (a) and (b) are represented in the three aggregate demand functions in the Keynesian cross diagram of panel (c). The lowest interest rate i_1 has the highest level of both planned investment spending i_1 and net exports NX_1 and hence the highest aggregate demand function Y_1^{ad}. Point 1 in panel (d) shows the resulting equilibrium level of output Y_1, which corresponds to interest rate i_1. As the interest rate rises to i_2, both planned investment spending and net exports fall, to I_2 and NX_2, so equilibrium output falls to Y_2. Point 2 in panel (d) shows the lower level of output Y_2, which corresponds to interest rate i_2. Finally, the highest interest rate i_3 leads to the lowest level of planned investment spending and net exports and hence the lowest level of equilibrium output, which is plotted as point 3.

The line connecting the three points in panel (d), the *IS* curve, shows the combinations of interest rates and equilibrium aggregate output for which aggregate output produced equals aggregate demand.[7] The negative slope indicates that higher interest rates result in lower planned investment spending and net exports and hence lower equilibrium output.

What the *IS* Curve Tells Us   The *IS* curve traces out the points at which the total quantity of goods produced equals the total quantity of goods demanded. It describes points at which the goods market is in equilibrium. For each given level of the interest rate, the *IS* curve tells us what aggregate output must be for the goods market to be in equilibrium. As the interest rate rises, planned investment spending and net exports fall, which in turn lowers aggregate demand; aggregate output must be lower in order for it to equal aggregate demand and satisfy goods market equilibrium.

The *IS* curve is a useful concept because output tends to move toward points on the curve that satisfy goods market equilibrium. If the economy is located in the area to the right of the *IS* curve, it has an excess supply of goods. At point B, for example, aggregate output Y_1 is greater than the equilibrium level of output Y_3 on the *IS* curve. This excess supply of goods results in unplanned inventory accumulation, which causes output to fall toward the *IS* curve. The decline stops only when output is again at its equilibrium level on the *IS* curve.

If the economy is located in the area to the left of the *IS* curve, it has an excess demand for goods. At point A, aggregate output Y_3 is below the equilibrium level of output Y_1 on the *IS* curve. The excess demand for goods results in an unplanned decrease in inventory, which causes output to rise toward the *IS* curve, stopping only when aggregate output is again at its equilibrium level on the *IS* curve.

---

[7]The *IS* was so named by Sir John Hicks because in the simplest Keynesian framework with no government sector, equilibrium in the Keynesian cross diagram occurs when investment spending *I* equals saving *S*.

Significantly, equilibrium in the goods market does not produce a unique equilibrium level of aggregate output. Although we now know where aggregate output will head for a given level of the interest rate, we cannot determine aggregate output because we do not know what the interest rate is. To complete our analysis of aggregate output determination, we need to introduce another market that produces an additional relationship that links aggregate output and interest rates. The market for money fulfills this function with the *LM* curve. When the *LM* curve is combined with the *IS* curve, a unique equilibrium that determines both aggregate output and the interest rate is obtained.

Equilibrium in the Market for Money: The *LM* Curve

Just as the *IS* curve is derived from the equilibrium condition in the goods market (aggregate output equals aggregate demand), the *LM* curve is derived from the equilibrium condition in the market for money, which requires that the quantity of money demanded equal the quantity of money supplied. The main building block in Keynes's analysis of the market for money is the demand for money he called *liquidity preference*. Let us briefly review his theory of the demand for money (discussed at length in Chapters 5 and 21).

Keynes's liquidity preference theory states that the demand for money in real terms M^d/P depends on income Y (aggregate output) and interest rates i. The demand for money is positively related to income for two reasons. First, a rise in income raises the level of transactions in the economy, which in turn raises the demand for money because it is used to carry out these transactions. Second, a rise in income increases the demand for money because it increases the wealth of individuals who want to hold more assets, one of which is money. The opportunity cost of holding money is the interest sacrificed by not holding other assets (such as bonds) instead. As interest rates rise, the opportunity cost of holding money rises, and the demand for money falls. According to the liquidity preference theory, the demand for money is positively related to aggregate output and negatively related to interest rates.

Deriving the *LM* Curve   In Keynes's analysis, the level of interest rates is determined by equilibrium in the market for money, at which point the quantity of money demanded equals the quantity of money supplied. Figure 22-8 depicts what happens to equilibrium in the market for money as the level of output changes. Because the *LM* curve is derived holding the money supply at a fixed level, it is fixed at the level of $\overline{M}$, in panel (a).[8] Each level of aggregate output has its own money demand curve because as aggregate output changes, the level of transactions in the economy changes, which in turn changes the demand for money.

When aggregate output is Y_1, the money demand curve is $M^d(Y_1)$. It slopes downward because a lower interest rate means that the opportunity cost of holding money is lower, so the quantity of money demanded is higher. Equilibrium in the market for money occurs at point 1, at which the interest rate is i_1. When aggregate output is at the higher level Y_2, the money demand curve shifts rightward to $M^d(Y_2)$ because the higher level of output means that at any given interest rate, the quantity of money demanded is higher. Equilibrium in the market for money now occurs at point 2, at which the interest rate is at the higher level of i_2. Similarly, a still higher level of aggregate output, Y_3, results in an even higher level of the equilibrium interest rate, i_3.

---

[8]As pointed out in earlier chapters on the money supply process, the money supply is positively related to interest rates, and so the M^s curve in panel (a) should actually have a positive slope. The M^s curve is assumed to be vertical in panel (a) in order to simplify the graph, but allowing for a positive slope leads to identical results.

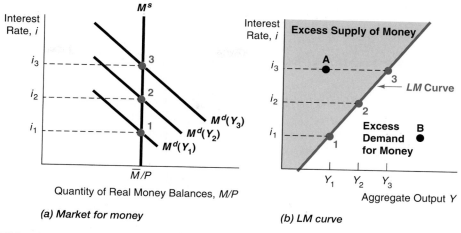

(a) Market for money   **(b) LM curve**

FIGURE 22-8   Deriving the *LM* Curve

Panel (a) shows the equilibrium levels of the interest rate in the market for money that arise when aggregate output is at Y_1, Y_2, and Y_3. Panel (b) plots the three levels of the equilibrium interest rate i_1, i_2, and i_3 corresponding to these three levels of output; the line that connects these points is the *LM* curve.

Panel (b) plots the equilibrium interest rates that correspond to the different output levels, with points 1, 2, and 3 corresponding to the equilibrium points 1, 2, and 3 in panel (a). The line connecting these points is the *LM* curve, which shows the combinations of interest rates and output for which the market for money is in equilibrium.[9] The positive slope arises because higher output raises the demand for money and thus raises the equilibrium interest rate.

What the *LM* Curve Tells Us   The *LM* curve traces out the points that satisfy the equilibrium condition that the quantity of money demanded equals the quantity of money supplied. For each given level of aggregate output, the *LM* curve tells us what the interest rate must be for there to be equilibrium in the market for money. As aggregate output rises, the demand for money increases and the interest rate rises, so that money demanded equals money supplied and the market for money is in equilibrium.

Just as the economy tends to move toward the equilibrium points represented by the *IS* curve, it also moves toward the equilibrium points on the *LM* curve. If the economy is located in the area to the left of the *LM* curve, there is an excess supply of money. At point A, for example, the interest rate is i_3 and aggregate output is Y_1. The interest rate is above the equilibrium level, and people are holding more money than they want to. To eliminate their excess money balances, they will purchase bonds, which causes the price of the bonds to rise and their interest rate to fall. (The inverse relationship between the price of a bond and its interest rate is discussed in Chapter 4.) As long as an excess supply of money exists, the interest rate will fall until it comes to rest on the *LM* curve.

If the economy is located in the area to the right of the *LM* curve, there is an excess demand for money. At point B, for example, the interest rate i_1 is below the equilibrium level, and people want to hold more money than they currently do. To acquire this money, they will sell bonds and drive down bond prices, and the

---

[9]Hicks named this the *LM* curve to indicate that it represents the combinations of interest rates and output for which money demand, which Keynes denoted as *L* to represent liquidity preference, equals money supply *M*.

interest rate will rise. This process will stop only when the interest rate rises to an equilibrium point on the *LM* curve.

ISLM APPROACH TO AGGREGATE OUTPUT AND INTEREST RATES

Now that we have derived the *IS* and *LM* curves, we can put them into the same diagram (Figure 22-9) to produce a model that enables us to determine both aggregate output and the interest rate. The only point at which the goods market and the market for money are in simultaneous equilibrium is at the intersection of the *IS* and *LM* curves, point E. At this point, aggregate output equals aggregate demand (*IS*) and the quantity of money demanded equals the quantity of money supplied (*LM*). At any other point in the diagram, at least one of these equilibrium conditions is not satisfied, and market forces move the economy toward the general equilibrium, point E.

To learn how this works, let's consider what happens if the economy is at point A, which is on the *IS* curve but not the *LM* curve. Even though at point A the goods market is in equilibrium, so that aggregate output equals aggregate demand, the interest rate is above its equilibrium level, so the demand for money is less than the supply. Because people have more money than they want to hold, they will try to get rid of it by buying bonds. The resulting rise in bond prices causes a fall in interest rates, which in turn causes both planned investment spending and net exports to rise, and thus aggregate output rises. The economy then moves down along the *IS* curve, and the process continues until the interest rate falls to i^* and aggregate output rises to Y^*—that is, until the economy is at equilibrium point E.

If the economy is on the *LM* curve but off the *IS* curve at point B, it will also head toward the equilibrium at point E. At point B, even though money demand equals money supply, output is higher than the equilibrium level and exceeds aggregate demand. Firms are unable to sell all their output, and unplanned inven-

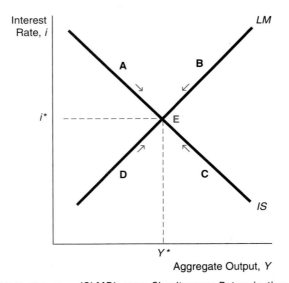

FIGURE 22-9   *ISLM* Diagram: Simultaneous Determination of Output and the Interest Rate

Only at point E, where the interest rate is i^* and output is Y^*, is there equilibrium simultaneously in both the goods market (as measured by the *IS* curve) and the market for money (as measured by the *LM* curve). At other points, such as A, B, C, or D, one of the two markets is not in equilibrium, and there will be a tendency to head toward the equilibrium, point E.

tory accumulates, prompting them to cut production and lower output. The decline in output means that the demand for money will fall, lowering interest rates. The economy then moves down along the *LM* curve until it reaches equilibrium point E.

Study Guide

To test your understanding of why the economy heads toward equilibrium point E at the intersection of the *IS* and *LM* curves, see if you can provide the reasoning behind the movement to point E from points such as C and D in the figure.

We have finally developed a model, the *ISLM* model, which tells us how both interest rates and aggregate output are determined when the price level is fixed. Although we have demonstrated that the economy will head toward an aggregate output level of Y^*, there is no reason to assume that at this level of aggregate output the economy is at full employment. If the unemployment rate is too high, government policymakers might want to increase aggregate output to reduce it. The *ISLM* apparatus indicates that they can do this by manipulating monetary and fiscal policy. We will conduct an *ISLM* analysis of how monetary and fiscal policy can affect economic activity in the next chapter.

SUMMARY

1. In the simple Keynesian framework in which the price level is fixed, output is determined by the equilibrium condition in the goods market that aggregate output equals aggregate demand. Aggregate demand equals the sum of consumer expenditure, planned investment spending, government spending, and net exports. Consumer expenditure is described by the consumption function, which indicates that consumer expenditure will rise as disposable income increases. Keynes's analysis shows that aggregate output is positively related to autonomous consumer expenditure, planned investment spending, government spending, and net exports and negatively related to the level of taxes. A change in any of these factors leads, through the expenditure multiplier, to a multiple change in aggregate output.

2. The *ISLM* model determines aggregate output and the interest rate for a fixed price level using the *IS* and *LM* curves. The *IS* curve traces out the combinations of the interest rate and aggregate output for which the goods market is in equilibrium, and the *LM* curve traces out the combinations for which the market for money is in equilibrium. The *IS* curve slopes downward because higher interest rates lower planned investment spending and so lower equilibrium output. The *LM* curve slopes upward because higher aggregate output raises the demand for money and so raises the equilibrium interest rate.

3. The simultaneous determination of output and interest rates occurs at the intersection of the *IS* and *LM* curves, where both the goods market and the market for money are in equilibrium. At any other level of interest rates and output, at least one of the markets will be out of equilibrium, and forces will move the economy toward the general equilibrium point at the intersection of the *IS* and *LM* curves.

KEY TERMS

aggregate demand, p. 497

aggregate demand function, p. 501

"animal spirits", p. 504

autonomous consumer expenditure, p. 498

consumer expenditure, p. 496

consumption function, p. 498

disposable income, p. 498

expenditure multiplier, p. 502

fixed investment, p. 499

government spending, p. 497

inventory investment, p. 499

IS curve, p. 511

LM curve, p. 511

marginal propensity to consume, p. 498

net exports, p. 497

planned investment spending, p. 497

QUESTIONS AND PROBLEMS

Questions marked with an asterisk are answered at the end of the book in an appendix, "Answers to Selected Questions and Problems."

1. Calculate the value of the consumption function at each level of disposable income in Table 22-1 if $a = 100$ and $mpc = 0.9$.

*2. Why do companies cut production when they find that their unplanned inventory investment is greater than zero? If they didn't cut production, what effect would this have on their profits? Why?

3. Plot the consumption function $C = 100 + 0.75Y$ on graph paper.
   a. Assuming no government sector, if planned investment spending is 200, what is the equilibrium level of aggregate output? Show this equilibrium level on the graph you have drawn.
   b. If businesses become more pessimistic about the profitability of investment and planned investment spending falls by 100, what happens to the equilibrium level of output?

*4. If the consumption function is $C = 100 + 0.8Y$ and planned investment spending is 200, what is the equilibrium level of output? If planned investment falls by 100, how much does the equilibrium level of output fall?

5. Why are the multipliers in Problems 3 and 4 different? Explain intuitively why one is higher than the other.

*6. If firms suddenly become more optimistic about the profitability of investment and planned investment spending rises by $100 billion, while consumers become more pessimistic and autonomous consumer spending falls by $100 billion, what happens to aggregate output?

7. "A rise in planned investment spending by $100 billion at the same time that autonomous consumer expenditure falls by $50 billion has the same effect on aggregate output as a rise in autonomous con-

sumer expenditure alone by $50 billion." Is this statement true, false, or uncertain? Explain your answer.

*8. If the consumption function is $C = 100 + 0.75Y$, $I = 200$, and government spending is 200, what will be the equilibrium level of output? Demonstrate your answer with a Keynesian cross diagram. What happens to aggregate output if government spending rises by 100?

9. If the marginal propensity to consume were 0.5, how much would government spending have to rise in order to raise output by $1000 billion?

*10. Suppose that government policymakers decide that they will change taxes to raise aggregate output by $400 billion, and $mpc = 0.5$. By how much will taxes have to be changed?

11. What happens to aggregate output if both taxes and government spending are lowered by $300 billion and $mpc = 0.5$? Explain your answer.

*12. Will aggregate output rise or fall if an increase in autonomous consumer expenditure is matched by an equal increase in taxes?

13. If a change in the interest rate has no effect on planned investment spending, trace out what happens to the equilibrium level of aggregate output as interest rates fall. What does this imply about the slope of the *IS* curve?

*14. Using a supply and demand diagram for the market for money, show what happens to the equilibrium level of the interest rate as aggregate output falls. What does this imply about the slope of the *LM* curve?

15. "If the point describing the combination of the interest rate and aggregate output is not on either the *IS* or the *LM* curve, the economy will have no tendency to head toward the intersection of the two curves." Is this statement true, false, or uncertain? Explain your answer.

Chapter 23

Monetary and Fiscal Policy in the *ISLM* Model

PREVIEW   Since World War II, government policymakers have tried to promote high employment without causing inflation. If the economy experiences a recession such as the one that occurred at the time of Iraq's invasion of Kuwait in 1990, policymakers have two principal sets of tools that they can use to affect aggregate economic activity: *monetary policy,* the control of interest rates or the money supply, and *fiscal policy,* the control of government spending and taxes.

The *ISLM* model can help policymakers predict what will happen to aggregate output and interest rates if they decide to increase the money supply or increase government spending. In this way, *ISLM* analysis enables us to answer some important questions about the usefulness and effectiveness of monetary and fiscal policy in influencing economic activity.

But which is better? When is monetary policy more effective than fiscal policy at controlling the level of aggregate output, and when is it less effective? Will fiscal policy be more effective if it is conducted by changing government spending rather than changing taxes? Should the monetary authorities conduct monetary policy by manipulating the money supply or interest rates?

In this chapter we use the *ISLM* model to help answer these questions and to learn how the model generates the aggregate demand curve featured prominently in the aggregate demand and supply framework (examined in Chapter 24), which is used to understand changes not only in aggregate output but in the price level as well. Our analysis will show why economists focus so much attention on topics such as the stability of the demand for money function and whether the demand for money is strongly influenced by interest rates.

First, however, let's examine the *ISLM* model in more detail to see how the *IS* and *LM* curves developed in Chapter 22 shift and the implications of these shifts. (We continue to assume that the price level is fixed so that real and nominal quantities are the same.)

FACTORS THAT CAUSE THE *IS* CURVE TO SHIFT

You have already learned that the *IS* curve describes equilibrium points in the goods market—the combinations of aggregate output and interest rate for which aggregate output produced equals aggregate demand. The *IS* curve shifts whenever a change in autonomous factors (independent of aggregate output) occurs that is unrelated to the interest rate. (A change in the interest rate that affects equilibrium aggregate output only causes a movement along the *IS* curve.) We have already identified five candidates as autonomous factors that can shift aggregate demand and hence affect the level of equilibrium output. We can now ask how changes in each of these factors affect the *IS* curve.

1. *Changes in Autonomous Consumer Expenditure.* A rise in autonomous consumer expenditure shifts aggregate demand upward and shifts the *IS* curve to the right (Figure 23-1). To see how this shift occurs, suppose that the *IS* curve is initially at IS_1 in panel (a) and a huge oil field is discovered in Alberta, perhaps containing more oil than in Saudi Arabia. Consumers now become more optimistic about the future health of the economy, and autonomous consumer expenditure rises. What happens to the equilibrium level of aggregate output as a result of this rise in autonomous consumer expenditure when the interest rate is held constant at i_A?

   The IS_1 curve tells us that equilibrium aggregate output is at Y_A when the interest rate is at i_A (point A). Panel (b) shows that this point is an equilibrium in the goods market because the aggregate demand function Y_1^{ad} at an interest rate i_A crosses the 45° line $Y = Y^{ad}$ at an aggregate output level of Y_A. When autonomous consumer expenditure rises because of the oil discovery, the aggregate demand function shifts upward to Y_2^{ad} and equilibrium output rises to $Y_{A'}$. This rise in equilibrium output from Y_A to $Y_{A'}$ when the interest rate is i_A is plotted in panel (a) as a movement from point A to point A'. The same analysis can be applied to every point on the initial IS_1 curve; therefore, the rise in autonomous consumer expenditure shifts the *IS* curve to the right from IS_1 to IS_2 in panel (a).

   A decline in autonomous consumer expenditure reverses the direction of the analysis. For any given interest rate, the aggregate demand function shifts downward, the equilibrium level of aggregate output falls, and the *IS* curve shifts to the left.

2. *Changes in Investment Spending Unrelated to the Interest Rate.* In Chapter 22 we learned that changes in the interest rate affect planned investment spending and hence the equilibrium level of output, but this change in investment spending merely causes a movement along the *IS* curve and not a shift. A rise in planned investment spending unrelated to the interest rate (say, because companies become more confident about investment profitability after the Alberta oil discovery) shifts the aggregate demand function upward, as in panel (b) of Figure 23-1. For any given interest rate, the equilibrium level of aggregate output rises, and the *IS* curve will shift to the right, as in panel (a).

   A decrease in investment spending because companies become more pessimistic about investment profitability shifts the aggregate demand function downward for any given interest rate; the equilibrium level of aggregate output falls, shifting the *IS* curve to the left.

3. *Changes in Government Spending.* An increase in government spending will also cause the aggregate demand function at any given interest rate to shift upward, as in panel (b). The equilibrium level of aggregate output rises at any given interest rate, and the *IS* curve shifts to the right. Conversely, a decline in

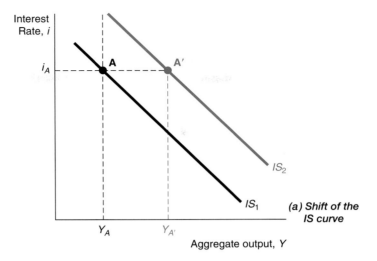

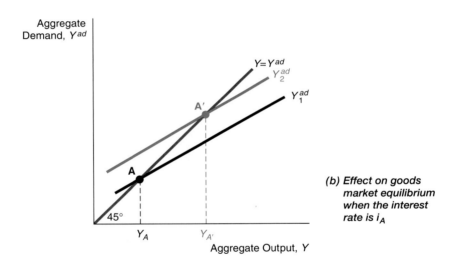

FIGURE 23-1   Shift in the *IS* Curve

The *IS* curve will shift from IS_1 to IS_2 as a result of (1) an increase in autonomous consumer spending, (2) an increase in planned investment spending due to business optimism, (3) an increase in government spending, (4) a decrease in taxes, or (5) an increase in net exports that is unrelated to interest rates. Panel (b) shows how changes in these factors lead to the rightward shift in the *IS* curve using a Keynesian cross diagram. For any given interest rate (here i_A), these changes shift the aggregate demand function upward and raise equilibrium output from Y_A to $Y_{A'}$.

government spending shifts the aggregate demand function downward, and the equilibrium level of output falls, shifting the *IS* curve to the left.

4. *Changes in Taxes*. Unlike changes in other factors that directly affect the aggregate demand function, a decline in taxes shifts the aggregate demand function by raising consumer expenditure and shifting the aggregate demand function upward at any given interest rate. A decline in taxes raises the equilibrium level of aggregate output at any given interest rate and shifts the *IS* curve to the right (as in Figure 23-1). Recall, however, that a change in taxes has a smaller effect on aggregate demand than an equivalent change in

government spending. So for a given change in taxes, the *IS* curve will shift less than for an equal change in government spending.

A rise in taxes lowers the aggregate demand function and reduces the equilibrium level of aggregate output at each interest rate. Therefore, a rise in taxes shifts the *IS* curve to the left.

5. *Changes in Net Exports Unrelated to the Interest Rate.* As with planned investment spending, changes in net exports arising from a change in interest rates merely cause a movement along the *IS* curve and not a shift. An autonomous rise in net exports unrelated to the interest rate—say because Canadian-made clothes become more chic than French-made clothes—shifts the aggregate demand function upward and causes the *IS* curve to shift to the right, as in Figure 23-1. Conversely, an autonomous fall in net exports shifts the aggregate demand function downward, and the equilibrium level of output falls, shifting the *IS* curve to the left.

FACTORS THAT CAUSE THE *LM* CURVE TO SHIFT

The *LM* curve describes the equilibrium points in the market for money—the combinations of aggregate output and interest rate for which the quantity of money demanded equals the quantity of money supplied. Whereas five factors can cause the *IS* curve to shift (changes in autonomous consumer expenditure, planned investment spending unrelated to the interest rate, government spending, taxes, and net exports unrelated to the interest rate), only two factors can cause the *LM* curve to shift: autonomous changes in money demand and changes in the money supply. How do changes in these two factors affect the *LM* curve?

1. *Changes in the Money Supply.* A rise in the money supply shifts the *LM* curve to the right, as shown in Figure 23-2. To see how this shift occurs, suppose that the *LM* curve is initially at LM_1 in panel (a) and the Bank of Canada conducts open market purchases that increase the money supply. If we consider point A, which is on the initial LM_1 curve, we can examine what happens to the equilibrium level of the interest rate, holding output constant at Y_A.

Panel (b), which contains a supply and demand diagram for the market for money, depicts the equilibrium interest rate initially as i_A at the intersection of the supply curve for money M_1^s and the demand curve for money M^d. The rise in the quantity of money supplied shifts the supply curve to M_2^s, and, holding output constant at Y_A, the equilibrium interest rate falls to $i_{A'}$. In panel (a), this decline in the equilibrium interest rate from i_A to $i_{A'}$ is shown as a movement from point A to point A'. The same analysis can be applied to every point on the initial LM_1 curve, leading to the conclusion that at any given level of aggregate output, the equilibrium interest rate falls when the money supply increases. Thus LM_2 is below and to the right of LM_1.

Reversing this reasoning, a decline in the money supply shifts the *LM* curve to the left. A decline in the money supply results in a shortage of money at points on the initial *LM* curve. This condition of excess demand for money can be eliminated by a rise in the interest rate, which reduces the quantity of money demanded until it again equals the quantity of money supplied.

2. *Autonomous Changes in Money Demand.* The theory of asset demand outlined in Chapter 5 indicates that there can be an autonomous rise in money demand (not caused by a change in the price level, aggregate output, or the interest rate). For example, an increase in the volatility of bond returns would make bonds riskier relative to money and would increase the quantity of money demanded at any given interest rate, price level, or amount of

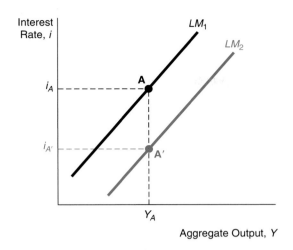

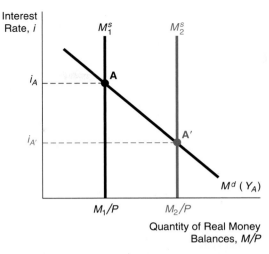

(a) Shift of the LM curve

(b) Effect on the market for money when aggregate output is constant at Y_A

FIGURE 23-2   Shift in the *LM* Curve from an Increase in the Money Supply
The *LM* curve shifts to the right from LM_1 to LM_2 when the money supply increases because, as indicated in panel (b), at any given level of aggregate output (say, Y_A), the equilibrium interest rate falls (point A to A′).

aggregate output. The resulting autonomous increase in the demand for money shifts the *LM* curve to the left, as shown in Figure 23-3. Consider point A on the initial LM_1 curve. Suppose that a massive financial panic occurs, sending many companies into bankruptcy. Because bonds have become a riskier asset, people want to shift from holding bonds to holding money; they will hold more money at all interest rates and output levels. The resulting increase in money demand at an output level of Y_A is shown by the shift of the money demand curve from M_1^d to M_2^d in panel (b). The new equilibrium in the market for money now indicates that if aggregate output is constant at Y_A, the equilibrium interest rate will rise to $i_{A'}$, and the point of equilibrium moves from A to A′.

Conversely, an autonomous decline in money demand would lead to a rightward shift in the *LM* curve. The fall in money demand would create an excess supply of money, which is eliminated by a rise in the quantity of money demanded from a decline in the interest rate.

CHANGES IN EQUILIBRIUM LEVEL OF THE INTEREST RATE AND AGGREGATE OUTPUT

You can now use your knowledge of factors that cause the *IS* and *LM* curves to shift for the purpose of analyzing how the equilibrium levels of the interest rate and aggregate output change in response to changes in monetary and fiscal policies.

Response to a Change in Monetary Policy

Figure 23-4 illustrates the response of output and interest rate to an increase in the money supply. Initially, the economy is in equilibrium for both the goods market and the market for money at point 1, the intersection of IS_1 and LM_1. Suppose that at the resulting level of aggregate output Y_1, the economy is suffering from an unemployment rate of 10%, and the Bank of Canada decides it should try to raise output and reduce unemployment by raising the money supply. Will the Bank's change in monetary policy have the intended effect?

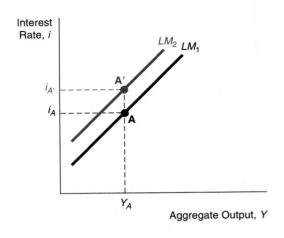

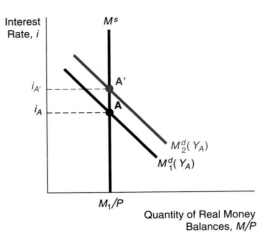

(a) Shift in the LM curve

(b) Effect on the market for money when aggregate output is constant at Y_A

FIGURE 23-3 Shift in the *LM* Curve When Money Demand Increases
The *LM* curve shifts to the left from LM_1 to LM_2 when money demand increases because, as indicated in panel (b), at any given level of aggregate output (say, Y_A), the equilibrium interest rate rises (point A to A').

The rise in the money supply causes the *LM* curve to shift rightward to LM_2, and the equilibrium point for both the goods market and the market for money moves to point 2 (intersection of IS_1 and LM_2). As a result of an increase in the money supply, the interest rate declines to i_2, as we found in Figure 23-2, and aggregate output rises to Y_2; the Bank's policy has been successful in improving the health of the economy.

For a clear understanding of why aggregate output rises and the interest rate declines, think about exactly what has happened in moving from point 1 to point 2. When the economy is at point 1, the increase in the money supply (rightward shift of the *LM* curve) creates an excess supply of money, resulting in a decline in the interest rate. The decline causes investment spending and net exports to rise, which in turn raises aggregate demand and causes aggregate output to rise. The excess supply of money is eliminated when the economy reaches point 2 because both the rise in output and the fall in the interest rate have raised the quantity of money demanded until it equals the new higher level of the money supply.

A decline in the money supply reverses the process; it shifts the *LM* curve to the left, causing the interest rate to rise and output to fall. Accordingly, ***aggregate output is positively related to the money supply;*** aggregate output expands when the money supply increases and falls when it decreases.

Response to a Change in Fiscal Policy

Suppose that the Bank of Canada is not willing to increase the money supply when the economy is suffering from a 10% unemployment rate at point 1. Can the federal government come to the rescue and manipulate government spending and taxes to raise aggregate output and reduce the massive unemployment?

The *ISLM* model demonstrates that it can. Figure 23-5 depicts the response of output and the interest rate to an expansionary fiscal policy (increase in government spending or decrease in taxes). An increase in government spending or a decrease in taxes causes the *IS* curve to shift to IS_2, and the equilibrium point for both the goods market and the market for money moves to point 2 (intersection of IS_2 with LM_1). The result of the change in fiscal policy is a rise in aggregate

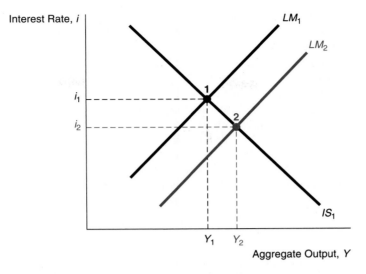

FIGURE 23-4 Response of Aggregate Output and the Interest Rate to an Increase in the Money Supply

The increase in the money supply shifts the *LM* curve to the right from LM_1 to LM_2; the economy moves to point 2, where output has increased to Y_2 and the interest rate has declined to i_2.

output to Y_2 and a rise in the interest rate to i_2. Note the difference in the effect on the interest rate between an expansionary fiscal policy and an expansionary monetary policy. In the case of an expansionary fiscal policy, the interest rate rises, whereas in the case of an expansionary monetary policy, the interest rate falls.

Why does an increase in government spending or a decrease in taxes move the economy from point 1 to point 2, causing a rise in both aggregate output and the

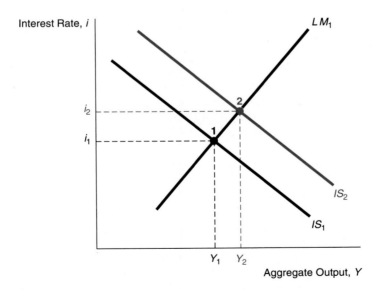

FIGURE 23-5 Response of Aggregate Output and the Interest Rate to an Expansionary Fiscal Policy

Expansionary fiscal policy (a rise in government spending or a decrease in taxes) shifts the *IS* curve to the right from IS_1 to IS_2; the economy moves to point 2, aggregate output increases to Y_2, and the interest rate rises to i_2.

interest rate? An increase in government spending raises aggregate demand directly; a decrease in taxes makes more income available for spending and raises aggregate demand by raising consumer expenditure. The resulting increase in aggregate demand causes aggregate output to rise. The higher level of aggregate output raises the quantity of money demanded, creating an excess demand for money, which in turn causes the interest rate to rise. At point 2, the excess demand for money created by a rise in aggregate output has been eliminated by a rise in the interest rate, which lowers the quantity of money demanded.

A contractionary fiscal policy (decrease in government spending or increase in taxes) reverses the process described in Figure 23-5; it causes aggregate demand to fall, which shifts the *IS* curve to the left and causes both aggregate output and the interest rate to fall. ***Aggregate output and the interest rate are positively related to government spending and negatively related to taxes.***

Study Guide

As a study aid, Table 23-1 indicates the effect on aggregate output and interest rates of a change in the seven factors that shift the *IS* and *LM* curves. In addition, the table provides schematics describing the reason for the output and interest-rate response. *ISLM* analysis is best learned by practicing applications. To get this practice, you might try to develop the reasoning for your own Table 23-1 in which all the factors decrease rather than increase, or answer Problems 9, 10, and 11 at the end of this chapter.

APPLICATION | *The Policy Mix and German Unification*

So far we have looked at fiscal and monetary policy in isolation and showed how each one works. In practice, however, fiscal and monetary policies are used together and the combination of the two is known as the **policy mix**.

For example, following the 1990 unification of West Germany and East Germany, the German government sharply increased government spending and transfers in order to revive eastern Germany. In terms of the *ISLM* model of Figure 23-6, this resulted in a large rightward shift of the *IS* curve from IS_1 to IS_2 and moved the German economy from point 1 to point 2, thereby raising aggregate output.

The German central bank (Bundesbank) saw these developments and feared that they would result in inflation. The Bundesbank concluded that economic activity should be slowed and adopted accordingly a tight monetary policy. In terms of the *ISLM* model of Figure 23-6, it shifted the *LM* curve to the left from LM_1 to LM_2 in order to increase interest rates and slow down the level of activity. Thus, the policy mix moved the German economy to point 3 and resulted in fast growth (from the fiscal expansion) and high interest rates (from the tight monetary policy).

In fact, the Bundesbank due to its financial leadership was accused of forcing interest rates to higher levels than they might otherwise have been in Europe as well as in the rest of the world.

Bundesbank
www.bundesbank.de

TABLE 23-1   Effects from Factors That Shift the *IS* and *LM* Curves

Factor	Autonomous Change in Factor	Response	Reason	
Consumer expenditure, C	↑	$Y\uparrow$, $i\uparrow$	$C\uparrow \Rightarrow Y^{ad}\uparrow \Rightarrow$ *IS* shifts right	
Investment, I	↑	$Y\uparrow$, $i\uparrow$	$I\uparrow \Rightarrow Y^{ad}\uparrow \Rightarrow$ *IS* shifts right	
Government spending, G	↑	$Y\uparrow$, $i\uparrow$	$G\uparrow \Rightarrow Y^{ad}\uparrow \Rightarrow$ *IS* shifts right	
Taxes, T	↑	$Y\downarrow$, $i\downarrow$	$T\uparrow \Rightarrow C\downarrow \Rightarrow Y^{ad}\downarrow \Rightarrow$ *IS* shifts left	
Net exports, NX	↑	$Y\uparrow$, $i\uparrow$	$NX\uparrow \Rightarrow Y^{ad}\uparrow \Rightarrow$ *IS* shifts right	
Money supply, M^s	↑	$Y\uparrow$, $i\downarrow$	$M^s\uparrow \Rightarrow i\downarrow \Rightarrow$ *LM* shifts right	
Money demand, M^d	↑	$Y\downarrow$, $i\uparrow$	$M^d\uparrow \Rightarrow i\uparrow \Rightarrow$ *LM* shifts left	

Note: Only increases (↑) in the factors are shown. The effect of decreases in the factors would be the opposite of those indicated in the "Response" column.

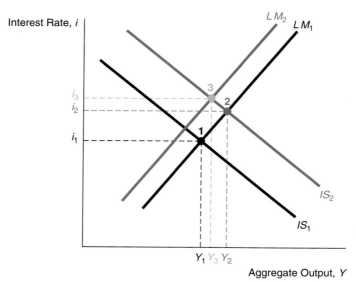

FIGURE 23-6 The Policy Mix and German Unification

The fiscal expansion led to a rightward shift of the IS curve from IS_1 to IS_2 and moved the German economy from point 1 to point 2, thereby raising both the interest rate and aggregate output. The Bundesbank's tight money policy led to a leftward shift of the LM curve from LM_1 to LM_2 and moved the economy to point 3. Thus, the policy mix resulted in fast growth and high interest rates.

EFFECTIVENESS OF MONETARY VERSUS FISCAL POLICY

Our discussion of the effects of fiscal and monetary policy suggests that a government can easily lift an economy out of a recession by implementing any of a number of policies (changing the money supply, government spending, or taxes). But how can policymakers decide which of these policies to use if faced with too much unemployment? Should they decrease taxes, increase government spending, raise the money supply, or do all three? And if they decide to increase the money supply, by how much should it be increased? Economists do not pretend to have all the answers, and although the *ISLM* model will not clear the path to aggregate economic bliss, it can help policymakers decide which policies may be most effective under certain circumstances.

Monetary Policy Versus Fiscal Policy: The Case of Complete Crowding Out

The *ISLM* model developed so far in this chapter shows that both monetary and fiscal policy affect the level of aggregate output. To understand when monetary policy is more effective than fiscal policy, we will examine a special case of the *ISLM* model in which money demand is unaffected by the interest rate (money demand is said to be interest-inelastic) so that monetary policy affects output but fiscal policy does not.

Consider the slope of the *LM* curve if the demand for money is unaffected by changes in the interest rate. If point 1 in panel (a) of Figure 23-7 is such that the quantity of money demanded equals the quantity of money supplied, then it is on the *LM* curve. If the interest rate rises to, say, i_2, the quantity of money demanded is unaffected, and it will continue to equal the *unchanged* quantity of money supplied only if aggregate output remains *unchanged* at Y_1 (point 2). Equilibrium in the market for money will occur at the same level of aggregate output regardless of the interest rate, and the *LM* curve will be vertical, as shown in both panels of Figure 23-7.

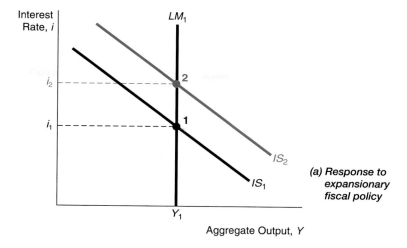

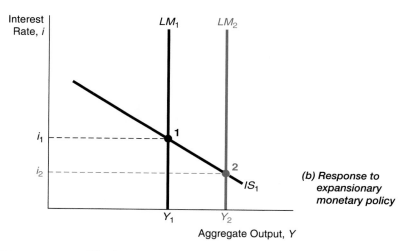

FIGURE 23-7   Effectiveness of Monetary and Fiscal Policy When Money Demand Is Unaffected by the Interest Rate

When the demand for money is unaffected by the interest rate, the *LM* curve is vertical. In panel (a), an expansionary fiscal policy (increase in government spending or a cut in taxes) shifts the *IS* curve from IS_1 to IS_2 and leaves aggregate output unchanged at Y_1. In panel (b), an increase in the money supply shifts the *LM* curve from LM_1 to LM_2 and raises aggregate output from Y_1 to Y_2. Therefore, monetary policy is effective, but fiscal policy is not.

Suppose that the economy is suffering from a high rate of unemployment, which policymakers try to eliminate with either expansionary fiscal or monetary policy. Panel (a) depicts what happens when an expansionary fiscal policy (increase in government spending or cut in taxes) is implemented, shifting the *IS* curve to the right from IS_1 to IS_2. As you can see in panel (a), the fiscal expansion has no effect on output; aggregate output remains at Y_1 when the economy moves from point 1 to point 2.

In our earlier analysis, expansionary fiscal policy always increased aggregate demand and raised the level of output. Why doesn't that happen in panel (a)? The answer is that because the *LM* curve is vertical, the rightward shift of the *IS* curve raises the interest rate to i_2, which causes investment spending and net exports to fall enough to offset completely the increased spending of the expansionary fiscal policy. Put another way, increased spending that results from expansionary fiscal policy has *crowded out* investment spending and net exports, which decrease because of the rise in the interest rate. This situation in which expansionary fiscal policy does not lead to a rise in output is frequently referred to as a case of **complete crowding out**.[1]

Panel (b) shows what happens when the Bank of Canada tries to eliminate high unemployment through an expansionary monetary policy (increase in the money supply). Here the *LM* curve shifts to the right from LM_1 to LM_2 because at each interest rate, output must rise so that the quantity of money demanded rises to match the increase in the money supply. Aggregate output rises from Y_1 to Y_2 (the economy moves from point 1 to point 2), and expansionary monetary policy does affect aggregate output in this case.

We conclude from the analysis in Figure 23-7 that if the demand for money is unaffected by changes in the interest rate (money demand is interest-inelastic), monetary policy is effective but fiscal policy is not. An even more general conclusion can be reached: ***the less interest-sensitive money demand is, the more effective monetary policy is relative to fiscal policy***.

Because the interest sensitivity of money demand is important to policymakers' decisions regarding the use of monetary or fiscal policy to influence economic activity, the subject has been studied extensively by economists and has been the focus of many debates. Findings on the interest sensitivity of money demand were discussed in Chapter 21.

APPLICATION   *Targeting Money Supply Versus Interest Rates*

In the 1970s and early 1980s, central banks in many countries pursued a strategy of monetary targeting—that is, they used their policy tools to hit a money supply target (tried to make the money supply equal to a target value). However, as we saw in Chapter 18, many of these central banks abandoned monetary targeting in the 1980s to pursue interest-rate targeting instead because of the breakdown of the stable relationship between the money supply and economic activity. The *ISLM* model has important implications for which variable a central bank should target and we can apply it to explain why central banks have abandoned monetary targeting for interest-rate targeting.[2]

As we saw in Chapter 18, when the Bank of Canada attempts to hit a money supply target, it cannot at the same time pursue an interest-rate target; it can hit one target or the other but not both. Consequently, it needs to know which of these two targets will produce more accurate control of aggregate output.

In contrast to the textbook world you have been inhabiting, in which the *IS* and *LM* curves are assumed to be fixed, the real world is one of great uncertainty

Bank of Canada
www.bankofcanada.ca

---

[1]When the demand for money is affected by the interest rate, the usual case in which the *LM* curve slopes upward but is not vertical, some crowding out occurs. The rightward shift of the *IS* curve also raises the interest rate, which causes investment spending and net exports to fall somewhat. However, as Figure 23-5 indicates, the rise in the interest rate is not sufficient to reduce investment spending and net exports to the point where aggregate output does not increase. Thus expansionary fiscal policy increases aggregate output, and only partial crowding out occurs.

[2]The classic paper on this topic is William Poole, "The Optimal Choice of Monetary Policy Instruments in a Simple Macro Model," *Quarterly Journal of Economics* 84 (1970): 192–216. A less mathematical version of his analysis, far more accessible to students, is contained in William Poole, "Rules of Thumb for Guiding Monetary Policy," in *Open Market Policies and Operating Procedures: Staff Studies* (Washington, D.C.: Board of Governors of the Federal Reserve System, 1971).

in which *IS* and *LM* curves shift because of unanticipated changes in autonomous spending and money demand. To understand whether the Bank of Canada should use a money supply target or an interest-rate target, we need to look at two cases: first, one in which uncertainty about the *IS* curve is far greater than uncertainty about the *LM* curve, and another in which uncertainty about the *LM* curve is far greater than uncertainty about the *IS* curve.

The *ISLM* diagram in Figure 23-8 illustrates the outcome of the two targeting strategies for the case in which the *IS* curve is unstable and uncertain and so it fluctuates around its expected value of *IS** from *IS'* and *IS''*, while the *LM* curve is stable and certain so it stays at *LM**. Since the central bank knows that the expected position of the *IS* curve is at *IS** and desires aggregate output of *Y**, it will set its interest-rate target at *i** so that the expected level of output is *Y**. This policy of targeting the interest rate at *i** is labelled "Interest-Rate Target."

How would the central bank keep the interest rate at its target level of *i**? Recall from Chapter 18 that the central bank can hit its interest-rate target by buying and selling bonds when the interest rate differs from *i**. When the *IS* curve shifts out to *IS''*, the interest rate would rise above *i** with the money supply unchanged. To counter this rise in interest rates, however, the central bank would need to buy bonds just until their price is driven back up so that the interest rate comes back down to *i**. (The result of these open market purchases, as we have seen in Chapters 15 and 16, is that the monetary base and the money supply rise until the *LM* curve shifts to the right to intersect the *IS''* curve at *i**—not shown in the diagram for simplicity.) When the interest rate is below *i**, the central bank needs to sell bonds to lower their price and raise the interest rate back up to *i**. (These open market sales reduce the monetary base and the money supply until the *LM* curve shifts to the left to intersect the *IS* curve at *IS'*—again not shown in the diagram.) The result of pursuing the interest-rate target is that aggregate output fluctuates between Y'_I and Y''_I in Figure 23-8.

If, instead, the central bank pursues a money supply target, it will set the money supply so that the resulting *LM* curve *LM** intersects the *IS** curve at the

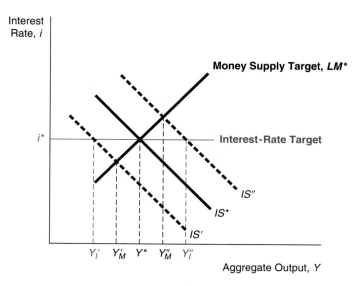

FIGURE 23-8 Money Supply and Interest-Rate Targets When the *IS* Curve Is Unstable and the *LM* Curve Is Stable

The unstable *IS* curve fluctuates between *IS'* and *IS''*. The money supply target produces smaller fluctuations in output (Y'_M to Y''_M) than the interest rate targets (Y'_I to Y''_I). Therefore, the money supply target is preferred.

desired output level of Y^*. This policy of targeting the money supply is labelled "Money Supply Target." Because it is not changing the money supply and so keeps the *LM* curve at *LM**, aggregate output will fluctuate between Y'_M and Y''_M for the money supply target policy.

As you can see in the figure, the money supply target leads to smaller output fluctuations around the desired level than the interest-rate target. A rightward shift of the *IS* curve to *IS''*, for example, causes the interest rate to rise, given a money supply target, and this rise in the interest rate leads to a lower level of investment spending and net exports and hence to a smaller increase in aggregate output than occurs under an interest-rate target. Because smaller output fluctuations are desirable, the conclusion is that *if the IS curve is more unstable than the LM curve, a money supply target is preferred*.

The outcome of the two targeting strategies for the case of a stable *IS* curve and an unstable *LM* curve caused by unanticipated changes in money demand is illustrated in Figure 23-9. Again, the interest-rate and money supply targets are set so that the expected level of aggregate output equals the desired level Y^*. Because the *LM* curve is now unstable, it fluctuates between *LM'* and *LM''* even when the money supply is fixed, causing aggregate output to fluctuate between Y'_M and Y''_M. The interest-rate target, by contrast, is not affected by uncertainty about the *LM* curve because it is set by the central bank's adjusting the money supply whenever the interest rate tries to depart from i^*. When the interest rate begins to rise above i^* because of an increase in money demand, the central bank again just buys bonds, driving up their price and bringing the interest rate back down to i^*. The result of these open market purchases is a rise in the monetary base and the money supply. Similarly, if the interest rate falls below i^*, the central bank sells bonds to lower their price and raise the interest rate back to i^*, thereby causing a decline in the monetary base and the money supply. The only effect of the fluctuating *LM* curve, then, is that the money supply fluctuates more as a result of the interest-rate target policy. The outcome of the interest-rate target is that output will be exactly at the desired level with no fluctuations.

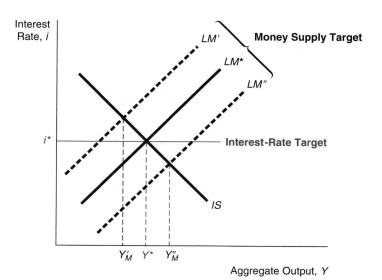

FIGURE 23-9 Money Supply and Interest-Rate Targets When the *LM* Curve Is Unstable and the *IS* Curve Is Stable

The unstable *LM* curve fluctuates between *LM'* and *LM''*. The money supply target then produces bigger fluctuations in output (Y'_M to Y''_M) than the interest-rate target (which leaves output fixed at Y^*). Therefore, the interest-rate target is preferred.

Since smaller output fluctuations are desirable, the conclusion from Figure 23-9 is that *if the LM curve is more unstable than the IS curve, an interest-rate target is preferred*.

We can now see why many central banks decided to abandon monetary targeting for interest-rate targeting in the 1980s. With the rapid proliferation of new financial instruments whose presence can affect the demand for money (see Chapter 21), money demand (which is embodied in the *LM* curve) became highly unstable in many countries. Thus central banks in these countries recognized that they were more likely to be in the situation in Figure 23-9 and decided that they would be better off with an interest-rate target than a money supply target.[3]

ISLM MODEL IN THE LONG RUN

So far in our *ISLM* analysis, we have been assuming that the price level is fixed so that nominal values and real values are the same. This is a reasonable assumption for the short run, but in the long run the price level does change. To see what happens in the *ISLM* model in the long run, we make use of the concept of the **natural rate level of output** (denoted by Y_n), which is the rate of output at which wages and the price level have no tendency to rise or fall (this is the full employment level of output). When output is above the natural rate level, the booming economy will cause prices to rise; when output is below the natural rate level, the slack in the economy will cause prices to fall.

Because we now want to examine what happens when the price level changes, we can no longer assume that real and nominal values are the same. The spending variables that affect the *IS* curve (consumer expenditure, investment spending, government spending, and net exports) describe the demand for goods and services and are *in real terms*; they describe the physical quantities of goods that people want to buy. Because these quantities do not change when the price level changes, a change in the price level has no effect on the *IS* curve, which describes the combinations of the interest rate and aggregate output *in real terms* that satisfy goods market equilibrium.

Figure 23-10 shows what happens in the *ISLM* model when output rises above the natural rate level, which is marked by a vertical line at Y_n. Suppose that initially the *IS* and *LM* curves intersect at point 1, where output $Y = Y_n$. Panel (a) examines what happens to output and interest rates when there is a rise in the money supply. As we saw in Figure 23-2, the rise in the money supply causes the *LM* curve to shift to LM_2, and the equilibrium moves to point 2 (the intersection of IS_1 and LM_2), where the interest rate falls to i_2 and output rises to Y_2. However, as

---

[3]It is important to recognize, however, that the crucial factor in deciding which target is preferred is the *relative* instability of the *IS* and *LM* curves. Although the *LM* curve has been unstable recently, the evidence supporting a stable *IS* curve is also weak. Instability in the money demand function does not automatically mean that money supply targets should be abandoned for an interest-rate target. Furthermore, the analysis so far has been conducted assuming that the price level is fixed. More realistically, when the price level can change so that there is uncertainty about expected inflation, the case for an interest-rate target is less strong. As we learned in Chapters 4 and 5, the interest rate that is more relevant to investment decisions is not the nominal interest rate but the real interest rate (the nominal interest rate minus expected inflation). Hence when expected inflation rises, at each given nominal interest rate, the real interest rate falls and investment and net exports rise, shifting the *IS* curve to the right. Similarly, a fall in expected inflation raises the real interest rate at each given nominal interest rate, lowers investment and net exports, and shifts the *IS* curve to the left. Since in the real world expected inflation undergoes large fluctuations, the *IS* curve in Figure 23-9 will also have substantial fluctuations, making it less likely that the interest-rate target is preferable to the money supply target.

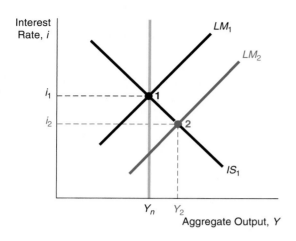

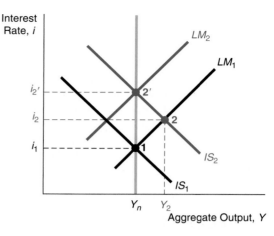

(a) Response to a rise in the money supply M

(b) Response to a rise in government spending G

FIGURE 23-10   The *ISLM* Model in the Long Run

In panel (a), a rise in the money supply causes the *LM* curve to shift rightward to LM_2, and the equilibrium moves to point 2, where the interest rate falls to i_2 and output rises to Y_2. Because output at Y_2 is above the natural rate level Y_n, the price level rises, the real money supply falls, and the *LM* curve shifts back to LM_1; the economy has returned to the original equilibrium at point 1. In panel (b), an increase in government spending shifts the *IS* curve to the right to IS_2, and the economy moves to point 2, at which the interest rate has risen to i_2 and output has risen to Y_2. Because output at Y_2 is above the natural rate level Y_n, the price level begins to rise, real money balances M/P begin to fall, and the *LM* curve shifts to the left to LM_2. The long-run equilibrium at point 2' has an even higher interest rate at $i_{2'}$, and output has returned to Y_n.

we can see in panel (a), the level of output at Y_2 is greater than the natural rate level Y_n, and so the price level begins to rise.

In contrast to the *IS* curve, which is unaffected by a rise in the price level, the *LM* curve is affected by the price level rise because the liquidity preference theory states that the demand for money *in real terms* depends on real income and interest rates. This makes sense because money is valued in terms of what it can buy. However, the money supply that you read about in newspapers is not the money supply in real terms; it is a nominal quantity. As the price level rises, the quantity of money *in real terms* falls, and the effect on the *LM* curve is identical to a fall in the nominal money supply with the price level fixed. The lower value of the real money supply creates an excess demand for money, causing the interest rate to rise at any given level of aggregate output, and the *LM* curve shifts back to the left. As long as the level of output exceeds the natural rate level, the price level will continue to rise, shifting the *LM* curve to the left, until finally output is back at the natural rate level Y_n. This occurs when the *LM* curve has returned to LM_1, where real money balances M/P have returned to the original level and the economy has returned to the original equilibrium at point 1. The result of the expansion in the money supply in the long run is that the economy has the same level of output and interest rates.

The fact that the increase in the money supply has left output and interest rates unchanged in the long run is referred to as **long-run monetary neutrality**. The only result of the increase in the money supply is a higher price level, which has increased proportionally to the increase in the money supply so that real money balances M/P are unchanged. Long-run monetary neutrality is generally consistent with time series data from actual economies (Box 23-1).

Panel (b) looks at what happens to output and interest rates when there is expansionary fiscal policy such as an increase in government spending. As we saw

BOX 23·1

International Evidence on Long-Run Monetary Neutrality

Over the years, the long-run neutrality proposition has been investigated in a large number of studies, often with conflicting results. In a recent paper, Apostolos Serletis and Zisimos Koustas argue that meaningful long-run monetary neutrality tests depend on the time series properties of the variables, and they test the long-run neutrality of money proposition using recent, state-of-the-art advances in the field of applied econometrics. In doing so, they use the Backus and Kehoe data set, consisting of over one hundred years of annual observations on real output and money for ten countries: Australia, Canada, Denmark, Germany, Italy, Japan, Norway, Sweden, the United Kingdom, and the United States.

Their results show that the data are supportive of the proposition that money is neutral in the long run.[4] The same authors find sup-port for the long-run neutrality of money using weighted monetary aggregates for the U.S. economy.[5] As already noted in Chapter 3, weighted monetary aggregates represent a significant advance over simple sum measures of money.

However, international evidence on another important long-run neutrality proposition, the Fisher effect, seems to provide little support to the hypothesis that fully anticipated inflation has a unit effect on nominal interest rates.[6] The preponderance of the evidence suggests that anticipated inflation has less than a unit effect on nominal interest rates, and thus reduces real interest rates even in the longest of runs.

The apparent contradiction of the two types of long-run-neutrality results represents a puzzle that needs to be addressed by future theoretical and empirical research.

---

earlier, the increase in government spending shifts the *IS* curve to the right to IS_2, and in the short run the economy moves to point 2 (the intersection of IS_2 and LM_1), where the interest rate has risen to i_2 and output has risen to Y_2. Because output at Y_2 is above the natural rate level Y_n, the price level begins to rise, real money balances M/P begin to fall, and the *LM* curve shifts to the left. Only when the *LM* curve has shifted to LM_2 and the equilibrium is at point 2′, where output is again at the natural rate level Y_n, does the price level stop rising and the *LM* curve come to rest. The resulting long-run equilibrium at point 2′ has an even higher interest rate at $i_{2'}$ and output has not risen from Y_n. Indeed, what has occurred in the long run is complete crowding out. The rise in the price level, which has shifted the *LM* curve to LM_2, has caused the interest rate to rise to $i_{2'}$, causing investment and net exports to fall enough to offset the increased government spending completely. What we have discovered is that even though complete crowding out does not occur in the short run in the *ISLM* model (when the *LM* curve is not vertical), it does occur in the long run.

Our conclusion from examining what happens in the *ISLM* model from an expansionary monetary or fiscal policy is that ***although monetary and fiscal policy can affect output in the short run, neither affects output in the long***

---

[4]See Apostolos Serletis and Zisimos Koustas, "International Evidence on the Neutrality of Money." *Journal of Money, Credit and Banking* 30 (1998): pp. 1-25. For details regarding the Backus and Kehoe data set, see David K. Backus and Patrick J. Kehoe, "International Evidence on the Historical Properties of Business Cycles." *American Economic Review* 82 (1992): pp. 864-888.

[5]See Apostolos Serletis and Zisimos Koustas, "Monetary Aggregation and the Neutrality of Money." *Economic Inquiry* 39 (2001): pp. 124-138.

[6]See Zisimos Koustas and Apostolos Serletis, "On the Fisher Effect." *Journal of Monetary Economics* 44 (1999): pp. 105-130.

run. Clearly, an important issue in deciding on the effectiveness of monetary and fiscal policy to raise output is how soon the long run occurs. This is a topic that we explore in the next chapter.

ISLM MODEL AND THE AGGREGATE DEMAND CURVE

We now examine further what happens in the *ISLM* model when the price level changes. When we conduct the *ISLM* analysis with a changing price level, we find that as the price level falls, the level of aggregate output rises. Thus we obtain a relationship between the price level and quantity of aggregate output for which the goods market and the market for money are in equilibrium, called the **aggregate demand curve**. This aggregate demand curve is a central element in the aggregate supply and demand analysis of Chapter 24, which allows us to explain changes not only in aggregate output but also in the price level.

Deriving the Aggregate Demand Curve

Now that you understand how a change in the price level affects the *IS* and *LM* curves, we can analyze what happens in the *ISLM* diagram when the price level changes. This exercise is carried out in Figure 23-11. Panel (a) contains an *ISLM* diagram for a given value of the nominal money supply. Let us first consider a price level of P_1. The *LM* curve at this price level is $LM(P_1)$, and its intersection with the *IS* curve is at point 1, where output is Y_1. The equilibrium output level Y_1 that occurs when the price level is P_1 is also plotted in panel (b) as point 1. If the price level rises to P_2, then *in real terms* the money supply has fallen. The effect on the *LM* curve is identical to a decline in the nominal money supply when the price level is fixed. The *LM* curve will shift leftward to $LM(P_2)$. The new equilibrium level of output has fallen to Y_2 because planned investment and net exports fall when the interest rate rises. Point 2 in panel (b) plots this level of output for price level P_2. A further increase in the price level to P_3 causes a further decline in the real money supply, leading to a further decline in planned investment and net exports, and output declines to Y_3. Point 3 in panel (b) plots this level of output for price level P_3.

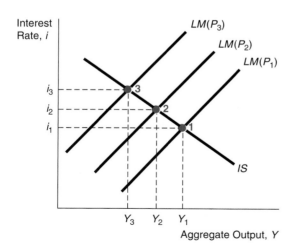

(a) ISLM diagram

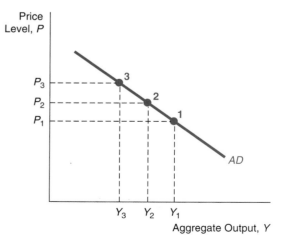

(b) Aggregate demand curve

FIGURE 23-11 Deriving The Aggregate Demand Curve

The *ISLM* diagram in panel (a) shows that as the price level rises from P_1 to P_2 to P_3, the *LM* curve shifts to the left, and equilibrium output falls. The combinations of the price level and equilibrium output from panel (a) are then plotted in panel (b), and the line connecting them is the aggregate demand curve *AD*.

The line that connects the three points in panel (b) is the aggregate demand curve *AD*, and it indicates the level of aggregate output consistent with equilibrium in the goods market and the market for money at any given price level. This aggregate demand curve has the usual downward slope because a higher price level reduces the money supply in real terms, raises interest rates, and lowers the equilibrium level of aggregate output.

Factors That Cause the Aggregate Demand Curve to Shift

ISLM analysis demonstrates how the equilibrium level of aggregate output changes for a given price level. A change in any factor (except a change in the price level) that causes the *IS* or *LM* curve to shift causes the aggregate demand curve to shift. To see how this works, let's first look at what happens to the aggregate demand curve when the *IS* curve shifts.

Shifts in the *IS* Curve   Five factors cause the *IS* curve to shift: changes in autonomous consumer spending, changes in investment spending related to business confidence, changes in government spending, changes in taxes, and autonomous changes in net exports. How changes in these factors lead to a shift in the aggregate demand curve is examined in Figure 23-12.

Suppose that initially the aggregate demand curve is at AD_1 and there is a rise, for example, in government spending. The *ISLM* diagram in panel (b) shows what then happens to equilibrium output, holding the price level constant at P_A. Initially, equilibrium output is at Y_A at the intersection of IS_1 and LM_1. The rise in government spending (holding the price level constant at P_A) shifts the *IS* curve to the right and raises equilibrium output to $Y_{A'}$. In panel (a), this rise in equilibrium output is shown as a movement from point A to point A', and the aggregate demand curve shifts to the right (to AD_2).

The conclusion from Figure 23-12 is that ***any factor that shifts the IS curve shifts the aggregate demand curve in the same direction***. Therefore, "animal spirits" that encourage a rise in autonomous consumer spending or planned

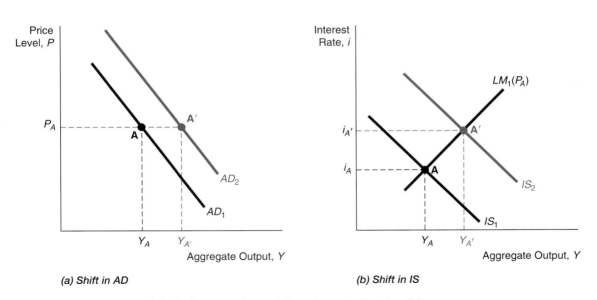

(a) Shift in AD   **(b) Shift in IS**

FIGURE 23-12   Shift in the Aggregate Demand Curve from a Shift in the *IS* Curve

Expansionary fiscal policy, a rise in net exports, or more optimistic consumers and firms shift the *IS* curve to the right in panel (b), and at a price level of P_A equilibrium output rises from Y_A to $Y_{A'}$. This change in equilibrium output is shown as a movement from point *A* to point *A'* in panel (a); hence the aggregate demand curve shifts to the right, from AD_1 to AD_2.

investment spending, a rise in government spending, a fall in taxes, or an autonomous rise in net exports—all of which shift the *IS* curve to the right—will also shift the aggregate demand curve to the right. Conversely, a fall in autonomous consumer spending, a fall in planned investment spending, a fall in government spending, a rise in taxes, or a fall in net exports will cause the aggregate demand curve to shift to the left.

Shifts in the *LM* Curve   Shifts in the *LM* curve are caused by either an autonomous change in money demand (not caused by a change in *P*, *Y*, or *i*) or a change in the money supply. Figure 23-13 shows how either of these changes leads to a shift in the aggregate demand curve. Again, we are initially at the AD_1 aggregate demand curve, and we look at what happens to the level of equilibrium output when the price level is held constant at $P_{A'}$. A rise in the money supply shifts the *LM* curve to the right and raises equilibrium output to $Y_{A'}$. This rise in equilibrium output is shown as a movement from point A to point A' in panel (a), and the aggregate demand curve shifts to the right.

Our conclusion from Figure 23-13 is similar to that of Figure 23-12. ***Any factor that shifts the LM curve shifts the aggregate demand curve in the same direction.*** Therefore, a decline in money demand and an increase in the money supply, both of which shift the *LM* curve to the right, also shift the aggregate demand curve to the right. The aggregate demand curve will shift to the left, however, if the money supply declines or money demand rises.

You have now derived and analyzed the aggregate demand curve—an essential element in the aggregate demand and supply framework that we examine in Chapter 24. The aggregate demand and supply framework is particularly useful because it demonstrates how the price level is determined and enables us to examine factors that affect aggregate output when the price level varies.

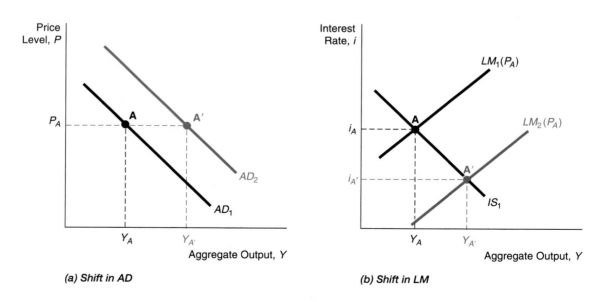

FIGURE 23-13   Shift in the Aggregate Demand Curve from a Shift in the *LM* Curve
A rise in the money supply or a fall in money demand shifts the *LM* curve to the right in panel (b), and at a price level of $P_{A'}$ equilibrium output rises from Y_A to $Y_{A'}$. This change in equilibrium output is shown as a movement from point A to point A' in panel (a); hence the aggregate demand curve shifts to the right, from AD_1 to AD_2.

SUMMARY

1. The *IS* curve is shifted to the right by a rise in autonomous consumer spending, a rise in planned investment spending related to business confidence, a rise in government spending, a fall in taxes, or an autonomous rise in net exports. A movement in the opposite direction of these five factors will shift the *IS* curve to the left.

2. The *LM* curve is shifted to the right by a rise in the money supply or an autonomous fall in money demand; it is shifted to the left by a fall in the money supply or an autonomous rise in money demand.

3. A rise in the money supply raises equilibrium output but lowers the equilibrium interest rate. Expansionary fiscal policy (a rise in government spending or a fall in taxes) raises equilibrium output but, in contrast to expansionary monetary policy, also raises the interest rate.

4. The less interest-sensitive money demand is, the more effective monetary policy is relative to fiscal policy.

5. The *ISLM* model provides the following conclusion about the conduct of monetary policy. When the *IS* curve is more unstable than the *LM* curve, pursuing a money supply target provides smaller output fluctuations than pursuing an interest-rate target and is preferred; when the *LM* curve is more unstable than the *IS* curve, pursuing an interest-rate target leads to smaller output fluctuations and is preferred.

6. The conclusion from examining what happens in the *ISLM* model from an expansionary monetary or fiscal policy is that although monetary and fiscal policy can affect output in the short run, neither affects output in the long run.

7. The aggregate demand curve tells us the level of aggregate output consistent with equilibrium in the goods market and the market for money for any given price level. It slopes downward because a lower price level creates a higher level of the real money supply, lowers the interest rate, and raises equilibrium output. The aggregate demand curve shifts in the same direction as a shift in the *IS* or *LM* curve; hence it shifts to the right when government spending increases, taxes decrease, "animal spirits" encourage consumer and business spending, autonomous net exports increase, the money supply increases, or money demand decreases.

KEY TERMS

QUESTIONS AND PROBLEMS

Questions marked with an asterisk are answered at the end of the book in an appendix, "Answers to Selected Questions and Problems."

1. If taxes and government spending rise by equal amounts, what will happen to the position of the *IS* curve? Explain this with a Keynesian cross diagram.

*2. What happened to the *IS* curve during the Great Depression when investment spending collapsed? Why?

3. What happens to the position of the *LM* curve if the Bank of Canada decides that it will decrease the money supply to fight inflation and if, at the same time, the demand for money falls?

*4. "An excess demand for money resulting from a rise in the demand for money can be eliminated only by a rise in the interest rate." Is this statement true, false, or uncertain? Explain your answer.

In Problems 5–13, demonstrate your answers with an *ISLM* diagram.

5. Suppose that the Bank of Canada wants to keep interest rates from rising when the government sharply increases military spending. How can the Bank do this?

*6. Evidence indicates that lately the demand for money has become quite unstable. Why is this finding important to monetary policymakers?

7. "As the price level rises, the equilibrium level of output determined in the *ISLM* model also rises." Is this statement true, false, or uncertain? Explain your answer.

*8. What will happen to the position of the aggregate demand curve if the money supply is reduced when government spending increases?

9. An equal rise in government spending and taxes will have what effect on the position of the aggregate demand curve?

*10. If money demand is unaffected by changes in the interest rate, what effect will a rise in government spending have on the position of the aggregate demand curve?

Using Economic Analysis to Predict the Future

11. Predict what will happen to interest rates and output if a stock market crash causes autonomous consumer expenditure to fall.

*12. Predict what will happen to interest rates and aggregate output when there is an autonomous export boom.

13. If a series of defaults in the bond market make bonds riskier and as a result the demand for money rises, predict what will happen to interest rates and aggregate output.

Chapter 24

Aggregate Demand and Supply Analysis

PREVIEW In earlier chapters we focused considerable attention on monetary policy because it touches our everyday lives by affecting the prices of the goods we buy and the quantity of available jobs. In this chapter we develop a basic tool, aggregate demand and supply analysis, which will enable us to study the effects of money on output and prices. **Aggregate demand** is the total quantity of an economy's final goods and services demanded at different price levels. **Aggregate supply** is the total quantity of final goods and services that firms in the economy want to sell at different price levels. As with other supply and demand analyses, the actual quantity of output and the price level are determined by equating aggregate demand and aggregate supply.

Aggregate demand and supply analysis will enable us to explore how aggregate output and the price level are determined. (The "Following the Financial News" box indicates when data on aggregate output and the price level are published.) Not only will the analysis help us interpret recent episodes in the business cycle, but it will also enable us to understand the debates on how economic policy should be conducted.

AGGREGATE DEMAND

The first building block of aggregate supply and demand analysis is the **aggregate demand curve**, which describes the relationship between the quantity of aggregate output demanded and the price level when all other variables are held constant. **Monetarists** (led by Milton Friedman) view the aggregate demand curve as downward-sloping with one primary factor that causes it to shift—changes in the quantity of money. **Keynesians** (followers of Keynes) also view the aggregate demand curve as downward-sloping, but they believe that changes in government spending and taxes or in consumer and business willingness to spend can also cause it to shift.

Monetarist View of Aggregate Demand

The monetarist view of aggregate demand links the quantity of money M with total nominal spending on goods and services $P \times Y$ (P = price level and Y = aggregate real output or, equivalently, aggregate real income). To do this it uses the concept of the **velocity of money**: the average number of times per year that a dollar is spent on final goods and services. More formally, velocity V is calculated by dividing nominal spending $P \times Y$ by the money supply M:

$$V = \frac{P \times Y}{M}$$

Suppose that the total nominal spending in a year was $2 trillion and the money supply was $1 trillion; velocity would then be $2 trillion/$1 trillion = 2. On average, the money supply supports a level of transactions associated with 2 times its value in final goods and services in the course of a year. By multiplying both sides by M, we obtain the **equation of exchange**, which relates the money supply to aggregate spending:

$$M \times V = P \times Y \tag{1}$$

At this point, the equation of exchange is nothing more than an identity; that is, it is true by definition. It does not tell us that when M rises, aggregate spending will rise as well. For example, the rise in M could be offset by a fall in V, with the result that $M \times V$ does not rise. However, Friedman's analysis of the demand for money (discussed in detail in Chapter 21) suggests that velocity varies over time in a predictable manner unrelated to changes in the money supply. With this analysis, the equation of exchange is transformed into a theory of how aggregate spending is determined and is called the **modern quantity theory of money**.

To see how the theory works, let's look at an example. If velocity is predicted to be 2 and the money supply is $1 trillion, the equation of exchange tells us that aggregate spending will be $2 trillion (2 × $1 trillion). If the money supply doubles to $2 trillion, Friedman's analysis suggests that velocity will continue to be 2 and aggregate spending will double to $4 trillion (2 × $2 trillion). Thus Friedman's modern quantity theory of money concludes that ***changes in aggregate spending are determined primarily by changes in the money supply***.

Deriving the Aggregate Demand Curve   To learn how the modern quantity theory of money generates the aggregate demand curve, let's look at an example in which we measure aggregate output in trillions of 1996 dollars, with the price level in 1996 having a value of 1.0. As just shown, with a predicted velocity of 2 and a money supply of $1 trillion, aggregate spending will be $2 trillion. If the price level is given at 2.0, the quantity of aggregate output demanded is $1 trillion because aggregate spending $P \times Y$ then continues to equal 2.0 × $1 trillion = $2 trillion, the value of $M \times V$. This combination of a price level of 2.0 and aggregate output of 1 is marked as point A in Figure 24-1. If the price level is given as 1.0 instead, aggregate output demanded is $2 trillion (point B), so aggregate spending continues to equal $2 trillion (= 1.0 × 2 trillion). Similarly, at an even lower price level of 0.5, the quantity of output demanded rises to $4 trillion, shown by point C. The curve connecting these points, marked AD_1, is the aggregate demand curve, given a money supply of $1 trillion. As you can see, it has the usual downward slope of a demand curve, indicating that as the price level falls (everything else held constant), the quantity of output demanded rises.

Shifts in the Aggregate Demand Curve   In Friedman's modern quantity theory, changes in the money supply are the primary source of the changes in aggregate spending and shifts in the aggregate demand curve. To see how a change in the money supply shifts the aggregate demand curve in Figure 24-1, let's look at what happens when the money supply increases to $2 trillion. Now aggregate spending rises to 2 × $2 trillion = $4 trillion, and at a price level of 2.0, the quantity of aggregate

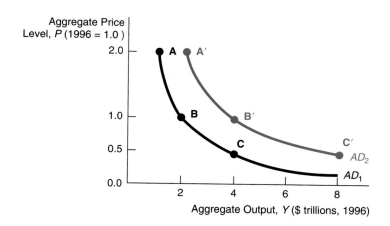

FIGURE 24-1   Aggregate Demand Curve

An aggregate demand curve is drawn for a *fixed* level of the money supply. A rise in the money supply from $1 trillion to $2 trillion leads to a shift in the aggregate demand curve from AD_1 to AD_2.

output demanded will rise to \$2 trillion so that 2.0×2 trillion $=$ \$4 trillion. Therefore, at a price level of 2.0, the aggregate demand curve moves from point A to A'. At a price level of 1.0, the quantity of output demanded rises from \$2 to \$4 trillion (from point B to B'), and at a price level of 0.5, output demanded rises from \$4 to \$8 trillion (from point C to C'). The result is that the rise in the money supply to \$2 trillion shifts the aggregate demand curve outward to AD_2.

Similar reasoning indicates that a decline in the money supply lowers aggregate spending proportionally and reduces the quantity of aggregate output demanded at each price level. Thus a decline in the money supply shifts the aggregate demand curve to the left.

Keynesian View of Aggregate Demand

Rather than determining aggregate demand from the equation of exchange, Keynesians analyze aggregate demand in terms of its four component parts: **consumer expenditure**, the total demand for consumer goods and services; **planned investment spending**,[1] the total planned spending by business firms on new machines, factories, and other inputs to production, plus planned spending on new homes; **government spending**, spending by all levels of government (federal, provincial, and local) on goods and services (paper clips, computers, computer programming, missiles, government workers, and so on); and **net exports**, the net foreign spending on domestic goods and services, equal to exports minus imports. Using the symbols C for consumer expenditure, I for planned investment spending, G for government spending, and NX for net exports, we can write the following expression for aggregate demand Y^{ad}:

$$Y^{ad} = C + I + G + NX \tag{2}$$

Aggregate Demand Curve Keynesian analysis, like monetarist analysis, suggests that the aggregate demand curve is downward-sloping because a lower price level ($P\downarrow$), holding the nominal quantity of money (M) constant, leads to a larger quantity of money in real terms (in terms of the goods and services that it can buy, $M/P\uparrow$). The larger quantity of money in real terms ($M/P\uparrow$) that results from the lower price level causes interest rates to fall ($i\downarrow$), as suggested in Chapter 5. The resulting lower cost of financing purchases of new physical capital makes investment more profitable and stimulates planned investment spending ($I\uparrow$). Because, as shown in Equation 2, the increase in planned investment spending adds directly to aggregate demand ($Y^{ad}\uparrow$), the lower price level leads to a higher level of aggregate demand ($P\downarrow => Y^{ad}\uparrow$). Schematically, we can write the mechanism just described as follows:

$$P\downarrow \Rightarrow M/P\uparrow \Rightarrow i\downarrow \Rightarrow I\uparrow \Rightarrow Y^{ad}\uparrow$$

Another mechanism that generates a downward-sloping aggregate demand curve operates through international trade. Because a lower price level ($P\downarrow$) leads to a larger quantity of money in real terms ($M/P\uparrow$) and lower interest rates ($i\downarrow$), Canadian dollar bank deposits become less attractive relative to deposits denominated in foreign currencies, thereby causing a fall in the value of dollar deposits relative to other currency deposits (a decline in the exchange rate, denoted by $E\downarrow$). The lower value of the dollar, which makes domestic goods cheaper relative to foreign goods, then causes net exports to rise ($NX\uparrow$), which in turn increases aggregate demand ($Y^{ad}\uparrow$):

$$P\downarrow \Rightarrow M/P\uparrow \Rightarrow i\downarrow \Rightarrow E\downarrow \Rightarrow NX\uparrow \Rightarrow Y^{ad}\uparrow$$

---

[1] Recall that economists restrict use of the word *investment* to the purchase of new physical capital, such as a new machine or a new house, which adds to expenditure.

The mechanisms described also indicate why Keynesian analysis suggests that changes in the money supply shift the aggregate demand curve. For a given price level, a rise in the money supply causes the real money supply to increase ($M/P\uparrow$), which leads to an increase in aggregate demand, as shown. Thus an increase in the money supply shifts the aggregate demand curve to the right (as in Figure 24-1) because it lowers interest rates and stimulates planned investment spending and net exports. Similarly, a decline in the money supply shifts the aggregate demand curve to the left.[2]

In contrast to monetarists, Keynesians believe that other factors (manipulation of government spending and taxes, changes in net exports, and changes in consumer and business spending) are also important causes of shifts in the aggregate demand curve. For instance, if the government spends more ($G\uparrow$) or net exports increase ($NX\uparrow$), aggregate demand rises, and the aggregate demand curve shifts to the right. A decrease in government taxes ($T\downarrow$) leaves consumers with more income to spend, so consumer expenditure rises ($C\uparrow$). Aggregate demand also rises, and the aggregate demand curve shifts to the right. Finally, if consumer and business optimism increases, consumer expenditure and planned investment spending rise ($C\uparrow$, $I\uparrow$), again shifting the aggregate demand curve to the right. Keynes described these waves of optimism and pessimism as "**animal spirits**" and considered them a major factor affecting the aggregate demand curve and an important source of business cycle fluctuations.

The Crowding-Out Debate

You have seen that both monetarists and Keynesians agree that the aggregate demand curve is downward-sloping and shifts in response to changes in the money supply. However, monetarists see only one important source of movements in the aggregate demand curve—changes in the money supply—while Keynesians suggest that other factors—fiscal policy, net exports, and "animal spirits"—are equally important sources of shifts in the aggregate demand curve.

Because aggregate demand can be written as the sum of $C + I + G + NX$, it might appear that any factor affecting one of its components must cause aggregate demand to change. Then it would seem that a fiscal policy change such as a rise in government spending (holding the money supply constant) would necessarily shift the aggregate demand curve. Because monetarists view changes in the money supply as the only important source of shifts in the aggregate demand curve, they must be able to explain why the foregoing reasoning is invalid.

Monetarists agree that an increase in government spending will raise aggregate demand if the other components of aggregate demand, C, I, and NX, remain unchanged after the government spending rise. They contend, however, that the increase in government spending will *crowd out* private spending (C, I, and NX), which will fall by exactly the amount of the government spending increase. For example, an increase of $50 billion in government spending might be offset by a decline of $30 billion in consumer expenditure, $10 billion in investment spending, and $10 billion in net exports. This phenomenon of an exactly offsetting movement of private spending to an expansionary fiscal policy, such as a rise in government spending, is called **complete crowding out**.

How might complete crowding out occur? When government spending increases ($G\uparrow$), the government has to finance this spending by competing with private borrowers for funds in the credit market. Interest rates will rise ($i\uparrow$), increasing the cost of financing purchases of both physical capital and consumer

---

[2]A complete demonstration of the Keynesian analysis of the aggregate demand curve is given in Chapters 22 and 23.

goods and lowering net exports. The result is that private spending will fall ($C\downarrow$, $I\downarrow$, $NX\downarrow$), and so aggregate demand may remain unchanged. This chain of reasoning can be summarized as follows:

$$G\uparrow \Rightarrow i\uparrow \Rightarrow C\downarrow, I\downarrow, NX\downarrow$$

Therefore, $C + I + G + NX = Y^{ad}$ is unchanged.

Keynesians do not deny the validity of the first set of steps. They agree that an increase in government spending raises interest rates, which in turn lowers private spending; indeed, this is a feature of the Keynesian analysis of aggregate demand (see Chapters 22 and 23). However, they contend that in the short run only **partial crowding out** occurs—some decline in private spending that does not completely offset the rise in government spending.

The Keynesian crowding-out picture suggests that when government spending rises, aggregate demand does increase, and the aggregate demand curve shifts to the right. The extent to which crowding out occurs is the issue that separates monetarist and Keynesian views of the aggregate demand curve. We will discuss the evidence on this issue in Chapter 25.

AGGREGATE SUPPLY

The key feature of aggregate supply is that as the price level increases, the quantity of output supplied increases *in the short run*. Figure 24-2 illustrates the positive relationship between quantity of output supplied and price level. Suppose that initially the quantity of output supplied at a price level of 1.0 is $4 trillion, represented by point A. A rise in the price level to 2.0 leads, in the short run, to an increase to $6 trillion in the quantity of output supplied (point B). The line AS_1 connecting points A and B describes the relationship between the quantity of output supplied in the short run and the price level and is called the **aggregate supply curve**; as you can see, it is upward-sloping.

To understand why the aggregate supply curve slopes upward, we have to look at the factors that cause the quantity of output supplied to change. Because the goal of business is to maximize profits, the quantity of output supplied is determined by the profit made on each unit of output. If profit rises, more output will be produced, and the quantity of output supplied will increase; if it falls, less output will be produced, and the quantity of output supplied will fall.

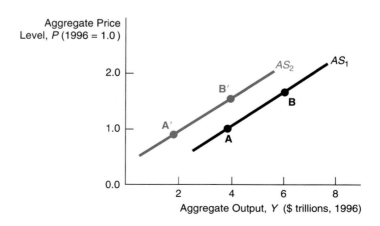

FIGURE 24-2   Aggregate Supply Curve in the Short Run

A rise in the costs of production shifts the supply curve leftward from AS_1 to AS_2.

Profit on a unit of output equals the price for the unit minus the costs of producing it. In the short run, costs of many factors that go into producing goods and services are fixed; wages, for example, are often fixed for periods of time by labour contracts (sometimes as long as three years), and raw materials are often bought by firms under long-term contracts that fix the price. Because these costs of production are fixed in the short run, when the overall price level rises, the price for a unit of output will be rising relative to the costs of producing it, and the profit per unit will rise. Because the higher price level results in higher profits in the short run, firms increase production, and the quantity of aggregate output supplied rises, resulting in an upward-sloping aggregate supply curve.

Frequent mention of the *short run* in the preceding paragraph hints that the aggregate supply curve (AS_1 in Figure 24-2) may not remain fixed as time passes. To see what happens over time, we need to understand what makes the aggregate supply curve shift.

Shifts in the Aggregate Supply Curve

We have seen that the profit on a unit of output determines the quantity of output supplied. If the cost of producing a unit of output rises, profit on a unit of output falls, and the quantity of output supplied falls. To learn what this implies for the position of the aggregate supply curve, let's consider what happens at a price level of 1.0 when the costs of production increase. Now that firms are earning a lower profit per unit of output, they reduce production, and the quantity of aggregate output supplied falls from $4 (point A) to $2 trillion (point A′). Applying the same reasoning at point B indicates that aggregate output supplied falls to point B′. What we see is that ***the aggregate supply curve shifts to the left when costs of production increase and to the right when costs decrease***.

EQUILIBRIUM IN AGGREGATE SUPPLY AND DEMAND ANALYSIS

The equilibrium level of aggregate output and the price level will occur at the point where the quantity of aggregate output demanded equals the quantity of aggregate output supplied. However, in the context of aggregate supply and demand analysis, there are two types of equilibrium: short-run and long-run.

Equilibrium in the Short Run

Figure 24-3 illustrates an equilibrium in the short run in which the quantity of aggregate output demanded equals the quantity of output supplied, that is, where the aggregate demand curve *AD* and the aggregate supply curve *AS* intersect at point E. The equilibrium level of aggregate output equals Y^*, and the equilibrium price level equals P^*.

As in our earlier supply and demand analyses, equilibrium is a useful concept only if there is a tendency for the economy to head toward it. We can see that the economy heads toward the equilibrium at point E by first looking at what happens when we are at a price level above the equilibrium price level P^*. If the price level is at P'', the quantity of aggregate output supplied at point D is greater than the quantity of aggregate output demanded at point A. Because people want to sell more goods and services than others want to buy (a condition of *excess supply*), the prices of goods and services will fall, and the aggregate price level will drop. This decline in the price level will continue until it has reached its equilibrium level of P^* at point E.

When the price level is below the equilibrium price level, say at P', the quantity of output demanded is greater than the quantity of output supplied. Now the price level will rise because people want to buy more goods than others want to

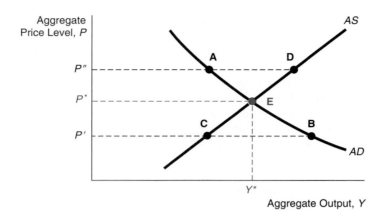

FIGURE 24-3 Equilibrium in the Short Run

Equilibrium occurs at point E at the intersection of the aggregate demand curve *AD* and the aggregate supply curve *AS*.

sell (a condition of *excess demand*). This rise in the price level will continue until it has again reached its equilibrium level of P^* at point E.

Equilibrium in the Long Run

Usually in supply and demand analysis, once we find the equilibrium at which the quantity demanded equals the quantity supplied, there is no need for additional discussion. In *aggregate* supply and demand analysis, however, that is not the case. Even when the quantity of aggregate output demanded equals the quantity supplied, forces operate that can cause the equilibrium to move over time. To understand why, we must remember that if costs of production change, the aggregate supply curve will shift.

The most important component of production costs is wages (approximately 70% of production costs), which are determined in the labour market. If the economy is booming, employers will find that they have difficulty hiring qualified workers and may even have a hard time keeping their present employees. In this case, the labour market is tight because the demand for labour exceeds the supply; employers will raise wages to attract needed workers, and this raises the costs of production. The higher costs of production lower the profits per unit of output at each price level, and the aggregate supply curve shifts to the left (see Figure 24-2).

By contrast, if the economy enters a recession and the labour market is slack because demand for labour is less than supply, workers who cannot find jobs will be willing to work for lower wages. In addition, employed workers may be willing to make wage concessions to keep from losing their jobs. Therefore, in a slack labour market in which the demand for labour is less than the supply, wages and hence costs of production will fall, profits per unit of output will rise, and the aggregate supply curve will shift to the right.

Our analysis suggests that the aggregate supply curve will shift depending on whether the labour market is tight or slack. How do we decide which it is? One helpful concept is the **natural rate of unemployment**, the rate of unemployment to which the economy gravitates in the long run at which demand for labour equals supply. (A related concept is the **NAIRU**, the **nonaccelerating inflation rate of unemployment**, the rate of unemployment at which there is no tendency for inflation to change.) Many economists believe that the rate is currently around 7%. When unemployment is at, say, 4%, below the natural rate of unemployment, the labour market is tight; wages will rise, and the aggregate supply curve will shift leftward. When unemployment is at, say, 8%, above the natural rate of unemployment, the labour market is slack; wages will fall, and the aggregate supply curve will shift rightward. Only when unemployment is at the natural rate will no pressure exist from the labour market for wages to rise or fall, so the aggregate supply need not shift.

The level of aggregate output produced at the natural rate of unemployment is called the **natural rate level of output**. Because, as we have seen, the aggregate supply curve will not remain stationary when unemployment and aggregate output differ from their natural rate levels, we need to look at how the short-run equilibrium changes over time in response to two situations: when equilibrium is initially below the natural rate level and when it is initially above the natural rate level.

In panel (a) of Figure 24-4, the initial equilibrium occurs at point 1, the intersection of the aggregate demand curve AD and the initial aggregate supply curve AS_1. Because the level of equilibrium output Y_1 is greater than the natural rate level Y_n, unemployment is less than the natural rate, and excessive tightness exists in the labour market. This tightness drives wages up, raises production costs, and shifts the aggregate supply curve to AS_2. The equilibrium is now at point 2, and

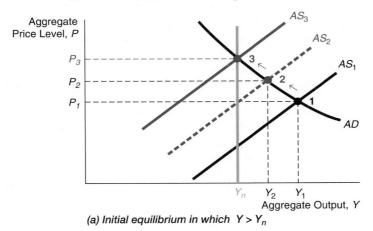

(a) Initial equilibrium in which $Y > Y_n$

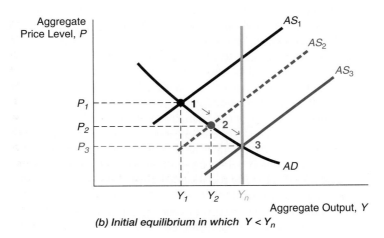

(b) Initial equilibrium in which $Y < Y_n$

FIGURE 24-4   Adjustment to Long-Run Equilibrium in Aggregate Supply and Demand Analysis

In both panels, the initial equilibrium is at point 1 at the intersection of AD and AS_1. In panel (a), $Y_1 > Y_n$, so the aggregate supply curve keeps shifting to the left until it reaches AS_3, where output has returned to Y_n. In panel (b), $Y_1 < Y_n$, so the aggregate supply curve keeps shifting to the right until output is again returned to Y_n. Hence in both cases, the economy displays a self-correcting mechanism that returns it to the natural rate level of output.

output falls to Y_2. Because aggregate output Y_2 is still above the natural rate level, Y_n, wages continue to be driven up, eventually shifting the aggregate supply curve to AS_3. The equilibrium reached at point 3 is on the vertical line at Y_n and is a long-run equilibrium. Because output is at the natural rate level, there is no further pressure on wages to rise and thus no further tendency for the aggregate supply curve to shift.

The movements in panel (a) indicate that the economy will not remain at a level of output higher than the natural rate level because the aggregate supply curve will shift to the left, raise the price level, and cause the economy to slide upward along the aggregate demand curve until it comes to rest at a point on the vertical line through the natural rate level of output Y_n. Because the vertical line through Y_n is the only place at which the aggregate supply curve comes to rest, this vertical line indicates the quantity of output supplied in the long run for any given price level. We can characterize this as the **long-run aggregate supply curve**.

In panel (b), the initial equilibrium at point 1 is one at which output Y_1 is below the natural rate level. Because unemployment is higher than the natural rate, wages begin to fall, shifting the aggregate supply curve rightward until it comes to rest at AS_3. The economy slides downward along the aggregate demand curve until it reaches the long-run equilibrium point 3, the intersection of the aggregate demand curve AD and the long-run aggregate supply curve at Y_n. Here, as in panel (a), the economy comes to rest when output has again returned to the natural rate level.

A striking feature of both panels of Figure 24-4 is that regardless of where output is initially, it returns eventually to the natural rate level. This feature is described by saying that the economy has a **self-correcting mechanism**.

An important issue for policymakers is how rapidly this self-correcting mechanism works. Many economists, particularly Keynesians, believe that the self-correcting mechanism takes a long time, so the approach to long-run equilibrium is slow. This view is reflected in Keynes's often quoted remark, "In the long run, we are all dead." These economists view the self-correcting mechanism as slow because wages are inflexible, particularly in the downward direction when unemployment is high. The resulting slow wage and price adjustments mean that the aggregate supply curve does not move quickly to restore the economy to the natural rate of unemployment. Hence when unemployment is high, these economists (called **activists**) are more likely to see the need for active government policy to restore the economy to full employment.

Other economists, particularly monetarists, believe that wages are sufficiently flexible that the wage and price adjustment process is reasonably rapid. As a result of this flexibility, adjustment of the aggregate supply curve to its long-run position and the economy's return to the natural rate levels of output and unemployment will occur quickly. Thus these economists (called **nonactivists**) see much less need for active government policy to restore the economy to the natural rate levels of output and unemployment when unemployment is high. Indeed, monetarists advocate the use of a rule whereby the money supply or the monetary base grows at a constant rate so as to minimize fluctuations in aggregate demand that might lead to output fluctuations. We will return in Chapter 26 to the debate about whether using active government policy to keep the economy near full employment is beneficial.

Shifts in Aggregate Demand

You are now ready to analyze what happens when the aggregate demand curve shifts. Our discussion of the Keynesian and monetarist views of aggregate demand indicates that six factors can affect the aggregate demand curve: the money supply, government spending, net exports, taxes, consumer optimism, and business optimism—the last two ("animal spirits") affecting willingness to spend. The possible effect on the aggregate demand curve of these six factors is summarized in Table 24-1.

SUMMARY

TABLE 24-1   Factors That Shift the Aggregate Demand Curve

Factor	Change	Shift in the Aggregate Demand Curve
Money supply, M	↑	P — $AD_1 \to AD_2$ ... Y
Government spending, G	↑	P — $AD_1 \to AD_2$ ... Y
Taxes, T	↑	P — $AD_2 \leftarrow AD_1$ ... Y
Net exports, NX	↑	P — $AD_1 \to AD_2$ ... Y
Consumer optimism, C	↑	P — $AD_1 \to AD_2$ ... Y
Business optimism, I	↑	P — $AD_1 \to AD_2$ ... Y

Note: Only increases (↑) in the factors are shown. The effect of decreases in the factors would be the opposite of those indicated in the "Shift" column. Note that monetarists view only the money supply as an important cause of shifts in the aggregate demand curve.

Figure 24-5 depicts the effect of a rightward shift in the aggregate demand curve caused by an increase in the money supply ($M\uparrow$), an increase in government spending ($G\uparrow$), an increase in net exports ($NX\uparrow$), a decrease in taxes ($T\downarrow$), or an

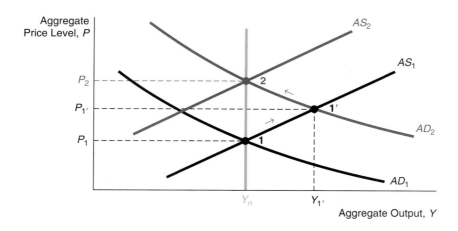

FIGURE 24-5 Response of Output and the Price Level to a Shift in the Aggregate Demand Curve

A shift in the aggregate demand curve from AD_1 to AD_2 moves the economy from point 1 to point 1'. Because $Y_{1'} > Y_n$, the aggregate supply curve begins to shift leftward, eventually reaching AS_2, where output returns to Y_n and the price level has risen to P_2.

increase in the willingness of consumers and businesses to spend because they become more optimistic ($C\uparrow$, $I\uparrow$). The figure has been drawn so that initially the economy is in long-run equilibrium at point 1, where the initial aggregate demand curve AD_1 intersects the aggregate supply AS_1 curve at Y_n. When the aggregate demand curve shifts rightward to AD_2, the economy moves to point 1', and both output and the price level rise. However, the economy will not remain at point 1' because output at $Y_{1'}$ is above the natural rate level. Wages will rise, eventually shifting the aggregate supply curve leftward to AS_2, where it finally comes to rest. The economy thus slides up the aggregate demand curve from point 1' to point 2, which is the point of long-run equilibrium at the intersection of AD_2 and Y_n. *Although the initial short-run effect of the rightward shift in the aggregate demand curve is a rise in both the price level and output, the ultimate long-run effect is only a rise in the price level.*

Shifts in Aggregate Supply

Not only can shifts in aggregate demand be a source of fluctuations in aggregate output (the business cycle), but so can shifts in aggregate supply. Factors that cause the aggregate supply curve to shift are the ones that affect the costs of production: (1) tightness of the labour market, (2) expectations of inflation, (3) workers' attempts to push up their real wages, and (4) changes in the production costs that are unrelated to wages (such as energy costs). The first three factors shift the aggregate supply curve by affecting wage costs; the fourth affects other costs of production.

Tightness of the Labour Market Our analysis of the approach to long-run equilibrium has shown us that when the labour market is tight ($Y > Y_n$), wages and hence production costs rise, and when the labour market is slack ($Y < Y_n$), wages and production costs fall. The effects on the aggregate supply curve are as follows. *When aggregate output is above the natural rate level, the aggregate supply curve shifts to the left; when aggregate output is below the natural rate level, the aggregate supply curve shifts to the right.*

Expected Price Level Workers and firms care about wages in real terms, that is, in terms of the goods and services that wages can buy. When the price level increases, a worker earning the same nominal wage will be able to buy fewer goods and services. A worker who expects the price level to rise will thus demand a higher nominal wage in order to keep the real wage from falling. For example, if Chuck the Construction Worker expects prices to increase by 5%, he will want a wage increase of at least 5% (more if he thinks he deserves an increase in real wages). Similarly, if Chuck's employer knows that the houses he is building will rise in value at the same rate as inflation (5%), he will be willing to pay Chuck 5% more. An increase in the expected price level leads to higher wages, which in turn raise the costs of production, lower the profit per unit of output at each price level, and shift the aggregate supply curve to the left (see Figure 24-2). Therefore, ***a rise in the expected price level causes the aggregate supply curve to shift to the left. The greater the expected increase in price level (that is, the higher the expected inflation), the larger the shift.***

Wage Push   Suppose that Chuck and his fellow construction workers decide to strike and succeed in obtaining higher real wages. This wage push will then raise the costs of production, and the aggregate supply curve will shift leftward. ***A successful wage push by workers will cause the aggregate supply curve to shift to the left.***

Changes in Production Costs Unrelated to Wages   Changes in technology and in the supply of raw materials (called **supply shocks**) can also shift the aggregate supply curve. A negative supply shock, such as a reduction in the availability of raw materials (like oil), which raises their price, increases production costs and shifts the aggregate supply curve leftward. A positive supply shock, such as unusually good weather that leads to a bountiful harvest and lowers the cost of food, will reduce production costs and shift the aggregate supply curve rightward. Similarly, the development of a new technology that lowers production costs, perhaps by raising worker productivity, can also be considered a positive supply shock that shifts the aggregate supply curve to the right.

The effect on the aggregate supply curve of changes in production costs unrelated to wages can be summarized as follows. ***A negative supply shock that raises production costs shifts the aggregate supply curve to the left; a positive supply shock that lowers production costs shifts the aggregate supply curve to the right.***[3]

Study Guide | As a study aid, factors that shift the aggregate supply curve are listed in Table 24-2.

Now that we know what factors can affect the aggregate supply curve, we can examine what occurs when they cause the aggregate supply curve to shift leftward, as in Figure 24-6. Suppose that the economy is initially at the natural rate level of output at point 1 when the aggregate supply curve shifts from AS_1 to AS_2

---

[3]Developments in the foreign exchange market can also shift the aggregate supply curve by changing domestic production costs. As discussed in more detail in Chapter 7, an increase in the value of the dollar makes foreign goods cheaper in Canada. The decline in prices of foreign goods and hence foreign factors of production lowers Canadian production costs and thus raises the profit per unit of output at each price level in Canada. An increase in the value of the dollar therefore shifts the aggregate supply curve to the right. Conversely, a decline in the value of the dollar, which makes foreign factors of production more expensive, shifts the aggregate supply curve to the left.

TABLE 24-2 Factors That Shift the Aggregate Supply Curve

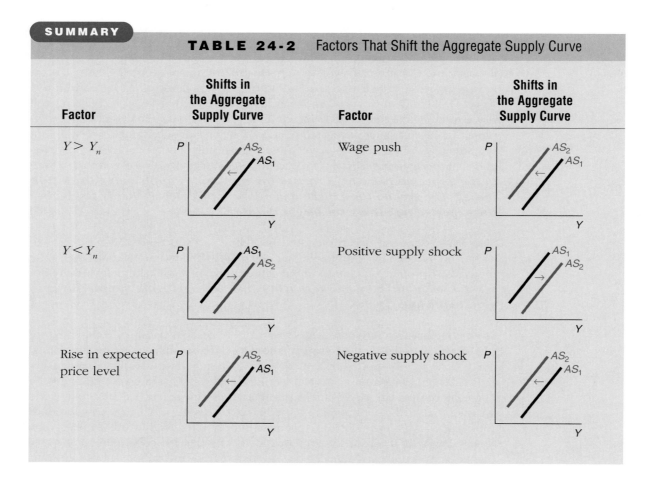

Factor	Shifts in the Aggregate Supply Curve	Factor	Shifts in the Aggregate Supply Curve
$Y > Y_n$		Wage push	
$Y < Y_n$		Positive supply shock	
Rise in expected price level		Negative supply shock	

because of a negative supply shock (a sharp rise in energy prices, for example). The economy will move from point 1 to point 2, where the price level rises but aggregate output *falls*. A situation of a rising price level but a falling level of aggregate output, as pictured in Figure 24-6, has been labelled *stagflation* (a combination of the words *stagnation* and *inflation*). At point 2, output is below the natural rate level, so wages fall and shift the aggregate supply curve back to where it was initially at AS_1. The result is that the economy slides down the aggregate demand curve AD_1 (assuming that the aggregate demand curve remains in the same position), and the economy returns to the long-run equilibrium at point 1. ***Although a leftward shift in the aggregate supply curve initially raises the price level and lowers output, the ultimate effect is that output and price level are unchanged (holding the aggregate demand curve constant).***

Shifts in the Long-Run Aggregate Supply Curve: Real Business Cycle Theory and Hysteresis

To this point we have assumed that the natural rate level of output Y_n and hence the long-run aggregate supply curve (the vertical line through Y_n) are given. However, over time, the natural rate level of output increases as a result of economic growth. If the productive capacity of the economy is growing at a steady rate of 3% per year, for example, this means that every year Y_n will grow by 3% and the long-run aggregate supply curve at Y_n will shift to the right by 3%. To simplify the analysis when Y_n grows at a steady rate, Y_n and the long-run aggregate supply curve are drawn as fixed in the aggregate demand and supply diagrams. Keep in mind, however, that the level of aggregate output pictured in these diagrams is actually best thought of as the level of aggregate output relative to its normal rate of growth (trend).

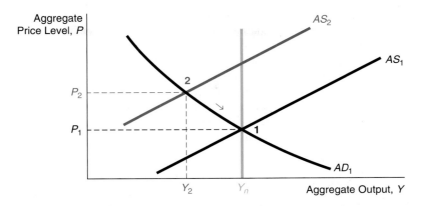

FIGURE 24-6   Response of Output and the Price Level to a Shift in Aggregate Supply

A shift in the aggregate supply curve from AS_1 to AS_2 moves the economy from point 1 to point 2. Because $Y_2 < Y_n$, the aggregate supply curve begins to shift back to the right, eventually returning to AS_1, where the economy is again at point 1.

The usual assumption when conducting aggregate demand and supply analysis is that shifts in either the aggregate demand or aggregate supply curve have no effect on the natural rate level of output (which grows at a steady rate). Movements of aggregate output around the Y_n level in the diagram then describe short-run (business cycle) fluctuations in aggregate output. However, some economists take issue with the assumption that Y_n is unaffected by aggregate demand and supply shocks.

One group, led by Edward Prescott of the University of Minnesota, has developed a theory of aggregate economic fluctuations called **real business cycle theory** in which aggregate supply (real) shocks do affect the natural rate level of output Y_n. This theory views shocks to tastes (workers' willingness to work, for example) and technology (productivity) as the major driving forces behind short-run fluctuations in the business cycle because these shocks lead to substantial short-run fluctuations in Y_n. Shifts in the aggregate demand curve, say as a result of changes in monetary policy, by contrast, are not viewed as being particularly important to aggregate output fluctuations. Because real business cycle theory views most business cycle fluctuations as resulting from fluctuations in the natural rate level of output, it does not see much need for activist policy to eliminate high unemployment. Real business cycle theory is highly controversial and is the subject of intensive research.[4]

Another group of economists disagrees with the assumption that the natural rate level of output Y_n is unaffected by aggregate demand shocks. These economists contend that the natural rate level of unemployment and output are subject to **hysteresis**, a departure from full employment levels as a result of past high unemployment.[5] When unemployment rises because of a reduction of aggregate demand that shifts the AD curve leftward, the natural rate of unemployment is viewed as rising above the full employment level. This could occur because the unemployed become discouraged and fail to look hard for work or because employers may be reluctant to hire workers who have been unemployed for a

[4]See Charles Plosser, "Understanding Real Business Cycles," *Journal of Economic Perspectives* (1989): 51–77, for a nontechnical discussion of real business cycle theory.

[5]For a further discussion of hysteresis, see Olivier Blanchard and Lawrence Summers, "Hysteresis in the European Unemployment Problem," *NBER Macroeconomics Annual*, 1986, 1, ed. Stanley Fischer (Cambridge, Mass.: M.I.T. Press, 1986), pp. 15–78.

long time, seeing it as a signal that the worker is undesirable. The outcome is that the natural rate of unemployment shifts upward after unemployment has become high, and Y_n falls below the full employment level. In this situation, the self-correcting mechanism will be able to return the economy only to the natural rate levels of output and unemployment, not to the full employment level. Only with expansionary policy to shift the aggregate demand curve to the right and raise aggregate output can the natural rate of unemployment be lowered (Y_n raised) to the full employment level. Proponents of hysteresis are thus more likely to promote activist, expansionary policies to restore the economy to full employment.

Study Guide | Aggregate supply and demand analyses are best learned by practicing applications. In this section, we have traced out what happens to aggregate output when there is an increase in the money supply or a negative supply shock. Make sure you can also draw the appropriate shifts in the aggregate demand and supply curves and analyze what happens when other variables such as taxes or the expected price level change.

Conclusions

Aggregate demand and supply analysis yields the following conclusions (under the usual assumption that the natural rate level of output is unaffected by aggregate demand and supply shocks):

1. A shift in the aggregate demand curve—which can be caused by changes in monetary policy (the money supply), fiscal policy (government spending or taxes), international trade (net exports), or "animal spirits" (business and consumer optimism)—affects output only in the short run and has no effect in the long run. Furthermore, the initial change in the price level is less than is achieved in the long run, when the aggregate supply curve has fully adjusted.

2. A shift in the aggregate supply curve—which can be caused by changes in expected inflation, workers' attempts to push up real wages, or a supply shock—affects output and prices only in the short run and has no effect in the long run (holding the aggregate demand curve constant).

3. The economy has a self-correcting mechanism, which will return it to the natural rate levels of unemployment and aggregate output over time.

APPLICATION | *Explaining Past Business Cycle Episodes*

Aggregate supply and demand analysis is an extremely useful tool for analyzing aggregate economic activity; we will apply it to several business cycle episodes. To simplify our analysis, we always assume, in this application and the next, that aggregate output is initially at the natural rate level.

The United States During the Vietnam War Buildup, 1964–1970

America's involvement in Vietnam began to escalate in the early 1960s, and after 1964, the United States was fighting a full-scale war. Beginning in 1965, the resulting increases in military expenditure raised government spending, while at the same time the Federal Reserve increased the rate of money growth in an attempt to keep interest rates from rising. What does aggregate supply and demand analysis suggest should have happened to aggregate output and the price level in the United States as a result of the Vietnam War buildup?

The rise in government spending and the higher rate of money growth would shift the aggregate demand curve to the right (shown in Figure 24-5). As a result,

Federal Reserve
www.federalreserve.gov

aggregate output would rise, unemployment would fall, and the price level would rise. Table 24-3 demonstrates that this is exactly what happened. The unemployment rate fell steadily from 1964 to 1969, remaining well below what economists now think was the natural rate of unemployment during that period (around 5%), and inflation began to rise. As Figure 24-5 predicts, unemployment would eventually begin to return to the natural rate level because of the economy's self-correcting mechanism. This is exactly what we saw occurring in 1970, when the inflation rate rose even higher and unemployment increased.

Negative Supply Shocks, 1973–1975 and 1978–1980

In 1973, the Canadian and world economies were hit by a series of negative supply shocks. As a result of the oil embargo stemming from the Arab–Israeli war of 1973, the Organization of Petroleum Exporting Countries (OPEC) was able to engineer a quadrupling of oil prices by restricting oil production. In addition, a series of crop failures throughout the world led to a sharp increase in food prices. These events caused the aggregate supply curve in Canada to shift sharply leftward, and as the aggregate demand and supply diagram in Figure 24-6 predicts, both the price level and unemployment began to rise dramatically (see Table 24-4).

The 1978–1980 period was almost an exact replay of the 1973–1975 period. By 1978, the economy had just about fully recovered from the 1973–1974 supply shocks when poor harvests and a doubling of oil prices (as a result of the overthrow of the shah of Iran) again led to another sharp leftward shift of the aggregate supply curve. The pattern predicted by Figure 24-6 played itself out again—inflation and unemployment both shot upward (see Table 24-4).

OPEC
www.opec.org

TABLE 24-3   Unemployment and Inflation in the United States During the Vietnam War Buildup, 1964–1970

Year	Unemployment Rate (%)	Inflation (Year to Year) (%)
1964	5.0	1.3
1965	4.4	1.6
1966	3.7	2.9
1967	3.7	3.1
1968	3.5	4.2 ·
1969	3.4	5.5
1970	4.8	5.7

Source: Economic Report of the President.

TABLE 24-4   Unemployment and Inflation in Canada During the Negative Supply Shock Periods, 1973–1975 and 1978–1980

Year	Unemployment Rate (%)	Inflation (Year to Year) (%)	Year	Unemployment Rate (%)	Inflation (Year to Year) (%)
1973	5.6	9.4	1978	8.3	6.5
1974	5.3	14.6	1979	7.4	9.5
1975	6.9	10.3	1980	7.5	10.9

Source: Statistics Canada, CANSIM Series D44950 and D15612.

APPLICATION | *Predicting Future Economic Activity*

Now let's see what will happen to aggregate output and the price level if certain events that have a reasonable probability of occurring in the near future actually do occur.

NAFTA, WTO, and the Elimination of Trade Barriers

World Trade Organization
www.wto.org

International agreements, such as the North American Free Trade Agreement (NAFTA) among Canada, the United States, and Mexico, together with the provisions in the World Trade Organization (WTO), have been gradually eliminating trade barriers such as tariffs and import quotas. What might we predict will happen to output and the price level in Canada as foreign countries eliminate barriers to exports of Canadian goods?

Our aggregate supply and demand analysis of the elimination of barriers to exports of Canadian goods would be that pictured in Figure 24-5. The elimination of trade barriers would cause Canadian net exports to rise, leading to a rightward shift of the aggregate demand curve, which would initially raise aggregate output and the price level (increasing inflation) in Canada. In the long run, however, aggregate output would return to its natural rate level, and the price level would stop rising, so the increase in inflation would be only temporary.

Reduction in EU Subsidies

European Union
www.europa.eu.int

Currently, one of the objectives of the European Union (EU) is to reach agreement on new rules to limit spending such as, for example, farm subsidies and regional subsidies. What effect will such cuts have on the EU economy?

The reduction in spending would probably lead to a leftward shift of the aggregate demand curve. The outcome would be opposite that pictured in Figure 24-5: the price level would fall, lowering the inflation rate, and aggregate output would also fall at first; in the long run, however, aggregate output would return to the natural rate level.

Canada's Next Big Resource Boom

Canada was founded on resource exports and even today earns about 25% of its annual income from resources. Currently, we export non-renewable resources such as oil and gas, but within a decade we will be exporting large quantities of fresh water to the United States and many other countries around the world. What effect will water exports have on the Canadian economy?

Water exports will lead to a rightward shift in the aggregate demand curve. The outcome would be that pictured in Figure 24-5. The price level would rise (increasing inflation) and aggregate output would also rise at first. In the long run, however, aggregate output would return to the natural level.

SUMMARY

1. The aggregate demand curve indicates the quantity of aggregate output demanded at each price level, and it is downward-sloping. Monetarists view changes in the money supply as the primary source of shifts in the aggregate demand curve. Keynesians believe that not only are changes in the money supply important to shifts in the aggregate demand curve, but so are changes in fiscal policy (government spending and taxes), net exports, and the willingness of consumers and businesses to spend ("animal spirits").

2. In the short run, the aggregate supply curve slopes upward because a rise in the price level raises the profit earned on each unit of production, and the quantity of output supplied rises. Four factors can cause the aggregate supply curve to shift: tightness of the labour market as represented by unemployment relative to the natural rate, expectations of inflation, workers' attempts to push up their real wages, and supply shocks unrelated to wages that affect production costs.

3. Equilibrium in the short run occurs at the point where the aggregate demand curve intersects the aggregate supply curve. Although this is where the economy heads temporarily, it has a self-correcting mechanism, which leads it to settle permanently at the long-run equilibrium where aggregate output is at its natural rate level. Shifts in either the aggregate demand or the aggregate supply curve can produce changes in aggregate output and the price level.

KEY TERMS

activist, p. 550

aggregate demand, p. 541

aggregate demand curve, p. 541

aggregate supply, p. 541

aggregate supply curve, p. 546

"animal spirits", p. 545

complete crowding out, p. 545

consumer expenditure, p. 544

equation of exchange, p. 542

government spending, p. 544

hysteresis, p. 555

Keynesian, p. 541

long-run aggregate supply curve, p. 550

modern quantity theory of money, p. 543

monetarist, p. 541

natural rate level of output, p. 549

natural rate of unemployment, p. 548

net exports, p. 544

nonaccelerating inflation rate of unemployment (NAIRU), p. 548

nonactivist, p. 550

partial crowding out, p. 546

planned investment spending, p. 544

real business cycle theory, p. 555

self-correcting mechanism, p. 550

supply shock, p. 553

velocity of money, p. 542

QUESTIONS AND PROBLEMS

Questions marked with an asterisk are answered at the end of the book in an appendix, "Answers to Selected Questions and Problems."

1. Given that a monetarist predicts velocity to be 5, graph the aggregate demand curve that results if the money supply is $400 billion. If the money supply falls to $50 billion, what happens to the position of the aggregate demand curve?

*2. Milton Friedman states, "Money is all that matters to nominal income." How is this statement built into the aggregate demand curve in the monetarist framework?

3. Suppose that government spending is raised at the same time that the money supply is lowered. What will happen to the position of the Keynesian aggregate demand curve? The monetarist aggregate demand curve?

*4. Why does the Keynesian aggregate demand curve shift when "animal spirits" change, but the monetarist aggregate demand curve does not?

5. If the dollar increases in value relative to foreign currencies so that foreign goods become cheaper in Canada, what will happen to the position of the aggregate supply curve? The aggregate demand curve?

*6. "Profit-maximizing behaviour on the part of firms explains why the aggregate supply curve is upward-sloping." Is this statement true, false, or uncertain? Explain your answer.

7. If huge budget deficits cause the public to think that there will be higher inflation in the future, what is likely to happen to the aggregate supply curve when budget deficits rise?

*8. If a pill were invented that made workers twice as productive but their wages did not change, what would happen to the position of the aggregate supply curve?

9. When aggregate output is below the natural rate level, what will happen to the price level over time if the aggregate demand curve remains unchanged? Why?

*10. Show how aggregate supply and demand analysis can explain why both aggregate output and the price level fell sharply when investment spending collapsed during the Great Depression.

11. "An important difference between monetarists and Keynesians rests on how long they think the long run actually is." Is this statement true, false, or uncertain? Explain your answer.

Using Economic Analysis to Predict the Future

*12. Predict what will happen to aggregate output and the price level if the Bank of Canada increases the money supply at the same time that the government implements an income tax cut.

13. Suppose that the public believes that a newly announced anti-inflation program will work and so lowers its expectations of future inflation. What

will happen to aggregate output and the price level in the short run?

*14. Predict the effect of an increase in the goods and services tax (GST) on both the aggregate supply and demand curves and on aggregate output and the price level.

15. When there is a decline in the value of the dollar, some experts expect this to lead to a dramatic improvement in the ability of Canadian firms to compete abroad. Predict what would happen to output and the price level in Canada as a result.

Chapter 25

Transmission Mechanisms of Monetary Policy: The Evidence

PREVIEW   Since 1980, the Canadian economy has been on a roller coaster, with output, unemployment, and inflation undergoing drastic fluctuations. At the start of the 1980s, inflation was running at double-digit levels, and the recession of 1980 was followed by one of the shortest economic expansions on record. After a year, the economy plunged into the 1981–1982 recession, the most severe economic contraction in the postwar era—the unemployment rate climbed to over 10%, and only then did the inflation rate begin to come down to around the 5% level by early 1984.

For several years following 1984, the Canadian economy enjoyed robust growth, with the inflation rate falling to around 3% and the unemployment rate to around 8% by early 1990. With the Iraqi invasion of Kuwait in the summer of 1990 and the collapse in consumer confidence in the United States, the Canadian economy again plunged into recession. The recovery that began in 1992 was initially weak, not only by historical standards but also by comparison with the robust recovery of the U.S. economy. However, subsequent growth in the Canadian economy sped up, lowering the unemployment rate to around 6% in 2000. In light of large fluctuations in aggregate output (reflected in the unemployment rate) and inflation, and the economic instability that accompanies them, policymakers face the following dilemma: what policy or policies, if any, should be implemented to reduce output and inflation fluctuations in the future?

To answer this question, monetary policymakers must have an accurate assessment of the timing and effect of their policies on the economy. To make this assessment, they need to understand the mechanisms through which monetary policy affects the economy. In this chapter we examine empirical evidence on the effect of monetary policy on economic activity. We first look at a framework for evaluating empirical evidence and then use this framework to understand why there are still deep disagreements on the importance of monetary policy to the economy. We then go on to examine the transmission mechanisms of monetary policy and evaluate the empirical evidence on them to better understand the role that monetary policy plays in the economy. We will see that these monetary transmission mechanisms emphasize the link between the financial system (which we studied in the first three parts of this book) and monetary theory, the subject of this part.

FRAMEWORK FOR EVALUATING EMPIRICAL EVIDENCE

To develop a framework for understanding how to evaluate empirical evidence, we need to recognize that there are two basic types of empirical evidence in economics and other scientific disciplines. **Structural model evidence** examines whether one variable affects another by using data to build a model that explains the channels through which this variable affects the other; **reduced-form evidence** examines whether one variable has an effect on another simply by looking directly at the relationship between the two variables.

Suppose that you were interested in whether drinking coffee leads to heart disease. Structural model evidence would involve developing a model that analyzed data on how coffee is metabolized by the human body, how it affects the operation of the heart, and how its effects on the heart lead to heart attacks. Reduced-form evidence would involve looking directly at whether coffee drinkers tend to experience heart attacks more frequently than non–coffee drinkers.

How you look at the evidence—whether you focus on structural model evidence or reduced-form evidence—can lead to different conclusions. This is particularly true for the debate between monetarists and Keynesians. Monetarists tend to focus on reduced-form evidence and feel that changes in the money supply are more important to economic activity than Keynesians do; Keynesians, for their part, focus on structural model evidence. To understand the differences in their views about the importance of monetary policy, we need to look at the nature of the two types of evidence and the advantages and disadvantages of each.

Structural Model Evidence

The Keynesian analysis discussed in Chapter 24 is specific about the channels through which the money supply affects economic activity (called the **transmission mechanisms of monetary policy**). Keynesians typically examine the effect of money on economic activity by building a **structural model**, a description of how the economy operates using a collection of equations that describe the behaviour of firms and consumers in many sectors of the economy. These equations then show the channels through which monetary and fiscal policy affect aggregate output and spending. A Keynesian structural model might have behavioural equations that describe the workings of monetary policy with the following schematic diagram:

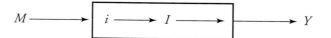

The model describes the transmission mechanism of monetary policy as follows: the money supply M affects interest rates i, which in turn affect investment spending I, which in turn affects aggregate output or aggregate spending Y. The Keynesians examine the relationship between M and Y by looking at empirical evidence (structural model evidence) on the specific channels of monetary influence, such as the link between interest rates and investment spending.

Reduced-Form Evidence

Monetarists do not describe specific ways in which the money supply affects aggregate spending. Instead, they examine the effect of money on economic activity by looking at whether movements in Y are tightly linked to (have a high correlation with) movements in M. Using reduced-form evidence, monetarists analyze the effect of M on Y as if the economy were a black box whose workings cannot be seen. The monetarist way of looking at the evidence can be represented by the following schematic diagram, in which the economy is drawn as a black box with a question mark:

Now that we have seen how monetarists and Keynesians look at the empirical evidence on the link between money and economic activity, we can consider the advantages and disadvantages of their approaches.

Advantages and Disadvantages of Structural Model Evidence

The structural model approach, used primarily by Keynesians, has the advantage of giving us an understanding of how the economy works. If the structure is correct—if it contains all the transmission mechanisms and channels through which monetary and fiscal policy can affect economic activity—the structural model approach has three major advantages over the reduced-form approach.

1. Because we can evaluate each transmission mechanism separately to see whether it is plausible, we will obtain more pieces of evidence on whether money has an important effect on economic activity. If we find important effects of monetary policy on economic activity, for example, we will have more confidence that changes in monetary policy actually cause the changes in economic activity; that is, we will have more confidence in the direction of causation between M and Y.

2. Knowing how changes in monetary policy affect economic activity may help us predict the effect of M on Y more accurately. For example, expansions in the money supply might be found to be less effective when interest rates are low. Then, when interest rates are higher, we would be able to predict that an expansion in the money supply would have a larger impact on Y than would otherwise be the case.

3. By knowing how the economy operates, we may be able to predict how institutional changes in the economy might affect the link between M and Y. Because of the rapid pace of financial innovation, the advantage of being able to predict how institutional changes affect the link between M and Y may be even more important now than in the past.

These three advantages of the structural model approach suggest that this approach is better than the reduced-form approach *if we know the correct structure of the model*. Put another way, structural model evidence is only as good as the structural model it is based on; it is best only if all the transmission mechanisms are fully understood. This is a big *if*, as failing to include one or two relevant transmission mechanisms for monetary policy in the structural model might result in a serious underestimate of the impact of M on Y.

Monetarists worry that many Keynesian structural models may ignore the transmission mechanisms for monetary policy that are most important. For example, if the most important monetary transmission mechanisms involve consumer spending rather than investment spending, the Keynesian structural model (such as the $M\uparrow \Rightarrow i\downarrow \Rightarrow I\uparrow \Rightarrow Y\uparrow$ one we used earlier), which focuses on investment spending for its monetary transmission mechanism, may underestimate the importance of money to economic activity. In other words, monetarists reject the interpretation of evidence from many Keynesian structural models because they believe that the channels of monetary influence are too narrowly defined. In a sense, they accuse Keynesians of wearing blinders that prevent them from recognizing the full importance of monetary policy.

Advantages and Disadvantages of Reduced-Form Evidence

The main advantage of reduced-form evidence over structural model evidence is that no restrictions are imposed on the way monetary policy affects the economy. If we are not sure that we know what all the monetary transmission mechanisms are, we may be more likely to spot the full effect of M on Y by looking at whether movements in Y correlate highly with movements in M. Monetarists favour reduced-form evidence because they believe that the particular channels through which changes in the money supply affect Y are diverse and continually changing. They contend that it may be too difficult to identify all the transmission mechanisms of monetary policy.

The most notable objection to reduced-form evidence is that it may misleadingly suggest that changes in M cause changes in Y when that is not the case. A basic principle applicable to all scientific disciplines, including economics, states that ***correlation does not necessarily imply causation***. The fact that the movement of one variable is linked to another doesn't necessarily mean that one variable *causes* the other.

Suppose, for example, you notice that wherever criminal activity abounds, more police patrol the street. Should you conclude from this evidence that police patrols cause criminal activity and recommend pulling police off the street to lower the crime rate? The answer is clearly no, because police patrols do not cause criminal activity; criminal activity causes police patrols. This situation is called **reverse causation** and can lead to misleading conclusions when interpreting correlations (see Box 25-1).

The reverse causation problem may be present when examining the link between money and aggregate output or spending. Our discussion of the conduct of monetary policy in Chapter 18 suggested that when the Bank of Canada has an interest-rate or a reserves target, higher output might lead to a higher money supply. If most of the correlation between M and Y occurs because of the Bank's interest-rate target, controlling the money supply will not help control aggregate output because it is actually Y that is causing M rather than the other way around.

Another facet of the correlation–causation question is that an outside factor, yet unknown, could be the driving force behind two variables that move together. Coffee drinking might be associated with heart disease not because coffee drinking causes heart attacks but because coffee drinkers tend to be people who are under a lot of stress and the stress causes heart attacks. Getting people to stop drinking coffee, then, would not lower the incidence of heart disease. Similarly, if there is an unknown outside factor that causes M and Y to move together, controlling M will not improve control of Y.

Conclusions

No clear-cut case can be made that reduced-form evidence is preferable to structural model evidence or vice versa. The structural model approach, used primarily by Keynesians, offers an understanding of how the economy works. If the structure is correct, it predicts the effect of monetary policy more accurately, allows predictions of the effect of monetary policy when institutions change, and provides more confidence in the direction of causation between M and Y. If the structure of the model is not correctly specified because it leaves out important transmission mechanisms of monetary policy, it could be very misleading.

Perils of Reverse Causation

A Russian Folk Tale. A Russian folk tale illustrates the problems that can arise from reverse causation. As the story goes, there once was a severe epidemic in the Russian countryside and many doctors were sent to the towns where the epidemic was at its worst. The peasants in the towns noticed that wherever doctors went, many people were dying. So to reduce the death rate, they killed all the doctors.

Were the peasants better off? Clearly not.

The reduced-form approach, used primarily by monetarists, does not restrict the way monetary policy affects the economy and may be more likely to spot the full effect of *M* on *Y*. However, reduced-form evidence cannot rule out reverse causation, whereby changes in output cause changes in money, or the possibility that an outside factor drives changes in both output and money. A high correlation of money and output might then be misleading because controlling the money supply would not help control the level of output.

Armed with the framework to evaluate empirical evidence we have outlined here, we can now use it to evaluate the empirical debate between monetarists and Keynesians on the importance of money to the economy. This debate has its roots in differing views of the main causes of the Great Depression of the 1930s, especially as it occurred in the United States. The Great Depression was created in the United States and transmitted quickly to Canada and the rest of the world. By understanding the different interpretations of the causes of the Great Depression in the United States, you will have a better understanding of the role that central banks and commercial banks play in the economy.

EARLY KEYNESIAN EVIDENCE ON THE IMPORTANCE OF MONEY

Although Keynes proposed his theory for analyzing aggregate economic activity in 1936, his views reached their peak of popularity among economists in the 1950s and early 1960s, when the majority of economists had accepted his framework. Although Keynesians currently believe that monetary policy has important effects on economic activity, the early Keynesians of the 1950s and early 1960s characteristically held the view that *monetary policy does not matter at all* to movements in aggregate output and hence to the business cycle.

Their belief in the ineffectiveness of monetary policy stemmed from three pieces of structural model evidence:

1. During the Great Depression, interest rates on Canadian and U.S. government securities fell to extremely low levels. Early Keynesians viewed monetary policy as affecting aggregate demand solely through its effect on nominal interest rates, which in turn affect investment spending; they believed that low interest rates during the Depression indicated that monetary policy was easy because it encouraged investment spending and so could not have played a contractionary role during this period. Seeing that monetary policy was not capable of explaining why the worst economic contraction in history had taken place, they concluded that changes in the money supply have no effect on aggregate output—in other words, that money doesn't matter.

2. Early empirical studies found no linkage between movements in nominal interest rates and investment spending. Because early Keynesians saw this

link as the channel through which changes in the money supply affect aggregate demand, finding that the link was weak also led them to the conclusion that changes in the money supply have no effect on aggregate output.

3. Surveys of businesspeople revealed that their decisions on how much to invest in new physical capital were not influenced by market interest rates. This evidence further confirmed that the link between interest rates and investment spending was weak, strengthening the conclusion that money doesn't matter. The result of this interpretation of the evidence was that most economists paid only scant attention to monetary policy until the mid-1960s.

---

*Study
Guide*

Before reading about the objections that were raised against early Keynesian interpretations of the evidence, use the ideas on the disadvantages of structural model evidence to see if you can come up with some objections yourself. This will help you learn to apply the principles of evaluating evidence discussed earlier.

Objections to Early Keynesian Evidence

University of Chicago
www.uchicago.edu

While Keynesian economics was reaching its ascendancy in the 1950s and 1960s, a small group of economists at the University of Chicago, led by Milton Friedman, adopted what was then the unfashionable view that money *does* matter to aggregate demand. Friedman and his disciples, who later became known as *monetarists,* objected to the early Keynesian interpretation of the evidence on the grounds that the structural model used by the early Keynesians was severely flawed. Because structural model evidence is only as good as the model it is based on, the monetarist critique of this evidence needs to be taken seriously.

In 1963, Friedman and Anna Schwartz published their classic monetary history of the United States, which showed that contrary to the early Keynesian beliefs, monetary policy during the Great Depression was not easy; indeed, it had never been more contractionary.[1] Friedman and Schwartz documented the massive bank failures of this period and the resulting decline in the money supply—the largest ever experienced in the United States. Hence monetary policy could explain the worst economic contraction in U.S. history, and the Great Depression could not be singled out as a period that demonstrates the ineffectiveness of monetary policy.

A Keynesian could still counter Friedman and Schwartz's argument that money was contractionary during the Great Depression by citing the low level of interest rates. But were these interest rates really so low? Although interest rates on government securities and high-grade corporate bonds were low during the Great Depression, interest rates on lower-grade bonds rose to unprecedented high levels during the sharpest part of the contraction phase (1930–1933). By the standard of these lower-grade bonds, then, interest rates were high and monetary policy was tight.

There is a moral to this story. Although much aggregate economic analysis proceeds as though there is only *one* interest rate, we must always be aware that there are *many* interest rates, which may tell different stories. During normal times, most interest rates move in tandem, so lumping them all together and looking at one representative interest rate may not be too misleading. But that is not always so. Unusual periods (like the Great Depression), when interest rates on different securities begin to diverge, do occur. This is exactly the kind of situation in which a structural model (like the early Keynesians') that looks at only the interest rates on a low-risk security such as a Canadian government Treasury bill or bond can be very misleading.

---

[1]Milton Friedman and Anna Jacobson Schwartz, *A Monetary History of the United States, 1867–1960* (Princeton, N.J.: Princeton University Press, 1963).

There is a second, potentially more important reason why the early Keynesian structural model's focus on nominal interest rates provides a misleading picture of the tightness of monetary policy during the Great Depression. In a period of deflation, when there is a declining price level, low *nominal* interest rates do not necessarily indicate that the cost of borrowing is low and that monetary policy is easy—in fact, the cost of borrowing could be quite high. If, for example, the public expects the price level to decline at a 10% rate, then even though nominal interest rates are at zero, the real cost of borrowing would be as high as 10%. (Recall from Chapter 4 that the real rate equals the nominal rate, 0, minus the expected rate of inflation, −10%, so the real rate equals 0 − (−10%) = 10%.)

You can see in Figure 25-1 that this is exactly what happened during the Great Depression in the United States. Real interest rates on U.S. Treasury bills were far higher during the 1931–1933 contraction phase of the Depression than was the case throughout the next 40 years.[2] As a result, movements of *real* interest rates indicate that contrary to the early Keynesians' beliefs, monetary policy was extremely tight during the Great Depression. Because an important role for monetary policy during this depressed period could no longer be ruled out, most economists were forced to rethink their position regarding whether money matters.

Monetarists also objected to the early Keynesian structural model's view that a weak link between nominal interest rates and investment spending indicates that

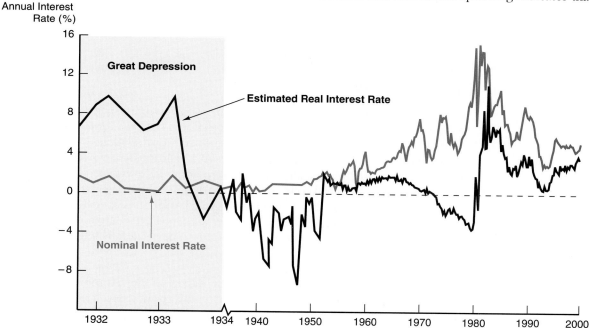

FIGURE 25-1 Real and Nominal Interest Rates on Three-Month Treasury Bills, 1931–2000

Source: Nominal rates from www.bog.frb.fed.us/releases/H15/data/a/tbaa3m.txt. The real rate is constructed using the procedure outlined in Frederic S. Mishkin, "The Real Interest Rate: An Empirical Investigation," *Carnegie-Rochester Conference Series on Public Policy* 15 (1981): 151–200. This involves estimating expected inflation as a function of past interest rates, inflation, and time trends and then subtracting the expected inflation measure from the nominal interest rate.

---

[2]In the 1980s, real interest rates rose to exceedingly high levels, approaching those of the Great Depression period. Research has tried to explain this phenomenon, some of which points to monetary policy as the source of high real rates in the 1980s. For example, see Oliver J. Blanchard and Lawrence H. Summers, "Perspectives on High World Interest Rates," *Brookings Papers on Economic Activity* 2 (1984): 273–324; and John Huizinga and Frederic S. Mishkin, "Monetary Policy Regime Shifts and the Unusual Behaviour of Real Interest Rates," *Carnegie-Rochester Conference Series on Public Policy* 24 (1986): 231–274.

investment spending is unaffected by monetary policy. A weak link between *nominal* interest rates and investment spending does not rule out a strong link between *real* interest rates and investment spending. As depicted in Figure 25-1, nominal interest rates are often a very misleading indicator of real interest rates—not only during the Great Depression but in later periods as well. Because real interest rates more accurately reflect the true cost of borrowing, they should be more relevant to investment decisions than nominal interest rates. Accordingly, the two pieces of early Keynesian evidence indicating that nominal interest rates have little effect on investment spending do not rule out a strong effect of changes in the money supply on investment spending and hence on aggregate demand.

Monetarists also assert that interest-rate effects on investment spending might be only one of many channels through which monetary policy affects aggregate demand. Monetary policy could then have a major impact on aggregate demand even if interest-rate effects on investment spending are small, as was suggested by the early Keynesians.

Study Guide   As you read the monetarist evidence presented in the next section, again try to think of objections to the evidence. This time use the ideas on the disadvantages of reduced-form evidence.

EARLY MONETARIST EVIDENCE ON THE IMPORTANCE OF MONEY

In the early 1960s, Milton Friedman and his followers published a series of studies based on reduced-form evidence that promoted the case for a strong effect of money on economic activity. In general, reduced-form evidence can be broken down into three categories: *timing evidence,* which looks at whether the movements in one variable typically occur before another; *statistical evidence,* which performs formal statistical tests on the correlation of the movements of one variable with another; and *historical evidence,* which examines specific past episodes to see whether movements in one variable appear to cause another. Let's look at the monetarist evidence on the importance of money that falls into each of these three categories.

Timing Evidence   Monetarist timing evidence reveals how the rate of money supply growth moves relative to the business cycle. The evidence on this relationship was first presented by Friedman and Schwartz in a famous paper published in 1963.[3] Friedman and Schwartz found that in every business cycle they studied over nearly a century, the money growth rate always turned down before output did. On average, the peak in the rate of money growth occurred 16 months before the peak in the level of output. However, this lead-time could vary, ranging from a few months to more than two years. The conclusion that these authors reached on the basis of this evidence is that money growth causes business cycle fluctuations, but its effect on the business cycle operates with "long and variable lags."

Timing evidence is based on the philosophical principle first stated in Latin as *post hoc, ergo propter hoc,* which means that if one event occurs after another, the

[3]Milton Friedman and Anna Jacobson Schwartz, "Money and Business Cycles," *Review of Economics and Statistics* 45, Suppl. (1963): 32–64.

second event must have been caused by the first. This principle is valid only if we know that the first event is an *exogenous* event, an event occurring as a result of an independent action that could not possibly be caused by the event following it or by some outside factor that might affect both events. If the first event is exogenous, when the second event follows the first we can be more confident that the first event is causing the second.

An example of an exogenous event is a controlled experiment. A chemist mixes two chemicals; suddenly his lab blows up and he with it. We can be absolutely sure that the cause of his demise was the act of mixing the two chemicals together. The principle of *post hoc, ergo propter hoc* is extremely useful in scientific experimentation.

Unfortunately, economics does not enjoy the precision of hard sciences like physics or chemistry. Often we cannot be sure that an economic event, such as a decline in the rate of money growth, is an exogenous event—it could have been caused, itself, by an outside factor or by the event it is supposedly causing. When another event (such as a decline in output) typically follows the first event (a decline in money growth), we cannot conclude with certainty that one caused the other. Timing evidence is clearly of a reduced-form nature because it looks directly at the relationship of the movements of two variables. Money growth could lead output, or both could be driven by an outside factor.

Because timing evidence is of a reduced-form nature, there is also the possibility of reverse causation, in which output growth causes money growth. How can this reverse causation occur while money growth still leads output? There are several ways in which this can happen, but we will deal with just one example.[4]

Suppose that you are in a hypothetical economy with a very regular business cycle movement, plotted in panel (a) of Figure 25-2, that is four years long (four years from peak to peak). Let's assume that in our hypothetical economy, there is reverse causation from output to the money supply, so movements in the money supply and output are perfectly correlated; that is, the money supply M and output Y move upward and downward at the same time. The result is that the peaks and troughs of the M and Y series in panels (a) and (b) occur at exactly the same time; therefore, no lead or lag relationship exists between them.

Now let's construct the rate of money supply growth from the money supply series in panel (b). This is done in panel (c). What is the rate of growth of the money supply at its peaks in years 1 and 5? At these points, it is not growing at all; the rate of growth is zero. Similarly, at the trough in year 3, the growth rate is zero. When the money supply is declining from its peak in year 1 to its trough in year 3, it has a negative growth rate, and its decline is fastest sometime between years 1 and 3 (year 2). Translating to panel (c), the rate of money growth is below zero from years 1 to 3, with its most negative value reached at year 2. By similar reasoning, you can see that the growth rate of money is positive in years 0 to 1 and 3 to 5, with the highest values reached in years 0 and 4. When we connect all these points together, we get the money growth series in panel (c), in which the peaks are at years 0 and 4, with a trough in year 2.

Now let's look at the relationship of the money growth series of panel (c) with the level of output in panel (a). As you can see, the money growth series consistently has its peaks and troughs exactly one year before the peaks and troughs of the output series. We conclude that in our hypothetical economy, the

---

[4]A famous article by James Tobin, "Money and Income: *Post Hoc, Ergo Propter Hoc,*" *Quarterly Journal of Economics* 84 (1970): 301–317, describes an economic system in which changes in aggregate output cause changes in the growth rate of money but changes in the growth rate of money have no effect on output. Tobin shows that such a system with reverse causation could yield timing evidence similar to that found by Friedman and Schwartz.

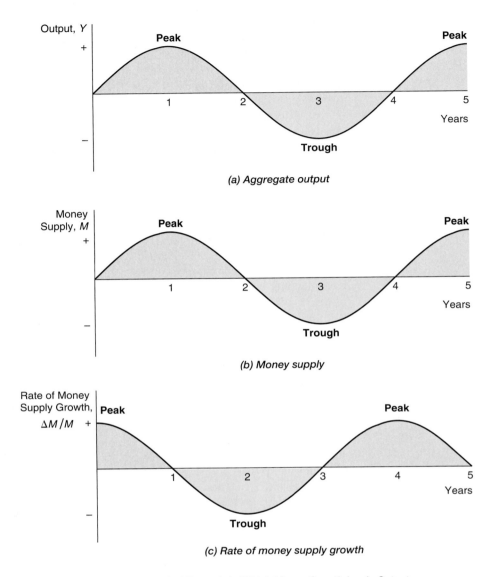

(a) Aggregate output

(b) Money supply

(c) Rate of money supply growth

FIGURE 25-2   Hypothetical Example in Which Money Growth Leads Output

Although neither *M* nor *Y* leads the other (that is, their peaks and troughs coincide), $\Delta M/M$ has its peaks and troughs one year ahead of *M* and *Y*, thus leading both series. (Note that *M* and *Y* in the panels are drawn as movements around a positive average value; a plus sign indicates a value above the average, and a minus sign indicates a value below the average, not a negative value.)

rate of money growth always decreases one year before output does. This evidence does not, however, imply that money growth *drives* output. In fact, by assumption, we know that this economy is one in which causation actually runs from output to the level of money supply, and there is no lead or lag relationship between the two. Only by our judicious choice of using the *growth rate* of the money supply rather than its *level* have we found a leading relationship.

This example shows how easy it is to misinterpret timing relationships. Furthermore, by searching for what we hope to find, we might focus on a variable, such as a growth rate, rather than a level, which suggests a misleading relationship. Timing evidence can be a dangerous tool for deciding on causation.

Stated even more forcefully, "one person's lead is another person's lag." For example, you could just as easily interpret the relationship of money growth and output in Figure 25-2 to say that the money growth rate lags output by three years—after all, the peaks in the money growth series occur three years after the peaks in the output series. In short, you could say that output leads money growth.

We have seen that timing evidence is extremely hard to interpret. Unless we can be sure that changes in the leading variable are exogenous events, we cannot be sure that the leading variable is actually causing the following variable. And it is all too easy to find what we seek when looking for timing evidence. Perhaps the best way of describing this danger is to say, "timing evidence may be in the eyes of the beholder."

Statistical Evidence

Monetarist statistical evidence examines the correlations between money and aggregate output or aggregate spending by performing formal statistical tests. Again in 1963 (obviously a vintage year for the monetarists), Milton Friedman and David Meiselman published a paper that proposed the following test of a monetarist model against a Keynesian model.[5] In the Keynesian framework, investment and government spending are sources of fluctuations in aggregate demand, so Friedman and Meiselman constructed a "Keynesian" autonomous expenditure variable A equal to investment spending plus government spending. They characterized the Keynesian model as saying that A should be highly correlated with aggregate spending Y, while the money supply M should not. In the monetarist model, the money supply is the source of fluctuations in aggregate spending, and M should be highly correlated with Y, while A should not.

A logical way to find out which model is better would be to see which is more highly correlated with Y: M or A. When Friedman and Meiselman conducted this test for many different periods of U.S. data, they discovered that *the monetarist model wins!*[6] They concluded that monetarist analysis gives a better description than Keynesian analysis of how aggregate spending is determined.

Several objections were raised against the Friedman–Meiselman evidence:

1. The standard criticisms of this reduced-form evidence are the ones we have already discussed. Reverse causation could occur, or an outside factor might drive both series.

2. The test may not be fair because the Keynesian model is characterized too simplistically. Keynesian structural models commonly include hundreds of equations. The one-equation Keynesian model that Friedman–Meiselman tested may not adequately capture the effects of autonomous expenditure. Furthermore, Keynesian models usually include the effects of other variables. By ignoring them, the effect of monetary policy might be overestimated and the effect of autonomous expenditure underestimated.

3. The Friedman–Meiselman measure of autonomous expenditure A might be constructed poorly, preventing the Keynesian model from performing well. For example, orders for military hardware affect aggregate demand before they appear as spending in the autonomous expenditure variable that Friedman and Meiselman used. A more careful construction of the

---

[5]Milton Friedman and David Meiselman, "The Relative Stability of Monetary Velocity and the Investment Multiplier," in *Stabilization Policies,* ed. Commission on Money and Credit (Upper Saddle River, N.J.: Prentice-Hall, 1963), pp. 165–268.

[6]Friedman and Meiselman did not actually run their tests using the Y variable because they felt that this gave an unfair advantage to the Keynesian model in that A is included in Y. Instead, they subtracted A from Y and tested for the correlation of $Y - A$ with M or A.

autonomous expenditure variable should take account of the placing of orders for military hardware. When the autonomous expenditure variable was constructed more carefully by critics of the Friedman–Meiselman study, they found that the results were reversed: the Keynesian model won.[7] A more recent postmortem on the appropriateness of various ways of determining autonomous expenditure does not give a clear-cut victory to either the Keynesian or the monetarist model.[8]

Historical Evidence

The monetarist historical evidence, found in Friedman and Schwartz's *A Monetary History,* has been very influential in gaining support for the monetarist position. We have already seen that the book was extremely important as a criticism of early Keynesian thinking, showing as it did that the Great Depression was not a period of easy monetary policy and that the depression could be attributed to the sharp decline in the money supply from 1930 to 1933 resulting from bank panics. In addition, the book documents in great detail that the growth rate of money leads business cycles because it declines before every recession. This timing evidence is, of course, subject to all the criticisms raised earlier.

The historical evidence contains one feature, however, that makes it different from other monetarist evidence we have discussed so far. Several episodes occur in which changes in the money supply appear to be exogenous events. These episodes are almost like controlled experiments, so the *post hoc, ergo propter hoc* principle is far more likely to be valid. If the decline in the growth rate of the money supply is soon followed by a decline in output in these episodes, much stronger evidence is presented that money growth is the driving force behind the business cycle.

One of the best examples of such an episode is the increase in reserve requirements in the United States in 1936–1937, which led to a sharp decline in the money supply and in its rate of growth. The increase in reserve requirements was implemented because the Federal Reserve wanted to improve its control of monetary policy; it was not implemented in response to economic conditions. We can thus rule out reverse causation from output to the money supply. Also, it is hard to think of an outside factor that could have driven the Fed to increase reserve requirements and that could also have directly affected output. Therefore, the decline in the money supply in this episode can probably be classified as an exogenous event with the characteristics of a controlled experiment. Soon after this experiment, the very severe U.S. recession of 1937–1938 occurred. We can conclude with confidence that in this episode, the change in the money supply due to the Fed's increase in reserve requirements was indeed the source of the business cycle contraction that followed.

A Monetary History also documents other historical episodes, such as the bank panic of 1907 and other years in which the decline in money growth again appears to have been an exogenous event. The fact that recessions have frequently followed apparently exogenous declines in money growth is very strong evidence that changes in the growth rate of the money supply do have an impact on aggregate output. Recent work by Christina and David Romer, both of the University of California, Berkeley, applies the historical approach to more recent data using more sophisticated statistical techniques and also finds that monetary policy shifts have had an important impact on the aggregate economy.[9]

University of California, Berkeley
www.berkeley.edu

---

[7]See, for example, Albert Ando and Franco Modigliani, "The Relative Stability of Monetary Velocity and the Investment Multiplier," *American Economic Review* 55 (1965): 693–728.

[8]See William Poole and Edith Kornblith, "The Friedman-Meiselman CMC Paper: New Evidence on an Old Controversy," *American Economic Review* 63 (1973): 908–917.

OVERVIEW OF THE MONETARIST EVIDENCE

Where does this discussion of the monetarist evidence leave us? We have seen that because of reverse causation and outside-factor possibilities, there are some serious doubts about the conclusions that can be drawn from timing and statistical evidence alone. However, some of the historical evidence in which exogenous declines in money growth are followed by business cycle contractions does provide stronger support for the monetarist position. When historical evidence is combined with timing and statistical evidence, the conclusion that money does matter seems warranted.

As you can imagine, the economics profession was quite shaken by the appearance of the monetarist evidence, as up to that time most economists believed that money does not matter at all. Monetarists had demonstrated that this early Keynesian position was probably wrong, and it won them a lot of converts. Recognizing the fallacy of the position that money does not matter does not necessarily mean that we must accept the position that money is *all* that matters. Many Keynesian economists shifted their views toward the monetarist position, but not all the way. Instead, they adopted an intermediate position compatible with the Keynesian aggregate supply and demand analysis described in Chapter 24. They allowed that money, fiscal policy, net exports, and "animal spirits" all contributed to fluctuations in aggregate demand. The result has been a convergence of the Keynesian and monetarist views on the importance of money to economic activity. However, proponents of a new theory of aggregate fluctuations called *real business cycle theory* are more critical of the monetarist reduced-form evidence that money is important to business cycle fluctuations because they believe there is reverse causation from the business cycle to money (see Box 25-2).

TRANSMISSION MECHANISMS OF MONETARY POLICY

After the successful monetarist attack on the early Keynesian position, economic research went in two directions. One direction was to use more sophisticated monetarist reduced-form models to test for the importance of money to economic activity.[10] The second direction was to pursue a structural model approach and to develop a better understanding of channels (other than interest-rate effects on investment) through which monetary policy affects aggregate demand. In this section we examine some of these channels, or *transmission mechanisms*, beginning with interest-rate channels because they are the key monetary transmission mechanism in the Keynesian *ISLM* and *AD/AS* models you have seen in Chapters 22, 23, and 24.

Traditional Interest-Rate Channels

The traditional Keynesian view of the monetary transmission mechanism can be characterized by the following schematic showing the effect of a monetary expansion:

$$M\uparrow \Rightarrow i_r\downarrow \Rightarrow I\uparrow \Rightarrow Y\uparrow \tag{1}$$

---

[9]Christina Romer and David Romer, "Does Monetary Policy Matter? A New Test in the Spirit of Friedman and Schwartz," *NBER Macroeconomics Annual, 1989,* 4, ed. Stanley Fischer (Cambridge, Mass.: M.I.T. Press, 1989), 121–170.

[10]The most prominent example of more sophisticated reduced-form research is the so-called St. Louis model, which was developed at the Federal Reserve Bank of St. Louis in the late 1960s and early 1970s. It provided support for the monetarist position but is subject to the same criticisms of reduced-form evidence outlined in the text. The St. Louis model was first outlined in Leonall Andersen and Jerry Jordan, "Monetary and Fiscal Actions: A Test of Their Relative Importance in Economic Stabilization," Federal Reserve Bank of St. Louis *Review* 50 (November 1968): 11–23.

BOX 25·2

Real Business Cycle Theory and the Debate on Money and Economic Activity

New entrants to the debate on money and economic activity are advocates of *real business cycle theory,* which states that real shocks to tastes and technology (rather than monetary shocks) are the driving forces behind business cycles. Proponents of this theory are critical of the monetarist view that money matters to business cycles because they believe that the correlation of output with money reflects reverse causation; that is, the business cycle drives money, rather than the other way around. An important piece of evidence they offer to support the reverse causation argument is that almost none of the correlation between money and output comes from the monetary base, which is controlled by the monetary authorities.* Instead, the money–output correlation stems from other sources of money supply movements that, as we saw in Chapters 15 and 16, are affected by the actions of banks, depositors, and borrowers from banks and are more likely to be influenced by the business cycle.

*Robert King and Charles Plosser, "Money, Credit and Prices in a Real Business Cycle," *American Economic Review* 74 (1984): 363–380; Charles Plosser, "Understanding Real Business Cycles," *Journal of Economic Perspectives* 3 (Summer 1989): 51–78.

where $M\uparrow$ indicates an expansionary monetary policy leading to a fall in real interest rates ($i_r\downarrow$), which in turn lowers the cost of capital, causing a rise in investment spending ($I\uparrow$), thereby leading to an increase in aggregate demand and a rise in output ($Y\uparrow$).

Although Keynes originally emphasized this channel as operating through businesses' decisions about investment spending, the search for new monetary transmission mechanisms recognized that consumers' decisions about housing and **consumer durable expenditure** (spending by consumers on durable items such as automobiles and refrigerators) also are investment decisions. Thus the interest-rate channel of monetary transmission outlined in Equation 1 applies equally to consumer spending, in which I represents residential housing and consumer durable expenditure.

An important feature of the interest-rate transmission mechanism is its emphasis on the *real* rather than the nominal interest rate as the rate that affects consumer and business decisions. In addition, it is often the real *long*-term interest rate and not the short-term interest rate that is viewed as having the major impact on spending. How is it that changes in the short-term nominal interest rate induced by a central bank result in a corresponding change in the real interest rate on both short- and long-term bonds? The key is the phenomenon known as *sticky prices*, the fact that the aggregate price level adjusts slowly over time, meaning that expansionary monetary policy, which lowers the short-term nominal interest rate, also lowers the short-term *real* interest rate. The expectations hypothesis of the term structure described in Chapter 6, which states that the long-term interest rate is an average of expected future short-term interest rates, suggests that the lower real short-term interest rate leads to a fall in the real long-term interest rate. These lower real interest rates then lead to rises in business fixed investment, residential housing investment, inventory investment, and consumer durable expenditure, all of which produce the rise in aggregate output.

The fact that it is the real interest rate rather than the nominal rate that affects spending provides an important mechanism for how monetary policy can stimulate the economy, even if nominal interest rates hit a floor of zero during a deflationary episode. With nominal interest rates at a floor of zero, an expansion in the money supply ($M\uparrow$) can raise the expected price level ($P^e\uparrow$) and hence expected inflation ($\pi^e\uparrow$), thereby lowering the real interest rate ($i_r = i - \pi^e\downarrow$) even when the nominal interest rate is fixed at zero and stimulating spending through the interest-rate channel:

$$M\uparrow \Rightarrow P^e\uparrow \Rightarrow \pi^e\uparrow \Rightarrow i_r\downarrow \Rightarrow I\uparrow \Rightarrow Y\uparrow \tag{2}$$

This mechanism thus indicates that monetary policy can still be effective even when nominal interest rates have already been driven down to zero by the monetary authorities. Indeed, this mechanism is a key element in monetarist discussions of why actual economies were not stuck in a liquidity trap (in which increases in the money supply may not be sufficient to lower interest rates, discussed in Chapter 21) during the Great Depression and why expansionary monetary policy could have prevented the sharp decline in output during that period.

Some economists, such as John Taylor of Stanford University, take the position that there is strong empirical evidence for substantial interest-rate effects on consumer and investment spending through the cost of capital, making the interest-rate monetary transmission mechanism a strong one. His position is highly controversial, and many researchers, including Ben Bernanke of Princeton University and Mark Gertler of New York University, believe that the empirical evidence does not support strong interest-rate effects operating through the cost of capital.[11] Indeed, these researchers see the empirical failure of traditional interest-rate monetary transmission mechanisms as having provided the stimulus for the search for other transmission mechanisms of monetary policy.

These other transmission mechanisms fall into two basic categories: those operating through asset prices other than interest rates and those operating through asymmetric information effects on credit markets (the so-called **credit view**). (All these mechanisms are summarized in the schematic diagram in Figure 25-3.)

Stanford University
www.stanford.edu

Princeton University
www.princeton.edu

New York University
www.nyu.edu

Other Asset Price Channels

As we saw earlier in the chapter, a key monetarist objection to the Keynesian analysis of monetary policy effects on the economy is that it focuses on only one asset price, the interest rate, rather than on many asset prices. Monetarists envision a transmission mechanism in which other relative asset prices and real wealth transmit monetary effects onto the economy. In addition to bond prices, two other asset prices receive substantial attention as channels for monetary policy effects: foreign exchange and equities (stocks).

Exchange Rate Effects on Net Exports With the growing internationalization of economies throughout the world and the advent of flexible exchange rates, more attention has been paid to how monetary policy affects exchange rates, which in turn affect net exports and aggregate output.

This channel also involves interest-rate effects because, as we saw in Chapter 7, when domestic real interest rates fall, domestic dollar deposits become less attractive relative to deposits denominated in foreign currencies. As a result, the

---

[11]See John Taylor, "The Monetary Transmission Mechanism: An Empirical Framework," *Journal of Economic Perspectives* 9 (Fall 1995): 11–26, and Ben Bernanke and Mark Gertler, "Inside the Black Box: The Credit Channel of Monetary Policy Transmission," *Journal of Economic Perspectives* 9 (Fall 1995): 27–48.

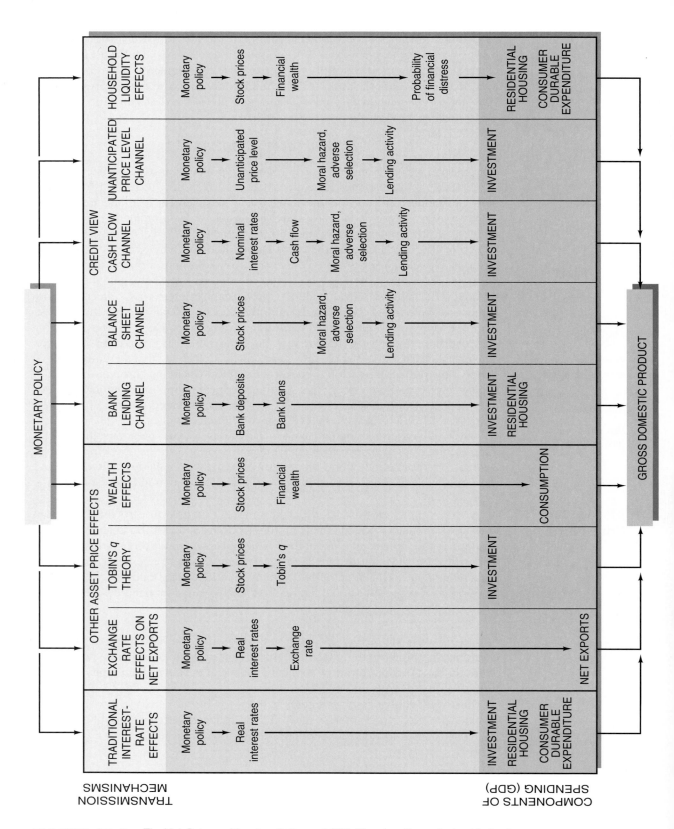

FIGURE 25-3 The Link Between Monetary Policy and GDP: Monetary Transmission Mechanisms

value of dollar deposits relative to other currency deposits falls, and the dollar depreciates (denoted by $E\downarrow$). The lower value of the domestic currency makes domestic goods cheaper than foreign goods, thereby causing a rise in net exports ($NX\uparrow$) and hence in aggregate output ($Y\uparrow$). The schematic for the monetary transmission mechanism that operates through the exchange rate is

$$M\uparrow \Rightarrow i_r\downarrow \Rightarrow E\downarrow \Rightarrow NX\uparrow \Rightarrow Y\uparrow \qquad (3)$$

Recent research has found that this exchange rate channel plays an important role in how monetary policy affects the domestic economy.[12]

Tobin's *q* Theory   James Tobin developed a theory, referred to as *Tobin's q Theory*, that explains how monetary policy can affect the economy through its effects on the valuation of equities (stock). Tobin defines q as the market value of firms divided by the replacement cost of capital. If q is high, the market price of firms is high relative to the replacement cost of capital, and new plant and equipment capital is cheap relative to the market value of firms. Companies can then issue stock and get a high price for it relative to the cost of the facilities and equipment they are buying. Investment spending will rise because firms can buy a lot of new investment goods with only a small issue of stock.

Conversely, when q is low, firms will not purchase *new* investment goods because the market value of firms is low relative to the cost of capital. If companies want to acquire capital when q is low, they can buy another firm cheaply and acquire old capital instead. Investment spending, the purchase of new investment goods, will then be very low. Tobin's q theory gives a good explanation for the extremely low rate of investment spending during the Great Depression. In that period, stock prices collapsed and q fell to unprecedented low levels.

The crux of this discussion is that a link exists between Tobin's q and investment spending. But how might monetary policy affect stock prices? Quite simply, when monetary policy is expansionary, the public finds that it has more money than it wants and so gets rid of it through spending. One place the public spends is in the stock market, increasing the demand for stocks and consequently raising their prices.[13] Combining this with the fact that higher stock (equity) prices (P_e) will lead to a higher q and thus higher investment spending I leads to the following transmission mechanism of monetary policy:[14]

$$M\uparrow \Rightarrow P_e\uparrow \Rightarrow q\uparrow \Rightarrow I\uparrow \Rightarrow Y\uparrow \qquad (4)$$

(Note that P_e represents the price of equity, whereas P^e, in an earlier schematic, represents the expected price level.)

---

[12]For example, see Ralph Bryant, Peter Hooper, and Catherine Mann, *Evaluating Policy Regimes: New Empirical Research in Empirical Macroeconomics* (Washington, D.C.: Brookings Institution, 1993), and John B. Taylor, *Macroeconomic Policy in a World Economy: From Econometric Design to Practical Operation* (New York: Norton, 1993).

[13]See James Tobin, "A General Equilibrium Approach to Monetary Theory," *Journal of Money, Credit, and Banking* 1 (1969): 15–29. A somewhat more Keynesian story with the same outcome is that the increase in the money supply lowers interest rates on bonds so that the yields on alternatives to stocks fall. This makes stocks more attractive relative to bonds, so demand for them increases, raises their price, and thereby lowers their yield.

[14]An alternative way of looking at the link between stock prices and investment spending is that higher stock prices lower the yield on stocks and reduce the cost of financing investment spending through issuing equity. This way of looking at the link between stock prices and investment spending is formally equivalent to Tobin's q approach; see Barry Bosworth, "The Stock Market and the Economy," *Brookings Papers on Economic Activity* 2 (1975): 257–290.

Wealth Effects In their search for new monetary transmission mechanisms, researchers also looked at how consumers' balance sheets might affect their spending decisions. Franco Modigliani was the first to take this tack, using his famous life cycle hypothesis of consumption. **Consumption** is spending by consumers on nondurable goods and services.[15] It differs from *consumer expenditure* in that it does not include spending on consumer durables. The basic premise of Modigliani's theory is that consumers smooth out their consumption over time. Therefore, what determines consumption spending is the lifetime resources of consumers, not just today's income.

An important component of consumers' lifetime resources is their financial wealth, a major component of which is common stocks. When stock prices rise, the value of financial wealth increases, thereby increasing the lifetime resources of consumers, and consumption should rise. Considering that, as we have seen, expansionary monetary policy can lead to a rise in stock prices, we now have another monetary transmission mechanism:

$$M\uparrow \Rightarrow P_e\uparrow \Rightarrow \text{wealth} \uparrow \Rightarrow \text{consumption} \uparrow \Rightarrow Y\uparrow \qquad (5)$$

Modigliani's research found this relationship to be an extremely powerful mechanism that adds substantially to the potency of monetary policy.[16]

The wealth and Tobin's q channels allow for a general definition of equity, so the Tobin q framework can also be applied to the housing market, where housing is equity. An increase in house prices, which raises their prices relative to replacement cost, leads to a rise in Tobin's q for housing, thereby stimulating its production. Similarly, housing and land prices are extremely important components of wealth, and so rises in these prices increase wealth, thereby raising consumption. Monetary expansion, which raises land and housing prices through the Tobin's q and wealth mechanisms described here, thus leads to a rise in aggregate demand.

Credit View

Dissatisfaction with the conventional stories that interest-rate effects explain the impact of monetary policy on expenditures on durable assets has led to a new explanation based on the problem of asymmetric information in financial markets (see Chapter 8). This explanation, referred to as the *credit view*, proposes that two types of monetary transmission channels arise as a result of information problems in credit markets: those that operate through effects on bank lending and those that operate through effects on firms' and households' balance sheets.[17]

Bank Lending Channel The bank lending channel is based on the analysis in Chapter 8, which demonstrated that banks play a special role in the financial system because they are especially well suited to solve asymmetric information problems in credit markets. Because of banks' special role, certain borrowers will not have access to the credit markets unless they borrow from banks. As long as there is no perfect substitutability of retail bank deposits with other sources of funds, the bank

---

[15]Consumption also includes another small component, the services that a consumer receives from the ownership of housing and consumer durables.

[16]See Franco Modigliani, "Monetary Policy and Consumption," in *Consumer Spending and Money Policy: The Linkages* (Boston: Federal Reserve Bank, 1971), pp. 9–84.

[17]Recent surveys of the credit view can be found in Ben Bernanke, "Credit in the Macroeconomy," Federal Reserve Bank of New York *Quarterly Review*, Spring 1993, pp. 50–70; Ben Bernanke and Mark Gertler, "Inside the Black Box: The Credit Channel of Monetary Policy Transmission," *Journal of Economic Perspectives* 9 (Fall 1995): 27–48; Stephen G. Cecchetti, "Distinguishing Theories of the Monetary Transmission Mechanism," Federal Reserve Bank of St. Louis *Review* 77 (May-June 1995): 83–97; and R. Glenn Hubbard, "Is There a 'Credit Channel' for Monetary Policy?" Federal Reserve Bank of St. Louis *Review* 77 (May-June 1995): 63–74.

lending channel of monetary transmission operates as follows. Expansionary monetary policy, which increases bank reserves and bank deposits, increases the quantity of bank loans available. Because many borrowers are dependent on bank loans to finance their activities, this increase in loans will cause investment (and possibly consumer) spending to rise. Schematically, the monetary policy effect is

$$M\uparrow \Rightarrow \text{bank deposits} \uparrow \Rightarrow \text{bank loans} \uparrow \Rightarrow I\uparrow \Rightarrow Y\uparrow \qquad (6)$$

An important implication of the credit view is that monetary policy will have a greater effect on expenditure by smaller firms, which are more dependent on bank loans, than it will on large firms, which can access the credit markets directly through stock and bond markets (and not only through banks).

Balance Sheet Channel   Like the bank lending channel, the balance sheet channel also arises from the presence of asymmetric information problems in credit markets. In Chapter 8, we saw that the lower the net worth of business firms, the more severe the adverse selection and moral hazard problems in lending to these firms. Lower net worth means that lenders in effect have less collateral for their loans, and so potential losses from adverse selection are higher. A decline in net worth, which raises the adverse selection problem, thus leads to decreased lending to finance investment spending. The lower net worth of businesses also increases the moral hazard problem because it means that owners have a lower equity stake in their firms, giving them more incentive to engage in risky investment projects. Since taking on riskier investment projects makes it more likely that lenders will not be paid back, a decrease in businesses' net worth leads to a decrease in lending and hence in investment spending.

Monetary policy can affect firms' balance sheets in several ways. Expansionary monetary policy ($M\uparrow$), which causes a rise in equity prices ($P_e\uparrow$) along lines described earlier, raises the net worth of firms and so leads to higher investment spending ($I\uparrow$) and aggregate demand ($Y\uparrow$) because of the decrease in adverse selection and moral hazard problems. This leads to the following schematic for one balance sheet channel of monetary transmission:

$$M\uparrow \Rightarrow P_e\uparrow \Rightarrow \text{adverse selection} \downarrow, \text{moral hazard} \downarrow \Rightarrow \text{lending} \uparrow \Rightarrow I\uparrow \Rightarrow Y\uparrow \quad (7)$$

Cash Flow Channel   Another balance sheet channel operates through its effects on *cash flow,* the difference between cash receipts and cash expenditures. Expansionary monetary policy, which lowers nominal interest rates, also causes an improvement in firms' balance sheets because it raises cash flow. The rise in cash flow causes an improvement in the balance sheet because it increases the liquidity of the firm (or household) and thus makes it easier for lenders to know whether the firm (or household) will be able to pay its bills. The result is that adverse selection and moral hazard problems become less severe, leading to an increase in lending and economic activity. The following schematic describes this additional balance sheet channel:

$$M\uparrow \Rightarrow i\downarrow \Rightarrow \text{cash flow} \uparrow \Rightarrow \text{adverse selection} \downarrow,$$
$$\text{moral hazard} \downarrow \Rightarrow \text{lending} \uparrow \Rightarrow I\uparrow \Rightarrow Y\uparrow \qquad (8)$$

An important feature of this transmission mechanism is that it is *nominal* interest rates that affect firms' cash flow. Thus this interest-rate mechanism differs from the traditional interest-rate mechanism discussed earlier in which it is the real rather than the nominal interest rate that affects investment. Furthermore, the short-term interest rate plays a special role in this transmission mechanism because it is interest payments on short-term rather than long-term debt that typically have the greatest impact on households' and firms' cash flow.

A related mechanism involving adverse selection through which expansionary monetary policy that lowers interest rates can stimulate aggregate output involves the credit-rationing phenomenon. As we discussed in Chapter 9, credit rationing occurs in cases where borrowers are denied loans even when they are willing to pay a higher interest rate. This is because individuals and firms with the riskiest investment projects are exactly the ones who are willing to pay the highest interest rates, for if the high-risk investment succeeds, they will be the primary beneficiaries. Thus higher interest rates increase the adverse selection problem, and lower interest rates reduce it. When expansionary monetary policy lowers interest rates, less risk-prone borrowers make up a higher fraction of those demanding loans, and so lenders are more willing to lend, raising both investment and output, along the lines of parts of the schematic in Equation 8.

Unanticipated Price Level Channel A third balance sheet channel operates through monetary policy effects on the general price level. Because in industrialized countries debt payments are contractually fixed in nominal terms, an unanticipated rise in the price level lowers the value of firms' liabilities in real terms (decreases the burden of the debt) but should not lower the real value of the firms' assets. Monetary expansion that leads to an unanticipated rise in the price level ($P\uparrow$) therefore raises real net worth, which lowers adverse selection and moral hazard problems, thereby leading to a rise in investment spending and aggregate output as in the following schematic:

$$M\uparrow \Rightarrow \text{unanticipated } P\uparrow \Rightarrow \text{adverse selection } \downarrow,$$
$$\text{moral hazard } \downarrow \Rightarrow \text{lending } \uparrow \Rightarrow I\uparrow \Rightarrow Y\uparrow \tag{9}$$

The view that unanticipated movements in the price level have important effects on aggregate demand has a long tradition in economics. It is the key feature in the debt-deflation view of the Great Depression we outlined in Chapter 8.

Household Liquidity Effects Although most of the literature on the credit channel focuses on spending by businesses, the credit view should apply equally well to consumer spending, particularly on consumer durables and housing. Declines in bank lending induced by a monetary contraction should cause a decline in durables and housing purchases by consumers who do not have access to other sources of credit. Similarly, increases in interest rates cause a deterioration in household balance sheets because consumers' cash flow is adversely affected.

Another way of looking at how the balance sheet channel may operate through consumers is to consider liquidity effects on consumer durable and housing expenditures—found to have been important factors during the Great Depression.[18] In the liquidity effects view, balance sheet effects work through their impact on consumers' desire to spend rather than on lenders' desire to lend. Because of asymmetric information about their quality, consumer durables and housing are very illiquid assets. If, as a result of a bad income shock, consumers needed to sell their consumer durables or housing to raise money, they would expect a big loss because they could not get the full value of these assets in a distress sale. (This is just a manifestation of the lemons problem described in Chapter 8.) In contrast, if consumers held financial assets (such as money in the bank, stocks, or bonds), they could easily sell them quickly for their full market value and raise the cash. Hence if consumers expect a higher likelihood of finding

---

[18]Frederic S. Mishkin, "The Household Balance Sheet and the Great Depression," *Journal of Economic History* 38 (1978): 918–937.

themselves in financial distress, they would rather be holding fewer illiquid consumer durable or housing assets and more liquid financial assets.

A consumer's balance sheet should be an important influence on his or her estimate of the likelihood of suffering financial distress. Specifically, when consumers have a large amount of financial assets relative to their debts, their estimate of the probability of financial distress is low, and they will be more willing to purchase consumer durables or housing. When stock prices rise, the value of financial assets rises as well; consumer durable expenditure will also rise because consumers have a more secure financial position and a lower estimate of the likelihood of suffering financial distress. This leads to another transmission mechanism for monetary policy, operating through the link between money and equity prices:[19]

$$M \uparrow \Rightarrow P_e \uparrow \Rightarrow \text{financial assets} \uparrow \Rightarrow \text{likelihood of financial distress} \downarrow$$

$$\Rightarrow \text{consumer durable and housing expenditure} \uparrow \Rightarrow Y \uparrow \qquad (10)$$

The illiquidity of consumer durable and housing assets provides another reason why a monetary expansion, which lowers interest rates and thereby raises cash flow to consumers, leads to a rise in spending on consumer durables and housing. A rise in consumer cash flow decreases the likelihood of financial distress, which increases the desire of consumers to hold durable goods or housing, thus increasing spending on them and hence aggregate output. The only difference between this view of cash flow effects and that outlined in Equation 8 is that it is not the willingness of lenders to lend to consumers that causes expenditure to rise but the willingness of consumers to spend.

Why Are Credit Channels Likely to Be Important?

There are three reasons to believe that credit channels are important monetary transmission mechanisms. First, a large body of evidence on the behaviour of individual firms supports the view that credit market imperfections of the type crucial to the operation of credit channels do affect firms' employment and spending decisions.[20] Second, there is evidence that small firms (which are more likely to be credit-constrained) are hurt more by tight monetary policy than large firms, which are unlikely to be credit-constrained.[21] Third, and maybe most compelling, the asymmetric information view of credit market imperfections at the core of the credit channel analysis is a theoretical construct that has proved useful in explaining many other important phenomena, such as why many of our financial institutions exist, why our financial system has the structure that it has, and why financial crises are so damaging to the economy (all topics discussed in Chapter 8). The best support for a theory is its demonstrated usefulness in a wide range of applications. By this standard, the asymmetric information theory supporting the existence of credit channels as an important monetary transmission mechanism has much to recommend it.

APPLICATION   *National Monetary Policy and Differential Regional Effects*

Our analysis thus far has assumed a uniform national monetary effect. In reality, however, there are quite pronounced regional disparities across a geographically

---

[19]See Frederic S. Mishkin, "What Depressed the Consumer? The Household Balance Sheet and the 1973–1975 Recession," *Brookings Papers on Economic Activity* 1 (1977): 123–164.

[20]For a survey of this evidence, see Hubbard, "Is There a 'Credit Channel'?" (note 17).

[21]See Mark Gertler and Simon Gilchrist, "Monetary Policy, Business Cycles, and the Behaviour of Small Manufacturing Firms," *Quarterly Journal of Economics* 109 (May 1994): 309–340.

large and diversified country like Canada, meaning that monetary policy actions may have differential effects on regional economic activity. In fact, as Gerald Carlino and Robert DeFina (1998) argue, regional differences in the mix of interest-sensitive industries and in the proportion of large and small borrowers underscores the complexity of conducting a national monetary policy.[22]

There is, at present, little evidence on the issue of whether Canadian monetary policy has differential effects on regional economic activity. Empirical evidence on this issue may aid policymakers in their consideration of regional economic conditions in the formulation of national monetary policy.

LESSONS FOR MONETARY POLICY

What useful implications for central banks' conduct of monetary policy can we draw from the analysis in this chapter? There are four basic lessons to be drawn.

1. ***It is dangerous always to associate the easing or tightening of monetary policy with a fall or a rise in short-term nominal interest rates.***
   Because most central banks use short-term nominal interest rates, typically the interbank rate, as the key operating instrument for monetary policy, there is a danger that central banks and the public will focus too much on short-term nominal interest rates as an indicator of the stance of monetary policy. Indeed, it is quite common to see statements that always associate monetary tightenings with a rise in the interbank rate and monetary easings with a decline in the rate. This view is highly problematic because movements in nominal interest rates do not always correspond to movements in real interest rates, and yet it is typically the real and not the nominal interest rate that is an element in the channel of monetary policy transmission. For example, we have seen that during the contraction phase of the Great Depression in the United States, short-term interest rates fell to near zero and yet real interest rates were extremely high. Short-term interest rates that are near zero therefore do not indicate that monetary policy is easy if the economy is undergoing deflation, as was true during the contraction phase of the Great Depression. As Milton Friedman and Anna Schwartz have emphasized, the period of near-zero short-term interest rates during the contraction phase of the Great Depression was one of highly contractionary monetary policy rather than the reverse.

2. ***Other asset prices besides those of short-term debt instruments contain important information about the stance of monetary policy because they are important elements in various monetary policy transmission mechanisms.*** As we have seen in this chapter, economists have come a long way in understanding that other asset prices besides interest rates have major effects on aggregate demand. The view in Figure 25-3 that other asset prices, such as stock prices, foreign exchange rates, and housing and land prices, play an important role in monetary transmission mechanisms is held by both monetarists and Keynesians. Furthermore, the discussion of such additional channels as those operating through the exchange rate, Tobin's *q*, and wealth effects provides additional reasons why other asset prices play such an important role in the monetary transmission mechanisms. Although there are strong disagreements among economists

---

[22]Gerald Carlino and Robert DeFina, "The Differential Regional Effects of Monetary Policy," *The Review of Economics and Statistics* 80 (November 1998): 572-587.

about which channels of monetary transmission are the most important—not surprising, given that economists, particularly those in academia, always like to disagree—they do agree that other asset prices play an important role in the way monetary policy affects the economy.

The view that other asset prices besides short-term interest rates matter has important implications for monetary policy. When we try to assess the stance of policy, it is critical that we look at other asset prices besides short-term interest rates. For example, if short-term interest rates are low or even zero and yet stock prices are low, land prices are low, and the value of the domestic currency is high, monetary policy is clearly tight, *not* easy.

3. ***Monetary policy can be highly effective in reviving a weak economy even if short-term interest rates are already near zero.*** We have recently entered a world where inflation is not always the norm. Japan, for example, recently experienced a period of deflation, when the price level was actually falling. One common view is that when a central bank has driven down short-term nominal interest rates to near zero, there is nothing more that monetary policy can do to stimulate the economy. The transmission mechanisms of monetary policy described here indicate that this view is false. As our discussion of the factors that affect the monetary base in Chapter 15 indicated, expansionary monetary policy to increase liquidity in the economy can be conducted with open market purchases, which do not have to be solely in short-term government securities. For example, purchases of foreign currencies, like purchases of government bonds, lead to an increase in the monetary base and in the money supply. This increased liquidity helps revive the economy by raising general price-level expectations and by reflating other asset prices, which then stimulate aggregate demand through the channels outlined here. Therefore, monetary policy can be a potent force for reviving economies that are undergoing deflation and have short-term interest rates near zero. Indeed, because of the lags inherent in fiscal policy and the political constraints on its use, expansionary monetary policy is the key policy action required to revive an economy experiencing deflation.

4. ***Avoiding unanticipated fluctuations in the price level is an important objective of monetary policy, thus providing a rationale for price stability as the primary long-run goal for monetary policy.*** As we saw in Chapter 18, central banks in recent years have been putting greater emphasis on price stability as the primary long-run goal for monetary policy. Several rationales have been proposed for this goal, including the undesirable effects of uncertainty about the future price level on business decisions and hence on productivity, distortions associated with the interaction of nominal contracts and the tax system with inflation, and increased social conflict stemming from inflation. The discussion here of monetary transmission mechanisms provides an additional reason why price stability is so important. As we have seen, unanticipated movements in the price level can cause unanticipated fluctuations in output, an undesirable outcome. Particularly important in this regard is that, as we saw in Chapter 8, price deflations can be an important factor leading to a prolonged financial crisis, as occurred during the Great Depression. An understanding of the monetary transmission mechanisms thus makes it clear that the goal of price stability is desirable because it reduces uncertainty about the future price level. Thus the price stability goal implies that a negative inflation rate is at least as undesirable as too high an inflation rate. Indeed, because of the threat of financial crises, central banks must work very hard to prevent price deflations.

SUMMARY

1. There are two basic types of empirical evidence: reduced-form evidence and structural model evidence. Both have advantages and disadvantages. The main advantage of structural model evidence is that it provides us with an understanding of how the economy works and gives us more confidence in the direction of causation between money and output. However, if the structure is not correctly specified because it ignores important monetary transmission mechanisms, it could seriously underestimate the effectiveness of monetary policy. Reduced-form evidence has the advantage of not restricting the way monetary policy affects economic activity and so may be more likely to capture the full effects of monetary policy. However, reduced-form evidence cannot rule out the possibility of reverse causation or an outside driving factor, which could lead to misleading conclusions about the importance of money.

2. The early Keynesians believed that money does not matter because they found weak links between interest rates and investment and because low interest rates on government securities convinced them that monetary policy was easy during the worst economic contraction in history, the Great Depression. Monetarists objected to this interpretation of the evidence on the grounds that (a) the focus on nominal rather than real interest rates may have obscured any link between interest rates and investment, (b) interest-rate effects on investment might be only one of many channels through which monetary policy affects aggregate demand, and (c) by the standards of real interest rates, monetary policy was extremely contractionary during the Great Depression.

3. Early monetarist evidence falls into three categories: timing, statistical, and historical. Because of reverse causation and outside-factor possibilities,

some serious doubts exist regarding conclusions that can be drawn from timing and statistical evidence alone. However, some of the historical evidence in which exogenous declines in money growth are followed by recessions provides stronger support for the monetarist position that money matters. As a result of empirical research, Keynesian and monetarist opinion has converged to the view that money does matter to aggregate economic activity and the price level. However, Keynesians do not agree with the monetarist position that money is *all* that matters.

4. The transmission mechanisms of monetary policy include traditional interest-rate channels that operate through the cost of capital and affect investment; other asset price channels such as exchange rate effects, Tobin's q theory, and wealth effects; and the credit view channels—the bank lending channel, the balance sheet channel, the cash flow channel, the unanticipated price level channel, and household liquidity effects.

5. Four lessons for monetary policy can be drawn from this chapter: (a) It is dangerous always to associate monetary policy easing or tightening with a fall or a rise in short-term nominal interest rates; (b) other asset prices besides those on short-term debt instruments contain important information about the stance of monetary policy because they are important elements in the monetary policy transmission mechanisms; (c) monetary policy can be highly effective in reviving a weak economy even if short-term interest rates are already near zero; and (d) avoiding unanticipated fluctuations in the price level is an important objective of monetary policy, thus providing a rationale for price stability as the primary long-run goal for monetary policy.

KEY TERMS

consumer durable expenditure, p. 574

consumption, p. 578

credit view, p. 575

reduced-form evidence, p. 562

reverse causation, p. 564

structural model, p. 562

structural model evidence, p. 562

transmission mechanisms of monetary policy, p. 562

QUESTIONS AND PROBLEMS

Questions marked with an asterisk are answered at the end of the book in an appendix, "Answers to Selected Questions and Problems."

1. Suppose that a researcher is trying to determine whether jogging is good for a person's health. She examines this question in two ways. In method A, she looks to see whether joggers live longer than nonjoggers. In method B, she looks to see whether jogging reduces cholesterol in the bloodstream and lowers blood pressure; then she asks whether lower cholesterol and blood pressure prolong life. Which of these two methods will produce reduced-form evidence and which will produce structural model evidence?

2. If research indicates that joggers do not have lower cholesterol and blood pressure than nonjoggers, is it still possible that jogging is good for your health? Give a concrete example.

3. If research indicates that joggers live longer than nonjoggers, is it possible that jogging is not good for your health? Give a concrete example.

*4. Suppose that you plan to buy a car and want to know whether a General Motors car is more reliable than a Ford. One way to find out is to ask owners of both cars how often their cars go into the shop for repairs. Another way is to visit the factory producing the cars and see which one is built better. Which procedure will provide reduced-form evidence and which structural model evidence?

*5. If the GM car you plan to buy has a better repair record than a Ford, does this mean that the GM car is necessarily more reliable? (GM car owners might, for example, change their oil more frequently than Ford owners.)

*6. Suppose that when you visit the Ford and GM car factories to examine how the cars are built, you only have time to see how well the engine is put together. If Ford engines are better built than GM engines, does that mean that the Ford will be more reliable than the GM car?

7. How might bank behaviour (described in Chapter 16) lead to causation running from output to the money supply? What does this say about evidence that finds a strong correlation between money and output?

*8. What operating procedures of the Bank of Canada (described in Chapter 18) might explain how movements in output might cause movements in the money supply?

9. "In every business cycle in the past 100 years, the rate at which the money supply is growing always decreases before output does. Therefore, the money supply causes business cycle movements." Do you agree? What objections can you raise against this argument?

*10. How did the research strategies of Keynesian and monetarist economists differ after they were exposed to the earliest monetarist evidence?

11. In the 1973–1975 recession, the value of common stocks in real terms fell by nearly 50%. How might this decline in the stock market have affected aggregate demand and thus contributed to the severity of this recession? Be specific about the mechanisms through which the stock market decline affected the economy.

*12. "The cost of financing investment is related only to interest rates; therefore, the only way that monetary policy can affect investment spending is through its effects on interest rates." Is this statement true, false, or uncertain? Explain your answer.

13. Predict what will happen to stock prices if the money supply rises. Explain why you are making this prediction.

*14. Franco Modigliani found that the most important transmission mechanisms of monetary policy involve consumer expenditure. Describe how at least two of these mechanisms work.

15. "The monetarists have demonstrated that the early Keynesians were wrong in saying that money doesn't matter at all to economic activity. Therefore, we should accept the monetarist position that money is all that matters." Do you agree? Why or why not?

Chapter 26

Money and Inflation

Since the early 1960s, when the inflation rate hovered between 1 and 2%, the economy has suffered from higher and more variable rates of inflation. By the late 1960s, the inflation rate had climbed beyond 4%, and by 1974, it reached the double-digit level. After moderating somewhat during the 1975–1978 period, it shot above 10% in 1980 and 1981, slowed to around 3% from 1982 to 1990, and declined further to around 2% in the late 1990s. Inflation, the condition of a continually rising price level, has become a major concern of politicians and the public, and how to control it frequently dominates the discussion of economic policy.

How do we prevent the inflationary fire from igniting and end the roller-coaster ride in the inflation rate of the past 30 years? Milton Friedman provides an answer in his famous proposition that "inflation is always and everywhere a monetary phenomenon." He postulates that the source of all inflation episodes is a high growth rate of the money supply: simply by reducing the growth rate of the money supply to low levels, inflation can be prevented.

In this chapter we use aggregate demand and supply analysis from Chapter 24 to reveal the role of monetary policy in creating inflation. You will find that as long as inflation is defined as the condition of a continually and rapidly rising price level, monetarists and Keynesians both agree with Friedman's proposition that inflation is a monetary phenomenon.

But what *causes* inflation? How does inflationary monetary policy come about? You will see that inflationary monetary policy is an offshoot of other government policies: the attempt to hit high employment targets or the running of large budget deficits. Examining how these policies lead to inflation will point us toward ways of preventing it at minimum cost in terms of unemployment and output loss.

MONEY AND INFLATION: EVIDENCE

The evidence for Friedman's statement is straightforward. **Whenever a country's inflation rate is extremely high for a sustained period of time, its rate of money supply growth is also extremely high.**

Consider the inflation experienced in Latin America from 1989 to 1999. A popular belief is that something structural in the Latin American economies (say, militant labour unions or unstable political systems) causes high inflation. In reality, the experience of inflation in Latin America is varied; some Latin American countries, such as Chile, had average annual inflation rates below 20% during this period, while others, such as Argentina, Brazil, and Peru, suffered from inflation rates exceeding 100%.

The graph in Box 26-1, which plots the inflation rates for Latin American countries against the growth rates of their money supply, reveals that the countries with very high inflation also have the highest rates of money growth. Evidence for the Latin American countries, as well as countries elsewhere in the world (see Figure 1-6), seems to support the proposition that extremely high inflation is the result of a high rate of money growth. Keep in mind, however, that you are looking at reduced-form evidence, which focuses solely on the correlation of two variables: money growth and the inflation rate. As with all reduced-form evidence, reverse causation (inflation causing money supply growth) or an outside factor that drives both money growth and inflation could be involved.

How might you rule out these possibilities? First, you might look for historical episodes in which an increase in money growth appears to be an exogenous event; a high inflation rate for a sustained period following the increase in money growth would provide strong evidence that high money growth is the driving force behind the inflation. Luckily for our analysis, such clear-cut episodes—hyperinflations (extremely rapid inflations with inflation rates exceeding 50% per month)—have occurred, the most notorious being the German hyperinflation of 1921–1923.

German Hyperinflation, 1921–1923

In 1921, the need to make reparations and reconstruct the economy after World War I caused the German government's expenditures to greatly exceed revenues. The government could have obtained revenues to cover these increased expenditures by raising taxes, but that solution was, as always, politically unpopular and would have taken much time to implement. The government could also have financed the expenditure by borrowing from the public, but the amount needed was far in excess of its capacity to borrow. There was only one route left: the printing press. The government could pay for its expenditures simply by printing more currency (increasing the money supply) and using it to make payments to the individuals and companies that were providing it with goods and services. As shown in Figure 26-1, this is exactly what the German government did; in late 1921, the money supply began to increase rapidly, and so did the price level.

In 1923, the budgetary situation of the German government deteriorated even further. Early that year, the French invaded the Ruhr because Germany had failed to make its scheduled reparations payments. A general strike in the region then ensued to protest the French action, and the German government actively supported this "passive resistance" by making payments to striking workers. As a result, government expenditures climbed dramatically, and the government printed currency at an even faster rate to finance this spending. As displayed in Figure 26-1, the result of the explosion in the money supply was that the price level blasted off, leading to an inflation rate for 1923 that exceeded 1 million percent!

The invasion of the Ruhr and the printing of currency to pay striking workers fit the characteristics of an exogenous event. Reverse causation (that the rise in the price level caused the French to invade the Ruhr) is highly implausible, and it is hard to imagine a third factor that could have been a driving force behind both inflation and the explosion in the money supply. Therefore, the German hyperinflation qualifies as a "controlled experiment" that supports Friedman's proposition that inflation is a monetary phenomenon.

Inflation and Money Growth Rates in Latin America, 1989–1999

This graph plots for a group of Latin American countries the average inflation rate over the period 1989–1999 against the average money growth rate over the same period. It demonstrates that high inflation in these countries is generally associated with a high rate of money growth. (Countries such as Brazil and Nicaragua do not appear in the graph because their data were unavailable for the 1989–1999 period.)

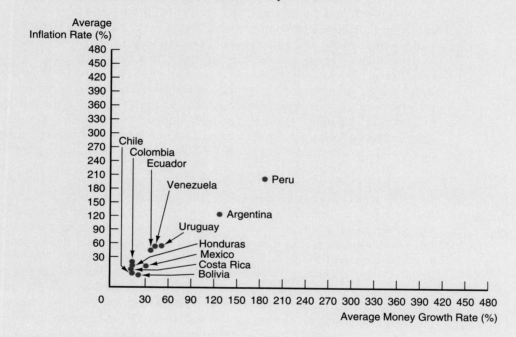

Source: *International Financial Statistics.*

Recent Episodes of Rapid Inflation

Although recent rapid inflations have not been as dramatic as the German hyperinflation, many countries in the 1980s and 1990s experienced rapid inflations in which the high rates of money growth can also be classified as exogenous events. For example, of all Latin American countries in the decade from 1989 to 1999, Argentina, Brazil, and Peru had both the highest rates of money growth and the highest average inflation rates. However, in the last couple of years, inflation in these countries has been brought down considerably.

The explanation for the high rates of money growth in these countries is similar to the explanation for Germany during its hyperinflation. The unwillingness of Argentina, Brazil, and Peru to finance government expenditures by raising taxes led to large budget deficits (sometimes over 15% of GDP), which were financed by money creation.

That the inflation rate is high in all cases in which the high rate of money growth can be classified as an exogenous event (including episodes in Argentina, Brazil, Peru, and Germany) is strong evidence that high money growth causes high inflation.

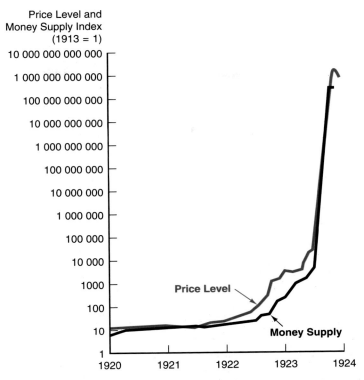

FIGURE 26-1 Money Supply and Price Level in the German Hyperinflation
Source: Frank D. Graham, *Exchange, Prices and Production in Hyperinflation: Germany, 1920–25* (Princeton, N.J.: Princeton University Press, 1930), pp. 105–106.

MEANING OF INFLATION

You may have noticed that all the empirical evidence on the relationship of money growth and inflation discussed so far looks only at cases in which the price level is continually rising at a rapid rate. It is this definition of inflation that Friedman and other economists use when they make statements such as "Inflation is always and everywhere a monetary phenomenon." This is not what your friendly newscaster means when reporting the monthly inflation rate on the nightly news. The newscaster is only telling you how much, in percentage terms, the price level has changed from the previous month. For example, when you hear that the monthly inflation rate is 1% (12% annual rate), this merely indicates that the price level has risen by 1% in that month. This could be a one-shot change, in which the high inflation rate is merely temporary, not sustained. Only if the inflation rate remains high for a substantial period of time (greater than 1% per month for several years) will economists say that inflation has been high.

Accordingly, Milton Friedman's proposition actually says that upward movements in the price level are a monetary phenomenon *only* if this is a sustained process. When *inflation* is defined as a continuing and rapid rise in the price level, most economists, whether monetarist or Keynesian, will agree with Friedman's proposition that money alone is to blame.

VIEWS OF INFLATION

Now that we understand what Friedman's proposition means, we can use the aggregate supply and demand analysis learned in Chapter 24 to show that large and persistent upward movements in the price level (high inflation) can occur only if there is a continually increasing money supply.

Monetarist View First, let's look at the outcome of a continually increasing money supply using monetarist analysis (Figure 26-2). Initially, the economy is at point 1, with output at the natural rate level and the price level at P_1 (the intersection of the aggregate demand curve AD_1 and the aggregate supply curve AS_1). If the money supply increases steadily over the course of the year, the aggregate demand curve shifts rightward to AD_2. At first, for a very brief time, the economy may move to point $1'$ and output may increase above the natural rate level to Y', but the resulting decline in unemployment below the natural rate level will cause wages to rise, and the aggregate supply curve will quickly begin to shift leftward. It will stop shifting only when it reaches AS_2, at which time the economy has returned to the natural rate level of output on the long-run aggregate supply curve.[1] At the new equilibrium, point 2, the price level has increased from P_1 to P_2.

If the money supply increases the next year, the aggregate demand curve will shift to the right again to AD_3, and the aggregate supply curve will shift from AS_2 to AS_3; the economy will then move to point $2'$ and then 3, where the price level has risen to P_3. If the money supply continues to grow in subsequent years, the economy will continue to move to higher and higher price levels. As long as the money supply grows, this process will continue, and inflation will occur.

Do monetarists believe that a continually rising price level can be due to any source other than money supply growth? The answer is no. In monetarist analysis, the money supply is viewed as the sole source of shifts in the aggregate demand curve, so there is nothing else that can move the economy from point 1 to 2 to 3 and beyond. ***Monetarist analysis indicates that rapid inflation must be driven by high money supply growth.***

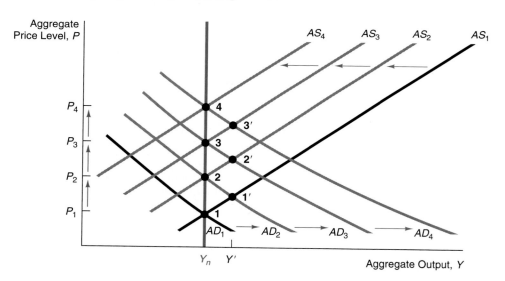

FIGURE 26-2 Response to a Continually Rising Money Supply

A continually rising money supply shifts the aggregate demand curve to the right from AD_1 to AD_2 to AD_3 to AD_4, while the supply curve shifts to the left from AS_1 to AS_2 to AS_3 to AS_4. The result is that the price level rises continually from P_1 to P_2 to P_3 to P_4.

---

[1]In monetarist analysis, the aggregate supply curve may immediately shift leftward toward AS_2 because workers and firms may expect the increase in the money supply, so expected inflation will be higher. In this case, the movement to point 2 will be very rapid, and output need not rise above the natural rate level. (Further support for this scenario, from the theory of rational expectations, is discussed in Chapter 28.)

Keynesian View   Keynesian analysis indicates that the continually increasing money supply will have the same effect on the aggregate demand and supply curves that we see in Figure 26-2. The aggregate demand curve will keep on shifting to the right, and the aggregate supply curve will keep shifting to the left.[2] The conclusion is the same one that the monetarists reach: a rapidly growing money supply will cause the price level to rise continually at a high rate, thus generating inflation.

Could a factor other than money generate high inflation in the Keynesian analysis? The answer is no. This result probably surprises you, for in Chapter 24 you learned that Keynesian analysis allows other factors besides changes in the money supply (such as fiscal policy and supply shocks) to affect the aggregate demand and supply curves. To see why Keynesians also view high inflation as a monetary phenomenon, let's examine whether their analysis allows other factors to generate high inflation in the absence of a high rate of money growth.

Can Fiscal Policy By Itself Produce Inflation?   To examine this question, let's look at Figure 26-3, which demonstrates the effect of a one-shot permanent increase in government expenditure (say, from \$500 billion to \$600 billion) on aggregate output and the price level. Initially, we are at point 1, where output is at the natural rate level and the price level is P_1. The increase in government expenditure shifts the aggregate demand curve to AD_2, and we move to point 1′, where output is above the natural rate level at $Y_{1'}$. The aggregate supply curve will begin to shift leftward, eventually reaching AS_2, where it intersects the aggregate demand curve AD_2 at point 2, at which output is again at the natural rate level and the price level has risen to P_2.

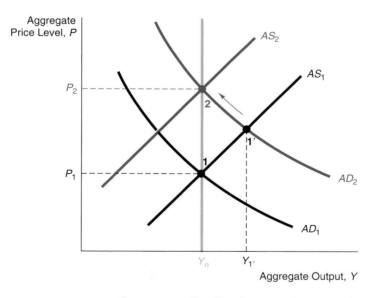

FIGURE 26-3   Response to a One-Shot Permanent Increase in Government Expenditure

A one-shot permanent increase in government expenditure shifts the aggregate demand curve rightward from AD_1 to AD_2, moving the economy from point 1 to point 1′. Because output now exceeds the natural rate level Y_n, the aggregate supply curve eventually shifts leftward to AS_2, and the price level rises from P_1 to P_2, a one-shot permanent increase but not a continuing increase.

---

[2]The only difference in the two analyses is that Keynesians believe that the aggregate supply curve would shift leftward more slowly than monetarists do. Thus Keynesian analysis suggests that output might tend to stay above the natural rate longer than monetarist analysis does.

The net result of a one-shot permanent increase in government expenditure is a one-shot permanent increase in the price level. What happens to the inflation rate? When we move from point 1 to 1′ to 2, the price level rises, and we have a positive inflation rate. But when we finally get to point 2, the inflation rate returns to zero. We see that the one-shot increase in government expenditure leads to only a *temporary* increase in the inflation rate, not to an inflation in which the price level is continually rising.

If, however, government spending increased continually, we *could* get a continuing rise in the price level. It appears, then, that Keynesian analysis could reject Friedman's proposition that inflation is always the result of money growth. The problem with this argument is that a continually increasing level of government expenditure is not a feasible policy. There is a limit on the total amount of possible government expenditure; the government cannot spend more than 100% of GDP. In fact, well before this limit is reached, the political process would stop the increases in government spending. As revealed in the continual debates over balanced budgets and government spending, both the public and politicians have a particular target level of government spending they deem appropriate; although small deviations from this level might be tolerated, large deviations would not. Indeed, public and political perceptions impose tight limits on the degree to which government expenditures can increase.

What about the other side of fiscal policy, taxes? Could continual tax cuts generate an inflation? Again the answer is no. The analysis in Figure 26-3 also describes the price and output response to a one-shot decrease in taxes. There will be a one-shot increase in the price level, but the increase in the inflation rate will be only temporary. We can increase the price level by cutting taxes even more, but this process would have to stop—once taxes reach zero, they can't be reduced further. We must conclude, then, that **Keynesian analysis indicates that high inflation cannot be driven by fiscal policy alone**.[3]

Can Supply-Side Phenomena by Themselves Produce Inflation?

Because supply shocks and workers' attempts to increase their wages can shift the aggregate supply curve leftward, you might suspect that these supply-side phenomena by themselves could stimulate inflation. Again, we can show that this suspicion is incorrect.

Suppose that there is a negative supply shock—for example, an oil embargo—that raises oil prices (or workers could have successfully pushed up their wages). As displayed in Figure 26-4, the negative supply shock shifts the aggregate supply curve from AS_1 to AS_2. If the money supply remains unchanged, leaving the aggregate demand curve at AD_1, we move to point 1′, where output $Y_{1'}$ is below the natural rate level and the price level $P_{1'}$ is higher. The aggregate supply curve will now shift back to AS_1 because unemployment is above the natural rate, and the economy slides down AD_1 from point 1′ to point 1. The net result of the supply shock is that we return to full employment at the initial price level, and there is no continuing inflation. Additional negative supply shocks that again shift the aggregate supply curve leftward will lead to the same outcome. The price level

---

[3]The argument here demonstrates that "animal spirits" also cannot be the source of inflation. Although consumer and business optimism, which stimulates their spending, can produce a one-shot shift in the aggregate demand curve and a temporary inflation, it cannot produce continuing shifts in the aggregate demand curve and inflation in which the price level rises continually. The reasoning is the same as before: consumers and businesses cannot continue to raise their spending without limit because their spending cannot exceed 100% of GDP.

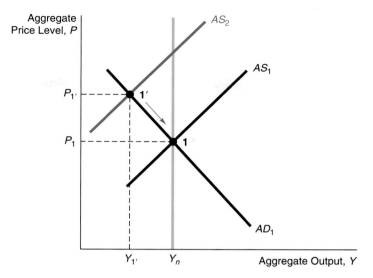

FIGURE 26-4   Response to a Supply Shock
A negative supply shock (or a wage push) shifts the aggregate supply curve leftward to
AS_2 and results in high unemployment at point 1'. As a result, the aggregate supply curve
shifts back to the right to AS_1, and the economy returns to point 1, where the price level
has returned to P_1.

will rise temporarily, but inflation will not result. The conclusion that we have
reached is the following: ***supply-side phenomena cannot be the source of
high inflation***.[4]

Summary

Our aggregate demand and supply analysis shows that Keynesian and monetarist
views of the inflation process are not very different. Both believe that high inflation can occur only with a high rate of money growth. Recognizing that by inflation we mean a continuing increase in the price level at a rapid rate, most
economists agree with Milton Friedman that "inflation is always and everywhere a
monetary phenomenon."

ORIGINS OF INFLATIONARY MONETARY POLICY

Although we now know *what* must occur to generate a rapid inflation—a high rate
of money growth—we still can't understand *why* high inflation occurs until we
have learned how and why inflationary monetary policies come about. If everyone agrees that inflation is not a good thing for an economy, why do we see so
much of it? Why do governments pursue inflationary monetary policies? Since
there is nothing intrinsically desirable about inflation and since we know that a
high rate of money growth doesn't happen of its own accord, it must follow that
in trying to achieve other goals, governments end up with a high money growth
rate and high inflation. In this section we will examine the government policies
that are the most common sources of inflation.

---

[4]Supply-side phenomena that alter the natural rate level of output (and shift the long-run aggregate
supply curve at Y_n) can produce a permanent one-shot change in the price level. However, this resulting one-shot change results in only a temporary inflation, not a continuing rise in the price level.

High Employment Targets and Inflation

The first goal most governments pursue that often results in inflation is high employment. Two types of inflation can result from an activist stabilization policy to promote high employment: **cost-push inflation**, which occurs because of negative supply shocks or a push by workers to get higher wages, and **demand-pull inflation**, which results when policymakers pursue policies that shift the aggregate demand curve to the right. We will now use aggregate demand and supply analysis to examine how a high employment target can lead to both types of inflation.

Cost-Push Inflation In Figure 26-5, the economy is initially at point 1, the intersection of the aggregate demand curve AD_1 and the aggregate supply curve AS_1. Suppose that workers decide to seek higher wages either because they want to increase their real wages (wages in terms of the goods and services they can buy) or because they expect inflation to be high and wish to keep up with inflation. The effect of such an increase (similar to a negative supply shock) is to shift the aggregate supply curve leftward to AS_2.[5] If government fiscal and monetary policy remains unchanged, the economy would move to point 1′ at the intersection of the new aggregate supply curve AS_2 and the aggregate demand curve AD_1. Output would decline to below its natural rate level Y_n, and the price level would rise to $P_{1'}$.

What would activist policymakers with a high employment target do if this situation developed? Because of the drop in output and resulting increase in unemployment, they would implement policies to raise the aggregate demand curve to AD_2 so that we would return to the natural rate level of output at point 2 and price level P_2. The workers who have increased their wages have not fared too badly. The government has stepped in to make sure that there is no excessive unemployment, and they have achieved their goal of higher wages. Because the government has, in effect, given in to the demands of workers for higher wages, an activist policy with a high employment target is often referred to as an **accommodating policy**.

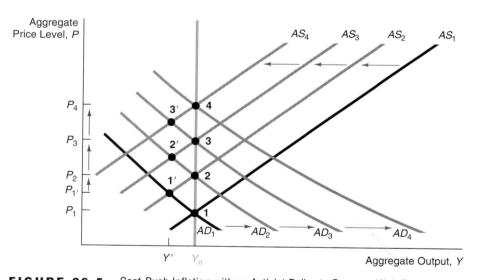

FIGURE 26-5 Cost-Push Inflation with an Activist Policy to Promote High Employment

In a cost-push inflation, the leftward shifts of the aggregate supply curve from AS_1 to AS_2 to AS_3 and so on cause a government with a high employment target to shift the aggregate demand curve to the right continually to keep unemployment and output at their natural rate levels. The result is a continuing rise in the price level from P_1 to P_2 to P_3 and so on.

---

[5]The cost-push inflation we describe here might also occur as a result of either firms' attempts to obtain higher prices or negative supply shocks.

The workers, having eaten their cake and had it too, might be encouraged to seek even higher wages. In addition, other workers might now realize that their wages have fallen relative to their fellow workers', and because they don't want to be left behind, these workers will seek to increase their wages. The result is that the aggregate supply curve shifts leftward again, to AS_3. Unemployment develops again when we move to point 2′, and the activist policies will once more be used to shift the aggregate demand curve rightward to AD_3 and return the economy to full employment at a price level of P_3. If this process continues, the result will be a continuing increase in the price level—a cost-push inflation.

What role does monetary policy play in a cost-push inflation? A cost-push inflation can occur only if the aggregate demand curve is shifted continually to the right. In Keynesian analysis, the first shift of the aggregate demand curve to AD_2 could be achieved by a one-shot increase in government expenditure or a one-shot decrease in taxes. But what about the next required rightward shift of the aggregate demand curve to AD_3, and the next, and the next? The limits on the maximum level of government expenditure and the minimum level of taxes would prevent the use of this expansionary fiscal policy for very long. Hence it cannot be used continually to shift the aggregate demand curve to the right. But the aggregate demand curve *can* be shifted continually rightward by continually increasing the money supply, that is, by going to a higher rate of money growth. Therefore, ***a cost-push inflation is a monetary phenomenon because it cannot occur without the monetary authorities pursuing an accommodating policy of a higher rate of money growth***.

Demand-Pull Inflation The goal of high employment can lead to inflationary monetary policy in another way. Even at full employment, unemployment is always present because of frictions in the labour market, which make it difficult to match workers with employers. An unemployed autoworker in Windsor may not know about a job opening in the oil industry in Calgary or, even if he or she did, may not want to move or be retrained. So the unemployment rate when there is full employment (the natural rate of unemployment) will be greater than zero. If policymakers set a target for unemployment that is too low because it is less than the natural rate of unemployment, this can set the stage for a higher rate of money growth and a resulting inflation. Again we can show how this can happen using an aggregate supply and demand diagram (Figure 26-6).

If policymakers have an unemployment target (say 4%) that is below the natural rate (estimated to be 7% currently), they will try to achieve an output target greater than the natural rate level of output. This target level of output is marked Y_T in Figure 26-6. Suppose that we are initially at point 1; the economy is at the natural rate level of output but below the target level of output Y_T. To hit the unemployment target of 4%, policymakers enact policies to increase aggregate demand, and the effects of these policies shift the aggregate demand curve until it reaches AD_2 and the economy moves to point 1′. Output is at Y_T, and the 4% unemployment rate goal has been reached.

If the targeted unemployment rate were at the natural rate level, there would be no problem. However, because at Y_T the 4% unemployment rate is below the natural rate level, wages will rise and the aggregate supply curve will shift leftward to AS_2, moving the economy from point 1′ to point 2. The economy is back at the natural rate of unemployment but at a higher price level of P_2. We could stop there, but because unemployment is again higher than the target level, policymakers would again shift the aggregate demand curve rightward to AD_3 to hit the output target at point 2′, and the whole process would continue to drive the economy to point 3 and beyond. The overall result is a steadily rising price level—an inflation.

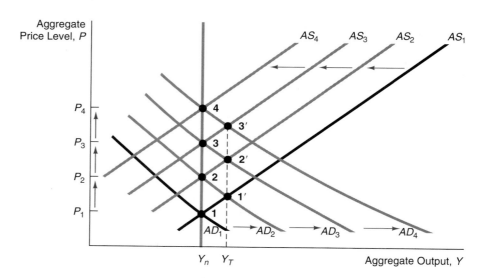

FIGURE 26-6 Demand-Pull Inflation: The Consequence of Setting Too Low an Unemployment Target

Too low an unemployment target (too high an output target of Y_T) causes the government to shift the aggregate demand curve rightward from AD_1 to AD_2 to AD_3 and so on, while the aggregate supply curve shifts leftward from AS_1 to AS_2 to AS_3 and so on. The result is a continuing rise in the price level known as a demand-pull inflation.

How can policymakers continually shift the aggregate demand curve rightward? We have already seen that they cannot do it through fiscal policy because of the limits on raising government expenditures and reducing taxes. Instead they will have to resort to expansionary monetary policy: a continuing increase in the money supply and hence a high money growth rate.

Pursuing too high an output target or, equivalently, too low an unemployment rate is the source of inflationary monetary policy in this situation, but it seems senseless for policymakers to do this. They have not gained the benefit of a permanently higher level of output but have generated the burden of an inflation. If, however, they do not realize that the target rate of unemployment is below the natural rate, the process that we see in Figure 26-6 will be well under way before they realize their mistake.

Because the inflation described results from policymakers pursuing policies that shift the aggregate demand curve to the right, it is called a *demand-pull inflation*. In contrast, a *cost-push inflation* occurs when workers push their wages up. Is it easy to distinguish between them in practice? The answer is no. We have seen that both types of inflation will be associated with higher money growth, so we cannot distinguish them on this basis. Yet as Figures 26-5 and 26-6 demonstrate, demand-pull inflation will be associated with periods when unemployment is below the natural rate level, whereas cost-push inflation is associated with periods when unemployment is above the natural rate level. To decide which type of inflation has occurred, we can look at whether unemployment has been above or below its natural rate level. This would be easy if economists and policymakers actually knew how to measure the natural rate of unemployment; unfortunately, this very difficult research question is still not fully resolved by the economics profession. In addition, the distinction between cost-push and demand-pull inflation is blurred because a cost-push inflation can be initiated by a demand-pull inflation. When a demand-pull inflation produces higher inflation rates, expected inflation will eventually rise and cause workers to demand higher wages so that their real wages do not fall. In this way, demand-pull inflation can eventually trigger cost-push inflation.

Budget Deficits and Inflation

Our discussion of the evidence on money and inflation suggested that budget deficits are another possible source of inflationary monetary policy. To see if this could be the case, we need to look at how a government finances its budget deficits.

Government Budget Constraint   Because the government has to pay its bills just as we do, it has a budget constraint. There are two ways we can pay for our spending: raise revenue (by working) or borrow. The government also enjoys these two options: raise revenue by levying taxes or go into debt by issuing government bonds. Unlike us, however, it has a third option. The government can create money and use it to pay for the goods and services it buys.

Methods of financing government spending are described by an expression called the **government budget constraint**, which states the following: the government budget deficit *DEF,* which equals the excess of government spending *G* over tax revenue *T,* must equal the sum of the change in the monetary base ΔMB and the change in government bonds held by the public ΔB. Algebraically, this expression can be written as

$$DEF = G - T = \Delta MB + \Delta B \tag{1}$$

To see what the government budget constraint means in practice, let's look at the case in which the only government purchase is a $100 million supercomputer. If the government convinces the electorate that such a computer is worth paying for, it will probably be able to raise the $100 million in taxes to pay for it, and the budget deficit will equal zero. The government budget constraint then tells us that no issue of money or bonds is needed to pay for the computer because the budget is balanced. If taxpayers think that supercomputers are too expensive and refuse to pay taxes for them, the budget constraint indicates that the government must pay for it by selling $100 million of new bonds to the public or by printing $100 million of currency to pay for the computer. In either case, the budget constraint is satisfied; the $100 million deficit is balanced by the change in the stock of government bonds held by the public (ΔB = $100 million) or by the change in the monetary base (ΔMB = $100 million).

The government budget constraint thus reveals two important facts. ***If the government deficit is financed by an increase in bond holdings by the public, there is no effect on the monetary base and hence on the money supply. But, if the deficit is not financed by increased bond holdings by the public, the monetary base and the money supply increase.***

There are several ways to understand why a deficit leads to an increase in the monetary base when the public's bond holdings do not increase. The simplest case is when the government issues currency to finance its deficit. Financing the deficit is then very straightforward. The government just pays for the spending that is in excess of its tax revenues with new currency. Because this increase in currency adds directly to the monetary base, the monetary base rises and the money supply with it through the process of multiple deposit creation described in Chapters 15 and 16.

In Canada, however, and in many other countries, the government does not have the right to issue currency to pay for its bills. In this case, the government must finance its deficit by first issuing bonds to the public to acquire the extra funds to pay its bills. Yet if these bonds do not end up in the hands of the public, the only alternative is that they are purchased by the central bank. For the government bonds not to end up in the hands of the public, the central bank must conduct an open market purchase, which, as we saw in Chapters 15 and 16, leads to an increase in the monetary base and in the money supply. This method of financing government spending is called **monetizing the debt** because, as the two-step process described indicates, government debt issued to finance government spending has been removed from the hands of the public and has been replaced by high-powered money. This method of financing, or the more direct method when a government just issues the currency directly, is also, somewhat inaccurately, referred to as **printing money** because high-powered money (the monetary base) is created in the process. The use of the word *printing* is misleading because what is essential to this method of financing government spending is not the actual printing of money but rather the issuing of monetary liabilities to the public after the money has been printed.

We thus see that a budget deficit can lead to an increase in the money supply if it is financed by the creation of high-powered money. However, earlier in this chapter you have seen that inflation can develop only when the stock of money grows continually. Can a budget deficit financed by printing money do this? The answer is yes, if the budget deficit persists for a substantial period of time. In the first period, if the deficit is financed by money creation, the money supply will rise, shifting the aggregate demand curve to the right and leading to a rise in the price level (see Figure 26-2). If the budget deficit is still present in the next period, it has to be financed all over again. The money supply will rise again, and the aggregate demand curve will again shift to the right, causing the price level to rise further. As long as the deficit persists and the government resorts to printing money to pay for it, this process will continue. *Financing a persistent deficit by money creation will lead to a sustained inflation.*

A critical element in this process is that the deficit is persistent. If temporary, it would not produce an inflation because the situation would then be similar to that shown in Figure 26-3, in which there is a one-shot increase in government expenditure. In the period when the deficit occurs, there will be an increase in money to finance it, and the resulting rightward shift of the aggregate demand curve will raise the price level. If the deficit disappears next period, there is no longer a need to print money. The aggregate demand curve will not shift further, and the price level will not continue to rise. Hence the one-shot increase in the money supply from the temporary deficit generates only a one-shot increase in the price level, and no inflation develops.

To summarize, *a deficit can be the source of a sustained inflation only if it is persistent rather than temporary and if the government finances it by creating money rather than by issuing bonds to the public*.

If inflation is the result, why do governments frequently finance persistent deficits by creating money? The answer is the key to understanding how budget deficits may lead to inflation.

Budget Deficits and Money Creation in Other Countries   Although Canada has well-developed money and capital markets in which huge quantities of its government bonds, both short- and long-term, can be sold, this is not the situation in many developing countries. If developing countries run budget deficits, they cannot finance them by issuing bonds and must resort to their only other alternative, printing money. As a result, when they run large deficits relative to GDP, the money supply grows at substantial rates, and inflation results.

Earlier we cited Latin American countries with high inflation rates and high money growth as evidence that inflation is a monetary phenomenon. The Latin American countries with high money growth are precisely the ones that have persistent and extremely large budget deficits relative to GDP. The only way to finance the deficits is to print more money, so the ultimate source of their high inflation rates is their large budget deficits.

In all episodes of hyperinflation, huge government budget deficits are also the ultimate source of inflationary monetary policies. The budget deficits during hyperinflations are so large that even if a capital market exists to issue government bonds, it does not have sufficient capacity to handle the quantity of bonds that the government wishes to sell. In this situation, the government must also resort to the printing press to finance the deficits.

Budget Deficits and Money Creation in Canada   So far we have seen why budget deficits in some countries must lead to money creation and inflation. Either the deficit is huge, or the country does not have sufficient access to capital markets in which it can sell government bonds. But neither of these scenarios seems to describe the situation in Canada. True, Canada's deficits were large in the 1980s and early 1990s, but even so, the magnitude of these deficits relative to GDP was small compared to the deficits of countries that have experienced hyperinflations. The federal government deficit as a percentage of GDP reached a peak of 6.5% in 1985, whereas Argentina's budget deficit sometimes exceeded 15% of GDP. Furthermore, since Canada has a well-developed government bond market, it can issue large quantities of bonds when it needs to finance its deficit.

Whether the budget deficit can influence the monetary base and the money supply or not depends critically on how the Bank of Canada chooses to conduct monetary policy. If the Bank pursues a policy goal of preventing high interest rates (a possibility, as we have seen in Chapter 18), many economists contend that a budget deficit will lead to the printing of money. Their reasoning, using the supply and demand analysis of the bond market in Chapter 5, is as follows: when the government issues bonds to the public, the supply of bonds rises (from B_1^s to B_2^s in Figure 26-7), causing interest rates to rise from i_1 to i_2 and bond prices to fall. If the Bank of Canada considers the rise in interest rates undesirable, it will buy bonds to prop up bond prices and reduce interest rates. The net result is that the government budget deficit can lead to Bank of Canada open market purchases, which raise the monetary base (create high-powered money) and raise the money supply. If the budget deficit persists so that the quantity of bonds supplied keeps on growing, the upward pressure on interest rates will continue, the Bank will purchase bonds again and again, and the money supply will continually rise, resulting in an inflation.

Harvard University
www.harvard.edu

Economists such as Robert Barro of Harvard University, however, do not agree that budget deficits influence the monetary base in the manner just described. Their analysis (which Barro named **Ricardian equivalence** after the nineteenth-century British economist David Ricardo) contends that when the government runs deficits and issues bonds, the public recognizes that it will be subject to higher taxes in the future to pay off these bonds. The public then saves more in anticipation of these future taxes, with the net result that the public demand for bonds increases to match the increased supply. The demand curve for bonds shifts rightward to B_R^d in Figure 26-7, leaving the interest rate unchanged at i_1. There is now no need for the Bank of Canada to purchase bonds to keep the interest rate from rising.

To sum up, although high inflation is "always and everywhere a monetary phenomenon" in the sense that it cannot occur without a high rate of money growth, there are reasons why this inflationary monetary policy might come about. The two underlying reasons are the adherence of policymakers to a high employment target and the presence of persistent government budget deficits.

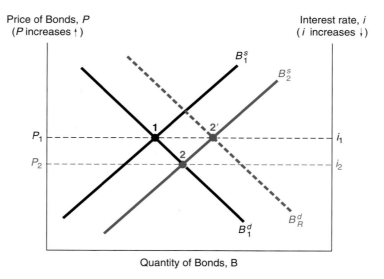

FIGURE 26-7 Interest Rates and the Government Budget Deficit

When the government issues bonds to finance the budget deficit, the supply curve for bonds shifts rightward from B_1^s to B_2^s. Many economists take the position that the equilibrium moves to point 2 because the bond demand curve remains unchanged, with the result that the bond price falls from P_1 to P_2 and the interest rate rises from i_1 to i_2. Adherents of Ricardian equivalence, however, suggest that the demand curve for bonds also increases to B_R^d, moving the equilibrium to point 2', where the interest rate is unchanged at i_1. (Note that P and i increase in opposite directions. P on the left vertical axis increases as we go up the axis, whereas i on the right vertical axis increases as we go down the axis.)

APPLICATION | *Explaining the Rise in Canadian Inflation, 1960–1980*

Now that we have examined the underlying sources of inflation, let's apply this knowledge to understanding the causes of the rise in Canadian inflation from 1960 to 1980.

Figure 26-8 documents the rise in inflation in those years. At the beginning of the period, the inflation rate is less than 2% at an annual rate; by the late 1970s, it is averaging around 8%. How does the analysis of this chapter explain this rise in inflation?

The conclusion that inflation is a monetary phenomenon is given a fair amount of support by the period from 1960 through 1980. As Figure 26-8 shows, in this period there is a close correspondence between movements in the inflation rate and the monetary growth rate from two years earlier. (The money growth rates are from two years earlier because research indicates that a change in money growth takes that long to affect the inflation rate.) The rise in inflation from 1960 to 1980 can be attributed to the rise in the money growth rate over this period. But you have probably noticed that in 1979–1980, the inflation rate is well above the money growth rate from two years earlier. You may recall from Chapter 24 that temporary upward bursts of the inflation rate in those years can be attributed to supply shocks from oil and food price increases that occurred in 1978–1980.

However, the linkage between money growth and inflation after 1980 is not at all evident in Figure 26-8, and this explains why in 1982 the Bank of Canada announced that it would no longer use M1 as a basis to set monetary policy (see

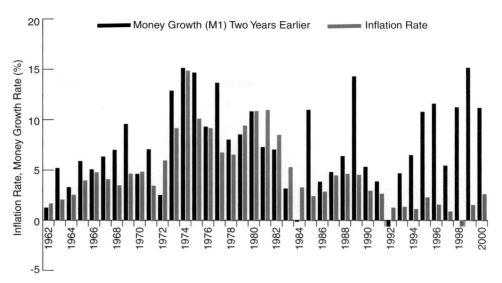

FIGURE 26-8 Inflation and Money Growth, 1960–2000

Source: Statistics Canada, CANSIM Series B1627 and D15612.

Chapter 18). The breakdown of the relationship between money growth and inflation is the result of substantial gyrations in velocity in the 1980s and 1990s (documented in Chapter 21). For example, the early 1980s was a period of rapid disinflation (a substantial fall in the inflation rate), yet the money growth rates in Figure 26-8 do not display a visible downward trend. (The disinflationary process in the 1980s will be discussed in another application later in this chapter.) Although some economists see the 1980s and 1990s as evidence against the money–inflation link, others view this as an unusual period characterized by large fluctuations in interest rates and by rapid financial innovation that made the correct measurement of money far more difficult (see Chapter 3). In their view, this period was an aberration, and the close correspondence of money and inflation is sure to reassert itself. However, this has not yet occurred.

What is the underlying cause of the increased rate of money growth that we see occurring from 1960 to 1980? We have identified two possible sources of inflationary monetary policy: government adherence to a high employment target and budget deficits. Let's see if budget deficits can explain the move to an inflationary monetary policy by plotting the ratio of government debt to GDP in Figure 26-9. This ratio provides a reasonable measure of whether government budget deficits put upward pressure on interest rates. Only if this ratio is rising might there be a tendency for budget deficits to raise interest rates because the public is then being asked to hold more government bonds relative to their capacity to buy them. Surprisingly, over the course of the 20-year period from 1960 to 1980, this ratio was falling, not rising. Thus Canadian budget deficits in this period did not raise interest rates and so could not have encouraged the Bank of Canada to expand the money supply by buying bonds. Therefore, Figure 26-9 tells us that we can rule out budget deficits as a source of the rise in inflation in this period.

We have ruled out budget deficits as the instigator; what else could be the underlying cause of the higher rate of money growth and more rapid inflation in the 1960s and 1970s? Figure 26-10, which compares the actual unemployment rate to the natural rate of unemployment, shows that the economy was experiencing unemployment below the natural rate in all but three years between 1964 and

Debt (% of GDP)

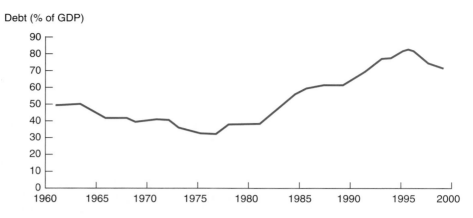

FIGURE 26-9   Government Debt-to-GDP Ratio, 1960–2000
Source: Statistics Canada, CANSIM Series D162201 and D14841.

1974. This suggests that in 1964–1974, the Canadian economy was experiencing the demand-pull inflation described in Figure 26-6.[6]

Policymakers apparently pursued policies that continually shifted the aggregate demand curve to the right in trying to achieve an output target that was too high, thus causing the continual rise in the price level outlined in Figure 26-6. This occurred because policymakers, economists, and politicians had become committed in the mid-1960s to full employment. Most economists today agree that the natural rate of unemployment was substantially higher in this period, on the order of 5 to 6%, as shown in Figure 26-10. The result of the inappropriate unemployment target was the beginning of the most sustained inflationary episode in Canadian history.

After 1975, the unemployment rate was regularly above the natural rate of unemployment, yet inflation continued. It appears that we have the phenomenon of a cost-push inflation described in Figure 26-5 (the impetus for which was the earlier demand-pull inflation). The persistence of inflation can be explained by the

Unemployment Rate (%)

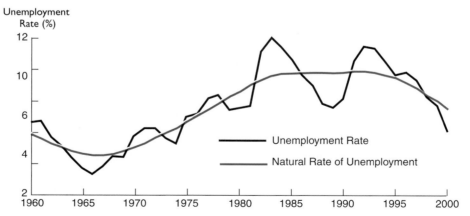

FIGURE 26-10   Unemployment and the Natural Rate of Unemployment, 1960–2000
Source: Statistics Canada, CANSIM Series D44950 and *Historical Statistics of Canada.*

[6]Our estimates of the natural rate of unemployment are based on the methodology suggested by Finn E. Kydland and Edward C. Prescott, "Business Cycles: Real Facts and a Monetary Myth," Federal Reserve Bank of Minneapolis *Quarterly Review* (Spring 1990): 3-18. Although this method can produce reasonable estimates of the natural rate of unemployment, such estimates are subject to a great deal of uncertainty and disagreement amongst economists.

public's knowledge that government policy continued to be concerned with achieving high employment. With a higher rate of expected inflation arising initially from the demand-pull inflation, the aggregate supply curve in Figure 26-5 continued to shift leftward, causing a rise in unemployment that policymakers would try to eliminate by shifting the aggregate demand curve to the right. The result was a continuation of the inflation that had started in the 1960s.

ACTIVIST/NONACTIVIST POLICY DEBATE

All economists have similar policy goals—they want to promote high employment and price stability—and yet they often have very different views on how policy should be conducted. Activists regard the self-correcting mechanism through wage and price adjustment (see Chapter 24) as very slow and hence see the need for the government to pursue active, accommodating, discretionary policy to eliminate high unemployment whenever it develops. Nonactivists, by contrast, believe that the performance of the economy would be improved if the government avoided active policy to eliminate unemployment. We will explore the activist/nonactivist policy debate by first looking at what the policy responses might be when the economy experiences high unemployment.

Responses to High Unemployment

Suppose that policymakers confront an economy that has moved to point 1′ in Figure 26-11. At this point, aggregate output $Y_{1'}$ is lower than the natural rate level, and the economy is suffering from high unemployment. Policymakers have two viable choices. If they are nonactivists and do nothing, the aggregate supply curve will eventually shift rightward over time, driving the economy from point 1′ to point 1, where full employment is restored. The accommodating, activist alternative is to try to eliminate the high unemployment by attempting to shift the aggregate demand curve rightward to AD_2 by pursuing expansionary policy (an increase in the money supply, increase in government spending, or lowering of taxes). If policymakers could shift the aggregate demand curve to AD_2 instantaneously, the economy would immediately move to point 2, where there is full employment. However, several types of lags prevent this immediate movement from occurring.

1. The *data lag* is the time it takes for policymakers to obtain the data that tell them what is happening in the economy. Accurate data on GDP, for example, are not available until several months after a given quarter is over.

2. The *recognition lag* is the time it takes for policymakers to be sure of what the data are signalling about the future course of the economy. For example, to minimize errors, the government will not declare the economy to be in recession until at least six months after it has determined that one has begun.

3. The *legislative lag* represents the time it takes to pass legislation to implement a particular policy. The legislative lag does not exist for most monetary policy actions such as open market operations. It can, however, be quite important for the implementation of fiscal policy, when it can sometimes take six months to a year to get legislation passed to change taxes or government spending.

4. The *implementation lag* is the time it takes for policymakers to change policy instruments once they have decided on the new policy. Again, this lag is unimportant for the conduct of open market operations because the Bank of Canada's trading desk can purchase or sell bonds almost immediately upon being told to do so. Actually implementing fiscal policy may

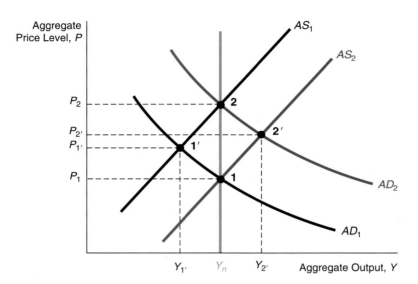

FIGURE 26-11 The Choice Between Activist and Nonactivist Policy

When the economy has moved to point 1', the policymaker has two choices of policy: the nonactivist policy of doing nothing and letting the economy return to point 1 or the activist policy of shifting the aggregate demand curve to AD_2 to move the economy to point 2.

take time, however; for example, getting government agencies to change their spending habits takes time, as does changing tax tables.

5. The *effectiveness lag* is the time it takes for the policy actually to have an impact on the economy. An important element of the monetarist viewpoint is that the effectiveness lag for changes in the money supply is long and variable (from several months to several years). Keynesians usually view fiscal policy as having a shorter effectiveness lag than monetary policy (fiscal policy takes approximately a year until its full effect is felt), but there is substantial uncertainty about how long this lag is.

Activist and Nonactivist Positions

Now that we understand the considerations that affect decisions by policymakers on whether to pursue an activist or nonactivist policy, we can examine when each of these policies would be preferable.

Case for an Activist Policy Activists, such as the Keynesians, view the wage and price adjustment process as extremely slow. They consider a nonactivist policy costly because the slow movement of the economy back to full employment results in a large loss of output. However, even though the five lags described above result in a delay of a year or two before the aggregate demand curve shift to AD_2, the aggregate supply curve moves very little during this time. The appropriate path for policymakers to pursue is thus an activist policy of moving the economy to point 2 in Figure 26-11.

Case for a Nonactivist Policy Nonactivists, such as the monetarists, view the wage and price adjustment process as more rapid than activists do and consider nonactivist policy less costly because output is soon back at the natural rate level. They suggest that an activist, accommodating policy of shifting the aggregate demand curve to AD_2 is costly because it produces more volatility in both the price level and output. The reason for this volatility is that the time it takes to shift the aggregate demand curve to AD_2 is substantial, whereas the wage and price adjustment process is more rapid. Hence before the aggregate demand curve shifts to the right, the aggregate supply curve will have shifted rightward to AS_2, and the economy will have moved from point $1'$ to point 1, where it has returned to the natural rate level of output Y_n. After adjustment to the AS_2 curve is complete, the shift of the aggregate demand curve to AD_2 finally takes effect, leading the economy to point $2'$ at the intersection of AD_2 and AS_2. Aggregate output at Y_2 is now greater than the natural rate level ($Y_2 > Y_n$), so the aggregate supply curve will now shift leftward back to AS_1, moving the economy to point 2, where output is again at the natural rate level.

Although the activist policy eventually moves the economy to point 2 as policymakers intended, it leads to a sequence of equilibrium points—$1'$, 1, $2'$, and 2—at which both output and the price level have been highly variable. Output overshoots its target level of Y_n, and the price level falls from $P_{1'}$ to P_1 and then rises to $P_{2'}$ and eventually to P_2. Because this variability is undesirable, policymakers would be better off pursuing the nonactivist policy, which moved the economy to point 1 and left it there.

Expectations and the Activist/ Nonactivist Debate

Our analysis of inflation in the 1970s demonstrated that expectations about policy can be an important element in the inflation process. Allowing for expectations about policy to affect how wages are set (the wage-setting process) provides an additional reason for pursuing a nonactivist policy.

Do Expectations Favour a Nonactivist Approach?

Does the possibility that expectations about policy matter to the wage-setting process strengthen the case for a nonactivist policy? The case for an activist policy states that with slow wage and price adjustment, the activist policy returns the economy to full employment at point 2 far more quickly than it takes to get to full employment at point 1 under nonactivist policy. However, the activist argument does not allow for the possibility (1) that expectations about policy matter to the wage-setting process and (2) that the economy might initially have moved from point 1 to point $1'$ because an attempt by workers to raise their wages or a negative supply shock shifted the aggregate supply curve from AS_2 to AS_1. We must therefore ask the following question about activist policy: will the aggregate supply curve continue to shift to the left after the economy has reached point 2, leading to cost-push inflation?

The answer to this question is yes *if* expectations about policy matter. Our discussion of cost-push inflation in Figure 26-5 suggested that if workers know that policy will be accommodating in the future, they will continue to push their wages up, and the aggregate supply curve will keep on shifting leftward. As a result, policymakers are forced to accommodate the cost push by continuing to shift the aggregate demand curve to the right to eliminate the unemployment that develops. The accommodating, activist policy with its high employment target has the hidden cost or disadvantage that it may well lead to inflation.[7]

The main advantage of a nonaccommodating, nonactivist policy, in which policymakers do not try to shift the aggregate demand curve in response to the cost push, is that it will prevent inflation. As depicted in Figure 26-4, the result of an upward push on wages in the face of a nonaccommodating, nonactivist policy will be a period of unemployment above the natural rate level, which will eventually shift the aggregate supply curve and the price level back to their initial positions. The main criticism of this nonactivist policy is that the economy will suffer protracted periods of unemployment when the aggregate supply curve shifts leftward.

---

[7]The issue that is being described here is the time-inconsistency problem described in Chapter 20.

Workers, however, would probably not push for higher wages to begin with if they knew that policy would be nonaccommodating, because their wage gains will lead to a protracted period of unemployment. A nonaccommodating, nonactivist policy may have not only the advantage of preventing inflation but also the hidden benefit of discouraging leftward shifts in the aggregate supply curve that lead to excessive unemployment.

In conclusion, ***if workers' opinions about whether policy is accommodating or nonaccommodating matter to the wage-setting process, the case for a nonactivist policy is much stronger***.

Do Expectations About Policy Matter to the Wage-Setting Process?   The answer to this question is crucial to deciding whether activist or nonactivist policy is preferred and so has become a major topic of current research for economists, but the evidence is not yet conclusive. We can ask, however, whether expectations about policy do affect people's behaviour in other contexts. This information will help us know if expectations regarding whether or not policy is accommodating are important to the wage-setting process.

As any good negotiator knows, convincing your opponent that you will be nonaccommodating is crucial to getting a good deal. If you are bargaining with a car dealer over price, for example, you must convince him that you can just as easily walk away from the deal and buy a car from a dealer on the other side of town. This principle also applies to conducting foreign policy—it is to your advantage to convince your opponent that you will go to war (be nonaccommodating) if your demands are not met. Similarly, if your opponent thinks that you will be accommodating, he will almost certainly take advantage of you (for an example, see Box 26-2). Finally, anyone who has dealt with a two-year-old child knows that the more you give in (pursue an accommodating policy), the more demanding the child becomes. People's expectations about policy *do* affect their behaviour. Consequently, it is quite plausible that expectations about policy also affect the wage-setting process.[8]

Rules Versus Discretion: Conclusions

Carnegie-Mellon University
www.carnegiemellon. edu

The following conclusions can be generated from our analysis. Activists believe in the use of discretionary policy to eliminate excessive unemployment whenever it develops because they view the wage and price adjustment process as sluggish and unresponsive to expectations about policy. Nonactivists, by contrast, believe that a discretionary policy that reacts to excessive unemployment is counter-productive because wage and price adjustment is rapid and because expectations about policy can matter to the wage-setting process. Nonactivists thus advocate the use of a policy rule to keep the aggregate demand curve from fluctuating away from the trend rate of growth of the natural rate level of output. Monetarists, who adhere to the nonactivist position and who also see money as the sole source of fluctuations in the aggregate demand curve, in the past advocated a policy rule whereby the Bank of Canada keeps the money supply growing at a constant rate. This monetarist rule is referred to as a **constant-money-growth-rate rule**. Because of the misbehaviour of velocity of M1 and M2, monetarists such as Bennett McCallum and Alan Meltzer of Carnegie-Mellon University now advocate a rule for the growth of the monetary base that is adjusted for past velocity changes.

---

[8]A recent development in monetary theory, new classical macroeconomics, strongly suggests that expectations about policy are crucial to the wage-setting process and the movements of the aggregate supply curve. We will explore why new classical macroeconomics comes to this conclusion in Chapters 27 and 28, when we discuss the implications of the rational expectations hypothesis, which states that expectations are formed using all available information, including expectations about policy.

B O X   2 6 · 2

Perils of Accommodating Policy

The Terrorism Dilemma. A major dilemma confronting foreign policy in recent years is whether to cave in to the demands of terrorists when they are holding hostages. Because our hearts go out to the hostages and their families, we might be tempted to pursue an accommodating policy of giving in to the terrorists to bring the hostages safely back home. However, pursuing this accommodating policy is likely to encourage terrorists to take hostages in the future.

The terrorism dilemma illustrates the principle that opponents are more likely to take advantage of you in the future if you accommodate them now. Recognition of this principle, which demonstrates the perils of accommodating policy, explains why governments in countries such as the United States and Israel have been reluctant to give in to terrorist demands even though it has sometimes resulted in the death of hostages.

As our analysis indicates, an important element for the success of a nonaccommodating policy rule is that it be *credible*. The public must believe that policymakers will be tough and not accede to a cost push by shifting the aggregate demand curve to the right to eliminate unemployment. In other words, government policymakers need credibility as inflation-fighters in the eyes of the public. Otherwise, workers will be more likely to push for higher wages, which will shift the aggregate supply curve leftward after the economy reaches full employment at a point such as point 2 in Figure 26-11 and will lead to unemployment or inflation (or both). Alternatively, a credible, nonaccommodating policy rule has the benefit that it makes a cost push less likely and thus helps prevent inflation and potential increases in unemployment. The following application suggests that recent historical experience is consistent with the importance of credibility to successful policymaking.

APPLICATION | *Importance of Credibility to the Bank of Canada's Victory over Inflation*

In the period from 1965 through the 1970s, policymakers had little credibility as inflation-fighters—a well-deserved reputation, as they pursued an accommodating policy to achieve high employment. As we have seen, the outcome was not a happy one. Inflation soared to double-digit levels, while the unemployment rate remained high. To wring inflation out of the system, the Bank of Canada under governor Gerald Bouey put the economy through two back-to-back recessions in 1980 and 1981–1982 (see Chapter 19). (The data on inflation, money growth, and unemployment in this period are shown in Figures 26-8 and 26-10.) Only after the 1981-1982 recession—the most severe in the postwar period, with unemployment above the 10% level—did Bouey establish credibility for the Bank of Canada's anti-inflation policy. By the end of 1983, inflation was running at a rate of less than 5%.

From November 1982 to January 1988, the primary objective of the Bank of Canada was price stability in the longer term and inflation containment in the shorter term. This policy, however, was carried out without intermediate targets or a specified path to the longer-term goal. In January 1988, John Crow, the governor of the Bank of Canada, announced that the Bank would subsequently pursue an objective of price stability. One indication of the Bank of Canada's credibility came in 1991 when the Bank and the Department of Finance jointly announced inflation targets. This convinced the public and the markets that if inflation reared its head, the Bank of Canada would pursue a nonaccommodating policy of quashing it. Workers and firms did not raise wages and prices, which would have led to both inflation and unemployment. The success of the Bank's anti-inflation policy has been continuing to date—the inflation rate has been running at a rate of less than 3%. The Bank of Canada's triumph over inflation was achieved because it obtained credibility the hard way; it earned it.

SUMMARY

1. Milton Friedman's famous proposition that "inflation is always and everywhere a monetary phenomenon" is supported by the following evidence. Every country that has experienced a sustained, high inflation has also experienced a high rate of money growth.

2. Aggregate demand and supply analysis shows that Keynesian and monetarist views of the inflation process are not very different. Both believe that high inflation can occur only if there is a high rate of money growth. As long as we recognize that by inflation we mean a rapid and continuing increase in the price level, almost all economists agree with Friedman's proposition.

3. Although high inflation is "always and everywhere a monetary phenomenon" in the sense that it

cannot occur without a high rate of money growth, there are reasons why inflationary monetary policy comes about. The two underlying reasons are the adherence of policymakers to a high employment target and the presence of persistent government budget deficits.

4. Activists believe in the use of discretionary policy to eliminate excessive unemployment whenever it occurs because they view wage and price adjustment as sluggish and unresponsive to expectations about policy. Nonactivists take the opposite view and believe that discretionary policy is counterproductive. In addition, they regard the credibility of a nonaccommodating (nonactivist) anti-inflation policy as crucial to its success.

KEY TERMS

accommodating policy, p. 594

constant-money-growth-rate rule, p. 606

cost-push inflation, p. 594

demand-pull inflation, p. 594

government budget constraint, p. 597

monetizing the debt, p. 597

printing money, p. 598

Ricardian equivalence, p. 599

QUESTIONS AND PROBLEMS

Questions marked with an asterisk are answered at the end of the book in an appendix, "Answers to Selected Questions and Problems."

1. "There are frequently years when the inflation rate is high and yet money growth is quite low. Therefore, the statement that inflation is a monetary phenomenon cannot be correct." Comment.

*2. Why do economists focus on historical episodes of hyperinflation to decide whether inflation is a monetary phenomenon?

3. "Since increases in government spending raise the aggregate demand curve in Keynesian analysis, fiscal policy by itself can be the source of inflation." Is this statement true, false, or uncertain? Explain your answer.

*4. "A cost-push inflation occurs as a result of workers' attempts to push up their wages. Therefore, inflation does not have to be a monetary phenomenon." Is this statement true, false, or uncertain? Explain your answer.

5. "Because government policymakers do not consider inflation desirable, their policies cannot be the source of inflation." Is this statement true, false, or uncertain? Explain your answer.

*6. "A budget deficit that is only temporary cannot be the source of inflation." Is this statement true, false, or uncertain? Explain your answer.

7. How can the Bank of Canada's desire to prevent high interest rates lead to inflation?

*8. "If the data and recognition lags could be reduced, activist policy would more likely be beneficial to the economy." Is this statement true, false, or uncertain? Explain your answer.

9. "The more sluggish wage and price adjustment is, the more variable output and the price level are when an activist policy is pursued." Is this statement true, false, or uncertain? Explain your answer.

*10. "If the public believes that the monetary authorities will pursue an accommodating policy, a cost-push inflation is more likely to develop." Is this statement true, false, or uncertain? Explain your answer.

11. Why are activist policies to eliminate unemployment more likely to lead to inflation than nonactivist policies?

*12. "The less important expectations about policy are to movements of the aggregate supply curve, the stronger the case is for activist policy to eliminate unemployment." Is this statement true, false, or uncertain? Explain your answer.

13. If the economy's self-correcting mechanism works slowly, should the government necessarily pursue an activist policy to eliminate unemployment?

*14. "To prevent inflation, the Bank of Canada should follow Teddy Roosevelt's advice: 'Speak softly and carry a big stick.'" What would the Bank's "big stick" be? What is the statement trying to say?

Chapter 27

Theory of Rational Expectations
and Efficient Capital Markets

PREVIEW

Throughout our discussion of the many facets of money, banking, and financial markets, you may have noticed that the subject of expectations keeps cropping up. If consumers expect that they will be richer in the future, for example, they spend more today, and aggregate output will increase; if banks expect deposit outflows to occur, they increase their holdings of excess reserves, which causes the money supply to fall; and if participants in the capital markets expect interest rates to rise and anticipate capital losses on long-term bonds, they will decrease their demand for long-term bonds, and the bond prices will fall. Expectations influence the behaviour of all participants in the economy and have a major impact on economic activity.

The *theory of rational expectations* attempts to explain how economic agents form their expectations. It is at the centre of many recent debates about how monetary policy and fiscal policy should be conducted (discussed in Chapter 28). In addition, when this theory is applied to financial markets, where it is called the *theory of efficient capital markets* (or, more simply, *efficient markets theory*), it has important implications about what factors determine securities prices and how these prices move over time.

In this chapter we examine the basic reasoning behind the theory of rational expectations and apply it to financial markets. In addition to helping us understand the factors that influence the formation of business and consumer expectations, rational expectations theory explains some puzzling features of the operation and behaviour of financial markets. You will see, for example, that it explains why changes in stock prices are unpredictable and why listening to a stockbroker's hot tips may not be a good idea.

Theoretically, rational expectations theory should be a powerful tool for analyzing behaviour. But to establish that it is *in reality* a useful tool, we must compare the theory with the data. Does the empirical evidence support the theory? Although the evidence is somewhat mixed and is very controversial, it indicates that for many purposes, this theory is a good starting point for analyzing expectations.

ROLE OF EXPECTATIONS IN ECONOMIC ACTIVITY

It is difficult to think of any sector of the economy in which expectations exert no influence on the effects of policy and the way markets behave. To point up the critical role of expectations in influencing economic activity, it might be useful to list the various avenues in which they have come into play in our study of money, banking, and financial markets.

Study Guide

Before you read on, try to list examples from this book in which expectations influence economic behaviour and then compare your list to the examples that follow. This is an excellent way for you to review how the material we have studied so far fits together.

1. *Asset demand and the determination of interest rates.* Because expectations of returns are an important factor in determining the quantity of an asset people demand, expectations are central to the behaviour of asset prices in a financial market (Chapter 5). For example, we have seen that expectations of inflation have a major impact on bond prices and interest rates through the Fisher effect. The speed with which expectations of inflation respond to a higher rate of money growth is an important factor determining whether interest rates rise or fall when money growth increases.

2. *Risk and term structure of interest rates.* Expectations are also central in the determination of the risk and term structure of interest rates (Chapter 6). Expectations about the likelihood of bankruptcy are probably the most important factors in determining the risk structure of interest rates. Expectations of future short-term interest rates play a central role in determining long-term interest rates.

3. *Foreign exchange rates.* Recall that the exchange rate is the price of one asset (deposits denominated in the domestic currency) in terms of another (deposits denominated in the foreign currency). Thus the expected returns on foreign deposits relative to domestic deposits are a central element in the determination of foreign exchange rates (Chapter 7). Because expected appreciation or depreciation of the domestic currency affects the expected return on foreign deposits relative to domestic deposits, expectations about the price level, inflation, tariffs and quotas, import and export demand, and the money supply play an important role in determining the exchange rate. In addition, expectations that a central bank is about to devalue or revalue its domestic currency are a key feature of a speculative attack on a currency (Chapter 19).

4. *Asymmetric information and financial structure.* Expectations are what make the asymmetric information problems of adverse selection and moral hazard we encountered in Part III important in determining financial structure. Financial intermediaries engage in information collection because they have expectations that adverse selection will occur, that is, that the least desirable credit risks will be the most likely to seek loans. Similarly, expectations that borrowers will increase moral hazard by taking on too much risk are what drive financial institutions to take steps to limit moral hazard

through monitoring and enforcement of restrictive covenants. The greater the expectations of the effects of adverse selection and moral hazard, the greater the efforts of financial institutions to engage in activities to reduce these asymmetric information problems and hence the greater the impact of asymmetric information on our financial structure.

5. *Financial innovation.* Because financial institutions are concerned with the future profitability of the new financial instruments they issue, expectations about interest-rate movements and the nature of the regulatory environment in the future affect financial innovation (Chapters 9 and 10). Furthermore, in deciding which regulations to impose on financial markets, regulators must guess how financial institutions will behave in response to new regulations. The result can be a complicated game between the regulators and the regulated in which each tries to outguess the other.

6. *Bank asset and liability management.* Banks' decisions about which assets to hold are influenced by their expectations about the returns, risk, and liquidity of various assets (Chapter 9). Their decisions about which liabilities to assume are influenced by their expectations about the future cost of taking on various liabilities. In addition, because banks must manage liquidity to remain solvent, expectations about deposit outflows will affect their decisions about whether to hold more or fewer liquid assets.

7. *The money supply process.* As you will recall from Chapters 15 and 16, depositor behaviour and bank behaviour are important in the money supply process. Depositors' decisions to hold currency versus demand or time deposits are affected primarily by expectations of the relative returns on these assets. Banks' decisions about excess reserves and borrowing from the Bank of Canada are influenced by their expectations of the returns they can earn on loans. In addition, the amount of excess reserves is affected by bankers' expectations concerning depositor outflows.

   The role of expectations in bank panics and the resulting declines in the money supply are especially important (Chapter 16). Depositors' expectations that a bank or banks are in trouble cause them to withdraw deposits, which in turn causes banks to fail, which causes more banks to fail. Bankers' expectations of deposit outflows make the situation even worse because their scramble for liquidity and the resulting increase in excess reserves can lead to more bank failures. The net result of this process is that the currency–chequable deposits ratio and excess reserves rise, causing a sharp drop in the money supply.

8. *Bank of Canada.* The Bank's expectations of inflation and the state of the economy affect the targets it sets for monetary policy. Its expectations of short-term interest rates can be a factor in the procedures it uses to control the money supply (Chapter 18).

9. *Demand for money.* Because money is just another asset, its expected return relative to other assets is an important factor in determining its demand (Chapter 21). Expectations about the level of lifetime resources (usually represented by permanent income) are frequently thought to be another major determinant of the demand for money.

10. *Aggregate demand.* Expectations play a prominent role in determining aggregate demand. Our discussion of the *ISLM* model (Chapters 22 and 23) and the transmission mechanisms of monetary policy (Chapter 25) reveals that consumer expenditure is related to consumers' expectations of the

future resources available to them and of the likelihood of financial distress. Investment spending depends on firms' expectations of future profits from investment projects as well as expectations about the cost of financing the project. It is no wonder that Keynes emphasized "animal spirits" (expectations) as a major factor driving aggregate demand and the business cycle.

11. *Aggregate supply and inflation.* Analysis of the aggregate supply curve (Chapter 24) indicated that workers' expectations about inflation and the likely response of government policy to unemployment affect the position of the aggregate supply curve. Expectations about inflation and government policy influence workers' willingness to push wages higher, and so these expectations play a central role in cost-push inflation, whereby the aggregate supply curve shifts farther and farther to the left (Chapter 26). The public's expectations of government policy, which are affected by the credibility of government policymakers, have implications for the desirability of pursuing activist or nonactivist policies.

In conclusion, expectations are important in every sector of the economy through their effects on policy and market behaviour. Next we outline the theory of rational expectations, currently the most widely used theory to describe the formation of business and consumer expectations.

THEORY OF RATIONAL EXPECTATIONS

In the 1950s and 1960s, economists regularly viewed expectations as formed from past experience only. Expectations of inflation, for example, were typically viewed as being an average of past inflation rates. This view of expectation formation, called **adaptive expectations**, suggests that changes in expectations will occur slowly over time as past data change.[1] So if inflation had formerly been steady at a 5% rate, expectations of future inflation would be 5% too. If inflation rose to a steady rate of 10%, expectations of future inflation would rise toward 10%, but slowly. In the first year, expected inflation might rise only to 6%; in the second year, to 7%; and so on.

Adaptive expectations have been faulted on the grounds that people use more information than just past data on a single variable to form their expectations of that variable. Their expectations of inflation will almost surely be affected by their predictions of future monetary policy as well as by current and past monetary policy. In addition, people often change their expectations quickly in the light of new information. To meet these objections to adaptive expectations, John Muth developed an alternative theory of expectations, called **rational expectations**, which can be stated as follows: ***expectations will be identical to optimal forecasts (the best guess of the future) using all available information***.[2]

---

[1] More specifically, adaptive expectations, say of inflation, are written as a weighted average of past inflation rates:

$$\pi_t^e = (1 - \lambda)\sum_{j=0}^{\infty}\lambda^j \pi_{t-j}$$

where π_t^e = adaptive expectation of inflation at time t

π_{t-j} = inflation at time $t - j$

λ = a constant between the values of 0 and 1

[2] John Muth, "Rational Expectations and the Theory of Price Movements," *Econometrica* 29 (1961): 315–335.

What exactly does this mean? To explain it more clearly, let's use the theory of rational expectations to examine how expectations are formed in a situation that most of us encounter at some point in our lifetime: our drive to work. Suppose that when Joe Commuter travels when it is not rush hour, it takes an average of 30 minutes for his trip. Sometimes it takes him 35 minutes, other times 25 minutes, but the average non-rush-hour driving time is 30 minutes. If, however, Joe leaves for work during the rush hour, it takes him, on average, an additional 10 minutes to get to work. Given that he leaves for work during the rush hour, the best guess of the driving time—the **optimal forecast**— is 40 minutes.

If the only information available to Joe before he leaves for work that would have a potential effect on his driving time is that he is leaving during the rush hour, what does rational expectations theory allow you to predict about Joe's expectations of his driving time? Since the best guess of his driving time using all available information is 40 minutes, Joe's expectation should also be the same. Clearly, an expectation of 35 minutes would not be rational because it is not equal to the optimal forecast, the best guess of the driving time.

Suppose that the next day, given the same conditions and the same expectations, it takes Joe 45 minutes to drive because he hits an abnormally large number of red lights, and the day after that he hits all the lights right and it takes him only 35 minutes. Do these variations mean that Joe's 40-minute expectation is irrational? No, an expectation of 40 minutes' driving time is still a rational expectation. In both cases, the forecast is off by 5 minutes, so the expectation has not been perfectly accurate. However, the forecast does not have to be perfectly accurate to be rational—it need only be the *best possible* given the available information; that is, it has to be correct *on average,* and the 40-minute expectation meets this requirement. Since there is bound to be some randomness in Joe's driving time regardless of driving conditions, an optimal forecast will never be completely accurate.

The example makes the following important point about rational expectations. ***Even though a rational expectation equals the optimal forecast using all available information, a prediction based on it may not always be perfectly accurate.***

What if an item of information relevant to predicting driving time is unavailable or ignored? Suppose that on Joe's usual route to work there is an accident that causes a two-hour traffic jam. If Joe has no way of ascertaining this information, his rush-hour expectation of 40 minutes' driving time is still rational because the accident information is not available to him for incorporation into his optimal forecast. However, if there was a radio or TV traffic report about the accident that Joe did not bother to listen to or heard but ignored, his 40-minute expectation is no longer rational. In light of the availability of this information, Joe's optimal forecast should have been two hours and 40 minutes.

Accordingly, there are two reasons why an expectation may fail to be rational:

1. People might be aware of all available information but find it takes too much effort to make their expectation the best guess possible.

2. People might be unaware of some available relevant information, so their best guess of the future will not be accurate.

Nonetheless, it is important to recognize that if an additional factor is important but information about it is not available, an expectation that does not take account of it can still be rational.

Formal Statement of the Theory

We can state the theory of rational expectations somewhat more formally. If X stands for the variable that is being forecast (in our example, Joe Commuter's driving time), X^e for the expectation of this variable (Joe's expectation of his driving time), and X^{of}

for the optimal forecast of X using all available information (the best guess possible of his driving time), the theory of rational expectations then simply says

$$X^e = X^{of} \tag{1}$$

That is, the expectation of X equals the optimal forecast using all available information.

Rationale Behind the Theory

Why do people try to make their expectations match their best possible guess of the future using all available information? The simplest explanation is that it is costly for people not to do so. Joe Commuter has a strong incentive to make his expectation of the time it takes him to drive to work as accurate as possible. If he underpredicts his driving time, he will often be late to work and risk being fired. If he overpredicts, he will, on average, get to work too early and will have given up sleep or leisure time unnecessarily. Accurate expectations are desirable, and there are strong incentives for people to try to make them equal to optimal forecasts by using all available information.

The same principle applies to businesses. Suppose that an appliance manufacturer, say General Electric, knows that interest-rate movements are important to the sales of appliances. If GE makes poor forecasts of interest rates, it will earn less profit because it might produce either too many appliances or too few. There are strong incentives for GE to acquire all available information to help it forecast interest rates and use the information to make the best possible guess of future interest-rate movements.

The incentives for equating expectations with optimal forecasts are especially strong in financial markets. In these markets, people with better forecasts of the future get rich. The application of the theory of rational expectations to financial markets (where it is called **efficient markets theory**) is thus particularly useful.

Implications of the Theory

Rational expectations theory leads to two commonsense implications for the forming of expectations that are important in the analysis of the aggregate economy.

1. *If there is a change in the way a variable moves, the way in which expectations of this variable are formed will change as well.* This tenet of rational expectations theory can be most easily understood through a concrete example. Suppose that Keynes was correct in believing that interest rates move in such a way that they tend to return to a "normal" level in the future (Chapter 21). If today's interest rate is high relative to the normal level, an optimal forecast of the interest rate in the future is that it will decline to the normal level. Rational expectations theory would imply that when today's interest rate is high, the expectation is that it will fall in the future.

   Suppose now that the way in which the interest rate moves changes so that when the interest rate is high, it stays high. In this case, when today's interest rate is high, the optimal forecast of the future interest rate, and hence the rational expectation, is that it will stay high. Expectations of the future interest rate will no longer indicate that the interest rate will fall. The change in the way the interest-rate variable moves has therefore led to a change in the way that expectations of future interest rates are formed. The rational expectations analysis here is generalizable to expectations of any variable. Hence when there is a change in the way any variable moves, the way in which expectations of this variable are formed will change too.

2. *The forecast errors of expectations will on average be zero and cannot be predicted ahead of time.* The forecast error of an expectation is

$X - X^e$, the difference between the realization of a variable X and the expectation of the variable; that is, if Joe Commuter's driving time on a particular day is 45 minutes and his expectation of the driving time is 40 minutes, the forecast error is 5 minutes.

Suppose that in violation of the rational expectations tenet, Joe's forecast error is not, on average, equal to zero; instead, it equals 5 minutes. The forecast error is now predictable ahead of time because Joe will soon notice that he is, on average, 5 minutes late for work and can improve his forecast by increasing it by 5 minutes. Rational expectations theory implies that this is exactly what Joe will do because he will want his forecast to be the best guess possible. When Joe has revised his forecast upward by 5 minutes, on average, the forecast error will equal zero so that it cannot be predicted ahead of time. Rational expectations theory implies that forecast errors of expectations cannot be predicted.

EFFICIENT MARKETS THEORY: RATIONAL EXPECTATIONS IN FINANCIAL MARKETS

While the theory of rational expectations was being developed by monetary economists, financial economists were developing a parallel theory of expectation formation in financial markets. It led them to the same conclusion as that of the rational expectations theorists: expectations in financial markets are equal to optimal forecasts using all available information.[3] Although financial economists gave their theory another name, calling it the *theory of efficient capital markets* or *efficient markets theory,* in fact their theory is just an application of rational expectations to the pricing of securities.

Efficient markets theory is based on the assumption that prices of securities in financial markets fully reflect all available information. You may recall from Chapter 4 that the rate of return from holding a security equals the sum of the capital gain on the security (the change in the price) plus any cash payments, divided by the initial purchase price of the security:

$$RET = \frac{P_{t+1} - P_t + C}{P_t} \tag{2}$$

where
RET = rate of return on the security held from time t to $t + 1$ (say the end of 2000 to the end of 2001)

P_{t+1} = price of the security at time $t + 1$, the end of the holding period

P_t = price of the security at time t, the beginning of the holding period

C = cash payment (coupon or dividend payments) made in the period t to $t + 1$

Let's look at the expectation of this return at time t, the beginning of the holding period. Because the current price P_t and the cash payment C are known at the beginning, the only variable in the definition of the return that is uncertain is the price next period, P_{t+1}.[4] Denoting the expectation of the security's price at the end of the holding period as P_{t+1}^e, the expected return RET^e is

---

[3]The development of efficient markets theory was not wholly independent of the development of rational expectations theory in that financial economists were aware of Muth's work.

[4]There are cases where C might not be known at the beginning of the period, but that does not make a substantial difference to the analysis. We would in that case assume that not only price expectations but also the expectations of C are optimal forecasts using all available information.

$$RET^e = \frac{P^e_{t+1} - P_t + C}{P_t}$$

Efficient markets theory also views expectations of future prices as equal to optimal forecasts using all currently available information. In other words, the market's expectations of future securities prices are rational, so that

$$P^e_{t+1} = P^{of}_{t+1}$$

which in turn implies that the expected return on the security will equal the optimal forecast of the return:

$$RET^e = RET^{of} \tag{3}$$

Unfortunately, we cannot observe either RET^e or P^e_{t+1}, so the rational expectations equations by themselves do not tell us much about how the financial market behaves. However, if we can devise some way to measure the value of RET^e, these equations will have important implications for how prices of securities change in financial markets.

The supply and demand analysis of the bond market developed in Chapter 5 shows us that the expected return on a security (the interest rate in the case of the bond examined) will have a tendency to head toward the equilibrium return that equates the quantity demanded to the quantity supplied. Supply and demand analysis enables us to determine the expected return on a security with the following equilibrium condition: the expected return on a security RET^e equals the equilibrium return RET^*, which equates the quantity of the security demanded to the quantity supplied; that is,

$$RET^e = RET^* \tag{4}$$

The academic field of finance explores the factors (risk and liquidity, for example) that influence the equilibrium returns on securities. For our purposes, it is sufficient to know that we can determine the equilibrium return and thus determine the expected return with the equilibrium condition.

We can derive an equation to describe pricing behaviour in an efficient market by using the equilibrium condition to replace RET^e with RET^* in the rational expectations equation (Equation 3). In this way we obtain

$$RET^{of} = RET^* \tag{5}$$

This equation tells us that ***current prices in a financial market will be set so that the optimal forecast of a security's return using all available information equals the security's equilibrium return***. Financial economists state it more simply: in an efficient market, a security's price fully reflects all available information.

Rationale Behind the Theory

Let's see what the efficient markets condition means in practice and why it is a sensible characterization of pricing behaviour. Suppose that the equilibrium return on a security, say Nortel common stock, is 10% at an annual rate, and its current price P_t is lower than the optimal forecast of tomorrow's price P^{of}_{t+1} so that the optimal forecast of the return at an annual rate is 50%, which is greater than the equilibrium return of 10%. We are now able to predict that, on average, Nortel's return would be abnormally high. This situation is called an **unexploited profit opportunity** because, on average, people would be earning more than they should, given the characteristics of that security. Knowing that, on average, you can earn such an abnormally high rate of return on Nortel because $RET^{of} > RET^*$, you would buy more, which would in turn drive up its current price P_t relative to the expected future price P^{of}_{t+1}, thereby lowering RET^{of}. When the current price has risen sufficiently so that RET^{of} equals RET^* and the efficient markets condition (Equation 5) is satisfied, the buying of Nortel will stop, and the unexploited profit opportunity will have disappeared.

Similarly, a security for which the optimal forecast of the return is -5% while the equilibrium return is 10% ($RET^{of} < RET^*$) would be a poor investment because, on average, it earns less than the equilibrium return. In such a case, you would sell the security and drive down its current price relative to the expected future price until RET^{of} rose to the level of RET^* and the efficient markets condition is again satisfied. What we have shown can be summarized as follows:

$$RET^{of} > RET^* \rightarrow P_t\uparrow \rightarrow RET^{of}\downarrow$$
$$RET^{of} < RET^* \rightarrow P_r\downarrow \rightarrow RET^{of}\uparrow$$
$$\text{until}$$
$$RET^{of} = RET^*$$

Another way to state the efficient markets condition is this: ***in an efficient market, all unexploited profit opportunities will be eliminated***.

An extremely important factor in this reasoning is that ***not everyone in a financial market must be well informed about a security or have rational expectations for its price to be driven to the point at which the efficient markets condition holds***. Financial markets are structured so that many participants can play. As long as a few keep their eyes open for unexploited profit opportunities, they will eliminate the profit opportunities that appear because in so doing, they make a profit. The theory of efficient markets makes sense because it does not require everyone in a market to be cognizant of what is happening to every security.

Stronger Version of Efficient Markets Theory

Many financial economists take efficient markets theory one step further in their analysis of financial markets. Not only do they define efficient markets as those in which expectations are rational, that is, equal to optimal forecasts using all available information, but they also add the condition that an efficient market is one in which prices reflect the true fundamental (intrinsic) value of the securities. Thus in an efficient market, all prices are always correct and reflect **market fundamentals** (items that have a direct impact on future income streams of the securities). This stronger view of market efficiency has several important implications in the academic field of finance. First, it implies that in an efficient capital market, one investment is as good as any other because the securities' prices are correct. Second, it implies that a security's price reflects all available information about the intrinsic value of the security. Third, it implies that security prices can be used by managers of both financial and nonfinancial firms to assess their cost of capital (cost of financing their investments) accurately and hence that security prices can be used to help them make the correct decisions about whether a specific investment is worth making or not. The stronger version of market efficiency is a basic tenet of much analysis in the finance field.

EVIDENCE ON EFFICIENT MARKETS THEORY

Early evidence on efficient markets theory was quite favourable to it, but in recent years, deeper analysis of the evidence suggests that the theory may not always be entirely correct. Let's first look at the earlier evidence in favour of the theory and then examine some of the more recent evidence that casts some doubt on it.

Evidence in Favour of Market Efficiency

Evidence in favour of market efficiency has examined the performance of investment analysts and mutual funds, whether stock prices reflect publicly available information, the random-walk behaviour of stock prices, and the success of so-called technical analysis.

Performance of Investment Analysts and Mutual Funds   We have seen that one implication of efficient markets theory is that when purchasing a security, you cannot expect to earn an abnormally high return, a return greater than the equilibrium return. This implies that it is impossible to beat the market. Many studies shed light on whether investment advisers and mutual funds (some of which charge steep sales commissions to people who purchase them) beat the market. One common test that has been performed is to take buy and sell recommendations from a group of advisers or mutual funds and compare the performance of the resulting selection of stocks with the market as a whole. Sometimes the advisers' choices have even been compared to a group of stocks chosen by throwing darts at a copy of the financial page of the newspaper tacked to a dartboard. The *Wall Street Journal,* for example, has a regular feature called "Investment Dartboard" that compares how well stocks picked by investment advisers do relative to stocks picked by throwing darts. Do the advisers win? To their embarrassment, the dartboard beats them as often as they beat the dartboard. Furthermore, even when the comparison includes only advisers who have been successful in the past in predicting the stock market, the advisers still don't regularly beat the dartboard.

In studies of mutual fund performance, mutual funds are separated into groups according to whether they had the highest or lowest profits in a chosen period. When their performance is compared to that in a subsequent period, the mutual funds that did well in the first period do not beat the market in the second.[5]

The conclusion from the study of investment advisers and mutual fund performance is this: ***having performed well in the past does not indicate that an investment adviser or a mutual fund will perform well in the future***. This is not pleasing news to investment advisers, but it is exactly what the theory of efficient markets predicts. It says that some advisers will be lucky and some will be unlucky. Being lucky does not mean that a forecaster actually has the ability to beat the market. (An exception that proves the rule is discussed in Box 27-1.)

Do Stock Prices Reflect Publicly Available Information?   Efficient markets theory predicts that stock prices will reflect all publicly available information. Thus if information is already publicly available, a positive announcement about a company will not, on average, raise the price of its stock because this information is already reflected in the stock price. Early empirical evidence also confirmed this conjecture from efficient markets theory: favourable earnings announcements or announcements of stock splits (a division of a share of stock into multiple shares, which is usually followed by higher earnings) do not, on average, cause stock prices to rise.[6]

Wall Street Journal
www.wallstreetjournal. com

---

[5]An early study that found that mutual funds do not outperform the market is Michael C. Jensen, "The Performance of Mutual Funds in the Period 1945–64," *Journal of Finance* 23 (1968): 389–416. Further studies on mutual fund performance are Mark Grimblatt and Sheridan Titman, "Mutual Fund Performance: An Analysis of Quarterly Portfolio Holdings," *Journal of Business* 62 (1989): 393–416, and R. A. Ippolito, "Efficiency with Costly Information: A Study of Mutual Fund Performance, 1965–84," *Quarterly Journal of Economics* 104 (1989): 1–23.

[6]Ray Ball and Philip Brown, "An Empirical Evaluation of Accounting Income Numbers," *Journal of Accounting Research* 6 (1968): 159–178, and Eugene F. Fama, Lawrence Fisher, Michael C. Jensen, and Richard Roll, "The Adjustment of Stock Prices to New Information," *International Economic Review* 10 (1969): 1–21.

BOX 27·1

An Exception That Proves the Rule

Ivan Boesky. Efficient markets theory indicates that investment advisers should not have the ability to beat the market. Yet that is exactly what Ivan Boesky was able to do until 1986, when he was charged by the U.S. Securities and Exchange Commission with making unfair profits (rumoured to be in the hundreds of millions of dollars) by trading on inside information. In an out-of-court settlement, Boesky was banned from the securities business, fined $100 million, and sentenced to three years in jail. (After serving his sentence, Boesky was released from jail in 1990.) If the stock market is efficient, can the SEC legitimately claim that Boesky was able to beat the market? The answer is yes.

The most successful of the so-called *arbs* (short for *arbitrageurs*), Ivan Boesky made hundreds of millions in profits for himself and his clients by investing in the stocks of firms that were about to be taken over by other firms at an above-market price. Boesky's continuing success was assured by an arrangement whereby he paid cash (sometimes in a suitcase) to Dennis Levine, an investment banker who had inside information about when a takeover was to take place because his firm was arranging the financing of the deal. When Levine found out that a firm was planning a takeover, he would inform Boesky, who would then buy the stock of the company being taken over and sell it after the stock had risen.

Boesky's ability to make millions year after year in the 1980s is an exception that proves the rule that financial analysts cannot continually outperform the market; yet it supports the efficient markets claim that only information *unavailable to the market* enables an investor to do so. Boesky profited from knowing about takeovers before the rest of the market; this information was known to him but unavailable to the market.

Random-Walk Behaviour of Stock Prices The term **random walk** describes the movements of a variable whose future changes cannot be predicted (are random) because, given today's value, the variable is just as likely to fall as to rise. An important implication of efficient markets theory is that stock prices should approximately follow a random walk; that is, *future changes in stock prices should, for all practical purposes, be unpredictable.* The random-walk implication of efficient markets theory is the one most commonly mentioned in the press because it is the most readily comprehensible to the public. In fact, when people mention the "random-walk theory of stock prices," they are in reality referring to efficient markets theory.

The case for random-walk stock prices can be demonstrated. Suppose that people could predict that the price of Happy Feet Corporation (HFC) stock would rise 1% in the coming week. The predicted rate of capital gains and rate of return on HFC stock would then be over 50% at an annual rate. Since this is very likely to be far higher than the equilibrium rate of return on HFC stock ($RET^{of} > RET^*$), the theory of efficient markets indicates that people would immediately buy this stock and bid up its current price. The action would stop only when the predictable change in the price dropped to near zero so that $RET^{of} = RET^*$.

Similarly, if people could predict that the price of HFC stock would fall by 1%, the predicted rate of return would be negative ($RET^{of} < RET^*$), and people would immediately sell. The current price would fall until the predictable change in the price rose back to near zero, where the efficient markets condition again holds. Efficient markets theory suggests that the predictable change in stock prices will be near zero, leading to the conclusion that stock prices will generally follow a random walk.[7]

Financial economists have used two types of tests to explore the hypothesis that stock prices follow a random walk. In the first, they examine stock market records to see if changes in stock prices are systematically related to past changes and hence could have been predicted on that basis. The second type of test examines the data to see if publicly available information other than past stock prices could have been used to predict changes. These tests are somewhat more stringent because additional information (money supply growth, government spending, interest rates, corporate profits) might be used to help forecast stock returns. Early results from both types of tests generally confirmed the efficient markets view that stock prices are not predictable and follow a random walk.[8]

Technical Analysis   A popular technique used to predict stock prices, called *technical analysis*, is to study past stock price data and search for patterns such as trends and regular cycles. Rules for when to buy and sell stocks are then established on the basis of the patterns that emerge. The theory of efficient markets suggests that technical analysis is a waste of time. The simplest way to understand why is to use the random-walk result derived from efficient markets theory that holds that past stock price data cannot help predict changes. Therefore, technical analysis, which relies on such data to produce its forecasts, cannot successfully predict changes in stock prices.

Two types of tests bear directly on the value of technical analysis. The first performs the empirical analysis described earlier to evaluate the performance of any financial analyst, technical or otherwise. The results are exactly what efficient markets theory predicts. Technical analysts fare no better than other financial analysts; on average, they do not outperform the market, and successful past forecasting does not imply that their forecasts will outperform the market in the future. The second type of test (first performed by Sidney Alexander) takes the rules developed in technical analysis for when to buy and sell stocks and applies them to new data.[9] The performance of these rules is then evaluated by the profits that would have been made using them. These tests also discredit technical analysis. It does not outperform the overall market.

---

[7]Note that the random-walk behaviour of stock prices is only an *approximation* derived from efficient markets theory. It would hold exactly only for a stock for which an unchanged price leads to its having the equilibrium return. Then, when the predictable change in the stock price is exactly zero, $RET^{of} = RET^*$.

[8]The first type of test, using only stock market data, is referred to as a test of *weak-form efficiency* because the information that can be used to predict stock prices is restricted to past price data. The second type of test is referred to as a test of *semistrong-form efficiency* because the information set is expanded to include all publicly available information, not just past stock prices. A third type of test is called a test of *strong-form efficiency* because the information set includes insider information, known only to the managers (directors) of the corporation, as when they plan to declare a high dividend. Strong-form tests do sometimes indicate that insider information can be used to predict changes in stock prices. This finding does not contradict efficient markets theory because the information is not available to the market and hence cannot be reflected in market prices. In fact, there are strict laws against using insider information to trade in financial markets. For an early survey on the three forms of tests, see Eugene F. Fama, "Efficient Capital Markets: A Review of Theory and Empirical Work," *Journal of Finance* 25 (1970): 383–416.

[9]Sidney Alexander, "Price Movements in Speculative Markets: Trends or Random Walks?" *Industrial Management Review,* May 1961, pp. 7–26, and Sidney Alexander, "Price Movements in Speculative Markets: Trends or Random Walks? No. 2," in *The Random Character of Stock Prices,* ed. Paul Cootner (Cambridge, Mass.: MIT Press, 1964), pp. 338–372.

APPLICATION | *Should Foreign Exchange Rates Follow a Random Walk?*

Efficient markets theory can be used to show that foreign exchange rates, like stock prices, should generally follow a random walk. To see why this is the case, consider what would happen if people could predict that a currency would appreciate by 1% in the coming week. By buying this currency, they could earn a greater than 50% return at an annual rate, which is likely to be far above the equilibrium return for holding a currency. As a result, people would immediately buy the currency and bid up its current price, thereby reducing the expected return. The process would stop only when the predictable change in the exchange rate dropped to near zero so that the optimal forecast of the return no longer differed from the equilibrium return. Likewise, if people could predict that the currency would depreciate by 1% in the coming week, they would sell it until the predictable change in the exchange rate was again near zero. Efficient markets theory therefore implies that future changes in exchange rates should, for all practical purposes, be unpredictable; in other words, exchange rates should follow random walks. This is exactly what empirical evidence finds.[10]

Evidence Against Market Efficiency

All the early evidence supporting efficient markets theory appeared to be overwhelming, causing Eugene Fama, a prominent financial economist, to state in his famous 1970 survey of the empirical evidence on efficient markets theory, "The evidence in support of the efficient markets model is extensive, and (somewhat uniquely in economics) contradictory evidence is sparse."[11] However, in recent years, the theory has begun to show a few cracks, referred to as *anomalies*, and empirical evidence indicates that efficient markets theory may not always be generally applicable.

Small-Firm Effect One of the earliest reported anomalies in which the stock market did not appear to be efficient is called the *small-firm effect*. Many empirical studies have shown that small firms have earned abnormally high returns over long periods of time, even when the greater risk for these firms has been taken into account.[12] The small-firm effect seems to have diminished in recent years but is still a challenge to the theory of efficient markets. Various theories have been developed to explain the small-firm effect, suggesting that it may be due to rebalancing of portfolios by institutional investors, tax issues, low liquidity of small-firm stocks, large information costs in evaluating small firms, or an inappropriate measurement of risk for small-firm stocks.

January Effect Over long periods of time, stock prices have tended to experience an abnormal price rise from December to January that is predictable and hence

---

[10]See Richard A. Meese and Kenneth Rogoff, "Empirical Exchange Rate Models of the Seventies: Do They Fit Out of Sample?" *Journal of International Economics* 14 (1983): 3–24.

[11]Eugene F. Fama, "Efficient Capital Markets: A Review of Theory and Empirical Work," *Journal of Finance* 25 (1970): 383–416.

[12]For example, see Marc R. Reinganum, "The Anomalous Stock Market Behaviour of Small Firms in January: Empirical Tests of Tax Loss Selling Effects," *Journal of Financial Economics* 12 (1983): 89–104; Jay R. Ritter, "The Buying and Selling Behaviour of Individual Investors at the Turn of the Year," *Journal of Finance* 43 (1988): 701–717; and Richard Roll, "Vas Ist Das? The Turn-of-the-Year Effect: Anomaly or Risk Mismeasurement?" *Journal of Portfolio Management* 9 (1988): 18–28.

inconsistent with random-walk behaviour. This so-called **January effect** seems to have diminished in recent years for shares of large companies but still occurs for shares of small companies.[13] Some financial economists argue that the January effect is due to tax issues. Investors have an incentive to sell stocks before the end of the year in December because they can then take capital losses on their tax return and reduce their tax liability. Then when the new year starts in January, they can repurchase the stocks, driving up their prices and producing abnormally high returns. Although this explanation seems sensible, it does not explain why institutional investors such as private pension funds, which are not subject to income taxes, do not take advantage of the abnormal returns in January and buy stocks in December, thus bidding up their price and eliminating the abnormal returns.[14]

Market Overreaction   Recent research suggests that stock prices may overreact to news announcements and that the pricing errors are corrected only slowly.[15] When corporations announce a major change in earnings, say a large decline, the stock price may overshoot, and after an initial large decline, it may rise back to more normal levels over a period of several weeks. This violates efficient markets theory because an investor could earn abnormally high returns, on average, by buying a stock immediately after a poor earnings announcement and then selling it after a couple of weeks when it has risen back to normal levels.

Yale University
www.yale.edu

Excessive Volatility   A phenomenon closely related to market overreaction is that the stock market appears to display excessive volatility; that is, fluctuations in stock prices may be much greater than is warranted by fluctuations in their fundamental value. In an important paper, Robert Shiller of Yale University found that fluctuations in the S&P 500 stock index could not be justified by the subsequent fluctuations in the dividends of the stocks making up this index. There has been much subsequent technical work criticizing these results, but Shiller's work, along with research finding that there are smaller fluctuations in stock prices when stock markets are closed, has produced a consensus that stock market prices appear to be driven by factors other than fundamentals.[16]

Mean Reversion   Some researchers have also found that stock returns display **mean reversion**. Stocks with low returns today tend to have high returns in the future, and vice versa. Hence stocks that have done poorly in the past are more likely to do well in the future because mean reversion indicates that there will be a predictable positive change in the future price, suggesting that stock prices are not a random walk. Other researchers have found that mean reversion is not nearly as strong in data after World War II and so have raised doubts

---

[13]For example, see Donald B. Keim, "The CAPM and Equity Return Regularities," *Financial Analysts Journal* 42 (May–June 1986): 19–34.

[14]Another anomaly that makes the stock market seem less than efficient is the fact that the *Value Line Survey*, one of the most prominent investment advice newsletters, has produced stock recommendations that have yielded abnormally high returns on average. See Fischer Black, "Yes, Virginia, There Is Hope: Tests of the Value Line Ranking System," *Financial Analysts Journal* 29 (September–October 1973): 10–14, and Gur Huberman and Shmuel Kandel, "Market Efficiency and Value Line's Record," *Journal of Business* 63 (1990): 187–216. Whether the excellent performance of the *Value Line Survey* will continue in the future is, of course, a question mark.

[15]Werner De Bondt and Richard Thaler, "Further Evidence on Investor Overreaction and Stock Market Seasonality," *Journal of Finance* 62 (1987): 557–580.

[16]Robert Shiller, "Do Stock Prices Move Too Much to Be Justified by Subsequent Changes in Dividends?" *American Economic Review* 71 (1981): 421–436, and Kenneth R. French and Richard Roll, "Stock Return Variances: The Arrival of Information and the Reaction of Traders," *Journal of Financial Economics* 17 (1986): 5–26.

about whether it is currently an important phenomenon. The evidence on mean reversion remains controversial.[17]

Chaos and Fractals   Some researchers have also found evidence of chaotic dynamics in asset prices. The possible existence of **chaos** could be exploitable and even invaluable, as it implies that profitable, nonlinearity-based trading rules exist at least in the short run, and provided the actual generating mechanism is known. Prediction, however, over long periods is all but impossible, due to a property of chaos known as sensitive dependence on initial conditions.[18]

In related literature, the famous mathematician Benoit Mandelbrot of Yale University has introduced complex geometric patterns in the description of financial markets, similar to those that describe the shapes of coastlines, ferns, and galaxies throughout the cosmos. Mandelbrot argues that charts of asset prices are **fractal curves** and applies many powerful tools of mathematical and computer analyses to explain how such prices soar and plummet.[19]

Recently there has been considerable criticism of the existing research on nonlinear dynamics in economics and finance. However, as William Barnett of Washington University in St. Louis and Apostolos Serletis of the University of Calgary report, "in the field of economics, it is especially unwise to take a strong opinion (either pro or con) in that area of research. Contrary to popular opinion within the profession, there have been no published tests of chaos 'within the structure of the economic system,' and there is very little chance that any such tests will be available in this field for a very long time. Such tests are simply beyond the state of the art."[20]

Washington University
www.washu.edu

University of Calgary
www.ucalgary.ca

Overview of the Evidence on Efficient Markets Theory

As you can see, the debate on efficient markets theory is far from over. The evidence seems to suggest that efficient markets theory may be a reasonable starting point for evaluating behaviour in financial markets. However, there do seem to be important violations of market efficiency that suggest that efficient markets theory may not be the whole story and so may not be generalizable to all behaviour in financial markets.

[17]Evidence for mean reversion has been reported by James M. Poterba and Lawrence H. Summers, "Mean Reversion in Stock Prices: Evidence and Implications," *Journal of Financial Economics* 22 (1988): 27–59; Eugene F. Fama and Kenneth R. French, "Permanent and Temporary Components of Stock Prices," *Journal of Political Economy* 96 (1988): 246–273; and Andrew W. Lo and A. Craig MacKinlay, "Stock Market Prices Do Not Follow Random Walks: Evidence from a Simple Specification Test," *Review of Financial Studies* 1 (1988): 41–66. However, Myung Jig Kim, Charles R. Nelson, and Richard Startz, in "Mean Reversion in Stock Prices? A Reappraisal of the Evidence," *Review of Economic Studies* 58 (1991): 515–528, question whether some of these findings are valid. For an excellent summary of this evidence, see Charles Engel and Charles S. Morris, "Challenges to Stock Market Efficiency: Evidence from Mean Reversion Studies," *Federal Reserve Bank of Kansas City Economic Review,* September–October 1991, pp. 21–35. See also N. Jegadeesh and Sheridan Titman, "Returns to Buying Winners and Selling Losers: Implications for Stock Market Efficiency," *Journal of Finance* 48 (1993): 65–92, which shows that mean reversion also occurs for individual stocks.

[18]Evidence for chaotic dynamics on financial data has been reported by José A. Scheinkman and Blake Lebaron, "Nonlinear Dynamics and Stock Returns," *Journal of Business* 62 (1989): 311-337; Murray Frank and Thanasis Stengos, "Measuring the Strangeness of Gold and Silver Rates of Return," *Review of Economic Studies* 56 (1989): 553-567; and Apostolos Serletis and Periklis Gogas, "Chaos in East European Black-Market Exchange Rates," *Research in Economics* 51 (1997): 359-385.

[19]See, for example, Benoit B. Mandelbrot, "A Multifractal Walk down Wall Street," *Scientific American* February (1999): 70-73.

[20]William A. Barnett and Apostolos Serletis, "Martingales, Nonlinearity, and Chaos," *Journal of Economic Dynamics and Control* 24 (2000): 703-724.

| APPLICATION | *Practical Guide to Investing in the Stock Market* |

Efficient markets theory has numerous applications to the real world. It is especially valuable because it can be applied directly to an issue that concerns many of us: how to get rich (or at least not get poor) in the stock market. (The "Following the Financial News" box shows how stock prices are reported daily.) A practical guide to investing in the stock market, which we develop here, provides a better understanding of the use and implications of efficient markets theory.

FOLLOWING THE FINANCIAL NEWS

Stock Prices

Stock prices are published daily in most daily newspapers. *The Globe and Mail: Report on Business* provides quotations for companies listed on the Toronto and Montreal stock exchanges and the Canadian Venture Exchange in Canada as well as for companies listed on the New York, Nasdaq, and American stock exchanges in the United States. The stocks' prices are quoted in the following format (companies listed on the Toronto exchange are used as an example):

52 Week high	low	Stock	Sym	Div	High	Low	Close	Chg	Vol (100s)	Yield	P/E ratio
20.95	13.60	♣Noranda	NOR	0.80	14.25	13.80	14.25	+0.35	4937	5.6	11.9
11.50	7.00	♣Normndy	NDY	0.60	8.25	7.85	8.00	+0.15	27	7.5	11.1
46.00	4.00	Norsat Intl	NII		9.60	8.50	8.50	-1.25	95		
124.5	40.87	♣Nortel Net	NT	.113	75.00	69.85	71.55	-24.50	5108134	0.2	

Source: The Globe and Mail: Report on Business, October 26, 2000, p. B28. Reprinted with permission.

The following information is included in each column. Nortel Networks (Nortel Net) common stock is used as an example.

52-week high: Highest price of a share in the past 52 weeks: 124.50 for Nortel Networks stock
52-week low: Lowest price of a share in the past 52 weeks: 40.87 for Nortel Networks stock
Stock: Company name: Nortel Net for Nortel Networks
Sym: Symbol that identifies company: NT
Div: Annual dividends (excluding special dividends): .113 for Nortel Networks stock
High: Highest price of a share that day: 75.00
Low: Lowest price of a share that day: 69.85

Close: Closing price (last price) that day: 71.55
Chg: Change in the closing price from the previous day: -24.50
Vol (100s): Number of shares (in hundreds) traded that day: 5108134
Yield %: Yield expressed as a percentage, calculated by dividing annual dividends by today's closing price: .2% (=.113/71.55) for Nortel Networks stock.
P/E ratio: Price-earnings ratio; the stock price divided by the amount the corporation earned per share over the past year. The P/E ratio is not shown if greater than 100.

♣indicates that free annual or quarterly reports are available

Should You Hire an Ape as Your Investment Adviser?

The *San Francisco Chronicle* came up with an amusing way of evaluating how successful investment advisers are at picking stocks. They asked eight analysts to pick five stocks at the beginning of the year and then compared the performance of their stock picks to those chosen by Jolyn, an orangutan living at Marine World/ Africa in Vallejo, California. Consistent with the results found in the "Investment Dartboard" feature of the *Wall Street Journal,* Jolyn beat the investment advisers as often as they beat her. Given this result, you might be just as well off hiring an orangutan as your investment adviser as you would hiring a human being!

**How Valuable
Are Published
Reports by
Investment
Advisers?**

Suppose you have just read in the *Globe and Mail: Report on Business* that investment advisers are predicting a boom in oil stocks because an oil shortage is developing. Should you proceed to withdraw all your hard-earned savings from the bank and invest them in oil stocks?

Efficient markets theory tells us that when purchasing a security, we cannot expect to earn an abnormally high return, a return greater than the equilibrium return. Information in newspapers and in the published reports of investment advisers is readily available to many market participants and is already reflected in market prices. So acting on this information will not yield abnormally high returns, on average. As we have seen, the empirical evidence for the most part confirms that recommendations from investment advisers cannot help us outperform the general market. Indeed, as Box 27-2 suggests, human investment advisers in San Francisco do not on average even outperform an orangutan!

Probably no other conclusion is met with more scepticism by students than this one when they first hear it. We all know or have heard of somebody who has been successful in the stock market for a period of many years. We wonder, how could someone be so consistently successful if he or she did not really know how to predict when returns would be abnormally high? The following story, reported in the press, illustrates why such anecdotal evidence is not reliable.

A get-rich-quick artist invented a clever scam. Every week, he wrote two letters. In letter A, he would pick team A to win a particular football game, and in letter B, he would pick the opponent, team B. A mailing list would then be separated into two groups, and he would send letter A to the people in one group and letter B to the people in the other. The following week he would do the same thing but would send these letters only to the group who had received the first letter with the correct prediction. After doing this for ten games, he had a small cluster of people who had received letters predicting the correct winning team for every game. He then mailed a final letter to them, declaring that since he was obviously an expert predictor of the outcome of football games (he had picked winners ten weeks in a row) and since his predictions were profitable for the recipients who bet on the games, he would continue to send his predictions only if he were paid a substantial amount of money. When one of his clients figured out what he was up to, the con man was prosecuted and thrown in jail!

What is the lesson of the story? Even if no forecaster is an accurate predictor of the market, there will always be a group of consistent winners. A person who has done well regularly in the past cannot guarantee that he or she will do well in the future. Note that there will also be a group of persistent losers, but you rarely hear about them because no one brags about a poor forecasting record.

Should You Be Sceptical of Hot Tips?

Suppose your broker phones you with a hot tip to buy stock in the Happy Feet Corporation (HFC) because it has just developed a product that is completely effective in curing athlete's foot. The stock price is sure to go up. Should you follow this advice and buy HFC stock?

Efficient markets theory indicates that you should be sceptical of such news. If the stock market is efficient, it has already priced HFC stock so that its expected return will equal the equilibrium return. The hot tip is not particularly valuable and will not enable you to earn an abnormally high return.

You might wonder, though, if the hot tip is based on new information and would give you an edge on the rest of the market. If other market participants have gotten this information before you, the answer is no. As soon as the information hits the street, the unexploited profit opportunity it creates will be quickly eliminated. The stock's price will already reflect the information, and you should expect to realize only the equilibrium return. But if you are one of the first to gain the new information (as Ivan Boesky was—see Box 27-1), it can do you some good. Only then can you be one of the lucky ones who, on average, will earn an abnormally high return by helping eliminate the profit opportunity by buying HFC stock.

Do Stock Prices Always Rise When There Is Good News?

If you follow the stock market, you might have noticed a puzzling phenomenon: when good news about a stock, such as a particularly favourable earnings report, is announced, the price of the stock frequently does not rise. Efficient markets theory and the random-walk behaviour of stock prices explain this phenomenon.

Because changes in stock prices are unpredictable, when information is announced that has already been expected by the market, the stock price will remain unchanged. The announcement does not contain any new information that should lead to a change in stock prices. If this were not the case and the announcement led to a change in stock prices, it would mean that the change was predictable. Because that is ruled out in an efficient market, **stock prices will respond to announcements only when the information being announced is new and unexpected.** If the news is expected, there will be no stock price response. This is exactly what the evidence we described earlier, which shows that stock prices reflect publicly available information, suggests will occur.

Sometimes an individual stock price declines when good news is announced. Although this seems somewhat peculiar, it is completely consistent with the workings of an efficient market. Suppose that although the announced news is good, it is not as good as expected. HFC's earnings may have risen 15%, but if the market expected earnings to rise by 20%, the new information is actually unfavourable, and the stock price declines.

Efficient Markets Prescription for the Investor

What does the theory of efficient markets recommend for investing in the stock market? It tells us that hot tips, investment advisers' published recommendations, and technical analysis—all of which make use of publicly available information—cannot help an investor outperform the market. Indeed, it indicates that anyone without better information than other market participants cannot expect to beat the market. So what is an investor to do?

Efficient markets theory leads to the conclusion that such an investor (and almost all of us fit into this category) should not try to outguess the market by constantly buying and selling securities. This process does nothing but boost the income of brokers, who earn commissions on each trade.[21] Instead, the investor should pursue a "buy and hold" strategy—purchase stocks and hold them for long periods of time. This will lead to the same returns, on average, but the investor's net profits will be higher because fewer brokerage commissions will have to be paid.

---

[21]The investor may also have to pay capital gains taxes on any profits that are realized when a security is sold—an additional reason why continual buying and selling does not make sense.

It is frequently a sensible strategy for a small investor, whose costs of managing a portfolio may be high relative to its size, to buy into a mutual fund rather than individual stocks. Because efficient markets theory indicates that no mutual fund can consistently outperform the market, an investor should not buy into one that has high management fees or that pays sales commissions to brokers but rather should purchase a no-load (commission-free) mutual fund that has low management fees.

As we have seen, the evidence indicates that it will not be easy to beat the prescription suggested here, although some of the anomalies to efficient markets theory suggest that an extremely clever investor (which rules out most of us) may be able to outperform a buy-and-hold strategy.

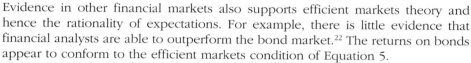

EVIDENCE ON RATIONAL EXPECTATIONS IN OTHER MARKETS

Evidence in other financial markets also supports efficient markets theory and hence the rationality of expectations. For example, there is little evidence that financial analysts are able to outperform the bond market.[22] The returns on bonds appear to conform to the efficient markets condition of Equation 5.

University of Toronto
www.utoronto.ca

Rationality of expectations is, however, much harder to test in markets other than financial markets because price data that reflect expectations are not as readily available. The most common tests of rational expectations in these markets make use of survey data on the forecasts of market participants. For example, one well-known study by James Pesando of the University of Toronto used a survey of inflation expectations collected from prominent economists and inflation forecasters.[23] In that survey, these people were asked what they predicted the inflation rate would be over the next six months and over the next year. Because rational expectations theory implies that forecast errors should on average be zero and cannot be predicted, tests of the theory involve asking whether the forecast errors in a survey could be predicted ahead of time using publicly available information. The evidence from Pesando's and subsequent studies is mixed. Sometimes the forecast errors cannot be predicted, and at other times they can. The evidence is not as supportive of rational expectations theory as the evidence from financial markets.

Does the fact that forecast errors from surveys are often predictable suggest that we should reject rational expectations theory in these other markets? The answer is not necessarily. One problem with this evidence is that the expectations data are obtained from surveys rather than from actual economic decisions of market participants. That is a serious criticism of this evidence. Survey responses are not always reliable because there is little incentive for participants to tell the truth. For example, when people are asked in surveys how much television they watch, responses greatly underestimate the actual time spent. Neither are people very truthful about the shows they watch. They may say they watch ballet on public television, but we know they are actually watching Vanna White turn letters on *Wheel of Fortune* instead, because it, not ballet, gets high ratings. How many people will admit to being regular watchers of *Wheel of Fortune?*

A second problem with survey evidence is that a market's behaviour may not be equally influenced by the expectations of all the survey participants, making

---

[22]See the discussion in Frederic S. Mishkin, "Efficient Markets Theory: Implications for Monetary Policy," *Brookings Papers on Economic Activity* 3 (1978): 707–768, of the results in Michael J. Prell, "How Well Do the Experts Forecast Interest Rates?" *Federal Reserve Bank of Kansas City Monthly Review,* September–October 1973, pp. 3–15.

[23]James Pesando, "A Note on the Rationality of the Livingston Price Expectations," *Journal of Political Economy* 83 (1975): 845–858.

survey evidence a poor guide to market behaviour. For example, we have already seen that prices in financial markets often *behave* as if expectations are rational even though many of the market participants do not have rational expectations.[24]

Proof is not yet conclusive on the validity of rational expectations theory in markets other than financial markets. One important conclusion, however, that is supported by the survey evidence is that ***if there is a change in the way a variable moves, there will be a change in the way expectations of this variable are formed as well.***

APPLICATION | *What Does the Stock Market Crash of 1987 Tell Us About Rational Expectations and Efficient Markets?*

Many economists have suggested that the October 19, 1987, stock market crash should make us question the validity of efficient markets and rational expectations. They do not believe that a rational marketplace could have produced such a massive swing in share prices. To what degree should the stock market crash make us doubt the validity of rational expectations and efficient markets theory?

Nothing in rational expectations theory rules out large one-day changes in stock prices. A large change in stock prices can result from new information that produces a dramatic change in optimal forecasts of the future valuation of firms. Some economists have pointed out that there are many possible explanations for why rational expectations of the future value of firms dropped dramatically on October 19, 1987: moves in the U.S. Congress to restrict corporate takeovers, the disappointing performance of the U.S. trade deficit, failure to reduce the budget deficit substantially, increased fears of inflation, and increased fears of financial distress in the banking industry. Other economists doubt whether these explanations are enough to explain the stock market drop because none of these market fundamentals seems important enough.

One lesson from the Black Monday stock market crash appears to be that factors other than market fundamentals may have had an effect on stock prices. The crash of 1987 has therefore convinced many economists that the stronger version of efficient markets theory, which states that asset prices reflect the true fundamental (intrinsic) value of securities, is incorrect. They attribute a large role in determination of stock prices to market psychology and to the institutional structure of the marketplace. However, nothing in this view contradicts the basic reasoning behind rational expectations or efficient markets theory—that market participants eliminate unexploited profit opportunities. Even though stock market prices may not always solely reflect market fundamentals, this does not mean that rational expectations do not hold. As long as the stock market crash was unpredictable, the basic lessons of the theory of rational expectations hold.

Some economists have come up with theories of what they call *rational bubbles* to explain events such as the stock market crash. A **bubble** is a situation in which the price of an asset differs from its fundamental market value. In a rational bubble, investors can have rational expectations that a bubble is occurring because the asset price is above its fundamental value but continue to hold the asset anyway. They might do this because they believe that someone else will buy

---

[24]There is some fairly strong evidence for this proposition. For example, Frederic S. Mishkin, "Are Market Forecasts Rational?" *American Economic Review* 71 (1981): 295–306, finds that although survey forecasts of short-term interest rates are not rational, the bond market *behaves* as if the expectations of these interest rates are rational.

the asset for a higher price in the future. In a rational bubble, asset prices can therefore deviate from their fundamental value for a long time because the bursting of the bubble cannot be predicted and so there are no unexploited profit opportunities.

However, other economists believe that the stock market crash of 1987 suggests that there may be unexploited profit opportunities and that the theory of rational expectations and efficient markets theory may be fundamentally flawed. The controversy over whether capital markets are efficient or expectations are rational continues.

SUMMARY

1. Expectations are important to almost all economic behaviour.

2. The theory of rational expectations states that expectations will not differ from optimal forecasts (the best guesses of the future) using all available information. Rational expectations theory makes sense because it is costly for people not to have the best forecast of the future. The theory has two important implications: (a) If there is a change in the way a variable moves, there will be a change in the way expectations of this variable are formed, too, and (b) the forecast errors of expectations are unpredictable.

3. Efficient markets theory is the application of rational expectations to the pricing of securities in financial markets. Current security prices will fully reflect all available information because in an efficient market, all unexploited profit opportunities are eliminated. The elimination of unexploited profit opportunities necessary for a financial market to be efficient does not require that all market participants be well informed and have rational expectations.

4. The evidence on efficient markets theory is quite mixed. Early evidence on the performance of investment analysts and mutual funds, whether stock prices reflect publicly available information, the random-walk behaviour of stock prices, and the success of so-called technical analysis was quite favourable to efficient markets theory. In recent years, however, evidence on the small-firm effect, the January effect, the Value Line Survey, market overreaction, excessive volatility, mean reversion,

and chaotic dynamics suggests that the theory may not always be entirely correct. The evidence seems to suggest that efficient markets theory may be a reasonable starting point for evaluating behaviour in financial markets but may not be generalizable to all behaviour in financial markets.

5. Efficient markets theory indicates that hot tips, investment advisers' published recommendations, and technical analysis cannot help an investor outperform the market. The prescription for investors is to pursue a buy-and-hold strategy—purchase stocks and hold them for long periods of time. Empirical evidence generally supports these implications of efficient markets theory in the stock market.

6. Although the evidence supporting rational expectations in financial markets is strong, the evidence in other markets is more mixed. However, even for these other markets, there is support for the rational expectations conclusion that a change in the way a variable moves will change the way that expectations of the variable are formed.

7. The stock market crash of 1987 has convinced many economists that the stronger version of efficient markets theory, which states that asset prices reflect the true fundamental (intrinsic) value of securities, is not correct. It is less clear that the stock market crash shows that rational expectations theory is wrong. Even if the stock market was driven by factors other than fundamentals, the crash does not clearly demonstrate that expectations were not rational as long as the crash could not have been predicted.

KEY TERMS

adaptive expectations, p. 613

bubble, p. 629

chaos, p. 624

efficient markets theory, p. 615

fractal curve, p. 624

January effect, p. 623

market fundamentals, p. 618

mean reversion, p. 623

optimal forecast, p. 614

random walk, p. 620

rational expectations, p. 613

unexploited profit opportunity, p. 617

QUESTIONS AND PROBLEMS

Questions marked with an asterisk are answered at the end of the book in an appendix, "Answers to Selected Questions and Problems."

*1. "Forecasters' predictions of inflation are notoriously inaccurate, so their expectations of inflation cannot be rational." Is this statement true, false, or uncertain? Explain your answer.

2. "Whenever it is snowing when Joe Commuter gets up in the morning, he misjudges how long it will take him to drive to work. Otherwise, his expectations of the driving time are perfectly accurate. Considering that it snows only once every ten years where Joe lives, Joe's expectations are almost always perfectly accurate." Are Joe's expectations rational? Why or why not?

*3. If a forecaster spends hours every day studying data to forecast interest rates but his expectations are not as accurate as predicting that tomorrow's interest rates will be identical to today's interest rate, are his expectations rational?

4. "If stock prices did not follow a random walk, there would be unexploited profit opportunities in the market." Is this statement true, false, or uncertain? Explain your answer.

*5. In Chapter 25 you studied why stock prices might rise when the money supply rises. Does this mean that when you see that the money supply has risen sharply in the past week, you should go out and buy stocks? Why or why not?

6. If the public expects a corporation to lose $5 a share this quarter and it actually loses $4, which is still the largest loss in the history of the company, what does efficient markets theory say will happen to the price of the stock when the $4 loss is announced?

*7. If I read in the *Globe and Mail: Report on Business* that the "smart money" on Bay Street expects stock prices to fall, should I follow that lead and sell all my stocks?

8. If my broker has been right in her five previous buy and sell recommendations, should I continue listening to her advice?

*9. Can a person with rational expectations expect the price of IBM to rise by 10% in the next month?

10. "If most participants in the stock market do not follow what is happening to the monetary aggregates, prices of common stocks will not fully reflect information about them." Is this statement true, false, or uncertain? Explain your answer.

*11. "An efficient market is one in which no one ever profits from having better information than the rest." Is this statement true, false, or uncertain? Explain your answer.

12. If higher money growth is associated with higher future inflation and if announced money growth turns out to be extremely high but is still less than the market expected, what do you think would happen to long-term bond prices?

*13. "Foreign exchange rates, like stock prices, should follow a random walk." Is this statement true, false, or uncertain? Explain your answer.

14. Can we expect the value of the dollar to rise by 2% next week if our expectations are rational?

*15. "Human fear is the source of stock market crashes, so these crashes indicate that expectations in the stock market cannot be rational." Is this statement true, false, or uncertain? Explain your answer.

Chapter 28

Rational Expectations: Implications for Policy

After World War II, economists, armed with Keynesian models (such as the *ISLM* model) that described how government policies could be used to manipulate employment and output, felt that activist policies could reduce the severity of business cycle fluctuations without creating inflation. In the 1960s and 1970s, these economists got their chance to put their policies into practice (see Chapter 26), but the results were not what they had anticipated. The economic record for that period is not a happy one. Inflation accelerated, the rate often climbing above 10%, while unemployment figures deteriorated from those of the 1950s.[1]

In the 1970s and 1980s, economists, including Robert Lucas of the University of Chicago and Thomas Sargent of Stanford University and the University of Chicago, used rational expectations theory to examine why activist policies appear to have performed so poorly. Their analysis cast doubt on whether macroeconomic models can be used to evaluate the potential effects of policy and on whether policy can be effective when the public *expects* that it will be implemented. Because the analysis of Lucas and Sargent has such strong implications for the way policy should be conducted, it has been labelled the *rational expectations revolution*.[2]

This chapter examines the analysis behind the rational expectations revolution. We start first with the Lucas critique, which indicates that because expectations are important in economic behaviour, it may be quite difficult to predict what the outcome of an activist policy will be. We then discuss the effect of rational expectations on the aggregate demand and supply analysis developed in Chapter 24 by exploring three models that incorporate expectations in different ways.

A comparison of all three models indicates that the existence of rational expectations makes activist policies less likely to be successful and raises the issue of credibility as an important element affecting policy outcomes. With rational expectations, an essential ingredient to a successful anti-inflation policy is the

---

[1]Some of the deterioration can be attributed to supply shocks in 1973–1975 and 1978–1980.

[2]Other economists who have been active in promoting the rational expectations revolution are Robert Barro of Harvard University, Bennett McCallum of Carnegie-Mellon University, Edward Prescott of the University of Minnesota, and Neil Wallace of Pennsylvania State University.

credibility of the policy in the eyes of the public. The rational expectations revolution is now at the centre of many of the current debates in monetary theory that have major implications for how monetary and fiscal policy should be conducted.

THE LUCAS CRITIQUE OF POLICY EVALUATION

In his famous paper "Econometric Policy Evaluation: A Critique," Robert Lucas presented an argument that had devastating implications for the usefulness of conventional **econometric models** (models whose equations are estimated with statistical procedures) for evaluating policy.[3] Economists developed these models for two purposes: to forecast economic activity and to evaluate the effects of different policies. Although Lucas's critique had nothing to say about the usefulness of these models as forecasting tools, he argued that they could not be relied on to evaluate the potential impact of particular policies on the economy.

Econometric Policy Evaluation

To understand Lucas's argument, we must first understand econometric policy evaluation: how econometric models are used to evaluate policy. For example, we can examine how the Bank of Canada uses its econometric model in making decisions about the future course of monetary policy. The model contains equations that describe the relationships among hundreds of variables. These relationships are assumed to remain constant and are estimated using past data. Let's say that the Bank wants to know the effect on unemployment and inflation of a decrease in the overnight rate from 5% to 4%. It feeds the new, lower overnight rate into a computer that contains the model, and the model then provides an answer about how much unemployment will fall as a result of the lower overnight rate and how much the inflation rate will rise. Other possible policies, such as a rise in the overnight rate by one percentage point, might also be fed into the model. After a series of these policies have been tried out, the policymakers at the Bank can see which policies produce the most desirable outcome for unemployment and inflation.

Lucas's challenge to this procedure for evaluating policies is based on a simple principle of rational expectations theory. *The way in which expectations are formed (the relationship of expectations to past information) changes when the behaviour of forecasted variables changes.* So when policy changes, the relationship between expectations and past information will change, and because expectations affect economic behaviour, the relationships in the econometric model will change. The econometric model, which has been estimated with past data, is then no longer the correct model for evaluating the response to this policy change and may consequently prove highly misleading.

Example: The Term Structure of Interest Rates

The best way to understand Lucas's argument is to look at a concrete example involving only one equation typically found in econometric models: the term structure equation. The equation relates the long-term interest rate to current and past values of the short-term interest rate. It is one of the most important equations in Keynesian econometric models because the long-term interest rate, not the short-term rate, is the one believed to have an impact on aggregate demand.

In Chapter 6 we learned that the long-term interest rate is related to an average of expected future short-term interest rates. Suppose that in the past, when the short-term rate rose, it quickly fell back down again; that is, any increase was tem-

---

[3] *Carnegie-Rochester Conference Series on Public Policy* 1 (1976): 19–46.

porary. Because rational expectations theory suggests that any rise in the short-term interest rate is expected to be only temporary, a rise should have only a minimal effect on the average of expected future short-term rates. It will cause the long-term interest rate to rise by a negligible amount. The term structure relationship estimated using past data would then show only a weak effect on the long-term interest rate of changes in the short-term rate.

Suppose the Bank of Canada wants to evaluate what will happen to the economy if it pursues a policy that is likely to raise the short-term interest rate from a current level of 5% to a permanently higher level of 8%. The term structure equation that has been estimated using past data will indicate that there will be just a small change in the long-term interest rate. However, if the public recognizes that the short-term rate is rising to a permanently higher level, rational expectations theory indicates that people will no longer expect a rise in the short-term rate to be temporary. Instead, when they see the interest rate rise to 8%, they will expect the average of future short-term interest rates to rise substantially, and so the long-term interest rate will rise greatly, not minimally as the estimated term structure equation suggests. You can see that evaluating the likely outcome of the change in Bank of Canada policy with an econometric model can be highly misleading.

The term structure example also demonstrates another aspect of the Lucas critique. The effects of a particular policy depend critically on the public's expectations about the policy. If the public expects the rise in the short-term interest rate to be merely temporary, the response of long-term interest rates, as we have seen, will be negligible. If, however, the public expects the rise to be more permanent, the response of long-term rates will be far greater. ***The Lucas critique points out not only that conventional econometric models cannot be used for policy evaluation but also that the public's expectations about a policy will influence the response to that policy.***

The term structure equation discussed here is only one of many equations in econometric models to which the Lucas critique applies. In fact, Lucas uses the examples of consumption and investment equations in his paper. One attractive feature of the term structure example is that it deals with expectations in a financial market, a sector of the economy for which the theory and empirical evidence supporting rational expectations are very strong. The Lucas critique should also apply, however, to sectors of the economy for which rational expectations theory is more controversial because the basic principle of the Lucas critique is not that expectations are always rational but rather that the formation of expectations changes when the behaviour of a forecasted variable changes. This less stringent principle is supported by the evidence in sectors of the economy other than financial markets.

NEW CLASSICAL MACROECONOMIC MODEL

We now turn to the implications of rational expectations for the aggregate demand and supply analysis we studied in Chapter 24. The first model we examine that views expectations as rational is the *new classical macroeconomic model* developed by Robert Lucas and Thomas Sargent, among others. In the new classical model, all wages and prices are completely flexible with respect to expected changes in the price level; that is, a rise in the expected price level results in an immediate and equal rise in wages and prices because workers try to keep their *real* wages from falling when they expect the price level to rise.

This view of how wages and prices are set indicates that a rise in the expected price level causes an immediate leftward shift in the aggregate supply curve, which leaves real wages unchanged and aggregate output at the natural rate (full-employment) level if expectations are realized. This model then suggests that anticipated policy has no effect on aggregate output and unemployment; only unanticipated policy has an effect.

Effects of Unanticipated and Anticipated Policy

First, let us look at the short-run response to an unanticipated (unexpected) policy such as an unexpected increase in the money supply.

In Figure 28-1, the aggregate supply curve AS_1 is drawn for an expected price level P_1. The initial aggregate demand curve AD_1 intersects AS_1 at point 1, where the realized price level is at the expected price level P_1 and aggregate output is at the natural rate level Y_n. Because point 1 is also on the long-run aggregate supply curve at Y_n, there is no tendency for the aggregate supply to shift. The economy remains in long-run equilibrium.

Suppose the Bank of Canada suddenly decides the unemployment rate is too high and so makes a large bond purchase that is unexpected by the public. The money supply increases, and the aggregate demand curve shifts rightward to AD_2. Because this shift is unexpected, the expected price level remains at P_1 and the aggregate supply curve remains at AS_1. Equilibrium is now at point 2', the intersection of AD_2 and AS_1. Aggregate output increases above the natural rate level to $Y_{2'}$ and the realized price level increases to $P_{2'}$.

If, by contrast, the public expects that the Bank of Canada will make these open market purchases in order to lower unemployment because they have seen it done in the past, the expansionary policy will be anticipated. The outcome of such anticipated expansionary policy is illustrated in Figure 28-2. Because expectations are rational, workers and firms recognize that an expansionary policy will shift the aggregate demand curve to the right and will expect the aggregate price level to rise to P_2. Workers will demand higher wages so that their real earnings will remain the same when the price level rises. The aggregate supply curve then

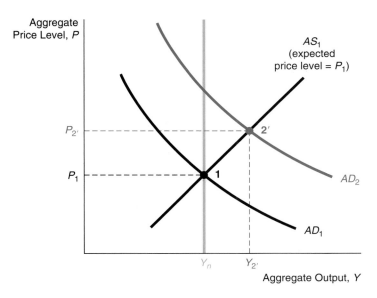

FIGURE 28-1   Short-Run Response to Unanticipated Expansionary Policy in the New Classical Model

Initially, the economy is at point 1 at the intersection of AD_1 and AS_1 (expected price level $= P_1$). An expansionary policy shifts the aggregate demand curve to AD_2, but because this is unexpected, the aggregate supply curve remains fixed at AS_1. Equilibrium now occurs at point 2'—aggregate output has increased above the natural rate level to $Y_{2'}$, and the price level has increased to $P_{2'}$.

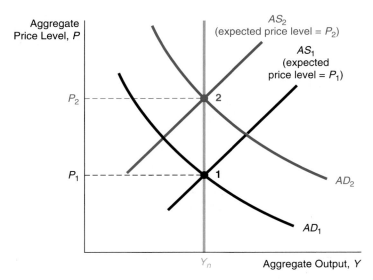

FIGURE 28-2 Short-Run Response to Anticipated Expansionary Policy in the New Classical Model

The expansionary policy shifts the aggregate demand curve rightward to AD_2, but because this policy is expected, the aggregate supply curve shifts leftward to AS_2. The economy moves to point 2, where aggregate output is still at the natural rate level but the price level has increased to P_2.

shifts leftward to AS_2 and intersects AD_2 at point 2, an equilibrium point where aggregate output is at the natural rate level Y_n and the price level has risen to P_2.

The new classical macroeconomic model demonstrates that aggregate output does not increase as a result of anticipated expansionary policy and that the economy immediately moves to a point of long-run equilibrium (point 2) where aggregate output is at the natural rate level. Although Figure 28-2 suggests why this occurs, we have not yet proved why an anticipated expansionary policy shifts the aggregate supply curve to exactly AS_2 (corresponding to an expected price level of P_2) and hence why aggregate output *necessarily* remains at the natural rate level. The proof is somewhat difficult and is dealt with in Box 28-1.

The new classical model has the word *classical* associated with it because when policy is anticipated, the new classical model has a property that is associated with the classical economists of the nineteenth and early twentieth centuries: aggregate output remains at the natural rate level. Yet the new classical model allows aggregate output to fluctuate away from the natural rate level as a result of *unanticipated* movements in the aggregate demand curve. The conclusion from the new classical model is a striking one: ***anticipated policy has no effect on the business cycle; only unanticipated policy matters***.[4]

This conclusion has been called the **policy ineffectiveness proposition** because it implies that one anticipated policy is just like any other; it has no effect on output fluctuations. You should recognize that this proposition does not rule out output effects from policy changes. If the policy is a surprise (unanticipated), it will have an effect on output.[5]

---

[4]Note that the new classical view in which anticipated policy has no effect on the business cycle does not imply that anticipated policy has no effect on the overall health of the economy. For example, the new classical analysis does not rule out possible effects of anticipated policy on the natural rate of output Y_n, which can benefit the public.

[5]Thomas Sargent and Neil Wallace, "'Rational' Expectations, the Optimal Monetary Instrument, and the Optimal Money Supply Rule," *Journal of Political Economy* 83 (1975): 241–254, first demonstrated the full implications of the policy ineffectiveness proposition.

Proof of the Policy Ineffectiveness Proposition

The proof that in the new classical macroeconomic model aggregate output *necessarily* remains at the natural rate level when there is anticipated expansionary policy is as follows. In the new classical model, the expected price level for the aggregate supply curve occurs at its intersection with the long-run aggregate supply curve (see Figure 28-2). The optimal forecast of the price level is given by the intersection of the aggregate supply curve with the anticipated aggregate demand curve AD_2. If the aggregate supply curve is to the right of AS_2 in Figure 28-2, it will intersect AD_2 at a price level lower than the expected level (at the intersection of this aggregate supply curve and the Y_n

line). The optimal forecast of the price level will then not equal the expected price level, thereby violating the rationality of expectations. A similar argument can be made to show that when the aggregate supply curve is to the left of AS_2, the assumption of rational expectations is violated. Only when the aggregate supply curve is at AS_2 (corresponding to an expected price level of P_2) are expectations rational because the optimal forecast equals the expected price level. As we see in Figure 28-2, the AS_2 curve implies that aggregate output remains at the natural rate level as a result of the anticipated expansionary policy.

Can an Expansionary Policy Lead to a Decline in Aggregate Output?

Another important feature of the new classical model is that an expansionary policy, such as an increase in the rate of money growth, can lead to a *decline* in aggregate output if the public expects an even more expansionary policy than the one actually implemented. There will be a surprise in the policy, but it will be negative and drive output down. Policymakers cannot be sure if their policies will work in the intended direction.

To see how an expansionary policy can lead to a decline in aggregate output, let us turn to the aggregate supply and demand diagram in Figure 28-3. Initially we are at point 1, the intersection of AD_1 and AS_1; output is Y_n, and the price level is P_1. Now suppose that the public expects the Bank of Canada to increase the money supply in order to shift the aggregate demand curve to AD_2. As we saw in Figure 28-2, the aggregate supply curve shifts leftward to AS_2 because the price level is expected to rise to P_2. Suppose that the expansionary policy engineered by the Bank of Canada actually falls short of what was expected so that the aggregate demand curve shifts only to $AD_{2'}$. The economy will move to point 2' the intersection of the aggregate supply curve AS_2 and the aggregate demand curve $AD_{2'}$. The result of the mistaken expectation is that output falls to $Y_{2'}$, while the price level rises to $P_{2'}$ rather than P_2. An expansionary policy that is less expansionary than anticipated leads to an output movement directly opposite to that intended.

Study Guide

Mastering the new classical macroeconomic model, as well as the new Keynesian model in the next section, requires practice. Make sure that you can draw the aggregate demand and supply curves that explain what happens in each model when there is a contractionary policy that is (1) unanticipated, (2) anticipated, and (3) less contractionary than anticipated.

Implications for Policymakers

The new classical model, with its policy ineffectiveness proposition, has two important lessons for policymakers. It illuminates the distinction between the effects of anticipated versus unanticipated policy actions, and it demonstrates that

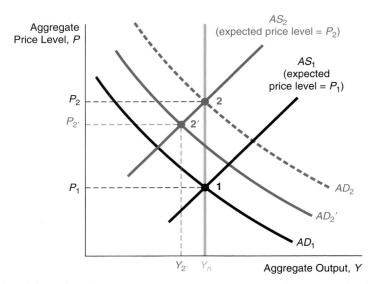

FIGURE 28-3 Short-Run Response to an Expansionary Policy That Is Less Expansionary Than Expected in the New Classical Model

Because the public expects the aggregate demand curve to shift to AD_2, the aggregate supply curve shifts to AS_2 (expected price level = P_2). When the actual expansionary policy falls short of the public's expectation (the aggregate demand curve merely shifts to $AD_{2'}$), the economy ends up at point 2', at the intersection of $AD_{2'}$ and AS_2. Despite the expansionary policy, aggregate output falls to $Y_{2'}$.

policymakers cannot know the outcome of their decisions without knowing the public's expectations regarding them.

At first you might think that policymakers can still use policy to stabilize the economy. Once they figure out the public's expectations, they can know what effect their policies will have. There are two catches to such a conclusion. First, it may be nearly impossible to find out what the public's expectations are, given that the public consists of about 30 million citizens. Second, even if it were possible, policymakers would run into further difficulties because the public has rational expectations and will try to guess what policymakers plan to do. Public expectations do not remain fixed while policymakers are plotting a surprise—the public will revise its expectations, and policies will have no predictable effect on output.[6]

Where does this lead us? Should the Bank of Canada and other policymaking agencies pack up, lock the doors, and go home? In a sense, the answer is yes. The new classical model implies that discretionary stabilization policy cannot be effective and might have undesirable effects on the economy. Policymakers' attempts to use discretionary policy may create a fluctuating policy stance that leads to unpredictable policy surprises, which in turn cause undesirable fluctuations around the natural rate level of aggregate output. To eliminate these undesirable fluctuations, the central bank and other policymaking agencies should abandon discretionary policy and generate as few policy surprises as possible.

As we saw in Figure 28-2, even though anticipated policy has no effect on aggregate output in the new classical model, it *does* have an effect on the price level. The new classical macroeconomists care about anticipated policy and suggest that policy rules be designed so that the price level will remain stable.

---

[6]This result follows from one of the implications of rational expectations. The forecast error of expectations about policy (the deviation of actual policy from expectations of policy) must be unpredictable. Because output is affected only by unpredictable (unanticipated) policy changes in the new classical model, policy effects on output must be unpredictable as well.

NEW KEYNESIAN MODEL

In the new classical model, all wages and prices are completely flexible with respect to expected changes in the price level; that is, a rise in the expected price level results in an immediate and equal rise in wages and prices. Many economists who accept rational expectations as a working hypothesis do not accept the characterization of wage and price flexibility in the new classical model. These critics of the new classical model, called *new Keynesians,* object to complete wage and price flexibility and identify factors in the economy that prevent some wages and prices from rising fully with a rise in the expected price level.

Long-term labour contracts are one source of rigidity that prevents wages and prices from responding fully to changes in the expected price level (called *wage–price stickiness*). For example, workers might find themselves at the end of the first year of a three-year wage contract that specifies the wage rate for the coming two years. Even if new information appeared that would make them raise their expectations of the inflation rate and the future price level, they could not do anything about it because they are locked into a wage agreement. Even with a high expectation about the price level, the wage rate will not adjust. In two years, when the contract is renegotiated, both workers and firms may build the expected inflation rate into their agreement, but they cannot do so immediately.

Another source of rigidity is that firms may be reluctant to change wages frequently even when there are no explicit wage contracts because such changes may affect the work effort of the labour force. For example, a firm may not want to lower workers' wages when unemployment is high because this might result in poorer worker performance. Price stickiness may also occur because firms engage in fixed-price contracts with their suppliers or because it is costly for firms to change prices frequently. All of these rigidities (which diminish wage and price flexibility), even if they are not present in all wage and price arrangements, suggest that an increase in the expected price level might not translate into an immediate and complete adjustment of wages and prices.

Although the new Keynesians do not agree with the complete wage and price flexibility of the new classical macroeconomics, they nevertheless recognize the importance of expectations to the determination of aggregate supply and are willing to accept rational expectations theory as a reasonable characterization of how expectations are formed. The model they have developed, the *new Keynesian model,* assumes that expectations are rational but does not assume complete wage and price flexibility; instead, it assumes that wages and prices are sticky. Its basic conclusion is that unanticipated policy has a larger effect on aggregate output than anticipated policy (as in the new classical model). However, in contrast to the new classical model, the policy ineffectiveness proposition does not hold in the new Keynesian model: anticipated policy *does* affect aggregate output and the business cycle.

Effects of Unanticipated and Anticipated Policy

In panel (a) of Figure 28-4, we look at the short-run response to an unanticipated expansionary policy for the new Keynesian model. The analysis is identical to that of the new classical model. We again start at point 1, where the aggregate demand curve AD_1 intersects the aggregate supply curve AS_1 at the natural rate level of output and price level P_1. When the Bank of Canada pursues its expansionary policy of purchasing bonds and raising the money supply, the aggregate demand curve shifts rightward to AD_2. Because the expansionary policy is unanticipated, the expected price level remains unchanged, leaving the aggregate supply curve unchanged. Thus the economy moves to point U, where aggregate output has increased to Y_U and the price level has risen to P_U.

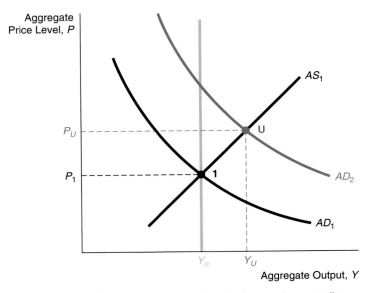

(a) Response to an unanticipated expansionary policy

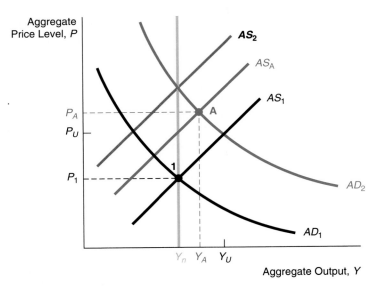

(b) Response to an anticipated expansionary policy

FIGURE 28-4   Short-Run Response to Expansionary Policy in the New Keynesian Model

The expansionary policy that shifts aggregate demand to AD_2 has a bigger effect on output when it is unanticipated than when it is anticipated. When the expansionary policy is unanticipated in panel (a), the short-run aggregate supply curve does not shift, and the economy moves to point U so that aggregate output increases to Y_U and the price level rises to P_U. When the policy is anticipated in panel (b), the short-run aggregate supply curve shifts to AS_A (but not all the way to AS_2 because rigidities prevent complete wage and price adjustment), and the economy moves to point A so that aggregate output rises to Y_A (which is less than Y_U) and the price level rises to P_A (which is higher than P_U).

In panel (b), we see what happens when the Bank's expansionary policy that shifts the aggregate demand curve from AD_1 to AD_2 is anticipated. Because the expansionary policy is anticipated and expectations are rational, the expected price level increases, causing wages to increase and the aggregate supply curve to shift to the left. Because of rigidities that do not allow *complete* wage and price adjustment, the aggregate supply curve does not shift all the way to AS_2 as it does in the new classical model. Instead, it moves to AS_A, and the economy settles at point A, the intersection of AD_2 and AS_A. Aggregate output has risen above the natural rate level to Y_A, while the price level has increased to P_A. **Unlike the new classical model, in the new Keynesian model anticipated policy does have an effect on aggregate output.**

We can see in Figure 28-4 that Y_U is greater than Y_A, meaning that the output response to unanticipated policy is greater than to anticipated policy. It is greater because the aggregate supply curve does not shift when policy is unanticipated, causing a lower price level and hence a higher level of output. We see that **like the new classical model, the new Keynesian model distinguishes between the effects of anticipated versus unanticipated policy, with unanticipated policy having a greater effect.**

Implications for Policymakers

Because the new Keynesian model indicates that anticipated policy has an effect on aggregate output, it does not rule out beneficial effects from activist stabilization policy, in contrast to the new classical model. It does warn the policymaker that designing such a policy will not be an easy task because the effects of anticipated and unanticipated policy can be quite different. As in the new classical model, to predict the outcome of their actions, policymakers must be aware of the public's expectations about those actions. Policymakers face similar difficulties in devising successful policies in both the new classical and new Keynesian models.

COMPARISON OF THE TWO NEW MODELS WITH THE TRADITIONAL MODEL

To obtain a clearer picture of the impact of the rational expectations revolution on our analysis of the aggregate economy, we can compare the two rational expectations models (the new classical macroeconomic model and the new Keynesian model) to a model we call, for lack of a better name, the *traditional model.* In the traditional model, expectations are *not* rational. That model uses adaptive expectations (mentioned in Chapter 27), expectations based solely on past experience. The traditional model views expected inflation as an average of past inflation rates. This average is not affected by the public's predictions of future policy; hence predictions of future policy do not affect the aggregate supply curve.

First we will examine the short-run output and price responses in the three models. Then we will examine the implications of these models for both stabilization and anti-inflation policies.

Study Guide

As a study aid, the comparison of the three models is summarized in Table 28-1. You may want to refer to the table as we proceed with the comparison.

Short-Run Output and Price Responses

Figure 28-5 compares the response of aggregate output and the price level to an expansionary policy in the three models. Initially, the economy is at point 1, the intersection of the aggregate demand curve AD_1 and the aggregate supply curve AS_1. When the expansionary policy occurs, the aggregate demand curve shifts to AD_2. If the expansionary policy is *unanticipated,* all three models show the same short-run output response. The traditional model views the aggregate supply curve

TABLE 28-1   The Three Models

Model	Response to Unanticipated Expansionary Policy	Response to Anticipated Expansionary Policy	Can Activist Policy Be Beneficial?	Response to Unanticipated Anti-inflation Policy	Response to Anticipated Anti-inflation Policy	Is Credibility Important to Successful Anti-inflation Policy?
Traditional model	$Y\uparrow, P\uparrow$	$Y\uparrow, P\uparrow$ by same amount as when policy is unanticipated	Yes	$Y\downarrow, \pi\downarrow$	$Y\downarrow, \pi\downarrow$ by same amount as when policy is unanticipated	No
New classical macroeconomic model	$Y\uparrow, P\uparrow$	Y unchanged, $P\uparrow$ by more than when policy is unanticipated	No	$Y\downarrow, \pi\downarrow$	Y unchanged, $\pi\downarrow$ by more than when policy is unanticipated	Yes
New Keynesian model	$Y\uparrow, P\uparrow$	$Y\uparrow$ by less than when policy is unanticipated, $P\uparrow$ by more than when policy is unanticipated	Yes, but designing a beneficial policy is difficult	$Y\downarrow, \pi\downarrow$	$Y\downarrow$ by less than when policy is unanticipated, $\pi\downarrow$ by more than when policy is unanticipated	Yes

Note: π represents the inflation rate.

as given in the short run, while the other two view it as remaining at AS_1 because there is no change in the expected price level when the policy is a surprise. Hence when policy is *unanticipated*, all three models indicate a movement to point 1', where the AD_2 and AS_1 curves intersect and where aggregate output and the price level have risen to Y_1, and P_1, respectively.

The response to the *anticipated* expansionary policy is, however, quite different in the three models. In the traditional model in panel (a), the aggregate supply curve remains at AS_1 even when the expansionary policy is anticipated because adaptive expectations imply that anticipated policy has no effect on expectations and hence on aggregate supply. It indicates that the economy moves to point 1', which is where it moved when the policy was unanticipated. The traditional model does not distinguish between the effects of anticipated and unanticipated policy: both have the same effect on output and prices.

In the new classical model in panel (b), the aggregate supply curve shifts leftward to AS_2 when policy is anticipated because when expectations of the higher price level are realized, aggregate output will be at the natural rate level. Thus it indicates that the economy moves to point 2; aggregate output does not rise, but prices do, to P_2. This outcome is quite different from the move to point 1' when policy is unanticipated. The new classical model distinguishes between the short-run effects of anticipated and unanticipated policies: anticipated policy has no

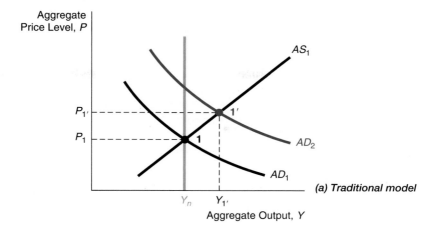

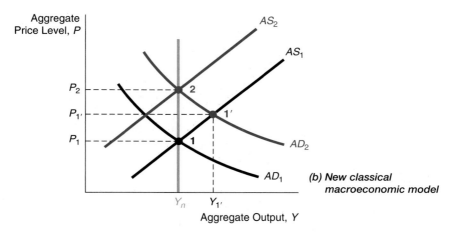

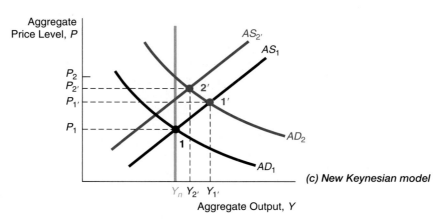

FIGURE 28-5   Comparison of the Short-Run Response to Expansionary Policy in the Three Models

Initially, the economy is at point 1. The expansionary policy shifts the aggregate demand curve from AD_1 to AD_2. In the traditional model, the expansionary policy moves the economy to point 1′ whether the policy is anticipated or not. In the new classical model, the expansionary policy moves the economy to point 1′ if it is unanticipated and to point 2 if it is anticipated. In the new Keynesian model, the expansionary policy moves the economy to point 1′ if it is unanticipated and to point 2′ if it is anticipated.

effect on output, but unanticipated policy does. However, anticipated policy has a bigger impact than unanticipated policy on price level movements.

The new Keynesian model in panel (c) is an intermediate position between the traditional and new classical models. It recognizes that anticipated policy affects the aggregate supply curve, but due to rigidities such as long-term contracts, wage and price adjustment is not as complete as in the new classical model. Hence the aggregate supply curve shifts only to $AS_{2'}$ in response to anticipated policy, and the economy moves to point $2'$, where output at $Y_{2'}$ is lower than the Y_1 level reached when the expansionary policy is unanticipated. But the price level at $P_{2'}$ is higher than the level P_1 that resulted from the unanticipated policy. Like the new classical model, the new Keynesian model distinguishes between the effects of anticipated and unanticipated policies: anticipated policy has a smaller effect on output than unanticipated policy but a larger effect on the price level. However, in contrast to the new classical model, anticipated policy does affect output fluctuations.

Stabilization Policy

The three models have different views of the effectiveness of *stabilization policy,* policy intended to reduce output fluctuations. Because the effects of anticipated and unanticipated policy are identical in the traditional model, policymakers do not have to concern themselves with the public's expectations. This makes it easier for them to predict the outcome of their policy, an essential matter if their actions are to have the intended effect. In the traditional model, it is possible for an activist policy to stabilize output fluctuations.

The new classical model takes the extreme position that activist stabilization policy serves to aggravate output fluctuations. In this model, only unanticipated policy affects output; anticipated policy does not matter. Policymakers can affect output only by surprising the public. Because the public is assumed to have rational expectations, it will always try to guess what policymakers plan to do.

In the new classical model, the conduct of policy can be viewed as a game in which the public and the policymakers are always trying to outfox each other by guessing the other's intentions and expectations. The sole possible outcome of this process is that an activist stabilization policy will have no predictable effect on output and cannot be relied on to stabilize economic activity. Instead it may create a lot of uncertainty about policy that will increase random output fluctuations around the natural rate level of output. Such an undesirable effect is exactly the opposite of what the activist stabilization policy is trying to achieve. The outcome in the new classical view is that policy should follow a nonactivist rule in order to promote as much certainty about policy actions as possible.

The new Keynesian model again takes an intermediate position between the traditional and the new classical models. Contrary to the new classical model, it indicates that anticipated policy *does* matter to output fluctuations. Policymakers can count on some output response from their anticipated policies and can use them to stabilize the economy.

In contrast to the traditional model, however, the new Keynesian model recognizes that the effects of anticipated and unanticipated policy will not be the same. Policymakers will encounter more uncertainty about the outcome of their actions because they cannot be sure to what extent the policy is anticipated or not. Hence an activist policy is less likely to operate always in the intended direction and is less likely to achieve its goals. The new Keynesian model raises the possibility that an activist policy could be beneficial, but uncertainty about the outcome of policies in this model may make the design of such a beneficial policy extremely difficult.

Anti-inflation Policies

So far we have focused on the implications of these three models for policies whose intent is to eliminate fluctuations in output. By the end of the 1970s, the high inflation rate (then over 10%) helped shift the primary concern of policymakers to the reduction of inflation. What do these models have to say about anti-inflation policies designed to eliminate upward movements in the price level? The aggregate demand and supply diagrams in Figure 28-6 will help us answer the question.

Suppose that the economy has settled into a sustained 10% inflation rate caused by a high rate of money growth that shifts the aggregate demand curve so that it moves up by 10% every year. If this inflation rate has been built into wage and price contracts, the aggregate supply curve shifts so as to rise at the same rate. We see this in Figure 28-6 as a shift in the aggregate demand curve from AD_1 in year 1 to AD_2 in year 2, while the aggregate supply curve moves from AS_1 to AS_2. In year 1, the economy is at point 1 (intersection of AD_1 and AS_1); in the second year, the economy moves to point 2 (intersection of AD_2 and AS_2), and the price level has risen 10%, from P_1 to P_2. (Note that the figure is not drawn to scale.)

Now suppose that a new Bank of Canada governor is appointed who decides that inflation must be stopped. He convinces the Bank's Board of Directors to stop the high rate of money growth so that the aggregate demand curve will not rise from AD_1. The policy of halting money growth immediately could be costly if it led to a fall in output. Let's use our three models to explore the degree to which aggregate output will fall as a result of an anti-inflation policy.

First, look at the outcome of this policy in the traditional model's view of the world in panel (a). The movement of the aggregate supply curve to AS_2 is already set in place and is unaffected by the new policy of keeping the aggregate demand curve at AD_1 (whether the effort is anticipated or not). The economy moves to point 2′ (the intersection of the AD_1 and AS_2 curves), and the inflation rate slows down because the price level increases only to $P_{2'}$ rather than P_2. The reduction in inflation has not been without cost: output has declined to $Y_{2'}$, which is well below the natural rate level.

In the traditional model, estimates of the cost in terms of lost output for each 1% reduction in the inflation rate are around 4% of a year's real GDP. The high cost of reducing inflation in the traditional model is one reason why some economists are reluctant to advocate an anti-inflation policy of the sort tried here. They question whether the cost of high unemployment is worth the benefits of a reduced inflation rate.

If you adhere to the new classical philosophy, you would not be as pessimistic about the high cost of reducing the inflation rate. If the public *expects* the monetary authorities to stop the inflationary process by ending the high rate of money growth, it will occur without any output loss. In panel (b), the aggregate demand curve will remain at AD_1, but because this is expected, wages and prices can be adjusted so that they will not rise, and the aggregate supply curve will remain at AS_1 instead of moving to AS_2. The economy will stay put at point 1 (the intersection of AD_1 and AS_1), and aggregate output will remain at the natural rate level while inflation is stopped because the price level is unchanged.

An important element in the story is that the anti-inflation policy be anticipated by the public. If the policy is *not* expected, the aggregate demand curve remains at AD_1, but the aggregate supply curve continues its shift to AS_2. The outcome of the unanticipated anti-inflation policy is a movement of the economy to point 2′. Although the inflation rate slows in this case, it is not entirely eliminated as it was when the anti-inflation policy was anticipated. Even worse, aggregate output falls below the natural rate level to $Y_{2'}$. An anti-inflation policy that is unanticipated, then, is far less desirable than one that is.

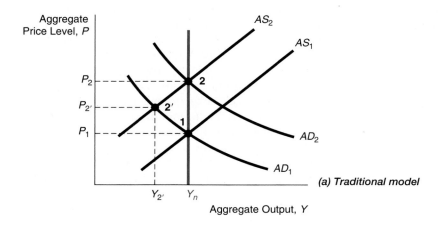

(a) Traditional model

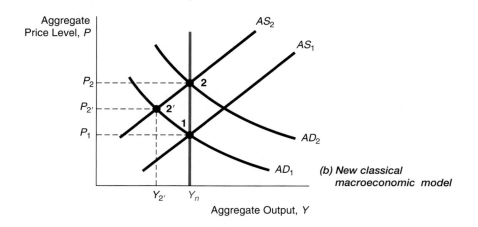

(b) New classical macroeconomic model

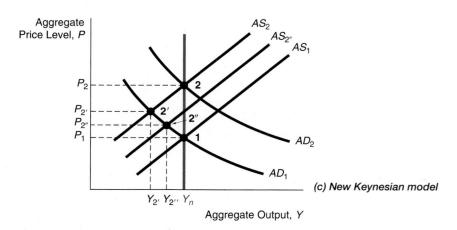

(c) New Keynesian model

FIGURE 28-6 Anti-inflation Policy in the Three Models

With an ongoing inflation in which the economy is moving from point 1 to point 2, the aggregate demand curve is shifting from AD_1 to AD_2 and the short-run aggregate supply curve from AS_1 to AS_2. The anti-inflation policy, when implemented, prevents the aggregate demand curve from rising, holding it at AD_1. (a) In the traditional model, the economy moves to point 2' whether the anti-inflation policy is anticipated or not. (b) In the new classical model, the economy moves to point 2' if the policy is unanticipated and to point 1 if it is anticipated. (c) In the new Keynesian model, the economy moves to point 2' if the policy is unanticipated and to point 2'' if it is anticipated.

The new Keynesian model in panel (c) also leads to the conclusion that an unanticipated anti-inflation policy is less desirable than an anticipated one. If the policy of keeping the aggregate demand curve at AD_1 is *not* expected, the aggregate supply curve will continue its shift to AS_2, and the economy moves to point 2', at the intersection of AD_1 and AS_2. The inflation rate slows, but output declines to $Y_{2'}$, well below the natural rate level.

If, by contrast, the anti-inflation policy is *expected,* the aggregate supply curve will not move all the way to AS_2. Instead it will shift only to $AS_{2''}$ because some wages and prices (but not all) can be adjusted, so wages and the price level will not rise at their previous rates. Instead of moving to point 2' (as occurred when the anti-inflation policy was not expected), the economy moves to point 2'', the intersection of the AD_1 and $AS_{2''}$ curves. The outcome is more desirable than when the policy is unanticipated—the inflation rate is lower (the price level rises only to $P_{2''}$ and not P_2), and the output loss is smaller as well ($Y_{2''}$ is higher than $Y_{2'}$).

Credibility in Fighting Inflation

Both the new classical and new Keynesian models indicate that for an anti-inflation policy to be successful in reducing inflation at the lowest output cost, the public must believe (expect) that it will be implemented. In the new classical view of the world, the best anti-inflation policy (when it is credible) is to go "cold turkey." The rise in the aggregate demand curve from AD_1 should be stopped immediately. Inflation would be eliminated at once with no loss of output *if the policy were credible.* In a new Keynesian world, the cold-turkey policy, *even if credible,* is not as desirable because it will produce some output loss.

John Taylor, a proponent of the new Keynesian model, has demonstrated that a more gradual approach to reducing inflation may be able to eliminate inflation without producing a substantial output loss.[7] An important catch here is that this gradual policy must somehow be made credible, which may be harder to achieve than a cold-turkey anti-inflation policy, which demonstrates immediately that the policymakers are serious about fighting inflation. Taylor's contention that inflation can be reduced with little output loss may be overly optimistic.

Incorporating rational expectations into aggregate supply and demand analysis indicates that a successful anti-inflation policy must be credible. Evidence that credibility plays an important role in successful anti-inflation policies is provided by the dramatic end of the Bolivian hyperinflation in 1985 (Box 28-2). But establishing credibility is easier said than done. You might think that an announcement by policymakers at the Bank of Canada that they plan to pursue an anti-inflation policy might do the trick. The public would expect this policy and would act accordingly. However, that conclusion implies that the public will believe the policymakers' announcement. Unfortunately, that is not how the real world works.

Our historical review of Bank of Canada policymaking in Chapter 18 suggests that the Bank has not always done what it set out to do. In the early 1970s, the Bank accommodated inflationary shocks by raising the rate of growth of monetary aggregates, thereby forming expectations of rising inflation. When in 1975 the Bank adopted a gradual anti-inflation policy, the public had no reason to believe in such a policy. As Robert Lucas of the University of Saskatchewan argues, "For various reasons, including the caution of the Bank in moving too quickly for fear of generating large increases in the unemployment rate in the transition to lower inflation, the policy was a failure."[8]

University of
Saskatchewan
www.usask.ca

---

[7]John Taylor, "The Role of Expectations in the Choice of Monetary Policy," in *Monetary Policy Issues in the 1980s* (Kansas City: Federal Reserve Bank, 1982), pp. 47–76.

[8]Robert F. Lucas, "The Bank of Canada and Zero Inflation: A New Cross of Gold?" *Canadian Public Policy* 15 (1989): 84-93.

Ending the Bolivian Hyperinflation

Case Study of a Successful Anti-inflation Program. The most remarkable anti-inflation program in recent times was implemented in Bolivia. In the first half of 1985, Bolivia's inflation rate was running at 20 000% and rising. Indeed, the inflation rate was so high that the price of a movie ticket often rose while people waited in line to buy it. In August 1985, Bolivia's new president announced his anti-inflation program, the New Economic Policy. To rein in money growth and establish credibility, the new government took drastic actions to slash the budget deficit by shutting down many state-owned enterprises, eliminating subsidies, freezing public sector salaries, and collecting a new wealth tax. The finance ministry was put on a new footing; the budget was balanced on a day-by-day basis. Without exceptions, the finance minister would not authorize spending in excess of the amount of tax revenue that had been collected the day before.

The rule of thumb that a reduction of 1% in the inflation rate requires a 4% loss of a year's aggregate output indicates that ending the Bolivian hyperinflation would have required halving Bolivian aggregate output for 1600 years! Instead, the Bolivian inflation was stopped in its tracks within one month, and the output loss was minor (less than 5% of GDP).

Certain hyperinflations before World War II were also ended with small losses of output using policies similar to Bolivia's,* and a more recent anti-inflation program in Israel that also involved substantial reductions in budget deficits sharply reduced inflation without any clear loss of output. There is no doubt that credible anti-inflation policies can be highly successful in eliminating inflation.

*For an excellent discussion of the end of four hyperinflations in the 1920s, see Thomas Sargent, "The Ends of Four Big Inflations," in *Inflation: Causes and Consequences,* ed. Robert E. Hall (Chicago: University of Chicago Press, 1982), pp. 41–98.

Wilfrid Laurier University
www.wlu.ca

Such episodes reduced the credibility of the Bank of Canada in the eyes of the public and, as predicted by the new classical and new Keynesian models, had serious consequences. For example, when the Bank embarked on a very restrictive monetary policy in the summer of 1981, following the Federal Reserve Board of the United States, it was successful in generating a significant decline in the inflation rate (from 12 to 4 percent), but it initiated the most severe recession in the post-World War II period. Clearly, unless some method of restoring credibility to anti-inflation policy is achieved, eliminating inflation will be a costly affair because such policy will be unanticipated.

Recently, however, the Bank of Canada acquired considerable credibility. When the Bank and the Department of Finance jointly announced inflation targets in 1991, they were clearly credible. In fact, as David Johnson of Wilfrid Laurier University argues in a recent paper, this particular announcement had little effect on the level of inflation in the short run, but the subsequent revision of inflation targets and the 1993 change in governor (from governor Crow to governor Theissen) were handled in such a way that the Bank's anti-inflation policy turned out to be successful.[9]

[9]David R. Johnson, "Expected Inflation in Canada 1988-1995: An Evaluation of Bank of Canada Credibility and the Effect of Inflation Targets," *Canadian Public Policy* 23 (1997): 233-258.

The Canadian government can play an important role in establishing the credibility of anti-inflation policy. We have seen that large budget deficits may help stimulate inflationary monetary policy, and when the government and the Bank of Canada announce that they will pursue a restrictive anti-inflation policy, it is less likely that they will be believed *unless* the federal government demonstrates fiscal responsibility. Another way to say this is to use the old adage "Actions speak louder than words." When the government takes actions that will help the Bank of Canada adhere to anti-inflation policy, the policy will be more credible. Unfortunately, this lesson has sometimes been ignored by politicians in both Canada and other countries.

A P P L I C A T I O N | *Credibility and Budget Deficits*

The Reagan administration in the United States was strongly criticized for creating huge budget deficits by cutting taxes in the early 1980s. In the Keynesian framework, we usually think of tax cuts as stimulating aggregate demand and increasing aggregate output. Could the expectation of large budget deficits have helped create a more severe recession in 1981–1982 after the Federal Reserve implemented an anti-inflation monetary policy?

Some economists answer yes, using diagrams like panels (b) and (c) of Figure 28-6. They claim that the prospect of large budget deficits made it harder for the public to believe that an anti-inflationary policy would actually be pursued when the Fed announced its intention to do so. Consequently, the aggregate supply curve would continue to rise from AS_1 to AS_2 as in panels (b) and (c). When the Fed actually kept the aggregate demand curve from rising to AD_2 by slowing the rate of money growth in 1980–1981 and allowing interest rates to rise, the economy moved to a point like 2′ in panels (b) and (c), and much unemployment resulted. As our analysis in panels (b) and (c) of Figure 28-6 predicts, the inflation rate did slow substantially, falling below 5% by the end of 1982, but this was very costly: unemployment in the United States reached a peak of 10.7%.

If the Reagan administration had actively tried to reduce deficits instead of raising them by cutting taxes, what might have been the outcome of the anti-inflation policy? Instead of moving to point 2′, the economy might have moved to point 2″ in panel (c)—or even to point 1 in panel (b), if the new classical macroeconomists are right. We would have had an even more rapid reduction in inflation and a smaller loss of output. No wonder some economists were so hostile to Reagan's budget policies!

Although many economists agree that the Fed's anti-inflation program lacked credibility, especially in its initial phases, not all of them agree that the Reagan budget deficits were the cause of that lack of credibility. The conclusion that the Reagan budget deficits helped create a more severe recession in 1981–1982 is controversial.

Reagan is not the only head of state who ran large budget deficits while espousing an anti-inflation policy. Britain's Margaret Thatcher preceded Reagan in this activity, and economists such as Thomas Sargent assert that the reward for her policy was a climb of unemployment in Britain to unprecedented levels.[10]

---

[10]Thomas Sargent, "Stopping Moderate Inflations: The Methods of Poincaré and Thatcher," in *Inflation, Debt, and Indexation,* ed. Rudiger Dornbusch and M. H. Simonsen (Cambridge, Mass.: MIT Press, 1983), pp. 54–96, discusses the problems that Thatcher's policies caused and contrasts them with more successful anti-inflation policies pursued by the Poincaré government in France during the 1920s.

IMPACT OF THE RATIONAL EXPECTATIONS REVOLUTION

The theory of rational expectations has caused a revolution in the way most economists now think about the conduct of monetary and fiscal policies and their effects on economic activity. One result of this revolution is that economists are now far more aware of the importance of expectations to economic decision-making and to the outcome of particular policy actions. Although the rationality of expectations in all markets is still controversial, most economists now accept the following principle suggested by rational expectations: expectation formation will change when the behaviour of forecasted variables changes. As a result, the Lucas critique of policy evaluation using conventional econometric models is now taken seriously by most economists. The Lucas critique also demonstrates that the effect of a particular policy depends critically on the public's expectations about that policy. This observation has made economists much less certain that policies will have their intended effect. An important result of the rational expectations revolution is that economists are no longer as confident in the success of activist stabilization policies as they once were.

Has the rational expectations revolution convinced economists that there is no role for activist stabilization policy? Those who adhere to the new classical macroeconomics think so. Because anticipated policy does not affect aggregate output, activist policy can lead only to unpredictable output fluctuations. Pursuing a nonactivist policy in which there is no uncertainty about policy actions is then the best we can do. Such a position is not accepted by many economists because the empirical evidence on the policy ineffectiveness proposition is mixed. Some studies find that only unanticipated policy matters to output fluctuations, while other studies find a significant impact of anticipated policy on output movements.[11] In addition, some economists question whether the degree of wage and price flexibility required in the new classical model actually exists.

The result is that many economists take an intermediate position that recognizes the distinction between the effects of anticipated versus unanticipated policy but believe that anticipated policy can affect output. They are still open to the possibility that activist stabilization policy can be beneficial, but they recognize the difficulties of designing it.

The rational expectations revolution has also highlighted the importance of credibility to the success of anti-inflation policies. Economists now recognize that if an anti-inflation policy is not believed by the public, it may be less effective in reducing the inflation rate when it is actually implemented and may lead to a larger loss of output than is necessary. Achieving credibility (not an easy task in that policymakers often say one thing but do another) should then be an important goal for policymakers. To achieve credibility, policymakers must be consistent in their course of action.

The rational expectations revolution has caused major rethinking about the way economic policy should be conducted and has forced economists to recognize that we may have to accept a more limited role for what policy can do for us. Rather than attempting to fine-tune the economy so that all output fluctuations are eliminated, we may have to settle for policies that create less uncertainty and thereby promote a more stable economic environment.

---

[11]Studies with findings that only unanticipated policy matters include Thomas Sargent, "A Classical Macroeconometric Model for the United States," *Journal of Political Economy* 84 (1976): 207–237; Robert J. Barro, "Unanticipated Money Growth and Unemployment in the United States," *American Economic Review* 67 (1977): 101–115; and Robert J. Barro and Mark Rush, "Unanticipated Money and Economic Activity," in *Rational Expectations and Economic Policy,* ed. Stanley Fischer (Chicago: University of Chicago Press, 1980), pp. 23–48. Studies that find a significant impact of anticipated policy are Frederic S. Mishkin, "Does Anticipated Monetary Policy Matter? An Econometric Investigation," *Journal of Political Economy* 90 (1982): 22–51, and Robert J. Gordon, "Price Inertia and Policy Effectiveness in the United States, 1890–1980," *Journal of Political Economy* 90 (1982): 1087–1117.

SUMMARY

1. The simple principle (derived from rational expectations theory) that expectation formation changes when the behaviour of forecasted variables changes led to the famous Lucas critique of econometric policy evaluation. Lucas argued that when policy changes, expectation formation changes; hence the relationships in an econometric model will change. An econometric model that has been estimated on the basis of past data will no longer be the correct model for evaluating the effects of this policy change and may prove to be highly misleading. The Lucas critique also points out that the effects of a particular policy depend critically on the public's expectations about the policy.

2. The new classical macroeconomic model assumes that expectations are rational and that wages and prices are completely flexible with respect to the expected price level. It leads to the policy ineffectiveness proposition that anticipated policy has no effect on output; only unanticipated policy matters.

3. The new Keynesian model also assumes that expectations are rational but views wages and prices as sticky. Like the new classical model, the new Keynesian model distinguishes between the effects from anticipated and unanticipated policy: antici-pated policy has a smaller effect on aggregate output than unanticipated policy. However, anticipated policy does matter to output fluctuations.

4. The new classical model indicates that activist policy can only be counterproductive, while the new Keynesian model suggests that activist policy might be beneficial. However, since both indicate that there is uncertainty about the outcome of a particular policy, the design of a beneficial activist policy may be very difficult. A traditional model in which expectations about policy have no effect on the aggregate supply curve does not distinguish between the effects of anticipated or unanticipated policy. This model favours activist policy because the outcome of a particular policy is less uncertain.

5. If expectations about policy affect the aggregate supply curve, as they do in the new classical and new Keynesian models, an anti-inflation policy will be more successful (will produce a faster reduction in inflation with smaller output loss) if it is credible.

6. The rational expectations revolution has forced economists to be less optimistic about the effective use of activist stabilization policy and has made them more aware of the importance of credibility to successful policymaking.

KEY TERMS

econometric model, p. 633

policy ineffectiveness proposition, p. 636

QUESTIONS AND PROBLEMS

Questions marked with an asterisk are answered at the end of the book in an appendix, "Answers to Selected Questions and Problems."

1. If the public expects the Bank of Canada to pursue a policy that is likely to raise short-term interest rates permanently to 12% but the Bank does not go through with this policy change, what will happen to long-term interest rates? Explain your answer.

*2. If consumer expenditure is related to consumers' expectations of their average income in the future, will an income tax cut have a larger effect on consumer expenditure if the public expects the tax cut to last for one year or for ten years?

Use an aggregate supply and demand diagram to illustrate your answer in all the following questions.

3. Having studied the new classical model, the new governor of the Bank of Canada has thought up a surefire plan for reducing inflation and lowering unemployment. He announces that the Bank will lower the rate of money growth from 10% to 5%, but the Bank actually keeps the rate of money growth at 10%. If the new classical view of the world is correct, can his plan achieve the goals of lowering inflation and unemployment? How? Do you think his plan will work? If the traditional model's view of the world is correct, will the governor's surefire plan work?

*4. "The costs of fighting inflation in the new classical and new Keynesian models are lower than in the traditional model." Is this statement true, false, or uncertain? Explain your answer.

5. The new classical model is sometimes characterized as an offshoot of the monetarist model because the two models have similar views of aggregate supply. What are the differences and similarities between the monetarist and new classical views of aggregate supply?

*6. "The new classical model does not eliminate policymakers' ability to reduce unemployment because they can always pursue policies that are more expansionary than the public expects." Is this statement true, false, or uncertain? Explain your answer.

7. What principle of rational expectations theory is used to prove the proposition that stabilization policy can have no predictable effect on aggregate output in the new classical model?

*8. "The Lucas critique by itself casts doubt on the ability of activist stabilization policy to be beneficial." Is this statement true, false, or uncertain? Explain your answer.

9. "The more credible the policymakers who pursue an anti-inflation policy, the more successful that policy will be." Is this statement true, false, or uncertain? Explain your answer.

*10. Many economists are worried that a high level of budget deficits may lead to inflationary monetary policies in the future. Could these budget deficits have an effect on the current rate of inflation?

Using Economic Analysis to Predict the Future

11. Suppose that a treaty is signed limiting armies throughout the world. The result of the treaty is that the public expects military and hence government spending to be reduced. If the new classical view of the economy is correct and government spending does affect the aggregate demand curve, predict what will happen to aggregate output and the price level when government spending is reduced in line with the public's expectations.

12. How would your prediction differ in Problem 11 if the new Keynesian model provides a more realistic description of the economy? What if the traditional model provides the most realistic description of the economy?

*13. The governor of the Bank of Canada announces that over the next year, the rate of money growth will be reduced from its current rate of 10% to a rate of 2%. If the governor is believed by the public but the Bank actually reduces the rate of money growth to 5%, predict what will happen to the inflation rate and aggregate output if the new classical view of the economy is correct.

*14. How would your prediction differ in Problem 13 if the new Keynesian model provides a more accurate description of the economy? What if the traditional model provides the most realistic description of the economy?

15. If, in a surprise victory, a new government is elected to office that the public believes will pursue inflationary policy, predict what might happen to the level of output and inflation even before the new government comes into power. Would your prediction differ depending on which of the three models—traditional, new classical, and new Keynesian—you believed in?

GLOSSARY

accommodating policy An activist policy in pursuit of a high employment target. **594**

activist An economist who views the self-correcting mechanism through wage and price adjustment to be very slow and hence sees the need for the government to pursue active, discretionary policy to eliminate high unemployment whenever it develops. **550**

adaptive expectations Expectations of a variable based on an average of past values of the variable. **613**

advances See *overdraft loans.*

adverse selection The problem created by asymmetric information *before* a transaction occurs: The people who are the most undesirable from the other party's point of view are the ones who are most likely to want to engage in the financial transaction. **32**

aggregate demand The total quantity of output demanded in the economy at different price levels. **497, 541**

aggregate demand curve A relationship between the price level and the quantity of aggregate output demanded when the goods and money markets are in equilibrium. **536, 541**

aggregate demand function The relationship between aggregate output and aggregate demand that shows the quantity of aggregate output demanded for each level of aggregate output. **501**

aggregate income The total income of factors of production (land, labour, capital) in the economy. **14**

aggregate output The total production of final goods and services in the economy. **7**

aggregate price level The average price of goods and services in an economy. **8**

aggregate supply The quantity of aggregate output supplied by the economy at different price levels. **541**

aggregate supply curve The relationship between the quantity of output supplied in the short run and the price level. **546**

American option An option that can be exercised at any time up to the expiration date of the contract. **312**

"animal spirits" Waves of optimism and pessimism that affect consumers' and businesses' willingness to spend. **504, 545**

annual percentage rate The actual rate of return. **67**

annuities Financial contracts under which a customer pays an annual premium in exchange for a future stream of annual payments beginning at a set age, say 65, and ending when the person dies. **280**

appreciation Increase in a currency's value. **4, 135**

arbitrage Elimination of a riskless profit opportunity in a market. **304**

asset management The acquisition of assets that have a low rate of default and diversification of asset holdings to increase profits. **194**

asset market approach An approach of determining asset prices using stocks of assets rather than flows. **86**

asset A financial claim or piece of property that is a store of value. **2**

asymmetric information The unequal knowledge that each party to a transaction has about the other party. **31**

autonomous consumer expenditure The amount of consumer expenditure that is independent of disposable income. **498**

balance of payments A bookkeeping system for recording all payments that have a direct bearing on the movement of funds between a country and foreign countries. **427**

balance sheet A list of the assets and liabilities of a bank (or firm) that balances: Total assets equal total liabilities plus capital. **185**

balance-of-payments crisis A foreign exchange crisis stemming from problems in a country's balance of payments. **438**

bank failure A situation in which a bank cannot satisfy its obligations to pay its depositors and other creditors and so goes out of business. **251**

bank holding companies Companies that own one or more banks. **227**

Bank of Canada (the Bank) Canada's central bank. **10**

bank panic The simultaneous failure of many banks, as during a financial crisis. **176**

bank rate The interest rate the Bank of Canada charges to members of the Canadian Payments Association. **196, 344**

bank supervision (prudential supervision) Overseeing who operates banks and how they are operated. **255**

banker's risk The risk of not holding enough reserves to make immediate and larger than normal cash payments to liability holders. **190**

banks Financial institutions that accept money deposits and make loans (such as commercial banks, savings and loan associations, and credit unions). **6**

base money The sum of the Bank of Canada's monetary liabilities (notes outstanding and bank settlement balances) and coins outstanding. Also called *monetary base.* **328**

basis point One one-hundredth of a percentage point. **68**

bearer deposit notes Debt instruments in bearer form, meaning that the buyer's name is neither recorded in the issuer's books nor on the security itself. **22**

Big Six The six largest chartered banks that together hold over 92% of the assets in the industry. **224**

Board of Directors of the Bank of Canada A board with fifteen members (including the governor) that is responsible for the management of the Bank. **326**

Board of Governors of the Federal Reserve System A board with seven governors (including the chairman) that plays an essential role in decision making within the Federal Reserve System. **335**

bond A debt security that promises to make payments periodically for a specified period of time. **2**

branches Additional offices of banks that conduct banking operations. **220**

Bretton Woods system The international monetary system in use from 1945 to 1971 in which exchange rates were fixed and the U.S. dollar was freely convertible into gold (by foreign governments and central banks only). **431**

brokerage firms Firms that participate in securities markets as brokers, dealers, and investment bankers. **297**

brokered deposits Deposits that enable depositors to circumvent the $100 000 limit on federal deposit insurance by breaking up a large deposit into smaller packages of less than $100 000 at each bank so that the total amount deposited is fully insured. **271**

brokers Agents for investors who match buyers with sellers. **20**

bubble A situation in which the price of an asset differs from its fundamental market value. **629**

budget deficit The excess of government expenditure over tax revenues. **10**

business cycles The upward and downward movement of aggregate output produced in the economy. **7**

call Feature found on a debt instrument that allows it to be redeemed on specified notice. **27**

call option An option contract that provides the right to buy a security at a specified price. **313**

Canadas Securities issued by the federal government. **28**

capital account An account that describes the flow of capital between the U.S. and other countries. **429**

capital adequacy management A bank's decision about the amount of capital it should maintain and then acquisition of the needed capital. **194**

capital market A financial market in which longer-term debt (generally with original maturity of greater than one year) and equity instruments are traded. **21**

capital mobility A situation in which foreigners can easily purchase a country's assets and the country's residents can easily purchase foreign assets. **143**

cash flow The difference between cash receipts and cash expenditures. **176**

cash setting The management of participants' settlement balances by means of shifting government deposits between the government's account at the Bank of Canada and the government's accounts at the participating financial institutions. **396**

cash reserves See *vault cash.*

central bank The government agency that oversees the banking system and is responsible for the amount of money and credit supplied in the economy; in Canada, the Bank of Canada. **10, 220**

central bank independence Advocates of central bank independence find that inflation performance is found to be the best for countries with the most independent central banks. **339**

chaos A nonlinear deterministic process that looks random. **624**

closed-end fund A mutual fund in which a fixed number of nonredeemable shares are sold at an initial offering, then traded in the over-the-counter market like common stock. **291**

coinsurance A situation in which only a portion of losses are covered by insurance, so that the insured suffers a percentage of the losses along with the insurance agency. **266**

collateral Property that is pledged to the lender to guarantee payment in the event that the borrower is unable to make debt payments. **160**

commodity money Money made up of precious metals or another valuable commodity. **47**

compensating balance A required minimum amount of funds that a firm receiving a loan must keep in a chequing account at the lending bank. **205**

complete crowding out The situation in which expansionary fiscal policy, such as an increase in government spending, does not lead to a rise in output because there is an equal offsetting movement in private spending. **530, 545**

consol (perpetuity) A perpetual bond with no maturity date and no repayment of principal that periodically makes fixed coupon payments. **63**

constant-money-growth-rate rule A policy rule advocated by monetarists whereby the central bank keeps the money supply growing at a constant rate. **606**

consumer durable expenditure Spending by consumers on durable items such as automobiles and household appliances. **574**

consumer expenditure The total demand for (spending on) consumer goods and services. **496, 544**

consumption Spending by consumers on non-durable goods and services (including services related to the ownership of homes and consumer durables). **578**

consumption function The relationship between disposable income and consumer expenditure. **498**

costly state verification Monitoring a firm's activities, an expensive process in both time and money. **169**

cost-push inflation Inflation that occurs because of the push by workers to obtain higher wages. **594**

coupon bond A credit market instrument that pays a fixed interest payment every year until the maturity date, when a specified final amount is repaid. **58**

coupon rate The dollar amount of the yearly coupon payment expressed as a percentage of the face value of a coupon bond. **58**

credit rationing A lender's refusing to make loans even though borrowers are willing to pay the stated interest rate or even a higher rate or restricting the size of loans made to less than the full amount sought. **205**

credit risk The risk arising from the possibility that the borrower will default. **194**

credit view Monetary transmission mechanisms operating through asymmetric information effects on credit markets. **575**

creditor A holder of debt. **173**

currency board A monetary regime in which the domestic currency is backed 100% by a foreign currency (say dollars) and in which the note-issuing authority, whether the central bank or the government, establishes a fixed exchange rate to this foreign currency and stands ready to exchange domestic currency at this rate whenever the public requests it. **452**

currency swap The exchange of a set of payments in one currency for a set of payments in another currency. **319**

currency union A group of countries that share a common currency. **440**

current account An account that shows international transactions involving currently produced goods and services. **428**

current yield An approximation of the yield to maturity that equals the yearly coupon payment divided by the price of a coupon bond. **66**

dealers People who link buyers with sellers by buying and selling securities at stated prices. **20**

debt-currency swap The form of debt conversion where the debt denominated in foreign currency is converted into domestic currency. **237**

debt-debt swap The form of debt conversion where banks holding the debt of one less developed country (LDC) exchange it for the debt of another LDC. **237**

debt deflation A situation in which a substantial decline in the price level sets in, leading to a further deterioration in firms' net worth because of the increased burden of indebtedness. **177**

debt-equity swap The form of debt conversion where the debt is converted into the equity of public and private domestic enterprises. **237**

deductible The fixed amount by which the insured party's loss is reduced when a claim is paid off. **285**

default risk The chance that the issuer of a debt instrument will be unable to make interest payments or pay off the face value when the instrument matures. **114**

default A situation in which the party issuing a debt instrument is unable to make interest payments or pay off the amount owed when the instrument matures. **22**

default-free bonds Bonds with no default risk, such as Canada bonds. **114**

defensive open market operations Open market operations intended to offset movements in other factors that affect the monetary base (such as changes in government deposits with the Bank of Canada or changes in float). **388**

defined-benefit plan A pension plan in which benefits are set in advance. **286**

defined-contribution plan A pension plan in which benefits are determined by the contributions into the plan and their earnings. **286**

demand curve A curve depicting the relationship between quantity demanded and price when all other economic variables are held constant. **82**

demand-pull inflation Inflation that results when policymakers pursue policies that shift the aggregate demand curve. **594**

demutualization The process of converting a life insurance company into a stock company. **278**

deposit outflows Losses of deposits when depositors make withdrawals or demand payment. **194**

deposit rate ceiling Restriction on the maximum interest rate payable on deposits. **215**

depreciation Decrease in a currency's value. **4, 135**

desired excess reserves See *desired reserves.*

desired reserve ratio The fraction of deposits that banks desire to keep as reserves. **190, 345**

desired reserves Reserves that are held to meet the banks' desire that for every dollar of deposits, a certain fraction should be kept as reserves. **190, 345**

devaluation Resetting of the fixed value of a currency at a lower level. **433**

direct clearers Members of the Canadian Payments Association who participate directly in the Automated Clearing Settlement System (ACSS) and maintain a settlement account at the Bank of Canada. **381**

dirty float See *managed float regime.* **423**

discount bond A credit market instrument that is bought at a price below its face value and whose face value is repaid at the maturity date; it does not make any interest payments. Also called a *zero-coupon bond.* **58**

discount rate The interest rate that the Federal Reserve charges banks on discount loans. **395**

disintermediation A reduction in the flow of funds into the banking system that causes the amount of financial intermediation to decline. **215**

disposable income Total income available for spending, equal to aggregate income minus taxes. **498**

dividends Periodic payments made by equities to shareholders. **20**

dollarization The adoption of a sound currency, like the U.S. dollar, as a country's money. **453**

drawdowns Transfers of government deposits from the government's accounts with the direct clearers to the government's account with the Bank of Canada. **396**

dual banking system The system in the United States in which banks supervised by the federal government and banks supervised by the states operate side by side. **221**

duration analysis A measurement of the sensitivity of the market value of a bank's assets and liabilities to changes in interest rates. **207**

dynamic open market operations Open market operations that are intended to change the level of reserves and the monetary base. **388**

econometric model A model whose equations are estimated using statistical procedures. **633**

economies of scale The reduction in transaction costs per dollar of transaction as the size (scale) of transactions increases. **31**

efficient markets theory The application of the theory of rational expectations to financial markets. **615**

electronic money (e-money) Money that is stored electronically. **49**

endowment insurance See *permanent insurance.*

equation of exchange The equation $MV = PY$, which relates nominal income to the quantity of money. **474, 542**

equities Claims to share in the net income and assets of a corporation (such as common stock). **20**

equity capital See *net worth.*

equity multiplier *(EM)* The amount of assets per dollar of equity capital. **200**

Eurobonds Bonds denominated in a currency other than that of the country in which they are sold. **28**

Eurocurrencies A variant of the Eurobond, which are foreign currencies deposited in banks outside the home country. **28**

Eurodollars U.S. dollars that are deposited in foreign banks outside the United States or in foreign branches of U.S. banks. **28**

European option An option that can be exercised only at the expiration date of the contract. **312**

excess demand A situation in which quantity demanded is greater than quantity supplied. **85**

excess reserves Reserves in excess of desired reserves. **345**

excess supply A situation in which quantity supplied is greater than quantity demanded. **84**

Exchange Fund Account The fund that holds Canada's official foreign exchange assets. **328, 343, 397**

exchange rate The price of one currency in terms of another. **133**

exchange rate overshooting A phenomenon whereby the exchange rate changes by more in the short run than it does in the long run when the money supply changes. **152**

exchange rate union A group of countries that agree to fix exchange rates among themselves while floating jointly against the currencies of countries outside the union. **440**

exchanges Secondary markets in which buyers and sellers of securities (or their agents or brokers) meet in one central location to conduct trades. **21**

exercise price The price at which the purchaser of an option has the right to buy or sell the underlying financial instrument. Also known as the *strike price.* **312**

expectations theory The proposition that the interest rate on a long-term bond will equal the average of the short-term interest rates that people expect to occur over the life of the long-term bond. **121**

expected return The return on an asset expected over the next period. **80**

expenditure multiplier The ratio of a change in aggregate output to a change in investment spending (or autonomous spending). **502**

fallen angels Investment-grade securities whose rating has fallen to junk levels. **116**

face value A specified final amount paid to the owner of a coupon bond at the maturity date. Also called *par value.* **58**

Federal Open Market Committee (FOMC) The committee that makes decisions regarding the conduct of open market operations; composed of the seven members of the Board of Governors of the Federal Reserve System, the president of the Federal Reserve Bank of New York, and the presidents of four other Federal Reserve banks on a rotating basis. **335**

Federal Reserve Banks The 12 district banks in the Federal Reserve System. **335**

Federal Reserve System (the Fed) The central banking authority responsible for monetary policy in the United States. **335**

fiat money Paper currency decreed by a government as legal tender but not convertible into coins or precious metal. **47**

financial crisis A major disruption in financial markets that is characterized by sharp declines in asset prices and the failures of many financial and nonfinancial firms. **174**

financial derivatives Instruments that have payoffs that are linked to previously issued securities, used as risk reduction tools. **300**

financial engineering The process of researching and developing new products and services that would meet customer needs and prove profitable. **211**

financial futures A futures contract in which the standardized commodity is a particular type of financial instrument. **302**

financial futures option An option in which the underlying instrument is a futures contract. Also called a *futures option*. **312**

financial intermediaries Institutions (such as banks, insurance companies, mutual funds, pension funds, and finance companies) that borrow funds from people who have saved and then make loans to others. **6**

financial intermediation The process of indirect finance whereby financial intermediaries link lender-savers and borrower-spenders. **31**

financial markets Markets in which funds are transferred from people who have a surplus of available funds to people who have a shortage of available funds. **1**

financial panic The widespread collapse of financial markets and intermediaries in an economy. **38**

Fisher effect The outcome that when expected inflation occurs, interest rates will rise; named after economist Irving Fisher. **94**

fixed bank rate regime System whereby the central bank can change the bank rate on any business day. **431**

fixed exchange rate regime A regime in which central banks buy and sell their own currencies to keep their exchange rates fixed at a certain level. **392**

fixed investment Spending by firms on equipment (computers, airplanes) and structures (factories, office buildings) and planned spending on residential housing. **499**

fixed-payment loan A credit market instrument that provides a borrower with an amount of money that is repaid by making a fixed payment periodically (usually monthly) for a set number of years. **58**

floating bank rate regime The bank rate is tied to a specific market interest rate. **394**

foreign bonds Bonds sold in a foreign country and denominated in that country's currency. **28**

foreign exchange intervention An international financial transaction in which a central bank buys or sells currency to influence foreign exchange rates. **423**

foreign exchange market The market in which exchange rates are determined. **3, 133**

foreign exchange rate The price of one country's currency in terms of another's. See also *exchange rate*. **3**

forward contract An agreement by two parties to engage in a financial transaction at a future (forward) point in time. **300**

forward exchange rate The exchange rate for a forward transaction. **135**

forward transaction A transaction that involves the exchange of bank deposits denominated in different currencies at some specified future date. **135**

four pillar approach Regulation of the banking industry by institution (banking, brokerage, trusts, and insurance), versus regulation by function. **228**

fractal A complex geometric figure characterized by self similarity. **624**

free banking A concept that permitted the organization of a bank by any group that met certain established criteria concerning the amount of equity capital and maintenance of reserves. **221**

free-rider problem The problem that occurs when people who do not pay for information take advantage of the information that other people have paid for. **164**

fully funded Describing a pension plan in which the contributions to the plan and their earnings over the years are sufficient to pay out the defined benefits when they come due. **287**

futures option See *financial futures option*.

gap analysis A measurement of the sensitivity of bank profits to changes in interest rates, calculated by subtracting the amount of rate-sensitive liabilities from the amount of rate-sensitive assets. **207**

globalization The growing integration and interdependence of national economies. **415**

gold standard A regime under which a currency is directly convertible into gold. **222, 430**

Governing Council of the Bank of Canada A council with six members (including the governor) that is responsible for the management of the Bank. **327**

government budget constraint The requirement that the government budget deficit equal the sum of the change in the monetary base and the change in government bonds held by the public. **597**

government deposit transfers The transfer (by the Bank of Canada) of government deposits between the government's deposit account with the Bank of Canada and the government's deposit accounts with the direct clearers. **345**

government spending Spending by all levels of government on goods and services. **497, 544**

gross domestic product (GDP) The value of all final goods and services produced in the economy during the course of a year. **14**

group life insurance Insurance sold to a group of people under a single policy. **279**

hedge To protect oneself against risk. **301**

hedge fund A special type of mutual fund that engages in "market-neutral strategies." **292**

high-powered money The monetary base. **347**

hyperinflation An extreme inflation in which the inflation rate exceeds 50% per month. **46**

hysteresis A departure from full employment levels as a result of past high unemployment. **555**

incentive-compatible Having the incentives of both parties to a contract in alignment. **171**

income The flow of earnings. **44**

indebtedness In describing a country, the total amount it has borrowed from banks. **237**

indexed bond A bond whose interest and principal payments are adjusted for changes in the price level, and whose interest rate thus provides a direct measure of a real interest rate. **76**

indirect clearers Members of the Canadian Payments Association who do not maintain a settlement account at the Bank of Canada, but retain a direct clearer to represent them in the clearing and settlement process. **381**

individual life insurance Insurance sold one policy at a time. **279**

inflation The condition of a continually rising price level. **8**

inflation rate The rate of change of the price level, usually measured as a percentage change per year. **8**

initial public offering (IPO) A stock whose firm is issuing it for the first time. **296**

insolvent A situation in which the value of a firm's or bank's assets has fallen below its liabilities; bankrupt. **178**

institutional investors Institutional investors–mutual funds and pension funds–are important players in Canadian financial markets; they are also the predominant players in the stock markets, with over 70% of the total daily volume in the stock market due to their trading. **291**

items in transit (float) Items in the process of collection. **189**

interbank deposits Deposits made at other banks. **189**

interest parity condition The observation that the domestic interest rate equals the foreign interest rate plus the expected appreciation in the foreign currency. **144**

interest rate The cost of borrowing or the price paid for the rental of funds (usually expressed as a percentage per year). **2**

interest-rate forward contract A forward contract that is linked to a debt instrument. **300**

interest-rate futures contract A futures contract that is linked to a debt instrument. It is similar to an interest-rate forward contract. **302**

interest-rate risk The possible reduction in returns associated with changes in interest rates. **72, 194**

interest-rate swap A financial contract that allows one party to exchange (swap) a set of interest payments for another set of interest payments owned by another party. **319**

intermediate target Any of a number of variables, such as monetary aggregates or interest rates, that have a direct effect on employment and the price level and that the central bank seeks to influence. **406**

International Monetary Fund (IMF) The international organization created by the Bretton Woods agreement whose objective is to promote the growth of world trade by making loans to countries experiencing balance-of-payments difficulties. **431**

international policy coordination Agreements among countries to enact policies cooperatively. **415**

international reserves Central bank holdings of assets denominated in foreign currencies. **423**

inventory investment Spending by firms on additional holdings of raw materials, parts, and finished goods. **499**

inverted yield curve A yield curve that is downward-sloping. **119**

investment banks Firms that assist in the initial sale of securities in the primary market. **20**

***IS* curve** The relationship that describes the combinations of aggregate output and interest rates for which the total quantity of goods produced equals the total quantity demanded (goods market equilibrium). **511**

January effect An abnormal rise in stock prices from December to January. **623**

junk bonds Bonds with ratings below Baa (or BBB) that have a high default risk. **116**

Keynesian A follower of John Maynard Keynes who believes that movements in the price level and aggregate output are driven by changes not only in the money supply but also in government spending and fiscal policy and who does not regard the economy as inherently stable. **541**

Large Value Transfer System (LVTS) An electronic, net settlement system for the transfer of large-value payments. **380**

law of one price The principle that if two countries produce an identical good, the price of this good should be the same throughout the world no matter which country produces it. **137**

lender of last resort Provider of reserves to financial institutions when no one else would provide them in order to prevent a financial crisis. **224, 390**

leverage ratio A bank's capital divided by its assets. **254**

liabilities IOUs or debts. **18**

liability management The acquisition of funds at low cost to increase profits. **194**

liquid Easily converted into cash. **20**

liquidity management The decisions made by a bank to maintain sufficient liquid assets to meet the bank's obligations to depositors. **194**

liquidity preference framework A model developed by John Maynard Keynes that predicts the equilibrium interest rate on the basis of the supply of and demand for money. **99**

liquidity preference theory John Maynard Keynes's theory of the demand for money. **478**

liquidity premium theory The theory that the interest rate on a long-term bond will equal an average of short-term interest rates expected to occur over the life of the long-term bond plus a positive term (liquidity) premium. **125**

liquidity The relative ease and speed with which an asset can be converted into cash. **46, 80**

LM **curve** The relationship that describes the combinations of interest rates and aggregate output for which the quantity of money demanded equals the quantity of money supplied. **511**

load funds Open-end mutual funds sold by salespeople who receive a commission that is paid at the time of purchase and is immediately subtracted from the redemption value of the shares. **292**

loan commitment A bank's commitment (for a specified future period of time) to provide a firm with loans up to a given amount at an interest rate that is tied to some market interest rate. **204**

loan sale The sale under a contract (also called a secondary loan participation) of all or part of the cash stream from a specific loan, thereby removing the loan from the bank's balance sheet. **208**

loanable funds framework Determining the equilibrium interest rate by analyzing the supply of and demand for bonds (loanable funds). **86**

loanable funds The quantity of loans. **86**

long position A contractual obligation to take delivery of an underlying financial instrument. **301**

long-run aggregate supply curve The quantity of output supplied in the long run at any given price level. **550**

long-run monetary neutrality See *monetary neutrality.*

long-term With reference to a debt instrument, having a maturity of ten years or more. **19**

LVTS See *Large Value Transaction System.*

LVTS participants Members of the Canadian Payments Association (CPA) who participate in the LVTS and maintain a settlement account at the Bank of Canada. **380**

M1 The narrowest measure of money that the Bank of Canada reports, MI includes currency, personal chequing accounts, and current accounts. **51**

M1+ M1, plus other assets that have cheque-writing features—all chequable notice deposits at chartered banks, TMLs, and CUCPs. **51**

M1++ M1+, plus all non-chequable notice deposits at chartered banks, TMLs, and CUCPs. **51**

M2 Adds to M1 money market deposit accounts, money market mutual fund shares, small-denomination time deposits, savings deposits, overnight repurchase agreements, and overnight Eurodollars. **51**

M2+ Includes M2 plus deposits at near banks, life insurance company annuities, and money market mutual funds. **52**

M2++ Adds to M2+ Canada Savings Bonds and non-money market mutual funds. **52**

M3 Adds to M2 large-denomination time deposits, long-term repurchase agreements, and institutional money market fund shares. **51**

macro hedge A hedge of interest-rate risk for a financial institution's entire portfolio. **305**

managed float regime The current international financial environment in which exchange rates fluctuate from day to day but central banks attempt to influence their countries' exchange rates by buying and selling currencies. Also known as a *dirty float.* **423**

margin requirement A sum of money that must be kept in an account (the margin account) at a brokerage firm. **308**

marginal propensity to consume The slope of the consumption function line that measures the change in consumer expenditure resulting from an additional dollar of disposable income. **498**

marked to market Repriced and settled in the margin account at the end of every trading day to reflect any change in the value of the futures contract. **308**

market equilibrium A situation occurring when the quantity that people are willing to buy (demand) equals the quantity that people are willing to sell (supply). **84**

market fundamentals Items that have a direct impact on future income streams of a security. **618**

maturity Time to the expiration date (maturity date) of a debt instrument. **19**

mean reversion The phenomenon that stocks with low returns today tend to have high returns in the future, and vice versa. **623**

medium-term With reference to a debt instrument, having a maturity of one to ten years. **19**

medium of exchange Anything that is used to pay for goods and services. **44**

micro hedge A hedge for a specific asset. **305**

modern quantity theory of money The theory that changes in aggregate spending are determined primarily by changes in the money supply. **543**

monetarism A theory that emphasizes the importance of money in the economy, but opposes the use of activist stabilization policy. **412**

monetarist A follower of Milton Friedman who sees changes in the money supply as the primary source of movements in the price level and aggregate output and who views the economy as inherently stable. **541**

monetary aggregates The various measures of the money supply used by the central bank (M1, M2, and M3). **51**

monetary base See *base money.*

monetary conditions Determined by the level of short-term interest rates and the exchange rate of the Canadian dollar. **386**

monetary neutrality A proposition that in the long run, a percentage rise in the money supply is matched by the same percentage rise in the price level, leaving unchanged the real money supply and all other economic variables such as interest rates. **151**

monetary policy The management of the money supply and interest rates. **10**

monetary theory The theory that relates changes in the quantity of money to changes in aggregate economic activity and the price level. **8, 473**

monetizing the debt A method of financing government spending whereby the government debt issued to finance government spending is removed from the hands of the public and is replaced by high-powered money instead. Also called *printing money.* **597**

money Anything that is generally accepted in payment for goods or services or in the repayment of debts. **6**

money centre banks Large banks in key financial centres. **198**

money market A financial market in which only short-term debt instruments (generally those with original maturity of less than one year) are traded. **21**

money multiplier A ratio that relates the change in the money supply to a given change in the monetary base. **363**

moral hazard The risk that one party to a transaction will engage in behaviour that is undesirable from the other party's point of view. **33**

multilateral netting The LVTS process by which only the net credit or debit position of each participant vis-à-vis all other participants is calculated for settlement, thereby reducing the need for a large amount of settlement balances. **380**

multiple deposit creation The process whereby, when the Bank of Canada supplies the banking system with $1 of additional reserves, deposits increase by a multiple of this amount. **354**

municipal bonds (municipals) Securities issued by municipal governments. **28**

NAIRU (nonaccelerating inflation rate of unemployment) The rate of unemployment when demand for labour equals supply, consequently eliminating the tendency for the inflation rate to change. **420, 548**

national banks Federally chartered banks in the U.S. **221**

natural rate level of output The level of aggregate output produced at the natural rate of unemployment at which there is no tendency for wages or prices to change. **533, 549**

natural rate of unemployment The rate of unemployment consistent with full employment at which the demand for labor equals the supply of labour. **403, 548**

net exports Net foreign spending on domestic goods and services, equal to exports minus imports. **497, 544**

net worth The difference between a firm's assets (what it owns or is owed) and its liabilities (what it owes). Also called *equity capital.* **167**

no-load funds Mutual funds sold directly to the public on which no sales commissions are charged. **292**

nominal anchor A nominal variable such as the inflation rate, an exchange rate, or the money supply that monetary policymakers use to tie down the price level. **447**

nominal interest rate An interest rate that does not take inflation into account. **74**

nonaccelerating inflation rate of unemployment See *NAIRU.* **420, 548**

nonactivist An economist who believes that the performance of the economy would be improved if the government avoided active policy to eliminate unemployment. **550**

nonbank banks Limited-service banks that either do not make commercial loans or do not take in deposits. **227**

nonborrowed monetary base The monetary base minus discount loans. **368**

notional principal The amount on which interest is being paid in a swap arrangement. **319**

off-balance-sheet activities Bank activities that involve trading financial instruments and the generation of income from fees and loan sales, all of which affect bank profits but are not visible on bank balance sheets. **208, 254**

official reserve transactions balance The current account balance plus items in the capital account. **429**

open interest The number of contracts outstanding. **305**

open market operations The Bank of Canada's buying or selling of bonds in the open market. **329, 347**

open market purchase A purchase of bonds by the Bank of Canada. **348**

open market sale A sale of bonds by the Bank of Canada. **348**

open-end fund A mutual fund in which shares can be redeemed at any time at a price that is tied to the asset value of the fund. **291**

operating band The Bank's operational objective is to keep the overnight rate within an operating band of 50 basis points. **381**

operating target Any of a set of variables, such as reserve aggregates or interest rates, that the Bank of

Canada seeks to influence and that are responsive to its policy tools. **406**

opportunity cost The amount of interest (expected return) sacrificed by not holding an alternative asset. **100**

optimal forecast The best guess of the future using all available information. **614**

option A contract that gives the purchaser the option (right) to buy or sell the underlying financial instrument at a specified price, called the exercise price or strike price, within a specific period of time (the term to expiration). **312**

over-the-counter (OTC) market A secondary market in which dealers at different locations who have an inventory of securities stand ready to buy and sell securities "over the counter" to anyone who comes to them and is willing to accept their prices. **21**

overdraft loans Borrowings from the Bank of Canada. **188**

overnight interest rate The interest rate at which participants borrow and lend overnight funds to each other in the money market. **24, 381**

par value See *face value*.

partial crowding out The situation in which an increase in government spending leads to a decline in private spending that does not completely offset the rise in government spending. **546**

payments system The method of conducting transactions in the economy. **47**

perpetuity See *consol*.

permanent life insurance An insurance policy that has a constant premium throughout the life of the policy. **279**

Phillips curve theory A theory suggesting that changes in inflation are influenced by the state of the economy relative to its production capacity, as well as to other factors. **420**

planned investment spending Total planned spending by businesses on new physical capital (machines, computers, apartment buildings) plus planned spending on new homes. **497, 544**

policy ineffectiveness proposition The conclusion from the new classical model that anticipated policy has no effect on output fluctuations. **636**

policy mix The combination of fiscal and monetary policies used together. **526**

political business cycle A business cycle caused by expansionary policies before an election. **338**

premium The amount paid for an option contract. **312**

present discounted value See *present value*. **60**

present value Today's value of a payment to be received in the future when the interest rate is *i*. **58**

primary dealers Government securities dealers, operating out of private firms or commercial banks, with whom the Bank of Canada's open market desk trades. **389**

primary market A financial market in which new issues of a security are sold to initial buyers. **20**

principal–agent problem A moral hazard problem that occurs when the managers in control (the agents) act in their own interest rather than in the interest of the owners (the principals) due to different sets of incentives. **168**

printing money See *monetizing the debt*.

provincial bonds (provincials) Securities issued by provincial governments. **28**

prudential supervision See *bank supervision*.

put option An option contract that provides the right to sell a security at a specified price. **313**

quantity theory of money The theory that nominal income is determined solely by movements in the quantity of money. **475**

quotas Restrictions on the quantity of foreign goods that can be imported. **140**

random walk The movements of a variable whose future changes cannot be predicted (are random) because the variable is just as likely to fall as to rise from today's value. **620**

rate of capital gain The change in a security's price relative to the initial purchase price. **71**

rate of return See *return*.

rational expectations Expectations that reflect optimal forecasts (the best guess of the future) using all available information. **613**

real business cycle theory A theory that views real shocks to tastes and technology as the major driving force behind short-run business cycle fluctuations. **555**

real interest rate The interest rate adjusted for expected changes in the price level (inflation) so that it more accurately reflects the true cost of borrowing. **74**

real money balances The quantity of money in real terms. **479**

real terms Terms reflecting actual goods and services one can buy. **74**

recession A period when aggregate output is declining. **7**

redemption See *call*.

redeposits Transfers of government deposits from the Bank of Canada to the direct clearers. **396**

reduced-form evidence Evidence that examines whether one variable has an effect on another by simply looking directly at the relationship between the two variables. **562**

registered bonds The name of the owner appears on the bond certificate and is also recorded at the Bank of Canada. **27**

regulatory capital Financial institutions are required by regulatory authorities to hold this capital to protect depositors, policyholders, and liability guarantors. **40**

Regulation Q The regulation under which the Federal Reserve System had the power to set maximum interest rates that banks could pay on time deposits. **215**

regulatory forbearance Regulators' refraining from exercising their right to put an insolvent bank out of business. **263**

reinsurance An allocation of the portion of the insurance risk to another company in exchange for a portion of the insurance premium. **282**

repo See *Special Purchase and Resale Agreements.*

required reserves Reserves that are held to meet the central bank's requirement that for every dollar of deposits at a bank, a certain fraction must be kept as reserves. **346**

reserve currency A currency, such as the U.S. dollar, that is used by other countries to denominate the assets they hold as international reserves. **432**

reserves (total cash reserves) Banks' settlement balances with the Bank of Canada plus currency that is physically held by banks (vault cash). **190, 345**

restrictive covenants Provisions that restrict and specify certain activities that a borrower can engage in. **160**

return on assets *(ROA)* Net profit after taxes per dollar of assets. **200**

return on equity *(ROE)* Net profit after taxes per dollar of equity capital. **200**

return The payments to the owner of a security plus the change in the security's value, expressed as a fraction of its purchase price. More precisely called the *rate of return.* **69**

revaluation Resetting of the fixed value of a currency at a higher level. **434**

reverse causation A situation in which one variable is said to cause another variable when in reality the reverse is true. **564**

reverse repo See *Sale and Repurchase Agreements.*

Ricardian equivalence Named after the nineteenth-century British economist David Ricardo, it contends that when the government runs deficits and issues bonds, the public recognizes that it will be subject to higher taxes in the future in order to pay off these bonds. **599**

risk premium The spread between the interest rate on bonds with default risk and the interest rate on default-free bonds. **114**

risk structure of interest rates The relationship among the various interest rates on bonds with the same term to maturity. **113**

risk The degree of uncertainty associated with the return on an asset. **80**

Sale and Repurchase Agreements (SRAs). The Bank of Canada's sale of government securities to primary dealers with an agreement to repurchase them one business day later. **346**

Schedule I banks Comprised of the Big Six, together with the Laurentian Bank of Canada and the Canadian Western Bank. **225**

Schedule II banks Include three domestic Schedule II banks, Citizen Bank (owned by Vancity Savings), First Nations Bank (owned by the Toronto Dominion Bank), and Manulife Bank (owned by Manulife Insurance), and 36 subsidiaries (i.e., separate Canadian legal entities) of foreign banks. **225**

Schedule III banks Foreign banks allowed to branch directly into Canada, under certain restrictions. **225**

seasoned issue A stock issued for sale for which prior issues currently sell in the market. **296**

secondary market A financial market in which securities that have previously been issued (and are thus secondhand) can be resold. **20**

secondary reserves Short-term U.S. government and agency securities held by banks. **190**

secured debt Debt guaranteed by collateral. **160**

securitization The process of transforming illiquid financial assets into marketable capital market instruments. **242**

security A claim on the borrower's future income that is sold by the borrower to the lender. Also called a *financial instrument.* **2**

segmented markets theory A theory of term structure that sees markets for different-maturity bonds as completely separated and segmented such that the interest rate for bonds of a given maturity is determined solely by supply of and demand for bonds of that maturity. **124**

seignorage The revenue a government receives by issuing money. **222, 455**

self-correcting mechanism A characteristic of the economy that causes output to return eventually to the natural rate level regardless of where it is initially. **550**

settlement balances Deposits held by directly clearing members of the Canadian Payments Association at the Bank of Canada. They are also known as *clearing balances.* **40, 188, 345**

share draft account An account at a credit union that is similar to a NOW account. **244**

short position A contractual obligation to deliver an underlying financial instrument. **301**

short sale Involves borrowing a security from an investor or another financial institution for a fixed time period and selling it in the market with the intention of repurchasing it when it is due to be returned to the lender. **188**

short-term With reference to a debt instrument, having a maturity of one year or less. **19**

simple deposit multiplier The multiple increase in deposits generated from an increase in the banking system's reserves in a simple model in which the behavior of depositor and bank plays no role. **358**

simple loan A credit market instrument providing the borrower with an amount of funds that must be repaid to the lender at the maturity date along with an additional payment (interest). **58**

sources of the base The factors that determine the monetary base. **347**

sovereign loans Loans to foreign governments and their agencies in the less developed countries. **235**

special drawing rights (SDRs) An IMF-issued paper substitute for gold that functions as international reserves. **435**

Special Purchase and Resale Agreements (SPRAs). The Bank of Canada's purchase of government securities from primary dealers with an agreement to resell them one business day later. **344**

specialist A dealer-broker operating in an exchange who maintains orderly trading of the securities for which he or she is responsible. **297**

spot exchange rate The exchange rate for a spot transaction. **135**

spot transaction The predominant type of exchange rate transaction, involving the immediate exchange of bank deposits. **135**

standing facilities Refers to the Bank of Canada standing ready to lend to or borrow from a participant to bring their settlement balances to zero at the end of the banking day. **382**

state banks State-chartered banks in the U.S. **221**

sterilized foreign exchange intervention A foreign exchange intervention with an offsetting open market operation that leaves the monetary base unchanged. **425**

stock option An option on an individual stock. **312**

stock A security that is a claim on the earnings and assets of a corporation. **2**

store of value A repository of purchasing power over time. **46**

strike price See *exercise price*.

structural model A description of how the economy operates, using a collection of equations that describe the behaviour of firms and consumers in many sectors of the economy. **562**

structural model evidence Evidence that examines whether one variable affects another by using data to build a model illustrating the channels through which this variable affects the other. **562**

supply curve A curve depicting the relationship between quantity supplied and price when all other economic variables are held constant. **84**

supply shock Any change in technology or the supply of raw materials that can shift the aggregate supply curve. **553**

swap A financial contract that obligates one party to exchange (swap) a set of payments it owns for a set of payments owned by another party. **319**

sweep account An arrangement in which any balances above a certain amount in a corporation's chequing account at the end of a business day are "swept out" of the account and invested in overnight repos that pay the corporation interest. **215**

systemic risk The risk to the entire payments system due to the inability of one financial institution to fulfill its payment obligations in a timely fashion. **380**

T-account A simplified balance sheet with lines in the form of a T that lists only the changes that occur in balance sheet items starting from some initial balance sheet position. **191**

tariffs Taxes on imported goods. **140**

Taylor rule Economist John Taylor's monetary policy rule that explains how the federal funds rate target is set. **420**

temporary life insurance An insurance policy with a premium that is matched every year to the amount needed to insure against death during the period of the term. **279**

term deposit receipts (term notes) Non-negotiable CDs issued in denominations ranging from $5000 to $100 000 and with maturities of 1 day to 5 years. **23**

term structure of interest rates The relationship among interest rates on bonds with different terms to maturity but with the same risk of default. **113**

theory of asset demand The theory that the quantity demanded of an asset is (1) usually positively related to wealth, (2) positively related to its expected return relative to alternative assets, (3) negatively related to the risk of its return relative to alternative assets, and (4) positively related to its liquidity relative to alternative assets. **81**

theory of purchasing power parity (PPP) The theory that exchange rates between any two currencies will adjust to reflect changes in the price levels of the two countries. **138**

time-inconsistency problem The problem that occurs when monetary policymakers conduct monetary policy in a discretionary way and pursue expansionary policies that are attractive in the short run but lead to bad long-run outcomes. **448**

total cash reserves See *reserves*.

trade balance The difference between merchandise exports and imports. **428**

transaction costs The time and money spent trying to exchange financial assets, goods, or services. **31**

transmission mechanisms of monetary policy The channels through which the money supply affects economic activity. **562**

trustees The power to serve as the representative of a person or corporation. **231**

underfunded Describing a pension plan in which the contributions and their earnings are not sufficient to pay out the defined benefits when they come due. **287**

underwriters Investment banks that guarantee prices on securities to corporations and then sell the securities to the public. **296**

underwriting Guaranteeing prices on securities to corporations and then selling the securities to the public. **20**

unemployment rate The percentage of the labour force not working. **7**

unexploited profit opportunity A situation in which an investor can earn a higher than normal return. **617**

unit of account Anything used to measure value in an economy. **45**

unsecured debt Debt not guaranteed by collateral. **160**

unsterilized foreign exchange intervention A foreign exchange intervention in which a central bank allows the purchase or sale of domestic currency to affect the monetary base. **425**

uses of the base The items accounting for use of the monetary base (Bank of Canada notes outstanding, bank settlement balances, and coins not held by the Bank of Canada). **347**

vault cash (cash reserves) Currency that is physically held by banks and stored in vaults overnight. **188**

velocity of money The rate of turnover of money; the average number of times per year that a dollar is spent in buying the total amount of final goods and services produced in the economy. **474, 542**

venture capital firm A financial intermediary that pools the resources of its partners and uses the funds to help entrepreneurs start up new businesses. **169**

virtual bank A bank that has no building but rather exists only in cyberspace. **213**

wealth All resources owned by an individual, including all assets. **80**

World Bank The International Bank for Reconstruction and Redevelopment, an international organization that provides long-term loans to assist developing countries in building dams, roads, and other physical capital that would contribute to their economic development. **431**

yield curve A plot of the interest rates for particular types of bonds with different terms to maturity. **119**

yield on a discount basis The measure of interest rates by which dealers in bill markets quote the interest rate on Treasury bills. Also known as the *discount yield.* **67**

yield to maturity The interest rate that equates the present value of payments received from a credit market instrument with its value today. **60**

zero-coupon bond See *discount bond.*

ANSWERS TO SELECTED QUESTIONS AND PROBLEMS

Chapter 1 Why Study Money, Banking, and Financial Markets?

2. The data in Figures 1-1, 1-2, 1-3, and 1-4 suggest that real output, the inflation rate, and interest rates would all fall.

4. You might be more likely to buy a house or a car because the cost of financing them would fall, or you might be less likely to save because you earn less on your savings.

6. No. It is true that people who borrow to purchase a house or a car are worse off because it costs them more to finance their purchase; however, savers benefit because they can earn higher interest rates on their savings.

8. They channel funds from people who do not have a productive use for them to people who do, thereby resulting in higher economic efficiency.

10. The lower price for a firm's shares means that it can raise a smaller amount of funds, and so investment in facilities and equipment will fall.

12. It makes foreign goods more expensive, so British consumers will buy fewer foreign goods and more domestic goods.

14. In the mid- to late 1970s and in the early 1980s and 1990s, the value of the dollar was low, making travel abroad relatively more expensive; thus it was a good time to vacation in Canada and see the Canadian Rockies. With the rise in the dollar's value in the late 1980s, travel abroad became relatively cheaper, making it a good time to visit the Tower of London.

Chapter 2 An Overview of the Financial System

1. The share of IBM stock is an asset for its owner because it entitles the owner to a share of the earnings and assets of IBM. The share is a liability for IBM because it is a claim on its earnings and assets by the owner of the share.

3. Yes, because the absence of financial markets means that funds cannot be channeled to people who have the most productive use for them. Entrepreneurs then cannot acquire funds to set up businesses that would help the economy grow rapidly.

5. This statement is false. Prices in secondary markets determine the prices that firms issuing securities receive in primary markets. In addition, secondary markets make securities more liquid and thus easier to sell in the primary markets. Therefore, secondary markets are, if anything, more important than primary markets.

7. Because you know your family member better than a stranger, you know more about the borrower's honesty, propensity for risk taking, and other traits. There is less asymmetric information than with a stranger and less likelihood of an adverse selection problem, with the result that you are more likely to lend to the family member.

9. Loan sharks can threaten their borrowers with bodily harm if borrowers take actions that might jeopardize their paying off the loan. Hence borrowers from a loan shark are less likely to increase moral hazard.

11. Yes, because even if you know that a borrower is taking actions that might jeopardize paying off the loan, you must still stop the borrower from doing so. Because that may be costly, you may not spend the time and effort to reduce moral hazard, and so the problem of moral hazard still exists.

13. Because the costs of making the loan to your neighbour are high (legal fees, fees for a credit check, and so on), you will probably not be able to earn 5% on the loan after your expenses even though it has a 10% interest rate. You are better off depositing your savings with a financial intermediary and earning 5% interest. In addition, you are likely to bear less risk by depositing your savings at the bank rather than lending them to your neighbour.

15. Increased discussion of foreign financial markets in the Canadian press and the growth in markets for international financial instruments such as Eurodollars and Eurobonds.

Chapter 3 What Is Money?

2. Since the orchard owner likes only bananas but the banana grower doesn't like apples, the banana grower will not want apples in exchange for his bananas, and they will not trade. Similarly, the chocolatier will not be willing to trade with the banana grower because she does not like bananas. The orchard owner will not trade with the chocolatier because he doesn't like chocolate. Hence in a barter economy, trade among these three people may well not take place because in no case is there a double coincidence of wants. However, if money is introduced into the economy, the orchard owner can sell his apples to the chocolatier and then use the money to buy bananas from the banana grower. Similarly, the banana grower can use the money she receives from the orchard owner to buy chocolate from the chocolatier, and the chocolatier can use the money to buy apples from the orchard owner. The result is that the need for a double coincidence of wants is eliminated,

and everyone is better off because all three producers are now able to eat what they like best.

4. Because a cheque was so much easier to transport than gold, people would frequently rather be paid by cheque even if there was a possibility that the cheque might bounce. In other words, the lower transactions costs involved in handling cheques made people more willing to accept them.

6. Because money was losing value at a slower rate (the inflation rate was lower) in the 1950s than in the 1970s, it was then a better store of value, and you would have been willing to hold more of it.

9. Money loses its value at an extremely rapid rate in hyperinflation, so you want to hold it for as short a time as possible. Thus money is like a hot potato that is quickly passed from one person to another.

11. Not necessarily. Although the total amount of debt has predicted inflation and the business cycle better than M1, M1+, M1++, M2, M2+, M2++, or M3, it may not be a better predictor in the future. Without some theoretical reason for believing that the total amount of debt will continue to predict well in the future, we may not want to define money as the total amount of debt.

13. M1 contains the most liquid assets. M2++ is the largest measure.

15. Revisions are not a serious problem for long-run movements of the money supply because revisions for short-run (one-month) movements tend to cancel out. Revisions for long-run movements, such as one-year growth rates, are thus typically quite small.

Chapter 4   Understanding Interest Rates

1. Less. It would be worth $1/(1 + 0.20) = \$0.83$ when the interest rate is 20%, rather than $1/(1 + 0.10) = \$0.91$ when the interest rate is 10%.

3. $\$1100/(1 + 0.10) + \$1210/(1 + 0.10)^2 + \$1331/(1 + 0.10)^3 = \$3000$.

5. $\$2000 = \$100/(1 + i) + \$100/(1 + i)^2 + \dots + \$100/(1 + i)^{20} + \$1000/(1 + i)^{20}$.

7. 14.9%, derived as follows: The present value of the $2 million payment five years from now is $\$2/(1 + i)^5$ million, which equals the $1 million loan. Thus $1 = 2/(1 + i)^5$. Solving for i, $(1 + i)^5 = 2$, so that $i = \sqrt[5]{2} - 1 = 0.149 = 14.9\%$.

9. If the one-year bond did not have a coupon payment, its yield to maturity would be ($1000 – $800)/$800 = $200/$800 = 0.25 = 25%. Since it does have a coupon payment, its yield to maturity must be greater than 25%. However, because the current yield is a good approximation of the yield to maturity for a 20-year bond, we know that the yield to maturity on this bond is approximately 15%. Therefore, the one-year bond has a higher yield to maturity.

11. You would rather own the Treasury bill because it has a higher yield to maturity. As the example in

the text indicates, the discount yield's understatement of the yield to maturity is substantial. Thus the yield to maturity on the one-year bill would perhaps be greater than 9%, the yield to maturity on the one-year Canada bond.

13. No. If interest rates rise sharply in the future, long-term bonds may suffer such a sharp fall in price that their return might be quite low, possibly even negative.

15. The economists are right. They reason that nominal interest rates were below expected rates of inflation in the late 1970s, making real interest rates negative. The expected inflation rate, however, fell much faster than nominal interest rates in the mid-1980s, so nominal interest rates were above the expected inflation rate and real rates became positive.

Chapter 5   The Behaviour of Interest Rates

2. (a) More, because your wealth has increased; (b) more, because it has become more liquid; (c) less, because its expected return has fallen relative to Air Canada stock; (d) more, because it has become less risky relative to stocks; (e) less, because its expected return has fallen.

4. (a) More, because they have become more liquid; (b) more, because their expected return has risen relative to stocks; (c) less, because they have become less liquid relative to stocks; (d) less, because their expected return has fallen; (e) more, because they have become more liquid.

6. When the Bank of Canada sells bonds to the public, it increases the supply of bonds, thus shifting the supply curve B^s to the right. The result is that the intersection of the supply and demand curves B^s and B^d occurs at a higher equilibrium interest rate, and the interest rate rises. With the liquidity preference framework, the decrease in the money supply shifts the money supply curve M^s to the left, and the equilibrium interest rate rises. The answer from the loanable funds framework is consistent with the answer from the liquidity preference framework.

8. When the price level rises, the quantity of money in real terms falls (holding the nominal supply of money constant); to restore their holdings of money in real terms to their former level, people will want to hold a greater nominal quantity of money. Thus the money demand curve M^d shifts to the right, and the interest rate rises.

11. Interest rates would rise. A sudden increase in people's expectations of future real estate prices raises the expected return on real estate relative to bonds, so the demand for bonds falls. The demand curve B^d shifts to the left, and the equilibrium interest rate rises.

13. In the loanable funds framework, the increased riskiness of bonds lowers the demand for bonds.

The demand curve B^d shifts to the left, and the equilibrium interest rate rises. The same answer is found in the liquidity preference framework. The increased riskiness of bonds relative to money increases the demand for money. The money demand curve M^d shifts to the right, and the equilibrium interest rate rises.

15. Yes, interest rates will rise. The lower commission on stocks makes them more liquid than bonds, and the demand for bonds will fall. The demand curve B^d will therefore shift to the left, and the equilibrium interest rate will rise.

17. The interest rate on corporate bonds will rise. Because people now expect interest rates to rise, the expected return on long-term corporate bonds will fall, and the demand for these bonds will decline. The demand curve B^d will therefore shift to the left, and the equilibrium interest rate will rise.

19. Interest rates will rise. When bond prices become volatile and bonds become riskier, the demand for bonds will fall. The demand curve B^d will shift to the left, and the equilibrium interest rate will rise.

Chapter 6 The Risk and Term Structure of Interest Rates

2. Canadian Treasury bills have lower default risk and more liquidity than negotiable CDs. Consequently, the demand for Treasury bills is higher, and they have a lower interest rate.

4. True. When bonds of different maturities are close substitutes, a rise in interest rates for one bond causes the interest rates for others to rise because the expected returns on bonds of different maturities cannot get too far out of line.

6. (a) The yield to maturity would be 5% for a one-year bond, 6% for a two-year bond, 6.33% for a three-year bond, 6.5% for a four-year bond, and 6.6% for a five-year bond. (b) The yield to maturity would be 5% for a one-year bond, 4.5% for a two-year bond, 4.33% for a three-year bond, 4.25% for a four-year bond, and 4.2% for a five-year bond. The upward-sloping yield curve in (a) would be even steeper if people preferred short-term bonds over long-term bonds because long-term bonds would then have a positive liquidity premium. The downward-sloping yield curve in (b) would be less steep and might even have a slight positive upward slope if the long-term bonds have a positive liquidity premium.

8. The flat yield curve at shorter maturities suggests that short-term interest rates are expected to fall moderately in the near future, while the steep upward slope of the yield curve at longer maturities indicates that interest rates further into the future are expected to rise. Because interest rates and expected inflation move together, the yield curve suggests that the market expects inflation to fall moderately in the near future but to rise later on.

10. The cost of borrowing increases, since the return demanded by investors rises to compensate them for the greater probability of default.

12. Lower brokerage commissions for corporate bonds would make them more liquid and thus increase their demand, which would lower their risk premium.

14. You would raise your predictions of future interest rates because the higher long-term rates imply that the average of the expected future short-term rates is higher.

Chapter 7 The Foreign Exchange Market

2. False. Although a weak currency has the negative effect of making it more expensive to buy foreign goods or to travel abroad, it may help domestic industry. Domestic goods become cheaper relative to foreign goods, and the demand for domestically produced goods increases. The resulting higher sales of domestic products may lead to higher employment, a beneficial effect on the economy.

4. It predicts that the value of the yen will fall 5% in terms of dollars.

6. Even though the Japanese price level rose relative to the American, the yen appreciated because the increase in Japanese productivity relative to American productivity made it possible for the Japanese to continue to sell their goods at a profit at a high value of the yen.

8. The pound depreciates but overshoots, declining by more in the short run than in the long run. Consider Britain the domestic country. The rise in the money supply leads to a higher domestic price level in the long run, which leads to a lower expected future exchange rate. The resulting expected depreciation of the pound raises the expected return on foreign deposits, shifting RET^F to the right. The rise in the money supply lowers the interest rate on pound deposits in the short run, which shifts RET^D to the left. The short-run outcome is a lower equilibrium exchange rate. However, in the long run, the domestic interest rate returns to its previous value, and RET^D shifts back to its original position. The exchange rate rises to some extent, although it still remains below its initial position.

10. The dollar will depreciate. A rise in nominal interest rates but a decline in real interest rates implies a rise in expected inflation that produces an expected depreciation of the dollar that is larger than the increase in the domestic interest rate. As a result, the expected return on foreign deposits rises by more than the expected return on domestic deposits. RET^F shifts rightward more than RET^D, so the equilibrium exchange rate falls.

12. The dollar will depreciate. An increased demand for imports would lower the expected future exchange rate and result in an expected appreciation of the foreign currency. The higher resulting expected return on foreign deposits shifts the RET^F schedule to the right, and the equilibrium exchange rate falls.

14. The contraction of the European money supply will increase European interest rates and raise the future value of the euro, both of which will shift RET^F (with Europe as the foreign country) to the right. The result is a decline in the value of the dollar.

Chapter 8 An Economic Analysis of Financial Structure

2. Financial intermediaries develop expertise in such areas as computer technology so that they can inexpensively provide liquidity services such as chequing accounts that lower transaction costs for depositors. Financial intermediaries can also take advantage of economies of scale and engage in large transactions that have a lower cost per dollar per transaction.

4. Standard accounting principles make profit verification easier, thereby reducing adverse selection and moral hazard problems in financial markets and hence making them operate better. Standard accounting principles make it easier for investors to screen out good firms from bad firms, thereby reducing the adverse selection problem in financial markets. In addition, they make it harder for managers to understate profits, thereby reducing the principal–agent (moral hazard) problem.

6. Smaller firms that are not well known are the most likely to use bank financing. Since it is harder for investors to acquire information about these firms, it will be hard for the firms to sell securities in the financial markets. Banks that specialize in collecting information about smaller firms will then be the only outlet these firms have for financing their activities.

8. Yes. The person who is putting her life savings into her business has more to lose if she takes on too much risk or engages in personally beneficial activities that don't lead to higher profits. So she will act more in the interest of the lender, making it more likely that the loan will be paid off.

10. True. If the borrower turns out to be a bad credit risk and goes broke, the lender loses less because the collateral can be sold to make up any losses on the loan. Thus adverse selection is not as severe a problem.

12. The separation of ownership and control creates a principal-agent problem. The managers (the agents) do not have as strong an incentive to maximize profits as the owners (the principals). Thus the managers might not work hard, might engage in wasteful spending on personal perks, or might pursue business strategies that enhance their personal power but do not increase profits.

14. A stock market crash reduces the net worth of firms and so increases the moral hazard problem. With less of an equity stake, owners have a greater incentive to take on risky projects and spend corporate funds on items that benefit them personally. A stock market crash, which increases the moral hazard problem, thus makes it less likely that lenders will be paid back. So lending and investment will decline, creating a financial crisis in which financial markets do not work well and the economy suffers.

Chapter 9 The Banking Firm and the Management of Financial Institutions

2. The rank from most to least liquid is (c), (b), (a), (d).

4. Reserves drop by $500. The T-account for the First Bank is as follows:

First Bank			
Assets		**Liabilities**	
Reserves	−$500	Chequable deposits	−$500

6. The bank would rather have the balance sheet shown in this problem because after it loses $50 million due to deposit outflow, the bank would still have excess reserves of $5 million: $50 million in reserves minus desired reserves of $45 million (10% of the $450 million of deposits). Thus the bank would not have to alter its balance sheet further and would not incur any costs as a result of the deposit outflow. By contrast, with the balance sheet in Problem 5, the bank would have a shortfall of reserves of $20 million ($25 million in reserves minus the desired reserves of $45 million). In this case, the bank will incur costs when it raises the necessary reserves through the methods described in the text.

8. No. When you turn a customer down, you may lose that customer's business forever, which is extremely costly. Instead, you might go out and borrow from other banks, corporations, or the Bank of Canada to obtain funds so that you can make the customer loans. Alternatively, you might sell negotiable CDs or some of your securities to acquire the necessary funds.

10. It can raise $1 million of capital by issuing new stock. It can cut its dividend payments by $1 million, thereby increasing its retained earnings by $1 million. It can decrease the amount of its assets so that the amount of its capital relative to its assets increases, thereby meeting the capital requirements.

12. Compensating balances can act as collateral. They also help establish long-term customer relationships, which make it easier for the bank to collect information about prospective borrowers, thus reducing the adverse selection problem. Compensating balances help the bank monitor the activities of a borrowing firm so that it can prevent the firm from taking on too much risk, thereby not acting in the interest of the bank.

14. The assets fall in value by $8 million (= $100 million $\times$ -2% $\times$ 4 years) while the liabilities fall in value by $10.8 million (= $90 million $\times$ -2% $\times$ 6 years). Since the liabilities fall in value by $2.8 million more than the assets do, the net worth of the bank rises by $2.8 million. The interest-rate risk can be reduced by shortening the maturity of the liabilities to a duration of four years or lengthening the maturity of the assets to a duration of six years. Alternatively, you could engage in an interest-rate swap, in which you swap the interest earned on your assets with the interest on another bank's assets that have a duration of six years.

Chapter 10 Banking Industry: Structure and Competition

2. (a) The Office of the Superintendent of Financial Institutions (OSFI), the Bank of Canada, and the CDIC; (b) the OSFI and provincial banking authorities; (c) provincial banking authorities.

4. Improvements in technology made it easier for investors to screen out bad from good credit risks. This made it easier for corporations to issue long-term debt securities as in the junk bond market, and also to raise funds by issuing short-term debt securities like commercial paper.

6. The Big Six were severely punished in the early 1980s when the recession hit hard the less developed countries. When Argentina, Brazil, Mexico, and Peru threatened to default on their loans, the banks chose to make more loans to enable them to service their debts, instead of declaring these countries in default and acknowledging losses. This increased the indebtedness of these countries and led to a number of debt conversion schemes (such as debt-debt swaps, debt-currency swaps, and debt-equity swaps) to alleviate their debt service obligations.

8. To introduce more competition into the Canadian financial services industry.

10. No, because the Saudi-owned bank is subject to the same regulations as the Canadian-owned bank.

12. The rise in inflation and the resulting higher interest rates on alternatives to chequable deposits meant that banks had a big shrinkage in this low-cost way of raising funds. The innovation of money market mutual funds also meant that the banks lost deposit account business.

14. The growth of the commercial paper market and the development of the junk bond market meant that corporations were now able to issue securities rather than borrow from banks, thus eroding the competitive advantage of banks on the lending side. Securitization has enabled other financial institutions to originate loans, again taking away some of the banks' loan business.

Chapter 11 Economic Analysis of Banking Regulation

2. There would be adverse selection because people who might want to burn their property for some personal gain would actively try to obtain substantial fire insurance policies. Moral hazard could also be a problem because a person with a fire insurance policy has less incentive to take measures to prevent a fire.

4. Regulations that restrict banks from holding risky assets directly decrease the moral hazard of risk taking by the bank. Requirements that force banks to have a large amount of capital also decrease the banks' incentives for risk taking because banks now have more to lose if they fail. Such regulations will not completely eliminate the moral hazard problem because bankers have incentives to hide their holdings of risky assets from the regulators and to overstate the amount of their capital.

6. The S&L crisis did not occur until the 1980s because interest rates stayed low before then, so S&Ls were not subjected to losses from high interest rates. Also, the opportunities for risk taking were not available until the 1980s, when legislation and financial innovation made it easier for S&Ls to take on more risk, thereby greatly increasing the adverse selection and moral hazard problems.

8. FIRREA provided funds for the S&L bailout, created the Resolution Trust Corporation to manage the resolution of insolvent thrifts, eliminated the Federal Home Loan Bank Board and gave its regulatory role to the Office of Thrift Supervision, eliminated the FSLIC and turned its insurance role and regulatory responsibilities over to the FDIC, imposed restrictions on thrift activities similar to those in effect before 1982, increased the capital requirements to those adhered to by commercial banks, and increased the enforcement powers of thrift regulators.

10. Risk-based insurance premiums reduce the moral hazard incentives for banks to take on higher risk, in the form of lower capital or riskier assets. The problem with risk-based insurance premiums is that it is difficult to determine the amount of risk that the financial institution is taking.

12. Eliminating or limiting the amount of deposit insurance would help reduce the moral hazard of excessive risk taking on the part of banks. It

would, however, make bank failures and panics more likely, so it might not be a very good idea.

14. The economy would benefit from reduced moral hazard; that is, banks would not want to take on too much risk because doing so would increase their deposit insurance premiums. The problem is, however, that it is difficult to monitor the degree of risk in bank assets because often only the bank making the loans knows how risky they are.

Chapter 12 Nonbank Financial Institutions

1. Because there would be more uncertainty about how much they would have to pay out in any given year, life insurance companies would tend to hold shorter-term assets that are more liquid.

3. Because benefits paid out are set to equal contributions to the plan and their earnings.

5. False. Government pension plans are often underfunded. Many pension plans for both federal and provincial employees are not fully funded.

7. Because the bigger the policy, the greater the moral hazard—the incentive for the policyholder to engage in activities that make the insurance payoff more likely. Because payoffs are costly, the insurance company will want to reduce moral hazard by limiting the amount of insurance.

9. Because interest rates on loans are typically lower at banks than at finance companies.

11. Because you do not have to pay a commission on a no-load fund, it is cheaper than a load fund, which does require a commission.

13. Government loan guarantees may be very costly because like any insurance, they increase moral hazard. Because the banks and other institutions making the guaranteed loans do not suffer any losses if the loans default, these institutions have little incentive not to make bad loans. The resulting losses to the government can be substantial.

15. No. Investment banking is a risky business because if the investment bank cannot sell a security it is underwriting for the price it promised to pay the issuing firm, the investment bank can suffer substantial losses.

Chapter 13 Financial Derivatives

2. You would enter into a contract that specifies that you will sell the $25 million of bonds at a price of 110 one year from now.

4. You have a loss of 6 points, or $6000, per contract.

6. You would buy $100 million worth (1000 contracts) of the call long-term bond option with a delivery date of one year in the future and with a strike price that corresponds to a yield of 8%. This means that you would have the option to buy the long bond with the 8% interest rate, thereby making sure that you can earn the 8%. The disadvantage of the options contract is that you have to pay

a premium that you would not have to pay with a futures contract. The advantage of the options contract is that if the interest rate rises and the bond price falls during the next year, you do not have to exercise the option and so will be able to earn a higher rate than 8% when the funds come in next year, whereas with the futures contract, you have to take delivery of the bond and will only earn 8%.

8. You have a profit of 1 point ($1000) when you exercise the contract, but you have paid a premium of $1500 for the call option, so your net profit is -$500, a loss of $500.

10. Because for any given price at expiration, a lower strike price means a higher profit for a call option and a lower profit for a put option. A lower strike price makes a call option more desirable and raises its premium and makes a put option less desirable and lowers its premium.

12. It would swap interest on $42 million of fixed-rate assets for the interest on $42 million of variable-rate assets, thereby eliminating its income gap.

14. You would hedge the risk by buying 80 DM futures contracts that mature 3 months from now.

Chapter 14 Structure of Central Banks and the Bank of Canada

1. The primary motivation for the formation of the Bank of Canada was political. As the Great Depression undermined faith in the existing market economy and inflation blamed on the concentrated banking industry, support was given to the idea of a central bank.

3. The Bank Act was amended in 1967 to give the ultimate responsibility for monetary policy to the government. In practice, however, the Bank of Canada does essentially control monetary policy. In the event of a disagreement between the Bank and the government, the minister of finance can issue a directive that the Bank must follow.

5. After governor Coyne tendered his resignation in 1961 and Louis Rasminsky became the third governor of the Bank of Canada, upon assuming office he issued a public statement making clear his views regarding the division of responsibility between the Bank and the government. The matter rested until 1967 when the Bank of Canada Act was amended to confirm that the minister of finance and the governor of the Bank of Canada should consult regularly on monetary policy.

7. True. Assuming that politicians are driven by the need to win the next election, they are likely to seek short-run solutions to problems like high unemployment and interest rates. For example, they are likely to increase money growth in order to reduce unemployment and interest rates in the short run. In the long run, however, such policies will lead to more inflation.

9. By not renewing the governor's appointment when it expires.

11. False. Maximizing one's welfare does not rule out altruism. Operating in the public interest is clearly one objective of the Bank of Canada. The theory of bureaucratic behaviour only points out that other objectives, such as maximizing power, also influence Bank decision making.

13. False. The Bank is still subject to political pressure because the government might not renew the governor's appointment when it expires. Also, if the Bank is performing badly, the minister of finance can issue a directive that the Bank must follow.

15. During the first 60 or so years of Confederation there was little need for a central bank in what was a scattered and mainly rural economy. The branch bank network, influenced by the British tradition, was sufficient to serve the banking needs of the small, scattered, rural settlements.

Chapter 15   Multiple Deposit Creation and the Money Supply Process

2. Reserves are unchanged, but the monetary base falls by $2 million, as indicated by the following T-accounts:

Irving the Investor

Assets		Liabilities
Currency	−$2 million	
Securities	+$2 million	

Bank of Canada

Assets		Liabilities	
Securities	−$2 million	Currency	−$2 million

3. Reserves increase by $50 million, but the monetary base increases by $100 million, as the T-accounts for the five banks and the Bank of Canada indicate:

Five Banks

Assets		Liabilities	
Reserves	+$50 million	Advances	+$100 million
		Deposits	−$50 million

Bank of Canada

Assets		Liabilities	
Advances	+$100 million	Reserves	+$50 million
		Currency	+$50 million

5. The T-accounts are identical to those in the sections "Deposit Creation: The Single Bank" and "Deposit Creation: The Banking System" except that all the entries are multiplied by 10 000 (that is, $100 becomes $1 million). The net result is that chequable deposits rise by $10 million.

7. The $1 million Bank of Canada purchase of bonds increases reserves in the banking system by $1 million, and the total increase in chequable deposits is $10 million. The fact that banks buy securities rather than make loans with their excess reserves makes no difference in the multiple deposit creation process.

9. Reserves in the banking system fall by $1000, and a multiple contraction occurs, reducing chequable deposits by $10 000.

11. The level of chequable deposits falls by $50 million. The T-account of the banking system in equilibrium is as follows:

Banking System

Assets		Liabilities	
Reserves	−$5 million	Chequable deposits	−$50 million
Securities	+$5 million		
Loans	−$50 million		

13. The $1 million holdings of excess reserves means that the bank has to reduce its holdings of loans or securities, thus starting the multiple contraction process. Because the desired reserve ratio is 10%, chequable deposits must decline by $10 million.

15. The deposit of $100 in the bank increases its reserves by $100. This starts the process of multiple deposit expansion, leading to an increase in chequable deposits of $1000.

Chapter 16   Determinants of the Money Supply

1. Uncertain. As the formula in Equation 4 indicates, if r_D is greater than 1, the money multiplier can be less than 1. In practice, however, r_D is less than 1 and the money multiplier is greater than 1.

3. The money supply fell sharply because when c rose, there was a shift from one component of the money supply (chequable deposits) with more multiple expansion to another (currency) with less. Overall multiple deposit expansion fell, leading to a decline in the money supply.

5. There would be a shift from one component of the money supply (chequable deposits) with less multiple expansion to another (traveller's cheques) with more. Multiple expansion therefore increases, and the money supply increases.

7. With a lower desired reserve ratio for time deposits, a shift from chequable deposits (with less multiple expansion) to time deposits (with

more multiple expansion) increases the total amount of deposits and raises M2+.

9. Both the Bank's purchase of $100 million of bonds (which raises the monetary base) and the lowering of r_D (which increases the amount of multiple expansion and raises the money multiplier) lead to a rise in the money supply.

11. The Bank's sale of $1 million of bonds shrinks the monetary base by $1 million, and the reduction of advances also lowers the monetary base by another $1 million. The resulting $2 million decline in the monetary base leads to a decline in the money supply.

13. A rise in expected inflation would increase interest rates (through the Fisher effect), which would in turn cause r_D to fall and the volume of advances to rise. The fall in r_D increases the amount of reserves available to support chequable deposits so that deposits and the money multiplier will rise. The rise in advances causes the monetary base to rise. The resulting increase in the money multiplier and the monetary base leads to an increase in the money supply.

15. The money supply would fall because banks would need to hold more reserves, making fewer reserves available to support deposits. Moreover, abolishing central bank lending would reduce the volume of advances, which would also cause the monetary base and the money supply to fall.

Chapter 17 The Framework for the Implementation of Monetary Policy and the Tools of Monetary Policy

1. The increase in government deposits at the Bank of Canada will reduce bank settlement balances. To counteract this effect, the manager will undertake a defensive open market purchase.

3. As we saw in Chapter 15, when the government's deposits at the Bank fall, the monetary base increases. To counteract this increase, the manager would undertake an open market sale.

5. It suggests that defensive open market operations are far more common than dynamic operations because repurchase agreements are used primarily to conduct defensive operations to counteract temporary changes in the monetary base.

7. The monetary base and the money supply would increase indefinitely. Banks could borrow at the lower bank rate and then lend the proceeds at a higher interest rate. Hence banks would make a profit on every dollar borrowed from the Bank, so they would continue to borrow indefinitely—which would in turn increase the monetary base indefinitely.

9. This statement is incorrect. The CDIC would not be effective in eliminating bank panics without central bank lending to troubled banks in order to keep bank failures from spreading.

11. Usually yes, since declines in the bank rate occur because the operating band for the overnight rate has been lowered.

13. In a repo, the Bank of Canada buys government of Canada securities from participants with an agreement to resell them on the next business day. The Bank pays for the repos by crediting the participant's account at the Bank, thereby increasing settlement balances. This increase in settlement balances puts downward pressure on the overnight interest rate, as banks would have to borrow less to meet their settlement requirements. In a reverse repo, the Bank of Canada sells government of Canada securities with an agreement to buy them back on the next day. When the Bank sells these securities, it debits the participant's account at the Bank, thereby reducing settlement balances. This reduction in settlement balances puts upward pressure on the overnight rate, as banks would have to borrow more to meet their settlement requirements.

15. Open market operations are more flexible, reversible, and faster to implement than the other tool.

Chapter 18 Conduct of Monetary Policy: Goals and Targets

1. Disagree. Some unemployment is beneficial to the economy because the availability of vacant jobs makes it more likely that a worker will find the right job and that the employer will find the right worker for the job.

3. True. In such a world, hitting a monetary target would mean that the Bank of Canada would also hit its interest target, or vice versa. Thus the Bank could pursue both a monetary target and an interest-rate target at the same time.

5. The Bank of Canada can control the interest rate on three-month Treasury bills by buying and selling them in the open market. When the bill rate rises above the target level, the Bank would buy bills, which would bid up their price and lower the interest rate to its target level. Similarly, when the bill rate falls below the target level, the Bank would sell bills to raise the interest rate to the target level. The resulting open market operations would of course affect the money supply and cause it to change. The Bank would be giving up control of the money supply to pursue its interest-rate target.

7. Disagree. Although *nominal* interest rates are measured more accurately and more quickly than the money supply, the interest-rate variable that is of more concern to policymakers is the *real* interest rate. Because the measurement of real interest rates requires estimates of expected inflation, it is not true that real interest rates are necessarily measured more accurately and more quickly than

the money supply. Interest-rate targets are therefore not necessarily better than money supply targets.

9. When the Bank raises the operating band the monetary base declines and this reduces the money supply. In the opposite case, when the Bank lowers the operating band, it encourages banks to borrow reserves. The increase in reserves increases the monetary base and ultimately leads to an increase in the money supply.

11. When the economy enters a recession, interest rates usually fall. If the Bank is targeting interest rates, it tries to prevent a decline in interest rates by selling bonds, thereby lowering their prices and raising interest rates to the target level. The open market sale would then lead to a decline in the monetary base and in the money supply. The decline in interest rates would also cause excess reserves to rise.

13. The Bank may prefer to control interest rates rather than the money supply because it wishes to avoid the conflict with the government that occurs when interest rates rise. The Bank might also believe that interest rates are actually a better guide to future economic activity.

Chapter 19 The International Financial System

2. The purchase of dollars involves a sale of foreign assets, which means that international reserves fall and the monetary base falls. The resulting fall in the money supply causes interest rates to rise and RET^D to shift to the right while it lowers the future price level, thereby raising the future expected exchange rate, causing RET^F to shift to the left. The result is a rise in the exchange rate. However, in the long run, the RET^D curve returns to its original position, and so there is overshooting.

4. Because other countries often intervene in the foreign exchange market when the United States has a deficit so that U.S. holdings of international reserves do not change. By contrast, when Canada has a deficit, it must intervene in the foreign exchange market and buy Canadian dollars, which results in a reduction of international reserves for Canada.

6. Two francs per dollar.

8. A large balance-of-payments surplus may require a country to finance the surplus by selling its currency in the foreign exchange market, thereby gaining international reserves. The result is that the central bank will have supplied more of its currency to the public, and the monetary base will rise. The resulting rise in the money supply can cause the price level to rise, leading to a higher inflation rate.

10. In order to finance the deficits, the central bank in these countries might intervene in the foreign exchange market and buy domestic currency, thereby implementing a contractionary monetary policy. The result is that they sell off international reserves and their monetary base falls, leading to a decline in the money supply.

12. When other countries buy U.S. dollars to keep their exchange rates from changing vis-à-vis the dollar because of the U.S. deficits, they gain international reserves and their monetary base increases. The outcome is that the money supply in these countries grows faster and leads to higher inflation throughout the world.

14. There are no direct effects on the money supply because there is no central bank intervention in a pure flexible exchange rate regime; therefore, changes in international reserves that affect the monetary base do not occur. However, monetary policy can be affected by the foreign exchange market because monetary authorities may want to manipulate exchange rates by changing the money supply and interest rates.

Chapter 20 Monetary Policy Strategy: The International Experience

4. First is that the exchange-rate target directly keeps inflation under control by tying the inflation rate for internationally traded goods to that found in the anchor country to which its currency is pegged. Second is that it provides an automatic rule for the conduct of monetary policy that helps mitigate the time-inconsistency problem. Third, it has the advantage of simplicity and clarity.

6. With a pegged exchange rate, speculators are sometimes presented with a one-way bet in which the only direction for a currency to go is down in value. In this case, selling the currency before the likely depreciation gives speculators an attractive profit opportunity with potentially high expected returns. As a result, they jump on board and attack the currency.

8. The long-term bond market can help reduce the time-inconsistency problem because politicians and central banks will realize that pursuing an overly expansionary policy will lead to an inflation scare in which inflation expectations surge, interest rates rise, and there is a sharp fall in long-term bond prices. Similarly, they will realize that overly expansionary monetary policy will result in a sharp fall in the value of the currency. Avoiding these outcomes constrains policymakers and politicians so time-inconsistent monetary policy is less likely to occur.

10. A currency board has the advantage that the central bank no longer can print money to create inflation, and so it is a stronger commitment to a fixed exchange rate. The disadvantage is that it is still subject to a speculative attack, which can lead to a sharp contraction of the money supply. In

addition, a currency board limits the ability of the central bank to play a lender-of-last-resort role.

12. Monetary targeting has the advantage that it enables a central bank to adjust its monetary policy to cope with domestic considerations. Furthermore, information on whether the central bank is achieving its target is known almost immediately.

14. Inflation-targeting central banks engage in extensive public information campaigns that include the distribution of glossy brochures, the publication of *Monetary Policy Report*–type documents, making speeches to the public, and continual communication with the elected government.

16. Uncertain. If the relationship between monetary aggregates and the goal variable, say inflation, is unstable, then the signal provided by the monetary aggregates is not very useful and is not a good indicator of whether the stance of monetary policy is correct.

18. With a nominal GDP target, a decline in projected real output growth would automatically imply an increase in the central bank's inflation target. This increase would tend to be stabilizing because it would automatically lead to an easier monetary policy. Nominal GDP targeting does suffer from potential confusion about what nominal GDP is and from the political complications that arise because nominal GDP requires the announcement of a potential GDP growth path.

20. All allow a central bank to pursue an independent monetary policy that can focus on domestic considerations.

Chapter 21 The Demand for Money

1. Velocity is approximately 10 in 2001, 11 in 2002, and 12 in 2003. The rate of velocity growth is approximately 10% per year.

3. Nominal GDP declines by approximately 10%.

5. The price level quadruples.

7. False. The two approaches differ in that Fisher's rules out any possible effect of interest rates on the demand for money, whereas the Cambridge approach does not.

9. The demand for money will decrease. People would be more likely to expect interest rates to fall and therefore more likely to expect bond prices to rise. The increase in the expected return on bonds relative to money will then mean that people would demand less money.

11. Money balances should average one-half of Grant's monthly income because he would hold no bonds, since holding them would entail additional brokerage costs but would not provide him with any interest income.

13. True. Because bonds are riskier than money, risk-averse people would be likely to want to hold both.

15. In Keynes's view, velocity is unpredictable because interest rates, which have large fluctuations, affect the demand for money and hence velocity. In addition, Keynes's analysis suggests that if people's expectations of the normal level of interest rates change, the demand for money changes. Keynes thought that these expectations moved unpredictably, meaning that money demand and velocity are also unpredictable. Friedman sees the demand for money as stable, and because he also believes that changes in interest rates have only small effects on the demand for money, his position is that the demand for money, and hence velocity, is predictable.

Chapter 22 The Keynesian Framework and the *ISLM* Model

2. Companies cut production when their unplanned inventory investment is greater than zero because they are then producing more than they can sell. If they continue at current production, profits will suffer because they are building up unwanted inventory, which is costly to store and finance.

4. The equilibrium level of output is 1500. When planned investment spending falls by 100, the equilibrium level of output falls by 500 to 1000.

6. Nothing. The $100 billion increase in planned investment spending is exactly offset by the $100 billion decline in autonomous consumer expenditure, and autonomous spending and aggregate output remain unchanged.

8. Equilibrium output of 2000 occurs at the intersection of the 45° line $Y = Y^{ad}$ and the aggregate demand function $Y^{ad} = C + I + G = 500 \div 0.75Y$. If government spending rises by 100, equilibrium output will rise by 400 to 2400.

10. Taxes should be reduced by $400 billion because the increase in output for a $T decrease in taxes is $T; that is, it equals the change in autonomous spending $mpc \times T$ times the multiplier $1/(1 - mpc)$ = $(mpc \times T)[1/(1 - mpc)] = 0.5T[1/(1 - 0.5)] = 0.5T/0.5 = T$.

12. Rise. The fall in autonomous spending from an increase in taxes is always less than the change in taxes because the marginal propensity to consume is less than 1. By contrast, autonomous spending rises one-for-one with a change in autonomous consumer expenditure. So if taxes and autonomous consumer expenditure rise by the same amount, autonomous spending must rise, and aggregate output also rises.

14. When aggregate output falls, the demand for money falls, shifting the money demand curve to the left, which causes the equilibrium interest rate to fall. Because the equilibrium interest rate falls when aggregate output falls, there is a positive association between aggregate output and the equilibrium interest rate, and the *LM* curve slopes up.

Chapter 23 Monetary and Fiscal Policy in the *ISLM* Model

2. When investment spending collapsed, the aggregate demand function in the Keynesian cross diagram fell, leading to a lower level of equilibrium output for any given interest rate. The fall in equilibrium output for any given interest rate implies that the *IS* curve shifted to the left.

4. False. It can also be eliminated by a fall in aggregate output, which lowers the demand for money and brings it back into equality with the supply of money.

6. The *ISLM* model gives exactly this result. The tax cuts shifted the *IS* curve to the right, while tight money shifted the *LM* curve to the left. The interest rate at the intersection of the new *IS* and *LM* curves is necessarily higher than at the initial equilibrium, and aggregate output can be higher.

8. Because it suggests that an interest-rate target is better than a money supply target. The reason is that unstable money demand increases the volatility of the *LM* curve relative to the *IS* curve, and as demonstrated in the text, this makes it more likely that an interest-rate target is preferred to a money supply target.

10. The effect on the aggregate demand curve is uncertain. A rise in government spending would shift the *IS* curve to the right, raising equilibrium output for a given price level. But the reduction in the money supply would shift the *LM* curve to the left, lowering equilibrium output for a given price level. Depending on which of these two effects on equilibrium output is stronger, the aggregate demand curve could shift either to the right or to the left.

12. No effect. The *LM* curve would be vertical in this case, meaning that a rise in government spending and a rightward shift in the *IS* curve would not lead to higher aggregate output but rather only to a rise in the interest rate. For any given price level, therefore, equilibrium output would remain the same, and the aggregate demand curve would not shift.

Chapter 24 Aggregate Demand and Supply Analysis

2. Because the position of the aggregate demand curve is fixed if nominal income ($P \times Y$) is fixed, Friedman's statement implies that the position of the aggregate demand curve is completely determined by the quantity of money. This is built into the monetarist aggregate demand curve because it shifts only when the money supply changes.

4. The Keynesian aggregate demand curve shifts because a change in "animal spirits" causes consumer expenditure or planned investment spending to change, which then causes the quantity of aggregate output demanded to change at any given price level. In the monetarist view, by contrast, a change in "animal spirits" has little effect on velocity, and aggregate spending ($P \times Y$) remains unchanged; hence the aggregate demand curve does not shift.

6. True. Given fixed production costs, firms can earn higher profits by producing more when prices are higher. Profit-maximizing behaviour on the part of firms thus leads them to increase production when prices are higher.

8. The aggregate supply curve would shift to the right because production costs would fall.

10. The collapse in investment spending during the Great Depression reduced the quantity of output demanded at any given price level and shifted the aggregate demand curve to the left. In an aggregate demand and supply diagram, the equilibrium price level and aggregate output would then fall, which explains the decline in aggregate output and the price level that occurred during the Great Depression.

12. Both the increase in the money supply and the income tax cut will increase the quantity of output demanded at any given price level and so will shift the aggregate demand curve to the right. The intersection of the aggregate demand and aggregate supply curve will be at a higher level of both output and price level in the short run. However, in the long run, the aggregate supply curve will shift leftward, leaving output at the natural rate level, but the price level will be even higher.

14. Because goods would cost more, the national sales tax would raise production costs, and the aggregate supply curve would shift to the left. The intersection of the aggregate supply curve with the aggregate demand curve would then be at a higher level of prices and a lower level of aggregate output; aggregate output would fall, and the price level would rise.

Chapter 25 Transmission Mechanisms of Monetary Policy: The Evidence

4. Seeing which car is built better produces structural model evidence because it explains why one car is better than the other (that is, how the car is built). Asking owners how often their cars undergo repairs produces reduced-form evidence because it looks only at the correlation of reliability with the manufacturer of the car.

5. Not necessarily. If GM car owners change their oil more frequently than Ford owners, GM cars would have better repair records even though they are not more reliable cars. In this case, it is a third factor, the frequency of oil changes, that leads to the better repair record for GM cars.

6. Not necessarily. Although the Ford engine might be built better than the GM engine, the rest of the GM car might be better made than the Ford. The

result could be that the GM car is more reliable than the Ford.

8. If the Bank of Canada has interest-rate targets, a rise in output that raises interest rates might cause the Bank to buy bonds and bid up their price in order to drive interest rates back down to their target level (see Chapter 5). The result of these open market purchases would be that the increase in output would cause an increase in the monetary base and hence an increase in the money supply. In addition, a rise in output and interest rates would cause reserves to fall (because excess reserves would fall). If the Bank has a reserves target, the increase in aggregate output will then cause the Bank to increase the money supply because it believes that money is tight.

10. Monetarists went on to refine their reduced-form models with more sophisticated statistical procedures, one outcome of which was the St. Louis model. Keynesians began to look for transmission mechanisms of monetary policy that they may have ignored.

12. False. Monetary policy can affect stock prices, which affect Tobin's *q,* thereby affecting investment spending. In addition, monetary policy can affect loan availability, which may also influence investment spending.

14. There are three mechanisms involving consumer expenditure. First, a rise in the money supply lowers interest rates and reduces the cost of financing purchases of consumer durables, and consumer durable expenditure rises. Second, a rise in the money supply causes stock prices and wealth to rise, leading to greater lifetime resources for consumers and causing them to increase their consumption. Third, a rise in the money supply that causes stock prices and the value of financial assets to rise also lowers people's probability of financial distress, and so they spend more on consumer durables.

Chapter 26 Money and Inflation

2. Because hyperinflations appear to be examples in which the increase in money supply growth is an exogenous event, the fact that hyperinflation occurs when money growth is high is powerful evidence that a high rate of money growth causes inflation.

4. False. Although workers' attempts to push up their wages can lead to inflation if the government has a high employment target, inflation is still a monetary phenomenon because it cannot occur without accommodating monetary policy.

6. True. If financed with money creation, a temporary budget deficit can lead to a onetime rightward shift in the aggregate demand curve and hence to a onetime increase in the price level. However, once the budget deficit disappears, there is no

longer any reason for the aggregate demand curve to shift. Thus a temporary deficit cannot lead to a continuing rightward shift of the aggregate demand curve and therefore cannot produce inflation, a continuing increase in the price level.

8. True. The monetarist objection to activist policy would no longer be as serious. The aggregate demand curve could be quickly moved to AD_2 in Figure 26-11, and the economy would move quickly to point 2 because the aggregate supply curve would not have as much time to shift. The scenario of a highly variable price level and output would not occur, making an activist policy more desirable.

10. True, if expectations about policy affect the wage-setting process. In this case, workers and firms are more likely to push up wages and prices because they know that if they do so and unemployment develops as a result, the government will pursue expansionary policies to eliminate the unemployment. Therefore, the cost of pushing up wages and prices is lower, and workers and firms will be more likely to do it.

12. True. If expectations about policy have no effect on the aggregate supply curve, a cost-push inflation is less likely to develop when policymakers pursue an activist accommodating policy. Furthermore, if expectations about policy do not matter, pursuing a nonaccommodating, nonactivist policy does not have the hidden benefit of making it less likely that workers will push up their wages and create unemployment. The case for an activist policy is therefore stronger.

14. The Bank's big stick is the ability to let unemployment develop as a result of a wage push by not trying to eliminate unemployment with expansionary monetary policy. The statement proposes that the Bank should pursue a nonaccommodating policy because this will prevent cost-push inflation and make it less likely that unemployment develops because of workers' attempts to push up their wages.

Chapter 27 Theory of Rational Expectations and Efficient Capital Markets

1. False. Expectations can be highly inaccurate and still be rational because optimal forecasts are not necessarily accurate: A forecast is optimal if it is the best possible even if the forecast errors are large.

3. No, because he could improve the accuracy of his forecasts by predicting that tomorrow's interest rates will be identical to today's. His forecasts are therefore not optimal, and he does not have rational expectations.

5. No, you shouldn't buy stocks because the rise in the money supply is publicly available information that will be already incorporated into stock prices.

So you cannot expect to earn more than the equilibrium return on stocks by acting on the money supply information.

7. No, because this is publicly available information and is already reflected in stock prices. The optimal forecast of stock returns will equal the equilibrium return, so there is no benefit from selling your stocks.

9. No, if the person has no better information than the rest of the market. An expected price rise of 10% over the next month implies an annual return on IBM stock of more than 100%, which certainly exceeds its equilibrium return. This would mean that there is an unexploited profit opportunity in the market, which would have been eliminated in an efficient market. The only time that the person's expectations could be rational is if the person had information unavailable to the market that allowed the person to beat the market.

11. False. The people with better information are exactly those who make the market more efficient by eliminating unexploited profit opportunities. These people can profit from their better information.

13. True in principle. Foreign exchange rates are a random walk over a short interval such as a week because changes in the exchange rate are unpredictable. If a change were predictable, large unexploited profit opportunities would exist in the foreign exchange market. If the foreign exchange market is efficient, these unexploited profit opportunities cannot exist, and so the foreign exchange rate will approximately follow a random walk.

15. False. Although human fear may be the source of stock market crashes, that does not imply that there are unexploited profit opportunities in the market. Nothing in rational expectations theory rules out large changes in stock prices as a result of fears on the part of the investing public.

Chapter 28 Rational Expectations: Implications for Policy

2. A tax cut that is expected to last for ten years will have a larger effect on consumer expenditure than one that is expected to last only one year. The reason is that the longer the tax cut is expected to last, the greater its effect on expected average income and consumer expenditure.

4. True, if the anti-inflation policy is credible. As shown in Figure 28-6, if anti-inflation policy is believed (and hence expected), there is no output loss in the new classical model (the economy stays

at point 1 in panel b), and there is a smaller output loss than would otherwise be the case in the new Keynesian model (the economy goes to point 2″ rather than point 2′ in panel c).

6. Uncertain. It is true that policymakers can reduce unemployment by pursuing a more expansionary policy than the public expects. However, the rational expectations assumption indicates that the public will attempt to anticipate policymakers' actions. Policymakers cannot be sure whether expansionary policy will be more or less expansionary than the public expects and hence cannot use policy to make a predictable impact on unemployment.

8. True, because the Lucas critique indicates that the effect of policy on the aggregate demand curve depends on the public's expectations about that policy. The outcome of a particular policy is therefore less certain in Lucas's view than if expectations about it do not matter, and it is harder to design a beneficial activist stabilization policy.

10. Yes, if budget deficits are expected to lead to an inflationary monetary policy and expectations about monetary policy affect the aggregate supply curve. In this case, a large budget deficit would cause the aggregate supply curve to shift more to the left because expected inflation would be higher. The result is that the increase in the price level (the inflation rate) would be higher.

13. The aggregate supply curve would shift to the left less than the aggregate demand curve shifts to the right; hence at their intersection, aggregate output would rise and the price level would be higher than it would have been if money growth had been reduced to a rate of 2%.

14. Using the traditional model, the aggregate supply curve would continue to shift leftward at the same rate, and the smaller rightward shift of the aggregate demand curve because money supply growth has been reduced would mean a smaller increase in the price level and a reduction of aggregate output. In the new Keynesian model, the effect of this anti-inflation policy on aggregate output is uncertain. The aggregate supply curve would not shift leftward by as much as in the traditional model because the anti-inflation policy is expected, but it would shift to the left by more than in the new classical model. Hence inflation falls, but aggregate output may rise or fall, depending on whether the aggregate supply curve shifts to the left more or less than the aggregate demand curve shifts to the right.

INDEX